THE OXFORD HANDBOOK OF

MANAGEMENT INFORMATION SYSTEMS

THE OXFORD HANDBOOK OF

MANAGEMENT

INFORMATION

SYSTEMS

CRITICAL PERSPECTIVES AND NEW DIRECTIONS

Edited by

ROBERT D. GALLIERS

and

WENDY L. CURRIE

OXFORD
UNIVERSITY PRESS

OXFORD
UNIVERSITY PRESS

Great Clarendon Street, Oxford OX2 6DP

Oxford University Press is a department of the University of Oxford.
It furthers the University's objective of excellence in research, scholarship,
and education by publishing worldwide in

Oxford New York

Auckland Cape Town Dar es Salaam Hong Kong Karachi
Kuala Lumpur Madrid Melbourne Mexico City Nairobi
New Delhi Shanghai Taipei Toronto

With offices in

Argentina Austria Brazil Chile Czech Republic France Greece
Guatemala Hungary Italy Japan Poland Portugal Singapore
South Korea Switzerland Thailand Turkey Ukraine Vietnam

Oxford is a registered trade mark of Oxford University Press
in the UK and in certain other countries

Published in the United States
by Oxford University Press Inc., New York

British Library Cataloguing in Publication Data
Data available

Library of Congress Cataloguing in Publication Data
Data available

Typeset by SPI Publisher Services, Pondicherry, India
Printed in Great Britain
on acid-free paper by
MPG Books Group, Bodmin and King's Lynn

ISBN 978-0-19-958058-3

1 3 5 7 9 10 8 6 4 2

Acknowledgements

We gratefully acknowledge all the many contributors to this book, not least the authors of each of the chapters who so willingly gave of their time to make this Handbook a reality. We recognize that book chapters are not a high priority given the many demands placed on the academy these days: university rankings and accreditation exercises have seen to that. We also acknowledge their patience in the long gestation period that was needed to bring this collection to completion. We fervently hope that they will be pleased with the fruits of their collective labours, and that this collection will serve as a strong foundation for the development of the still emergent field that is management information systems (MIS).

We also wish to make special mention of our late colleague, Heinz Klein, whose many contributions to our field will be sorely missed. His untimely death, in June 2008, meant that he would not see his contribution in published form. May this Handbook serve as something of a memorial to him and his work.

Special mention should also be made of David Musson, the commissioning editor for this Handbook. He, and his former colleague, Matthew Derbyshire, were hugely encouraging and supportive, and we thank them for their faith in our ability to bring this collection of disparate contributions together into a coherent whole. More recently, we have had Emma Lambert, Carol Bestley and Joy Mellor supporting us in bringing the book to publication. We thank them in addition.

Support in our own institutions was and is crucial too, and we want to acknowledge with profound thanks, Diane Whelan and Maria Skaletsky in particular.

We, the editors, together with the publisher would like to thank:

Elsevier, for permission to reprint as Chapter 17: M. C. Lacity, S. A. Khan, and L. P. Willcocks, 'A review of the IT outsourcing literature: Insights for Practice'. From *The Journal of Strategic Information Systems* 18 (3), 130–46. Copyright 2009 by Elsevier B.V.

and to acknowledge:

Palgrave Macmillan and the authors, for some of the material to be found in Chapter 18 by Jacky Swan, which was first published in: S. Newell, M. Robertson, H. Scarbrough, and J. Swan, *Managing Knowledge Work and Innovation*, 2nd edition, Houndmills, Basingstoke: Palgrave Macmillan, 2009. Copyright 2009 by S. Newell, M. Robertson, H. Scarbrough, and J. Swan.

Bob Galliers and Wendy Currie

CONTENTS

PART III RETHINKING THEORY
IN MIS PRACTICE

PART IV RETHINKING MIS PRACTICE IN A BROADER CONTEXT

LIST OF CONTRIBUTORS

THE EDITORS

Bob Galliers was appointed as Bentley University's inaugural University Distinguished Professor in July 2009. He served as Bentley's Provost and Vice President for Academic Affairs for seven years following his arrival in July 2002, during which time he lead Bentley's development to become the USA's first business university. Bentley is accredited by EQUIS and AACSB International, and has recently been elected as the USA's first full member of EDAMBA, the European doctoral consortium in Management and Business Administration. Previously Professor of Information Systems and Research Director in the Department of Information Systems at the London School of Economics (LSE), he retains his connection with the LSE as Visiting Professor. He is also Visiting Professor at the Australian School of Business, UNSW; King's College, London; the University of Witwatersrand, Johannesburg; and Brunel Business School, Brunel University. Before joining LSE, Galliers served as Lucas Professor of Business Management Systems and Dean of Warwick Business School, UK, and earlier as Foundation Professor and Head of the School of Information Systems at Curtin University, Australia. He holds an AB (honours) degree in Economics from Harvard University; a Master's with distinction in Management Systems from Lancaster University; a Ph.D. in Information Systems from the LSE, and an Honorary Doctor of Science degree from Turku School of Economics & Business Administration, Finland. He is the editor-in-chief of the *Journal of Strategic Information Systems*, and a fellow of the British Computer Society (FBCS); the Association for Information Systems (FAIS), and the Royal Society of Arts (FRSA). He was President of the AIS in 1999. Galliers has had published over seventy articles in many leading international journals, three of which have received best paper awards. He also has eleven books to his name, including the fourth edition of the best seller, *Strategic Information Management: Challenges and Strategies in Managing Information Systems* (Routledge, 2009); *Exploring Information Systems Research Approaches: Readings and Reflections* (Routledge, 2007); *Rethinking Management Information Systems* (Oxford University Press, 1999), and *IT and Organizational Transformation* (Wiley, 1998). His work has been cited over 3,000 times. His research is transdisciplinary in nature, focusing primarily on information systems strategizing and organizational innovation; knowledge management, and intra- and extra-organizational impacts of ICT.

Wendy L. Currie combines academic, business, and charity (not-for-profit) roles. She currently holds a professorial post at the University of Greenwich Business School and was formerly Professor at Warwick Business School. She holds a Ph.D in Management and a B.Sc. in Sociology. Her research focuses on the intersection between international policy and technology with particular emphasis on cross-national comparisons on the adoption and diffusion of information and communications technology. Her current research projects include a large-scale study of eHealth across the twenty-seven European Union member states supported by Microsoft and a coalition of partners including Accenture, GE, and Phillips. Other projects are looking at regulation, compliance, and auditing using ICT in the financial services sector. Another study has focused on an eight-year (longitudinal) analysis of the National Programme for Information Technology (NPfIT) in the UK National Health Service. She has obtained research funding from the European Union, EPSRC, ESRC, and from industry. In 2005, she set up the M.Sc. Information Systems and Management course at Warwick Business School, which aims to promote the 'university apprentice' scheme by placing students in organizations as interns. The course is now a leader in this market and is currently expanding each year. Currie is on the editorial board of ten academic journals and regularly publishes her research work. She currently serves as Hon Treasurer for the Fellowship of Postgraduate Medicine charity and is a Trustee of the Cardiovascular Research Trust. She regularly consults on the interface between business, management and technology and has recently completed assignments with Microsoft, Mouchel, 7 Layer, Deloitte, the Church of England, and Barclays Capital.

CONTRIBUTORS

Chrisanthi Avgerou is Professor of Information Systems at the London School of Economics and Political Science. Her main research interests concern the relationship of ICT to organizational change and the role of ICT in socio-economic development. She is chairperson of the IFIP Technical Committee 9 on Social Implications of Information Technology and she chaired the IFIP WG 9.4 group on computers in developing countries from 1996 till 2003. Among her recent publications are *Information Systems and Global Diversity*, *The Social Study of Information and Communication Technology: Innovation, Actors, and Contexts*, and *The Oxford Handbook of Information and Communication Technologies* all published by Oxford University Press.

Pierre Berthon holds the Clifford F. Youse Chair of Marketing and Strategy at Bentley University. Berthon has held academic positions at Columbia University in the USA, Henley Management College, Cardiff University, and University of Bath in the UK. He has also taught or held visiting positions at Rotterdam School of Management, Copenhagen Business School, Norwegian School of Economics and Management, Cape

Town Business School, University of Cape Town, and Athens Laboratory of Business Administration. His research focuses on the interaction of technology, corporate strategy, and consumer behaviour, and has appeared in journals such as *Sloan Management Review, California Management Review, Information Systems Research, Technological Forecasting and Social Change, Journal of the Academy of Marketing Science, Journal of Business Research, Journal of International Marketing, Long Range Planning, Business Horizons, European Management Journal, Journal of Interactive Marketing, Journal of Information Technology, Information Systems Review, Journal of Business Ethics, Marketing Theory*, and others.

Yolande E. Chan is Professor, MIS, and Director, The Monieson Centre at the School of Business at Queen's University in Canada. She holds a Ph.D. from the Richard Ivey School of Business, an M.Phil. in Management Studies from Oxford University, and SM and SB degrees in Electrical Engineering and Computer Science from MIT. She is a Rhodes Scholar. Prior to joining Queen's, she worked with Andersen Consulting (now Accenture). Dr Chan conducts research on strategic alignment, knowledge management, and information privacy. She serves on editorial boards and has published findings in several leading MIS journals.

Peter Checkland is Emeritus Professor of Systems at Lancaster University. After fifteen years in industry he started teaching and researching at Lancaster. Seeking a better approach to complex management problems, he led the thirty-year programme of action research which yielded Soft-Systems Methodology and the distinction between 'hard' and 'soft' systems thinking. His work has received many honours, including four honorary doctorates, the Beale Medal of the OR Society, the gold medal of the UK Systems Society, the 'Pioneer' award of the International Council on Systems Engineering, and a Fellowship from the American Systems Engineering Honor Society.

Philip DesAutels is a researcher at Bentley University and Director of Academic Evangelism at Microsoft. He holds M.S. and B.S. degrees in Industrial and Management Engineering from Rensselaer Polytechnic Institute. Prior to Microsoft, Philip was founder and CTO of Ereo, an image retrieval search company. He worked as Chief Scientist for Excite@Home and as a researcher on the staff of the World Wide Web consortium as well as with IBM, Anderson Consulting, and John Hancock. As a Peace Corps volunteer, he served in Uzbekistan, where he lectured, established a micro-lending programme, and installed part of the country's first email infrastructure. Philip serves as the Chair of the Globe Award for Sustainable Innovation. In addition, he serves as a board member and adviser to numerous NGOs. His research interests lie in the areas of sustainability, the future of sustainable business, and society and technology and he has published research in the areas of operations research, marketing, and information systems.

Brian Donnellan is a lecturer in Information Systems at NUI Galway. His Ph.D. was entitled 'Knowledge Management Systems for New Product Development'. His research interests lie primarily in the area of knowledge management systems, a broad area which encompasses the use of information systems to support knowledge management, innovation, new product development, and technology management. He has been successful in a number of research funding proposals from the Irish government and the EU. He has been actively involved in a two-year (2004–5) STREP project under the EU FP6 programme. The consortium aims at introducing, analysing, and supporting the use of Open Data Standards (ODS) and Open Source (OS) software for personal productivity and document management in European Public Administrations and comprises universities and public administrations in Ireland, Italy, UK, Denmark, Belgium, and Hungary. He has spent twenty years working in industry. His most recent position was in Analog Devices Inc. (ADI), the European R&D centre of a US electronics company with headquarters in Boston. While at ADI his responsibilities included management of the Knowledge Management Business Process and management of engineering computer services for New Product Development Teams.

Rudy Hirschheim is the Ourso Family Distinguished Professor of Information Systems in the E. J. Ourso College of Business, Louisiana State University. He has previously been on the faculties of the University of Houston, Templeton College Oxford (UK), London School of Economics (UK), and McMaster University (Canada). He has held visiting appointments at Monash University (Australia), University of New South Wales (Australia), University of Bayreuth (Germany), University of Jyvaskyla (Finland), University of Warwick (UK), University of Linz (Austria), and University of Paris-Dauphine (France). He is past Senior Editor for the *Journal of the Association for Information Systems* and on the editorial boards of the journals: *Information and Organization*; *Information Systems Journal*; *Journal of Strategic Information Systems*; *Journal of MIS*; and *Journal of Information Technology*; and has previously been on the boards of: *European Journal of Information Systems* and *MIS Quarterly*. He was VP for Publications for the Association for Information Systems. In 2006, he was awarded an honorary doctorate from the University of Oulu (Finland). And in 2007, he was made 'Fellow' of the Association for Information Systems. His research interests relate to IT management, especially outsourcing.

Debra Howcroft is Professor of Technology and Organizations at Manchester Business School and a member of the ESRC-funded Centre for Research on Socio-Cultural Change (CRESC). Broadly, her research interests are concerned with the drivers and consequences of socio-economic restructuring in a global context.

Fernando Ilharco is Assistant Professor of the Catholic University of Portugal, Lisbon, where he is Director of the Ph.D. in Communication Sciences Programme. He holds a Ph.D. from the London School of Economics and Political Science (LSE), Department of Information Systems, 2002, and an M.B.A. from the business school of the Catholic

University of Portugal (1993). Since his Ph.D., Ilharco has been publishing regularly in academic journals and books. His areas of interest are (i) ICT and Society and (ii) Leadership and Organizational Theory, both informed by phenomenological lenses. For ten years he kept a regular column on societal issues on *Público*, a leading Portuguese reference newspaper.

Lucas D. Introna is Professor of Technology, Organization, and Ethics at Lancaster University. His research interest is the social study of information technology and its consequences for society. In particular he is concerned with the ethics and politics of technology. He also has an active interest in business and research ethics. He is co-editor of *Ethics and Information Technology*, associate editor of *Information Systems Research*, and a founding member of the International Society for Ethics and Information Technology (INSEIT) <http://www.lums.lancs.ac.uk/owt/profiles/119/>.

Blake Ives holds the C. T. Bauer Chair in Business Leadership at the Bauer College of Business at the University of Houston. He is the past Director of Research for the Society for Information Management's Advanced Practice Council and a former Director of the Information Systems Research Center at the University of Houston. Blake is a past president of the Association for Information Systems, a fellow of the Association for Information Systems, and a past editor-in-chief of the *MIS Quarterly*. He currently serves on a number of editorial boards including as Senior Editor of *MISQ Executive* and a member of the board of the *Communications of the Association for Computing Machinery* (CACM). He has held distinguished fellowships at the Harvard Business School, Oxford University, and IBM. According to Google Scholar, his scholarly research has been cited close to 5,000 times. His work includes publications in, among others, *Management Science, MIS Quarterly, Information Systems Research, Communications of the ACM, MISQ Executive, Decision Sciences, Organization Science*, and the *Sloan Management Review*.

Matthew Jones is a university lecturer in Information Management at the Judge Business School and the Department of Engineering at the University of Cambridge. He previously held postdoctoral positions at the University of Reading and the University of Cambridge where he was involved in the development of computer-based models for public policy decision-making. His current research interests are concerned with the social and organizational aspects of the design and use of information systems, especially in healthcare settings, the relationship between technology and organizational and social change, and theoretical and methodological issues in Information Systems research.

Shaji Khan is a Ph.D. candidate in business administration with information systems emphasis at the University of Missouri-St Louis. His research interests include collective mindfulness and its impact on IS performance, outsourcing, knowledge sharing and transfer, user involvement and IS success, user innovativeness, agent-based modelling, and entrepreneurship. He has published in the *International Journal of Entrepreneurship and Innovation*, as well as in the conference proceedings of AMCIS, Academy of Management Annual Meetings (AOM), and Babson-Nankai International Entrepreneurship Research Conference. He also has extensive IS related industry experience working in positions such as senior systems analyst, web developer, and IS manager and still maintains an active interest in his entrepreneurial IT venture.

Heinz Karl Klein (1940–2008) was a professor and scholar who made fundamental contributions to the philosophical foundations of the field of Information Systems, and the subfields of systems development, data modelling, and interpretive research in information systems. He is a widely cited scholar in these areas <http://en.wikipedia.org/wiki/Heinz_Klein-cite_note-0>. Dr Klein earned his Dipl.Kfm. (equivalent of an MBA) and Ph.D. from the Faculty of Business Administration, University of Munich. In 1998, he received an honorary doctorate from the University of Oulu for his academic contributions to the development of information systems research in Finland. He received the Paper of the Year award for 1999 from *MIS Quarterly*. From 2001 to 2004 he was a doctoral programme director at Temple University. In his last years he was Invited Chair at Salford University, and Adjunct Professor at the School of Management of the State University of New York at Binghamton. He also held a variety of research and teaching appointments at major research universities in Germany, Canada, Finland, Denmark, New Zealand, and South Africa. His mentoring of doctoral students and junior faculty produced several nationally and internationally renowned university professors.

Mary C. Lacity is Professor of Information Systems and an International Business Fellow at the University of Missouri-St Louis. Her current research focuses on global outsourcing of business and IT services. She was the recipient of the 2008 Gateway to Innovation Award sponsored by the IT Coalition and Society for Information Management and the 2000 World Outsourcing Achievement Award sponsored by PricewaterhouseCoopers and Michael Corbett and Associates. She has published twelve books, most recently *China's Emerging Outsourcing Capabilities* (Palgrave, 2010, co-editors Leslie Willcocks and Yingqin Zheng) and *Information Systems Outsourcing: Theory and Practice* (Palgrave, 2009; coauthor: Leslie P. Willcocks). She is Senior Editor of the *Journal of Information Technology*, Co-editor of the Palgrave Series: Work, Technology, and Globalization, and on the editorial boards for *MIS Quarterly Executive, Journal of Strategic Information Systems, Strategic Outsourcing: An International Journal*, and *Journal of the Association for Information Systems (JAIS)*.

Eleni Lioliou is currently pursuing her Ph.D. research at LSE. Her research has been funded by the Karelia Foundation, Leventis Foundation, and the LSE. She holds a B.Sc., a B.A., an M.Litt., an M.Sc., and an M.Phil. She has worked as a research assistant for the LSE, University of Warwick and the University of Loughborough, as well as a teaching assistant at the LSE, London Business School, University College London, and the Cass

Business School. Her research interest revolves around IT outsourcing and offshoring, governance, control as well as the Foucauldian approach into the study of ICTs.

M. Lynne Markus is the John W. Poduska, Sr., Professor of Information and Process Management at Bentley University. Professor Markus's research interests include IT governance, the organizational architectures of multinational enterprises, data and process standardization, and interorganizational information sharing and systems. She is the author or editor of five books and over 100 other scholarly publications, two of which have received the Association for Information Systems (AIS) Publication of the Year award. She was named a fellow of the AIS in 2004 and received the AIS LEO Award for Exceptional Lifetime Achievement in Information Systems in 2008.

John Mingers is Professor of Operational Research and Information Systems at Kent Business School, and Director of Research. Prior to this, he was at Warwick Business School. His research interests include the development of theory concerning the nature of information, meaning and knowledge; the use of systems methodologies in problem situations, particularly the mixing of different methods within an intervention (multi-methodology); the development of critical realism as an underpinning philosophy for information systems; research metrics and autopoiesis and its applications. He has published the only comprehensive study of autopoiesis, *Self-Producing Systems: Implications and Applications of Autopoiesis*, and has also edited *Information Systems: An Emerging Discipline?* (with Prof. Frank Stowell), *Social Theory and Philosophy for Information Systems* (with Prof. Leslie Willcocks), *Multimethodology: The Theory and Practice of Combining Management Science Methodologies* (with Tony Gill), and *Rational Analysis for a Problematic World* (with Prof. Jonathan Rosenhead). His latest monograph is *Realizing Systems Thinking: Knowledge and Action in Management Science*. He has published widely in journals including *Information Systems Research, Information Systems Journal, JORS, Information and Organization,* and *The Sociological Review*. He is an academician of the Academy of the Social Sciences. He joined the Editorial Board of *MIS Quarterly* in 2010.

Nathalie Mitev is a senior lecturer at the London School of Economics, held previous positions at Salford University and City University, and has been teaching information systems (IS) for the last twenty years. She holds several French postgraduate degrees, an M.B.A. and a Ph.D. Her research interests focus on IS and organizational change, and she has researched IS in the travel, health, small business, and construction industries. She has applied theories from the sociology of technology to analysing IS failures.

Sue Newell is the Cammarata Professor of Management, Bentley University, USA, and a part-time Professor of Information Management at Warwick University, UK. She has a B.Sc. and Ph.D. from Cardiff University, UK. Sue's research focuses on understanding the relationships between innovation, knowledge, and organizational networking (ikon), primarily from an organizational theory perspective. She was one of the founding members of ikon, a research centre based at Warwick University. Her research emphasizes a critical, practice-based understanding of the social aspects of innovation, change, knowledge management, and inter-firm networked relations. Sue has published over eighty-five journal articles in the areas of organization studies, management, and information systems, as well as numerous books and book chapters. Administratively, Sue is the Director of the Ph.D. at Bentley and led the effort to design, develop, and implement two new Ph.D.s, one in Business and one in Accountancy. In terms of teaching Sue has taught at all levels—undergraduate, graduate, post-graduate, and executive—and focuses on designing innovative courses that emphasize the practical relevance of solid theoretical foundations.

Amy Ray currently serves as Trustee Chair in the Information Process and Management Department at Bentley University. Dr. Ray teaches, consults, and conducts research in information security, with special interests in interorganizational systems and processes, particularly in healthcare. Dr. Ray has worked extensively with leaders in the healthcare and consumer packaged goods industries and has taught a variety of information security courses in executive and university education programmes. She has received numerous grants, including grants from Symantec and NSF to complete security and other practice-oriented research. Her research appears in numerous scholarly MIS journals including the *Journal of Management Information Systems*, *Information and Management*, the *Journal of Information Systems*, and *the Journal of Strategic Information Systems* as well as several scholarly accounting journals.

Blaize Horner Reich worked for many years in the IT industry as a practitioner, project manager, and consultant before developing an academic career. She is currently a board member for several academic journals and a corporate director. Dr. Reich has been published in many journals, including *MIS Quarterly*, *Journal of Information Technology*, *Journal of Management Information Systems*, and the *Journal of Strategic Information Systems*. Her current IT project research focuses on knowledge management and modelling performance. Her IT governance work focuses on managing risk and attaining business-IT alignment.

Simon Rogerson is Professor and Director of the Centre for Computing and Social Responsibility at De Montfort University. He researches into the ethical issues of new technologies. He is Europe's first Professor in Computer Ethics. He received the 2000 IFIP Namur Award and 2005 was awarded the SIGCAS Making-a-Difference Award by the ACM. He conceived and co-directs the ETHICOMP conference series. He is Chair of Council and VP of IMIS and a member of the Ethics Strategic Panel of BCS.

Gabriele Piccoli is Professor of Information Systems in the Management of Technology and Strategy department at the Grenoble École de Management. Prior to moving to Grenoble, Prof. Piccoli was Associate Professor of Information Systems at Cornell University (USA) and subsequently Associate Professor of Applied Economics at the

University of Sassari. Prof. Piccoli began his career as an Assistant Professor at Cornell in 2000, receiving indefinite tenure at the School of Hotel Administration and Hospitality Management upon his promotion to Associate Professor in 2006. Prof. Piccoli is the author of the book *Information Systems for Managers: Text and Cases*, published by John Wiley & Sons. His recent research interests span strategic information systems and the use of information systems to enable customer service. This work has appeared in leading Information Systems and applied journals, including *MIS Quarterly*, *Decision Sciences Journal*, *Communications of the ACM*, *Harvard Business Review*, and *MIS Quarterly Executive*.

Leyland F. Pitt is Professor of Marketing, Segal Graduate School of Business, Simon Fraser University, Vancouver, Canada, and is Senior Research Fellow of the Leeds University Business School in the United Kingdom. He has also taught on executive and M.B.A. programmes at major international business schools such as the University of Chicago, Columbia University, and London Business School. His work has been accepted for publication by such journals as *Information Systems Research*, *Journal of the Academy of Marketing Science*, *Sloan Management Review*, *California Management Review*, *Communications of the ACM*, and *MIS Quarterly* (for which he also served as Associate Editor).

Dr Carsten Sørensen lectures on Information Systems and Innovation in the Department of Management at the London School of Economics and Political Science, United Kingdom. He studies how ICT shapes and is shaped by emerging working practices and organizational forms and has, since 2001, studied enterprise mobility (<mobility.lse.ac.uk>). Carsten has since 1990 worked on and managed a range of large EU, Swedish, and UK research projects. He has published broadly within Information Systems and is Senior Editor for the *Information Systems Journal*. Carsten is actively engaged with executive education and has consulted for a range of organizations. He can be reached at <www.carstensorensen.com>.

Bernd Carsten Stahl is Professor of Critical Research in Technology in the Centre for Computing and Social Responsibility at De Montfort University, Leicester, UK. His interests cover philosophical issues arising from the intersections of business, technology, and information. This includes the ethics of computing and critical approaches to information systems.

Jacky Swan is Professor in Organizational Behaviour at Warwick Business School, University of Warwick, Associate Dean (Ph.D. Programme) and Director of the Innovation Knowledge and Organizational Networks (IKON) research centre. Her research interests are in linking innovation and networking to processes of managing knowledge across different industry sectors and national contexts. Of late she has been Principal Investigator on research projects looking at the translation of knowledge into medical practice via clinical trials and commissioning decisions. She is co-author of *Managing Knowledge Work and Innovation* (Palgrave, 2009).

Eileen M. Trauth is Professor of Information Sciences & Technology at the Pennsylvania State University. She has affiliate professorships in Women's Studies, Labor Studies & Employee Relations, International Affairs, and Management & Organization. Dr. Trauth's research is concerned with societal, cultural, and organizational influences on information technology and the information technology professions with a special focus on the role of diversity and social inclusion. She has published nine books and over 150 scholarly papers on her work on gender and social inclusion, the information economy, qualitative research methods, critical theory, global informatics, information policy, information management, telecommunications policy, and information systems skills.

Mike Wade is Associate Professor of Management Information Systems at the Schulich School of Business, York University, Toronto, where he also holds the position of Academic Director of the Kellogg-Schulich Executive M.B.A. Programme. He received a Ph.D. from the Ivey Business School at the University of Western Ontario. Professor Wade has worked extensively with public and private sector organizations to further an understanding of the strategic use of information systems for sustainable competitive advantage. He has lived and worked in seven countries across four continents and consulted for top international organizations including Cisco Systems, Microsoft, and IBM. His research has appeared in journals such as *MIS Quarterly*, *Strategic Management Journal*, and the *Communications of the ACM*. He is Senior Editor at the *Journal of the AIS* and Associate Editor at *ISR*. Professor Wade has co-authored four books in the areas of Information Systems, eCommerce, and Management Theory.

Erica Wagner is an associate professor in the Department of Management at Portland State University's School of Business. She earned her Ph.D. from the London School of Economics and has an undergraduate degree in accounting. She has previously taught at Cornell University and the London School of Economics. Her research interests focus on the ways software is 'made to work' within different organizational contexts, with particular emphasis on how work practices are designed into artefacts, standard processes, and methods of accounting. Her research has been published in a variety of outlets including *The Journal of the Association for Information Systems*, *Information and Organization*, *Communications of the ACM*, and the *Journal of Strategic Information Systems*. Dr Wagner's paper entitled 'The Creation of "Best practice" Software: Myth, Reality and Ethics', was awarded 'Best Research Paper 2006' by leading scholars in her field. In addition, she was one of four faculty members across Cornell University to receive a three-year grant from the National Science Foundation's (NSF) Digital Government project (2005) on Natural Language Processing Support for eRulemaking. While at Cornell University she also won two awards related to her teaching: The Merrill Presidential Scholar award for Outstanding Educator and the Faculty Innovation in Teaching Grant.

Geoff Walsham is Professor of Management Studies (Information Systems) at Judge Business School, University of Cambridge. In addition to Cambridge, he has held academic posts at the University of Lancaster in the UK where he was Professor of Information Management, the University of Nairobi in Kenya, and Mindanao State University in the Philippines. His teaching and research is focused on the question: are we making a better world with information and communication technologies? He was one the early pioneers of interpretive approaches to research on information systems.

Richard Watson is the J. Rex Fuqua Distinguished Chair for Internet Strategy in the Terry College of Business at the University of Georgia. He has published nearly 150 journal articles and given invited presentations in more than thirty countries. His current research focuses on Energy Informatics. He is a consulting editor for John Wiley & Sons, a former President of AIS, a visiting professor at the University of Agder in Norway, and co-leads the Global Text Project.

Cynthia Clark Williams is the Director of the Harold S. Geneen Institute of Corporate Governance at Bentley University and an assistant professor of management. She holds a Ph.D. from the honours programme at Boston University and an M.A. from Northwestern University. Her research interests are primarily in the areas of ethics, corporate disclosures, and governance. Her research has been published in *MIS Quarterly*, *Business Ethics Quarterly*, *Business & Society*, and the *Case Research Journal* to name a few. She teaches courses in strategy and social issues in management.

Leslie Willcocks is Professor of Technology Work and Globalization at the London School of Economics and Political Science, head of the Information Systems and Innovation group, and director of The Outsourcing Unit there. He is known for his work on global sourcing, information management, IT evaluation, e-business, organizational transformation, as well as for his practitioner contributions to many corporations and government agencies. He holds visiting chairs at Erasmus, Melbourne, and Sydney universities and is Associate Fellow at Templeton, University of Oxford. He has been Editor-in-Chief of the *Journal of Information Technology* for the last twenty years, and is Joint Series Editor, with Mary C. Lacity, of the Palgrave book series *Technology Work and Globalization*. He has co-authored thirty-one books, including most recently *Major Currents in Information Systems* (Sage, 2008, with Allen Lee), and *Global Sourcing of Business and IT Services* (Palgrave, 2006, with Mary C. Lacity). He has published over 180 refereed papers in journals such as *Harvard Business Review*,*Sloan Management Review*, *MIS Quarterly*, *MISQ Executive*, *Journal of Management Studies*, *Communications of the ACM*, *and Journal of Strategic Information Systems*.

PART I

··

SETTING THE SCENE

··

In this volume, *The Oxford Handbook of Management Information Systems: Critical Perspectives and New Directions*, we include twenty-six chapters by leading scholars in the field. We present this body of work in four parts, including Setting the Scene (Part I), Theoretical and Methodological Perspectives in MIS (Part II), Rethinking Theory in MIS Practice (Part III), and Rethinking MIS Practice in a Broader Context (Part IV).

In the opening chapter to this volume, Lynne Markus provides valuable insights into the development of the MIS field, considering how changing technology has posed a series of important challenges to organizations and individuals. This is followed by a chapter by Rudy Hirschheim and Heinz K. Klein (1940–2008) where they trace five decades of the information systems academic field. They divide the decades into four eras from 1964 to 1974, 1975 to 1984, 1985 to 1994, and from 1995 onwards. They include important developments in technology, research themes, schools of thought, education and the curriculum, and infrastructural advancements and the launch of professional societies. This historical overview is critically important for gaining a wide appreciation of how the information systems field has developed from the early 1960s to the present day.

....

CHAPTER 1

HISTORICAL REFLECTIONS ON THE PRACTICE OF INFORMATION MANAGEMENT AND IMPLICATIONS FOR THE FIELD OF MIS

....

M. LYNNE MARKUS

A HANDBOOK is meant to provide concise and current coverage of essential topics in an area of knowledge. On these criteria, the *Oxford Handbook of Management Information Systems* succeeds admirably. This Handbook gives the reader an expertly guided tour through the contemporary management information systems (MIS) landscape—the leading social theories applied in studies of MIS, the major concerns of contemporary information management practice, and the larger social issues in which information technology (IT) is implicated at present.

Even the weightiest handbooks have little space to spare for history, although this one starts with an in-depth look at the history of the Information Systems academic field (Hirschheim and Klein, this volume). Therefore, it seems opportune to use this introductory chapter to comment on the evolution of the practice of information management. In the pages that follow, I briefly characterize three co-evolving trends in the practice of information management: the professionalization of management and information management, the externalization of IT work, and the transformation of in-house IT services. These trends are likely to continue unfolding for some years to come, leading to new opportunities and challenges for the field of MIS.

THE PROFESSIONALIZATION OF MANAGEMENT AND INFORMATION MANAGEMENT

In many ways, the history of information technology is the history of management professionalism. (See Swan in this volume.) For example, the concept of the economic order quantity (EOQ) and the formulas for calculating it were developed in the early 1900s, but the concept was not widely applied in practice until the 1960s, when companies began developing software that automated its computation. In other cases, the attempt to apply computing power to organizational tasks stimulated the invention of new management practices. Some years ago, I had a conversation with a man who had programmed one of the first manufacturing control programs in the early 1960s. He explained that, at that time, the 'bill of materials' concept was unknown (in his organization, at least); he and his colleagues and clients had to invent (or possibly reinvent) the concept in the process of building their system.

As time went on, management ideas such as EOQ and the bill of materials diffused among organizations via many channels: personnel movements, professional societies, management education, research organizations, and the growing software and professional services industry. Whether or not these new ideas actually constitute 'best practices' (Wagner and Newell in this volume), they have become institutionalized as beliefs about the best ways for people in organizations to do things (Currie in this volume). Furthermore, encoding these beliefs in software often imbues them with the force of law. It is now impossible to do many things in organizations without information systems. Business rules are increasingly captured in black-box analytic engines that few, if any, people can understand or override. As one CIO recently asserted: 'There are no more business processes any more; the system *is* the business process'.

Whereas formerly the systems that codified management ideas were 'home-grown' and unique to the cultures and practices of individual organizations, they are increasingly 'off-the-shelf' packages or services that themselves have the aura of 'best practice' standards. Accountants, planners, marketers, human resources specialists, and financial analysts are all expected to know how to use certain 'best of breed' IT applications in doing their work. These experts in turn urge their organizations to adopt the applications, reinforcing transorganizational understandings about how the practice of management is to be done. Thus, the growing use of standard software contributes to the shaping of practitioners' identities and their identification with the communities of practitioners outside their organizations. In addition, driven in part by the relentless process of releasing software 'upgrades', packaged software use promotes the ongoing development of professional knowledge and standardized practices.

Professionalism supported and reinforced by IT has also accelerated in the information management domain. Professional associations such as the Association for Computing Machinery (ACM), the Association for Information Technology Professionals (formerly the Data Processing Management Institute and originally the National

Machine Accountants Association), and the Society for Information Management date back to the 1950s and 1960s. But the last two decades have seen a profound and rapid increase in the professionalism of the major IT-related occupations: IT operations, software development, project management, and the general management of the IT function.

The first book describing the methods of the IT Infrastructure Library (ITIL), which sought to codify practices related to the management of IT services, was published in 1989. Although widely adopted in Europe, ITIL was virtually unknown in the US until 2000, when ITIL v.2 was released and consultants began organizing US conferences and training. By 2006, however, CIO magazine was able to report that 'most [US] companies' were using ITIL, at least to some extent (Lynch 2006). The Capability Maturity Model (CMM), which defined a process for continuous improvement in software engineering, was first released in 1991. By 2004, large US organizations letting contracts for outsourced software development reportedly considered Level 5 (the highest level) of CMM assessment 'a condition for getting into the game'; as a result, some unscrupulous software providers were claimed to exaggerate their ratings in order to qualify for contracts (Koch 2004). The Project Management Institute (PMI) released the first version of its 'Book of Knowledge' in 1996. By 2005, PMI certification was considered a sign of a 'well qualified' IT project manager (Meyer 2005). Other IT professionalism initiatives include the IT Financial Management Association, founded in 1988, the Control Objectives for Business and Related Information Technology (COBIT), first published in 1996, and the IT Governance Institute, established in 1998. Today, every area of IT-related practice is supported by professional associations, trained practitioners, and IT applications that teach, standardize and enforce, or automate prescribed professional behaviours.

In summary, information technology has contributed to the professionalization of management over the last fifty years. In addition, information management itself has been professionalized—a process supported and reinforced by the use of IT—significantly during the last two decades. As a result, whereas the practice of information management was originally a craft occupation with practices customized by individuals and organizations, its increasing professionalization gives information management a transorganizational character. Among other consequences, professionalism facilitates the movement of IT workers among IT-using organizations. It also promotes externalization, discussed below. By externalization, I mean the movement of IT professionals out of IT-using organizations and into organizations that specialize in the provision of IT services. (See Lacity and Willcocks in this volume.)

THE EXTERNALIZATION OF IT WORK

The practice of information management evolved the way it did because of how it got started. Although executives at IBM reportedly saw little commercial potential in the first computers, large organizations disagreed and began to order them in the early 1950s. (Hirscheim and Klein, this volume, cited the introduction of the LEO—the Lyons Electronic Office—in 1951.) However, using the analogy of purchased consumer goods, the computing machines delivered to these pioneering users required more than a little assembly and came with few operating instructions. Furthermore, there was no pool of knowledgeable and experienced IT staff who could be employed to help. Basically, it was up to the organizations that bought computers to figure out how to train people to apply computers to business tasks. In the process, computer-using organizations began developing the procedures and methods that have since become the professional standards described in the preceding section.

It did not take long, however, for a market in software and services to emerge. The market was arguably launched by IBM's decision to unbundle software and services from its hardware sales in 1969. This move was motivated by the US Department of Justice's antitrust proceedings against the company. By the time those proceedings ended in 1982, the heyday of mainframes and of computer hardware generally was drawing to a close. Owing in no small part to the strategic vision of Bill Gates at Microsoft (incorporated in 1981), software soon generated the largest share of the profits in the information technology space. (Around 2000 Microsoft faced its own antitrust proceedings in the US and Europe over its bundling of the browser and search tools with the operating system.) IBM languished but was later turned around by Lou Gerstner (hired in 1993), who, among other transformative measures, emphasized IT services such as outsourcing.

Outsourcing IT operations and software maintenance had become a booming business since 1989, when a poorly performing Eastman Kodak Company shocked the business community by announcing its intention to outsource all IT activities. Similar major contracts were also being made in Europe. In the five years that followed, more than sixty organizations let major outsourcing contracts (Caldwell 1995). The decision to outsource IT was consistent with the business ideology of the time, in which 'sticking to our core business' and 're-engineering business processes to drive business value' were familiar mantras. Recall that Michael Hammer and Thomas Davenport published highly influential articles on business process re-engineering nearly simulta-neously in 1990.

The outsourcing movement was also likely spurred by the recession of 1990–1, when for the first time middle managers and white collar workers were laid off in massive numbers—victims of what the press erroneously called 're-engineering'. By the time the value of the Internet for delivering services became clear (Amazon was founded in 1995), the IT and business process outsourcing trend was well established. To empha-size this growing market, IBM launched its Global Business Systems division in 1996. Software vendors began promoting 'application hosting' and 'software-as-a-service'. For instance, start-up Salesforce.com first offered its customer relationship manage-ment software on a services basis in 1999; today its Force.com—an enterprise system development environment offered as a service—has become a phenomenon. The current popular vision is 'cloud computing', in which organizations are expected to access computing power and applications services that are distributed 'on the grid'. Although the services market suffered some deflation from the dot-com crash in 2000, it has continued to grow—much of it 'off-shore'. By 2004, IBM was promoting 'services science' as an emerging academic discipline.

While the services market was building steam, the market for corporate enterprise software applications exploded. Until the early 1990s, many large organizations had the policy of building all applications in house, and companies that wrote software target-ing large enterprises struggled. The tide began to turn in the early-middle 1990s, for several reasons. First, many companies were disappointed in their re-engineering efforts because of the inflexibility of their legacy systems. Their newly redesigned processes could not be implemented, since their custom-built systems were too expen-sive to change. Second, by the middle of the decade, the 'Year 2000 (Y2K) problem' finally came into general public awareness. Although IT specialists had been warning for years that legacy software programmed with two-digit date fields was vulnerable to failure at the turn of the millennium, their requests for funding to rewrite information systems fell on deaf ears in the aftermath of the 1990–1 recession. When corporate executives finally began to acknowledge Y2K risks, they also recognized the risks and expense of trying to rewrite the mass of legacy code with a tight and fixed deadline. Still another impetus for the purchase of packaged software was the impending launch of the Euro currency in 2002, which required major changes to legacy systems.

In the face of inflexible systems, the Y2K problem, and the Euro launch, implement-ing enterprise resource planning (ERP) system packages suddenly seemed the answer. (See Wagner and Newell in this volume.) ERP system vendors made presentations to CEOs and Boards of Directors, who sometimes concluded deals over the objections of their in-house IT staffs. By 1998, SAP was acknowledged the clear winner in the enterprise software space, and the consulting arms of leading consulting firms, which had grown tremendously from their enterprise system implementation services, began to sever their relationships with their audit partners. In 2001, Andersen Consulting became Accenture and made its initial public offering.

Enterprise software and the related services got another growth spurt as a result of notorious accounting scandals at Enron (2001) and WorldCom (2002). The US passed its Sarbanes–Oxley legislation in 2002, mandating evidence of rigorous internal con-trols, and many other countries soon followed suit. Enterprise software vendors argued that their systems had been thoroughly vetted; new enterprise systems were sold to manage compliance with Sarbanes–Oxley legislation.

Although many large companies continue to run enterprise systems (packaged or home-grown) in-house, the trend toward outsourcing appears to be increasing. The recession of 2001–3 and the current economic crisis undoubtedly deserve some credit. Although outsourcing may not reduce IT costs in the short run, it can allow companies to 'monetize' their IT investments and exchange fixed for variable costs. Other motiva-tions can also be discerned. Despite the recession, North American and European companies have experienced local shortages of skilled IT labour, while vast talent pools can be found overseas. Some Western companies have set up their own IT operations abroad, but others do not want to acquire the skills required to manage offshore IT personnel. These companies turn to IT service providers with their access to overseas talent and their managerial expertise. Current technologies allow IT service providers to run systems and processes for their clients in distant locations, if not seamlessly, at least with acceptable levels of reliability and quality.

Another outsourcing driver is the desire of many executives to achieve business agility, of which one type is the ability to grow quickly—and shrink quickly—as business conditions require. Appropriately designed outsourcing relationships can leverage the resources and capabilities of IT services providers to achieve that goal. The leading exemplar of outsourcing for scale is Bharti Airtel's outsourcing contract with IBM (IBM 2005), rumoured to have exceeded $2 billion. The Indian company's partnership with IBM, which gives IBM incentives to propose process changes and new automation that will improve Airtel's effectiveness, has allowed the telecommunications company to grow at phenomenal rates. Interestingly, while a number of Indian IT companies have entered the ranks of the world's largest IT service providers, IBM has become the largest provider of IT services to companies in India.

Observing these trends, more than a few high-tech analysts have predicted the demise of in-house IT operations. In 1987, a *Sloan Management Review* article proclaimed that the IS organization would 'wither away' as a result of outsourcing (Dearden 1987). In 2003, Nicholas Carr outraged the information management and MIS communities with a *Harvard Business Review* article entitled 'IT doesn't matter' (Carr 2003). In a recent book, *The Big Switch*, Carr argued that in-house IT organizations may survive in some form, but 'they will have little left to do after the bulk of business computing shifts out of private data centers and into "the cloud"' (Carr 2008: 118). To assess the plausibility of Carr's claim it is helpful to know to know what typically happens when IT services are performed in-house—the topic discussed next.

THE TRANSFORMATION IN IN-HOUSE IT SERVICES

The starting point for a discussion of in-house IT services is the changes that have occurred in organizational design and functioning over the last two decades. Although it may seem too obvious to mention, business has globalized considerably since the early 1990s (see Walsham in this volume), when the UN Council on Trade and Development began publishing data on the largest transnational enterprises. Although sceptics claim that most businesses are much less global than is commonly thought (Rugman and Verbeke 2004), there is little doubt that transnational business activity has increased substantially (Dunning, Fujita, and Yakova 2007) and continues to increase, according to the latest reports.

To a great extent, large corporations increased their global reach through mergers and acquisitions (M&A). An unprecedented boom of M&A activity began around 1995 and has continued almost unabated since then. There was an understandable fall-off in M&A activity during the 2001–2 recession, but it picked up shortly thereafter. Again, the current recession has put a damper on M&A activity, but many analysts expect it to resume as the economic situation improves. The scale of this activity is such that one scholar was motivated to ask in 2001 whether 'most of us [will] be working for giant enterprises by 2028' (Pryor 2001). Whether or not that will be the case, there is little doubt that the largest companies are huge: Siemens, for example, approaches 500,000, and Wal-Mart 1,000,000, employees worldwide. There are smaller countries!

Interestingly, while some organizations are growing larger, others appear to be shrinking as a result of outsourcing, virtual organizing, radical decentralization, and business networks connected by market and clan relations (see, for example, Malone 2004). Although evidence of the trend toward organizational unbundling is harder to come by, striking examples can be found. It seems possible that both giant enterprises and disaggregated networked enterprises can flourish side by side. A few years ago, a report from a leading consulting firm predicted that most industry segments would support only 3–5 global competitors: intermediate-sized companies would vanish, leaving a large number of regional or local players. Not explored in the report was the possibility that smaller organizations could band together to offer global business services that are comparable in scale and scope to those of the largest integrated organizations.

In a less well-noticed trend, organizations of all sizes in a number of different industries are getting together to develop standards, and sometimes also technologies and information services providers, to support joint business processes. For example, spearheaded by the Mortgage Bankers Association of America, organizations in all segments of the mortgage industry have come together to develop MISMO information systems and business process standards that enable electronic data exchange and 'all-electronic' mortgages (Markus et al. 2006). A related development was the creation of a new organization, MERS, to streamline the trading of loans by electronic means. This trend may accelerate the externalization of IT—not just to IT services providers as discussed earlier—but also to industry consortia governed by industry members.

Returning to the theme of globalization, one can see that transnational organizations are not only getting larger, they are changing how they manage their global operations. The multi*divisional* organizational form, first designed in the early twentieth century, has been the norm for multi-product, multi-market companies since the 1970s. However, in recent years, analysts have noted a distinct movement toward a different form they call the multi*dimensional* organization, which attempts to manage synergies across business units as well as the profitability of each (cf. Bartlett 1982; Galbraith 2000; Strikwerda and Stoelhorst 2009).

The management philosophy of multidivisional enterprises is one of decentralization. Each business unit is responsible for the profit and loss of some self-contained area of business activity. Therefore, the belief is, business unit managers need to control all activities—such as information systems—that contribute to the bottom line. The role of corporate headquarters in such an enterprise is to define the scope of the units' activities and to allocate capital to them. The strength of the multidivisional enterprise is its ability to accommodate different product technologies and different market demands. Its weakness is its tendency to promote competition among business units with overlapping technologies or markets.

The disadvantages of the multidivisional form became apparent to global organizations as a result of two previously discussed trends. First, as the customers of multidivisional enterprises themselves globalized, they demanded to be treated as single global entities. Second, multidivisional enterprises began to emphasize services and bundled 'solutions' of diverse products and services. Both trends required much greater coordination among formerly autonomous business units.

Global account management was plausibly the first major sign of change in the structure and functioning of multidivisional organizations (Yip and Masden 1996). In addition to products and markets, global organizations created new units, roles, and coordination mechanisms to ensure that business units cooperated in serving global, 'corporate' customers. And many enterprises found that they needed to manage even more organizational dimensions, including business processes, technologies, and projects. IBM, said to be one of the world's most complex organizations, manages six organizational dimensions (Galbraith 2009) as a 'globally integrated enterprise' (Palmisano 2006).

Managing the multidimensional organization involves, among other things, planning and performance measurement and reporting for each dimension as well as coordination of the interactions among the dimensions. That in turn requires a much more influential role for corporate headquarters, for information systems, and for the IT management function, than is common in the multidivisional organization (Goold and Campbell 2002). For the decentralized, multidivisional organization, MIS—meaning both integrated information systems and centralized control of information systems via a staff group—has been called 'a mirage' (Dearden 1972). But for the 'integrated', multidimensional organization, globally integrated (or at least *standardized*) enterprise systems and the shared services and planning organizations needed to support them are considered necessities. (See Galliers, Chan and Reich, Wagner and Newell, and Newell and Williams in this volume.)

The shared services organization for activities such as accounting and management information systems is not a new concept. One of the first documented cases of shared services was a finance unit in GE Canada in 1984 (Applegate 1989), and shared provision of IT services was described as the 'centrally-decentralized IS organization' in a 1990 *Harvard Business Review* article (von Simson 1990). Although shared services units superficially resemble simple centralization, they are distinguished by a strong customer service orientation, a menu of standardized service offerings, professional service-level agreements, and (occasionally) market-like pricing schemes—often institutionalized through adoption of ITIL practices. These arrangements are said to provide significant organizational benefits in terms of cost and service quality without infringing on business unit autonomy for product or market decisions. For example, accounting units are reported today to spend 40 per cent less on financial activities than they did in 1992 (Hackett Group 2009). Perhaps more significant than cost and service quality improvements, however, is the role that shared services units and standardized systems play in supporting the management of multidimensional organizations, such as Procter & Gamble (P&G) and Nestlé.

In the late 1990s, in response to serious performance problems, P&G announced a major organizational restructuring plan that set up global business units for various product families (Piskorski and Spadini 2007). As part of this reorganization, P&G created its Global Business Services division to provide more than seventy shared business services to all operating units from three worldwide locations. The division's first priority was to consolidate and standardize the majority of the company's information systems on a single shared SAP system. The services supported by this platform included not only traditional administrative processes such as human resource benefits, desktop IT support, and expense reporting, but also a number of business activities such as demand management, shopper intelligence, and packaging design (Weill, Soh, and Sia 2007). In 2002, P&G claimed to have received $500 million in savings since implementing ITIL discipline in its Global Business Services division four years previously (Dubie 2002).

Nestlé followed a similar course a few years later. In April 2000, the company's chief financial officer approved a $2.4 billion 'attempt to force its confederation of global businesses to operate as if they were a single entity'. As at P&G, significant changes in how Nestlé was structured and managed included a common global information system (also SAP) and a global shared services unit to provide standardized business processes throughout the company (Steinert-Threlkeld 2006). Both organizations subsequently outsourced major portions of these shared services to external service providers.

Procter & Gamble and Nestlé exhibit the convergence of trends discussed above: IT professionalism, externalization of IT work, and organizational design changes that have led to changes in the design of the organization as a whole and of the information management function. Thus, it appears that, in multidimensional organizations, organization design and governance are co-evolving with changes in IT and its governance.

Will all global enterprises follow a similar course? That seems unlikely, as far as outsourcing is concerned: organizations in which IT forms the product or a core service delivery mechanism (e.g. organizations in financial services, information products and services, research and high technology, transportation, etc.) are likely to retain at least the most strategic parts of their information management capabilities in house. In addition, some large enterprises undoubtedly have the scale to provide in-house information services as efficiently and professionally as external service providers. In 2008, for example, Intel had 5,700 IT employees (Intel 2008) for enterprise support in addition to the IT professionals involved in creating the IT-related company's products and services.

Furthermore, it is likely that many organizations will choose not to pursue consolidation and standardization of information technology and IT services to the extent that Procter & Gamble and Nestlé do. For example, The Dow Chemical Company has internationalized as much by joint ventures as by mergers and acquisitions. Having early decided to integrate and standardize its systems and business processes on an SAP platform, Dow Chemical later sought a more 'federated' approach for IT-enabled business with its joint ventures (Ross and Beath 2005). Some observers now believe that most large organizations will have several IT platforms, some managed in house, some externalized to service providers 'in the cloud', and some managed on a shared basis by industry consortia and professional associations.

Regardless of where and by whom IT and business process services are provided, organizations that use these services will need to continue managing their consumption, if not also their design and the related organizational changes. The roles of in-house IT professionals are shifting away from traditional activities of system design and operations; roles such as vendor management, customer relationship management, process redesign, and organizational change management are becoming more important. Central management and professionalism of IT staff appear to be increasing. IT staff concerned with 'enterprise systems' are less likely than formerly to report to business unit heads. Many in-house IT jobs are starting to resemble those of the client management personnel of external service providers. In-house IT services may not be 'withering away', but it is clear that they are changing.

THE FIELD OF MIS

What does this all mean for the academic field of MIS? Hirschheim and Klein (this volume) have traced the history of the Information Systems field; now those of us in the field must chart its future course. The simple answer is that MIS needs to change, although how the field should change is a topic for debate.

MIS is a field that arose to address the needs of organizations that began to apply computers at a time when external service providers and professional IT staff were few or non-existent. Reckoning from when the ENIAC computer was built (1946) and the LEO (Lyon's Electronic Office) introduced (1951), information technology is around 65 five years old today. The practice of information management arguably dates from the mid-1950s when computers were first used for commercial purposes. About ten years later, forty years ago, the field of MIS emerged through the teachings and writings of scholars such as C. W. Churchman, G. B. Davis, B. Langefors, E. Mumford, and F. Land. (See Hirschheim and Klein, this volume.)

The early concerns of information management practice and MIS scholarship centred on the development of information systems. The first MIS scholars tackled the challenges of building software applications and organizational processes in ways that would reliably meet the needs of clients and workers. That this was (and remains) a difficult task is nicely captured in the adage 'software is hard'. Yet, this problem no longer dominates MIS scholarship, as the contents of this volume attest. Yes, organizations still need to strategize about deploying specific IT applications to achieve business value and competitive advantage. (See Chan and Reich, and Wade, Piccoli, and Ives in this volume.) But software increasingly comes prepackaged as enterprise systems or outsourced services. As a result, software development has generally become the headache of specialist IT vendors and service providers; the organizations that use their services have different headaches now.

The field of MIS can adapt to the evolving trends in professionalization, externalization, and organizational information management in either, or both, of two ways. First, while continuing to focus on our historical constituency—organizations that use IT— we can de-emphasize the technical activities of applications development and infrastructure design and service provision and increase our attention to strategic considerations and the management of external information services and IT service providers, as the editors of this Handbook have done. Here, we may need to explicitly differentiate the information management requirements of different kinds of organizations, such as smaller enterprises that completely externalize their IT services, larger enterprises that collaborate with external partners in the provision of their IT services, and companies that deliver IT-based products and services to external customers that largely provision IT in house. Second, we can shift our focus from the needs of companies that use IT to the needs of companies that provide IT services. This would require an emphasis on entrepreneurship in the IT industry, for example the development, pricing, and support of commercial IT products and services (such as the mobile IT services discussed by Sørensen in this volume) and client or customer management. Many of the topics analysed in each stream would be the same, but the point of view and the practices emphasized would differ. Finally, we can attempt to combine both approaches. This would involve front-and-centre awareness that technology continues to evolve, creating opportunities and challenges for organizations that use IT products and services as well as for the companies that provide them. For example, the rise in Web 2.0 technologies creates both technical and organizational integration issues with which IT-using companies are currently struggling. Similarly, many large organizations like Procter & Gamble and Nestlé have just finished creating integrated enterprise system architectures and may now have to learn how to disassemble them into multiple, coordinated architectures comprising 'cloud' offerings and industry platforms in addition to in-house systems.

This volume suggests that the MIS field is predominantly taking the first course. Whether or not we turn more toward the second or the third, this brief historical excursion suggests that it is time for the MIS field and for information management practitioners to assess and possibly re-engineer our own 'legacy processes', not just those of other areas of management.

References

Applegate, L. M. (1989). *GE Canada: Designing a New Organization*. Boston, MA: Harvard Business School Case 9-189-138.

Bartlett, C. A. (1982). 'How Multinational Organizations Evolve', *Journal of Business Strategy*, 3(1): 20–32.

Caldwell, B. (1995). 'Outsourcing Megadeals: More than 60 Huge Contracts Signed since 1989 Prove They Work', *InformationWeek*, 6 November.

Carr, N. C. (2003). 'IT Doesn't Matter', *Harvard Business Review*, May: 41–9.

——(2008). *The Big Switch: Rewiring the World, From Edison to Google*. New York: W. W. Norton & Company.

Dearden, J. (1972). 'MIS is a Marriage', *Harvard Business Review*, 50(1): 90–9.

——(1987). 'The Withering away of the IS Organization', *Sloan Management Review*, 28(4): 87–91.

Dubie, D. (2002). 'Procter & Gamble Touts IT Services Model, Saves $500 Million', *Computerworld*, 1 October, <http://www.computerworld.com/s/article/74762/Procter_Gamble_touts_IT_services_model_saves_500_million?taxonomyId=14&pageNumber=1>, accessed 18 August 2009.

Dunning, J. H., Fujita, M., and Yakova, N. (2007). 'Some Macro-Data on the Regionalization/Globalisation Debate: A Comment on the Rugman/Verbeke Analysis', *Journal of International Business Studies*, 38: 177–99.

Galbraith, J. R. (2000). *Designing the Global Corporation*. San Francisco: Jossey-Bass.

——(2009). *Designing Matrix Organizations that Actually Work: How IBM, Procter & Gamble, and Others Design for Success*. San Francisco: Jossey-Bass.

Goold, M., and Campbell, A. (2002). *Designing Effective Organizations*. San Francisco, CA: Jossey-Bass.

Hackett Group. (2009). *Hackett Study: Finance Shared Services Now Standard Approach; Shared Services as a Cost-Cutting Tool Shows Dramatic Expansion*, 21 February, <http://www.thehackettgroup.com/about/alerts/alerts_2009/alert_02172009.jsp>, accessed 18 August 2009.

IBM. (2005). *Bharti Airtel: End-to-end Business Transformation Provides Flexibility for Rapid Growth*, 20 January <http://www-935.ibm.com/services/us/index.wss/casestudy/imc/a1008559?cntxt=a1000414>, accessed 18 August 2009.

Intel. (2008). *IT@Intel 2008 Information Technology Performance Report*, <http://download.intel.com/it/pdf/IT_2008_apr.pdf>, accessed 19 August 2009.

Koch, C. (2004). 'Software Quality: Bursting the CMM Hype', CIO.com, 1 March, <http://www.cio.com/article/32138/Software_Quality_Bursting_the_CMM_Hype>, accessed 5 August 2009.

Lynch, C. G. (2006). 'Management Report: Most Companies Adopting ITIL Practices', CIO.com, 1 March, <http://www.cio.com/article/17921/Management_Report_Most_Companies_Adopting_ITIL_Practices>, accessed 5 August 2009.

Malone, T. W. (2004). *The Future of Work: How the New Order of Business Will Shape Your Organization, Your Management Style and Your Life*. Boston, MA: Harvard Business School Press.

Markus, M. L., Steinfield, C., Wigand, R. T., and Minton, G. (2006). 'Industry-wide IS Standardization as Collective Action: The Case of the US Residential Mortgage Industry', *MIS Quarterly*, 30, Special Issue: 439–65.

Meyer, N. D. (2005). 'Understanding the Project Management Office', CIO.com, 25 September, <http://www.cio.com/article/12263/Understanding_the_Project_Management_Office>, accessed 5 August 2009.

Palmisano, S. J. (2006). 'The Globally Integrated Enterprise', *Foreign Affairs*, 85(3): 127–36.

Piskorski, M. J., and Spadini, A. L. (2007). *Procter & Gamble: Organization 2005 (A)*. Boston: Harvard Business School Case 9-707-519.

Pryor, F. L. (2001). 'Will Most of Us Be Working for Giant Enterprises by 2028?', *Journal of Economic Behavior and Organization*, 44: 363–82.

Ross, J. W., and Beath, C. M. (2005). *The Federated Broker Model at The Dow Chemical Company: Blending World Class Internal and External Capabilities*. Cambridge, MA: MIT Sloan CISR W.P. 355.

Rugman, A. M., and Verbeke, A. (2004). 'A Perspective on Regional and Global Strategies of Multinational Enterprises', *Journal of International Business Studies*, 35(1): 3–19.

Steinert-Threlkeld, T. (2006). 'Nestlé Pieces it Together', *Baseline*, January: 37–52.

Strikwerda, J., and Stoelhorst, J. W. (2009). 'The Emergence and Evolution of the Multidimensional Organization', *California Management Review*, 51(4): 11–31.

von Simson, E. M. (1990). 'The "Centrally Decentralized" IS Organization', *Harvard Business Review*, July–August: 158–62.

Weill, P., Soh, C., and Sia, S. K. (2007). *Governance of Global Shared Solutions at Procter & Gamble*. Cambridge, MA: MIT Sloan CISR Research Briefing, 7(3A).

Yip, G., and Masden, T. (1996). 'Global Account Management: The New Frontier in Relationship Marketing', *International Marketing Review*, 13(3): 24–42.

CHAPTER 2

···

TRACING THE HISTORY OF THE INFORMATION SYSTEMS FIELD

···

RUDY HIRSCHHEIM AND HEINZ K. KLEIN

'Those who do not know history are condemned to repeat it'
(Santayana)

INTRODUCTION

···

THE field of Information Systems (IS) has been around since the 1960s and has been evolving ever since. It formed from the nexus of computer science, management and organization theory, operations research, and accounting (Davis and Olson 1985: 13–14).[1] Each of these areas or disciplines brought a unique perspective to the application of computers to organizations, but each was also far broader in orientation. None focused specifically on the application of computers in organizations.

Because of its roots in multiple disciplines, it is hardly surprising that the field of IS is broad and embodies many themes and areas. Nor is it surprising that there is considerable disagreement about what the field actually includes and does not include, and what its core features are.[2] Mason and Mitroff (1973), for example, in their classic framework of IS, characterize the core components to be: psychological type (of the user), class of problems to be solved, organizational context, method of evidence generation and guarantor of evidence, and mode of presentation of the output. Ives, Hamilton, and Davis (1980) define IS in terms of five environments (external, organization, user, IS development, and IS operations), three processes (user, IS development, and IS operations), and an information subsystem. Lyytinen (1987) divides the field into nine components: the information system itself, IS operations environment,

IS development environment, user environment, organizational environment, external environment, use process, development process, and operations process. Swanson and Ramiller (1993) discuss the field in terms of the broad areas people write papers on: computer-supported cooperative work, information and interface, decision support and knowledge-based systems, systems projects, evaluation and control, users, economics and strategy, introduction and impact, and IS research. Others have used co-citation analyses to identify intellectual subfields upon which IS draws (cf. Culnan 1986, 1987; Culnan and Swanson 1986; Cheon, Lee, and Grover 1992). Culnan (1986) for instance, noted the existence of three categories of 'referents' upon which IS draws: fundamental theory (e.g. systems science); related applied disciplines (e.g. accounting, computer science, finance, management, and operations research); and underlying disciplines (anthropology, political science, psychology, sociology). Keen (1987) categorized the field in terms of the problem areas each historical era chose to focus on. For example, in the early 1970s the focus was on 'managing systems development, design methodologies, economics and computers'. In the mid-1970s the focus changed to 'decision support, managing organizational change, and implementation'. In the early 1980s the focus was on 'productivity tools, data base management, personal computing, organizational impacts of technology, and office technology'. And in the mid-1980s, it changed to 'telecommunications, competitive implications of information technology, expert systems, impact of IT on the nature of work' (Keen 1987: 1).[3]

Keen (1987: 3) goes on further to articulate what he thinks the mission of the field is:

> The mission of Information Systems research is to study the effective design, delivery, use and impact of information technologies in organizations and society. The term 'effective' seems key. Surely the IS community is explicitly concerned with improving the craft of design and the practice of management in the widest sense of both those terms. Similarly, it looks at information technologies in their context of real people in real organizations in a real society.

The growth of IS field over the past four decades has manifested itself in many ways. For example, as the field has grown, new specialties and research communities have emerged, and the level of research has increased dramatically. New journals, new conferences, new departments, and new IS programmes are indicative of the dramatic growth of the field.[4] We have witnessed the generation of a wealth of literature in information systems. On the whole, this literature can be characterized as diverse and pluralistic. There is diversity of problems addressed; diversity of theoretical foundations and 'referents'; and diversity of research methodologies (Benbasat and Weber 1996). Consider, for example, the phenomenon of IS implementation. It has been examined from such diverse perspectives as technical implementation (DeMarco 1978; Gane and Sarson 1979), planned change models of Lewin and Schein (Alter and Ginzberg 1978; Keen and Scott-Morton 1978), political theories (Wilensky 1967; Bardach 1977; Keen 1981; Newman and Rosenberg 1985), action learning (Argyris and Schon 1978; Kolb 1984; Heiskanen 1994), Marxist economic theory (Nygaard 1975; Sandberg 1985) and institutional economics (Alchian and Demsetz 1972; Williamson 1975;

Kemerer 1992; Heikkila 1995). To make matters worse, there are probably as many conflicting messages about what constitutes 'good IS implementation' as there are perspectives. Regardless of whether diversity is considered a blessing (e.g. Robey 1996; Galliers 2003) or a curse (e.g. Benbasat and Weber 1996), it is widely accepted as a hallmark of the field (Cooper 1988; Alavi, Carlson, and Brooke 1989; Banville and Landry 1989; Keen 1991; Orlikowski and Baroudi 1991; Swanson and Ramiller 1993; Markus 1997; Hirschheim and Klein 2003; King and Lyytinen 2006; Klein and Hirschheim 2008).

Beyond the field's diversity in terms of its multidisciplinary base, it is possible to note its development as it moves through different historical stages. For example, the earliest stage of the field might be thought of as the 'data-processing' period where IS was mainly treated as a tool to automate clerical work. During this time organizations adopted IS for the purpose of helping to automate tasks and reducing costs. Next came the stage when IS was used as a supporting tool to facilitate management in decision making. This was known as the period of 'management support' and embraced tools such as DSS, GSS, TPS, ES, etc., when organizations began to realize that IS added value to not only operations but also the management of organizations. As perhaps an extension to 'management support' came the period where IS was seen to help situate organizations in a competitive position against others in the marketplace. Many organizations believed IS functioned as a competitive weapon (Ives and Learmonth 1984) and could be used to increase their competitiveness (McFarlan 1981; Porter and Millar 1985; Clemons 1986), improve productivity (Hitt and Brynjolfsson 1996) and enhance performance (Brynjolfsson and Hitt 1996). Indeed, IS is thought to be strategic in today's organizations and executives speak of the importance of aligning their business strategy with IS strategy (Venkatraman 1991; Henderson and Venkatraman 1992; Chan et al. 1997; Sabherwal, Hirschheim, and Goles 2001).[5]

With such extensive development and advancement in the IS field, one would expect the field to have established a strong position in both practice and academia. However, that is not the case. Instead, the IS field continues to struggle (Mingers and Stowell 1997; Checkland and Holwell 1998; Benbasat and Zmud 2003; King and Lyytinen 2006). It continues to face questions about its identity and its legitimacy. Today, more than forty years after its conception, researchers in the field raise questions regarding 'whether IS is in crisis' (Hirschheim and Klein 2003), and 'what would happen if the IS field goes away?' (Markus 1999). In response to the dilemma faced by the field, IS researchers have tried to articulate 'what is IS' and 'how IS differs from other disciplines such as Computer Science and Management'. Early researchers such as Blumenthal (1969), Davis (1974), and Langefors (1974) provided conceptualizations of IS. But no agreement was ever reached and this helps to explain why we have such difficulty defining even today what IS is or is not. Other researchers such as Gorry and Scott Morton (1971), Mason and Mitroff (1973), Ives, Hamilton, and Davis (1980), and Nolan and Wetherbe (1980) attempted to categorize IS research and its boundaries through the development of frameworks. Again, numerous conflicting frameworks were proposed during different eras leading to the lack of a tacit agreement on the core of the field. It also explains why in fact, at various times different names such as MIS, IT, IS, DSS, information management, information science, etc., have been proposed to label the IS field (cf. Avgerou, Siemer, and Bjorn-Andersen 1999; Davis 2000), because each framework's architects thought to have discovered the true core of IS, but later the majority of IS researchers recognized that the new framework shed light on just another aspect of the proverbial elephant: the whole Gestalt of the field remained elusive. Such work shows continuous efforts to define and redefine IS to reflect the evolving boundaries of the field testifying that we still cannot define the field's identity in simple terms.

Thus, despite significant and seemingly continuous efforts toward defining the boundary of the IS field, the boundary remains fluid. On the one hand, such fluidity provides the field with the strength and flexibility to allow a wide variety of ideas to enter the field (Robey 1996; Davis 2000; Galliers 2003; Hirschheim and Klein 2003). On the other hand, this characteristic has led to what Banville and Landry (1989) describe as a 'fragmented adhocracy' where researchers adopt 'piece-meal research tactics' (Hirschheim, Klein, and Lyytinen 1996) and work on a wide variety of topics that are often quite disjointed (Bjørn-Andersen 1984; Benbasat and Weber 1996). The diversity ranges from the problems and topics addressed to the theoretical foundations and reference disciplines used to guide IS research and to the methods used in collecting, analysing, and interpreting data (Benbasat and Weber 1996). Such diversity often makes the field look disorganized (Lucas 1999) and raises the question of whether research in the IS field has contributed to a cumulative research tradition (Keen 1980). The 'fluid boundary' of the field also introduces the possibility of the field being dispersed into other disciplines, particularly in Business schools (Lucas 1999). Some Deans of Business schools contend that there is no need for a separate area of IS study (Lucas 1999; Watson, Sousa, and Junglas 2000). They argue that since IS is a service function to other organizational units such as Management and Marketing, research in IS should naturally occur within the context of problems faced by these business areas. As such, the study of IS should be taught as a service course by other fields. In fact, other disciplines in Business schools are already offering what might be perceived as 'IS courses'. For example, some Marketing departments offer courses in e-Commerce and data-mining, while Accounting departments offer courses in Accounting Information Systems.

The first step in trying to understand and resolve these issues is to step back and reflect on the history of the IS field. This chapter attempts to look at factors and events that led to the birth of the IS field, and traces how the field has changed over time and evolved to what it is today. It is hoped that IS researchers will make use of our work to help sort out what has happened in the IS field over the past forty years. Such an understanding would facilitate IS researchers in (1) answering the question 'what is IS?', (2) differentiating the IS field from other disciplines, and (3) developing a sense of an 'IS identity'.[6]

THE HISTORY OF IS

Since its inception in the mid-1960s (Davis 2000), the IS field has made significant progress. In order to capture the most significant changes of the last forty years, this section will divide IS history into four eras:[7] first era (1964–74), second era (1975–84), third era (1985–94), and fourth era (1995 onward), and discuss each era in turn. The delineation of these eras on first sight may appear to be somewhat arbitrary, but they are carefully chosen based on two principal considerations: *technology shifts* and *theoretical shifts*. The first aspect distinguishes eras by major changes of 'the nature of the technology and how it has been applied and managed' (DeSanctis, Dickson, and Price 2000; Hevner, Berndt, and Studnicki 2000). To some extent this aspect also captures what happened in industry (Davis 2000) and to a limited extent the technological changes in industry also reflect significant changes in academic eras. However, the academic evolution of IS has also been driven by internal forces, independently of and sometimes even in contradiction to industry trends. An example of the latter might be the concern with participatory system development or with proposing quality of work life as a major requirement for IS user acceptance (cf. Mumford 1983). Thus, an equally important aspect for determining era boundaries surrounds the theoretical shifts in thinking (cf. Mitroff 1983) within academia. Therefore, to characterize each era, the major development and advancements in (1) technology and (2) theory (including the typical research themes, influential school of thoughts, and research methodologies) are described first. This is followed by highlights of other significant events that can help to understand the flavour and '*Zeitgeist*' (spirit of) each era. These are (3) the emergence of IS degree programmes and professional societies plus (4) infrastructure advancements, in particular the establishment of peer refereed IS journals and of national and international of conferences, which are still influential.

First Era (1964–74)

After the first computer ('electronic calculator') applications with a business flavour had succeeded (with Lyon's Electronic Office (LEO) in 1951 and various logistics systems),[8] special IS groups or departments began to emerge in organizations at the beginning of this era. It is therefore typically taken to mark the beginning of MIS or IS as a discipline in business schools as opposed to the establishment of computer science concerned primarily with technology. At that time, the management of organizations saw the need for consolidating a variety of disparate processing functions each using incompatible hardware and software. The introduction of third-generation computers, in particular the 360 series computers by IBM in 1964, however, created an awareness of the need for standard platforms. The 360 computer series—followed by the development of integrated circuits and eventually, microprocessors—pushed along the advancement in information technologies. With an increase in the use of IS in organizations, academics began to see the need for formal IS education. The first university programme in business computing was developed by Börje Langefors at the Royal Institute of Technology and the University of Stockholm in Sweden in 1965 (Galliers and Whitley 2007). In 1967, Gordon Davis and Gary Dickson formed the first MIS programme in the USA at the University of Minnesota. At the same time, Frank Land introduced an information systems programme at the LSE in London. Concomitantly, several schools of thoughts emerged to lay the foundation of future IS research. These schools of thought included Churchman's systems thinking, Langefors's infological approach, Teichroew's automation concept, and Emery's socio-technical thinking. Formal curriculum guidelines were also formulated during this era by both the ACM and IFIP/BCS. Research efforts in this era concentrated on defining and conceptualizing IS. Researchers also studied decision support systems, information systems development, and human computer interface. As both industry and academics paid more attention to IS, several professional societies that were tangential to the IS field also began to attribute small parts of their activities to serve the needs of the emerging IS community.

Technology

IS organizations first appeared at the beginning of this era as organizations began using computers. During this time, the focus of organizations shifted slowly from mere automation of basic business processes of the 1950s and the early 1960s to consolidating control within the data processing function. To achieve that, organizations centralized their IS function to consist of routine data processing operations, with some inventory management and transaction processing systems. This function was, in most cases, led by the manager of computer operations who reported to the Controller of Accounting. There were few users, with most concentrated in Engineering and Accounting departments. The Engineering users performed CPU-intensive applications for number crunching, while the accounting users had I/O-intensive operations primarily for report generation. These users were relatively computer literate and could communicate well with computer personnel. Nearly all computing systems were developed internally by corporate programming staffs using an Assembler language or a standardized programming language such as COBOL or FORTRAN. These development processes tended to be highly technical and the systems usually took very long to develop and were very costly.

Mainframes were the dominant computers used in organizations as they had more speed and power to run complicated business transactions. However, each new model mainframe required new hardware and software. As a result, the computers were not compatible with each other. In 1964, the nature of the market changed when IBM introduced its 360 family of compatible computer systems. The 360 series introduced the notion of integrated, uniform computer system architecture across organizations, and highlighted the importance of software that was compatible across different platforms. The 360 series allowed organizations the alternative of purchasing low-capability models for business data processing. Along with IBM computers, new technologies such as the integrated circuit and microprocessor were also evolving. Gordon Moore, a co-founder of Intel, noted that integrated circuit density was doubling every year and predicted that by the end of this era all circuits of a mainframe could be implemented on a single chip. His observation was later known as the Moore's Law. In addition, the introduction of database technology, the development of direct-access storage devices (DASD) and the innovations in the realm of data communications (i.e. the Ethernet in 1973) allowed data transmission to extend outside the computer room for the first time, thus making networking a reality. All these innovations led to the decrease in the cost of hardware and software and therefore improved the cost/performance ratio of computing. Nonetheless, the rising corporate costs for computing drew the concern of senior management (cf. Somogyi and Galliers 1987).

Schools of Thought

During this era, many schools of thought emerged. They were the bases for what IS fundamentally was, and have greatly influenced the research direction and perspective of IS. They also span the range of technical and social IS camps. One of the earliest schools of thought can be attributed to C. West Churchman. Churchman, a philosopher at the University of California, Berkeley, is well known for his conceptualization of 'inquiring systems' that was founded on the systems approach.[9] He argues that in order for one to conceptualize a problem, one has to conduct an inquiry. This inquiry will address the nature of the problem and will collect information about the problem. According to Churchman, there are five types of inquiry systems: Leibnizian IS, Lockean IS, Kantian IS, Hegelian IS, and Singerian–Churchman IS. Each of these systems is distinct from the others and as a result, each will have a different representation of a problem and will produce different kinds of information. In addition, each of the systems will also have different methods to verify the content of the information produced. Churchman's thoughts on systems concept and inquiry systems were recorded in his (1971) and (1979) seminal works on *The Design of Inquiring Systems: Basic Concepts of Systems and Organization* and *The Systems Approach and Its Enemies* respectively.[10] Churchman's thoughts had great influence on early work in the area of IS development. Moreover, with the drive toward globalization, his thoughts will likely become even more useful as organizations start building global IS that are large and complex in nature.

Daniel Teichroew, at the University of Michigan, adopted a technical conceptualization of IS. He was concerned with the development of computer-based information processing systems by using the computer itself in the process, and by applying management science techniques to the problem. In the mid-1960s, he saw the need to build a system that would facilitate system developers in their work and decided to develop such tools to automate systems development. He envisioned a set of routines that would interact to automatically build computer systems. Teichroew's idea took shape in the form of a research project called the ISDOS project. This project involved the building of many pieces of software to automate systems development. However, only two of the major pieces were ever fully developed and implemented. These pieces were the Systems Optimization and Design Algorithm (SODA) and the Problem Statement Language/Problem Statement Analyzer (PSL/PSA). Fundamentally, Teichroew, was concerned was the automation of IS design including software generation from an exact 'problem statement' (expressed in PSL) using AI techniques. When this proved impossible the research moved to supporting the specification process, i.e. IS modelling. For Teichroew an IS was whatever could be specified consistently in a repository.[11] Even though Teichroew's ideas were never fully developed, his ideas were instrumental in the eventual development of CASE tools.

At about the same time, researchers in Europe began a stream of research based on hard systems thinking. Bjőre Langefors, an influential figure in Scandinavia countries, developed a rather theoretical view of IS from the system approach. He applied this view into his work on 'systemeering'[12] where he pioneered the infological approach to ISD. The basic idea of this approach is to differentiate between an 'infological problem' (i.e. what information should the system provide in order to satisfy users' information needs) and a 'datalogical problem' (i.e. how should the information and system be structured using IT) (Langefors 1974). His Infological equation was insightful: $I = i(D, S, t)$ where

I = the information produced by the system
D = the date made available by system processes
S = the recipient's prior knowledge and experience (world-view)
t = the time period during which interpretation process occurs
i = the interpretation process that produces information for a recipient based on both the data and the recipient's prior knowledge and experience.

Langefors's equation recognized that information is not simply the result of algorithmic processing. Rather, information included the result of prior knowledge and experience of the individual receiving the results of the processing data. As such, no two individuals would receive exactly the same information from one data processing. However, the equation acknowledged the fact that individuals having similar prior experience and knowledge could possibly share meaningful interpretations of the same data. Even though Langefors's work was criticized as being too rigid and mechanical (Kling and Scacchi 1982; Morgan 1986), his work paved the way for the dominance of Scandinavian research among the European IS research communities in the 1970s and the early 1980s. Such dominance explains why Langefors and Scandinavian researchers were key players in founding IFIP TC8 (Technical Committee of Information Systems). Langefors's ideology on the infological approach has also become the foundation for other approaches to ISD in the Scandinavian research community (Iivari and Lyytinen 1999).

In the late 1960s, Sherman Blumenthal undertook the task of documenting a process for the development and use of computer-based information systems for business organizations. His book *Management Information Systems: A Framework for Planning and Development* published in 1969 was most likely the first detailed North American treatment of the subject and might have rivalled Langefors work had Blumenthal lived long enough to finish his book and promote his ideas. In the end he died before the book was finished and it was left up to one of his colleagues to complete it. The result was bittersweet. While the book was indeed a comprehensive attempt at the development of IS theory, it never quite lived up Blumenthal's claim that his ideas were 'the long awaited intelligent, scientific approach to determining an organization's information needs and developing the kind of system that is responsive to sound decision making'. It would be more accurate to characterize Blumenthal's ideas primarily as a modular, incremental design strategy of building reporting and control information systems on top of transaction-based systems. His implied IS 'theory' was that of a parametric feedback loop hierarchy of the type envisioned by Forrester's Industrial Dynamics.

In the early 1960s, Emery and Trist began to work on extending previous thinking on hard systems. While studying the British coal industry, they found that existing thoughts on system development could not fully explain the phenomena they observed in their study. They contended system thinking was technical in nature and could not explain the impacts of systems on the work environment. They argued that in order to better understand the complete picture, one needs to also look at the social dimensions of the system. They used the term 'social-technical system' (STS) to capture the need to consider jointly social and technical issues in systems design (DeGreene 1973). The ideology of Emery and Trist has been very influential in Europe. In the early 1970s, Mumford took the idea of STS and applied it to the design and development of computer systems. This idea emphasizes the relationship between the technical systems and the social system and the necessity for working with both when designing a new production system. In the late 1970s and early 1980s, the focus of attention shifted from STS design and development towards STS implementation. This resulted in the emergence of 'participative design' that emphasized the importance of user participation in system development process, cf. Land and Hirschheim (1983).

At Lancaster University, a group of researchers led by Peter Checkland began to provide consulting services at British Aircraft Corporation during the 1970s. During his research in the company, Checkland found that 'hard system thinking' as applied in the 1960s by Churchman, Ackoff, and others in the Operations Research community could not explain many incidents that occurred in the company. Instead, he found that the complexity of the world not only made it difficult for hard systems to define their objectives precisely, it also made the results produced at the end of the project irrelevant. He therefore saw the need to find an explanation for the phenomena in the British Aircraft Corporation. By combining the sociological and philosophical ideas of Weber and Husserl respectively, Checkland added a phenomenological twist to the traditional hard systems thinking to introduce his famous Soft System Methodology (SSM) (Checkland 1972, 1981, 1999). The SSM is a learning system that provides a way of conceptualizing the social processes that a particular group of people is involved in within a particular organizational context. It stresses the importance of differentiating the various meanings attributed by individuals to the same phenomena. When applying SSM to IS, Checkland refers to IS as a *'meaning attribution system* in which people select certain data and get them processed to make them *meaningful in a particular context* in order to *support people who are engaged in purposeful action* [italics added]' (Checkland 1999: 53). To further understand the 'meaning attribution system' or the 'human activity system', Checkland proposed a seven-stage methodology (Checkland and Scholes 1990). His methodology has been adopted and adapted in a number of other approaches, cf. Schäfer et al.'s (1987) 'FAOR' and Avison and Wood-Harper's (1990) 'Multiview'. (See Stowell (1995) for a review of the contribution of Soft Systems Methodology to IS.)

Another research stream was begun by Gordon Davis and his colleagues at the University of Minnesota. This stream is not as theoretical as previous schools; rather it was the first truly empirical research stream in IS history. Davis, often referred to as the 'father of the [IS] field' in the USA (Sipior 1997), has been instrumental in the conceptualization, development, and advancement of the field of IS. In the 1960s when the field focused on data processing (DP), Davis envisioned the value and the need to extend DP to include an understanding of managers, organizations, information, systems (in general), and computer systems (in particular). He saw the need to add a business-oriented perspective to the notion of DP. To accomplish this, Davis envisioned a formal programme for teaching IS. In 1967, Davis and his colleagues (mainly Gary Dickson) began the first formal academic degree programmes (Ph.D.) in MIS in the United States at the University of Minnesota. Following the establishment of the programme, Davis and Dickson saw the need to have a close relationship with practitioners. To promote and facilitate such a relationship, they established the University of Minnesota Management Information Systems Research Center (MISRC) in 1968. Davis and Dickson have had significant impact on IS research, and what constitutes 'valid' IS research. Their interest in IS analysis and the behavioural aspects associated with it led them to conceive a series of laboratory experiments to develop a knowledge base about IT specifically on the topic of the relationship between the decision, the decision maker, and the IS supporting the decision. This proved to be very successful and has had a major impact on the field resulting in forming the foundation of the Decision Support Systems (DSS) research stream that continued into the mid-1980s (DSS research will be discussed next in the era of the 1970s). These experiments, best known as the Minnesota Experiments, resulted in a series of publications, the most famous of which was the paper by Dickson, Senn, and Chervany (1977) summarizing a set of ten experiments that were conducted over a period of eight years to examine the nature of IS on decision-making behaviours. These experiments are all firmly rooted in the empirical camp and are classically functionalist in orientation.

Table 2.1 summarizes the key 'Schools of Thought' and how each conceived of what an information systems was.

Research Themes

In this era, researchers put a great deal of effort into describing why IS was different from other disciplines. Dickson (1968: 17), for example, saw IS as a way to

Table 2.1 Key schools of thought

Original school of thought	Concept of information systems
Langefors (1966, 1973)	datalogical and infological systems
Blumenthal (1969)	reporting and control systems
Teichroew (1972, 1974); Yourdon (1978)	formal specified technical systems
Churchman (1971)	inquiry systems
Dickson (1968, 1981); Davis (1974)	behavioural systems
Mumford (1974); Mumford and Henshall (1978); Bostrom and Heinen (1977)	socio-technical systems
Checkland (1972, 1981)	human activity systems

'integrate . . . these techniques [e.g. operations research, systems analysis, integrated data processing and management] and to provide the analytical frames of reference and the methodologies necessary to meet the new management requisites'. Gordon Davis also saw the need to extend the notion of DP to include an understanding of managers, organizations, information, and computer systems. He intended to provide and define the idea of MIS in his classic book, *Management Information Systems: Conceptual Foundations, Structure and Development*. He defined IS as '[an] integrated, man/machine system for providing information to support the operations, management, and decision-making functions in an organization. The system utilizes computer hardware and software, manual procedure, management and decision models, and a data base' (Davis 1974: 5). Davis's book was the first textbook in the IS field. Other significant books that provided topical coverage of IS included Gregory and Van Horn (1960), Sharpe (1969), Sanders (1970), Li (1972), Coleman and Riley (1973), and Davis and Everest (1976).

Besides books, many framework articles appeared during this time period attempting to define IS by providing templates to guide the direction of research in the 1970s and into the 1980s. Mason and Mitroff (1973), for example, characterized IS from an individual perspective where they saw IS as composed of five main components: (1) the psychological type of the individual, (2) the classes of problems to be solved, (3) the method of evidence generation, (4) the organizational context, and (5) the mode of presentation of the output. Gorry and Scott-Morton (1971) argued that 'IS should exist only to support decisions' and suggested that IS should be looked at from a decision-making perspective. Lucas (1973) took an organizational approach and developed a model of the impact of situational, personal, and attitudinal variables on the systems usage and systems users. Chervany, Dickson, and Kozar (1972) proposed the relationship between decision outcomes and several input variables. Young (1968) developed a detailed model of organization as an adaptive total system and proposed that problems within organizations be treated with a 'total systems' approach. He therefore proposed a structure for 'total management information systems'.[13] Note that these early conceptual definitions of IS focused on 'elements making up the system of information storage and processing and the applications supported by the system . . . [These definitions] were based on the interaction of information technology, information systems, organizational systems, and individuals and groups employing or affected by the systems' (Davis 2000: 72–3).

While some were very enthusiastic about IS, some were not. Ackoff (1967), for example, outlined his concerns about the nature of IS. In his article *Management Misinformation Systems*, Ackoff warned against the widespread but false assumptions about IS. He argued that these false assumptions had led to major deficiencies in the resulting systems. Similarly, Tolliver (1971) presented his myths on pitfalls resulting from management being oversold on the advantages and capabilities of computers. Dearden (1972), in his article *MIS is a Mirage*, took a highly sceptical view of the MIS idea. Specifically, he questioned the existence of the systems approach as an independent field of specialization and doubted the practical feasibility of an integrated IS in supplying the needs of organizations. Brooker (1965) refuted the 'total systems approach' proposed by Young (1968) by arguing that systems theory functions were not the only analytical tool needed to explain and predict an organization's total performance. Instead, he proposed a 'human-oriented' theory of business. The disagreement between the supporting and the dissenting views of the IS field resulted in a series of debates on the efficacy of IS (Rappaport 1968; Emery and Sprague 1972). Nevertheless, overall, both IS academics and practitioners were generally enthusiastic about the emergence of IS.

The way IS researchers conceptualized IS (i.e. as a supporting tool in decision making as shown in the various definitions presented above) along with the series of laboratory experiments conducted in Minnesota formed the foundation of the DSS research stream[14] in the mid-1970s. The conceptual thinking of DSS was mostly influenced by early work of Michael Scott Morton (1971), Peter Keen (Keen and Scott Morton 1978), and John Bennett (1983). This line of thinking integrated behavioural decision making and cognitive science with ideas from mathematical modelling and operations research. Early DSS research sought to explain how to build an effective decision support system and whether a DSS actually improved decision quality and decision performance (Sprague 1980; Sprague and Carlson 1982). They argued that an unstructured decision process could be structured with the appropriate system. As the research developed, studies attempted to link the user's cognitive style to the design of a DSS as the decision maker who helped to design the system would ultimately be using the system (Zmud 1979). This issue was debated during the late 1970s and into the 1980s, with Huber and Robey debating the issue in *Management Science* in 1983. Individual and design characteristics were also debated throughout the development of DSS research in the attempt to determine how these features affected decision-making effectiveness. Mixed results have been found in the area of DSS, but researchers continued to investigate the linkage between design and individual characteristics and decision-making effectiveness. Researchers also continued to study how to reduce effort using DSS capabilities and guide efforts toward a favourable decision (Todd and Benbasat 1992, 1999).

Closely related to DSS research and Minnesota research has been the study of human-computer interactions. This stream of research seeks to understand how to build a system that is easy to use. Various results such as hypertext, ergonomics, screen displays, and graphical output emerged from this research (Shackel 1997). This research stream continues to undertake studies on how to develop systems that can empower users and present information in a manner that is relevant to the audience.

In addition, researchers also continued to show interest in studying the IS development (ISD) process. Research in this area was greatly influenced by Churchmanian 'hard' systems thinking. Many studies were conducted to examine each step of the Systems Development Life Cycle (SDLC) or the 'waterfall model' of the systems development processes (Daniels and Yeates 1971; Avison and Fitzgerald 1999). These studies focused on the technical dimensions of SDLC. However, this technical SDLC method has been criticized for failing to meet the needs of management, for its instability across the whole process, and for its inflexibility (Avison and Fitzgerald 1995). Research in ISD continued into the 1980s and 1990s (the research will be discussed under each of the era respectively).

Education/curriculum

During this era, IS grew outside of its shell of the 1950s and early 1960s where its main function was the automation of clerical tasks. IS now became more than simply a data processing tool; organizations began looking at IS as a potential tool to support decision making in organizations. As a result, the tasks performed by computers became more complex. Organizations began to realize that many individuals hired for IS jobs did not have the formal educational background adequate for their positions. The few who knew how to do IS jobs accumulated much of their knowledge through experience, most of which was mainly technical in nature. These individuals did not have an understanding of the integration between technology and organizations. As a consequence, organizations feared that as they grew more and more complex in the future, a point would be reached where these few individuals with experience would not have the knowledge and the skills required to perform their jobs efficiently and effectively. Even though other academic disciplines at that time offered courses related to computers, these courses were too specific in nature. For example, while Computer Sciences offered courses that emphasized algorithmic problem solving and Management offered courses on decision making based on the available data, neither of these programmes was designed to equip students with both the technical and the organizational knowledge required to perform an IS job.

ACM determined that the only way to solve the problem was to formulate a formal guideline of IS courses for higher education. However, there were no governmental college accreditation procedures in the USA that would govern such a process. So, the ACM formed a committee to draft and make recommendations for an IS programme appropriate for an entry-level position. The members of the committee included Dan Teichroew, Robert Ashenhurst, Dan Couger, Gordon Davis, James McKenney, Russell Armstrong, Robert Benjamin, John Lubin, Howard Morgan, and Frederic Tonge. After extensive discussions with representatives from industry and educational institutions, the first ACM graduate curriculum for IS was published in 1972 (Ashenhurst 1972). This curriculum attempted to add a new perspective to the IS field by integrating the IS knowledge (technically oriented) with organizational knowledge (managerially oriented) (Davis 1974). The curriculum report provided detailed course outlines for major new courses necessary for a professional programme in systems design, and recommended new fields of specialization for IS in existing educational programmes. In the following year, the ACM published the curriculum for an undergraduate IS degree programme under the leadership of Daniel Cougar (Cougar 1973). An updated version of the ACM curriculum was later published in 1982 (Nunamaker, Cougar, and Davis 1982). It should be noted that the ACM curriculum was only intended to provide guidance for the design of an IS programme with the expectation that individual schools would modify the specific courses to reflect their own identity. Even when schools stated that they were following the ACM curriculum, the ACM did not accredit the programmes nor attempt to enforce compliance of its guidelines. However, it should be noted that this was the first formal guideline marking the beginning of a shared educational format.

Besides the higher educational institutions in the USA, academic institutions in Europe also faced the same issue of the lack of formal educational guidelines for an IS degree. In 1968, the IFIP Technical Committee for Education (TC3) and the IFIP Administrative Data Processing Group (IAG) initiated a working group to prepare a suitable curriculum for an IS degree. Again, the objective was to provide an educational guideline that would prepare individuals for a professional career as information analysts and system designers. This curriculum was designed to accommodate individuals with different educational backgrounds and experiences. The curriculum was also designed in such a way that institutions in different countries could adopt it. However, unlike the curriculum proposed by the ACM, the IFIP/BCS curriculum required students to have practical experience as part of the programme. After six years of effort, the completed report was finally published in 1974 under the title 'An International Curriculum for Information System Designers' (Buckingham et al. 1987). In 1987, a revised version of the curriculum was published. Schools such as the London School of Economics, the Royal Military College of Science (Shrivenham), Hatfield Polytechnic, and North Staffordshire Polytechnic were the early adopters of the IFIP/BCS curriculum.

In addition to the formalization of degree guidelines, IS academics also began to recognize the importance of conducting research in the IS field. Besides the Minnesota school discussed above, the Massachusetts Institute of Technology (MIT) also formed its own Center for Information Systems Research (CISR) in 1974. Similar to the mission of MISRC, the mission of CISR was 'to develop concepts and frameworks... [that would] help executives address the IT-related challenges of leading increasingly dynamic, global, and information-intensive organizations'. Compared to the research at Minnesota, which was highly laboratory oriented at that time, most of the work at MIT was field-based research aimed at studying the management and use of IT in organizations (Canning 1979). Around the same time, other programmes also began at the University of Michigan, University of Pennsylvania, New York University, the University of California at Los Angeles, and the University of Colorado at Colorado Springs.

Infrastructure Advancements: Professional Societies

Prior to 1964, societies that were tangentially related to IS existed. These included the Institute of Management Science (TIMS), the Academy of Management, and the Association for Computing Machinery (ACM). During this era, other societies such as the Data Processing Management Association (DPMA), the Association for Systems Management (ASM), and the Society for Management Information Systems (SMIS) emerged to serve practitioners. At the same time, the American Institute for Decision Sciences (AIDS)[15] and the IFIP technical committee 8 (TC8)[16] were formed to serve academics. While IS was only a small subset of the overall activities in AIDS, it was the main focus in IFIP TC8. Specifically, IFIP TC8 was dedicated to promoting cooperation worldwide among IS researchers in studying IS-related issues and to increase understanding among practitioners about IS.

Second Era (1975–84)

In this second era, technological advancement continued to soar. The major advancement was the introduction of PCs (personal computers) by IBM. With the introduction of PCs, organizations began to distribute their computing/processing powers across organizations as the hardware cost of PCs was much cheaper compared to mainframes. Nevertheless, the operational costs continued to make leading organizations question the value of IT investment. Researchers began to conduct research to find out whether IS provided competitive advantage to organizations and whether user participation during systems development improved the success of systems implementation. In addition, the IS field held its first conferences (IRIS and ICIS), published its first IS journal (*MIS Quarterly*), and raised the issue of the need for new research methodologies.

Technology

In this era, business units other than the accounting and the engineering departments began to compete for computer resources. As the range of users broadened, organizations took a stronger management orientation to their traditionally technical-oriented approach to IS operations. They tried to address and satisfy user requirements by forming steering committees. Many organizations also began to involve users in their systems development projects where these users would help in determining application requirements as well as monitoring the deliverability of IT systems as developments took place (DeMarco 1978; Gane and Sarson 1979). Later, some users even took charge of IS projects. However, corporate level strategies for IT were not very well developed. Nor for that matter was there much discussion about alignment of IT with business strategy. Rather, individual functions or departments were developing IT applications of critical importance to their particular areas.

Computing technology had also evolved to the point where new processing options became available. Midrange and mini computers had arrived to enable organizations to process some applications locally. Still, most organizations relied on corporate mainframes for most core business applications. However, in 1981, the reliance on mainframe computers shifted with IBM's introduction of PCs. PCs made desktop computing a real possibility. These computers had open architectures and were available at lower individual unit cost compared to mainframes. As a result, organizations began to replace mainframes with PCs and used PCs to distribute processing power throughout their organizations. Organizations also began to redesign their business processes based on the new distributed computing architectures. While organizations continued to develop their own systems in-house, some commercial, externally developed software packages now became available.

Research themes

During this era, the effort to define the IS field continued. Nolan (1979), for example, presented a stage growth model of IS.[17] The model contained six stages: initiation, contagion, control, integration, database administration, and maturity. Ives, Hamilton, and Davis (1980) defined IS in terms of five IS environments (external, organization, user, IS development, and IS operations), three processes (user, IS development, and IS operations), and an information subsystem. Nolan and Wetherbe (1980) defined IS as an 'open system (technology) which transforms data, requests for information, and organizational resources (inputs) into information (outputs) in the context of an organization (environment of MIS) and provides a feedback system', while Keen (1987) categorized the IS field in terms of problem areas that each historical era (from the 1970s to the 1980s) chose to focus on. While these researchers tried to define IS from the perspective of different research areas, other researchers chose to search for the identity through the identification of reference disciplines. Culnan (1986, 1987), for instance, conducted co-citation analyses and identified three categories of 'referents' that IS research drew on. These referents were fundamental theory (e.g. systems science), related applied disciplines (e.g. management, finance), and underlying disciplines (e.g. sociology, psychology). However, one important point worth noting here was that the scope of the research in identifying the IS field expanded beyond those of the 1960s and 1970s. Whereas earlier frameworks (such as Mason and Mitroff, and Gorry and Scott-Morton) stopped with the identification of research areas, frameworks that surfaced in the 1980s evaluated the contribution of IS research. For example, Ives, Hamilton, and Davis (1980) categorized 331 doctoral dissertations into their framework while Nolan and Wetherbe (1980) tested their framework with samples from the IS literature.

In addition to working on defining the field, IS researchers also conducted research on a variety of diverse topics. One of these topics focused on examining the organizational impact of IT. As DeLone and McLean (1992) discussed the relationships between different surrogates for IS success, researchers have attempted to use a variety of dependent variables of 'success' at this level; the most famous being the group of researchers who attempted to determine the impact of IT on an organization's competitive advantage (Ives and Learmonth 1984; McFarlan 1984; Porter and Millar 1985; Rackoff, Wiseman, and Ullrich 1985; Clemons 1986). The concept of 'competitive advantage' originated at the Harvard Business School by Michael Porter. He proposed that in order for organizations to achieve competitive advantage, they could adopt two different strategies: (1) being a cost leader or (2) being a differentiator (Porter 1980). Research in this area has found that IT can function as a competitive weapon. However, IT in itself does not implicitly lead to the desired outcome. Rather, it is management's ability to conceive of, develop, and exploit IT applications that leads to a sustainable competitive advantage (Ives and Learmonth 1984; McFarlan 1984; Porter and Millar 1985). Further research has also concluded that the use of IT allows organizations to change their competitive boundaries in the marketplace (Parsons 1983; Cash and Konsynski 1985) and create organizational structures that are more nimble and able to adapt to the external environment more quickly (Huber 1990). This last result has initiated a widely debated issue on the causal link between the presence of IT and organizational change (Markus and Robey 1988). Some researchers argued for a direct link while others argued for a contingency view. Another research stream that studies organizational impact is research on the effect of IT on the economic performance of organizations (Mahmood and Mann 1993; Hitt and Brynjolfsson 1996). Researchers attempted to assess IT value through performance metrics such as return on investment (ROI) and market share. Results found in this area around this time show primarily no correlation between IT investment and improved performance (Barua and Mukhopadhyay 2000). This led Roach (1988, 1989) to coin the term 'IT productivity paradox' to capture the conflicting results. This research stream on IT productivity continued into the 1990s (additional discussion will be presented under the section on 'the era after the 1990s').

Participative design was another area of interest during the 1980s (Mumford 1981; Ives and Olson 1984; Hirschheim 1985; Cavaye 1995). This stream of research originated in the social-technical school led by Emery in the 1960s. Here, researchers such as Enid Mumford, Rudy Hirschheim, Frank Land, and Robert Bostrom applied the original STS ideas through user participation. Specifically, they studied how user participation during the systems development process led to a successful system implementation. While this research had mixed empirical results, it was clear that user involvement and participation are important in the systems development process. This research also tried to identify factors that increase involvement and participation and argued that by increasing involvement and participation, users will be more likely to accept and be satisfied with the system. To measure end-user satisfaction, a variety of researchers developed scales (Bailey and Pearson 1983; Ives, Olson, and Baroudi 1983;

Doll and Torkzadeh 1988) that assess the satisfaction of users. While user participation research around this time focused on the traditional system development process, in the 1990s research expanded to include the areas of the Internet and e-commerce.

Along the lines of user participation (i.e. focusing on individual users), a stream of research that studied user acceptance emerged in the late 1980s. This research, based mainly on Davis's (1989) Technology Acceptance Model (TAM), posits that users will intend to use a system based upon its perceived usefulness and perceived ease of use. This model has been investigated over the years in a variety of contexts using a number of technologies and has been found to predict up to 40 per cent of intentions to use (Davis and Venkatesh 2000). Other researchers in this area have attempted to refine what it means to 'use' a system (DeSanctis and Poole 1994; Chin, Gopal, and Salisbury 1997), arguing that the faithfulness of use is important as well. Besides user acceptance, Rogers's (1983) diffusion of innovation has also formed a considerable body of IS research in the study of IT diffusion. Specifically, researchers studied the rate, pattern, and factors that determine an organization's decision to adopt a particular innovation (Moore and Benbasat 1991; Fichman 2000).

In the area of ISD research, various sociological perspectives emerged to explain issues in ISD research. This is in contrast with the primarily technically focused perspective of the 1970s. These sociological perspectives come from Checkland's SSM, Emery's social-technical approach, and Kling's interactionist approach. Researchers such as Hirschheim, Klein, Iivari, and Lyytinen have done considerable work in this area (cf. Hirschheim, Klein, and Lyytinen 1995).

Research methodology

In 1984, researchers began expressing their concerns over research methods in IS. They questioned the adequacy of traditional research methods in investigating social needs and problems in IS research. To address this issue, IFIP Working Group 8.2[18] organized a colloquium that was held at the Manchester Business School in 1984. The conference, chaired by Enid Mumford, allowed researchers to 'look critically at the kinds of research associated up to now with information sciences, and ... [to discuss] the need for new approaches' (Fitzgerald et al. 1985). It also allowed researchers to 'call into question the notion of research in information systems being a science, in the same sense as research in the physical or natural sciences, and to ask whether the scientific research methodology is the only relevant methodology for information systems research or indeed whether it is an appropriate one at all' (Fitzgerald et al. 1985: 2). This colloquium not only marked a milestone in the effort to inaugurate additional research approaches that are needed to explain and understand IS (Lee, Liebenau, and DeGross 1997), it also demonstrated the willingness of IS researchers to appreciate the different approaches to IS research (Mumford et al. 1985).[19]

Education/curriculum

In 1981, a curriculum called the Data Processing Management Association (DPMA) Computer IS curriculum was published by DPMA Education Foundation (Adams and

Athey 1981). This curriculum had the same objective as the ACM and IFIP/BCS curricula, that is to provide a structure for an IS degree. The DPMA curriculum, however, differed from previous curricula in that it was initiated by practitioners who in turn defined the skills and education required for an entry-level position of data processing personnel. As such, it tended to be narrow and focused only on skill sets related to data processing. It also differed from the ACM curriculum as it required schools that adopt its curriculum to follow the structure without any modification. This requirement explained why the curriculum only had a significant impact on data processing education at the undergraduate level but not at the graduate level (Davis 2000). Also since this curriculum employed strict rules, it provided certification to schools that met the requirements of the curriculum.

Infrastructure advancements: conferences

The late 1970s and early 1980s marked another significant milestone in the history of IS, with the advent of the first IS conferences. In 1978, the first conference solely for the IS discipline[20]—Information Systems Research in Scandinavia (IRIS)—was launched. Primarily a Finnish event, the conference soon became Scandinavian, with increasing numbers of non-Scandinavians attending (Iivari and Lyytinen 1999). This was quickly followed by the first International Conference on Information Systems (ICIS),[21] which was held in Philadelphia, Pennsylvania, in 1980. The conference was supported by SMIS, TIMS, and ACM to serve primarily IS academicians along with invited IS practitioners. The objective of the conference was to provide a direction to IS research as it moved into the 1980s. Many significant issues were addressed during this conference. Peter Keen (Keen 1980), for example, stressed the importance of building a cumulative research tradition. To that extent, he urged researchers to identify the dependent variable of IS research and clarify the reference disciplines of the IS field. Davis (1980) discussed the roles of publication for tenure and promotion for IS academics while Dickson, Benbasat, and King (1980) identified problems, challenges, and opportunities for IS research. Their advice and concerns later became the subject of discussions and research for some time. While most conferences have been held in North America (mainly in the USA, with the exception of 1994 and 1997 in Canada), ICIS is internationally oriented and has been held in Europe (Denmark in 1990, the Netherlands in 1995, Finland in 1998, and Spain in 2002) and Australia (in 2000). It is to be held in Shanghai, China, in 2011. Today, ICIS attracts over a thousand leading academicians worldwide. Researchers welcome the conference as the presentations and panel discussions held during the conference provide a single place for researchers to get together to share and exchange their research ideas and knowledge. Through these interactions, researchers stimulate each other's thinking and nurture their research relationships. In addition to the presentations and panel discussions, ICIS has also organized various activities to guide newcomers in the field. For example, ICIS has doctoral consortia where Ph.D. students in their dissertation stage can get together to discuss their research areas and interests. ICIS also has junior faculty workshops where newly graduated Ph.D. students and assistant professors can discuss the problems they face in the process of building their careers. Recent ICIS sessions have brought together senior faculty to discuss and plan the direction of the IS field. All these activities are useful in building and shaping the future of the IS field.

Infrastructure advancements: journals

As more and more research was being conducted in the IS field, IS researchers began producing more articles and thus needed more journal space to publish their scholarly work. Until 1977, there was no publication outlet that was IS specific. Instead, IS researchers had to depend on journals that belonged to other disciplines such as *Management Science, Communications of the ACM (CACM)*, and *Academy of Management Journal* to get their IS articles published. As a result, some researchers were pressured to 'force-fit' their work to suit the style and themes of the particular journal[22] (Keen 1980: 10). Even then, many manuscripts were rejected because they did not fit closely enough with the focus of a particular journal. Facing these problems IS academicians saw the need to have a journal of their own. SMIS, which was short on products and services to offer its members at that time, welcomed the idea of a journal. So, with SMIS needing a service and product for its members and MISRC wanting to be the home for a journal in the IS area, the first journal that belonged to the IS field—*MIS Quarterly (MISQ)* was born. Gary Dickson, the founding editor of *MISQ*, stated in his first editorial note that MISQ 'attempts to break the new ground in the information systems field' (1977: p. iii) by providing a vehicle of communication for IS communities (Dickson 1982). During the early days of *MISQ*, there were two target audiences, the IS academics and the practitioners. However, the focus tended to be on practitioners[23] as the primary source of funding at that time came from SMIS, a society with primarily IS practitioners. Yet, *MISQ* strived to satisfy the need of both audiences by creating a two-section journal, one on Application and the other on Theory and Research. Dickson stated that the goal of *MISQ* was 'to be managerially oriented [to] . . . offer something of benefit to the practitioner . . . [and] at the same time . . . to provide a vehicle for the researchers working in the information systems field to communication with each other and with practitioners' (1977: p. iii). Over the years, *MISQ* has shifted its target audience from practitioners to academics. It has maintained its quality and reputation as the top IS journal of the field, highly regarded both within and outside the IS field (Jackson and Nath 1989; Gillenson and Stutz 1991; Walstrom, Hardgrave, and Wilson 1995) as well as both within North America and abroad (Chen and Hirschheim 2004).

Besides *MISQ*, another IS-oriented journal published by Elsevier Science, *Information and Management (I&M)*, emerged in 1977. *I&M* evolved from *Management Datamatics*, which in turn came from *Management Informatics*.[24] This journal had a new editorial focus and tended to have a more European flavour. In 1984, the *Journal of Management Information Systems* also began publication.

Third Era (1985–94)

During this era, IS began to gain more ground in organizations with the creation of separate IS departments. Another area where IS made an important leap was in the establishment of AIS (the Association for Information Systems), a professional society to represent the IS academic community. Furthermore, regional conferences, topic-specific conferences, and topic-specific journals also emerged and that helped researchers in the study of some specific research topics in IS. Research themes that emerged in this era included GDSS, IT value, and outsourcing.

Technology

This is the era where PC hardware, software, and telecommunications evolved rapidly. New products were continually being introduced with each more appealing than its predecessors. This phenomenon further improved the price/performance ratio of computer devices. As a result, many business units resorted to purchasing their own hardware and software to suit their departmental needs. This trend led to new problems of data incompatibility, connectivity, and integrity across functional departments. The dire need to provide improved access to corporate DP resources to users all over the organization and organization-wide connectivity led to the creation of separate IS departments. This IS department was responsible for maintaining organization-wide data, applications, and computer architecture as well as developing new systems for future needs. The head of the department was given the title of CIO. As competition became stiffer and profit margins shrank, organizations looked to outside vendors for IS solutions. At the same time, they began to align their corporate strategies with their IT strategies.

Research themes

In terms of research, the era saw the emergence of new research topics in addition to research areas from the previous era. New topics included implementation, strategy alignment, and outsourcing. The research stream on IT productivity continued the tradition of economics-based research of the 1980s. Contrary to the negative results found earlier, more recent research showed that IT significantly improves productivity. Nonetheless contradicting results continue. Researchers argue that the reason behind the contradicting results is due to the fact that economics-based approaches cannot pinpoint where and how IT impacts are created and where management action may be needed to increase the payoff from IT investments (Barua Kriebel, and Mukhopadhyay 1995; Barua and Mukhopadhyay 2000). Another perspective on measuring the value of IT progressed concurrently and independently. This perspective took the 'process-model' orientation and proposed a multiple dimensional approach to study IT value creation (Kauffman and Kriebel 1988; Banker and Kauffman 1991). This perspective can be seen as a complement to the earlier economics-based approach. Specifically, this perspective analyses the impact of IT and other factors through a network of relationships between various variables of interest.

The research stream that began in DSS shifted into the area of GDSS at the beginning of this era. The focus of GDSS is individual users and groups within organizations (Kramer and King 1988). Two universities, the University of Arizona and the University of Minnesota, have contributed significantly to the development of GDSS. However, each university adopted different research philosophies and methods when studying GDSS. The University of Arizona adopted the EMS model proposed by Jay Nunamaker, Alan Dennis, Benn Konsynski, Doug Vogel, Joe Valacich, and colleagues (1988). This model was grounded in an engineering world-view and believed that group performance and behaviour could be improved by imposing an efficient structure on the group through specific processes and technologies. The University of Minnesota, on the other hand, adopted the Adaptive Structuration Theory (AST) framework proposed by Michael Scott Poole and Gerardine DeSantics. This framework, grounded in a traditional social science world-view, believes that since each group appropriates technology in a unique way, it is important to understand how groups interact with and adopt technology. Even though early research in GDSS produced inconsistent results (Gray, Vogel, and Beauclair 1990; Rao and Jarvenpaa 1991), GDSS had been found to have impacts on some aspects of group processes and outcomes (Dennis et al. 1988; Nunamaker, Chen, and Purdin 1991). While the traditional focus of GDSS was to support management decision making, this research expanded into other types of technologies and users.

With the concern for various technical and sociological issues that arose as technologies were being introduced in organizations, researchers began studying the issue of IT implementation. This research stream stems mostly from a process-based view (Kwon and Zmud 1987), arguing that there are stages that the process of implementing technology progresses through. Cooper and Zmud (Cooper and Zmud 1990) present a famous model of implementation that includes the stages of initiation, adoption, adaptation, acceptance, routinization, and infusion. The implementation process has also been viewed from a variety of perspectives including politics (Markus 1983), a change perspective (Zmud and Cox 1979), a factor-based view (Zmud 1979; Aggarwal 1995), and social system view (Bostrom and Heinen 1977; Robey 1987).

As organizations got frustrated with the uncertainty of their IT investment and were faced with problems in their IT implementation, they began looking for a less expensive way to get the job done. They looked outside their organizations to vendors for solutions. With Kodak pioneering the first outsourcing contract, many organizations began to adopt the belief that outside vendors whose core competence was in IT would be able to provide more cost efficient and effective services (Loh and Venkatraman 1992). This trend initiated an outsourcing research stream that sought to understand various outsourcing issues such as motivation (Lacity and Hirschheim 1993; Hirschheim and Lacity 2000), scope (Gupta and Gupta 1992; Benko 1993), performance (Arnett and Jones 1994; Loh and Venkatraman 1995), insourcing-or-outsourcing (Reponen 1993; Meyer 1994), contract (Fitzgerald and Willcocks 1994) and partnership (Klepper, 1995; Grover,

Cheon, and Teng 1996). Recent research in this area has expanded to include offshore outsourcing (Rajkumar and Dawley 1998; Rajkumar and Mani 2001), backsourcing (Hirschheim 1998; Falaleeva 2003) and the study of the vendors' perspective (Fitzgerald and Willcocks 1994; Clark, Zmud, and McGray 1995).[25]

The decision to outsource shows a shift in IS strategy in organizations. Complemented by previous research on IT value and IT competitiveness, researchers began to study how to align business strategy and IT strategy (Henderson and Venkatraman 1992; Brown and Magill 1994; Chan et al. 1997; Sabherwal, Hirschheim, and Goles 2001), how IT and business units relate and formulate strategy (Sambamurthy and Zmud 1999), how business and IT plan (Teo and King 1999), and how IT accomplishes its tasks (Sambamurthy and Zmud 1998).

Research methodology

In this era IS researchers continued to pay attention to the importance of the state of IS research. In response, Harvard Business School organized a research colloquium discussing the state of IS as a field of study. A steering committee comprising James Cash, James McKenney, Warren McFarlan, Jack Rockart, Jay Nunamaker, Gordon Davis, and Richard Mason identified five subject areas that needed further attention. One of these subject areas was 'research methodology': qualitative research, experimental research, survey research, mathematical models, and software systems demonstrations. The methodology colloquia resulted in the publication of three volumes of research on qualitative research methods, survey research methods, and experimental research methods respectively.

In addition to the Harvard Business School colloquium, IFIP also continued its previous efforts to address issues on qualitative research. Another colloquium was held in Copenhagen in 1990 and the result was documented in the book, *IS Research: Contemporary Approaches and Emergent Tradition* (Nissen, Klein, and Hirschheim 1991).

Education/curriculum

As technology developed and requirements for skill level changed in organizations, academics also tried to ensure that they equipped future IS professionals with current and necessary skill sets. In 1987, a revised version of the IFIP/BCS curriculum was published. This revised curriculum updated the previous curriculum published in 1974 (Buckingham et al. 1987).

Infrastructure advancements: professional societies

As the IS field grew more diverse, IS research communities saw the need for a professional society to represent the field.[26] Such a need was first spelled out in an editorial authored by the first five editors-in-chief of the *MISQ* in March of 1993. IS communities envisioned the professional society providing a shared vision that would unify the diverse communities (Dickson et al. 1993). They also envisioned a society that would provide the leadership needed to lead the IS field (Dickson et al. 1993). Based on the hard work of many individuals, in 1994, the premier international association for IS academics, AIS, was formed. AIS has a governance structure that represents three international regions: (1) Americas, (2) Europe and Africa, and (3) Asia and the Pacific. Its leadership comes from various regions and rotates annually—Bill King (from the USA in 1995), Niels Bjorn-Anderson (from Europe in 1996), Ron Weber (from Asia/Pacific in 1997), Gordon Davis (from the USA in 1998), Bob Galliers (Europe/Africa in 1999), Michael Vitale (from Australia in 2000), Blake Ives (from the USA in 2001), Philip Ein-Dor (from Europe in 2002), K. K. Wei (from Asia/Pacific in 2003), Rick Watson (from the USA in 2004), Claudia Loebbecke (from Europe in 2005), Michael Myers (from Asia/Pacific in 2006), Dennis Galletta (from the USA in 2007), David Avison (from Europe 2008), Bernard Tan (from Asia/Pacific in 2009), and Joey George (from the USA in 2010).

Since its inception, AIS has worked to improve the IS field. For example, it publishes two electronic journals—*Communications of the Association for Information Systems* (*CAIS*) and *Journal of the Association for Information Systems* (*JAIS*). *CAIS* publishes tutorials, comments, and pedagogical articles that fall outside traditional research. *JAIS*, on the other hand, publishes traditional research articles. These electronic journals have moved the field into a different mode of publication. They lift the concern of limited journal space and reduces the turnaround time for the review process.[27]

AIS offers various other services to its members. The AIS-ICIS placement service, for example, provides a very useful service to both the institutions and Ph.D. candidates searching for jobs. AIS e-library provides access to AIS journals (*CAIS* and *JAIS*), AIS conference proceedings (both ICIS and AMCIS), and *MIS Quarterly*. AIS also sponsors the establishment of Special Interest Groups (SIGs). These groups bring together researchers who are interested in specific research areas and allow them the opportunity to exchange knowledge and ideas and to form a close relationship with each other. The focus of these groups includes, but is not limited to, human-computer interaction, E-business, knowledge management, cognitive research, Internet and network security, process automation, and management and agent-based IS, outsourcing, philosophy, etc. In addition, AIS forms loose affiliations with other international organizations such as SIGMIS, TC8 (IFIP), and INFORMS (formerly called TIMS and then ORSA/TIMS). It also runs ICIS and AMCIS and supports PACIS (Pacific-Asia Conference on Information Systems) and ECIS.

Apart from providing services to its members, AIS also works towards recognizing significant contribution by individuals to the IS field. In 1999, under Bob Galliers's leadership, it established two awards, (1) the LEO award for lifetime achievement and (2) Fellow of the AIS award, which are to be presented annually at ICIS. The former, which is the highest honour in the IS field, is presented to a very small number of truly outstanding individuals who have devoted themselves to the ongoing development of the IS field over the years; the latter recognizes major contributions made by individuals in national, regional, and international settings.

As envisioned by the committees who formed AIS, today AIS is recognized as *the* academy for the IS field. Through its various services, AIS has established an

administrative and legal structure for managing the IS community. It has also established a formalized political voice to lead the direction of IS research and IS education.

In addition to AIS, the launch of the ISWorld Net in 1994 marked another significant
milestone for the IS field. ISWorld was formed under the vision of Blake Ives. Today, it
is the premier communication and cooperation vehicle for the field. It provides various
resources such as information related to research, teaching, and professional activities;
an online directory of IS faculty members,[28] links (i.e. portal) to country-specific pages
and discussion lists. In 1998, ISWorld formed an alliance with AIS.[29] Such an alliance
unifies and coordinates the services provided to the IS community.

Infrastructure advancements: conferences

This era saw the emergence of a number of regional conferences. The European
Conference on Information Systems (ECIS), for example, was first held in 1993. As
noted by Galliers and Whitley (2007), the formation of ECIS can be traced back to two
independent initiatives to run a primarily European conference in IS. The first was led
by Dan Remenyi, then at Henley Management College, while the second arose from
discussions following the publication of the *European Journal of Information Systems*
by the UK's Operational Research Society. The editors of *EJIS* were based at the LSE
at the time, and Edgar Whitley began working with the OR Society to organize a
European conference that mirrored the new journal's focus. Having learned of both
initiatives, Frank Land worked to ensure that the merger of the two initiatives and ECIS
was born and held at Henley Management College. With the foundation of the
Association for Information Systems (AIS) in 1994, PACIS and ECIS were recognized
as regional AIS conferences and the Americas Conference on Information Systems
(AMCIS) was established to complement these already existing conferences. The
brainchild of Frank Land and Bob Galliers, the UK Academy for Information Systems
(UKAIS) was a separate but related development, and pre-dated AIS by a year. The first
Australasian Conference on Information Systems (ACIS) was held in 1990 while the
first Pacific-Asia Conference on Information Systems (PACIS) was held in 1993. Both
conferences have the objective of serving the interest of IS scholars from Australasia
and from the Asia Pacific Region respectively.[30] The first AMCIS was held in 1995 in
Pittsburgh, PA. Other conferences focusing on specific research areas are also being
held. Examples of these types of conferences are the International Conference on
Outsourcing of Information Services (ICOIS), the European Conference on e-Government, and the International Conference on Electronic Commerce.

Infrastructure advancements: journals

During this era, the number of professionals with an IS degree and the number of
programmes offering IS degrees increased dramatically. Concomitantly, the production of IS research by academics brought with it the need for more publication outlets.
With *MISQ* being the only high-quality IS-oriented journal, researchers began to seek
additional high-quality publication outlets. During ICIS in 1985, Chris Bullen, the
Chair of the TIMS College on IS, organized an informal discussion that led to the

establishment of an Ad Hoc Committee to investigate the need for a new journal. This committee was chaired by Bill King. Other members of the committee included Gordon Davis, E. Burton Swanson, Omar El Sawy, George Huber, Charles Kriebel, Robert Rouse, and Michael Treacy. The committee conducted a survey to 400 randomly selected IS faculties and received 196 responses that showed substantial support for a new journal. In the following ICIS, King and Bullen led a discussion to refine the idea of publishing a new IS journal. In the same year, King and Bullen formally proposed the idea to TIMS Council meeting in 1986. The proposal was approved and *Information Systems Research (ISR)* was established. It was published by the Institute for Operations Research and the Management Sciences (INFORMS, formerly TIMS)[31] and began publishing papers in 1990. *ISR* took a different focus from the early *MISQ*. It targeted research communities and focused on publishing 'theoretical and empirical works'. *ISR* publishes a variety of articles including 'those of organizational application of IT, conceptual work in IS, how different literatures may be jointly drawn upon to explain significant IS phenomena, theoretical analysis where the connection to IS practice is a strong one, good qualitative as well as quantitative, empirical research' (Swanson 1990). *ISR* is generally considered as the IS field's other top journal.

In Europe, several journals emerged to serve those whose research interests are broader than the more orthodox positivist camp which dominates IS research in North America. These journals included the *Journal of Information Technology (JIT)* published in 1986, the *European Journal of Information Systems (EJIS)*, the *Journal of Information Systems (JIS)*,[32] *Information & Organization* (formerly *Accounting, Management and Information Technologies*), and *Journal of Strategic Information Systems* which all started publishing in 1991. In Scandinavia, the *Scandinavian Journal of Information Systems (SJIS)* began publishing in 1988 as a place for Scandinavian researchers to publish their work. In Australia, the *Australian Journal of Information Systems (AJIS)* was formed in 1993. *AJIS* has now has changed its name to *Australasian Journal of Information Systems* to better reflect the wider arena of its author base.

Many topic-specific journals have emerged to serve the interests of particular research areas. For example, *Decision Support Systems* began in 1985 to support the DSS community, and the *Journal of Global Information Management* (JGIM) began in 1993 to serve the community whose interests lie in the area of global IT management and cross-cultural research.

Fourth Era (1995 Onwards)

This era marks a significant shift of IS technology and the business environment. The commercialization of the Internet enables new methods of communication and new ways of conducting business that were not possible in the previous eras. The Internet allows the dissemination of knowledge to different parts of the world regardless of time and space. Due to this changing environment, organizations started to modify their business strategies to take advantage of the new technological opportunities afforded by the Internet. Additionally, more focus was placed on aligning IS strategy with business strategy. As the focus of organizations shifted, new research topics emerged. Researchers now focus their attention in areas such as knowledge management, the Internet, virtual teams, and e-commerce. With globalization, researchers are encouraged to look at the areas of cross-cultural research and IS in developing countries. Further, IS communities are also becoming more receptive of interpretive research methods.

Technology

As organizations entered the mid-1990s, the focus turned from the invention and development of new technologies to reaching a 'critical mass' of this 'Internet age' (Hevner, Berndt, and Studnicki 2000). The commercialization of the Internet in 1995 dramatically changes the environment organizations compete in. The Internet provides a stage of connectivity where organizations are networked and constantly connected to their customers and suppliers. This eliminates previous concerns for differences in time and space. All these changes dissolve traditional organizational boundaries and make the traditional 'bricks-and-mortar' business model obsolete. In order to compete with new forms of organizations such as Amazon.com and eBay, many existing organizations are now re-engineering and consolidating their operations to move towards networked organizations. Intranets and extranets were developed to further support the re-engineering process. As the price/performance ratio for technology continues to improve, the use of PCs becomes pervasive within organizations. Organizations now equip their employees with various mobile technologies such as laptop computers, digital assistants (PDAs), mobile phones, etc., that allow their employees to extend their work beyond the formal workplace. Organizations have also shifted their focus to provide better services to their customers. To that end, they customize services and products to meet individual needs. The pervasiveness of technology means more challenges for IT managers to manage the widely distributed technologies, IT personnel, and users. The recent collapse of the 'dotcoms' tightens up the IT job markets and raises some questions of the viability of IS. Nonetheless, it is believed that technological advances will continue to push the world towards ubiquitous computing (Lyytinen and Yoo 2002).

Research themes

Most of the themes studied by researchers extended from the previous eras. However, the commercialization of the Internet began the streams of research that surrounds the Internet. Research in this area ranges from the investigation of general use of the Internet to the more specific business adoption of the Internet (i.e. e-commerce). These include the study of the adoption of the Internet/e-commerce (Iacovou, Benbasat, and Dexter 1995; Tan and Teo 2000; Chau and Jim 2002), the implementation of the Internet (Purba 2002), and the value and performance of the Internet (Applegate, McFarlan and McKenney 1996; Armstrong and Hagel 1996; Bakos and Nault 1997; Chatfield and Yetton 2000).

Globalization that began to expand during this era encouraged researchers to pay attention to environments other than one's home country. As a result, cross-cultural research in IT (Tricker 1999; Hunter and Beck 2000; Myers and Tan 2002; Straub et al. 2002) began to emerge. Generally, researchers investigated similar research topics as when they were focusing within one environment, except now researchers had to take into consideration the differences in culture. In addition, cross-cultural researchers began to pay more attention to IT in developing countries (Avgerou 2002; Heeks 2002; Walsham and Sahay 2006).

Both the commercialization of the Internet and the emergence of the phenomena of globalization bring another research stream: the study of virtual organizations and virtual teams (Saunders 2000). Researchers study issues such as the factors affecting the effectiveness of virtual teams (Jarvenpaa, Knoll, and Leidner 1984; Brandon and Pratt 1999; Duarte and Snyder 1999) and the performance of virtual teams (Citurs and Yoo 1999; Furst, Blackburn, and Rosen 1999). Further, with the changes in the business environment and strategy, organizations began to understand the significant implications of managing organizational knowledge. Researchers have also begun to pay more attention to the area of knowledge management (Davenport and Prusack 1997; Alavi and Leidner 1999; Alavi 2000) and IT personnel (Ang and Slaughter 2000).

Research methodology

This era further developed the state of IS research methodology. Prior to this era, IS research was primarily grounded on functionalist philosophical assumptions. Research that adopted this assumption was conducted using positivist research methods such as laboratory experiments and survey research methods, and was analysed using quantitative analysis. Interpretive research was virtually non-existent (Galliers and Land 1987; Orlikowski and Baroudi 1991; Alavi and Carlson 1992). However, this era marks tremendous progress in terms of the field's acceptance of interpretive research methods. In 1997, IFIP 8.2 held another colloquium in Philadelphia. The purpose of the colloquium was to take a 'self-reflective' and 'evaluative' stance to examine qualitative research and its history within the IS field (Lee, Liebenau, and DeGross 1997). Again, in 2000, IFIP 8.2 held another colloquium in Aalborg for qualitative researchers to discuss the issues they faced in their research. It was concluded from these two colloquia that the IS community is becoming more understanding and appreciative of other philosophical assumptions such as the interpretive and critical research paradigm and more journals are beginning to publish qualitative research. MISQ, for example, has devoted a special issue to address qualitative research (Markus and Lee 1999, 2000). Further, there have been publications of books on qualitative research. For example, an edited book on 'Qualitative Research in IS' by Eileen Trauth was published in 2001. In addition, conferences have also begun to organize workshops and panel discussions on qualitative research (Cash and Lawrence 1989; Nissen et al. 1991; Lee, Liebenau, and DeGross 1997; Myers and Walsham 1998; Trauth 2001). ICIS in the year 2001 had a specific panel discussion on confessional research (i.e. ethnography research). More recently, IFIP 8.2 held its fourth research colloquium on 'IS Research Methodologies' in Manchester (a twenty-year anniversary of the first Research Methods conference) to explore the progress of alternative research approaches (Kaplan et al. 2004).

Education/curriculum

In terms of curriculum, AIS, as the professional association of the IS community, took an active role in revising the existing curriculum. To that extent, AIS worked with ACM and AITP (formerly DPMA) to revise the curriculum. The result is the IS 1997 report that was published in the Winter 1997 issue of *Database*.

Infrastructure advancements: journals

As in the end of the previous era, many topic-specific journals have emerged to serve the interests of newly emerging research areas. For example, in the year 2000, the *Journal of Electronic Commerce Research* was published to serve researchers who study issues surrounding electronic commerce, while the *E-Journal on Information Systems in Developing Countries* (*EJISDC*) was established to publish research originating in developing countries. Additionally, *Information Systems Frontiers*—a more general IS journal—came on stream. *MIS Quarterly*, in an attempt to address the needs to be more 'practical', started publishing a new journal—*MISQ Executive*—which specifically focuses on more applied articles. It in many ways competes with journals such as *Sloan Management Review* and *California Management Review*. This era also saw a change in *Communications of the ACM*, previously a key publication outlet for scholarly IS research which morphed into an outlet for short articles appealing to the wider practitioner and academic computing communities.

Discipline critiques

Recently, the field has started to question its very existence and a rich debate has ensured. Markus (1999) openly wonders: 'what happens if the IS field as we know it goes away?' For her, the field is at a crossroads. On the one hand, it could become one of the most important areas for business since no organization can ignore the inexorable development and application of new information technology and expect to survive. On the other hand, there is a move to emasculate and devolve the field, moving IS tasks and skills into the business functions and/or overseas. Lucas (1999) supports Markus' concern noting that the migration of IS skills to other business disciplines is occurring. Hirschheim and Klein (2003) suggest another reason the skills are disappearing: the dramatic increase in the 'offshoring' of IS jobs to places like India, China, and Russia. Whether these concerns are real has been the subject of much debate; cf. Watson, Rosemann, and Stewart (1999); Benbasat and Zmud (2003), the special issue of the *Communications of the AIS* (Volume 12, 2003), and several papers appearing in *Journal of the AIS* commenting on the Benbasat and Zmud position (DeSanctis 2003; Galliers 2003; Robey 2003; Ives et al. 2004; Lyytinen and King 2004).

Another aspect of disciplinary critique which has also been widely debated involves the issue of *relevancy*. Markus (1997), in her IFIP8.2 keynote address, argued that one of the directions the field should take is 'the appreciation of practicality in IS research'. She felt that researchers in the IS field need to complement theoretical research with 'rigorous research that describes and evaluates what is going on in practice'. This was underscored by the conference theme of ICIS97 with its emphasis on 'the issue of relevance and relationship of IS research to practice' (Kumar 1997: p. xvii). In 1999, the editor-in-chief of *MISQ*, Allen Lee, announced a renewed thrust aimed 'at better imbuing rigorous research with the element of relevance to managers, consultants, and other practitioners' (Lee 1999a: p. viii). The discussions presented in Applegate and King (1999), Benbasat and Zmud (1999), Lyytinen (1999), and Lee (1999b) supported this thrust. In March 2001, *Communications of the AIS* (Volume 6) had a special issue on 'Relevancy'. The interest in the topic of relevance vs. rigour continues even more recently (King and Lyytinen 2006).[33]

DISCUSSION

The IS field has made significant progress since the 1960s and has, in the view of some, 'fully emerged as a discipline in its own right' (Baskerville and Myers 2002). Many universities now offer an IS degree at both the undergraduate and graduate levels. In fact, the number of degree programmes has increased tremendously over the years as a result of the growing need for IS skills in industry (Watson, Rosemann, and Stewart 1999; Abraham et al. 2006). The field has also tried to educate the business community as a whole on what it needs to know about IS (Ives et al. 2002).

The IS field has also begun to accumulate its own distinctive subject matter and now studies a wide range of issues surrounding technology within an organizational context. Examples of research themes that have emerged are DSS, GDSS, organizational impact of IS, user acceptance, ISD, IS implementation, outsourcing, etc. A cumulative research tradition is also evident as current and previous IS research have served as a foundation for further IS research. The field has also begun to embrace different research perspectives in addition to the traditional positivist stance. Compared to the time when the field first began, the IS field is now more receptive to interpretive, action, and critical research. An indication of this is *MISQ*'s publication of a *Special Issue on Intensive Research in Information Systems* over three volumes (Markus and Lee 1999; Markus 2000). Further, the IS field has produced well-known scholars. These scholars have published a variety of exemplar articles that are highly influential and widely cited. Markus's (1983) article on *Power, Politics and MIS Implementation*, for example, has been cited more than 200 times since 1993 by researchers from a variety of disciplines such as communication, human resources, organization change management, sociology, manufacturing, medical informatics, and urban planning (Baskerville and Myers 2002).

Moreover, the field has journals such as *MISQ* and *ISR* that publish IS-oriented articles. These two journals have grown in quality over the years and have established reputations as top IS scholarly journals both within and outside the field (Watson, Rosemann, and Stewart 1999). The same can also be said of newer journals such as *JAIS* and *JMIS* as well as the more 'European' journals such as *EJIS, ISJ, JSIS, JIT,* and *Information and Organization*. Indeed, the field of IS has become truly global with IS conferences and journals being produced across the globe. Each of these regions has its own history of IS, some of which have been well documented (cf. Avgerou, Siemer, and Bjorn-Andersen 1999; Iivari and Lyytinen 1999; Galliers and Whitley 2007; Gable, Gregor, and Smyth 2008).[34]

The field has its own international society (AIS) that functions as a 'political voice' for the IS community. AIS has provided leadership and various services that are contributing to the unification and the development of the field. Further, the field has other services such as special work groups and ISWorld that equip IS researchers with better resources. Collectively, these form an excellent communication network for IS scholars to interact with each other, to share knowledge, and to build research relationships.

The IS community has set its own standards and procedures to measure the performance of IS academics. For example, journal rankings are used to measure the quality of publications. This measurement, while not perfect, is in turn used for tenure and promotion purposes. The IS community recognizes and supports the establishment of such standards as a way to make the tenure and promotion process more transparent.

But whilst the field has achieved a certain level of maturity, there is considerable diversity amongst its members in terms of research interests, research communities, and beliefs about what belongs and does not belong in the field (Klein and Hirschheim 2008). Such diversity can be seen as valuable if we see it as evidence of past progress. Only by knowing and understanding the many streams which have shaped the current landscape can we collectively prepare for the field's future even if we cannot agree what the best future or futures might be. Perhaps a shared sense of history is more effective in helping with bridging the communication gaps than with obtaining consensus on preferred forms of knowledge creation. Isn't it easier for all of us to agree on what has been accomplished by the field in the past than on what we should do in the future for advancing knowledge creation?

By seeing alternative visions of the discipline's future against a *shared historical backdrop*, each of us can obtain a sense of the larger meaning of our individual contributions and a better understanding of the potential contribution of the work of others. We believe that a better grasp of IS history is a more feasible strategy for improving mutual understanding between differing communities. The field would benefit in addressing its current and future issues if we could align our perspectives at least about *past* accomplishments even if we continue to disagree about current and future research priorities and strategy. This would not only nurture identity-forming discussions about historical controversies but also facilitate boundary spanning amongst the field's diverse communities for the following reasons. (1) Historical analyses lead to shared concepts, (2) a shared history makes communications easier across boundaries, (3) a shared history forms emotional bonds and commitments, and (4) historical awareness supports reflection and critical distance to the present helping to divorce discussions from personality conflicts and various forms of dogmatism. We hope our attempt at offering an IS history will help the field develop such a shared understanding. It is long overdue.

ACKNOWLEDGEMENT

We are indebted to Siew Fan Wong for her assistance in gathering much of the material for the four eras identified in this chapter.

NOTES

1. Another area that is often thought to be significant for the growth of IS is systems theory. Additionally, disciplines such as psychology, anthropology, economics, sociology, political cal science, and architecture are considered to have had an impact on the IS field.
2. Or indeed whether there is a 'core' at all (cf. Lyytinen and King 2004). See also Lyytinen and King (2006) and Weber (2006).
3. A similar historical analysis can be found in Friedman and Cornford (1989), who specifically focus on the evolution and growth of the systems analyst and the systems analysis function.
4. Although the field has been experiencing a decline of late in terms of IS majors (cf. George, Valacich, and Valor 2005; Hirschheim et al. 2007).
5. On the other hand, the explosive growth of IT outsourcing might suggest otherwise (cf. Lacity and Hirschheim 1993; Dibbern et al. 2004).
6. It is somewhat surprising to us that the discipline of IS has few published reflective pieces tracing the historical roots of the field. We are not sure whether the field considers itself too young to need such a reflection or whether there simply are not enough 'old timers' around who could provide such a view. Whatever the case, we believe this to be a serious shortcoming of the IS discipline.
7. Note that this chapter does not discuss the era before 1964 as most of the academic work in IS only began during the mid-1960s.
8. See e.g. Caminer et al. (1998), Aris, Land, and Maller (2003), and Ferry (2003).
9. Systems thinking is a mode of inquiry which focuses on synthesis. At the core of systems thinking lies the concept of an 'adaptive whole'—a whole entity which can adapt and survive, within limits, in a changing environment.
10. Mitroff and Sagasti wrote an article in 1973 that summarized Churchman's idea on inquiry systems.

11. De facto this was very similar to what Yourdon (1978) tried to teach with manual specifications even though Teichroew claimed that the ISDOS project was independent of any specific methodology.
12. Systemeering is the early non-English word which refers to ISD.
13. Researchers such as Blumenthal have argued that the concept of 'total management information systems' commenced with a sometimes naive, sometimes sophisticated theory of the firm. Blumenthal said that attempts towards total MIS fell short of translating what is merely perspective and overview into something concrete, in the form of a comprehensive and integrated corporate-wide plan.
14. Research on IT support for decision making originated in the 1960s with the work by Herbert Simon, Allan Newell, and their colleagues. In fact, their work established a behavioural perspective on the relationship between IT and decision making. The development of management science and operations research around the same time frame provided the mathematical framework for DSS research.
15. AIDS was later changed to DSI.
16. TC8 was formed by IFIP. Among those who founded this society included Langefors and other Scandinavian communities who dominated the European IS community at that time.
17. Note that even though other researchers have found that Nolan's (1979) stage model is inconsistent with empirical studies, Nolan's model has been widely adopted by practitioners because it made sense and because it gave managers a tool for proactive control over the IS function.
18. Note that the area of interest and focus of IFIP Working Group 8.2 is the relationships and interactions between IS, IT, organizations, and society.
19. Even Davis said this colloquium altered his once only positivist view of IS research. He stated that now he believes a 'world-class scholar must be competent in both hypothesis testing using quantitative data and qualitative, interpretive methods using observations, interviews, and participations (2000: 80).
20. Before IRIS or ICIS, a popular conference which supported IS research was the Hawaiian International Conference on System Sciences (HICSS). While somewhat broader than just IS, it started in the late 1960s, and continues to bring together members of the IS community on an annual basis.
21. Note that the name ICIS came in the mid-1980s. Initially, the conference was simply called 'Conference on Information Systems'.
22. *Management Science*, for example, was mainly quantitative in orientation; *CACM* published computer science (technical material) *Academy of Management Journal/Academy of Management Review* published decision-making research or organizational studies. Periodicals such as *Datamation* and *Journal of Systems Management* were practitioner oriented.
23. Even though the primary referees of the articles published under the 'Theory and Research' section of *MISQ* were academicians, a practitioner referee was also on duty to make the judgement as to whether or not the articles had any practical value (Dickson 1982).
24. *Management Datamatics* and *Management Informatics* were no longer in publication.
25. See Lacity, Kahn, and Willcocks (2009) for a review.
26. During this time, there was no professional society that was IS oriented. Instead, IS communities joined other societies such as DSI, TIMS, etc.

27. For a paper journal, a turnaround time of two to three years is not atypical.
28. The Americas database online access was developed by Janice DeGross, David Naumann, and Jesper Johansson. Europe/Africa and Pacific/Asia directories were developed by Niels Bjørn-Andersen and Guy Gable.
29. Two main reasons that led to the formation of the alliance between ISWorld Net and AIS: (1) Lack of support to develop and maintain Web repositories and the list server and (2) Lack of resources to support the operations of ISWorld Net.
30. With the exception of PACIS, the rest of the conferences are held annually.
31. Note that at that time, the Institute for Operations Research and the Management Sciences (INFORMS) had already published many scholarly journals for specific areas. For example, *Management Science* was publishing OR-related articles; *Organization Science* was publishing organizational-related articles; and *Marketing Science* was publishing marketing-related articles.
32. *The Journal of Information Systems* has changed its name to *Information Systems Journal*.
33. An interesting anomaly of this 'call for relevancy' is that much European IS research is curiously considered by North Americans to be too practically focused and lacking in rigour. Many European and Australasian IS researchers have been quick to point out the irony in this relevancy plea by the North Americans.
34. In fact, the Gable, Gregor, and Smyth (2008) book might serve as a model of how the rest of the world could document its specific IS history.

REFERENCES

Ackoff, R. (1967). 'Management Misinformation Systems', *Management Science* (December): B147–56.

Adams, D. R., and Athey, J. H. (eds.) (1981). *DPMA Model Curriculum for Undergraduate Computer Information Systems Education*, DPMA, Park Ridge, USA (Document ED239584).

Aggarwal, S. (1995). 'Flexibility Management: The Ultimate Strategy', *Industrial Management*, 37(6): 20–6.

Alavi, M. (2000). 'Managing Organizational Knowledge', in R. W. Zmud (ed.), *Framing the Domains of IT Management: Projecting the Future . . . Through the Past*. Cincinnati, OH: Pinnaflex Educational Resources.

——and Carlson, P. (1992). 'A Review of MIS Research and Disciplinary Development', *Journal of Management Information Systems*, 8(4): 45–62.

———and Brooke, G. (1989). 'The Ecology of MIS Research: A Twenty Year Review', in J. I. DeGross, J. C. Henderson, and B. R. Konsynski (eds.), *Proceedings of the Tenth International Conference on Information Systems*, Boston, MA: MIT, 363–75.

——and Leidner, D. E. (1999), 'Knowledge Management Systems: Issues, Challenges, and Benefits', *Communications of the Association for Information Systems*, 1(7): 1–37.

Alchian, A., and Demsetz, H. (1972). 'Production, Information Costs and Economic Organizations', *American Economic Review*, 62(5): 777–95.

Alter, S., and Ginzberg, M. J. (1978). 'Managing Uncertainty in MIS Implementation', *Sloan Management Review*, 19: 23–31.

Ang, S., and Slaughter, S. (2000). 'The Missing Context of Information Technology Personnel: A Review and Future Directions for Research', in R. W. Zmud (ed.), *Framing the Domains of IT Management: Projecting the Future from the Past*. Cincinnati: Pinnaflex Educational Resources.

Applegate, L., and King, J. (1999). 'Rigor and Relevance: Careers on the Line', *MIS Quarterly*, 23(1): 17–18.

——McFarlan, W., and McKenney, J. (1996). *Corporate Information Management: Text and Cases*. Boston: Irwin/McGraw-Hill.

Argyris, C., and Schon, D. (1978). *Organizational Learning: A Theory of Action Perspective*. Reading: Addison-Wesley.

Aris, J., Land, F., and Maller, V. (eds.) (2003). 'Special issue: LEO Conference 2001', *Journal of Strategic Information Systems*, 12(4): 253–395.

Armstrong, A., and Hagel III, J. (1996). 'The Real Value of Online Communities', *Harvard Business Review* (May/June): 134–40.

Arnett, K. P., and M. C. Jones (1994). 'Firms that Choose Outsourcing: A Profile', *Information & Management*, 26: 179–88.

Ashenhurst, R. L. (1972). 'Curriculum Recommendations for Graduate Professional Programs in Information Systems', *Communications of the ACM*, 15(5): 364–98.

Avgerou, C. (2002). *Information Systems and Global Diversity*. Oxford: Oxford University Press.

——Siemer, J., and Bjorn-Andersen, N. (1999). 'The Academic Field of Information Systems in Europe', *European Journal of Information Systems*, 8(2): 136–53.

Avison, D. E. and Fitzgerald, G. (1995). *Information Systems Development: Methodologies, Techniques and Tools*. 2nd edn., New York: McGraw-Hill.

————(1999). 'Information Systems Development,' in W. L. Currie and R. D. Galliers (eds.), *Rethinking Management Information Systems: An Interdisciplinary Perspective*. New York: Oxford University Press, 250–78.

——and Wood-Harper, A. T. (1990). *MULTIVIEW: An Exploration in Information Systems Development*. London: Blackwell Scientific Publications.

Bailey, J., and Pearson, S. (1983). 'Development of a Tool for Measuring and Analyzing Computer User Satisfaction', *Management Science*, 29(5): 530–45.

Bakos, J. Y., and Nault, B. R. (1997). 'Ownership and Investment in Electronic Networks', *Information Systems Research*, 8(4): 321–41.

Banker, R., and Kauffman, R. (1991). 'Quantifying the Business Value of Information Technology: An Illustration of the "Business Value Linkage" Framework', *NYU working paper no. IS-91-21*, August.

Banville, C., and Landry, M. (1989). 'Can the Field of MIS be Disciplined?', *Communications of the ACM*, 32(1): 48–60.

Bardach, E. (1977). *The Implementation Game*. Cambridge, MA: MIT Press.

Barua A., Kriebel C., and Mukhopadhyay T. (1995). 'Information Technology and Business Value: An Analytic and Empirical Investigation', *Information Systems Research*, 7(4).

——and Mukhopadhyay, T. (2000). 'Information Technology and Business Performance: Past, Present, and Future', in R. W. Zmud, *Framing the Domains of IT Research: Projecting the Future through the Past*. Cincinnati, OH: Pinnaflex Educational Resources, 65–84.

Baskerville, R. L. and Myers, M. D. (2002). 'Information Systems as a Reference Discipline', *MIS Quarterly*, 26(1): 1–14.

Benbasat, I., and Weber, R. (1996). 'Rethinking Diversity in Information Systems Research', *Information Systems Research*, 7(4): 389–99.

——and Zmud, R. (1999). 'Empirical Research in Information Systems: The Practice of Relevance', *MIS Quarterly*, 23(1): 3–16.

————(2003). 'The Identity Crisis within the IS Discipline: Defining and Communicating the Discipline's Core Properties', *MIS Quarterly*, 27(2): 183–94.

Benko, C. (1992). 'If Information System Outsourcing is the Solution, What is the Problem?', *Journal of Systems Management*, 43(11): 32–5.

Bennett, J. (1983). *Building Decision Support Systems*. Reading: Addison-Wesley.

Bjorn-Andersen, N. (1984). 'Challenge to Certainty', in T. Bemelmans (ed.), *Beyond Productivity: Information Systems Development for Organizational Effectiveness*. North-Holland, Amsterdam: 1–8.

Blumenthal, S. C. (1969). *Management Information Systems: A Framework for Planning and Development*. Englewood Cliffs, NJ: Prentice-Hall.

Bostrom, R., and Heinen, S. (1977). 'MIS Problems and Failures: A Sociotechnical Perspective—Part I: The Causes', *MIS Quarterly*, 1(3): 17–32.

Brooker, W. (1965). 'The Total Systems Myth', in J. C. Wetherbe, V. T. Dock, and S. L. Mandell (1988) *Readings in Information Systems: A Managerial Perspective*. Eagan, MN: West Publishing.

Brown, C. V., and Magill, S. U. (1994). 'Alignment of the IS Function with the Enterprise: Toward a Model of Antecedents', *MIS Quarterly*, 18(4): 371–403.

Brynjolfsson, E., and Hitt, L. (1996). 'Paradox lost? Firm-Level Evidence of the Returns on Information Systems Spending', *Management Science*, 42: 541–58.

Buckingham, R. A., Hirschheim, R. A., Land, F. F., and Tully, C. J. (1987). 'Information Systems Curriculum: A Basis for Course Design', in R. A. Buckingham et al. (eds.), *Information Systems Education: Recommendations and Implementation*. Cambridge: Cambridge University Press, 14–133.

Caminer, D., Aris J., Hermon, P., and Land, F. (1998). *LEO: The Incredible Story of the World's First Business Computer*. New York: McGraw Hill.

Canning, R. C. (1979). 'The Analysis of User Needs', *EDP Analyzer*, 17(1).

Cash, J. I., and Konsynski, B. R. (1985). 'IS Redraws Competitive Boundaries', *Harvard Business Review*, 63(2): 134–42.

——and Lawrence, P. (eds.) (1989). *The Information Systems Research Challenge: Qualitative Research Methods—Vol. 1*. Boston, MA: Harvard University Press.

Cavaye, A. L. M. (1995). 'User Participation in System Development Revisited'. *Information & Management*, 28: 311–23.

Chan, Y. E., Huff, S. L., Barclay, D. W., and Copeland, D. G. (1997). 'Business Strategy Orientation, Information Systems Orientation and Strategic Alignment', *Information Systems Research*, 8(2): 125–50.

Chatfield, A., and Yetton, P. (2000). 'Strategic Payoffs from EDI as a Function of EDI Embeddedness', *Journal of Management Information Systems*, 16(4): 195–224.

Chau, Y. K., and Jim, C. F. (2002). 'Adoption of Electronic Data Interchange in Small and Medium Enterprise', *Journal of Global Information Management*, 10(4): 61–85.

Checkland, P. (1972). 'Towards a Systems-Based Methodology for Real-World Problem-Solving', *Journal of Applied Systems Engineering*, 3(2): 87–116.

——(1981). *Systems Thinking, Systems Practice*. Chichester: John Wiley & Sons.

——(1999). *Soft Systems Methodology: A Thirty Year Retrospective*. Chichester: John Wiley.

Checkland, P. and Holwell, S. (1998). *Information, Systems and Information Systems: Making Sense of the Field*. Chichester: John Wiley & Sons.

——and Scholes, J. (1990). *Soft Systems Methodology in Action*. Chichester: John Wiley & Sons.

Cheon, M., Lee, C., and Grover, V. (1992). 'Research in MIS—Points of Work and Reference: A Replication and Extension of the Culnan and Swanson Study', *Data Base*, 23(2): 21–9.

Chervany, N. L., Dickson, G. W., and Kozar, K. (1972). 'An Experimental Gaming Framework for Investigating the Influence of Management Information Systems on Decision Effectiveness', *MISRC Working Paper No. 71-12*, Management Information Systems Research Center, University of Minnesota, MN.

Chin, W. W., Gopal, A., and Salisbury, W. D. (1997). 'Advancing the Theory of Adaptive Structuration: The Development of a Scale to Measure Faithfulness of Appropriation', *Information Systems Research*, 8(4): 342–67.

Churchman, C. W. (1971). *The Design of Inquiring Systems*. New York: Basic Books.

——(1979). *The Systems Approach and Its Enemies*. New York: Basic Books.

Citurs, A. B., and Yoo, Y. (1999). 'Development of Expertise Coordination Patterns in Electronic Teams', Presented at the 1999 Academy of Management Meeting, Chicago, IL.

Clark, T. D., Zmud, R. W. and McCray, G. E. (1995). 'The Outsourcing of Information Services: Transforming the Nature of Business in the Information Industry', *Journal of Information Technology*, 10(4): 221–37.

Clemons, E. K. (1986), 'Information Systems for Sustaining Competitive Advantage', *Information & Management*, 3 (October): 131–6.

Coleman, R. J., and Riley, M. J. (eds.) (1973). *MIS: Management Dimensions*. San Francisco, CA: Holden Day.

Cooper, R. (1988). 'Review of Management Information Systems Research: A Management Support Perspective', *Information Processing & Management*, 24(1): 73–102.

——and Zmud, R. W. (1990). 'Information Technology Implementation Research: A Technology Diffusion Approach', *Management Science*, 36(2): 123–39.

Cougar, J. D. (1973). 'Curriculum Recommendations for Undergraduate Programs in Information Systems', *Communications of the ACM*, 16(12): 727–49.

Culnan, M. (1986). 'The Intellectual Development of Management Information Systems, 1972–1982: A Co-Citation Analysis', *Management Science*, 32(2): 156–72.

——(1987). 'Mapping the Intellectual Structure of MIS, 1980–1985: A Co-Citation Analysis', *MIS Quarterly*, 11(3): 341–53.

——and Swanson, E. B. (1986). 'Research in Management Information Systems, 1980–1984: Points of Work and Relevance', *MIS Quarterly*, 10(3): 286–301.

Daniels, A., and Yeates, D. A. (1971). *Basic Training in Systems Analysis*. 2nd edn, London: Pitman.

Davenport, T., and Prusack, L. (1997). *Information Ecology*. New York: Oxford University Press.

Davis, F. D. (1989). 'Perceived Usefulness, Perceived Ease of Use, and User Acceptance of Information Technology', *MIS Quarterly*, 13(3): 319–39.

——and Venkatesh, V. (2000). 'A Theoretical Extension of the Technology Acceptance Model: Four Longitudinal Field Studies', *Management Science*, 46(2): 186–204.

Davis, G. (1974). *Management Information Systems*. New York: McGraw-Hill.

——(1980). 'A Systematic Evaluation of Publications for Promotion of MIS Academics', *Proceedings of the First Conference on Information Systems*, Philadelphia.

——(1982). 'Strategies for Requirements Determination', *IBM Systems Journal*, 21(1): 4–30.

——(2000). 'Information Systems Conceptual Foundations: Looking Backward and Forward', in R. Baskerville, J. Stage, and J. DeGross (eds.), *Organizational and Social Perspectives on Information Technology*. Boston, MA: Kluwer Publishers, 61–82.

——and Everest, G. (eds.) (1976). *Readings in the Management of Information Systems*. New York: McGraw-Hill.

——and Olson, M. (1985). *Management Information Systems: Conceptual Foundations, Structure, and Development*, New York: McGraw-Hill.

Dearden, J. (1972). 'MIS is a Mirage', *Harvard Business Review* (January–February): 90–9.

DeGreene, K. (1973). *Sociotechnical Systems: Factors in Analysis, Design and Management*. Englewood Cliffs, NJ: Prentice-Hall.

DeLone, W. H., and McLean, E. R. (1992). 'Information Systems Success: The Quest for the Dependent Variable', *Information Systems Research*, 3: 60–95.

DeMarco, T. (1978). *Structured Analysis and Systems Specification*. New York: Yourdon Press.

Dennis, A., George, J., Jessup, L., Nunamaker, J., and Vogel, D. (1988). 'Information Technology to Support Electronic Meetings', *MIS Quarterly*, 12(4): 591–624.

DeSanctis, G. (2003). 'The Social Life of Information Systems Research', *Journal of the Association for Information Systems*, 4(7): 360–76.

——Dickson, G., and Price, R. (2000). 'Information Technology Management', in *Information Technology and the Future Enterprise: New Models for Managers*. Upper Saddle River, NJ: Prentice Hall.

——and Poole, M. S. (1994). 'Capturing the Complexity in Advanced Technology Use: Adaptive Structuration Theory', *Organization Science*, 5(2): 121–47.

Dibbern, J., Goles, T., Hirschheim, R., and Jayatilaka, B. (2004). 'Information Systems Outsourcing: A Survey and Analysis of the Literature', *Database*, 35(4): 6–102.

Dickson, G. (1968). 'Management Information-Decision Systems', *Business Horizons*, 11 (December): 17–26.

——(1981). 'Management Information Systems: Evolution and Status', in M. Yovits (ed.), *Advances in Computers*. New York: Academic Press.

——(1982). 'Management Information Systems: Evolution and Status', *MISRC Working Paper Series*, University of Minnesota, 81–02.

——Benbasat, I., and King, W. R. (1982). 'The MIS Area: Problems, Challenges, and Opportunities', *Data Base*, 14(1): 7–12.

——Senn, J. A., and Chervany, N. L. (1977). 'Research in Management Information Systems: The Minnesota Experiments', *Management Science*, 23: 913–23.

——Emery, J. C., Ives, B., King, W. R., and McFarlan, F. W. (1993). 'Professional Societies: A Service to Members and Professional Leadership', *MIS Quarterly*, 17(1): iii–vi.

Doll, W. J., and Torkzadeh, G. (1988). 'The Measurement of End-User Computing Satisfaction', *MIS Quarterly*, 12(2).

Emery, J., and Sprague, C. (1972). 'MIS: A Mirage or Misconception?', *Harvard Business Review*, 50(3): 22–3.

Falaleeva, N. (2003). 'Antecedents to Backsourcing', in *Proceedings of the Americas Conference on Information Systems*.

Ferry, G. (2003). *A Computer Called LEO: Lyons Teashops and the World's First Office Computer*. London: Fourth Estate.

Fichman, R. G. (2000). 'The Diffusion and Assimilation of Information Technology Innovations', in R. W. Zmud (ed.), *Framing the Domains of IT Management: Projecting the Future through the Past*. Cincinnati, OH: Pinnaflex Publishing, 105–28.

Fitzgerald, G., and Willcocks, L. P. (1994). 'Outsourcing Information Technology: Contracts and Client/Vendor Relationships', *Working Paper RDP94/10*. Oxford Institute of Information Management.

——Hirschheim, R., Mumford, E., and Wood-Harper, T. (1985). 'Information Systems Research Methodology: An Introduction', in E. Mumford, R. Hirschheim, G. Fitzgerald and T. Wood-Harper (eds.), *Research Methods in Information Systems*. Amsterdam: North Holland, 3–9.

Friedman, A., and Cornford, D. (1989). *Computer Systems Development: History, Organization and Implementation*. Chichester: John Wiley & Sons.

Furst, S., Blackburn, R., and Rosen, B. (1999). 'Virtual Team Effectiveness: A Proposed Research Agenda', *Information Systems Journal*, 9(4): 249–69.

Gable, G., Gregor, S., and Smyth, R. (eds.) (2008). *The Information Systems Academic Discipline in Australia*. Canberra: ANU Press.

Galliers, R. D. (2003). 'Change as Crisis of Growth? Toward a Trans-disciplinary view of Information Systems as a Field of Study', *Journal of the Association for Information Systems*. 4(6): 337–51.

——and Land, F. F. (1987). 'Choosing an Appropriate Information Systems Research Methodology', *Communications of the ACM*, 30(11): 900–2.

——and Meadows J. (2003). 'A Discipline Divided: Globalization and Parochialism in Information Systems Research', *Communications of the Association for Information Systems*, 11 (5): 108–17.

——and Whitley, E. (2007). '*Vive les differences?* Developing a Profile of European Information Systems Research as a Basis for International Comparison', *European Journal of Information Systems*, 16: 20–35.

Gane, C., and Sarson, T. (1979). *Structured Systems Analysis: Tools and Techniques*. Englewood Cliffs, NJ: Prentice Hall.

George, J., Valacich, J., and Valor, J. (2005). 'Does Information Systems Still Matter: Lessons for a Maturing Discipline', *Communications of the AIS*, 16: 219–32.

Gillenson, M. A., and Stutz, J. D. (1991). 'Academic Issues in MIS: Journals and Books', *MIS Quarterly*, 15(4): 447–52.

Gorry, G., and Scott-Morton, M. (1971). 'A Framework for Management Information Systems', *Sloan Management Review* (Fall): 55–70.

Gray, P., Vogel, D., and Beauclair, R. (1990). 'Assessing GDSS Empirical Research', *European Journal of Operational Research*, 46(2): 162–76.

Gregory, R., and Van Horn, R. (1960). *Automatic Data-Processing Systems*. Belmont, CA: Wadsworth.

Grover, V., Cheon, M. J., and Teng, J. T. C (1996). 'The Effect of Service Quality and Partnership on the Outsourcing of Information Systems Functions', *Journal of Management Information System*, 12: 89–116.

Gupta, U. G., and Gupta, A. (1992). 'Outsourcing the IS Function: Is It Necessary for Your Organisation?' *Information Systems Management* (Summer): 44–50.

Heeks, R. (2002). 'Information Systems and Developing Countries: Failure, Successes, and Local Improvisations', *The Information Society*, 18(2): 101–12.

Heikkila, J. (1995). 'The Diffusion of a Learning Intensive Technology into Organizations: The Case of PC Technology', Ph.D. Dissertation, Department of Computer Science, University of Tampere.

Heiskanen, A. (1994). 'Issues and Factors Affecting the Success and Failure of a Student Record System Development Process: A Longitudinal Investigation Based on Reflection-in-Action', Ph.D. Dissertation, Helsinki School of Economics and Business Administration, Helsinki.

Henderson, J., and Venkatraman, N. (1992). Strategic Alignment: A Model for Organizational Tranformation through Information Technology', in T. A. Kochan and M. E. Useem (eds.), *Transforming Organisations*. Oxford: Oxford University Press, 97–117.

Hevner, A. R., Berndt D. J., and Studnicki, J. (2000). 'Strategic Information Systems Planning with Box Structures', *IEEE Proceeding of the 33rd Hawaii International Conference on Systems Science*, Hawaii, January.

Hirschheim, R. (1985), 'User Experiences with and Assessment of Participative Systems Design', *MIS Quarterly*, 9(4): 295–303.

——(1998). 'Backsourcing: An Emerging Trend?', *Infoserver*, September, <http://www.out sourcing-academics.com/backsourcing.html>.

——and Klein, H. (2003). 'Crisis in the IS Field? A Critical Reflection on the State of the Discipline', *Journal of the Association for Information Systems*, 4(5): 237–93.

————and Lyytinen, K. (1995). *Information Systems Development and Data Modeling: Conceptual and Philosophical Foundations*. Cambridge: Cambridge University Press.

——————(1996). 'Exploring the Intellectual Structures of Information Systems Development: A Social Action Theoretic Analysis', *Accounting, Management and Information Technologies*, 6(1/2): 1–64.

——and Lacity, M. (2000). 'Information Technology Insourcing: Myths and Realities', *Communications of the ACM*, 43(2): 99–107.

——Newman, M., Loebeckke, C., and Valor, J. (2007). 'Offshoring and the Implications for the IS Discipline: Where Perception meets Reality', *Communications of the Association for Information Systems*, 20(51): 824–35.

Hitt, L., and Brynjolfsson, E. (1996). 'Productivity, Profit and Consumer Welfare: Three Different Measures of Information Technology's Value'. *MIS Quarterly* (June): 1–23.

Huber, G. P. (1983). 'Cognitive Style as a Basis for MIS and DSS Designs: Much Ado About Nothing?', *Management Science*, 29(5): 567–77.

——(1990). 'A Theory of the Effects of Advanced Information Technologies on Organizational Design, Intelligence, and Decision Making', *Academy of Management Review*, 15(1): 47–71.

Hunter, M. G., and Beck, J. E. (2000). 'Using Repertory Grids to Conduct Cross-Cultural Information Systems Research', *Information Systems Research*, 11: 93–101.

Iacovou, C. L., Benbasat, I., and Dexter, A. S. (1995). 'Electronic Data Interchange and Small Organizations: Adoption and Impact of Technology', *MIS Quarterly*, 19(4): 465–85.

Iivari, J., and Lyytinen, K. (1999). 'Research on Information Systems Development in Scandinavia', *Scandinavian Journal of Information Systems*, 10(1/2): 135–85.

Ives, B., Hamilton, S., and Davis, G. (1980). 'A Framework for Research in Computer-Based Management Information Systems', *Management Science*, 26(9): 910–34.

——and Learmonth, G. (1984). 'The Information System as a Competitive Weapon', *Communications of the ACM*, 27(12): 1193–201.

Ives, B., and Olsen, M. H. (1984). 'User Involvement and MIS Research: A Review of Research', *Management Science*, 30(5): 586–603.

——and Baroudi, J. (1983). 'The Measurement of User Information Satisfaction', *Communications of the CACM*, 26(10): 785–93.

——Valacich, J., Watson, R. T., Zmud. R. et al. (2002). 'What Every Business Student Needs to Know about Information Systems', *Communications of the Association for Information Systems*, 9.

——Parks, M. S., Porra, J., and Silva, L. (2004). 'Phylogeny and Power in the IS Domain: A Response to Benbasat and Zmud's Call for Returning to the IT Artifact', *Journal of the Association for Information Systems*, 5(3): 108–24.

Jackson, W. M., and Nath, R. (1989). 'Publication Patterns of MIS Researchers', *Interface*, 11 (2): 15–20.

Jarvenpaa, S., Knoll, K., and Leidner, D. (1998). 'Is Anybody Out There? Antecedents of Trust in Global Virtual Teams', *Journal of Management Information Systems*, 14(4): 29–64.

Kaplan, B., Truex, D., Wastell, D., Wood-Harper, T., and DeGross, J. (eds.) (2004). *Information Systems Research: Relevant Theory and Informed Practice*. Boston, MA: Kluwer Academic Publishers.

Kauffman, R. J., and Kriebel, C. H. (1988). 'Modeling and Measuring the Business Value of Information Technology', in *Measuring the Business Value of Information Technologies*. Washington, DC: ICIT Press.

Keen, P. (1980). 'MIS Research: Reference Disciplines and Cumulative Tradition', in E. McLean (ed.), *Proceedings of the First International Conference on Information Systems*, Philadelphia, 17–31.

——(1981). 'Information Systems and Organizational Change', *Communications of the ACM*, 24(1): 24–33.

——(1987). 'MIS Research: Current Status, Trends and Needs', in R. Buckingham, R. Hirschheim, F. Land, and C. Tully (eds.), *Information Systems Education: Recommendations and Implementation*. Cambridge: Cambridge University Press, 1–13.

——(1991). 'Relevance and Rigor in Information Systems Research: Improving Quality, Confidence, Cohesion, and Impact', in H. E. Nissen, H. K. Klein, and R. Hirschheim (eds.), *Information Systems Research: Contemporary Approaches and Emergent Traditions*. Amsterdam: North-Holland, 27–49.

——and Scott-Morton, M. (1978). *Decision Support Systems: An Organizational Perspective*. Reading, MA: Addison-Wesley.

Kemerer, C. (1992). 'How the Learning Curve Affects CASE Tool Adoption', *IEEE Software*, 9 (3): 23–6.

King, J., and Lyytinen, K. (eds.) (2006). *Information Systems: The State of the Field*. Chichester: J. Wiley & Sons.

Klein, H. K., and Hirschheim, R. (2008). 'The Structure of the IS Discipline Reconsidered: Implications and Reflections from a Community of Practice Perspective', *Information & Organization*, 18(4): 280–302.

Klepper, R. (1995). 'The Management of Partnering Development in I/S Outsourcing', *Journal of Information Technology*, 10(4): 248–57.

Kling, R., and Scacchi, W. (1982). 'The Web of Computing: Computer Technology as Social Organization', *Advances in Computers*, 21: 1–90.

Kolb, D. (1984). *Experiential Learning: Experience as the Source of Learning and Development*. Englewood Cliffs, NJ: Prentice Hall.

Kramer, K. L., and King, J. L. (1988). 'Computer-Based Systems for Cooperative Work and Group Decision Making', *ACM Computer Surveys*, 20: 329–380.

Kumar, K. (1997). 'Program Chair's Statement', in K. Kumar and J. DeGross (eds.), *Proceedings of the Eighteenth International Conference on Information Systems*, Atlanta, GA, 15–17 December 1997, xvii–xix.

Kwon, T. H. and Zmud, R. W. (1987). 'Unifying the Fragmented Models of Information Systems Implementation', in R. J. Boland and R. A. Hirschheim (eds.), *Critical Issues in Information Systems Research*. Chichester: John Wiley & Sons, 227–51.

Lacity, M., and Hirschheim, R. (1993). *Information Systems Outsourcing: Myths, Metaphors and Realities*. Chichester: J. Wiley & Sons.

——Khan, S. A., and Willcocks, L. P. (2009). 'A Review of the IT Outsourcing Literature: Insights for Practice', *Journal of Strategic Information Systems*, 18(3): 130–46.

Land, F., and Hirschheim, R. (1983). 'Participative Systems Design: Rationale, Tools and Techniques', *Journal of Applied Systems Analysis*, 10: 91–107.

Langefors, B. (1966). *Theoretical Analysis of Information Systems*. Lund: Studentlitteratur.

——(1973). *Theoretical Analysis of Information Systems*. Philadelphia, PA: Auerbach.

——(1974). 'Information Systems', in *Information Processing 74*. Amsterdam: North-Holland, 937–45.

Lee, A. (1999a). 'The MIS Field, the Publication Process, and the Future Course of MIS Quarterly', *MIS Quarterly*, 23(1): v–xi.

——(1999b). 'Rigor and Relevance in MIS Research: Beyond the Approach of Positivism Alone', *MIS Quarterly*, 23(1): 29–33.

——Liebenau, J., and DeGross, J. (eds.) (1997). *Information Systems and Qualitative Research*. London: Chapman & Hall.

Li, D. (ed.) (1972). *Design and Management of Information Systems*. Chicago, IL: SRA Publishers.

Loh, L., and Venkatraman, N. (1992). 'Diffusion of Information Technology Outsourcing: Influence Sources and the Kodak Effect', *Information Systems Research*, 3(4): 334–78.

————(1995). 'An Empirical Study of IT Outsourcing: Benefits, Risks and Performance Implications', *International Conference of Information Systems (ICIS)*, Amsterdam.

Lucas, H. (1999). 'The State of the Information Systems Field', *Communications of the AIS*, 5(1).

Lucas, H. C., Jr. (1973). 'A Descriptive Model of Information Systems in the Context of the Organization', Proceedings of the Wharton Conference on Research on Computers in Organizations, *Data Base* (Winter): 27–36.

Lyytinen, K. (1987). 'A Taxonomic Perspective of Information Systems Development: Theoretical Constructs and Recommendations', in R. Boland and R. Hirschheim (eds.), *Critical Issues in Information Systems Research*. Chichester: Wiley, 3–41.

——(1999). 'Empirical Research in Information Systems: On the Relevance of Practice in Thinking of IS Research', *MIS Quarterly*, 23(1): 25–7.

——and King, J. (2004). 'Nothing at the Center? Academic Legitimacy in the Field of Information Systems', *Journal of the Association for Information Systems*, 5(6).

————(2006). 'The Theoretical Core and Academic Legitimacy: A Response to Professor Weber', *Journal of the Association for Information Systems*, 7(10).

——and Yoo, Y. (2002). 'Introduction to the Special Issue on Issues and Challenges in Ubiquitous Computing', *Communications of the ACM*, 45(12) (December): 62–5.

McFarlan, F. W. (1981). 'Portfolio Approach to Information Systems', *Harvard Business Review* 59(5): 142–50.

McFarlan, F. W. (1984). 'Information Technology Changes the Way You Compete', *Harvard Business Review* (May–June): 98–103.

Mahmood, M., and Mann, G. (1993). 'Measuring the Organizational Impact of Information Technology Investment: An Exploratory Study', *Journal of Management Information Systems* 10(1): 97–122.

Markus, M. L. (1983). 'Power, Politics, and MIS Implementation', *Communications of the ACM* 26(6): 430–44.

——(1997). 'The Qualitative Difference in Information Systems Research and Practice', in A. Lee, J. Liebenau, and J. DeGross (eds.), *Information Systems and Qualitative Research*. London: Chapman & Hall, 11–27.

Markus, M. L. (1999). 'Thinking the Unthinkable: What Happens if the IS Field as We Know it Goes away?', in W. Currie and R. Galliers (eds.), *Rethinking MIS*. Oxford: Oxford University Press, 175–203.

——(2000). 'Special Issue on Intensive Research in Information Systems: Using Qualitative, Interpretive, and Case Methods to Study Information Technology—Second Installment, Foreword', *MIS Quarterly*, 24(3).

——and Lee, A. S. (1999). 'Special Issue on Intensive Research in Information Systems: Using Qualitative, Interpretive, and Case Methods to Study Information Technology; Forward', *MIS Quarterly*, 23(1): 1–2.

————(2000). 'Using Qualitative, Interpretive, and Case Methods to Study Information Technology', *MIS Quarterly*, 24(1).

——and Robey, D. (1988). 'Information Technology and Organizational Change: Causal Structure in Theory and Research', *Management Science*, 34(5): 583–98.

Mason, R., and Mitroff, I. (1973). 'A Program for Research on Management Information Systems', *Management Science*, 19(5): 475–87.

Meyer, N. D. (1994). 'A Sensible Approach to Outsourcing', *Information Systems Management* 11(4): 23–7.

Mingers, J., and Stowell, F. (eds.) (1997). *Information Systems: An Emerging Discipline?* Maidenhead: McGraw-Hill.

Mitroff, I. (1983). *Stakeholders of the Organisational Mind: Toward a New View of Organisational Policy Making*. London: Jossey-Bass.

——and Sagasti, F. (1973). 'Epistemology as General Systems Theory: An Approach to the Design of Complex Decision-Making Experiments', *Philosophy of Social Sciences*, 3: 117–34.

Moore, G., and Benbasat, I. (1991). 'Development of an Instrument to Measure the Perceptions of Adopting an Information Technology Innovation', *Information Systems Research*, 2(3): 192–222.

Morgan, G. (1986). *Images of Organizations*. London: Sage.

Mumford, E. (1974). 'Computer Systems and Work Design: Problems of Philosophy and Vision', *Personnel Review*, 3(2): 40–9.

——(1981). 'Participative Systems Design: Structure and Method', *Systems, Objectives, Solutions*, 1(1): 5–19.

——(1983). *Designing Human Systems: The ETHICS Method*. Manchester: Manchester Business School Press.

——and Henshall, D. (1978). *A Participative Approach to the Design of Computer Systems*. London: Associated Business Press.

——Hirschheim, R., Fitzgerald, G., and Wood-Harper, T. (eds.) (1985). *Research Methods in Information Systems*. Amsterdam: North-Holland.

Myers, M., and Walsham, G. (1998). 'Exemplifying Interpretive Research in Information Systems: An Overview', *Journal of Information Technology*, 13: 33–4.

——and Tan, F. B. (1997). 'Beyond Models of National Culture in Information Systems Research', *Journal of Global Information Management*, 10(1): 24–32.

Newman, M., and Rosenberg, D. (1985). 'Systems Analysts and the Politics of Organizational Control', *Omega*, 13(3): 393–406.

Nissen, H-K., Klein, H., and Hirschheim, R. (eds.) (1991). *Information Systems Research: Contemporary Approaches and Emergent Themes*. Amsterdam: North-Holland.

Nolan, R. L. (1979). 'Managing the Crises in Data Processing', *Harvard Business Review* (March–April): 115–26.

——and Wetherbe, J. C. (1980). 'Toward a Comprehensive Framework for MIS Research', *MIS Quarterly*, 4(2): 1–19.

Nunamaker, J., Chen, M., and Purdin, T. (1991). 'Systems Development in Information Systems Research', *Information Systems Research*, 7(3): 89–106.

——Cougar, J. D., and Davis, G. B. (1982). 'Information Systems Curriculum Recommendations for the 80's', Undergraduate and Graduate Programs: A Report of the ACM Curriculum Committee.

Nygaard, K. (1975). 'The Trade Unions New Users of Research', *Personnel Review*, 4(2).

Orlikowski, W., and Baroudi, J. (1991). 'Studying Information Technology in Organizations: Research Approaches and Assumptions', *Information Systems Research*, 2(1): 1–28.

Parsons, G. L. (1983). 'Information Techonology: A New Competitive Weapon', *Sloan Management Review*, 25(1).

Porter, M., and Millar, V. (1985). 'How Information Gives you Competitive Advantage', *Harvard Business Review*, 63(4): 149–60.

Purba, R. (2002). 'Greening the Supply Chain: A New Initiative in South East Asia', *International Journal of Operations and Production Management*, 22: 632–55.

Rackoff, N., Wiseman, C., and Ullrich, W. (1985). 'Information Systems for Competitive Advantage: Implementation of a Planning Process', *MIS Quarterly*, 9(4): 285–94.

Rajkumar, T. M., and Dawley, D. L. (1998). 'Problems and Issues in Offshore Development of Software', in L. P. Willcocks and M. C. Lacity (eds.,) *Strategic Sourcing of Information Systems: Perspectives and Practices*. Chichester: John Wiley & Sons Ltd, 369–86.

——and Mani, R. V. S. (2001). 'Offshore Software Development: The View from Indian Suppliers', *Information Systems Management* (Spring): 63–73.

Rao, V. S., and Jarvenpaa, S. L. (1991). 'Computer Support of Groups: Theory-Based Models for GDSS Research', *Management Science*, 37(10): 1347–62.

Rappaport, A. (1968). 'Management Information Systems: Another Perspective', *Management Science*, 15(4): B133–6.

Reponen, T. (1993). 'Strategic Information Systems: A Conceptual Analysis', *The Journal of Strategic Information Systems*, 2.

Roach, S. S. (1988). 'Technology and the Service Sector: America's Hidden Competitive Advantage', in B. Guile and J. B. Quinn (eds.), *Technology in Services*. Washington, DC: National Academy Press, 125–45.

——(1989). 'The Case of the Missing Technology Payback', *Tenth International Conference on Information Systems*. Boston, December.

Robey, D. (1983). 'Cognitive Style and DSS Design: A Comment on Huber's Paper', *Management Science*, 29(5): 580–2.

——(1987). 'Implementation and the Organizational Impacts of Information Systems', *Interfaces*, 17: 72–84.

——(1996). 'Diversity in Information Systems Research: Threat, Promise, and Responsibility', *Information Systems Research*, 7(4): 400–8.

——(2003). 'Identity, Legitimacy and the Dominant Research Paradigm: An Alternative Prescription for the IS Discipline', *Journal of the Association for Information Systems*, 4(7): 352–9.

Sabherwal, R., Hirschheim, R., and Goles, T. (2001). 'The Dynamics of Alignment: Insights from a Punctuated Equilibrium Model', *Organization Science*, 12(2): 179–97.

Sandberg, A. (1985). 'Socio-technical Design, Trade Union Strategies and Action Research', in E. Mumford, R. Hirschheim, G. Fitzgerald, and A. T. Wood-Harper (eds.), *Research Methods in Information Systems*. Amsterdam: North-Holland, 79–92.

Sanders, D. (1970). *Computers and Management: In a Changing Society*. New York: McGraw-Hill.

Saunders, C. (2000). 'Virtual Teams: Piecing Together the Puzzle', in R. Zmud (ed.), *Framing the Domain of IT Management: Projecting the Future through the Past*. Cincinnati, OH: Pinnaflex.

Schäfer, G. et al. (ed.) (1988). *Functional Analysis of Office Requirements: A Multiperspective Approach*. Chichester: Wiley.

Scott Morton, M. S. (1971). *Management Decision Systems: Computer-Based Support for Decision Making*. Boston, Mass.: Graduate School of Business Administration, Harvard University.

Shackel, B. (1997). 'Human-Computer Interaction: Whence and Whither', *Journal of the American Society for Information Science*, 48(11): 970–86.

Sharpe, W. (1969). *The Economics of Computers*. New York: Columbia University Press.

Sipior, J. C. (1997). 'Congratulations to our ACM Fellows'. *DATA BASE*, 28(1): 14–16.

Somogyi, E., and Galliers, R. (1987). 'Applied Information Technology: From Data Processing to Strategic Information Systems', *Journal of Information Technology*, 2(1): 30–41.

Sprague, R. (1980). 'A Framework for the Development of Decision Support Systems', *MIS Quarterly*, 4(4): 1–24.

——and Carlson, E. D. (1982). *Building Effective Decision Support Systems*. Englewood Cliffs, NJ: Prentice-Hall.

Stowell, F. (ed.) (1995). *Information Systems Provision: The Contribution of Soft Systems Methodology*. Maidenhead: McGraw-Hill.

Straub, D., Loch, K., Evaristo, R., Karahanna, E., and Strite, M. (2002). 'Toward a Theory-Based Measurement of Culture', *Journal of Global Information Management*, 10(1): 13–23.

Swanson, E. B. (1990). 'Distributed Decision Support Systems: A Perspective', *Proceedings of the 23rd Annual Hawaii International Conference on System Sciences*, 111: 129–36, Hawaii, January.

——and Ramiller, N. (1993). 'Information Systems Research Thematics: Submissions to a New Journal, 1987–1992', *Information Systems Research*, 4(4): 299–330.

Tan, M., and Teo, T. S. H. (2000). 'Factors Influencing the Adoption of Internet Banking', *Journal of the Association for Information Systems*, 1: 1–42.

Teichroew, D. (1972). 'A Survey of Languages for Stating Requirements for Computer Based Information Systems', *Proceedings of the Fall Joint Computer Conference*.

——(1974). 'Improvements in the System Life Cycle', *Information Processing 74*. Amsterdam: North-Holland.

Teo, T., and King, W. (1999). 'An Empirical Study of the Integration Business Planning and Information Systems Planning', *European Journal of Information Systems*, 8(3): 200–1.

Todd, P., and Benbasat, I. (1992). 'The Use of Information in Decision Making: An Experimental Investigation of the Impact of Computer-Based Decision Aids', *MIS Quarterly*, 16 (3): 373–93.

———(1999). 'Evaluating the Impact of DSS, Cognitive Effort, and Incentives on Strategy Selection', *Information Systems Research*, 10(4): 357.

Tolliver, E. M. (1971). 'Myths of Automated Management Systems', *Journal of Systems Management*, 22(3): 29–32.

Tricker, R. (1999). 'The Cultural Context of Information Management', in W. L. Currie and R. Galliers (eds.), *Rethinking Management Information Systems*. Oxford: Oxford University Press, 393–416.

Venkatraman, N. (1991). 'IT-induced Business Reconfiguration', in M. S. Scott-Morton (ed.), *The Corporation of the 1990s: Information Technology and Organizational Transformation*. New York: Oxford University Press, 122–58.

Walsham, G., and Sahay, S. (2006). 'Research on Information Systems for Developing Countries: Current Landscape and Future Prospects', *Information Technology and Development*, 12(1): 7–24.

Walstrom, K. A., Hardgrave, B. C., and Wilson, R. L. (1995). 'Forums for Management Information Systems Scholars', *Communications of the ACM*, 38(3): 93–102.

Watson, E., Rosemann, M., and Stewart, G. (1999). 'An Overview of Teaching and Research Using SAP R/3', in W. D. Haseman and D. L. Nazareth (eds.), *Proceedings of the 5th Americas Conference on Information Systems*, Milwaukee.

Watson, H. J., Sousa, R. D., and Junglas, I. (2000). 'Business School Deans Assess the Current State of the IS Academic Field', *Communications of the AIS*, 4.

Weber, R. (2006). 'Reach and Grasp in the Debate over the IS Core: An Empty Hand?' *Journal of the Association for Information Systems*, 7(10).

Wilensky, H. (1967). *Organizational Intelligence: Knowledge and Policy in Government and Industry*. New York: Basic Books.

Williamson, O. (1975). *Markets and Hierarchies: Analysis and Antitrust Implications*. New York: Free Press.

Young, S. (1968). 'Organization as a Total System', *California Management Review*, 10(3): 21–32.

Yourdon, E. (1978). *Modern Structured Analysis*. Englewood Cliffs, NJ: Prentice-Hall.

Zmud, R. (1979). 'Individual Difference and MIS Success: A Review of the Empirical Literature', *Management Science*, 25(10): 966–79.

——and Cox, J. F. (1979). 'The Implementation Process: A Change Approach'. *MIS Quarterly* (June): 35–43.

PART II

....

THEORETICAL AND
METHODOLOGICAL
PERSPECTIVES
IN MIS

....

PART II includes nine chapters which consider a variety of theoretical and methodological perspectives currently used in the MIS field. The intellectual antecedents of these theories are not found in the MIS field, but in the more traditional disciplines of, for example, sociology and philosophy. However, their relevance and applicability to MIS is without question. The various contributions can be treated as 'stand-alone' although each theory or methodology can be applied to a range of MIS-related practices, particularly if we consider the wider implications of the discipline to include societal and environmental factors.

This section begins with a chapter by Mingers (Chapter 3) raises important philosophical and practical issues in undertaking research in the pursuit of knowledge, including some of the questions and debates that are of interest within the philosophy of IS. Five themes are identified: being systemic, being critical and realist, being pluralist in approach, having a concern for truth and recognizing a variety of forms of knowledge. This chapter demonstrates the importance of philosophical and practical issues in research and the production of knowledge, and presents five propositions which are the hallmarks for producing rigorous and relevant research in a complex world. They include: adopting a systemic and holistic approach to the world; using critical realism as an underpinning philosophical perspective; employing multiple research methods to reflect the complexity of the real world; recognizing a variety of forms of knowledge; and accepting concomitantly the importance of truth or warrantability. It is interesting to contrast this chapter with our next chapter (4) by Checkland, who presents his seminal work on systems thinking and soft systems methodology, which has greatly influenced the development of the IS field. The chapter examines 'basic systems' ideas and what it means to do 'systems thinking'. A distinction is made between 'hard' and 'soft' systems thinking, both of which are relevant in the creation of an information system in a real-life situation. The development of the approach is discussed to show how the 'hard/soft' distinction in the use of systems ideas is linked to the Soft Systems Methodology (SSM) and how these ideas are relevant to the IS field. Delineating between hard/soft approaches to IS is noteworthy given that the European tradition in IS draws heavily from the philosophical writings of various scholars, as we shall see below.

The next seven chapters review leading theoretical perspectives including structuration theory, institutional theory, Foucault's ideas of techne and technology, critical theory, hermeneutics, phenomenology, and post-structuralism. We begin with a chapter by Jones that deals with structuration theory, which emerged as a significant development in European sociology in the late 1970s. The theory has its origins in Berger and Luckman's (1967) concept of the mutual constitution of society and individuals. Other strands of structurational analysis are found in the work of Bourdieu (1977), Bhaskar (1979), and Giddens (1991). In focusing on the contribution of Giddens, Jones points out that structuration is a general theory of social organization, and not one specific to IS, which has led to many studies in IS pursuing ideas and debates that are 'at odds' with the work of Giddens. As information systems are seen as social systems, which exist in social and organizational contexts that influence their development and use, and are also implicated in sustaining and changing these contexts, the theory potentially offers useful insights for the IS field. Jones shows that, in recent years, structuration has become an important theoretical lens for many scholars in the organizational and IS fields, with contributions from such leading IS scholars as Orlikowski and Robey (1991), DeSanctis and Poole (1994), and Orlikowski and Yates (1994).

In Chapter 6, Currie considers institutional theory as an important contribution to the IS field. Noting that institutional theory has its roots in core disciplines of sociology, economics, anthropology, and political science, its varied and complex concepts provide an interesting and relevant backdrop for understanding IS phenomena. This chapter provides an overview of institutional theory from the seminal papers of the 1970s to the more recent contributions which consider institutional change and deinstitutionalization. In the IS field, the 'organization' is often used as the primary unit of analysis, where researchers operationalize institutional concepts as a lens to interpret and analyse data. However, institutional theory also shows how macro-units of analysis, i.e. regulatory, legal, and policy frameworks, are also important in influencing and determining organizational and behavioural change. Equally, while institutional theory is traditionally concerned with stability and persistence, information technologies are often associated with rapid, and sometimes disruptive, societal and organizational changes. The more recent work in institutional theory which considers institutional entrepreneurship and change is therefore relevant for the IS field, particularly in understanding why many large-scale IT projects fail to become embedded in highly institutionalized contexts, for example, in the healthcare sector. Willcocks and Lioliou, in Chapter 7, continue our focus on theoretical perspectives by looking at the contribution of Michel Foucault's work, which they see as 'unjustly neglected' in the IS field. In particular, they assess Foucault's views of techne and technology and argue that IS could learn from a deeper Foucauldian genealogy. This chapter assumes a degree of familiarity with Foucault's main work, but not with its application to information and communications technology.

Stahl (Chapter 8) continues the theme of applying theory to IS research by focusing on the contribution of 'critical theory' or 'critical research'. This chapter presents an overview of the usage of critical theory in contemporary IS research and practice. The author follows Klein (2009) in using the term 'critical social information systems research' (CSISR) and reviews the growing body of work on CSISR to offer an in-depth understanding of the meaning and history of this tradition. CSISR is characterized by the intention to change social reality and promote emancipation, which is a departure from other research approaches and traditions. The CSISR discourse is influenced by the philosophical writings of Jürgen Habermas, particularly in the light of the ethical dimension of his work. See also Chapter 23. The chapter discusses problems of the approach and finishes with a critical reflection CSISR in general and this present narrative in particular.

In Chapter 9, Introna discusses the complex ideas surrounding hermeneutics which emerged as an interest in the IS field in the 1980s and 1990s through the work of Richard Boland. Hermeneutics is the study of interpretation theory, and includes the art of interpretation, as well as the theory and practice of interpretation. The author claims the theory involves the 'rendering meaningful of a text (object or phenomenon), which has become obscured or "distanced" in some way, thereby making it no longer immediately obvious'. Applied to the IS field, it is noteworthy that IT which is a repository of large amounts of data and information may lead to a form of distancing. A distinction is made between IS research and computer science research, since the former is largely a social science, 'in which researchers are always in some sense "distanced" from the social phenomena they are studying'. He continues with ideas in the philosophy of social science in Chapter 10, with an exploration of phenomenology, both in terms of its philosophical underpinnings and as a methodology. Phenomenology is widely used in management studies, notably in organizational analysis, and the core disciplines of anthropology, sociology, history, psychology, among many others. This chapter draws on literature on the phenomenological movement and its relevance to the IS field.

Our final chapter in Part II is by Mitev and Howcroft, who address an omission in IS research concerning the debate in social science on postmodernism and post-structuralism. They outline the fundamental arguments of this debate and draw attention to the relevant discussions and disputes. In so doing, they introduce the basic ideas surrounding Actor Network Theory (ANT) and show its origins in post-structuralist debates in the field of science and technology studies (STS).

The diverse theories and methodologies in Part II are intended to provide the reader with a flavour of past, present, and future ideas and debates which are relevant to the IS field. Implicit in these contributions is the notion that IS is not simply about the 'technical imperative' but incorporates a rich tapestry of issues and concerns which are central to social science. These theories and methods are therefore an invitation to IS academics to broaden their repertoire of perspectives and approaches in undertaking IS research, not least to provide greater depth in our understanding and appreciation of how information systems are influenced by, and seek to influence, actions, behaviours, and outcomes. Complementary readings to Part II of this volume are Mingers and Willcocks (2004) and Mansell et al. (2007).

REFERENCES

Berger, P. L., and Luckmann, T. (1979). *The Social Construction of Reality: A Treatise in the Sociology of Knowledge*. Harmondsworth: Penguin.

Bourdieu, P. (1977). *Outline of a Theory of Practice*. Cambridge: Cambridge University Press.

Bhaskar, R. (1979). *The Possibility of Naturalism*. Brighton: Harvester.

DeSanctis, G., and Poole, M. S. (1994). 'Capturing the Complexity in Advanced Technology Use: Adaptive Structuration Theory', *Organization Science*, 5(2): 121–47.

Giddens, A. (1991). 'Structuration Theory: Past, Present and Future', in C. G. A Bryant and D. Jary (eds.), *Giddens' Theory of Structuration: A Critical Appreciation*. London: Routledge, 201–21.

Klein, H. K. (2009). 'Critical Social IS Research Today: A Reflection of Past Accomplishments and Current Challenges', in C. Brooke (ed.), *Critical Management Perspectives on Information Systems*. Oxford: Butterworth Heinemann.

Mansell, R., Avgerou, C., Quah, D., and Silverstone, R. (2007). *The Oxford Handbook of Information and Communication Technologies*. Oxford: Oxford University Press.

Mingers, J., and Willcocks, L. P. (2004). *Social Theory and Philosophy for Information Systems*. New York: Wiley.

Orlikowski, W. J., and Robey, D. (1991). 'Information Technology and the Structuring of Organizations', *Information Systems Research*, 2(2): 143–9.

——and Yates, J. (1994). 'Genre Repertoire: Examining the Structuring of Communicative Practices in Organizations', *Administrative Science Quarterly*, 39: 541–74.

....

CHAPTER 3

THE TRUTH, THE WHOLE TRUTH, AND NOTHING BUT THE TRUTH: HIGH-QUALITY RESEARCH IN INFORMATION SYSTEMS

....

JOHN MINGERS

INTRODUCTION

....

OUR research careers usually begin by doing doctoral research. The objectives of a Ph.D. are clearly stated—'to make an original contribution to knowledge'—and this remains the primary objective of all research. From this simple statement it would seem that the nature of 'knowledge' is fundamental to conducting research. In order to be able to contribute to knowledge we need to understand what knowledge is; what distinguishes knowledge from mere opinion or belief; what kinds of things we can have knowledge of; and how we might acquire knowledge. However, when we look at textbooks that give guidance on methods for doing research, and this is one such, we rarely find much discussion of the nature of knowledge. An admittedly ad hoc survey of research methods books that are easily available to me shows that none has a chapter on knowledge and many do not even refer to it in the index (Bryman 2001; Bryman and Bell 2003; Easterby Smith, Thorpe, and Jackson 2008; Creswell 2009), a useful exception being Lee and Lings (2008). How can they tell us how to discover knowledge if they do not even tell us what it is?

This would not be so strange if knowledge were in fact a very straightforward matter that everyone would agree on but this is far from the case as the literature on epistemology or even knowledge management would show. 'Knowledge' is actually a highly contentious and much debated subject and this may be precisely why such books tend to ignore it—because any serious discussion would raise so many issues that the research methods themselves would become lost. The assumption is that if the methods are rigorously followed the result will be knowledge even if we cannot say precisely what knowledge is.

Interestingly, knowledge is not the only fundamental concept that dare not speak its name—another is *truth*. If we look at the literature of knowledge management then there is actually much discussion of the nature of knowledge, although perhaps little agreement. Surely a fundamental characteristic that distinguishes knowledge from belief or prejudice is that it is *true*—philosophically, knowledge has traditionally been defined as true, justified belief. Yet within the knowledge management literature, for example, there is almost no discussion of the nature of truth (Mingers 2008).

The aim of this chapter is to highlight some key themes that I believe are vital for producing rigorous contributions to knowledge in answer to questions that are of real significance today. These themes are not at the level of particular research methods, or even research paradigms, but concern the very scaffolding that underlies all research. To begin with we need to consider philosophy and the role that it should play in IS research. Broadly speaking, if science is reflective activity about the workings of the everyday world then philosophy of science is reflective activity about the workings of science itself. After this, I want to put forward five propositions concerning high-quality research. First, that we approach the world systemically or holistically. That is, that we recognize it is a complex web of interacting systems and that cutting it up reductionistically into small isolated chunks is likely to destroy the very relationships and interactions that actually matter. Second, that we adopt a particular philosophical position—critical realism—that offers a way out of the sterile battle between positivism and interpretivism that has so dogged IS research for many years (Mingers 2004a). Third, and following on from the first two, that we should be pluralist in our methodological approach. That is, we must recognize that the world is complex and multidimensional, and that the objects of our knowledge take on many forms—material, social, and cognitive—thus requiring a range of research methods. Fourth, that we need to be concerned with truth as a distinguishing characteristic of knowledge and recognize that truth itself has different forms dependent on the type of knowledge we wish to attain. This brings us full-circle back to knowledge itself and the fifth proposition which is that we can validly talk of 'knowing' many different things, and the differing natures of the objects of knowledge leads to different forms of knowledge and truth.

PHILOSOPHY AND IS RESEARCH

I would like to begin by giving a brief review of the role of philosophy with respect to IS research with the help of Figure 3.1 which draws in part on the ideas of both Bhaskar (1978) and Checkland (1999).

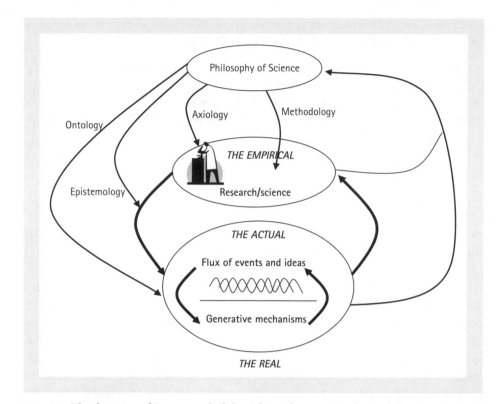

FIGURE 3.1 The domains of Science and Philosophy with respect to the Real, the Actual, and the Empirical

We can begin in the bottom of Figure 3.1 with the ongoing flux of events and ideas. Following Bhaskar, we can term this the domain of the Actual, the actual occurrences and non-occurrences of the everyday world. We can then see that these events are the manifestations of underlying mechanisms or systems, often unobservable, which through the interactions of their properties and powers generate the events. Bhaskar terms this the domain of the Real. We should note two things: that the events are part of the causal dance in that they can be triggers of the underlying mechanisms; and that human beings are also part of this picture, being powerful generative mechanisms.

Moving up Figure 3.1 we can see that science emerges as a domain of reflective action in which people try to understand and explain the workings of the everyday world. This involves observation and interrogation of the Actual and the Real, as well as attempts to test and validate theories and, in the case of action research, explicitly to bring about change. In Bhaskar's terms, this is the domain of the Empirical in which a small subset of all the actual events that occur is captured for scientific activity.

We can now move to another meta-level and consider the emergence of philosophy, more specifically the philosophy of science, as a domain of reflective action that considers the nature of science and research and, in particular, tries to offer guidance about how science can and/or should be carried out. The main philosophical questions that arise can be classified in terms of Mingers (2003a):

- *Ontology*: what kinds of objects or entities may be taken to exist, and what are their types of properties or forms of being?
- *Epistemology*: what is our relationship, as human beings, to the objects of our knowledge (including ourselves), and what distinguishes valid (i.e. true?) knowledge from belief or opinion?
- *Methodology*: given the first two, what methods should we use to acquire valid knowledge?
- *Axiology*: what are the purposes or values of science? What are the ethical or moral limits of science (if any?).

We can see from Figure 3.1 how these four elements relate to various aspects of the world and of science. The whole of Figure 3.1 constitutes what Bhaskar would call the domain of the Real.

A particular set of assumptions about these four questions can be called a paradigm (Kuhn 1970; Burrell and Morgan 1979). Kuhn originally used the term to describe the historical development of one set of theories (e.g. the theory of relativity) from another (e.g. Newtonian physics) but now, especially in the social sciences, paradigms are often seen to be coexisting. For much of the twentieth century the prevailing scientific paradigm was empiricism, more specifically positivism, which sees science as limited to explaining events that can be empirically observed. Events are expected to display regularities or patterns that can be explained as being particular instances of universal laws of the form 'given certain conditions, whenever event X occurs then event Y will occur'. Science is seen as the systematic observation of event regularities (Humean causality), the description of these regularities in the form of general laws, and the prediction of particular outcomes from the laws.

This view of science was extensively critiqued. The idea of pure, objective perception and observation was exploded by psychologists, sociologists, and philosophers; others showed that observational terms were not an atomistic picturing of reality but part of a pre-given linguistic structure—in short that all observation was theory dependent; and Popper (1959, 1969), based on Hume, rejected the possibility of verification and induction, replacing it with falsification and deduction. In response there developed the standard 'deductive-nomological (D-N)' or 'hypothetico-deductive' method.

This view leads to a much greater recognition of the social and psychological nature of scientific activity. The idea of paradigms replacing each other over time has developed, particularly within social science, to the idea of there being competing paradigms existent at the same time (e.g. positivist, interpretive, and critical). This is often combined with the claim that paradigms are incommensurable. Clearly, the Kuhnian view has major relativistic implications for empiricism. It highlights the constructed, conventional nature of scientific theorizing, and truth is that which is accepted by a scientific community rather than correspondence to some external reality. The incommensurability thesis is even more undermining since in makes it impossible to judge between paradigms or even assert that a later paradigm is actually superior to an earlier one.

There are also major philosophical debates concerning the nature of social science in relation to natural science that can only be sketched here. Broadly, there are three possible positions: (i) the *naturalist* view that there is one general approach to science that applies to all domains. Within this category, positivists hold that for anything to be scientific it must follow the canons of positivism/empiricism and thus be based on universal generalizations from empirical observations. (ii) The antithesis is the view that the social world is intrinsically different to the natural world, being constituted through language and meaning, and thus involves entirely different hermeneutic, phenomenological, or social constructivist approaches. The argument here would be the idealist one that ontologically social objects do not exist in the way physical ones do (i.e. as subject independent), and that epistemologically there is no possibility of facts or observations that are independent of actors, cultures, or social practices. (iii) The most radical position denies the possibility of objective or scientific knowledge at all, in either domain. Arguments here come from the strong sociology of knowledge programme; post-structuralists such as Foucault (1980), and more generally postmodernists (Best and Kellner 1991) who attempt to undermine even the most basic categories of modernist rationality.

In the rest of the chapter, I want to put forward five themes which I value in terms of generating significant and reliable knowledge: systems thinking, pluralism, critical realism, and truth and knowledge.

THE SYSTEMS APPROACH OR HOLISTIC THINKING

The systems approach at its most general involves deciding explicitly to employ systems concepts in theorizing and research. Some of the basic concepts are: a system as a collection of elements that are linked together such that the behaviour or characteristics of the whole depends on the relationships between the parts rather than the nature of the parts themselves; a boundary separating the system from its environment; subsystems and wider systems that form a nested hierarchy; multiple-cause relations and feedback loops; communication and control systems; the inevitable entanglement of the observer with the observed; and a commitment to holism rather than reductionism. Beyond these basic concepts there are many particular systems approaches that have been developed, for instance systems engineering, cybernetics, system dynamics, soft systems, General Systems Theory (GST), living systems theory, and complexity theory.

How does systems thinking relate to the philosophical questions and paradigms outlined above? It could be argued that it could be conceived of as a paradigm in its own right in the sense that it does have implications for each of the levels, but I think that it is actually orthogonal to the paradigms. That is, one can have positivist, interpretive, or critical versions of systems thinking just as one could also have such versions of non-systems thinking.

To what extent is the systems approach evident in the IS/IT literature? At one level one could say that systems thinking is at least implicit in most IS research. The discipline is called information *systems* after all, and I suspect that few researchers would say they were reductionists, or deny that they ultimately assume a systems approach. However, the number of papers that formally or explicitly claim to use systems theory is actually relatively small, leading Alter (2004), who argued for a systems thinking approach as opposed to a 'tool thinking' approach within IS, to title his paper 'Desperately Seeking Systems Thinking in the IS Discipline'.

We can find examples drawing on the main areas of systems thinking—complexity, GST, SSM, and cybernetics—although I have found nothing using system dynamics. Xu (2000) provides a reasonable overview. Beginning with general systems concepts and GST several authors are concerned with using ST to improve the integration of the discipline either overall (Mora et al. 2007); with regard to research methods (Mingers 2007); or in developing actual IS systems (Garrity 2001; Wainwright and Waring 2004). Porra, Hirschheim, and Parks (2005) examined the history of Texaco's IT function using GST, interestingly using several different 'lenses' thus showing that GST can be used in an interpretive manner, while Wennberg, Brandt, and Revay (2006) used GST to examine information security within Swedish pharmacies.

Complexity and chaos theory have also been used to provide new lenses with which to view organizations and information systems within them (Courtney et al. 2008). Vidal and Lacroux (1999) argue that complex society becomes decentred, away from a single decision maker with a particular problem towards a nexus of participants/organizations/problems. This means that an important function for an IS is *intermediation* between such elements, in particular between individuals, organizations, and reality. McBride (2005) uses complexity concepts such as 'strange attractors' and the 'edge of chaos' to better understand the history of the development of an IS strategy within the UK Probation Service. Samoilenko (2008) uses concepts such as 'fitness landscapes' and 'self-organization' to suggest improvements to ISD methodologies.

Finally we will consider the contribution of two related approaches—SSM and Churchman's dialectical inquiring systems. These are related in that Checkland (1999) drew on Churchman's work on dialectical systems in developing SSM. Churchman was one of the founding fathers of both OR and systems thinking and his major work was *The Design of Inquiring Systems* (Churchman 1971) which considered systems for generating knowledge from different philosophical perspectives, especially Hegelian and Singerian. This has led to a stream of work exploring these approaches within the context of DSS (Courtney 2001), e-business (Bajgoric 2006), and knowledge management (Richardson, Courtney, and Haynes 2006).

SSM has had a long history of application within information systems from one of Checkland's earliest papers (Checkland and Griffin 1970) through to one of his more recent books (Checkland and Holwell 1998). Considerable work was done on linking SSM to more conventional systems development methodologies (Mingers 1988; Stowell 1995; Bustard, He, and Wilkie 2000) particularly in the area of requirements definition. This has led to the generation of a range of specific IS development methodologies based primarily on SSM such as Multiview (Wood-Harper, Antill, and Avison 1985), SISTeM (Atkinson 2000), and CLIC (Champion, Stowell, and O'Callaghan 2005). We can also find examples of the use of SSM in specific areas such as information system failures (Yeo 2002) and the validation of IS (Petkova and Petkov 2003). Finally, SSM has been suggested as an alternative paradigm within information systems—Hirschheim, Iivari, and Klein (1997) suggest it as an alternative to the mainstream approaches such as structured systems design, and Vo, Chae, and Olson (2006) discuss three systems thinking approaches (SSM, Senge's *Fifth Discipline* (Senge 1990), and Mitroff and Linstone, *Unbounded Mind* (Mitroff and Linstone 1993)) as paradigms for developing IS education.

CRITICAL REALISM

Critical realism (CR) is a position within the philosophy of science that has been developed primarily by Roy Bhaskar over the last thirty years (Bhaskar 1978, 1979, 1993). In essence, it maintains a position that is opposed to both positivism (empiricism) and interpretivism (idealism) while accepting elements of both. CR strongly espouses ontological realism—i.e. the existence of a reality independent of our knowledge of it, yet also accepts epistemological relativism—i.e. that our knowledge of that reality will always be locally situated and provisional. Critical realism is becoming increasingly influential within information systems (Mutch 1999; Dobson 2001a, 2001b; Klein 2004; Mingers 2004b; Monod 2004; Pather and Remenyi 2004; Wikgren 2005; Longshore Smith 2006) and management more generally (Ackroyd and Fleetwood 2000; Reed 2001; Fleetwood and Ackroyd 2004; Contu and Willmott 2005; Hunt 2005; Mutch 2005; Reed 2005; Willmott 2005).

In fact, we can distinguish between Critical Realism (CR) and 'critical' 'realism'. What I mean is that CR is one specific philosophical approach but there are other ways of being both critical (e.g. critical hermeneutics (Myers 2004) or critical theory (Klein and Huynh 2004)) and realist (e.g. critical scientific realism (Niiniluoto 2002) or scientific realism (Hunt 2005)).

The idea of 'being critical' or of critique has a long history rooted in the work of both Kant and Marx. At its most general we can see it as a deep form of questioning, of refusing to take things for granted or accept the status quo (Mingers 2000). We can distinguish two main senses: one linked to epistemology and one to axiology in Figure 3.1. The first, Kantian idealist sense, is concerned with knowledge and the limits to or conditions of knowledge. Here we are questioning particular forms or types of knowledge; the explicit, or often implicit, assumptions made by particular theories; or indeed the transcendental limits of knowledge itself. The second, Marxist materialist sense, involves questioning the oppressive nature of society and its institutions and organizations. The two senses can be seen to come together in the work of Habermas (Habermas 1978, 1984, 1987) and later Foucault (Foucault 1988a, 1988b), who had epistemological concerns about the nature of knowledge and portrayed how knowledge was constituted and distorted by the operation of power within society.

Within IS there has been a long if somewhat thin line of critically inspired research based mainly on the work of Habermas going back to Mingers's (1980) comparison of Habermas and soft systems methodology, Mumford et al.'s (1985) exploration of alternative research approaches, and Lyytinen and Hirschheim's (1988) application of communicative action theory. Klein and Huynh (2004) provide a comprehensive coverage of Habermas's theory and its relevance for IS while Heng and de Moor (2003) and Sheffield (2004) are recent empirical studies. Foucault has been less well used although Zuboff's (1988) seminal book is inspired by his ideas. Willcocks (2004) provides an exceptionally clear introduction to Foucault's complex works and covers applications within IS and more broadly within management studies. There are other philosophers whose work falls within the critical realm but who have made less impact on information systems so far including Adorno (Probert 2004) and Callon and Latour (actor-network theory) (Walsham 1997; Mitev and Wilson 2004). Howcroft and Trauth (2005) have produced a handbook on critical research in information systems which covers theories as well as practical applications. There have been several recent empirical studies based on a critical realist perspective (Volkoff, Strong, and Elmes 2007; Bygstad 2008; Reimers and Johnson 2008; Wynn and Williams 2008).

All research is inevitably embedded within the messy real world of power, politics, and interest yet it is often described in papers as though it were pure and perfect. This is a delusion that we all collectively maintain. As authors we do it because we fear our papers will be rejected, and as referees/editors we do it because we fear the journal's reputation for rigorous research will be tarnished. In reality, however, as has been continually shown by the critical research discussed above, it is a fallacy to suppose that rigour comes from sanitized results; that facts can be divorced from values; or that research can be isolated from power and interest (Cordoba and Robson 2003; Doolin 2004; Backhouse, Hsu, and Silva 2006). It is much better to be open and explicit about the real context of the research so that readers can judge for themselves any potential effects or biases. A framework of questions for assisting this process can be found in Mingers (1997).

Ontological and Methodological Pluralism

We have seen how different paradigms developed within IS and other social science disciplines—positivism, interpretivism, critical, and perhaps postmodernist—and for a period these became like silos, each separate and isolated from the others (Burrell and Morgan 1979). Each paradigm developed its own research methods and research had to be conducted from within one paradigm. There were divisive debates between the paradigms (Mingers 2004a).

However, this polarization could not continue and it came to be recognized within social science generally that the world does not divide itself up neatly into hard and soft, quantitative and qualitative, and that to understand its full complexity we need to combine methods from a variety of perspectives. Tashakkori and Teddlie (1998) published one of the first methodology books entirely on mixed methods in social science based on many studies that had already been carried out, and Mingers and Gill (1997) published a book on 'multimethodology', i.e. combining management science methodologies. This movement has grown considerably with a new handbook of mixed methods (Tashakkori and Teddlie 2003); a new journal—*Journal of Mixed Methods Research*; and discussion of mixed methods in general research methodology textbooks, e.g. Bryman and Bell (2003).

There are several different positions with respect to mixed methods or multimethodology. My own view is a strong one in that I argue for plurality not just of methods but of all the four philosophical dimensions in Figure 3.1. Moreover, I suggest that this stance actually follows from both a systems perspective, seeing the world in a holistic way, and a critical realist perspective which accepts a plurality of objects of knowledge. To employ Habermas's (1984) model (discussed further below) we can say that communications and actions relate to three different 'worlds'—the objective or material world that consists of all actual or possible states of affairs; the social or normative world that consists of accepted and legitimate norms of behaviour; and the subjective or personal world that consists of individuals' emotions, feelings, and ideas. As human beings we have different epistemological access to each of these ontological domains: we *observe the* material world, we *participate in our* social world, and we each *experience 'my'* own personal world. This in turn generates the need for distinctive methodologies which then need to be combined together to synthesize our understanding of the whole. Finally, we have distinct axiological relations to the worlds (Habermas 1993), pragmatic with respect to the material world, moral for the social world, and ethical for the personal world.

This leads into the view that there are actually different forms or types of knowledge and that these are distinguished by different forms of truth (Mingers 2003b).

FORMS OF TRUTH

It is paradoxical that 'truth' is one of the great unspoken concepts of the IS literature. If we assume that the purpose of scholarly research is the generation of valid and reliable knowledge, and that truth is a central characteristic of valid knowledge, then we might expect that there should be discussion and debate about the nature of truth and procedures for discovering the truth. In fact, the subject is never mentioned in the IS literature, even in the literature on knowledge management where one might expect that a concern with the validity of knowledge was central. I searched the ISI Web of Knowledge using the very general key words 'information systems' and 'truth' going back to 1970. Amazingly only two proper IS papers were returned (Sheffield 2004; Zhou, Burgoon, and Twitchell 2004), neither of which had any sustained discussion of truth.

This situation could be explained if the concept of truth was essentially simple and uncontested yet this is actually far from the case. Differing positions in terms of ontology and epistemology inevitably lead to different views on the nature of truth, and even as to whether truth is a necessary or attainable characteristic of knowledge. The most common view, in Western philosophy, is that knowledge is *true, justified, belief* (TJB). These three conditions have been taken to be both necessary and sufficient for a proposition to count as knowledge. In other words, to validly assert 'I know that *p* . . .' implies:

1. You must sincerely believe that *p* is the case.
2. You must have justifiable grounds, evidence, or explanation for *p*.
3. *p* must, indeed, be true.

Although this sounds straightforward, there are in fact many problems with each condition as well as their conjunction. For instance, there is much debate about what would constitute proper justification for such a belief—empirical evidence, rational argument, personal experience, perception, or what? How in any case can we determine if something is actually true? More fundamentally, however, there are several different and competing theories of truth (see Mingers (2003b) for a fuller discussion and references).

Correspondence theories are the main and most obvious view of truth. They hold that truth (and falsity) is applied to propositions depending on whether the proposition corresponds to the way the world actually is. *Coherence theories* stress the extent to which a proposition is consistent with other beliefs, theories, and evidence that we have. The more that it fits in with other well-attested ideas the more we should accept it as true. This approach avoids the need for a direct comparison with 'reality'. However, it is more concerned with the justification of beliefs rather than their absolute truth. *Pragmatic theories* hold that truth is best seen in terms of how useful or practical a theory is—that which best solves a problem is the best theory. A version of this is instrumentalism, which holds that a theory is simply an instrument for making predictions, and has no necessary connection to truth at all. This also leads into consensus theories. An obvious argument against this view is that a *true* theory is likely to be most useful and powerful[1] and therefore should be an important component of a *useful* theory. *Consensus or discursive theories* hold that truth is that which results from a process of enquiry resulting in a consensus amongst those most fully informed—in the case of science, scientists. At one level, we can see that this must be the case if we accept with critical realism the impossibility of proving correspondence truth. But, today's accepted truth is usually tomorrow's discarded theory and so this does not guarantee truth. Finally there are *redundancy, deflationary, and performative theories* which argue, in different ways, that the whole concept of truth is actually redundant. If we say 'it is true that snow is white' we are saying no more than that 'snow is white', the two propositions will always have the same truth values and are therefore equivalent.

Turning now to critical realism, what view of truth does it espouse? The first thing to say is that the whole approach is fallibilist. That is, since CR accepts epistemic relativity, the view that all knowledge is ultimately historically and locally situated, it has to accept that theories can never be proved or known certainly to be true. Thus, if provable truth were to be made a necessary criterion for knowledge there could be no knowledge within critical realism.

Bhaskar does discuss the notion of truth and comes up with a multivalent view involving four components or dimensions (Bhaskar 1994: 62) that could apply to a judgment about the truth or falsity of something. The first level is sincerity or trustworthiness: truth as being that which is believed from a trustworthy source— 'trust me, I believe it, act on it'. Second is warranted or justified: based on evidence and justification rather than mere belief—'there's sound evidence for this'. Third is weak correspondence: corresponding to or at least being adequate to some intransitive object of knowledge. Whereas the first two dimensions are clearly in the transitive domain and strongly tied to language, this aspect moves beyond to posit some sort of relation between language and a referent. Finally, ontological and alethic: this level is the most controversial (Groff 2000) as it moves truth entirely into the intransitive domain. It is the truth of things in themselves, and their generative causes, rather than the truth of propositions. It is no longer tied to language although it may be expressed in language.

It is also interesting to consider Habermas's theories of knowledge and truth as his work has been applied within information systems. His first framework was known as the theory of knowledge-constitutive interests (KCI) (Habermas 1978). This suggested that humans, as a species, had needs for, or interest in, three particular forms of knowledge. The *technical* interest in moulding nature led to the empirical and physical sciences. For Habermas these were underpinned by a pragmatist philosophy of science (inspired by Peirce) and a consensus theory of truth. The *practical* interest in communication and mutual understanding led to the historical and interpretive sciences underpinned by a hermeneutic criterion of understanding. And the *emancipatory* interest in self-development and authenticity led to critical science which identified repressions and distortions in knowledge and in society. Its criterion of success was the development of insight and self-expression free from constraint.

This theory of transcendental interests was the subject of much criticism (see Mingers 1997 for a review), and Habermas later transmuted it into the theory of communicative action (TCA) (Habermas 1984, 1987). Utterances and, I would argue, actions as well raise certain validity claims that must, if challenged, be justified. These claims are *comprehensibility*, *truth*, *rightness*, and *truthfulness* (*sincerity*). This is premissed on the argument that utterances stand in relation to the three different 'worlds' discussed above. When such a claim is challenged, the process of justification must always be discursive or dialogical. That is there should ideally be a process of open debate unfettered by issues of power, resources, access, and so on until agreement is reached by the 'unforced force of the better argument' (Habermas 1974: 240), what Habermas calls the 'ideal speech situation'. Thus, Habermas held a consensus or discursive view of truth both in the moral or normative domain of what ought we to do, as well as in the material domain of external reality. To say of a proposition, 'it is true' is the same as saying of an action, 'it is right', namely *ideal, warranted assert-ability*.

However, more recently Habermas (2003) has returned to the issue of truth and now rejects his discursive theory for propositions about the material world in favour of one with an irreducible ontological (i.e. realist) component. In essence, Habermas now maintains that there is a substantive difference between the moral domain of normative validity which can only ever be established through discussion and debate within an ideal speech situation, and the domain of propositional truth where properly arrived at and justified agreement may still be proven wrong by later events. Our experience of living in and coping with the world shows us that even the most strongly held and well-justified views may turn out to be false.

> The experience of 'coping' accounts for two determinations of 'objectivity': the fact that the way the world is is not up to us; and the fact that it is the same for all of us. (Habermas 2003: 254)

Thus the whole question of truth is linked intimately with that of knowledge and thus with research and the whole scholarly and scientific enterprise.

KNOWLEDGE AND TRUTH

In this section, I want to put forward ideas about how the different forms of knowledge relate to truth. I argue that there is not one form of knowledge but several distinct types with different characteristics. These differ in terms of their nature, their source, their form of representation, and their criteria for validity. Truth as usually understood does not apply equally to all of them. The primary forms of knowledge that I distinguish are: performative knowledge—knowing how to do something; experiential knowledge—knowing, through one's own personal experience, a person, place, occurrence etc; propositional knowledge—knowing that some state of affairs is the case; and epistemological knowledge—knowing scientifically how and why something is the case. See Table 3.1 for a summary.

Actual human knowledge can never be certain or known to be correct (even an actually true theory could not be proved to be true). From a critical realist perspective, this is because we can never have pure unmediated access to the intransitive domain; from a Habermasian perspective, ultimate truth could only emerge from a never-ending, impossibly perfect discourse although now mediated by interactions with a constraining outer world. We therefore need to think of knowledge in terms of degrees of confidence and warrantability or justification rather than pure truth. We can link the different forms of knowledge with the different validity or truth claims.

Performative knowledge can best be judged by its actual success or failure. A claim to be able to do something, whether a physical skill or a social role, can only be vindicated by a performance. In some ways, this is actually quite close to Bhaskar's concept of alethic truth that I critiqued above. It is also related to ideas of tacit knowledge (Polanyi 1958; Nonaka and Takeuchi 1995) in that competent performers may well not be able to fully articulate how they perform. To demonstrate that one is a pianist by actually performing validates itself without need of propositions or assertions. Even here, there are of course degrees of performance and competence. We can also bring in here Habermas's validity claim of comprehensibility. Before a speech act or indeed any other social action can be judged it must be understood, that is it must be performed in a competent manner. Habermas draws on Chomsky's (1957) notion of a competent speaker of a language (Habermas 1979: 29) but this can be enlarged to cover all the aspects of performative knowledge.

Experiential knowledge must ultimately come down to a matter of Habermas's truthfulness or sincerity (normative-fiduciary in Bhaskar's terms) since it concerns a particular person's experiences or feelings. Of course, one does not just have to accept a person's discursive justification, one might try to discover or provide some sort of evidence or justification as well which could include documentary evidence—letters, photos, transcripts, etc., or corroboration from other people.

Propositional knowledge is explicit knowledge concerning the presence or absence of particular states of affairs—truth for Habermas, referential-expressive for Bhaskar. Here we can go beyond belief and even justification towards confirming a relation between the proposition and the intransitive world to which it refers. Indeed, if we follow Dretske (1981) we can see a direct *causal* relation between information and the knowledge that it generates. The information carried by a petrol gauge for example (which must be true to be information) leads us to know that the tank is nearly empty and so our knowledge in this case is true justified belief. Even so, we cannot finally prove our knowledge is true for we might be mistaken either in our interpretation of the sign (the gauge might actually read half-full), or in believing it was (true) information when in fact it was not (the gauge was faulty).

Table 3.1 Forms of Knowledge and Truth

Type of knowledge	Object of knowledge	Source of knowledge	Form of representation	Criteria for validity
Propositional I know it's raining I know there's a train at 3.00 I know there's someone at the door	States of affairs in the physical and social world. *To know that x*	Direct perception, receipt of information, communications, the media	Generally explicit and propositional although some may be tacit	*(Ontological) truth* Referential–expressive
Experiential I know her well I know the feeling I know I left my key there I know how the system works	People, places, events we know through personal experience. *To know x*	Personal experiences	Memories, some aspects of which may be tacit and embodied	*Sincerity* Normative-fiduciary Adequating
Performative I know how to ride I know how to read an X-Ray I know how to present	Skills, abilities, and competences. *To know how to do x*	Personal experience, learning, training	Embodied	*Competence, (Epistemic) rightness* Alethic
Epistemological I know what black holes are I know linear algebra	Reasons for the (non-) occurrence of things and events. *To know why x*	Formal methods of discovery e.g. in science	Explicit, discursive, 'objective', open to debate.	*Truth, rightness, sincerity* Ontological, alethic

Epistemological knowledge takes us to the realm of science where its primary characteristic is the huge effort in trying to ensure that the knowledge generated is reliable even whilst accepting that we can never be certain of it. This is ontological (incorporating a causal explanation) truth for Bhaskar. The key feature distinguishing this from propositional knowledge is the need to go beyond immediate appearances to form an underlying explanation of *why* might be as they appear. This is not confined to the material world but applies equally to Habermas's social and personal worlds. In the social world we are interested in explaining why certain norms or patterns of behaviour exist and are maintained, and perhaps why others are not. In the personal world we want to understand why a person behaves as they do, why they do certain things and not others.

Finally, I should say that in real-world situations and activities these different types of knowledge will typically be involved together and will interact with each other. To take just one example, suppose you are chairing a meeting. This will draw on propositional knowledge about particular facts and states of affairs; experiential knowledge of people, events, and practices; performative knowledge, perhaps of body language and physical gestures; and epistemological knowledge perhaps of economics or a particular industrial process.

CONCLUSIONS

The aim of this chapter has been to raise important philosophical and practical issues in research and the production of knowledge, and to argue for five propositions which are, I believe, the hallmarks for producing research that is both rigorous and relevant to the complexities and seriousness of the problems we face in the organizational world. These keys are: adopting a systemic and holistic approach to the world; using critical realism as an underpinning philosophical perspective; employing multiple research methods to reflect the complexity of the real-world; recognizing a variety of forms of knowledge; and accepting concomitantly the importance of truth or warrantability.

I would also argue that as well as each one being warranted in its own right, they also all interlock so that it is actually difficult to accept any one without also accepting the others. Taken together they form a more consistent, coherent, and comprehensive account of the philosophy and methodology of IS research than any other position.

ACKNOWLEDGEMENT

This chapter is developed from Mingers (2007).

NOTE

1. Although postmodernists argue that it is the theory that is deemed most powerful that is accepted as true.

REFERENCES

Ackroyd, S. and Fleetwood, S. (2000). *Realist Perspectives on Management and Organisations.* London: Routledge.

Alter, S. (2004). 'Desperately Seeking Systems Thinking in the Information Systems Discipline', in *International Conference on Information Systems 25.* Washington, DC: Association for Information Systems.

Atkinson, C. (2000). 'The "Soft Information Systems and Technologies Methodology": An Actor Network Contingency Approach to Integrated Development', *European Journal of Information Systems*, 9: 104–23.

Backhouse, J., Hsu, C., and Silva, L. (2006). 'Circuits of Power in Creating *de jure* Standards: Shaping an International Information Systems Security Standard', *MIS Quarterly*, 30: 413–38.

Bajgoric, N. (2006). 'Information Systems for e-Business Continuance: A Systems Approach', *Kybernetes*, 35: 632–52.

Best, S., and Kellner, D. (1991). *Postmodern Theory: Critical Interrogations.* New York: Guilford Press.

Bhaskar, R. (1978). *A Realist Theory of Science.* Hemel Hempstead: Harvester.

——(1979). *The Possibility of Naturalism.* Brighton: Harvester Press.

——(1993). *Dialectic: The Pulse of Freedom.* London: Verso.

——(1994). *Plato Etc.* London: Verso.

Bryman, A. (2001). *Social Research Methods.* Oxford: Oxford University Press.

—— and Bell, E. (2003). *Business Research Methods.* Oxford: Oxford University Press.

Burrell, G., and Morgan, G. (1979). *Sociological Paradigms and Organisational Analysis.* London: Heinemann.

Bustard, D., He, Z., and Wilkie, F. (2000). 'Linking Soft Systems and Use-Case Modelling through Scenarios', *Interacting with Computers*, 13: 97–110.

Bygstad, B. (2008). 'Information Infrastructure as Organization: A Critical Realist View', in *International Conference on Information Systems (ICIS2008).* Paris: Association for Information Systems.

Champion, D., Stowell, F., and O'Callaghan, A. (2005). 'Client-Led Information System Creation (CLIC): Navigating the Gap', *Information Systems Journal*, 15: 213–31.

Checkland, P. (1999). *Systems Thinking, Systems Practice: Includes a 30-Year Retrospective.* Chichester: Wiley.

——and Griffin, R. (1970). 'Management Information Systems: A Systems View', *Journal Systems Engineering*, 1: 29–42.

——and Holwell, S. (1998). *Information, Systems and Information Systems: Making Sense of the Field.* Chichester: Wiley.

Chomsky, N. (1957). *Syntactic Structures.* The Hague: Mouton.

Churchman, C. W. (1971). *The Design of Inquiring Systems.* New York: Basic Books.

Contu, A., and Willmott, H. (2005). 'You Spin Me Round: The Realist Turn in Organization and Management Studies', *Journal Management Studies*, 42: 1645–62.

Cordoba, J.-R., and Robson, W. (2003). 'Making the Evaluation of Information Systems Insightful: Understanding the Role of Power-Ethics Strategies', *Electronic Journal of Information Systems Evaluation*, 6: 55–64.

Courtney, J. F. (2001). 'Decision Making and Knowledge Management in Inquiring Organizations: Toward a New Decision-Making Paradigm for DSS', *Decision Support Systems*, 31: 17–38.

——Merali, Y., Paradice, D., and Wynn, E. (2008). 'On the Study of Complexity in Information Systems', *International Journal of Information Technologies and the Systems Approach*, 1: 37–47.

Creswell, J. (2009). *Research Design.* Los Angeles, CA: Sage.

Dobson, P. (2001a). 'Longitudinal Case Research: A Critical Realist Perspective', *Systemic Practice and Action Research*, 14: 283–96.

——(2001b). 'The Philosophy of Critical Realism: An Opportunity for Information Systems Research', *Information Systems Frontiers*, 3: 199–210.

Doolin, B. (2004). 'Power and Resistance in the Implementation of a Medical Management Information System', *Information Systems Journal*, 14: 343–62.

Dretske, F. (1981). *Knowledge and the Flow of Information.* Oxford: Blackwell.

Easterby Smith, M., Thorpe, R., and Jackson, P. (2008). *Management Research.* London: Sage.

Fleetwood, S., and Ackroyd, S. (eds.) (2004). *Critical Realist Applications in Organisation and Management Studies.* London: Routledge.

Foucault, M. (1980). *Power/Knowledge: Selected Interviews and Other Writings 1972–1977.* Brighton: Harvester Press.

——(1988a). 'Truth, Power, Self: An Interview with Michel Foucault', in L. Martin, H. Gutman, and P. Hutton (eds.), *Technologies of the Self: An Interview with Michel Foucault.* Amherst, MA: University of Massachusetts Press, 9–15.

——(1988b). 'What is Enlightenment?', in P. Rabinow (ed.), *The Foucault Reader.* London: Penguin, 32–50.

Garrity, E. (2001). 'Synthesizing User Centered and Designer Centered IS Development Approaches Using General Systems Theory', *Information Systems Frontiers*, 3: 107–21.

Groff, R. (2000). 'The Truth of the Matter: Roy Bhaskar's Critical Realism and the Concept of Alethic Truth', *Philosophy of the Social Sciences*, 30: 407–35.

Habermas, J. (1974). *Theory and Practice.* London: Heinemann.

——(1978). *Knowledge and Human Interests.* London: Heinemann.

——(1979). *Communication and the Evolution of Society.* London: Heinemann.

——(1984). *The Theory of Communicative Action, i: Reason and the Rationalization of Society.* London: Heinemann.

——(1987). *The Theory of Communicative Action, ii: Lifeworld and System: A Critique of Functionalist Reason.* Oxford: Polity Press.

——(1993). 'On the Pragmatic, the Ethical, and the Moral Employments of Practical Reason', in J. Habermas (ed.), *Justification and Application*, Cambridge: Polity Press, 1–17.

——(2003). *Truth and Justification.* Cambridge: Polity Press.

Heng, M., and de Moor, A. (2003). 'From Habermas's Communicative Theory to Practice on the Internet', *Information Systems Journal*, 13: 331–52.

Hirschheim, R., Iivari, J., and Klein, H. (1997). 'A Comparison of Five Alternative Approaches to Information Systems Development', *Australasian Journal of Information Systems*, 5: 3–29.

Howcroft, D., and Trauth, E. (eds.) (2005). *Handbook of Critical Information Systems Research: Theory and Application.* London: Edward Elgar.

Hunt, S. (2005). 'For Truth and Realism in Management Research', *Journal of Management Inquiry*, 14: 127–38.

Klein, H. (2004). 'Seeking the New and the Critical in Critical Realism: Déjà Vu?', *Information and Organization*, 14: 123–44.

——and Huynh, M. (2004). 'The Critical Social Theory of Jurgen Habermas and its Implications for IS Research', in J. Mingers and L. Willcocks (eds.), *Social Theory and Philosophy for Information Systems.* Chichester: Wiley, 157–237.

Kuhn, T. (1970). *The Structure of Scientific Revolutions.* Chicago: Chicago University Press.

Lee, N., and Lings, I. (2008). *Doing Business Research: A Guide to Theory and Practice.* London: Sage.

Longshore Smith, M. (2006). 'Overcoming Theory-Practice Inconsistencies: Critical Realism and Information Systems Research', *Information and Organization*, 16: 191–211.

Lyytinen, K., and Hirschheim, R. (1988). 'Information Systems as Rational Discourse: An Application of Habermas's Theory of Communicative Rationality', *Scandinavian Journal of Management Studies*, 4: 19–30.

McBride, N. (2005). 'Chaos Theory as a Model for Interpreting Information Systems in Organizations', *Information Systems Journal*, 15: 233–54.

Mingers, J. (1980). 'Towards an Appropriate Social Theory for Applied Systems Thinking: Critical Theory and Soft Systems Methodology', *Journal Applied Systems Analysis*, 7: 41–50.

——(1988). 'Soft Systems Methodology and Information Systems: A Comparison of Conceptual Models and Data Flow Diagrams', *Computer Journal*, 31: 376–79.

——(1997). 'Towards Critical Pluralism', in J. Mingers and A. Gill (eds.), *Multimethodology: Theory and Practice of Combining Management Science Methodologies.* Chichester: Wiley, 407–40.

——(2000). 'What is it to be Critical? Teaching a Critical Approach to Management Undergraduates', *Management Learning*, 31: 219–37.

——(2003a). 'A Classification of the Philosophical Assumptions of Management Science Methods', *Journal of the Operational Research Society*, 54: 559–70.

——(2003b). *Information, Knowledge and Truth: A Polyvalent View.* Report No. 77, Kent Business School, Canterbury.

——(2004a). 'Paradigm Wars: Ceasefire Announced, Who Will Set up the New Administration?', *Journal Information Technology*, 19: 165–71.

——(2004b). 'Re-establishing the Real: Critical Realism and Information Systems Research', in J. Mingers and L. Willcocks (eds.), *Social Theory and Philosophy for Information Systems.* London: Wiley, 372–406.

——(2007). 'Pluralism, Realism and Truth: The Keys to Knowledge in Information Systems Research', *International Journal of Information Technologies and the Systems Approach*, 1: 81–92.

——(2008). 'Management Knowledge and Knowledge Management: Realism and Forms of Truth', *Knowledge Management Research and Practice*, 6: 62–76.

——and Gill, A. (eds.) (1997). *Multimethodology: Theory and Practice of Combining Management Science Methodologies.* Chichester: Wiley.

Mitev, N., and Wilson, M. (2004). 'What We May Learn from the Social Shaping of Technology Approach', in J. Mingers and L. Willcocks (eds.), *Social Theory and Philosophy for Information Systems*. Chichester: Wiley, 329–71.

Mitroff, I., and Linstone, H. (1993). *The Unbounded Mind: Breaking the Chains of Traditional Business Thinking*. Oxford: Oxford University Press.

Monod, E. (2004). 'Einstein, Heisenberg, Kant: Methodological Distinctions and Conditions of Possibility', *Information and Organization*, 14: 105–21.

Mora, M., Gelman, O., Forgionne, G., Petkov, D., and Cano, J. (2007). 'Integrating the Fragmented Pieces of IS Research Paradigms and Frameworks: A Systems Approach', *Information Resources Management Journal*, 20: 1–22.

Mumford, E., Hirschheim, R., Fitzgerald, G., and Wood-Harper, T. (eds.) (1985). *Research Methods in Information Systems*. Amsterdam: North Holland.

Mutch, A. (1999). 'Information: A Critical Realist Approach', in T. Wilson and D. Allen (eds.), *Proceedings of the 2nd Information Seeking in Context*. London: Taylor Graham, 535–51.

——(2005). 'Critical Realism, Agency and Discourse: Moving the Debate Forward', *Organization*, 12: 781–6.

Myers, M. (2004). 'The Nature of Hermeneutics', in J. Mingers and L. Willcocks (eds.), *Social Theory and Philosophy for Information Systems*. Chichester: Wiley, 103–28.

Niiniluoto, I. (2002). *Critical Scientific Realism*. Oxford: Oxford University Press.

Nonaka, I., and Takeuchi, H. (1995). *The Knowledge-Creating Company: How Japanese Companies Create the Dynamics of Innovation*. Oxford: Oxford University Press.

Pather, S., and Remenyi, D. (2004). 'Some of the Philosophical Issues Underpinning Research on Information Systems: From Positivism to Critical Realism', in *SAICSIT 2004*. Prague: SAICSIT.

Petkova, O., and Petkov, D. (2003). 'A Holistic Approach towards the Validation and Legitimisation of Information Systems', *Kybernetes*, 32: 703–14.

Polanyi, M. (1958). *Personal Knowledge: Towards a Post-Critical Philosophy*. London: Routledge.

Popper, K. (1959). *The Logic of Scientific Discovery*. London: Hutchinson.

——(1969). *Conjectures and Refutations*. London: Routledge and Kegan Paul.

Porra, J., Hirschheim, R., and Parks, M. (2005). 'The History of Texaco's Corporate Information Function: A General Systems Theoretical Interpretation', *MIS Quarterly*, 29: 721–46.

Probert, S. (2004). 'Adorno: A Critical Theory for IS', in J. Mingers and L. Willcocks (eds.), *Social Theory and Philosophy for Information Systems*. Chichester: Wiley, 129–56.

Reed, M. (2001). 'Organization, Trust and Control: A Realist Analysis', *Organization Studies*, 22: 201–23.

——(2005). 'Reflections on the "Realist Turn" in Organization and Management Studies'. *Journal of Management Studies*, 42: 1621–44.

Reimers, K., and Johnson, R. (2008). 'The Use of an Explicitly Theory-Driven Data Coding Method for High-Level Theory Testing in IOS', in *International Conference on Information Systems (ICIS2008)*. Paris: Association for Information Systems.

Richardson, S., Courtney, J., and Haynes, J. (2006). 'Theoretical Principles for Knowledge Management System Design: Application to Pediatric Bipolar Disorder', *Decision Support Systems*, 42: 1321–37.

Samoilenko, S. (2008). 'Information Systems Fitness and Risk in IS Development: Insights and Implications from Chaos and Complex Systems Theories', *Information Systems Frontiers*, 10: 281–92.

Senge, P. (1990). *The Fifth Discipline: The Art and Practice of the Learning Organization.* London: Century Books.

Sheffield, J. (2004). 'The Design of GSS-Enabled Interventions: A Habermasian Perspective', *Group Decision and Negotiation*, 13: 415–35.

Stowell, F. (ed.) (1995). *Information Systems Provision: The Contribution of Soft Systems Methodology.* London: McGraw Hill.

Tashakkori, A., and Teddlie, C. (1998). *Mixed Methodology: Combining Qualitative and Quantitative Approaches.* London: SAGE Publications.

————(2003). *Handbook of Mixed Methods in Social and Behavioural Research.* Thousand Oaks, CA: Sage.

Vidal, P., and Lacroux, F. (1999). 'Complexity and Management: New Representations for Information Systems', in W. Baets (ed.), *A Collection of Essays on Complexity and Management.* Singapore: World Scientific Publishing Company.

Vo, H. V., Chae, B., and Olson, D. L. (2006). 'Integrating Systems Thinking into IS Education', *Systems Research and Behavioral Science*, 23: 107–21.

Volkoff, O., Strong, D., and Elmes, M. (2007). 'Technological Embeddedness and Organizational Change', *Organization Science*, 18: 832–48.

Wainwright, D., and Waring, T. (2004). 'Three Domains for Implementing Integrated Information Systems: Redressing the Balance between Technology, Strategic and Organisational Analysis', *International Journal of Information Management*, 24: 329–46.

Walsham, G. (1997). 'Actor-Network Theory and IS Research: Current Status and Future Prospects', in A. Lee, J. Liebenau and J. DeGross (eds.), *Information Systems and Qualitative Research.* London: Chapman Hall, 466–80.

Wennberg, L., Brandt, P., and Revay, P. (2006). 'Information Security: An Application of a Systems Approach', *Kybernetes*, 35: 786–96.

Wikgren, M. (2005). 'Critical Realism as a Philosophy and Social Theory in Information Science?', *Journal of Documentation*, 61: 11–22.

Willcocks, L. (2004). 'Foucault, Power/Knowledge and Information Systems: Reconstructing the Present', in J. Mingers and L. Willcocks (eds.), *Social Theory and Philosophy for Information Systems.* Chichester: Wiley.

Willmott, H. (2005). 'Theorising Contemporary Control: Some Post-structuralist Responses to some Critical Realist Questions', *Organization*, 12: 747–80.

Wood-Harper, T., Antill, L., and Avison, D. (1985). *Information Systems Definition: The Multiview Approach.* Oxford: Blackwell.

Wynn, D., and Williams, C. (2008). 'Critical Realism-Based Explanatory Case Study Research in Information Systems', in *International Conference on Information Systems (ICIS2008).* Paris: Association for Information Systems.

Xu, L. (2000). 'The Contribution of Systems Science to Information Systems Research', *Systems Research and Behavioral Science*, 17: 105–16.

Yeo, K. (2002). 'Critical Failure Factors in Information Systems Projects', *International Journal of Project Management*, 20: 241–6.

Zhou, L., Burgoon, J., and Twitchell, D. (2004). 'A Comparison of Classification Methods for Predicting Deception in Computer-Mediated Communication', *Journal of Management Information Systems*, 20: 139–65.

Zuboff, S. (1988). *In the Age of the Smart Machine: The Future of Work and Power.* New York: Basic Books.

CHAPTER 4

SYSTEMS THINKING AND SOFT SYSTEMS METHODOLOGY

PETER CHECKLAND

INTRODUCTION

EVERY organized process carried out to achieve some desirable end (of which the creation of an information system is an example) will take its form and content from some framework of ideas which are taken as given, and make the process meaningful for those who carry out the process or make use of its end product. This chapter examines ideas which underpin work on information systems (IS) namely systems ideas. It examines basic systems ideas and what it means to do 'systems thinking', and marks the distinction between 'hard' and 'soft' systems thinking, both of which are relevant to creating any real-world 'information system' in an organization. This is done through an account of the development of the approach which led to recognition of the 'hard/soft' distinction between these two linked but different ways of using systems ideas, namely Soft Systems Methodology (SSM). Finally it summarizes the implications of these ideas for illuminating and making sense of the field of IS as a whole.

Firstly, however, it may be useful to illustrate the degree of complexity of (human) situations in which information systems are developed.

During the joint Anglo-French effort to design, make, and sell the world's first supersonic passenger-carrying aircraft, Concorde, my group at Lancaster University were invited by a director of what was then the British Aircraft Corporation to take a 'systems engineering' approach to the Anglo-French Concorde Project. Our aim was to give advice on how the management of the project could be improved. This was at a time when the two pre-production aircraft, one in Bristol, one in Toulouse, were nearing completion, but had not yet flown. The Concorde project was, at the time, the subject of much public debate in the UK, since it was by then very apparent that it was going to take years longer to develop than originally thought and would cost many millions more than originally estimated. As we started the work, we took it as completely obvious, not to be questioned, that this was clearly an engineering project; and it seemed obvious too that this project was 'a system to create a supersonic passenger aircraft according to a defined technical specification, within a certain time, at a certain cost, and under the constraints that it must gain the certificate from the Civil Aviation Authority which will enable the public to fly in it, and that it must not unacceptably damage the environment'. We had the idea that we could model this activity, and work out from the models the information systems which would be required to support that activity. Then we could, in the light of the models, examine the project's real-world activity and information support, and work out how to improve them.

In the event we were amazed when our models seemed to bear no relation at all to real-world structures and activities and, most importantly, engendered little interest in the engineers and managers working on 'the Concorde project'. Our eventual hard-won learning was that there was in fact no 'project' in the accepted sense of the way the word is used in the management literature. Although the phrase 'the Concorde project' was on everyone's lips, used many times each day, project management as such was not at all in evidence; that is not how Concorde was created. It was created by a functional structure in which all the hydraulic engineers were in one department, all the electrical engineers in another, etc.

Realizing our mistake provided valuable learning for us. We were beginning to learn that there are great difficulties in an ill-formed and conceptually confused field like management (of which IS is a part) which stem from the fact that there is no agreed language available for serious discussion which is separate from everyday language. Physical chemists know exactly what they mean by 'entropy', or 'the Q-branch of an infra-red spectrum'. Would-be scholars in the management field, on the other hand, have no shared precise meaning for many of their relevant concepts, for example 'role', 'norm', 'culture', or 'information system'; all these terms are fuzzy as a result of their unreflective use in everyday chat. Serious work in management and in IS needs always to be aware of that.

In the Concorde work our initial mistake was due to the fact that we were thinking that when people used the phrase 'the Concorde project' they were actually referring to something in the British Aircraft Corporation which corresponded to an organized *project* in the full sense of the word. We were too ready to accept the everyday language phrase 'the Concorde project' as indicating that there actually was a project in existence, and that we could model it as *a system* and hence work out its necessary information support.

This example of the misleading use of the word 'project' in the British Aircraft Corporation at that time is an example of the untrustworthiness of casual everyday language in the management field. Unfortunately the problem is very much worse in that part of the broad field of management which uses the language of 'systems'.

Casually, in everyday talk we speak of 'the education system', 'the prison system', the 'transport system', etc., as if these were integrated coordinated wholes with each part contributing coherently to the performance of the whole. (To use the phrase 'the transport system' is, in the UK at the present time, almost to make a joke. The UK has no coherent system of transport, only an aggregate of structures and processes which deliver transport services in an uncoordinated way.) The word 'system' has been captured by everyday language to refer, without precision, to any large more-or-less connected entity.

For serious intellectual and scholarly purposes we need to separate 'system' from everyday language and use the word as a technical term; 'system' is, truly, the name of a concept: that of a complex whole which can adapt or be adapted to a changing environment and so remain viable through time.

With the proviso that the word 'system' be used in this serious sense, systems thinking can help to provide understanding and clarification of the whole field of IS. It is in order to try to dispel some of the confusion which results from the casual use of the word 'system' in everyday language, that this chapter will examine: the origins of systems thinking and the core ideas behind the concept 'system'; the development of 'soft' systems thinking in Soft Systems Methodology; and the implications of this for work in IS. It draws on earlier accounts including Checkland (1981, 1988, 1996), Checkland and Scholes (1990), Checkland and Haynes (1994), Checkland and Poulter (2006). (Checkland, 1996, an encyclopaedia article, includes an annotated bibliography.)

SYSTEMS THINKING: ORIGINS

Systems ideas emerged as a generalization of ideas about organisms which were developed within biology in the first half of the twentieth century. Where classical physics developed its core conceptualizations in the Newtonian revolution of the seventeenth century (to be modified by Einsteinian physics in the twentieth) and chemistry developed its core concepts ('elements', 'compounds', etc.) in the eighteenth and nineteenth centuries, biology was later in emerging as a science with an accepted conceptual framework. As the new science of biology was developed, its concern with living things led to many controversies over the nature of the living, and hence over the proper concerns of the new discipline. Much debate concerned the issue of *vitalism*: did living things, which to many were, intuitively, clearly 'more than the sum of their parts', possess some mysterious non-material component or directing spirit which characterized the living? (The spirit was even given a name, *entelechy*!) In the twentieth century the elucidation of molecular genetic mechanisms based upon DNA replication has finally resolved these debates. But within biology itself there was from the second half of the nineteenth century a strand of holistic thinking within the subject which argued that the degree of *organization* was the crucial characteristic of living organisms, rather than the presence of some metaphysical directing spirit.

The school of thought associated with these so-called 'organismic biologists', based on such work as Woodger's *Biological Principles* of 1929, focused upon the organism as the unit of analysis in biology, and developed ideas about the processes which characterize metabolism and self-reproduction in organisms. It was one of these organismic biologists, the Austrian Ludwig von Bertalanffy, who founded the systems movement by beginning to argue, in the late 1940s, that these ideas about organisms could be extended to complex wholes of any kind: to 'systems' (von Bertalanffy 1968; Gray and Rizzo 1973).

Since it was ideas about physically existing organisms which were generalized as ideas about 'systems' in general, it is perhaps not surprising that most people, taking their cue from everyday language, simply assume unquestioningly that *systems* exist in the world. It is the later history of the systems movement which has painfully established that *system* is, truly, the abstract concept of a whole which may or may not turn out to be useful as a descriptive device for making sense of real-world wholes. Unfortunately, from the very start of the work in the systems movement, Bertalanffy himself used the word promiscuously both as an abstract idea (i.e. epistemologically) and as a label-word (i.e. ontologically). (It may be remarked at this point that this chapter's title has the phrase 'Systems Thinking'—i.e. the *process* of thinking using systems ideas—rather than 'Systems Theory' precisely because the latter title would be taken by many to mean 'the theory *of* systems', taking as given the status of systems as 'things in the world'.)

But in spite of this confusion the concept *system* has been found to be useful as an explanatory device in many subject areas: including for example ecology, engineering, economics, anthropology, sociology, psychology, geography, as well as the natural sciences. In fact systems thinking has emerged as a meta-discipline and as a meta-language which can be used to talk *about* the subject matter of many different fields.

An example of the status of systems thinking as a meta-subject is shown by the emergence of cybernetics, which occurred at about the same time that Bertalanffy was advocating the development of general system(s) theory. The mathematician Norbert Wiener worked on mechanical/electrical computing machines to aim and fire anti-aircraft guns, the work representing an attempt to automate what the hunter after a moving quarry does intuitively. Wiener, with Bigelow, was developing feedback systems in which information about current performance modifies future performance. Excess feedback in such systems leads to oscillatory 'hunting' about the desired performance, which cannot then be tightly controlled. Wiener also worked with a Harvard medical scientist Rosenblueth, who was familiar with the pathological condition 'purpose tremor' in which the patient, in trying to pick up a simple object, overshoots and goes into uncontrollable oscillation. The similarity between the human and electro-mechanical cases suggests that these are two different manifestations of a notional control system which can be described as a general case applicable to many different embodiments. Wiener (1948) launched cybernetics as the general (meta-level) science of 'communication and control in man and machine', though Plato had already made the same point more than 2,000 years earlier in making an analogy between a helmsman steering a ship and a statesman steering the 'ship of state' (Checkland 1981: 82–6). Nowadays cybernetics is a subset of the broad area covered by systems thinking.

From its emergence in organismic biology, systems thinking has both developed core systems ideas and itself been developed in a number of different ways in different areas. The next sections summarize these developments.

SYSTEMS THINKING: CORE CONCEPTS

In the journal *Philosophy of Science* in 1955 it was announced that 'A Society for the Advancement of General Systems Theory is in the process of organization'. Behind this initiative were the biologist Bertalanffy, an economist (K. E. Boulding), a physiologist (R. W. Gerard), and a mathematician (A. Rapoport). Their idea was that there could be developed meta-level theory and models 'applicable to more than one of the traditional departments of knowledge'—just as, in the example given above, a single model of a feedback control system might give an account which can describe both the behaviour of electro-mechanical servo-mechanisms made by engineers and the behaviour called 'purpose tremor' in human patients. Surely the engineers and medical scientists would find this both intriguing and useful? The society referred to was the Society for General Systems Research, and it still exists, with a small membership, as the International Society for the Systems Sciences. But its original project, the development of a meta-level systems theory into whose language problems within many disciplines could be translated for solution—leading to an anticipated greater unification of the sciences—cannot be declared a success. The kind of meta-level problem solving envisaged by the pioneers has not occurred.

Rather, systems ideas have made contributions within many different subject areas. In this the original ideas of the protagonists of general system(s) theory have been vindicated to some extent. There is now a set of systems ideas which find application in many fields.

At the core of systems thinking is a concept which clearly derives very directly from our intuitive or casual knowledge of organisms: the concept of a whole entity which can adapt and survive, within limits, in a changing environment. This notion of 'the adaptive whole' is the central image in systems thinking, and the systems movement can be regarded as the attempt to explore the usefulness of this particular concept in many different fields. In order to understand and use this concept we need a handful of further ideas which, together with the idea of the adaptive whole, constitute the bedrock of systems thinking. (For more detailed discussion, see Checkland 1981: chs. 3 and 4.)

First, for an observer to choose to see some complex entity as a whole, separable from its environment, it must have properties which (for that observer at least) are properties of it as a single entity: so-called *emergent properties*. These are the properties which make the whole entity 'more than the sum of its parts'. This is not a mysterious concept, except to those New Age mystics who are drawn to the systems movement by a yearning for an elusive ill-defined holism. The parts of a bicycle, in a sack, are simply an aggregate. When assembled in the particular structure we call 'a bicycle', that entity has vehicular potential, which is an emergent property of the whole. In the structure of DNA, the laws of physical chemistry allow any sequence of the amino-acid residues which join the double helix. In order to explain experimental findings we have to invoke the idea that certain sequences constitute a 'code' which, in biological repro-duction, results in our having red hair or a large nose. The 'genetic code' is an emergent property of the amino-acid sequences. Another example: university degrees are awarded not by departments or courses but by the university as a single entity. The power to confer degrees is an emergent property of the institution as a whole, one which the institution itself invents.

Secondly, wholes having emergent properties may well have smaller wholes with their own emergent properties; for example, it is meaningful to think of a department of a university as having autonomous emergent properties (the resources and authority to put on a particular course, for example). Equally, the larger whole (the university) may be only a part in a yet larger whole (the university sector of higher education) with its own emergent properties . . . and so on. In other words systems thinking includes the idea of *layered structure*.

Thirdly, if our entity is to survive in environments which change, it must have available to it ways of finding out about its environments and ways of responding internally to them; it must have processes of *communication* and *control*, which may be automatic (control of core temperature in our bodies for example) or created by human beings (rules within a university, for example), depending on the kind of entity being considered.

These four ideas: emergent properties, layered structure, processes of communica-tion, and control, are the ideas needed to describe the basic concept of an adaptive whole. They are the core ideas of systems thinking, and have been used in different ways in many different fields, from engineering to economics, from geography to jurisprudence.

Broadly speaking, systems ideas have been used in three different areas: the study of wholes which Nature creates (often called 'natural systems'); the study of wholes designed by human beings ('designed systems') such as watches, radios, suspension bridges; and finally the study of human affairs, including such activities as governing, managing, designing, educating, etc. Obviously the three areas show many links. A landscape gardener, for example, enacts a human system of activity which interacts with, to modify, a natural system.

In general, work involving 'natural' and 'designed' wholes, are ones in which there is usually good mapping between the systems concepts and the observed real world. Not surprisingly these are areas in which the everyday use of the word 'system' does not lead to too many intellectual difficulties. It is in these cases possible to forget that systems are always, *fundamentally*, abstract concepts which may or may not map real entities. Here there are reasonable grounds for equating an entity in the real world (e.g. 'the natural drainage system of the Rhine Valley') with the systems description of it. It is from this kind of work that the use of *system* as a mere label for something in the real world derives.

But such easy mapping is much more problematical in the third broad area of application, that of human affairs. In the 1960s the main development of systems thinking in this area skirted round and managed to avoid this problem by focusing on arrangements to meet goals or objectives declared in advance to be desirable. If a carefully defined objective could be taken as given then a 'system' to meet the objective could be *engineered*. This adoption of the notion of goal seeking was the approach which characterized the post-war developments arising from the success of operational research in the Second World War. Bell Telephones formalized their approach to the development of new technology in 'systems engineering' (Hall 1962); RAND Corporation developed 'systems analysis' (Optner 1973). As mainframe computers were developed the same thinking was adopted to provide an approach to designing and establishing a computer system. (This was reasonable in the early days when computers were used only to transfer to a machine the transaction processing previously done by clerks; but the thinking behind early computer systems analysis became increasingly inappropriate as the technology developed, as this book illustrates.)

This thinking about achieving a declared objective characterizes the first major use of systems thinking within human affairs. It is essentially *systematic* in character. The approaches just referred to consist of examining and selecting one among a number of alternative systems to achieve an objective which is defined as desirable at the start and is taken as given. It is thus limited to the subset of situations in which objectives are undisputed, so that the problems are those of 'how to do it?' not problems of 'what to do?' This is mainly the case in situations which relate to technology.

This idea of creating systems to meet a desirable objective, now thought of as 'Hard' Systems Thinking, has been very successful, and it is the characteristic core of most post-Second World War 'management science'. However, a great many managerial problem situations cannot be reduced to goal-seeking. The reduction does work well in technological situations, and Systems Engineering is now a well-developed field with its own journals, professional associations, methodology, and techniques. But for most managers, at every level, most of the time, the managerial task is to cope with ill-defined, dynamic, multifaceted situations in which objectives are unclear, and many different interests clamour for attention. Such situations entail problems often described as 'wicked', in that just when you think you are on top of them they reveal new aspects which demand attention and call for rethinking.

It was in seeking a way of coping with this type of situation that a different, broader way of using systems ideas emerged, different, that is, from assuming that the world out there contains systems whose objectives can be defined, enabling the systems to be engineered to achieve them. The broader way of using the basic systems ideas (now known as 'Soft' Systems Thinking) came out of a programme of action research in real-world situations which was carried out over a period of thirty years at Lancaster University. It broadened the scope of systems thinking and also led to useful ways of thinking about the field of information systems as a whole. These developments are described in the next sections of this chapter.

THE DEVELOPMENT OF SOFT SYSTEMS THINKING AND SOFT SYSTEMS METHODOLOGY

The Research Context

The context which enabled the development of Soft Systems Thinking was the creation of a postgraduate Department of Systems Engineering at Lancaster University in the late 1960s. The Department was founded by Professor Gwilym Jenkins (the well-known statistician), and the present writer joined him in 1969. After fifteen years as first a technologist, then a manager of research in the new industry of making wholly synthetic fibres, I decided to start a new career when Jenkins explained to me that he intended to interpret the word 'engineering' in the Department's name in the broader sense in which the word can be used. In the English language you can 'engineer' a meeting with someone, or 'engineer' the release of hostages, as well as 'engineer' a chemical plant. Also, after an interesting and illuminating time in a giant corporation (ICI Ltd) I was intrigued by—and thoroughly agreed with—Jenkins's idea that the way to further develop systems engineering was to work in real-world problem situations outside the University, in organizations large and small in both public and private sectors. This strategy became possible because we found ourselves recruiting Masters students of average age around 30, mature people who were at a point in their lives when they were rethinking who they were and what future direction their careers might take. Jenkins and I also agreed that just as whatever ideas we have in our head influence the experience we acquire in the world, ultimately it is the experience of the world which is the source of the ideas. In the relation between the two (as shown in Figure 4.1) what is most important is neither the ideas nor the experience but the arrows: *the cycle between the two*, the mutual influence which leads to each creating the other. Asked by Professor Jenkins to take over the lead in establishing the Department's research programme, I felt that, given mature students, we could use them in a programme of action research in organizations in ways which would not be possible with fresh graduates. After a few years we supplemented this effort by persuading the University to allow us to establish a university-owned consultancy company, ISCOL Ltd. This enabled us to undertake projects at any time and of any length, i.e. not restricted by the timings of the one-year Masters degree. Some of our best students

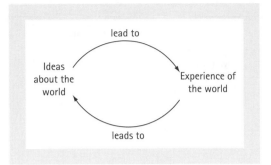

FIGURE 4.1 Ideas about the world and experience of it steadily create each other

stayed on after the Masters course to work for a year or two as ISCOL consultants. The Company structure was simple. Each year ISCOL Ltd. gave its surplus to a charity, namely its owner Lancaster University! Over the twenty years in which the Company existed the University received nearly £500,000 from ISCOL. The size of the surplus was not crucially important from our point of view, as long as there was a surplus to ensure continuity. What was most important was that we had here an overall mechanism in which each and every research project—whether from the Masters course or from ISCOL—was one unit within an overall coherent strategy. Also, in the action research approach (Checkland and Holwell 1998a) researchers do not simply observe or collect data from outside organizations, they *take part* in the work going on to solve problems or to bring about improvements. This ensured that each of the 300+ projects carried out during the life of the programme had the potential to make its own contribution to the research learning as a whole, adding to the cumulative experience and helping to develop the ideas.

The Research Process

The initial research idea was to take Systems Engineering (SE) as developed by Bell Telephone Laboratories, and described in Arthur Hall's classic book *A Methodology for Systems Engineering* (1962), and try to apply it outside the area for which it had been developed, namely situations in which desirable new technical systems were developed. Our aim was to test it in messy general management situations, ones in which the option of taking some defined objective as given was not available. Whatever happened, we would learn from the experience gained as we cycled many times round the cycle shown in Figure 4.2. This shows a cycle of three elements: methodology; use; and learning from use, which itself may then modify the declared methodology. We were breaking into that cycle by taking SE as given.

We quickly found that classic SE was not rich enough to cope with the complexity found in problematical management situations. Two early experiences illustrate this. In

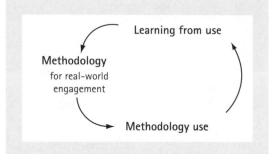

FIGURE 4.2 The concept behind the development of Soft Systems Methodology

the Anglo-French work on Concorde mentioned in the Introduction to this chapter, we were initially thinking, like systems engineers, that we could work from a tightly defined objective related to the work going on in Bristol and Toulouse: creating the world's first supersonic passenger-carrying jet aircraft. This was not wrong but it was naive. As well as being an engineering project Concorde had a significant political aspect. Britain and France signed a treaty (no less) to do the joint work at a time when the French President was vetoing British entry into the European Common Market. From the British perspective this work constituted a political as well as an engineering project, one which aimed to show what a good European partner the UK could be. To engage richly with the situation it was necessary to embrace both the engineering and the politics. This realization was seen eventually as a key experience in the development of Soft Systems Methodology.

Also in the early years of the programme, on a very different scale, in a small carpet-making company, the owner/managing director said at the start of the work 'I know I need to do more than live from day to day in this Company; I want you to make me plan.' Seeking to impress him quickly with our practicality, work began in an area which we thought could rather easily be improved, namely production planning. But no, he did not want that; nor did he want to take up other suggestions we made. This was very frustrating. Eventually it was possible to make sense of this situation by recognizing the managing director's unstated fear: that his firm might become more profitable and begin to grow—which would change both it and his lifestyle. In saying 'make me plan' he really wanted to ensure that his firm remained viable but did not change. He did not look for greater wealth; he wanted to make sure he preserved a pleasant lifestyle which enabled him to play golf on two mid-week afternoons every week. Such is the real complexity of human affairs, something which often surprises graduates of MBA courses.

Learning from experiences of this kind brought the realization that SE methodology would not survive unscathed in the cycle of Figure 4.2 when applied to typical management, rather than technical situations. In the end the experiences led to a methodology so enriched that it acquired its own name: Soft Systems Methodology (SSM). As SSM emerged it was also realized that the modelling of activity systems,

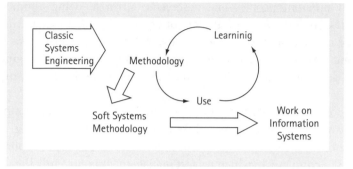

FIGURE **4.3** The outcome of the Action Research Programme

which had become a feature of SSM, also led to a highly relevant approach to work on information systems (IS), as indicated in Figure 4.3.

This arose from the fact that for each activity in an activity model you can ask: 'What information would be required to do this activity; and what information would be generated by doing it?' Thus activity models can be a coherent (arguable, discussable) source of information models. This has led to much use of SSM in the IS field, a development which was not anticipated from the start of the research; it was a welcome bonus from the action research experience.

THE NATURE OF SSM

Doing research is always a confusing experience when you are in the middle of it, and the research which established SSM and Soft Systems Thinking was no exception. However, the Action Research process, in which the research object is the real-world experience itself, *requires* reflection upon the experience, and this supplies a structure through which the learning can emerge to be captured explicitly (Checkland and Holwell 1988a).

Over a period of some years it became clear that the methodology emerging from reflection on dealing with 'wicked' management problem situations took a more subtle view of human affairs than the goal-seeking view which underlies classic SE and most Management Science. This new view will be set out succinctly at this point rather than being left to emerge later in this discussion. (This will better serve the present purpose, which is to provide a clear account of the shape of SSM, explain the difference between 'hard' and 'soft' systems thinking, and, finally, argue the relevance of SSM to work in the IS field.)

Every human situation will always contain people who interpret the perceived real world differently from each other. Every such situation will contain different world-views, that is to say different mental structures which cause the world to be seen differently by different people—one observer's 'terrorist' being another's 'freedom fighter'. In the Concorde work the absence of organized project management stemmed from a senior management world-view that world-class engineering was best ensured by organizing professional engineers in peer groups: hydraulic engineers in one department, electrical engineers in another, etc.; hence the functional organizational structure.

However, world-views, though often hard to change, are never completely static; they change over time, often remarkably quickly, as a result of changing experience or sudden crisis. The 'British Aircraft Corporation' which developed Concorde is now 'BAE Systems', a company in which project management is currently the unquestioned norm. Similarly, when we wished to set up ISCOL Ltd. in Lancaster University there was much opposition to the idea. Had the decision been in the hands of Senate we would not have been allowed to go ahead, since the idea of bringing in money for services rendered was thought by some academics to be somehow improper. Luckily the decision was in the hands of the University Council, which contains people from outside the University, and that body allowed us to establish ISCOL Ltd. Nowadays, although universities are not—by private sector standards—noticeably dynamic organizations, university Deans urge academics to think of anything they could do which would bring in money, and encourage them to do it vigorously. World-views do change!

Finally, human situations will always contain people trying to act purposefully—deliberately, consciously, with intent—this being one of the core characteristics which makes us human. Whether we work in giant corporations or in small firms, and whether in the private or the public sector, it is always the case that people try to take purposeful action, though the purpose might well be in dispute and the intentional action may well be mixed with random thrashing about. There is never any shortage of that in human affairs. These three characteristics: different world-views; changing world-views; would-be purposeful action, provide an image of human situations which underpins SSM. They lead to the shape of the approach.

In making sense of the emergence of SSM from the action research experience four crucial points of learning can be identified. They established both the image of human situations just described and the overall shape of SSM. First came the realization that every research situation was characterized by would-be purposeful action. This led to the idea of making models of purposeful activity, and a way of doing this was worked out based on the basic systems ideas (emergent properties, a layered structure, and processes of communication and control). Not much progress could be made with this, however, until it was accepted that any such model could be built only on the basis of a declared world-view, since a number of world-views will be relevant to any contemplated purposeful action. For example a number of different models relevant to capturing the purposeful activity of a hospital could be built. Their content would depend upon the world-view selected, which could range among those attributed to doctors, nurses, managers, patients, government, the local community, etc.

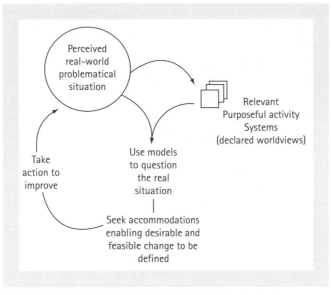

FIGURE 4.4 SSM's inquiring/learning system

These thoughts in combination led to the basic shape of the SSM process, which is shown in Figure 4.4. In this the concern is not with trying to define 'a problem', and certainly not 'a system' but lies in expressing 'a *situation* considered by some to be problematical'. Models of purposeful activity considered relevant to exploring the situation are built.

The models are used as a source of questions to ask of the situation addressed. This provides structure to a debate focused on some possible change which is both desirable and feasible—desirable, that is, given the models used, and feasible *culturally* for these particular people in this particular situation with their particular history and perspectives. The debate about change might be expected to find consensus, but in our experience that is the occasional special case. The norm in the human tribe is the need to find *accommodation*s among world-views in conflict. This entails finding versions of the situation which different people with different outlooks could nevertheless *live with*. The whole process is one of learning one's way to useful practical change; it needs to be constituted as a learning system. SSM provides many techniques to help in traversing this learning cycle. They will be mentioned in outline below, but first it is important to make some general points about the cycle as a whole:

- the process, which is action-oriented, is in principle *ongoing*, although developed in time-limited projects it can also be seen more generally as a way of going about the task of managing;
- the models, unlike most models in management science do not purport to describe anything in the real world, they are only *intellectual devices* which help

bring structure to debate about change; they are models of *ways of thinking about the real situation* each based on a particular world-view thought relevant to the particular situation;

• traversing the cycle is not a step-by-step process; rather, experienced users will be found doing work at many or all stages of the cycle during a use of the approach: for example, doing more finding out, building new models, comparing models with real-world activity, finding more relevant world-views; in general, reacting to the debate engendered, letting it speak, rather than confining it to any particular template;

• since each model is built according to a declared world-view, the use of the models to question the real situation raises the focus of debate from current specifics to the meta level: What world-views are being taken as given here? What alternatives are there? This is eye-opening in most situations; really sophisticated users of SSM use Figure 4.4, once it is internalized, as itself a sense-making model to bring clarity and understanding to the engagement with the situation; the best uses usually reveal the approach to be in the hands of people in the situation addressed, with facilitating help from someone with detailed knowledge of SSM.

As far as techniques are involved in SSM, they facilitate the activities surrounding the learning cycle in Figure 4.4. They all emerged in research experience and have been found to be consistently helpful. It is not relevant here to describe them in detail. (The most accessible source of detail is Checkland and Poulter (2006), an account of SSM written for people wishing to use the approach rather than agonize about its theory or its history.)

Finding out about the problematical situation is helped by representing it pictorially in 'Rich Pictures' and in three analyses. The rationale for drawing Rich Pictures is that the complexity in real life is always a nexus of interacting relationships, and relationships are better represented in pictures than in linear prose. The three analyses (One, Two, and Three) supplement the pictures, covering: examination of the intervention in the situation (One); the social flavour of the situation in terms of roles, norms, and values (Two); and the 'commodities' which embody power in the situation—how they are acquired, used, defended, relinquished etc. (Three). This finding out is a source both of ideas for models likely to be insightful and for an understanding of what kind of change might be feasible in the situation. (In the Concorde work described above, the introduction of a project management approach was culturally infeasible at that time in the British Aircraft Corporation.)

The model building in SSM, since it entails forming only *concepts* of a defined purposeful activity (not descriptions of part of the real world), is a straightforward application of logical thinking, once a well-formulated account of the activity (a 'Root Definition' in SSM) has been made. The core of this kind of model building is the realization that any purposeful activity can be expressed as a transformation process T which converts an input into an output. (At one level: 'unpainted garden fence' into 'painted garden fence', at another: 'health care needs of the citizens of Oslo' into 'those

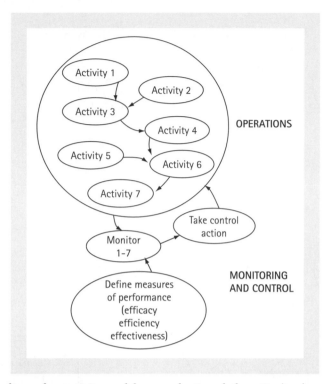

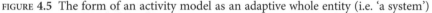

FIGURE **4.5** The form of an activity model as an adaptive whole entity (i.e. 'a system')

needs met'). Model building is then a matter of assembling the activities necessary to obtain the input to T, the activities to transform it, and the activities to dispose of T's output. These activities, linked by arrows which express the dependency of one activity upon another, represent the model's operational activities. To this we add activities of monitoring the operational activities in order to take control action if necessary. This meets the requirements of a system as an adaptive whole and gives a structure like that in Figure 4.5.

Figure 4.6 shows an activity model built using the IKEA mission statement as if it were a Root Definition.

It is not by chance that Figure 4.5 has seven activities in the operational part of the model. It has been found very useful always to represent the transformation process initially in around '7±2' activities, this expression coming from George Miller's well-known 1968 paper in cognitive psychology ('The Magical Number 7±2'). This suggests, from laboratory experiments, that the human brain may have the capacity to cope with this many concepts simultaneously. Any of that initial cluster of activities in a model can always itself become the source of a Root Definition and a more detailed model. (For example a single activity: 'Obtain raw material X' could itself be expanded into a model in its own right whose activities would include such items as 'Find

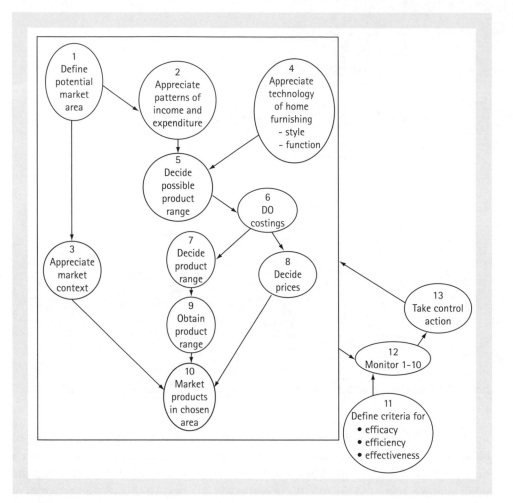

FIGURE **4.6** An SSM-style activity model built from the concept in the IKEA mission statement: marketing home furnishing items of good function and style at prices low enough to enable a majority of people to buy them

suppliers', 'Ascertain their reliability', 'Compare prices', etc. This stems from the layered nature of the core systems concept of an adaptive whole.)

In order to help create purposeful models of this kind SSM provides several guide-lines from experience. Having thought of a combination of world-view and purposeful activity relevant to exploring the problem situation, express it in the PQR formula: do P, by Q, in order to contribute to the higher-level aim R—for example 'paint the garden fence, by hand painting, in order to improve the appearance of the property'. This answers the questions, What?, How?, and Why? (Note that in Figure 4.6 the Root Definition used is of the kind: do P to help achieve R, missing out the 'how' and with R only implied as 'run a successful business'.) Then expand consideration of the purposeful concept using the CATWOE mnemonic, where T and W are the transformation process and world-view, and the other elements enrich this further. C (for the metaphor 'customer') answers the question: who would be most affected by the outcome of this transformation process? A (for 'actor(s)') addresses the question: who would carry out these activities? O (for 'owner(s)') covers: who could stop this transformation, and E ('environmental constraints' on T) asks: what does this process have to take as 'given' from outside itself—for example, is there a finite budget or timescale, or perhaps legal constraints which have to be met? Answering these questions ensures a rich Root Definition from which the operational part of the model can be constructed. It also allows the other part of the model—the monitoring and control activity—to be completed. (Note that the IKEA mission statement (Figure 4.6) could be enriched by using CATWOE and PQR.)

Since no two human situations are ever identical, a particular model might have some highly specific measure of performance, for example ethics or aesthetics. However there are three criteria which are always relevant, and defining them for a particular model always leads to insights. In asking what criteria enable performance to be monitored, we are asking how might T fail, and we need criteria for each of three kinds of failure. There might be failure to deliver the output from the input—we need a criteria for *efficacy*. Quite separately the process might be using too much resource, even if it were efficacious—we need a criteria for *efficiency*. Thirdly, even if efficacious and efficient the process might not be contributing to some higher level or longer-term aim, since it is possible to do well something which is actually not worth doing at all—it might be *ineffective*. So we need to decide how efficacy, efficiency, and effectiveness (the '3 Es' in SSM) defined in this way, would be judged for the particular purposeful transformation in question.

Finally, it was realized in the course of the research that Root Definitions can be of two types, now called 'Primary Task' or 'Issue-based' (IB). PT definitions are models in which the purposeful activity model maps, in principle, some real-world structure—for example in a company with a functional organization structure we might make a model related to, say, production, in which case the model boundary would map onto the organization boundary of the production department. An IB definition on the other hand is a model of an activity which is relevant and important but is not itself captured in an organizational entity. For example, when working in the Petrochemical Division of ICI Ltd, it was found useful to make a model of 'a system to innovate in the petrochemical industry'. There was no 'innovation department' as such. Many of the activities in the model did in fact exist in the real situation but were spread between Research, Production, and Marketing Departments: the model boundary cut across the organizational boundaries. The general rule is: do not use only PT or IB models, use both. Not surprisingly, IB models stir up interest precisely because they cut across organization boundaries and hence impinge upon political realities in the organization in question. Figure 4.7 summarizes all of these guidelines which support the modelling process in SSM.

When it comes to using models to structure debate, exactly how this is done will depend very much on the norms and attitudes in the situation addressed, making

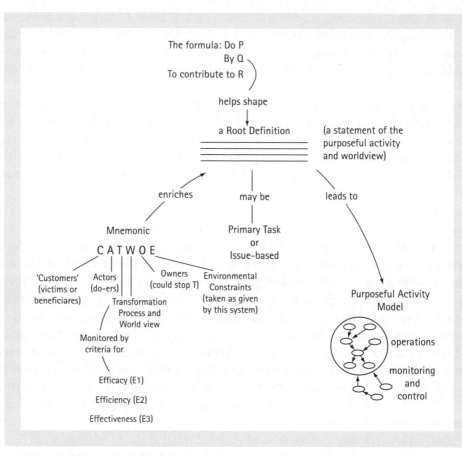

The formula: Do P
By Q
To contribute to R

helps shape

a Root Definition   (a statement of the
                            purposeful activity
                            and worldview)

enriches   may be   leads to

Mnemonic   Primary Task
                  or
C A T W O E   Issue-based

'Customers'   Actors   Owners   Environmental
(victims or   (do-ers)   (could stop T) Constraints
beneficiares)   (taken as given
               Transformation   by this system)   Purposeful Activity
               Process and   Model
               World view

Monitored by   operations
criteria for

Efficacy (E1)   monitoring
                                                               and
Efficiency (E2)   control

Effectiveness (E3)

FIGURE 4.7 Guidelines for building models of concepts of purposeful activity in Soft Systems Methodology

generalization difficult. In a project to rethink the role, structure, and information systems of a 600-strong Head Office department in the Shell Group, for example (described in detail in Checkland and Scholes 1990) the work was carried out in a sequence of two-day management workshops, making use of a standard way of tackling issues within the Shell culture. Day One aimed to end up with some relevant models, Day Two used the models to question the real world of the Head Office department and its ongoing interactions with its internal 'clients' in the Company.

Technically, comparing the models with the real situation is done by using the models as a source of questions to ask of the real world. It is of course also possible to ask, at a higher level, how the world-views associated with the models compare with the (normally unexamined) assumptions about the perceived world which characterize the situation being explored. The questioning can be informal—putting models on flip charts, for example, and having a discussion with reference to them—or can be carried out systematically. In this latter case it is a matter of asking, for each activity and link in a model questions such as: Does this exist in the real situation?, How is it manifest?, Is it regarded as satisfactory?, Is it essential?, By what criteria is it judged?, etc., etc.

As this kind of comparison proceeds the aim is always to think in terms of possible desirable change which is also feasible in the culture in question—change which different interests could live with and is acceptable within the local politics, or changes them. The change itself may be structural, procedural, or attitudinal, or a mix of all three. As ideas for a particular change emerge, it can be scrutinized in terms of what, who, how, when, etc., not forgetting an always relevant question: what *enabling* activity would be needed to bring about this change? In the UK's National Health Service, for example, it used to be the case that hospital consultants were very powerful indeed, though that has changed in recent years. When work in the NHS using SSM started, no change in a UK hospital could be made if powerful consultants did not support it. The enabling activity was: gain consultant support.

The aim of this necessarily brief account of SSM is to show that it is a well-established learning approach to real-world complexity. Based on the notions of usually unexamined, but in principle changeable world-views, together with the ubiquity in human affairs of an intention to act purposefully, it explores situations thought to be problematical, and learns its way to 'action to improve'. Its content was honed over thirty years in several hundred projects which were thought of as both practical interventions and as pieces of methodological research. A slow maturation led to a way of engaging with real situations which was very far from the classic systems engineering process of the 1960s with which it had started. It was only gradually recognized that a very significant intellectual step separated SSM from classic SE, a step which marks and establishes the distinction between 'hard' and 'soft' systems thinking. This is explained in the next section and leads to a final section which applies these ideas to the field of information systems.

'HARD' AND 'SOFT' SYSTEMS THINKING

Whenever you observe someone taking purposeful action in the everyday world it is always interesting to ask yourself: what ideas must they be taking as given if they assume that what they are doing is a sensible thing to do? Similarly, of any organized process of intervention in real situations we can ask ourselves: what must be the accepted assumptions behind this process? This question can be asked at two levels. There will be an assumed philosophical position reflected in the form of the intervention process, and there will be an assumed sociology reflecting a particular view of the nature of human society.

As SSM developed into a mature process it was gradually realized that it assumed both a different philosophy and a different sociology from those assumed at the start, namely the assumptions behind the classic Bell Telephone systems engineering process (Hall 1962) which had itself been taken as given at the start of the research. In common with most of the systems work done in the 1950s and 1960s, classic SE uses the word 'system' in the same way that it is used in everyday language. It is assumed to be a label-word for reified 'systems' which exist out there in the real world. The world is taken to contain multiple interacting systems which could be engineered to work better. (This is the same assumption found in RAND Corporation systems analysis (Hitch 1955), classic system dynamics (Forrester 1961), classic operational research (Rivett and Ackoff 1963) and the viable systems model (Beer 1972).) All of this work thus assumes a philosophy of positivism, the philosophy of natural science, and a process of goal-seeking/optimizing. Along with this goes a sociology of functionalism, in which each part of the system addressed plays its part in contributing to the achievement of system objectives. The viable systems model, for example, consists of a set of linked functional subsystems, each with an explicit role in the system as whole. This model is then mapped onto real-world organizations as if functionalism is the only way to conceptualize an organization. The world-view of this strand of thinking is thus that illustrated in the upper half of Figure 4.8 in which the observer sees systems in the real world which can be engineered to achieve their objectives.

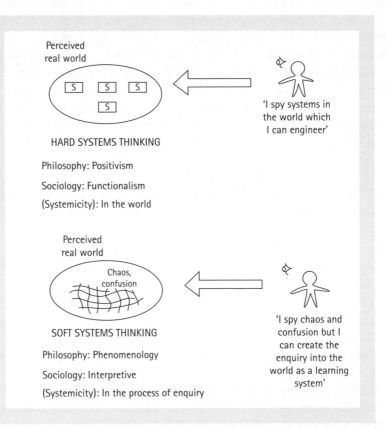

FIGURE **4.8** Hard and Soft system thinking (the former being a special case of the latter)

Once SSM had embraced the concept of alternative world-views—which can themselves change over time—together with the ubiquity in human settings of would-be purposeful action, its concept of social reality was that this was in a process of continuously being constructed and reconstructed in human talk and action (Checkland 1981: ch. 8). Positivism and functionalism do not cover this perception. Rather it is based on a Husserlian philosophy of phenomenology, in which what is prime is not the external world itself but our mental activity which engages with that reality, together with an interpretive sociology of the kind which Alfred Schutz derived from Husserl's philosophy (Schutz 1967, originally published in German in 1932). The lower half of Figure 4.8 illustrates the intellectual stance in which SSM sits. The observer sees in the world complexity and confusion, but can consciously organize *the process of engaging with the world* as a learning system. The difference between the upper and lower parts of Figure 4.8 lies in their attributions of systemicity (systemness). The upper observer assumes the world to be systemic, a set of linked systems. The other observer assumes that he or she can make the process of inquiry into the world systemic. This different attribution of systemicity is the crucial distinction between 'hard' and 'soft' systems thinking. (For more detailed discussion, see Checkland and Holwell 2004; and Checkland and Poulter 2006: Appendix A: SSM's Theory.)

Expressed in a different way: hard systems thinking uses the word 'system' ontologically; soft systems thinking, as in SSM, uses the word epistemologically, SSM providing an epistemology for making sense of experienced social reality. This defines the relation between 'hard' and 'soft'. The two are not necessarily separate. Within soft systems thinking the user has the freedom to decide that the chosen action-to-improve might be, in a particular case, to design and implement in the real situation a *system* to do something or other, with all of the work from the 1950s and 1960s available to help with this. Thus soft systems thinking does not throw away the earlier thinking: the hard stance is an occasional special case within the soft.

IMPLICATIONS OF SOFT SYSTEMS THINKING AND SOFT SYSTEMS

Methodology for Information Systems

Basic ideas

The provision of information was rarely absent from the issues involved in the several hundred projects of the SSM research programme. This is not surprising; information has long been a compelling issue in human affairs. The first printed book in Europe, the Gutenberg Bible, appeared in 1455, and by 1501 the Pope was suggesting to bishops that the control of printing should be considered in order to preserve the purity of the faith (Roberts 1980). Information is always potentially subversive, and control of it is a very common way of exercising power in modern organizations. So it is to be expected that the opening up of the mind entailed in soft systems thinking and SSM should be relevant to work in the field of information systems.

We can ignore the so-called 'information theory' developed from work done in the 1920s by communication engineers. Their concern as engineers was signal coding, transmitting, receiving, and decoding. The *context* of the messages sent was not of interest. To them 'I have just changed my socks' has the same status as 'I have just pressed the nuclear button.' One of the pioneers of the theory, Warren Weaver (in Shannon and Weaver 1949), describes as 'disappointing and bizarre' the fact that the theory 'has nothing to do with meaning'. But 'having meaning' is the usual connotation of the admittedly ambiguous concept: 'information'. Although there is no universally agreed sharp definition of 'information', there is broad agreement in the literature that 'information' is what you get when human beings attribute meaning to data in a particular context.

In fact we can make sense of the world of IS via a familiar but usually unremarked sequence of mental processes (Checkland and Holwell 1998b). At the start of the sequence are the uncountable millions of facts which we call *data* (from the Latin 'dare', to give). These are the world's givens. In the first process we pay attention to a very small subset of all the items of data, the ones of interest to us in our contexts. Unfortunately we do not have a word for this subset of items of data which we focus on, have an interest in, or pay attention to. The word *capta* suggests itself—from the Latin 'capere', to take—and would be useful since the selection of capta from a mass of data is a crucial process both for individuals and organizations. It shapes their creation of meaning. For example a random item of data which could no doubt be obtained quickly from the internet is: the temperature today in Tucson, Arizona. I have no current interest in this. But if I were travelling to Tucson tomorrow and was packing my bag, I might well promote this item to the category capta, and find out the current temperature in Tucson. This item of capta would immediately be processed into the next category, *information*, since it would have acquired meaning in terms of the context of my packing of clothes for the trip. Over time the next process operates. Collections of structurally linked data or capta attain a more permanent status and can survive for a period (possibly a long period) over time: they constitute structures of *knowledge*; for example: plate tectonics, or the history of rock climbing in Colorado. Finally we may add a process in which some knowledge can achieve the higher status we call 'wisdom'. This has no agreed definition but implies a combination of experience-based knowledge which can provide insightful judgements.

Understanding these processes is the business of the IS field, and we may note that at the heart of the sequence: data/capta/information/knowledge/wisdom is the creation of what are usually called 'information systems'. This is a rather loose everyday-language expression. More precisely, in terms of the above discussion, information systems are actually 'capta-processing systems' which—the designer intends—yield desired information. *Users* of the system, of course, may attribute a meaning to the processed capta different from that intended by the system designer. For example, a system tabulating student marks on a university degree course, intended to help classify degree grades at an Examination Board meeting, may be seen by lecturers as revealing unequal and unfair teaching loads. In this lies much of the complexity, and the interest, of work in the IS field. But the starting point at least is clear: define the capta which will yield the desired information.

Creating information systems

When it comes to thinking about the process of designing and implementing information systems some very basic systems thinking is helpful. Suppose that some purposeful human action is conceptualized in an SSM-style activity model, model A. Suppose that this action is served, supported, or helped by some other purposeful activity which could be conceptualized in another model, model B. Now it is clear that model B could not be built until model A is available. This is because what counts as the service, support, or help provided by B would entirely depend upon how A has been described. In general: if one system serves another then the system which serves can only be conceptualized when an account of the system served is available. Now, no one creates information systems for their own sake. They are service systems, created to serve or support people taking purposeful action. Thus an information system can be conceptualized properly only after prior careful conceptualization of the purposeful activity served. Therefore well-thought-out work to create an information system has to begin by defining the real-world purposeful action which the information system will support, not by considering data, capta, or information, and especially not by considering IT.

Subtlety is then added to this process by the fact that a real-world purposeful action can always be looked at according to various different world-views. For example, the information systems needed to support a manufacturing operation will be very different if that operation is conceptualized in terms of maximizing production efficiency, rather than in terms of meeting a market need. Also, additional subtlety comes from the fact that the sophistication of modern IT makes it possible to think of new purposeful activities, ones not possible without the technology, and also new kinds of information system which would not be possible without the capabilities of today's technology. The general situation is therefore that shown in Figure 4.9. Expression of intended purposeful action makes it possible to define the needed IS support, which is realizable through IT. The dotted feedback then acknowledges the role of modern IT in extending the possibilities both of real-world action and its information support. System design logically calls for iteration among the elements in Figure 4.9.

Back in the real world, every reader of this book will have experienced instances in which organizations have purchased computers and/or off-the-shelf systems and only then asked themselves what they are going to use them for. Once that is decided they usually wish they had bought a rather different system. Sometimes major problems of this kind become public knowledge, for example: the failure of the £75 million Taurus project of the London Stock Exchange; the abandonment of the London ambulance system after twenty-four hours of chaos; the criticism by the UK Audit Commission of

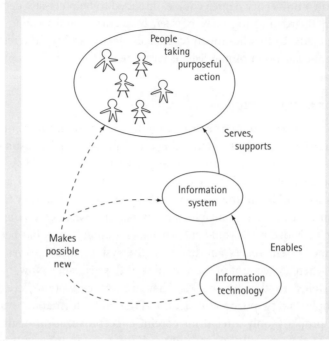

FIGURE 4.9 The concept of IT-based information support of purposeful action

the expenditure of £106 million on would-be integrated hospital support systems which yielded identifiable benefits of £3.3 million. Such failures emphasize the need for clear basic thinking relevant to the provision of information systems.

The argument here is that systems thinking, especially soft systems thinking and SSM can provide a way of conceptualizing the social processes in which, in a particular organizational context, a particular group of people can conceptualise their world and hence the purposeful action they wish to undertake. That provides the basis for ascertaining what informational support is needed by those who undertake that action. Then it becomes appropriate to ask how modern information technology can both provide that support, and also enrich the thinking about possible action and possible information systems. (For more extensive discussion of the relation between SSM and IS see Checkland and Holwell 1998b.)

CONCLUSION

One of the strongest impulses of human beings is to dispel uncertainty by attributing meaning to what they perceive—even if this entails believing (temporarily) that the earth is flat. We are meaning-creating animals, which means that at the core of the IS field is the human process of attributing meaning to what we perceive, in our contexts. We continuously create information in order to feel more comfortable, more in control of our perceived world. Sometimes this process is captured in formal 'information systems' involving, nowadays, sophisticated IT. But the technology can never take over the human act of attributing meaning. This means that IS can never become a purely technical field. Work within it—whether practice or research—will always exhibit a steady symbiotic interaction between human aspects and technical support.

This chapter argues that the human/social/technical interaction can be conceptualized and helped by Soft Systems Thinking and Soft Systems Methodology. The latter embodies a view of the nature of human groups: not only organizations, but also less formal groups such as teams, task forces, or groups of friends. It sees them as information-creating-and-exchanging groups who create an ongoing story or narrative which makes sense of them and their unfolding history. This has been expressed, as below, for a group of family doctors working in a medical practice, but it applies equally to all organizations and reasonably stable human groups:

> Oral history studies of general practice show that GPs have a very clear sense of the narrative that underpins the development of their practice. The ebb and flow of partners, memorable employees and past significant events blend together to build a coherent narrative that engenders a sense of belonging within the participants. (Checkland 2003)

Soft Systems Thinking and Soft Systems Methodology offer a means of uncovering the narratives which sustain human groups, and hence enable us to grasp their (changing) ideas about their relevant purposeful action and the information support it will require. This makes both approaches highly relevant to the related human, social, and technical issues which characterize, and will continue to characterize, the IS field.

References

Beer, S. (1972). *Brain of the Firm*. London: Allen Lane.

Checkland, K. (2003). 'Changing the Lens: Widening the Approach to Primary Care Research', *Journal of Health Services Research and Policy*, 8(4): 248–50.

Checkland, P. (1981). *Systems Thinking, Systems Practice*. Chichester: Wiley.

——(1988). 'OR and the Systems Movement', *Journal of the Operational Research Society*, 34 (8): 661–75.

——(1996). 'Systems and Systems Thinking', in M. Warner (ed.), *International Encyclopaedia of Business and Management*. London: International Thomson Business Press.

Checkland, P., and Haynes, M. (1994). 'Varieties of Systems Thinking: The Case of Soft Systems Methodology', *System Dynamics Review*, 10(2–3): 189–97.

—— and Holwell, S. (1998a). 'Action Research: Its Nature and Validity', *Systemic Practice and Action Research*, 11(1): 9–21.

————(1998b). *Information, Systems, and Information Systems*. Chichester: Wiley.

Checkland, P., and Holwell, S. (2004). 'Classic OR and Soft OR: An Asymmetric Complementarity', in Pidd (2004).

—— and Poulter, J. (2006). *Learning for Action: A Short Definitive Account of Soft Systems Methodology and its Use for Practitioners, Teachers and Students.* Chichester: Wiley.

—— and Scholes, J. (1990). *Soft Systems Methodology in Action.* Chichester: Wiley.

Forrester, J. (1961). *Industrial Dynamics* (Cambridge, MA: MIT Press).

Gray, W., and Rizzo, N. D. (1973). *Unity through Diversity: A Festschrift for Ludwig von Bertalanffy.* New York: Gordon & Breach.

Hall, A. D. (1962). *A Methodology for Systems Engineering.* Princeton: Van Nostrand.

Hitch, C. J. (1955). 'An Appreciation of Systems Analysis', in Optner (1973).

Miller, G. A. (1968). *The Psychology of Communication.* Harmondsworth: Pelican.

Optner, S. L. (ed.) (1973). *Systems Analysis.* Harmondsworth: Penguin.

Pidd, M. (ed.) (2004). *Systems Modelling: Theory and Practice.* Chichester: Wiley.

Rivett, P., and Ackoff, R. L. (1963). *A Manager's Guide to Operational Research.* Chichester: Wiley.

Roberts, J. M. (1980). *The Penguin History of the World.* London: Penguin.

Schutz, A. (1967). *The Phenomenology of the Social World.* Evanston, IL: Northwestern University Press.

Shannon, C. E., and Weaver, W. (1949). *The Mathematical Theory of Communication.* Urbana, IL: University of Illinois Press.

Von Bertalanffy, L. (1968). *General System Theory.* New York: Braziller.

Wiener, N. (1948). *Cybernetics.* Cambridge, MA: MIT Press.

CHAPTER 5

....

STRUCTURATION THEORY

....

MATTHEW JONES

INTRODUCTION
....

STRUCTURATION theory emerged as a significant development in European sociology in the late 1970s. Urry (1982) traced its origins to Berger and Luckman's (1979) concept of the mutual constitution of society and individuals, and identified several different strands of structurational analysis including the work of Bourdieu (1977), Bhaskar (1979), and Giddens. In the IS context, however, it is only Giddens that has received any significant attention and his work will therefore be the focus of this chapter.

It should be emphasized at the outset that structuration is a general theory of social organization rather than a theory specific to IS. To the extent, however, that IS are seen as social systems, existing in social and organizational contexts that influence their development and use, and are also implicated in sustaining and changing these contexts, then structuration offers potentially significant insights on IS phenomena as this chapter will seek to illustrate.

This view would seem to be borne out by the claim of Poole and DeSanctis (2004: 207) that structuration had become the 'theoretical lens of choice for most scholars' in the overlap of research on information systems and organizations in the preceding decade. Whether this choice was always based on a close reading of Giddens's work, however, would seem less clear. Certainly, a number of the structurational studies in the IS field adopt perspectives that are significantly at odds with the ideas Giddens has presented. The purpose of this chapter will therefore be to present a summary of key features of Giddens's structuration theory and some criticisms that have been made of these and to discuss its use in the IS field in the light of these features.

It should also be acknowledged, however, that, in attempting to summarize structuration and the debates it has engendered in a few pages, there is a risk of Giddens's ideas being distorted. This is exacerbated by the quantity of Giddens's writing (he is the author of more than forty books and many more articles), which has provided plenty of opportunity for subtle restatement of the main tenets of his position, and by the wide range of sources on which he draws in developing the theory (often, it must be said, providing in the process a most concise and telling précis of others' work). Combined with his adoption of deliberately idiosyncratic definitions of certain key terms and a fluency of expression that can sometimes seem to cover up for a lack of precision in the statement of his own position on particular issues, a concise exposition, even in Giddens's own words, is not easily arrived at. This has not escaped the notice of his critics, for example (Bernstein 1989: 27) describes him as 'foxlike' and notes his tendency, in the face of difficult problems, to 'introduce a plethora of distinctions and schemas' which, while illuminating, often fail to be sufficiently specific about the criteria of their applicability. For this reason, the current chapter will make perhaps more than usual use of quotations, both from Giddens and those who have drawn on his work, to enable readers to reach their own conclusions, although of course this cannot be an adequate substitute for a detailed consultation of the original sources.

STRUCTURATION THEORY

A Brief Sketch of Giddens's Theory

Giddens has described structuration theory as 'an attempt to transcend, without discarding altogether' (Giddens 1981: 26) competing traditions in social theory and philosophy between those who consider social phenomena as products of the action of human 'agents' in the light of their subjective interpretation of the world, and others who see them as caused by the influence of 'objective', exogenous social structures. Giddens identifies the first of these traditions with interpretive sociologies, such as Schutz's phenomenology, Garfinkel's ethnomethodology, and post-Wittgensteinian language philosophy, which, he argues, are 'strong on action, but weak on structure' (Giddens 1993: 4), having little to say on issues of 'constraint, power and large-scale social organisation' (ibid.). The other tradition he identifies with 'naturalistic' sociology (a term he prefers to the 'more diffuse and ambiguous label "positivism"' (Giddens 1993: 1)), in particular functionalism (especially as developed by Parsons), but also structuralism and (in some accounts) post-structuralism. These approaches, particularly functionalism, he argues, are 'strong on structure, but weak on action' (Giddens 1993: 4), underplaying the importance of human agency, and imputing purposes, reasons, and needs to society rather than to individuals.

Giddens attempts to 'square this circle' by proposing that structure and agency be viewed, not as independent and conflicting elements, but as a mutually interacting *duality*. Thus social structure is seen as being drawn on by human agents in their actions, while the actions of humans in social contexts serve to produce, and reproduce, the social structure.

More specifically, Giddens identifies three dimensions of structure, drawing from earlier work of Durkheim, Marx, and Weber, which he describes as signification,

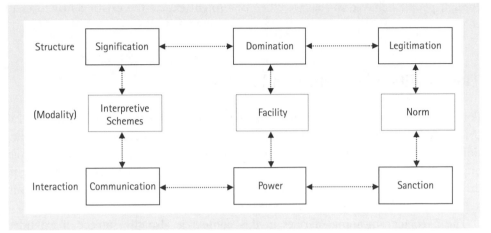

FIGURE 5.1 The dimensions of the duality of structure (after Giddens 1984: 29)

domination, and legitimation. These are seen as interacting through *modalities* of, respectively, interpretive schemes, resources, and norms, with human action of communication, power, and sanctions as shown in Figure 5.1. The separation of these dimensions is simply for analytical convenience, however, since they are, in practice, intimately interlinked. For example the operation of norms depends upon power relationships for their effectiveness and are deployed through symbolic and linguistic devices.

An everyday example may help to illustrate these concepts, albeit at the cost of presenting structuration in a rather more mechanistic way than might be desirable. Thus, when buying an item at a shop we draw on structures of signification which tell us that items have prices and that we may expect these to be displayed on or near them and that the pieces of paper or metal (money) in our pockets are valid forms of exchange for these items. Our interpretive scheme allows us to translate the symbols on the price tag into an idea of how much money we will need to buy them. Similarly we draw on structures of domination that indicate that money gives you the right to acquire the item and expect the shopkeeper to hand over the item in exchange for the money. There are also structures of legitimation which define the appropriate norms of exchange in the particular cultural context—in Britain we usually do not haggle over the price and would expect to receive sanctions if we tried to take the item without paying. In acting in the established way we reinforce these existing structures. For example, in proffering the appropriate amount of money for the items we reproduce the structure of signification, in receiving the item in exchange for the money the structure of domination is reproduced, in paying the ticket price for the goods we reinforce the structure of legitimation. In each instance, however, there is the possibility (since we are active agents) that we may fail to reproduce the structure. We could argue with the shopkeeper over the meaning of the symbols on the price tag, arm-wrestle with them to decide the right to acquire the item, or take the item without paying. If enough people behaved in that way then one might expect the existing structures to change.

The Duality of Structure and its Status

For Giddens the duality of structure refers to the 'essential recursiveness of social life, as constituted in social practices: structure is both medium and outcome of the reproduction of practices' (Giddens 1979: 69). His emphasis is therefore on structuration as an ongoing process rather than structure as a static property of social systems. In order to drive this home, Giddens adopts quite specific and non-standard meanings for certain key terms (Giddens 1979: 66) (see Table 5.1).

The particular meaning of rules in this context is also the subject of extended discussion (Giddens 1984: 17–23) in which Giddens distinguishes between the 'rules of social life [which are] techniques or generalisable procedures applied in the enactment/reproduction of social practices' and 'formulated rules', such as those of a game or a bureaucracy, which are 'codified interpretations of rules rather than rules as such' (Giddens 1984: 21). As an illustration of the type of rules he is referring to Giddens cites the mathematical formula $an = n2 + n - 1$. As he stresses, this does not mean that 'social life can be reduced to a set of mathematical principles' (Giddens 1984: 20), but that the formula provides a rule for how to carry on in any given situation (n) and that an individual may be able to state the formula without understanding its meaning or observe a sequence of numbers that obey it without being able to describe the principle involved. Two types of resources are also distinguished: allocative, which involve 'transformative capacity generating command over objects, goods or material phenomena' and authoritative, which involve 'transformative capacity generating commands over persons or actors' (Giddens 1984: 33).

Giddens's definition of structure leads him to describe it as a 'virtual order' of transformative relations that only exists when instantiated in the practices of social actors and in the memory traces of knowledgeable human agents (Giddens 1984: 17). For Giddens, therefore, even apparently material allocative resources (such as land) which 'might seem to have a 'real existence' ... become resources only when incorporated within processes of structuration' (Giddens 1984: 33).

Table 5.1 Giddens's key terms

STRUCTURE	Rules and resources, organized as properties of systems. Structure only exists as 'structural properties'.
SYSTEM	Reproduced relations between actors or collectivities, organized as regular social practices.
STRUCTURATION	Conditions governing the continuity or transformation of structures, and therefore the reproduction of systems.

This idea, that structure is virtual, has attracted particular controversy, leading some critics to identify Giddens as an idealist (Porpora 1989; Sewell 1992). For Sewell (1992), for example, Giddens's conflation of rules and resources is ontologically inconsistent. Although rules (or conceptual schemas as he prefers to call them) may be virtual, he argues, resources always have a material basis. Layder (1987) also argues that Giddens's complete rejection of any objectivist element in his ontological position is both unnecessary and theoretically problematic, while New (1994) argues that Giddens's view that structure is causally generative implies that it is real. Arguing that these critiques have their own problems and are based on a misreading of Giddens, however, Stones (2005) proposes a revised account of structuration, consistent with Giddens's writings, that he calls 'strong structuration'. In particular he distinguishes, analytically, between external and internal structures (the conditions of action and the dispositions and conjuncturally specific knowledge of external structures) that, he suggests are present, but under-elaborated and under-explained, in Giddens's own account.

Clearly, it is not possible within this chapter to resolve these debates. For the present purposes, however, it will suffice to note the central position of Giddens's distinctive concept of structure to the claims of structuration theory and that a plausible defence of Giddens's treatment of structure is possible.

Knowledgeability, Agency, and Constraint

A further important corollary of Giddens's account of structure is the knowledgeability of social actors. This may include 'unconscious sources of cognition' (Giddens 1979: 5) as well as those at level of practical consciousness embodied in what actors know 'about how to "go on" in the multiplicity of contexts of social life' (Giddens 1983) and at the discursive level, at which they are able to provide explanations for them (Giddens 1984: 7). Individuals are thus seen to be continuously engaged in reflexive monitoring of conduct, rather than as the 'cultural' or 'structural dopes...of stunning mediocrity' (Giddens 1979: 52) suggested by traditional views of structure as constraint on action. This has important implications for the understanding of social action, as 'every member of society must know...a great deal about the workings of that society by virtue of his or her participation in it' (Giddens 1979: 250). Giddens uses the term 'discursive penetration' to describe this awareness of social actors of their engagement in social reproduction and production. This leads, he argues to a 'double hermeneutic' whereby the concepts that sociological observers describe are already constituted as meaningful by social actors and can themselves become elements of the actors' understanding of their own condition.

This knowledgeability of social actors might seem to suggest that they are always in control of action. Giddens avoids this however by emphasizing the unacknowledged conditions and unintended consequences of action. Thus 'the production or constitution of society is a skilled accomplishment of its members, but one that does not take place under conditions that are either wholly intended or wholly comprehended by them' (Giddens 1993: 108).

For a number of critics (e.g. Callinicos 1985; Porpora 1989; Archer 1990), however, Giddens's treatment of agency is inappropriately voluntaristic (unacknowledged conditions and unanticipated consequences notwithstanding). In particular they question Giddens's contention that structure is not simply constraining, but is also enabling, and that, except in situations where they have been drugged and manhandled by others, human agents always 'have the possibility of doing otherwise' (Giddens 1989: 258). Thus 'the seed of change is there in every act which contributes towards the reproduction of any "ordered" form of social life' (Giddens 1993: 108). This is linked to a relational model of power based on a dialectic of control whereby the operation of power relationships relies upon the compliance of subordinates.

Giddens's critics, however, suggest that it does not make sense to argue that structural constraint simply places 'limits upon the feasible range of options open to an actor in a given circumstance' (Giddens 1984: 177). Individuals, such as a landless peasant at the start of the capitalist era, they argue, had effectively only one feasible option if they wished to survive, to sell their labour-power. Archer (1995) therefore proposes a morphogenetic approach in which constraint and action operate sequentially, while Layder (1985: 146) argues for a notion of structural power which is 'not simply a negotiable outcome of routine and concrete interactions and relationships' in the specific context. Barbalet (1987), in particular, criticizes Giddens's assumption that material existents (which, as we shall see, are a potentially significant issue in relation to a structurational theory of information systems) cannot be social structural resources in power relations. Similarly Storper (1985) argues that 'the *durée* of the material, although not imposing absolute constraints on system change, does mean that at any moment not everything is possible'.

Critics of Giddens also question his view that social order is produced and reproduced entirely through individual action. Focusing on the dependency of social structure on agency, some, such as Harré (1983), suggest that in well-ordered institutions, such as monasteries, social rules may dominate social reproduction and that individual structurational agency is thus insignificant or even absent. Others argue that all aspects of structure may not be equally amenable to agency, suggesting that there may be a 'differentiated (and thus limited) topography for the exercise of agency rather than an endlessly recursive plain' (Storper 1985: 419), or that some structural constraints may be 'relatively independent' (Layder 1987).

Giddens, however, does not accept these views, suggesting that the alternative to his conception of agency is a form of determinism. All sanctions, he argues, no matter how oppressive and comprehensive, even the threat of death, carry no weight without the acquiescence of those threatened with them, in this case the individual's wish not to die (Giddens 1984: 175). Again, this is not the place to resolve these debates, but it is important to note that Giddens's account of structuration leads him to adopt a particularly strong view of the knowledgeability and agency of social actors, that has potentially significant methodological implications for researchers drawing on Giddens's work, as will be discussed further below.

Time, Routines, and Time/Space Distantiation

Time, for Giddens, is one of the central, but frequently neglected, topics of social science and each of his major writings gives considerable attention to it. In particular, he identifies (Giddens 1994: 28) three intersecting planes of temporality involved in every moment of structuration—*durée* (the temporality of daily experience), Heidegerrian *dasein* (the temporality of the life-cycle, being-unto-death), and Braudel's *longue durée* (the temporality of institutions). In this way, he argues, structuration ties together the individual and institutional levels of social practice and points to the recursive nature of social life.

The idea of structure being continuously produced and reproduced through action also leads to another significant aspect of structuration, that of routinization. Giddens argues that routine is 'integral to the continuity of the personality of the agent . . . and to the institutions of society' (Giddens 1984: 60). In particular, individuals acquire ontological security through their engagement in predictable routines and encounters. Because these encounters are also constitutive of social institutions they enable the continuity of social life, the classic sociological 'problem of order'. Giddens permits a distinction between two levels of integration, or regularized relations of relative autonomy and dependence, between social practices. The first is defined as 'social integration' and refers to 'systemness', in terms of the definition given above, at the level of face-to-face interaction, while the second, 'system integration', refers to systemness on the level of relations between social systems or collectivities (Giddens 1979: 76). What this highlights, apart from the differentiation of micro and macro spheres of sociological analysis, is the significance of space and presence in social relations. This forms an important strand of Giddens's later analysis of modernity (see the section below entitled 'Other, Related Writing of Giddens'), drawing on the work of time-geographers. From an IS standpoint this is particularly significant in view of the role of IT in the changing temporal and spatial character of modern organizations.

The Role of Theory and its Relationship to Empirical Research

The final aspect of structuration to be considered will be its relevance to empirical research, where some critics, such as Gregson (1989) have suggested that it operates at too high a level of generality to provide guidance in specific empirical settings. Giddens, himself, also shows a certain ambivalence about the appropriate use of his ideas, presenting various statements of the principles and features of a 'structurationist programme of research' in different works (Giddens 1984: 281–4; Giddens 1989: 300; Giddens 1991b: 311) and in Giddens (1983), Giddens (1984: Chapter 6), and Giddens (1991a: 213–18) he discusses various attempts by researchers to use structuration in empirical research projects. At the same time he frequently states that structuration is not intended as a concrete research programme (Giddens 1983: 77) and that his principles 'are essentially procedural and do not supply concepts useful for the actual prosecution of research' (Giddens 1990b: 311). He is also critical of those who 'have attempted to import structuration theory *in toto* into their given area of study', preferring those 'in which concepts, either from the logical framework of structuration theory, or other aspects of my writings, are used in a sparing and critical fashion' (Giddens 1991b: 213). Another favoured description of the role of structuration in empirical research is the use of principles derived from it as 'sensitising devices' or to 'provide an explication of the logic of research into human social activities and cultural products' (Giddens 1991b: 213).

Craib (1992: 108) suggests that this is because the focus of structuration is primarily ontological: 'it tells us what sort of things are out there in the world, not what is happening to or between them; it does not give us anything to test or to find out', or, as Archer puts it, structuration is 'fundamentally non-propositional'. This is effectively acknowledged by Giddens (1989: 295) in his distinction between theory, as a generic category, and *theories*, or explanatory generalization. Structuration, he argues, is clearly of the first type. A number of authors have therefore suggested that structuration is best considered as a meta-theory, a way of thinking about the world rather than as an empirically testable explanation of social behaviour, indeed Weaver and Gioia (1994) propose it as *the* integrating meta-theory for organizational studies (although this is contested by DeCock and Rickards (1995)).

Another significant feature of structuration theory in relation to empirical research is Giddens's post-empiricist and anti-positivist methodological stance (Bryant and Jary 1991). Thus, in Giddens (1984: 344–5) he states that there are no universal laws of human social conduct (equivalent to those in the natural sciences), and argues further that 'The idea that with further research such laws will eventually be uncovered is, at best, markedly implausible'. Hence social generalizations can only ever be 'historical', i.e. temporally and spatially circumscribed. He also rejects, as a form of determinism, what he describes as 'event causality' (Giddens 1993: 91) that presupposes 'laws' of invariant connection.

While for Giddens, this means that 'all social science is irretrievably hermeneutic' (Giddens 1993: 13), this does not imply that 'technically-sophisticated, hard-edged' methods can make no contribution to social research (Giddens 1991b: 219). Indeed in Giddens (1994) he specifically states that 'I do not try to wield a methodological scalpel... there is [nothing] in the logic or the substance of structuration theory which would somehow prohibit the use of some specific research technique, such as survey methods, questionnaires or whatever'. Rather, he argues that 'the intellectual claims of sociology do not rest distinctively upon [hard-edged research]. All social research in my view, no matter how mathematical or quantitative, presumes ethnography' (Giddens 1991b: 219). This is not to say that ethnography is the only valid form of structurational research, but that all social research depends on an underlying deep understanding of the phenomena it seeks to study.

Other, Related Writings of Giddens

The breadth of application of structuration theory means that it has implications across the entire range of social phenomena and Giddens has explored these in a number of works that followed his initial exposition of structuration in the 1970s and 80s. Several aspects of this research may be argued to deserve serious consideration in the IS field, especially as Giddens considers them to be a continuation of the structurational project (Bryant and Jary 2001: 6)).

In *The Consequences of Modernity* (Giddens 1990a), for example, Giddens characterizes the current era as one of 'high' modernity (rather than some form of postmodernity) which acquires its dynamism through the separation of time and space, the development of disembedding mechanisms, and the reflexive appropriation of knowledge. As we have seen, time and space are significant features of structuration, and Giddens argues that the two are becoming increasingly separated. Whereas in premodern societies time might have been measured by the movement of the sun relative to the features of a specific locale, or even by a public clock, in modern society time throughout the world follows a common, abstract, and standardized order. Space is also dislocated from place as the common physical environment of interaction in premodern societies gives way to interactions between individuals widely separated from any situation of face-to-face interaction, whether communicating over a telephone or corresponding with friends or customers in another country. In this, IT, not least the Internet, may be seen to have a potentially significant role.

The concept of disembedding refers to the 'lifting out' of social relations from specific contexts and their 'restructuring across indefinite spans of time-space' (Giddens 1990a: 21) and is viewed, with reflexivity, as a major source of the globalizing character of modernity. Disembedding is seen as being achieved by two forms of 'abstract systems': symbolic tokens, pre-eminently money, and 'expert systems', here seen as 'systems of technical accomplishment or professional expertise' (Giddens 1990a: 27) such as those involved in designing a software programme or in medical diagnosis. Individuals, who cannot hope to acquire all the necessary technical expertise to understand how these 'expert systems' work, nevertheless have to trust in their enduring and generalized efficacy. Thus, even if Giddens adopts a non-standard definition of the term 'expert system', IS are likely to be implicated in many of these disembedding mechanisms.

The reflexive appropriation of knowledge describes the way in which knowledge about social practices comes to be drawn upon in their reproduction. For example, concepts of the information society, such as information poverty or the virtual organization, help us to make sense of and talk about the way that society is perceived to be changing. This knowledge is not uniformly appropriated however and certain groups may be better placed to draw on it in the pursuit of sectional interests.

These ideas are taken forward in *Modernity and Self Identity* (Giddens 1991b), predominantly at the level of the individual. Here the focus is on how modernity contributes to a reflexivity of the self which Giddens links with existential anxiety and the problematization of identity. Electronic media are seen as an inseparable component of modernity, contributing to a 'collage effect', whereby news about the world becomes a patchwork of unconnected events not linked to any particular sense of place, and to the increasing intrusion of distant events into everyday life. They are also identified as contributing to the plurality of lifestyle choices that individuals face.

STRUCTURATION AND IS

In their own review of structuration theory and IS research, which analysed more than 330 studies, Jones and Karsten (2008) identified nine earlier review papers. It would therefore seem unnecessary to duplicate these efforts here. Rather the focus will be on exploring the distinctive character of structurational research in the IS field and on some particular issues that structuration presents in the IS context.

In order to appreciate the particular ways in which IS researchers have used structuration, however, some understanding of structurational research in the more general management field would seem to be required, as this may be considered the context from which structurational IS studies emerged. Thus the use of structuration theory by management researchers, while following that in sociology, pre-dated its significant uptake in the IS field by almost a decade, with many of the early IS-related papers employing structuration being published in management journals.

Structuration in Management Research

Ranson, Hinings, and Greenwood (1980) is widely identified as one of the first attempts to utilize structuration in the management literature. Their discussion of organizational structure cites Bourdieu and Giddens and emphasizes the continual production and reproduction of structure through the action of organizational members. They also suggest, however, that structures, 'embody and become constitutive of . . . provinces of meaning' which are mediated by contingent size, technology, and environment and that 'the influence of structural constraints upon organizational structuring can be quite independent of an individual's perception of them' (p. 11). As Willmott (1981) argued, such claims are inconsistent with Giddens and are based on a functionalist model of organization that structuration had sought to transcend.

Another widely cited early study is Riley (1983), who employed structuration in an analysis of organizational culture, with a focus on 'organizational symbols and language that embody political intentions or display the trappings of political power' (p. 418). Issues of power were also taken up in another significant stream of structurational analysis by Knights, Willmott, and others (e.g. Knights and Willmott 1985; Willmott 1987; and Knights and Willmott 1989). In the management field, therefore, structurational research had an important critical component.

While this early literature, although drawing on some empirical evidence, had a primarily theoretical focus, structuration was also used in a few case studies such as that of Smith (1983) on the pure-bred beef business. A similar mix of theoretical and empirical papers is found in the accounting literature, with Roberts and Scapens (1985) using structuration to propose a reorientation of accounting research, while Macintosh and Scapens (1990) used it to analyse a longitudinal case study of accounting practice, arguing that management accounting systems constitute interpretive schemes, communicate norms and values, and support management control. Boland (1996), however, argued that, in basing their explanation on shared meanings and values, Macintosh and Scapens had misinterpreted Giddens, ignoring the agency of individual managers and the way in which they created meaning for themselves from the accounting reports.

As Whittington (1992) argued, therefore, in reviewing forty-seven structurational papers in leading management journals in the 1980s, management researchers' early use of Giddens's work was characterized by selective use of his ideas and, in some cases, by their misinterpretation. Some of these misinterpretations could be highly influential, moreover, giving rise to a substantial secondary literature, the majority of which cited only earlier management papers. Giddens, Whittington (1992: 707) concluded, therefore, had 'still not been fully put into action' in the management literature.

Subsequent reviews of structuration in management research suggest that this picture may not have changed significantly. Thus Pozzebon (2004) showed that in the eighteen structurational papers published in the strategic management field between 1995 and 2000, Giddens's ideas were rarely the primary theoretical foundation. Rather, structuration was used as a 'broad framework' to complement other theories, especially institutionalism. The predominantly theoretical orientation of structurational research in organization studies and the consequent paucity of empirical work was also noted by Pozzebon and Pinsonneault (2005).

Structuration and IS Research

In contrast to other management fields, Pozzebon and Pinsonneault (2005) showed that IS structurational research has had a much stronger emphasis on empirical studies. Indeed they identify a cumulative tradition of empirical structurational studies in the

IS field that they suggest may provide lessons for other management researchers. Although Jones and Karsten (2008) also reported more than 80 per cent of empirical papers among those they reviewed, they remained more doubtful about whether these constituted a cumulative tradition, noting the fragmentation and lack of co-citation of different strands of this research (often reflecting their differing philosophical orientations). Nevertheless it would seem that IS structurational research has had a particular emphasis on empirical studies.

Empirical Structurational IS Research

Nearly half of the 331 studies reviewed by Jones and Karsten (2008) involved the straightforward empirical application of structuration theory, that is, they employed structurational concepts to address IS-related phenomena, with about half of these being general applications of the theory as a whole (typically characterized in terms of the duality of structure and its dimensions). Such papers often seek to illustrate the insights offered by structuration on particular IS processes such as strategy formation (Walsham and Waema 1994), IS development (Sillince and Mouakket 1997), or IS implementation (Montealegre 1997), or in particular application domains, such as agro-informatics (Leeuwis 1993), real estate firms (Crowston, Sawyer, and Wigand 2001), or healthcare (Lehoux et al. 2002). Many of the early structurational IS studies (e.g. Barley's widely cited study of the implementation of computed tomography scanners in two hospitals (Barley 1986)) were of this type and a steady stream of such papers has continued to be published over the years. While initially valuable in demonstrating the relevance of structuration theory in IS research and establishing the empirical tradition in the field, however, it is unclear how further studies 'applying' structuration theory in toto, which do not extend or challenge existing accounts, necessarily advance our understanding of either structuration theory or IS.

More consistent with Giddens's preference for 'sparing and critical' use of structuration (Giddens 1991b: 213), there has also been a continuing stream of papers employing particular aspects of the theory, such as its treatment of agency and constraint (e.g. Nandhakumar and Jones 1997) or time and temporality (Barrett and Scott 2004), to address IS phenomena, as well as a smaller number of studies exploring the use of concepts, such as self-identity (Thompson 1989) and disembedding (Ellingsen and Monteiro 2003) from Giddens's later writings. In both cases, however, the relatively small number of studies and their selective treatment of Giddens's ideas has meant that IS researchers have addressed only a limited range of his concepts, leaving considerable opportunities for further contributions. As was observed of management researchers' use of structuration, therefore, it would also appear to have 'exercised a substantial, if rather peculiar, influence' (Whittington 1992: 707) in the IS field.

Theoretical Developments

If IS structurational research has been notable for its empirical orientation, this does not mean that it has had nothing to say from a theoretical perspective. Indeed, the structurational IS literature includes two significant theoretical contributions, Poole and DeSanctis's 'Adaptive Structuration Theory' (AST) (Poole and DeSanctis 1990; DeSanctis and Poole 1994) and Orlikowski's 'Duality of Technology' (Orlikowski 1992), and later works that have sought to develop and apply an IS-specific version of structuration that overcomes what are perceived to be its limitations in the IS context. While there is not the space in this chapter to provide a detailed account of these authors' positions, some important features of their treatment of structuration deserve attention.

Adaptive Structuration Theory

Responding to what they perceived to be IS researchers' enduring concern with the 'structuring properties of technology', Poole and DeSanctis identified structuration theory as providing a potentially valuable 'focus on structure and on the processes by which structures are used and modified over time' (Poole and DeSanctis 2004: 208). 'There are at least two aspects of structuration theory that are not developed by Giddens but are essential to address in order for empirical study of structuration to proceed for IS', they argued however (Poole and DeSanctis 2004: 210). These were identified as the role of technology (as 'structuration theory does not include technology') and the application of 'deterministic reasoning within the recursive logic of the theoretical arguments'.

AST, therefore, considers technologies as social structures that can be described in terms of their structural features (examples of which are cited, in the context of Group Decision Support Systems, as anonymous recording of ideas and voting algorithms) and their spirit (defined as the 'general intent with regards to values and goals underlying a given set of structural features') (DeSanctis and Poole 1994: 126). Structural features are seen to correspond to Giddens's structures of signification and domination, while spirit is associated with structures of legitimation. Using these extra constructs, it is argued, AST can be used to establish propositions of the form: 'Given advanced information technology and other sources of social structure n_1 to n_k and ideal appropriation processes, and decision processes that fit the task at hand, then desired outcomes of advanced information technology will result' (DeSanctis and Poole 1994: 131).

Thus AST, Poole and DeSanctis (2004: 216) argue, can be used to advance a programme of what they describe as 'functional' structurational research that develops testable models which represent IS phenomena as a 'network of causal, moderating, and correlational relationships among abstract variables'. While many of the AST studies of Poole, DeSanctis, and colleagues have adopted this approach, as has almost all the substantial secondary AST literature (much of which does not cite Giddens), Poole and DeSanctis (2004: 217) also identify a second type of structurational research that they term 'constitutive'. 'Underlying every variable and relationship in a causal analysis is a process of social construction responsible for making it an active force in the social system', they argue, and constitutive analysis can be used to study 'the interpretive processes that figure in the operation of causal relationships'. For Poole and DeSanctis, 'Functional' and 'Constitutive' analyses 'complement and buttress one another to provide a comprehensive picture of structuration processes' (Poole and DeSanctis 2004: 218).

As Poole and DeSanctis (2004) acknowledge, their conception of structuration is at odds with Giddens in several respects: structure is considered to be separable from action and potentially capable of being embedded in technology; causal logics that can 'explain variance in behaviours and predict outcomes' are introduced; and they advocate an agenda for structurational IS research predominantly focused on quantification, constructs, and relationships and testable models. AST itself also interprets a number of Giddens's concepts, such as structure, dialectic of control, structures of signification, domination, and legitimation in idiosyncratic ways and introduces new concepts such as 'spirit' and 'faithfulness' of 'appropriation moves' (DeSanctis and Poole 1994) that are not evidently derived from Giddens's work. While, therefore, AST has undoubtedly been influential in IS structurational research (contributing to more than 20 per cent of the papers reviewed by Jones and Karsten (2008)) it has not necessarily advanced this research in ways that are well aligned with Giddens's account of structuration. For Poole and DeSanctis (2004: 218) this is unavoidable if structuration is to fit with 'mainstream views in the IS field'. Jones and Karsten (2008), however, argue that there is considerable scope for advancing structurational IS research in ways that do not involve the a priori rejection of key tenets of Giddens's position.

Orlikowski's duality of technology and practice lens

The potential for such critical, but sympathetic use of Giddens's work is perhaps illustrated by the evolution of the structurational research of Wanda Orlikowski. Her early papers in this area included a case study applying structuration theory to explore the contradictory implications of the implementation of CASE tools for forms of control in a software consulting firm (Orlikowski 1993b); the development and illustration of structurationally informed frameworks for investigating the interaction of human actors and social structure during IS development and use (Orlikowski and Robey 1991) and, perhaps best known, her 'duality of technology' study (Orlikowski 1992). Presented by Bryant and Jary (2001: 48) as an exemplar of the use of structuration, this set out a 'structurational model of technology' (Figure 5.2) that sought to insert technology into Giddens's structure/agency duality.

In Orlikowski (1992: 403) technology is defined as 'material artifact' (although it is claimed, paradoxically, that this does not imply an 'exclusive focus on technology as a physical object'), that is 'created and changed by human action, yet it is also used by humans to accomplish some action'. This is termed the 'duality of technology'. Technology is thus seen as 'interpretively flexible', even if this is not always recognized due to the 'time-space discontinuity' of design and use of IS which 'typically' occur in

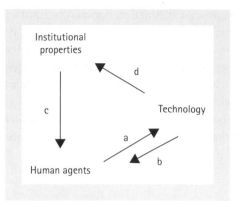

FIGURE 5.2 The structurational model of technology (Orlikowski 1992)

different organizations (those of the vendor and customer). Interpretive flexibility is not considered to be infinite, however, being constrained by the material characteristics of the technology and the institutional contexts of its design and use, and the power, knowledge, and interests of the relevant actors. In particular, technology is seen as reinforcing or transforming the institutional properties of organizations (arrow 'd' in Figure 5.2). For example, 'when users conform to the technology's embedded rules and resources' (i.e. structures in Giddens's terms) it is argued, 'they unwittingly sustain the institutional structures in which the technology is deployed' (Orlikowski 1992: 411).

Compared to AST, Orlikowski's model is much more evidently aligned with Giddens's account of structuration, and Orlikowski (1992) frequently shows a subtle appreciation of Giddens's work. In a number of respects, however, the duality of technology also departs significantly from Giddens. Thus, the definition of technology as material artefact, existing outside the duality of structure and agency and acting unilaterally on institutional properties, is ontologically inconsistent. Similarly, to suggest that structure may be somehow embedded in technology is to separate it from agency and hence to turn Giddens's carefully constructed duality back into a dualism.

In subsequent papers analysing genres of organizational communication (Yates and Orlikowski 1992) and cases of incremental and radical change in systems development (Orlikowski 1993a) electronic mail and conferencing technology in a Japanese R&D project group (Orlikowski, Okamura, and Fujimoto 1995), use of Lotus Notes in two consultancies (Orlikowski et al. 1995), and organizational transformation in the customer support function at a software company (Orlikowski 1996), the structurational model of Orlikowski (1992) was not significantly developed or applied, rather there was greater emphasis on improvisation, enactment, and practices. This trend may be seen as culminating in a significant restatement of Orlikowski's structurational approach in her 'Practice lens' paper (Orlikowski 2000). Contrary to her earlier account, Orlikowski (2000) argues that technologies do not become stabilized after development, but are continuously open to modification and new uses, and that structures, as Giddens understands them, cannot be embodied in technology, but are enacted and emergent through users' situated practices. She thus proposes a distinction between technology as artefact, 'the bundle of material and symbol properties packaged in some socially-recognisable form', e.g. hardware, software, techniques, and technology-in-practice, 'the specific structure routinely enacted as we use the specific machine, technique, appliance, device, or gadget in recurrent ways in our everyday situated activities' (Orlikowski 2000: 408). This practice perspective has subsequently been applied in studies of temporal structuring (Orlikowski and Yates 2002), in a globally distributed high-tech organization, and technology-mediated network relations (Schultze and Orlikowski 2004).

Other theoretical contributions

Although the work of DeSanctis, Poole, and Orlikowski has been highly influential in promoting structurational research in the IS field (at least as indicated by the secondary literature citing them) they have not been the only IS researchers to engage theoretically with structuration. Thus Jones and Karsten (2008) identify a group of IS papers seeking to extend structuration through the use of other theories such as Actor Network Theory (e.g. Braa and Hedberg 2002), Unger's formative contexts (e.g. Ciborra and Lanzara 1994) and Luhmann's autopoiesis (e.g. Holmer-Nadesan 1997). A number of authors have also offered critiques of structuration drawing on approaches such as Actor Network Theory (e.g. Monteiro and Hanseth 1995) and Critical Realism (e.g. Dobson 2001). The issues raised in these papers reflect a number of the themes identified in the earlier discussion of the key features of stucturation. The final section of this chapter therefore draws these together to present a critical assessment of structuration's contribution and potential in the IS field.

ISSUES IN THE USE OF STRUCTURATION IN IS RESEARCH

The Materiality of Technology

As was explained in the introduction to this chapter, Giddens makes almost no reference in his extensive writings to technology or to IS phenomena. Indeed, when pressed on this point he remarked 'technology does nothing, except as implicated in the actions of human beings' (Giddens and Pierson 1998: 2). This has led some authors to argue that Giddens and some structurational IS researchers neglect technology, treating it as a 'mere occasion for structuring, without any activity or specificity of its own' (Berg 1998: 466).

While it may be the case, as Monteiro and Hanseth (1995) have argued, that IS researchers employing structuration theory have often failed to be sufficiently specific about the technologies they are studying, it is not clear that this is necessarily because more detailed and fine-grained analysis would be inconsistent with Giddens (as Monteiro and Hanseth acknowledge). Contrary to the claim of Poole and DeSanctis (2004), Giddens does not deny the materiality of the physical world, nor does he deny that physical contexts may be 'strongly relevant to the possibilities and constraints open to any individual or group' (Giddens and Pierson 1998: 82). Rather his argument is that this materiality is only socially consequential when drawn upon by human agents in their practices. That Giddens has paid little attention to these consequences, rather than indicating a failing of structuration may, as Jones and Karsten (2008) argue, therefore represent a significant opportunity for IS scholars to contribute to structurational research by remedying this neglect. Recent work by Orlikowski, for example, has begun, through the concept of sociomateriality, to seek to give a much more central place to 'the material forms and spaces through which humans act and interact' in our understanding of contemporary organizing. While not explicitly drawing on her previous structurational research, it can be seen as extending ideas developed in Orlikowski (2000).

Agency and Flexibility

Another criticism made of structurational IS research is that it shows a bias towards flexible forms of technology and to organizational settings in which actors have considerable autonomy in their use of this technology. Thus, empirical studies employing structuration predominantly focus on cases such as consultants' use of collaborative technologies or the use of software tools by IS developers rather than shopfloor workers' use of production planning systems or call centre agents' use of automated call distribution systems, giving a misleading impression of the scope of individual agency in IS use.

While arguments, such as that of Orlikowski (2000: 405), linking the need for a practice-based structurational approach with the increasing prevalence of 'internet-worked and reconfigurable technology (such as groupware and the Web)' in contemporary organizations might seem to support this view, it is not clear, again, that this association is a necessary corollary of structuration theory. Indeed, it might be argued that it would be particularly valuable for structurational researchers to study the scope of agency in apparently highly controlled settings.

Narrow Focus

The apparent bias in the systems and settings studied by IS researchers employing structuration may be seen as symptomatic of a general narrowness of focus. Thus, notwithstanding structuration's argument for the interconnectedness of societal institutions and individual action, IS research using structuration has adopted a predominantly intra-organizational focus, with the influence of broader social forces receiving less attention. Although, as Orlikowski and Barley (2001) argue, the neglect of societal influences is widespread in IS research this would seem a particular failing in structurational research, the remedying of which (as Whittington (2006) argues in respect of practice research in the strategy field) would bring it into closer alignment with the work of Giddens on which it claims to be based.

The intra-organizational focus also means that much structurational research in the IS field excludes significant aspects of Giddens's writing that are arguably of considerable relevance to the IS researcher. These include Giddens's later work on modernity, self-identity, and the risk society as well as the broader implications of his work on, for example, temporality and knowledgeability. To echo Whittington's observation regarding management researchers' use of structuration, therefore, while Giddens's may have had a major influence on IS research, much of his directly relevant work has been neglected and his ideas have been interpreted in what could be considered a 'peculiarly limited sort of way' (Whittington 1992: 698).

Selective Use

It is not just that IS researchers have been selective in the aspects of Giddens's work that they have employed, but they have also been selective in their use of the concepts they have taken from his work. While in some cases (e.g. Poole and DeSanctis 2004) this has reflected a deliberate decision to reject what are perceived to be problematic features of Giddens's position in an IS context, such as his 'virtual' concept of structure or his objections to positivism and determinism, in others it is not clear that such a conscious choice has been made. Rather, superficial correspondence of terminology is seen as indicative of deeper conceptual equivalence without awareness of potentially significant differences in the underlying theoretical position. This would seem particularly the case with the substantial secondary structurational literature, where the modified version of structuration presented by IS authors often appears to be taken for the original.

This is not to suggest that this 'pick and mix' approach to theory cannot, in the right hands, lead to insightful analysis which remains true to Giddens's principles (i.e. retains the meta-theoretical assumptions of structuration whether explicated or not), but that there is a risk that structurational concepts may be incorporated into frameworks which may contradict key tenets of Giddens's account, or which juxtapose them with incompatible concepts from other writers. Contractor and Eisenberg (1990) provide an example of this in which Giddens's duality of structure is paired with an approach based on Archer's morphogenetic principles in the analysis of computer-mediated communication. Unfortunately, as Archer and Giddens have both forcefully argued in Clark, Modgil, and Modgil (1990), their positions are fundamentally different; structure cannot be both a duality and a dualism, and the combination of the two approaches would therefore suggest a lack of appreciation of the underlying positions.

CONCLUSION

Despite the breadth and complexity of Giddens's writing, the absence of almost any reference in his work to information systems (or to contemporary phenomena in which they are seen to be implicated), and the arguably voluntarist and idealist stance that he adopts (that is seen as making it difficult to account for the materiality of technology), IS researchers have shown a continuing interest in structuration theory, especially in empirical studies, for more than twenty-five years. What is more, as Jones and Karsten (2008) show, this interest has proved to be more than a passing fashion with an average of more than twenty-seven structurational IS papers having been published each year for the past decade, with numbers running at the highest levels in the most recent years they reviewed. Indeed there is some evidence (e.g. Jones 2000; Poole and DeSanctis 2004) to suggest that Giddens may be the most frequently cited social theorist in the IS field. There would therefore seem good evidence that structuration has achieved a high level of recognition, at least among organizational IS researchers (whether or not they consider it their 'theoretical lens of choice' (Poole and DeSanctis 2004: 207)). What these citations tell us about the influence of Giddens's work on IS research is more debatable, however.

Thus structuration has been widely seized upon to support non-dualist accounts of IS phenomena and to legitimate attention to the influence of the social and the scope of human agency in IS contexts. In this respect it may be considered to have exerted a positive, if rather non-specific influence on the field. What is much less clear, however, is whether these accounts, especially those reliant on secondary sources, have fully recognized the implications of Giddens's particular position, such that they might be considered to offer a specifically structurational analysis rather than one that just employs structurational terminology toward ends that may be inconsistent with Giddens's objectives and approach in developing the theory. The narrow scope of much IS structurational research, while arguably not atypical of IS research as a whole, would also seem to suggest that significant opportunities may have been missed in the use of this rich and broad-ranging theory.

While this might seem a negative assessment of structuration's contribution to the IS field, it can also be seen as an indication that, as Jones and Karsten (2008) argue, there remains considerable potential for IS researchers to pursue work that engages positively, but not uncritically, with the distinctive character of structuration theory and that explores the full range of Giddens's oeuvre. A priority in this respect might be the development of a clearer account of the position of materiality in structuration, as has already been noted, not least to counter claims, such as those of Poole and DeSanctis (2004), that structuration is unable to address technology.

The opportunities for structurational IS research need not be restricted to enhancing existing accounts, however, but may also support new directions. Thus, structuration would seem well-aligned with the recent 'practice turn' in social and management research (Schatzki, Knorr Cetina, and von Savigny 2001; Whittington 2006). While Orlikowski (2000) illustrated some of structuration's potential in this area, the implications of practice theory, as Reckwitz (2002) argues, go considerably further in developing aspects of structuration, such as practical consciousness and routinization, that have typically been neglected in IS research. Other new avenues for IS research may be supported by aspects of Giddens's non-structurational writings that have been similarly neglected in the IS literature to date. His concepts, such as disembedding, expert systems, and the reflexivity of the self, for example, would seem particularly pertinent in understanding the role of IS in contemporary problems in global financial markets.

This is not intended to suggest that structuration is uniquely placed among social theories to address IS phenomena, or that the criticisms made of its use in the IS field are without foundation. Rather the claim is that, despite the substantial IS literature drawing on structuration theory, its contribution to IS research may not have been exhausted yet.

REFERENCES

Archer, M. (1990). 'Human Agency and Social Structure: A Critique of Giddens', in J. Clark, C. Modgil, and J. Modgil (eds.), *Anthony Giddens: Consensus and Controversy*. Brighton: Falmer Press, 73–84.

——(1995). *Realist Social Theory: The Morphogenetic Approach*. Cambridge: Cambridge University Press.

Barbalet, J. M. (1987). 'Power, Structural Resources and Agency', *Current Perspectives in Social Theory*, 8: 1–24.

Barley, S. R. (1986). 'Technology as an Occasion for Structuring: Evidence from Observation of CT Scanners and the Social Order of Radiology Departments', *Administrative Science Quarterly*, 31: 78–108.

Barrett, M., and Scott, S. (2004). 'Electronic Trading and the Process of Globalization in Traditional Futures Exchanges: A Temporal Perspective', *European Journal of Information Systems*, 13(1): 65–79.

Berg, M. (1998). 'The Politics of Technology: On Bringing Social Theory into Technological Design', *Science, Technology and Human Values*, 23(4): 456–91.

Berger, P. L., and Luckmann, T. (1979). *The Social Construction of Reality: A Treatise in the Sociology of Knowledge*. Harmondsworth: Penguin.

Bernstein, R. J. (1989). 'Social Theory as Critique', in D. Held and J. B. Thompson (eds.), *Social Theory of Modern Societies: Anthony Giddens and his Critics*. Cambridge: Cambridge University Press, 19–33.

Bhaskar, R. (1979). *The Possibility of Naturalism*. Brighton: Harvester.

Boland, R. J. (1996). 'Why Shared Meanings Have No Place in Structuration Theory: A Reply to Scapens and Macintosh', *Accounting, Organizations and Society*, 21(7/8): 691–7.

Bourdieu, P. (1977). *Outline of a Theory of Practice*. Cambridge: Cambridge University Press.

Braa, J., and Hedberg, C. (2002). 'The Struggle for District-Based Health Information Systems in South Africa', *The Information Society*, 18(2): 113–27.

Bryant, C. G. A., and Jary, D. (1991). 'Introduction: Coming to Terms with Anthony Giddens', in C. G. A. Bryant and D. Jary (eds.), *Giddens' Theory of Structuration: A Critical Appreciation*. London: Routledge.

——(2001) *The Contemporary Giddens: Social Theory in a Globalizing Age*. Basingstoke: Palgrave.

Callinicos, A. (1985). 'Anthony Giddens: A Contemporary Critique', *Theory and Society*, 14(2): 133–66.

Ciborra, C. U., and Lanzara, G. F. (1994). 'Formative Contexts and Information Technology: Understanding the Dynamics of Innovation in Organizations', *Accounting, Management & Information Technologies*, 4(2): 61–86.

Clark, J., Modgil, C., and Modgil, J. (1990). *Anthony Giddens: Consensus and Controversy*. Brighton: Falmer Press.

Cohen, I. (1989). *Structuration Theory: Anthony Giddens and the Constitution of Social Life*. Basingstoke: Macmillan.

Contractor, N. S., and Eisenberg, E. M. (1990). 'Communication Networks and New Media in Organizations', in J. Fulk and C. Steinfeld (eds.), *Organizations and Communication Technology*. Beverly Hills, CA: Sage, 143–73.

Craib, I. (1992). *Anthony Giddens*. London: Routledge.

Crowston, K., Sawyer, S., and Wigand, R. (2001). 'Investigating the Interplay between Structure and Information and Communications Technology in the Real Estate Industry', *Information Technology and People*, 14(2): 163–83.

DeCock, C., and Rickards, T. (1995). 'Of Giddens, Paradigms and Philosophical Garb', *Organization Studies*, 16(4): 699–704.

DeSanctis, G., and Poole, M. S. (1994). Capturing the Complexity in Advanced Technology Use: Adaptive Structuration Theory', *Organization Science*, 5(2): 121–47.

Dobson, P. J. (2001). 'The Philosophy of Critical Realism: An Opportunity for Information Systems Research', *Information Systems Frontiers*, 3(2): 199–210.

Ellingsen, G., and Monteiro, E. (2003). 'Mechanisms for Producing a Working Knowledge: Enacting, Orchestrating and Organizing', *Information and Organization*, 13(3): 203–29.

Giddens, A. (1979). *Central Problems in Social Theory*. Basingstoke: Macmillan.

——(1981). *A Contemporary Critique of Historical Materialism: Power, Property and the State*. London: Macmillan.

——(1983). 'Comments on the Theory of Structuration', *Journal for the Theory of Social Behaviour*, 13: 75–80.

——(1984). *The Constitution of Society*. Cambridge: Polity.

——(1989). 'A Reply to my Critics', in D. Held and J. B. Thompson (eds.), *Social Theory of Modern Societies: Anthony Giddens and his Critics*. Cambridge: Cambridge University Press, 249–301.

Giddens, A. (1990a). *The Consequences of Modernity*. Cambridge: Polity.

——(1990b). 'Structuration Theory and Sociological Analysis', in J. Clark, C. Modgil, and J. Modgil (eds.), *Anthony Giddens: Consensus and Controversy*. Brighton: Falmer Press, 297–315.

——(1991a). *Modernity and Self-Identity*. Cambridge: Polity.

——(1991b). 'Structuration Theory: Past, Present and Future', in C. G. A. Bryant and D. Jary (eds.), *Giddens' Theory of Structuration: A Critical Appreciation*. London: Routledge, 201–21.

——(1993). *New Rules of Sociological Method*. 2nd edn., Cambridge: Polity.

——(1994). *A Contemporary Critique of Historical Materialism*. 2nd edn., Basingstoke: Macmillan.

——and Pierson, C. (1998). *Conversations with Anthony Giddens*. Cambridge: Polity.

Gregson, N. (1989). 'On the Ir(relevance) of Structuration Theory to Empirical Research', in D. Held and J. B. Thompson (eds.), *Social Theory of Modern Societies: Anthony Giddens and his Critics*. Cambridge: Cambridge University Press, 235–48.

Harré, R. (1983). 'Commentary from an Ethogenic Standpoint', *Journal for the Theory of Social Behaviour*, 13: 69–73.

Held, D., and Thompson, J. B. (eds.), *Social Theory of Modern Societies: Anthony Giddens and his Critics*. Cambridge: Cambridge University Press.

Holmer-Nadesan, M. (1997). 'Essai: Dislocating (Instrumental) Organizational Time', *Organization Studies*, 18(3): 481–510.

Jones, M. R. (2000). 'The Moving Finger: The Use of Social Theory in WG8.2 Conference Papers, 1975–1999', in R. Baskerville, J. Stage, and J. I. DeGross (eds.), *Organizational and Social Perspectives on Information Technology*. Boston, MA: Kluwer Academic Publishers, 15–31.

——and Karsten, H. (2008). 'Giddens's Structuration Theory and Information Systems Research', *MIS Quarterly*, 32(1): 127–57.

Knights, D., and Willmott, H. (1985). 'Power and Identity in Theory and Practice', *Sociological Review*, 33(1): 22–46.

————(1989). 'Power and Subjectivity at Work: From Degradation to Subjugation in Social Relations', *Sociology*, 23(4): 535–58.

Layder, D. (1985). 'Power, Structure and Agency', *Journal for the Theory of Social Behaviour*, 15: 131–49.

——(1987). 'Key Issues in Structuration Theory: Some Critical Remarks', *Current Perspectives in Social Theory*, 8: 25–46.

Leeuwis, C. (1993). 'Towards a Sociological Conceptualization of Communication in Extension Science: On Giddens, Habermas and Computer-Based Communication Technologies in Dutch Agriculture', *Sociologia Ruralis*, 33(2): 281–305.

Lehoux, P., Sicotte, C., Denis, J. L., Berg, M., and Lacroix, A. (2002). 'The Theory of Use behind Telemedicine: How Compatible with Physicians' Clinical Routines?', *Social Science & Medicine*, 54(6): 889–904.

Macintosh, N. W., and Scapens, R. W. (1990). 'Structuration Theory in Management Accounting', *Accounting Organizations and Society*, 15(5): 455–77.

Montealegre, R. (1997). 'The Interplay of Information Technology and the Social Milieu', *Information Technology and People*, 10(2): 106–31.

Monteiro, E., and Hanseth, O. (1995). 'Social Shaping of Information Infrastructure: On Being Specific about the Technology', in W. J. Orlikowski, G. Walsham, M. R. Jones, and

J. I. DeGross (eds.), *Information Technology and Changes in Organizational Work*. London: Chapman & Hall, 325–43.

Nandhakumar, J., and Jones, M. R. (1997). 'Designing in the Dark: The Changing User-Developer Relationship in Information Systems Development', *Proceedings of ICIS*, Atlanta, GA, 75–86.

New, C. (1994). 'Structure Agency and Social Transformation', *Journal for the Theory of Social Behaviour*, 24(3): 197–205.

Orlikowski, W. J. (1992). 'The Duality of Technology: Rethinking the Concept of Technology in Organizations', *Organization Science*, 3(3): 398–427.

——(1993a). 'Learning from Notes: Organizational Issues in Groupware Implementation', *The Information Society*, 9(3): 237–50.

——(1993b). 'CASE Tools as Organizational Change: Investigating Increment', *MIS Quarterly*, 17(3): 309–40.

——(1996). 'Improvising Organizational Transformation over Time: A Situated Change Perspective', *Information Systems Research*, 7(1): 63–92.

——(2000). 'Using Technology and Constituting Structures: A Practice Lens for Studying Technology in Organizations', *Organization Science*, 11(4): 404–28.

——and Barley, S. R. (2001). 'Technology and Institutions: What can Research on Information Technology and Research on Organizations Learn from Each Other?', *MIS Quarterly*, 25(2): 145–65.

——and Robey, D. (1991). 'Information Technology and the Structuring of Organizations', *Information Systems Research*, 2(2): 143–69.

——and Yates, J. (2002). 'It's about Time: Temporal Structuring in Organizations', *Organization Science*, 13(6): 684–700.

——————Okamura, K., and Fujimoto, M. (1995). 'Shaping Electronic Communication: The Metastructuring of Technology in the Context of Use', *Organization Science*, 6(4): 423–44.

Poole, M. S., and DeSanctis, G. (1990). 'Understanding the Use of Group Decision Support Systems: The Theory of Adaptive Structuration', in J. Fulk and C. Steinfeld (eds.), *Organizations and Communication Technology*. Beverley Hills, CA: Sage Publications, 173–93.

——————(2004). 'Structuration Theory in Information Systems Research: Methods and Controversies', in M. E. Whitman and A. Woszcynski (eds.), *Handbook of Information Systems Research*. Hershey, PA: Idea Group, 206–49.

Porpora, D. (1989). 'Four Concepts of Social Structure', *Journal for the Theory of Social Behaviour*, 19(2): 195–211.

Pozzebon, M. (2004). 'The Influence of a Structurationist View on Strategic Management Research', *Journal of Management Studies*, 41(2): 247–72.

——and Pinsonneault, A. (2005). 'Challenges in Conducting Empirical Work Using Structuration Theory: Learning from IT Research', *Organization Studies*, 26(9): 1353–76.

Ranson, S., Hinings, B., and Greenwood, R. (1980). 'The Structuring of Organizational Structures', *Administrative Science Quarterly*, 25: 1–17.

Reckwitz, A. (2002). 'Toward a Theory of Social Practices: A Development in Culturalist Theorizing', *European Journal of Social Theory*, 5(2): 243–63.

Riley, P. (1983). 'A Structurationist Account of Political Culture', *Administrative Science Quarterly*, 28: 414–37.

Roberts, J., and Scapens, R. (1985). 'Accounting Systems and Systems of Accountability: Understanding Accounting Practices in their Organisational Contexts', *Accounting, Organizations and Society*, 10(4): 443–56.

Schatzki, T., Knorr Cetina, K. D., and von Savigny, E. (2001). *The Practice Turn in Contemporary Theory*. London: Routledge.

Schultze, U., and Orlikowski, W. J. (2004). 'A Practice Perspective on Technology-Mediated Network Relations: The Use of Internet-Based Self-Serve Technologies', *Information Systems Research*, 15(1): 87–106.

Sewell, William H., Jr. (1992). 'A Theory of Structure: Duality, Agency and Transformation', *American Journal of Sociology*, 98(1): 1–29.

Sillince, J. A. A., and Mouakket, S. (1997). 'Varieties of Political Process during Systems Development', *Information Systems Research*, 8(4): 368–98.

Smith, C. W. (1983). 'A Case Study of Structuration: The Pure-Bred Beef Business', *Journal for the Theory of Social Behaviour*, 13: 3–18.

Stones, R. (2005). *Structuration Theory*. Basingstoke: Palgrave Macmillan.

Storper, M. (1985). 'The Spatial and Temporal Constitution of Social Action: A Critical Reading of Giddens', *Environment and Planning D: Society and Space*, 3: 407–24.

Thompson, J. B. (1989). 'The Theory of Structuration', in D. Held and J. B. Thompson (eds.), *Social Theory of Modern Societies: Anthony Giddens and his Critics*. Cambridge: Cambridge University Press, 56–76.

Urry, J. (1982). 'Duality of Structure: Some Critical Issues', *Theory, Culture and Society*, 1(2): 100–6.

Walsham, G., and Waema, T. (1994). 'Information Systems Strategy and Implementation: A Case Study of a Building Society', *ACM Transactions on Information Systems*, 12(2): 150–73.

Weaver, G. R., and Gioia, D. A. (1994). 'Paradigms Lost: Incommensurability *vs* Structurationist Inquiry', *Organization Studies*, 15(4): 565–90.

Whittington, R. (1992). 'Putting Giddens into Action: Social Systems and Managerial Agency', *Journal of Management Studies*, 29(6): 693–712.

——(2006). 'Completing the Practice Turn in Strategy Research', *Organization Studies*, 27(5): 613–34.

Willmott, H. (1981). 'The Structuring of Organizational Structure: A Note', *Administrative Science Quarterly*, 26: 470–4.

——(1987). 'Studying Managerial Work: A Critique and a Proposal', *Journal of Management Studies*, 24(3): 249–70.

Yates, J., and Orlikowski, W. J. (1992). 'Genres of Organizational Communication: A Structurational Approach to Studying Communication and Media', *Academy of Management Review*, 17(2): 299–326.

CHAPTER 6

INSTITUTIONAL THEORY OF INFORMATION TECHNOLOGY

WENDY L. CURRIE

INTRODUCTION

INSTITUTIONAL theory offers a rich and diverse conceptualization of information technology (IT). In various expressions of the theory, a common theme is that the activities of developing and using IT are subject to social pressures, sometimes from external sources such as production and user organizations, professions, and government agencies, other times from legitimated rules and logics embodied within the technologies. These institutional pressures push individuals, groups, and organizations to take intentional or unintentional actions such as conforming to technology mandates, adopting popular innovations, and modifying business practices to fit technology, all possibly leading to increased opportunities for social approval or legitimacy. Since institutional pressures operate conjointly or despite any particular actor's considerations of economic and technical utility, institutional theory draws attention away from the economic-rationalistic perspective, now dominating the research and practice in Information Systems, toward the social nature of IT. Actors may make instrumentally rational choices among various options to develop and/or use IT. Nonetheless, institutional theory holds that the boundary of such rationality is socially constructed, and if legitimated and taken for granted as a social fact, operates and persists even beneath the level of consciousness. Institutional analysis thus aims to understand how legitimated social facts are socially constructed and what consequences they bring about. Conducted frequently and naturally at supra-individual levels, institutional analysis differs from atomistic economic analysis in that properties of the social construction process cannot be reduced to aggregations of individual actors' characteristics, motives, and interests. As a result of its distinctive perspective, institutional theory provides understanding of phenomena not so well explained by economic-rationalist models, such as the wide adoption and acceptance of IT innovations seemingly suboptimal in economic and technical terms.

While institutional theory is gaining increasing attention in IS research, it is still a relatively novel theoretical perspective in IS. Most IS studies using the institutional perspective focus on the organization as the unit of analysis, where institutional concepts are operationalized as a lens to interpret and analyse data. Another approach is to use the organizational field as the level of analysis to extend our theoretical and empirical understanding of institutional processes and effects across industries, sectors, and organizations. Thus far applications of the theory by IS scholars demonstrate both narrow and broad interpretations, perhaps because these scholars come from diverse disciplinary and research traditions, or because institutional theorists have tended to stress their differences more than agreements, or because institutional theory is inherently difficult to explicate as 'it taps taken-for-granted assumptions at the core of social action' (Zucker 1987: 443).

Given the rich history and complexity of institutional theory and its current state in IS research, this chapter has three objectives. First, it seeks to provide IS scholars, regardless of their prior exposure to institutional theory, with an overview of the theory, focusing on the most vibrant stream—the new or neo-institutionalism in organizational analysis. We demonstrate the explicit and implicit points of disagreement among institutional theorists and also articulate common themes, principles, processes, and elements of the theory that they share. This effort helps IS researchers stay up to date on the development of institutional theory as we theorize, operationalize, and refine institutional concepts for IS research and the wider academic community. Second, we present a review of the IS studies which have applied institutional theory. We critically evaluate the theoretical and empirical strengths and weaknesses of this body of work, and caution against a tendency to simplify institutional concepts into one-dimensional constructs without appreciating the ontological and epistemological antecedents of institutionalism. Finally, we offer a research agenda for the IS field to embrace the institutional perspective and develop an *institutional theory of IT*.

FOUNDATIONS OF INSTITUTIONAL THEORY

The publication of the New Institutionalism in Organizational Analysis (Powell and DiMaggio 1991) and Institutions and Organizations (Scott 1995) signified the renaissance in the study of institutions in social sciences (DiMaggio and Powell 1991). These influential books show that institutionalism is a highly complex paradigm with contributions delineated across disciplines (e.g. economics, sociology, political science, history, and ecology) and time spans (e.g. 'old' and 'new' institutionalism). This chapter is rooted in the new institutionalism in organizational studies (primarily in sociology) because this is the most vibrant and established research stream of institutionalism. Central concepts such as institution, institutionalization, deinstitutionalism, and reinstitutionalization add further complexity as they incorporate both macro- and micro-dimensions.

Scott (2001: 49) gives five definitions of institution, stressing they are, 'multi-faceted, durable, social structures, made up of symbolic elements, social activities, and material resources'. Jepperson (1991) gives sixteen examples of an institution, including, marriage, formal organization, academic tenure, and the corporation. Institutionalization, is thus the process by which an institution attains a stable and durable state or property. Deinstitutionalization is a departure from institutionalization, which represents 'the process by which the legitimacy of an established or institutionalized organizational practice erodes or discontinues' (Oliver 1992: 564). A further concept, reinstitutionalization, is an 'exit from one institutionalization, and entry into another institutional form, organized around different principles or rules' (Jepperson 1991: 152).

As DiMaggio and Powell (1991: 1) point out, institutional analysis was used in the work of Emile Durkheim in the nineteenth century where he studied 'social facts as things'. Later in the twentieth century, Selznick (1957: 16–17) provided a classic insight that to 'institutionalize is to infuse with value beyond the technical requirements of the task at hand'. This suggested an impediment to effective task performance where the goals of the organization were subverted, thus drawing a distinction between institutional and task elements at the levels of the environment and organization. This dichotomy of macro- and micro-phenomena identified in old institutionalism continues in the new institutionalism, thus extending the breadth and depth of institutional theory where conceptual and empirical challenges continue. A significant challenge is defining institution as both a theoretical concept and construct for empirical investigation. Associated with such complexity and diversity of institutional forms, the notion of institution is more easily understood by reviewing institutionalists' seminal work and trying the analytical tools institutionalists developed.

Three classic papers are among those that represent the essence of neo-institutionalism. These papers introduce the central concepts within institutional theory. The central argument of Meyer and Rowan's (1977) paper was that formal organizational structures emerge as reflections of rationalized myths and rules. Using abstract language, they suggest,

> Institutional rules function as myths which organizations incorporate, gaining legitimacy, resources, stability, and enhanced survival prospects. Organizations whose structures become isomorphic with the myths of the institutional environment, in contrast with those primarily structured by the demands of technical production and exchange, decrease internal coordination and control in order to maintain legitimacy. Structures are decoupled from each other and from ongoing activities. (p. 340)

In the same year, Zucker (1977) examined institutionalization in the context of cultural persistence. She was critical of traditional approaches to institutionalization that overlooked this issue. Three levels of institutionalization on three aspects of cultural persistence were identified. They were: generational uniformity of cultural understanding, maintenance of these understandings, and resistance to change of these understandings. Zucker found strong support for the prediction that, 'the greater the degree of institutionalization, the greater the generational uniformity, maintenance, and resistance to change of cultural understandings' (p. 276).

Further development of institutional concepts was found in DiMaggio and Powell's (1983) influential paper that examined the link between institutional isomorphism and rationality. These authors posed the question: 'What makes organizations so similar' (DiMaggio and Powell 1983: 147)? They argued that 'the engine' of rationalization and bureaucratization had shifted from the competitive marketplace to the state and the professions. They were interested to examine the 'startling homogeneity of organizational forms and practices'. Developing the concept of the organizational field, which they defined as 'those organizations that, in the aggregate, constitute a recognized area of institutional life' (DiMaggio and Powell 1983: 148) they contended that, once a set of organizations becomes a field, a paradox emerges in that 'rational actors make their organizations increasingly similar as they try to change them' (p. 147). The authors developed three distinctive isomorphic processes: coercive, mimetic, and normative to explain institutional isomorphism. Coercive isomorphism results from both formal and informal pressures exerted on organizations by powerful entities such as the state and by cultural expectations in the organization's environment. Mimetic isomorphism derives from uncertainty. This occurs when organizational technologies are poorly understood, goals are ambiguous, or when the environment creates symbolic uncertainty. These factors encourage organizations to model themselves after other organizations. Normative pressures stem largely from professionalization, which means the collective struggle of members of an occupation to define the conditions and methods of their work. This is to control 'the production of producers' and to establish a cognitive base and legitimacy for their occupational autonomy.

In an early review paper on institutional theories of organization, Zucker (1987) presented environment and organization as two distinct theoretical approaches to institutionalization. The *environment-as-institution* perspective posits that institutions exist in an organization's environment as social facts. The basic institutional process is the reproduction or copying of environmental social facts at the organizational level. The *organization-as-institution* perspective contends that institutions arise within the organization. The central institutional process is thus generation—the creation of new institutional elements at the organization level. Reproduction is therefore a consequence of institutionalization rather than a cause. Addressing the question, 'What is the meaning of institutional?' (p. 445), Zucker (1987) presented two defining elements shared by theoretical approaches to institutionalization in organizations. They include, (a) a rule-like, social fact quality of an organized pattern of action (exterior) and (b) an embedding in formal structures, such as formal aspects of organizations that are not tied to particular actors or situations (nonpersonal/objective)' (p. 444). As a departure from earlier contributions on institutional theory where conceptions were 'tautological', 'descriptive', or 'untestable', Zucker (1987) contended that neo-institutional theory viewed institutionalization as a variable that separated 'its causes from the major consequence' (p. 444). Her review of institutional theory proclaimed that much of the empirical work examined the theory piecemeal, and seldom tested the causal predictions and that research on causes of institutionalization had been 'eclipsed by study of its consequences or outcomes'.

Since the publication of these seminal papers on institutional theory, further work has greatly enhanced the theoretical and empirical development of the field. In the following four subsections, we organize scholarly work on institutional theory into four broad areas, drawing from Scott's (1995) study, which delineates the societal, sectoral, organizational, and individual dimensions of institutionalism. In each area, we delineate the key theoretical contributions and methodological challenges. We illustrate the changing fashions within institutional theory, particularly as contributions for the past three decades are depicted as 'new institutionalism' (DiMaggio and Powell 1991) presenting an intellectual departure from the old institutionalism of Selznick (1949), Perrow (1986), and colleagues. The criteria for classifying publications are (a) their main title, and/or (b) their substantive content (see Appendix A). We recognize that some contributions may span two or more categories or theoretical perspectives, but our primary purpose for this exercise is to demonstrate the scale and scope of institutionalist literature, rather than to provide a definitive classification system.

Construction, Maintenance, and Diffusion

The construction, maintenance, and diffusion of institutional arrangements are exemplified by a number of studies that adopt either variance or process models. Zucker (1977) observed that institutionalization is both a property and a process variable. As a property variable, institution is observed as an entity. This may be a cultural, political, or social system that exhibits one or more features or properties. Variance theories view institutions as entities. They examine their characteristics, view them as abstract independent or dependent variables, and endeavour to establish their causal relations to other variables. Precursor (independent) variables determine the values of outcome (dependent) variables (Scott 1995).

Process theories examine a series of occurrences of events rather than a set of closely defined variables (Mohr 1982). In process theories, time is important, particularly, the time ordering of events that may be delineated into sequences that make up different eras. For example, a conceptual model by Tolbert and Zucker (1996) delineates the component processes of institutionalization into three distinct stages: habitualization, objectification, and sedimentation. This framework provides a conceptual tool for understanding the different stages of the institutionalization process, where innovation may become institutionalized (sedimentation) or fail to move through the various stages, remaining at the habitualized stage. Theoretical models of this nature are useful for conceptualizing innovation as a process, but the extent to which the various stages are empirically distinct can only be verified through longitudinal research.

To a large extent, it is arbitrary to distinguish the properties and processes used to create institutions from those that may change them. The literature, however, shows a distinction in that some studies examine the conditions and processes which give rise to new rules and practices (institutional creation), while others examine the beliefs, norms, and practices which become threatened over time and lead to deinstitutionalization. Studies concerned with institution building or creation are found in many disciplines (e.g. ecology, economics, political science, sociology, and history) and focus on different units of analysis (e.g. societal, sector, field, population, organization, and interpersonal) (Scott 1995). The topics of these studies have included: conditions that give rise to new institutional arrangements (Suchman 1995), cultural-cognitive aspects of institutionalism (DiMaggio 1991a), social construction of knowledge (Mizruchi and Fein 1999), and institutionalization through discourse (Phillips, Lawrence, and Hardy 2004).

In conjunction with the work on institutional construction, institutional theorists further examine how institutions are maintained and diffused. Zucker (1977) argued that the traditional approaches to institutionalization do not provide an adequate explanation of cultural persistence. Nearly two decades later, Scott (1995) similarly observed that institutional theory has paid little attention to the issue of institutional persistence, with many scholars disagreeing over the mechanisms that underlie stability. According to Scott (1995), three broad conceptions of institution influence views on maintenance. They include: regulatory view, which emphasizes rational and conscious control efforts concerning interests, agency and power, and the deployment of sanctions (DiMaggio 1988), normative view, which emphasizes the stabilizing influence of shared norms, and cultural-cognitive view, which emphasizes the unconscious, taken-for-granted assumptions about social reality.

These three institutional views also help explain the diffusion of innovations, an ever-interesting phenomenon previously examined primarily from the communication of information perspective (Rogers 2003). Regulative mandates demand compliances, forcing more social actors to adopt innovations faster than without such mandates (Tolbert and Zucker 1983). Normative pressures push innovations through formal or informal ties among actors in social networks such as profession, community, industry associations. However, normative pressures based on relational ties in social networks can only explain a fraction of the diffusion process (Strang and Soule 1998). As Strang and Meyer (1994) argued, 'when the diffusion process is socially meaningless, as in the spread of measles, physical contact may be all that is required for transmission to occur. When adoptions are socially meaningful acts, it is common to think of actors as making different choices cognitively available to each other, developing shared understandings and exploring the consequences of innovation through each other's experience' (p. 101). According to this view, cultural-cognitive processes can 'theorize' an innovation as an efficient means to an end considered important by actors belonging to socially constructed categories. It is this theorization that helps diffuse, legitimate, and institutionalize innovations (Strang and Meyer 1994; Tolbert and Zucker 1996). Finally, the regulative, normative, and cultural-cognitive processes are not mutually exclusive. They may be interdependent. For example, recent institutional research has found that regulatory activities often depend on normative and cognitive elements as actors negotiate, interpret, and socially construct the meaning of laws and regulations based on normative and cultural-cognitive considerations (Dobbin and Sutton 1998; Edelman, Ugger, and Erlanger 1999).

Organizational Fields and Institutional Logics

The concept of organizational field is now well established in institutional theory and extends beyond the notion of organization as a single entity. DiMaggio and Powell (1983) asserted that, 'By organizational field, we mean those organizations that, in the aggregate, constitute a recognized area of institutional life: key suppliers, resource and product consumers, regulatory agencies, and other organizations that produce similar services or products' (p. 148). These authors suggested that the structure of the organizational field must be defined on the basis of empirical investigation and cannot be determined a priori. At a more abstract level, the authors claimed, 'fields only exist to the extent that they are institutionally defined'. They identified four parts in the process of institutional definition or structuration: (1) an increase in the extent of interaction among organizations in the field; (2) the emergence of sharply defined inter-organizational structures of domination and patterns of coalition; (3) an increase in the information load with which organizations in the field must contend; (4) and the development of a mutual awareness among participants in a set of organizations that they are involved in a common enterprise (DiMaggio and Powell 1983: 148). Similarly, Scott (2001: 84) offered another abstract definition: 'The notion of field connotes the existence of a community of organizations that partakes of a common meaning system and whose participants interact more frequently and fatefully with one another than with actors outside of the field'.

The concept of organizational field focuses upon a macro, interorganization analysis. Within institutional theory, the concept of the organizational field has continued to gain ground and differs in its unit of analysis from sectoral or population approaches since it includes 'the totality of relevant actors' (DiMaggio and Powell 1983: 148). Research studies used the concept of organizational field to examine field structure (DiMaggio 1986), task environment relationships (Oliver 1997), and institutional entrepreneurship in emerging fields (Maguire, Hardy, and Lawrence 2004).

Closely aligned with the concept of organizational field is institutional logics defined as 'sets of 'material' practices and symbolic constructions which constitute a field's organizing principles and which are available to organizations and individuals to elaborate' (Friedland and Alford 1991: 248). They 'provide the formal and informal rules of action, interaction, and interpretation that guide and constrain decision makers in accomplishing the organization's tasks and in obtaining social status, credits, penalties and rewards in the process' (Ocasio 1997) and the 'cognitive maps or the belief systems that are carried by individuals located in an organizational field to embed meaning to their activities' (Scott et al. 2000: 20).

Many studies examine the relationship between traditional institutional logics and emerging logics in fields such as the craft industry (Thornton 2002), healthcare (Scott et al. 2000; Reay and Hinings 2005; Currie and Guah 2007), and higher education publishing (Thornton and Ocasio 1999). Others examine how innovations at the periphery of the radio broadcasting field exerted influences that migrated to the core of the field once new practices were shown to be effective (Leblebici et al. 1991). This study showed how the existing social structure of the field shaped the efficacy of non-routine action.

Organizational Structure, Performance, and Choice

Neo-institutionalism views institutionalization as occurring at the societal, sectoral, field, and inter-organizational levels, where the primary focal lens is on how organizational forms, structural components, performance outcomes, and individual choices become institutionalized. Many studies on institutional processes examine the effects on specific organizations (Scott 2001). A distinction is made between formal and informal structures of an organization; the former being the 'blueprint' for activities that comprise the rationalized formal structure that is more likely to arise in highly institutionalized contexts.

The classic paper by Meyer and Rowan (1977) argued that the formal structures of many organizations reflect the myths of their institutional environments, rather than the demands of their work activities. Formal organizational structures arise as reflections of rationalized institutional rules that contribute to the expansion and growing complexity of these structures. Institutional rules serve as myths which organizations incorporate into their formal structure to gain legitimacy, scarce resources, stability, and enhanced prospects of long-term survival. Organizations where structures become isomorphic with the myths of the institutional environment, rather than those structured by the demands of technical production and exchange, act to decrease internal coordination and control as a means of maintaining legitimacy. Such isomorphism results in formal structures becoming decoupled from technical/informal structures and from ongoing activities (Meyer and Rowan 1977).

From this influential paper, the concepts of isomorphism, legitimacy, and decoupling became central in neo-institutionalist work. As the old institutionalism saw organizations as organic wholes, the new institutionalism viewed organizations 'loosely coupled arrays of standardized elements' (DiMaggio and Powell 1991: 14). Neo-institutionalism emphasizes the 'homogeneity of organizations' and the 'stability of institutionalized components' (DiMaggio and Powell 1991: 14) and institutional isomorphism (DiMaggio and Powell

1983; Meyer and Rowan 1977). Institutionalization was seen as a phenomenological process, where social relationships and actions exhibit a taken-for-granted quality, and a state of affairs where 'shared cognitions determine what actions are possible and what has meaning' (Zucker 1983: 2).

Neo-institutionalism examines rationality at the level of the formal structure, rather than at the individual actor level. It attributes the 'diffusion of departments and operating procedures to inter-organizational influences, conformity, and the persuasiveness of cultural accounts, rather than to the functions they are intended to perform' (DiMaggio and Powell 1991: 13). Conflicts arise between conformity to institutionalized rules and efficiency criteria. Attempts to coordinate and control activity to promote efficiency will undermine ceremonial conformity, which will, in turn, reduce the support and legitimacy in the organization. To maintain conformity, organizations that reflect institutional rules will seek to 'buffer their formal structures from the uncertainties of technical activities by becoming loosely coupled, building gaps between their formal structures and actual work activities' (Meyer and Rowan 1977: 340–1). Institutionalists who examine change across organizational fields and within organizations have more recently used the concept of decoupling. Greenwood and Hinings (1996) hypothesize that radical change in tightly coupled institutional fields is likely to be revolutionary, unlike in loosely coupled fields (which is more common) and likely to be evolutionary. We will examine institutional change in the next section.

An important debate within institutional theory concerns the relationship between institutional and rational choice arguments, which are often seen as diametrically opposed (DiMaggio 1991b). Rational choice models have played a significant role in social science both in the understanding of designing institutions and the how they serve the individual and collective interests of institutional actors. These models are invariably used to empirically test the dysfunctional features of institutions, since this is a prominent issue in understanding institutional outcomes. Rational choice theorists are interested in individual and collective goal-orientated, purposive behaviour, and also non-rational and even irrational choices, without which, the rational choice thesis becomes a tautology.

A fundamental criticism of rational choice models embraces a wider criticism of functionalist premises in social science. This contends that we cannot claim to have explained the origin of an institution simply by reference to the functionality of the institution. A tension in rational choice theory is between individual rationality and institutional inefficiency. Institutional actors (individual or collective) may exhibit non-instrumental and non-rational behaviour that produces unintended consequences. They may also consciously pursue institutional goals and outcomes that are not conducive to efficient task performance. Based on these observations, many institutionalists express serious criticisms of rational choice perspectives since they exaggerate issues of choice and agency, while overlooking important institutional influences emanating from the societal, sectoral and field levels (Greenwood and Hinings 2006).

As a 'radical retreat from society' rational choice theories are criticized for adopting the premise that the actions and behaviour of instrumental, rational individuals are the primary cause of institutional arrangements. Public-choice theory, agency theory, rational-actor models, and the new institutional economics all adopt this premiss. Rational choice theorists perceive organizational arrangements, 'whether party, state, family or firm—from the rationality of individuals in exchange, each attempting to maximise his or her utility by exchanging scarce, usually material resources' (Friedland and Alford 1991: 232).

On closer examination of the broader social science literature, however, the dichotomy between institutional and rational actor accounts is oversimplified. While functional institutionalism tends to overstate the role of institutional actors and undermine the societal and field influences on organizational outcomes, the two perspectives are not necessarily diametrically opposed. Jepperson (1991: 158) points out that 'self-proclaimed rational-choice arguments often feature institutional constraints (in connection with opportunity costs) as central causes and institutional arguments often invoke adaptive responses to change in institutional conditions'. So rather than treating the perspectives as competing paradigms, 'they might represent competing ways to invoke institutional effects, or reflect disagreements about proper micro-foundations or micro-effects, to mention just two alternatives'.

The literature shows that institutional theorists from across the disciplines make different assumptions about individual choice and what determines social action. In the sociological theory of the twentiethth century, Max Weber defined social action to emphasize the importance of meanings individuals attach to their own and others' behaviour. Weber distinguished between action and behaviour that was rational, non-rational, or irrational. More recently, the new economic institutionalism, such as the transaction cost economics (TCEs) of Williamson (1975) is grounded in rational individual choice, where the defining feature is the attempt to explain behaviour as a result of the instrumental choices of individual or collective actors in pursuit of their goals. New economic institutionalism is seen as being applicable for the study of regulation. This activity is described as one, 'carried on between and among actors seeking to gain greater efficiency (or arbitrate differences across systems to avoid friction) through cooperation... The search for solutions to common problems that cannot be resolved unilaterally leads to the adoption of new structures that reflect the assumptions of the 'new economic' institutionalism' (Reich 2000: 503). Game theorists similarly adopt an atomistic view that emphasizes how individual and collective actors engaged in behaviour to maximize outcomes, having assimilated all the relevant data and information to inform their decision making (Miller 2000). They seek to explain how cooperation and efficiency results from the instrumental behaviour of individuals (Axelrod 1981). Political scientists tend to pay more attention to the effects of institutions than to issues of institutional origins and change. The consequence has been a marked tendency to 'fall back on implicit or explicit functional accounts, in which the effects of institutions explain the presence of those institutions' (Pierson 2000: 475).

While neo-institutional analysts in economics and political science embrace rational choice theory, Simon's (1997) bounded rationality thesis has been highly influential by demonstrating that, despite the presumption that actors intend to be rational, they are bounded by the limitations of the information they possess. Neo-institutional theorists who embrace this and related models tend to view institutions primarily as regulative frameworks. In this context, individual or collective actors design institutions to resolve perceived or real problems of social dysfunction (e.g. financial misconduct) where regulation carries with it the reward of incentives or the threat of sanctions.

Neo-institutional theorists at the other end of the spectrum tend to emphasize the cultural-cognitive influences on behaviour as opposed to regulative and normative influences. Phenomenologists (Schütz 1967) and ethnomethodologists (Garfinkel 1967) reject rational actor accounts, even those which emphasize bounded rationality, as they believe action and behaviour are influenced by power relations and political structures where conflict is likely to produce unintended consequences. Phenomenologists and ethnomethodologists, like rational choice theorists, treat the individual as the unit of analysis, yet reject the notion of an explicit theory of individual behaviour when they examine institutional structure and performance outcomes. Sociological perspectives in neo-institutional theory, particularly those from phenomenology and ethnomethodology, perceive the limitation of embracing a narrow, functionalist rational choice framework as an oversimplification, where action and behaviour are examined as a means-ends relationship. As opposed to emphasizing the role of the individual, many neo-institutional theorists sympathetic to phenomenology and ethnomethodology adopt an organicist rather than an atomistic view of institutions, where 'the essential characteristics of any element are seen as outcomes of relations with other entities. Actors in interaction constitute social structures, which, in turn, constitute actors. The products of prior interactions—norms, rules, beliefs, resources—provide the situational elements that enter into individual decision making' (Scott 2001: 67).

Institutional Change

While much of the prior work by institutional theorists has viewed institutionalism as a source of stability and order (Zucker 1977; Strang and Meyer 1993), recent work has considered how institutions undergo change (Scott 2001; Greenwood and Hinings 2006). Over the past two decades, neo-institutionalists have increasingly adopted process-oriented methods to examine institutional change in a diverse range of fields. The complexity of political, regulatory, and technical changes at the societal, sectoral, field, and organizational levels have made institutional change and adaptation a central issue for institutionalists (Greenwood and Hinings 1996). The literature exhibits a diverse range of studies from across the social science disciplines using a number of institutionalist theories, with most studies examining the processes of institutionalization, rather than deinstitutionalziation, or reinstitutionalization (Greenwood, Suddaby, and Hinings 1996).

Observing how institutional forces exert changes in markets, Haveman (1993) combined organizational ecology and neo-institutional theory to explain the process of diversification. She focused on how the structure of markets affects the rate of market entry. Using the density-dependency model of competition and legitimization to study organizational founding and failure, the study found legitimation of new markets for loan associations by the presence of successful thrifts is balanced by competitive or crowding effects. Neo-institutional arguments were found to be insufficient for explaining market entry. To counter this, the author recommended incorporating concepts of competition from organizational ecology to help explain why rates of market entry do not continue to rise as successful firm market density rises.

Davis, Diekmann, and Tinsley (1994) examined the decline and fall of the conglomerate firm in the 1980s, which they conceptualized as the deinstitutionalization of an organizational form. The conglomerate firm in the 1980s was composed of several unrelated businesses and was the dominant corporate form in the United States. A decade later, this form had become deinstitutionalized. Using comprehensive time-series data from the 1980s on a population of the largest industrial firms in the USA, the authors demonstrated that deinstitutionalization was the result of two processes. First, diversified firms were taken over at a high rate and their unwanted parts were typically sold off. Second, the less diversified firms that survived rejected the strategy of conglomerate growth. These authors suggested the aggregate result was that by 1990, the largest industrial firms in the USA had become much less diversified.

Another study by Sine and David (2003) examined environmental jolts and entrepreneurial opportunity in the US electric power industry over a forty-year period. These authors found that environmental jolts mobilize actors to reformulate institutions, resulting in increased entrepreneurial activity. Their study found that, when the institutional environment was stable, incumbent organizational forms and embedded logics present formidable obstacles to entrepreneurial activity. Environmental jolts, however, catalyse search processes and motivate the evaluation of current institutional logics. In the case of the electric power industry, environments of abundance and regulation resulted in homogeneity of organizational structures and strategies, and few entrepreneurial opportunities. Environments marked by scarcity and crisis, however, witnessed heavy scrutiny of existing institutional arrangements that eroded their taken-for-grantedness and symbolic value, resulting in opportunities for entrepreneurial action.

At the field level, many studies consider process-oriented change. Scott et al. (2000) examined the transformation in healthcare systems in the San Francisco Bay Area over a fifty-year period. As one of the most comprehensive studies on an organizational field, the authors identified competing institutional logics, each of which illustrated a specific time period. Recognizing that rapid change is not usually a characteristic attributed to healthcare, as hospitals display highly institutionalized structures and practices, the authors used a longitudinal case-based research method to examine large-scale government supported innovation. They found that, despite strong pressures for isomorphism, healthcare had become a more complex environment over the past two decades, as new entrants in the form of external service providers, and changing roles of healthcare consumers (including patients) all conspired to alter a previously stable institutional setting.

Another study examined the role of professional associations in the highly institutionalized organizational field of accounting. The authors presented their work as a case study of the profession to show how it underwent major change over a twenty-year period. The setting was the professional business services field in Alberta, Canada, that plays a significant role in legitimating change. A six-stage model of institutional change was developed which commenced with social, technological, or regulatory jolts which precipitate deinstitutionalization, possibly leading to the next stage of reinstitutionalization. The authors extended the ideas of Strang and Mayer (1993) who suggested that for practices to become widely adopted, they have to become 'theorized', which is 'the development and specification of abstract categories and the elaboration of chains of cause and effect' (Greenwood, Suddaby, and Hinings 1996: 60). This study found that professional associations that act as regulatory agencies played a significant part in theorizing change by endorsing local innovations and shaping their diffusion.

Since the concept of deinstitutionalization is central to institutional change, institutionalists have called for more research that departs from the traditional focus on institutional persistence and stability, to understand the processes of evolutionary or revolutionary institutional change. Prior research suggests that government regulations and policies are most likely to deinstitutionalize organizational practices due to the threat of coercion that accompanies the legal enforcement of government mandates (DiMaggio and Powell 1983; Scott 2001). Government imposed health and financial regulations are two examples.

One of the most comprehensive frameworks on deinstitutionalization processes is by Oliver (1992). This study delineates three antecedents of deinstitutionalization that may erode or discontinue an institutionalized organizational activity or practice. First, political pressures show that institutionalized practices come under threat, erosion, or displacement when the utility or legitimacy of such practices is seriously called into question. Political conditions that delegitimate organizational practices may occur as a result of a performance crisis. Second, functional pressures are those that arise from perceived problems in performance levels associated with institutionalized practices. The potential for innovative pressures and performance problems to deinstitutionalize enduring organizational practices is related to technical or functional considerations that tend to compromise or raise doubts about the instrumental value of an institutionalized practice. Third, social pressures are associated with differentiation of groups and the existence of heterogeneous divergent or discordant beliefs and practices. Social pressures that precipitate deinstitutionalization explain many of the conditions under which organizations are neither pro-active agents of deinstitutionalization nor centrally intent on abandoning or rejecting particular institutional traditions.

Oliver (1992) gives three reasons why an examination of the consequences and causes of deinstitutionalization is important. First, deinstitutionalization explains a broad range of changes in organizations that an institutional perspective has traditionally neglected, including challenges to the institutional status quo, the abandonment of habits and customs, and the deterioration of organizational consensus around the value of institutionalized activity. Second, the causes of deinstitutionalization explain when institutional pressures are least likely to exert an enduring influence on organizations. Institutional theorists have tended to emphasize the cultural persistence of institutionalized organizational forms and process (Zucker 1977; Scott 1987; Zucker 1987). The potential for deinstitutionalization of organizational activities calls into question the stability and longevity of institutional values and practices, suggesting instead that under a variety of predictable conditions, institutionalized processes or practices will be vulnerable to challenge, reassessment, or rejection. Third, deinstitutionalization describes the conditions under which institutional rules and expectations fail in their predicted effects on organizations. Therefore, an examination of deinstitutionalizing pressures may help to clarify the boundary conditions of institutional explanations and, by so doing, shed light on the conditions or organizational contexts within which institutional explanations might be most relevant or powerful. Finally, institutional theory has been increasingly criticized for its lack of attention to political processes as well as other non-institutional factors in shaping the responses of organizations to institutional pressures.

In a similar vein to criticisms by institutional theorists about rational-choice theories, the traditional focus on institutional creation, maintenance, and stability has underplayed important issues of human agency (DiMaggio 1988; Oliver 1991). Scott (2001) addressed this issue by developing a framework that incorporated top-down and bottom-up processes of institutional creation and diffusion. This multi-level framework incorporates societal institutions, fields, organizations, and actors. Change processes are more fruitfully examined by research designs that incorporate multiple levels of analysis since social action and structure occupies a duality that each serves to constrain and empower the other. Scott (2001: 203) asserts that, 'social structures themselves are nested, groups within organizations or networks of organizations, organizations within fields, fields within broader societal and trans-societal systems. Although every study can not attend to all levels, analysts should be aware of them and craft designs to include critical actors and structures engaged in maintaining and transforming institutions'.

One study that explicitly linked agency and institutional theory examined sales compensation policies of fifty-four retail speciality stores (Eisenhardt 1988). Using a range of variables, including the programmability of a job, span of control, uncertainty, type of merchandize, and the age of a store, the author found that both theoretical perspectives were necessary for explaining retail compensation policies. The contribution of agency theory was a more balanced view of performance contingency pay, which suggested that firms prefer pay based on behaviours and use pay based on outcomes only when behaviours are difficult to measure. The contribution of institutional theory was the recognition that founding conditions and simple industry traditions play an important role in determining compensation policies. The author recommended that a combination of agency and institutional theory variables for future research would strengthen both theoretical perspectives and increase understanding of phenomena.

The relationship between agency and institutions has been picked up by a more recent stream of institutional research, which seeks to tackle the so-called 'paradox of embedded agency' (DiMaggio and Powell 1991; Holm 1995; Seo and Creed 2002). Garud, Hardy, and Maguire (2007: 961) describe the paradox as follows: 'if actors are embedded in an institutional field and subject to regulative, normative and cognitive processes that structure their cognitions, define their interests and produce their identities, how are they able to envision new practices and then subsequently get others to adopt them?' Among attempts to solve the theoretical puzzle, most notable is the 'institutional entrepreneurship' perspective, drawing insights from institutional theory and entrepreneurship research. Institutional entrepreneurship is defined as the 'activities of actors who have an interest in particular institutional arrangements and who leverage resources to create new institutions or to transform existing ones' (Maguire, Hardy, and Lawrence 2004: 657). Institutional entrepreneurship enables us to concentrate on how interested actors conspire to influence their institutional contexts by formulating strategies to influence regulatory, market, or technical change (Lawrence and Suddaby 2006).

By reintroducing agency and interests into institutional analysis, research on institutional entrepreneurship has revealed mechanisms and strategies used by the institutional entrepreneurs to create or transform institutions. For example, in a study of Sun Microsystems' efforts to establish its Java technology as an industry standard, Garud, Jain, and Kumaraswamy (2002) find that Sun mobilized a broad set of partners including systems assemblers, software firms, and component manufacturers with an open systems strategy. As Sun's partners, their support of the Java platform does not prevent them from competing with one another on the Java products they produce. To legitimate Java's write-once, run-everywhere platform, Sun coined the slogan, 'The network is the computer.' This slogan justified programmers' efforts to write software for the Internet, rendering obsolete Microsoft's desktop-centric view of computing.

The linking of multiple theoretical perspectives has further been explored between structuration processes and institutional theory. Both theories contend that institutions and actions are linked and that institutionalization is a dynamic and ongoing process (Barley and Tolbert 1997). These authors assert that institutionalists have pursued an empirical agenda that has largely ignored how institutions are created, altered and reproduced because process models of institutionalization are immature. Conversely, structuration theory remains a process theory of such abstraction that it has produced few empirical studies (see Chapter 5). Presenting a discussion of their similarities, the authors argue why a fusion of the two theories would enhance institutional theory by developing a model of institutionalization as a structuration process.

LIMITATIONS OF NEO-INSTITUTIONALISM

Here, we offer a brief critique of neo-institutionalism by discussing concerns about its lack of theoretical clarity and the shortcomings of variance and process accounts. Often in these accounts, researchers either oversimplify institutional constructs or fail to explain the processes of institutional creation and change. Notwithstanding neo-institutional concerns about the dominance of strategic choice (Goodrick and Salancik 1996) and rational-actor models (DiMaggio and Powell 1991), institutionalism invites many criticisms about its theoretical and empirical shortcomings. These criticisms relate to both variance and process approaches to institutionalization.

While new institutionalism has been influential in identifying the limitations of rationalization, it is criticized for not adequately explaining how 'the pool of social ideas, instrumental orientations and schemes (i.e. the rationalized environment) is translated into the specific administrative patterns encountered in particular organizations or populations of organizations' (Hasselbladh and Kallinikos 2000: 699). Neo-institutionalism underplays the 'social construction of rationalization', that it conceptualizes as structural isomorphism (Hasselbladh and Kallinikos 2000: 700). The end state of institutionalization is not diffusion of rationalized beliefs and practices. Instead, 'institutionalization is sustained and given meaning and direction through its capacity to constitute distinctive forms of actor-hood'. This is contingent on cultural-cognitive factors where 'ideas are elaborated, and rendered solid and durable' (Hasselbladh and Kallinikos 2000: 700).

Others criticize neo-institutionalism for treating institutions as independent variables and the primary unit of analysis. Many institutionalists examine the regulative, normative, and cultural-cognitive factors that influence institutions, but it is also imperative to include the 'properties of the supra-individual'. While institutionalists recognize that institutional outcomes are not reducible to 'aggregations or direct consequences of individuals' attributes or motives' (DiMaggio and Powell 1991: 8), their lack of attention to human agency has often produced an 'over-socialised' account of organizational behaviour (DiMaggio 1988).

These criticisms suggest that theoretical concepts used by institutionalists are too idealistic and broad to inform empirical enquiry. But, whereas researchers using variance models attempt to resolve this problem by simplifying institutional concepts or constructs to obtain rigour and clarity in their research design, others using a process-oriented approach also simplify the complexities of institutionalization using multi-stage models. A common problem identified in process models is a lack of empirical verification of how one stage in the institutionalization process gives way to another. Also, theorists need to explain why some processes lead to institutionalization while others do not. This is particularly relevant in the area of innovation studies.

Since variance and process studies may fail to adequately explain the effects or processes of institutionalization, calls are made to broaden the institutionalist perspective still further (Greenwood et al. 2007). However, extending research designs through developing more complex multi-level and multi-stage models presents even greater challenges, both theoretically and empirically.

Given that many institutional accounts focus on the outcome of social construction (e.g. by observing a particular institution such as education), researchers are encouraged to abandon the 'bird's eye view of the field, and come closer to the social and

cognitive means and procedures underlying rationalized beliefs and schemes of action'
(Hasselbladh and Kallinikos 2000: 700). Some argue that institutional accounts have
become associated with notions that organizations are not concerned with task performance, and are instead only concerned with issues of legitimacy. This form of 'institutionalization of the institutional perspective' is dismissed by Powell (1991) who argues
that studies often highlight 'specific findings at the expense of the basic argument that
institutional pressures stem from more general societal wide processes of rationalization' (p. 190). An important insight is that, 'if organizations can manipulate the
symbols they present to the external environment, then they must also be adept at
producing and controlling the symbolic elements as well' (ibid.). Much of this misunderstanding is caused by the lack of clarity in some of the original statements by neo-
institutionalists.

INSTITUTIONAL THEORY AND INFORMATION SYSTEMS RESEARCH

Our discussion of the broad literature of neo-institutionalism provides a critical
foundation for understanding and appreciating the diversity of scholarly contributions
from a range of disciplines and some of the limitations of this complex theory. Our
primary analytic focus is sociological perspectives on neo-institutionalism from the
sub-field of organization studies (OS). Recognizing the complementary nature of OS
and IS, scholars have called for a closer intellectual relationship between the two fields
(Orlikowski and Barley 2001). King et al. (1994) suggest that new institutionalism
provides a strong base for understanding the role of institutions in IT innovation.
These ideas were embraced by other scholars who called for more 'research that
embraces the importance of simultaneously understanding the role of human agency
as embedded in institutional contexts as well as the constraints and affordances of
technologies as material systems' (Orlikowski and Barley 2001: 158). Recently, a special
issue of the *Journal of Applied Behavioral Science* was published to encourage more
active engagement between OS and IS, particularly as the former is explicitly interested
in technology-enabled change, while the latter examines the growing sophistication
and diversity of specific technical artefacts, and how they impact organizations and the
wider society (Barrett, Grant, and Wailes 2006).

In parallel, others call for closer synergies between IS and other theoretical perspectives
from OS, including structuration (Barley 1986; Orlikowski and Robey 1991; Orlikowski
1992; DeSanctis and Poole 1994; Barley and Tolbert 1997), agency theory (Orlikowski
1996; Weick 1998; Boudreau and Robey 2005), anthropological approaches (Wareham
2002), and discourse analysis (Doolin 2003). Extending the use of research methods is
further recommended to include interpretive approaches (Walsham 1993) and more

specifically, phenomenology (Mingers 2001) and ethnomethodology (Ross and Chiasson 2005).

We acknowledge that institutional theory in IS research is a relatively new phenomenon and is gaining momentum. The IS literature reveals an eclectic approach by researchers to using institutionalist perspectives. Yet most contributions treat neo-institutionalism as a single theory and play down its multi-disciplinary and conceptually ambiguous nature. In this regard, institutional theory is deployed as a 'lens' to examine the relationships between constructs delineated from, for example, organizational fields, isomorphism and institutional logics, using either variance or process approaches.

In the IS literature, researchers tend to study institution as a process (institutionalization) and an entity (with institutional effects). Theoretical and empirical preferences of IS researchers tend to determine the choice of environmental and organizational variables in the research design. For example, we found fewer studies on IT as a process of institutionalization. The majority of studies looked at the institutional effects on IT, often using institutional concepts piecemeal (Mignerat and Rivard 2005). Many studies on institutional effects on IT used the three mechanisms of institutional isomorphism: coercive, mimetic, and normative developed by DiMaggio and Powell (1983).

The common unit of analysis was the level of the organization rather than the wider environmental (societal, sectoral, field) or individual (agency) levels. Paradoxically, while many IS researchers use organization as the focal point in their research, many variance and process studies examine the cause/effect relationships between IT-related constructs (e.g. adoption intention, department size, assimilation) without relating them to the higher environmental and interorganizational levels. This is problematic both theoretically and empirically since institutional theory emphasizes the criticality of using multi-level analysis in the research design.

We further identify seven broad categories where IS researchers have used institutionalist perspectives. They include: technology and institutions, innovation, industrial sectors, adoption and diffusion, strategy and outsourcing, applications development and implementation, and knowledge-based work. We recognize that some of these classifications reflect current fashion in the IS field.

King et al. (1994) are among the first to employ the new institutional approach in IS research. They note three characteristics of neo-institutionalism that focus attention to institutional factors for understanding innovation. First, they cautioned against treating institutions and technology as two separate categories of environmental influence. Thus, the 'technical/institutional divide classified as 'technical' for-profit organizations operating in a marketplace where production efficiency was the key goal, and as 'institutional' non-profit and public organizations operating in a context of law and procedure, where legitimacy of process is as important as the goal' (p. 146). They suggest the new institutional approach takes both efficiency and legitimacy as significant factors in all organizations. The second characteristic of neo-institutionalism, according to King et al. (1994), is the shift of the subject of institutional analysis from organizations with legal authority or geographic proximity to organizations competing or trading with each other. Third, the authors point out that neo-institutionalism does not assume institutions as monolithic and inflexible. To the contrary, institutions can and do change.

We recognize that identifying and delineating the boundaries of institutionalist perspectives within IS research from other disciplines poses challenges. One observation is that IS studies adopting institutional theory span many academic journals. The aggregate body of work further incorporates multi-levels of analysis, with contributions examining societal, market and sectoral level institutional forces (Cousins and Robey 2005; Hu and Quan 2006; Salmeron and Bueno 2006) and social and cultural-cognitive forces (Kaye and Little 1996; Damsgaard and Scheepers 1999; Nicolaou 1999). Orlikowski and Barley (2001) recommended IS researchers adopt institutional theory to investigate how institutions influence the design, use, and consequences of technologies, either within or across organizations. Instead of focusing on lower level analysis of development, use and management of IS, they suggested researchers study the regulative processes, normative systems, and cultural frameworks that shape the design and use of IS.

Regulatory and normative approaches have been used by King et al. (1994) to integrate institutional theory with economic history to theoretically explain the role of governmental institutions in IT innovation. They articulated dimensions related to institutional interventions through influences and regulations that augment supply-push and demand-pull for IT innovation. Building on this work, Montealegre (1999) examined policy-related institutional actions in four developing countries to explain the Internet adoption to provide technological services at the national level. Similarly, Ang and Cummings (1997) examined factors that moderate the effects of institutional influences on IS outsourcing decisions in the banking industry focusing on peer and federal regulators.

Cultural-cognitive approaches place greater emphasis on individual agency. Swanson and Ramiller (2004) adopted a cognitive perspective to introduce the concept of mindful innovation with IT. They argued that a firm is 'mindful in innovating with IT when it attends to an innovation with reasoning grounded in its own organizational facts and specifics' (p. 559). They contrasted this with mindless innovation where a firm's actions 'betray a lack of attention to organizational specifics' (p. 563).

Variance models are developed by several IS researchers who use survey-based methods to test theoretical constructs. Teo, Wei, and Benbasat (2003) used institutional theory as a lens to understand the factors that enable the adoption of interorganizational systems. Their research model tested how mimetic, coercive and normative pressures existing in an institutionalized environment, could influence organizational predisposition toward an information technology-based interorganizational linkage. Findings suggested that all three institutional pressures had a significant influence on organizational intention to adopt financial electronic data interchange. The authors claim their findings indicate that organizations are embedded in institutional networks and call for more research into the institutional pressures on the adoption of IT innovations. Employing similar methods, Liang et al. (2007) found significant evidence of institutional effects of coercive, mimetic, and normative pressures on the assimilation of enterprise systems in organizations.

Another study using a variance approach considers the institutionalization of IT budgeting in the financial services sector. Hu and Quan (2006) examined the influences of institutional pressures from a firm's external environment on the corporate IT budgeting processes. Using firm-level IT and financial data of publicly traded companies in the financial sector, the authors found one of the most significant sources of influence on an firm's average IT budget was the IT spending level of the perceived industry leaders. They concluded that IT budgeting processes have been at least partially institutionalized.

Process models are increasingly used by IS researchers to examine institutional change and deinstitutionalization. Swanson and Ramiller (1997) developed a theoretical model to understand the cultural-cognitive institutional processes that drive the adoption and diffusion of IT innovations. The authors introduce the notion of 'organizing vision', which serves three important functions in the creation and promulgation of IT innovations: interpretation of the innovations, legitimation of the need for innovations, and mobilization of material resources to support the innovations. The production and dissemination of organizing visions is an integral part of the institutionalization process of IT innovations.

Currie (2004) used the organizing vision model to interpret data from a five-year study on the adoption and diffusion of application service provider (ASP) technology. Using a process-oriented analysis, she observed that over time, the initial hype surrounding ASP was replaced by scepticism and distrust, as powerful institutional interests in the form of technology firms, industry analysts, and IT consultancies were ultimately unsuccessful in their attempts to disseminate ASP throughout the wider business and not-for-profit IS user communities. This study builds on ideas where rhetoric and reality in large-scale innovation and change programmes can be conceptualized as management fashions (Abrahamson 1996). Innovations that are widely diffused and taken-for-granted within society are described as institutionalized. Conversely, those that pose a disruptive threat or become distrusted, fail to gain traction and become abandoned. To explain such success or failure, Wang and Swanson (2007) employed institutional entrepreneurship to study how interested organizational actors (institutional entrepreneurs) struggled to institutionalize professional services automation (PSA). They found that, for institutional entrepreneurs to launch an IT innovation toward institutionalization, it is crucial to develop a relative coherent organization vision for the innovation and mobilize a driver community to create and maintain the industrial infrastructure for the innovation.

In summary, our review of institutional theory in IS research enables us to offer the following insights. First, the dominant view among IS scholars is the recognition that institutions reside in the environment and they shape the development and use of IT. Exactly how this occurs is not well articulated, since most of the literature focuses upon the institutional effects on IT, rather than how such institutions come into being (e.g. the process of institutionalization) or disappear over time (deinstitutionalization).

Second, the IT-as-institution perspective is dominated by multivariate empirical studies that examine regulative, normative, and cultural-cognitive effects on IT adoption and diffusion, yet restrict the unit of analysis to the level of the organization. This approach rarely considers the larger dynamic where institutionalization processes or effects may vary among organizations within and across fields, sectors, and markets (Thatcher, Brower, and Mason 2006). Third, many studies adopt an atomistic or reductionist approach where institutional concepts are simplified for the purposes of empirical clarity and precision. While this is pursued for the purposes of methodological rigour, we suggest that some concepts are not amenable to simple reductionism. For example, the concept of isomorphism is widely used in the OS literature, albeit with varying definitions (Greenwood et al. 2007). Imported by IS academics, we suggest that caution needs to be applied in using isomorphism to measure cause and effect relationships in either static or stage models. Fourth, IS researchers rarely discuss the theoretical and empirical antecedents of institutional theory which resides in reference disciplines including sociology, economics, political science, and anthropology. Many studies present institutional theory as new to the IS field. While this is not problematic in itself, the failure to convey the wider intellectual tradition of the theory may lead to misinterpretation within the IS community and confusion about the relationship between institutionalism and other theoretical perspectives.

AN INSTITUTIONAL AGENDA
FOR IS RESEARCH

In proposing a research agenda for IS which embraces institutionalism, we reiterate prior calls from King et al. (1994) who recognized that institutional factors are 'ubiquitous and essential components' (p. 141) for understanding and explaining IT innovations, and Orlikowski and Barley's (2001) contention that institutionalism offers IT researchers 'a vantage point for conceptualizing the digital economy as an emergent, evolving, embedded, fragmented, and provisional social production that is shaped as much by cultural and structural forces as by technical and economic ones' (p. 154).

While institutionalism has gained momentum in the OS field, IS has seen the publication of a steady stream of research papers over the past decade, most of which deploy institutional concepts as a lens to interpret data rather than offering new theoretic insights. An explanation for the reluctance to adopt institutionalism as a theoretical perspective for empirical investigation, we argue, may derive from the shortcomings we have identified above. Also, the dominance in positivist research methodology (e.g. surveys and experiments) compared with interpretivist methods (case studies and ethnographies) may preclude some scholars from deploying institutionalist concepts that are ill-defined and amorphous. Another reason suggests that IT research is predominantly concerned with the development, use, and management of information systems where researchers focus on lower levels of analysis rather than how 'regulative processes, normative systems, and cultural frameworks shape the design and use of technical systems' (Orlikowski and Barley 2001: 153). This is less common where researchers observe fewer demarcation boundaries between IS and OS, for example.

The current trend in the IS field to isolate the IT artefact within an organizational setting reflects a wider trend in social science from the 1970s, which has seen a shift from asking 'big questions' about society and organizations in favour of producing 'narrowly orientated research in the idiom of normal science'. This is witnessed in contingency theoretic formulations and much of the mainstream OS, where 'organizations have become codified and packaged into standard research strategies rational-functionalism and economic determinism' (Lounsbury and Ventresca 2003: 462). While the new institutionalism is explicitly anti-reductionist and rejects the causal primacy of efficiency or narrow self interest, the use of institutional theory to inform research enquiry needs to take into account how institutions influence IT within and across organizations (Orlikowski and Barley 2001), and how IT itself may be an institution. So given the pervasiveness and importance of IT and its relevance in contemporary organizational change, it is noteworthy that OS scholars interested in change have not addressed IT in a more explicit and systematic fashion (Barrett, Grant, and Wailes 2006) and equally that IS researchers underplay the importance of politically and socially constructed realities in shaping the processes and effects of IT.

Calls to expand institutionalist research come from within and beyond the IS community. However, a broadened institutional approach has some limitations (Powell 1991), not least because multiple definitions of institution rarely offer convincing accounts of the processes and effects of institutionalization (Greenwood et al. 2007). Researchers therefore need to avoid becoming 'thrown into a field of research that has almost no limits, and also few directions about what is more or less important or relevant . . . (where) almost all aspects of social life become a possible research object' (Hasselbladh and Kallinikos 2000: 702).

Recognizing the potential advantages and disadvantages in using institutionalism as a mainstream theoretical perspective in IS, we identify five challenges for IS researchers concerning theory development and empirical investigation. First, institutionalism embodies powerful and complex concepts and ideas that provide a firm foundation for designing variance and process models. Researchers need to fully engage with the neo-institutional literature, not merely from OS, but also from sociology, economics, and political science to gain a wide appreciation of the intellectual antecedents of this complex theoretical approach. Institutional concepts are not axiomatic and need to be carefully defined in any research design. Since many IS researchers may not possess a wide knowledge of institutionalism, they will not extend the theory by treating concepts as axiomatic. IS research needs to *discover the scope conditions under which institutional explanations may or may not hold in the numerous complex and dynamic contexts of IT development and use.*

Second, earlier neo-institutionalism accounts have focused on stability and persistence, and more recently on institutional change and deinstitutionalization (Greenwood and Hinings 2006). IS researchers need to *develop robust research designs which address issues of how and why institutions emerge, transform, and vanish*. Detailed ethnographic studies that reveal how institutional practices come to be legitimated coupled with large-scale, longitudinal studies that explore the staying power of institutional arrangements will greatly contribute to the body of research on institutionalization (Powell 1991). Archival data can also be collected, analysed, and measured to study paths of institutionalization (Colyvas and Powell 2006) and monitor institutional stability and change. Third, IS researchers should continue to focus on a *range of core sectors of the economy*, such as government, health, manufacturing, and finance since many studies have traditionally investigated institutionalism in the public, not-for-profit, or highly regulated sectors (Powell 1991). Although studies have emerged on specific sectors, we suggest that differentiating between not-for-profit and for-profit sectors is becoming increasingly outdated. We suggest that macro-institutional analysis shows that reality is infused with shared values and interests between public (state) and private (capital) sectors, particularly in the light of increased IT outsourcing where external firms engage with highly institutionalized organizational settings, an example being the market initiatives in healthcare (Scott et al. 2000).

Fourth, institutionalism needs to *embrace a multi-level analysis* to avoid criticisms that it pays too much attention to institutional forces emanating from the societal and interorganizational levels and not enough attention to the role of individuals in shaping their institutional environment. Research needs to embrace 'the importance of simultaneously understanding the role of human agency as embedded in institutional contexts as well as the constraints and affordances of technologies as material systems' (Orlikowski and Barley 2001: 158). Recent work on institutional entrepreneurship addresses some of these limitations and demonstrates how individuals and groups serve to both stabilize and change habitualized behaviours (Lawrence and Suddaby 2006). Research could examine the role of 'technical champions' as a type of institutional entrepreneur, as many IS accounts pay scant attention to the institution-building activities that shape individual and group behaviour within and across networks, organizations, and fields.

Fifth, the shortcomings of institutionalism may be overcome by a *multi-theory approach* to empirical investigation. Combining institutional theory with structuration theory, agency theory, discourse analysis, and critical management perspectives, for example, may provide a powerful foundation from which new and exciting insights may arise. For example, Barley and Tolbert (1997) proposed that a fusion of institutional theory and structuration theory makes it possible to theorize institutionalization as a structuration process. While organization theorists routinely use a multi-theory approach, we caution against a tendency in the IS literature to adopt a 'pick n mix' approach to theory, as key concepts and terms can become lost in translation.

Our review of institutional research in IS has also allowed us to identify two broad questions specific to IT research. First, *what unique challenges and opportunities do*

IT innovations face in an institutional environment? The creation, diffusion, and maintenance of institutions are primarily based on information that social actors collect, process, and transfer (Zucker 1977). New information technologies, by definition, bring new information, relationships, or processes in information management, inevitably disrupting existing institutions—taken-for-granted incentive systems based on existing information, relationships, and processes. For this reason, *IT innovations naturally entail institutional changes* and thus *understanding IT phenomena requires an institutional theory of IT*. To develop an institutional theory of IT, researchers must go beyond the organizational level analysis of institutional effects to investigate multiple levels and sources of institutional change. We recognize this is a serious challenge since research enquiry that isolates the management of IT in an organizational setting is less complex and contentious than studies that encapsulate a multi-level and multi-variate analysis linking policy, process, practice, and people. Research output that conveys neutral and apolitical accounts of values and interests has greater 'facticity', since 'participants are able to tell researchers much more succinctly how they interact with technological artifacts', rather than research on the management of information which takes into account 'the social constructions that constitute information' (Thatcher, Brower, and Mason 2006: 449). But while studying IT as an artefact is less controversial, it is also 'less important in shaping behaviour than are structuration activities at higher levels of analysis' (ibid. 449). Extending research enquiry beyond the organization is therefore likely to generate richer and more analytical accounts of the interplay between regulatory, normative, and cultural cognitive influences on IT development, implementation, and management.

The second broad question we raise is: *how do institutional changes synchronize with technological changes*? Institutionalists characteristically portray the institutional/technical dichotomy and argue both the institutional and technical priorities 'impinge on' a social actor at the same time (Zucker 1987). DiMaggio and Powell (1991) recognized that environmental changes (including technological change) frequently outpace institutional changes and social actors' adaptation and that suboptimal institutions can persist for an extended period of time and rarely reflect current political, economic, and technological forces. On the other hand, Brown and Duguid (2000: 84) warned against the argument that 'society falls behind while technology streaks ahead.' As IT advances at 'exponential' speed, it is worth asking whether and how institutions and technology can remain or become in synch. While we caution against using a false dichotomy between institution and IT, we recognize that IT-enabled change may disrupt existing working practices leading to deinstitutionalization. In this regard, our *IT-as-institution* perspective is therefore useful in that it recognizes that the adoption and assimilation of new IT *in use* is essentially the institutionalization process, which culminates with the new IT as a new or transformed institution.

CONCLUSION

This chapter demonstrates that institutional theory is increasingly used by IS researchers, although the relationship between the core theoretic concepts with other management fields is not well articulated in the IS literature. Reviewing the seminal papers on neo-institutional theory reveals that interorganizational and field level units of analysis are used in disciplines such as sociology and economics, for example, but the majority of IS studies deploy the organization (business unit, site, department) to analyse institutional concepts. Institutionalization, however, is both a multi-level process and an outcome. The separation of institution and technology in some areas of the literature suggests a false dichotomy, particularly as IT may also be conceptualized as an institution. We therefore posit the concept of IT-as-institution to convey the complex relationship between IT with higher-level institutional forces and influences. Indeed, studying IT in isolation of macro-environmental and organizational factors and, more importantly, ignoring the complex interrelationships between them, is unlikely to produce theoretic insights of any real significance or impact. This has serious implications for the future of IS as a critical discipline in business and information schools.

IS researchers need to study how and why environmental and organizational processes and effects influence IT adoption and diffusion, for example; and how core ideas, such as legitimacy, taken-for-grantedness, isomorphism, and institutional logics can explicate pathways to institutionalization and deinstitutionalization. This is important since institutionalization is driven by self-reinforcing feedback dynamics that serve to create stability and persistence, yet may also be receptive to exogenous and endogenous 'jolts' acting as a catalyst for institutional change. We recognize that using a multi-level analysis to study IS practice using an institutional perspective is complex particularly as institutions may be viewed as the 'ongoing product of a series of integrated and semi-autonomous social fields, each of which has a distinct history, logic and structure' (Lawrence and Suddaby 2006: 248–9).

In conclusion, we urge IS researchers to extend their theoretical repertoire, not by attempting to generate 'new theories for IS', but to recognize that existing theories, such as institutionalism, have rich and diverse intellectual antecedents which are not amenable to simple reductionism. By broadening the level of analysis to include interorganizations and fields, IS researchers will be able to recognize that IT adoption and diffusion at the organizational level is inextricably linked to macro-environmental factors, such as government policy, corporate strategy, market dynamics, and the like. To understand IS outcomes in healthcare, for example, is not reducible to simple survey or case study analysis on individual priorities and preferences at single sites, since deeply engrained institutional behaviours play a key role in determining what is either possible or not possible in practical terms. In sum, this chapter has covered a wide range of neo-institutional literature to give a flavour of the depth and breadth of this complex theory. We hope that IS researchers will seek out this literature to enrich our knowledge of how institutionalism can encourage deeper insights into the multi-faceted phenomenon of information management and technology.

Appendix A   Selected Studies in Institutional Research from Reference Disciplines, Especially Organizational Sociology

Category	Theoretical Perspective	Context	Reference
Institutional Theory	Institutions Institutionalism Institutionalization	• New institutionalism: organizational factors in political life • Formal structure as myth and ceremony • Role of institutionalization in cultural persistence • The iron cage revisited • Organizations as institutions • Organizational environments: ritual and rationality • Institutional theories of organizations • Adolescence of Institutional Theory • Institutional patterns and organizations • Rediscovering institutions • Three pillars of institutions • Virtues of the old institutionalism • New institutionalism in organizational analysis	March and Olsen 1976 Meyer and Rowan 1977 Zucker 1977 DiMaggio and Powell 1983 Zucker 1983 Meyer, Rowan, and Scott 1983 Zucker 1987 Scott 1987 Zucker 1988a March and Olsen 1989 Scott 1995 (2nd edn. 2001) Stinchcombe 1997 Powell and DiMaggio 1991
Construction, Maintenance, and Diffusion	Variance and process models Creation, maintenance, and stability	• Variance and process theories of institutionalization • Component processes of institutionalization • Cultural cognitive aspects of institutionalism • Conditions for new institutional arrangements • Narrative mode of knowing • Social construction of organizational knowledge • Temporal dynamics of institutionalization • Multitheory approach to the cognitive underpinnings of institutional persistence and change	Mohr 1982 Tolbert and Zucker 1996 DiMaggio 1991b. Suchman 1995 Czarniawska 1997 Mizruchi and Fein 1999 Lawrence, Winn, and Jennings 2001 George, Sitkin, and Barden 2006 Greenwood and Suddaby 2006 Philips, Lawrence, and Hardy 2004

Diffusion	• Institutional entrepreneurship in mature fields	
	• Discourse and institutions	
	• Diffusion in organizations and social movements	Strang and Soule 1998
	• Institutional conditions for diffusion	Strang and Meyer 1993
	• Adoption of institutionally contested organizational practices	Sanders and Tuschke 2007
Organizational Fields and Institutional Logics	Organization Fields	
	• Structural analysis of organizational fields	DiMaggio 1986
	• The institutional context of industry creation	Aldrich and Fiol 1994
	• Institutional entrepreneurship in emerging fields	Fligstein 2002
	• Conceptualizing organizational fields	Scott 1994
	Industry creation, markets, sociocultural and political explanations	
	• Political-cultural approach to market institutions	Fligstein 1996
	• Institutional and task environment relationships in the Canadian Construction Industry	Oliver 1997
	• Institutional Change in the Healthcare System	Scott et al. 2000
	• Institutionalist account of European Integration	Maguire, Hardy, and Lawrence 2004
	• Differentiation of institutional space: organizational forms in the New York welfare sector	Mohr and GuerraPearson 2006
	Institutional Logics	
	• Cultural framing and institutional integration	Hirsch 1986
	• Symbols, practices, and institutional contradictions	Friedland and Alford 1991
	• Historical contingency of power in higher educational publishing in the USA	Thornton and Ocasio 1999
		Thornton 2002
		Blatter 2003
	• Conflict and conformity in institutional logics in the craft industry	Reay and Hinings 2005
		Currie and Guah 2007

(continued)

Appendix A (Continued)

Category	Theoretical Perspective	Context	Reference
Organizational Structure, Performance, and Choice	Formal and informal structures, governance, and strategic processes	• Logics and change in transboundary spaces • Competing logics in Healthcare in Alberta, Canada • Dominant logics in Healthcare in the UK, National Health Service • Social structure and organizations • Institutional sources of change in the formal structure of organizations • Governance structures in large law firms • Politics of bureaucratic structures • Strategic responses to institutional processes	Stinchcombe 1965 Tolbert and Zucker 1983 Tolbert and Stern 1989 Moe 1990 Oliver 1992
	Decoupling and Loose coupling	• Educational organizations as loosely coupled systems • Formal and informal organizations • Institutional and technical sources of organization structure • Power and decoupling in the healthcare system • Substance and symbolism in CEOs' long-term incentive plans	Weick 1976 March and Olsen 1976 Meyer, Scott, and Deal 1981 Covaleski, Dirsmith, and Michelman 1993 Westphal and Zajac 1994
	Isomorphism	• Resource dependence and institutional environments • Mimetic isomorphism and entry to new markets • Coercive, mimetic, and normative isomorphism • Symbolic isomorphism and organizational names	Tolbert 1985 Haveman 1983 Mizruchi and Fein 1999 Gynn and Abzug 2002

Legitimacy	• Organizational legitimacy: social values and organizational behaviour	Dowling and Pfeffer 1975
		Meyer and Scott 1983
	• Centralization and legitimacy problems in local government	Scott 1990
		Suchman 1995b
	• Symbols and Organizations	Kraatz and Zajac 1996
	• Strategic and institutional approaches to managing legitimacy	Ruef and Scott 1998
		Suddaby and Greenwood 2005
	• Causes and consequences of illegitimate organizational change	Maitless 2005
	• Multidimensional model in organizational legitimacy	
	• Rhetorical strategies of legitimacy	
	• Social processes of organizational sense making	
Strategic Choice and Rational Actor	• Organization structure, environment, and performance	Child 1972
		Goodrick and Salancick 1996
	• Organizational discretion in responding to institutional practices	
Institutional Change	• Understanding strategic change: the contribution of archetypes	Greenwood and Hinings 1993
		Greenwood and Hinings 1996
	• Interaction of organizational context and organizational action	Meyer, Brooks, and Goes 1990
		Clemens and Cook 1999
	• Organizational responses to discontinuous change	Hoffman 1999
		Lounsbury 2002
	• Politics and institutionalism: explaining durability and change	Greenwood, Suddaby, and Hinings 2002
		DeHolan and Philips 2002
	• Institutional evolution and change	Sine and David 2003

(continued)

Appendix A (Continued)

Category	Theoretical Perspective	Context	Reference
		• Institutional transformation and status mobility	Rao, Monin, and Durand 2003
		• Role of professional associations in the transformation of institutionalized fields	Dacin, Goldstein, and Scott 2002
		• Institutional management and organizational change	Seo and Creed 2002
		• Environmental jolts and entrepreneurial opportunity in the US electric power industry	Sherer and Lee 2002
		• Institutional change in Toque Ville Nouvelle cuisine	
		• Institutional theory and institutional change	
		• Institutional contradictions, praxis, and institutional change	
		• Institutional change in large law firms	
	Deinstitutionalization	• Decline and fall of the conglomerate firm in the 1980s	Davis, Diekmann, and Tinsley 1994
		• Interest and agency in institutional theory	DiMaggio 1988
		• Antecedents of Deinstitutionalization	Oliver 1992
			Tolbert and Sine 1999

Agency	• Determinants of organizational compliance with institutional pressures	Eisenhardt 1988
	• Agency and institutional theory perspectives to explore the sales compensation policies in retail	DiMaggio 1988
	• Interest and agency in institutional theory	
Rational Choice	• Theory of institutional change and economic history of the Western World	North 1983
	• New economics of organization	Moe 1984
	• How institutions think	Douglas 1986
	• Institutionalization of rational organization	Powell 1985
Structuration Processes	• Adaptive structuration theory	DeSanctis and Poole 1994
	• Links between action and institution	Barley and Tolbert 1997
	• Action, structure, and contradiction in social theory	Giddens 1979
	• Bureaucratization without centralization	Meyer et al. 1988

REFERENCES

Abrahamson, E. (1996). 'Management Fashion, Academic Fashion, and Enduring Truths', *Academy of Management Review*, 21(3): 616–18.

Ang, S., and Cummings, L. L. (1997). 'Strategic Response to Institutional Influences on Information Systems Outsourcing', *Organization Science*, 8(3): 235–56.

Axelrod, R. (1981). 'The Emergence of Cooperation among Egoists', *American Political Science Review*, 75(2): 305–18.

Barley, S. R. (1986). 'Technology as an Occasion for Structuring: Evidence from Observations of CT Scanners and the Social Order of Radiology Departments', *Administrative Science Quarterly*, 31(1): 78–108.

—— and Tolbert, P. S. (1997). 'Institutionalization and Structuration: Studying the Links between Action and Institution', *Organization Studies*, 18(1): 93–117.

Barrett, M., Grant, D., and Wailes, N. (2006). 'ICT and Organizational Change: Introduction to the Special Issue', *The Journal of Applied Behavioral Science*, 42(1): 6–22.

Boudreau, M.-C., and Robey, D. (2005). 'Enacting Integrated Information Technology: A Human Agency Perspective', *Organization Science*, 16(1): 3–18.

Brown, J. S., and Duguid, P. (2000). *The Social Life of Information*. Boston, MA: Harvard Business School Press.

Colyvas, J. A., and Powell, W. W. (2006). 'Roads to Institutionalization: The Remaking of Boundaries between Public and Private Science', in B. M. Staw (ed.), *Research in Organizational Behaviour: An Annual Series of Analytical Essays* 27. Amsterdam: Elsevier.

Cousins, K. C., and Robey, D. (2005). 'The Social Shaping of Electronic Metals Exchanges: An Institutional Theory Perspective', *Information Technology & People*, 18(3): 212–29.

Currie, W. L. (2004). 'The Organizing Vision of Application Service Provision: A Process-Oriented Analysis', *Information and Organization*, 14(4): 237–67.

—— and Guah, M. W. (2007). 'Conflicting Institutional Logics: A National Programme for IT in the Organisational Field of Healthcare', *Journal of Information Technology*, 22(3): 235–47.

Czarniawska, B. (1997). *Narrating the Organization: Dramas of Institutional Identity*. Chicago, IL: University of Chicago Press.

Damsgaard, J., and Scheepers, R. (1999). 'Power, Influence and Intranet Implementation: A Safari of South African Organizations', *Information Technology & People*, 12(4): 333–58.

Davis, G. F., Diekmann, K. A., and Tinsley, C. H. (1994). 'The Decline and Fall of the Conglomerate Firm in the 1980s: The Deinstitutionalization of an Organizational Form', *American Sociological Review*, 59(4): 547–70.

DeSanctis, G., and Poole, M. S. (1994). 'Capturing the Complexity in Advanced Technology Use: Adaptive Structuration Theory', *Organization Science*, 5(2): 121–47.

DiMaggio, P. (1986). 'Structural Analysis of Organizational Fields: A Blockmodel Approach', in B. M. Staw and L. L. Cummings (eds.), *Research in Organization Behaviour*, 8. Greenwich, CT: JAI Press, 355–70.

——(1988). 'Interest and Agency in Institutional Theory', in L. G. Zucker (ed.), *Institutional Patterns and Organizations: Culture and Environment*. Cambridge, MA: Ballinger, 3–21.

——(1991a). 'Constructing an Organizational Field as a Professional Project: U.S. Art Museums, 1920–1940', in W. W. Powell and P. DiMaggio (eds.), *The New Institutionalism in Organizational Analysis*. Chicago, IL: University of Chicago Press, 267–92.

——(1991b). 'Social Structure, Institutions and Cultural Goods: The Case of the US', in P. Bourdieu and J. Coleman (eds.), *Social Theory for a Changing Society*. Boulder, CO: Westview Press, 133–55.

——and Powell, W. W. (1983). 'The Iron Cage Revisited: Institutional Isomorphism and Collective Rationality in Organizational Fields', *American Sociological Review*, 48(2): 147–60.

———(1991). 'Introduction', in W. W. Powell and P. DiMaggio (eds.), *The New Institutionalism in Organizational Analysis*. Chicago, IL: University of Chicago Press, 1–38.

Dobbin, F. R., and Sutton, J. R. (1998). 'The Strength of a Weak State: The Rights Revolution and the Rise of Human Resources Management Divisions', *American Journal of Sociology*, 104(2): 441–76.

Doolin, B. (2003). 'Narratives of Change: Discourse, Technology and Organization', *Organization*, 10(4): 751–70.

Edelman, L. B., Uggen, C., and Erlanger, H. S. (1999). 'The Endogeneity of Legal Regulation: Grievance Procedures as Rational Myth', *American Journal of Sociology*, 105(2): 406–54.

Eisenhardt, K. M. (1988). 'Agency- and Institutional-Theory Explanations: The Case of Retail Sales Compensation', *Academy of Management Journal*, 31(3): 488–511.

Friedland, R., and Alford, R. R. (1991). 'Bringing Society Back In: Symbols, Practices, and Institutional Contradictions', in W. W. Powell and P. DiMaggio (eds.), *The New Institutionalism in Organizational Analysis*. Chicago, IL: University of Chicago Press, 232–63.

Garfinkel, H. (1967). *Studies in Ethnomethodology*. Englewood Cliffs, NJ: Prentice-Hall.

Garud, R., Hardy, C., and Maguire, S. (2007). 'Institutional Entrepreneurship as Embedded Agency: An Introduction to the Special Issue', *Organization Studies*, 28(7): 957–69.

——Jain, S., and Kumaraswamy, A. (2002). 'Institutional Entrepreneurship in the Sponsorship of Common Technological Standards: The Case of Sun Microsystems and Java', *Academy of Management Journal*, 45(1): 196–214.

George, E., Sitkin, S., and Barden, J. (2006). 'Cognitive Underpinnings of Institutional Persistence and Change: A Framing Perspective', *Academy of Management Review*, 31: 347–65.

Goodrick, E., and Salancik, G. R. (1996). 'Organizational Discretion in Responding to Institutional Practices: Hospitals and Cesarean Births', *Administrative Science Quarterly*, 41(1): 1–28.

Gosain, S. (2004). 'Enterprise Information Systems as Objects and Carriers of Institutional Forces: The New Iron Cage?', *Journal of the Association for Information Systems*, 5(4): 151–82.

Greenwood, R., and Hinings, C. R. (1996). 'Understanding Radical Organizational Change: Bringing Together the Old and the New Institutionalism', *Academy of Management Review*, 21(4): 1022–54.

Greenwood, R., and Hinings, C. R. (2006). 'Radical Organizational Change', in S. R. Clegg, C. Hardy, and W. R. Nord (eds.), *The Sage Handbook of Organization Studies*. Thousand Oaks, CA: Sage, 814–42.

Greenwood, R., and Suddaby, R. (2006). 'Institutional Entrepreneurship in Mature Fields: The Big Five Accounting Firms', *Academy of Management Journal*, 49: 27–48.

———and Hinings, C. R. (1996). 'Theorizing Change: The Role of Professional Associations in the Transformation of Institutionalized Fields', *Academy of Management Journal*, 45(1): 58–80.

——Oliver, C., Sahlin, K., and Suddaby, R. (eds) (2007). *Handbook of Organizational Institutionalism*. Thousand Oaks, CA: Sage.

Hasselbladh, H., and Kallinikos J. (2000). 'The Project of Rationalization: A Critique and Reappraisal of Neo-institutionalism in Organization Studies', *Organization Studies*, 21(4): 697–720.

Haveman, H. A. (1993). 'Follow the Leader: Mimetic Isomorphism and Entry into New Markets', *Administrative Science Quarterly*, 38(4): 593–627.

Holm, P. (1995). 'The Dynamics of Institutionalization: Transformation Processes in Norwegian Fisheries', *Administrative Science Quarterly*, 40(3): 398–422.

Hu, Q., and Quan, J. (2006). 'The Institutionalization of IT Budgeting: Empirical Evidence from the Financial Sector', *Information Resources Management Journal*, 19(1): 84–97.

Jepperson, R. L. (1991). 'Institutions, Institutional Effects, and Institutionalism', in W. W. Powell and P. DiMaggio (eds.), *The New Institutionalism in Organizational Analysis*. Chicago, IL: University of Chicago Press, 143–63.

Kaye, R., and Little, S. E. (1996). 'Global Business and Cross-Cultural Information Systems Technical and Institutional Dimensions of Diffusion', *Information Technology & People*, 9(3): 30–54.

King, J. L., Gurbaxani, V., Kraemer, K. L., McFarlan, F. W., Raman, K. S., and Yap, C. S. (1994). 'Institutional Factors in Information Technology Innovation', *Information Systems Research*, 5(2): 139–69.

Lawrence, T. B., and Suddaby, R. (2006). 'Institutions and Institutional Work', in S. R. Clegg, C. Hardy, T. B. Lawrence, and W. R. Nord (eds.), *The Sage Handbook of Organizational Studies*. Thousand Oaks, CA: Sage, 215–54.

Lawrence, T., Winn, M. I., and Jennings, P. D. (2001). 'The Temporal Dynamics of Institutionalization', *Academy of Management Review*, 25: 625–44.

Leblebici, H., Salancik, G. R., Copay, A., and King, A. (1991). 'Institutional Change and the Transformation of Interorganizational Fields: An Organizational History of the U.S. Radio Broadcasting Industry', *Administrative Science Quarterly*, 36(3): 333–63.

Liang, H., Saraf, N., Hu, Q., and Xue, Y. (2007). 'Assimilation of Enterprise Systems: The Effect of Institutional Pressures and the Mediating Role of Top Management', *MIS Quarterly*, 31(1): 59–87.

Lounsbury, M., and Ventresca, M. (2003). 'The New Structuralism in Organizational Theory', *Organization*, 10(3): 457–80.

Maguire, S., Hardy, C., and Lawrence, T. B. (2004). 'Institutional Entrepreneurship in Emerging Fields: HIV/AIDS Treatment Advocacy in Canada', *Academy of Management Journal*, 47(5): 657–79.

March, J. G., and Olsen, J. P. (1976). *Ambiguity and Choice in Organizations*. Bergen: Universitetsforlaget.

——(1989). *Rediscovering Institutions: The Organizational Basis of Politics*. New York: Free Press.

Meyer, J. W., and Rowan, B. (1977). 'Institutionalized Organizations: Formal Structure as Myth and Ceremony', *American Journal of Sociology*, 83(2): 340–63.

——and Scott, W. R. (1983). *Organizational Environments: Ritual and Reality*. Thousand Oaks, CA: Sage Publications.

Mignerat, M., and Rivard, S. (2005). 'Positioning the Institutional Perspective in Information Technology Research', HEC Montréal.

Miller, G. (2000). 'Rational Choice and Dysfunctional Institutions', *Governance: An International Journal of Policy and Administration*, 13(4): 535–47.

Mingers, J. (2001). 'Embodying Information Systems: The Contribution of Phenomenology', *Information and Organization*, 11(2): 103–28.

Mizruchi, M. S., and Fein, L. C. (1999). 'The Social Construction of Organizational Knowledge: A Study of the Uses of Coercive, Mimetic, and Normative Isomorphism', *Administrative Science Quarterly*, 44(4): 739–77.

Mohr, L. B. (1982). *Explaining Organizational Behavior*. San Francisco, CA: Jossey-Bass.

Montealegre, R. (1999). 'A Temporal Model of Institutional Interventions for Information Technology Adoption in Less-Developed Countries', *Journal of Management Information Systems*, 16(1): 207–32.

Nicolaou, A. I. (1999). 'Social Control in Information Systems Development', *Information Technology & People*, 12(2): 130–47.

Ocasio, W. (1997). 'Towards an Attention-Based View of the Firm', *Strategic Management Journal*, 18 (Special Issue SI): 187–206.

Oliver, C. (1991). 'Strategic Responses to Institutional Processes', *Academy of Management Review*, 16(1): 145–79.

—— (1992). 'The Antecedents of Deinstitutionalization', *Organization Studies*, 13(4): 563–88.

——(1997). 'The Influence of Institutional and Task Environment Relationships on Organizational Performance: The Canadian Construction Industry', *Journal of Management Studies*, 34(1): 99–124.

Orlikowski, W. J. (1992). 'The Duality of Technology: Rethinking the Concept of Technology in Organizations', *Organization Science*, 3(3): 398–427.

——(1996). 'Improvising Organizational Transformation over Time: A Situated Change Perspective', *Information Systems Research*, 7(1): 63–92.

——and Barley, S. R. (2001). 'Technology and Institutions: What Can Research on Information Technology and Research on Organizations Learn from Each Other?', *MIS Quarterly*, 25(2): 145–65.

——and Robey, D. (1991). 'Information Technology and the Structuring of Organizations', *Information Systems Research*, 2(2): 143–69.

Perrow, C. (1986). *Complex Organizations: A Critical Essay*. 3rd edn., New York: Random House.

Phillips, N., Lawrence, T. B., and Hardy, C. (2004). 'Discourse and Institutions', *Academy of Management Review*, 29(4): 635–52.

Pierson, P. (2000). 'The Limits of Design: Explaining Institutional Origins and Change', *Governance: An International Journal of Policy and Administration*, 13(4): 475–99.

Porter, K., Whittington, K. B., and Powell, W. W. (2005). 'The Institutional Embeddedness of High-Tech Regions: Relational Foundations of the Boston Biotechnology Community', in S. Breschi and F. Malerba (eds.), *Clusters, Networks, and Innovation*. Oxford: Oxford University Press, 261–96.

Powell, W. W. (1991). 'Expanding the Scope of Institutional Analysis', in W. W. Powell and P. DiMaggio (eds.), *The New Institutionalism in Organizational Analysis*. Chicago, IL: University of Chicago Press, 183–203.

—— and DiMaggio, P. (1991). *The New Institutionalism in Organizational Analysis*. Chicago, IL: University of Chicago Press.

Reay, T., and Hinings, C. R. (2005). 'The Recomposition of an Organizational Field: Health Care in Alberta', *Organization Studies*, 26: 351–84.

Reich, S. (2000). 'The Four Faces of Institutionalism: Public Policy and a Pluralistic Perspective', *Governance: An International Journal of Policy and Administration*, 13(4): 501–22.

Rogers, E. M. (2003). *Diffusion of Innovations*. 5th edn., New York: Free Press.

Ross, A., and Chiasson, M. W. (2005). 'A Call to (Dis)Order: An Ethnomethodological Study of Information Technology "Disruptions" in the Courtroom', *Information and Organization*, 15(3): 203–27.

Salmeron, J. L., and Bueno, S. (2006). 'An Information Technologies and Information Systems Industry-Based Classification in Small and Medium-Sized Enterprises: An Institutional View', *European Journal of Operational Research*, 173(3): 1012–25.

Sanders, W. G., and Tuschke, A. (2007). 'The Adoption of Institutionally Contested Organizational Practices: The Emergence of Stock Option Pay in Germany', *Academy of Management Journal*, 50: 33–57.

Schütz, A. (1967). *Phenomenology of the Social World*, trans. F. Lehnert and G. Walsh. Evanston, IL: Northwestern University Press.

Scott, W. R. (1987). 'The Adolescence of Institutional Theory', *Administrative Science Quarterly*, 32(4): 493–511.

——(1995). *Institutions and Organizations*. Thousand Oaks, CA: Sage.

——(2001). *Institutions and Organizations*. 2nd edn., Thousand Oaks, CA: Sage.

——Ruef, M., Mendel, P. J., and Caronna, C. A. (2000). *Institutional Change and Healthcare Organizations: From Professional Dominance to Managed Care*. Chicago, IL: University of Chicago Press.

Selznick, P. (1949). *TVA and the Grass Roots: A Study in the Sociology of Formal Organization*. New York: Harper & Row.

——(1957). *Leadership in Administration*. Evanston, IL: Row, Peterson.

Seo, M.-G., and Creed, W. E. D. (2002). 'Institutional Contradictions, Praxis, and Institutional Change: A Dialectical Perspective', *Academy of Management Review*, 27(2): 222–47.

Simon, H. A. (1997). *Administrative Behavior: A Study of Decision-Making Processes in Administrative Organization*. 4th edn., New York: Free Press.

Sine, W. D., and David, R. J. (2003). 'Environmental Jolts, Institutional Change, and the Creation of Entrepreneurial Opportunity in the US Electric Power Industry', *Research Policy*, 32(2): 185–207.

Stinchcombe, A. L. (1997). 'On the Virtues of the Old Institutionalism', *Annual Review of Sociology*, 23: 1–18.

Strang, D., and Meyer, J. W. (1993). 'Institutional Conditions for Diffusion', *Theory and Society*, 22(4): 487–511.

————(1994). 'Institutional Condition for Diffusion', in W. R. Scott and J. W. Meyer (eds.), *Institutional Environments and Organizations: Structural Complexity and Individualism*. Newbury Park, CA: Sage, 100–12.

—— and Soule, S. A. (1998). 'Diffusion in Organizations and Social Movements: From Hybrid Corn to Poison Pills', in J. Hagan and K. S. Cook (eds.), *Annual Review of Sociology*, 24, Palo Alto, CA: Annual Reviews, 265–90.

Suchman, M. C. (1995). 'Localism and Globalism in Institutional Analysis: The Emergence of Contractual Norms in Venture Finance', in W. R. Scott and S. Christensen (eds.), *The Institutional Construction of Organizations: International and Longitudinal Studies*. Thousand Oaks, CA: Sage, 39–63.

Swanson, E. B., and Ramiller, N. C. (1997). 'The Organizing Vision in Information Systems Innovation', *Organization Science*, 8(5): 458–74.

————(2004). 'Innovating Mindfully with Information Technology', *MIS Quarterly*, 28(4): 553–83.

Teo, H. H., Wei, K. K., and Benbasat, I. (2003). 'Predicting Intention to Adopt Interorganizational Linkages: An Institutional Perspective', *MIS Quarterly*, 27(1): 19–49.

Thatcher, J. B., Brower, R. S., and Mason, R. M. (2006). 'Organizational Fields and the Diffusion of Information Technologies within and across the Nonprofit and Public Sectors', *The American Review of Public Administration*, 36(4): 437–54.

Thornton, P. H. (2002). 'The Rise of the Corporation in a Craft Industry: Conflict and Conformity in Institutional Logics', *Academy of Management Journal*, 45(1): 81–101.

———— and Ocasio, W. (1999). 'Institutional Logics and the Historical Contingency of Power in Organizations: Executive Succession in the Higher Education Publishing Industry, 1958–1990', *American Sociological Review*, 105(3): 801–43.

Tolbert, P. S., and Zucker, L. G. (1983). 'Institutional Sources of Change in the Formal Structure of Organizations: The Diffusion of Civil Service Reform, 1880–1935', *Administrative Science Quarterly*, 28(1): 22–39.

————(1996). 'The Institutionalization of Institutional Theory', in S. R. Clegg, C. Hardy, and W. Nord (eds.), *Handbook of Organization Studies*. Thousand Oaks, CA: Sage Publications, 175–90.

Walsham, G. (1993). *Interpreting Information Systems in Organizations*. New York: Wiley.

Wang, P., and Swanson, E. B. (2007). 'Launching Professional Services Automation: Institutional Entrepreneurship for Information Technology Innovations', *Information and Organization* 17(2): 59–88.

Wareham, J. (2002). 'Anthropologies of Information Costs: Expanding the Neo-Institutional View', *Information and Organization*, 12(4): 219–48.

Weick, K. E. (1998). 'Improvisation as a Mindset for Organizational Analysis', *Organization Science*, 9(5): 543–55.

Williamson, O. E. (1975). *Markets and Hierarchies: Analysis and Antitrust Implications*. New York: Free Press.

Zucker, L. G. (1977). 'The Role of Institutionalization in Cultural Persistence', *American Sociological Review*, 42(5): 726–43.

————(1983). 'Organizations as Institutions', in S. B. Bacharach (ed.), *Advances in Organizational Theory and Research*. Greenwich, CT: JAI Press.

————(1987). 'Institutional Theories of Organization', *Annual Review of Sociology*, (13): 443–64.

Zucker, L. G. (1988). *Institutional Patterns and Organizations: Culture and Environment*. Cambridge, MA: Ballinger.

CHAPTER 7

....

'EVERYTHING IS DANGEROUS': RETHINKING MICHEL FOUCAULT AND THE SOCIAL STUDY OF ICT

....

LESLIE P. WILLCOCKS AND ELENI A. LIOLIOU

INTRODUCTION

....

DESPITE the considerable cross-disciplinary influence of Foucault's work, he is, this chapter argues, unjustly neglected in the study of information and communication technologies (ICTs), especially in the Information Systems field (IS). We argue for the abiding relevance of Foucault's oeuvre.[1] His thinking on techne and technology is reviewed, and a critique of his relative neglect in the IS 'discipline' provided. The chapter then critically evaluates and illustrates how he can and has been used in the study of ICTs in IS, organization, management, and surveillance studies, and more recently by those studying governmentality, network society, techno-bodies, and cyberspace. We conclude by pointing to the potential for utilizing Foucault in deconstructing the growing interest in ICT-supported knowledge management and related systems, and understanding control in liquid modernity.

Given Foucault's massive influence across so many other diverse disciplines and areas of intellectual endeavour, it is surprising to find Foucauldian methods and concepts discussed so little, let alone digested and used in the Information Systems field.[2] However, there are also many academics who work on information and communication technology (ICT) related issues from adjacent or associated perspectives, and sometimes consciously connect with the IS community. These include researchers in organization studies (e.g. Burrell 1998; Clegg 1998); sociology (e.g. Lyon 1993;

Bauman 1999); cultural studies (e.g. Haraway 1991; Hayles 1999); philosophy of technology (e.g. Dreyfus and Rabinow 1983; Introna 1997; Feenberg 2002), innovation studies (Grint and Willcocks 1995; Bloomfield et al. 1997); strategic management (Knights and Murray 1994; McKinley and Starkey 1998), and critical accounting (e.g. Morgan and Willmott 1993; Miller and Rose 2008). Foucault has been much more influential amongst these latter groupings.

Here we will assess Foucault's views of techne and technology and why the relative neglect of his work in the IS field. We pinpoint this as ironic given that the celebrated ICT study by Zuboff (1988) is so influenced by Foucault, but explain the neglect through a brief genealogy of the IS 'discipline'. We argue that IS attempts to discipline itself could learn from a deeper Foucauldian genealogy, as attempted in part by Introna (2001). The chapter then illustrates where Foucauldian perspectives, concepts, and methods have been applied; and with what results. This section particularly illustrates effective applications of Foucauldian perspectives on ICTs in IS, organization, management, and surveillance studies. The final section argues against the view that Foucault has become less relevant with moves to liquid modernity (Bauman 1999) network society (Munro 2000), and new forms of technology and techno-bodies (Best and Kellner 2001). Instead we argue that Foucault's work has an abiding importance, and can become even more relevant to the study of ICTs.

This chapter assumes a degree of familiarity with Foucault's main work, but not with its application to ICTs. A detailed account of the broader intellectual career and work of Foucault can be found in Willcocks (2004). Before we begin, it is important to stress the provisionality of Foucault's ideas and the fact that Foucault himself was far from being a systematic thinker. He quite deliberately described his practices as 'analytical work' rather than theory, and his analysis of power relations as 'not a theory, but rather a way of theorizing practice' (Kritzman 1988). Somewhere Foucault refers to Nietzche's observation that while thinkers are always shooting arrows into the air, the key thing is for others to pick them up and shoot them in another direction.[3] If the unfinished, open-ended character of his work creates some difficulties for its reception and use, then it also leaves open the possibility of creative applications of his ideas. (We ourselves, for example, are developing an approach linking governmentality, power relations, and constitution of the self as a way of studying organizations and their use of external services). We must recognize throughout that Foucault himself would expect from others a development, not mere replication of his work.

FOUCAULT: TECHNE AND TECHNOLOGY

Foucault himself wrote little directly about information and communications technologies (ICT), and indeed little about technological artefacts and tools, though he recognized that the technologies he was interested in were physical in part, for example in the architecture of prisons, schools, the clinic. However, he did write much about procedures, techniques, processes, and behavioural/disciplinary technologies, for example the confession, the examination, prison rehabilitation regimes, and 'technologies of the self'. This may well have led to his relative neglect amongst ICT researchers, though a similar omission does not seem to have done any harm to the reception of the work of Giddens and Habermas, for example (Mingers and Willcocks 2004). Part of this may well be that Foucault comes less packaged, with fewer schemas that are easy to adopt. That said, some of his work, especially the image of the Panopticon, has been translated directly into, for example, studies of surveillance technologies (Lyon 1994, 2003), of the use of information and databases (Poster 1990), and of discipline, information use, and technologies at work (Zuboff 1988; Webster 2005).

However, Foucault's contribution can be much richer than this. For example, Foucault was well aware, not least from his reading of Heidegger, of the long-term, 'greatest danger' (Heidegger's phrase) from technology, as well as from Weberian rationalization (though Foucault (1983) prefers to investigate 'specific rationalities'), and the disciplining and normalization inherent in bio-power. Had he lived into the so-called 'Information Age' he might well have made the connections between these and the key roles of media-, military-, and work-based information and communication technologies forming this present danger, arising, in Heidegger's 'essence of technology' (1977) and in Virilio's (2002) view, as technocratic thinking and imagination become social imagination itself. A Foucauldian perspective leads to a key question here:

> We have been able to see what forms of power relation were conveyed by various technologies (whether we are speaking of productions with economic aims, or institutions whose goal is social regulation, or of techniques of communication) . . . What is at stake, then, is this: How can the growth of capabilities be disconnected from the intensification of power relations? (M. Foucault: 'What is Enlightenment', in Rabinow 1984)

From the early 1970s the word *technology* is increasingly to be found in Foucault's writings. The word is usually used in phrases such as 'technologies of power', 'political technology of the body', 'disciplinary technologies', and 'technologies of the self'. Foucault often elides the word technology with those of techne and also technique, but power always resides in his concept of technology whether referring to behavioural technologies, or to technology as architectures, buildings, physical artefacts, and how space is defined and used. Foucault rarely seeks to define his use of the word technology. In an interview called 'Space, Knowledge, and Power' (Rabinow 1984), while discussing the study of architecture, Foucault offers, somewhat elliptically, the following:

> What interests me more is to focus on what the Greeks called techne, that is to say, a practical rationality governed by a conscious goal. . . . The disadvantage of this word techne, I realize is its relation to the word 'technology' which has a very specific meaning . . . one thinks of hard technology, the technology of wood, of fire, of electricity. Whereas government is also a function of technology: the government of individuals, the government of souls, the government of the self by the self, the government of families, the government of children and so on.

An interesting contrast can be made with Heidegger who was interested in the products and tools of the *natural sciences*, and focused on 'the essence of technology', or what Dreyfus calls technicity, that is the new technocratic thinking and style of practices that have emerged, distinguished from the technological devices these practices produce and sustain. For Foucault, too, to judge technology by its tools and its production is to miss the point. In his later work, however, he is looking at modern *human sciences*, the practices and power relations by which they are founded, the knowledge and behavioural technologies they produce, and how these operate, allied to structures, designed space, and use of tools and artefacts. Moreover the operation of these new methods (technologies?) of power 'is not ensured by right but by technique, not by law but by normalization, not by punishment but by control' (Foucault 1978).

Furthermore, these technologies of power function anonymously—they are implemented by everyone and no one—and autonomously—for, as Foucault once commented in an interview: 'while people know what they do, and may know why they do what they do, they do not know what what they do does.' Given this distinctive, historically recent blending of knowledges, disciplinary technologies and bio-power, power/knowledge emerges as the key concept in Foucault' philosophy of modern technology. However this philosophy of technology is particularistic. Unlike Heidegger, he does not attempt a general account of the 'essence' of modern technology, but rather reveals specific histories of technological practices overlooked in other accounts of modern forms of power.

Several points occur here. Firstly, it is important to stress that Foucault does not deny that technologies of power/knowledge can have beneficial features: 'my point is not that everything is bad, but everything is dangerous . . . if everything is dangerous, then we always have something to do' (Foucault 1983). Secondly, especially in his later work, Foucault indicates that modern subjects can and do subvert the conditions of their own subjectivity. In the later volumes of *The History of Sexuality*, for example the individual is increasingly positioned as the personal space where both active and passive, and regulated and resistant possibilities for human agency surface in the context of material practices (Katz 2001). The self-subjectivation practices, or 'technologies of the self' as Foucault calls them, take on a more active, used dimension, less geared to relations of power and discourse, more geared to bending force back on itself, and so to self's work on the self. One can begin to read Haraway's (1991) cyborg manifesto: 'I would rather be a cyborg than a goddess' into the direction Foucault's work was taking.

Thirdly, Deleuze (1995) stresses that Foucault was one of the first to say that we have been shifting from disciplinary societies to what Deleuze calls *control societies*. These no longer operate by, for example, physically confining people but through continuous control and instant communication enabled by developments in material technology. In this rendering what has been called 'information society' can also be read as control society. If this is correct, then Foucault's power/knowledge, discourse, bio-power, and governmentality remain as thoroughly applicable concepts, as Foucault intended them to. Moreover, Deleuze points out that if each kind of society corresponds to a particular machine, e.g simple mechanical for sovereign societies, thermo-dynamic machines for disciplinary societies, and cybernetic machines and computers for control societies, then: 'the machines don't explain anything, you have to analyze the collective arrangements of which the machines are just one component'. In other words, the machines do not determine different kinds of society, but do express the social forms capable of producing them and making use of them. And of course, as we argue later, the shift to new forms of society can be exaggerated, as we have seen in the rhetorics of post-modernism, and on the Internet, digital and knowledge economies.

FOUCAULT: 'GHOST' IN THE AUTOMATE/INFORMATE DEBATE

While Foucault never wrote explicitly about ICTs, one book he might have written on the subject is, ironically, given the relative neglect of Foucault's work in the area, the most cited and celebrated in the whole of the IS field, namely Zuboff's 1988 book *In the Age of the Smart Machine*. The most cited aspect of Zuboff (1988) is its major premiss. ICTs can be designed and applied to automate or informate work. The former option builds on ICT, potential for speed and consistency, but creates deskilled blue and white collar jobs, minimizes job satisfaction, can displace physical labour, and increases the decision-making, discretion, and remoteness of management. Informating, on the other hand, derives from the enormous transparency given by ICT-assisted information generated from an organization's underlying production and administrative processes. Informating enables much greater ICT potential to be exploited, and more commercial advantage to be gained.

Undoubtedly, changes in technology greatly increase what is possible. But, Zuboff argues, what subsequently happens depends on transformations, profound discontinuities in fact, in how knowledge, authority, and technique are managed, and implies a comprehensive conscious strategy. The dilemma is posed by Zuboff as a stark and ultimately political question. Will managers move from drivers of largely bodily labour to drivers of learning? Do and will managers utilize ICT to support, and even reinforce, existing political, social, and organizational structures and processes, or transform these and their own positions within them in order to gain the full pay-offs from ICT investments?

In all this, though not heavily referenced, the influence of Foucault is quite striking. Zuboff's concept of power is not exactly that of Foucault's but, for her, power is a key concept, does circulate, and is intimately related to skills and types of knowledge. Like Foucault, she downplays conspiracy, and instead stresses contingency and expediency in how things turn out. Her approach in taking a long-run historical perspective on the labouring body and skill in production and white-collar work, on managerial authority (called by her 'the spiritual dimension of power'), and in presenting ICT as a potential discontinuity—all these echo the shape of Foucault's work in many places. In many ways Zuboff maps a long-run, complex, Foucault-like discourse on management, work, technology, and struggles, into which ICTs are finding their way. Foucault is also influential in Zuboff's concentration on technique, which she calls the material dimension of power. The debt then becomes explicit in the related two chapter headings, namely 'The Information Panopticon' and 'Panoptic Power and The Social Text'. Her focus on bio-power and the microphysics of power—how power produces bodies and mind—is also the Foucault of *Discipline and Punish*. Interestingly here, in her excellent research methodology, she gives a central place to phenomenology—a move Foucault would have needed to make if he had wanted to explore bio-power further at the material level in institutional settings. The automate/informate dilemma is also one that points, Foucauldian-like, to 'the present danger': will we reinforce present disciplinary, panoptic tendencies through ICT applications, or will we take up other options the new boost in power and possibilities these technologies can offer. Ultimately the pessimism in her findings, and to some extent her conclusions also remind one of Foucault's own dilemmas with disciplinary/bio-power.

But something interesting then happens to the direction which the informate/automate debate takes. As Zuboff's book becomes a bestseller, its Foucauldian influences and themes fall away almost completely, and the automate/informate dilemma comes to be posed as a choice for managers and, indeed capitalist societies to make. Partly this is because of how the book is sold, with a simplified central message, an 'informate' challenge, indeed, that Zuboff asks managers to step up to in her last chapter. But interestingly, there is some inconsistency between, on the one hand, the rich historical discourse and constraints she describes, and, on the other, the levels of active *choice* she then assumes for managers.

In practice, Zuboff's work becomes adopted by the Harvard Business School where she was, at the time, an associate professor. Harnessing the School's reputational effects and its powerful marketing and self-referencing capability, the book's public messages are pushed into certain directions rather than others. In fact, arguably, the book is used to support Harvard's own 'can do' 'born again' transformative philosophy of management, in which a dichtomous before/after, from/to message is transmitted to trainee managers and businesses alike. Simple, powerful messages are likely to be more influential than the twists and turns of a long, rich, and complex book that most have probably read about, rather than read all the way through. Power/knowledge circulates, people, institutions, and documents are its relays—knowledge and power produce each other indeed.

Ultimately the meaning of Zuboff's book is diluted and rendered complementary to, for example, Walton (1989), also a product of Harvard. Walton's work goes on to figure prominently in another book highly influential in IS, namely the *Corporation of the 1990s* (Scott Morton 1991). This proceeds to offer dichotomous thinking in contrasting bad/good 'control' versus 'commitment' strategies in ICT use, and, in an un-Foucauldian manner, fails to problematize commitment strategies and their political and control implications. A more informed view here is provided by Townley (1993) and Deetz

(1998) who see the cultural or normative controls that operate as alternatives to bureaucratic rules and direct supervision as new technologies of power developed within knowledge-intensive organizations.

A related, influential development has been the neo-Zuboffian 'don't automate, obliterate' message of Hammer and Champy's writings on re-engineering the corporation, with heavy use of ICTs. Grint and Willcocks (1995) point out that Hammer and Champy work with a negative, unitary view of power, and while the objective of re-engineering is ostensibly to render the corporation a-political, in fact successful re-engineering, supported by labour 'empowerment' strategies, is designed to make managerial power and control more complete. The inherently political agenda is signalled by the marked violence in the language used, the dismissal of 'resistance to change', the determination to banish social, cultural, and historical issues by starting with a blank sheet of paper, the use of management-determined ICT designs to support the shape and process of the transformed corporation. On this view 'informate' is too small a step, and 'transformate' is necessary (see also Scott Morton 1991), but only a more radical view of power relations would seek to fully problematize the intentions, approaches, and outcomes. Those in IS studying such phenomena could more than usefully adopt Foucauldian concepts and modes of analysis.

FOUCAULT AND DISCIPLINING 'INFORMATION SYSTEMS'

Ironically, again, the Foucauldian elements of Zuboff's book have been remarkably *uninfluential* in Information Systems, a relatively immature discipline crying out for applicable theory. But Zuboff's influence, taught as she has been on every conceivable type of IS programme (certainly in the period between 1988 and 2000), has hardly stretched to the founding of a Foucauldian school of IS. Despite her demonstration of his applicability, why *not* Foucault now?

The operational word here may will be discipline. For decades a string of scholars and articles have registered 'discipline anxiety' for IS. This comes from its relative newness as an area of study and its hybridity, based as it is on an amalgamation of computer science, operational research, management studies, economics, organization studies, strategic management, to name a few. The definitional phrase that comes to mind is the one Richard Whitley used for management studies: a fragmented adhocracy. How to discipline, and gain intellectual respectability for a knowledge field lacking discipline?

A natural tendency is to look to another accepted reference discipline for already approved methods, procedures, standards, for definitions of what qualifies as knowledge and truth. One unfortunate outcome in IS is that methods and approaches have often been adopted uncritically (that is, failing to address the debates that surround them in their own discipline, e.g transaction cost theory in economics), or may be inappropriate for the specific research task. This can lead to unnecessary defensive polarities developing, and an over-expectation on what a particular approach can deliver.

For historical reasons—not least because of the hard, technology component of IS, the general dominance of the procedures of the natural sciences infiltrating into the social sciences, the large influence of North American academic practices in IS—the IS tendency has been to focus on quantitative, statistics-based methods and procedures derived from natural sciences. The rise of IS as a discipline has yet to be charted satisfactorily, and may well benefit from a Foucauldian analysis. IS awaits its genealogist, though Introna (2001) makes a thought-provoking start in his paper on evolving regimes of truth from 1977 to 2000 at one of the major IS journals, namely *MIS Quarterly*. He shows the mechanisms used to produce truth, and how contingent they were. Also how, through intentional and unintentional moves, these regimes of truth were continually shifting, opening spaces for certain types of research to become legitimate, and others not. It is a matter of some pertinence here that the widespread acceptance of certain types of qualitative, interpretative, and case research into major IS journals has been a relatively recent phenomenon. In such an unstable situation, given their cross-disciplinarity, and provisional methods, Foucauldian-type studies, at best, could only be marginal to how the IS discipline has been developing.

The debate on what would constitute IS as a discipline has been running for some time. Post-2000, faced with the sheer rising diversity in research methods being adopted in the field, there has been renewed 'discipline anxiety' and fresh debates in several major IS journals over establishing the rules, procedures for what counts as knowledge, and how it can be legitimately produced. Introna (2003) makes an interesting Foucauldian intervention in pointing out that what constitutes acceptable research methods, processes for producing the truth, and a definable knowledge base are not matters of what is right or rationally superior, but are inherently political questions from the start. Moreover participants are not just disciplining others in the process of creating 'the IS discipline', but also disciplining themselves. Introna (2003) also points out that if IS proceeds to constitute itself as a regime of truth then it will need to follow Foucault (in Gordon 1980) in establishing five things. These are:

- the types of discourse it accepts and makes function as true
- mechanisms and instances that enable one to distinguish true and false statements
- means by which each is sanctioned
- techniques and procedures accorded value in the acquisition of truth
- status of those charged with saying what counts as true.

On these counts, one would suggest that if IS is not yet externally or even self-regarded as a discipline, it has been remarkably successful at disciplining itself, and that this process deserves much more detailed, perhaps Foucauldian study.

ASSESSING FOUCAULT'S USE IN IS STUDIES

Having said all this, some within IS have made a strong case for Foucault, and indeed have used aspects of his work. Introna (1997) effectively utilizes Foucault's power/ knowledge in harness with Clegg's (1989) conceptualization of circuits of power, in order to explicate several case studies of ICT implementation and use. Furthermore, Cordoba and Robson (2003) used Foucault's ideas on power/knowledge and ethics to develop a more critical understanding of the information systems evaluation process. The authors demonstrated that Foucault's theorization provides an alternative under-standing of information systems evaluation as a process of continuous tension between power, discourses, and ethics.

A study that tried to analyse information technology and surveillance through Foucault's theorization was carried out by Humphreys (2006). The author identified different marketing practices and Internet technologies employed by 'Amazon.com' as sight-technologies of power aiming to surveillance and individuation. Against this background, he argued that these technologies play an active role in constructing the consumer as an 'object of knowledge' and shaping consumer agency. More recently, Avgerou and McGrath (2007) in their study of a social security organization in Greece, drew on Foucault's work on power/knowledge and the aesthetics of existence to challenge the technical rationality underpinning IS organizational change and innova-tion. The authors went beyond the mere consideration of technical IS rationalities and underlined the role of social processes in explaining IS organizational change and innovation. Following this line, they argued that 'the rational techniques of IS practice and the power dynamics of an organization and its social context are closely inter-twined, requiring each other to be sustained' (Avgerou and McGrath 2007).

Brooke (2002a, 2002b), in discussing what it means to be ' critical' in IS research (see also Chapter 8), argues that Foucault can be used to move beyond the Habermasian framework employed in earlier IS work. As a related point, initially Habermas was presented somewhat uncritically in IS, but there has grown up a healthy critique of his use which Foucault's work can readily fuel (Klein and Huynh 2004). Indeed, Foucault challenges an idea central to critical theory when he suggests that relations of power are not something bad in themselves, nor something from which one can or must be emancipated. Foucault also argues that any production of knowledge contains within itself the potential for contradictory outcomes. If this is useful then, nevertheless, the scientific and positivistic heritage of IS does tend to favour adoption of approaches that are more easily 'modelled', and any line of research seeking to use a normatively articulated framework will tend to favour a Habermasian approach rather than a Foucauldian one. But when it comes to applying critical theory, who guards the guards? From a Foucauldian perspective, it is not enough to apply particular methodological frameworks, we also have to subject them to ongoing critique, and Foucault's work supplies means for doing this.

Davies has also sought to apply Foucault in several pieces of empirical research. For example, Davies and Mitchell (1994) adopted a research perspective that sought to understand technology formation as a power-knowledge object used within a socio-political context, but also looking at 'how technological forms affect the predomination of discourse of power, allowing for the "truth" of an object's utility value to emerge as a product of its own structural form and the value of the form according to the group world-view adopting it'. The authors argue, with Burrell (1998), that Foucault's genealogical method, focus on history, and concept of power/knowledge are of high relevance to studying organizational forms currently emerging, particularly in relation to the control of information effects induced by the increasing reliance upon information technologies within organizations.

While Davies and Mitchell do not adopt Foucault as comprehensively as they might, they do demonstrate how his work on the regulatory nature of discourse within contextual histories can be used productively in IS studies, in this case that of IT manipulation in an Australian state government department. Following Foucault, they point to the constraining regulations by which discourse are inevitably tied. They take three interacting forms, shown in Figure 7.1.

The three principles of exclusion are immediately external to a discourse and define and legitimize meaning and rationality within discourse. The three principles of limitation operate to classify order and distribute the discourse to allow for and to deal with irruption and unpredictability. Finally the three principles of communication

EXCLUSION

Prohibition	Division	Truth Power
Taboos	*Legitimate participation*	*True vs false*

LIMITATION

Commentary	Rarefaction	Disciplines
Meaning rules maintained	*Identity rules maintained*	*Belief rules maintained*

COMMUNICATION

Societies of Discourse	Social Appropriation	Systems of Regulation and Control
Social group	*Maintain or modify*	*Production and manipulation*

FIGURE 7.1 Principles of Discourse Regulation (after Foucault)

create the ritual framework (akin to an ideology) of the context of any discourse, with the ritual framework being more dominating than the merely external principles.

While these constructs may seem somewhat abstracted, the researchers do bring them to life in applying them to a concrete case, namely the purchasing of office support systems. By applying all the concepts, the research shows how one system is adopted in preference to another, predominantly through the prior regulations of discourse supporting the continuance of the superior technical knowledge and power of the IT function. The researchers successfully show how applying Foucauldian principles to analysing the discursive context of IT use in an organization can provide in-depth insight into the role of power and politics, and whether IT is used augmentatively to reinforce the status quo, or transformatively.

A later Foucauldian study of an ICT needs analysis project was also carried out by Davies, as Harvey (1998). The study usefully demonstrates how the history of power relations in an IT decision context influenced discourses regarding the acceptability of solutions. Historical dominance was demonstrated through how visibility was controlled, how counter-discourses were silenced, and how surveillance was applied. What is interesting in this study, that of Zuboff (1988) and of Davies and Mitchell (1994) is how they all extend and enhance interpretive research methods through using Foucault. Indeed, though interpretivism was never a direction in which Foucault himself was heading, Doolin (1998) argues that this is a necessary move in order to counter potential shortcomings in the treatment of technology in interpretive research on information systems.

For our purposes, Doolin (1998) is more useful in illustrating this theme of information systems as a calculative and disciplinary technology. He does so by reference to his own Foucauldian study of power relations and effects involving the deployment of a hospital 'case-mix' IS. A case-mix system is an IS which links detailed information on individual patient clinical activity with associated costs, for use by managers and service providers as a basis for contracting and for revealing the relative efficiency of clinical resource usage. The intention is to place clinical activity under scrutiny, and to persuade clinicians to conform to ' normal' work practices. Potentially Doolin found that the IS could increase hospital management control directly and indirectly. Direct control was attempted by monitoring and making visible the financial implications of clinical decisions. Managers could then use the information to make stronger truth claims in their attempts to contain clinical resource usage. Surveillance through the system also had the potential to engender a degree of self-control in clinicians' behaviour, leading to rational decision making and more efficient usage of resources.

However, following Foucault, resistance by the clinicians was always possible. Disciplinary technologies such as comparative surveillance IS are not exclusively constraining, but instead open up a new discursive space for action. In practice clinicians often appropriated and manipulated the information and rhetoric of the system, diverting disciplinary practices to their own ends, principally in arguing for more resources. Indeed some senior clinicians explored the possibilities offered by the case-mix system in assuming new roles as clinician managers. However, the IS increased the transparency of professional knowledge, expertise, and work processes. Its deployment provided management with the technology and the rational justification for increased intervention in medical practice. Moreover, case-mix information became the currency of debate, the principal medium through which claims to legitimacy and control were processed. Taking a Foucauldian view, Doolin points out that in reproducing the practices associated with the case-mix IS, clinicians internalized the norms and values inherent in the particular discourse in which case-mix is grounded, opening up the possibility of their self-control as self-disciplined subjects. Thus IS utilization could have more subtle power effects than deliberate strategies to modify clinical behaviour through strengthening general management in or imposing computerized surveillance. In a similar vain, Ball and Wilson (2000) studied the computer-based performance monitoring in two UK call centres and demonstrated how panoptic technologies of power were enmeshed with discourses which produced and reproduced relations of power and resistance in the work place.

More recently, Lioliou and Willcocks (2009) illustrate the relevance of Foucault's latter work on governance to the study of IT outsourcing arrangements. More specifically the authors demonstrate how Foucault's concept of 'governmentality' illuminates on the interplay between contractual and relational forms of IT outsourcing governance and its effects on the venture. With reference to the work of Rose and Miller (1992) as well as Bulkeley, Watson, and Hudson (2007), the authors organized their results in terms of 'programs' and 'technologies of government' and used key ideas from the governmentality literature for analysis. Their preliminary findings illustrated: (1) how the contract and the apparatus of governance it entails create visibility and transparency that not only renders the outsourcing relationship amenable to government and intervention, but also facilitates trust and collaboration among the outsourcing partners; (2) the role of the contract in the retention and diffusion of the spirit of the venture; (3) the role of governance mechanisms in the reduction for the need of authoritative surveillance; and (4) the need for the standardization of governance processes.

These illustrative studies demonstrate how Foucault's work can be utilized creatively and productively in the IS field. Indeed IS as a discipline may learn a great deal more on the applicability of Foucault if it addresses more seriously the altogether more developed debate and application of his work to be found in Organization Studies and associated areas (OS/MS).

FOUCAULT AND ICTS IN ORGANIZATION AND MANAGEMENT STUDIES

Foucault has had a long-standing presence in sociology and OS/MS because his concepts and contribution have such clear applicability to researching work organizations. Moreover, from the early 1980s as ICTs became increasingly used in organizations, it became a necessary move to embrace the analysis of how they are utilized and embedded in the social bodies, practices, and institutional arrangements of organizations. The same argument can be made from the perspective of Information Systems studies, of course, but, one suspects, its engineering/computer science origins led to a greater focus on the technology artefact. Discipline anxiety led to the adoption of more scientistic and 'rigorous' reference disciplines, while those rising to powerful positions in the IS field tended not to espouse approaches, especially unsystematic ones, they had not themselves been trained in.

The maturity of OS/MS Foucauldian debate and use is well demonstrated in the articles collected by McKinlay and Starkey (1998) and Carter, McKinlay, and Rowlinson (2000). These carry penetrating papers that seek to critique, develop, and utilize Foucault's work in for example human resource management (see also Townley 1993), power and politics in organizations and production, managing managers, accounting, reading organizational analysis into Foucault, developing a Foucauldian historical dimension in the study of organizations, the relationships between discipline and desire, the epistemic nature of management, and the need to deconstruct management studies underpinned, like influencing disciplines, as they are by rationality, agency, and causality.

Foucault has also done much to breathe new life into labour process theory, not least in OS/MS researchers emphasizing how individual subjectivities and identities are constructed and reconstructed through discourses operating in the workplace (Knights 1990; Knights and Vurdubakis 1994). There has also been an expansion of the concept of power (Clegg 1989, 1998), with Hardy and O'Sullivan (1998) positioning Foucault as providing the fourth dimension of power, extending the three defined by Steven Lukes. All this illustrates a strong Foucauldian pedigree in OS/MS, and one that is directly applicable to any work in IS where ICTs are studied in organizational contexts.

Even more pertinent to our purposes is the OS/MS accumulated evidence gained from applying Foucault to the study of information and communication technologies. Many of these attempts focus on new managerial technologies aimed to broaden the scope and deepen the intensity of the managerial gaze, but, Foucault-like, invariably with complex, often unanticipated outcomes. Surveillance, control, and legitimation is facilitated by giving complex, ambiguous phenomena 'hard' numerical values (Morgan and Willmott 1993), for example in ICT use in activity-based costing systems where the managerial gaze extends into supplier networks and market information. ICTs facilitate enumeration, which can underpin categorization, and thus what is made visible. Such technologies privilege formal quantitative information, aiding in the construction of calculative realities (Bloomfield and Coombs 1992).

However, developments in ICTs to monitor and scrutinize can also facilitate panopticon-like control, making individuals within an organization both calculable and calculating with respect to their own actions. For example, Sewell and Wilkinson (1992) investigate these propensities in the context of JIT manufacturing and Total Quality Control regimes. They point to the development of what Webster and Robins (1993) call 'a panopticon without walls', where responsibility can become delegated to groups, but individuals become enlisted in their own control through their belief that they are subject to constant electronic surveillance through collected, retained, and disseminated information. McKinley and Starkey (1998) also point to how the extension of JIT supplier relationships accelerates the concentration, widens the scope and speed of corporate knowledge acquisition, and that this is knowledge combined with economic power that is not reciprocal; 'there is no parallel gaze by consumers or supplier companies into the internal transaction costs of the organization'. Webster and Robins (1993) suggest also that these developments are not restricted to the labour process or the factory but are more societal, to the point where one can speak of a more generalized 'Social Taylorism' made more possible through information and communication technologies.

Bloomfield, Knights, Wilmott, and colleagues have done much important work in developing Foucauldian studies of ICTs and organization. It is not possible to do justice to the richness of their work but good examples can be found in Bloomfield and Coombs (1992), Bloomfield et al. (1997), and Knights, Murray, and Willmott (1997). A particularly representative work is that of Knights and Murray (1994). This book has the great merit of providing a real in-depth theoretical and empirical examination of the politics of systems development. In the theory sections it provides a Foucauldian-informed critique of the major theoretical perspectives on ICT development and implementation. From this, Knights and Murray then develop a political processual model of organizational change. At its centre stands politics as Foucauldian power/knowledge relations enacted in specific conditions of possibility, the social construction of which is also part of an organization's political processes.

Knights and Murray also supply the useful definition of ICT Foucault never provided (see above), in order to inform their Foucauldian analysis. They see ICT as a set of human and non-human artefacts, processes and practices ordinarily directed towards modifying or transforming natural and social phenomena in pursuit of human purposes. This involves:

- technological artefacts, such as computers, hardware
- technological knowledge, particularly systems development skills
- technological workers and managers engaged in particular systems development, and IS specialists
- the culture of technology—signs, symbols and values brought to bear in discussing, using and developing technology.

In this analytical framework, the organization is likened to a pinball machine. While recognizing the limitations of the analogy, the researchers suggest that the political process stands in the middle of the machine and is bombarded by steel balls energized in different parts of the organization. These bounce against the motor of political process and are shot back to bounce against other conditions of the organization. Though a little uncritical of Foucault, as opposed to every other theoretical approach, Knights and Murray (1994) do provide, as they show in their case study, operationalizable analytical tools that can be very useful to ICT researchers.

Foucault, ICTs, and Surveillance

Perhaps the most obvious and influential use of Foucault has been in surveillance studies, not just in manufacturing and service work organizations, but across society at large, including in all manner of institutional settings. There is a large literature on the theme of ICT roles in surveillance, with Lyon (1988) and Dandeker (1990) being representative of a number of writers in the late 1980s discussing the 'electronic panopticon', the 'carceral computer' and 'the electronic eye'. Poster (1984) is also influenced enough by Foucault to posit an emerging 'mode of information' by whose social conduits and databases members of developed economies are organized and controlled.

Webster (2005) also links surveillance technologies with the nation state's 'governmentality' role over security needs, rights, and duties of its citizens. For him, the panopticon is not an exact metaphor. Following Giddens, a lot of surveillance information does feed back to people and allow them to reflexively monitor their own position, prospects, and lifestyles. He is drawn instead to De Landa's (1991) depiction of the 'machine vision' of military surveillance where power and the accumulation of information are intimately connected, manifested in things like telecommunications interceptions, satellite observations, and automatic intelligence. De Landa sees the military dream of machine vision as an extension of earlier panoptic techniques. Now humans and their eyes do not have to physically operate in the surveillance tower. Moreover surveillance has extended from the optical to the non-optical regions of the electro-magnetic spectrum. Not just computing and telecommunications, but the discovery of infrared and ultraviolet radiation, radar, radio, and microwave technology have opened new resources to be exploited as well as new zones to be policed. De Landa offers the word 'Panspectron' to communicate the ambition of total surveyability vested in the 'new non-optical intelligence-acquisition machine'. This is a highly pertinent issue, not least for IS studies, if De Landa is correct in suggesting that, historically, earlier technologies developed in the military have been transmitted through a series of relays to the civilian worlds.

Lyon (1988) registers related concerns in his early work on the rise of information society. He suggests that dreams of electronic democracy must be tempered with a recognition of technological and political realities. He recognizes, even for the late 1980s, that the 'carceral computer' is 'a present reality, both in direct state administration and control, and in the potential for linkage with private databases'. However, as yet the dangers had not been sufficiently recognized or resisted by citizens, and some predictions of total social control by computers may be ahistorical 'in that past technological dystopias have not come into being, and may also be based on inadequate social theories'.

If Lyon (1988) points to the 'present danger', then the subsequent direction much of his work takes suggests that in his estimation, with rising use of ICT, the danger has become very real. Thus Lyon (1994) is entitled *The Electronic Eye: The Rise of*

Surveillance Society. For him the most socially pervasive question raised by the new technologies has become the garnering of personal information to be stored, matched, retrieved, processed, marketed, and circulated using powerful computer databases and related technologies. His position is that the electronic eye may well blink benignly, but important questions must be asked about under what circumstances and by what criteria the current computer-aided surveillance capability may also become undemocratic, coercive, impersonal, even inhuman.

In later work and edited volumes, Lyon and colleagues provide rich detailed studies of these and related questions (see for example Lyon and Zureik 1996; Lyon 2003). In all this, it becomes difficult not to read the influence and relevance of Foucault's work, amongst others. Thus, in these volumes some take the phenomenon of electronic surveillance as contributing to a postmodern condition in which several 'virtual selves' circulate within networked databases, independent of their Cartesian counterparts who use credit cards and are identified by social insurance numbers (Lyon and Zureik 1996). This raises questions of how identity and selves are constructed, sorted, and controlled, privately and publicly. In the same volume Mowshowitz sees the widespread use of databases promoting 'endogenous' forms of social control, where virtual individuality, group conformity, and other-directedness will reside in the data themselves. For Poster, databases have become the new text in Foucault's sense of discourse.

In all this, researchers point also to limitations in both Foucault's work and in applying it to surveillance studies. Thus Gandy, writing on 'Coming to Terms with the Panoptic Sort' enlists also Giddens's synthesis of Marxian, Weberian, and Foucauldian theory to emphasize surveillance as a modern institution, and the role of the 'dialectic of control' and knowledgeable human agents in all surveillance situations (Lyon and Zureik 1996). Zureik (in Lyon 2003) concludes that surveillance in the work place is ubiquitous and increasingly based on network control technologies. He suggests that the concept of panoptic power is important, but that more than one theoretical perspective is needed to analyse how in specific contexts empowerment and disempowerment, skilling and deskilling, control and autonomy exist, and indeed can coexist, depending on technological deployment, gender, and authority structures (but see also Knights and Murray above).

Lyon (1993) asks: in what ways does electronic surveillance display panoptic features? He finds plenty of evidence of ICT being used to accumulate coded information for the internal pacification of nation states. Also for panoptic control within work places, including what Zuboff calls 'anticipatory conformity', where standards of management had been internalized by employees. He also cites evidence of the spillover of panoptic surveillance into society at large in the establishment of, for example, more 'efficient' network marketplaces, something that Poster (1990) refers to as a 'Superpanopticon', because the panoptic has few technical limitations.

But, partly following Giddens, Lyon also sees analysts of electronic surveillance picking up from Foucault a relatively undifferentiated view of power and panopticism, and therefore of panopticism's ICT-facilitated spread across different types of institutions. At the same time he concedes that the reality of contemporary electronic surveillance is that, increasingly, disciplinary networks do, for example, connect employment with civil status, or consumption with policing. But if Poster's 'Super-panopticon' is accurate, nevertheless does it impose Foucault-type norms, incorporate bio-power, discipline subjects? Maybe, Lyon suggests, all it can do is provide a structure, and one within which real choices are still made. Ultimately Lyon finds the Panopticon wanting as an explanatory concept. Electronic surveillance does contribute to social control via invisible inspection and categorization. But seeing the Panopticon in a 'totalizing' way deflects attention from other modes of social ordering (Lyon 2003). Lyon (1993) also comments that Foucault's failure to admit any basis of 'outrage' against the Panopticon inhibits the development of a properly critical theory of electronic surveillance.

Maybe one of the mistakes in contemporary surveillance theory, as in other disciplines, is to represent Foucault's work too one-sidedly by the Panopticon and its admittedly strong metaphorical power. As we have seen, Foucault is much richer than this. For example, in summarizing his own work Foucault defined four major types of technologies, each a matrix of practical reason, each associated with a certain type of domination (Deetz 1998). Foucault presents technologies of production, of sign systems, of power, and technologies of self. He also suggests that these may interplay in particular sites. He also worked with a generic mode of discipline, of which the panoptic represents merely one type. One way forward for electronic surveillance studies may well be to readdress Foucault's work more fully. In addition Dandeker (1990) suggests that, given the uneasy relations in Foucault between an idealist history of knowledge, class struggle, and the functional or technical imperatives of modern societies, his insights may be used to complement those generated by other, especially Weberian, strands of social theory.

From Mode of Information to Network Society and Cyberstudies

In this final section, we look briefly at Foucault's abiding relevance in the face of developments of ICTs and their uses in the twenty-first century. Poster (1984, 1990, 1995) was amongst the first to suggest that Foucault provides key ideas (on signification, power/knowledge, subjectification, discourse) for the development of a critical theory of the newly emerging 'mode of information'. Poster suggests that the reversal of priorities Marx saw in the factory whereby the dead (machines) dominate the living (workers) is being increasingly extended by the computer to the realm of knowledge. He usefully posits three stages in the mode of information:

- Face-to-face, orally mediated exchange characterized by symbolic correspondences;
- Written exchanges mediated by print, characterized by the representation of signs;
- Electronically mediated exchange, characterized by informational simulations.

Given the attributes and applications of ICT, an increasing, distinctive characteristic in the latter electronic stage is that the self becomes decentred, dispersed, and multiplied in continuous instability. If Poster (1990) subsequently utilizes several postmodernist thinkers to analyse the emerging mode of information, he finds how information is structured and used through databases, and their relation to society best disclosed by Foucault's analysis of discourse: 'the linguistic quality of the database, its implications for politics, can best be captured by a theory, like Foucault's, that problematizes the interdependence of language and action.' As we have seen, Poster sees electronic circuits of communication and the databases they generate constituting a Superpanopticon, a system of surveillance without walls, windows, towers, or guards.

New ICTs used in surveillance result in a qualitative change in the microphysics of power. However, he observes, technological change, is only part of the process. The populace, through social security cards, drivers' licences, and in their consumerist activites, for example, have been disciplined to surveillance and participating in the process. For Poster (1990, 1995), when Foucauldian discourse analysis is applied to the new mode of information, it yields the uncomfortable discovery that the populace participates in its own self-constitution as subjects of the normalizing gaze of the Superpanopticon. Moreover, databases are seen often not as a threat to a centred individual or a threat to privacy, but as the multiplication of the individual, the constitution of an additional self, one that may be acted upon to the detriment of the 'real' self without that 'real' self ever being aware of what is happening. For Poster, then, while recognizing the deficiencies of Foucault's work, the concepts and methods for exploring discourse, subjectification, disciplining, knowledge, and power relations remain key to critical study of ICTs, and indeed the Internet (Poster 2001) in the emerging mode of information they facilitate. While the genealogy of information and communications technologies has yet to be written, Foucault, as Poster (1990) recognizes, provides a considerable amount of the groundwork needed.

Munro (2000) also recognizes how Foucault has been drawn upon to analyse the power relations involved in computer information systems. As a partial corrective, he argues not that disciplinary modalities of power have disappeared, but that they are subject to infiltration and mutation where ICTs are transforming social relationships and allowing other forms of power to be brought to bear. The examples he includes are how the Human Genome project is bringing to bear bio-technologies such as genetic screening and cloning. He also cites Deleuze's (1995) depiction of moves towards a 'control' society, e.g from schools to continuing education, from prisons to electronic tagging. Also new forms of 'resistance' are possible, e.g computer piracy and viruses, sabotage of information databases. Also new social divisions are developing, including the information haves and have-nots. Also new institutions, consisting of series of connected nodes or stations that work by circulating information flows as much as wealth and goods. He points to the power of networks and how these new institutions do not rely on enclosure or visual surveillance. Instead power operates through the regulation of flows rather than the imposition of exercises (Deleuze 1995).

Munro posits the rise of network power in contrast to panoptic power. The differentiation he makes is along the dimensions of techniques, space, time, and the body. At the level of technique, power relations become more centred on access to and control over information and the electronic text. Time-space constraints disappear, with real time and connected nodes creating new circuits of power. Following Virilio, the body becomes motile, that is more dependent on communications prosthetics e.g mobile phone, portable computer. Whereas the docile body was the object of disciplinary power, the prosthetic body is the object of network power.

Munro argues that sticking doggedly to Foucault's original conceptualizations of disciplinary power can lead to errors in analysis in these new conditions. Bauman (1991, 1999) also recognizes Foucault as seminal in the study of disciplinary societies and their technologies but posits less relevance for control technologies in the changed conditions of liquid modernity. However, while Bauman argues that seduction tends to replace panoptic forms of control, he does posit that large parts of the population still require close control. Moreover Bauman and Munro probably underestimate the extent to which the new ICTs themselves are conditioned in the first place, and may subsequently be infiltrated by disciplinary power (Finlay 1987a, 1987b). Munro's is a good formulation, but over-dichotomous in its presentation of developments. And as with computer surveillance studies, his argument also relies on not granting to Foucauldian analysis the full richness of Foucault's ideas and formulations.

In contrast, in documenting what they call 'changes in the technoscape' Robins and Webster (1999) argue that the information revolution does not represent a profound break from the past, but a continuation of capitalism in many similar forms. Moreover, the prevailing virtual culture 'lacks critical edge with respect to the capitalist dynamics of the network society' (see also Feenberg 2002). If this is the case, then not only is Foucault not outdated, as some have suggested, but means of critical questioning such as he provides are vitally needed in the study of contemporary ICTs.

In looking at contemporary developments one can trace Foucault's influence into work on bio-power and technology. Best and Kellner (2001) argue otherwise and point out that while Foucault (1970) heralded the 'death of man' and the coming of post-humanism, he saw this as a merely conceptual transformation from one episteme to another, whereas the shift to post-humanism is also a *material* matter of new technologies erasing the boundaries between biology and technology. They argue that Foucault provides no analysis of information and communications technologies, and little consideration of the hybrid landscape of techno-bodies. However, Best and Kellner have to concede that Foucault considers both the enmeshment of the body in systems of discipline and surveillance, and ethical technologies of the self that cultivate 'new passions and new pleasures'.

Hayles (1999) rightly points out that the absorption of embodiment into discourse imparted interpretive power to Foucault, but also limited his analysis in significant ways. The universalization of the Foucauldian body is a direct result of concentrating on discourse rather than embodiment. Building on Foucault's work while going beyond it requires understanding how embodiment moves in conjunction with inscription, technology, and ideology. But, as we have seen, this is something that Zuboff's work largely achieves, while Sofoulis (2002) rightly points out Foucault's influence on Haraway (1991) and her subsequent development of his notions of bio-power and bio-politics in her post-Foucauldian notions of the 'informatics of domination' and 'techno-biopower'. Quinby (1999) has also reorientated Foucault's work on subject formation. She uses it to develop how 'technoppression' can occur in the pursuit of the programmed perfection enabled by digital and biotechnologies. A Foucauldian perspective is useful in questioning the race to human bodily perfection through technological means.

Finally, one can point to some interest in Foucault's work amongst those studying the Internet. The questioning here is whether the Internet, and 'cyberspace', is or will become a form of more intensive control and power relations—precisely Foucault's concern registered at the head of this chapter. The literature so far tends to have different interests and emphases. Three examples need suffice. Thus Aycock (1997) is interested in applying the later Foucault and his notions of technologies of the self to examine how on-line identities can be fashioned. Winokur (2003) applies yet again the concept of the panopticon, and concludes that the codes of cyberspace are not clearly a disciplinary discourse. Boyle (1997) is interested in legal issues, surveillance, levels of censorship, and the development of digital libertarianism. He argues that digital libertarianism is often blind to the effects of private power, but also the state's own power in cyberspace. In practice he finds that the state can often use privatized enforcement and state-backed technologies to evade some of the supposed practical and constitutional restraints on the exercise of legal power over the Net. He also argues that technical solutions to these dilemmas are neither as neutral nor as benign as they are often perceived to be.

CONCLUSION

In providing a critical review, this chapter has argued for the abiding relevance of Foucault's work and the usefulness of incorporating and developing further his thinking into contemporary studies of ICTs. This should be done as a critical act in three senses. Firstly, Foucault should not be applied uncritically. Following Barratt (2003), he should be worked with rather than copied. This chapter accepts the provisional, unfinished nature of many of his concepts and formulations, but also demonstrates how these can, and have been addressed in the study of ICTs, for example with the use of ethnography (Zuboff 1988), and, we would argue, through social construction approaches. Secondly, Foucault has been shown to be a critical weapon usable in an IS field not over-full of such tools (the same is not argued for OS/MS which have been much more critically aware). Moreover, as in the case of the Foucault-Habermas debates for example (Ashenden and Owen 1999), Foucault can be used to sharpen our critique of other, explicit or implicit social theories and philosophies perhaps borrowed from reputationally stronger reference disciplines, and used uncritically in a relatively new IS field. Finally, as we saw, Foucault can be employed in the ongoing debate over the nature of, and what it is to construct, an IS, or any other discipline.

Fundamentally Foucault reminds us, uncomfortably, of our epistemological frailty and ontological uncertainties, and from this can sensitize us to how much human use of ICT is a will towards control, certainty, and 'knowledge' in the face of considerable risk and ambivalence. If he does not deal explicitly with ICTs as hardware and software, he does provide a useful corrective against narrow definitions of technology and ICT applications. Instead of privileging material technology, he privileges the behavioural and social technologies encoded and embedded in material technologies. This provides an important corrective to recent 'digital economy' rhetorics about the transformative power of ICTs in themselves. Furthermore, his work suggests that all participate in the technologies that surround us, whether these are invisible or visible, whether we know it or not. Despite how he is generally presented, Foucault also urges us to acknowledge indeterminacy. There is, for example, nothing inevitable about technology trajectories.

Finally, while Foucault's work still awaits the further application it deserves in ICT studies, it is strange that his theorizations of knowledge, power, and discourse have not been utilized more productively in, for example, deconstructing knowledge management and related systems. In the ICT context knowledge awaits its genealogist, and this may be one of the richer veins yet to emerge from Foucault's potentially important contributions to the ongoing study of information and communication technologies and their applications as part of organizations. However, this is only one way forward and Foucault himself indicated how he would see his work being used 'a kind of tool box which others can rummage through to find a tool which they can use however they wish in their own area . . . I don't write for an audience, I write for users not readers' (quoted in Defert, Ewart, and Lagrange 1994).

Foucauldian studies on ICT will be more fundamentally distinguished by their critical intent, realized through their historical dimension, pursuing Foucault's concern to problematize the inevitability of the present and question how things have turned out to be as they are and not otherwise. He sought to create a history of the different modes by which human beings are made subjects. More particularly his work is concerned with studying classification, dividing, and self-subjectification practices across three fields of subjectivity, namely the body, population, and the individual (Foucault 1983). Since his death in 1984 we have seen an enormous growth in ICT capabilities, and their rising incursion into all aspect of life in the developed economies. Foucault's remit remains abidingly important and he leaves us with a 'toolbox' to help us confront a fundamental guiding question: how indeed can the growth of technological capabilities be disconnected from the intensification of power relations?

Notes

1. This chapter draws upon unpublished work by Eleni Lioliou and on a less developed, earlier paper by L. Willcocks, 'Michel Foucault in The Social Study of ICTs: Critique and Reappraisal', *Social Science Computer Review*, 24(3) (2006) Fall Special Issue.
2. 'Information Systems' here refers to those academics, researchers, teachers, students, and indeed practitioners who gravitate around conferences such as ICIS, ECIS, HICSS, PACIS, ACIS, tend to be members of the Association for Information Systems or related/similar bodies, write research papers and books consciously within an IS 'discipline', and publish in a self-defined group of 'IS' journals that may be global, regional, or national in stretch.
3. The remark applies easily to Foucault's own complex relationship to and usage of many thinkers, but especially of Nietzche and Heidegger: 'My whole philosophical development was determined by my reading of Heidegger. But I recognise that Nietzche prevailed over him' (Foucault (1985) Final Interview, *Raritan*, 8). Reading Nietzche through Heidegger's account of Nietzche may have been particularly influential. See Babich (2009).

References

Ashenden, S., and Owen, D. (eds.) (1999). *Foucault Contra Habermas: Recasting the Dialogue between Genealogy and Critical Theory*. London: Sage.

Avgerou, C., and McGrath, K. (2007). 'Power, Rationality, and the Art of Living through Socio-Technical Change', *MIS Quarterly*, 31(2): 295–315.

Aycock, A. (1997). Technologies of the Self': Foucault and Internet Discourse', *Journal of Computer Mediated Communication*, 1(2): 25–38.

Babich, B. (2009). 'A Philosophical Shock: Foucault Reading Nietzche, Reading Heidegger', in C. G. Prado (ed.), *Foucault's Legacy*. New York: Continuum.

Ball, K., and Wilson, D. (2000). 'Power, Control and Computer-Based Performance Monitoring: Reportoires, Resistance and Subjectivities', *Organization Studies*, 21(3): 539–65.

Barratt, E. (2003). 'Foucault, HRM, and the Ethos of the Critical Management Scholar', *Journal of Management Studies*, 40(5): 1069–87.

Bauman, Z. (1991). *Intimations of Postmodernity*. London: Routledge.

——(1999). *Globalization: The Human Consequences*. Cambridge: Polity Press.

Best, S., and Kellner, D. (2001). *The Postmodern Adventure: Science Technology and Cultural Studies at the Third Millenium*. London: Routledge.

Bloomfield, B., and Coombs, R. (1992). 'Information Technology, Control and Power: The Centralization and Decentralization Debate Revisited', *Journal of Management Studies*, 29(4): 459–84.

——— Knights, D., and Littler, D. (eds.) (1997). *Information Technology and Organizations*. Oxford: Oxford University Press.

Boyle, J. (1997). 'Foucault in Cyberspace: Surveillance, Sovereignty and Hard-wired Censors', *Cincinnati Law Review*. Cited in <wcl.american.edu/pub/faculty/boyle>.

Brooke, C. (2002a). 'What Does it Mean to Be "Critical"' in IS Research? *Journal of Information Technology*, 17(2): 49–58.

Brooke, C. (2002b). 'Critical Perspectives on Information Systems: An Impression of the Research Landscape', *Journal of Information Technology*, 17(4): 271–85.

Bulkeley, H., Watson, M., and Hudson, R. (2007). 'Modes of Governing Municipal Waste', *Environment and Planning*, 39: 2733–53.

Burrell, G. (1998). 'Modernism, Postmodernism and Oganizational Analysis: The Contribution of Michel Foucault', in A. McKinley and K. Starkey (eds.), *Foucault, Management and Organization Theory*. London: Sage.

Carter, C., McKinlay, A., and Rowlinson, M. (eds.) (2000). 'Special Issue and Introduction: Foucault, Management and History', *Organization*, Special Issue, 9(4): 515–26.

Clegg, S. (1989). *Frameworks of Power*. London: Sage.

——(1998). 'Foucault, Power and Organizations', in A. McKinley and K. Starkey (eds.), *Foucault, Management and Organization Theory*. London: Sage.

Cordoba, J., and Robson, W. (2003). 'Making the Evaluation of Information Systems Insightful: Understanding the Role of Power-Ethics Strategies', *Electronic Journal of Information Systems Evaluation*, 6(2): 55–64.

Dandeker, C. (1990). *Surveillance, Power and Modernity*. Cambridge: Polity Press.

Davies, L., and Mitchell, G. (1994). 'The Dual Nature of the Impact of IT on Organizational Transformations', in R. Baskerville, S. Smithson, O. Ngwenyama, and J. DeGross (eds.), *Transforming Organizations with Information Technology*. North Holland: Elsevier Science.

Deetz, S. (1998). '(Re)constructing the Modern Organization', in A. McKinley and K. Starkey (eds.), *Foucault, Management and Organization Theory*. London: Sage.

Defert, D., Ewald, F., and Lagrange, J. (eds.) (1994). *Dits et Ecrits 1954–1988*, vols. i–iv. Paris: Gallimard.

De Landa, M. (1991). *War in the Age of Intelligent Machines*. New York: Swerve Editions.

Deleuze, G. (1995). *Negotiations: 1972–1990*. New York: Columbia University Press.

Doolin, B. (1998). 'Information Technology as a Disciplinary Technology: Being Critical in Interpretive Research in Information Systems', *Journal of Information Technology*, 13(4): 301–12.

Dreyfus, H., and Rabinow, P. (1983). *Michel Foucault: Beyond Structuralism and Hermeneutics*. 2nd edn., Chicago, IL: University of Chicago Press.

Feenberg, A. (2002). *Transforming Technology: A Critical Theory Revisited*. Oxford: Oxford University Press.

Finlay, M. (1987a). 'Technology as Practice: And (So) What about Emancipatory Interest', *Canadian Journal of Political and Social Theory*, 11(1–2): 198–214.

——(1987b). *Powermatics: A Discursive Critique of New Communications Technology*. London: Routledge, Kegan & Paul.

Foucault, M. (1970). *The Order of Things: An Archaeology of the Human Sciences*. London: Tavistock. Original French version 1966.

——(1978). *The History of Sexuality*, i: *An Introduction*. New York: Pantheon Books. Original French version 1976.

——(1983). 'The Subject and Power', in H. Dreyfus. and P. Rabinow (eds.), *Michel Foucault: Beyond Structuralism and Hermeneutics*. 2nd edn., Chicago, IL: University of Chicago Press.

——(1996). *Foucault Live: Collected Interviews 1961–84*. New York: Semiotexte.

Gordon, C. (ed.) (1980). *Foucault: Power/Knowledge*. Selected Interviews and Other Writings 1972–7. Brighton: Harvester.

Grint, K., and Willcocks, L. (1995). 'Business Process Reengineering in Theory and Practice: Paradise Regained?', *New Technology Work and Employment*, 10(2): 99–109.

Haraway, D. (1991). *Cyborgs and Women: The Reinvention of Nature*. New York: Routledge.

Hardy, C., and Leiba-O'Sullivan, S. (1998). 'The Power behind Empowerment: Implications for Research and Practice', *Human Relations*, 51: 451–85.

Hayles, K. (1999). *How We Became Posthuman*. Chicago, IL: University of Chicago Press.

Harvey, L. (1998). 'Visibility, Silencing and Surveillance in an IT Needs Analysis Project', in T. Larsen, L. Levine, and DeGross, J. (eds.), *Information Systems: Current Issues and Future Challenges*. North Holland: Elsevier Science.

Heidegger, M. (1977). *The Question Concerning Technology and Other Essays*. New York: Harper Row.

Humphreys, A. (2006). 'The Consumer as Foucauldian Object of Knowledge', *Social Science Computer Review*, 24(3): 296–309.

Introna, L. (1997). *Management, Information and Power*. London: Palgrave.

——(2001). 'Truth and its Politics: Evolving Regimes of Truth at the MISQ', in D. Howcroft and A. Adam (eds.), *(Re)defining Critical Research in Information Systems*, Proceedings of the CRIS Workshop, University of Salford (July), 45–55.

——(2003). 'Disciplining Information Systems: Truth and its Regimes', *European Journal of Information Systems*, 12: 235–40.

Katz, S. (2001). 'Michel Foucault', in A. Elliott and B. Turner (eds.), *Profiles in Social Theory*. London: Sage.

Knights, D. (1990). 'Subjectivity, Power and the Labour Process', in D. Knights and H. Willmott (eds.), *Labour Process Theory*. London: Macmillan.

——and Murray, F. (1994). *Managers Divided: Organizational Politics and Information Technology Management*. Chichester: Wiley.

————and Willmott, H. (1997). 'Networking as Knowledge Work: A', in B. Bloomfield, R. Coombs, D. Knights, and D. Littler (eds.), *Information Technology and Organizations*. Oxford: Oxford University Press.

——and Vurdubakis, T. (1994). 'Foucault, Power, Resistance and All That', in J. Jermier, D. Knights, and W. Nord (eds.), *Resistance and Power in Organizations*. London: Routledge.

Klein, H., and Hunyh, M. (2004). 'The Critical Theory of Jurgen Habermans and its Implications for IS Research', in J. Mingers and L. Willcocks (eds.), *Social Theory and Philosophy for Information Systems*. Chichester: Wiley.

Kritzmann, L. (ed.) (1988). *Foucault: Politics, Philosophy, Culture: Interviews and Other Writings 1977–84*. New York: Routledge.

Lioliou, E., and Willcocks, L. (2009). 'IT Outsourcing Governance: How Contractual and Relational Elements Shape the Outsourcing Venture', *Global Sourcing Workshop*, Keystone, CO, 21–5 March.

Lyon, D. (1988). *The Information Society: Issues and Illusions*. Cambridge: Polity Press.

——(1993). 'An Electronic Panopticon? A Sociological Critique of Surveillance Society', *Sociological Review*, 41(4): 653–78.

——(1994). *The Rise of Surveillance Society*. Cambridge: Polity Press.

——(ed.) (2003). *Surveillance as Social Sorting*. London: Routledge.

——and Zureik, E. (eds.) (1996). *Computers, Surveillance and Privacy*. Minneapolis, MN: University of Minnesota Press.

McKinley, A., and Starkey, K. (eds.) (1998). *Foucault, Management and Organization Theory*. London: Sage.

Miller, P., and Rose, N. (2008). *Governing the Present: Administering Economic, Social and Personal Life*. Chichester: Wiley.

Mingers, J., and Willcocks, L. (eds.) (2004). *Social Theory and Philosophy for Information Systems*. Chichester: Wiley.

Morgan, G., and Willmott, H. (1993). 'The "New" Accounting Research: On Making Accounting More Visible', *Accounting, Audibility and Accountability Journal*, 6(4): 3–36.

Munro, I. (2000). 'Non-Disciplinary Power and the Network Society', *Organization*, 7(4): 679–95.

Poster, M. (1984). *Foucault, Marxism and History: Mode of Production versus Mode of Information*. Cambridge: Polity Press.

——(1990). *The Mode of Information: Poststructuralism and Social Context*. Cambridge: Polity Press.

——(1995). *The Second Media Age*. Cambridge: Polity Press.

——(2001). *What's The Matter with the Internet*. Minneapolis, MN: University of Minnesota Press.

Quinby, L. (1999). *Millenial Seduction*. Ithaca, NY: Cornell University Press.

Rabinow, P. (ed.) (1984). *The Foucault Reader*. London: Penguin.

Robins, K., and Webster, F. (1999). *Times of the Technoculture: From the Information Society to the Virtual Life*. London: Routledge.

Rose, N., and Miller, P. (1992). 'Political Power beyond the State: Problematics of Government', *British Journal of Sociology*, 43(2): 173–205.

Sakolosky, R. (1992). 'Disciplinary Power and the Labour Process', in A. Sturdy, D. Knights, and H. Willmott (eds.), *Skill and Consent: Contemporary Studies in the Labour Process*. London: Routledge.

Scott Morton, M. (ed.) (1991). *The Corporation of the 90s*. New York: Oxford University Press.

Scranton, P. (1995). 'Determinism and Indeterminacy in the History of Technology', in M. Smith and L. Marx (eds.), *Does Technology Drive History*. London: MIT Press.

Sewell, G., and Wilkinson, B. (1992). '"Someone to Watch over Me" Surveillance: Discipline and the Just-In-Time Labour Process', *Sociology*, 26(2): 271–89.

Sofoulis, Z. (2002). 'Cyberquake: Haraway's Manifesto', in D. Tofts, A. Jonson, and A. Cavallaro (eds.), *Prefiguring Cyberculture: An Intellectual History*. Cambridge, MA: MIT Press.

Townley, B. (1993). 'Foucault, Power/Knowledge and its Relevance for Human Resource Management', *Academy of Management Review*, 18(3): 518–45.

——(2000). 'Managing with Modernity', *Organization*, 9(4): 549–73.

Virilio, P. (2002). *Ground Zero*. London: Verso.

Walton, R. (1989). *Up and Running*. Boston, MA: Harvard Business School Press.

Webster, F. (2005). *Theories of the Information Society*. 2nd edn., London: Routledge.

——and Robins, K. (1993). '"I'll Be Watching over You": Comment on Sewell and Wilkinson', *Sociology*, 27(2): 243–52.

Willcocks, L. (2004). 'Foucault, Power/Knowledge and Information Systems: Reconstructing the Present', in J. Mingers and L. Willcocks (eds.), *Social Theory and Philosophy for Information Systems*. Chichester: Wiley.

Winokur, M. (2003). 'The Ambiguous Panopticon: Foucault and the Codes of Cyberspace', *CTheory.Net* (March): 1–29.

Zuboff, S. (1988). *In the Age of the Smart Machine: The Future of Work and Power*. New York: Basic Books.

··

CHAPTER 8

CRITICAL SOCIAL INFORMATION SYSTEMS RESEARCH

··

BERND STAHL

INTRODUCTION

··

THE term 'critical' has many different meanings. This chapter concentrates on a particular tradition, which is sometimes called 'critical theory' or 'critical research'. Even critical theory in the sense of the word used here has a long history going back to the ancient Greeks (Harvey 1990). This chapter gives an overview of the usage of the term in current information systems (IS) research and practice. In order to avoid ambiguities and to render it clear that this chapter addresses a particular research tradition, the chapter follows Klein (2009) in using the term 'critical social information systems research' (CSISR).

The chapter describes the main ideas of critical social research and its relevance in IS. It reviews the literature on CSISR in order to provide the reader with an in-depth understanding of the meaning and history of this tradition. At the same time it moves beyond the literature in suggesting that CSISR is characterized by one main feature, namely the intention to change social reality and promote emancipation, which sets it apart from other research approaches and traditions. This central feature can explain most if not all of the characteristics of CSISR which are discussed below. One notable consequence arising from the emancipatory intention is the ethical implication of CISIR. The overview of characteristics and definitions of CSISR is supplemented by a discussion of dominant topics, questions of methodology, and theory. Despite the wealth of theories that inform CSISR, one can identify some main lines of thought and the present chapter concentrates on the work of Jürgen Habermas which has influenced large parts of the CSISR discourse. The brief review of Habermas's work leads to a discussion of the ethical properties of CSISR. Habermas's writings provides a suitable ethical theory that can support CSISR. The chapter discusses problems of the approach and finishes with a critical reflection CSISR in general and this present narrative in particular.

Definitions and Characteristics of CSISR

Due to its long history, changing scope and wide range of areas of application it is difficult to find one specific definition of critical research that would satisfy all scholars engaged in it (Brooke 2002a). One can argue that critical theory is not really a theory at all but rather a collection of interlinked principles (Howcroft and Trauth 2004), which renders it even more difficult to define clearly. The typical approach is therefore to collect a number of characteristics that in most cases apply to critical work (Basden 2002). This chapter will follow that established approach but, instead of simply listing the different characteristics, it will argue that there is a hierarchy of importance and that the core characteristic of critical research in general and of CSISR in particular is linked to the emancipatory intent to change social reality. The other characteristics discussed below are only relevant insofar as they provide theoretical support or practical ways of implementing the emancipatory intention.

Critical Intention: Change Social Reality to Promote Emancipation

Emancipation is an ongoing and central theme within critical research, which is relatively independent of particular issues, topics, theories, or methodologies (Howcroft and Trauth 2004). This links directly to the intention to facilitate change. Critical social theory aims to 'bring about real change in the human condition' (Lee 1991: 276). This intention to change reality is based on the recognition of the problems caused or perpetuated by the status quo, of structural contradictions and existing restrictions, oppressions, and domination (Orlikowski and Baroudi 1991). The starting point of the critical approach is thus not to gain an unbiased view of an external reality but the perception that the reality we live in is not perfect and can be improved (Klein and Myers 1999). There is thus an important aspect that refers directly to the researcher's motivation for doing research and his or her perception of the world. To put it differently, 'critical stance is focused on what is wrong with the world rather than what is right' (Walsham 2005b: 112).

What is wrong about the world from the critical perspective is that human beings are not given the opportunity to live the best possible lives they could or to achieve their potential (Klein and Huynh 2004: 163). The term 'emancipation' denotes the attempt to give people this opportunity, to allow them to live up to their potential. CSISR tends to focus on the specific way in which information systems can have alienating or emancipating effects (Cecez-Kecmanovic 2005).

This aim of promoting emancipation raises a range of questions and issues. The most obvious one is that of the definition of emancipation. The definition of emancipation alluded to in the preceding paragraph is somewhat problematic because of its open nature. There are many attempts to provide a more detailed definition. Hirschheim, Klein, and Lyytinen (1995: 83), for example, define emancipation as 'all conscious attempts of human reason to free us from pseudo-natural constraints'. Hirschheim and Klein (1994: 98) suggest that emancipation has a psychological and an organizational dimension. It is plausible to assume that alienating circumstances can be found in the environment as well as the agent. Emancipation therefore needs to address issues of 'false or unwarranted beliefs, assumptions, and constraints' (Ngwenyama and Lee 1997: 151). Waring (2004) seems to suggest that emancipation is about avoiding or overcoming conflict. In any event, it is difficult to clearly describe what constitutes emancipation. Attempts to define it substantively run the risk of turning into a dictatorship of the intellectual (Stahl 2006), whereas more procedural approaches can lead to outcomes that the critical researcher can view as undesirable (Broadbent and Laughlin 1997).

Given that the central aim of promoting emancipation may be practically problematic and epistemologically impossible to ascertain, critical scholars tend to focus on more modest goals which are nevertheless conducive to emancipation. In a first step they typically aim to lay the groundwork of social change by exposing the status quo from an unorthodox position. CSISR therefore needs to come to a sound understanding of social reality, often going beyond the perceptions of the individuals who are involved in the situation. Restricting and alienating conditions need to be understood in a first step (Varey, Wood-Harper, and Wood 2002) in order to then be exposed as such. An underlying assumption of this approach is that individuals, in many cases members of organizations, fail to see that alternative social realities are conceivable. Once these are pointed out, they are nevertheless capable of apprehending them and using their newly found view of the world to develop to their own advantage (Cecez-Kecmanovic 2005). Exposing alienation, domination, and oppression implies a challenge that contains the opportunity to overcome them (Howcroft and Trauth 2008).

Given the exposure of problems of the status quo, a range of possibilities of addressing these and changing social reality are conceivable. Many of these (e.g. political revolutions) raise problems in their own right and contain the seed to different forms of alienation and oppression. Critical scholars therefore usually aim to bring about change in a non-violent way that is sensitive to the perceptions and preferences to the people affected, without necessarily accepting the extant world-views. In practice this means that the aim of change is realized by contributing to 'transformative redefinitions' (Alvesson and Deetz 2000). Such transformative redefinitions that allow alternative views of social realities that are more emancipatory than the status quo need to be co-created with the individuals and organizations in question (Cecez-Kecmanovic, Klein, and Brooke 2008).

The critical intention to change social reality and promote emancipation is the core defining feature of most critical research. It sets it apart from other research which is purely descriptive. Based on the belief that social reality can and should be improved, the concept of emancipation provides the focal point of CSISR. This chapter argues that all other characteristics of critical research require the critical intention to change social reality in order to be coherent. At the same time, the emancipatory intention is based on a number of assumptions and has consequences for a variety of important aspects of research. These constitute the other characteristics of CSISR which are elaborated below.

Ontological Assumptions of CSISR

The emancipatory intention is not logically or necessarily tied to a particular ontology. It is arguably conceivable to promote emancipation in a world-view based on an objective and observer-independent reality. However, in practical terms, critical scholars in management and information systems tend to rely on non-objectivist views of the world (Alvesson and Willmott 2003). This is one aspect in which they set themselves apart from most mainstream scholars in the same fields of study. One of the reasons why CSISR scholars are sceptical of an objectivist ontology is that it can be used to hide and remove from discussion the causes of alienation (Lee 1991). The dominant ontological position adopted by critical scholars is that of social constructivism or constructionism (Gergen 1999). The relevance of this ontological position is that it gives a foundation for the process of transformative redefinition. Only if reality is socially constructed can there be a point in trying to develop alternative construction (Saravanamuthu 2002a). At the same time, however, critical scholars realize that there are limits to the ability to construct and reconstruct reality. Alternative realities are possible but they are constrained by accepted views and perceptions which are often difficult to change (Myers and Avison 2002). The constructionist ontology thus raises problems because it has to contend with the existence of an external reality, which may be open to social intervention but which also has a prima facie objective existence. This can raise significant problems for critical research because it limits the possibility of social change.

One area where CSISR scholars pay particular attention to ontology is the question of the nature of technology. There has been some debate with the field of information systems in general what the role is of technological artefacts and how they can be theorized appropriately (Orlikowski and Lacono 2001; Ives et al. 2004). This debate is partly linked to the question of the ontological nature of technology and technological artefacts. There is probably no simple version of the ontology of technology that all critical scholars subscribe to. They are, however, united in their general rejection of a simplistic technological determinism (Cecez-Kecmanovic 2005). This rejection is based on the empirically well-supported view that identical technological artefacts can lead to vastly different social and organizational consequences (Doherty, Coombs, and Loan-Clarke 2006). While this raises complex questions whether the ontological nature of technology is flexible or only our interpretation of this nature (Cadili and Whitley 2005), the consequence remains that CSISR scholars are generally open to constructivist views of technology, such as those proposed by proponents of the social shaping of technology (SST) or the social construction of technology (SCOT) (Howcroft, Mitev, and Wilson 2004).

Epistemology of CSISR

There is a close relationship between ontology as the philosophical discipline concerned with the nature of being and epistemology as its sister discipline concerned with knowledge. It is thus not surprising that relevant epistemological positions in CSISR correspond with the dominant non-objectivist ontology. Critical scholars view knowledge as socially constructed, grounded in history, and strongly linked to theory (Orlikowski and Baroudi 1991). Research cannot be an independent description of an external reality but is a process of co-creation of relevant knowledge in which researcher and respondents are engaged simultaneously (Trauth and Howcroft 2006).

Given these thoughts, it is not surprising that critical scholars are close in many respects to phenomenological ideas. They consider the life-worlds of actors as important and realize that issues of oppression or emancipation need to be understood from the point of view of agents (Ngwenyama and Lee 1997). While the external world has a certain amount of stability beyond individual perceptions (otherwise all alienation or oppression could be overcome by appropriate redefinitions of the individual's world-view), it can only be described appropriately with reference to the multitude of perceptions that constitute it. The phenomenological approach has therefore been described as particularly conducive to critical work (Moreno 2004).

As a consequence of these epistemological assumptions, critical theorists tend to have a complex understanding of truth. A simple correspondence relationship between statements and external facts that characterizes the commonsense understanding of truth does not suffice. Truth is temporal and context bound. It is always being negotiated and dependent on viewpoints and theories (Chua 1986). These are positions that raise a number of fundamental questions with regards to approaches and validity of critical research, some of which are discussed below. Critical researchers typically claim that openness and transparency with regards to such positions are an important feature of the approach, which supports the claim to academic integrity. Moreover, as critical research is interested in changing social reality and therefore can easily turn into political practice, it is less important to follow general expectations of research and more important to be open about strengths and weaknesses of the position.

Totality and Historicity

Totality is often described as another characteristic of critical work. The concept of totality has a long and diverse philosophical tradition. In the context of CSISR it usually means that things cannot be split up and treated as isolated elements but that all things need to be understood in the context of all relationships they entertain (cf. Orlikowski and Baroudi 1991). In research practice this means that the artificial limitation of observations to particular aspects is always recognized as problematic. It may be necessary for pragmatic reasons to focus on particular issues or variables but these are always recognized to be parts of other contexts. The study of a specific information system in a particular organization, usually done by investigation of a range of data sources, can always be supplemented by an observation of the socio-economic context within which this organization works but also by the cultural environment and many other aspects.

An important part of the context that is implied in the concept of totality is that of the historical situation from which the research has developed. In order to understand the role of IS in organizations and societies and to improve understanding of alienation or emancipation, it is important to be aware of the historical roots of the current situation. This has direct links to the question of the concept of technology and interpretive flexibility. If the researcher is to understand why a particular interpretation of technology has become dominant, then historical knowledge of earlier systems, or relationships between employees and management and other relevant issues is helpful. Only such historical awareness can provide the breadth of understanding necessary to facilitate a successful redefinition of alienating circumstances.

The concept of totality can also serve as a link to phenomenological epistemology in that it reminds us that there are other aspects that need to be considered when trying to understand why a certain technology may alienate or emancipate individuals. An important aspect here is the fact of the embodied nature of humans and human understanding, a topic addressed by research inspired by existential phenomenology in Heidegger's tradition. Much mainstream research in computer sciences and information systems neglects this crucial fact and therefore cannot provide suitable concepts to understand alienation, for example when it occurs due to disabilities that are simply not captured by abstract and objectivist accounts of reality (Adam and Kreps 2006).

Reflexivity

A final characteristic of CSISR worth mentioning is that of reflexivity (Kvasny and Richardson 2006; Richardson and Robinson 2007). The brief attempt to outline and characterize CSISR so far has shown that in many cases the critical approach raises as many or more problems than it resolves. It does not provide a simple and algorithmic way forward. In fact, it often serves to create problems or at least raise awareness of them and explicitly refuses to be used as a problem-solving tool. Critical research is non-functional in that it often questions the very legitimacy of existing problem-solving approaches.

The critical approach therefore requires scholars to be aware of the issues raised by their approach and to consider ways of addressing them. Reflexivity is the term that is often used to describe this awareness. It extends to the entire research, including research question, motivation, assumptions, outcomes, and methods. Reflexivity means that critical scholars intentionally and expressly question their own views, their beliefs, and values and own up to their agendas and intentions (Cecez-Kecmanovic 2001). Reflexivity is thus very much about the application of critical thoughts to themselves. Where critical research is about questioning assumptions and beliefs and raising awareness of problems, these activities are aimed at the critical research process itself (Doolin and McLeod 2005).

CENTRAL CONCEPTS AND TOPICS OF CSISR

The critical intention to change social reality and further emancipation explains the characteristics of CSISR and at the same time gives rise to a set of important figures of thought that pervade critical thinking. They also inspire research in certain topics, notably those that have a direct bearing on the possibility of emancipation.

Ideology and Hegemony

Two central ideas worth exploring in more detail because of their relevance for critical thinking are ideology and hegemony. Ideologies are particular and dominant world-views that advantage some and disadvantage others (McLellan 1995; Freeden 2003; Hawkes 2003). Ideologies are not simply falsehoods. Rather, they constitute central parts of the shared world-view of a society or group (Stewart and Gosain 2006). As such they can often even be supported by empirical evidence (Gouldner 1976). They are accepted by that group or society as correct descriptions of reality. However, from a critical perspective they can be seen as partial and alienating. Good examples of ideologies are the stereotypes linked to race and gender. Such stereotypes, if generally accepted, structure the actions available to members of a particular race or gender, which can be oppressive. Not surprisingly, much CSISR work concentrates on such ideologies (Kvasny and Trauth 2002; Wheeler 2005; Howcroft and Trauth 2008). Critical scholars can provide alternative descriptions and conceptualizations that allow different understandings, which allow for a higher degree of emancipation.

This should not be misunderstood as positing that there is an ideology-free way of understanding the world and that criticalists have found the golden path to it. Ideologies are part of all collective constructions of reality and therefore a necessary consequence of a social constructivist world-view. They may even have positive consequences when they allow for the development of positive views of experiences (McAulay, Doherty, and Keval 2002). What critical thinking has to offer to address ideologies is reflexivity. Being open to question one's own assumptions means that one has the ability to recognize where these assumptions have ideological and alienating qualities and thus prevent emancipation. It also means that alternative concepts and views can be developed which overcome these problems. Addressing ideology is not a simple solution but an ongoing process which pervades critical research.

Ideologies can only persist if they evade critical questioning and analysis. They must blend into the background in order to remain stable. The mechanism by which this is achieved is sometimes called hegemony. Hegemony renders ideology invisible, often by rending it natural and beyond discussion. The concept of hegemony is closely linked to Gramsci's work whose main question was why people acquiesced to the oppression they were subjected to (Kincheloe and McLaren 2005).

There are many ways in which technology and information systems can have ideological qualities and hegemonic functions. Ideologies may be socially accepted views such as the legitimacy of hierarchical management or of the imperative of profit maximization. Technology can then serve as hegemonic means by supporting and rendering invisible such ideologies (Feenberg 1999; Saravanamuthu 2002a). At the same time, technology itself can have an ideological status, for example when technology is equated with progress and progress is assumed to be unquestionably desirable or when technology embodies contested social regulations, for example through digital rights management. Hegemonic means to uphold the ideological quality of technology can then be drawn from the environment in the form of customs, agreements, or the law (Thomson 1987).

Topics of CSISR

The emancipatory intention and the problem of achieving it in the light of ideology and hegemony give rise to a set of topics that critical scholars tend to be interested in. Havey (1990: 2) mentions the classics of class, gender, and race, which are central in CSISR as well. However, this chapter will concentrate on power, rationality, capitalism and the IS discipline itself, which are topics frequently addressed by current work in the area.

Power and control

Being subjected to oppressive power relationships is one of the main reasons for lack of emancipation. At the same time information systems can represent power relationships, arise from power struggles, and can effect changes in power structures. It is therefore not surprising that issues of power form a central topic of CSISR. Power is also one of the less visible aspects of IS, often hidden in technological features and not explicitly reflected upon by those affected by it. The critical approach is therefore well suited to research power issues (Doolin 1998).

Researching power in IS raises the question of a definition of the term. Critical scholars are aware that such a definition is difficult and may hide its own ideological baggage. Criticalists therefore tend to use a broad definition, such as Giddens's view that power 'is the capacity to achieve outcomes' (Giddens 1984: 257). Such a wide view captures most aspects of power and allows extending the lens of power to a range of issues where no direct exertion of force is recognizable. Power pervades relationships, organizations, knowledge structures, and is continually negotiated (Bloomfield and Coombs 1992).

A related concept is that of control. It has long been established that IS are 'subsystems of control systems' (Ackoff 1967: 150). Control may be a better term than power because of its more positive connotation. At the same time, it is easy to argue that IS are often designed to control people and processes. Control is a central concept in the management literature and it has formal and informal aspects, both of which are reflected in IS (Kohli and Kettinger 2004).

From the critical perspective control as well as power is not necessarily bad or problematic. The question of interest to CSISR scholars is how existing power and control structures are affected by technology. There is no simple equation between IS and control but a complex interplay between them (Bloomfield and Coombs 1992; Feenberg 1993). One can also observe that traditional control mechanisms aimed at behaviour are replaced by output-oriented control, which relies on the internalization of control mechanisms, which can be supported by IS (Jackson, Gharavi, and Klobas 2006). This type of control is closely linked to surveillance and self-surveillance, which lends itself to interpretations using a Foucauldian lens (see Chapter 7), which is of theoretical interest to critical scholars (Zirkle and Staples 2005).

The interest in power furthermore means that critical scholars have an interest in the political manifestations of power and their influence on technology. Given the emancipatory intent, engaging in political activities can be viewed as an important and sometimes necessary aspect of critical research (Saravanamuthu 2002b). This raises issues of what counts as political activities and at what point research turns into political activism (Richardson 2005).

The ongoing interest in power and control does not imply that critical scholars have a simplistic view of power. They are aware that power is always contextual and continually negotiated. The Foucauldian tradition of critical work has sharpened the awareness of the fact that all power can lead to resistance and that power is always a reciprocal relationship (Doolin 1998). Resistance and subsequent IS failure are recognized topics in mainstream IS research (Sauer 1993). Whereas resistance is typically described as a problem to be overcome in such research, the critical perspective tends to be more interested in the legitimacy and processes of resistance (Wilson 2002). Understanding the processes that lead to negative perceptions and eventually resistance is helpful in describing where IS are oppressive or emancipatory and therefore of high interest to critical scholars (Lapointe and Rivard 2005; Alvarez 2008).

Rationality

A central concern of critical research is to understand why oppressive and alienating structures are upheld. One of the main hegemonic mechanisms that serve this purpose in current western societies and particularly in commercial organizations is the prevailing rationality. This problematic rationality, sometimes called 'purposive rationality' is the means-ends oriented view of rationality, which accepts given ends and concentrates exclusively on the question which means are required to achieve these ends. As a consequence of the adoption of purposive rationality organizational goals are no longer questioned and are in a position to override all other concerns (Klein and Lyytinen 1985). This is problematic because emancipatory concerns are pushed aside but also because it portrays a view of reality that is not tenable (Kumar, van Dissel, and Bielli 1998; Avgerou and McGrath 2007). Walsham (1992: 41) has called this the 'myth of rationality in contemporary business organizations'. This myth has the purpose of legitimizing authority and thereby power and control. It serves the hegemonic purpose of hiding the fact that managerial decisions are always involved, contested, negotiated, and embodied (Introna 1997; Ciborra 2002; Avgerou 2005).

This purposive rationality is prevalent in both of the areas that much IS research is built upon, namely business and technology (Probert 2004). Purposive rationality can have ideological as well as hegemonic attributes. It serves as an ideology by projecting a desirable description of social reality in which people are meant to be 'rational'. Such a rationality and social choices based on it leave some people better off than others, which is one of the definitions of ideology. In addition purposive rationality is a strong vehicle of hegemony. It can be used to define which questions can legitimately be asked in an organizational context and thereby hide the fact that other questions may be just as pertinent. It is thus an instrument of power that serves to hide power behind a veil of accepted discursive practices (Paterson 2007). The critical perspective allows demonstrating that apparently neutral purposive rationality has in fact a political nature and that this political nature needs to be exposed.

Capitalism

A core issue that critical research has traditionally been interested in and that is of ongoing concern for CSISR is that of the capitalist constitution of society. Critical research has strong roots in Marxism which explains some of the traditional scepticism of market mechanisms. It is important to note, however, that very few critical scholars in IS today are Marxist in a strong sense and want to overthrow capitalism. Historical experience indicates that this may lead to more than problematic consequences. Moreover, it has been remarked that there are aspects of capitalism which are emancipatory and a fundamental change of the economic constitution of society may not be desirable (Thrift 2005). The general drift of CSISR scholars is therefore to investigate how IS support the pathologies of capitalism and how they can be used to overcome these.

A traditional topic of critique of capitalism is that it produces or at least is conducive to class societies. The struggle between capital and labour is perceived as a serious issue to be addressed. Saravanamuthu (2002a) points out that IS play a role in this struggle. The struggle between capital and labour is seen to be problematic because it perpetuates a conflict-oriented constitution of society that necessarily leads to winners and losers, often to the exploitation of workers, and therefore limits emancipatory ideas (Orlikowski and Baroudi 1991). One way of addressing such problems is to use IS to support workers and help trades unions (Robinson 2006).

An ongoing concern is that of the role of managers in organizations. While criticalists don't typically deny the need to coordinate work and activities, the dominance of managers is often seen as problematic. The traditional depiction of managers as heroes is problematic because it is based on the purposive rationality criticized earlier (Stahl 2005). Managerial power struggles can cause problems for those lower down in the organizational hierarchy (McAulay, Doherty, and Keval 2002). But the problem goes beyond these predictable issues. Managers themselves are oppressed by the unrealistic expectations levelled at them, which they often find impossible to fulfil (Introna 1997). And the whole construct of the rational leader may not even be conducive to the success of the organization and the optimal use it could make of technology (Zuboff 1988).

Capitalism furthermore leads to commodification, which stands for the change of an entity into a tradable commodity. Commodification often is accompanied by reification whereby a contested and negotiated social issue becomes a thing. Commodification often serves as a means of hegemony because it removes issues or entities from discourses. Commodification is not necessarily bad but it can be problematic where it renders entities subject to commercial contracts which are not universally accepted as such. Brooke (2002a), for example, cites the example of the human genome, which, partly through the use of ICT, has turned into a marketable commodity. Further examples include classics such as work (Greenhill and Wilson 2006) but also complex and abstract issues such as information itself (Attias 2004).

Digital divides

One area where the injustices of the current capitalist system are highly visible and where IS have the potential to greatly improve or exacerbate the situation is that of digital divides (Parayil 2005). Digital divides are often and misleadingly described as technological problems. The contribution of critical scholars to digital divides debates can be to show that it needs to be understood in the context of global capitalism. It is worth pointing out that digital divides issues are often couched in ideological terms and rely on a deterministic view of technology. Critical views can point out the problem of defining and measuring digital divides (McSorley 2003). Digital divides are furthermore directly linked to power differences (Keniston 2001).

Similar and related issues tend to arise from other uses of IS in development. Digital divides are normally expressions of social divides, be they within or between countries, and the IS use for development is in many cases based on the idea that this can overcome divides (Walsham 2001). Critical theorists have applied relevant theories to such problems, such as post-colonialism (Mayasandra, Pan, and Myers 2006). Due to the oppressive nature of developmental differences and the potential of IS to address these, it has been suggested that IS researchers in the area should adopt a broadly critical approach to their work (Walsham 2005b).

Critical analysis of the IS discipline

There are many more topics that critical scholars work on and that would be worth describing. For the sake of brevity, the last part of this section is concerned with the way critical scholarship has made a contribution to the development of the IS discipline itself. An ongoing theme of the application of critical theory to the IS discipline is its emancipatory potential. Computers and information technology can easily be envisaged as reducing power differences and improving the transparency of business processes (Lyytinen and Hirschheim 1988). This could lead to more liberated working practices, which would allow employees to contribute to the design of their work and help them reach their potential. In doing so, emancipatory IS would maximize the knowledge and input of employees, thus strengthening the organization. The emancipatory potential would not only affect employees but also management (Argyris 1971). However, the emancipatory potential of IS goes beyond commercial and organizational applications. They could be used to support governance structures in politics and civil society that would allow a more participatory regime and strengthen democratic forms of governance in NGOs, governments, and even internationally (Heng and de Moor 2003; Janson and Cecez-Kecmanovic 2005).

Despite this emancipatory potential, the ambivalent nature of IS is such that the oppressive uses of such technology often overshadow the emancipatory ones (Klein and Huynh 2004). Moreover, the idea of emancipation and traditional views of computer-based systems are often 'at odds with each other' (Dhillon and Backhouse 2001). The cause of a lack of emancipation is typically a lack of interest in emancipation, which leads to the choice of systems whose emancipatory potential has never even been considered. In order to overcome this, IS will thus need to engage in larger discourses that go beyond its traditional boundaries (Porra 1999).

The emancipatory potential of IS and its frequent lack of realization mean that criticalists need to look at the discipline itself if they are to be successful in moving emancipation onto the agenda. They do this by reinterpreting important phenomena such as IS failure (Brooke and Maguire 1998; Wilson and Howcroft 2002) and by offering alternative views and theories (Howcroft, Mitev, and Wilson 2004). They engage in internal discourses and expose ideological assumptions and attempt to contribute to new avenues for the discipline, for example by showing the managerialist assumptions of IS (Richardson and Robinson 2007), pointing out the politics involved in publishing (Introna 2003; Introna and Whittaker 2004), or analysing current debates such as the debate about rigour versus relevance in IS (Lyttinen and King 2004). This type of engagement with the IS discipline shows the reflexivity of IS research and can be understood as an attempt to improve the chances of emancipation through IS by engaging with other research traditions and underlining the implicit emancipatory promises that IS holds.

METHODOLOGIES OF CSIR

Research in IS as in most other social sciences needs to show (empirical) relevance and findings, if it is to be accepted. This raises the question of how data should be collected and analysed, a question that is represented by the discourse surrounding the notion of methodology. The issue of methodology represents a central problem of CSISR, partly because there is no such thing as a critical methodology (McGrath 2005). The problem goes beyond this, however, because the very idea of methodology is problematical from the critical perspective. This is caused by the ontological and epistemological stances espoused by criticalists and by the emancipatory intention of CSISR (Brooke 2002b).

An important connotation of the term methodology is that it provides an objective way of collecting data about the world, which will lead to an adequate description of the phenomena in question. Critical scholars tend to reject the implicit distinction between values and facts (Ngwenyama 1991). An even more substantial problem arises from the emancipatory intention to change social reality. This intention itself implies a value judgement about reality which is prior to empirical research. It is based on a particular world-view and thus informs all empirical research. The characterization of extant social relationships as problematic raises the question of the purpose of empirical critical research. If reality is to be changed, then how can knowledge about its current form inform us? Knowledge of perceptions of respondents using IS may be informative in a variety of ways but they cannot tell critical scholars in what way to steer changes.

The very idea of empirical research is thus problematic in CSISR, which may explain why no strong tradition of methodology has emerged. There are nevertheless widely shared views of methodology in CSISR. The most prominent one is the opposition to dominant positivism (Cecez-Kecmanovic 2001; Probert 2004). Criticalists object to the apparent objectivity of positivist research, which often uses quantitative measures to come to the appearance of exactness, which is rarely appropriate in social situations. The objectivist belief that social reality is independent of the observer and naive truth theories that are implied in positivism are rejected, and the ideological quality of positivist research, which can marginalize other voices is underlined. Positivist research adopts the purposive rationality rejected by critical research and thereby turns into a hegemonic tool for upholding the status quo (Cecez-Kecmanovic 2001).

Given this rejection of the positivist tradition, it is no surprise that CSISR scholars tend to be closer to the main alternative to positivism in IS, namely interpretivism. Interpretivism shares the social constructivist view of critical research. Interpretive data collection and analysis methods are therefore more suitable for critical research. This has led to the situation where the dividing line between critical and interpretive research has become fuzzy (Walsham 2005b) and a range of scholars have started to use terms such as 'critical interpretivism' (Pozzebon 2004; Doolin and McLeod 2005: 244). Like interpretivists, criticalists rely on hermeneutics and phenomenology to understand the meaning of social phenomena. There are, however, important differences between critical and interpretivist approaches to research. Interpretivists tend to concentrate on the individual or group perception of reality and are often not concerned with the greater social context, including issues such as class or the economic constitution of society. Hermeneutic analysis and theoretical critique can develop a dynamic interplay (Myers 2004) but this is not guaranteed. Also, the emancipatory agenda is not necessarily linked to the basics of interpretivism, which explains why there can be non-critical interpretive research. In practice one can divide two types of empirical critical social research in IS: language oriented and practice oriented.

Language-Oriented Methodologies

Language-oriented data collection methods are based on the constructivist tenet that reality is socially constructed using the medium of language. Critical research interested in obstacles to emancipation therefore needs to pay attention to the use of language that can embody or obfuscate ideology and hegemony, which lead to alienation and oppression. An important task of language-oriented empirical critical research is therefore to engage in ideology critique. The aim of ideology critique is to expose ideologies and show how they are produced and reproduced (Schultze and Leidner 2002). Ideology critique includes a critique of the ideologies of critical research (Castells 2000).

One established way of exploring linguistic issues from a critical perspective is to engage in critical discourse analysis (CDA). Critical IS scholars can draw on a rich body of literature on CDA (Fairclough 1993, 1995, 2003; Chouliarki and Fairclough 1999). There is significant research employing different approaches to CDA in order to critique aspects of IS. Thompson (2002), for example, exposes issues of power and financial interests in IS for development. Alvarez (2008) explores the role of power and control in an enterprise system, whereas Stahl (2007a) demonstrates how terms such as privacy and security can be used for ideological purposes.

A related stream of research investigates how linguistic constructs such as metaphors are used to promote particular views and thereby strengthen ideological positions. Examples include the use of the word 'virus' to denote self-replicating programs or 'piracy' for unauthorized copying of files. Both terms have normative connotations, they contain assumptions and lead to practical consequences that can empower some and disempower others (Klang 2003). While linguistic means can be used to disguise ideology, they can equally well be used by critical scholars to expose ideologies. Marcuse (2002: 194) pointed out that modern technology contains characteristics of 'magic, witchcraft and ecstatic surrender'. This theme has been taken up by critical IS scholars who have shown that unexpected reinterpretations of IS in terms of magic and myth may offer better understanding than the apparent economically rational mainstream view (Hirschheim and Newman 1991; Kaarst-Brown and Robey 1999). Other metaphors used by IS scholars and meant to overcome current discursive closures include biological ones (Porra 1999), as well as alternative descriptions of managerial activities as tinkering and bricolage (Ciborra 2000) or even as a chimpanzee's tea party (Drummond and Hodgson 2003).

Practice-Oriented Methodologies

While such language-based research and deconstruction of current discourses has the advantage of being able to expose ideological views and discursive closure (Watson and Wood-Harper 1996), it is often not clear whether and how it leads to manifest changes in the status quo. Critical scholars therefore also employ methods of research that allow them to directly engage in the research environment with the aim to actively promote emancipation. When engaging in practical activities to support emancipation using IS, critical researchers are faced with the problem or the blurry boundary between research, consulting, and political activism. In order to gain acceptance as researchers it is thus advisable to employ methods that allow describing such work in terms of research. The most prominent way of doing this is to use the label of action research. Action research can be seen as a reaction to a perception of social science research as being wedded to the status quo. In particular the Scandinavian tradition of action research was positioned as an attempt to overcome this and introduce democracy in the work place (Sandberg 1985). Action research is not the only conceivable research method that would lend itself to practice-oriented critical research in IS but it is the one with the most established links to critical theory. The interventionist nature to action research dovetails with the emancipatory intent of CSISR (Trauth 2001). A basic tenet of action research is that the respondents are co-constructors of knowledge and that the research process should allow them to reflect on their situation and improve it (Jönsson 1991; Oates 2004). Action research can be used to leverage the research process to ameliorate the lives of the people under investigation (Cushman and Klecun 2006) or, to put it differently, to help them in their emancipatory aims.

A Theoretical Basis of CSISR: The Theory of Communicative Action and Discourse Ethics

There is a range of theories that critical scholars in IS can draw on. Any theory that allows identifying critical concerns and promoting emancipation can count as a suitable one for critical research (Cecez-Kecmanovic, 2005). This includes theoretical approaches such as postmodernism, post-colonialism, queer theory, and many others. Critical theory can also be defined in a more narrow sense in which it refers specifically to theories developed following Marx and particularly in the Frankfurt School tradition

(Wiggershaus 1995; Falconer 2008). Despite the considerable number of theorists who are linked to the different generations of the Franfkurt school, the application of this narrower definition in CSISR refers mostly to one theoretical body, namely that developed by Jürgen Habermas. Habermas's work has dominated CSISR to the point where this perspective 'has become largely synonymous with the critical in IS' (Marcon, Chiasson, and Gopal 2004: 145). This chapter will concentrate on Habermas's work and its role in CSISR, mindful of the fact that there are other appropriate critical theories that CSISR can draw upon, some of which are discussed elsewhere in this book (cf. Wilcock and Lioliou's discussion of Foucault, Chapter 7 in this volume).

Habermas's Theory of Communicative Action

Habermas has developed an impressive body of work during his still ongoing research career. It is not possible to do him justice in the short space available here. This chapter will briefly outline some of the notable features of his work that have influenced research in IS. His main work developing much of his early writing and preparing later work is the Theory of Communicative Action (TCA) (Habermas 2006a). The central question that Habermas discusses is how human beings can and should collaborate. The starting point is the anthropological observation that humans need to collaborate to survive and prosper. Each human has his or her individual life-world, a term Habermas borrows from phenomenology, but life-worlds overlap due to socialization and communication. Communication is also required for collaboration. Habermas distinguishes different types of action based on communication which can serve different purposes. The most desirable type is that of communicative action. Communicative action is characterized by the ability and willingness of the interlocutors to listen to each other and accept each other as equally dignified beings.

In the course of communicative action people raise validity claims. Each utterance carries claims to truth, normative rightness, and authenticity. Such claims can be disputed by interlocutors. This is the point where discourses begin. Discourses are the forums in which contentious validity claims can be raised, attacked, and defended. Discourses can cover all of the validity claims, which means that they have epistemological functions (i.e. related to the truth of an argument), ethical functions (i.e. related to the normative acceptability of a statement), as well as performative ones (i.e. related to the authenticity of the speaker). The aim of engaging in discourses is to achieve a consensus on the contentious validity claim. This consensus is carried by the better argument. In order for discourses to be successful, they need to be held in an environment where all participants are willing and able to listen to each other and rationally argue about the problem in question. This is what Habermas calls the ideal speech situation. This ideal speech situation is counterfactual because it is never really achieved. Its function in the TCA is transcendental, which means that it is the condition of the possibility of discourses. Only when interlocutors believe that the other participants in discourses are willing and capable of reacting to their utterances in a rational and meaningful way, will there be a point in engaging in the discourse.

Habermas has developed these central ideas of the TCA in a number of directions. A direct result of the TCA is the crystallization of his views on ethics, which he calls discourse ethics (Habermas 2006c, 1983). He has also taken these ideas to analyse other aspects of social life such as the law (Habermas 2006d) and, most notably, political theory. His TCA can be seen as a theoretical basis of a social and democratic society and Habermas is a frequent participant of current political issues (Goode 2005; Habermas 2006b).

Habermas's influence on CSISR is hard to overestimate. His work offers a valid theoretical foundation that allows identifying and addressing issues of emancipation (Cecez-Kecmanovic, Janson, and Brown 2002). Discourses are the place where oppressive issues can be raised and exposed. At the same time, conditions of extant discourses can contribute to oppression. This can be pointed out using the TCA. Information systems can be described as means of communication and there is thus an obvious link between IS and the TCA. IS can be conducive to communication in that they increase the reach and participation in discourses but they can also limit the content and transmission of communication. The TCA has served as a guiding idea for the use and development of IS in a number of ways. One important aspect of this is the recognition that the experts' view cannot claim legitimacy without being open to scrutiny of other stakeholders. This has led to the emphasis of participation in IS research and development, where the critical approach has been linked to other existing participative work (Mumford and Henshall 1978; Lyytinen and Klein 1985; Hirschheim and Klein 1994; Mumford 2003; Stahl 2007b). Due to its democratic background, the TCA also lends itself to non-commercial IS application, particularly those that promote democratic participation (Heng and de Moor 2003).

There are limitations to the use of TCA in general and more specifically in IS. Habermas does not specifically analyse technology, much less information technology, which renders the applicability of some of his terms and ideas (e.g. the life-world versus system debate) problematic (Feenberg 2004). There are also more general questions, for example about the relationship between real and ideal discourses or the status of the ideal speech situation (Silva 2005). Some of these issues are discussed below.

DISCOURSES AND THE ETHICS OF CSISR

One aspect of critical research that is rarely addressed in CSISR but that pervades all critical work is that of ethics. The main feature of critical work, the attempt to improve the status quo and to promote emancipation, requires an ethical premiss. The intention to change is normative. It can be translated into a normative statement such as 'one should emancipate'. Such a normative premiss cannot be deduced from descriptive research. Instead, it is embedded in the very idea of the critical approach and precedes and influences all empirical work. Ethics is thus a fundamental building block of the critical approach. CSISR scholars on occasion acknowledge the ethical quality of their work. There are ethical issues related to the topics and objects of critical research, for example in power, rationality, and others (Varey, Wood-Harper, and Wood 2002). In addition, the relationship between researcher and respondent as co-creator of knowledge contains ethical aspects (Trauth and Howcroft 2006). The characteristic of reflexivity requires openness about moral stances (Cecez-Kecmanovic 2005).

Despite this ethical relevance of CSISR, there is little explicit recognition of the problems arising in conjunction with it. Stahl (2008a, 2008b) argues that there are several aspects of ethics in CSISR that deserve closer attention. These include the question of the shared 'good life' that criticalists aim for, the issue of norms and rules they deem supportive of emancipation, but also issues of theoretical identification of ethical issues and justification of norms. These are important issues that critical scholars need to take into account if they want to avoid inconsistencies developing in their approach. At the same time they require a familiarity with philosophical ethics that not all CSISR scholars have.

Habermas's work offers a suitable ethical approach that can give answers to these questions, which may be a further explanation of his ongoing popularity among criticalists. While most of the reception of his work centres on the TCA and his sociological work, discourse ethics is deeply interlinked with this and should thus be easy to import into IS (Adam 2005). Discourse ethics offers a range of advantages that render it useful for CSISR. It is based on Kantian ethics but overcomes its reliance on individual rationality. Discourse ethics is procedural, which means that it does not make substantive prescriptions on the nature of moral rules or ways of achieving emancipation. It is participative and offers guidelines on how participation can be structured. Its reliance on discourses means that the communicative features of IS can be used to their potential. Despite these advantages, there is currently very little work that incorporates discourse ethics into IS but interest seems to be developing (Mingers and Walsham 2008).

Questions and Reflections

Having introduced and discussed the aims, characteristics, and approach of CSISR, this chapter now reflects on problems and critique of the approach. Reflexivity has been shown to be a defining feature of critical research. This chapter does not represent a critical piece of research, rather a review article on the topic. As a paper in the critical tradition, it should nevertheless be open to question about the critical approach in general and the specific assumptions of this text in particular.

Intrinsic Problems in the Critical Approach

There are a number of intrinsic problems related to critical research and its application in IS. Research in the critical traidition is better characterized by its diversity and tensions than by commonalities (Cecez-Kecmanovic, Klein, and Brooke 2008). Many of the central terms are hard to define. For example, this chapter has argued that emancipation is at the heart of critical work but it has to concede that this is difficult and theoretically complex, hard to assess in practice and empirical research. Despite the central nature of emancipation, it is unlikely that criticalists would easily agree on what counts as emancipation and how researchers can contribute to it. A related ongoing issue is the question whether and how practical change is achievable. Many of the substantial social changes that critical theorists are interested in are furthermore beyond the reach of individuals or limited groups and require fundamental change in social relationships. In order to change labour relationships to become more democratic and participative, for example, external pressure may have to be brought to bear on the economic system (Mumford 2006). An added problem is that emancipatory progress can be reversed (Beekman and Mumford 1994; Mumford 2003). Criticalists have also been accused of ignoring their own advice by relying on traditional figures of thought (e.g. one-dimensional views of managers (Orlikowski and Baroudi 1991)) or trying to decree emancipation in a top-down manner (Brigham and Introna 2007).

In addition, there are a number of problems of the Habermasian stream of critical research that cause considerable debate within the CSISR community. The TCA is often perceived as an attempt to safeguard ideas of enlightenment that are no longer tenable. The idea that there is a privileged kind of rationality, namely communicative rationality, which overcomes the limits of purposive rationality has been doubted. Members of the critical community with affinity to 'postmodern' views which doubt the possibility of grand narrative have strongly questioned the possibility of an alternative conception of rationality. The application of the Habermasian conception of critical research has as a consequence been harshly criticized as totalizing and just another oppressive ideology (Wilson 1997). This problem goes to the heart of some of the internal debate among critical scholars, such as the one between Habermas and Foucault (Kelly 1994; Ashenden and Owen 1999). While such critique is understandable and there is a danger of emancipatory work turning into oppression (Stahl 2006), this view overlooks the necessity of taking a normative stance if change is to be achieved. Giving up the hope that there is a positive conception of rationality that overcomes current oppression renders the critical intention to promote emancipation impotent. Also, critics need to understand that Habermas's views are not substantively prescriptive, i.e. they do not tell us what to do. What Habermas aims to do is provide a framework that would allow us to come to an acceptable shared understanding of how we want to live our individual and collective lives. The procedural nature of the Habermasian approach ensures that all totalizing aspects it may contain can be opened to discourses and consequently addressed.

THE ROLE OF CSISR IN IS

Another open question of CSISR concerns its relationship with other approaches recognized in IS. As indicated earlier, much critical research arose from an opposition to the established approaches, notably to positivism. This opens a link to the paradigm debate in IS. Depending on one's definition of paradigms, one can argue that critical research and positivist research are compatible or incommensurable. While the epistemological and ontological assumptions of critical research are probably incommensurable with positivist assumptions (Stahl 2007c), the definition of CSISR in this chapter does not necessarily lead to this conclusion. If critical research is about emancipation, then there is no reason why a positivist approach could not be used to achieve this. Indeed, given the apparent scientific legitimacy of critical research, one can argue that critical scholars should employ positivist methods and arguments in order to be heard.

Another debate within the field of IS, one with more relevance to critical research, is that on rigour versus relevance, which is a core debate surrounding the nature and self-definition of the field (Benbasat and Weber 1996; Benbasat and Zmud 1999, 2003; Lyytinen and King 2004; Klein and Rowe 2008). While this debate revolves mostly about the question what relevance means and whether IS research is useful for managers, the issue of relevance has a particular undertone for critical research. Given its interventionist intention, critical research arguably requires practical consequences. This raises the difficult question of what counts as impact and how to measure it. Whatever the definition, there seems to be a perception of a lack of impact of CSISR (Lyytinen 1992; McGrath 2005; Frank 2006). A particular concern here is the apparent lack of empirical research which is seen as an obstacle to practical impact (Cecez-Kecmanovic, Klein, and Brooke 2008; Howcroft and Trauth 2008), even though Richardson and Robinson (2007) shed doubt on the extent of the problem. The problem may thus not be a lack of relevance and impact but a lack of visibility of the critical tradition in IS.

To some degree this discussion of relevance and impact of CSISR may be less important than it appears at first sight. Focusing on relevance in terms of measurable and direct impact on current practices runs the risk of implicitly accepting the positivist and linear view of the role of research. As Giddens (1984: 257) points out, the 'formulation of critical theory is not an option; theories and findings in the social sciences are likely to have practical (and political) consequences regardless of whether or not the sociological observer or policy-maker decides that they can be "applied" to a given practical issue.' A look at the IS research landscape also shows that this view is convincing. While the dominance of positivist, functionalist, and managerialist research in IS is hard to doubt, one also needs to acknowledge that alternative views have gained legitimacy. It is now possible to publish work in highly regarded IS journals that doubts the beneficial nature of technology, that questions the rationality of managers, and that emphasizes the lack of emancipation resulting from the use of IS. Furthermore, there is a significant body of work that points to the weaknesses of prevailing orthodoxy and recommends critical work as a way of overcoming its short-comings (Siponen 2005). Using the Habermasian lens outlined in this chapter, one can view CSISR as one type of contribution to the ongoing discourse in IS. As a discursive contribution, the critical perspective has to show that its validity claims can be supported by good arguments. It then stands to reason that it will prevail over less convincing arguments. The way that such discourses work is difficult, maybe impossi-ble to predict. One important mechanism in which academic discourses gain relevance is via their influence on students during teaching. Criticalists should not forget the importance of this often under-valued role of academic activity. At the same time, criticalists need to be sufficiently savvy to the ways of the world and use their conceptual apparatus to understand how their own discipline works and use this understanding to their advantage. One cannot overestimate the importance of academic institutions such as conference journals, etc. and critical scholars need to follow Walsham's (2005a) advice and actively engage in contributing to such institutions to ensure that the critical view continues to gain legitimacy.

The Self-Application of Critical Research

This last point leads to the role of the present chapter and a reflection of the identity and status of CSISR. This chapter can be read as a contribution to the ongoing struggle for legitimacy in IS. Its inclusion in the *Oxford Handbook* bestows legitimacy to the critical approach. At the same time such legitimacy raises problems of its own. By being recognized as legitimate, critical research can turn into a different type of orthodoxy and thus into the very thing it aims to overcome. To use a different terminology, one could argue that a chapter such as the present one shows that critical scholars have been successful in building a new regime of truth, that they are now holders of power. This is a position that many critical scholars may find unpalatable but that, given the analysis of social structures that criticalists engage in, may be recognized as unavoidable.

So what is the difference between the critical and the alternative regimes of truth? The main difference is in the focal attention to emancipation. Emancipation is not limited to the respondents in empirical research but also extends to the researchers themselves. Critical academics need to realize the rules of the academic games they engage in but they do not have to take them for granted and are encouraged to change them where they become oppressive. This may require gaining power first, but with the aim of using power to improve the status quo. While this noble goal may be forgotten on an individual level, the reflective nature of the critical approach means that asking for it will remain a constant feature. Critical research can thus not turn into the new orthodoxy, at least not without substantially changing its nature. This does not mean that all questions are answered. Quite to the contrary, substantial conceptual and empirical issues remain open. However, this should be seen as a motivator for more members of the IS community to engage in critical research, explore questions of emancipation, debate the ethical question where IS should be heading, question prevailing orthodoxy and conventional wisdom, and thereby contribute to a lively community which views beyond the immediate and the obvious and aims to contribute to a better life in modern technology-oriented societies.

REFERENCES

Ackoff, R. L. (1967). 'Management Misinformation Systems', *Management Science*, 14(4): 147–56.

Adam, A. (2005). 'Against Rules: The Ethical Turn in Information Systems', in D. Howcroft and E. Trauth (eds.), *Handbook of Critical Information Systems Research: Theory and Application*. Cheltenham: Edward Elgar, 123–31.

——and Kreps, D. (2006). 'Enabling or Disabling Technologies? A Critical Approach to Web Accessibility', *Information Technology and People*, 19(3): 203.

Alvarez, R. (2008). 'Examining Technology, Structure and Identity during an Enterprise System Implementation', *Information Systems Journal*, 18(2): 203–24. doi: 10.1111/j.1365-2575.2007.00286.x.

Alvesson, M., and Deetz, S. A. (2000). *Doing Critical Management Research*. London: Sage Publications Ltd.

——and Willmott, H. (2003). *Studying Management Critically*. London: Sage Publications Ltd.

Argyris, C. (1971). 'Management Information Systems: The Challenge to Rationality and Emotionality', *Management Science*, 17(6): 275–92.

Ashenden, S., and Owen, D. (1999). *Foucault Contra Habermas: Recasting the Dialogue between Genealogy and Critical Theory*. London: Sage Publications Ltd.

Attias, B. A. (2004). 'Technology and the Great Refusal: The Information Age and Critical Social Theory', in D. Tabachnick and T. Koivukoski (eds.), *Globalization, Technology, and Philosophy*. Albany, NY: State University of New York Press, 43–56.

Avgerou, C. (2005). 'Doing Critical Research in Information Systems: Some Further Thoughts', *Information Systems Journal*, 15(2): 103–9.

——and McGrath, K. (2007). 'Power, Rationality, and the Art of Living through Socio-Technical Change', *MIS Quarterly*, 31(2): 295–315.

Basden, A. (2002). 'The Critical Theory of Herman Dooyeweerd?', *Journal of Information Technology*, 17: 257–69. doi: 10.1080/0268396022000017770.

Beekman, G. J., and Mumford, E. (1994). *Tools for Change and Progress: A Socio-Technical Approach to Business Process Re-engineering*. Leiden: CSG Publications.

Benbasat, I., and Weber, R. (1996). 'Research Commentary: Rethinking Diversity in Information Systems Research', *Information Systems Research*, 7(4): 389.

——and Zmud, R. W. (2003). 'The Identity Crisis within the IS Discipline: Defining and Communicating the Discipline's Core Properties', *MIS Quarterly*, 183–94.

————(1999). 'Empirical Research in Information Systems: The Practice of Relevance', *MIS Quarterly*, 23(1): 3–16.

Bloomfield, B. P., and Coombs, R. (1992). 'Information Technology, Control and Power: The Centralization and Decentralization Debate Revisited', *Journal of Management Studies*, 29 (4): 459–84.

Brigham, M., and Introna, L. D. (2007). 'Invoking Politics and Ethics in the Design of Information Technology: Undesigning the Design', *Ethics and Information Technology*, 9 (1): 1–10.

Broadbent, J., and Laughlin, R. (1997). 'Developing Empirical Research: An Example Informed by a Habermasian Approach', *Accounting, Auditing and Accountability Journal*, 10 (5): 622–48. doi: 10.1108/09513579710194027.

Brooke, C. (2002a). 'Critical Perspectives on Information Systems: An Impression of the Research Landscape', *Journal of Information Technology*, 17(4): 271–83.

——(2002b). 'What Does it Mean to be 'Critical' in IS Research?' *Journal of Information Technology*, 17: 49–57.

——and Maguire, S. (1998). 'Systems Development: A Restrictive Practice?', *International Journal of Information Management*, 18(3): 165–80.

Cadili, S., and Whitley, E. A. (2005). 'On the Interpretative Flexibility of Hosted ERP Systems', *Journal of Strategic Information Systems*, 14(2): 167–95.

Castells, M. (2000). *End of Millennium, iii: The Information Age–Economy, Society and Culture.* 2nd edn., Oxford: WileyBlackwell.

Cecez-Kecmanovic, D. (2001). 'Doing Critical IS Research: The Question of Methodology', in E. M. Trauth (ed.), *Qualitative Research in IS: Issues and Trends.* Illustrated edn., Hershey, PA: IGI Publishing, 141–62.

——(2005). 'Basic Assumptions of the Critical Research Perspectives in Information Systems', in D. Howcroft and E. Trauth (eds.), *Handbook of Critical Information Systems Research: Theory and Application.* Cheltenham: Edward Elgar Publishing Ltd., 19–46.

——Janson, M., and Brown, A. (2002). 'The Rationality Framework for a Critical Study of Information Systems', *Journal of Information Technology*, 17(4): 215–27. doi: 10.1080/0268396022000017752.

——Klein, H. K., and Brooke, C. (2008). 'Exploring the Critical Agenda in Information Systems Research', *Information Systems Journal*, 18(2): 123–35. doi: 10.1111/j.1365-2575.2008.00295.x.

Chouliarki, L., and Fairclough, N. (1999). *Discourse in Late Modernity: Rethinking Critical Discourse Analysis.* Edinburgh: Edinburgh University Press.

Chua, W. F. (1986). 'Radical Developments in Accounting Thought', *The Accounting Review*, 61(4): 601–32.

Ciborra, C. (2002). *The Labyrinths of Information: Challenging the Wisdom of Systems.* Oxford: Oxford University Press.

——(2000). *From Control to Drift: The Dynamics of Corporate Information Infrastructures.* Oxford: Oxford University Press.

Cushman, M., and Klecun, E. (2006). 'How (Can) Nonusers Engage with Technology: Bringing in the Digitally Excluded', in E. Trauth, D. Howcroft, T. Butler, B. Fitzgerald, and J. DeGross (eds.), *Social Inclusion, Societal and Organizational Implications for Information Systems: IFiP TC8 WG 8.2 International Working Conference, July 12–15, 2006, International Federation for Information Processing.* New York: Springer, 347–64.

Dhillon, G., and Backhouse, J. (2001). 'Current Directions in IS Security Research: Towards Socio-organizational Perspectives', *Information Systems Journal*, 11(2): 127–53.

Doherty, N. F., Coombs, C. R., and Loan-Clarke, J. (2006). 'A Re-conceptualization of the Interpretive Flexibility of Information Technologies: Redressing the Balance between the Social and the Technical', *European Journal of Information Systems*, 15(6): 569–82.

Doolin, B. (1998). 'Information Technology as Disciplinary Technology: Being Critical in Interpretive Research on Information Systems', *Journal of Information Technology*, 13(4): 301–11.

——and McLeod, L. (2005). 'Towards Critical Interpretivism in IS Research', in D. Howcroft and E. Trauth (eds.), *Handbook of Critical Information Systems Research: Theory and Application*. Cheltenham: Edward Elgar Publishing Ltd., 244–71.

Drummond, H., and Hodgson, J. (2003). 'The Chimpanzees' Tea Party: A New Metaphor for Project Managers', *Journal of Information Technology*, 18(3): 151–8.

Fairclough, N. (1993). 'Critical Discourse Analysis and the Marketization of Public Discourse: The Universities', *Discourse and Society*, 4(2): 133–68.

——(1995). *Critical Discourse Analysis: The Critical Study of Language*. London: Longman.

——(2003). *Analysing Discourse: Textual Analysis for Social Research*. 1st edn., London: Routledge.

Falconer, D. (2008). 'A Demographic and Content Survey of Critical Research in Information Systems for the Period 2001–2005', *Communications of the AIS*, 2008, 22: 547–68.

Feenberg, A. (1993). *Critical Theory of Technology*. New York: Oxford University Press.

——(1999). *Questioning Technology*. 1st edn., London: Routledge.

——(2004). 'Looking Backward, Looking Forward', in D. Tabachnick and T. Koivukoski (eds.), *Globalization, Technology, and Philosophy*. Albany, NY: State University of New York Press, 93–105.

Frank, U. (2006). *Towards a Pluralistic Conception of Research Methods in Information Systems Research*. Duisburg: ICB.

Freeden, M. (2003). *Ideology: A Very Short Introduction*. Oxford: Oxford University Press.

Gergen, K. (1999). *An Invitation to Social Construction*. 1st edn., London: Sage Publications Ltd.

Giddens, A. (1984). *The Constitution of Society: Outline of the Theory of Structuration*. Cambridge: Polity.

Goode, L. (2005). *Jurgen Habermas: Democracy and the Public Sphere*. London: Pluto Press.

Gouldner, A. W. (1976). *The Dialectic of Ideology and Technology: The Origins, Grammar and Future of Ideology*. London: Macmillan.

Greenhill, A., and Wilson, M. (2006). 'Haven or Hell? Telework, Flexibility and Family in the e-Society: A Marxist Analysis', *European Journal of Information Systems*, 15(4): 379–88.

Habermas, J. (1983). *Moralbewußtsein und kommunikatives Handeln*. Frankfurt a.M.: Suhrkamp.

——(2006a). *Theorie des kommunikativen Handelns*, 6th edn. Frankfurt a.M.: Suhrkamp.

——(2006b). *Die Neue Unübersichtlichkeit: Kleine Politische Schriften V*. Frankfurt a.M.: Suhrkamp.

——(2006c). *Erläuterungen zur Diskursethik*. 4th edn., Frankfurt a.M.: Suhrkamp.

——(2006d). *Faktizität und Geltung: Beiträge zur Diskurstheorie des Rechts und des demokratischen Rechtsstaates*. 3rd edn., Frankfurt a.M.: Suhrkamp.

Harvey, L. (1990). *Critical Social Research*. London: Unwin Hyman.

Hawkes, D. (2003). *Ideology*. 2nd edn., London: Routledge.

Heng, M. S. H., and de Moor, A. (2003). 'From Habermas's Communicative Theory to Practice on the Internet', *Information Systems Journal*, 13(4): 331–52.

Hirschheim, R., and Klein, H. K. (1994). 'Realizing Emancipatory Principles in Information Systems Development: The Case for ETHICS', *Management Information Systems Quarterly*, 18(1): 83–109.

——and Lyytinen, K. (1995). *Information Systems Development and Data Modeling: Conceptual and Philosophical Foundations*. Cambridge: Cambridge University Press.

——and Newman, M. (1991). 'Symbolism and Information Systems Development: Myth, Metaphor and Magic', *Information Systems Research*, 2(1): 29–62.

Howcroft, D., Mitev, N., and Wilson, M. (2004). 'What We May Learn from the Social Shaping of Technology Approach', in J. Mingers and L. P. Willcocks (eds.), *Social Theory and Philosophy for Information Systems*. Chichester: Wiley, 329–71.

——and Trauth, E. M. (2004). 'The Choice of Critical Information Systems Research', in B. Kaplan, D. Truex, D. Wastell, A. Wood-Harper, and J. DeGross (eds.), *Information Systems Research: Relevant Theory and Informed Practice*. Boston, MA: Springer, 196–211; retrieved 21 January 2009 from <http://dx.doi.org/10.1007/b115738>.

——(2008). 'The Implications of a Critical Agenda in Gender and IS Research', *Information Systems Journal*, 18(2): 185–202. doi: 10.1111/j.1365-2575.2008.00294.x.

Introna, L. D. (1997). *Management, Information and Power: A Narrative of the Involved Manager*. London: Palgrave Macmillan.

——(2003). 'Disciplining Information Systems: Truth and its Regimes', *European Journal of Information Systems*, 12(3): 235–40.

——and Whittaker, L. (2004). 'Truth, Journals, and Politics: The Case of the MIS Quarterly', in B. Kaplan, D. Truex, D. Wastell, A. Wood-Harper, and J. DeGross (eds.), *Information Systems Research: Relevant Theory and Informed Practice*. Boston, MA: Springer, 103–20; retrieved 21 January 2009 from <http://dx.doi.org/10.1007/b115738>.

Ives, B., Parks, M. S., Porra, J., and Silva, L. (2004). 'Phylogeny and Power in the IS Domain: A Response to Benbasat and Zmud's Call for Returning to the IT Artifact', *Journal of the Association for Information Systems*, 5(3), 108–24.

Jackson, P., Gharavi, H., and Klobas, J. (2006). 'Technologies of the Self: Virtual Work and the Inner Panopticon', *Information Technology and People*, 19(3): 219–43. doi: 10.1108/09593840610689831.

Janson, M., and Cecez-Kecmanovic, D. (2005). 'Making Sense of e-Commerce as Social Action', *Information Technology and People*, 18(4), 311–42.

Jönsson, S. (1991). 'Action Research', in H. Nissen, H. K. Klein, and R. Hirschheim (eds.), *Information Systems Research: Contemporary Approaches and Emergent Traditions*. Amsterdam: North Holland, 371–96.

Kaarst-Brown, M. L., and Robey, D. (1999). 'More on Myth, Magic and Metaphor', *Information Technology and People*, 12(2): 192–217.

Kelly, M. (1994). *Critique and Power: Recasting the Foucault/Habermas Debate*. Cambridge, MA: MIT Press.

Keniston, K. (2001). 'Language, Power, and Software', in C. Ess and F. Sudweeks (eds.), *Culture Technology Communication: Towards an Intercultural Global Village*, SUNY series in computer-mediated communication. Albany, NY: State University of New York Press, 283–306.

Kincheloe, J. L., and McLaren, P. (2005). 'Rethinking Critical Theory and Qualitative Research', in N. K. Denzin and Y. S. Lincoln (eds.), *The SAGE Handbook of Qualitative Research*. 3rd edn., Thousand Oaks, CA: Sage Publications, 305–42.

Klang, M. (2003). 'A Critical Look at the Regulation of Computer Viruses', *International Journal of Law and Information Technology*, 11(2): 162–83.

Klein, H. K. (2009). 'Critical Social IS Research Today: A Reflection of Past Accomplishments and Current Challenges', in C. Brooke (ed.), *Critical Management Perspectives on Information Systems*. Oxford: Butterworth Heinemann.

——and Huynh, M. Q. (2004). 'The Critical Social Theory of Jürgen Habermas and its Implications for IS Research', in J. Mingers and L. P. Willcocks (eds.), *Social Theory and Philosophy for Information Systems*. Chichester: Wiley, 157–237.

——and Lyytinen, K. (1985). 'The Poverty of Scientism in Information Systems', in E. Mumford, R. Hirschheim, G. Fitzgerald, and T. Wood-Harper (eds.), *Research Methods in Information Systems: IFIP Colloquium Proceedings*. Amsterdam: North-Holland Publishing Co., 131–61.

——and Myers, M. D. (1999). 'A Set of Principles for Conducting and Evaluating Interpretive Field Studies in Information Systems', *MIS Quarterly*, 23(1): 67–93.

——and Rowe, F. (2008). 'Marshaling the Professional Experience of Doctoral Students: A Contribution to the Practical Relevance Debate', *MIS Quarterly*, 32(4): 675–86.

Kohli, R., and Kettinger, W. J. (2004). 'Informating the Clan: Controlling Physicians' Costs and Outcome', *MIS Quarterly*, 28(3): 363–94.

Kumar, K., van Dissel, H. G., and Bielli, P. (1998). 'The Merchant of Prato—Revisited: Toward a Third Rationality of Information Systems', *MIS Quarterly*, 22: 199–226.

Kvasny, L., and Richardson, H. (2006). 'Critical Research in Information Systems: Looking Forward, Looking Back', *Information Technology and People*, 19(3): 196.

——and Trauth, E. M. (2002). 'The Digital Divide at Work and Home: The Discourse about Power and Underrepresented Groups in the Information Society', in E. H. Wynn, E. A. Whitley, M. D. Myers, and J. I. DeGross (eds.), *Global and Organizational Discourse about Information Technology (International Federation for Information Processing)*. New York: Springer, 273–91.

Lapointe, L., and Rivard, S. (2005). 'A Multilevel Model of Resistance to Information Technology Implementation', *MIS Quarterly*, 29(3): 461–91.

Lee, A. S. (1991). 'Architecture as a Reference Discipline for MIS', in H. Nissen, H. K. Klein, and R. Hirschheim (eds.), *Information Systems Research: Contemporary Approaches and Emergent Traditions*. Amsterdam: North-Holland, 573–92.

Lyytinen, K. (1992). 'Information Systems and Critical Theory', in M. Alvesson and H. Willmott (eds.), *Critical Management Studies*. London: Sage Publications Ltd., 159–80.

——and Hirschheim, R. (1988). 'Information Systems as Rational Discourse: An Application of Habermas' Theory of Communicative Action', *Scandinavian Journal of Management*, 4(1/2): 19–30.

——and King, J. L. (2004). 'Nothing at the Center? Academic Legitimacy in the Information Systems Field', *Journal of the Association for Information Systems*, 5(6): 220–46.

——and Klein, H. K. (1985). 'The Critical Theory of Jürgen Habermas as a Basis for a Theory of Information Systems', in E. Mumford, R. Hirschheim, G. Fitzgerald, and T. Wood-Harper (eds.), *Research Methods in Information Systems: IFIP Colloquium Proceedings*. Amsterdam: North-Holland, 219–36.

McAulay, L., Doherty, N., and Keval, N. (2002). 'The Stakeholder Dimension in Information Systems Evaluation', *Journal of Information Technology*, 17(4): 241–55.

McGrath, K. (2005). 'Doing Critical Research in Information Systems: A Case of Theory and Practice not Informing each other', *Information Systems Journal*, 15(2): 85–101.

McLellan, D. (1995). *Ideology*. 2nd edn., Buckingham: Open University Press.

McSorley, K. (2003). 'The Secular Salvation Story of the Digital Divide', *Ethics and Information Technology*, 5(2): 75–87.

Marcon, T., Chiasson, M., and Gopal, A. (2004). 'The Crisis of Relevance and the Relevance of Crisis: Renegotiating Critique in Information Systems Scholarship', in B. Kaplan, D. Truex, D. Wastell, A. Wood-Harper, and J. DeGross (eds.), *Information Systems Research: Relevant Theory and Informed Practice*. Boston, MA: Springer, 143–59; retrieved 21 January 2009, from <http://dx.doi.org/10.1007/b115738>.

Marcuse, H. (2002). *One-Dimensional Man: Studies in the Ideology of Advanced Industrial Society*. 1st edn., London: Routledge.

Mayasandra, R., Pan, S. L., and Myers, M. D. (2006). 'Viewing Information Technology Outsourcing Organizations through a Postcolonial Lens', in E. Trauth, D. Howcroft, T. Butler, B. Fitzgerald, and J. DeGross (eds.), *Social Inclusion, Societal and Organizational Implications for Information Systems: IFiP TC8 WG 8.2 International Working Conference, July 12–15, 2006, International Federation for Information Processing*. New York: Springer, 381–96.

Mingers, J., and Walsham, G. (2008). 'Towards Ethical Information Systems: The Contribution of Discourse Ethics', in *ICIS 2008 Proceedings*. Paris: AIS; retrieved from <http://aisel.aisnet.org/icis2008/176/>.

Moreno, V. (2004). 'Realizing Emancipatory Ideals in Phenomenological IS Research', in *Proceedings of the Tenth Americas Conference on Information Systems*. New York: AIS, 4361–7.

Mumford, E. (2003). *Redesigning Human Systems*. Hershey, PA: IGI Publishing.

——(2006). 'The Story of Socio-technical Design: Reflections on its Successes, Failures and Potential', *Information Systems Journal*, 16(4): 317–42.

——and Henshall, D. (1978). *Participative Approach to Computer Systems Design*. London: Associated Business Press.

Myers, M. D. (2004). 'Hermeneutics in Information Systems Research', in J. Mingers and L. P. Willcocks (eds.), *Social Theory and Philosophy for Information Systems*. Chichester: Wiley, 103–28.

——and Avison, D. (2002). 'An Introduction to Qualitative Research in Information Systems', in M. D. Myers and D. E. Avison (eds.), *Qualitative Research in Information Systems: A Reader*. London: Sage Publications Ltd.

Ngwenyama, O. K. (1991). 'The Critical Social Theory Approach to Information Systems: Problems and Challenges', in H. Nissen, H. K. Klein, and R. Hirschheim (eds.), *Information Systems Research: Contemporary Approaches and Emergent Traditions*. Amsterdam: North-Holland, 267–80.

——and Lee, A. S. (1997). 'Communication Richness in Electronic Mail: Critical Social Theory and the Contextuality of Meaning', *MIS Quarterly*, 21(2): 145–67.

Oates, B. J. (2004). 'Action Research: Time to Take a Turn?', in B. Kaplan, D. Truex, D. Wastell, A. Wood-Harper, and J. DeGross (eds.), *Information Systems Research: Relevant Theory and Informed Practice*. Boston: Springer, 315–33; retrieved 21 January 2009, from <http://dx.doi.org/10.1007/b115738>.

Orlikowski, W. J., and Baroudi, J. J. (1991). 'Studying Information Technology in Organizations: Research Approaches and Assumptions', *Information Systems Research*, 2(1): 1–28.

——and Iacono, C. S. (2001). 'Research Commentary: Desperately Seeking the "IT" in IT Research—A Call to Theorizing the IT Artifact', *Information Systems Research*, 12(2): 121.

Parayil, G. (2005). 'The Digital Divide and Increasing Returns: Contradictions of Informational Capitalism', *The Information Society*, 21(1): 41–51.

Paterson, B. (2007). 'We Cannot Eat Data: The Need for Computer Ethics to Address the Cultural and Ecological Impacts of Computing', in S. Hongladarom and C. Ess (eds.), *Information Technology Ethics: Cultural Perspectives*. Hershey, PA: Idea Group Reference, 153–68.

Porra, J. (1999). 'Colonial Systems', *Information Systems Research*, 10(1): 38–69.

Pozzebon, M. (2004). 'Conducting and Evaluating Critical Interpretive Research: Examining Criteria as a Key Component in Building a Reserarch Tradition', in B. Kaplan, D. Truex, D. Wastell, A. Wood-Harper, and J. DeGross (eds.), *Information Systems Research: Relevant Theory and Informed Practice*. Boston, MA: Springer, 275–92; retrieved 21 January 2009 from <http://dx.doi.org/10.1007/b115738>.

Probert, S. K. (2004). 'Adorno: A Critical Theory for IS Research', in J. Mingers and L. P. Willcocks (eds.), *Social Theory and Philosophy for Information Systems*. Chichester: Wiley, 129–56.

Richardson, H. (2005). 'Consuming Passion in the "Global Knowledge Economy"', in D. Howcroft and E. Trauth (eds.), *Handbook of Critical Information Systems Research: Theory and Application*. Cheltenham: Edward Elgar Publishing Ltd., 272–98.

——and Robinson, B. (2007). 'The Mysterious Case of the Missing Paradigm: A Review of Critical Information Systems Research 1991–2001', *Information Systems Journal*, 17(3): 251–70.

Robinson, B. (2006). 'CYBERSOLIDARITY: Internet-Based Campaigning and Trade Union Internationalism', in E. Trauth, D. Howcroft, T. Butler, B. Fitzgerald, and J. DeGross (eds.), *Social Inclusion, Societal and Organizational Implications for Information Systems: IFiP TC8 WG 8.2 International Working Conference, July 12-15, 2006, International Federation for Information Processing)*. New York: Springer, 123–35.

Sandberg, A. (1985). 'Socio-Technical Design, Trade Union Strategies and Action Research', in E. Mumford, R. Hirschheim, G. Fitzgerald, and T. Wood-Harper (eds.), *Research Methods in Information Systems: IFIP Colloquium Proceedings*. Amsterdam: North-Holland, 79–92.

Saravanamuthu, K. (2002a). 'Information Technology and Ideology', *Journal of Information Technology*, 17: 79–87.

——(2002b). 'The Political Lacuna in Participatory Systems Design', *Journal of Information Technology*, 17: 185–98.

Sauer, C. (1993). *Why Information Systems Fail: A Case Study Approach*. Henley-on-Thames: Alfred Waller Ltd.

Schultze, U., and Leidner, D. E. (2002). 'Studying Knowledge Management in Information Systems Research: Discourses and Theoretical Assumptions', *MIS Quarterly*, 26(3): 213–42.

Silva, L. O. (2005). 'Theoretical Approaches for Researching Power and Information Systems: The Benefit of a Machiavellian View', in D. Howcroft and E. Trauth (eds.), *Handbook of Critical Information Systems Research: Theory and Application*. Cheltenham: Edward Elgar Publishing Ltd., 47–69.

Siponen, M. T. (2005). 'Analysis of Modern IS Security Development Approaches: Towards the Next Generation of Social and Adaptable ISS Methods', *Information and Organization*, 15(4): 339–75.

Stahl, B. C. (2005). 'The Obituary as Bricolage: The Mann Gulch Disaster and the Problem of Heroic Rationality', *European Journal of Information Systems*, 14(5): 487–91. doi: DOI 10.1057/palgrave.ejis.3000560.

——(2006). 'Emancipation in Cross-cultural IS Research: The Fine Line between Relativism and Dictatorship of the Intellectual', *Ethics and Information Technology*, 8(3): 97–108.

——(2007a). 'Privacy and Security as Ideology', *IEEE Technology and Society Magazine*, 26(1): 35.

——(2007b). 'ETHICS, Morality and Critique: An Essay on Enid Mumford's Socio-technical Approach', *Journal of the Association for Information Systems*, 8(9), 479–90.

——(2007c). 'Positivism or Non-Positivism—Tertium Non Datur: A Critique of Philosophical Syncretism in IS Research', in R. Sharman, R. Kishore, and R. Ramesh (eds.), *Ontologies: A Handbook of Principles, Concepts and Applications in Information Systems*. New York: Springer, 115–42.

——(2008a). *Information Systems: Critical Perspectives*. Routledge Studies in Organization and Systems. London: Routledge.

——(2008b). 'The Ethical Nature of Critical Research in Information Systems', *Information Systems Journal*, 18(2): 137–63.

Stewart, K. J., and Gosain, S. (2006). 'The Impact of Ideology on Effectiveness in Open Source Software Development Teams', *MIS Quarterly*, 30(2): 291–314.

Thompson, M. (2002). 'ICT, Power, and Developmental Discourse: A Critical Analysis', *The Electronic Journal of Information Systems in Developing Countries*, 20: 347.

Thomson, A. (1987). 'Critical Legal Education in Britain', in P. Fitzpatrick and A. Hunt (eds.), *Critical Legal Studies*. Oxford: Blackwell, 183–97.

Thrift, N. J. (2005). *Knowing Capitalism*. London: Sage Publications.

Trauth, E. M. (2001). 'Choosing Qualitative Methods in IS Research: Lessons Learned', in E. M. Trauth (ed.), *Qualitative Research in IS: Issues and Trends*. Hershey, PA: IGI Publishing, 271–87.

——and Howcroft, D. (2006). 'Critical Empirical Research in IS: An Example of Gender and the IT Workforce', *Information Technology and People*, 19(3): 272.

Varey, R. J., Wood-Harper, T., and Wood, B. (2002). 'A Theoretical Review of Management and Information Systems Using a Critical Communications Theory', *Journal of Information Technology*, 17: 229–39.

Walsham, G. (1992). *Interpreting Information Systems in Organizations*. Chichester: John Wiley and Sons.

——(2001). *Making a World of Difference: IT in a Global Context*. Chichester: John Wiley and Sons.

——(2005a). 'Development, Global Futures and IS Research: A Polemic', *Journal of Strategic Information Systems*, 14(1): 5–15.

——(2005b). 'Learning about Being Critical', *Information Systems Journal*, 15(2) : 111–17. doi: 10.1111/j.1365-2575.2004.00189.x.

Waring, T. (2004). 'From Critical Theory into Information Systems Practice: A Case Study of a Payroll-Personnel System', in B. Kaplan, D. Truex, D. Wastell, A. Wood-Harper, and J. DeGross (eds.), *Information Systems Research: Relevant Theory and Informed Practice*. Boston: Springer, 555–75; retrieved 21 January 2009 from <http://dx.doi.org/10.1007/1-4020-8095-6_30>.

Watson, H., and Wood-Harper, T. (1996). 'Deconstruction Contexts in Interpreting Methodology', *Journal of Information Technology*, 11(1): 59–70. doi: 10.1080/026839696345432.

Wheeler, D. L. (2005). 'Gender Matters in the Internet Ages Voices from the Middle East', in M. Torseth and C. Ess (eds.), *Technology in a Multicultural and Global Society*. Trondheim: Norwegian University of Science and Technology, 27–42.

Wiggershaus, R. (1995). *The Frankfurt School: Its History, Theory and Political Significance*. New York: Polity Press.

Wilson, F. A. (1997). 'The Truth is Out There: The Search for Emancipatory Principles in Information Systems Design', *Information Technology and People*, 10(3): 187–204. doi: 10.1108/09593849710178207.

Wilson, M. (2002). 'Rhetoric of Enrollment and Acts of Resistance: Information Technology as Text', in E. H. Wynn, E. A. Whitley, M. D. Myers, and J. I. DeGross (eds.), *Global and Organizational Discourse about Information Technology (International Federation for Information Processing)*. Dordrecht: Springer, 225–48.

——and Howcroft, D. (2002). 'Re-conceptualising Failure: Social Shaping Meets IS Research', *European Journal of Information Systems*, 11(4): 236–50.

Zirkle, B., and Staples, W. G. (2005). 'Electronic Monitoring in the Workplace: Controversies and Solutions', in J. Weckert (ed.). Hershey, PA: Idea Group Publishing, 79–100.

Zuboff, S. (1988). *In the Age of the Smart Machine: The Future of Work and Power*. New York: Basic Books.

CHAPTER 9

HERMENEUTICS AND
MEANING-MAKING IN
INFORMATION SYSTEMS

LUCAS D. INTRONA

INTRODUCTION

IT is rather surprising that hermeneutics only came to the attention of the Information Systems (IS) community in the 1980s and early 1990s, mostly through the work of Richard Boland (1985, 1987, 1991, and 1993). Why is this surprising? It is surprising because hermeneutics is about the rendering meaningful of a text (object or phenomenon), which has become obscured or 'distanced' in some way, thereby making it no longer immediately obvious. One would imagine that the transformation of large amounts of data into measures, reports, etc., by information technology in organizations, would have constituted such a process of 'distancing' and hence call for, or at least point to, the need for hermeneutics. Moreover, since IS research (in contrast to computing research) is essentially a social science, in which researchers are always in some sense 'distanced' from the social phenomena they are studying, one would have imagined that hermeneutics would also have emerged earlier as relevant for IS researchers.

How can one explain this late arrival, as it were, of hermeneutics? One answer to this question is the fact that computers were early on rather narrowly framed, or conceived of, as large calculating machines that were merely automating calculations (transforming one set of numbers into another set of numbers) in a more or less innocent or obvious way. The use of these numbers for decision making, etc., was not seen as properly in the domain of the computer experts. As such we see an emphasis on the design of transformation rules or computer programs (and information defined in terms of these algorithmic transformations). This separation became increasingly untenable as the importance of the user and the use-context impinged on the attempt to objectively define the 'right' set of transformations. In terms of research methodology one can also explain the late arrival of hermeneutics by reference to the total dominance of positivism in the field until at least the late 1980s (indeed, which in some form or another still dominates the field). These explanations are undeniably helpful but they do not yet help us understand why it is that the understanding of information systems, and research phenomena, in this algorithmic and positivistic sense was so obviously correct for the early IS research community. How is it that they did not sense or problematize this 'distance' that would have made hermeneutics emerge as a possible answer? This is where we need to look to understand why hermeneutics is relevant—one might even suggest unavoidable—for the discipline.

For these early researchers and system developers the numbers on the screen (or in the computer-generated report) and the numbers on the Likert scale of the research questionnaire were direct expressions of the world as such. Hence, there was, for them, never a 'distance' to be breached, in some way or another. For them these numbers were immediately obvious as 'mirrors of the reality' (Rorty 1979) they were supposed to stand for or represent. Differently stated one might say that for them these numbers were basic 'facts' that did not need further elaboration as such—the facts 'spoke for themselves', as it were. Obviously, the way these facts became incorporated into the organizational decision-making and use context was an issue but this was not seen as the sort of problem with which these early researchers and the developers ought to concern themselves as such. This was a matter of politics, a problem for managers and society more generally. For them the facts were the facts, and how they were valued and used were located in a different domain, a domain that ought to be clearly separated form the objective world of facts. In other words for them the fact/value divide was obvious and they were squarely on the side of facts.

Studies in the use of information by managers as well as an ongoing critique of positivism by qualitative researchers made this divide or dualism less and less tenable (Mintzberg 1973; Boland 1985, 1987, 1991, and 1993). For example Boland in his 1993 paper 'Accounting and the Interpretive Act' demonstrated that managers use all sorts of contextual cues and prejudices (or prejudgements) to make sense, and come to particular understandings, about supposedly objective accounting facts—i.e. that the facts did not in the end speak for themselves. He showed that the managers made the facts speak through a creative and subtle process of ongoing 'meaning making'. In other words they found themselves indeed in some way 'distanced' from the reality those accounting facts were supposed to mirror or represent; as such they had to somehow make these facts contemporaneous to their own concerns, situation, and so forth. More specifically stated, those facts (by the very virtue of their existence) implicated a world or context, yet, the implicated world or context, to which the facts refer, is not given in the facts as such—hence the need for some process of recontextualization or reorientation. Given these results it was obvious to Boland and others in the IS research community (such as Winograd and Flores 1986; Lee 1994; Myers 1995; Introna 1997; and others) that there was a need for an explanation (or theory) that would account for this recontextualization or 'meaningful making' process—i.e. it was obvious to them that there was a need for hermeneutics.

Besides the pioneering work of Richard Boland there have been a number of papers in the IS literature which were more or less located within the hermeneutic tradition. For example, there is the early work by Winograd and Flores (1986) that made use of a Heideggerian hermeneutics to study interpretation and how this is situated in managerial work (especially with regard to speech acts). Myers (1994, 1995) also showed how hermeneutics can be used to make sense of failed IT implementations as well as suggesting it as a basis for a more general theory of implementation. Lee (1994) used hermeneutics to demonstrate the richness and social complexity of e-mail communication. Introna (1997) showed how managers draw on hermeneutics as an ongoing meaning making process in dealing with organizational texts. Others, such as Butler (1998) and Klein and Myers (1999) have made arguments for hermeneutics as an important part of the interpretive research tradition. Although all of this work is encouraging, it is still rather disappointing (and surprising) that hermeneutics have essentially remained on the periphery of the information systems qualitative research community. Our suggestion would be that this is due to the fact that there is still not a sufficient understanding and appreciation of the important contribution that hermeneutics can make, both methodologically and theoretically.

The purpose of this chapter is to introduce IS researchers to the field of hermeneutics. Given the scope of this chapter, this must be seen as merely a rough outline sketch, a useful starting point (or orientation). For a more in-depth treatment of the subject refer to Palmer (1969), Bleicher (1980), or Schmidt (2006).

This chapter is structured as follows. We start by sketching out a brief history of hermeneutics. We highlight and acknowledge that hermeneutics, as the art or practice of interpretation, is an intellectual tradition that goes back to early Greek philosophy—indeed it has a long and illustrious history. We proceed to indicate that the question of hermeneutics emerges in moments of 'breakdown' or distanciation where the text is rendered strange or obscure and seemingly in need of interpretation. Next we suggest that there are different views as to what it is that is being 'recovered' in the process of interpretation. There are those who argue that a text has an objective meaning (the original author's intentions) and those that argue that the meaning is situated and relative. We proceed to propose that the development of hermeneutics can be characterized as a gradual expansion of the nature of the 'text' to be interpreted: from the notion of obscure (often religious) texts through to seemingly obscure texts (such as art and music) through to everyday life and the self/other as a text; or from a methodology for interpreting obscure texts to an ontology of social life as fundamentally hermeneutic. In this movement of hermeneutics we put forward the work of three particular authors: Gadamer, Heidegger, and Ricoeur. We show how they, in their own particular but related way, understood the significance of hermeneutics, its constitutive nature, as well as what it was supposed to achieve. We close the chapter with some conclusions and implications for IS researchers—both for their research practice and their objects of study.

A VERY BRIEF EARLY HISTORY
OF HERMENEUTICS

Most simply put, hermeneutics is the art or practice of interpretation. The origin of the word hermeneutics lies in the Greek verb *hermeneuein*, generally translated as 'to interpret'. Palmer (1969: 13) explains that the verb *hermeneuein* and the noun *hermeneia* are derived from the name of the wing-footed messenger-god Hermes, which was supposed to take the language of gods and make it accessible to mere mortals. Thus, Hermes is associated with the function of transmuting what is beyond human understanding into a form that humans could grasp. The various forms of the word suggest the process of bringing a text, a thing, a situation, or a concept from unintelligibility to intelligibility.

The history of the use of the word 'hermeneutics' goes back a long way. Indeed, it can be traced back to the Socratic philosophers. In the course of the Middle Ages and the Renaissance, hermeneutics emerges in the theological tradition as a branch of biblical studies. Within this tradition hermeneutics referred to a set of principles/rules used to interpret the Bible and other sacred texts. Later, the use of the word broadened to refer to non-biblical texts where the meaning was seen as 'hidden' or obscure and therefore not apparently obvious. To be sure the history of hermeneutics can be characterized, or understood, by this *gradual expansion of the phenomena deemed somehow 'obscure' and in need of interpretation* as well as the nature of the outcome of such a process of interpretation. Let us briefly review a few of the 'early' fathers of hermeneutics before we consider some of the more recent work relevant to our purpose.

Schleiermacher (1799–1834) was a philosopher who conceived hermeneutics as being the science or art of understanding. Schleiermacher contended that the principles of understanding remain the same, whether the aim is to understand a legal document, religious scriptures, or a work of literature. As Palmer (1969: 86) points out, for Schleiermacher understanding as an art has the intention of *re-experiencing the mental processes of the author of the text*—the recovery of the authorial intentions. One might say that it is, in a sense, the reverse of composition, for it starts with the fixed and finished expression and goes back to the mental life from which such expressions arose. The interpretation is the result of two interacting processes of interpretation; the one is a grammatical (or philological) interpretation of the text and its structure, the other is in a sense a psychological interpretation of the author and authorial intentions. For Schleiermacher the psychological interpretation is a reconstruction of the thinking processes of the author within his or her total life-context.

The philosopher and literary historian *Wilhelm Dilthey* (1833–1911) saw in hermeneutics the foundation for the *Geisteswissenschaften* (humanities and social sciences). Dilthey believed that the use of the techniques of the natural sciences, or 'positivistic' techniques, to study the human sphere was invalid. In opposition to these approaches, he sought a way to use concrete, historical, and lived experience as the basis for understanding the *Geisteswissenschaften*. Although he rejected positivistic techniques, he still believed the requirement of objectivity to be of paramount importance. In hermeneutics he saw the methodological basis for understanding the phenomenon of humankind. As Palmer (1969: 101) explains:

> The problem of understanding man [human kind] was for Dilthey one of recovering a consciousness of the 'historicity' of our own existence which is lost in the static categories of science. We experience life not in the mechanical ahistorical categories of science but in complex, individual moments of 'meaning,' of direct experience of life as a totality and in loving grasp of the particular. These units of meaning require the context of the past and the horizon of the future expectations; they are intrinsically temporal and finite, and they are to be understood in terms of these dimensions that is, historically.

Dilthey believed the key word for human studies was *understanding*, as opposed to explaining. Natural sciences, he suggested, must *explain* nature, human studies on the other hand must *understand* humanity in its expression of life, in its creation of meaning, and in the complete experience of life within a comprehensive historical context. Human *experience*, and the understanding thereof, is for Dilthey the basic unit of meaning in the methodology of human studies. When referring to the concept 'experience', Dilthey uses the German word *Erlebnis* which can be more accurately translated as 'immediately lived experience'. Palmer (1969: 107) explains it in the following manner: 'In other words, a meaningful experience of a painting, for instance, may involve many encounters separated by time and still be called an "experience" (*Erlebnis*).' *Erlebnis* should not be seen as the 'content' of a reflexive act of consciousness, for then it would be something of which one is conscious. *Erlebnis* is rather the ongoing act of experiencing as such; it is the direct contact with life which we call 'lived experience'. It is clear from the above that Dilthey saw the 'text' to be interpreted as the *Erlebnis* or ongoing 'lived experience' of human beings as the most concrete connection with life itself. If one is to succeed in understanding this text, one could make sense of, or understand, human beings in their human way of being, which is for him the task of human studies or *Geisteswissenschaften*. Dilthey's contribution, focusing on life (via *Erlebnis*) as the 'text' to be interpreted, prepared the way for Heidegger and Gadamer, whose views will be discussed in the sections below. However, before we do this it might be useful to pause and reflect on the emergence of the need for interpretation and the possible outcome (and the status of the outcome) of such an interpretive process.

On the Need for Meaning Making/Interpretation

Interpretation and 'breakdown'

Why is interpretation necessary? Maybe, as a first step, one could start with a traditional *functionalist* model of communication. Put simply, a sender (author) encodes a message in symbols, words, or signs to communicate to the receiver something which the sender feels the receiver ought to know. On receiving this text the receiver must somehow 'unlock' or interpret the symbols, words, or signs so as to understand or attribute the 'correct' meaning to the communicated symbols, words, or signs. If the message is correctly interpreted we say the message was understood; the concept of 'meaning' and 'correctness' is purposefully left open at this stage of the discussion. Now it is obvious to many that this communication process is subject to many sources of 'disturbance' that may undermine its success. Some of the sources—which in itself can be debated—of disturbances could be: a limited set of symbols to communicate an unlimited set of intentions or meanings. There may not be a word, symbol, or sign available to which both the sender and receiver would attach the same meaning to encode a meaning that they wish to communicate; a time lapse between sending and receiving—the elapsed time may be seconds or even centuries (as is the case in the Bible or the Koran); a changing (evolving) set of relationships between words, symbols, or signs and the meanings they refer to; different frames of reference or contexts used by sender and receiver in the communication process; and so forth.

These disturbances can cause the communication process to 'break down' or fail. It is in such instances that one could argue for the need of some sort of 'interpretation' process to correct the 'failed' communication process. This seems sensible, yet, it could also be argued that all communication is inherently 'failed' communication and thus in need of interpretation—i.e. that all communication is disturbed in some way or another. It is possible to suggest that all these forms of disturbances (listed above) are more or less present in all forms of communication and signification. This is perhaps why Gadamer (1989: 350) claims that 'all understanding is [already] interpretation'—we will take up this suggestion below.

How does this interpretation in moments of distancing or breakdown happen? What is *it* that is understood? Is understanding always, in some way, the 'recovery' of meaning, or the author's intentions? In the discussion to follow, the symbols, words, signs involved in the process will be referred to as the 'text' that is in need of interpretation. The 'text' could be a spoken text, a written text, or even an enacted 'text' (i.e. actions)—indeed, as was suggested above, the development of hermeneutics can be seen as a progressive expansion of what is considered 'text' in the process of interpretation. It is obviously true that there are definite differences involved in the interpretation of these different types of 'texts' (or *text analogues* as they are often referred to), yet it is also true, or so argues Gadamer, that there is always a common set of principles involved, namely hermeneutics.

On the 'what' of the 'recovery' process

Before thinking through the interpretation 'process' it may be useful to step back and highlight a more fundamental, and often implicit issue. What is the intention, aim, or object of the interpretive process? Or differently stated: what is *it* that is recovered? These questions can be located in a broader context of the ongoing debate between objectivism and relativism. Objectivism is the basic conviction that there is some more or less permanent, ahistorical matrix or framework to which one can ultimately appeal in order to determine the correctness or truth of any claim (to reality). Relativism is the basic conviction that the determination of the correctness or truth of a claim to reality is always relative to some conceptual scheme, theoretical framework, paradigm, society, or culture.

Based on these definitions, the objectivist would say that when a text is interpreted, the text will have an intrinsically constant, and to large degree ahistorical meaning—often described as the original author's intentions. Thus, when two different persons from different historical periods attempt to understand the same text, they should both strive to unlock the objective, inherently there, meaning of the text. An objectivist would therefore argue that if they understand the text differently, then one or both of them were unsuccessful in retrieving the objective meaning of the text. Furthermore, the objectivist would say that an interpretation is correct or true if, and only if, the meaning that the interpreter attributes to the text is indeed the same, or corresponds to the meaning, that the author of the text intended in the creation of the text (the question whether it is possible for the author to 'know' what he or she intended will be discussed again below).

The relativist would contend that the meaning of a text evolves or changes as the historical, social, political, or moral context in which it is interpreted adapts and changes. Thus, in different historical contexts, different interpretations can legitimately be made. For example, Ricoeur (1981), whom we will discuss below, describes interpretation as a process of *appropriation* (rather than a re-enactment):

> The term 'appropriation' underlines two additional features [of interpretation]. One of the aims of all hermeneutics is to struggle against cultural [or any other contextual] *distance*. This struggle can be understood in purely temporal terms as a struggle against secular [linguistic] estrangement, or in more genuinely hermeneutical terms as a struggle against the estrangement of meaning itself, that is, from the system of values upon which the text is based. In this sense, interpretation 'brings together', 'equalises', renders 'contemporary and similar', thus genuinely making one's own what was initially alien. Above all, the characterisation of interpretation as appropriation is meant to underline the 'present' character of interpretation. (p. 159)

Through appropriation the interpreter renders the text relevant to the local, here and now—i.e. their own life-world. Indeed, the relativist would suggest that this is all that the interpreter can achieve—i.e. that we are always to a greater or lesser extent entrapped in our own context (prejudices, beliefs, values, etc.). It must however be noted that the relativist position does not mean that 'anything goes'. It merely states that the meaning is relative to a given context. The interpreter cannot remain ignorant or naive of this given context. The interpreter always has an obligation to show and make explicit (account for) how the meaning relates to, and derives from, the given context in a more or less compelling way.

In the section to follow this objectivist/relativist debate will always be implicitly or explicitly present in the discussion. Nevertheless, it can be argued that the work of

Heidegger (1962) and Wittgenstein (1967), which will emerge in the discussion, does offer some indication on how to overcome this Cartesian-based dualism by showing that we are always in a relational position with respect to text (object) and context in which they are each other's constitutive condition. There is no need (or point) to privileging the one or the other; they need and define each other.

From the discussion of the communication process above it seems that interpretation comes into play in moments of breakdown when the involved actor gets distanced from the involvement whole–the world shifts from being simply available and self-evident (ready-to-hand in Heidegger's (1962) terminology) to being unavailable (present-at-hand in Heidegger's (1962) terminology). In such moments of 'breakdown' we are often 'startled' as the world leaps forth in its unavailableness. For example a sign indicates something unexpected, or a person does something that does not make sense in a given context. How do we deal with this breakdown? We engage (often implicitly) in an interpretive process to restore the availability (or sense) of the world.

Interpretation and the 'Loss' of Meaning?

Interpreting obscure texts: art and music

In order to think through this notion of the 'recovery of sense or meaning' it may be helpful to start by examining some obvious examples of interpretive situations. A simple, and seemingly obvious, example is the interpretation of a work of art. When a painter paints a canvas, she is expressing meaning through the lines, texture, and colours (or signs) that she uses. If a person is confronted with this work of art, should one *only* strive to interpret or decode the meaning that the painter intended? How can we know what that is? It is such an ambiguous text. Clearly, it would seem limiting to most to suggest that the only possible meaning that can be construed from the work of art is that which the creator 'intended' at the time of creation. That is, if it is at all possible for the creator to determine for certain what she 'intended' as such. In interacting with the work the artist must also interpret or 'discover' what she intended, as she is also, in a sense, 'alienated' from the work as she completes it.

Is it not possible that the artist merely creates a medium from which many meanings can evolve or jump to life as each individual interprets the work of art 'for themselves'? It seems that even the creator can, at different times, interpret different meanings emanating from the work of art, and can in doing so, possibly discover more of herself, or of the subject of the work of art. Often one hears artists say of another's interpretation of their work, 'after hearing this interpretation I think I now have another, or even a better understanding of what I meant when I created the work of art', implying that the artists are in fact discovering more of themselves (or their subjects) through the interpretations of others. This reaction seems quite intelligible since most of the skills involved in creating the work of art, as well as the knowledge of the subject matter, are obviously quite tacit by nature.

Now one may say that this could be true for paintings, since painting is a unique type of expression where the signs (colour, texture, and lines) are very ambiguous and open to many different interpretations. However, if one looks at a music score, where the signs (notes, tempo, and rhythm) are much less ambiguous, there is still talk of different interpretations of the same piece of music, even talk of a 'good' or 'better' interpretation of a piece of music. This does not mean that one makes judgements based on private 'subjective' liking but that one does acknowledge that there can be different, sometimes conflicting judgements about the meaning of a piece of music. Did the composer in creating the music not merely create a spectrum of possibilities, some of which he may have been consciously aware of and some of which he may not have been consciously aware of? If this is true, then it is indeed possible that there may not be one 'correct' or 'right' interpretation. From this brief discussion of art and music we might conclude that the interpretation of art and music may not simply be a 'recovery' of lost meaning (due to breakdown). Rather, the interpretation of art or music is the 'making alive' of the text (art or music) in which *the interpreter seems actively involved*. It may however be argued that art and music are obviously tacit or inconspicuous by nature and therefore requires interpretation, but what about ordinary language? Surely, everyday language is much more clear-cut than art and music?

Interpretation and everyday language

In language, it seems, that we have a relatively clear-cut relation between the signifier (sign) and that signified, the word and that which it 'stands' for. Hence, one may want to argue that interpretation in situations of everyday language should pose much less of an interpretation problem than would art and music. Wittgenstein (1967) argues that this view of language is correct yet only for a very primitive language-game. If language were to function merely as clear and unambiguous pointers to objects (things, situations) in the world it will almost certainly break down in everyday use. Everyday language is not primitive–it is rich and subtle. It is 'constructed' intrinsically as part of *what we do*. Language is a game in which the 'language and the actions into which it is woven' are fused together. To speak a language is not to only to construct and utter grammatically good sentences. We always speak in a situation as part of doing whatever we are doing; speaking like doing is always already immersed in the situated practices in which it functions. We have 'lawyer-speak','nurse-speak','shopping-speak', 'fishing-speak', and so forth. These are many different 'forms of life' each with its own language-game. There is a way (words and rules for using these words) that the theatre nurse may use to say 'prepare this patient for the operating theatre' in the form of life called 'nursing'. It may be something like 'prep her!' Everyday language is a bricolage of the various language games we participate in as part of our everyday going about in the world.

In speaking, as part of doing in the world, we do not stop to decide the words and rules for their application. As socialized beings we always already know what to say/do because we participate in practices (including discursive practice) of the forms of life as part of our ongoing being-in-the-world. As Wittgenstein (1967) explains: 'So you are saying that human agreements decide what is true and what is false? [when speaking about something] It is what human beings say that is true and false; and they agree in the language they use. [But] that is not agreement in opinions but in form of life'. When, as part of the doing—within a form of life—the language-game breaks down, language will 'jump out' and require clarification or interpretation. However, it mostly does not, it mostly simply makes sense and is simply the way we speak inherently as part of ongoing practice. In situations of breakdown, however, language becomes a 'text' in need of interpretation. The important point is that the interpretive act cannot be severed from the form of life within which the language-game is constituted as a meaningful way of speaking and doing.

Gadamer (1989: 145), using different terminology, argues the same point:

> The difference between a literary work of art and any other text is not so fundamental. It is true that there is a difference between the language of poetry and the language of prose, and again between the language of poetic prose and of 'scientific' prose. These differences can certainly also be considered from the point of view of literary form. But the essential difference of these various 'languages' obviously lies elsewhere: namely, in the distinction between the claims of truth that each makes. All literary works *have a profound community* [forms of life] in that the linguistic form makes effective the significance of the contents to be expressed. In this light, the understanding of texts by, say, a historian is not so very different from the experience of art [or a paper in the language of mathematics]. And it is not mere chance that the concept of literature embraces not only works of literary art, but everything that has been transmitted in writing.

Taking what is said above and reflection on the aim of this chapter it becomes clear that the individual's engagement with an information system (as a particular type of text) is also an instance that requires interpretation. For example, the manager, considering a production report, is also to a greater or lesser extent 'distanced' from the form of life where the 'text' originates (the 'shop floor' as it is commonly referred to). The 'facts' in the report are constructed through the application of processing rules. As such it becomes disembedded from the form-of-life of the shop floor and needs to be re-embedded in the form-of-life of management. The manager must attempt to recontextualize it from 'shop floor-speak' into 'management-speak'. This might be more or less difficult to do. This problem of incommensurability of language-games, due to their rootedness in particular forms of life, will be a theme that will permeate all the discussions in some way or another as we proceed. In my opinion it is at the heart of the problem faced by all information systems in organizations—indeed it is at the heart of the virtualization process more generally. It is also at the heart of all social science research, including IS research.

To sum up: we mostly understand our actions and we understand our language because we already 'share' a world, we are always already in it. Interpretation becomes necessary in moments of breakdown, when as part of speaking and doing this tacit understanding breaks down. Interpretation is part of ongoing action as much as speaking is part of ongoing action. They are all rooted in forms of life, in our ongoing manner of being-in-the-world—we will return to this issue again below. To understand how this ongoing interpretive process happens we will now turn to three different authors: Gadamer, Heidegger, and Ricoeur. Each of these authors will take us on a slightly different path, which would lead to a different understanding of hermeneutics. Gadamer will emphasize the importance of our rootedness in tradition (our fore-understanding); Heidegger emphasizes the importance of our emersion in the world as being that we already understand the world in a particular way; and Ricoeur emphasizes the need to be critical of exactly that tradition and rootedness in which we already find ourselves when we interpret.

GADAMER AND HERMENEUTIC UNDERSTANDING

In the discussion above, on the interpretive situation, it was argued that interpretation comes into play when a certain 'distancing', 'fissure', or 'breakdown' occurs. It was suggested that in interpretive situations such as trying to understand art or music this distancing seems to be relatively self-evident. It was also argued, with reference to the work of Wittgenstein on language, that even the meaning of everyday language is not as self-evident as it seems. Indeed its self-evidence originates in its embeddedness in everyday forms of life, for those immersed in it, that is. However, when we encounter the form of life from the outside (as an outsider) then the meaning of the language is not self-evident at all and might require significant amount of interpretation. Now that we have a sense of the interpretive situation we can turn more specifically to the idea of interpretation, and the 'process' of interpretation, as articulated by Gadamer (1989)—see also Wranke (1987) for a good introduction to Gadamer.

Interpretation as the Appropriation of Meaning

For Gadamer a text is a text only to a reader; one is a reader only if a text is being read. For him there is an I/Other relationship in the act of understanding. In the confrontation of the I and Other there always occurs, to some degree, a fusion of worlds or horizons. In interpreting a 'text' the interpreter (the I) must 'reroot' it in the horizon or world of the author (the Other), yet do this exactly from within the world in which the interpreter (the I) is already fully immersed in. Since the text is just a series of movements, sounds, or letters of ink on paper it has no intrinsic 'already there' context attached to it. The meaning of a text is therefore, in principle, *always incomplete*. Simply put: the text does not 'speak for itself'. The meaning of the text rather comes into being or is constituted *by the very act of interpretation* or understanding itself; by the different interpreters as they bring to bear their own horizons, points of view, or forms of life on the text. Gadamer (1989: 146) explains it as follows:

> As we were able to show that the being of the work of art is play which needs to be perceived by the spectator in order to be completed, so it is universally true of texts that only in the process of understanding is the *dead trace of meaning* transformed back into living meaning. . . . Is this true also of the understanding of any text? Is the meaning of all texts realised only when they are understood? In other words, does understanding belong to the meaning of a text just as being heard belongs to the meaning of music? Understanding must be conceived as part of the process of coming into being of meaning, in which the significance of all statements—those of art and those of everything else that has been transmitted—is formed and made complete.

But if every interpreter completes the meaning of the text then the result will be a very partial and prejudiced understanding of the text. For Gadamer it is important that we make explicit the role of our fore-understanding and 'prejudices' (or prejudgments) in the interpretive process. The word prejudice here must not be seen in the normally held negative sense. Gadamer uses it merely to describe the 'first stab' or initial understanding or interpretation that the interpreter must *necessarily* make because we are always already immersed in our prejudices. This 'first stab' understanding or prejudice will, however, become negative if the interpreter does not continually open herself to the potentiality of new understanding that may emerge. Does this mean that Gadamer is proclaiming a sort of subjectivism or a relativist approach to understanding? As Bernstein (1983: 125) concludes: 'For it would seem that if the meaning of a work of art or text is affected by, or conditioned by, the understanding of its meaning, then there does not seem to be any meaning that has "objective" integrity, that is "there" in the work of art or text to be understood.'

This is, however, not the case. What Gadamer is saying is that one can simply not escape from one's prejudices (a better translation of the German word *Vorurteil* that Gadamer uses would be 'prejudgment', i.e. the anticipation of meaning which may or may not be substantiated by further experience). Gadamer's point would seem to be that anything new can *only* be understood in terms of what one already 'knows'. The first 'default' understanding is based on that which we, as beings already immersed in a particular world, would tend to imagine—or what one already knows or the tradition within which one finds oneself. If the process of understanding stops after the first step then, yes, it is purely subjective. But if one continually opens oneself to the text and continually re-evaluates one's understanding against the text, and other interpretations of the text, then one will be able to render its meaning more 'complete'. How then will one know that one is not 'misunderstanding' the text? Gadamer (1989) uses the example of using a word in everyday language. He suggests that one cannot continually misunderstand the use of a word 'without its affecting the meaning of the whole, so we cannot hold blindly to our own fore-meanings [and prejudgements] of the thing if we would understand the meaning of another.' In other words the interpretive process is always situated in a referential whole in which a limited range of meanings will make sense. What we ought to do, according to Gadamer (1989: 238), is to 'remain open to the meaning of the other person or text. But this openness always includes our placing the other meaning in a relation with the whole of our own meanings or ourselves in relation to it. . . . Thus there is a criterion here also. The hermeneutical task becomes automatically a questioning of things and is always in part determined by this.' The hermeneutical task therefore is a delicate process of using one's own bias (fore-meanings) yet staying open for the possibility that the text may challenge these very same fore-meanings that were the stepping stone for entering it in the first place. That is why 'the hermeneutically trained mind must be sensitive to the text's quality and newness. But this kind of sensitivity involves neither "neutrality" in the matter of the object, nor the extinction of one's self, but rather the conscious assimilation of one's own fore-meanings and prejudices—an ongoing fusion of horizons. The important thing is to be aware of one's own bias, so that the text may present itself in all its newness and thus be able to assert its own truth against one's own fore-meanings [prejudices].'

The above description by Gadamer suggests that there is some sort of iterative process involved in understanding. When one is confronted with a text, the first iteration starts with our 'fore-meanings' and prejudices. These 'fore-meanings' are continually re-evaluated in terms of the meanings that come to the fore in the text. In these iterations, the meaning of the text becomes more and more 'complete' through the iterative process of understanding. This iterative process is known as the hermeneutic circle.

The Hermeneutic Circle

The hermeneutic circle is one of the most important conceptual contributions of hermeneutics. The hermeneutic circle expresses the principle that understanding is situated in the relation between the part and the whole; that one must understand the parts from the whole and the whole from the parts. Differently stated, there is an *ongoing co-constitutive* relation between the parts and the whole. Gadamer (1989: 259) explains it as follows: 'The anticipation of meaning in which the whole is envisaged becomes explicit understanding in that the parts, that are determined by the whole, themselves also determine this whole.' The hermeneutic circle is not a 'vicious' or a subjective circle. It is neither formal nor necessarily 'methodological'; it is rather a necessary condition for anything to make sense at all. We always find ourselves already in the hermeneutic circle where the whole (horizon of significance) is already 'projected' onto the text (part), based on the form of life within which one is situated—i.e. the 'living context' from which one seeks to understand. In the hermeneutic circle, one continually adjusts one's point of view, perspective, or horizon, always within one's own tradition and situation, in an effort to fuse these points of view, perspectives, or horizons in order to achieve, or rather, maintain understanding. Through the ongoing fusion of horizons the meaning of the text, and the form of life, is maintained and kept alive. The hermeneutic circle is acknowledged by many diverse authors such as Kuhn (1977: p. xii) in his effort to understand the physics of Aristotle and Feyerabend (1993: 251) in describing what he called the 'anthropological method'.

The hermeneutic circle is, in a sense, an evolutionary process of understanding. It starts with something known and evolves to something new, or previously unknown. In the movement to and fro the 'harmony of all the details with the whole is the criterion of correct understanding. The failure to achieve this harmony means the understanding has failed' (Gadamer 1989: 259). Using the notion of the hermeneutic circle one can understand the importance of multiple perspectives—or the ongoing fusion of horizons as Gadamer would say. The first perspective (or horizon) is based on one's current understanding or prejudices. The interpretation process will try and render it coherent with the whole within which the interpretive process is situated. If this is not possible the perspective (or horizon) must be 'relocated' for a different understanding to emerge. The new horizon/perspective is again projected onto the text from which emerges a new meaning and thus an expansion of the possible under-standing of the text. This process of repeated and reiterated projection of perspectives/horizons onto the text (and their ongoing fusion) will expand the interpreter's under-standing of the text. However, this process, as explained above, requires an ongoing *openness* to the possibilities thrown up by the text and the context. The more the process is reiterated (the fusion of horizons achieved), the more comprehensible the text becomes and the 'greater' the interpreter's understanding of the text becomes. However, if the process is prematurely terminated (the interpreter closes herself to the possibilities of the text), then the interpretation and thus the understanding of the text is incomplete and to a degree subjective (one might say prejudged or prejudiced, or even dogmatic). It is clear that subjectivity itself is not a choice. It is in reality always a given. The degree of subjectivity is a choice. Subjectivity is an essential ingredient in the interpretive process. It is the interpreter's task to use it but also to struggle against and beyond it, to the never-ending horizon of alternative interpretations (understanding). One might describe this process as an ongoing dialogue between the interpreter and the text.

If the notion of the hermeneutic circle (and the fusion of horizons) is applied to the dialogical situation, the power of dialogue clearly emerges. In the above description, the responsibility of projecting the new perspective onto the text lies with the interpreter. In a dialogue, each partner in the dialogue injects a new perspective/horizon which locates both participants in a hermeneutical circle. Dialogue essentially ensues when two interlocutors from different perspectives engage to understand (or create) a common text by means of the hermeneutical circle. If successful, the conclusion of the dialogue should take the participants beyond their original points of view in the sense that these are either transformed, consolidated, or questioned by the encounter with the Other (or alternative perspectives) put forward by the interlocutor.

Interpretation and *Erlebnis*

Erlebnis (lived experience) is a very important concept for Gadamer. Hegel (in Gadamer 1989: 318) describes lived experience as follows: 'The principle of experience contains the infinitely important element that in order to accept a content as true, the man himself must be present or, more precisely, he must find the content in unity and combined with the certainty of himself.' Thus, lived experience is what grounds and in a sense guarantees the interpretive process.

Erlebnis is not merely an experience such as knowing or remembering that 'something has happened to me sometime and somewhere'—a sort of cluster of facts ordered in time and space that I am able to recall. *Erlebnis* has a 'condensing, intensifying meaning. If something is called or considered an *Erlebnis*, that means it is rounded into the unity of a significant whole . . . Every experience is taken out of the continuity of life and at the same time related to the whole of one's life. . . . Because it is itself within the whole of life, *the whole of life is present in it too*' (Gadamer: 1989, 66–9, emphasis added). *Erlebnis* is in a sense the whole in which the part, being interpreted, is already significant.

Very important to *Erlebnis* is the ongoing openness of the interpreter to other possibilities. To truly live experience, the interpreter cannot be dogmatic. Dogmatism forecloses the ongoing possibility of experience to be experienced as such. Thus, central to lived experience is a definite 'not-ness' character. One can only experience something if it is *not* as one assumed it would be. This 'not-ness' opens one to the possibility of experiencing. Experience can be unsettling, as an element of disillusionment is always to a lesser or greater degree involved. As Aeschylus, a Greek tragedian says, '*through suffering [we] learn*'. Experience puts one face to face with the reality of the finiteness of human existence for it is in experience that the limits of expectation are shown up.

Ongoing lived experience (*Erlebnis*) is the significant whole—the form of life, the involvement whole—that provides the ongoing horizon for interpretation to be possible at all. Hence, for Gadamer, every hermeneutic interpretation is always rooted in an already significant situated whole, life as given in ongoing lived experience.

HEIDEGGER, UNDERSTANDING, AND BEING-IN-THE-WORLD

In discussing Gadamer's notion of hermeneutic understanding above it was clear that interpretation is seen as a process of appropriation (not recovery) of meaning *in* the situation as part of ongoing lived experience. The appropriation becomes necessary in moments of breakdown when the interpreter is somehow distanced or alienated from the world (text). Interpretation is the 'way' to dissolve this distance and render the text 'alive' or meaningful again—i.e. makes it available in the ongoing world of situated practice. To put it simply: for Gadamer (1989: 389) understanding *occurs as an integral part of the ongoing* interpretive process or practice. For Gadamer this understanding is never complete, i.e. the interpreter can never leave the hermeneutic circle. Heidegger

(1962) revolutionized the concept of 'understanding' by moving it from the end of the hermeneutic process to the beginning. According to him we do not understand because we have made an interpretation, rather understanding is a necessary condition for interpretation to happen at all. The aim of the interpretive process is, for Heidegger, to bring to light the interpreter's already understood prior understanding.

From Heidegger's perspective the notion of 'distance'—as present in Gadamer's work—has the potential to reinstate the Cartesian dualism, of the 'removed' observer. For Heidegger *understanding is a primordial existential condition of the human being immersed in the world* (the human way of being which he refers to as *Dasein*—which literally means the 'there' or place of being). Understanding is not something we come to by dissolving the distance. To be *in* the world means to always already understand such a world. Our involvement in the world always already assumes such a prior understanding. As Kockelmans (1972: 16) explains: 'Man's interpretation does not throw a meaning over some "naked" thing that is present-at-hand, nor does it place a value on it. The intramundane thing that is encountered as such in the original understanding, which is characteristic of man's concernful dealing with things, already possesses a reference that is implicitly contained in man's co-understanding of the world and thus can be articulated by interpretation.' If interpretation does not lead to or restore understanding, what is the function of interpretation then? Before trying to answer this question we need to articulate more precisely Heidegger's notion of understanding.

Understanding as Already Being Projected

For Heidegger, as stated above, understanding is a primordial existential structural feature of human (or *Dasein's*) existence; 'to exist is essentially, even if not only, to understand' (Heidegger 1982: 276). Differently stated: understanding is a necessary (or transcendental) condition for a human being to be 'a human being'. This primordial understanding does not imply some cognitive content (picture or idea in our heads) about something or some situation, or to grasp it thematically, but rather, it refers to the necessary mode of being which is characteristic of humans as beings-in-the-world. In this original understanding *Dasein* manifests itself as 'being able to', as a being that always already has a range of possibilities to be. To understand a situation is to already have a particular comportment towards the possibilities present within this situated involvement whole. Hence, understanding has the existential structure of 'projection' (Heidegger 1962: 184–5). As projection, understanding makes the possibilities within the referential whole 'stand out' as simply meaningfully available, simply present to be enacted. In coping in the world *Dasein* continually presses forth into these possibilities and in so doing creates leeway for movement (or room for manoeuvring as Dreyfus (1991) puts it). This leeway for movement is the space of possibilities, the clearing that both opens up, and limits, *what obviously makes sense to do*. Let us consider an example. When I walk into the lecture theatre (as a lecturer) I do not encounter the room as strange (i.e. in need of interpretation). The room is mostly familiar and the sort of activities that it makes sense to do is immediately obvious and self-evident for me as a lecturer. Thus I, as a lecturer, am already familiar with (i.e. understand) lecturing, lecture theatres, and the sort of meaningful things that it makes sense to do there. Indeed, I am already comported to, and in, this evolvement whole in a particular way since I am not simply randomly entering the room, I am entering *in order to* give a lecture. In this comportment the computer and the projector already make sense because I already have my PowerPoint presentation on a memory stick, and so forth. I, as a lecturer, entering the room am already projected into the possibilities that are suggested there. They already make sense to me. I already understand them; as such I simply go about doing what lecturers do when they enter a lecture theatre in order to teach. However, being thrown into-the-world means that *Dasein* is also always limited to a space of sensible possibilities which it already understands or is projected onto, and is necessarily tied into the involvement whole that it is already *involved in*. This space of possibilities, this room for manoeuvre, *Dasein* 'knows' without reflection for it is the commonsense background of concerned or engaged circumspection implied in being involved in the world (of lecturing for example). What then is the meaning of interpretation in this context?

Understanding and Interpretation

In interpretation understanding 'does not become something different. It becomes itself' (Heidegger 1962: 188). We can only interpret that which we already understand. In interpretation we do not acquire additional information about what is already understood, rather interpretation is the 'working-out of possibilities [already] projected in understanding' (Heidegger 1962: 189). In understanding we already have a primordial sense or reference in our already situated form of life—an already there network of 'for-the-sake-of-which's' or an already there network of 'in-order-to's' about ourselves, and our 'tools', in the referential whole. However, this primordial understanding can be further interpreted in such a way that the simply available ready-at-hand world comes explicitly into that sight which understands it. This is accomplished by the 'taking apart', as it were, of the 'in-order-to's' that is already circumspectively understood, and concern ourselves with that which becomes visible through this process. This 'in-order-to' that is now explicitly understood has the structure of something *as* something—as a thing for doing this or that. For example, *as* a projector for projecting images, in-order-to explain something. Interpretation, therefore, is the laying out, the making explicit, *as* this or that, of something already understood in its 'in-order-to' as this or that. The 'as' structure constitutes the interpretation; it makes up the structure of the explicitness of something that is understood (Heidegger 1962: 189). If asked 'what is this?', we can answer (explain or interpret), it is something that functions as this or that—we 'see' it as an X (as a chair or as a table or as a pointer) in-order-to do something, or be in a certain way within that involvement whole. This is why Heidegger argues that in interpretation understanding does not become something else; it becomes itself; it makes explicit its own possibilities to be *as* this or that.

Let me try and illustrate these notions through a very simple example of a computer 'mouse'. I understand the 'mouse' in using it to point at various places on the screen in-order-to open files, open applications, select menu options, print, select text, etc.; in-order-to write letters, maintain my disk space, do Internet searches, etc.; for-the-sake-of getting my work done; for-the-sake-of being a good academic. In understanding the 'mouse' I already 'know' the space of possibilities that it *makes sense* to use it for, since I am involved in the referential whole (doing things on my computer) of which it is an 'in-order-to'. I know that I am 'able-to' use it to point and execute. Yet, I may not have made this explicit, although it is in principle always possible. If someone were to point at the mouse on my table and say, 'What is this?', I might explain (interpret) by responding, 'It is a something normally used *as a pointing thing*; to point at menus, icons, etc. to activate them in order to get things done, like opening files, or selecting text.' In this explanation I have made explicit what I already knew, not as an idea in my head, but as an 'in-order-to' that is always already embedded in an involvement whole that makes it significant, and which I may call 'working on my computer'.

Meaning and Meaningful

According to the objectivist model of communication words, symbols, signs, texts, etc. 'have' a meaning as such. In the communication process this meaning may 'get lost'. The purpose of the interpretation process is to 'recover' this meaning. When this recovery has happened, we say that we now understand. Thus, in this way of thinking understanding is merely a matter of linking the signifiers (words or pointers) to the signified (things or ideas of things) in a way commensurate to that of the speaker or sender (the author). Interpretation in this context would be to correct any muddled signifier/signified relationships. This notion of understanding is also implied when we say the computer 'understands' my input—i.e. the computer performed the action I intended it to perform when I issued the command. The computer established the same relationship between the signifier (the command) and the signified (the action to be performed) that I, the sender, had in mind when I 'talked' to it through the medium of the keyboard. Wittgenstein (1967), as was suggested above, argues that this view of understanding may be correct in a limited sense. For him, however, it is an example of a very primitive language-game; one that is not very useful for thinking about the complexities of everyday language. The idea that words or signs have stable and persisting associations linked to them is simply too static a view of everyday language. The meaning of a sign is not a 'meaning-body, an entity which determines its use. A sign becomes meaningful not through being associated with an object, but rather through having a rule-governed use' (Wittgenstein 1967: 432). The sign does not have an intrinsic meaning, the sign by itself is 'dead': 'What gives it life?—In use it is alive' (Wittgenstein 1967: 431–2). One might suggest that his argument is that we do not use language to convey meaning as such. We do not have an idea and then convey it by carefully selecting the words that best represent it. We use language as part of doing. Using language and doing things is like using a tool and doing things. It does not make much sense to talk about using a tool without thinking about doing something. What I 'mean' by an utterance is linked to a language-game (a set of signs and rules for applying them), which is linked to a form of life (a practical everyday doing of something). Therefore, 'a sign is meaningful depends on whether there is an established use [in a language-game], whether it can be employed to perform meaningful linguistic acts [in a form of life]; what meaning it has depends on how it can be used. The meaning of a word is its use in the language' (Wittgenstein 1967: 43). I understand the meaning of a word, sign, text because I can use it appropriately as part of some doing.

Heidegger would agree with Wittgenstein's analysis but he would go one step further. He argues that the primordial origin of our 'seeing' anything as meaningful is our presence in the world. Meaningfulness 'is first of all a mode of presence in virtue of which every entity of the world is discovered'. Meaning is not something we 'inject' into a meaningless world. Since our existential structure is that of *being-in*, the referential whole (the worldhood of world) is always already meaningful. We uncover this meaning as an implicit part of our ongoing engagement, or skilful coping, in the world as beings that are always already projected in the world we are already in. Thus words, signs do not 'have' meaning. They are only meaningful as part of ongoing activity in the referential whole that is my world.

This notion of meaning may best be made explicit through the computer mouse example. The words 'mouse' and 'point' do not 'have' meanings. If you were to say 'point the mouse to the "open file" icon' then this statement will only mean something as part of 'working on my computer' in-order-to get something done. The meaning is not that I can assign an object to the word 'mouse' and an action to the word 'point', etc. The meaning is that there is significance in the request to 'point the mouse and click on that file' in this form of life called working together on a computer in order to get something done. In this involvement whole the meaning of the request is already 'present'. It is already understood as that which it is for those engaged in the world of working together on a computer.

A criticism that can be levelled at both Gadamer and Heidegger is that they have an uncritical hermeneutics. Gadamer puts a lot of emphasis in the importance of prejudice, tradition, and the fusion of horizons without making it clear that those traditions may indeed be normatively problematic. Heidegger likewise provides a fascinating account of how our being-in-the-world grounds our understanding and interpretation without making it clear that the self-evidentness of such immersion in the world might be problematic in as much as it might limit our ability to reflect and be critical of it. For a critical hermeneutics we need to turn to the work of Ricoeur (and indeed further on to the work of Michel Foucault).

RICOEUR AND THE HERMENEUTICS
OF SUSPICION

For Ricoeur (1970, 1976) the recovery or appropriation of the meaning of the text is not an end point it is rather just the beginning. Ricoeur argues that in the text there is always a *surplus of meaning* that refers (mostly unintentionally) not only to what the author intended to say (the task of the hermeneutics of the faith) but also to the prejudices, traditions, and world-views that are drawn upon and assumed by the author in constructing the text (the task of the hermeneutics of suspicion). Thus, he argues that if meaning is grounded in a world then that world is also communicated as an implicit part of the coming into being of the text.

Ricoeur gives an account of this 'double meaning' by drawing on the notion of the metaphor. Ricoeur (1976) believes that intrinsic to metaphor is both an 'is like' element and an 'is not' element. The 'is like' element is used to convey the obvious meaning of the metaphor, while the 'is not' element indicates that the referent of the metaphor is not to be found in its literal expression. This tension between the 'is' and 'is not' implicates or projects 'a world in front of the text' which is the true metaphorical referent. It is therefore as important to understand the world the text assumes or projects for its meaning as it is to understand the text as such. Indeed, according to him, these two levels of interpretation cannot be separated. Thus, a hermeneutics of suspicion refers to the method of interpreting texts cautiously, aware that the surface-level meaning of a text may be an unconscious effort to conceal the political interests which benefit some at the expense of others. The task of the hermeneutics of suspicion is to strip off the surface to expose those interests.

According to Ricoeur interpretation therefore always involves at least a double reading. We must first read the text in the hermeneutics of faith which calls for the suspension of disbelief by the reader in which the text becomes the world which we inhabit when reading it. As such the reading tries to *understand* the text in its own terms. The hermeneutics of faith must then be followed by a hermeneutics of suspicion where the world assumed by the text is made explicit in order to reveal or explain the relationships of power, conflicts, and interests implicated in it. As Ricoeur (1970: 27) explains: 'Hermeneutics seems to me to be animated by this double motivation: willingness to suspect, willingness to listen; vow of rigor, vow of obedience.' Thus, for Ricoeur understanding and explaining are two essential dialectical moves in the process of interpretation. Understanding without explanation is blind and explanation without understanding is empty. Like Ricoeur, Habermas (1970) argues that texts are derived from social relations of power and domination, and these oppressive aspects are implicitly concealed in texts. He proposes dialogical engagement or a discourse ethics to 'surface' these implicit or explicit attempts to enforce a particular world onto the reader.

MEANING AND INFORMATION SYSTEMS:
SOME CONCLUSIONS

The very brief introduction to hermeneutics we have outlined above provides us with plenty of intellectual resources to take into account when thinking about information systems in organizations, as well as the researching of these phenomena in practice. We will outline some of these potential lines of thought as indicative and suggestive of the possibilities that hermeneutics might have for IS. We hope this will be enough to motivate the reader to take a serious interest in hermeneutics.

Let us take as an example the claim of Gadamer that there is an essential *I/Other relationship* in the act of interpretation and understanding. One can quickly gloss over this somewhat abstract claim without appreciating the profound implications of it. What Gadamer is claiming is that we are always in a position of essential strangeness (or otherness) when confronted with a text (or a text analogue—i.e. spoken words or actions). According to him there is always a level of 'otherness' in the text/text analogue that simply cannot be overcome, irrespective of how many times we go through the hermeneutic circle. In other words there is ultimately no frame of reference, context, concept, idea, or theory that will render this otherness comprehensible—interpretation meets its limit in the otherness of the other. This of course is not a weakness this is exactly the vital strength that sustains the ongoing dialogical movement of interpretation.

This essential strangeness/otherness is particularly important when one thinks of Giddens's (1984: 284) notion of the *double hermeneutic*—that is to say his claim that social scientists construct interpretations of subjects' texts (or text analogues) who have already constructed interpretations of themselves as they try to account for, or make sense of, their own practices. In other words it is not only the social scientists that are in some sense 'distanced' from the social practices that they are studying, the subjects themselves (and their practices) are not obviously transparent to themselves either. As subjects in the world we are continually trying to interpret and make sense of ourselves—we are also strangers or 'other' to ourselves, forever struggling against ongoing estrangement. Thus, the assumption that the actors involved in the practices self-evidently 'know the facts' can be questioned. Clearly, as competent actors they are able to produce an interpretation of themselves and the world as they encounter it. But in this interpretation or 'meaning making' process they are also struggling against an essential estrangement which they ultimately cannot overcome. Moreover, as with any act of interpretation, they will tend to draw upon their own prejudices (or prejudgements) in constructing these texts (or text analogues). As such the dialogical movement of the hermeneutic circle is essential in making these prejudices visible so that the actors may also potentially move beyond their own interpretations of themselves. In addition, in struggling to make sense of themselves the social actors also often adopt the interpretations of social scientist, of their practices, in accounting for those practices (just recall all the use of management-speak by social actors in organizations such as resistance to change, strategizing, leadership, innovating, and so forth). In this dialogical movement the question of whose (or which) text/account ought to be privileged is not a trivial question at all. This is not to say that every interpretation is equally legitimate (a subjectivist claim). It is rather to say that the validity of an account must be subject to an ongoing dialogical hermeneutic which continually evaluates it against the referential whole within which it is claimed to be valid.

For Heidegger human existence is fundamentally hermeneutic. Skilled and competent social actors know and understand the world in which they are involved. As already projected beings-in-the-world their possibilities for action (for being what they are as businessmen, teachers, carpenters, etc.) are immediately available to them in their world. For them the world mostly makes sense and is obvious and available, or ready-to-hand as Heidegger will say. Thus, as they go about their daily lives this available world tends not to show up as problematic or needing explaining. Indeed if asked to explain this world they would also need to enter into an interpretive hermeneutic process. In making sense of their own actions they also battle against a certain level of estrangement. In constructing their accounts, explanations, and the like, their own actions, behaviours, or practices are not simply an 'open book' that they can merely read out aloud. Accounting for their actions requires a different comportment to doing it. It is often only in 'breakdowns' when the actions or practices are suspended, and the actor can 'step back' (when the world becomes present-at-hand in Heidegger's terms) that such accounts or explanations can be produced *as a hermeneutic achievement*. In this hermeneutic process the social actor may attempt to offer alternative formulations or expressions of what (and why) things are the way they are. In these efforts of 'trying out' different expression or formulations the actor will inevitably feel more or less satisfied with the degree to which the expressions (accounts or explanations) capture the actuality of their way of being. In other words there always tends to be a sense in which there is an otherness (even to themselves) that they can never quite capture; something left out that always seems to require further elaboration and explanation—something extraordinary that is never quite graspable. It seems that there are always elements of our experience that defy our accounts and explanations of them. In trying to deal with this otherness they face the same conditions that any interpretive process has to deal with. They would tend to make use of their taken-for-granted assumptions, prejudices, and the like. They would have to go through multiple iterations, continually evaluating their expressions against the coherency of their own lived experience (*Erlebnis*). Thus, they require an ongoing hermeneutic dialogue grounded in lived experience, but which always acknowledges its own situatedness and incompleteness. This is true for researchers as well as organizational actors. The subjects of our research are struggling with their own otherness as much as we are struggling to make sense of them and their practices. Such an ongoing hermeneutic dialogue is fundamental to ongoing human existence. It is not only something that we are engaged in for time to time, it is the way we are—that is why Heidegger claims that we *are* fundamentally hermeneutic beings (it is an ontological claim). It is worth remembering that all accounting systems (including computerized information systems, reports, Ph.D. theses, etc.) embody an essential otherness that defies explication and explanation. In ongoing everyday activity organizational actors, through ongoing hermeneutic dialogue, continually struggle to account for themselves (to themselves and to others).

Ricoeur reminds us that in the interpretation of texts (or text analogues) there is always the obligation to do a 'double reading'. We must first read the text (or text analogue) in the hermeneutics of faith (or one might also say hermeneutics of fidelity). We must attempt to take the text (or text analogue) in its own terms, from its own perspective or point of view. We must suspend, to the degree that it is possible, our own prejudices and try and imagine why the text is the way it is. What are the conditions of possibility for a text to express what it expresses in the way that it expresses it? We must however, also immediately, engage in the hermeneutics of suspicion where the taken-for-granted world assumed by the text for its meaning is made explicit in order to reveal the assumptions, prejudices, relationships of power, conflicts, and interests implicated in it. Without the hermeneutics of suspicion the interpretation will be naive and without the hermeneutics of faith the interpretation will be cynical. Naivety and cynicism are short cuts that try to avoid the hard and truly difficult labour of double reading required for a vital hermeneutics. We can easily see the implications for researchers and organizational actors of this requirement for an ongoing double reading. Maintaining the simultaneity of faith/fidelity and suspicion is an ongoing struggle in the dialogical movement of interpretation.

We have now outlined a few conclusions and implications of hermeneutics for Information Systems researchers and organizational practices that they study. These are merely indicative and tentative. Nevertheless, it is hoped that they will inspire researchers in the field to make the effort to engage with hermeneutics as an important and valuable intellectual tradition.

REFERENCES

Bernstein, R. J. (1983). *Beyond Objectivism and Relativism: Science, Hermeneutics and Praxis.* Oxford: Basil Blackwell.

Bleicher, J. (1980). *Contemporary Hermeneutics: Hermeneutics as Method, Philosophy and Critique.* London: Routledge & Kegan Paul.

Boland, R. J. (1985). 'Phenomenology: A Preferred Approach to Research on Information Systems', in E. Mumford, R. Hirschheim, G. Fitzgerald, and A. T. Wood-Harper (eds.), *Research Methods in Information Systems.* Amsterdam: North-Holland, 193–201.

—— (1987). 'The In-formation of Information Systems', in R. J. Boland and R. A. Hirschheim (eds.), *Critical Issues in Information Systems Research.* New York: John Wiley & Sons, 363–94.

—— (1991). 'Information System Use as a Hermeneutic Process', in H.-E. Nissen, H. K. Klein, and R. A. Hirschheim (eds.), *Information Systems Research: Contemporary Approaches and Emergent Traditions.* Amsterdam: North-Holland, 439–64.

Boland, R. J. (1993). 'Accounting and the Interpretive Act', *Accounting, Organisations and Society*, 18(2/3): 125–46.

Butler, T. (1998). 'Towards a Hermeneutic Method for Interpretive Research in Information Systems', *Journal of Information Technology*, 13: 285–300.

Dreyfus, H. (1991). *Being-in-the-World: A Commentary on Heidegger's Being and Time, Division I*. Cambridge, MA: MIT Press.

Feyerabend, P. (1993). *Against Method*. 3rd edn., London: Verso.

Gadamer, H.-G. (1989). *Truth and Method*. 2nd rev. edn. trans. and rev. J. Weinsheimer and D. G. Marshall. London: Sheed & Ward.

Giddens, A. (1984). *The Constitution of Society: Outline of the Theory of Structuration*. Cambridge: Polity.

Habermas, J. (1985 [1970]). 'Hermeneutics and the Social Sciences', in K. Mueller-Vollmer (ed.), *The Hermeneutics Reader*. Oxford: Basil Blackwell, 293–319.

Heidegger, M. (1962). *Being and Time*. Oxford: Blackwell.

—— (1982). *The Basic Problems of Phenomenology*. Bloomington: Indiana University Press.

Introna, L. D. (1997). *Management, Information and Power*. London: Macmillan.

Klein, H. K., and Myers, M. D. (1999). 'A Set of Principles for Conducting and Evaluating Interpretive Field Studies in Information Systems', *MIS Quarterly*, 23(1): 67–94.

Kockelmans, J. J. (1972). *On Heidegger and Language*. Evanston, IL: Northwestern University Press.

Kuhn, T. S. (1977). *The Essential Tension: Selected Studies in Scientific Tradition and Change*. Chicago, IL: University of Chicago Press.

Lee, A. S. (1994). 'Electronic Mail as a Medium for Rich Communication: An Empirical Investigation Using Hermeneutic Interpretation', *MIS Quarterly*, 18(2): 143–57.

Mintzberg, H. (1973). *The Nature of Managerial Work*. New York: Harper & Row.

Myers, M. D. (1994). 'A Disaster for Everyone to See: An Interpretive Analysis of a Failed IS Project', *Accounting, Management and Information Technologies*, 4(4): 185–201.

—— (1995). 'Dialectical Hermeneutics: A Theoretical Framework for the Implementation of Information Systems', *Information Systems Journal*, 5(1): 51–70.

Palmer, R. E. (1969). *Hermeneutics: Interpretation Theory in Schleiermacher, Dilthey, Heidegger and Gadamer*. Evanston, IL: Northwestern University Press.

Ricoeur, P. (1970). *Freud and Philosophy: An Essay on Interpretation*. Trans. D. Savage, New Haven, CT: Yale University Press.

—— (1976). *Interpretation Theory: Discourse and the Surplus of Meaning*. Fort Worth, TX: Texas Christian University Press.

—— (1981). *Hermeneutics and the Human Sciences*. Trans. J. B. Thompson. Cambridge: Cambridge University Press.

Rorty, R. (1979). *Philosophy and the Mirror of Nature*. Princeton: Princeton University Press.

Schmidt, L. K. (2006). *Understanding Hermeneutics*. Stocksfield: Acumen Publishing.

Winograd, T., and Flores, F. (1986). *Understanding Computers and Cognition: A New Foundation for Design*. Reading, MA: Addison Wesley.

Wittgenstein, L. (1967). *Philosophical Investigations*. Oxford: Blackwell.

Wranke, G. (1987). *Gadamer: Hermeneutics, Tradition and Reason*. Stanford, CA: Stanford University Press.

CHAPTER 10

....

PHENOMENOLOGY, SCREENS, AND *SCREENNESS*: RETURNING TO THE WORLD ITSELF

....

LUCAS D. INTRONA AND
FERNANDO M. ILHARCO

INTRODUCTION

....

PHENOMENOLOGY, as a philosophical underpinning, as well as a method of investigation, is currently used in a wide range of fields, such as organization studies, management, anthropology, sociology, history, design, media studies and communication sciences, psychology, psychiatry, biology, mathematics, philosophy, education, and so forth. It has also been used in Information Systems (IS) research.[1] The authors have also, for several years now, been using a phenomenological approach to account for the phenomenon of the 'screen' (Introna and Ilharco 2000, 2004a, 2004b, 2006; Ilharco 2008; Introna, Ilharco, and Fäy 2008). As with many other methodological approaches the phenomenological method has a number of core central traits, which have been used in all phenomenological investigations. In this chapter we attempt to follow the traditional phenomenological approach as synthesized in Spiegelberg (1994). In our discussion and analysis we tend to draw only on the literature of the phenomenological movement. We hope that our exclusively phenomenological approach will provide a significant theoretical and methodological contribution to the IS field. This is timely as the phenomenological movement is currently experiencing a new growth period as is clear from the recent publication of a number of introductory works in the field (e.g. Moran 2000; Sokolowski 2000; Cerbone 2006; Glendinning 2007).

Phenomenology, as an approach, belongs to the most primary human need—that is, to return to a world already known, a world where phenomena have their meaning as such. As such we would claim that phenomenology can be seen as a radical answer to the ongoing ideological standoff between a sort of positive naturalism—which argues for general objective accounts of the world as directly given through our observations— and an interpretive approach—which argues for the importance of ongoing socially shared, subjective meaning. In this standoff phenomenology aims, rather, at returning to the world as it is, before analysis, science, theories, and interpretations are applied to its a posteriori understanding. Phenomenology provides a radical answer by showing that meaning is not an idiosyncratic subjectively constructed 'inner' domain, but rather an ongoing, objective public domain of *necessary* relations or references. More formally put, for phenomenology, meaning is not 'in' the thing (word, object, action, event, subject, etc.). Rather, it is 'in' the nexus of *necessary relations or references* for the thing (word, object, action, event, subject, etc.) *to be what it is already taken as*, when taken up in our ongoing activity in everyday life. More succinctly put: the meaning is in the world itself and it is to this world that we must 'return' (prior to any conceptualizing, theorizing, etc.). It is this radical insight that we hope to make clear through this chapter. It is also this radical insight that a widely cited commentator such as Leedy (1997: 161) seems to miss when he defines phenomenology, incorrectly, within the subjectivist paradigm—as 'a research method that attempts to understand *participants' perspectives and views* of social realities' (emphasis added).

To the things, themselves!, phenomenology's motto, introduced by Edmund Husserl (1859–1938), the founder of phenomenology, grounds phenomenology's meaning in the self-evident primacy of the world (Heidegger 1962; Husserl 1970a). This fundamental insight reminds us that whatever *is* already is within a nexus of relationships, the world itself. This is precisely what enables it to become manifest to us as this or that particular being. This phenomenal being—in accordance with Heidegger's (1962) phenomenology of humanness—is its meaning. What something is, as this or that being, is not a substance but is rather the totality of references implied in its being (Heidegger 1962). Thus, the referential context provides, or grounds, its meaning— only within a referential context can something come forth as something. This 'as something' (Heidegger 1962) is the meaning that opens up, for each of us, a world as a world, our own being as human, an organization as an organization, a screen as a screen, and so forth. This necessary and grounding account of our way of being human is primary to all theories and methods; it is nothing other than the pointing out of the world itself.

'Objective' features of things, their present-at-hand characteristics (Heidegger 1962), that is, their observed, decontextualized, analysed, and fragmented presence, reveal themselves to us only within a larger, meaningful context, which cannot itself be explained in terms of its present-at-handness. 'The astronomer determines that a certain star is millions of kilometres away from the sun. That is correct, but it means something to the astronomer and to the rest of us only if we can relate it back to the lifeworld in which three kilometres are a gentle afternoon stroll, and thirty kilometres are a good day's hike' (Polt 1999: 59). A computer technician measures the surface of a screen to be 27 centimetres wide and 21 centimetres high, or the resolution as a certain number of pixels. So what? What do these facts mean? What is their relevance? These measurements would be meaningless, and the technician would never have bothered finding them out, if they were not already meaningful in the world in which she exists, lives, and works as a technician—life comes first, the world is already there. As beings-in-the-world (Heidegger 1962), we have always and already understood things and events on the basis of their already established places in the referential whole, that is our immediate involvement with that world (Heidegger 1962). 'Objective', present-at-hand distances are understood, interpreted, and assumed on the basis of my *having been* (Heidegger 1962). An 'objective' distance per se has no meaning. Its meaning only appears on the basis of my life as a *having been*.

This 'world that is', that which is most evident to us, is the referential context within which we intend to account for the phenomenon screen. Kant (1985) considered it a scandal that a proof of existence of the external world had not yet been produced. Heidegger (1962) regarded it as a scandal that such a proof was searched for at all. For who we ourselves are—and the world we seek to understand—cannot be stripped out of that very world. We—and the world we seek to understand—are revealed only as 'beings-in-the-world' (Heidegger 1962). Our phenomenological analysis of the phenomenon 'screen' below is grounded in this approach. It calls for nothing more than a return to what phenomena already are in-the-world, that is, to return to the world itself. As Glendinning (2007: 16) summarizes so well:

> What the phenomenologist aims at, then, is not a theory of this or that phenome-non—a theory which would be characterised by its distinctive positions and ex-tractable theses—but an effort to come reflectively to terms with something that is, in some way, already 'evident'. It is in this sense a work of explication, elucidation, explication or description of something we, in some way, already understand or with which we are already, in some way familiar, but which, for some reason we cannot get into clear focus for ourselves without more ado.

Before proceeding we must note that there are many different ways in which one could 'do' phenomenology. One could, for example, explicitly follow the phenomeno-logical method, as we will in the analysis of the screen below. Nevertheless, one could also 'do' it in other ways, such as applying the results of previous phenomenological analysis, or using phenomenological assumptions and insights as grounding principles for one's work; there is simply not just 'one way' to use phenomenology.

This chapter endeavours to provide a coherent straightforward account of phenom-enology, discussing its central concerns and concepts, making some contrasts within the phenomenology movement, and providing a brief discussion of the phenomeno-logical method. We will also show the value of the phenomenological approach and method by doing a phenomenological analysis of the phenomenon 'screen' and pre-senting a critical assessment of it. We will conclude the chapter by pointing to some existing work in phenomenology that may serve as examples of how phenomenology may be used to inform future research. This is an ambitious task for one chapter and as such many important issues may have to be left unaccounted. Nevertheless, we hope the chapter will serve as a basis from which those interested can engage the literature of the phenomenology movement.

PHENOMENOLOGY: MOVEMENT AND APPROACH

There is no simple answer to the question of what phenomenology is. We can say, as Husserl did, that phenomenology is 'a return to the things themselves'. But such a cryptic saying only means something if we understand that the meaning of 'return', 'things', and 'themselves' here has some very specific meanings for the phenomenologist. How then will we proceed? One could, for example, give a historical answer by starting with a discussion of Husserl's (1964, 1969, 1970a, 1970b, 1995) main works, including his indebtedness to Brentano, and then show how this work was transformed by Heidegger and reinterpreted by Merleau-Ponty, Sartre, and Levinas amongst others. This was done in the massive, now classic, work by Spiegelberg (1994 [1959]) and more recently in the excellent, very readable, account by Dermot Moran (2000) and Glendinning (2007). We could also give an exposition of the 'key concepts' and 'method' of phenomenology, as was done so well by Sokolowski (2000). We will not take either of these routes. We will rather present the distinctiveness of phenomenology by developing an account of the claim that phenomenology is a *transcendental* approach to our understanding of the world. In the ongoing evolution of phenomenology the meaning and source of the 'transcendental' becomes transformed, redefined, and reinterpreted by the various proponents. Nevertheless, through the notion of 'transcendental' we can relate phenomenology to other approaches and explain why we believe it to be valuable and necessary for the IS community. We hope to present this discussion in a simple manner with minimal recourse to the technicality of the phenomenological lexicon. To do this in a manner that will show the distinctiveness of phenomenology, without becoming simplistic, will certainly not be an easy task. We must also emphasize that this is a very brief account and that any serious engagement with phenomenology requires a more in-depth study for which the references provided at the end of the chapter are a good guide.

PHENOMENOLOGY'S CENTRAL IDEA

Phenomenology is a transcendental approach to our understanding of the world *as given and taken in ongoing experience*. To understand what this might mean let us turn to a very mundane situation of experiencing something in the course of our everyday life. Let us take as our example our experience with a typical chair, standing in front of our table in our office. What makes it possible for us to experience it—take it to be, see it, refer to it, etc.—*as a chair* rather than as a something else? This may sound like a strange question. However, we must be careful to note that the chair—or any other object for that matter—is always only *given* to our senses as unordered sensations[2] and only in its aspect, or one-sidedness. When we stand in 'front' of it the 'back' is not given to our senses as such. When we stand at the back the front is hidden from our senses. As far as our direct sensory encounter is concerned we are always only given the unordered flux of perturbations of 'one side' of the chair at any particular time—i.e. our senses operate in an unordered flux of one-dimensionality. Yet when we approach the chair we do not *take* it as a confusing flux of sensation, or as one side of a chair, rather, we take it in its fullness of being, as that which it already is, a chair to sit on, stand on, and so forth. Thus, we can ask: what is it that allows us to *take* it in its fullness, *as a chair*, even though we are only always, at any particular point in time, sensually *given* an unordered flux of an aspect of it?

Phenomenology will answer that it is the 'already there' *sense* that I have of chairs that allows me to take it as a chair, rather than as something else. This 'sense' emerged through my many situated experiences with a multiplicity of 'chair' objects—some made of wood, some of plastic, some of steel—in many different situations—in the bedroom, in the kitchen, outside on the patio, etc. Thus, through all these various situated and ongoing experiences some 'sense' of what the object chair is—how to take it, see it, refer to it, and use it—remained sufficiently stable in order for me to have ongoing situated experiences of chairs 'as chairs', rather than as some unordered flux of an aspect of something. This *ongoing sense* we have of the world means that every experience we have of things, as the thing that they are, can never be wholly unprecedented, as if from scratch. If this was the case then our ongoing experience of the world will be deeply perplexing and confusing. However, this is in fact not our normal experience; rather we experience the world as mostly meaningful and familiar. Thus, in and through all our previous experiences with extended objects and chairs some sense 'remained', became sedimented in some way, which now provides the ongoing horizon or minimal condition of possibility for our ongoing 'taking' of this chair that we are now approaching to sit on 'as a chair' rather as something else. Let us suspend for the moment what this 'remainder' is and how it came about.

In phenomenology we refer to this ongoing persisting sense or 'remainder', that which constitutes the ongoing possibility for the taken extended object to be experienced 'as a chair', as the *transcendental* domain. More formally expressed we could say, 'the transcendental is that which *constitutes*, and thereby renders the empirical possible' (Mohanty 1970: 52). For the more philosophically minded it is important to make a distinction between Kant's (1787 [1965]) and Husserl's (1964, 1970a, 1970b) use of the notion of the 'transcendental'. For Kant—the originator of the notion—the transcendental is the *a priori categories of mind*—such as sensation and judgement—that makes cognition possible as such. *For Husserl the transcendental is the active, directed, ongoing life of consciousness that is the necessary condition for our ongoing experience of the world to be meaningful as such.*[3]

It is now possible to say that phenomenology, as a transcendental critique, was developed to question the assumptions of naturalism or empiricism that starts with a world of 'already there' objects without asking the question: how is it possible to experience the object (a chair) as the object that it is, 'as a chair', in the first instance (Mohanty 1970, 1997). Thus, an empirically based science—such as positivism—does not start with that which is *given*—as the world is only given as an unordered flux and in its aspect or one-sidedness—but rather with that which is *always and already constituted*—the world of objects already taken as such by us. Positive empiricists then pose the question 'how can we know these objects' without realizing that the very possibility of experiencing the objects, as such and such an object, already implies a meaningful epistemic encounter that has its source elsewhere. This 'elsewhere' is the already active, already directed, ongoing life of consciousness. It is this active ongoing structural correlation—one can almost say ongoing structuration in Giddens's (1984) terms—of conscious life and the world that is the 'remainder' which we have suspended above and to which we will now turn to in our discussion of Husserl's work.

HUSSERLIAN PHENOMENOLOGY

For Husserl consciousness—note we are referring here to embodied consciousness rather than a disembodied 'mind'—is not some pre-existing blank slate, space, or memory capacity 'in our heads' (an internal *subject* dimension) that somehow 'records' or captures a stream of sensations or representations of the world out there (an external *object* dimension), which it then somehow makes sense of. Rather, embodied conscious-ness, to be conscious at all, is already an active meaning giving directedness towards, and in, the world. To be conscious is always and already[4] to be conscious of *something as this or that something*. Consciousness is always and already an act—an already active *taking* of the given world—which implies, as necessary, some already available sense or meaning that renders such an act possible and meaningful. As conscious beings our relationship with the world is not some passive disinterested simply 'standing before' the world, being bombarded by an ongoing stream of confusing and unordered sensations. On the contrary, as we go about daily life (even if we sit passively in a chair) we find ourselves as always already *experiencing* the world in its fullness and the objects surrounding us *as something in particular*—as boring, interesting, hard, soft, a tree, a chair, a knife, useful, red, blue, cold, round, far, near, etc. However, such experiencing of the world 'as something' already suggests some simultaneously present sense (unity, or meaning, or in Husserl's language a *noema*) of that which is being experienced—as interesting, hard, tree, chair, soft, useful, cold, far, and near—that is the necessary condition or transcendental possibility for such an experience to be possible in the first place. Husserl (1969: 233–4) formulates this fundamental ongoing unity of consciousness and the world in ongoing experience as follows:

> But experience is not an opening through which a world, existing prior to all experience, shines into a room of consciousness; it is not a mere taking of something alien to consciousness into consciousness.... Experience is the performance in which for me, the experiencer, the experienced being 'is there', and is [already] there as what it is, with the whole content and the mode of being that experience itself, by the performance going on in its intentionality, attributes to it.

To make this discussion a bit more specific let us consider the experience of listening to music—as opposed to encountering objects discussed above. First, we have to note that music is never *given* to us *as music*. It is *given* to our senses as a flux of unordered[5] sounds. However, when we hear sounds we never *take* them—in ongoing experience— simply as a stream of unrelated sounds, rather we find ourselves already listening to them *as something*—music, a cry for help, a car braking, some construction noise, etc. '[W]e do not [ever] hear pure meaningless sounds' (Dreyfus 1991: 218). 'We hear the door shut in the house and never hear acoustical sensations or even mere sounds' (Heidegger 1971: 26). As Heidegger argues: 'What we "first" hear is never noises or complexes sounds, but the creaking wagon, the motorcycle... It requires a very artificial and complicated frame of mind to "hear" a "pure noise"' (Heidegger 1962: 207). The things themselves, in their meaningfulness, are much closer to us than all sensations (Heidegger 1971: 26). Thus, listening, the taking of sound as music, or a cry for help, or an accident, etc., implies an already there *sense* of what 'music', 'a cry for help' or 'an accident' is, that makes it possible for me to take these sounds as this or that, rather than as a mere flux of unordered sounds.

Furthermore, in order to listen to music, as music, I do not only listen, but this listening to music is also already informed by an ongoing *sense* (unity or *noema*) of movement, rhythm, tone, scale, style, and so forth. This ongoing active unity or *noema* provides an ongoing temporal horizon that enables me, in the experience of listening (the now), to simultaneously 'retain' the sounds I no longer hear (the past), and in anticipation 'fill in' the sounds I am not yet hearing, yet anticipate (the future). Thus, as a phenomenological being I find myself listening to music, not merely hearing sounds.

To sum up: our ongoing, always already directed experience (*noesis* in Husserl's terms) of the world as meaningful (as this or that), which was previously given as a flux of unordered sensation in its one-dimensionality, has as its necessary condition an ongoing transcendental structural correlation or unity (*noema*) which is immediately and wholly implicated in the ongoing experience *but distinct from it*. In all the situated experiences of chairs the given aspects of particular chairs varied (and could vary infinitely) but the persisting *noematic* sense remained identical.[6] The immediate and simultaneous presence of the identical (*noema*) in the ongoing act of experiencing (*noesis*) the chair through its aspects, possibilities, and past experiences is what Husserl refers to as the *intentionality* of consciousness. The always already intentful directedness of consciousness (*noesis*) has as a necessary condition an already present direction or structural orientation (*noema*), for its directedness to be meaningful rather than random and confused. As mentioned, this state of affairs is itself evident, as we tend to experience our ongoing engagement with the world as mostly meaningful rather than confused and meaningless. The ongoing noematic structure of consciousness is *both medium and outcome* of the intentional activity of consciousness, simultaneously directing and synthesizing. As such it is active and temporal rather than static and atemporal—it is not a Platonic ideal form. Thus, contrary to the view of the positivists, intentional consciousness is not a subjectively constructed inner and private domain that must be 'eliminated' but rather it is an always already *public mind* that exists as a completely immanent—wholly present, never absent—ongoing and necessary structural correlation with the world (Sokolowski 2000: 14).

So far we have tended to concentrate only on the experience of a particular object or event in our discussion—the chair and listening to music—however, these objects and events already exist in a *referential whole* in which things refer to each other in such a manner as to constitute a meaningful whole. For example, our experience of the pen on the table already refers to some sort of writing surface like paper, and the pen and paper refers to the possibility of writing or drawing, which refer to the possibility of communicating, which refers to the need for communication, etc. In this referential whole, where things refer to each other or imply each other, the meaning of something emerges as the nexus of necessary relationships that constitute something as that which it is, a pen in this case. Husserl refers to this as the *external horizon* (or in his later work as the 'life world'). We always *experience* the world within this unfolding horizon of references—its meaning.

Thus, for phenomenology the meaning or sense of something—the phenomena as such—is not the outcome of subjective choices (likes, dislikes, values, beliefs, etc.) but rather the outcome of the ongoing nexus of necessary relationships that serve as the transcendental condition of the active ongoing already meaning-giving consciousness. As such the intentionality of consciousness implies an *immediate* relationship between consciousness (the subject) and the world (the object)—an ongoing structural unity— that renders the experience of the world possible in the first place. The theory of the intentionality of consciousness—and human existence—is phenomenology's fundamental contribution.[7] All phenomenologists take some version of this doctrine or theory as self-evident and central to any phenomenological approach. Before we move on we must note that, although we have concentrated on perception—of a chair and music—in our discussion, the intentional nature of the active meaning-giving consciousness is implied in all forms of cognition such as judging, representing, planning, deciding, remembering, imagining, and so forth.

For Husserl the fundamental task of phenomenology is to *describe* and give an account of the necessary *noematic structural unity* of intentional consciousness—to describe the phenomena as such. For example, if we want to understand the phenomenological meaning of chairs as such—evident in all our experiences of it—we cannot answer this question by looking at this or that particular empirical chair. To our senses the chair can only be known in its 'one-sidedness,' or in its 'many-sidedness' in a sequence of observations, but never simultaneously in its 'all-sidedness'. Yet phenomenologically the 'essential' meaning of the chair—its 'sit-upon-ability'—is not known perspectivally. As Merleau-Ponty (1962: 67) explains: 'I see the next-door house from a certain angle, but it would be seen differently from the right bank of the Seine, or from the inside, or again from an aeroplane: the house itself is none of these appearances: it is, as Leibniz said, the geometrized projection of these perspectives and of all possible perspectives, that is, the perspectiveless position from which all can be derived, the house seen from nowhere.' The house, as phenomenon, is the disclosure of that which, lying hidden, is always implicit as horizons, that is, as the totality of perspectives. '[T]he house itself is not the house seen from nowhere, but the house seen from everywhere. The completed object is translucent, being shot through from all sides by an infinite number of present scrutinies which intersect in its depths leaving nothing hidden' (Merleau-Ponty 1962: 69).

To give an account of its essential meaning, as a 'sit-upon-able', we need to give an account of the ongoing noematic structural unity of consciousness and the world that makes such an experience possible through all our diverse 'chair experiences'—hence Husserl's famous saying we must 'return to the things [structural unity] themselves'. How do we 'return to the things themselves', i.e. gain access to the ongoing noematic structural correlation of consciousness and the world? How do we turn consciousness back upon itself? Obviously, this is very difficult to do—and Husserl claims that we will always be perpetual beginners.

According to Husserl we can achieve it by a cumulative process of suspension, referred to as the *epoché* ('suspension of judgement' in ancient Greek philosophy). In every suspension (*epochç*) there is a simultaneous event of reduction—from the Latin *reducere*, 'to lead back'—taking place. In Husserl's (1964, 1970b) work there are a number of suspensions and reductions described, however, we will only distinguish two different levels of reduction here. The first is the *phenomenological reduction*, which is the suspension of the natural attitude and all its suppositions. The second is what is referred to as the *eidetic reduction* (from the Latin root *eidos*, 'essence'), which is the suspension of the empirical world in grasping the essential structural unity of consciousness as such. We will not discuss these reductions here in detail. For a very accessible discussion the reader is referred to the excellent introduction by Sokolowski (2000). Nevertheless, it is worth stating clearly that through the phenomenological and eidetic reduction 'we look *at* what we normally look *through*' (Sokolowski 2000: 50) and as such we 'reach an understanding of the [ongoing] performance of subjectivity. The world is not something that simply exists. The world appears, and the structure of this appearance is conditioned and made possible by subjectivity [the ongoing intentional correlation of self and world]' (Zahavi 2003: 52). When we do the phenomenological analysis of the screen below this form of phenomenological and essential reflection will become clearer. Let us now turn to Heidegger (incidentally a student of Husserl).

HEIDEGGER AND INTENTIONALITY
AS BEING-IN-THE-WORLD

The eidetic reduction as the possibility of a 'direct' access to a domain of pure or absolute transcendental consciousness is the most controversial aspect of Husserl's phenomenology. Most phenomenologists after Husserl rejected it. It should also be noted that he also started to turn away from it in his final work *The Crisis of the European Sciences* (1970). Indeed, one can take the work of Heidegger, Merleau-Ponty, and Sartre as a direct existential critique of Husserl's transcendental enquiry (Kockelmans 1967). This enquiry towards the ideal structures of consciousness is often referred to as transcendental idealism. In contrast to this Heidegger (1962) insisted that the transcendental is always and already grounded in the ongoing practical activity in the world of everyday life.[8] For him 'all consciousness, all knowledge, all human undertakings, are drawn on an ever present substratum: the world, a world that is always already-there, radically primary' (Thevenaz 1962: 84). Likewise, for Merleau-Ponty (1962) the mind is not a pure intentional structure of consciousness but rather an embodied and always already situated mind.[9] He would argue that our scientific systems of orientation in time and space have their condition of possibility in our being a body—a lived body that is the ongoing horizon of orientation and meaning. For example, for him language already has its source, horizon of meaning, in the gesture.

Heidegger argued that early Husserl did not really break with the Cartesian dualism in as much as he still located the source of meaning in the structure of consciousness, *in the mind* as it were; in today's terms we might say that Heidegger criticized Husserl for his cognitivist tendencies, i.e. reducing meaning to some content in the mind. In contrast to this Heidegger argued that we cannot 'bracket out' the world of everyday practical activity, the referential whole, as this is exactly the ongoing source of all meaning—the ongoing being[10] of beings. One could argue that Heidegger abandoned Husserl's project—as Dreyfus (1991) does—or one could argue that Heidegger extended the work of Husserl, as Moran (2000) and Zahavi (2003) do—a position we would tend to take.

Heidegger's brilliant insight, articulated in division one of *Being and Time*, is that our intentional relationship with the world is *not epistemic*—as Husserl assumed—but *rather practical and ontological*. By this he means that we do not tend to encounter chairs 'as chairs' in the way Husserl describes but we rather tend to encounter them as 'possibilities for', such as 'a possibility for sitting down' or 'for standing on to reach higher' or 'for facing somebody', and so forth. Furthermore, the chair is a 'possibility for' (what Heidegger called an 'in-order-to') only within an already present referential whole where other things refer to it, as a 'possibility for', and it refers to them. Thus, for Heidegger the transcendental domain is not 'purified' consciousness but rather the ongoing, unfolding referential whole in which every thing is what it is—has its being. To describe this radically extended transcendental domain Heidegger uses the notion of *being-in-the-world*.[11] Heidegger argues that we humans (which he calls *Dasein*) exist in an ongoing structural openness towards the world in which the self and the world is always already a unity, a being-in-the-world (Heidegger 1982: 297). Thus, we human beings (*Dasein*) are this unity, we are always and already beings-in-the-world—we have this unity as our ongoing being.

Let us consider an example. Whenever we find ourselves or take note of ourselves, we find ourselves *already engaged in practical everyday activity* in which things show up as 'possibilities for' our practical intentions. We should first take note of the fact that our human nature is always one in which the things we encounter already *matter* in some way or another—even if it matters only as useless, boring, or irrelevant. This is what Heidegger means when he claims that our way of being is that we always and already *care*. It is impossible for us—as always already immersed or 'thrown-into' the world humans—to take a wholly disinterested stance in and towards the world (Heidegger 1962: 176). Thus, Heidegger transforms Husserl's notion of intentionality by insisting that 'intentionality must be understood in terms of the structural features of *Dasein*, specially *Dasein's* transcendence, that is, the fact that *Dasein* is already somehow beyond itself, already dwelling in the world, among things, and not locked up in the privacy of its own consciousness as the representationalist, Cartesian picture assumes' (Moran 2000: 42).

When we encounter tools they already matter in some way or another. However, these tools *are tools* for this or that purpose only in as much as they already refer to other tools, which also already refer to them as their transcendental condition for being this or that tool. Note that when using the notion 'refer' here, it is used in the sense of a *necessary relation or reference* for the tool to be what it already is *taken* to be when taken up in practical activity. The laptop we are working on, to be a laptop, rather than a piece of assembled plastic and silicone, refers to application programs, which refer to operating systems, which refer to hardware, which refer to a power supply—all of which refer to suppliers, which refer to maintenance services, and so forth. Dreyfus (1991: 62) calls this recursively defining, necessary nexus of relations, the *tool or equipment whole*.

When we take up these tools, as tools, we do not take them up for their own sake, we take them up with an already present reference to our projects.[12] We do not simply bang on keys, we use the laptop to type, in-order-to write this chapter, to do e-mail, to surf the web, etc. Moreover, the writing of this chapter refers to the possibility of a book, of which it would be a part. This book refers to editors, which refers to potential publishers, which refer to a potential audience, which refer to research, which refer to further possibilities, etc. Furthermore, the writing of this chapter also refers to the publication of our work, which refers to a publication record, which refers to academic status, which refers to the possibility for promotion, and so forth. Heidegger (1962: 118) calls this recursively defining and necessary nexus of projects, or for-the-sake-of relations, the *involvement whole*. The equipment whole and the involvement whole refer to each other and sustain each other as an ongoing referential whole, horizon of meaning, Heidegger calls 'the world'.[13] We humans (*Dasein*) dwell in the world in which the world is mostly familiar (it is simply already evidently there, 'ready-to-hand' in Heidegger's terminology). The phenomenological meaning of the world—in the case of our analysis below, the screen—can only be understood within the always already defining referential whole, the world itself.

Now sometimes the world 'breaks down' and then we tend to encounter it as objects or events *as such*—it becomes occurrent or present-to-hand in Heidegger's (1962) terminology. When we type and the key gets stuck then we notice it 'as a key', otherwise we merely type. If it remains stuck the computer becomes occurrent 'as a broken laptop'. However, as we start to take it apart, in an attempt to fix it, it recedes back into the background as something I am fixing. The point of Heidegger's account is 'that things show up for us or are encountered *as what they are* only against a background of familiarity, competence, and concern that carves out a system of related roles [recursively defining references] into which things fit. Equipmental things *are* the roles [recursively defining references] into which they are cast by skilled users of them, and skilled users *are* the practical roles [recursively defining references] into which they [become] cast themselves' (Hall 1993: 132). Thus, our relation with the world is ontological in as much as the world already shows up, or reveals itself to us, as it already is, in and through our ongoing project-edness, or comportments. However, to see this we need to suspend our natural attitude and take up a phenomenological attitude in which we can 'trace' and 'retrace' the referential whole that is the *transcendental* condition for the world to reveal itself as that which it already is.

This transformation of the transcendental by Heidegger, as wells as the work of Merleau-Ponty and Sartre, amongst others, has become described as *existential phenomenology* as opposed to the *transcendental phenomenology* of Husserl. Although we tend to follow the major steps of the Husserlian phenomenological method our detailed analysis within these steps is based more on Heideggerian existential phenomenology. We will give a brief outline of this method in the section below.

THE PHENOMENOLOGICAL METHOD

Like any other method the phenomenological method of investigation is realized through a methodological circle, however phenomenology strives to accept and to proceed only within the primacy of human *experience as experienced*, i.e. our ongoing intentional structural correlation with the world. As mentioned, our investigation into the phenomenological meaning of the *screen* below follows the traditional phenomenological method as developed and applied by Husserl and Heidegger, and synthesized by Spiegelberg (1975, 1994). Nevertheless, minor changes were needed to incorporate some of the existential critique developed by Heidegger and others. The main adaptation we introduce to Spiegelberg's synthesis of the method is the role of the traditional etymological critique. We consider the phenomenological account of the etymology of the words not merely as a step in the first phase of the method, but rather as a whole second phase in its own right. Such an adaptation, which to some extent is only recognition of an important and recurrent phenomenological practice, is clearly supported by the phenomenological investigations of Heidegger (1962, 1977, 1978). The phenomenological method we apply in the phenomenological analysis of the screen below is therefore structured in the following four[14] phases:

1. Describing the phenomenon
2. Analysing the etymology
3. Performing the reduction
4. Investigating the essence

It is important to stress the implicit unity when considering these four sequential phases. The phases are united in the basic purpose of 'giving us a fuller and deeper grasp' of the phenomenon (Spiegelberg 1975: 57), which can only be achieved if all four phases are applied fully. It ought to be clear how the essential concepts of phenomenology, discussed above, relate to the method as we proceed. Nevertheless, this relationship will be explained further as we apply the method to our analysis below. Let us very briefly characterize each of the four phases of the method with reference to our analysis of the phenomenon of the screen to be presented below.[15]

Phase 1—*Describing the Phenomenon Screen*. This phase aims at returning to the screen as primarily and directly experienced. The purpose is to describe the external horizon of the phenomenon as intuitively and as free as possible from our presuppositions. We are not looking for data in order to explain some preliminary hypothesis, nor are we trying to make sense of some previous intellectual construction about screens. Our central aim is not to explain but to *describe* the screen, as it is, in our ongoing activity in the world.

Phase 2—*Analysing the Etymology of Screen*. We shall trace back the origins of the word 'screen'. This analysis is not designed to bring back the meaning of the word per se, but rather to bring forth the meaning of the 'thing' itself, i.e. of screen, in the antepredicative life of consciousness. In our analysis we will also provide an account of the etymology of the word 'display' as closely related to screen.

Phase 3—*Performing the Phenomenological Reduction upon Screen*. In this phase we perform the phenomenological reduction upon the consolidated findings of the first two phases. The reduction will aim to *bracket out* the incidental aspects of particular examples of screens in order to reach some essential description of the phenomenon 'screen'. This bracketing process will be guided by our intentional experience of the screening of screens in our everyday encounters with screens.

Phase 4—*Investigating the Essence of Screen*. This phase aims at reaching the elements strictly necessary for the phenomenon screen to be what it is. This phase proceeds from the reduced phenomenon of screen presented in the previous phase. It proceeds by stripping it of those elements that in spite of being common to all appearances of screen are not strictly necessary. In the analysis the technique of free variation will be used as well as relating and contrasting the phenomenon of screen with closely related phenomena.

The analysis of the phenomenon of the screen, presented below, will proceed by carefully following the phases outlined above. Because the flow of the analysis is a way into the phenomenon of the screen, and a method of argumentation (Merleau-Ponty 1962; Heidegger 1977; Husserl 1995), we will, as we proceed phase by phase, add some further discussion of the method where appropriate. In this manner we aim to limit repetition, and improve the effectiveness of the discussion. Nevertheless, it must be pointed out that the always-provisional nature of the phenomenological method is such that it tends to lead to some repetition of formulations as well as the reconsideration of statements and positions previously taken. We also want to reiterate that following the explicit phenomenological method—outlined above and applied below—is just *one* way to do phenomenology.

A PHENOMENOLOGY OF THE SCREEN: AN EXAMPLE

In a strict phenomenological manner, following Husserl's counsel (Husserl 1964, 1970a, 1995), this phenomenological analysis will initially set aside important research that addresses directly or indirectly the phenomenon screen (e.g. McLuhan 1962, 1964, 1967; Idhe 1990, 2002; Sobchack 1991, 1994, 1999; Heim 1993, 1999; Manovich 1995, 2001).

The odds are that when reading this chapter you will have nearby, not one, but maybe even several screens. Whether at the workplace, at home relaxing with the family, travelling, or engaged in entertainment, a growing majority of people find themselves increasingly in front of screens—television (TV) screens, personal computer (PC) screens, mobile phone screens, palmtop computer displays, and so forth. It is unlikely that the pervasiveness of screens in contemporary life will be disputed. However, as an example of this fact it is worth noting that the funeral of Princess Diana in August 1997 was followed by an estimated TV audience of 2,500 million (ABC 1999), which represents more than 40 per cent of the world's population. What is the meaning of our increasing interactions with screens? In this section we want to demonstrate the importance of phenomenology as an approach and method for enabling us to answer the question of the meaning of screens, in its ongoing screening of our world. We will aim to show that this seemingly 'innocent' technology has powerful ontological implications for our understanding of its pervasive presence in organizations and everyday life.

Describing the Phenomenon Screen (Phase 1)

Let us start our analysis by exploring a description of the screen, qua screen. As a phenomenological analysis, we do not intend to direct our reflection to the *content* displayed on any particular screen as such, but rather to the meaning of the screen in its ongoing screening. The screen as we encounter it when we look at it as a screen when watching a movie, or the news or search for a place on Google maps, and so forth. Thus, the focus of our investigation is the screen as a nexus of relationships that provides a concrete way of relating ourselves to and in the world when we find ourselves before a screen.

It is rather surprising what we encounter from the start. When trying to describe a screen, a computer screen or a television screen, we immediately note that we never seem to look at a screen as a 'screen'. We rather tend to look at screens by attending to that which appears on them. What seems evident when looking at a screen is the content presented on that screen—the text, images, colours, graphics, and so on—not the screening of the screen. To try and look at a screen, and see it as a screen, not taking into account the particular content it presents, and all the references with which that same content already appears to us, is apparently not an easy task. We are not familiar with this type of encounter with a screen. Rather in our familiarity with screens or displays they tend to reveal themselves as things—perhaps surfaces—which function in particular contexts and for particular purposes. That is to say, we simply use screens as we act and relate ourselves to and in the world, mainly within a familiar organizational or institutional context. In the natural attitude screens are familiar 'places', simply there for our use. This familiarity may even lead us to think that the question of the meaning of the screen is odd and perhaps an 'intellectualization' of something quite ordinary. We note this strangeness as we proceed—that is, that although we are intimately familiar with screens we tend not to see screens in their screening, i.e. qua screens. As we move towards suspending the natural attitude and take up the phenomenological attitude—looking at the screen in its screening—what do we note?

Screens in screening present, show, exhibit, what is supposed to be *relevant 'data'* in each context, be it a spreadsheet while working at office, or a schedule while walking in the airport, or a movie while watching TV. The screen, in screening, finds itself at the centre of the activity. In showing it attracts our attention, often also our physical presence, as it locates our activity. It is often the focus of our concerns in that environment, be it at office working, or be it at home watching the news. Apparently the screen enters our ongoing activity and engagement in the world—as a screen—when we attend to it by turning it on. When we push the 'on' button the screen locates our attention, we sit down, quit—physically or cognitively—other activities we may have been performing to watch the screen, as it is the place, the location, where what is relevant or supposedly relevant for us at that particular time is happening. Indeed we rely on it as a transparent simply there *ready-to-hand* thing that is simply available to shape, affect, and mediate our own ongoing activity and engagement in the world (Heidegger 1962).

However, we must note that this screening of the screen—as involving, shaping, and mediating our activities—does not sometimes happen, and sometimes not. It is not only *when* we turn it 'on' that the screening of the screen is present. On the contrary, *that* we push the 'on' button means precisely that the screening of the screen—its pervasive transparent possibilities—are already suggested and present there in our ongoing activity, our world.[16] In the horizon of our ongoing everyday life—in its dynamic nexus of relationships—other activities and things already refer to it, already suggesting its meaningfulness. For example we organize our desk around our computer and our living room around our TV. We locate screens where they are visible. We have for example barcodes, text messages, notices at airports, and URLs that continually direct us towards the screen. Thus, even if this or that particular screen is off, we are already relying and basing ourselves, and our possibilities—the references in which we dwell—on the already present *screenhood* of screens. We will return to this point below.

From our initial attempt at 'seeing' the screen, as it screens (or looking at what we normally look through) we note that a screen gathers the attention of the people that surround it. The actions of those people are already directly shaped by the presence of the turned on screens, by the kind of content presented, and by the understanding people surrounding them implicitly assume of that content. The phenomenological description above of a screen points to the notions of *showing relevant data for and about each particular situation, of calling for attention, of suggesting relevance, of acting as mediation between ourselves and the world, and of gathering and locating what is appropriate in each particular context*. We now have a first phenomenological description of some of the central meanings of the screening of the screen. It is worth noting at this point that the description of the screen above is also valid for what we know as displays—for example as we find in palmtop displays. In the analysis we will aim to show that there is no fundamental phenomenological difference between a screen and what we refer to as a display[17]—they both have their meaning in-the-world in ongoing screening.

In the next section we will expand our investigation by doing a phenomenological analysis of the etymology of the word 'screen' and the word 'display'. In this phase we will attempt to trace and 'uncover' the paths of meaning of these words by juxtaposing them with the description already given above.

Analysing the Etymology of 'Screen' (Phase 2)

When doing an etymology of the word 'screen' it is not the intention of phenomenology to argue that a particular meaning of the word screen has a definitive superiority, or is the 'real' meaning. What is decisive is that the tracing back of the evolution of the meaning of the word 'screen' enables us somehow to make more evident the realm of *necessary* relations/references in which the word 'speaks' and maintains its meaning. As Heidegger (1977: 159) states:

> What counts, rather, is for us, in reliance on the early meaning of a word and its changes, to catch sight of the realm pertaining to the matter in question into which the word speaks. What counts is to ponder that essential realm as the one in which the matter named through the word moves.

Thus, although our phenomenological analysis does share some concerns with linguistic analysis, it goes beyond it. This analysis is not destined to 'bring back' the historical original meaning of the words screen and display, but rather to bring forth 'the [phenomenological] meaning of the thing itself, around which the acts of naming and expression took shape' (Merleau-Ponty 1962: p. xv).

Screens: calling for attention

'Screen' looks like a rather simple word. It is both a noun and a verb and its contemporary plurality of meanings can be brought together along three main themes: *projecting/ showing* (e.g. TV screen), *hiding/protecting* (e.g. fireplace screen), *and testing/selecting* (e.g. screening the candidates) (OPDT 1997: 681–2). What are the meanings that bind this plurality together?

The origins of the word 'screen' can be traced back to the fourteenth century. According to the *Merriam Webster Dictionary* (MW) the contemporary English word 'screen' evolved from the Middle English word *screne*, from the Middle French *escren*, and from the Middle Dutch *scherm*. It is a word akin to the Old High German (eighth century) words *skirm*, which meant shield, and *skrank*, which meant a barrier of some kind. The word screen also suggests another interesting signification, further away from us in history. It is a word 'probably akin' (MW) to the Sanskrit (1000 BC)[18] words *carman*, which meant 'skin', and *kränti*, which signifies 'he injures' (MW). These are possible meanings from which the Middle Age words evolved. The Sanskrit clue suggests that the notions of protection, shield, barrier, separation arose, possibly within the older Proto-Indo-European language, as metaphors of the concept of skin—possibly that of human (or animal) skin.

Let us now suggest a very brief sketch of the chronological etymological relations these words seem to have. A barrier or a protection is something raised over and against another something. This 'other' something faces the barrier, as the wind faces the *windscreen* of a car, which means that the screen protects against something, to be excluded, that moves towards it. That which is moving towards the screen could have been understood as a projection (from the Latin word *projectare*, which meant 'to throw forward') over a surface—just like the arrows and bullets were projected over the shields, or like the heat is projected onto the fireplace screen. The screen protects and shelters (just as a skin . . .) because it receives and holds the projection of that which is not to be received 'inside' the cover that the screen provides. But what happens when something stopped by the screen is allowed to pass through? The answer is that it was screened. This means that it was permitted to pass through that barrier, or that it simply passed through it. The screen as a barrier is now understood as a 'system for detecting [for example] disease, ability, attribute' (OPDT 1997: 681–2). This interpretation links, or so we hope, the three central themes of meaning attached to the word screen: hiding/protecting, projecting/showing, and testing/selecting (ibid.). Is there a central intent, distinction, or feature, common to all these specific meanings of the word screen? We would suggest that the central intent is 'demands for our attention'[19] as summarized in Table 10.1.

Table 10.1 The central intent of the multiple meanings of 'screen'

Projecting/showing (e.g. TV screen)	Projecting and showing assumes a target or audience whose attention is to be captured. Without such audience (target) showing (projecting) will not make sense.	Calls for the attention of audience/to target
Hiding/protecting (e.g. fireplace screen)	Hiding and protecting assumes something to be excluded from attention. Without exclusion from attention hiding would not make sense.	Calls for the exclusion from attention
Testing/selecting (e.g. screening the candidates)	Testing and selecting assumes the attention of those that 'select and test'. Without such attention selecting cannot be said to 'select'.	Calls for the attention of those selecting

From Table 10.1 it seems reasonable to propose that the central intent of the multiple meanings of 'screen' is *the presumed necessary attention* implied in *ongoing screening*, for screening to make sense. We summarize this meaning as *'calling for attention'*. We now turn our attention to the etymology of the word 'display', which is often used as a synonym for screen with regard to information technology devices, and which we will claim to have the same intentional meaning as screen.

Displaying: clear agreement

The word 'display' entered the English language as a verb in the fourteenth century, and as a noun in the seventeenth century (MW). As a verb display means 'to put or spread before the view' (e.g. *display* the flag), 'to make evident' (e.g. *displayed* great skill), 'to exhibit ostentatiously' (e.g. he liked to *display* his erudition) (MW). As a noun it means 'a setting or presentation of something in open view' (e.g. a fireworks *display*), 'a clear sign or evidence', an exhibition (e.g. a *display* of courage), an 'ostentatious show', 'an eye-catching arrangement by which something is exhibited' (MW). These notions of showing, in open view, and making evident are central to the word display. What are the necessary conditions for making sense of these diverse meanings? It seems that the central intent is some sense of apparentness, immediately clear to all. Such apparentness has as its condition of possibility the idea of *already there agreement*. For example we say 'it is evident to all present here' meaning it is impossible for anyone present to disagree with what is taken to be apparent. They in turn are linked to the idea of 'unfolding' and of some sort of agreement.

The work done in this step leads to an idea that is in an important way quite close to the one we had at the end of the previous step. This is the idea of screen as the bringing forth of (or calling forth for) attention and thereby implying evident relevance, since 'calling for attention' always implies the supposition, correctly or incorrectly, of some evident relevance. This 'evidence' 'relevance', and 'attention'—emerging from the etymological analysis above—points towards the idea of some already operating *agreement* (implicit or explicit) as its constitutive condition. If the 'attention' mentioned is our attention, as those before the screen, to what does 'evidence', 'relevance', and 'agreement' refer? Is the issue of evidence, relevance, and agreement a matter of the *content* of that which is on the screen or does screen in its fundamental meaning (or screening) already presume them?

Performing the Phenomenological Reduction on Screen (Phase 3)

At this point we must recall that to recover in some way the essential meaning of the screen, as revealed in screening, we must turn our reflection to the phenomenon as it reveals itself from the ongoing structural correlation of self and world. It is now important that we suspend—as a methodological condition of our analysis—the necessity of any particular empirical examples of this or that screen. Performing the phenomenological reduction does this. This means reducing the phenomenon screen to its ongoing appearance in the horizon of the already situated intentionality, disregarding characteristics that we value in it as a particular empirically 'existent' thing, while attempting to preserve its meaning as fully as possible.

As we perform the phenomenological reduction it is important to note that this intentional 'object', the screen in our already situated consciousness, in its 'screening', is *not* some pure isolated and abstract thing that has meaning in itself as such. For us to grasp the meaning of the screen as screening, we need to have already presumed its world—i.e. nexus of relationships without which it would not have any meaning as such. Thus, the screen, in its essential meaning, always already refers to its functioning in a world in which it makes sense, because it, and the other things and activities in the world mutually refer to each other as meaningful. The reduction is a return exactly to this *horizon of meaning*.

Having suspended the supposition of the necessary existence in any particular empirical screen we note that any screen, to make sense as a screen, still seems to require as necessary 'a calling for attention'. Without this 'calling for our attention', screens would no longer be screens, merely surfaces or objects. Thus screens, in their screening, seem to be promises of bringing to make evident what is relevant, while simultaneously hiding their claimed physical being behind that same relevance. We see that screens, in screening, function in the flow of our ongoing activity in the world, that is, transparently as simply there ready-to-hand beings (Heidegger 1962). Because the content displayed always 'shows up' within our ongoing activity whole it is already presumed relevant data—that is, data deserving our attention. The reduced phenomenon of screen appears as something devised to attract—or rather that *already* has—our attention and situate our action in the ongoing activity of our world of work, entertainment, travel, etc. This reflection can be made clearer by realizing the kind of difficulty one has to go through in order to imagine a situation in which screens do not present relevant data at all. For example experiencing a PC monitor at the NY Stock Exchange showing the ongoing schedule of the trains of some Asian city; or the display of the cash registers of a supermarket showing air traffic control data. These 'screens' may have an initial curiosity value but will quickly become ornaments in the background—they simply do not screen. These cases demonstrate the difficulty to imagine these surfaces *as screens* because in order to do so we would need to abandon the essential meaning of the screen, yet still force ourselves to use that same essence to understand an object that looks as if it has lost its meaning as a screen.

Screens display relevant data for us within the involvement whole in which we relate ourselves to the world. The data on screens grab our attention within our *particular* involvement whole (Heidegger 1962) in which it refers to our activities and our activities refer to it—within a particular 'form of life'.[20] For example, we can imagine what a man from the fifteenth century might think when confronted with a screen of an Automatic Teller Machine (ATM). That surface which we refer to as a 'screen' would merely be a potentially curious object for him. It would not be a 'screen' because he does not already dwell in a world—referential whole—that would render it meaningful as such. The screen would not be a 'screen' for him as it would not call for his attention, it and the content displayed 'on' it would not seem relevant as it is *not already* a screen for him; he would simply not recognize it in its essential meaning. However, for us, who already dwell in the world of bank accounts, the screen in screening is already calling for our attention as a possibility to see my 'bank balance', or to withdraw cash from my account, for example. The data on the screen refer to me, refer to my residence, my transactions, my financial status, my overdraft facility, and so forth; these in turn refer to other aspects of my ongoing activity in the world and they refer to it—Can I afford to buy something or not? Has my salary been deposited? etc.

Thus, screens in screening claim an ongoing meaning in-the-world as focal interpretive surfaces, presenting, making evident, relevant data for our involvement and action in the world. Screens promise to make evident our ongoing activity in-the-world, because they present an already interpreted and selected 'screened' world to us. This screened world is already consistent with our ongoing involvement in that world, within our form-of-life. Thus, foremost and primarily screens do not 'show' the data that appear 'on' the screen, but rather *a form of life as such*.

This phenomenological reduced description of screen shows how closely intertwined the ideas of 'attention', 'relevance', and 'world' are in the essential meaning of the screen—as such it also suggests references to notions of some necessary agreement. However, this is not enough for a fully phenomenological characterization of the phenomenon screen. In order to reach the essential meaning of the screening of screens we must now try to reach beyond this common ground to identify the *strictly necessary* references for the phenomenon screen to be what it *is*.

Investigating the Essential Meaning of the Screen (Phase 4)

To gain access to the essential meaning of the screen is not to generalize. As mentioned above generalization, as a process, already presupposes the existence of some essential meaning for its operation. Moreover, as is evident from our analysis thus far, the notion of 'essence' we use accounts for some grounded and historical way of unfolding that evolves and changes in-the-world (Heidegger 1962, 1977). As such, it does not point to some supposed static concept, object, or Platonic idea. Rather we take the investigation of the essence of the screen, in recognition of the work of Heidegger, to be an attempt to uncover the fundamental meanings, the grounding references, and the main and decisive contours as it were, of the growing and pervading presence of screens in our contemporary world.

The way in which screens are screens in-the-world of ongoing activity is of course common to all screens. Nevertheless, it is common not only to the examples analysed but to *all* potential examples of that phenomenon, because the essence is such that without it there is no phenomenon. Imagination, 'by discovering what one can and what one cannot imagine' (Hammond, Howarth, and Keat 1991: 76), is the key to the continuation of our analysis. This analysis aims to strip out of our preliminary phenomenon of screening those elements that in spite of being common are not necessary for a screen to be screening. Since we have a pervasive and ongoing experience with screens we now no longer need empirical observation for discovering the answers we need. Rather, in every new variation in imagination we know the object we describe is an object of that same kind, a screen, if we recognize it as such, as a screen. Thus, the implicit criterion of recognition—*my ability to recognize the object as the object it is*—is the decisive way of this essential *eidetic* reduction (Spiegelberg 1975, 1994; Husserl 1995, 1970a).

Firstly, we note that the same surface can be considered a screen and not considered a screen even if it displays the same data, as is clear from our example of the ATM above. If we have a mirror, with the size and shape of a screen, it displays data—the images it reflects—but we do not consider it to be a screen but a mirror. Nonetheless, we can equally have a screen displaying exactly the same image as the mirror and consider it a screen and not a mirror. So, what is the criterion that is implicit in this imagined experience? Mirrors *reflect*, screens *present*. This means the kind of data displayed by these different objects have diverse origins. In the case of mirrors it is merely reflecting back what it receives. However, in presentation there operates a fundamental process of ordering. Presentation always assumes a theme, in the way that a jigsaw puzzle, to be a jigsaw puzzle, assumes a whole that will be its ordering criterion.

Furthermore, the presumed theme of the presentation derives its meaning from an ongoing horizon of activity that already renders it meaningful as a relevant presentation. As Wittgenstein (1967: 88) argued, words do not refer to something because we agreed it, rather they already have meaning because we share a *form of life*—a meaningful ongoing activity whole. Conversely, the screen has meaning, not because we have agreed its content, but because in screening it necessarily assumes an already understood meaningful activity whole as its condition of possibility—one could say its already present organizing theme. Thus, we can say that the meaningfulness of the data presented on screens does not depend on the perceiving subject's perspective as such—i.e. it is not a matter of an interpretation as such—but rather on the *form of life* in which it already functions as meaningful. Screens present meaningful data, that is, data that were previously already selected in accordance with an already implied meaningful whole and therefore they gather and locate the attention of the people surrounding them. In watching, one could of course disagree with the relevance of this or that particular data being presented on the screen, but that evaluation itself already suggests a horizon of meaning in which such judgements would make sense.

Screens are not mirrors in that they do not reflect whatever they face. They are a presentation of what is already relevant within the flow of our purposeful action. However, we must also note that in selecting for presentation, in displaying—thus in making relevant or evident—other possibilities are *necessarily always implicitly exclud- ed*. Thus, the screen, as screen, conceals and filters in its revealing. For this to be the case, there is the logical necessity of a *previously agreed grounding* on the basis of which something can be filtered, can be *screened*, at all. To reveal implies to conceal; they both mean to filter, that is, to screen. The revealing and concealing of screening implies an already there, implicitly and fundamentally shared and agreed form of life, on the basis of which the things on the screen become constituted as meaningful and the way the world is (Heidegger 1962). We must emphasize that our discussion refers to screens, qua screens, which collect and attract attention. The agreement, implied in them, refers to some shared *ontological* understanding about the 'make-up' of the world, which is the basis on which our own actions with respect to screens gain their references and significance. Obviously, it does not mean that one has to agree with the terms, conditions, analysis, or format of what is displayed. The agreement is only with regard to the referential whole within which the screen is a screen—i.e. attracts our attention and directs our ongoing activity in that form of life. Thus, by the term 'ontological' here we are referring to the idea that the agreement implied by relevance and attention already suggest that we have agreed to take the world *to be in the terms it is being presented*. For example we see the news on television *as* the 'news' and take it to be referring to actual events, or we see the arrival time of the train on the monitor and take it to refer to the actual possibility of a train arriving at that time, or we see the numbers on the ATM screen to be the actual amount of money we have to spend, etc.

It is worthwhile to note that the screen as such is first and primordially seeing, watching, perceiving with the eyes. We, as human beings, have a structural tendency to assume the primacy of seeing. Seeing, according to Heidegger (1962: 214), is 'a peculiar way of letting the world be encountered by us in perception'. In *everyday practical activity* the human sense of sight performs a central role in our involvement in-the-world (Heidegger 1962). What is at stake in this supremacy of seeing, so to speak, is not a characteristic or feature of humans, but an ontological conception of being human *in which cognition is conceived as seeing*. This fundamental conception, the ontological primacy of seeing, grounds the way in which screens gain ontological importance as screens—rather than as mere dynamic surfaces.

This priority of seeing, in which cognition is understood as seeing, and thus seeing as the access to truth, can be traced back to the early Greek thought of Parmenides (Heidegger 1962: 215) and especially in the work of Aristotle (1998) as presented in his treatise *Metaphysics*. Saint Augustine also noted this priority of 'seeing'—this correspondence between seeing and cognition. In this regard Heidegger (1962: 215) refers to Saint Augustine's work from *The Confessions*:

> We even use this word 'seeing' for the other senses when we devote them to cognizing (. . .) We not only say 'See how that shines' (. . .), but we even say 'See how that sounds', 'See how that is scented', 'See how that tastes', 'See how hard that is' (. . .) Therefore the experience of the senses in general is designated as the 'lust of the eyes'; for when the issue is one of knowing something, the other senses, by a certain resemblance, take to themselves the function of seeing—a function in which the eyes have priority. (Saint Augustine quoted in Heidegger 1962: 215–16)

The power of the ontological suggestions 'on' screens is evident when we realize that we live in a tradition in which to see is to believe and what is believed is what is true. This priority of seeing, the primacy of the human sense of vision over the other senses, is a thesis defended by McLuhan (1962, 1964). He claimed that the phonetic alphabet, invented more than 4,000 years ago, was the technology that brought about that primacy, introducing us into a world dominated by vision-based patterns, modes, and equilibriums. This priority of seeing, in which cognition is understood as seeing, and thus seeing as the access to truth, gets revealed in a particular way in screens. In the phenomenon screen, seeing is not merely being aware of a surface. The very watching of the screen as screen implies an already present ontological agreement about the nature of the world; a world that is relevant (and true) to us that share it, in and through the screening of the screen. This is an important hint if we are to understand the power of screens in contemporary organizations and society.

In the phenomenon screen, seeing is not merely being aware of a surface. The very watching of the screen as it screens implies an already there ontological agreement about the nature of the world—as a world that is relevant (and true) to us that share it, in and through the screens we face. Screens, in their screening, already have the attention of those surrounding them because they are focal points of already agreement, because what is displayed already relies on a context of a fundamental already present agreement. It is exactly this already agreement that we depend on as managers, users, train drivers, and so forth, when we turn to the screen to reveal our world to us.

To conclude, the phenomenological meaning (Heidegger 1962, 1977) of screen qua screen reveals itself as already ontological agreement. It is this already agreement that calls for our attention, attracts us, makes us look at the screen in its screen-ness, *and simultaneously condemns to forgetfulness that which was already agreed upon*, precisely because it is not an agreement but an already agreement. This already agreement is a form of life in which the screens can be said to be, in a very profound way, its *skin*. As already agreement, the thinking, the bargaining, the transacting, the negotiating, that typically precede an agreeing emerge as pre-emptively excluded. It is because this concealed meaning of 'already agreement' is the essential background of 'relevance' and 'calling for attention' that the screen does not show itself, but rather hides itself, as it pursues its way in the world. This is where we started. We noted that we do not tend to look at screens in its screening but rather at what appears on their surface. As such screens 'screen' our world: concealing and spreading this already agreement. Indeed it is important to underscore the ongoing *concealing and spreading* of meaning in screening, made possible by the necessary *already agreement* of ongoing screening.

We must emphasize that this analysis of ours only provides the preliminary outlines of a full phenomenology of screens. It still requires further critical consideration to expose suppositions yet to be scrutinized. It also needs more imaginative variation to extend the analysis to other realms of screens, and so forth. Nevertheless we hope that it does serve as a useful illustration of the potential of phenomenology to move us beyond this or that screen, or the way this or that person interprets screens, to the essential meaning of screens as they function in the world of everyday meaningful activity.

Some Empirical Conclusions on the Screening of Screens

Unfortunately space will not allow us to explore all the possible empirical consequences and implications of our analysis. Nevertheless, we will offer here, for illustrative purposes, some brief comments to point out the empirical relevance of our phenomenological findings.

The power of *already agreement* can, for example, be seen with regard to our general view of television in everyday life. We often refer to people without television as 'living in another world'. As Fry (1993: 13) puts it, the 'television has arrived as the context' and those people without one seem to be out of that context. The power of television to reinforce what is presented just by the presentation itself has important consequences in our daily lives: 'all that is important is revealed on television while all that is so revealed on television acquires some authority' (Adams 1993: 59). But this power does not belong to the essence of television but rather to the essence of screens. This is also evident from the fact that the kind of data about us that appear on a screen, at the bank, at the office, at the medical doctor, at a public department, are often taken as more valid and trustworthy than ourselves—as many of us may have found out to our dismay. Indeed from our understanding of the screening of screens it is clear that this primacy of that which is on the screen over that which is not on the screen seems to be an issue that needs to be taken into account while designing new systems. Seemingly trivial decisions about entities and attributes to be included/excluded in the database have important ontological consequences for how we will understand our world. Indeed, these decisions will function as ontological references as they become presented on screens, and will as such mediate the manner in which we relate to and in that world.

It is possible to imagine all sorts of implications of our analysis for the importance of screening: for example, the importance of the *form of life* in establishing screens when managing change. And, for example, the power of screened information in creating 'facts' through screening as such. Due to space constraints we will not pursue these here. Let us turn now to some critical comments and limitations of phenomenology.

SOME CRITICAL COMMENTS AND LIMITATIONS OF PHENOMENOLOGY

Phenomenology, like all other approaches, has been criticized from various quarters. We will review some of these criticisms and indicate how other approaches emerged or are related to these criticisms.

Phenomenology is often criticized for scholasticism and obscurantism. Critics argue that authors in phenomenology have an excessive tendency to refer back to ancient Greek masters for authority as well as using strange formulations and technical terminology that serves only to hide, obscure, or circumvent the debate about its limits and possibilities. There is no doubt that the texts that form the canon of phenomenology are very difficult to access. This may be because it is often read in English as a translation from German or French, which does not always translate well. But more than this, the authors often use ordinary language in a unique and technical manner. This becomes necessary because our normal way of speaking is in the idiom of the 'natural attitude'—which is by its very nature dualistic. For example in our use of nouns, verbs, and adjectives we construct sentences that make us 'see' the world as populated with bounded objects (nouns) that do certain things (verbs) and 'have' certain characteristics or attributes (adjectives). So when Heidegger claims that humans are beings-in-the-world we would normally tend to think of humans as having 'being-in-the-world-ness' as an attribute. However, Heidegger, means precisely to say that being-in-the-world is what we are, as such; we are never *not* beings-in-the-world—self and world is a unity from the start, never not a unity. The difference between these two interpretations is profound. Thus, quite paradoxically, phenomenology needs a 'formal' language to talk about something we all informally already experience, in the background, as it were. However, because this background is *in the background* we do not talk about; it 'is not what we usually deal with and have words for, so to talk of it requires a special vocabulary' (Dreyfus 1991: 7).

Phenomenology in general, and Husserl's transcendental phenomenology in particular, is often criticized as being solipsistic. By this they mean that phenomenology reduces the reality of the world to some content in consciousness (the mind), i.e. that the account of phenomenology implies that we are ultimately 'locked up' in our own consciousness. This is a partial reading and understanding of phenomenology as argued by Sokolowski (2000) and Zahavi (2003). Because phenomenology takes subjectivity seriously and describes the world 'as experienced' does not mean that reality is the product of the inescapable mind. Nor did Husserl's transcendental reduction—the return to the things themselves—imply that the 'source' of reality is somehow 'locked up' in purified consciousness. Both of these views misses the radical innovation of phenomenology, namely the immediate, always already there, unity of the self and the world. For Husserl, as noted above, consciousness is not a subjectively constructed, inner and private domain, that must be 'eliminated' but rather it is an always already *public mind* that exists as a completely immanent—wholly present, never absent— ongoing structural correlation with the world (Sokolowski 2000: 14). As Zahavi (2003: 46) argues: 'To perform the *epochç* and the reduction is not to abstain from an investigation of the real world in order to focus on mental content and representation . . . The *epochç* and the reduction do not involve an *exclusive turn toward inwardness*, and they do not *imply any loss*' (emphasis added). One could, perhaps, argue that Husserl is solipsistic in his descriptive methodology, in as much as he does want to give an account of the things themselves through a reduction to the noematic structure of consciousness (Moran 2000: 178). Equally, Heidegger argued that the essence of being human is that we are beings that are always and already in-the-world—when we become aware of the world we are already there, committed to things, doing things, expecting things, and so forth. This already 'thereness' is the structural unity of world and self, which is the horizon—referential whole—within which things stand out as meaningful. This unity means that it does not make sense to talk about some meaning 'in the mind'. In this same vein we can see that the debate about idealism and realism does not appeal to phenomenology as it draws on a distinction phenomenology sees as meaningless or at least not very helpful. Having said this, it must be acknowledged that the fact that phenomenology operates from the first person perspective, the world 'as experienced', does make it weak with respect to its account of intersubjectivity. Heidegger's account of the intersubjective dimension as 'being-with' is acknowledged to be less innovative than his other work. Also the work of Schutz and Luckmann (1973) on intersubjectivity has not had the impact one might have expected. Nevertheless, the influence of phenomenology in the work of social theorists such as Giddens (1984) is widely acknowledged.

Phenomenology is often criticized as being ahistorical, or of not taking history seriously enough. This comment is often made together with the claim that phenomenology is an essentialist approach to understanding the world. We will discuss these two claims together. There is no doubt that phenomenology is essentialist, this is exactly its enormous potential. However, what phenomenology sees as 'essential' is different from the general interpretation of the notion.[21] Most often essentialism is seen within the context of Platonic essences or ideal forms, which are really existing timeless abstract entities of which physical objects are imperfect copies—or less starkly put, some timeless entity that is the real remainder once we remove the incidental and idiosyncratic. The Platonic need for transcending the specific and the incidental strips the object of its historicity. More significant for phenomenology is the Aristotelian notion of essence, namely, those properties that are essential or necessary without which things could not exist or be the things that they are. The phenomenological notion of essence is closer to the Aristotelian notion, in placing the emphasis on the 'necessary conditions (not properties!) for a being to be what it is'—however, it is also radically different, especially in the existential phenomenology of Heidegger. For Heidegger the essence is not 'in' the object but rather already in-the-world—i.e. in the ongoing referential whole that provided the ongoing necessary references for the thing to be what it is already taken to be. The chair is 'a chair' because of all the references, the referential whole or world, that refers to it as such and to which it refers as such. Furthermore, this referential whole is the whole that it is because it exists within the horizon of finite temporal human existence, of memory, activity, and anticipation. The unity of self and world is a unity only within finite human temporality. That is why Heidegger's major work is called *Being and Time*, being (essence) does not exist outside human time. Indeed it would be extremely difficult, we would argue impossible, to give an account of everyday life without recourse to some form of phenomenological essentialism. A response to the perceived essentialism, as well as the inadequate intersubjective account in phenomenology, which nevertheless emerged from phenomenology, is *ethnomethodology* (Garfinkel 1967). For ethnomethodology the world is as it appears in the natural attitude. They argue that we, as phenomenologists, should not assume to have some privileged access to a world 'more real' than it appears to normal everyday persons doing everyday things—for them there is nothing to be gained through the phenomenological attitude. With this in mind they proceed to examine the everyday practices by which actors make the ongoing ordinary life possible. We would argue that this response may be valid if directed towards early Husserlian phenomenology, but is certainly not valid with respect to existential phenomenology. We cannot peruse this debate here—refer to Rogers (1983) for a detailed discussion of the debate between phenomenology and ethnomethodology.

The most severe critique of phenomenology, in particular Husserlian phenomenology, comes from the deconstructivist movement, in particular from Derrida (1973). Derrida argues that phenomenology still mostly operates within the 'metaphysics of presence' that characterizes the Western philosophical tradition. By this he means the metaphysical assumption that that which is present to me now as such and such a thing is the same as when that same thing was present to me earlier on. Or, differently stated, that there is an *ongoing self-evident presence* that guarantees every re-presentation of every previous present thing as such. For example: if I look at the cup in front of me, look away, and then back at the cup, how will I know that it is indeed the same cup? What provides the ongoing temporal horizon for me to take the cup to be the same cup as some moments before? Derrida argues that 'this supposed self-presence is actually the *result of a repeated substitution*. As such, its ground is a nonpresence. Its basis is the absence that allows the substitute to take the place of what it substitutes for' (Mensch 2001: 5, emphasis added). Thus, the supposedly self-evident presence operates on the ongoing recalling of what is not present (absence) to guarantee itself here and now.

Heidegger realized this, and his later work is indeed a response to this and also the starting point for Derrida's project of *deconstruction*. It must also be said that the deconstruction project also eventually finds itself in a sort of 'metaphysics of absence or otherness', always deferring to a beyond that will never be a presence as such; this is evident in the work of Derrida (1973) and, in particular, the work of Levinas (1991). We will not explore this debate further here—refer to Mensch (2001) and Lawlor (2002) for a detailed discussion of the relationship between deconstruction and phenomenology.

We will note that this lack of self-presence, and the need for repeated substitution, identified by Derrida, is also the key to the *hermeneutics* project. The hermeneutics project, which started with the problem of interpreting ancient texts, moved progressively towards this idea of a fundamental always already distanciation at the heart of all ongoing experience, i.e. the need to continually 'bring back to the present' what has always already 'slipped away' into the past (Ricoeur 1981). Thus, we find that we are not at all transparent to ourselves, and as such we are continuously interpreting and making sense of our own ongoing presence in the world—in a sense we, and all other human beings, are always an obscure text in need of ongoing interpretation and self-interpretation.

Now that we have outlined some of the critiques against phenomenology and indicated some of the approaches that emanated from this critique we will turn to a brief discussion of some work in phenomenology that may be relevant to the IS community.

REFLECTIONS ON EXISTING WORK IN PHENOMENOLOGY

Albert Borgmann (1984) uses Heidegger's (1977) critique of modern technology—as presented in his famous essay 'The Question Concerning Technology'—to argue that we need to find a 'free' relation to technology. In his essay Heidegger argues that the essence of modern technology is *Gestell* (often translated as 'enframing'). By this he means that modern technology always already frames our relation to the world in a particular way. He argues that this particular way is one in which everything (even humans) are framed, or rather revealed, as 'resources-for' this or that project. Borgmann agrees with Heidegger's analysis of modern technology in arguing that modern technology reveals the world for us as 'devices'. By this he means that modern technology as devices *hides* the referentiality of the world—the worldhood of the world—upon which they depend. They do not disclose the multiplicity of necessary conditions for them to be what they are taken to be. In fact just the opposite, they try and hide the necessary effort for them to be available for use. Thus, a thermostat on the wall that we simply set at a comfortable temperature now replaces the process of chopping wood, building the fire, and maintaining it. Our relationship with the environment is now reduced to, and disclosed to us as a control that we simply set to our liking. In this way devices de-world our relationship with things, in Heidegger's terminology. By relieving us of the burden of making and maintaining fires our relationship with the world becomes disclosed in a new way—as one of disengagement. The world of things is not something to be engaged in, it is rather simply available for consumption. Against such a disengaging relationship with things in the world Borgmann argues for the importance of focal practices based on focal things. Focal things solicit our full and engaging presence. We can think of the focal practice of preparing and enjoying a meal with friends or family as opposed to a solitary consumption of a fast food meal. If one takes Borgmann's analysis seriously we might conclude that we, as contemporary humans surrounded by devices, are doomed to increasingly relate to the world in a disengaged manner. This might be so Borgmann argues, however, it is also possible to have a free relation with technology—also modern technology—if we imbed it in focal practices rather than use it, or accept it, as devices. Otherwise we will, as Heidegger (1977) argued, become the devices of our devices.

Phenomenology's critical contribution with respect to technology is not just at the general level as developed by Borgmann. Hurbert Dreyfus (1993) used it to develop a devastating critique of the artificial intelligence (AI). His work resulted in a complete reorientation of AI, of which the most prominent is perhaps the current 'embodied' paradigm (Steels and Brooks 1995). Dreyfus, using Heidegger's work, argued against a representationalist approach to cognition and action. He argued that we do not have representations in our mind that guide or direct our actions in the world. Rather, as skilled actors in-the-world we draw upon tools 'as possibilities for' without having first to conceptualize the tool, the task, and the relationship between them—as assumed in a representationalist account. To put it rather bluntly: skilled action is mindless. Suchman (1987), an ethnomethodologist, also uses this type of Heideggarian argument to show that we do not make plans and then execute it. Rather the plan only becomes relevant as resources that can be drawn upon in situated action when things start to break down.

The work of Dreyfus and Suchman has important implications for IS design and use. For example, organizational actors do not have plans, strategies, or goals in their heads that they then implement in action. Rather, as skilled actors they draw on events, reports, and communications as 'possibilities for', without having to conceptualize explicitly the strategy, the information, and relationship between them. This was also demonstrated clearly in the work of Ciborra (2000). It is also clear to see that if we take the work of Heidegger seriously, we would tend to think very differently about the role methodology plays in the design process (Winograd and Flores 1986; Rathswohl 1991; Introna and Whitley 1997).

Phenomenology may also help us to think very differently about the way in which organizational actors use information in decision making, as argued by Winograd and Flores (1986) and Introna (1996). For example, Introna (1996) argues that managers in the world already understand what they need to do and most often use information systems to find ways to articulate and make sense of what they already know. He argues with Heidegger that interpretation can only be based on an already present sense or understanding and not the other way around, as assumed. This claim makes sense if we see that interpretation is the 'unravelling' of the referential whole already present as the necessary condition of meaningful ongoing skilful action. Interpretation, and the information to support that, often becomes necessary in moments of breakdown when managers are asked to explain themselves. Likewise, Winograd and Flores (1986) argue that managers find themselves in networks of commitments—Heidegger's notion of thrownness—within which the question is not 'what should we do' but rather 'what is possible' given my already there network of commitments—the already there network of commitments that constitute the manager as 'a manager'. Managers in the world find themselves 'always already oriented to a certain direction of possibilities' in which 'relevance always comes from a pre-orientation within a background' (pp. 147–9). For the manager-in-the-world the information system is just one of the references in a dense, ongoing, referential whole that continuously locates and dislocates possibilities for action.

More generally, phenomenology has also interrogated phenomena such as cyberspace and its relation to embodiment. In his thoughtful book *Designing Information Technology in the Postmodern Age* Coyne (1995) argues that cyberspace is not an ontological world—mere 'information does not make worlds or space' (p. 177). It is the concerns of everyday life, the people we talk to, the community we are part of and the things that occupy our attention that makes a world. In a similar vein Dreyfus (2001: 90) argues that:

> Our body, including our emotions, plays a crucial role in our being able to make sense of things so as to see what is relevant, our ability to let things matter to us and to acquire skills, our sense of the reality of things, our trust in other people, and finally, our capacity for making unconditional commitments that gives meaning to our lives. It would be a serious mistake to think we could do without these embodied capacities [and practices]—to rejoice that the World Wide Web offers us a chance to become more and more disembodied, detached ubiquitous minds leaving our situated, vulnerable bodies behind.

Don Idhe (2002: 15) also concludes that virtual bodies 'are thin and never attain the thickness of flesh'. In the end when we switch the computer off we are still enmeshed in our daily entanglements, our thrownness, in which we have to make the mundane things work. The 'shortcutting' of the ordinary embodied and situated world through the virtual—the fantasy of the virtual organization, will always eventually have to be made 'real', or grounded, in the thick reality of everyday embodied practices—the world as such. We need to accept that the representation is not the world, the map is not the territory.

Ihde (1990) suggests through his phenomenological analysis of human/technology relationships that we embody technology such as screens. He uses the example of wearing eyeglasses. In wearing my eyeglasses I do not only see through them, they also become 'see through'. In being that which they are, they already withdraw into my own bodily sense as part of the ordinary way I experience my surrounding. Our phenomenology of screens suggests that screens are not just embodied they are also in a sense already enworlded. By this we mean they are not simply a way we look at the world (as representation of the world for example) but they already imply and draw upon a way of living. Hence, like the eyeglasses, they withdraw into our sense of what is relevant, or is not relevant, as part of our ongoing way of being. In this sense screens are embodied but also simultaneously hermeneutic (in Ihde's terminology). Although I might fix my focus on the text or images on the screen, what I actually see is not the screen itself but rather immediately and simultaneously the world it already refers to, the activities, people, or things already implied in the text and images on the screen. As we increasingly draw on screens they withdraw to become for us immediately and already the world itself. However, these hermeneutic possibilities and withdrawal will only take place if the screen is already a screen for us. It is this prior screenness that our analysis brings to the fore.

It is our argument that phenomenology offers a rich and subtle range of possibilities for IS researchers. However, phenomenology itself requires a commitment to scholarship and thoughtful thinking, which is always difficult in a world often requiring ready-made solutions rather than thoughtful interpretations.

FINAL COMMENTS

Returning to our opening argument. In concluding that the phenomenological meaning (Heidegger 1962, 1977) of screen, qua screen, is an ontological agreement, which we express as already agreement, we stress that our approach is entirely phenomenological. We did not try to take into account any other possible perspectives or approaches in presenting our phenomenology of the screen. That being said, our analysis presented above only provides a rather preliminary outline of a full phenomenology of screens. It still requires further critical consideration to expose suppositions yet to be scrutinized. Indeed the work of others such as Sobchack (1991, 1994, 1999) might be taken up fruitfully in extending our analysis to include, for example, the experience of watching screens. In addition our present analysis tends to privilege information technology based screens. Some additional analysis is necessary to extend it even further. Furthermore, the Heideggerian ontology as well as the methodological approach of the investigation has set its boundaries—clearly other orientations are possible, especially in non-Western terms. Even within phenomenology we might have chosen other paths such as the pragmatic phenomenology of Ihde (1990, 1993, 2002) or the ontological phenomenology of Ingarden (1989). Given the path we have taken we believe we have shown that the screen is an important phenomenon in contemporary life that merits further elaboration and analysis. We believe as well to have shown the potential and possibilities of phenomenology in research in the social sciences in general and in the area of information systems in particular.

As we indicated in the introduction, phenomenology is a response to all forms of empirical and psychological reductionism as well as idealistic theoretical reductionism. Empiricism is based on highly inappropriate suppositions, according to phenomenology. For the empiricists the facts of the world 'speak for themselves', they are given to us as that which they are, for example, a chair as a 'chair' and an attitude as an 'attitude'. In other words the objects, events, states, etc. that we observe are simply *given* to our senses as that which they are rather than being constituted through our consciousness of them. Their meaning is already inscribed on their very surfaces, as it were. The world is simply as revealed through our natural attitude. With this supposition in hand they then proceed to describe, measure, and account for the ongoing world in these 'given' terms. These evident given facts are captured through observation and then constructed into various explanations and theories of the world. Through this process of 'theory-making'—which is the 'stuff' of positivism—they proceed to cloak the world with all sorts of theoretical meanings divorced of any sense of actuality—leading many to describe the theory of IS as irrelevant and meaningless, divorced of practice. Against this view phenomenology argues that the world is always already meaningful. That we already observe this or that thing in the world requires as a necessary condition an already present horizon of meaning in which 'this' or 'that' show up as such. The task of phenomenology is to give an account of this necessary horizon of meaning. Through phenomenology we can give an account of the nexus of relationships (in consciousness and in the world) that constitute these meanings as such. Such an account can provide an entirely new foundation from which to direct empirical investigations of the world. Since phenomenology is guided by experience, as experienced, and nothing besides, it will maintain its actuality. Phenomenology is not against empirical investigation. Nor is phenomenology denying that the world exists separate from our experience of it—i.e. phenomenology is not anti-realist. It argues rather that such empirical investigation will only make sense if grounded in the world, in the nexus of relationships or horizon of meaning, that make such an investigation meaningful in the first place. The 'real world' of relevance is not merely speaking to more managers if such speaking is not grounded in the world of ongoing and active meaning.

A second supposition of the empirical reductionism—in a sense required by the first supposition—is that things have meaning *in themselves*. As said above their meaning is already inscribed on their very surfaces as such. This supposition leads to a decontextualization of meaning and a reconstruction of meaning through theory making as mentioned above. This leads to a theoretical world which is the form of life of scientists—which is a legitimate location of study in its own right. For existential phenomenology the meaning of the thing is always and already in the nexus of relationships of the world. We can only understand managers, 'as managers', by understanding and analysing the nexus of relationships that constitute the manager, and which the manager continues to draw upon in order to be 'a manager'. The manager is what she is only in the ongoing involvement whole of 'being a manager in the organization'. Thus, meaning-making of active consciousness is always and already 'grounded' in the world of ongoing activity. Interpretation of phenomena is not arbitrary or idiosyncratic. Every phenomenological attempt to give an interpretation of something can only be grounded in the world where it has its being, its meaning. Thus, in phenomenology, contrary to the criticism often levelled at interpretivism, not anything goes. Phenomenological interpretation is not the uncovering of the subject's private mind (this is psychological reductionism). It is not just another interpretation, or the endless proliferation of interpretations. Interpretivism that is not grounded in phenomenology can indeed be seen as psychologism—and there are quite a bit of so-called interpretive studies in IS that are of this nature.

The challenge of this chapter to the IS community is to take phenomenology seriously as a path towards meaningful analysis, theory, and research. With phenomenology we may be able to face our 'crisis' of rigorous and relevant (Keen 1991; Benbasat and Zmud 1999); rigorous, as we ground ourselves only in the things themselves—ongoing being-in-the-world as the completely immanent—wholly present, never absent—ongoing structural correlation with the world; relevant, as our ultimate authority is the ever-present horizon of meaning, which is the world itself.

NOTES

1. See e.g. Dreyfus 1982, 1993; Boland 1983, 1985, 1991, 1993; Winograd and Flores 1986; Zuboff 1988; Boland and Day 1989; Introna 1993, 1997; Kjaer and Madsen 1995; Ciborra 1997, 1998, 2000; Haynes 1997; Introna and Whitley 1997; Porra 1999; Introna and Ilharco 2000, 2004a, 2004b, 2006; Mingers 2001; Whittaker 2001; Ilharco 2002; Introna and Whittaker 2002; Brigham and Introna 2006; Croon Fors 2006.

2. We must note that it is not given to us as an extended object. To take it as an object we need to already have separated it from its immediate surroundings and background. Furthermore, to take it as extended we need to already have assumed spatiality. Thus, any taking of an object, even in its aspect, already requires, as necessary, a familiarity with the world as its condition of possibility.

3. It is important to state that Husserl's work is characterized by an earlier period and a later period. In the earlier period Husserl was more interested in the formal structures of consciousness (this work is often referred to as *transcendental phenomenology*). However in his later work especially *The Crisis of the European Sciences* Husserl (1970) shifts towards a more *genetic phenomenology* where he emphasizes the active, historical consciousness rooted in the life world. In our discussion and analysis we will tend to focus on this later Husserl rather than the earlier Husserl. It is also the later Husserl that creates the bridge to Heidegger, which is important in our use of phenomenology as an *existential phenomenology* when we analyse the phenomenon 'screen' below.

4. The term 'always and already' will be used frequently and is used in a very specific manner. By this term we mean 'always already' in the sense that it is impossible to find a starting point as such—some point where it all started as it were. At any point in the past that we may find it is already active and busy. Furthermore, the 'always already' refers to

the fact that it is not sometimes active and sometimes not. Rather it is 'always already' active, engaged, and directed. Refer to Heidegger's (1962) introduction of the term in *Being and Time*.

5. As mentioned above, even the possibility of experiencing sound 'as sound' implies a horizon of temporality that can hold together in the 'now' what has gone before and anticipate what is yet to come.

6. We must note that the *noemata* are not simply generalizations. The process of generalization itself already presupposes the existence of a *noema* since, for example 'the abstraction of the general idea "red" [or chair] is arrived at by leaving out of account all those respects in which several red [chair] objects differ in order to hold on to that respect in which they are similar. But the concept of similarity (or even respect) which is in question here itself presupposes the very comprehension (of the essence of "red" [chair]) which it is supposed to account for' (Macann 1993: 9).

7. For an excellent in-depth discussion of Husserl's theory of intentionally refer to Gurwitsch (1967, 1982).

8. For excellent introductions to Heiddegger's thought refer to Polt (1999) and King (2001).

9. Refer to Monika Langer's (1989) and John Mingers' (2001) commentary for a good introduction to Merleau-Ponty's work.

10. For Heidegger 'being' is not a substance but the ongoing unfolding of the referential whole that reveals something as what it is, its ongoing phenomenological meaning. Thus, for him being is a *process* not a substance. It would be better to write it as be-ing but this becomes awkward.

11. Heidegger uses the hyphens in being-in-the-world to indicate the ongoing structural unity of self and world so that we would not slip back into a natural language in which we speak of the self without immediately implying also an already there meaningful world. This is a bit awkward but it is important to signal.

12. We must note that we as humans do not take up projects in a similar way that we do not take up things as objects. Our projects are always already part of our being-in-the-world. We are always ahead of ourselves. When we get up in the morning we already anticipate the day ahead. When we get into our cars we already anticipate the journey. To put it rather abstractly, we are always and already project-ed as a necessary condition of what we already are—as academics, managers, etc. We did not decide to take up the project to write this chapter so much as we found ourselves writing this chapter as that which already made sense for us as academics to do.

13. Refer to Polt (1999: ch. 3) for a very accessible account of Heidegger's notion of world.

14. Elsewhere we have discussed the method as having five seven phases (Introna and Ilharco 2000). This is more in line with Spiegelberg's discussion. However, due to space constraints and considerations of pragmatic use of the method we will limit ourselves here to only four fundamental phases. These will serve as a consistent way to apply phenomenology.

15. Unfortunately, due to space limitations we cannot provide a detailed discussion here. We hope that the analysis of the screen will make the method clear. Also, refer to Spiegelberg's (1994: 677–719) account for more detail.

16. Take careful note again that when we use the term 'world' or 'in-the-world' in our analysis we are using it in the phenomenological sense, i.e. the nexus or referential whole in which things refer to each other as already meaningful—as explained above (Heidegger 1962).

17. Indeed other words we use to refer to screens, such as output device, dumb terminal, cathode ray tube, liquid crystal display, flat panel display, and so forth, are multiple modes of showing particular aspects, functionalities, or perspectives of screens. They are all phenomenologically related to the phenomenon 'screen'.

18. Sanskrit—the language in which 'The Vedas', the oldest sacred texts, are written—was an early form of an Indo-Aryan language, dating from around 1000 BC. The Indo-Aryan languages are supposed to derive from the hypothetical Proto-Indo-European language (before 3000 BC) from which also could have evolved Slavic, Baltic, Classical Greek, Latin, Germanic, and other families of languages. Old High German, Middle English, and Middle Dutch, belong to the *West* branch of the Germanic family. Middle French belongs to the Italic (Latin) family (Crystal 1987).

19. Elsewhere we have demonstrated this central intent through sound analysis. Due to space limitations we will not pursue such an analysis here (Introna and Ilharco 2000).

20. The notion of 'form of life' that we use here refers to a familiar and meaningful ongoing activity whole in which things already appears as meaningful and therefore does not require elaboration by those participating in the form of life—somewhat akin to Wittgenstein's (1967) notion of form of life.

21. For an excellent discussion on the phenomenological notion of essence refer to the work of Mohanty (1997, 1970).

REFERENCES

ABC (1999). *ABC News* <http://archive.abcnews.go.com/sections/world/1997/97diana.html>, accessed 29 December 1999.

Adams, P. (1993). 'In TV: On "Nearness", on Heidegger and on television', in T. Fry (ed.), *RUA TV? Heidegger and the Televisual*. Sydney: Power Institute of Fine Arts.

Aristotle (1998). *The Metaphysics,* trans. Hugh Lawson-Tancred. London: Penguin Books.

Baudrillard, J. (2002). *Screened Out*. London: Verso.

Benbasat, I. and Zmud, R. (1999). 'Empirical Research in Information Systems: The Practice of Relevance', *Management Information Systems Quarterly*, 23(1): 3–16.

Boland, R. J. (1983). 'The In-formation of Information Systems', in R. J. Boland and R. A. Hirschheim (eds.), *Critical Issues in Information Systems Research*. New York: John Wiley & Sons, 363–94.

—— (1985). 'Phenomenology: a Preferred Approach to Research on Information Systems', in E. Mumford et al. (eds.), *Research Methods in Information Systems*. Amsterdam: Elsevier Science Publishers B.V., 193–201.

—— (1991). 'Information System Use as a Hermeneutic Process', in H.-E. Nissen, H. K. Klein, and R. A. Hirschheim (eds.), *Information Systems Research: Contemporary Approaches and Emergent Traditions*. Amsterdam: North-Holland, 439–64.

—— (1993). 'Accounting and the Interpretive Act', *Accounting, Organisations and Society*, 18(2/3): 125–46.

—— and Day, W. F. (1989). 'The Experience of System Design: A Hermeneutic of Organizational Action', *Scandinavian Journal of Management*, 5(2): 87–104.

Brigham, M., and Introna, L. D. (2006). 'Hospitality, Improvisation and Gestell: A Phenome-nology of Mobile Information', *Journal of Information Technology*, 21(3): 140–53.

Borgmann, A. (1984). *Technology and the Character of Contemporary Life*. Chicago, IL: University of Chicago Press.

Cerbone, D. R. (2006). *Understanding Phenomenology*. Chesham: Acumen Publishing.

Ciborra C. (1997). 'De Profundis? Deconstructing the Concept of Strategic Alignment', Working paper, Department of Informatics, University of Oslo, Oslo, Norway.

—— (1998). 'From tool to *Gestell*', *Information Technology and People*, 11(4): 305–27.

—— (2000). *From Control to Drift: The Dynamics of Corporate Information Infrastructure*. Oxford: Oxford University Press.

Coyne, R. (1995). *Designing Information Technology in the Post-modern Age: From Method to Metaphor*. Cambridge, MA: MIT Press.

Croon Fors, A. (2006). *Being-with Information Technology: Critical Explorations beyond Use and Design*. Ph.D. thesis, Department of Informatics, Umeå University, Sweden.

Derrida, J. (1973). 'Speech and Phenomena', in *Speech and Phenomena and Other Essays on Husserl's Theory of Signs*, trans. David Allison. Evanston, IL: Northwestern University Press.

Dreyfus, H. (1982). *What Computers Can't Do: The Limits of Artificial Reason*. New York: Harper & Row.

—— (1991). *Being-in-the-World: A Commentary on Heidegger's Being and Time, Division I*. Cambridge, MA: MIT Press.

—— (1993). *What Computers Still Can't Do: A Critique of Artificial Reason*. Cambridge, MA: MIT Press.

—— (2001). *On the Internet*. New York: Routledge.

Fry, T. (1993). *RUA TV? Heidegger and the Televisual*. Sydney: Power Publications.

Garfinkel, H. (1967). *Studies in Ethnomethodology*. Englewood Cliffs, NJ: Prentice-Hall.

Giddens, A. (1984). *The Constitution of Society*. Berkeley, CA: University of California Press.

Glendinning, S. (2007). *In the Name of Phenomenology*. London: Routledge.

Gurwitsch, A. (1967). 'Intentionality, Constitution, and Intentional Analysis', in J. Kockel-mans (ed.), *Phenomenology*. New York: Anchor Books, Doubleday and Co, 118–37.

—— (1982). 'Husserl's Theory of the Intentionality of Consciousness', in H. Dreyfus (ed.), *Husserl's Intentionality and Cognitive Science*. Cambridge, MA: MIT Press, 59–71.

Hall, H. (1993). 'Intentionality and World: Division I of Being and Time', in Charles Guignon (ed.), *The Cambridge Companion to Heidegger*. Cambridge: Cambridge University Press.

Hammond, M., Howarth, J., and Keat, R. (1991). *Understanding Phenomenology*. Oxford: Blackwell.

Haynes, J. D. (1997). 'Meaning as Perspective: A Phenomenology of Information Systems'. Unpublished Ph.D. thesis, Bond University, Queensland.

Heidegger, M. (1962). *Being and Time*. Oxford: Blackwell.

—— (1971). *Poetry, Language, and Thought*, trans. Peter D. Hertz. New York: Harper.

—— (1977). *The Question Concerning Technology and Other Essays*. New York: Harper Torchbooks.

—— (1978). 'On the Essence of Truth', *Basic Writings*. London: Routledge

—— (1982). *The Basic Problems of Phenomenology*. Bloomington: Indiana University Press.

Heim, M. (1993). *The Metaphysics of Virtual Reality*. New York: Oxford University Press.

—— (1999). *Electric Language*. New York: Yale Universtity Press.

Husserl, E. (1964). *The Idea of Phenomenology*. The Hague: Martinus Nijhoff.

—— (1969). *Formal and Transcendental Logic*. The Hague: Martinus Nijhoff.

—— (1970a). *The Crisis of European Sciences and Transcendental Phenomenology: An Introduction to Phenomenological Philosophy*. Evanston, IL: Northwestern University Press.

—— (1970b). *Logical Investigations*. New York: Humanities Press.

—— (1995). *Cartesian Meditations: An Introduction to Phenomenology*. Dordrecht: Kluwer Academic Publishers.

Ihde, D. (2002). *Bodies in Technology*. Minneapolis: University of Minnesota Press.

—— (1990). *Technology and the Lifeworld: From Garden to Earth*. Bloomington: Indiana University Press.

—— (1993). *Philosophy of Technology—An Introduction*. New York: Paragon House.

Ilharco, F. M. (2002). 'Information Technology as Ontology'. Unpublished Ph.D. thesis, London School of Economics.

—— (2008). 'A catarse do fogo: a simbologia do fogo nos ecrãs da televisão', *Comunicação & cultura*, 5. Lisbon: FCH UCP.

Ingarden, R. (1989). *The Ontology of the Work of Art*, trans. R. Meyer with J. T. Goldthwait. Ohio, OH: Ohio University Press.

Introna, L. D. (1993). 'Information: A Hermeneutic Perspective', in *Proceedings of the First European Conference of Information Systems*. Henley-on-Thames, 171–9.

—— (1997). *Management, Information and Power*. London: Macmillan.

—— and Ilharco, F. M. (2000). 'The Screen and the World: A Phenomenological Investigation into Screens and our Engagement in the World', in R. Baskerville et al. (eds.), *Organizational and Social Perspectives on Information Technology*. Dordrecht: Kluwer Academic Publishers, 295–319.

———— (2004a). 'Phenomenology, Screens and the World: A Journey through Phenomenology with Husserl and Heidegger', in J. Mingers and L. Willcocks (eds.), *Social Theory and Philosophy for Information Systems*. London: Wiley & Sons.

————(2004b). 'The Ontological Screening of Contemporary Life: A Phenomenological Analysis of Screens', *European Journal of Information Systems*, 13(3): 221–34.

————(2006). 'On the Meaning of Screens: Towards a Phenomenological Account of Screenness', *Human Studies*, 29(1).

———— and Fäy, E. (eds.) (2008). *Phenomenology, Organisation and Technology*. Lisbon: Universidade Católica Editora.

—— and Whitley, E. A. (1997). 'Against Method-ism', *Information Technology and People*, 10(1): 31–45.

—— and Whittaker, L. (2002). 'The Phenomenology of Information Systems Evaluation: Overcoming the Subject Object Dualism', in E. H. Wynn et al. (eds.), *Global Organisational Discourse about Information Technology*. Dordrecht: Kluwer Academic Publishers, 155–75.

Kant, I. (1965). *Critique of Pure Reason*, trans. Norman Kemp Smith. New York: St Martin's Press.

Keen, P. (1991). 'Relevance and Rigor in Information Systems Research: Improving Quality, Confidence Cohesion and Impact', in H.-E. Nissen, H. Klein, and R. Hirschheim (eds.), *Information Systems Research: Contemporary Approaches & Emergent Traditions*. Amsterdam: North-Holland, 27–49.

King, M. (2001). *A Guide to Heidegger's Being and Time*, ed. John Llewelyn. Albany, NY: State University of New York Press.

Kjaer, A., and Madsen, K. H. (1995). 'Participatory Analysis of Flexibility', *Communications of the ACM*, 38(5): 53–60.

Kockelmans, J. (1967). *Phenomenology*. New York: Anchor Books, Doubleday and Co.

Langer, M. (1989). *Merleau-Ponty's Phenomenology of Perception: A Guide and Commentary*. Basingstoke: Macmillan Press.

Lawlor, L. (2002). *Derrida and Husserl: The Basic Problem of Phenomenology*. Bloomington, IN: Indiana University Press.

Leedy, P. D. (1997). *Practical Research: Planning and Design*. 6th edn., Englewood Cliffs, NJ: Prentice-Hall, Inc.

Levinas, E. (1991[1974]). *Other than Being or Beyond Essence*. Dordrecht: Kluwer Academic Publisher.

Macann, C. (1993). *Four Phenomenological Philosophers: Husserl, Heidegger, Sartre, Merleau-Ponty*. London: Routledge.

McLuhan, M. (1962). *The Gutenberg Galaxy*. Toronto: University of Toronto Press.

—— (1994) [1964]. *Understanding Media*. Cambridge, MA: MIT Press.

—— (2001) [1967]. *The Medium is the Massage*. Corte Madera, CA: Gingko Press.

Manovich, L. (1995). 'An Archaeology of a Computer Screen', NewMediaTopia, Soros Center for the Contemporary Arts, Moscow.

—— (2001). *The Language of New Media*. Chicago, IL: MIT Press.

Mensch, J. R. (2001). 'Derrida-Husserl: Towards a Phenomenology of Language', *Archai: New Journal for Philosophy and Phenomenological Research*, 1–66.

Merleau-Ponty, M. (1962). *Phenomenology of Perception*. London: Routledge.

Mingers, J. (2001). 'Embodying Information Systems: The Contribution of Phenomenology', *Information and Organization*, 11(2): 103–28.

Mohanty, J. (1970). *Phenomenology and Ontology*. The Hague: Martinus Nijhoff.

—— (1997). *Phenomenology: Between Essentialism and Transcendental Philosophy*. Evanston, IL: Northwestern University Press.

Moran, D. (2000). *Introduction to Phenomenology*. London: Routledge.

MW (1999, 2000). *Merriam Webster Dictionary* <http://www.m-w.com>.

OPDT (1997). *Oxford Paperback Dictionary & Thesaurus*, ed. Julia Elliot. Oxford: Oxford University Press.

Polt, R. (1999). *Heidegger: An Introduction*. London: UCL Press.

Porra, J. (1999).'Colonial Systems', *Information Systems Research*, 10(1): 38–69.

Rathswohl, E. J. (1991). 'Applying Don Idhe's Phenomenology of Instrumentation as a Framework for Designing Research in Information Science', in H.-E. Nissen, H. K. Klein, and R. A. Hirschheim (eds.), *Information Systems Research: Contemporary Approaches and Emergent Traditions*. Amsterdam: North-Holland, 421–38.

Ricoeur, P. (1981). *Hermeneutics and the Human Sciences*. Cambridge: Cambridge University Press.

Rogers, M. F. (1983). *Sociology, Ethnomethodology, and Experience: A Phenomenological Critique*. Cambridge: Cambridge University Press.

Schutz, A., and Luckmann, T. (1973).*The Structures of the LifeWorld*. Evanston, IL: Northwestern University Press.

Sobchack, V. (1991). *The Address of the Eye: A Phenomenology of Film Experience*. Princeton, NJ: Princeton University Press.

——(1994). 'The Scene of the Screen: Envisioning Cinematic and Electronic "Presence"', in H. U. Gumbrecht and K. L. Pfeiffer (eds.), *Materialities of Communication*. Stanford, CA: Stanford University Press, 83–106.

—(1999). 'Toward a Phenomenology of Nonfictional Film Experience', in J. M. Gaines and M. Renov (eds.), *Collecting Visible Evidence*. Minneapolis, MN: University of Minnesota Press, 243–54.

Sokolowski, R. (2000). *Introduction to Phenomenology*. Cambridge: Cambridge University Press.

Spiegelberg, H. (1975). *Doing Phenomenology*. The Hague: Martinus Nijhoff.

—(1994). *The Phenomenological Movement—A Historical Introduction*. 3rd rev. edn., Dordrecht: Kluwer Academic Publishers.

Steels, L., and Brooks, R. (eds.) (1995). *Building Situated Embodied Agents: The Alife Route to AI*. New Haven, CT: Lawrence Erlbaum Associates.

Suchman, L. (1987). *Plans and Situated Action: The Problem of Human-Machine Communication*. Cambridge: Cambridge University Press.

Thevenaz, P. (1962). *What is Phenomenology and Other Essays*, ed. and trans. J. M. Edie. London: Merlin Press.

Whittaker, L. (2001). 'Information Systems Evaluation: A Post Dualist Interpretation'. Unpublished Ph.D. thesis, University of Pretoria.

Winograd, T., and Flores, F. (1986). *Understanding Computers and Cognition: A New Foundation for Design*. Reading, MA: Addison Wesley.

Wittgenstein, L. (1967). *Philosophical Investigations*. Oxford: Blackwell.

Zahavi, D. (2003). *Husserl's Phenomenology*. Stanford, CA: Stanford University Press.

Zuboff, S. (1988). *In the Age of the Smart Machine*. New York: Basic Books.

....

CHAPTER 11

POST-STRUCTURALISM, SOCIAL SHAPING OF TECHNOLOGY, AND ACTOR-NETWORK THEORY: WHAT CAN THEY BRING TO IS RESEARCH?

....

NATHALIE MITEV AND DEBRA HOWCROFT

INTRODUCTION

....

MANY social theories have been used to analyse information systems, for instance: Foucault's postmodernist concept of power/knowledge (Knights and Murray 1997; Willcocks 2004); institutionalization (Silva and Backhouse 1997); structuration theory (Orlikowski 1992; Walsham 1993; Jones, Orlikowski, and Munir 2004); social shaping of technology (SST, Wilson and Howcroft 2003) and social construction of technology (SCOT) (Howcroft, Mitev, and Wilson 2004); critical realism (Mingers 2004); gender theories (Adam, Howcroft, and Richardson 2001); ir/rationality (Drummond 1996); Bourdieu's notion of habitus (Richardson 2003; Kvasny 2006), and actor-network theory (ANT) (Monteiro and Hanseth 1996). Nevertheless, there is overall limited reference in IS research to one of the most fundamental debates that has taken place in the social sciences over the last thirty years: that of postmodernism/post-structuralism. In this chapter we aim to address this omission by outlining this debate and highlighting relevant discussions and disputes. We do so in order to provide a clear understanding of ANT as it originates from post-structuralist debates in the field of science and technology studies (STS).

We begin by summarizing some of the key debates that are of relevance within post-structuralism and constructivism more specifically in management and organizational studies, which have addressed these debates more fully than IS research. Next, we outline STS, pointing out the debates between weak and strong constructivism and the relationship between SST, SCOT, and ANT. Then, some important ANT concepts are introduced before considering the use of ANT within IS research. The difficulties in using ANT are outlined and we argue that these are due to a lack of exposure to post-structuralism in IS research, as compared with other related disciplines such as organization theory and critical management studies. The next section asks whether it is possible for ANT to be critical on its own and suggests that consideration of efforts by scholars in related fields to combine ANT with critical social analysis may be a worthwhile pursuit for scholars of information systems. Finally, we warn that using ANT without a sound understanding of its post-structuralist roots can reduce it to a technicist and/or managerialist agenda and overlook its radical potential.

POST-STRUCTURALISM AND CONSTRUCTIVISM

In the 1980s, some organization theorists rejected positivism and started using post-structuralist approaches to carry out a critical study of topics such as power (Clegg 1989) or management as disciplinary control of the subject, using Foucauldian theory (see Chapter 7 in this volume). Rejection of positivism is not automatically a move towards social critique, just as to be a positivist is not automatically to be devoid of critical concern, but there is some linkage. At the very least, a recognition of the socially constructed nature of social arrangements points to their contingency and the possibility of their reconstruction along different lines. This is an important critical element of post-structuralism of which ANT is an example.

In their classic paper on critical theory and postmodernism in management studies, Alvesson and Deetz (1996) consider that a sophisticated critique comes from post-structuralism/postmodernism, which points to the agent-subject as crucial to critical analysis. Post-structuralism comes in different versions, some of which are argued to be reactionary as they undermine progress and emancipation. One of the most important tenets is the centrality of discourse where the constitutive powers of language are emphasized and 'natural' objects are viewed as discursively produced. This idea grew out of the linguistic turn in French structuralist philosophy. This fights the objectivists on the one hand with their science aimed at predicting/controlling nature and people, and humanists (or interpretivists) on the other for privileging the individual's reported experience and a naive version of human freedom. Through language, constructionism denies both the objectivist claim of objective truth, and the humanists' essentialist claims which miss the social/linguistic politics of experience. The Foucauldian version views discourses as systems of thought which are contingent upon, as well as informing, material practices. For example, 'corporate strategy' discourses have power effects, including the sustaining and enhancement of the prerogatives of management, the generation of a sense of personal security for managers, the expression of a gendered masculinity (see Chapter 21 in this volume), and the facilitation and legitimization of the exercise of power. These practices linguistically and practically produce forms of subjectivity through particular power techniques. Unlike the humanist essentialist understanding of humans, the person in postmodernism is always social first.

Subjectivity is a process where the discursive production of the individual replaces the conventional essentialist understanding of people. The notion of the autonomous, self-determining individual is rejected as ethnocentric and privileging rationality, masculinity, vision, and control, and participating in the reproduction of domination through discourses. The postmodernist understanding of objects and subjects is non-dualistic. It is concerned with the apparent stability of objects and the difficulty of unpacking the full range of activities that produce particular objects and sustain them. The presence of objects is not unproblematic and they only become an object in a specific relation to a being from whom it can be such an object. The point of view creates the object. For instance, workers do not have objective properties but are constructed by sets of relational systems which are not simply in the world but are a human understanding of the world, are discursive or textual.

One aspect of post-structuralism that is of relevance concerns its critique of grand narratives and its emphasis on multiple voices and local politics over large-scale political projects. Examples of grand narratives can be the external world in empiricism, human nature in humanism, Marxism's class struggle, technical progress, or the market economy in management. Stories in organizations connect to grand narratives but different ones have a local situational character.

Other focal points in post-structuralism are the power/knowledge connection, simulation, and resistance. It is impossible to separate power from knowledge and as a result knowledge loses neutrality. For example, the discourse that produces a 'manager' both empowers and disempowers the group of individuals formed as that object. Power resides in the demarcations and the systems of discourse that sustain them, including material arrangements. The demarcations provide forms of normative behaviour supported by claims of knowledge. Simulation takes precedence over the 'real world' in contemporary social order, and signs (for instance information systems) have 'model' responses to a 'model' world. Much postmodernist research highlights resistance and indeterminacy rather than rationality, predictability, and order. The primary methods are deconstruction and resistance reading, and genealogy. Instead of getting it 'right', the point is to challenge guiding assumptions, fixed meanings and relations, and expose the search for unity and harmony that suppresses division and conflict.

Social constructivist approaches such as post-structuralism are based on the understanding that the search for grand narratives and universal foundations has failed because the traditional social science ontology that there is a real world 'out there' that can be known epistemologically is not valid. Structural functionalists assume that world conditions exist separately from people's interpretations of them; interpretivism aims to counteract this. Additionally, the social constructivist perspective aims to

subvert claims to objective knowledge about problems and expert status. The constructionist position emphasizes that the activities through which problems are constructed
are rhetorical and analyses them as a social process, that is, as located within their social
context (Holstein and Miller 1993; Gergen 2001).

Social constructivist research has included the construction of theories and accounts
of institutions and of technical artefacts. Social constructivism has spread to science
and technology studies which reject both technological and social determinism (or
essentialism). Major advocates such as Latour and Woolgar (1979), Bijker and Law
(1992), and Collins and Pinch (1993) argue that there is no such thing as a social
problem that does not have technological components; nor can there be a technological
problem that does not have social components. Any attempt to make such a division is
bound to fail.

Constructivism: Beyond Interpretivist Research

Interpretivism has been used for many years in IS research (Walsham 1993; Walsham
1995; Orlikowski et al. 1996). In contrast to positivist interpretations of organizational
processes, interpretive methods aim at producing an 'understanding of the context of
the information system, and the process whereby the information system influences
and is influenced by its context' (Walsham 1993: 5). Within the interpretive tradition,
the study of the interaction between information systems and organizations has led to
the development of many theoretical models (e.g. Markus 1983; Markus and Robey
1988) and is associated with the emergent perspective (indeterminate interactions
between technology and human actors) and process theory. This enables the exploration of the dynamic interplay among individuals, technology, and larger social structures. A form of constructivism is present in interpretivist IS research (see Orlikowski
and Baroudi 1991; Walsham 1993; Myers 1994; Orlikowski et al. 1996) in which two
pivotal notions are process and context. For instance, in Walsham's view of interpretivism, processes of change should be studied as interconnected or embedded levels of
analysis and broader contexts (such as economic, social, political, sectoral, structural,
and cultural).

There is also a strong link between interpretivism and the use of structuration theory
(see Chapter 5 in this volume). For example, Orlikowski (1992) uses Giddens's
structuration theory and proposes a structurational model of technology, which under-
scores its dual nature as objective reality and as a socially constructed product. The
interaction of technology and organizations is 'a function of the different actors and
socio-historical contexts implicated in its development and use' (Orlikowski 1992:
405). Giddens's structuration theory offers models of social action and structure
from individual to global levels: structure constrains actions, but at the same time,
human action serves to establish structure; modalities link action and structure.

However, Monteiro and Hanseth (1996) argue that conceptualizations of information systems based on Giddens's structuration theory, despite being very convincing, 'lack in precision regarding the specifics of the IS' (p. 326) and 'are not fine-grained enough with respect to the technology to form an appropriate basis for understanding' (p. 328). Instead, they claim that ANT is more effective for describing how minute, technical design decisions are interwoven with organizational issues and for being 'specific about the technology' (p. 330). In their study of information infrastructure standards, ANT proved useful in 'accounting for how standards acquire stability, how they become increasingly "irreversible"' (p. 327).

More broadly, constructivism goes a step further than interpretivism in exploring and blurring the boundaries between levels of analysis and distinctions between agency and structure. This is because of its post-structuralism. When applied to technology it not only emphasizes that the same technology has several meanings for different groups and that there is a variety of interests in the process of developing and using a technology, but it also underlines how information systems are intertwined with their social meanings, and are not independent entities to which the social is merely added. There has been growing interest in social constructivism in general on the part of IS researchers (Askenas and Westelius 2000; McAdam and McCreedy 2000; Sarker 2000; Huysman 2002), as well as in ANT specifically (Bloomfield and Vurdubakis 1994; Vidgen and McMaster 1996; Holmström and Stalder 2001; Nandhakumar and Vidgen 2001).

SCIENCE AND TECHNOLOGY STUDIES

In order to understand how the constructivist approach has developed with ANT, it is important to first summarize the larger field of STS in which the take-up of the constructivist paradigm, particularly by the sociology of scientific knowledge, has been very influential on ANT. One important proviso is to begin by stating that STS scholars are deeply divided on themes such as relativism or constructivism and that there are continuous debates on these issues. However, it is difficult to appreciate or participate in these debates without understanding how STS has changed with post-structuralism. A useful overview of this can be found in Bucchi (2004).

Historians of science have, for a long time, analysed the growing disciplinary specialization of science, particularly in the nineteenth century. Sociologists, notably Robert Merton in the 1930–40s, who in effect created the discipline of the sociology of science, started linking the institutionalization of science with other processes, e.g. industrialization, capitalism, or religion (Merton 1938). This work concentrated initially on the professionalization and institutionalization of scientific work, social codification of the scientist's role, values, and norms, and science as a social subsystem. It was groundbreaking in that science came to be seen as a social institution, not a protected activity with a sacred aura, but an object to be studied like any other social phenomenon. The 'normative structure of science' (Merton 1942) had as its primary concerns the organizational and functional aspects of science as an institution capable of self-regulation, understanding which values and norms guarantee the functioning of science (Merton 1973).

The next wave of sociologists of science (Mitroff 1974; Mulkay 1974) criticized the 'normative structure of science' view as an idealization that was more prescriptive than descriptive in its intent, of science as 'it should be'. They developed counter-norms which they claimed can also play a positive role in scientific inquiry: particularism (individual characteristics are factors which influence how work will be judged); inter-estedness (individual seeks to serve her/his own interests); individualism (property rights); and organized dogmatism (scientist believes in her/his own findings while doubting those of others). These were deemed to be more realistic in taking into account behaviours around secrecy, survival, misconduct, competition, inequality, and away from the initial idealized naive vision of science. Some of the concepts which originate from this are now in common use, such as 'gatekeepers' and 'invisible colleges'.

The contribution of these early authors was that they went beyond descriptive detailed histories and effected a conceptual leap to analyse science as a social institution. From then on, the bulk of the sociological literature on science has developed in opposition to the institutional approach.

The Sociology of Scientific Knowledge (SSK) is interdisciplinary (not just sociology) and in particular, it draws on the philosophy of science and post-structuralism. One major influence was Kuhn's structure of scientific revolutions (1962) which looks at the resistance raised by ideas, the possibility of seeing—or not seeing—the same objects in an entirely different manner by observing them with other conceptual and interpretive apparatuses or paradigmatic dimensions. Confirmation and credence to data which fit, judgement of objectivity, discarding of observations from theory, and of theory from observations are central themes. Science does not advance smoothly along a linear path but by abrupt leaps and discontinuities. The emergence of a paradigm signals that a research sector has consolidated itself into a scientific discipline. It is part of a paradigm's nature as a 'perceptive filter' to emphasize those features of reality that accord with it.

In the 1970s–80s Edinburgh SSK scholars (Bloor 1976; Barnes 1985; Shapin and Schaffer 1985; Pickering 1992) applied these post-structuralist principles in their studies of scientific work to highlight mechanisms of confirmation bias, i.e. the tendency to give greater importance to data which concur with one's theoretical model. Observation does discipline theory, but theory disciplines observation also. Observation reports may be discarded on theoretical grounds, just as theories may be discarded on observational grounds. Knowledge is the paramount social creation. SSK argues that science is not just empirically grounded, but that the social influences scientific beliefs. It opposes the institutional sociology of science approach and opens the black box of science which the institutional approach had left largely intact.

Scientists produce knowledge against the background of their culture's inherited knowledge, their collectively situated purposes, and the information they receive from natural reality. An important principle in SSK is the principle of symmetry, or how the social does not just explain failures but also successes, scientific controversies, and disputes. SSK explores causality (the conditions which bring about beliefs or states of knowledge) and is impartial about truth/falsity, rationality/irrationality, success/failure, in that both sides of these dichotomies require explanation. It is symmetrical in its explanation as the same types of cause explain true and false belief. This is a clear vision of science and technology as not exempt from social influences. Social factors like interests, political ideologies, and cultural features should not be brought to bear solely when knowledge jumps the rails of rationality or lapses into error. It is not that observation or data from experience are valueless, but that they do not suffice in themselves to bring about changes in beliefs.

This followed with the emergence of ANT in the 1980s–90s which probed even further inside scientific laboratory work (Latour and Woolgar 1979; Knorr-Cetina 1995) and adopted a more microsociological (Law 1986; Woolgar 1988; Callon 1991) and anthropological stance (Bruno Latour is an anthropologist of science). It no longer takes a scientific theory and sets it in relation to a specific historical and social context. Rather it delves into the process itself that leads to the formation of the theory, isolating its components and placing them under a magnifying glass. In order to carry out microsociological empirical studies, it drew heavily on other currents of sociological inquiry, in particular ethnomethodology (Garfinkel 1967). As a result it flanks the macrosociological and causal analysis with detailed inquiry into contingent processes, producing case studies with minute reconstruction. The scientific fact is no longer seen as the point of departure; it is now the point of arrival. Scientific knowledge is not only socially conditioned, instead it is—from the very beginning—constructed and consti- tuted through microsocial phenomena. Some of the findings proposed that a negotia- tion occurs across transepistemic networks (e.g. financiers, suppliers, policy makers) thereby criss-crossing scientific and 'non-scientific' considerations. Also playing a significant part in the construction of a scientific fact is the rhetorical dimension: discourse strategies, representation techniques, forms of data presentation, inscrip- tions, and devices.

Weak and Strong Constructivism: SST, SCOT, and ANT

Debates have raged regarding weak and strong constructivism. ANT is said to be a 'strong' form of constructivism. For instance, Callon, a major advocate of ANT, refuses to categorize the elements in a system or network 'when these elements are permanently interacting, being associated, and being tested by the actors who innovate' (Callon 1986: 11). Callon (1986, 1991) uses a higher abstraction, 'actors', that subsumes science, technology, economics, politics. 'Human' and 'non-human' actors are the heteroge- neous entities that constitute a network. By contrast, Bijker, Hughes, and Pinch (1987), advocates of SCOT (Social Construction of Technology) are 'weak' constructivists who preserve the social environment and argue that the social groups that constitute the social environment play a critical role in defining and solving the problems that arise during the development of an artefact. Problems are defined within the context of the meaning assigned by a social group or a combination of social groups. Because social groups define the problems of technological development, 'there is flexibility in the way things are designed, not one best way' (Bijker, Hughes, and Pinch 1987: 14). SCOT is criticized by ANT for its 'externalism', the view that the context is able to determine the content of scientific research (e.g. theoretical predispositions guide observation, not the other way round). SCOT's response is that the social component is always present and always constitutive of knowledge; but that is not the only component, there may be other natural causes.

It is important to understand these debates to grasp the strong form of constructivism embodied in ANT. It is not arguing the absence of material reality from scientific activities, rather it asks that 'reality' and 'nature' be considered as entities continually retranscribed from within scientific activities. The focus of interest is 'the process of transcription' (Knorr Cetina 1995: 149). Further, facts are seen as consequences rather than causes of scientific descriptions. In rejecting the structural approach to the relationship between science and society, the ethnographers of scientific knowledge render the social dimension more pervasive, but at the same time more difficult to identify: an 'invisible gas'.

ANT is fundamentally non-essentialist. It attempts to expand the explanatory capacity of the microsociological approaches to science and takes the argument further by looking at science 'in the making' and the construction of a scientific fact, which relies on a series of allies within and without the lab. 'A scientific statement can only acquire the status of fact or artefact if a complex network of actors pass it from hand to hand' (Bucchi 2004: 71). The fate of what we say and make is in later users' hands. ANT depicts support networks and disputes as a series of distinctions (society vs science, human vs non-human). Since the settlement of a controversy is the cause of Nature's representation not the consequence, we can never use the outcome—Nature—to explain how and why a controversy has been settled. If we cannot use Nature as the reason for solution of a controversy, symmetrically, neither can we use Society, because the stabilization of alliances and of social interests is the result of the controversy, not its starting point. It is not the regularity of the world that imposes itself on our senses but the regularity of our institutionalized beliefs that imposes itself on the world. The aim of ANT is to study present-day controversies, 'science in the making', not 'ready-made science' or closed controversies.

Other 'weaker' constructivist (or constructionist) approaches to science and technology studies, represented by SCOT and by SST (the Social Shaping of Technology, MacKenzie and Wajcman 1985, 1999) concentrate on the interpretive flexibility of experimental results, which may lend themselves to more than one interpretation. They focus on the mechanisms by which closure is achieved and they attempt to connect closure mechanisms with wider social structures. SCOT, which also borrows from SSK, seeks to reveal key points of ambiguity or controversies between competing scientific claims and how one interpretation prevails over others. One of its principles is that all knowledge claims must be treated 'symmetrically' and that the explanation for their creation and acceptance rests on social factors, not the natural world. They are not interested in abstract discussions of the causal relationship between the social dimension and scientific practice, instead, they aim to embed the former in the latter, inserting it through the breach opened up by interpretive flexibility (Collins 1983) which is a more modest aim.

SST, like organizational sociology, points to the socially contingent form of technology itself. It seeks to identify factors that influence the form or content of technology and the direction of technological innovation and argues that this should be interpreted within an analysis of the struggles and growth of 'systems' or 'networks' (Hughes 1999). But the more constructivist approach moves away from making distinctions among technical, social, economic, and political aspects of technological development and uses the 'seamless web', 'system', or 'actor-network' metaphors, which stress the importance of paying attention to the different but interlocking elements of physical artefacts, institutions, and their environments.

It is clear that STS research has developed alternatives to technologically deterministic explanations and to the essentialist perspectives which see technical capacity as inherent to the technology. SST and SCOT share the view that 'antecedent circumstances, i.e. design, manufacture and production, are said to be "built into" and/or "embodied" in the final product; the resulting technology is "congealed social relations"' (Willcocks and Grint 1997: 103). However, debates within STS regarding constructivism have raged for two decades (for instance between Latour and Collins, or between Grint and Woolgar (1997) and Kling, see McLoughlin (1997)). The extreme relativist approach is criticized for relegating the influence of broader social structure and the roles of competing stakeholder interests as 'superfluous to the analysis of technology' (McLoughlin and Harris 1997: 17). 'Strong' constructivism believes that sociologists of technology should not adjudicate between different claims and constructs of technical capacity. In strong constructivism, the process of technological change and its outcomes is seen as almost entirely locally constructed, negotiable, and contingent. Technical capacities are not fixed but indeterminate and open to interpretive flexibility, not only during conception, design, and development but also in use. The problem revolves around how technical capacities are perceived. The late Rob Kling deems technical capacities (of information systems specifically) influence how technology is used. Woolgar and Grint judge this as technicist and unacceptable and suggest that, ironically, it becomes technological determinism in that the 'artefact has a definitive character and effect' (Woolgar and Grint, quoted in McLoughlin 1997: 214). On the other hand, constructivists are criticized for denying a 'critical dimension' to social analysis and for their inability to challenge 'traditionally held views about the political neutrality of technologies and the links between social advantage and technological innovation' (Kling 1992: 351), and for their scepticism towards broader social and economic structures of power and interest. As expressed:

> These 'material' or 'structural' phenomena, just as with technological artefacts and systems, are it is insisted created anew by social actors within the context in which

they act . . . [It is suggested] that factors such as class, power and politics should be seen as 'effects' and not 'causes' of social action. (McLoughlin 1997: 216)

Sociologists are blamed for over-stressing social choice at the expense of technological influences. At the other end of the spectrum, constructivists are accused of seeking to eliminate any distinction between the social and the technical. It is not our intention to address the in/commensurability of paradigms and different theoretical approaches in this chapter; however, this debate highlights some important issues. Truex and Basker- ville (1998: 110) warn that 'in so borrowing concepts . . . that are not taken for granted, [one also] borrows the controversy'.

Some Important ANT Concepts

The Technical and the Social

ANT provides a way of looking at phenomena that does not see the technical and the social as separate and stable entities. Technical and social choices are constantly negotiated and constructed:

> The sociology of technology has borrowed from the sociology of science its programme—the analysis of the production of artefacts, as that of scientific facts—and some of its methods, whether in following scientists at work to describe the mechanisms by which they mobilise various entities, or in studying controver- sial cases to show how the social and the technical are allocated and constituted. (Akrich 1993: 35)

Technological innovation is viewed by Callon (1986, 1991) and Latour (1989, 1991) as an attempt to build and stabilize a diffuse system of networks of alliances composed of both human (social) and non-human (technical) entities. This corresponds to a breakdown of the clear divide between science and society. No project is purely technical, nor is it purely social. This enables the circumvention of technological determinism in which technical projects and innovations are seen as proceeding naturally unless they are actively stopped. This is replaced with the idea that things do not happen unless human and non-human actors make them happen. Callon (1991) contends that networks can rarely be cut up into simple descriptive frameworks and he suggests that when the clouds from Chernobyl spread over Europe and contaminated the Lapp reindeer, then the plant as actor gained the upper hand over the plant as intermediary. According to Callon (1991), this explains how the discourse presenting technology as an uncontrolled and autonomous force (Ellul 1965; Winner 1977) gained ground over discourse that had reduced it to being a mere instrument that people in society used for better or for worse.

One of the strengths of ANT is the systematic avoidance of what can be called 'methodological dualism': 'the making of a priori distinctions between what is "technical" and what is not' and is therefore by implication 'social' (Bloomfield and Vurdubakis 1997: 85). 'Rather than assuming that we are dealing with two separate, but related, ontological domains—technology and organisations—we propose to regard them as but phases of the same essential action' (Latour 1991: 129). The presumed separation between technology and organization is a sense-making device and acts as a means by which we orient ourselves in the world (Bloomfield and Vurdubakis 1994). Identities are negotiated through the deployment of various human and non-human intermediaries which thereby mediate the relationships between actors. Intermediaries are passed between actors. This can imply a distinction between actors who have agency and intermediaries who are seen as essentially passive. However, it should be noted that 'attributions of agency versus passivity are context-dependent and made for particular purposes' (Bloomfield and Vurdubakis 1997: 106). For instance, in their study of the use of IT in the NHS, Bloomfield and Vurdubakis (1997: 89) highlight the intermediation between the domain of technology and the (social) world of the organization, which is interlinked with the intermediation between the professional groups of management and clinicians, and their respective rationalities (medical/administrative). In addition to constituting/negotiating the boundary between the 'technical' and the 'social', the IT-review at the NHS is an 'intermediary device which effects translations between the worlds of management and medicine, the commercial ethos of management consultancy and the public service orientation of the NHS, and how each delineates what is technical and what is social' (Bloomfield and Vurdubakis 1997: 89).

Sociology of Translation

Latour's (1991) alternative to technological determinism is that things do not happen unless other actors make them happen. This implies that each actor who takes the project further may take it in a different direction than that intended by the previous actor. As the study of science has shown (Knorr-Cetina and Cicourel 1981: 37), to construe a certain representation of the world is in principle always at the same time 'a matter of truth *and* a matter of political strategy, that is imposing one's say and of instituting certain consequences *with* or *against* others' (original emphasis). Latour uses the term 'translation' to describe this effect, playing on both of its meanings. The innovation is translated or carried from one position to another in the sense of a mathematical manipulation; the innovation is also interpreted or transposed from one position to another in the linguistic sense of the word translation. Translation operates between actors: an actor gives a definition to another actor, imputes him/her/it/them with interests, projects, desires, strategies, reflexes, afterthoughts (Callon 1991). An actor might be the company that has conceived, produced, and distributed a machine, while another actor might be its users. The translation is regulated by conventions that are more or less local, and they are always revisable (Callon 1991). The final shape and position of the innovation is unlikely to be that of the original developers. In each stage of its life, the project is taken and adapted by the actors that become involved in it. Only in the rare case when the future users can be persuaded to follow the initial goals does the innovation proceed as originally planned. All too often, however, the issue becomes sidetracked and unintended effects occur.

In one stratagem to achieve a translation, the actor may suggest that it shares a 'common' problem with putative allies, that is, it may draw equivalence between its problem and the problems which preoccupy others. This is known as '*problématisation*' (Callon 1991). If the actor can convince the allies that it has the necessary skills, knowledge, or other resources to devise a solution to their 'common' problem, then it may come to be seen as indispensable. It will have translated both the allies and their problem. The original problem is renegotiated while the allies become actors with a network defined by their common ownership of the translated problem. The negotiation of the identities of the various actors inside and outside an actor-network ('*intéressement*') is an intrinsic part of network building. Intéressement is: 'the group of actions by which an entity . . . attempts to impose and stabilise the identity of the other actors it defines through its problématisation' (Callon 1986: 207–8). In order for an actor to secure or win the support of others (potential allies) it must in some way make itself indispensable to them by translating their interests and enrol them; it must become an '*obligatory passage point*' (Callon 1986) in their '*enrolment*'. A successful negotiation/ translation of an obligatory passage point is a condition of network *stabilization* (Latour 1989). The process which 'folds up' or stabilizes an entire network so as to transform it into a point in another network (which at the same time becomes more general and more encompassing) is the basis of the progressive passage from the micro-level to the macro-level.

Of particular interest are the related concepts of stability and irreversibility. Network building is a search for stability which is enabled to the extent that changes set in train during network construction become irreversible (Callon 1991), either because it would be too costly to reverse them or because to do so becomes unthinkable. According to Callon (1991), convergence and irreversibility of techno-economic networks are both involved in the acts of translation and the networks that they sometimes succeed in forming. Convergence is the degree of accord (alignment and coordination) engendered by a series of translations. Controversies are translation as betrayal. The network is constructed according to the translations' own logic. The more aligned and coordinated a network is, the more the actors work together without being under constant challenge (Callon 1991). A translation is irreversible in that it is impossible to return to a previous situation. Convergence can increase or decrease and the same holds for irreversibility. The impossibility for other (past or future) translations to develop and impose themselves is a battle, a fight that is never definitely won. *Irreversibilization*, taken as the predetermination of translations and as the impossibility of a return to competing translations, is synonymous with normalization. A network which irreversibilizes itself is a network that has become heavy with durable, *immutable devices* (frozen elements or 'black boxes') and inscriptions, norms of all sorts, and which as a result slips into a codified metrology and information system.

In ANT, technological innovation is viewed as an attempt to build and stabilize a diffuse system of allies composed of both human and non-human entities. It enables the circumvention of technological determinism in which technical projects and innovations proceed naturally unless they are actively stopped and replaces it with the idea that things do not happen unless human and non-human actors make them happen. Symmetry and translation are two fundamental constructivist notions which can bring insights into the critical analysis of IS.

IS and ANT

ANT has grown in popularity in many disciplines over the last ten years. Attempts to apply it in other disciplines can also be found, in for example (Law and Hassard 1999): sociology (Barry and Elam 1997), health ethics and policy (Berg 1997), ecology (Cussins 1997), history (Harris 1997), cultural studies (Hatt 1997), medical technology (Lehoux 1997), urban planning (Murdoch 1997), linguistics (G. Myers 1997), and geography (Soderstrom 1997). Applications of ANT to IS empirical research (Orlikowski et al. 1996) range from: the inscription of work in a classification scheme for nursing work (Bowker, Timmermans, and Star 1996); the process of translation in activity-based costing and accounting technology (Boland and Schultze 1996); the processes of inscription and translation in the role of standards in EDI systems in the Norwegian health sector (Monteiro and Hanseth 1996); the attempted translation of interests in a car parking system (Vidgen and McMaster 1996); how and why the attempts at translation and alignment of interests around the development and use of administrative geographic information systems in India were a relative failure (Walsham and Sahay 1999).

It is not sufficient to explain information systems by recourse to mere technical factors, nor by reference to the 'supposed effects of some powerful social forces which were always there but somehow mysteriously overlooked' (Bloomfield et al. 1997: 130). Instead, we can draw upon ANT to consider several of the processes inherent in the building of heterogeneous actor-networks. The sociology of translation can be used to describe actors involved at many different levels of analysis, their interpretations of the social and the technical, and how IS projects are carried forward or not by various agencies, rather than following a predetermined trajectory.

As a constructivist theory, ANT can be effective for describing how technical design solutions are interwoven with social issues (Monteiro and Hanseth 1996). Software devices can be seen as network elements which display strong properties of irreversibility and are immutable inscriptions across time and space (Walsham 1997). Also the notion of symmetry makes it possible to analyse how success and failure are socially constructed at local level:

[it prevents the assumptions] that the world can be understood as a set of distinct compartments, such as the technical, the managerial or the psychological . . . This locates responsibility in a specific compartment, and it builds a barrier between one compartment and the next . . . However, causes and responsibilities don't stop for very long in compartments and tend to move on . . . We need to be specific, modest, located in particular contexts and situations. (Law 2001: 3, 5, 6, 14)

It also prevents envisaging technology as neutral and seeing the problem as social, for instance, in terms of resistance by (usually other) actors to an unproblematic technology. The technology addresses *and* creates social problems, and social problems have technological elements and representations. This also avoids a social or political essentialism. We do not have to lapse into a simplistic determinism to acknowledge that a phenomenon is part of wider technological, economic, cultural, and policy environments. These contexts and their interpretation are socially constructed by actors, and are an important influence on techno-organizational change. External 'factors' are merely 'conditions of possibility' that 'make certain courses of action feasible while constraining or ruling out others' (Knights and Murray 1994: 39). While 'conditions of possibility' such as 'the market' frame organizational behaviour, actors construct at the local level the 'external forces' that they then respond to. 'A market exists only in as much as people believe that it exists and act accordingly. Similarly, a technological opportunity or constraint exists only in so much as people believe it to exist' (Knights and Murray 1994: 41). Accordingly, macro-structures do not determine micro-events (Knorr-Cetina 1981) and social processes exhibit chains of intended and unintended outcomes. Some human perspectives win over others in the construction of technologies and truths, some human actors go along with the will of other actors, and some humans resist being enrolled.

In a discussion of ANT and IS research, Walsham (1997) comments that some of this research either explains the technology at the expense of social interactions, or conversely portrays social interactions without giving detailed descriptions of the technological inscriptions. In addition he also outlines some of the existing criticisms and limitations of ANT and classifies them into four broad strands: limited analysis of social structures; amoral stance; the problem of generalized symmetry; and the problem of description. The next section will expand on the criticisms levelled by Walsham and draw on other authors' critiques of ANT, since these are relevant to information systems research in general.

DIFFICULTIES WITH ANT

Methodologically speaking, ANT is a valuable analytical device, offers a strong contribution to building a serious empirical base and 'ANT is both a theory and methodology combined' (Walsham 1997: 469). Yet ANT studies—like many STS studies—produce a veritable mass of detail which often lead to book-length outputs (Walsham 1997), such as Latour's (1992/1996) monograph on Aramis. IS research is often lacking in research-based books such as this, and studies based on constructivism could offer a contribution to interpretive IS research.

One area of interest is how to minimize treating innovations as single events or projects which separate from their antecedents, thereby not limiting ourselves to snapshot data, as with many 'business case studies'. However, such detailed studies are extremely labour intensive and time consuming. There are a number of methodological difficulties (Mitev 2009): determining what 'all' actors are; how to treat small (e.g. software) and large actors (e.g. the State) and their differences; knowing where one network starts and another begins, where they overlap and where to stop—ANT advocates claim that 'everything is a network' which sounds universalist and is rather vague and difficult to apply; how to relate the micro-local and the macro-global; and how to include social constructions in the analysis. In practice, one builds an account that selects and prioritizes actors and ranks their importance according to categories and constructs. Yet analytic purity comes at a high price. Social constructivists aim to be aware of the rhetorical devices that they—as well as other actors—use to construct textual realities, and that they offer understandings that are partisan and potentially contestable by others. Constructivism is a step further than interpretivism: it is not just gathering people's interpretations, but is also about being aware of the process of social construction of reality in order to probe tendencies to relate 'facts' as how things are (Holstein and Miller 1993) and question their 'naturalness', therefore adding criticality. But this is difficult to carry out and case study research routinely 'fails to attain a constructivist ideal of standards for evaluating research, standards which are challenging and possibly not even desirable' (Best 1993: 135).

'Tracing the actors' is a methodological shortcut which points to Latour's ethnomethodological tradition as an anthropologist of science (Latour 1993a). It consists of following scientists' traces in their everyday work and paying attention to the materiality of their activities, rather than starting from grand narratives about science and society. It also explains the conceptualization of actor-networks as assemblages of socio-material entities, such as scientists gathering soil samples in the Amazon jungle, transporting them back to their labs and transforming them into models and scientific articles, which then become actors in debates about the erosion of the Amazon forest (Latour 1999).

Ethnomethodological work is demanding and time consuming, requiring considerable resources or skills. In IS research there is limited evidence that ethnomethodology has been used to its full extent, aside from some ethnographic work by Harvey and Myers (1995; M. D. Myers 1997) and by Ngwenyama and colleagues (Ngwenyama et al. 1997).

There are some difficulties with constructivist approaches that have also been identified by other IS researchers (Stalder 1997; Nandhakumar and Vidgen 2001). Only relying on the configuration of the actor-networks for an explanation may not be enough. As Stalder (1997) comments: 'ANT's a priori that society is ontologically flat is an excellent starting point but a weak ending of the analysis'. In particular, treating actors equally is problematic. The ANT notion of the 'seamless web' supports an open-ended and inclusive approach to actors in the largest possible sense, more so than is usually the case in IS research. The notion of actor in ANT is difficult to handle since not all actors are equal. Critics have noted the lack of political and moral analysis which Walsham also raises as he asks: 'where do the moral judgments come from if not from ideas that transcend the situation?' He adds that political and ethical theories cannot come from the basis of the network alone (Walsham 1997: 475), although he is unclear as to where they should come from.

ANT has been criticized for concentrating on how things get done to the detriment of how broader social structures shape socio-material practices, for giving interesting accounts of local contingencies and material arrangements without taking into account macro-social structures. In response to these criticisms, Latour (1991) has replied that the actor-network methodology can be used to move between levels of analysis, that the macro-structure is made of the same 'stuff' as the micro-structure, and that macro-structures can be investigated with the same methodological tools as micro-structures.

The symmetry between human and non-human actors, which is related to the symmetry between the social and the technical, society and nature, politics and science, values and facts, has been criticized for having gone too far in erasing all distinctions and reducing people to the status of things, thereby removing intentionality. There are political implications of levelling human and non-human differences. The disregard for macro-structures has led to criticisms of ANT in particular and of strong social constructivism and relativism in general, for being amoral and apolitical in that it leads to the ignoring of political biases that can underlie the spectrum of choices for relevant actors (Winner 1993). Star (1991) refers to the 'networks of the powerful' and to how irreversible networks are only stable for some and discriminate against those who do not belong to the community of practice who form, use, and maintain the network. Latour responded to criticisms of apoliticism and moral relativism thus:

> Refusing to explain the closure of a controversy by its consequences does not mean that we are indifferent to the possibility of judgements that transcend the situation. For network analysis does not prevent judgement any more than it prevents differentiation. Efficiency, truth, profitability, and interest are simply properties of networks, not of statements. Domination is an effect not a cause. In order to make a diagnosis or a decision about the absurdity, the danger, the amorality, or the unrealism of an innovation, one must first describe the network. (Latour 1991: 130)

The argument put forward by Latour is that social constructivism is not in itself amoral and that describing the network is not only a prerequisite but the *only way* to get at explanations:

> The explanation emerges once the description is saturated; if we display a socio-technical network—defining trajectories by actants' association and substitution, defining actants by all the trajectories in which they enter, by following translations and, finally, by varying the observer's point of view—we have no need to look for

additional causes. Explanation is the stabilisation of a network. If one is capable of explaining effects of causes, it is because a stabilised network is already in place. (Latour 1991: 129)

This is related to the criticism that ANT is a method for describing, but not for explaining (Collins and Yearley 1992). Callon's answer (1991) is that explanations are only offered by networks which increase their convergence and irreversibility (an agreement getting firmer), and that the descriptions delivered by intermediaries turn into explanations (and even predictions). This leaves the question of how to explain the failure to converge in the case of divergent, reversible, and unstable networks, which consequently cannot offer an explanation, but maybe a series of conflicting explanations? If all explanations are the result of a stabilized network already in place, one assumes that one (and actors too?) could use explanations of other (previous?) stable overlapping and neighbouring networks, but then the problem is transposed to where does one stop?

Another difficult area is the macro-micro question. Its reformulation is one of the underpinnings of ANT in its adoption of a 'birds eye perspective to reconstruct the network of interrelated affairs' (Knorr-Cetina 1981: 33) and in its rejection of the macro as an explanation. 'The macro appears no longer as a *particular layer* of social reality *on top* of micro-episodes composed of their interrelation, their aggregation or their unforeseen effects. Rather, it is seen to reside *within* these micro-episodes where it results from the *structuring practices* of agents' (Knorr Cetina 1981: 34, original emphasis). Callon and Latour (1981: 277) also conceive of the macro as actively construed and pursued within micro-social action. They comment that micro-actors 'blow themselves up to a macro-size by making themselves the spokesmen of many others whose following they enlist, through their summary representations' (which Knorr-Cetina refers to as the representation hypothesis, p. 40). They go on to point out that the macro-order consists of micro-actors who have successfully translated other actors' wills into a single will for which they speak, and because of the forces on which it can rely.

Furthermore, structures do not simply reside in the actions of people, they exist in a network of heterogeneous material arrangements. Latour (1991: 129) urges us to abandon the divide between material infrastructure and social superstructure and claims that, when actors and points of view are aligned, we enter a stable definition of society that looks like domination ('society made durable'). However, Knorr-Cetina (1981: 41, original emphasis) remarks that, pushed to its extreme, this 'denies the existence of a macro-order *apart from* the macro-representations which are accomplished in micro-social action'. In this perspective, macro-structures are created by routine inferences, interpretation and summary procedures, and do not control micro-events (p. 51). In other words, the degree to which macro-structures control micro-events is a continual matter of controversy and struggle in social life (Knorr-Cetina 1981: 39).

Avoiding taking the macro-order at face value is a strong motivation and a sound basis for wanting to study its production in micro-social environments instead. Knorr-Cetina (1981: 40) argues that this does not 'neglect the issue of power which hides beneath everyday differentiations between "big" and "small" actors' and that, instead, it 'relocates and redresses questions of power'. On the other hand, she warns that a microscopic recording of face-to-face interaction may not allow us to grasp whatever is the whole of the matter, even if she contends that 'it may be enough to begin with [in order] to hear the macro-order tick' (Knorr-Cetina 1981: 42).

Other authors have suggested that transformations of social reality occur between levels. Duster (1981) studied income tax regulation and community-based pro-grammes dedicated to the enactment of this regulation, according to different levels of abstraction of social reality and enquiry, so as to 'challenge the microscopic nature of all events' (Duster 1981: 109). In his analytical framework, macro-phenomena consist of the effects of the unintended consequences of micro- or middle-range action. For Harré (1981: 139) it is the 'macro-order composed of such effects which acts as a selection environment for social action', for example by determining which of the 'micro-mutations of social life will take off and persist as a component of social change' (Harré 1981: 139). Harré proposes a theory of social change in which the notion of 'diffuse social influence from unknown structural properties of a macro-order' plays a part (Harré 1981: 158). Similarly, in Giddens's duality of structure, based on the tension between action theory and institutional analysis, rules and resources instan-tiated in social systems structure actors' actions; structural qualities generate social action and are reproduced through these actions. But knowledgeability and capability of social actors are 'bounded by unintended consequences of (previous) social actions which condition social reproduction' (Giddens 1981: 161).

Callon and Latour (1981), on the other hand, do not believe in a micro-macro distinction. They do not think that we draw closer to social reality by descending to micro-negotiations or by rising towards the macro-actors. Macro-actors are not more complex than micro-actors and are just micro-actors 'seated on black boxes' (Callon and Latour 1981: 299). They also, symmetrically, oppose the view that micro-negotia-tions are truer and more real than the abstract, distant structures of the macro-actors (Callon and Latour 1981: 300). Furthermore, 'by taking for granted differences in level and size between actors, [one] ratifies past, present and future winners . . . finding favour with the powerful' (ibid.).

The macro-micro question is obviously unresolved. ANT is complex and difficult to use, since describing actors and networks runs the risk of producing asocial, apolitical, ahistorical, and decontextualized accounts. There are examples of IS research (Sarker, Sarker, and Sidorova 2006) which apply ANT instrumentally, as a way of controlling and managing the formation of the actor-network. They understand and apply 'trans-lation' as an actual business process of change, to be undertaken, managed, and controlled in the 'right' direction. It can all too easily turn into a linear, graphical representation (e.g. with nodes and arrows between actors), especially when used by researchers with a systems background. As noted by Brooke (2002: 55): 'The positivist heritage of IS research will tend to favour the adoption of approaches that are more easily "modelled" or normatively articulated'.

CAN ANT PROVIDE A SOCIAL CRITIQUE ON ITS OWN?

When using ANT, it is difficult not to use pre-existing concepts and categories. Latour (1991) argues that macro-explanations can be drawn without them because they rely on other stabilized networks which are already in place, but these already constitute pre-existing concepts and categories. Studying microsociological phenomena leads to social orders which are irreversible, pre-existing, powerful networks. To avoid social determinism it is important to do this critically in order to 'de-naturalize' assumed orders but it is challenging and there is limited experience of doing this in IS research. Perhaps a useful constructivist idea for IS research is that the negotiation between the social and the technical is political and relates to bigger 'social orders'. This can centre on treatments of the social and the technical and their links with social orders and political intentionality (Willmott 1994; Wilson 2000). A typical example of a dominant social order is the technical orientation towards the world (Feenberg 2000) and how 'technological choices are guided by social interests and codes established by cultural and political struggles' (Feenberg 1995: 12).

These issues are continuously debated in social constructivism debates (e.g. Howard 2002; Woodhouse, Hess, and Breyman 2002; Sorensen 2004; Lynch and Cole 2005). The focus for strong constructivism remains on claims-making, but on the rhetorics rather than the socially and historically grounded actions of claimants. Weak constructivism acknowledges assumptions about objective conditions and treats the evaluation of problems claims as an important part of the analysis; it studies claims-making within its context of culture and social structure (Best 1993; Gubrium 1993). MacKenzie (1988) also asserts that, although the micro/macro distinction is a false dichotomy, traditional macro-sociology is more relevant politically than micro-sociology.

ANT has been combined with other social theories in IS research, for example technology drift theory (Holmström and Stalder 2001), autopoiesis (Stadler 1997), politics and power (Silva 1997; Mitev 2005, 2009). Hanseth and Monteiro (1998) in their study of health information systems have complemented ANT with: (a) new institutionalism, after Powell and DiMaggio, to understand how institutions become stable and reproduce themselves; and (b) with Bourdieu's theory of practice and his notion of 'habitus' to account for the stability of action. Other authors have combined Heidegger with ANT (Ciborra and Hanseth 1998), or drawn on Foucault to study computer networks in the financial services industry (Knights, Murray, and Willmott 1997). Doolin and Lowe (2002) also argue that ANT can contribute to critical IS research and critical IS research has, more broadly, explored several theoretical avenues (Howcroft and Trauth 2004; Howcroft and Trauth 2005).

To be critical, it is insufficient to study the succession of events only as either negotiated outcomes of power struggles or as a series of translations between local actors resulting in a set of networks. Political issues are often seen by management as 'amenable to a technical solution' (Fournier and Grey 2000: 11). A critical analysis therefore involves examining 'what is being done in the name of managerial performativity' (Fournier and Grey 2000: 17) and 'probing socially divisive forms of management theory and practices' (Alvesson and Willmott 1992). A critical analysis should emphasize the link that exists between the social production of knowledge and collective political action, particularly with regards to the technology.

> The specific symbolic power to impose the principles of construction of reality, in particular social reality, is a major dimension of political power . . . [A critical analysis] must show how the orientation toward reality characteristic of technology is combined with the realization of technology in the social world . . . [and combine] insights into the technical orientation toward the world, with constructivist insights into the social nature of technology. (Feenberg 2000: 233)

Post-structuralism as Social Critique

When comparing IS research with organization studies and critical management studies (Alvesson and Willmott 1992; Alvesson and Deetz 2000; Grey and Willmott 2005), we can see that hermeneutics and Habermassian theories have been dominant in IS research and have remained largely untouched by a post-structuralist critique. For example, hermeneutic and interpretive IS approaches have focused on 'hidden agendas' (Ngwenyama and Lee 1997), 'underlying sense' (Myers 1994), or 'deep structures' (Heracleous and Barrett 2001); they entail probing the 'depth model' underneath narratives. However, from a postmodernist perspective, notions of the text and the world behind it and 'the reader bound into the socially constructed world standing behind the text' (Lee 1994: 150) show a misunderstanding about social construction. Post-structuralists and constructivists (Dreyfus and Rabinow 1982) deny the existence of an 'underneath'. The assumption of a 'hidden' meaning of discourse and the hermeneutic reclamation of lost, 'real', or even 'true' meaning deny a radical form of social constructivism. And social constructivism is corrosive of depth assumptions of hermeneutics. (But see also Chapter 9 in this volume.)

> A critical analysis does not mean that the researcher should 'seek to evaluate critically . . . the totality of understandings by analysing the participants' understandings in terms of changing social structures' (Myers 1994: 57). Dividing the phenomenon into interpretations on the one hand, and structures on the other, is problematic. By attributing (a) the subjective, the interpretive, the 'socially constructed', and meaning to hermeneutics on the one hand, and (b) the objective, the historical and social reality to the 'critical' on the other hand, Myers overlooks the postmodernist conception of the subjective. This separation reflects respectively a modernist individualistic epistemology and an objectivist realist ontology. By contrast, constructivism is epistemologically about the intersubjective social construction of meaning and ontologically about the construction of social reality. It combines a social theory of knowledge with a postmodern intersubjective, not a

modernist individualistic, theory of action. Constructionism is a more 'local sort of unmasking' (Hacking 1999: 54), which is concerned with questions of power and control and showing how 'categories of knowledge are used in power relationships. (Hacking 1999: 58)

After Lyotard (1984), a performative intent in managerialist discourses develops knowledge that contributes to the production of maximum output for minimum input and means-ends calculation. It subordinates knowledge to the production of efficiency and contributes to the effectiveness of managerial practice by building 'better' models or understandings. Information systems feature prominently in these models or understandings. In non-critical study, 'performativity is taken as an imperative towards which all knowledge and practice must be geared and which does not require questioning . . . [on the other hand critical study] questions the alignment between knowledge, truth and efficiency and is concerned with performativity . . . in that it seeks to uncover what is being done in its name' (Fournier and Grey 2000: 17). For instance, critical IS research could instead question the discourse of empowerment and flexibility through the use of mobile ICTs (see Chapter 18 in this volume); point out that workers' commuting time is being translated into a 'wasted' resource; that the notion of workers' time is being redefined through the term 'flexibility' itself, for instance with boundaries between home and work getting blurred; that workers' knowledge is being instrumentalized into a constantly available repository; and it would explore the ways in which organizational practices and intersubjective rules are implicated in the construction of meaning and reproduction of flexible workers' new identities. One method for doing this is 'denaturalization'.

A social constructivist stance supports criticality in that the present is not determined by the nature or truth of things; it seeks to 'denaturalize' the apparent natural order of things; thereby questioning the inevitability of the social status quo, and positing as a preliminary the contingency of social orders. Intersubjective rules, and not some unchangeable truths or realities, give meaning to practices. Social construction is not a kind of idiosyncratic, individual, or subjective will to knowledge. Our interpretations are based on a shared system of codes and symbols, of languages, lifeworlds, and social practices. Socially constructed knowledge is a 'constitutive factor of social power and the concept of power provides a central link between the construction of knowledge and social order' (Guzzini 2000: 172).

Without considering postmodernist themes, research can become unreflective about elitism and conditions of power. Yet without incorporating some political thought postmodernism becomes esoteric. The postmodernist view of the human subject creates difficulties in developing political action. For instance, to challenge gender and race discrimination, people have to organize and reveal these inequities across social situations. But making that essentialist difference denies social constructionism. If one rejects an essentialist foundation and believes that more than local resistance is needed, some kind of combination between postmodernism and critical theory may well provide the best remaining option. There are ways to think about them both at once, though not necessarily through some new synthesis. One option is to conduct multiple interpretations of the same phenomenon from both critical theory and postmodern positions; or see both as useful for reflexivity rather than as theories directly relevant for guiding and interpreting studies of substantive matters. Further, many management theorists have deployed a number of 'postmodern' theoretical lenses in the same text, for instance, labour process theory and social constructivism (e.g. Lilley, Lightfoot, and Paulo Amaral 2004), despite their apparent incommensurability. Alvesson and Deetz (1996, see also Mitev 2006) argue that various paths are possible that address the middle ground between more traditional critical realist and hermeneutic epistemologies on the one hand and a postmodern philosophy on the other hand.

DISCUSSION AND CONCLUSIONS

Post-structuralism and ANT offer an essential starting point for a critical analysis of how things are not fixed, how boundaries move, and how distinctions are negotiated. Post-structuralist approaches are well suited to the task of critique, for instance in probing themes such as performativity and managerialism, two under-critiqued modernist concepts that are dominant in IS. Still, ANT is difficult to handle well and prone to being used mechanistically and instrumentalized. ANT's radical thinking, non-dualism, and symmetry about the social and the technical are very useful, but like many others concerned with ascribing intentionality to objects, the symmetry between human and non-human can be dangerous (McLean and Hassard 2004). It seems to have taken precedence in IS research over other more useful ANT concepts, such as 'inscription' or 'action at a distance', some having been used to good effect by IS researchers (e.g. Wilson 2002). The theoretical lens of ANT is useful in moving beyond the notion of 'context', overcoming the divide between the 'social' and the 'technical' and exploring how this boundary is socially and politically constructed. ANT is a useful methodological tracing device providing a powerful vocabulary and conceptual principles that help to include a wide range of actors and formulate corresponding translations. Only concentrating on translations across local actors runs the danger of remaining quite narrow, and analysis should broaden the scope to avoid either technologically or sociologically deterministic explanations.

The micro-macro question and the scope of investigation remain contentious issues. Getting at these core 'macro' issues is not facilitated by the tendency in some current applications of ANT in IS research to limit actors within the organizational sphere and include only 'key' powerful managerial actors, thereby missing the point of following as many actors as possible. Critical analyses should include the social and political aspects of the external context to the organization. It should not neglect the way in which organizations both reflect and reproduce broader social inequalities and hence the essentially contestable nature of organizational relations. IS research has a limited record in doing this, and, as a result, the radical potential of ANT due to its post-structuralism, becomes reduced to a more managerialist agenda (Hassard, Law, and

Lee 1999). For instance, identifying 'errors' and 'omissions' during enrolment or problematization; instrumentalizing ANT concepts into 'managing' or 'aligning' translation processes, like a re-engineering exercise, as if translations could (or should!) be controlled. The ANT emphasis on non-human actors is also picked up by IS researchers who are primarily concerned with putting IT in the centre, thus often bordering on technological determinism, which is far from ANT premises.

Bringing a critical perspective to IS research has been mainly carried out using Habermas over the last two decades or so (e.g. by Hirschheim and Klein (1994)). Doolin (1998) emphasizes the importance of developing a critical IS research agenda that goes beyond using Habermas. He suggests exploring the relationship of ANT, qualitative empirical work, and a critical approach. A political dimension can be added combining, for instance, Foucault or Clegg with ANT concepts (obligatory passage points, problematization, enrolment, intéressement). The mechanism by which local events and networks become 'macro' or global structures is key: ANT declares that they are the same thing, but it is not a simple additive or combinatorial process.

In a critique of Latour's (1993b) *We Have Never Been Modern*, Cohen (1997: 351) argues that: 'anthropological totality [as represented by ANT] may be said to replace historical totality . . . [and is] a functional universal [which] is an absorptive cultural "logic" . . . and negates modern time-differences'; and that: 'conditions of possibility are not made explicable if the network-model is transcendental' (p. 357). Other theoretical traditions within STS may be more historically oriented and could help solve these problems. Biagioli's *Science Studies Reader* (1999) includes, for instance, a range of papers on: the social construction of technology, sociology of science and technology, anthropology of science, social shaping of technology, ANT, history of technical innovation, cultural studies of science, and also 'large technological systems' which could be particularly relevant to the study of large information systems. Many of these theoretical themes preceded ANT and in fact were partly responsible for its initial conceptualization. The current interest with ANT in the IS research community runs the danger of applying it as a simplifying universal tool; and IS researchers may benefit from drawing on some of its predecessors. Harry Collins in particular (Collins and Evans 2002), an eminent sociologist of science, has suggested a 'third wave' in STS to reawaken a critical sociological position in order to reinject social analysis into science and technology studies, but without shattering the theoretical insights brought by post-structuralist and constructivist approaches (the second wave) such as ANT. This is an issue that should concern all IS researchers, whether they employ ANT or not.

References

Adam, A., Howcroft, D. A., and Richardson, H. (2001). 'Absent Friends? The Gender Dimension in IS Research', in N. L. Russo, B. Fitzgerald, and J. I. DeGross (eds.), *Realigning Research and Practice in Information Systems Development: The Social and Organizational*

Perspective, Proceedings of the IFIP Working Group 8.2 Conference, Boise, Idaho, ID, 27–29 July 2001. Boston: Kluwer Academic Publishers.

Akrich, M. (1993). 'Les Objets techniques et leurs utilisateurs', in *Les Objets dans l'action, Raisons pratiques*, vol. iv. Paris: Éditions de l'École des Hautes Études en Sciences Sociales.

Alvesson, M., and Deetz, S. (1996). 'Critical Theory and Postmodernism Approaches to Organizational Studies', in S. R. Clegg, C. Hardy, and W. R. Nord (eds.), *Handbook of Organization Studies*. Thousand Oaks, CA: Sage Publications, 191–217. [Reprinted in C. Grey and H. Willmott (2005), *Critical Management Studies: A Reader*. Oxford: Oxford University Press (Oxford Management Readers), 60–106.]

————(2000). *Doing Critical Management Research*. Thousand Oaks, CA: Sage Publications.

——and Willmott, H. (eds.) (1992). *Critical Management Studies*. Thousand Oaks, CA: Sage Publications.

Askenas, L., and Westelius, A. (2000). 'Five Roles of an Information System: A Social Constructionist Approach to Analyzing the Use of ERP Systems', in W. J. Orlikowski, S. Ang, P. Weill, H. C. Krcmar, and J. I. DeGross (eds.), *21st International Conference on Information Systems*. Brisbane: ICIS.

Barnes, B. (1985). *About Science*. Oxford: Blackwell.

Barry, A., and Elam, M. (1997). 'Actor Networks and the Problem of Empire', *Actor-Network Theory and After Workshop*. Centre for Social Theory and Technology, Keele University, 10–11 July.

Berg, M. (1997). 'Of(f) the Record: Technology, Politics, Theory', *Actor-Network Theory and After Workshop*. Centre for Social Theory and Technology, Keele University, 10–11 July.

Best, J. (1993). 'But Seriously Folks: The Limitations of the Strict Constructionist Interpretation of Social Problems', in J. A. Holstein and G. Miller (eds.), *Reconsidering Social Constructionism: Debates in Social Problems Theory*. New York: Aldine de Gruyter, 129–50.

Biagioli, M. (ed.) (1999). *The Science Studies Reader*. New York: Routledge.

Bijker, W. E., Hughes, T. P., and Pinch, T. (eds.) (1987). *The Social Construction of Technological Systems: New Directions in the Sociology and History of Technology*. Cambridge, MA: MIT Press.

——and Law, J. (eds.) (1992). *Shaping Technology/Building Society: Studies in Socio-technical Change*. Cambridge, MA: MIT Press.

Bloomfield, B. B., and Vurdubakis, T. (1994). 'Boundary Disputes: Negotiating the Boundary between the Technical and the Social in the Development of IT Systems', *Information Technology and People*, 7(1): 9–24.

————(1997). 'Paper Traces: Inscribing Organisations and Information Technology', in B. P. Bloomfield, R. Coombs, D. Knights, and D. Littler (eds.), *Information Technology and Organizations: Strategies, Networks and Integration*. Oxford: Oxford University Press, 85–111.

——Coombs, R., Owen J., and Taylor, P. (1997). 'Doctors as Managers: Constructing Systems and Users in the National Health Service', in B. P. Bloomfield, R. Coombs, D. Knights, and D. Littler (eds.), *Information Technology and Organizations: Strategies, Networks and Integration*. Oxford: Oxford University Press, 112–34.

Bloor, D. (1976). *Knowledge and Social Imagery*. London: Routledge and Kegan Paul (2nd edn., Chicago University Press, 1991).

Boland, R. J., and Schultze, U. (1996). 'From Work to Activity: Technology and the Narrative of Progress', in W. J. Orlikowksi, G. Walsham, M. R. Jones, and J. DeGross (eds.),

Information Technology and Changes in Organizational Work, proceedings of the IFIP WG8.2 working conference, Cambridge University, 7–9 December 1995. London: Chapman and Hall, 308–24.

Bowker, G. C., Timmermans, S., and Star, S. L. (1996). 'Infrastructure and Organizational Transformation: Classifying Nurses' Work', in W. J. Orlikowksi, G. Walsham, M. R. Jones, and J. DeGross (eds.), *Information Technology and Changes in Organizational Work*, proceedings of the IFIP WG8.2 working conference, Cambridge University, 7–9 December 1995, London: Chapman and Hall, 344–70.

Brooke, C. (2002). 'What does it Mean to be 'Critical' in IS Research?' *Journal of Information Technology*, 17(2): 49–57 (Special Issue on Critical Research in Information Systems).

Bucchi, M. (2004). *Science in Society: An Introduction to Social Studies of Science*. London: Routledge.

Callon, M. (1986). 'Some Elements of a Sociology of Translation: Domestication of the Scallops and the Fishermen of St Brieuc Bay', in J. Law (ed.), *Power, Action and Belief*. London: Routledge & Kegan Paul, 196–233.

—— (1991). 'Techno-economic Networks and Irreversibility', in J. Law, *A Sociology of Monsters: Essays on Power, Technology and Domination*. London: Routledge, 132–64.

—— and Latour, B. (1981). 'Unscrewing the Big Leviathan: How Actors Macro-structure Reality and how Sociologists Help them to do it', in K. Knorr-Cetina and A. V. Cicourel (eds.), *Advances in Social Theory and Methodology: Towards an Integration of Micro- and Macro-sociologies*. London: Routledge & Kegan Paul, 277–303.

Ciborra, C., and Hanseth, O. (1998). 'From Tool to Gestell: Agendas for Managing the Information Infrastructure', *Information Technology and People*, 11(4): 305–27.

Clegg, S. R. (1989). *Frameworks of Power*. London: Sage.

Cohen, S. (1997). 'Science Studies and Language Suppression: A Critique of Bruno Latour's We Have Never Been Modern', *Studies of History and Philosophy of Science*, 28(2): 339–61.

Collins, H. (1983). 'An Empirical Relativist Programme in the Sociology of Scientific Knowledge', in K. Knorr-Cetina and M. Mulkay (eds.), *Science Observed*. London: Sage, 85–113.

—— and Evans, R. (2002). 'The Third Wave of Science Studies', *Social Studies of Science*, 32(2): 235–96.

—— and Pinch, T. (1993). *The Golem: What Everyone Should Know about Science*. Cambridge: Cambridge University Press.

—— and Yearley, S. (1992). 'Journey into Space', in A. Pickering (ed.), *Science as Practice and Culture*. Chicago, IL: University of Chicago Press, 369–89.

Cussins, C. (1997). 'Local and Global Challenges from Biodiversity Conservation to the Idea of Centres of Calculation (Translation?)', *Actor-Network Theory and After Workshop*, Centre for Social Theory and Technology, Keele University, 10–11 July.

Doolin, B. (1998). 'Information Technology as Disciplinary Technology: Being Critical in Interpretive Research on Information Systems', *Journal of Information Technology*, 13: 301–11.

—— and Lowe, A. (2002). 'To Reveal is to Critique: Actor-Network Theory and Critical Information Systems Research', *Journal of Information Technology*, 17(2): 69–78 (Special Issue on Critical Research in Information Systems).

Dreyfus, H., and Rabinow, P. (1982). *Michel Foucault: Beyond Structuralism and Hermeneutics*. Brighton: Harvester Press.

Drummond, H. (1996). *Escalation in Decision-Making: The Tragedy of Taurus*. Oxford: Oxford University Press.

Duster, T. (1981). 'Intermediate Steps between Micro- and Macro-integration: The Case of Screening for Inherited Disorders', in K. D. Knorr-Cetina and A. V. Cicourel (eds.), *Advances in Social Theory and Methodology: Towards an Integration of Micro- and Macro-sociologies*. London: Routledge & Kegan Paul, 109–37.

Ellul, J. (1965). *The Technological Society*. London: Jonathan Cape.

Feenberg, A. (1995). 'Subversive Rationalization: Technology, Power and Democracy', in A. Feenberg and A. Hannay (eds.), *Technology and the Politics of Knowledge*. Bloomington and Indianapolis, IN: Indiana University Press, 3–22.

——(2000). 'Constructivism and Technology Critique: Replies to Critics', *Inquiry*, 43: 225–38.

Fournier, V., and Grey, C. (2000). 'At the Critical Moment: Conditions and Prospects for Critical Management Studies', *Human Relations*, 53(1): 7–32.

Garfinkel, H. (1967). *Studies in Ethnomethodology*. Englewood Cliffs, NJ: Prentice Hall.

Gergen, K. J. (2001). *Social Construction in Context*. London: Sage.

Giddens, A. (1981). 'Agency, Institution, and Time-Space Analysis', in K. D. Knorr-Cetina and A. V. Cicourel (eds.), *Advances in Social Theory and Methodology: Towards an Integration of Micro- and Macro-sociologies*. London: Routledge & Kegan Paul, 161–74.

Grey, C., and Willmott, H. (2005). *Critical Management Studies: A Reader*. Oxford Management Readers. Oxford: Oxford University Press.

Grint K., and Woolgar S. (1997). *The Machine at Work: Technology, Work and Organization*. Cambridge: Polity Press and Oxford: Blackwell.

Gubrium, J. F. (1993). 'For a Cautious Naturalism', in J. A. Holstein and A. Miller (eds.), *Reconsidering Social Constructionism: Debates in Social Problems Theory*. New York: Aldine de Gruyter, 89–102.

Guzzini, S. (2000). 'A Reconstruction of Constructivism in International Relations', *European Journal of International Relations*, 6(2): 147–82.

Hacking, I. (1999). *The Social Construction of What?* Cambridge, MA: Harvard University Press.

Hanseth, O., and Monteiro, E. (1998). 'Changing Irreversible Networks', in W. R. J. Baets (ed.), *Sixth European Conference on Information Systems*, 4–6 June 1998, Aix-en-Provence, 1123–39.

Harré, R. (1981). 'Philosophical Aspects of the Micro-macro Problem', in K. D. Knorr-Cetina and A. V. Cicourel (eds.), *Advances in Social Theory and Methodology: Towards an Integration of Micro- and Macro-sociologies*. London: Routledge and Kegan Paul, 139–60.

Harris, S. (1997). 'Long-Distance Corporations and the Role of Organized Travel in the Making of Early Modern Science: The Case of the Society of Jesus', *Actor-Network Theory and After Workshop*, Centre for Social Theory and Technology, Keele University, 10–11 July.

Harvey, L. J., and Myers, M. D. (1995). 'Scholarship and Practice: The Contribution of Ethnographic Research Methods to Bridging the Gap', *Information Technology and People*, 8(3): 13–27.

Hassard, J., Law, J., and Lee, N. (1999). 'Themed Section: Actor-Network Theory and Managerialism. Preface', *Organization*, 6(3): 385–90.

Hatt, G. (1997). 'Re-materialising the Body: Networks and Embodied Nodes', *Actor-Network Theory and AfterWorkshop*, Centre for Social Theory and Technology, Keele University, 10–11 July.

Heracleous, L., and Barrett, M. (2001). 'Organizational Change as Discourse: Communicative Actions and Deep Structures in the Context of Information Technology Implementation', *Academy of Management Journal*, 44(4): 755–78.

Hirschheim, R., and Klein, H. K. (1994). 'Realizing Emancipatory Principles in Information Systems Development: The Case of ETHICS', *MIS Quarterly*, 18(1): 83–109.

Holmström, J., and Stalder, F. (2001). 'Drifting Technologies and Multi-purpose Networks: The Case of the Swedish Cashcard', *Information and Organization*, 11: 187–206.

Holstein, J. A., and Miller, G. (1993). *Reconsidering Social Constructionism: Debates in Social Problems Theory*. New York: Aldine de Gruyter.

Howard, J. (2002). 'Toward a Reconstructivist Stance in Technology Studies', Rensselaer Polytechnic Institute, Troy, New York, August.

Howcroft, D. A., Mitev, N. N., and Wilson, M. (2004). 'What We May Learn from the Social Shaping of Technology Approach', in J. Mingers and L. Willcocks (eds.), *Social Theory and Philosophy for Information Systems*. Chichester: John Wiley & Sons, 329–71.

——and Trauth, E. M. (2004). 'The Choice of Critical Information Systems Research', in B. Kaplan, D. P. Truex III, D. Wastell, A. T. Wood-Harper, and J. I. DeGross (eds.), *Information Systems Research: Relevant Theory and Informed Practice*. Boston, MA: Kluwer Academic Publishers, 195–212.

————(2005). 'Choosing Critical IS Research', in *Handbook of Information Systems Research: Critical Perspectives on Information Systems Design, Implementation and Use*. London: Edward Elgar Publishing Ltd.

Hughes, T. P. (1999). 'The Evolution of Large Technological Systems', in M. Biagioli (eds.), *The Science Studies Reader*. New York: Routledge, 202–23.

Huysman, M. (2002). 'Organizational Learning through Communities of Practice: A Social Constructivist Approach', in H. Tsoukas, and N. Mylonopoulos (eds.), *Organizational Knowledge, Learning and Capabilities, 3rd European Conference*. Athens: Athens Laboratory of Business Administration, Athens University of Economics.

Jones, M., Orlikowski, W. J., and Munir, K. (2004). 'Structuration Theory and Information Systems: A Critical Reappraisal', in J. Mingers and L. Willcocks (eds.), *Social Theory and Philosophy for Information System*. Chichester: John Wiley & Sons, 297–328.

Kling, R. (1992). 'Audiences, Narratives and Human Values in Social Studies of Technology', *Science, Technology and Human Values*, 17(3): 349–65.

Knights, D., and Murray, F. (1994). *Managers Divided: Organisation Politics and Information Technology Management*. Chichester: J. Wiley & Sons.

————(1997). 'Markets, Managers and Messages: Managing Information Systems in Financial Services', in B. B. Bloomfield, R. Coombs, D. Knights, and D. Littler (eds.), *Information Technology and Organizations: Strategies, Networks and Integration*. Oxford: Oxford University Press, 36–56.

————and Willmott, H. (1997). 'Networking as Knowledge Work: A Study of Strategic Inter-organizational Development in the Financial Services Industry', in B. P. Bloomfield, R. Coombs, D. Knights, and D. Littler (eds.), *Information Technology and Organizations: Strategies, Networks and Integration*. Oxford: Oxford University Press, 137–80.

Knorr-Cetina, K. (1981). 'The Micro-sociological Challenge of Macro-sociology: Towards a Reconstruction of Social Theory and Methodology', in K. D. Knorr-Cetina and A. V. Cicourel (eds.), *Advances in Social Theory and Methodology: Towards an Integration of Micro- and Macro-sociologies*. London: Routledge and Kegan Paul 1–47.

—— (1995). 'Laboratory Studies: The Cultural Approach to the Study of Science', in S. Janasoff, G. E. Markle, J. C. Petersen, and T. Pinch (eds.), *Handbook of Science and Technology Studies*. Thousand Oaks, CA: Sage, 140–65.

—— and Cicourel, A. V. (eds.) (1981). *Advances in Social Theory and Methodology: Towards an Integration of Micro- and Macro-sociologies*. London: Routledge & Kegan Paul.

Kvasny, L. (2006). 'The Cultural (Re)production of Digital Inequality', *Information, Communication and Society* 9(2): 160–81.

Latour, B. (1989). *La Science en action: introduction à la sociologie des sciences*. Paris: Gallimard, Folio Essais. In English: *Science in Action: How to Follow Scientists and Engineers through Society*. Cambridge, MA: Harvard University Press.

——(1991). 'Technology is Society Made Durable', in J. Law (ed.), *A Sociology of Monsters: Essays on Power, Technology and Domination*. London: Routledge, 103–31.

——(1992). *Aramis ou l'amour des techniques*. Série Textes à l'Appui, Anthropologie des Sciences et des Techniques. Paris: Éditions La Découverte. In English: *Aramis, or the Love of Technology*, trans. C. Porter. Cambridge, MA: Harvard University Press, 1996.

——(1993a). 'Ethnography of a 'High-Tech' Case: About Aramis', in P. Lemonnier, *Technological Choices: Transformations in Material Culture since the Neolithic*. London: Routledge & Kegan Paul, 372–98.

——(1993b). *We Have Never Been Modern*. Cambridge, MA: Harvard University Press.

——(1999). *Pandora's Hope: Essays on the Reality of Science Studies*. Cambridge, MA: Harvard University Press.

—— and Woolgar, S. (1979). *Laboratory Life: The Construction of Scientific Facts*. Princeton, NJ: Princeton University Press (1986 revised edition with a new postcript and index).

Law, J. (ed.) (1986). *Power, Action and Belief*. London: Routledge & Kegan Paul.

——(2001). *Ladbroke Grove or How to Think about Failing Systems*. Lancaster: Centre for Science Studies, Department of Sociology, University of Lancaster.

—— and Hassard, J. (eds.) (1999). *Actor Network Theory: And After*. Oxford: Blackwell.

Lee, A. S. (1994). 'Electronic Mail as a Medium for Rich Communication: An Empirical Investigation Using Hermeneutic Interpretation', *MIS Quarterly*, 18(2): 143–57.

Lehoux, P. (1997). 'Screeching Normativity, or can Actor-Network Theory Be Relevantly (Mis)used in Evaluation of Medical Technology', *Actor-Network Theory and After Workshop*, Centre for Social Theory and Technology, Keele University, 10–11 July.

Lilley, S., Lightfoot, G., and Paulo Amaral, M. N. (2004). *Representing Organization: Knowledge, Management and the Information Age*. Oxford: Oxford University Press.

Lynch, M., and Cole, S. (2005). 'Science and Technology Studies on Trial: Dilemmas of Expertise', *Social Studies of Science*, 35(2): 269–311.

Lyotard, J.-F. (1984). *The Postmodern Condition: A Report on Knowledge*. Minneapolis, MN: University of Minnesota Press.

McAdam, R., and McCreedy, A. (2000). 'A Critique of Knowledge Management Using a Social Constructionist Model', *New Technology, Work and Employment*, 15: 155–68.

MacKenzie, D. (1988). *'Micro' Versus 'Macro' Sociologies of Science and Technology*. Edinburgh PICT (Programme on Information and Communication Technologies) Working Paper No. 2, Research Centre for Social Sciences. Edinburgh: Edinburgh University.

—— and Wajcman, J. (eds.) (1985). *The Social Shaping of Technology*. Milton Keynes: Open University Press.

————(eds.) (1999). *The Social Shaping of Technology*. 2nd edn., Buckingham: Open University Press.

McLean, C., and Hassard, J. (2004). 'Symmetrical Absence/Symmetrical Absurdity: Critical Notes on the Production of Actor-Network Accounts', *Journal of Management Studies*, 41 (3): 493–519.

McLoughin, I. (1997). 'Babies, Bathwater, Guns and Roses', in I. McLoughin and M. Harris (eds.), *Innovation, Organizational Change and Technology*. London: International Thomson Business Press, 207–21.

——and Harris, M. (eds.) (1997). *Innovation, Organizational Change and Technology*. London: International Thomson Business Press.

Markus, M. L. (1983). 'Power, Politics and MIS Implementation', *Communications of the ACM*, 26(6): 430–44.

——and Robey, D. (1988). 'Information Technology and Organizational Change: Causal Structure in Theory and Research', *Management Science*, 34(5): 583–97.

Merton, R. (1938). *Science, Technology and Society in Seventeenth Century England*. Bruges: St Catherine Press (4th edn., New York: Howard Fertig, 2001).

——(1942). 'The Normative Structure of Science', reproduced in Merton 1973.

——(1973). *The Sociology of Science: Theoretical and Empirical Investigations*. Chicago, IL: University of Chicago Press.

Mingers, J. (2004). 'Re-establishing the Real: Critical Realism and Information Systems', in J. Mingers and L. Willcocks (eds.), *Social Theory and Philosophy for Information Systems*. Chichester: John Wiley & Sons, 372–406.

Mitev, N. N. (2005). 'Are Social Constructivist Approaches Critical? The Case of IS Failure', in D. A. Howcroft and E. Trauth (eds.), *Handbook of Information Systems Research: Critical Perspectives on Information Systems Design, Implementation and Use*. London: Edward Elgar Publishing Ltd.

——(2006). 'Postmodernism and Criticality in Information Systems Research: What Critical Management Studies Can Contribute', *Social Science Computer Review*, 24(3): 310–25 (Special Issue on 'Applying Critical Theory to the Study of ICTs').

——(2009). 'In and out of Actor-Network Theory: An Incomplete Journey', *Information Technology and People* (Special Issue on 'Using Social Theory to Make Sense of Information Systems: Reflexive Essays').

Mitroff, I. (1974). 'Norms and Counter Norms in a Select Group of the Apollo Moon Scientists: A Case Study of the Ambivalence of Scientists', *American Sociological Review*, 39: 579–95.

Monteiro, E., and Hanseth, O.. (1996). 'Social Shaping of Information Infrastructure: On Being Specific about the Technology', in W. J. Orlikowski, G. Walsham, M. R. Jones, and J. DeGross (eds.), *Information Technology and Changes in Organizational Work*, Proceedings of the IFIP WG8.2 working conference, Cambridge University, 7–9 December 1995. London: Chapman & Hall, 325–43.

Mulkay, M. (1974). 'Conceptual Displacement and Migration in Science', *Science Studies*, 4: 205–34.

Murdoch, J. (1997). 'Asymmetrical Translations: Configurations and Disfigurements within the Geometries of Power', *Actor-Network Theory and After Workshop*, Centre for Social Theory and Technology, Keele University, 10–11 July.

Myers, G. (1997). 'Texts, Time and Action: Unfolding Leaflets', *Actor-Network Theory and After Workshop*, Centre for Social Theory and Technology, Keele University, 10–11 July.

Myers, M. D. (1994). 'Dialectical Hermeneutics: A Theoretical Framework for the Implementation of Information Systems', *Information Systems Journal*, 5: 51–70.

——(1997). 'Critical Ethnography in Information Systems', in A. S. Lee, J. Liebenau, and J. I. DeGross (eds.), *Information Systems and Qualitative Research*. London: Chapman and Hall, 276–300.

Nandhakumar, J., and Vidgen, R. (2001). 'Due Process and the Introduction of New Technology: The Institution of Video Teleconferencing', in N. L. Russo, B. Fitzgerald, and J. I. DeGross (eds.), *Realigning Research and Practice in Information Systems Development: The Social and Organizational Perspective.* Proceedings of the IFIP Working Group 8.2 Conference, Boise, Idaho, 27–9 July 2001. Boston, MA: Kluwer Academic Publishers.

Ngwenyama, O. K., and Lee, A. S. (1997). 'Communicative Richness in Electronic Mail: Critical Social Theory and the Contextuality of Meaning', *MIS Quarterly*, 21(2): 145–67.

——Harvey, L., Myers, M. D., and Wynn, E. (1997). 'Ethnographic Research in Information Systems: An Exploration of Three Alternative Approaches to Ethnography', *18th International Conference on Information Systems*, Panel 17, Association of Information Systems, Atlanta, 533–4.

Orlikowski, W. J. (1992). 'The Duality of Technology: Rethinking the Concept of Technology in Organizations', *Organization Science*, 3(3): 398–427.

——and Baroudi, J. J. (1991). 'Studying Information Technology in Organizations: Research Approaches and Assumptions', *Information Systems Research*, 2(1): 1–28.

——Walsham, G., Jones, M. R., and DeGross, J. (eds.) (1996). *Information Technology and Changes in Organizational Work.* Proceedings of the IFIP WG8.2 Working Conference, Cambridge University, 7–9 December 1995. London: Chapman & Hall.

Pickering, A. (1992). *Science as Practice and Culture.* Chicago, IL: University of Chicago Press.

Richardson, H. (2003). 'CRM in Call Centres: The Logic of Practice', in M. Korpela, R. Montealegre, and A. Poulymenakou (eds.), *Organizational Information Systems in the Context of Globalization*, IFIP WG8.2 and WG9.4 Conference on Information Systems Perspectives and Challenges in the Context of Globalization, 15–17 June, Athens. Boston, MA: Kluwer Academic Publishers, 69–84.

Sarker, S. (2000). 'Toward a Methodology for Managing Information Systems Implementation: A Social Constructivist Perspective', *Informing Science* 3: 195–205.

——Sarker, S., and Sidorova, A. (2006). 'Understanding Business Process Change Failure: An Actor-Network Perspective', *Journal of Management Information Systems*, 23(1): 51–86.

Shapin, S., and Schaffer, S. (1985). *Leviathan and the Air Pump: Hobbes, Boyle and the Experimental Life.* Princeton, NJ: Princeton University Press.

Silva, L. (1997). 'Power and Politics in the Adoption of Information Systems in Organisations: The Case of a Research Centre in Latin America', Ph.D. thesis, Department of Information Systems. London: London School of Economics.

——and Backhouse, J. (1997). 'Becoming Part of the Furniture: The Institutionalisation of Information Systems', in A. S. Lee, J. Liebenau, and J. I. DeGross (eds.), *Information Systems and Qualitative Research.* London: Chapman & Hall, 389–416.

Soderstrom, O. (1997). 'Geographers and the Visual: From Iconophilia to Expertise', *Actor-Network Theory and After Workshop*, Centre for Social Theory and Technology, Keele University, 10–11 July.

Sorensen, K. (2004). 'Cultural Politics of Technology: Combining Critical and Constructive Interventions?', *Science, Technology and Human Values*, 29(2): 184–90.

Stalder, F. (1999). 'Fluid Objects: Reconfiguring Money and the Limits of Actor-Network Theory', paper given at the Sociality/Materiality conference, Brunel University, 9–11 Sept.

Star, S. L. (1991). 'Power, Technologies and the Phenomenology of Conventions: On Being Allergic to Onions', in J. Law (ed.), *A Sociology of Monsters: Essays on Power, Technology and Domination.* London: Routledge.

Truex, D. P., and Baskerville, R. (1998). 'Deep Structure or Emergence Theory: Contrasting Theoretical Foundations for Information Systems Development', *Information Systems Journal*, 8: 99–118.

Vidgen, R., and McMaster, T. (1996). 'Black Boxes, Non-human Stakeholders and the Translation of IT', in W. J. Orlikowski, G. Walsham, M. R. Jones, and J. DeGross (eds.), *Information Technology and Changes in Organizational Work*. Proceedings of the IFIP WG8.2 Working Conference, Cambridge University, 7–9 December 1995. London: Chapman & Hall, 250–71.

Walsham, G. (1993). *Interpreting Information Systems in Organisations*. Chichester: John Wiley & Sons.

——(1995). 'The Emergence of Interpretivism in IS Research', *Information Systems Research*, 6(4): 376–94.

——(1997). 'Actor-Network Theory and IS Research: Current Status and Future Prospects', in A. S. Lee, J. Liebenau, and J. I. DeGross, *Information Systems and Qualitative Research*. London: Chapman & Hall, 466–80.

——and Sahay, S. (1999). 'GIS for District-Level Administration in India: Problems and Opportunities. *MIS Quarterly*, 23(1): 39–65 (Special Issue on Intensive Research in Information Systems).

Willcocks, L. P. (2004). 'Foucault, Power/Knowledge and Information Systems: Reconstructing the Present', in J. Mingers and L. Willcocks (eds.), *Social Theory and Philosophy for Information Systems*. Chichester: John Wiley & Sons, 238–96.

——and Grint, K. (1997). 'Re-inventing the Organization? Towards a Critique of Business Process Re-engineering', in I. McLoughlin and M. Harris (eds.), *Innovation, Organizational Change and Technology*. London: International Thomson Business Press, 87–110.

Willmott, H. (1994). 'Bringing Agency (back) into Organizational Analysis: Responding to the Crisis of (Post)modernity', in J. Hassard and M. Parker (eds.), *Towards a New Theory of Organizations*. London: Routledge, 87–130.

Wilson, M. (2000). 'Discussant's Comments Delivered on "Machine Agency as Perceived Autonomy: An Action Perspective", by J. Rose and D. Truex', in R. Baskerville, J. Stage, and J. I. DeGross (eds.), *Organizational and Social Perspectives on Information Technology*. IFIP TC8 WG8.2 International Working Conference, 9–11 June, Aalborg, Denmark. Boston, MA: Kluwer Academic Publishers, 371–88.

——(2002). 'Making Nursing Visible? Gender, Technology and the Care Plan as Script', *Information Technology and People*, 15(2): 139–58.

——and Howcroft, D. A. (2003). 'Re-conceptualising Failure: Social Shaping Meets IS Research', *European Journal of Information Systems*, 11: 236–50.

Winner, L. (1977). *Autonomous Technology. Technics out-of-control as a Theme in Political Thought*. Cambridge, MA: MIT Press.

——(1993). 'Upon Opening the Black Box and Finding it Empty: Social Constructivism and the Philosophy of Technology', *Science, Technology and Human Values*, 18(3): 362–78.

Woodhouse, E., Hess, D., and Breyman, S. (2002). 'Science Studies and Activism', *Social Studies of Science*, 32(2): 297–319.

Woolgar, S. (1988). *Knowledge and Reflexivity: New Frontiers in the Sociology of Knowledge*. London: Sage.

PART III

....

RETHINKING THEORY IN MIS PRACTICE

....

BUILDING on the conceptual treatment of the field of Information Systems that is the focus of Part II, Part III of the book turns its attention to some of the key issues associated with managing information systems in practice. Where possible, we reference relevant related material that appears in other chapters, both in this section of the book and elsewhere. In addition, relevant research—from cognate fields in addition to Information Systems—is cited, in line with the transdisciplinary approach adopted by the editors and many of the other contributors.

Part III begins with a chapter by Bob Galliers on the subject of IS strategy. He adopts the term IS *strategizing* with a view to giving emphasis to the *process* of strategy making. He views IS strategizing as an integral aspect of business strategy rather than adopting the more common view that the IS strategy should be *aligned* with the business strategy. The sometimes vexed topic of alignment is dealt with in detail in Chapter 13 that follows. Galliers draws on such concepts as a socio-technical infrastructure, exploration alongside exploitation—ambidexterity, to use Tushman's terminology (Tushman and O'Reilly 1996)—and knowledge sharing and creating (see also Chapter 20) to provide a rationale for the development of a framework that may be used by organizations in considering how to go about the strategizing process. Issues associated with sourcing considerations—the focus of Chapter 19—are incorporated, as are issues associated with IT governance more generally (see Chapter 16) and with improved organizational performance (cf. competitive advantage—the subject matter of Chapter 14). The chapter builds on, in part, his chapter (Galliers 2007) in the *Oxford Handbook of Information and Communication Technology* (Mansell et al. 2007).

As indicated above, Chapter 13 deals with the thorny issue of alignment. Written by Yolande Chan and Blaize Horner Reich, the chapter provides a comprehensive review of the IT alignment literature, noting that the topic is one of the major concerns of senior executives and IT practitioners alike. The authors build on their recent *Journal of Information Technology* article (Chan and Reich 2007) and present divergent views and new perspectives on alignment, first discussing the motivation for alignment research and moving on to provide a definition of alignment, given the range of perspectives to be found in the literature. They address such questions as: what creates alignment and what benefits can reasonably be expected as a result? In concluding, they highlight key implications for researchers and practitioners.

Chapter 14 considers sustainable competitive advantage on the back of IT. Written by Michael Wade, Gabe Piccoli, and Blake Ives, the chapter builds on and extends the comprehensive review provided by the authors in a recent *MISQ* article (Piccoli and Ives 2005). The authors first note that the term sustainability has two meanings in the IS literature: (1) 'the ability of a firm to use IT to maintain a competitive advantage over a period of time', and (2) the 'ethics and long lasting socio-environmental benefits' of IT. We deal with questions of ethics and 'green IT' elsewhere in the book (e.g. in Chapters 16 and 23, and 22, respectively). Here, the authors focus on the first meaning of the term. They make the key point that the factors that may assist in *gaining* an advantage are not necessarily those required to *sustain* that advantage. While much of the literature focuses on the former, relatively less has considered the means by which 'firms can hold on to a competitive advantage based on, or enabled by, IT'. Reasons for this include the need for longitudinal research, which is all too often missing from our major journals. In addition, they note the significant challenge in isolating the specific role played by IT in sustaining advantage as against other competing explanations. 'Unfortunately, the resultant scarcity of rigorous investigation and evidence is a contributing cause of the recurrence of attacks on the role of IT as a competitive resource' (Carr 2003). The chapter aims to redress the balance somewhat.

The next chapter—Chapter 15—is written by Erica Wagner and Sue Newell and turns our attention to enterprise systems. Building on the previous chapter's treatment of firms gaining competitive advantage on the back of IT, the authors make the point that this competitiveness is thought to be gained through enabling leaner production as a result of streamlining work flow with a view to increasing productivity, reducing costs, and improving decision quality and resource control. They note that this *perceived* ability to streamline and integrate business operations across an organization's value chain (Shanks and Seddon 2000) lead to enterprise systems becoming the most popular business software of the twentieth century (Robey, Ross, and Boudreau 2002). The central tenet of enterprise systems is that this integration will help to leverage organizational competitiveness through improving the way in which information is produced, shared, and managed across functions and locations, providing the administrative backbone that an organization needs (Davenport 1998), thereby avoiding the issues of incompatibility associated with so-called 'legacy' systems that focused on discrete functions in prior times. So much, then, for the received wisdom: the authors go on to point out that, while enterprise systems hold the *promise* of business integration across an organization, 'accomplishing this promise requires changes that affect an unprecedented amount of people across the enterprise'. Referring to the work of Aladwani (2002) and Scott and Wagner (2003), for example, they argue that the 'standardization of work practices across functional areas of the business is often difficult to achieve, with resistance from stakeholder groups being common' with organizational change being more problematic than first thought (Scott and Vessey 2002) and high levels of project failure being common (Robbins-Gioia 2001). Noting that, while 20 per cent of IT projects are abandoned prior to implementation (Cooke, Gelman, and Peterson 2001), this means that 80 per cent of enterprise system projects do at least go ahead. This leads them to suggest that the chapter might usefully refocus its attention away from looking at the *short-term* problems and opportunities associated with implementation towards understanding how organizations learn to exploit the functionality of these potentially powerful systems over the *long term*. Citing the work of Robey and Boudreau (1999), this perspective requires rethinking many of the assumptions about IT implementation and use—moving away from such simplistic notions as 'IT "drives", "forces" or even merely "enables" change' to exploring 'the complex relationship of reciprocal causality between IT and organization with the outcomes emergent and difficult to predict in advance' (e.g. Walsham 1993; Orlikowski 2000). This reorientation of our thinking leads to questions being raised concerning notions of 'best practice', consensus, user participation, and implementation. In so doing, the authors provide considerable food for thought in relation to some of the more taken-for-granted assumptions underpinning much of the mainstream literature on information systems more broadly.

This treatment of enterprise systems leads nicely into Chapter 16—a chapter that deals with IT governance issues more broadly. In it, Sue Newell and Cynthia Williams consider how decisions are made in organizations about IT. They note that how these decisions 'are made, who makes these decisions and what rules and norms guide decisions is a fundamental first step as this will likely influence whether the necessary organizational structures are put in place to support the strategic adoption and use of IT'. Calling on the more general corporate governance literature, they broaden the notion of IT governance commonly found in the mainstream literature on the subject by looking at the 'rights and responsibilities associated with the use, storage, retrieval and collection of data'. Corporate governance concerns itself 'with ensuring that there is correspondence between the interests of managers, as decision makers, and the interests of shareholders, as owners' (cf. Eisenhardt 1989). In other words, the authors take a broader stakeholder perspective in their treatment of the subject matter, and consider that IT governance is 'about ensuring that IT decisions are made in the interests of the long-term sustainability of the organization'. There is thus an ethical dimension (see also Chapter 22), to their treatment of the subject matter. They draw on work by the likes of Brundtland (1987) to incorporate sustainability criteria in measuring organizational success, referring to the 'triple-bottom line' concept coined by John Elkington (1994) to indicate that organizational performance should be measured according to three key criteria—social and environmental as well as financial. Thus, they argue that the decisions related to IT governance need to be aligned with these social, financial, and environmental considerations.

A key aspect of the 'rights and responsibilities associated with the use, storage, retrieval and collection of data' is the question of security, and this topic is the focus of Chapter 17 written by Amy Ray. Noting that notwithstanding the fact that while spending on security is increasing, so are security breaches, the author argues that it is high time to rethink current approaches to information security management. In light of this, the chapter considers 'how the growing sophistication of newer technologies demands new security management thinking beyond addressing individual vulnerabilities'. The chapter goes on to present ideas for improving IT security management efforts, including 'suggestions for more proactively identifying risks resulting from emergent use of these systems'. In doing so, this chapter bridges 'the gap between high level policy-based security management and low level technology-based security management to consider how more attention to technological and business processes may lead to improvements in information security management efforts'.

One of the newer technologies that have had major impacts on the way we need to think about the topic 'MIS' is the emergence in recent years of mobile information technology, and this is the focus of Chapter 18. Written by Carsten Sørensen, this chapter notes that mobile IT concerns the shrinking of computers, 'making them mobile or embedded into the environment, and establishing wireless connections to local—or global—information infrastructures'. Sørensen notes the amazing growth of one form of this technology, that of the mobile phone. There were approximately four billion such devices in the world in 2009 and that number is estimated to reach six billion by 2013. 'Such a phenomenon', he argues, 'clearly deserves to be studied and a growing body of research is exactly doing so.' But much of the debate on the topic 'tends to emphasize the technical opportunities or affordances at the cost of a more comprehensive analysis of how the social and the technical is co-constructed' and much of the research on the topic focuses on a single mobile technology—the mobile phone. This chapter aims to counter the fact that there is relatively little research that broadens the focus to include the range of mobile information technologies. Such arrangements may comprise 'more than one mobile phone, dedicated mobile email client, notebook computer with wireless Internet access, and perhaps peripheral equipment interacting with the devices in Personal Area Networks (PANs) such as Bluetooth headsets, cameras, photo printers, and speakers'. The chapter considers 'enterprise mobility' as an outcome of the use of mobile IT in and between organizations, and raises 'critical issues in our understanding the intersection between the individual experience with mobile IT at work and the organizational concern for efficiency'.

The increasing complexity associated with MIS in this day and age is also reflected in the subject matter that is the focus of Chapter 19: outsourcing. Written by two internationally renowned authorities on the topic—Mary Lacity and Leslie Willcocks, together with a colleague, Shaji Khan—this chapter, originally published in the *Journal of Strategic Information Systems* (Lacity, Khan, and Willcocks 2009), provides an overview of the many contributions that MIS research has made to practice. Ten aspects of IT outsourcing (ITO) are covered, namely: (1) determinants of IT outsourcing; (2) IT outsourcing strategy; (3) determinants of ITO success; (4) client capabilities; (5) supplier capabilities and perspectives; (6) relationship management; (7) global IT workforce issues; (8) offshore outsourcing; (9) application service provision; and (10) the future of global sourcing. The authors go on to note, however, that there remain 'five persistent, prickly issues that continue to plague ITO practice that still need our attention'. In dealing with the many contributions that have arisen from the mutual constituted nature of theory in and of practice, this chapter—and the others that make up Part III—serves as something of a metaphor for the Handbook as a whole, given our intention to provide both critical perspectives on and new directions for this important field of study. Paraphrasing Lacity and Willcocks: 'It is our hope that [the book] will serve to acknowledge the contributions of [MIS] researchers, to inform interested readers in the main findings of [MIS] research that assist practice, and to inspire future researchers to tackle unresolved challenges.'

REFERENCES

Aladwani, A. (2002). 'IT Project Uncertainty, Planning and Success: An Empirical Investigation from Kuwait', *Information Technology & People*, 15: 210–26.

Brundtland, G. H. (1987). *Our Common Future: Report of the World Commission on Environment and Development*. Oxford: Oxford University Press.

Carr, N. (2003). 'IT Doesn't Matter', *Harvard Business Review*, 81(5): 41–9.

Chan, Y. E., and Reich, B. H. (2007). 'IT Alignment: What Have We Learned?', *Journal of Information Technology*, 22: 297–315.

Cooke, D., Gelman, L., and Peterson, W. J. (2001). *ERP Trends* (Report No. R-1292-01-RR). New York: The Conference Board.

Davenport, T. (1998). 'Putting the Enterprise into the Enterprise System', *Harvard Business Review*, 76(4): 121–31.

Eisenhardt, K. M. (1989). 'Agency Theory: An Assessment and Review', *Academy of Management Review*, 14: 57–74.

Elkington, J. (1994). 'Towards the Sustainable Corporation: Win-Win-Win Business Strategies for Sustainable Development', *California Management Review*, 36(2): 90–100.

Galliers, R. D. (2007). 'On Confronting some of the Common Myths of Information Systems Strategy Discourse', in Mansell et al. 2007: 225–43.

Lacity, M. C., Khan, S. A., and Willcocks, L. P. (2009). 'A Review of the IT Sourcing Literature: Insights for Practice', *Journal of Strategic Information Systems*, 18(3): 130–46.

Mansell, R., Avgerou, C., Quah, D., and Silverstone, R. (eds.) (2007). *The Oxford Handbook of Information and Communication Technology*. Oxford: Oxford University Press.

Orlikowski, W. (2000). 'Using Technology and Constituting Structures: A Practice Lens for Studying Technology in Organizations', *Organization Science*, 11: 404–28.

Piccoli, G., and Ives, B. (2005). 'IT-Dependent Strategic Initiatives and Sustained Competitive Advantage: A Review and Synthesis of the Literature', *MIS Quarterly*, 29(4): 747–76.

Robbins-Gioia (2001). The Robbins-Gioia Survey at <http://www.robbinsgioia.com/>.

Robey, D., and Boudreau, M. (1999). 'Accounting for the Contradictory Organizational Consequences of Information Technology', *Information Systems Research*, 10: 167–85.

——Ross, J. W., and Boudreau, M. C. (2002). 'Learning to Implement Enterprise Systems: An Exploratory Study of the Dialectics of Change', *Journal of Management Information Systems*, 19: 17–46.

Scott, J., and Vessey, I. (2002). 'Managing Risks in Enterprise Systems Implementations', *Communications of the ACM*, 45(4): 74–81.

Scott, S. V., and Wagner, E. L. (2003). 'Networks, Negotiations, and New Times: The Implementation of Enterprise Resource Planning into an Academic Administration', *Information & Organization*, 13(4): 285–313.

Shanks, G., and Seddon, P. (2000). Editorial, *Journal of Information Technology*, 15: 243–4.

Tushman, M. L., and O'Reilly, C. (1996). 'Ambidextrous Organizations: Managing Evolutionary and Revolutionary Change', *California Management Review*, 38(1): 8–30.

Walsham, G. (1993). *Interpreting Information Systems in Organizations*. London: John Wiley & Sons.

CHAPTER 12

FURTHER DEVELOPMENTS IN INFORMATION SYSTEMS STRATEGIZING: UNPACKING THE CONCEPT

ROBERT D. GALLIERS

PROLOGUE: TOWARDS A REVISED FRAMEWORK FOR INFORMATION SYSTEMS STRATEGIZING

IN previous work (in particular, Galliers 2004, 2007a), an attempt was made to collect together aspects of recent thinking in organizational and information systems (IS) strategic thinking to develop a framework that would aid the process of IS strategizing. The problematic nature of key tenets of much of the mainstream IS strategy literature (i.e. issues of alignment, competitive advantage, and so-called knowledge management systems or 'best practice' solutions) was considered in the context of the development and strategic impact and use of information and communication technology (ICT) systems in and between organizations. *Inter alia*, it was noted that there are vexed issues associated with aligning dynamic information needs with a relatively static technology (see also Desouza 2006), and harnessing an increasingly commoditized technology to provide competitive advantage. This is at the heart of Carr's (2003, 2005) argument that 'IT Doesn't Matter'. But Carr misses the point. Crucially, it is the *use* to which ICT is put by organizations, and their capability and competencies in this regard, that are crucial, as is the key role that information can play in questioning, supporting, and informing the strategizing process. In relation to knowledge management and knowledge management systems in particular, questions were raised as to whether ICT systems could in fact capture and transfer knowledge, with the *process* of knowing and knowledge creation (e.g. Boland and Tenkasi 1995; Nonaka and Takeuchi 1995; Cook and Brown 1999; von Krogh, Ichijo, and Nonaka 2000) being highlighted. This orientation was set against the capture and transfer knowledge that is the focus of much of the mainstream literature on the topic, and the knowledge-based theory of the firm (Grant 1996; Spender 1996).

In attempting to synthesize these arguments with a view to developing a more holistic framework for IS strategizing, the socio-technical concept of an information architecture or infrastructure (e.g. Star and Ruhleder 1996; Monteiro 1998; Ciborra 2000; Hanseth 2004) provided a useful building block. In addition, it was argued that organizations should be 'ambidextrous' (Tushman and O'Reilly 1996) in that they should combine an ability to *explore* new opportunities as well as *exploit* current capabilities and technology. I argued that this ambidexterity can be facilitated by an environment—an information infrastructure or architecture—that provides a support-ive context for learning and interaction. I introduced each of these components in the context of a framework that is meant to be used as a sense-making (cf. Weick 1995) device, rather than a prescriptive tool.

Before proceeding to unpack the framework in greater detail than previously, I should first clarify how the term information systems (IS) is used here. As I have argued elsewhere (see e.g. Galliers 2003, 2006b), I view IS as neither being focused on the IT artefact (a technological perspective common in much of the literature) at one pole nor on knowledge sharing and creation at the other. I view IS as incorporating both aspects—as a socio-technical construct in other words, mutually constituted. There are two primary reasons for this. The first relates to the nature of data, information, and knowledge (Galliers and Newell 2003a, 2003b). The socio-technical infrastructure (e.g. Star and Ruhleder 1996; Ciborra 2000) depicted in Figure 12.1 comprises human beings who can make sense of data provided by both formal and informal systems via the application of their (situated) knowledge. In doing so, they turn data into purposeful information (see also Chapter 20). The second reason is to provide an otherwise missing link between the literatures on IS/IT strategy, on knowl-edge management, and on organizational strategies for change. Too often viewed as discrete, an underlying argument in this chapter is that the concepts emerging from these literatures should be viewed as complimentary and synergistic, as argued by Porter (2001), for example (see also Galliers et al. 1997). I shall refer to these other literatures in the course of this chapter in addition to providing a critical treatment of much of the IS strategy and planning literature.

I should also note that aspects of the IS, IT, and information management (IM) strategies first articulated by Michael Earl (1989), and developed further in Galliers (1991, 1999) as information, IT, and information services strategies—the combination forming the IS strategy as a whole—are incorporated into both the exploration and exploitation strategies of Figure 12.1. The *exploration* strategy takes more of an informal approach—Ciborra (1992, 1994, after Lévi-Strauss 1966) would call this tinkering or bricolage—as against the formal approaches of the kind identified by Earl (1993). These include what Earl terms business-led, method-driven, administra-tive (i.e. resource-focused) and technological approaches. His study led to the

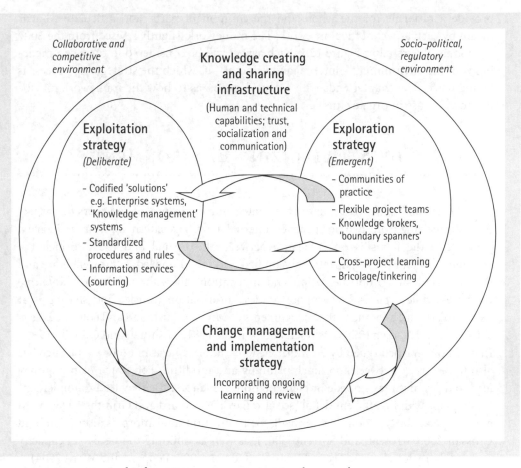

FIGURE 12.1 A revised information systems strategizing framework

conclusion that an organizational approach held most promise given its emphasis on process, integration, and, crucially, stakeholder involvement (see also Códoba 2009). The exploration strategy also takes into account the learning—or knowledge—that can emerge from communities of practice, boundary spanning individuals and flexible project teams (e.g. Tushman and Scanlan 1981; Lave and Wenger 1991; Wenger 1998; Hansen, Nohria, and Tierney 1999; Scheepers, Venkitachalam, and Gibbs 2004; Erden, von Krogh, and Nonaka 2008), including learning across projects (e.g. Newell and Edelman 2008). The *exploitation* strategy, as noted, is more formal in its approach and focuses more on codified 'solutions', standardized procedures, and standards. It also incorporates issues of how the information services function should be organized, including key sourcing issues (e.g. Lacity and Willcocks 2000).

In this chapter, then, I shall attempt to unpack the concept of the IS strategizing framework still further, by articulating, in greater depth, the literature that has informed its development. The aim is to ground the framework in the extant literature, provide a rationale for the whole and the component parts, and articulate what is meant by each aspect of the framework. The framework, slightly revised from the 2007 version, is illustrated in Figure 12.1. Each aspect will be considered in turn, commencing with the environment—internal and external—in which the strategizing process is taking place. The chapter ends with a consideration as to how the framework may be put to good use in organizations.

THE STRATEGIZING ENVIRONMENT

As indicated above, my treatment of the strategizing environment considers this aspect of IS strategizing from two perspectives: internal as well as external. From the *internal* perspective the focus is on a balance between the formal and the informal; the technological and the organizational; codified and tacit knowledge; the deliberate and the emergent, and implementation and innovation, all with the aim of *exploiting* resources while *exploring* new opportunities. Information transfer and sharing is at its core, very much in line with the arguments of Michael Tushman and colleagues (e.g. Tushman and Nadler 1978; Tushman and Scanlan 1981; Tushman and O'Reilly 1996). In addition, and as argued by Newkirk, Lederer, and Srinavasan (2003), a balance has also to be struck between too much planning and too little. Too much planning may lead to delay and may impede implementation, while too little may lead to implementation plans with insufficient detail (see also Earl 1993; Ward and Griffiths 1996; Ward and Peppard 2002). Room has to made for innovation and improvisation (Vera and Crossan 2005; Crossan and Sorrenti 2007), as well as building the necessary capacity and capability for change (Teece, Pisano, and Shuen 1997; Peppard and Ward 2004)— organizational characteristics that 'enable an organization to conceive, choose and implement strategies' (Barney 1997). This, too, is where the knowledge creating and sharing infrastructure plays a significant role, as detailed below.

The *external* environment should take account of the institutional context (see Chapter 6) in which the organisation operates—including the socio-political and regulatory environment, and cultural nuances in different parts of the organization, especially in multinational arrangements, for example (Finnegan and Longaigh 2002; Mohdzain and Ward 2007; David et al. 2008). In relation to the latter, there has been increasing focus in the literature on subsidiaries (e.g. Gupta and Govindarajan 2000; O'Donnell 2000), for example, given growing globalization (e.g. Walsham 2001; Sheth and Sisodia 2007; Galliers 2007b; Oshri, van Fenema, and Kotlarsky 2008), with Finnegan and colleagues (2003) noting the impact of different cultures and power relationships of external stakeholders, and Ives and colleagues (1993) highlighting the potential of resistance from foreign subsidiaries and the disparity in the IT infrastructure and available products in different parts of the world. The effects of trust in virtual communities may also be significant (Jarvenpaa and Leidner 1999; Ridings, Gelen, and Arinze 2002). Depending on particular circumstances, these are the kind of considerations that need to be taken into account. Also of potential relevance is the work on issues associated with integrating IS after mergers and acquisitions (McKiernan and Merali 1993, 1995; Brown and Renwick 1996; Giacomazzi et al. 1997), with Wijnhoven and colleagues (2006) developing a variant of Henderson and Venkatraman's (1999) alignment model to take account of the extent of integration: from complete integration to mere coexistence. All this is in addition to the analysis of the competitive forces (e.g. Porter 2001) and the cooperative—or conflictual—arrangements (e.g. Webster 1995) at play.

One final point: in earlier work (Galliers 1991, 1993, 1999 in particular), and as noted above, I proposed an IS strategizing framework that was closely linked to a business strategy. The business strategy was considered to exist outside the boundary of the IS strategy—that is, in its internal environment. The link, it was argued, should be a strong one, with the information strategy feeding off, and feeding into, the business strategy. The information strategy, in my terms, was concerned with the information needed not only to *support* but also to *question* the business strategy. For example, are assumptions that underpin the strategy being borne out? It should be noted that the business strategy is absent from Figure 12.1, however. This is not an oversight. In line with Porter's (2001: 78) argument, the revised IS strategy is a significant aspect of the overall business strategy, it is integrated into it. In an earlier reflection on the subject (Galliers 2007a: 238, emphasis added), I reinterpreted a passage from Porter's article, as follows:

> The next stage of strategy evolution will involve a shift in thinking from business strategy and knowledge strategy, to Information Systems strategising. By *integrating* Information Systems considerations into the discourse on business and knowledge strategy, the resultant thinking and practice will become mutually constituted and significantly more robust.

It is with this in mind that the IS strategizing framework is presented without explicit mention of the business strategy, and with which the knowledge creating and sharing infrastructure is introduced to provide the oxygen needed for what should be seen as a dynamic, ongoing, and iterative process.

THE KNOWLEDGE CREATING AND SHARING INFRASTRUCTURE

In a previous work, I described the knowledge creating and sharing infrastructure in terms of an information architecture (Galliers 2004: 255–6). This was meant to connote an enabling socio-technical environment for both the *exploitation* of knowledge (efficiency) and the *exploration* of knowledge (innovation) in line with Tushman's concept of ambidexterity (Tushman and O'Reilly 1996). There are elements here, too, of what Boland and Tenkasi (1995) term communities of knowing. I shall unpack the exploitation and exploration strategies that play an important role in the IS strategizing concept in the sections that follow, but it is important to note at this stage that this socio-technical environment is meant to enable and facilitate the strategizing process by ensuring that the necessary human and technical capabilities are in place (cf. Peppard and Ward 2004), not only within the organization but with key partners, such as in sourcing arrangements (Beulen, van Fenema, and Currie 2005).

As noted previously (Galliers 2004), the concept of an information infrastructure has developed over time. In the 1980s and 1990s, the term information infrastructure usually connoted the standardization of corporate ICT, systems, and data, with a view to reconciling centralized processing and distributed applications. So, the question would need to be asked whether the necessary technologies are in place to support the enterprise moving forward. Increasingly, however, the concept has come to relate to the human infrastructure in addition. For example, what roles and skills are required, not just in terms of developing and delivering information systems—increasingly in a distributed environment (Kotlarsky and Oshri 2005)—but also in their management (Galliers and Leidner 2009)? Weill and Ross (2004) talk in terms of IT governance in commenting on some of these issues. As already noted, trust plays an important role here too (Kanawattanachai and Yoo 2002; Sambamurthy and Jarvenpaa 2002), with a team atmosphere needing to be in place (Zárraga and Bonache 2005). Additionally, the means by which alternative stakeholder concerns are taken into account (Códoba 2009) is an important consideration, bearing in mind that implicit in many of the more formal approaches to strategizing is the assumption that individuals can make stated organizational objectives their own (Willmott 1993), with questions of power (Foucault 1984) often being left unconsidered. As noted earlier, Star and Ruhleder (1996) talk of infrastructures in terms of their embeddedness, transparency, reach, links with conventions of practice, and installed base. An information infrastructure should thus be viewed as heterogeneous in nature.

The concept is further refined here by introducing ideas related to knowledge creating and sharing, building on earlier work by Nonaka, von Krogh, and colleagues (e.g. Nonaka 1991, 1994; Nonaka et al. 1994; von Krogh, Ichijo, and Nonaka 2000; Nonaka and Toyama 2003; Nonaka, von Krogh, and Voepel 2006; Nonaka and von Krogh 2007; Erden, von Krogh, and Nonaka 2008), and to project learning (Kotnour 1999; Salas, Burke, and Cannon-Bowers 2000; Schindler and Epplerm 2003; Scarbrough et al. 2004) and cross-project learning capability (Newell and Edelman 2008), bearing in mind the 'stickiness' of knowledge (von Hippel 1994; Szulanski 1996; Szulanski and Jensen 2004), and the resultant need for boundary spanning activity (Tushman and Scanlan 1981). The creation of a dynamic capability (Zollo and Winter 2002; Winter 2003) in this regard is key. According to Zollo and Winter (2002: 340), dynamic capabilities are 'a learned and stable pattern of collective activity through which the organization systematically generates and modifies its operating routines in pursuit of effectiveness'.

Previously, issues of exploration and exploitation have tended to be considered as being in opposition to each other (March 1991). Increasingly, however, we see different ICT initiatives such as ERP and KM systems being implemented in tandem in an attempt to foster the simultaneous development of organizational efficiency and flexibility (Newell et al. 2003)—hence the need to view the exploration and exploitation strategies as being mutually constituted and reinforcing (cf. Cook and Brown 1999). Formal 'organisation memory' IS (Nevo and Wand 2005) will certainly have their place, but so will means by which knowing is facilitated and by which knowledge can flow, even in distributed teams (Carmel 1999; Desouza and Evaristo 2004) or in multinational locations (Gupta and Govindarajan 2000; Oshri, van Fenema, and Kotlarsky 2008).

THE EXPLOITATION STRATEGY

The process of exploitation bears many of the hallmarks of mainstream and earlier thinking on IS strategy. For example, much of earlier and even recent practice follows what might be termed a deterministic path of technology exploitation (cf. Earl 1993). Thus, Lederer and Sethi (1988), for example, speak of strategic information systems planning as 'the process whereby an organization determines a portfolio of computer-based applications to help it achieve its business objectives'. In a later work, Lederer and colleagues (Newkirk, Lederer, and Srinavasan 2003) detail such planning phases as strategic awareness; situation analysis; strategy conception; strategy formulation, and strategy implementation. This is the deliberate—as compared to the emergent—strategy of which Mintzberg speaks (Mintzberg and Waters 1985). A deliberate attempt is made to identify and develop ICT applications that both support and question the organization's strategic vision, and current need for information and expertise (Segars and Grover 1999). Here, we find both the IS and IT strategies that Earl (1989) proposes. It is likely that Enterprise Systems (e.g. Howcroft, Newell, and Wagner 2004, 2005) and so-called KMS (e.g. Leidner 2000), and standardized procedures for adopting ICT products, hiring ICT personnel, and developing customized applications will each contribute to this exploitation strategy. Indeed, organizational routines can be a source of connections and improved understandings according to Feldman and Rafaeli (2002). And in line with the models introduced in Galliers (1991, 1999), an aspect of this strategy will relate to the organizational arrangements for IS/IT services, including sourcing considerations (cf. Lacity and Willcocks 2000; Carmel and Agarwal 2002, for example). Policies on such issues as risk, security, and confidentiality will also need to be considered in this context (e.g. Backhouse et al. 2005).

THE EXPLORATION STRATEGY

With respect to the exploration aspects of IS strategizing, here the emphasis is much more on issues associated with situated learning (Lave and Wenger 1991), communities of practice (Wenger 1998) and of knowing (Boland and Tenkasi 1995), and cross-project learning (Newell and Edelman 2008), as noted in the above discussion on infrastructure. Ciborra and colleagues (Ciborra 2000) talk of drift in this context—as against control—but there is nonetheless a sense of direction and purpose associated with this activity. I therefore prefer the term emergence in this regard, but there is certainly a sense of bricolage (cf. Lévi-Strauss 1966) and tinkering at play here, to return to terms favoured by Ciborra (1992). Elements of what Lindblom (1959) termed 'muddling through' and of improvisation (Crossan and Sorrenti 1997; Vera and Crossan 2005) and innovation (Van der Gerben, van Beers, and Kleinknecht 2002) play an important part in addition. As noted, organizations are increasingly reliant on project teams whose membership may well be in flux and distributed. Considerations of trust (Sambamurphy and Jarvenpaa 2002), socialization (Ahuja and Galvin 2003), and learning from one project to another (e.g. Scarbrough et al. 2004) are key features at play here. The role of communities of practice (e.g. Wenger 1998) is crucial in knowledge creation as we have seen, as is the role of boundary spanning individuals (Tushman and Scanlan 1981), or what we might term knowledge brokers—(see also Lave and Wenger 1991; Hansen, Nohria, and Tierney 1999).

While the concept of the ambidextrous organization has been postulated (Tushman and O'Reilly 1996), and some empirical research has been conducted to test the thesis (e.g. He and Wong 2004), there remains little in the literature that might be of assistance to organizations in providing an enabling, supportive environment that might foster this sought-after 'ambidexterity'. Relating concepts of infrastructure introduced earlier in this chapter to the concept of ambidexterity would appear to hold some promise in this regard. Thus, the kind of socio-technical environment proposed by Star and Ruhleder (1996), Ciborra (2000), and Hanseth (2004), among others, would combine information and knowledge sharing services—both electronic and human—that would facilitate both exploitation *and* exploration of knowledge, together with the kind of flexibility necessary to enable appropriate responses to changing business imperatives. The development of different scenarios can be helpful in exploring alternative futures in this context (Galliers 1993, 2006a).

THE CHANGE MANAGEMENT STRATEGY

As previously (Galliers 2007a: 236–7), I have attempted to stress the importance of ongoing learning and review in the strategizing process. Improved understanding can lead to informed judgements being taken, with a view to further developments taking place—in terms of improved systems and processes (formal as well as informal) that may assist individual and collective activity and decision making, and organizational performance. Ongoing learning and review are central to the processual view of IS strategizing adopted here, given the unintended—as well as the intended—consequences arising from ICT implementations (Robey and Boudreau 1999); the dynamic nature of alignment (Sabherwal, Hirschheim, and Goles 2001)—the need for agility therefore (Desouza 2006), and the emergent nature of strategizing (Mintzberg and Waters 1985). Thus, the process of strategizing is one of visioning, planning, taking action, and assessing outcomes, all with an eye to changing circumstance and imperatives, *and* the actions of individuals and groups outside of, or irrespective of, any formal strategy process. Some means of measuring the impact on firm performance is key in this regard (Rivard, Raymond, and Verreault 2006).

I noted in the earlier work (Galliers 2007a) that there are a number of popular books on breakthrough change management focusing on the role of ICT (e.g. Lientz and Rea 2004) and on so-called transformational leaders (e.g. Anderson and Anderson 2001). The major features of this genre include prescriptive, deliberate approaches that suggest guaranteed, order-of-magnitude gains. Organizational realities suggest an alternative, incremental approach more akin to 'muddling through' (Lindblom 1959), however, as has been argued here. The incremental exploration of possibilities—the tinkering (Ciborra 1992) and bricolage (Lévi-Strauss 1966)—along with the more deliberate, analytical approaches that incorporate oversight of implementations and review of outcomes (e.g. Willcocks 2009) are what is envisaged here, with improvements in organizational performance in mind (Rivard, Raymond, and Verreault 2006). Exploration *and* exploitation (March 1991; Tushman and O'Reilly 1996) are therefore the name of the game, as is providing the appropriate organizational architecture for change (Nadler, Gerstein, and Shaw 1992) to revert to terminology introduced earlier in this chapter.

There is not an insignificant literature on the review process. For example, Venkatraman and Ramanujam (1987), Segars and Grover (1998), and Doherty, Marples, and Suhaimi (1999) are among those who have considered means by which IS strategy success may be measured. Venkatraman and Ramanujam, for example, stress the need for success measures in ongoing evaluation as a means to improve planning capability. Seddon, Graeser, and Willcocks (2002) consider this in terms of organizational effectiveness, while Kearns (2004) proposes a multi-objective, multi-criteria approach. Others, such as Kumar (1990) and Norris (1996), focus their attention on system evaluation, and others still call for emancipation as a key design principle (Wilson 1997). Whatever the focus, it should not be assumed that evaluation is an entirely objective issue. For example, Gwillim, Dovey, and Wieder (2005) consider the politics of post-implementation reviews, noting that few organizations undertake ex-post evaluation. As Walsham (1997) notes, without a formal evaluation policy, IT and business executives alike will act—perfectly rationally—in their own interests. The pre-eminence of individual interests in organizations is a point made clear by the likes of Handy (1995) and Schein (1997). Thus, Wagner and Newell (2007) emphasize the importance of participation in making further refinements (in this case with respect to enterprise systems) during the post-implementation period. Indeed, Matta and Ashkenas (2003) remind us that even good projects fail, particularly with respect to cross-functional projects. There is a danger in organizations failing to learn from different project experiences and reinventing the wheel (Lyttinen and Robey 1999; Kearns 2004). This, in part, stems from formal project reviews that are documented for others to consider at some future point in time (Schindler and Epplerm 2003), or at predetermined milestones

(Kotnour 1999). Drawing on this, Scarbrough and Swan (2001) make the point that the emphasis has tended to be on the supply rather than the demand for knowledge, and this is why Newell and Edelman (2008) emphasize the need to encourage teams to reflect and tell stories about their learning experiences (cf. Boland and Tenkasi 1995) in a way that comes alive and helps nurture a learning capability by providing context.

APPLYING THE FRAMEWORK

As I hope has been made abundantly clear, the framework presented in Figure 12.1 is not meant to be a prescriptive tool: it does not—and is not meant to—provide some kind of solution. It is presented as a sense-making (cf. Weick 1995) device, meant more as an aide-memoire, to be used to raise questions and facilitate discussion concerning the strategizing elements and connections that may or may not be in place in any particular organization. As already mentioned, the IS strategizing process envisaged here is a dynamic and iterative one based on learning and questioning. Assumptions need to be tested and a range of viewpoints sought—both from within and outside the organization. The framework can be used to help in this process of enquiry.

Thus, questions can be posed that may surface the presence—or absence—of key features that make up the framework. For example, is a knowledge creating and sharing infrastructure in place? How supportive is it in terms of both the human as well as the technical capabilities required to implement the strategy? Is there a greater emphasis on exploitation as against exploration? And if so, what impact does this appear to have on organizational performance? Do sourcing considerations form an integral part of the exploitation strategy process? Similarly, does cross-project learning form an integral part of the exploration aspects of strategizing? How does communication and under-standing materialize in and between virtual teams? To what extent does ongoing learning and review take place as part of the change management and implementation strategy? Are performance measures in place?

All these questions are merely illustrative of how the framework may be used in organizations. Certain of them, and certain aspects of the framework itself, may be more or less relevant and/or important depending on the differing circumstances in which different organizations in different locations in the world, at different stages of growth (Penrose 1959; Galliers and Sutherland 1991), and different sectors of the economy find themselves. An aspect of the framework's application that should be consistent, no matter what the circumstances, is its ongoing deployment as a learning tool. As already noted, the process of strategizing is an iterative one. While there may be a defined planning horizon, with particular targets being set for that particular time period, the questioning based on the framework and its various components should continue, at least periodically. The framework itself, and its component parts, may be adapted and developed in line with the particular and changing nature of the context in which it is being applied, but its use as a sense-making device should continue with a

view to improving organizational performance, exploiting organizational and technological capabilities, exploring new opportunities, with a view to continuous innovation.

Acknowledgements

This chapter builds on earlier work by the author—in particular: Galliers (1991, 1993, 1999, 2004, 2006, 2007); Galliers and Newell (2003); Newell et al. (2003).

References

Ahuja, M. K., and Galvin, J. E. (2003). 'Socialization in Virtual Groups', *Journal of Management*, 29: 161–85.

Anderson, D., and Anderson, L. A. (2001). *Beyond Change Management: Advanced Strategies for Today's Transformational Leaders*. San Francisco, CA: Jossey-Bass/Pfieffer.

Backhouse, J., Bener, A., Chauvidul, N., Wamala, F., and Willison, R. (2005). 'Risk Management in Cyberspace', in R. Mansell and B. Collins (eds.), *Trust and Crime in Information Societies*. Cheltenham: Edward Elgar, 349–79.

Barney, J. B. (1991). 'Firm Resources and Sustained Competitive Advantage', *Journal of Management*, 17(1): 99–120.

Beulen, E., van Fenema, P. C., and Currie, W. (2005). 'From Application Outsourcing to Infrastructure Management: Extending the Offshore Outsourcing Portfolio', *European Management Journal*, 25: 133–44.

Boland, R. J., and Tenkasi, R. (1995). 'Perspective Making and Perspective Taking in Communities of Knowing', *Organization Science*, 13: 442–55.

Brown, C., and Renwick, J. (1996). 'Alignment of the IS Organization: The Special Case of Corporate Acquisitions', *The DATABASE for Advances in Information Systems*, 27(4): 25–33.

Carmel, E. (1999). *Global Software Teams: Collaborating across Borders and Time Zones*. Saddle River, NJ: Prentice Hall PTR.

—— and Agarwal, R. (2002). 'The Maturation of Off-Shore Sourcing of Information Technology Work', *MISQE* 1: 65–77.

Carr, N. G. (2003). 'IT Doesn't Matter', *Harvard Business Review*, 81(5): 41–9.

—— (2005). 'The End of Corporate Computing', *MIT Sloan Management Review*, 46(3): 67–73.

Ciborra, C. U. (1992). 'From Thinking to Tinkering: The Grassroots of IT and Strategy', *Information Society*, 8: 297–309.

—— (1994). 'The Grassroots of IT and Strategy', in C. Ciborra and T. Jelassi (eds.), *Strategic Information Systems: A European Perspective*. Chichester: Wiley, 3–24.

—— (ed.) (2000). *From Control to Drift: The Dynamics of Corporate Information Infrastructures*. Oxford: Oxford University Press.

Códoba, J.-R. (2009). 'Critical Reflection in Planning Information Systems: A Contribution from Critical Thinking', *Information Systems Journal*, 19(2): 123–47.

Cook, S. D. N., and Brown, J. S. (1999). 'Bridging Epistemologies: The Generative Dance between Organizational Knowledge and Organizational Knowing', *Organization Science*, 10(4): 381–400.

Crossan, M. and Sorrenti, M. (1997). 'Making Sense of Improvisation', *Advances in Strategic Management*, 14: 155–80.

David, G., Chand, D., Newell, S., and Resende-Santos, J. (2008). 'Integrated Collaboration across Distributed Sites: The Perils of Process and the Promise of Practice', *Journal of Information Technology*, 23: 44–54.

Desouza, K. C. (ed.) (2006). *Agile Information Systems: Conceptualization, Construction, and Management*. Oxford: Butterworth-Heinemann.

——and Evaristo, J. R. (2004). 'Managing Knowledge in Distributed Projects', *Communications of the ACM*, 47: 87–91.

Doherty, N. F., Marples, C. G., and Suhaimi, A. (1999). 'The Relative Success of Alternative Approaches to Strategic Information Systems Planning: An Empirical Analysis, *Journal of Strategic Information Systems*, 8(3): 263–83.

Earl, M. J. (1989). *Management Strategies for Information Technology*. London: Prentice Hall.

——(1993). 'Experiences in Strategic Information Systems Planning', *MIS Quarterly*, 17(1): 1–24.

Erden, Z., von Krogh, G., and Nonaka, I. (2008). 'The Quality of Group Tacit Knowledge', *Journal of Strategic Information Systems*, 17(1): 4–18.

Feldman, M. S., and Rafaeli, A. (2002). 'Organizational Routines as Sources of Connections and Understandings', *Journal of Management Studies*, 39(3).

Finnegan, P., Galliers, R. D., and Powell, P. (2003). 'Applying Triple Loop Learning to Planning Electronic Trading Systems', *Information Technology and People*, 16(4): 461–83.

——and Longaigh, S. N. (2002). 'Examining the Effects of Information Technology on Control and Coordination Relationships: An Exploratory Study in Subsidiaries of Pan-national Companies', *Journal of Information Technology*, 17(3): 149–63.

Foucault, M. (1984). 'The Ethics of the Concern of Self as a Practice of Freedom', in P. Rabinow (ed.), *Michel Foucault: Ethics, Subjectivity and Truth: Essential Works of Foucault 1954–1984*. London: Penguin, 281–301.

Galliers, R. D. (1991). 'Strategic Information Systems Planning: Myths, Reality and Guidelines for Successful Implementation', *European Journal of Information Systems*, 1(1): 55–64.

——(1993). 'Towards a Flexible Information Architecture: Integrating Business Strategies, Information Systems Strategies and Business Process Redesign', *Journal of Information Systems*, 3(3): 199–213.

——(1999). 'Towards the Integration of e-Business, Knowledge Management and Policy Considerations within an Information Systems Strategy Framework', *Journal of Strategic Information Systems*, 8(3): 229–34.

——(2003). 'Change as Crisis or Growth? Toward a Trans-disciplinary View of Information Systems as a Field of Study—A Response to Benbasat and Zmud's Call for Returning to the IT Artifact', *Journal of the Association for Information Systems*, 4(6): 337–51.

——(2004). 'Reflections on Information Systems Strategizing', in C. Avgerou, C. Ciborra, and F. Land (eds.), *The Social Study of Information and Communication Technology: Innovation, Actors, and Contexts*. Oxford: Oxford University Press, 231–62.

——(2006a). 'Strategizing for Agility: Confronting Information Systems Inflexibility in Dynamic Environments', in K. De Souza (ed.), *Agile Information Systems*. Oxford: Butterworth Heinemann, 1–15.

——(2006b). '"Don't Worry, Be Happy ..." A Post-modernist Perspective on the Information Systems Domain', in J. King and K. Lyytinen (eds.), *Information Systems: The State of the Field*. Chichester: Wiley, 324–31.

——(2007a). 'On Confronting some of the Common Myths of Information Systems Strategy Discourse', in R. Mansell, C. Avgerou, D. Quah, and R. Silverstone (eds.), *The Oxford Handbook of Information and Communication Technology*. Oxford: Oxford University Press, 225–43.

——(2007b). 'IT and Globalization: Knowledge Creation and Sharing across Frontiers', in S. Dayal and M. Murphy (eds.), *Global Babel: Questions of Discourse and Communication in a Time of Globalization*. Newcastle: Cambridge Scholars Publishing.

——Jackson, M. C., and Mingers, J. (1997). 'Organization Theory and Systems Thinking: The Benefits of Partnership', *Organization*, 4(2): 269–78.

——and Leidner, D. E. (2009). *Strategic Information Management: Challenges and Strategies in Managing Information Systems*. 4th edn., New York: Routledge.

——and Newell, S. (2003a). 'Strategy as Data Plus Sense-Making', in S. Cummings and D. C. Wilson (eds.), *Images of Strategy*. Oxford: Blackwell, 164–96.

————(2003b). 'Back to the Future: From Knowledge Management to the Management of Information and Data', *Information Systems and e-Business Management*, 1(1): 5–13.

——and Sutherland, A. R. (1991). 'Information Systems Management and Strategy Formulation: The "Stages of Growth" Model Revisited', *Journal of Information Systems*, 1(2): 89–114.

Giacomazzi, F., Panella, C., Pernicci, B., and Sansomi, M. (1997). 'Information Systems Integration in Mergers and Acquisitions: A Normative Model', *Information and Management*, 32(6): 289–302.

Grant, R. M. (1996). 'Toward a Knowledge-Based Theory of the Firm', *Strategic Management Journal*, 17: 109–22.

Gupta, A. K., and Govindarajan, V. (2000). 'Knowledge Flows within Multinational Corporations', *Strategic Management Journal*, 21(4): 473–496.

Gwillim, D., Dovey, K., and Wieder, B. (2005). 'The Politics of Post-implementation Reviews', *Information Systems Journal*, 15(4): 307–19.

Handy, C. (1995). *Gods of Management*. 2nd edn., London: Arrow Books.

Hansen, M. T., Nohria, N., and Tierney, T. (1999). 'What's your Strategy for Managing Knowledge? *Harvard Business Review*, 77(2): 106–16.

Hanseth, O. (2004). 'Knowledge as Architecture', in C. Avgerou, C. Ciborra, and F. Land (eds.), *The Social Study of Information and Communication Technology: Innovation, Actors, and Contexts*. Oxford: Oxford University Press, 103–18.

Haspeslagh, P., and Jemison, D. (1991). *Managing Acquisitions: Creating Value through Corporate Renewal*. New York: The Free Press.

He, Z.-L., and Wong, P.-K. (2004). 'Exploration vs. Exploitation: An Empirical Test of the Ambidexterity Hypothesis', *Organization Science*, 15(4): 481–94.

Henderson, J. C., and Venkatraman, N. (1999). 'Strategic Alignment: Leveraging Information Technology for Transforming Organizations', *IBM Systems Journal*, 38(2/3): 472–84.

Hippel, E. von (1994). 'Sticky Information and the Locus of Problem Solving', *Implications for Innovation Science*, 40: 429–39.

Howcroft, D., Newell, S., and Wagner, E. (eds.) (2004). 'Special Issue: Understanding the Contextual Influences on Enterprise System Design, Implementation, Use and Evaluation', *Journal of Strategic Information Systems*, 13(4): 271–419.

Howcroft, D., Newell, S., and Wagner, E. (eds.) (2005). 'Special Issue: Understanding the Contextual Influences on Enterprise System Design, Implementation, Use and Evaluation, Part II', *Journal of Strategic Information Systems*, 14(2): 91–242.

Ives, B., Jarvenpaa, S. L., and Mason, R. O. (1993). 'Global Business Drivers: Aligning Information Technology to Global Business Strategy', *IBM Systems Journal*, 32(1): 143–61.

Jarvenpaa, S. L., and Leidner, D. E. (1999). 'Communication and Trust in Global Virtual Teams', *Organization Science*, 10: 791–815.

Kanawattanachai, P., and Yoo, Y. (2002). 'Dynamic Nature of Trust in Virtual Teams', *Journal of Strategic Information Systems*, 11: 187–213.

Kearns, G. S. (2004). 'A Multi-objective, Multi Criteria Approach for Evaluating IT Investments: Results from Two Case Studies', *Information Resources Management Journal*, 17(1): 37–62.

Kotlarsky, J., and Oshri, I. (2005). 'Social Ties, Knowledge Sharing and Successful Collaboration in Globally Distributed System Development Projects', *European Journal of Information Systems*, 14: 37–48.

Kotnour, T. (1999). 'A Learning Framework for Project Management', *Project Management Journal*, 30(1): 32–8.

Krogh, G. von, Ichijo, K., and Nonaka, I. (2000). *Enabling Knowledge Creation: How to Unlock the Mystery of Tacit Knowledge and Release the Power of Innovation*. New York: Oxford University Press.

Kumar, K. (1990). 'Post Implementation Evaluation of Computer Based Information Systems: Current Practices', *Communications of the ACM*, 33: 203–12.

Lacity, M. C., and Willcocks, L. (2000). *Global Information Technology Outsourcing: In Search of Business Advantage*. Chichester: Wiley.

Lave, J., and Wenger, E. (1991). *Situated Learning: Legitimate Peripheral Participation*. Cambridge: Cambridge University Press.

Lederer, A. L., and Sethi, V. (1988). 'The Implementation of Strategic Information Systems Planning Methodologies', *MIS Quarterly*, 12(3): 445–61.

Leidner, D. (ed.) (2000). 'Special Issue: Knowledge Management and Knowledge Management Systems', *Journal of Strategic Information Systems*, 9(2–3): 101–261.

Lévi-Strauss, C. (1966). *The Savage Mind*. London: Weidenfeld & Nicolson.

Lientz, B. P., and Rea, K. P. (2004). *Breakthrough IT Change Management: How to Get Enduring Change Results*. Oxford: Elsevier Butterworth Heinemann.

Lindblom, C. (1959). 'The Science of Muddling Through', *Public Administration Review*, 19(2): 79–88.

Luhmann, N. (1996). *Social Systems*. Stanford, CA: Stanford University Press.

Lyttinen, K., and Robey, D. (1999). 'Learning Failure in Information Systems Development', *Information Systems Journal*, 9(2): 85–101.

McKiernan, P., and Merali, Y. (1993). 'The Strategic Positioning of Information Systems in Post-acquisition Management', *Journal of Strategic Information Systems*, 2(2): 105–24.

————(1995). 'Integrating Information Systems after a Merger', *Long Range Planning*, 28(4): 54–62.

March, J. (1991). 'Exploration and Exploitation in Organizational Learning', *Organization Science*, 2(1): 71–86.

Matta, N., and Ashkenas, R. (2003). 'Why Good Projects Fail Anyway', *Harvard Business Review*, 81: 109–15.

Mintzberg, H., and Waters, J. A. (1985). 'Of Strategies, Deliberate and Emergent', *Strategic Management Journal*, 6(3): 257–72.

Mohdzain, M. B., and Ward, J. M. (2007). 'A Study of Subsidiaries' Views of Information Systems Planning in Multinational Organizations', *Journal of Strategic Information Systems*, 16(4): 324–52.

Monteiro, E. (1998). 'Scaling Information Infrastructure: The Case of the Next Generation IP in Internet', *The Information Society*, 14(3): 229–45.

Nadler, D., Gerstein, M., and Shaw, R. (1992). *Organizational Architectures: Designs for Changing Organizations.* San Francisco, CA: Jossey-Bass.

Nevo, D., and Wand, Y. (2005). 'Organizational Memory Information Systems: A Transactive Memory Approach', *DSS* 39: 549–62.

Newell, S., and Edelman, L. F. (2008). 'Developing a Dynamic Project-Learning and Cross-Project Learning Capability: Synthesizing Two Perspectives', *Information Systems Journal*, 18(6): 567–90.

——Huang, J. C., Galliers, R. D., and Pan, S. L. (2003). 'Implementing Enterprise Resource Planning and Knowledge Management Systems in Tandem: Fostering Efficiency and Innovation Complementarity', *Information and Organization*, 13(1): 25–52.

Newkirk, H. E., Lederer, A. L., and Srinavasan, C. (2003). 'Strategic Information Systems Planning: Too Little or too Much?', *Journal of Strategic Information Systems*, 12(3): 201–28.

Nonaka, I. (1991). 'The Knowledge-Creating Company', *Harvard Business Review*, 69(6): 96–104.

——(1994). 'A Dynamic Theory of Organizational Knowledge Creation', *Organization Science*, 5(1): 14–37.

——and von Krogh, G. (2007). 'Tacit Knowledge, Knowledge Conversations, and Leadership: From Critique to Advancement of Organizational Knowledge Theory'. Working paper, ETH Zurich, Switzerland.

————and Voepel, S. (2006). 'Organizational Knowledge Creation Theory: Evolutionary Paths and Future Advances', *Organization Studies*, 27(8): 1179–208.

——and Takeuchi, H. (1995). *The Knowledge-Creating Company: How Japanese Companies Create the Dynamics of Innovation.* Oxford: Oxford University Press.

——and Toyama, R. (2003). 'The Knowledge Creating Theory Revisited: Knowledge Creation as a Synthesizing Process', *Knowledge Management Research and Practice*, 1(1): 2–10.

——Byosiere, P., Borucki, C. C., and Konno, N. (1994). 'Organizational Knowledge Creation Theory: A First Comprehensive Test', *International Business Review*, 3: 337–51.

Norris, G. (1996). 'Post-investment Appraisal', in L. Willcocks (ed.), *Investing in Information Systems.* London: Chapman & Hall, 193–223.

O'Donnell, S. W. (2000). 'Managing Foreign Subsidiaries: Agents of Headquarters, or an Interdependent Network?', *Strategic Management Journal*, 21(5): 525–48.

Oshri, I., van Fenema, P., and Kotlarsky, J. (2008). 'Knowledge Transfer in Globally Distributed Teams: The Role of Transactive Memory', *Information Systems Journal*, 18(6): 567–90.

Penrose, E. T. (1959). *The Theory of the Growth of the Firm.* New York: Wiley.

Peppard, J., and Ward, J. (2004). 'Beyond Strategic Information Systems: Towards an IS Capability', *Journal of Strategic Information Systems*, 13(2): 167–94.

Porter, M. E. (2001). 'Strategy and the Internet', *Harvard Business Review*, 79(3): 63–78.

Ridings, C., Gelen, D., and Arinze, B. (2002). 'Some Antecedents and Effects of Trust in Virtual Communities', *Journal of Strategic Information Systems*, 11: 271–95.

Rivard, S., Raymond, L., and Verreault, D. (2006). 'Resource-Based View and Competitive Strategy: An Integrated Model of the Contribution of Information Technology to Firm Performance', *Journal of Strategic Information Systems*, 15(1): 29–50.

Robey, D., and Boudreau, M. C. (1999). 'Accounting for the Contradictory Organizational Consequences of Information Technology: Theoretical Directions and Methodological Implications', *Information Systems Research*, 10(2): 167–85.

Sabherwal, R., Hirschheim, R., and Goles, T. (2001). 'The Dynamics of Alignment: Insights from a Punctuated Equilibrium Model', *Organization Science*, 12(2): 179–97.

Salas, E., Burke, C. S., and Cannon-Bowers, J. A. (2000). 'Teamwork: Emerging Principles', *International Journal of Management Review*, 2: 339–56.

Sambamurthy, V., and Jarvenpaa, S. (eds.) (2002). Special Issue of *Journal of Strategic Information Systems* on Trust in the Digital Economy, 11(3–4): 183–346.

Scarbrough, H., and Swan, J. (2001). 'Explaining the Diffusion of Knowledge Management: The Role of Fashion', *British Journal of Management*, 12(1): 3–12.

—— Bresnen, M., Edelman, L. F., Laurent, S., Newell, S., and Swan, J. (2004). 'The Processes of Project-Based Learning: An Exploratory Study', *Management Learning*, 35(4): 491–506.

Scheepers, R., Venkitachalam, K., and Gibbs, M. R. (2004). 'Knowledge Strategy in Organizations: Refining the Model of Hansen, Nohria and Tierney', *Journal of Strategic Information Systems*, 13(3): 201–22.

Schein, E. (1997). *Organizational Culture and Leadership*. San Francisco, CA: Jossey-Bass.

Schindler, M., and Epplerm M. (2003). 'Harvesting Project Knowledge: A Review of Project Learning Methods and Success Factors', *International Journal of Project Management*, 21: 219–29.

Seddon, P., Graeser, V., and Willcocks, L. (2002). 'Measuring Organizational Effectiveness: An Overview and Opdate of Senior Management Perspectives', *Data Base for Advances in Information Systems*, 33: 11–27.

Segars, A. H., and Grover, V. (1998). 'Strategic Information Planning Success: An Investigation of the Construct and its Measurements', *MIS Quarterly*, 22(2), 139–63.

—— —— (1999). 'Profiles of Strategic Information Planning', *Information Systems Research*, 10(1): 87–97.

Sheth, J. N., and Sisodia, R. S. (2007). 'The Regional Face of Globalization', in S. Dayal and M. Murphy (eds.), *Global Babel: Questions of Discourse and Communication in a Time of Globalization*. Newcastle: Cambridge Scholars Publishing.

Spender, J. C. (1996). 'Making Knowledge the Basis of a Dynamic Theory of the Firm', *Strategic Management Journal*, 17: 45–62.

Star, S. L., and Ruhleder, K. (1996). 'Steps towards an Ecology of Infrastructure: Design and Access to Large Information Spaces', *Information Systems Research*, 7(1): 111–34.

Stehr, N. (1992). *Practical Knowledge: Applying the Social Sciences*. London: Sage Publications.

Szulanski, G. (1996). 'Exploring Internal Stickiness: Impediments to the Transfer of Best Practice within the Firm', *Strategic Management Journal*, 17(1): 27–43.

Teece, D. J., Pisano, G., and Shuen, A. (1997). 'Dynamic Capabilities and Strategic Management', *Strategic Management Journal*, 18(7): 509–33.

Tushman, M. L., and Nadler, D. A. (1978). 'Information Processing as an Integrating Concept in Organizational Design', *Academy of Management Review*, 3(3): 613–24.

—— and O'Reilly, C. (1996). 'Ambidextrous Organizations: Managing Evolutionary and Revolutionary Change', *California Management Review*, 38(1): 8–30.

——and Scanlan, T. (1981). 'Boundary Spanning Individuals: Their Role in Information Transfer and their Antecedents', *Academy of Management Journal*, 24(2): 289–305.

Van der Gerben, P., van Beers, C., and Kleinknecht, A (2002). 'Success and Failure of Innovation: A Literature Review', *International Journal of Innovation Management*, 7: 309–38.

Venkatraman, N., and Ramanujam, V. (1987). 'Planning System Success: A Conceptualization and Operational Model', *Management Science*, 33(6): 687–705.

Vera, D., and Crossan, M. (2005). 'Improvisation and Innovative Performance in Teams', *Organization Science*, 16(3): 203–24.

Wagner, E., and Newell, S. (2007). 'Exploring the Importance of Participation in the Post-implementation Period of an Enterprise System Project: A Neglected Area', *Journal of the Association for Information Systems*, 8(10): article 32.

Walsham, G. (1997). *Interpreting Information Systems in Organizations*. Chichester: Wiley.

——(2001). *Making a World of Difference: IT in a Global Context*. Chichester: Wiley.

Ward, J., and Griffiths, P. (1996). *Strategic Planning for Information Systems*. 2nd edn., Chichester: Wiley.

——and Peppard, J (2002). *Strategic Planning for Information Systems*. 3rd edn., Chichester: Wiley.

Webster, J (1995). 'Networks of Collaboration or Conflict? Electronic Data Interchange and Power in the Supply Chain', *Journal of Strategic Information Systems*, 4(1): 31–42.

Weick, K. E. (1995). *Sensemaking in Organizations*. Thousand Oaks, CA: Sage.

——and Roberts, K. H. (1993). 'Collective Mind in Organizations: Heedful Interrelating on Flight Decks', *Administrative Science Quarterly*, 38: 357–81.

Weill, P., and Ross, J. (2004). *IT Governance: How Top Performers Manage IT Decision Rights for Superior Results*. Boston, MA: Harvard Business School Press.

Wenger, E. (1998). *Communities of Practice: Learning, Meaning, and Identity*. Cambridge: Cambridge University Press.

Wijnhoven, T., Spil, T., Stegwee, R., and Fa, R. T. A. (2006). 'Post-merger IT Integration Strategies: An IT Alignment Perspective', *Journal of Strategic Information Systems*, 15(1): 5–28.

Willcocks, L. (2009). 'Evaluating the Outcomes of Information Systems Plans: Managing Information Technology Evaluation. Techniques and Processes', in R. D. Galliers and D. E. Leidner (eds.), *Strategic Information Management: Challenges and Strategies in Managing Information Systems*. 4th edn., New York: Routledge, 209–26.

Willmott, H. (1993). 'Strength is Ignorance; Slavery is Freedom: Managing Culture in Modern Organizations', *Journal of Management Studies*, 30: 515–62.

Wilson, F. (1997). 'The Truth is out there: The Search for Emancipator Principles in Information Systems Design', *Information Technology and People*, 10: 187–204.

Winter, S (2003). 'Understanding Dynamic Capabilities', *Strategic Management Journal*, 24: 991–5.

Zárraga, C., and Bonache, J (2005). 'The Impact of Team Atmosphere on Knowledge Outcomes in Self-Managed Teams', *Organization Studies*, 26(5): 661–81.

Zollo, M., and Winter, S (2002). 'Deliberate Learning and the Evolution of Dynamic Capabilties', *Organization Science*, 13: 339–51.

CHAPTER 13

RETHINKING BUSINESS–IT ALIGNMENT

YOLANDE E. CHAN AND BLAIZE HORNER REICH

INTRODUCTION

FOR decades, Business–IS/IT[1] alignment has appeared as a top concern for IT practitioners and company executives (Luftman, Kempaiah, and Nash 2006; Hiner 2008). In this chapter, we review the IT alignment literature, and suggest where future contributions might be made. Challenges to the value of alignment research, divergent views, and new perspectives on alignment are presented. Our goal is to be as inclusive of major alignment perspectives as possible. We first discuss the motivation for alignment research. Then we define alignment and present key aspects of the alignment construct. Next, we discuss alignment factors and processes. We address the questions: What creates alignment? What benefits can reasonably be expected? We close by providing reflections on the IT alignment research stream to date, suggesting new ways of thinking about IT alignment, and highlighting key implications for research and practice.

TO ALIGN OR NOT TO ALIGN: THAT IS THE QUESTION

For many years, researchers have drawn attention to the importance of alignment between business and IT (e.g. McLean and Soden 1977; Henderson and Sifonis 1988).

Early motivation for alignment emerged from a focus on strategic business planning and long-range IT planning (e.g. IBM 1981; King 1988). From a business perspective, planning was characterized as a top-down and a bottom-up process and departmental (e.g. IT) plans were created in support of corporate strategies. From an IT perspective, decisions on hardware and software had such significant cost and time implications that bureaucratic planning approaches were necessary. These conceptualizations have been enlarged over time and now research recognizes many points of alignment between business and IT.

The performance implications of alignment have been demonstrated repeatedly through surveys and case studies (e.g. Chan et al. 1997; Irani 2002; Leede, de Looise, and Alders 2002; Kearns and Lederer 2003). Simply put, most studies have supported the hypothesis that those organizations that successfully align their business strategy with their IT strategy will outperform those that do not. Alignment leads to more focused and strategic use of IT which, in turn, leads to increased performance (Chan, Sabherwal, and Thatcher 2006).

Some scholars have argued that the alignment literature fails to capture important phenomena and that in fact, alignment is not always desirable. The arguments have had several themes, including:

1) Alignment literature is mechanistic and fails to capture real life,
2) Alignment is not desirable if the business environment is rapidly changing, and
3) IT should often challenge the business, not follow it.

These arguments are described more fully below.

Ciborra[2] (1997) suggested that the alignment literature is too theoretical; that it is generated by the scientific method applied to the design of human affairs and computer systems. He recommended a Mintzberg-like approach, where researchers go to the field for insights (Mintzberg 1973). Other critics of IT alignment research argue that strategy is not a clear concept due to turbulent, unpredictable circumstances that leave managers muddling through, betting, and tinkering with their corporate strategies (Vitale, Ives, and Beath 1986).

Tightly coupled arrangements can have negative outcomes. That is, if the business environment suddenly changes and internal alignment is too tight, businesses may not be able to respond adequately and can stagnate. Furthermore, the use of technology itself is characterized by improvisations of various sorts (Ciborra 1996; Orlikowski 1996) and by unexpected outcomes. Working toward pre-specified or fixed outcomes may be unrealistic. Ciborra (1997) calls for an enlarged notion of alignment within a network of semi-autonomous (vs. harmonized and synchronized) actions.

One can also argue that it is necessary for IT to challenge the business, not simply implement its vision. Disagreement, friction, and conflict can be more desirable than reactive IT operations in order to achieve high business performance. This view suggests that researchers who believe that IT should simply support what the business is doing may be wasting their and others' time. Kearns and Lederer (2000) balance this view by arguing that while effective alignment of the IT plan with the business plan can provide competitive advantage, the opposite—aligning the business plan with the IT strategy in a 'tail wagging the dog' mode—is more likely to result in potential losses.

Levy (2000), using a resource-based perspective, reminds us that IT—even aligned IT—in and of itself is not strategic. In order for IT to be strategic, it must be valuable, unique, and difficult for competitors to imitate. Sauer and Burn (1997) warn that alignment can give rise to pathologies that require careful management if undesired business and IT costs are to be avoided. One example of pathology is when a company tries to align IT with business strategies that are not internally consistent.

Finally, Shpilberg et al. (2007) argue that a narrow focus on alignment under-estimates the complexity of systems, application, and infrastructure which address different business needs. They suggest that the focus should be on IT-powered growth, high IT project effectiveness and IT delivery, and only secondarily on IT alignment.

So should we abandon the study of alignment? The authors think not. Although there are theoretical and empirically based arguments suggesting that alignment may not always be a suitable goal, the practitioner community consistently ranks it as a top priority. The Society for Information Management conducts surveys to gauge the importance of various IT issues. In 2005 and in 2008, the number one management concern of all groups of respondents was alignment (Luftman, Kempaiah, and Nash 2006; Hiner 2008). Alignment was also ranked as the top management concern in 2004 and 2003, whereas it was ranked 9th in 1994; 7th in 1990; 5th in 1986; and 7th in 1983. It is clear that the issue of IT alignment has remained a high business priority for almost three decades.

From the authors' perspective, the issues noted above are challenges to the attain-ment of alignment, rather than reasons alignment should not be pursued or studied. In this chapter, we take the position that alignment is of value and contributes to organizational success. What we do not accept is that alignment is a static, single-dimensional construct or process, or that it is easy to attain. Our goal is to explore the many perspectives taken on alignment and to suggest ways in which academics and practitioners can integrate, build on, and apply what has been learned.

WHAT IS ALIGNMENT?

When asking focus group participants to define alignment, Campbell (2005) was given the following answer: 'Alignment is business and IT working together to reach a common goal.' Similarly, Abraham (2006) described alignment using a rowing analogy: 'Strategic alignment, is everyone rowing in the same direction.' The meaning in these practitioner-based perspectives is clear but imprecise. Researchers have developed a multiplicity of perspectives in their quest to create constructs that have face validity but at the same time can be measured and modelled. In the next section, we discuss the history, equivalent terms, dimensions, and levels of analysis that have been developed in the IT alignment research literature.

Alignment Definitions

Research conducted in the 1980s at MIT (Scott Morton 1991) served as an initial attempt to harness the strategic power of IT. The MIT model argues that revolutionary change involving IT investment can bring about substantial rewards as long as the key elements of strategy, technology, structure, management processes, and individuals and roles are kept in alignment. Baets (1992) and Henderson and Venkatraman (1992) refined these ideas, and developed models which defined alignment as the degree of fit and integration among business strategy, IT strategy, business infrastructure, and IT infrastructure. Other researchers have stressed the importance of matching business and IT capabilities (McKeen and Smith 2003) and appropriate and timely use of technology (King 1988; Luftman and Brier 1999).

Equivalent terms

In the literature, alignment also has been called fit (Chan 1992; Henderson and Venkatraman 1993), linkage (Reich 1993), and integration (Henderson and Venkatraman 1993). These terms and others (e.g. bridge (Ciborra 1997), harmony (Luftman, Papp, and Brier 1999), and fusion (Smaczny 2001)) are sometimes used interchangeably with alignment, although subtle differences exist (Avison et al. 2004).

The term 'fit' has an extensive research stream in the mathematical and strategic management literatures (e.g. see Edwards 1992). In the MIS literature, it has often been used to refer to the measurement of alignment (e.g. Bergeron, Raymond, and Rivard 2001). Although it may be argued that 'alignment' is now the dominant term in the IT literature, this cannot be said for the strategy literature where we also find extensive use of terms such as fit, congruence, and covariation.

Alignment dimensions

In the IT literature, several dimensions of alignment are clearly apparent: strategic, intellectual, structural, social, and cultural. In much of the literature, there is agreement that alignment between IT and business involves strategic and structural aspects that are interrelated (Chan 2001). Although significantly more attention is given to strategic IT alignment, both strategic alignment and structural alignment influence performance. In addition, alignment is contingent on many of the social and cultural aspects of an organization (Chan 2001).

Strategic and intellectual dimensions

Strategic alignment refers to the degree to which the business strategy and plans, and the IT strategy and plans, complement each other. Reich and Benbasat (2000) define intellectual alignment in terms of 'the state in which a high-quality set of interrelated IT and business plans exist.' With this perspective, it is difficult for alignment to occur if the business lacks a formal, documented plan (Vitale, Ives, and Beath 1986; Lederer and Mendelow 1989; Wang and Tai 2003).

Structural dimensions

Structural alignment refers to the degree of structural fit between IT and the business. Structural alignment is influenced by the location of IT decision-making rights, reporting relationships, (de)centralization of IT, and the deployment of IT personnel (Chan 2002). Pyburn (1983) found that IT is much more likely to be perceived as supporting the critical needs of the business when there are few levels between senior management and IT management.

Earl (1989) outlined five ideal IT arrangements: centralized, business unit, business venture, decentralized, and federal. Brown and Magill (1994) suggested a simpler structural typology involving IT structures that are centralized, decentralized, or hybrid. They provided evidence that each structure can be effective, given the right circumstances. Bergeron, Raymond, and Rivard (2001) found that increasing structural complexity alone has no impact on performance. That is, more complex IT structures are not necessarily superior. However, increasing structural complexity in conjunction with stronger IT management can increase growth and profitability.

Although the formal structure is most often researched, Chan (2001) found the informal structure (defined as 'relationship-based structures that transcend the formal division of labor and coordination of tasks') to be of great importance in improving IT alignment and performance. Chan's study suggested that scarce management time and resources are better spent on improving the informal organization than on aligning formal structures. At any point in time, formal organization and IT structures are unlikely to suffice. The complementary informal organization provides overlapped, reinforcing connections. Although less visible than the formal structure, it can be more malleable and paradoxically more enduring.

Social dimension

Reich and Benbasat (2000) define the social dimension of strategic alignment in terms of 'the state in which business and IT executives within an organizational unit understand and are committed to the business and IT mission, objectives, and plans.' They argue that researchers should study social and intellectual dimensions of alignment together to reveal the complexity and challenges of IT alignment.

There are many barriers to achieving both intellectual and social dimensions of alignment including the need for strong CEO–CIO relationships (Feeny, Edwards, and Simpson 1992). IT personnel and business staff must collaborate together at all levels of an organization. This is a prerequisite for high alignment. Yet this may be hindered by many issues such as the invisibility of the IT staff; communication barriers; history of IT/business relationships; attitudes of organization members to IT; shared domain knowledge; and leadership (Earl 1989; Campbell 2005).

Communication is often associated with understanding, which in turn increases the locus of comprehension. The argument exists that the typical IT person lacks good communication skills. Campbell (2005) suggested this might be a myth and pointed out that even if some IT personnel wanted to communicate they would not be allowed to. Sledgianowski and Luftman (2006) noted that for alignment business-IT communication should regularly occur and be pervasive throughout the organization. They argued that it should also be informal and should use appropriate methods such as email, videoconferencing, and face-to-face communications.

Cultural dimension

Pyburn (1983), in an early study on strategic IT issues, pointed out the importance of cultural fit between business and IT as a precondition for successful IS planning. Alignment needs to be culturally supported; otherwise, it is a never-ending quest. Tallon (2003) also emphasized culture, arguing that there needs to be a mind-set that encourages shared networks and common IT procurement policies, and an across-the-board willingness to give up best-of-breed systems that could be incompatible. He stated that the 'alignment paradox' cannot be avoided just by picking certain technologies and avoiding others. Flexibility and alignment take vigilance and smart management approaches.

Alignment is then fundamentally about cultural change and behaviour change (CIO Insight 2004). There has to be commitment from top management for alignment to work. People are not going to listen to what the CIO says as much as they are going to watch what the CIO does, and what the CIO's business partners do. IT personnel need to be skilled in the softer side of business which often does not go hand-in-hand with the engineering focus that IT professionals tend to have. Top management buy-in, proactive CIOs, and socially adept IT professionals are vital for making alignment a cultural phenomenon.

Levels of Analysis

Although the preceding definitions of alignment focus primarily on the organizational level, alignment should be present at many other levels, including the system level (Floyd and Woolridge 1990; Campbell 2005), project level (Jenkin and Chan 2006), and the individual/cognitive level (Tan and Gallupe 2006).

According to Floyd and Woolridge (1990), misalignment can often explain system implementation difficulties. Formal strategies are often only implemented at the upper levels of the organizations, yet strategy is carried out on the front line. Recognizing this problem, Bleistein, Cox, and Verner (2006) use requirements engineering to link higher-level strategic goals to lower-level, explicit organizational processes. Their model depicts alignment as the explicit connections to requirements made at adjacent levels between superordinate goals and subordinate goals.

Jenkin and Chan (2006) examine alignment at the project level. They define IT project alignment as the degree to which an IT project's deliverables are congruent with the organization's IT strategy and the project's objectives. Critical to project alignment is the project's response to change triggers. These triggers can be both internal (e.g. a mid-term project evaluation) and external (e.g. a change in the environment). Failure to respond to change triggers effectively leads to project misalignment which can trickle upwards, leading to overall IT strategic misalignment.

Tan and Gallupe (2006) operationalize alignment, at its most micro-level, as shared cognition between the business and IT executives. That is, the higher the level of cognitive commonality between business and IT executives, the higher the levels of IT-business alignment. This perspective has strong parallels with social alignment and shared knowledge discussed earlier (Reich and Benbasat 1996). Similarly Campbell (2005) suggests that the focus of alignment at the lower levels of an organization involves translating business unit goals into personal goals.

If one considers alignment to be a socially constructed concept, then users' satisfaction with IT service may be another aspect of alignment. Jia, Reich, and Pearson (2008), in a study of IT work groups and their corresponding users, found that a strong 'climate for service' within the IT groups was a better predictor of user satisfaction than was the level of competence of the IT group. Therefore, another level of alignment to consider is the work-group level.

It can be argued that both internal and external coherence must be examined (Henderson and Venkatraman 1993). Earl (1989) proposed an internal view of alignment in that IT strategy and infrastructure should be aligned with the applications and information within an organization. Externally, organizations must align their business and IT strategies with industry and technology forces. Denford (2009) demonstrated that internal alignment without external alignment often results in poor business performance.

Sledgianowski and Luftman (2006) recommended as an alignment best practice that organizations should leverage IT assets on an enterprise-wide basis to extend the reach (the IT extrastructure) of the organization into supply chains of customers and suppliers. Similarly, Galliers (2004) suggested that alignment is not just related to internal challenges, but also influences and is influenced by relationships with crucial partner organizations such as customers and suppliers.

ANTECEDENTS AND OUTCOMES OF ALIGNMENT

In the academic literature, alignment has been seen both as a construct to be measured at a single point in time (e.g. in a cross-sectional study using a variance or factor model) and as a process to be understood over time. In this section, we focus on factor models, highlighting antecedents of alignment over which managers have some control, and then turning our attention to outcomes that can be expected when alignment is achieved. In the section that follows, process models are described.

Antecedents to Alignment

We discuss antecedents to alignment in two groups. Background antecedents include shared knowledge, prior successful experience with IT, corporate culture, and locus of control. Visible foreground or behavioural antecedents include leadership approaches, planning, and communication styles. We acknowledge that these antecedents overlap and are interdependent.

Background antecedents

Reich and Benbasat (2000) found that two background factors—shared domain knowledge and IT implementation success—influenced foreground behaviours such as communication between IT and business executives and connections between IT and business planning. For example, when shared domain knowledge was high, communication between the two groups was strategic and frequent, and the result was a high level of alignment. These four factors were antecedents to short-term alignment but only shared domain knowledge was an antecedent to long-term alignment.

Other studies have also found that shared domain knowledge between IT and business people influence alignment (Teo and Ang 1999; Chan, Sabherwal, and Thatcher 2006). Van Der Zee and de Jong (1999) and CIO Insight (2004) raised the issue of the lack of a common 'language' between business and IT executives. They cited the need to build bridges so that both IT and business personnel are using the same terms, talking about the same topic, to assist with alignment in thought and action. Hunt (1993) found that in well-aligned firms, top management welcomes what can be done through IT, using their understanding of the particular business issues in their company and their imagination when conceiving IT-enabled business strategies.

Brown and Magill (1994) also found that a successful history of IT implementation, expressed as satisfaction with the management of technology and satisfaction with the use of technology, influenced the attainment of alignment.

In a study of organizational assumptions about IT, Kaarst-Brown and Robey (1999) found five separate cultural archetypes. In several of these archetypes, notably the 'fearful' and the 'controlled', managers felt that IT was not a benign force within the organization. Therefore, although managers cognitively knew what was needed to achieve IT alignment, practically they were reluctant to pursue it.

Campbell, Kay, and Avison (2005) suggested that when managers are confronted with a business challenge, they make decisions based on their locus of comprehension (understanding) and their locus of control (authority). Strategic alignment can be seen as an array of *bounded* choices made in order to resolve strategic ambiguity (Campbell 2005).

Foreground/leadership behaviours

Baker (2004) studied alignment as a function of leadership style and asked executives to indicate whether their company's management style was autocratic, collaborative, or indecisive. Most firms led by collaborative managers indicated that their company's IT was well aligned with the business strategy. On the other hand, managers in firms with autocratic or indecisive leadership reported a lower level of alignment.

Feeny, Edwards, and Simpson (1992) established the importance of the relationship between the CEO and the CIO. In the firms they examined with successful CEO–CIO relationships, the CEO perceived that IT was critical and had positioned IT as an agent of business transformation. The CIO promoted IT as an agent of business transformation and contributed well beyond the IT function. Although the specific attributes of CEOs and CIOs that foster alignment may have changed in recent years, their relationship is still a critical antecedent.

Another issue revolves around the existence and knowledge of the corporate strategy. Corporate strategy may be unknown by IT or undeveloped (Vitale, Ives, and Beath 1986; Lederer and Mendelow 1989; Reich and Benbasat 2000; Wang and Tai 2003). If known, strategies can be unclear and/or difficult to support (Baets 1992). In addition, formal business strategies are often ambiguous (Campbell 2005). Managers must understand the difference between espoused strategies, strategies in use, and managerial actions, many of which may be in conflict. These issues pose a significant challenge because most models of alignment presuppose an existing, clearly understandable business strategy to which an IT organization can align itself.

In a study of small manufacturers, Cragg, King, and Hussein (2002) found that many of the manufacturers had achieved a high degree of alignment between their business strategy and IT. While two-thirds of the sample had written a business plan, only a quarter had formalized their IT strategy. So while IT planning existed in small firms, much of it was carried out informally (Lefebvre and Lefebvre 1988).

Lederer and Mendelow (1989) found that coordination of the IT plan and the business plan were achieved in three dimensions (Shank, Niblock, and Sandals 1973): plan content, timing, and personnel. Chan, Sabherwal, and Thatcher (2006) found that planning sophistication and comprehensiveness led to an increase in shared knowledge which in turn affected alignment. The more sophisticated the planning process, the greater the likelihood of involvement of personnel from different areas of expertise. This in turn led to improved shared knowledge and ultimately alignment.

Luftman, Papp, and Brier (1999) examined the enablers and inhibitors of alignment. Their research highlighted that IT executives can directly impact project priority setting, IT knowledge of the business, and IT leadership. Factors under control of business leaders include IT involvement in strategy development and senior executive support for IT. Both business and IT leaders have to foster a close working relationship.

Outcomes of Alignment

Henderson and Venkatraman (1992) argued that strategic alignment can influence organizational transformation in a descriptive sense (i.e. by illustrating the value of emerging IT), prescriptive sense (i.e. by grounding cases in a theoretical framework and suggesting possible courses of action), and in a dynamic sense (i.e. by conceptualizing major relationships and interactions to be addressed over time). Technology influences the power and reach of organizations. High-performing organizations often have developed superior capabilities to harness and align IT (Scott Morton 1991). IT alignment is a management concern primarily because of its potential impact on firm performance. In this section, we focus on organization level outcomes.

Strategic IT alignment leads to increased profits for an organization, above and beyond what would be expected to be produced using only industry and strategy variables (Floyd and Woolridge 1990; Powell 1992; Cragg, Kind, and Hussin 2002). Yetton (1994) concluded that if the separation of business and IT was substantial, company performance suffered. This separation contributed to organization's failing to learn how to manage IT investments and extract value from them. Similarly, Sauer and Burn (1997) argued that when business decisions were made without consideration of IT, there was a risk of pathological or damaging outcomes.

However, not all empirical evidence concludes that alignment has direct or positive performance implications. Tallon (2003) found that while 70 per cent of companies reduced costs or improved sales and customer service after increasing strategic alignment, 30 per cent saw no improvement or even a decline. This was attributed to the failure of alignment to be achieved with some degree of flexibility. That is, companies locked themselves into an alignment plan (via investing in various technologies) that hindered their ability to react to change. Similarly, Palmer and Markus (2000) did not find a relationship between alignment and performance when examining the use of Quick Response technology in the retailing sector.

It has been argued that these negative or unclear results are due in part to a lack of control variables in the analyses. Chan, Sabherwal, and Thatcher (2006) and Denford (2009) found that factors such as industry, organizational size, and type of strategy all had an impact on the performance implications of alignment. Byrd, Lewis, and Bryan (2006) found that strategic alignment had a direct impact on performance as a moderator between IT investment and business performance. The real value in alignment was in leveraging the firm's IT investment, not simply just investing more in IT.

Contingencies

We have discussed antecedents and outcomes of IT alignment documented in the literature. However, contingency theory posits that there is no universally superior strategy or way to organize in a given context or environment (Venkatraman 1989); rather, the context and structure must fit together if an organization is to perform well (Drazin and Van den Ven 1985). Applied to IT alignment, contingency theory tells us that certain contextual and organizational factors fit together to facilitate alignment more so than others. Thus, certain business and IT factors, when combined in certain contexts, produce superior performance. We present several contingency perspectives in this section.

Industry

Alignment can be more difficult in industries with quick clock speeds, when there are economic downturns and scarce resources, with certain organizational strategies, and at certain points in the organizational life cycle. Peak, Guynes, and Kroon (2005, 2006) found that deregulation can serve as a powerful motivator for companies, in those industries, to align their IT with their business strategies. In their study, the increased competition that came with deregulation highlighted the importance of alignment. Tan (1995) found that IT is more responsive to business strategy in those organizations which emphasize innovation in their product and market strategies, as opposed to organizations operating in a relatively stable product/market area.

Organizational size

While very small firms may be well aligned because communication is high and individuals play multiple roles, medium-sized institutions frequently show less evidence of alignment. As organizations continue to grow in size and complexity, more formal planning processes are enacted to help ensure an integrated vision for IT. In larger organizations, managers more commonly introduce formal processes and structures to ensure alignment (Hale and Cragg 1996). Also, larger firms tend to have more slack which can be devoted for alignment purposes. Chan, Sabherwal, and Thatcher (2006) found that alignment increased as organization size increased, but only in business (as opposed to academic institutions). This result was explained by institutional theory as academic institutions tend to function similarly regardless of size.

Raymond, Pare, and Bergeron (1995) found that greater sophistication in the use of IT was significantly associated with better performance. However the results revealed the importance of size and environmental uncertainty as crucial contingency factors. Firms with larger sizes that perceived their environment to be more uncertain tended to have greater IT sophistication, which in turn allowed these firms to respond better to complexity or growth.

Strategic orientation

The Miles and Snow (1978) typology of business strategy, commonly used in the alignment literature, classifies businesses as either taking on a Prospector, Analyser, Defender, or Reactor strategy. Tan (1995) found that prospectors and defenders differ in the extent to which IT is explicitly considered in shaping business strategy. The more aggressive the business strategy, the more IT is explicitly viewed as a strategic tool.

Sabherwal and Chan (2001) found no significant relationship between alignment and performance in Defenders, whereas the alignment-performance relationship was observed for Prospectors and Analysers.

Croteau and Bergeron's (2001) study indicated the existence of a link between strategic activities, technological deployment, and organizational performance. This relationship, however, took different shapes depending on the type of business strategy. The study indicated that IT could enhance performance in companies using prospector or analyser strategies. Organizations with analyser strategies could make effective use of IT by encouraging personnel to read journals specific to IT, participating in professional associations, and being educated regarding the application of new technologies. Organizations with prospector strategies generally did not use technology as their primary driver and did not regularly scan the IT environment, but did recognize the importance of having the IT department participate in strategic meetings. Defender and reactor organizations, however, did not experience this relationship in the first place, and thus technology was less helpful for them. Similarly, Chan, Sabherwal, and Thatcher (2006) found that the type of business strategy had an impact on the importance of alignment. In their study, prospectors generally had lower levels of alignment than analysers, and were less affected by environmental uncertainty.

Turbulence

Environmental uncertainty, or the degree of change and instability in the firm's operating context, has an impact on alignment (Tallon and Pinsonneault 2005). In times of high environmental uncertainty, organizations have a higher need for information processing and information systems. It is expected that organizations will invest heavily in IT alignment during times of environmental uncertainty (Johnston and Carrico 1988; Gupta, Karimi, and Somers 1997) and organizations operating in uncertain environments may be able to derive greater benefits from IT (Sabherwal and Kirs 1994). So environmental turbulence affects the importance of IT alignment, the ease with which it is achieved, and the mechanisms for achieving it.

Vitale, Ives, and Beath (1986) found that turbulence associated with frequent changes in products, suppliers, customers, production processes, or competitive environment made top-down planning more difficult. Moreover, such turbulence decreased the utility of the top-down planning process as an instrument for identifying competitive applications of information technology. The authors suggested an adaptive planning approach, which is less concerned with higher-level, predetermined goals and more concerned with subtle incremental change and evolution.

Choe (2003) found that perceived environmental uncertainty had an indirect effect on IT strategic applications. In an uncertain environment, a high level of strategic applications and well-arranged facilitators of alignment could contribute more to the improvement of performance than in a stable environment.

In summary, this literature suggests that turbulence creates opportunities for IT to make a difference, but that a prepared and competent IT group and sophisticated management approaches are needed to capitalize on them.

PROCESS MODELS OF ALIGNMENT

Many studies of alignment have emphasized that alignment is a process rather than an end state (Parker, Benson, and Trainor 1988; MacDonald 1991; Niederman, Brancheau, and Wetherbe 1991; Baets 1992, 1996; Powell 1992; Broadbent and Weill 1993; Henderson and Venkatraman 1993; Norden 1993; Papp 1999; Rondinelli, Rosen, and Drory 2001). Van Der Zee and De Jong (1999) highlight a main challenge of relying on plans to guide alignment. Given that the business environment and technology change so quickly, once any large-scale IT plan has been enacted, there is a high probability that the plan and the technology are already obsolete. As Galliers (2004) noted, 'an issue that has remained relatively unchallenged and unquestioned is how to align ICT that is relatively fixed, once implemented in an organization, with a business strategy and associated information requirements that are constantly in need of adjustment'.

In this section, we review various process approaches to the study of alignment. We begin with the work that makes the general case that alignment is a process or journey that can never be completely achieved (ICEX 2004). We then turn to the research that outlines the factors that must be continually adjusted to keep the organization moving towards alignment. The final section discusses the research which proposes patterns of alignment that emerge over time in organizations. However, before addressing these three perspectives on the process of alignment, we review two schools of thought about alignment—the classic and the processual (Whittington 1993).

Classic vs. Processual Schools of Thought

Two perspectives on the relationship between strategy and technology emerge: the classical school and the processual approach (Whittington 1993). The classical school is based on a model of rational adaptation. The tenets of this approach are that (i) organizations are market-driven and constantly adapt to the changes and contingencies of the external environment, (ii) IT is a resource to be deployed according to the needs and pressures of that environment, and (iii) the relationship between strategy and IT has to do with recognizing the contingencies of the technology and its potential for application to business objectives (McFarlan 1984 referenced in Scarbrough 1998).

The processual school advocates a focus on internal and power issues. Strategy cannot be equated with the business plan as both can become meaningless and ineffective when implemented. The processual approach (i) rejects formal plans and methodologies as simply the tip of the organizational iceberg, (ii) exposes hidden social values, political interests, and structural inertia, and (iii) perceives the role of IT as a resource and an instrument for gaining power—not achieving adaptation.

Drawing on Burt's work on structural holes (1992), people gain power when they are part of relationships that span the holes in a network. Power is gained since network spanners broker the flow of information between people and control projects that bring people together. To the extent that IT spans holes in the organizational network, it can command power.

Alignment as Continuous Management of Specific Organizational Components

Much of the research on the process view of alignment suggests that certain structures, processes, and relationships need continual calibration. Many scholars have suggested this approach, differing only in the set of variables that need aligning.

Baets (1996) concluded that IT strategy alignment is a process, including business strategy, business organization, IT infrastructure, and IT strategy elements. Alignment is a collaborative process between all actors and divisions. Thus it is not enough to simply understand the factors involved in alignment; one must understand the inter-relationships among the factors.

Rondinelli, Rosen, and Drori (2001) studied multinational corporations and suggested that they should continuously readjust and realign four sets of strategic components—business strategy, market penetration decisions, management processes, and organizational structures.

ICEX (2004) identified the CIO as critical in achieving strategic alignment. Four critical responsibilities to be carried out by the CIO are building shared vision, building relationships, enhancing the CEO relationship, and proactive planning.

Sledgianowski and Luftman (2006) suggested monitoring alignment through the mechanism of service level agreements. They recommended having periodic formal assessments and reviews of service level agreements with both IT and business representation, and a formal process in place to make changes based on the results of the assessments.

Tallon (2007–8) advocated a 'value disciplines' perspective in which alignment is tight in critical processes but less tight in lower priority processes. He argued that the right type of alignment examines the particular mix of business processes, and has an individual process focus versus an overall business strategy-level focus.

In studying the actions that managers take, Hirschheim and Sabherwal (2001) demonstrated three trajectories that can occur in the process of alignment: paradoxical decisions, excessive transformations, and uncertain turnarounds. Pursuing alignment is complex and frequently chaotic (Rondinelli, Rosen, and Drori 2001).

Street (2006) developed measures for seven alignment capabilities: IS service matching, environmental IT scanning, assessing alignment, building stakeholder commitment, IT filtering, prioritizing IT resources, and strategic IT experiments.

Modelling Alignment over Time

There are several models of how alignment changes over time. These include stages of growth, lead–lag, and punctuated equilibrium models.

Stages of growth

Burn (1993) found that organizations change IT planning styles as they progress through stages of growth of IT usage. Further, different approaches to strategy are favoured by different organizational configurations. She suggested that transitions through this alignment model are characterized by periods of dynamic change which can be predicted at certain stages of growth. Organizations with strong correlations between IT planning styles and organizational strategies are perceived by the user groups to have the most satisfactory IT support.

Street (2006) provided a preliminary explanation of how the development of IT capabilities is associated with different IT alignment change patterns. In case studies, it was found that organizations go through four phases in alignment: punctuation, change, settling-in, and stability.

The lead–lag model

Burn suggested that there is an internal (functional) level of alignment, whereby internal processes and strategies are aligned and an external (strategic) level of alignment, in which industry, technology, and organizational strategies are aligned. These different levels of alignment suggest the need for a lead–lag model of IT strategy (Burn 1996, 1997).

This lead–lag model posits that organizations will alternate between IT leading change and IT catching up with change. The model is cyclical, at least for highly competitive industries characterized by rapid technological innovation, and cycles tend to be specific to particular organizational types and particular industries. According to Burn, most organizations follow a highly conservative and traditional approach to the alignment process and find difficulty in sustaining alignment. Not all organizations can follow the same path for organizational transformation through IT. As alignment is not a one-time process, knowing the cycles of change and the organizational position in relation to them will facilitate management of the alignment process.

Punctuated equilibrium

Sabherwal, Hirschheim, and Goles (2001) concluded that the punctuated equilibrium model can explain some aspects of IT alignment. According to this model, IT alignment goes through long periods of relative stability, or evolutionary change, interrupted by short periods of quick and extensive, or revolutionary, change. Their research differs from traditional evolutionary perspectives, however, by suggesting that during stable times, IT may not be properly aligned.

Sabherwal et al. suggested that changes in alignment are, for the most part, small and evolutionary. These changes may prevent catastrophes by controlling misalignments, but they inhibit moving to an altogether different pattern of alignment.

New Directions

What will IT alignment look like in 2020? By examining business and technology trends and trying to peer into the future, the following alignment challenges can be predicted.

Alignment in a Complex, Chaotic World

Ten years from now, what will business look like? Although this seems impossible to judge, it is likely to be even more complex than it is today. Certainly, there will be a greater need for agility, speed, and flexibility. Today's cloud computing, end-to-end-virtualized infrastructures, and service-oriented network platforms provide increased flexibility. Business–IT alignment will certainly involve responsiveness—the provision of IT capacity on demand, with IT resources being acquired and released as the business grows and shrinks in real time.

Dynamic IT capabilities (Chen, Sun, and Helms 2008) will be critical. Also critical will be IT people who have business backgrounds and can interpret the business chaos. Shared business–IT domain knowledge is likely to be even more important than it is today, as business and IT models keep changing and 'common ground' is hard to find. Thinking in terms of business–IT interactions and holistic business–IT systems may be increasingly important for timely responses to either business or IT paradigm shifts.

Alignment in Troubled Economic Times

The 2009 global economic downturn has affected business priorities and strategies. Executives are focused on the bottom line and commonly defer non-core opportunities. While this is likely to reduce misalignment because frivolous expenditures are unlikely to be made, it may also limit full alignment as opportunities are missed.

IT alignment in a global recession will likely focus on the use of IT for survival versus IT for expansion and growth. We anticipate that we will see a renewed emphasis on IT as a driver of efficiency ('doing more with less'). This will renew the focus on IT-enabled processes and restructuring. IT will be an integral part of the business strategy. In fact, IT is likely to be an integral part of the survival strategies of entire industries as supply chains are merged and made more competitive. As budgets are cut (including those allocated to the IT department and IT investments), organizations and industries may find IT-based economic solutions. Instead of IT being viewed as 'the plumbing' (Carr 2003), there will be no question that aligned IT matters.

Aligned IT will be smart IT. We anticipate that instead of financing large software purchases, organizations will be more likely to use 'pay as you go' approaches available in cloud computing service and software-as-a-service models. IT investments will have strategic significance. For instance, business intelligence (BI) systems will support better decision making at every level of the organization. Aligned IT will not be wasteful or flamboyant but disciplined and lean.

End-to-End Alignment

Other issues that are likely to emerge in the years to come involve seamless alignment across multinational firms and across industries. The challenges of obtaining maximum IT performance in the face of multiple partnerships, cultures, human resource policies, and preferred platforms will receive increased attention. Solid IT governance and standardized infrastructures will rise in importance.

As non-essential services are outsourced, and global enterprise-wide systems are streamlined, alignment issues will rear their heads. Managers will need to address alignment in a 'flat world' where IT levels opportunities, brings organizations together virtually as though they coexisted physically, and increases visibility and transparency of operations. Boundaryless, networked business environments will facilitate collaboration but increase challenges associated with social and technical alignment. Knowledge management systems and social networking tools may be critical tools to manage shared understanding.

One-to-one alignment will be demanded as IT is used to increase accountability, standardize and deliver services, and address environmental ('green') issues. IT will be aligned with a variety of stakeholder concerns—including those of shareholders, customers, and employers. As difficult business tradeoffs are made under intense IT-enabled scrutiny, stakeholder management systems that go beyond CRM systems will enable organizations to balance multiple, conflicting stakeholder demands. For instance, green IT will enable more efficient production and reduced energy footprints.

Alignment in an Information Overloaded World

We cannot close our 2020 discussions without addressing the increasing importance of knowledge strategies and management as business generates more data than individuals and organizations can process. For IT to remain aligned, knowledge engineering (organizing knowledge to produce desired results) must receive increased attention. In this information overloaded business world, data that are needed cannot be buried.

Information sourcing, integration, analysis, and selective reporting will be critical to organizations struggling with insufficient information absorptive capacities. Deciphering key trends, that is making sense of the data, will be critical for firms that seek to shape, as opposed to being victims of, their industries. Aligned IT will provide 'just in time' real time data at the speed of business.

CONCLUSION

Although we have already learned a great deal about alignment, the increasing complexity of our business and technology environments suggests that research will have to continuously innovate to be relevant. As the underlying organizations change their shape, size, and strategy, business–IT alignment will also change.

One issue of importance may stand in the way of research into alignment—and that is the lack of consensus about its essential nature and therefore the measures which should be used. For example, there are at least two distinct conceptualizations of alignment. The first conceptualizes alignment as an ongoing process, requiring certain IT management capabilities, encompassing specific actions and reactions and having discernible patterns over time. The second conceptualization is alignment as an end state, focusing on the antecedents, measures, and outcomes of alignment. These views are equally necessary—we need to be able to measure the state of alignment if we are to track it over time. And we must be able to describe and model alignment as a process in order to understand its true complexity. Therefore, research which links these two perspectives is likely to be the most difficult but the most beneficial.

Examining the Process of Alignment

In general, the process view of alignment has been under-represented in research to date, notwithstanding the widespread acknowledgement that alignment is an ongoing activity.

Ciborra (1997) concluded that we need a different style of research, a style that questions the core activity of management research and practice. To some extent, the work of Campbell (2005) has begun again 'at the beginning', employing grounded research techniques with the participants in alignment. This work questions the possibility of alignment, and sheds light on the ways that actors struggle with it. More grounded research like this is needed—work that questions the very possibility of alignment and allows the voices of the participants to be heard.

Similarly, Taxén (2005) has also broken away from the dichotomy between process and factor approaches to alignment, by taking a socio-technical lens to the subject. He defines alignment as coordination between work practices, with the goal being to achieve a common understanding among actors.

Information systems strategizing has both a location and temporal dimension (Adam 1990, cited in Galliers 2004)—the latter, in particular, being as yet under-researched. Galliers (2004) reminds us of the essential difficulty in trying to match a relatively fixed set of IT assets to a fast-moving business strategy. Researchers have insufficiently investigated the processes and nuances of alignment. Longitudinal research is needed to enrich and extend models such as lead-lag and punctuated equilibrium.

It may be time to take stock of our contingency theory-based alignment research. Is it leading us towards more understanding or merely to less generalizable theory, thus hindering the maturity of the field? More focused (vs. broad brush) investigations of alignment may be needed to go beyond 'motherhood/alignment is good' statements, and to explore subtleties concerning how, when, and where IT alignment really matters.

Alignment processes in entrepreneur-led firms are different from those found in larger bureaucracies (Street 2006) and small to medium-sized firms (Hale and Cragg 1996). Researchers are encouraged to focus on specific firm sizes and types to reveal the nature of alignment within firm types.

Examining Antecedents

We encourage researchers to explore the interrelationships among antecedents, to create archetypes and patterns that influence alignment. An example would be Van Der Zee and De Jong's (1999) challenge to understand the prerequisites for integrated IT and management in terms of culture, skills, and responsibilities.

Novel and extreme contexts should be explored as they evolve in the workplace—for example, what does alignment look like when IT development is all offshored? When there are no proprietary applications? When all computing power is rented?

New Theoretical Underpinnings

It has been argued by many a reviewer that current alignment research is largely a-theoretic. Because of its heavy reliance on the strategic management reference discipline and contingency theory (which some do not consider theory), it is not rich in the use of theories such as institutional theory, the resource-based view of the firm, and stakeholder theory. While we acknowledge that this is already changing, greater use of well-established theories in alignment research is needed. Use of theory may be the only way to anchor research in a changing world.

New Research Approaches

Chung, Rainer, and Lewis (2003) recommend that new research examine the recursive relationship between alignment and the extent of applications implementation and IT infrastructure flexibility. Street (2006) has begun this work, examining 'service gaps' as a measure of alignment.

More complex research tools and frameworks can be utilized. Even though there is some agreement that alignment is the congruence of business and IT strategy (and/or plans, understanding, or commitment), there has been little examination of the different loci of alignment. In a complex organization, there is alignment between corporate IT and corporate management, between corporate IT and business units, and within the business unit, between the IT group and the business unit management (Henderson and Venkatraman 1993; Reich 1993). Each locus of alignment is likely to have its own unique requirements, depending on alignment at the other loci. To understand alignment in a complex firm is a multi-level task requiring comprehensive analyses.

Implications for Practitioners

What have academics learned that could be useful to business managers and IT practitioners? Below we summarize the findings from IT research.

Shared governance

Alignment is one aspect of the governance of IT and, as such, should be a joint responsibility between IT and business executives as well as between executives and their board of directors. A clear understanding of the accountability shared between the board, CEO, CIO, and line business units should be established and reviewed periodically. Setting strategy, prioritizing projects, monitoring performance, and managing risk are four key alignment issues that need to be considered by the governance team.

Shared knowledge

Research points to the conclusion that shared governance rests on the existence of shared knowledge between business and IT people. There are many ways to achieve shared domain knowledge (e.g. cross-training IT people, rotating business leaders through IT roles) but this is an investment that it is critical to make in the long-term interests of successful, appropriate deployment of information technology within an organization. IT managers and their peers in the business need a clear plan to build and maintain shared knowledge between their domains.

A culture of success

At a deep level, organizations see themselves as either able to manage and use IT or not. Therefore, creating alignment between business and IT objectives is not just a matter of changing the CIO or implementing an IT steering committee. Over the long term, the culture and stories within the organization must move from those of failure and defeat to those of mastery and success. If IT is important to an organization's success, then everyone needs to take an active leadership role in making a collaborative environment work. Alignment is everyone's responsibility.

Focus

Several researchers have suggested that CIOs focus their alignment efforts on a subset of their portfolio—the areas that are likely to make the most impact on the firm. In light of current economic challenges, this seems to be good advice. IT is pervasive but this does not mean that it needs to be excellent throughout—only where it matters. Business and IT can use Pareto's principle to identify and then manage these key areas.

Organizational Value Chain

Performance research concludes that technology only influences organizational performance when it enables change in business processes. Therefore, the focus on strategy needs to be augmented with a focus on process and project—projects to enable change, and process as the medium through which value is realized. This may mean that the CIO is given responsibility for organizational transformation as well as the project office, but whatever the structural solution is, there needs to be alignment between these key pieces of the organizational value chain.

In closing, we observe that IT alignment remains an important but elusive goal, and is likely to become even more elusive in the decades to come. Much is well understood but there is much more to learn. We hope that this chapter has provided thought-provoking and helpful information for future alignment explorers and managers.

ACKNOWLEDGEMENTS

The authors are grateful to Dr Chris Sauer and the *Journal of Information Technology* for permitting the reuse of information published in the article, 'IT Alignment: What Have We Learned?', *Journal of Information Technology*, 22 (2007), 297–315. The authors thank research assistants Catherine Shea, Zorana Svedic, and Darius Tadaniewicz for their contributions to the original article, and the Social Sciences and Humanities Research Council of Canada for funding received.

NOTES

1. The terms IS and IT are used interchangeably.
2. We acknowledge with sadness the passing of Dr Claudio Ciborra in 2005. His contributions to the IT field were significant.

References

Abraham, G. A. (2006). 'Successful Organizational Leadership: Effective Execution through Strategic Management', *CEO Refresher*, 12(10.5).

Avison, D., Jones, J., Powell, P., and Wilson, D. (2004). 'Using and Validating the Strategic Alignment Model', *Strategic Information Systems*, 13: 223–46.

Baets, W. (1992). 'Aligning Information Systems with Business Strategy', *IS and Business Strategy Alignment*, 1(4): 205–13.

—— (1996). 'Some Empirical Evidence on IS Strategy Alignment in Banking', *Information and Management*, 30: 155–77.

Baker, E. H. (2004). 'Leading Alignment', *CIO Insight*, 1(45): 19–20.

Bergeron, F., Raymond, L., and Rivard, S. (2001). 'Fit in Strategic Information Technology Management Research: An Empirical Comparison of Perspectives', *International Journal of Management Science*, 29(2): 125–42.

Bleistein, S. J., Cox, K., and Verner, J. (2006). 'Validating Strategic Alignment of Organizational IT Requirements Using Goal Modeling and Problem Diagrams', *Journal of Systems and Software*, 79(3): 362–78.

Broadbent, M., and Weill, P. (1993). 'Improving Business and Information Strategy Alignment: Learning from the Banking Industry', *IBM Systems Journal*, 32(1): 162–79.

Brown, C. V., and Magill, S. L. (1994). 'Alignment of the IS Functions with the Enterprise: Toward a Model of Antecedents', *MIS Quarterly*, 18(4): 371–403.

Burn, J. M. (1993). 'Information Systems Strategies and the Management of Organizational Change: A Strategic Alignment Model', *Journal of Information Technology*, 8(4): 205–16.

—— (1996). 'IS Innovation and Organizational Alignment: A Professional Juggling Act', *Journal of Information Technology*, 11(1): 3–12.

—— (1997). 'A Professional Balancing Act: Walking the Tightrope of Strategic Alignment', in C. Sauer and P. W. Yetton (eds.), *Steps to the Future: Fresh Thinking on the Management of IT-Based Organizational Transformation*. 1st edn., San Francisco, CA: Jossey-Bass Publishers, 55–88.

Burt, R. S. (ed.) (1992). *Structural Holes: The Social Structure of Competition*. Cambridge, MA: Harvard University Press.

Byrd, A., Lewis, B. R., and Bryan, R. W. (2006). 'The Leveraging Influence of Strategic Alignment on IT Investment: An Empirical Examination', *Information and Management*, 43(3): 308–21.

Campbell, B. (2005). 'Alignment: Resolving Ambiguity within Bounded Choices', Paper presented at the Pacific Asia Conference on Information Systems, Bangkok, Thailand.

—— Kay, R., and Avison, D. (2005). 'Strategic Alignment: A Practitioner's Perspective', *Journal of Enterprise Information Management*, 18(5/6): 653–64.

Carr, N. G. (2003). 'IT Doesn't Matter', *Harvard Business Review*, 81(5): 41–9.

Chan, Y. E. (1992). 'Business Strategy, Information Systems Strategy, and Strategic Fit: Measurement and Performance Impacts'. Unpublished Ph.D. thesis, University of Western Ontario.

—— (2001). 'Information Systems Strategy, Structure and Alignment', in R. Papp (ed.), *Strategic Information Technology: Opportunities for Competitive Advantage*. 1st edn., Hershey, PA: Idea Group Publishing, 56–81.

—— (2002). 'Why Haven't We Mastered Alignment? The Importance of the Informal Organization Structure', *MIS Quarterly Executive*, 1(2): 97–112.

Chan, Y. E. and Reich, B. H. (2007). 'IT Alignment: What Have we Learned?', *Journal of Information Technology*, 22: 297–315.

—— Sabherwal, R., and Thatcher, J. B. (2006). 'Antecedents and Outcomes of Strategic IS Alignment: An Empirical Investigation', *IEEE Transactions on Engineering Management*, 51(3): 27–47.

—— Huff, S. L., Barclay, D. W., and Copeland, D. G. (1997). 'Business Strategic Orientation, Information Systems Strategic Orientation, and Strategic Alignment', *Information Systems Research*, 8(2): 125–50.

Chen, R.-S., Sun, C.-M., and Helms, M. (2008). 'Aligning Information Technology and Business Strategy with a Dynamic Capabilities Perspective: A Longitudinal Study of a Taiwanese Semiconductor Company', *International Journal of Information Management*, 28(5): 366–78.

Choe, J. (2003). 'The Effect of Environmental Uncertainty and Strategic Applications of IS on a Firm's Performance', *Information and Management*, 40(4): 257–68.

Chung, S. H., Rainer, R. K., Jr., and Lewis, B. R. (2003). 'The Impact of Information Technology Infrastructure Flexibility on Strategic Alignment and Applications Implementations', *Communications of the Association for Information Systems*, 11: 191–206.

Ciborra, C. U. (1996). *Groupware and Teamwork*. New York: John Wiley & Sons.

—— (1997). 'De Profundis? Deconstructing the Concept of Strategic Alignment', *Scandinavian Journal of Information Systems*, 9(1): 57–82.

CIO Insight Staff (2004). 'Is your Culture Hindering Alignment?', *CIO Insight*, 45(1): 65–75.

Cragg, P., King, M., and Hussin, H. (2002). 'IT Alignment and Firm Performance in Small Manufacturing Firms', *Journal of Strategic Information Systems*, 11(2): 109–32.

Croteau, A., and Bergeron, F. (2001). 'An Information Technology Trilogy: Business Strategy, Technological Deployment and Organizational Performance', *Journal of Strategic Information Systems*, 10(2): 77–99.

Denford, J. S. (2009). 'The Alignment of Knowledge Strategies'. Ph.D. thesis, Queen's School of Business, Queen's University.

Drazin, R., and van de Ven, A. H. (1985). 'Alternative Forms of Fit in Contingency Theory', *Administrative Science Quarterly*, 30(4): 514–39.

Earl, M. J. (1989). *Management Strategies for Information Technology*. London: Prentice Hall.

Edwards, J. R. (1992). 'The Study of Congruence in Organizational Behavior Research: Critique and a Proposed Alternative', *Organizational Behavior and Human Decision Processes*.

Feeny, D. F., Edwards, B. R., and Simpson, K. M. (1992). 'Understanding the CEO/CIO Relationship', *MIS Quarterly*, 16(4): 435–48.

Floyd, S. W., and Woolridge, B. (1990). 'Path Analysis of the Relationship between Competitive Strategy, Information Technology, and Financial Performance', *Journal of Management Information Systems*, 7(1): 47–64.

Galliers, R. D. (2004). 'Reflections on Information Systems Strategizing', in C. Avgerou, C. Ciborra, and F. Land (eds.), *The Social Study of Information and Communication Technology*. 1st edn., London: Oxford University Press, 231–62.

Gupta, Y. P., Karimi, J., and Somers, T. M. (1997). 'Alignment of a Firm's Competitive Strategy and Information Technology Management Sophistication: The Missing Link', *IEEE Transactions on Engineering Management*, 44: 399–413.

Hale, A., and Cragg, P. (1996). 'Business Process Reengineering in the Small Firm: A Case Study', *Journal of INFOR*, 34(1): 15–27.

Henderson, J. C., and Sifonis, J. G. (1988). 'The Value of Strategic IS Planning: Understanding Consistency, Validity, and IS Markets', *MIS Quarterly*, 12(2): 187–200.

—— and Venkatraman, N. (1992). 'Strategic Alignment: A Model for Organizational Transformation through Information Technology', in T. A. Kocham and M. Useem (eds.), *Transforming Organizations*. New York: Oxford University Press.

—— ——(1993). 'Strategic Alignment: Leveraging Information Technology for Transforming Organizations', *IBM Systems Journal*, 32(1): 4–16.

Hiner, J. (2008). 'SIM Survey 2008: Top 10 IT Management Concerns', <http://blogs.zdnet.com/BTL/?p=10844>, accessed 18 March 2009.

Hirschheim, R., and Sabherwal, R. (2001). 'Detours in the Path toward Strategic Information Systems Alignment', *California Management Review*, 44(1): 87–108.

Hunt, G. E. (1993). 'Management Challenges for Survival in the 1990s', *Journal of Information Technology*, 8(1): 43–9.

IBM (1981). *Business Systems Planning: Information Systems Planning Guide*. 3rd edn, EE 20–0527–3.

ICEX Inc. (2004). *ICEX Knowledge Kit for IT Strategic Alignment*. Boston: ICEX Inc. <http://www.itproductivity.org/ICEXitstrategicalignment.htm>.

Irani, Z. (2002). 'Information Systems Evaluation: Navigating through the Problem Domain', *Information & Management*, 40(1): 11–24.

Jenkin, T. A., and Chan, Y. E. (2006). 'Exploring the IS Project Alignment Construct', Queen's School of Business working paper.

Jia, R. Q., Reich, B. H., and Pearson, J. M. (2008). 'IT Service Climate: An Extension to IT Service Quality Research', *Journal of the Association for Information Systems*, 29(5): 294–320.

Johnston, H. R., and Carrico, S. R. (1988). 'Developing Capabilities to Use Information Strategically', *MIS Quarterly*, 12(1): 37–48.

Kaarst-Brown, M. L., and Robey, D. (1999). 'More on Myth, Magic and Metaphor: Cultural Insights into the Management of Information Technology in Organizations', *Information Technology and People*, 12(2): 192–218.

Kearns, G. S., and Lederer, A. L. (2000). 'The Effect of Strategic Alignment on the Use of IS-Based Resources for Competitive Advantage', *Journal of Strategic Information Systems*, 9(4): 265–93.

—— ——(2003). 'A Resource-Based View of Strategic IT Alignment: How Knowledge Sharing Creates Competitive Advantage', *Decision Sciences*, 34(1): 1–29.

King, W. R. (1988). 'How Effective is your Information Systems Planning?' *Long Range Planning*, 21(5): 103–12.

Lederer, A. L., and Mendelow, A. L. (1989). 'Coordination of Information Systems Plans with Business Plans', *Journal of Management Information Systems*, 6(2): 5–19.

Leede, J., de Looise, J. C., and Alders, B. (2002). 'Innovation, Improvement and Operations: An Exploration of the Management of Alignment', *International Journal of Technology Management*, 23(4): 353–68.

Lefebvre, L. A., and Lefebvre, E. (1988). 'Computerization of Small Firms: A Study of the Perceptions and Expectations of Managers', *Journal of Small Business and Entrepreneurship*, 1(3): 1–17.

Levy, D. L. (2000). 'Applications and Limitations of Complexity Theory in Organization Theory and Strategy', in J. Rabin, G. J. Miller, and W. B. Hildreth (eds.), *Handbook of Strategic Management*. 2nd edn., New York: Marcel.

Luftman, J., and Brier, T. (1999). 'Achieving and Sustaining Business–IT Alignment', *California Management Review*, 42(1): 109–22.

—— Kempaiah, R., and Nash, E. (2006). 'Key Issues for IT Executives 2005', *MIS Quarterly Executive*, 5(2): 81–101.

—— Papp, R., and Brier, T. (1999). 'Enablers and Inhibitors of Business–IT Alignment', *Communications of the Association for Information Systems*, 1: Article 11.

MacDonald, H. (1991). 'The Strategic Alignment Process', in M. S. Scott Morton (ed.), *The Corporation of the 1990s: Information Technology and Organizational Transformation*. London: Oxford University Press.

McFarlan, W. E. (1984). 'Information Technology Changes the Way You Compete', *Harvard Business Review*, 62(3): 98–103.

McKeen, J. D., and Smith, H. (2003). *Making IT Happen: Critical Issues in IT Management*. Chichester: Wiley.

McLean, E. R., and Soden, J. V. (1977). *Strategic Planning for MIS*. New York: Wiley.

Miles, R. E., and Snow, C. C. (1978). *Organizational Strategy, Structure, and Process*. New York: McGraw-Hill Book Co.

Mintzberg, H. (1973). *The Nature of Managerial Work*. New York: Harper & Row.

Niederman, F., Brancheau, J. C., and Wetherbe, J. C. (1991). 'Information Systems Issues for the 1990s', *MIS Quarterly*, 15(4): 475–500.

Norden, P. V. (1993). 'Qualitative Techniques in Strategic Alignment', *IBM Systems Journal*, 32(1): 180–97.

Orlikowski, W. (1996). 'Improvising Organisational Transformation over Time: A Situated Change Perspective', *Information Systems Research*, 7(1): 63–92.

Palmer, J. W., and Markus, M. L. (2000). 'The Performance Impacts of Quick Response and Strategic Alignment in Specialty Retailing', *Information Systems Research*, 11(3): 241–59.

Papp, R. (1999). 'Business–IT Alignment: Productivity Paradox Payoff?', *Industrial Management + Data Systems*, 99(8): 367–73.

Parker, M. M., Benson, R. J., and Trainor, H. E. (1988). *Information Economics: Linking Business Performance to Information Technology*. Englewood Cliffs, NJ: Prentice Hall.

Peak, D., Guynes, C. S., and Kroon, V. (2005). 'Information Technology Alignment Planning—A Case Study', *Information and Management*, 42(5): 635–49.

Powell, T. C. (1992). 'Organizational Alignment as Competitive Advantage', *Strategic Management Journal*, 13(2): 119–34.

Pyburn, P. J. (1983). 'Linking the MIS Plan with Corporate Strategy: An Exploratory Study', *MIS Quarterly*, 7(2): 1–14.

Raymond, L., Pare, G., and Bergeron, F. (1995). 'Matching Information Technology and Organizational Structure: An Empirical Study with Implications for Performance', *European Journal of Information Systems*, 4(1): 3–16.

Reich, B. H. (1993). 'Investigating the Linkage between Business and Information Technology Objectives: A Multiple Case Study in the Insurance Industry'. Unpublished Ph.D. thesis, University of British Columbia.

—— and Benbasat, I. (1996). 'Measuring the Linkage between Business and Information Technology Objectives', *MIS Quarterly*, 20(1): 55–81.

—— —— (2000). 'Factors that Influence the Social Dimension of Alignment between Business and Information Technology Objectives', *MIS Quarterly*, 24(1): 81–113.

Rondinelli, D., Rosen, B., and Drori, I. (2001). 'The Struggle for Strategic Alignment in Multinational Corporations: Managing Readjustment during Global Expansion', *European Management Journal*, 19(4): 404–16.

Sabherwal, R., and Chan, Y. E. (2001). 'Alignment between Business and IS Strategies: A Study of Prospectors, Analyzers, and Defenders', *Information Systems Research*, 12(1): 11–33.

—— Hirschheim, R., and Goles, T. (2001). 'The Dynamics of Alignment: Insights from a Punctuated Equilibrium Model', *Organization Science*, 12(2): 179–97.

—— and Kirs, P. (1994). 'The Alignment between Organizational Critical Success Factors and Information Technology Capability in Academic Institutions', *Decision Sciences*, 25(2): 301–30.

Sauer, C., and Burn, J. M. (1997). 'The Pathology of Strategic Management', in C. Sauer and P. W. Yetton (eds.), *Steps to the Future*. 1st edn., San Francisco, CA: Jossey-Bass.

Scarbrough, H. (1998). 'Linking Strategy and IT-Based Innovation: The Importance of the 'Management of Expertise', in R. D. Galliers and W. R. J. Baets (eds.), *Information Technology and Organizational Transformation: Innovation for the 21st Century Organization*. 2nd edn., Toronto: John Wiley & Sons, 19–36.

Scott Morton, M. S. (ed.) (1991). *The Corporation of the 1990s: Information Technology and Organizational Transformation*. London: Oxford University Press.

Shank, J. K., Niblock, E. G., and Sandalls, W. T., Jr. (1973). 'Balance Creativity and Practicality in Formal Planning', *Harvard Business Review*, 51(1): 87–95.

Shpilberg, D., Berez, S., Puryear, R., and Shah, S. (2007) 'Avoiding the Alignment Trap in Information Technology', *MIT Sloan Management Review*, 49(1): 51–8.

Sledgianowski, D., and Luftman, J. (2006). 'IT-Business Strategic Alignment Maturity: A Case Study', *Journal of Cases on Information Technology*, 7(2): 102–20.

Smaczny, T. (2001). 'Is an Alignment between Business and Information Technology the Appropriate Paradigm to Manage IT in Today's Organisations?', *Management Decision*, 39 (10): 797–802.

Street, C. T. (2006). 'Evolution in IS Alignment and IS Alignment Capabilities over Time: A Test of Punctuated Equilibrium Theory'. Unpublished Ph.D. thesis, Queen's University.

Tallon, P. P. (2003). 'Paul Tallon: The Alignment Paradox', *CIO Insight*, 1(47).

—— (2007–8). 'A Process-Oriented Perspective on the Alignment of Information Technology and Business Strategy', *Journal of Management Information Systems*, 24(3): 227–68.

—— and A. Pinsonneault, A. (2005). 'In Pursuit of Value: Reconceptualizing the Form and Function of Strategic IT Alignment under Environmental Dynamism'. Article under review at *Organization Science*, 2005.

Tan, F. B. (1995). 'The Responsiveness of Information Technology to Business Strategy Formulation: An Empirical Study', *Journal of Information Technology*, 10(3): 171–8.

—— and Gallupe, B. (2006). 'Aligning Business and Information Systems Thinking: A Cognitive Approach', *Engineering Management, IEEE Transactions*, 53(2): 223–37.

Taxén, L. A. (2005). 'Sociotechnical Approach towards Alignment', *Software Process Improvement and Practice*, 10: 427–39.

Teo, T. S. H., and Ang, J. S. K. (1999). 'Critical Success Factors in the Alignment of IS Plans with Business Plans', *International Journal of Information Management*, 19(1): 173–85.

Van Der Zee, J. T. M., and De Jong, B. (1999). 'Alignment is not Enough: Integrating Business and Information Technology Management with the Balanced Business Scorebard', *Journal of Management Information Systems*, 16(2): 137–56.

Venkatraman, N. (1989). 'The Concept of Fit in Strategy Research: Toward Verbal and Statistical Correspondence', *Academy of Management Review*, 14(3): 423–44.

Vitale, M. R., Ives, B., and Beath, C. M. (1986). 'Linking Information Technology and Corporate Strategy: An Organizational View', *Proceedings of the 7th International Conference on Information Systems*, San Diego, CA, 265–26.

Wang, E. T. G., and Tai, J. C. F. (2003). 'Factors Affecting Information Systems Planning Effectiveness: Organizational Contexts and Planning Systems Dimensions', *Information & Management*, 40(4): 287–303.

Whittington, R. (ed.) (1993). *What is Strategy—And Does it Matter?* Routledge Series in Analytical Management. London: Routledge.

Yetton, P. W. (1994). 'False Prophecies, Successful Practice and Future Directions in IT Management', *Proceedings of the IFIP TC8 Open Conference: Business Process Re-Engineering: Information Systems Opportunities and Challenges*, Queensland Gold Coast, Australia.

CHAPTER 14

IT-DEPENDENT STRATEGIC INITIATIVES AND SUSTAINED COMPETITIVE ADVANTAGE: A REVIEW, SYNTHESIS, AND AN EXTENSION OF THE LITERATURE

MICHAEL WADE, GABRIELE PICCOLI, AND BLAKE IVES

INTRODUCTION

It's *one thing to reach the top, another thing entirely to stay there.* Behind this familiar axiom is the understanding that the factors necessary to gain an advantage are not necessarily those required to sustain that advantage. A great deal of research has been conducted on how firms gain strategic advantage through the use of IT. By contrast, relatively little work has been done to study how firms can hold on to a competitive advantage based on, or enabled by, IT (Piccoli and Ives 2005). There are two reasons for this. First, since creating an advantage is temporally precedent to sustaining one, researchers have tended to focus on the prior condition. After all, why bother to worry about what to do once you achieve success if you never get there in the first place? The second reason is more pragmatic. Academic research seeks to be rigorous and generalizable and work on the sustainability of competitive advantage necessarily requires longitudinal approaches; such studies are typically expensive and time consuming to conduct. There is also a significant challenge in isolating the role of the IT-enabled resource in order to rule out competing explanations. These reasons make this type of research risky and costly. Unfortunately, the resultant scarcity of rigorous investigation and evidence is a contributing cause of the recurrence of attacks on the role of IT as a competitive resource (Carr 2003).

In our *MISQ Review* articles, we examined the issue of sustainability[1] from a conceptual point of view (Wade and Hulland 2004; Piccoli and Ives 2005). Our conclusions were similar in that we challenged the commonly held view that sustaining a competitive advantage based on IT was infeasible. We agreed that forward looking firms (and researchers) needed to start seriously thinking about IT strategies for maintaining positions of competitive advantage. In this chapter, we argue that strategic thinking about IT is more important than ever. The competitive landscape has shifted so that, in some respects, achieving and sustaining an advantage based on IT has become much more difficult—we will outline some of these challenges below. However, rather than regarding these challenges as the final death knell of IT's strategic value—an approach we have seen some companies and authors adopt—we argue that firms can achieve and sustain substantial IT-enabled benefits as long as they pay close attention to the strategic value of information systems *throughout* the planning process. Consideration of the strategic value of the IT value proposition needs to happen from the time the IT initiative is first conceived, through the implementation and acceptance processes, and continue once the advantage has been attained. In other words, it is during the design phase of any IT-dependent strategic initiative that the firm must first lay the groundwork for sustainability and it is the execution phase that presents the opportunity to continue to extend that sustainability. In both instances, understanding the role of IT in fostering sustainability is essential. In this update, we briefly discuss the theoretical framework for our work, including the resource-based view of the firm (RBV), the dynamic capabilities perspective, agility, and the notion of the IT-dependent strategic initiative. We then comment on the value of these approaches in light of current structural, economic, political, legal, and cultural conditions. We offer an evaluation of work to date, challenge some of the received wisdom, and propose a number of possible avenues for pushing forward our understanding of the conditions for sustainable IT-enabled competitive advantage.

THE RESOURCE-BASED VIEW AND THE SUSTAINABILITY OF IT-ENABLED COMPETITIVE ADVANTAGE

The resource-based view has found a great deal of traction within the IS field as a theory of competitive advantage. The RBV looks at the firm as a collection of resources. These resources, in turn, exhibit the following attributes to different degrees: value, rarity, imitability, and non-substitutability (see Figure 14.1). Competitive advantage can be created or sustained depending on the nature of these attributes (Penrose 1959; Barney 1991; Grant 1991). In general, empirical studies using RBV theory have displayed strong support for its tenets and conclusions (e.g. McGrath, MacMillan, and Venkataram 1995; Miller and Shamsie 1996; Zaheer and Zaheer 1997).

Resources that are valuable and rare can provide a temporary advantage (the competitive advantage creation phase in Figure 14.1). These attributes are ex-ante limits to competition. This advantage can be sustained over time to the extent that the resource resists imitation or substitution (the competitive advantage sustainability phase in Figure 14.1). These attributes are ex-post limits to competition. Three factors contribute to low imitability: unique firm history, causal ambiguity, and social complexity (Barney 1991). The role of history recognizes the importance of a firm's unique past, a past that other firms are unable to duplicate. For example, a firm might purchase a piece of land at one point in time that subsequently becomes very valuable (Ricardo 1966; Hirshleifer 1980). Causal ambiguity exists when the link between a resource and the competitive advantage it confers is poorly understood. This ambiguity may lie in uncertainty about *how* a resource leads to sustainable competitive advantage, or it may lie in lack of clarity about *which* resource (or combination of resources) leads to the advantage. Such ambiguity makes it extremely hard for competing firms to duplicate a resource or copy the way in which it is deployed (Lippman and Rumelt 1982; Dierickx and Cool 1989).

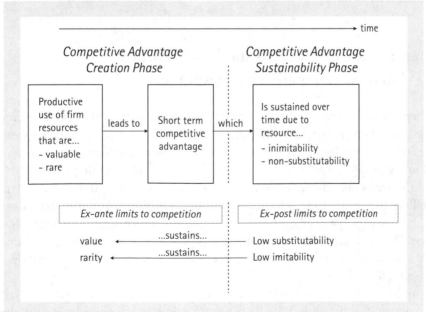

FIGURE **14.1** Sustainability and the resource-based view (modified from Wade and Hulland 2004)

Finally, social complexity refers to the multifarious relationships within the firm and between the firm and key stakeholders such as shareholders, suppliers, and customers (Hambrick 1987). The complexity of these relationships makes them difficult to manage, and even more difficult to imitate. An example of this is Walmart's logistics management system. Even if all the individual elements are in place, the relationships between the elements, and thus its complexity, would likely result in an imperfect substitute (Dierickx and Cool 1989). A resource has low substitutability if there are few, if any, strategically equivalent resources that are, themselves, rare and inimitable (Amit and Schoemaker 1993; Black and Boal 1994; Collis and Montgomery 1995). Firms may find, for example, that excellence in IT development, systems integration, or environmental scanning may be achieved through a number of equifinal paths. We will return to the question of substitutability in the later sections.

Imitability and rarity are logically linked to one another. As a resource is imitated, it becomes less rare. Similarly, as more substitutes are developed, a resource becomes less valuable. The RBV is a valuable enhancement to the Information Systems literature where it has long been argued that IS resources are valuable, but not rare, that they rarely resist imitation, and have multiple substitutes (Mata, Furst, and Barney 1995). Technological assets, for example, such as computer hardware and software, are often considered to be relatively easy to acquire and copy (Mata, Furst, and Barney 1995; Powell and Dent-Micallef 1997)—even though empirical validation of this seeming received wisdom awaits. Although various studies have examined how IS resources can potentially create competitive advantage for firms, very little of this work has looked at sustaining that advantage over time.

Dynamic Capabilities and the Sustainability of IT-Enabled Competitive Advantage

Another stream of research that has influenced IT strategic thinking revolves around dynamic capabilities. Dynamic capabilities address a commonly articulated weakness of the RBV—its fundamentally static nature. The resource-based view has been criticized for ignoring factors surrounding resources, instead assuming that they simply 'exist' (Stinchcombe 2000). Eisenhardt and Martin (2000: 1107) defined dynamic capabilities as 'Firm's processes that use resources—specifically the processes to integrate, reconfigure, gain and release resources—to match and even create market change. Dynamic capabilities thus are the organizational and strategic routines by which firms achieve new resource configurations as markets emerge, collide, split, evolve, and die.'

By acting as a buffer between core resources and a changing business environment, dynamic capabilities allow a firm to adjust its resource mix and thereby maintain the sustainability of the firm's competitive advantage that otherwise might be quickly eroded (Volberda 1996; Teece, Pisano, and Shuen 1997; Eisenhardt and

Martin 2000; Wade and Hulland 2004). Indeed, some research has suggested that IS resources may take on many of the attributes of dynamic resources, and thus may be particularly useful to firms operating in rapidly changing environments (Jarvenpaa and Leidner 1998). Thus, even when IS resources do not directly lead the firm to a position of competitive advantage, they may nonetheless be critical to the firm's longer-term competitiveness in unstable environments; particularly (or maybe 'but only') if they help it to develop, add, integrate, and release other key resources over time.

Agility and the Sustainability of IT-Enabled Competitive Advantage

A third literature stream closely related to dynamic capabilities is the research on agility. Agility is defined as the ability to detect opportunities for innovation and seize those competitive market opportunities by assembling requisite assets, knowledge, and relationships with speed and surprise (D'Aveni 1994; Goldman, Nagel, and Preiss 1995; Sambamurthy, Bharadwaj, and Grover 2003). Further, agility encompasses a firm's capabilities related to interactions with customers, orchestration of internal operations, and utilization of its ecosystem of external business partners (Sambamurthy, Bharadwaj, and Grover 2003). Firms that are agile have the ability to rapidly and effectively alter their strategies and approaches in the face of changing market conditions. IT can both aid and hinder agility depending on its structural conditions (Sambamurthy, Bharadwaj, and Grover 2003). For example, a rigid legacy system may impede a firm's ability to adapt to new market conditions. Further, when IT is deeply embedded within organizational systems and routines, it may become an impediment to change when those systems and routines need to be renewed. On the other hand, IT can be a strong facilitator of organizational agility. It can reduce switching and coordination costs, and quickly and cheaply combine with other resources to form new, better positioned resources (Evans and Wurster 2000). Agility is related to the concept of real options. In the context of IT, options confer the right, but not the obligation to obtain benefits from future IT initiatives (Fichman 2004). The holder of an option typically makes a small initial investment, holds it open until an opportunity arrives, and then exercises a choice to strike the option and capture the value inherent in that opportunity (Sambamurthy, Bharadwaj, and Grover 2003). Alternatively, if the option is shown to have no value, it is left to expire with little residual cost. IS resources can be used by firms to generate sets of options and strategies that can be pursued depending on the future nature of the competitive environment. These strategies would otherwise be very expensive and/or time consuming to develop from scratch.

IT-Dependent Strategic Initiatives

Complementing previous work on the RBV, dynamic capabilities, and agility is the stream of research that focuses on the individual initiative level. This complementary approach is important because, as an applied discipline, the Information Systems literature must be able to inform the design of technology-enabled initiatives and provide managerial guidance not only for aggregate IT investments, but also for the deployment of specific projects. To this end, the IT-dependent strategic initiative perspective provides a complete approach to evaluating the competitive potential of new technologies because it places them in the organizational context in which they are introduced and deployed. IT-dependent strategic initiatives represent 'identifiable competitive moves that depend on the use of IT to be enacted, and are designed to lead to sustained improvements in a firm's competitive position' (Piccoli and Ives 2005: 748). Moreover, the IT-dependent strategic initiative perspective complements the significant work to date on business value of IT and the complementary role of resources (Melville, Kraemer, and Gurbaxani 2004) to explain how IT 'does not contribute to firm performance in isolation, but instead contributes as part of an activity system that fosters the creation and appropriation of economic value' (Piccoli and Ives 2005: 766).

Central to the framework is the notion that firms compete on the basis of value propositions that they offer to their customers[2] and that competitive replication, in order to be successful, must enable competitors to produce a comparable value proposition. Producing a comparable value proposition is not equivalent to creating a comparable 'IT system' because the IT-dependent strategic initiatives underlying

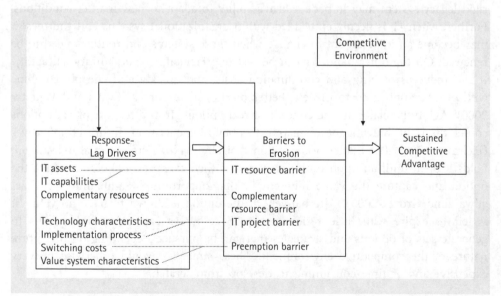

FIGURE 14.2 Response lag drivers (Piccoli and Ives 2005)

such value proposition depends on the characteristics of the technology itself as well as the characteristics of the implementing organization and the value network in which the firm operates (Piccoli and Ives 2005). These other components are organized in response lag drivers and, in turn, categorized in four barriers to erosion. Each of the barriers is briefly described below with some discussion of how they have evolved over time.

Barrier No. 1: IT resource barrier

An IT resource barrier is based on the fact that 'At any point in time, competing firms have a different endowment of IT resources at their disposal to identify, assemble, deploy, and use information technologies.' (Piccoli and Ives 2005: 752). Firms therefore can take advantage of IT resource heterogeneity to create value propositions that leverage their idiosyncrasies and thus may not be readily available to competing firms. IT resources can either be classified as IT assets—things the firm has—or IT capabilities—things the firms is able to do (Wade and Hulland 2004). By successfully erecting a strong IT resource barrier, a firm can foster resource inimitability (in RBV parlance) and, to the extent that the underlying resources create significant value, can generate a sustainable competitive advantage.

The true potential offered by the IT resource barrier for sustainable advantage has been the subject of considerable debate in the literature due to the commonly held assumption that IT resources are undifferentiated, fungible commodities, and, as such, cannot form the basis of differentiated strategic initiatives (Mata, Fuerst, and Barney 1995; Powell and Dent-Micalleff 1997; Carr 2003). While quite appealing at a theoretical level, this argument breaks down in the context of IT-dependent strategic initiatives. Supporting evidence for that position mostly comes in the form of archival research studies using highly aggregate definitions of IT investments (see Melville, Kraemer, and Gurbaxani 2004 for a review); this is countered by work demonstrating the significant response lag (Feeny and Ives 1990) associated with IT assets, such as IT infrastructure and data repositories (Pemberton, Stonehouse, and Barber 2001), as well as IT capabilities (Barton and Peters 1992; Bharadwaj 2000; Santhanam and Hartono 2003). Recent work contributes to the debate on the role of IT resources, as well as on the methodological implications of using aggregate measures for IT investments, by demonstrating that different classes of IT investments produce different impacts on organizations and, more importantly, that the manner in which such performance accrues varies significantly between different classes of IT investments (Aral and Weill 2007).

Looking at general trends that either reinforce or weaken the IT resources barrier, we suggest that a growing awareness for the competitive value of data and information (Piccoli and Watson 2008) and an increasing feasibility of urban sensing and pervasive computing (Cuff, Hansen, and Kang 2008) create an enhanced opportunity for organizations to strengthen their IT resource positions (e.g. IT infrastructure, IT repositories). Conversely, weakening the potential of this barrier to erosion is the growing incidence of IT outsourcing. Outsourcing has always been a part of business, yet the prevalence of IT outsourcing has increased substantially in recent years (Lacity, Will-cocks, and Rottman 2008). While IT outsourcing promises a number of efficiency and effectiveness benefits, it may also reduce the ability of organizations to foster strong internal IT capabilities. Moreover, if outsourcing becomes prevalent within an indus-try, the relevance of technical skills, and to some extent IT management skills, will likely decrease. For example, when an IT product or service is outsourced, the control over its use and management is reduced, and in some cases lost. This is particularly evident with software-as-a-service and some kinds of cloud computing arrangements where control over alignment and integration of the IT resource with current and future strategy is weakened.

Furthermore, in most outsourcing relationships, the firm has less control over the customization or the evolution of the IT resource. For sound business reasons, many outsourcing contracts are based on standard tools, platforms, and methodologies. Standardization can simplify data transfer, supply-chain integration, and ongoing system management, as well as providing a level of skill base consistency between the focal firm and the outsourcing partner. Standardization, however, prevents the firm from controlling the development of the IT resource. Finally, hiring external talent for either systems development or systems integration—talent that typically specializes in the firm's own industry and has likely worked on implementation projects for multiple firms within that industry—all but negates the development of internal IT capabilities other than relationship assets (Ross, Beath, and Goodhue 1996). Such relationship assets would remain quite relevant in the presence of outsourcing contracts, but would need to extend beyond the boundaries of the firm (Feeny and Willcocks 1998; Ranganathan and Balaji 2007). IT management skills, while remaining a relevant source of differentiation, would also need to evolve in the management of outsourcing relationships.

Barrier No. 2: Complementary resource barrier

Complementarity is central to the notion of the IT-dependent strategic initiative. A value proposition is created not by IT resources in isolation, but through the combination of IT and non-IT resources to form a composite IT-dependent strategic initiative. These prerequisite resources can form powerful barriers to the erosion of the firm's competitive advantage. That is,

> When a firm has access to co-specialized complementary assets that underpin the IT dependent strategic initiative, significant response lag can be created because imitation of the initiative is predicated on the ability to obtain the same (or equivalent) complementary resources. A compelling example was Dell's early exploitation of the World Wide Web via Dell Online. It strategically leveraged Dell's direct order business model, a distribution model that most PC manufacturers at the time did not have in place and would have a difficult time putting in place. To the extent that the technology is co-specialized to, and amplifies the value of, unique complementary resources, its mere imitation by competitors is not sufficient. (Piccoli and Ives 2005: 757)

Identifying and categorizing complementary resources is beyond the scope of this work. However, there is substantial research supporting the notion that IT investment can amplify the value of complementary resources (Wade and Hulland 2004) and we believe that complementary resources continue to hold significant potential for generating response lag and to make it difficult to overcome the leader's advantage. Through customization of the IT core, a firm can leverage its unique assets to form the basis of a sustainable advantage. However, in many industries, firms in search of efficiencies have reduced the contribution of idiosyncratic complementary resources and instead have utilized standardized commercial packages. These packages have made it more difficult for firms to pursue strategies of strategic differentiation. Consider the example of enterprise systems. Most contemporary enterprise systems are built on a 'best practices' model. The idea of software being organized around best practices is appealing to implementing firms. A vendor surveys a particular industry to identify the top performing firms and 'embeds superior practices' into its enterprise system design for the customer (i.e. the implementing firm) to deploy once the software is installed and configured. While the viability of this model is questioned (Wagner and Newell 2004; Wagner, Scott, and Galliers 2006), it is problematic even when successfully implemented as it tends to homogenize business practices within an industry. This homogenization becomes particularly dangerous in industries that have widely adopted software suites from a small number of vendors, such as pharmaceuticals and heavy manufacturing. From a competitive standpoint, it becomes more difficult for a firm to competitively differentiate when its business processes are based on the same underlying factors as its rivals (Davenport 1998). With organizational information systems, such as enterprise systems, this means that firms not only start to look similar in terms of technical infrastructure, but also on a business process level. As a consequence, firms find it more difficult to compete on the basis of their information systems, impeding their ability to gain, and in particular sustain any IT-based advantage. As we mentioned in the introduction, the value of a preliminary analysis of sustainability during initiative design can uncover opportunities to leverage idiosyncratic and valuable complementary resources.

Barrier No. 3: IT project barrier

The IT project barrier is the instantiation of the project at the core of the initiative. According to the IT-enabled strategic initiative perspective: 'Since IT-dependent strategic initiatives rely on an essential enabling IT core, they cannot be implemented until the necessary technology and associated information systems have been successfully deployed—the more time consuming and costly the process, the more resilient the IT project barrier' (Piccoli and Ives 2005: 759). However, many critics of the strategic value of IT mistakenly confuse the IT project for the IT-dependent strategic initiative. Consider a simple example. Multinational lodging companies, such as Marriott International, Accor Group, and Hyatt Hotels, compete fiercely on the dimension of customer service. In the pursuit of superior customer service and customer choice, they have introduced a number of IT-enabled service channels. A recent trend has been the introduction of brand-wide standard self-service kiosks across their affiliated properties to facilitate the check-in and check-out processes. An IT investment or IT project mentality, as assumed by critics of the strategic potential of IT (e.g. Carr 2003), suggests that this initiative will be easily imitated by competitors who have ready access to the kiosk technology. As that reasoning goes, the kiosks are fairly standardized hardware/software bundles that can be easily replicated and deployed by competitors. Conversely, an IT-dependent strategic initiative calls observers to take a broader look considering the impact of all four barriers to erosion. For example, the kiosk is an incremental interface to the chain's customer service system and, as such, it leverages the firm's own IT infrastructure and data repositories. These prerequisite IT resources are neither easily deployed nor fungible, making replication by competitors less than straightforward. Moreover, as demonstrated by the literature, the kiosk technology must fit with the brand's positioning and with customer characteristics (Parasuraman 2000). As a customer-facing service initiative, the implementing firm must recognize that the customer is also the technology user (Cenfetelli, Benbasat, and Al-Natour 2008) and, as a consequence, the potential to deliver the value proposition depends heavily on customer fit. For example, beyond general technology readiness and IT savvy of the intended customer-user, the degree of customer loyalty the brand enjoys will likely determine the success of the initiative. That is, hotels with a high percentage of returning customers will likely enjoy higher adoption rates, lower implementation costs per using customer, and a higher percentage of successful use by customers who have had more experience and therefore have become better users of the specific technology kiosk (see the pre-emption barrier for an explanation of the process by which co-specialized investments accrue).

The example of check-in kiosks is useful in showing how, even when a rather simple IT project represents the core of the IT-dependent strategic initiative, the question of sustainability is not straightforward. The example however can be misleading in that it appears to reinforce the 'IT is easily imitable' argument. But, not all IT is created equal and the IT project barrier charts the many response lag drivers that characterize the wide variety of IT projects that a firm can undertake. Discussion of these response lag drivers is beyond the scope of the present discussion. However, simply on intuitive grounds, we challenge the notion that IT projects cannot engender response lag and play a role in the sustainability of a competitive advantage. The information systems literature has played witness to countless project failures and it is hard to argue that an IT system is 'easily imitable' as much as it is not 'easily implementable'. That is, both custom development projects and off-the-shelf implementations still today are characterized by high failure rates (Light and Wagner 2006). Moreover, as we argued above, the contention that a firm can 'import' best practices and standard processes when it implements standardized software—thereby reducing the strategic differences with competitions—has also been questioned by information systems researchers (Wagner and Newell 2004; Wagner, Scott, and Galliers 2006). Thus, despite the prevalent rhetoric, the process of implementing large-scale organizational information systems remains an extremely complex endeavour. (See also Chapter 15 in this volume.)

We do recognize that the cycle of innovation and change in information technology has been speeding up over the last two decades and that this trend toward faster cycle technology development has increased competition in IT intensive industries (McAfee and Brynjolfsson 2008). A number of trends underlie this evolution. First, the increasing size and prominence of the software industry has accelerated the shift toward a 'buy and make' approach to systems development that eschews custom development in favour of configuration and customization of standard off-the-shelf software packages (Markus 2000). To the extent that the uniqueness and complexity of the technology core of an IT-dependent strategic initiative decreases, so does the strength of the IT project barrier in staving off erosion of competitive advantage. Second, the increasing trend toward software modularity and the use of web services allows for software to be organized into discrete elements that can be separated from surrounding code thus enabling software reuse. Modularity leads to more efficient reuse, as modules can be discretely stored and utilized as required. Large libraries of software modules exist, saving firms substantial amounts of development time and cost. While these software development approaches enhance efficiency and speed of software delivery, they may also make it harder for firms to build truly differentiated systems. Modular software design, reuse, open programming environments, standardized development tools and methodologies, all make it harder for firms to develop systems that resist replication, and thus reduce the ability of firms to gain or sustain advantages based on software applications.

While limited academic research has formally tested the impact of these trends on the strength of the IT project barrier, there is mounting evidence to suggest that in absolute terms the build and implementation phase of an IT project has been shrinking in size and risk over the years. Competitors still need to become aware of the specific characteristics of the IT core of the leader's IT-dependent strategic initiative. However, once aware and once they have taken a decision to react, competitors can move more quickly than before through the process of implementing the necessary IT core. From the perspective of the resource-based view, IT resources remain valuable, but we believe the 'window of scarcity and rareness' has shrunk significantly.

At this point we caution against misunderstanding the implication of the argument developed above, what we call the 'fallacy of relative terms'. In absolute terms, the speed of delivery of IT projects has increased over time. However, at a theoretical level, the process by which the IT project barrier operates to limit erosion of competitive advantage has not changed, despite faster IT project development cycles. In other words, IT projects that deliver functionalities that were cutting edge decades ago (e.g. American Airlines SABRE), can be designed and deployed today at a fraction of the cost, with lower risk and greater speed. Today's equivalent of SABRE, a system of unprecedented size and complexity in its time, is not an inventory and reservation system. A more theoretically accurate parallel may be Google's search engine, an application that is highly unique, complex, and innovative and despite significant scrutiny remains quite difficult to replicate. In other words, what constitutes a large, complex, risky project that is hard to replicate can only be expressed in relative terms.

In conclusion, we acknowledge that the relentless evolution of information technology has made it more and more viable for organizations of all kinds to purchase and deploy the IT core of IT-enabled strategic initiatives with increasing speed and accuracy. Standard solutions, such as ERP or CRM systems, at the same time, can limit, but not eliminate, the scope of opportunities to create inimitable IT enabled projects. However, we caution theorists and practitioners alike against dismissing the potential contribution of the IT project barrier to protect a firm's leadership position and the uniqueness of a value proposition rooted in an IT-enabled strategic initiative. The process by which the IT project barrier contributes to sustainability and the contribution of its response lag drivers remain viable. Moreover, the IT core of the IT-dependent strategic initiative may play a crucial developmental role that has, to date, remained largely unexplored.

Barrier No. 4: Pre-emption barrier

The first three barriers to erosion could be termed barriers to imitation, as they explain what prevents competitors from replicating a leader's initiative. The fourth barrier to erosion is concerned with whether, 'even after successful imitation has occurred, the leader's position of competitive advantage can be threatened' (Piccoli and Ives 2005). In other words, the pre-emption barrier seeks to understand under what circumstances *successful* replication of the IT project and its prerequisite resources still prevents the followers from being able to produce the same value proposition and erode the leader's advantage. Central to the discussion of the pre-emption barrier is the notion of switching costs. Historically, information systems research has focused on IT-based switching costs (Feeny and Ives 1990). Such switching cost may be rooted in specialized user interfaces, proprietary codes and scripts, or proprietary software interfaces for interoperability.

The same trends toward software modularity and open standards discussed above create pressure that is depressing the traditional barrier to erosion and the role of IT switching costs. For example, software management and delivery platforms, such as web services, tend to lower the role of co-specialized technology investments, thus making it simpler to swap functionalities and foster interoperability of diverse software programs. Moreover, as users have become increasingly comfortable with computer-based interfaces and generally more technology ready (Parasuraman 2000), we foresee the value of switching costs associated with interface design to mitigate over time— albeit much more slowly than many predict due to the powerful influence of human inertia and resistance to change. Finally, governmental institutions are seemingly more aware of the potential power position that control of technology platforms yield and, as a consequence, have enacted legislation that promotes open standards and bans or restricts the use of proprietary networks—as the mounting European pressure on Microsoft to open up Windows and Apple to open up its iTunes service attest (Keizer 2007).

Notwithstanding the above arguments we note that, as with the IT project barrier, critics of the role of IT as a strategic resource tend to focus on the IT project rather than the IT-enabled strategic initiative. This seemingly semantic difference is extremely powerful since, once we broaden our view of what constitutes a co-specialized investment, we find that significant potential for erecting barriers to erosion through prevention remain. First, it points to the continued viability of the development of switching costs associated with the value proposition enabled by the initiative rather than the technology itself. This condition is particularly evident in cases where the technology is the catalyst for the development of strong network effects characterized by exclusivity. In such a scenario, as the example of eBay Inc. shows, switching costs can become daunting and extremely powerful as a means for preventing erosion of competitive advantage.

As with the IT project barrier, we draw attention to the 'fallacy of relative terms'. The role of co-specialized investments and switching costs as a response lag driver can only be evaluated with respect to the specific IT-dependent strategic initiative with which they are associated. As such, even IT switching costs may have the ability to contribute to erosion of competitive advantage, even though their magnitude is generally decreasing. Take the example of business casual custom-made apparel, such as that offered by Lands' End with its Lands' End Custom IT-dependent strategic initiative (Piccoli, Bass, and Ives 2003). Customers who want to take advantage of the superior comfort of mass-customized garments spend the time to provide their measurements to Lands' End, investing a small amount of time to understand the Lands' End web interface, measuring themselves following the specific requirements of the Lands' End customization engine, and selecting specific options for their custom chinos or shirts. Having invested time, they have made a co-specialized investment—at least in part—to the Lands' End Custom initiative. While they will not encounter insurmountable barriers to repeating a similar procedure on the LL Bean website if LL Bean launched a comparable initiative, the key question is how much of an incentive would customers need in order to do so? Would they spend the time to understand the LL Bean interface and enter their data for a discount of $50? $25? $5? If the average cost of a pair of custom chinos is $70, then $5 represents a premium over 7 per cent. This simple thought experiment demonstrates how, even when switching costs are 'small' in the abstract, they are in fact substantial in relative terms. As such, if we extend our thought experiment, they offer significant opportunity to limit the erosion of a competitive advantage and a first mover advantage.

The Net Effect

In the previous pages we have discussed the state of the art in the research streams focused on the question of the role of information technology in the search for sustainable competitive advantage, with particular attention to the IT-enabled strategic initiative perspective. We have outlined a number of trends that we argue have affected, and continue to affect, the ability of firms to build and sustain competitive advantages based on IT-dependent strategic initiatives. Some of these trends weaken the power of IT-dependent strategic initiatives to sustain advantages while others strengthen it. However, what emerges clearly from our analysis is that, while the prevalent rhetoric indicates that IT is losing its strategic potential, i.e. by becoming more fungible and easily imitable, a broader perspective shows that the dynamics are more complex and—for academic research—far more interesting. We believe that by closely analysing the value propositions that are enabled by IT-dependent strategic initiatives, we see a deceptively high potential for IT to contribute to sustainable advantage and for information systems researchers to play a part in explaining how and why this process takes place.

RESEARCH AND MANAGERIAL IMPLICATIONS

Our analysis of the literature to date, within the framework presented above, confirms the value of a project level perspective and opens a series of avenues for future research attention. Focusing on research at the initiative level has a number of theoretical and practical advantages. First, it more accurately reflects organizational evaluation processes. Returning to the earlier example of lodging kiosks, we note how the major lodging firms, after evaluating the need to improve customer service, identified and evaluated a number of different possible options. Each of these options can be conceptualized as a strategic initiative and, to the extent that it requires IT at its core, as an IT-dependent strategic initiative. Before implementation, the firm assesses the viability of the kiosk-enabled solution to customer service improvement, and evaluates the potential return (i.e. value creation and appropriation) as well as the potential for defending it from competitors' imitation (i.e. the question of sustainability) in order to reap benefits over time. Thus, the analysis at the level of the IT-dependent strategic initiative has significant potential to inform practice as it enables management to evaluate the potential for the value proposition stemming from the initiative to resist imitation and substitution.

From a research standpoint, the IT-enabled strategic initiative perspective helps resolve one of the critical concerns associated with research on sustainability: namely, the parallelism between cause and effect. In other words, much of the business value of IT and sustainability literature has used highly aggregated measures for both the independent and dependent variables—respectively IT investments and financial performance (Ray, Barney, and Muhanna 2004). While this perspective is extremely valuable, it suffers from two main problems. On the one hand it does not allow researchers to identify the process by which the specific characteristics of individual IT investments contribute to performance (Aral and Weill 2007). On the other it may lead to conflicting findings as the outcome variables (i.e. financial performance) are far removed from the determinants (i.e. IT investments and complementary resources).

An IT-dependent strategic initiative perspective simultaneously appeases both of these concerns. By focusing on specific initiatives, it enables researchers to directly account for their nature and characteristics. Moreover, by using the initiative as the unit of analysis, researchers can identify the specific process-level outcome variables of interest and more precisely map the chain of causality to competitive effects. Finally, an IT-enabled strategic initiative perspective enables an analysis of the complementarities and interactions between specific components of a given initiative.

The main limitation of this approach stems from its very focus on a single initiative. Thus, it is not applicable to investigations of widely shared services and assets, such as IT infrastructure. Moreover, to the extent that some IT resources underpin multiple and widely different initiatives, the IT-dependent strategic initiative perspective might not be applicable. Thus, we note how this perspective is complementary to the resource-based view and the research stream on agility, with each best suited to a different set of research questions pertaining to the sustainability of IT-enabled competitive advantage. In the remainder of this section we draw a number of implications for research and practice.

Combinatorial Effects in IT-Enabled Strategic Initiatives

Despite theoretical arguments and case evidence that supports the IT-dependent strategic initiative perspective (Piccoli and Ives 2005; Aral and Weill 2007), the 'IT as a commodity' argument persists both in the popular press and in academic circles (Clemons and Row 1991; Mata, Fuerst, and Barney 1995; Powell and Dent-Micallef 1997; Carr 2003). For example, consider the notion that 'of all resources in the IT equation, human resources are probably the most neglected and difficult to master' (Powell and Dent-Micallef 1997: 395). While appealing on the surface, these arguments are misleading in that they fail to recognize the critical theoretical issue of relevance: explaining how IT and other resources interact to create superior IT-enabled strategic initiatives. Trying to isolate the single component that makes an initiative difficult to counter as in the argument that IT is an 'easy to master' commoditized technology, fails to recognize the value of combinatorial complexity and fit of the various components of an IT-enabled strategic initiative. Such a combinatorial approach seeks to explain how (not just whether) the IT resource 'combines' with other resources in order to leverage and amplify their effect, or to diminish it (Jeffers, Muhanna, and Nault 2008). Thus, it is the interaction between the technology and other resources that enables the formation of the firm's unique value proposition. Viewed as an interlocking set of activities and components (Rivkin 2000), IT-dependent strategic initiatives are more difficult to replicate than IT investments (Piccoli, Bass, and Ives 2003). It follows that the very same technology will have different effects in different organizations, even head-to-head competitors, not only with respect to implementation success (Orlikowski and Iacono 2001), but also with regard to competitive performance. Under these circumstances, the notion that IT is easily imitable loses applicability and appeal.

The combinatorial perspective is coherent with the IT-enabled strategic initiative perspective, but it has yet to be applied to the question of sustainability. We believe that there is great potential for research that takes a holistic approach and focuses on examining the interplay of the components of IT-dependent strategic initiatives, rather than seeking to isolate their effect on sustained advantage.

Effect Timing

Another question that remains unexplored in the literature pertains to the role of information technology and IT-enabled strategic initiatives in fostering the development of other assets and capabilities. Largely influenced by the emergence of the resource-based view, the strategic information systems literature appears to have assumed that the IT resource can be considered a strategic resource to the extent that it contributes to making it hard for competitors to replicate or substitute, or, as suggested by the IT-dependent strategic initiative perspective, the value proposition it underpins. However, the strategic role of information technology may need to be reconceptualized taking into account the timing of its effects. In other words, we may need to split the role that IT can play as a resource in a given initiative—the current definition of strategic—and its role in fostering the development of other resources and future strategic initiatives.

The literature is silent about this latter point. However, previous work has identified organizational learning and asset stock accumulation processes as critical in reinforcing and rejuvenating barriers to erosion (Piccoli and Ives 2005). For example, an IT resource is a prerequisite condition for the ability to collect valuable customer information and to build information repositories (Piccoli and Watson 2008). Extending this line of reasoning, beyond the notion of IT-dependent strategic initiatives, information technology may be conceptualized as the prerequisite resource for the development of strategic options (Fichman 2004) through the development of strategic assets. While little work to date has been done in this area, IT may indeed itself be a source of innovation as it fosters the firm's ability to experiment faster and at lower cost than ever before.

The Threat of Substitution

Perhaps the main limitation of the IT-dependent strategic initiative is that it focuses on the threat of imitation, rather than the threat of substitution. That is, the framework addresses the process by which an IT-enabled strategic initiative can resist erosion in the face of replication by competitors (Eisenhardt and Martin 2000). It is silent with respect to the process by which competitors can leapfrog a firm with a superior IT-enabled strategic initiative by substituting the leader's value proposition with a different initiative that better fulfils the same customer need or that evolves from first fulfilling another customer's need and then grows into, and beyond, the service provided by the original leader (Christensen 1997). An early investment in a relatively inflexible IT infrastructure can seriously hamper responsiveness and, therefore, subsequent extensions of the sustainable advantage. The resource-based view provides conceptual support for the importance of non-substitutability as a barrier to erosion. Yet, there is very little empirical evidence that seeks to test the properties of substitution. Part of the problem is that substitutability is inherently exogenous to the IT resource. One can examine whether or not an IT resource can be imitated by examining its component properties. However, it is much more difficult to assess the comparative level of non-substitutability. Yet, IT resources have strong substitutability properties. Consider how video conferencing has become a substitute for air travel, how the Internet and video games have become substitutes for television, and how the iPhone and its applications have impacted on so many products and services. More research on the notion of substitutability and its relationship to IT resources and IT-dependent strategic initiatives is clearly warranted.

CONCLUSION

Research questions regarding the strategic role of IT resources and IT projects in the firm's search for sustainable competitive advantage still remain largely unanswered. The lack of research is a surprising realization, given the centrality of the issue for academic research and the implications, both positive and negative, for information systems practice. Nonetheless, such a paucity of research attention has created fertile, though challenging, ground for Information Systems scholars to explore. Such research, at least in the initial stages, is likely to be case based and longitudinal, with researchers exploring IT-enabled moves, and countermoves, over a series of years. One lesson to emerge from our review for practitioners is to take great care in how 'strategic' systems are designed and used. Opportunities to create competitive advantages based on IT-dependent strategic initiatives are increasingly hard to come by, and as such, should be actively sought and exploited. Creating a sustainable competitive advantage should be a consideration from the moment a strategic initiative is proposed.

We acknowledge that changing economic conditions have strengthened the widely held view that IT is a commodity, and as such, has no place in the creation or sustaining of competitive advantage. In this chapter, we have outlined some of the trends that have led to this view. However, while we accept that IT assets may be undifferentiated, we reject the suggestion that IT-dependent strategic initiatives have no strategic value. In fact, we argue that these initiatives, when formed in projects with complementary organizational resources, can lead to powerful business benefits, and can further form strong barriers to advantage erosion. The key to success is to maintain a sustainability mindset throughout the IT strategic planning process.

NOTES

1. The term 'sustainability' has two meanings in the academic literature on information systems. One meaning refers to the ability of a firm to use IT to maintain a competitive advantage over a period of time. The second, more recent meaning refers to research associated with ethics and long-lasting socio-environmental benefits. Our use of the term 'sustainability' is consistent with the first meaning.
2. The framework encompasses both customer facing and internal initiatives. Given the focus of this chapter we discuss exclusively the former.

REFERENCES

Amit, R., and Schoemaker, P. J. H. (1993). 'Strategic Assets and Organizational Rent', *Strategic Management Journal* (14), 33–46.

Aral, S., and Weill, P. (2007). 'IT Assets, Organizational Capabilities & Firm Performance: How Resource Allocations and Organizational Differences Explain Performance Variation', *Organization Science*, 18(5): 1–18.

Barney, J. (1991). 'Firm Resources and Sustained Competitive Advantage', *Journal of Management*, 17(1): 99–120.

Barton, P. S., and Peters, D. H. (1992). 'The ASB Bank: An IT Case Study in Sustained Competitive Advantage', *Journal of Strategic Information Systems*, 1(3): 165–70.

Bharadwaj, A. S. (2000). 'A Resource-Based Perspective on Information Technology Capability and Firm Performance: An Empirical Investigation', *MIS Quarterly*, 24(1): 169–96.

Black, J. A. and Boal, K. B. (1994). 'Strategic Resources: Traits, Configurations and Paths to Sustainable Competitive Advantage', *Strategic Management Journal*, 15: 131–48.

Carr, N. (2003). 'IT Doesn't Matter', *Harvard Business Review*, 81(5): 41–9.

Cenfetelli, R., Benbasat, I., and Al-Natour, S., 'Addressing the What and How of Online Services: Positioning Supporting-Services Functionality and Service Quality for Business-to-Consumer Success', *Information Systems Research*, 19(2): 161–81.

Christensen, C. (1997). *The Innovator's Dilemma: When New Technologies Cause Great Firms to Fail.* Boston, MA: Harvard Graduate School of Business Press.

Clemons, E. K. and Row, M. C. (1991). 'Sustaining IT Advantage: The Role of Structural Differences', *MIS Quarterly*, 15(3): 275–92.

Collis, D. J., and Montgomery, C. A. (1995). 'Competing on Resources: Strategy in the 1990s', *Harvard Business Review*, 73(4): 118–28.

Cuff, D., Hansen, M., and Kang, J. (2008). 'Out of the Woods: Urban Sensing', *Communications of the ACM*, 51(3): 24–33.

D'Aveni, R. A. (1994). *Hypercompetition: Managing the Dynamics of Strategic Maneuvering.* New York: The Free Press.

Davenport, T. H. (1998). 'Putting the Enterprise into the Enterprise System', *Harvard Business Review*, 76(4): 121–31.

Dierickx, I., and Cool, K. (1989). 'Asset Stock Accumulation and Sustainability of Competitive Advantage', *Management Science*, 35: 1504–11.

Eisenhardt, K., and Martin, J. (2000). 'Dynamic Capabilities: What are They?', *Strategic Management Journal*, 21: 1105–21.

Evans, P. B., and Wurster, T. S. (2000). *Blown to Bits: How the New Economics of Information Transforms Strategy*. Cambridge, MA: Harvard Business School Press.

Feeny, D. F., and Ives, B. (1990). 'In Search of Sustainability: Reaping Long-Term Advantage from Investments in Information Technology', *Journal of Management Information Systems*, 7(1): 27–46.

—— and Willcocks, L. P. (1998). 'Core IS Capabilities for Exploiting Information Technology', *Sloan Management Review*, 39(3): 9–21.

Fichman, R. G. (2004). 'Real Options and IT Platform Adoption: Implications for Theory and Practice', *Information Systems Research*, 15(2): 132–54.

Goldman, S. L., Nagel, R. N., and Preiss, K. (1995). *Agile Competitors and Virtual Organizations: Strategies for Enriching the Customer*. New York: Van Nostrand Reinhold.

Grant, R. M. (1991). 'The Resource-based Theory of Competitive Advantage: Implications for Strategy Formulation', *California Management Review*, 33(1): 114–35.

Hambrick, D. (1987). 'Top Management Teams: Key to Strategic Success', *California Management Review*, 30: 88–108.

Hidding, G. (2001). 'Sustaining Strategic IT Advantage in the Information Age: How Strategy Paradigms Differ by Speed', *Journal of Strategic Information Systems*, 10: 201–22.

Hirshliefer, J. (1980). *Price Theory and Applications*. Englewood Cliffs, NJ: Prentice-Hall.

Jarvenpaa, S. L., and Leidner, D. E. (1998). 'An Information Company in Mexico: Extending the Resource-Based View of the Firm to a Developing Country Context', *Information Systems Research*, 9(4): 342–61.

Jeffers, P. I., Muhanna, W. A., and Nault, B. R. (2008). 'Interaction of IT and non-IT Resources on Process Coordination: An Exploratory Investigation', *Decision Sciences Journal*, 39(4): 703–35.

Keizer, G. (2007). 'Microsoft Gives in to Vista Search Change Demands', *Computerworld*, 20 June.

Lacity, M., Willcocks, L., and Rottman, J. (2008). 'Global Outsourcing of Back Office Services: Lessons, Trends and Enduring Challenges', *Strategic Outsourcing: An International Journal*, 1(1): 13–34.

Light, B., and Wagner, E. (2006). 'Integration in ERP environments: Rhetoric, Realities and Organisational Possibilities', *New Technology Work and Employment*, 21(3): 215–28.

Lippman, S., and Rumelt, R. (1982). 'Uncertain Imitability: An Analysis of Interfirm Differences in Efficiency under Competition', *Bell Journal of Economics*, 13: 418–38.

McAfee, A., and Brynjolfsson, E. (2008). 'Investing in the IT that Makes a Competitive Difference', *Harvard Business Review* (July–August).

McGrath, R. G., MacMillan, I. C., and Venkataraman, S. (1995). 'Defining and Developing Competence: A Strategic Process Paradigm', *Strategic Management Journal*, 16: 251–75.

Markus, M. L. (2000). 'Paradigm Shifts: E-Business and Business/Systems Integration', *Communications of the AIS*, 4(10).

Mata, F. J., Fuerst, W. L., and Barney, J. B. (1995). 'Information Technology and Sustained Competitive Advantage: A Resource-Based Analysis', *MIS Quarterly*, 19(4): 487–505.

Melville, N., Kraemer, K., and Gurbaxani, V. (2004). 'Review: Information Technology and Organizational Performance: An Integrative Model of IT Business Value', *MIS Quarterly*, 28(2).

Miller, D., and Shamsie, J. (1996). 'The Resource-Based View of the Firm in Two Environments: The Hollywood Firm Studios from 1936–1965', *Academy of Management Journal*, 39(3): 519–43.

Orlikowski, W. J., and Iacono, C. S. (2001). 'Research Commentary: Desperately Seeking the "IT" in IT Research—A Call to Theorizing the IT Artifact', *Information Systems Research*, 12(2): 121–34.

Parasuraman, A. (2000). 'Technology Readiness Index (TRI): A Multiple-Item Scale to Measure Readiness to Embrace New Technologies', *Journal of Service Research*, 2(4): 307–20.

Pemberton, J. D., Stonehouse, G. H., and Barber, C. E. (2001). 'Competing with CRS-Generated Information in the Airline Industry', *Journal of Strategic Information Systems*, 10(1): 59–75.

Peteraf, M. A. (1993). 'The Cornerstones of Competitive Advantage: A Resource-based View', *Strategic Management Journal*, 14: 179–91.

Piccoli, G., Bass, B., and Ives, B. (2003). 'Custom Made Apparel at Lands' End', *MIS Quarterly Executive*, 2(2): 74–85.

—— Feeny, D., and Ives, B. (2002). 'Creating and Sustaining IT-Enabled Competitive Advantage', in J. Luftman (ed.), *Competing in the Information Age: Strategic Alignment in Practice*. Oxford: Oxford University Press.

—— and Ives, B. (2005). 'IT-Dependent Strategic Initiatives and Sustained Competitive Advantage: A Review and Synthesis of the Literature', *MIS Quarterly*, 29(4): 747–76.

—— and Watson, R. (2008). 'Profit from Customer Data by Identifying Strategic Opportunities and Adopting the "Born Digital" Approach', *MIS Quarterly Executive*, 7(3): 113–22.

Powell, T. C., and Dent-Micalleff, A. D. (1997). 'Information Technology as Competitive Advantage: The Role of Human, Business, and Technology Resources', *Strategic Management Journal*, 18(5): 375–405.

Ranganathan, C., and Balaji, S. (2007). 'Critical Capabilities for Offshore Outsourcing of Information Systems', Working paper, Indiana University.

Ray, G., Barney, J. B., and Muhanna, W. A. (2004). 'Capabilities, Business Processes, and Competitive Advantage: Choosing the Dependent Variable in Empirical Tests of the Resource- Based View', *Strategic Management Journal*, 25(1): 23–37.

Ricardo, D. (1966). *Economic Essays*. New York: A. M. Kelly.

Rivkin, J. W. (2000). 'Imitation of Complex Strategies', *Management Science*, 46(6): 824–44.

Ross, J. W., Beath, C. M., and Goodhue, D. L., (1996). 'Develop Long-Term Competitiveness through IT Assets', *Sloan Management Review*, 38(1): 31–42.

Sambamurthy, V., Bharadwaj, A., and Grover, V. (2003). 'Shaping Agility through Digital Options: Reconceptualizing the Role of Information Technology in Contemporary Firms', *MIS Quarterly*, 27(2): 237–63.

Santhanam, R., and Hartono, E. (2003). 'Issues in Linking Information Technology Capability to Firm Performance', *MIS Quarterly*, 27(1): 125–53.

Stinchcombe, A. L. (2000). 'Social Structure and Organizations: A Comment', in J. Baum and F. Dobbins (eds.), *Economics Meets Sociology in Strategic Management: Advances in Strategic Management*. Greenwich, CT: JAI Press.

Teece, D. J., Pisano, G., and Shuen, A. (1997). 'Dynamic Capabilities and Strategic Management', *Strategic Management Journal*, 18(7): 509–33.

Volberda, H. W. (1996). 'Toward the Flexible Firm: How to Remain Vital in Hypercompetitive Environments', *Organization Science*, 7(4): 359–74.

Wade, M., and Hulland, J. (2004). 'Review: The Resource-Based View and Information Systems Research. Review, Extension and Suggestions for Future Research', *MIS Quarterly*, 28(1): 107–42.

Wagner, E., and Newell, S. (2004). '"Best" for whom? The Tension between "Best Practice" ERP Packages and Diverse Epistemic Cultures in a University Context', *Journal of Strategic Information Systems*, 13(4): 305–28.

—— Scott, S. V., and Galliers, R. D. (2006). 'The Creation of Best Practice Software: Myth, Reality and Ethics', *Information and Organization*, 16(3): 251–75.

Zaheer, A., and Zaheer, S. (1997). 'Catching the Wave: Alertness, Responsiveness, and Market Influence in Global Electronic Networks', *Management Science*, 43(11): 1493–509.

CHAPTER 15

CHANGING THE STORY SURROUNDING ENTERPRISE SYSTEMS TO IMPROVE OUR UNDERSTANDING OF WHAT MAKES ERP WORK IN ORGANIZATIONS

ERICA WAGNER AND SUE NEWELL

INTRODUCTION

ENTERPRISE Systems (ES) have been the most popular business software of the twentieth century (Robey, Ross, and Boudreau 2002). These packages are popular in organizations (Davenport 2000) because of their potential ability to streamline and integrate business operations across an organization's value chain (Shanks and Seddon 2000). ES work by integrating core business functions, including finance, logistics, and human resources, through the creation of a single system with a shared database (Lee and Lee 2000). This provides a powerful business system infrastructure for organizations. The idea is that this integration will help to leverage organizational competitiveness through improving the way in which valuable information is produced, shared, and managed across functions and locations, providing the administrative backbone for an organization (Davenport 1998). Historically in large, globally distributed organizations legacy systems were developed to meet a specific functional need but were not designed to 'talk with one another'. As such processes were redundant and data that resided in these functional systems had various formatting conventions and meaning attributed to each field. This made business and systems integration across the organization difficult. ES are implemented in an attempt to replace these legacy systems with a single tightly coupled enterprise-wide system.

ES, then, are seen as systems that support competitiveness through streamlining work flow in order to try to increase productivity, reduce costs, and improve decision quality and resource control, thereby enabling leaner production. To be effective, however, the integration of systems needs to be coupled with business integration, where business processes are streamlined across functions and departments. However, while ES hold the promise of business integration across an organization, accomplishing this promise requires changes that affect an unprecedented amount of people across the enterprise. In particular, the standardization of work practices across functional areas of the business is often difficult to achieve, with resistance from stakeholder groups being common (Aladwani 2002; Scott and Wagner 2003). Thus, many organizations that implement ES find that achieving the promise of this technologically enabled change is problematic (Scott and Vessey 2002). Indeed, today, ES are associated with high levels of project failure (Robbins-Gioia 2001). Nevertheless, while 20 per cent of IT projects are shut down prior to installation (Cooke, Gelman, and Peterson 2001), 80 per cent of implementations do at least go ahead. This suggests that our focus might usefully be turned from looking at the short-term problems and opportunities associated with an ES implementation project towards understanding how organizations learn to exploit the functionality of these potentially powerful systems over the long term.

In taking this longer-term view of ES, we will demonstrate in this chapter that it requires rethinking many of the assumptions about IT implementation and use. Our starting premiss for understanding the long-term relationship between an ES and an organization, is that we need to move away from the very simplistic notion that IT 'drives', 'forces', or even merely 'enables' change (Robey and Boudreau 1999). Instead, it is evident that we need to explore the complex relationship of reciprocal causality between IT and organization with the outcomes emergent and difficult to predict in advance (e.g. Walsham 1993; Orlikowski 2000). Moreover, we also need to explore how the institutional context (Scott 2000) influences this reciprocal relationship. In this chapter then, we will identify a number of themes that need to be rethought in relation to understanding the long-term relationship between and ES and the adopting organization. The themes include:

- Rethinking best practice—from best practice to negotiated practice
- Rethinking approaches to negotiation—from consensus to compromise
- Rethinking user participation—from pre- to post-implementation
- Rethinking implementation—from implementation/use to continuous cycles of configuration/customization/use.

We take each of these related themes in turn and examine them in this chapter. Before doing this we describe an ES case. We use this case throughout the chapter to illustrate the different issues that we deal with.

An ES Case Illustration

In the summer of 2002, Uni, an elite US university, began modernizing its administrative information systems through a two-year ES implementation. Uni was one of the first universities to select ES and chose to work with Vision Corporation in order to develop two software modules related to grants and contracts activities. That October the project structure was formed and functional teams were created with co-business and technical leaders. The composition of teams was mostly Uni middle-level managers from Central Administration whose permanent positions had been back-filled for the duration of the project. Although an experienced ES project manager had been hired, the real authority lay with the teams who communicated directly with Uni's newly appointed Vice President for Finance and Administration.

Once under way, the project team found that Vision's technical experts were not on-site as often as expected, leaving team members working with an incomplete software suite and having to imagine how the grants and contracts module would be integrated. Uni was concerned about the project's lack of progress after a year of high-level theorizing and very little technical development. They hired consultants to audit the readiness of the ES for its scheduled 'big bang' implementation in October 2004. Their findings caused Uni to modify expectations and switch to a phased implementation strategy. A revised deadline of July 2005 was set for the deployment of the integrated suite. Uni met this deadline in that the basic ES functionality was operational on the first day of the new fiscal year but the user interface and reporting environment still required significant development. The sub-optimal roll-out of the ES was complicated by user resistance to the grants and contracts design. The academic constituencies who had expectations of an improved working environment were unable to complete crucial administrative tasks. Faculty demanded changes in the ES's design as well as interim support for their administrators whose workload increased dramatically in the ES-enabled environment. For more than two years the project team was involved in post-implementation design changes before finally receiving buy-in from the academic community.

Below, two contentious episodes that nearly caused the derailment of Uni's ES project are described. These episodes have been selected because they illustrate the kinds of factions that one might typically come in contact with during large software projects where multiple stakeholder groups are involved in the implementation. The first episode adopts an internal-external perspective which is important to consider in light of the growing trend for contractual relationships between client organizations and external experts such as software vendors. Whereas the second episode concentrates on the goals of different organizational groups who share in the university mission but also have unique aims.

Uni-Vision Conflict

The Uni-Vision strategic partnership was created to benefit both parties through the development of a higher education ES suite. This product would form the basis of Uni's administrative infrastructure and would help Vision enter an untapped vertical market. Vision sought the industry expertise of Uni in order to help the software vendor modify their government/public sector ES product to meet university needs. The result would be the creation of a new product which both Uni and Vision would continue to fine-tune over time through migrations to new releases of the ES product. Through coordinated action Uni and Vision were expecting to achieve this common aim because alone neither had all the necessary skills to create a higher education enterprise solution.

However, during the first two years of the project Vision failed to become enrolled in the project to the extent that Uni expected—being largely absent from the project site. Moreover, Uni felt the level of resources provided by Vision to be inadequate and a misrepresentation of their partnership agreement, and struggled to move forward because of this. From Vision's perspective this resource allocation was understandable given that Uni represented one client within a small vertical market, which had limited growth opportunities; Vision staffed the project to reflect this. Vision approached development as a modification to their government package which they wanted to do in the most efficient manner possible so that they could see the highest return on investment given the market potential. Over time, those on the Uni team came to realize this. In contrast the project represented a major commitment for Uni in terms of time and resources and was a substantial capital investment that was expected to have long-term implications for their operation and governance.

When the original October 2004 deadline arrived Vision was still developing one of the modules and decided to completely redesign the other. Their absence, coupled with the failure to produce tangible products, led Uni team members to organize themselves more closely to one another and simultaneously reinterpret their relationship with Vision. Uni began considering alternative ways to achieve its goal given its reliance on Vision—what did Vision want and how best should Uni negotiate with them? It was clear that Vision needed discipline expertise with regards to university grants management; and Uni team members began to realize that their modernization initiative was more complex because of the partnership with Vision due to the vendor's need to create a marketable product. Uni had a well-respected grants management office that administered the external funding process for faculty. Uni was happy with the current operations of this office and their accompanying IS, however they lacked the ability to centrally manage the way in which faculty budgeted and spent their award dollars. So while Uni would have preferred to leave pre-awards out of the scope of the ES project, they realized that they were in an interdependent relationship with Vision who saw pre- and post-award activities as parts of the same process, both of which were necessary to develop as part of a higher education solution that would be sold to research institutions. Uni saw the potential to leverage their grants management expertise in order to obligate Vision for repayment to Uni sometime in the future.

As Uni began to reinterpret their partnership with Vision by seeking compromise, the VP decided to mediate divergent goals and beliefs by using his power and influence to get things done. The VP began by exerting his power over the project and hired an enterprise computing expert as Technical Director of Administrative Systems whose charge was to stop waiting for Vision and 'ramp up' the technical development. In addition to refocusing the project team through strong leadership, the VP and newly hired Director felt that it was necessary to give Vision an ultimatum. In-house technical expertise (internal 'geniuses') were mobilized to start creating an alternative solution and the threat was made that they would abandon Vision and go with the in-house solution.

The VP also made a personal visit to Vision headquarters where he indicated that there was indeed 'no free lunch' available for the vendor but rather they had an obligation to repay Uni for its commitment to developing the higher education product. While the project team 'geniuses' continued to develop an alternative solution for grant and labour functionality, Vision produced what they called 'essential' functionality in time for Uni's fiscal year 2005 and Uni chose not to drop Vision as a development partner. Their continued involvement with the vendor was directly related to their own interests for a robust product which they understood would only be achieved if they were able to influence Vision's behaviour and development trajectory by visiting the vendor and being involved in product functionality decisions, despite the costs involved.

Conflict between Academic Constituencies and Central Administration

During implementation, team members focused on professionalizing the university's administrative practices in order to ensure institutional governance and mediate financial and regulatory risk. This goal was spearheaded by the Financial Management (FM) team leader who persuaded project members of this agenda, and through coordinated action they purposely excluded legacy grants management practices (based on a commitment accounting approach) from the enterprise system design in preference for a corporate accounting approach based on time-phased budgeting interpreted as more rigorous. The FM team leader described the legacy system as 'old-fashioned' and likened it to a 'Quicken' solution (a simplistic software program for the management of personal finances). He excluded the possibility of other views in favour of quashing the old ways of working. In his mind, everyone should be on the same page—sharing common aims—or they had no place at the university. The content and tone of his message illustrates little respect for the different views across the university.

When the ES was rolled out to the Uni community it was met with resistance from academic administrators who were unable to inform their faculty members about the financial details of their grant and contract awards using the time-phased approach embedded in the ES. Faculty, in turn, became deeply unhappy about the ES because they were unable to receive the answers they needed in order to do their jobs effectively. At this time the project entered paralysis because the project team was unable to gain political support from the academic departments. It is in this moment of controversy that all parties involved realized the lack of common aims and began to consider how they might advance their particular interests.

Frustrated by this situation and cognizant of the increased stress levels of their staff, powerful faculty members reminded the VP of his official promise that the ES would improve university administrative practices for the entire community. Faculty and their administrators joined forces and used their power to secure a meeting with the Provost, VP, and project leadership where they gave an ultimatum threatening to build local systems and use the ES only as a data repository unless the legacy functionality replaced the time-phased approach. As a result of these meetings the project began to move out of paralysis. The legacy commitment accounting system remained live and new, 'bolt-on' tools were developed that customized the ES system, so that faculty needs were met. The expectation was that by appeasing faculty with regards to grants management, the ES as a whole would be more likely to succeed.

Compromising on system functionality was not something that the project team had envisioned having to do. However, the project team came to realize that if they were going to successfully move users out of shadow systems and into the integrated ES environment they were going to have to temper their hard-line approach. The team thus reprioritized their post-installation development activities and created a custo- mized piece of software that was bolted onto the ES software.

What Needs Rethinking?

We next consider some issues that we can rethink in relation to the adoption, implementation, and appropriation of packaged software that may be different to traditional IT systems that were custom-made for a particular context.

FROM BEST PRACTICE TO NEGOTIATED PRACTICE

Traditional IT systems were customized for particular contexts. However, ES are packages that supposedly embed 'best practices' (O'Leary 2000) so that the adopting organization is theoretically adopting the 'best practices' for a particular business process. However, this notion is problematic for a number of reasons. We can look at this from different theoretical perspectives including:

Institutional theory and the idea of competing institutional logics (cf. Chapter 6)—As Yoo, Lyytinen, and Brente (2007: 14) argue, ES represent 'a rationalization, encoding and abstraction of "best practices" that, while being congruent with the logics of particular areas of certain organizations can be in conflict with others'. In other words, 'best' is contextually and dynamically contingent so that what is considered to be the 'best' way of operationalizing a process in one context and at one point in time may be different in another context and time. This is because there is an institutional logic inherent in an ES that may align with what is considered best by one community of users but be at odds with what is considered best by another community. From an institutional theory perspective, the 'best' aspect of an ES is simply what is institutionally legitimated at a particular point in time—it is a fashion (Abrahamson 1996) that will be adopted because adopting a fashion legitimizes the wearer (i.e. the adopter). Moreover, an institutional theory perspective would alert us to the idea that there may be a disconnect between how the technology is supposed to operate and how it works in practice, because this theory identifies how there may be decoupling between systems that are adopted to conform to institutional pressures and the actual operating core of an organization (Meyer and Rowan 1977).

Practice theory and the idea of situated knowledge and learning —This perspective takes as a starting point the idea that knowledge is created and recreated through engagement in a practice within a particular field of relations, so there can actually be no such thing as a 'best practice'. As Cook and Brown (1999: 92) argue: 'A body of knowledge cannot be understood in and of itself, allowing it to be transferred unchanged from one context to another, without changes to its properties.' In other words, knowing and learning are constructed by relations among people (and objects) engaged in an activity. Thus, 'best' practice is always locally defined and moreover emergent and changing since practices are constantly changing so that there are always inconsistencies, even when it is supposedly the same practice. As Nicolini (2007: 894) says, 'pursuing the same thing necessarily produces something different', so that a singular best practice is a nonsense. Here we might think about ES users as performing in a play (rather than a film)—a play changes every time it is performed, because of subtle differences in terms of how the actors interact in the moment; unlike a film, which once shot can be rerun over and over again in an identical way.

Power and ability to impose definition—A power perspective views power and knowledge as indistinguishable because those with power have the ability to define what is perceived to be reality—what is valid knowledge. As a result knowledge is a product of power. Thus, an ES is simply the embodiment of the interests of those who have power. This, it can be argued, is why the ES 'best practices' emphasize efficiency and automated integration rather than, for example, empowerment and worker identity.

The problem of assuming that a 'best practice' exists and can be designed into software is illustrated in the Uni case. The project team, mostly composed of people from central administration, and the VP for Finance in particular, saw the introduction of the ES as an opportunity to move from what they saw as 'old-fashioned' and 'amateurish' practices accounting to what they considered a more corporate approach to budgeting. The initial stance of the Financial Management team was that others simply had to come around to their view of what was 'best' because they only tolerated one definition of this. However, faculty found the corporate approach did not meet their needs—it was not a 'best practice' from their perspective—and they ultimately rebelled against the design imposition, declaring that they would not use the ES unless their legacy accounting functionality was added back. In this case they were able to get the project team to go back and 'bolt on' the legacy functionality so that they could continue to manage their budgets in the way they considered 'best'.

This suggests that rather than seeing ES as embedding 'best practices' it would be better to see an ES as providing an opportunity for negotiated practice. Negotiated practice depends on first recognizing and then selectively accommodating competing views of what is 'best' by adopting a cooperative approach that includes being willing to compromise (see next section). Proactively managing this process, and identifying the critical areas where compromise is needed around what is 'best', will likely smooth out complex implementation efforts.

FROM CONSENSUS TO COMPROMISE

Organization by *common aims* or *reciprocity* (compromise) represent opposing ways in which problems are solved and goals achieved with the former being based on participants having the same goal and the latter on their wanting different things (Fuller 1978). In an organizational context it might be assumed that the best way to achieve change is through establishing common aims—all buying-in to a common vision. However, while organizations are built on common aims, it is dangerous to assume that all parties will want the same thing over time and that if different goals emerge it is just a matter of educating the dissenters so that they can 'see the truth' (Fuller 1978: 361). Moreover, the more stakeholders affected by a change initiative, the more challenging it is to create and maintain common interests due to the diffuse nature of the effort (Latour 1999) and due to differences in goals *and* beliefs about how best to approach and solve a particular problem (Pfeffer 1992). These differences are the inevitable result of specialization since this means there are groups with different backgrounds and training and so different 'thought worlds' (Dougherty 1992). The coexistence of these disparate views is particularly relevant when considering ES implementations as a major form of organizational change because the software's integrated design encourages the institutionalization of a dominant perspective (i.e. the best practice idea discussed above) across the organization while attempting to silence other ways of working (Wagner and Newell 2004). As a result ES implementations are notorious for attempting to imbue a social order that impacts power relations in a dictatorial manner—either all agree to the common vision or they keep their dissenting views to themselves.

However, given the existence of heterogeneous perspectives in an organization, Fuller (1978) argues that it is important that one is sceptical of organizing through common aims. Instead, he argues one should consider what the other party wants and how to best negotiate with them. This suggests that in situations of interdependence and divergence of goals and beliefs, it will be necessary to use power and influence to get things done (Pfeffer 1992). If power and influence are not used there will be a paralysis, reflecting 'an inability to mobilize sufficient political support and resources to take action' (Pfeffer 1992: 4). While it may be possible to move forward using hierarchical power to impose a particular decision, this will not in itself lead to successful problem solving, since as Pfeffer notes (1992: 19) 'a decision by itself changes nothing'. For example, while senior managers can dictate that particular ES functionality be implemented (e.g. the corporate budgeting method) this does not necessarily translate into ES use, since there are many ways in which users can resist using the ES, at least as it was intended (Bordreau and Robey 2005). Other means must, therefore, be found to mobilize action in these situations of interdependence and capitalizing on the norm of reciprocity is important. There is 'no free lunch' is an oft-quoted saying that defines the norm of reciprocity which implies that we are obligated to future repayments of favours, gifts, invitations, etc. received from others (Gouldner 1960). This is different from a straightforward exchange, based on a market transaction, since the returned favour is not explicitly specified. Rather, the favour implies a diffuse, generalized obligation for repayment sometime in the future. This norm facilitates transactions between individuals and groups over time and is extremely important in facilitating organizational change (Pfeffer 1992). In a decision-making situation it suggests that while each party must stand up for their goals and needs, they must at the same time be aware of the needs and goals of others because at some time in the future, each might want what the other party can give. Central to this form of working, then, is that each party involved has an understanding of what makes the other tick—what are their motivations and goals.

The focus on organizing by common aims was evident in the initial phase of the Uni case, where the common aim among the internal stakeholders was improved administrative efficiency and the common aim for the Uni-Vision partnership was the development of an ES system to modernize the administrative practices of higher education institutions. None of the parties possessed the skills to create these goals alone. However, by joining forces the entities expected to be able to create the desired solution by participating in organization by common aims. While the impetus for creating such relationships, either internally or externally is, therefore, common aims, over time the extent to which consensus is truly felt in more than name alone—where it informs the actions of those involved—will ebb and flow. Thus, during controversial episodes, the common aim among those involved did not prevent problems arising because of conflicting interests that threatened to derail the project; there was a real danger that the Uni-Vision partnership would be disbanded and that a system would be produced that faculty departments would not use. The only way to avoid these negative outcomes was for the parties to begin to negotiate on the basis of reciprocity rather than common aims.

For example, underneath the common aim of changing administrative practice the Financial Management leader developed a narrative around 'professionalizing practice' and was able to enrol the project team around this storyline. However, this meant that they designed the grant accounting functionality based on corporate budgeting techniques that were directly at odds with legacy faculty accounting methods. It was only during the post-implementation 'use phase' of the project that faculty interests surfaced through narratives of betrayal and demands for design modifications. While initially this opposing narrative was dismissed as 'amateurish', eventually it was recognized that ignoring the demands embedded in this narrative would not help in creating the working ES that all were seeking. The result was that the team worked with faculty to develop a hybrid ES involving post-installation customization. This hybrid was negotiated once the decision makers involved recognized reciprocal interests, and stopped trying to impose a common aim (the FM's vision). Similarly, the tension between Uni and Vision was resolved when both parties began to 'give a little', recognizing and accepting as legitimate the narratives of the other that were initially seen as unacceptable. For example, Uni came to realize that the market for a university-focused ES was actually very small for Vision, helping Uni to understand why Vision did not want to put too much effort into developing specialized functionality for this market. Realizing this, they then agreed to help Vision develop some functionality around grant applications that Uni itself did not need because they had their own more-than-adequate system in place, but which they recognized that Vision would need if they were going to sell the ES as a university-focused system. This led Vision to compromise on the timeline and put in the resources that were needed to meet the deadline that Uni was working towards.

While it is possible in such situations for one party to impose its design requirements as the 'common aim' through the use of hierarchical power, this approach is likely to be limited (Pfeffer 1981). For example, as the client in the relationship, Uni could have withdrawn from the partnership agreement with Vision. However, this would not have helped them to develop the integrated system that they sought. Similarly, the team could have insisted on sticking to the corporate budgeting approach, ignoring faculty demands for legacy accounting functionality. However, the likelihood of creating a stable post-implementation environment where employees actually used the software as intended was small (Boudreau and Robey 2005), especially given the setting where the use of absolute power is antithetical to the fiefdom-like structure of universities (Pollock 1999; Cornford 2000; Allen and Kern 2001). In such contexts, attempting to impose a software system on different users, without a consideration of their interests and demands, is likely to, at best, create a system that will be only partially used and, at worst, lead to complete system failure. Instead, what is important is to 'give a little' so that the demands of users are met, even though decision makers may believe that these demands are based on 'old thinking'. One way of enabling this compromise is to bring forward some of the valued legacy practices to ensure buy-in to the change. This may not be 'rational' from the perspective of the project team, in the sense that the underpinning legacy thinking may be unnecessary in the changed organizational context, but it is necessary to ensure the commitment and motivation of those who need to be enticed to use the system. Such 'irrationality', argues Brunnson (1985), is often the key to effective decision implementation in organizations.

In other words, achieving a working information system does not mean that consensus must be sought or achieved in all instances as is articulated in the principle of common aims. Rather, the important thing appears to be coordinating action that will allow goals to be achieved, even if this involves compromise along the way. Such compromise depends on reciprocity to produce social order and doesn't expect a shared aim as long as a solution can be negotiated. Moreover, this compromise is likely to occur in the post-implementation use phase, having implications therefore for the issue of user participation.

FROM PRE-IMPLEMENTATION TO POST-IMPLEMENTATION PARTICIPATION

User acceptance is seen to be the number one critical success factor for software projects, and user participation can help to achieve this (Mumford and Weir 1979; Mumford 1983, 1995, 2000; Davis and Olsen 1985). Moreover, user participation continues to be seen as critical in relation to ES implementation success (Holland and Light 1999; Parr, Shanks, and Darke 1999; Markus et al. 2000; Rosario 2000; Sumner 2000; Nah et al. 2001; Nah, Lau, and Kuang 2003). Participation has been described as 'institutionalized practice' (Howcroft and Wilson 2003) so ubiquitous is its emphasis within the IS literature, dating back to the early work of the Tavistock Institute in the UK. Mumford (1983), for example, assumed that it is important to create IS that take account of people's social as well as technical needs and that user participation is necessary to achieve this. However, we need to consider how this can be realized in the context of packaged software when users cannot actually be involved in software *design*, precisely because the design is relatively fixed by the package. Thus, historically early user participation was considered necessary in order to specify the system requirements; after all the system was being specifically designed for a particular group of users. However, today's off-the-shelf packages come embedded with 'best practices' which organizations are encouraged to adopt by vendors and consultants rather than change the package to follow users' existing practices. This raises questions about the importance and usefulness of user participation in the early stages of an ES project given that the system design is pre-specified and non-negotiable, at least if the adopting organization wants to follow vendor advice and implement the 'vanilla' system.

Based on such analysis, Wagner and Newell (2007) identified a series of limits to user participation during the initial configuration/customization phase including:

Legacy thinking. Users find it difficult during the early stages of requirements definition to see beyond their current practices and anticipate how things could be done differently if they had new tools to enable more integration within and across functions. This is because much work practice is rooted in everyday interactions (Suchman 1987) so that trying to appreciate a new way of working by just looking at the technical system is difficult. Add this to the users' limited technical knowledge (Beath and Orlikowski 1994) and it becomes understandable why, when users are involved in the configuration/customization phase, their main concern is that the new system will enable them to do what they did before—with 'as little change as possible'. Arguably, given such 'legacy thinking', user involvement during the design stage can actually restrict the potential for the new system to be used in transforming ways. This problem is not traditionally experienced in software development because bespoke software is being developed specifically to support organizational processes (even if these have been previously reengineered). This highlights a key difference between the traditional and packaged IS development lifecycle and the implications for user participation.

'Vanilla' implementation. Since the option to purchase software was first recognized in the literature so too was the question raised as to whether one should implement an unmodified ('vanilla') package, or enhance and customize the purchased package (Rands 1992). While the new generation ES packages do allow configuration options, the general advice from software companies and consultants is to avoid, as far as possible, customizations to the package (changes to the actual software code), and so go for a vanilla implementation. Given this context, does it not beg the question of the point of user involvement if users are not listened to because of the desire for a 'vanilla' implementation? Instead it may actually create frustration and resentment, thus eliminating one of the primary goals of participation: to reduce user resistance (Wong and Tate 1994). In the instances where 'vanilla' implementation is a project goal, user participation beyond the consultative level (informing users of what is happening rather than actively involving them in the process—Avison and Fitzgerald 1995) during the configuration/customization phase might in some circumstances be counter-productive. Of course, such a problem would not surface during traditional IS development.

Motivation. A final problem during the pre-implementation phase is actually getting users interested in participation throughout the initiative. Lack of engagement is a reflection of human nature, as depicted by the situated learning school, where we only become interested in something when it is salient to us and when we can actually begin to learn about the technology through practice and participation (Wenger 1998). Even genuine attempts involving users will fall short because of more pressing matters that are in front of them at the time (Wagner and Piccoli 2007). Users who are busy at work will have their attention captured by immediate responsibilities and the ES will remain low in salience, failing to fully engage their attention. In addition, a temporal element needs to be considered, involving the examination of how closely the content provided impacts on daily life. According to elaboration likelihood (Petty and Cacioppo 1986), individuals have to be both motivated and able to process information in order for it to become salient and move them into action. Thus, when an ES completion is imminent and the reality of new work practices becomes apparent, users begin to evaluate the new system more closely and significant issues are raised, often leading to user resistance and the need for post-implementation modifications. In the Uni case this problem was very evident—users may have shown up at meetings where the developing ES was described, but it was not until actual implementation that users actually started to raise questions about the functionality. This was a surprise to the project team leader who had, up until this point, assumed that all stakeholders were happy with the ES that was being developed.

Given these difficulties of user participation in the initial configuration/customization phase organizations should consider how users may be encouraged to participate in the post-implementation environment. If we take the notions of salience during situated learning as our point of departure with regards to the engagement of human resources during ES projects, then the framework for effective user participation changes. Modifications occur in the post-implementation period, when users finally become engaged in making the software work for them—in the context of their everyday situated learning from practice.

This leads us to question high levels of continuous user participation throughout the duration of the initiative, especially when consensus is so difficult to achieve given the political nature of organizations (Howcroft and Wilson 2003). Furthermore, the 'whole house' scope of ES implementations means that consensus participation (Mumford 1983) would require an unwieldy amount of user participation during pre-implementation (reflected in the discussion above about the importance of compromise rather than assuming common aims can be identified and maintained). Given the integrated nature of an ES, involving users from all the different areas is likely to lead to a situation where agreement is difficult, if not impossible, to achieve. Different groups will want different things included/excluded and if consensus is sought this is likely to lead to a stalemate (Wagner and Newell 2006) or to the development of a configuration that is initially seen to be 'perfect' and yet 'falls apart' in use. The issue here is that users (and designers) are attempting to create an ES that suits current demands, but ignore the fact that demands change rapidly today and/or that once a system is 'in use', users will in any case adapt/modify and develop 'work arounds' so that, through a process of situated learning, any system will change from its intended use pattern (Suchman 1987; Orlikowski 1996). Therefore, it may be more advantageous both in terms of resource time and eventual buy-in to find out how the basic system is used before deciding what customizations are going to add real value, beyond those that are initially agreed to be essential to accommodate unique organizational nomenclature.

This indicates that it may be sensible to treat the 'vanilla' system as a prototype—'simple and relatively quick to create, amend and rebuild' (Dearnley and Mayhew 1983: 41). From this perspective, the prototype is a system 'in use' (Avison and Fitzgerald

1995) that will continue to evolve as the organization does. This is in keeping with the idea of growth and emergence as opposed to design (Truex, Baskerville, and Klein 1999) where user acceptance will never be complete because organizations are constantly changing. As such, ES development needs to be seen as a continuous process of evolution with no final design being possible or warranted. User participation from this perspective may not be constrained to the pre-implementation phase but may also be considered in the context of use, both in terms of informal learning and improvisation (Orlikowski 1996) but also in terms of formal processes of continuous and iterative ES development.

FROM IMPLEMENTATION/USE TO CYCLES OF IMPLEMENTATION/USE

The above discussion suggests that an ES implementation is best not viewed as a one-time process but rather as a series of cycles of implementation/use with reflection and learning occurring during each cycle so that gradually the ES becomes more embedded and adapted to the particular context of use. In relation to an ES the implementation phase of the cycle involves making decisions about what to configure and what to customize. During the cycles of configuration/customization and use the reality of the new system certainly becomes salient and users will inevitably become more interested as they begin to learn from their situated practice. During these iterations users will really look at what the new system offers and be concerned about whether it makes their job easier or more difficult. Where the new system is seen to make their job difficult, there will be significant user resistance, as in Uni with time-phased budgeting. Two issues stand out if we see ES adoption as cycles of configuration/customization and use—selective engagement and resources allocation.

Selective Engagement

In the post-implementation environment it is much easier to engage users effectively. This does not necessarily imply that users should not be engaged in consultative participation during the initial configuration/customization phase of the implementation since this is in any case likely to be both politically important and necessary for the intelligence function of the project team (Kawalek and Wood-Harper 2002). What it does mean is that there are limits to user participation in the early stages of an ES implementation, as discussed above, while once they have to actually use the system and begin to learn about its advantages and limitations from their situated practice they are much more likely to want and be able to have their voices heard. At first consideration, thinking about involving users after installation of the software seems unrealistic and expensive but we can introduce the notion of selective engagement as an additional form of participation that would augment the existing levels of participation (Dearnley and Mayhew 1983; Mumford 1983; Avison and Fitzgerald 1995). Engaging users selectively in the post-implementation use phase is likely to be particularly important and productive in terms of creating a viable, working ES.

Others have shown that analysts don't do a good job of hearing users during requirements definition (Alvarez and Urla 2002). This is in part due to the storytelling approach users adopt when talking about their requirements where they share stories about their current activities and point out limitations, challenges, and highlights of their business practices. This is a reflection of the situated embeddedness of everyday work practices (Lave and Wenger 1991; Wenger 1998). However, analysts discount this information as superfluous and become frustrated when users cannot list their requirements in a more linear, rule-based manner. Analysts fail to recognize the extent to which rules of action do not proscribe practice, since each episode of action is unique and in some way dependent on the meaning that actors determine, rather than on predefined causal connections (Garfinkel 1986).

Despite the wisdom of conceptual modelling such as Soft Systems Methodology (Checkland 1981)—see Chapter 4—as an aid in information requirements determination (cf. Galliers 1987) many analysts still discount these 'stories' during pre-implementation. It is easier to 'hear' the users when there are tangible products/processes/functions to refer back to and users are working in the new environment. If users have migrated to the ES environment, they will likely tell stories about their experiences in that environment and highlight what they feel is lacking both in terms of what they used to have and of new functionality that might be incomplete. This is not to argue that requirements definition should be avoided during the initial configuration/customization phase. Indeed, this is necessary, both in terms of facilitating users to move away from 'legacy thinking' and the political necessities associated with system 'ownership'. Rather, this is to say that sticking more closely to the vanilla implementation may be preferable—as long as key actors are willing to engage selectively in the post-implementation engagement. Doing so will highlight that which is non-negotiable from the users' perspective and that which is not.

Determining non-negotiable requests is much easier in the post-implementation environment when users will highlight that which is most likely to lead to a rejection of the system. The power of an implemented system is not to be underestimated in terms of persuading users to make it work.

Resource Allocation

If we see implementation as a series of cycles of configuration/customization and use then it becomes important to ensure that resources are allocated to these cycles, rather than front-loading resources to the first cycle only. In addition, budgeting for post-implementation work efforts can aid in resource-intensive activities like data cleaning.

Of course, prior to 'go-live', it is important to try and clean up the data from legacy systems in order, for example, to avoid duplication of records. However, it is likely to be impossible or at least extremely time consuming to get the data completely 'clean'. As users actually use the system, they will be more focused and able, iteratively, to pick it up and rectify any problems with the data in order to gradually improve the database that everyone is working with.

CONCLUSIONS

In this chapter we have highlighted the problem of identifying 'best practice'. Instead we have advocated seeing the introduction of an ES as cycles of learning where practices are negotiated through time. This is because trying to figure out what is 'best' from the packaged software and 'best' from existing practice is going to be an iterative process that is unlikely to be easily worked through in advance of actual implementation and use. This is because users themselves need to participate in this decision process and for a number of reasons—legacy thinking, lack of engagement and motivation—this participation is going to be limited prior to actual implementation and situated learning through use. We therefore advocate seeing an ES in terms of an iterative experience life cycle where phases of configuration/customization and implementation/use will alternate cyclically, gradually helping to exploit the functionality of the software. Getting users to buy in to the final product and empowering them to take an active role in their work lives are goals of participation efforts (Mumford 1983). Post-implementation engagement is an effective way of garnering user interest and assistance, at least in respect of an ES. Given this iterative cycle of ES exploitation in the post-implementation period, finding ways to speed up and more effectively facilitate this iteration through user participation would seem to be a significant opportunity for organizations. The problem is that if the importance of this post-implementation user participation is not legitimized it is likely to be less effective and exploitation will be slower (just as post-build additions to one's house often get postponed) although adaptations will eventually happen (just as post-build tinkering with one's house happen). This post-implementation is particularly problematic in an ES implementation because members of the core project team who could usefully facilitate user participation during this period may not be available. This may be for a number of reasons—because the team has been disbanded, or because team members have left to take advantage of their ES implementation experience, or simply because, given the long duration of many ES projects, the project team is 'burnt out'.

In the earlier cycles, attempting to get users to appreciate and use all the potential functionality of the new system appears to be a mistaken or unrealistic target. A more realistic goal appears to be providing users with a system that makes their jobs not significantly more difficult and at the same time provides them with the prospect that they will be able to do even more in the future. This incremental or piecemeal approach to ES implementation (Robey, Ross, and Boudreau 2002) has been criticized because, in the post-implementation environment, resources are not typically provided to source the effort that is required to continue the development process. However, we argue that this is a matter of planning for resources to be available in the post-implementation environment, rather than a fundamental problem with the piecemeal approach. Indeed, we would argue, based on our research, that such an approach is likely to be more realistic and more successful, provided that these resources can be made available.

So what are the practical implications of our rethinking analysis? First, it suggests that it is important for managers to recognize ES as a long-term learning process where benefits will be emergent as users learn to appropriate the ES as part of their ongoing daily work practices in ways that help them to do their jobs better. This learning process is dependent on those involved recognizing that there is not one 'best' way to do something and that others will have alternative views of what is best. Negotiating practice through time as part of a learning orientation can help organizations exploit an ES for their unique benefit, rather than be straitjacketed into an ES. We might call this a 'sand-box' approach to ES implementation, since it recognizes the potential of learning from 'playing' with the system rather than training users to press certain buttons in a rote learning fashion that will severely restrict the ability to appropriate benefit over time.

Another implication is that, while IT-enabled organizational change involving partnerships and projects affecting multiple internal stakeholders, in their inception, are built on common aims, there will nevertheless be numerous controversial moments that are faced, when opposing voices emerge which indicate divergent opinions about how to achieve the common aims, or even different aims. How these controversies are dealt with is likely to be critical in relation to whether a working system is produced. In this respect our analysis indicates that it is important for managers to be aware of the emergence of opposing voices and not to dismiss or ignore them, however irrational they may appear from their particular perspective. In Uni, for example, the project implementation team was able to initially marginalize the dissenting voices about the problems of time-phased budgeting and design a system which ignored the concerns being expressed. However, in this case the dissension came from a powerful group in the organization and it became clear that it was not going to be possible to ignore them, at least if they wanted the ES to be fully used. Faculty in a university setting may be different in this respect from employees in other kinds of organization. Indeed, the departmental administrators had been unable to make their voices heard when they were expressing similar concerns and it was only the involvement of the faculty that finally led to functionality being added as a customization. In other organizational contexts, it may be easier to continue to ignore or dismiss the dissenting voices. This is likely to lead to a situation where the ES is implemented but remains under- or unused, explaining perhaps why many ES implementations do not meet expectations and often involve substantial employee workarounds.

A final implication of our rethinking of ES implementations is that in some organizations, as in Uni, select customizations will be necessary if the ES is to be made to work because these valued legacy practices cannot be met through configuration alone. This goes against all the advice about avoiding customization to ensure the benefits of upgrades, etc. (Alshawi, Themistocleous, and Almadani 2004). However, our findings indicate that customization to a system is sometimes necessary to achieving a working IS. In fact, if done strategically customization can ease tensions, and sustain employees' commitment and motivation through the complex transitional phases that are part of any organizational change initiative.

ACKNOWLEDGEMENTS

Ideas presented in this chapter have been previously published in the following publications: Wagner, E., and Newell, S. (2004). '"Best" for Whom? The Tension between Best Practice ERP Packages and the Epistemic Cultures of an Ivy League University', *Journal of Strategic Information Systems*, 13(4): 91–6.

———— (2006). 'Repairing ERP: Producing Social Order to Create a Working Information System', *Journal of Applied Behavioral Science*, 42(1): 40–57.

———— (2007). 'Exploring the Importance of Participation in the Post-implementation Period of an Enterprise System Project: A Neglected Area', *Journal of the Association for Information Systems*, 8(10): article 32.

REFERENCES

Abrahamson, E. (1996). 'Management Fashion', *Academy of Management Review*, 21: 254–85.

Aladwani, A. (2002). 'IT Project Uncertainty, Planning and Success: An Empirical Investigation from Kuwait', *Information Technology and People,* 15: 210–26.

Allen, D. K., and Kern, T. (2001). 'Enterprise Resource Planning Implementation: Stories of Power, Politics and Resistance', in N. L. Russo, B. Fitzgerald, and J. I. Degross (eds.), *Realigning Research and Practice in Information Systems Development: The Social and Organizational Perspective.* Boston, MA: Kluwer, 149–54.

Alshawi, S., Themistocleous, M., and Almadani, R. (2004). 'Integrating Diverse ERP Systems: A Case Study', *Journal of Enterprise Information Management*, 17(6): 454–62.

Alvarez, R., and Urla, J. (2002). 'Tell me a Good Story: Using Narrative Analysis to Examine Information Requirements Interviews during an ERP Implementation', *SIGMIS Database*, 33(1): 38–52.

Avison, D., and Fitzgerald, G. (1995). *Information Systems Development: Methodologies, Techniques and Tools.* 2nd edn., London: McGraw-Hill.

Beath, C., and Orlikowski, W. (1994). 'The Contradictory Structure of Systems Development Methodologies: Deconstructing the IS-User Relationships in Information Engineering', *Information Systems Research*, 5(4): 350–77.

Boudreau, M.-C., and Robey, D. (2005). 'Enacting Integrated Information Technology: A Human Agency Perspective', *Organization Science*, 16: 3–19.

Brunsson, N. (1985). *The Irrational Organization: Irrationality as the Basis for Organizational Action and Change*. New York: John Wiley.

Checkland, P. B. (1981). *Systems Thinking, Systems Practice*. Chichester: Wiley.

Cook, S. D. N., and Brown, J. S. (1999). 'Bridging Epistemologies: The Generative Dance between Organizational Knowledge and Organizational Knowing', *Organization Science*, 10: 381–400.

Cooke, D., Gelman, L., and Peterson, W. J. (2001). *ERP Trends* (Report No. R-1292-01-RR). New York: The Conference Board.

Cornford, J. (2000). 'The Virtual University is . . . the University Made Concrete?', *Information, Communication and Society*, 3: 508–25.

Davenport, T. (1998). 'Putting the Enterprise into the Enterprise System', *Harvard Business Review*, 76(4): 121–31.

—— (2000). *Mission Critical: Realizing the Promise of Enterprise Systems*. Boston, MA: Harvard Business School Press.

Davis, G., and Olsen, M. (1985). *Management Information Systems*. New York: McGraw-Hill.

Dearnley, P. A., and Mayhew, P. J. (1983). 'In Favor of System Prototypes and their Integration into the System Development Life Cycle', *Computer Journal*, 26(1).

Dougherty, D. (1992). 'Interpretive Barriers to Successful Product Innovation in Large Firms', *Organization Science*, 3: 179–202.

Fuller, L. L. (1978). 'The Forms and Limits of Adjudication', *Harvard Law Review*, 92: 394–404.

Galliers, R. D. (1987). *Information Analysis: Selected Readings*. Wokingham: Addison-Wesley.

Garfinkel, H. (ed.) (1986). *Ethnomethodological Studies of Work*. London: Routledge & Kegan Paul.

Gouldner, A. (1960). 'The Norm of Reciprocity: A Preliminary Statement', *American Sociological Review*, 25: 161–78.

Holland, C., and Light, B. (1999). 'A Critical Success Factors Model for ERP Implementation', *IEEE Software*, 16(3): 30–6.

Howcroft, D., and Wilson, M. (2003). 'Participation: "Bounded Freedom" or Hidden Constraints on User Involvement', *New Technology, Work and Employment*, 18(1): 2–19.

Kawalek, P., and Wood-Harper, A. T. (2002). 'The Finding of Thorns: User Participation in Enterprise System Implementation', *ACM SIGMIS DataBase*, 33(1): 13–22.

Latour, B. (1999). 'On Recalling ANT', in J. Law and J. Hassard (eds.), *Actor Network Theory and After*. Oxford: Blackwell Publishers, 15–25.

Lave, J., and Wenger, E. (1991). *Situated Learning: Legitimate Peripheral Participation*. Cambridge: Cambridge University Press.

Lee, Z., and Lee, J. (2000). 'An ERP Implementation Case Study from a Knowledge Transfer Perspective', *Journal of Information Technology*, 15: 281–8.

Markus, M. L., Axline, S., Petrie, D., and Tanis, C. (2000). 'Learning from Adopters' Experiences with ERP: Problems Encountered and Success Achieved', *Journal of Information Technology*, 15: 245–65.

Meyer, J., and Rowan, B. (1977). 'Institutionalized Organizations: Formal Structure as Myth and Ceremony', *American Journal of Sociology*, 83: 340–63.

Mumford, E. (1983). 'Participative Systems Design: Practice and Theory', *Journal of Occupational Psychology*, 4(1): 47–57.

—— (1995). *Effective Systems Design and Requirements Analysis*. Basingstoke: MacMillan.

——(2000). 'Socio-technical Design: An Unfulfilled Promise or a Future Opportunity? ', in R. Baskerville, J. Stage, and J. DeGross (eds.), *Organizational and Social Perspectives on Information Technology*. London: Kluwer, 33–46.

——and Weir, D. (1979). *Computer Systems in Work Design: The ETHICS Method*. New York: Wiley.

Nah, F. F., Lau J. L., and Kuang, J. (2001). 'Critical Factors for Successful Implementation of Enterprise Systems', *Business Process Management*, 7(3): 285–96.

——Zuckweller, K., and Lau, J. (2003). 'ES Implementation: Chief Information Officers' Perceptions of Critical Success Factors', *International Journal of Human-Computer Interactions*, 16(1): 5–22.

Newell, S., Huang, J., and Tansley, C. (2004). 'Social Capital and Knowledge Integration in an ES Project Team: The Importance of Bridging and Bonding', *British Journal of Management*, 15: 43–57.

——Cooprider, J., David, G., Edelman, L., and Logan, T. (2005). 'Analyzing Different Strategies to Enterprise System Adoption: Reengineering-Led versus Quick Deployment', *International Journal of Enterprise Information Systems*, 1(2): 1–16.

Nicolini, D. (2007). 'Stretching out and Expanding Medical Practices: The Case of Telemedicine', *Human Relations*, 60(6): 889–920.

O'Leary, D. E. (2000). *Enterprise Resource Planning Systems: Systems, Life Cycle, Electronic Commerce, and Risk*. Cambridge: Cambridge University Press.

Orlikowski, W. (1996). 'Improvising Organizational Transformation over Time: A Situated Change Perspective', *Information Systems Research*, 7(1): 63–92.

——(2000). 'Using Technology and Constituting Structures: A Practice Lens for Studying Technology in Organizations', *Organization Science*, 11: 404–28.

Parr, A., Shanks, G., and Darke, P. (1999). 'Identification of Necessary Factors for Successful Implementation of ERP Systems', in O. Ngwenyama, L. Introna, M. Myers, and J. DeCross (eds.), *New Information Technologies in Organizational Process*. Boston, MA: Kluwer Academic Publishers, 99–119.

Petty, R. E., and Cacioppo, J. T. (1986). *Communication and Persuasion: Central and Peripheral Routes to Attitude Change*. New York: Springer-Verlag.

Pfeffer, J. (1981). *Power in Organizations*. Marshfield, MA: Pitman.

——(1992). *Managing with Power: Politics and Influence in Organizations*. Cambridge, MA: Harvard Business School Press.

Pollock, N. (1999). ' "The Virtual University" as "Accurate and Timely Information" ', *Information, Communication and Society*, 3: 1–17.

Rands, T. (1992). 'The Key Role of Applications Software Make-or-Buy Decisions', *Journal of Strategic Information Systems*, 1(4): 215–23.

Robbins-Gioia (2001). The Robbins-Gioia Survey at <http://www.robbinsgioia.com/>.

Robey, D., and Boudreau, M. (1999). 'Accounting for the Contradictory Organizational Consequences of Information Technology', *Information Systems Research*, 10: 167–85.

——Ross, J. W., and Boudreau, M. C. (2002). 'Learning to Implement Enterprise Systems: An Exploratory Study of the Dialectics of Change', *Journal of Management Information Systems*, 19: 17–46.

Rosario, J. (2000). 'On the Leading Edge: Critical Success Factors in ERP Implementation Projects', *Business World*.

Scott, J., and Vessey, I. (2002). 'Managing Risks in Enterprise Systems Implementations', *Communications of the ACM*, 45(4): 74–81.

Scott, S. V., and Wagner, E. L. (2003). 'Networks, Negotiations, and New Times: The Implementation of Enterprise Resource Planning into an Academic Administration', *Information and Organization*, 13(4): 285–313.

Scott, W. R. (2000). *Institutions and Organizations*. London: Sage.

Shanks, G., and Seddon, P. (2000). Editorial. *Journal of Information Technology*, 15: 243–4.

Suchman, L. (1987). *Plans and Situated Actions: The Problem of Human/Machine Communication*. Cambridge: Cambridge University Press.

Sumner, M. (2000). 'Risk Factors in Enterprise-wide/ERP Projects', *Journal of Information Technology*, 15: 317–27.

Truex, D., Baskerville, R., and Klein, H. (1999). 'Growing Systems in Emergent Organizations', *Communications of the ACM*, 42(8): 117–23.

Wagner, E., and Newell, S. (2004). ' "Best" for Whom? The Tension between Best Practice ERP Packages and the Epistemic Cultures of an Ivy League University', *Journal of Strategic Information Systems*, 13(4): 305–28.

————(2006). 'Repairing ERP: Producing Social Order to Create a Working Information System', *Journal of Applied Behavioral Science*, 42(1): 40–57.

————(2007). 'Exploring the Importance of Participation in the Post-implementation Period of an ES Project: A Neglected Area', *Journal of the AIS*, 8(10): article 32.

——and Piccoli, G. (2007). 'A Call to Engagement: Moving beyond User Participation in Order to Achieve Successful Information Systems Design', *Communications of the ACM*, 50(12): 51–5.

Walsham, G. (1993). *Interpreting Information Systems in Organizations*. London: John Wiley & Sons.

Wenger, E. (1998). *Communities of Practice: Learning, Meaning and Identity*. Cambridge: Cambridge University Press.

Wong, E., and Tate, G. (1994). 'A Study of User Participation in Information Systems Development', *Journal of Information Technology*, 9: 51–60.

Yoo, Y., Lyytinen, K., and Brente, N. (2007). 'An Institutional Analysis of Pluralistic Responses to Enterprise Systems Implementations', *ICIS Proceedings*. Montreal, Canada.

CHAPTER 16

A MULTI-THEORETIC APPROACH TO IT GOVERNANCE: THE NEED FOR COMMITMENT AS WELL AS ALIGNMENT

SUE NEWELL AND CYNTHIA CLARK WILLIAMS

INTRODUCTION

IT investment accounts for a significant proportion of the operational budget and capital investment made by many organizations. For example, Computer Economics, which conducts annual surveys of IT spending, staffing, and technology trends, shows that while IT spending reduces in response to a slowdown in the economy, growth of IT operational budgets was still at 4 per cent in 2008, even when GDP was only growing at about 1 per cent (Computer Economics 2008/9). The same survey showed that organizations spent on average 1.5 per cent of revenue on IT in 2008, with median IT spending per user averaging $6,667. These figures demonstrate the importance of IT to contemporary business.

Since the importance of IT is not a hotly debated issue today, some have argued that IT is no longer of strategic significance for organizations (Carr 2003). From this perspective, IT is like water or electricity—it is essential to the running of a business but does not differentiate between businesses. It is just a commodity. However, given that studies also show that many IT projects are over budget and/or delivered late and more importantly perhaps fail to deliver on the expected business benefits, then exploiting the potential from one's IT investment would seem to be of major strategic significance for an organization. For example, the Standish Group, an organization that has studied the effectiveness of software projects since 1994, recently reported some improvement over the last fifteen years. In 1994, it reported that 16.2 per cent of software projects could be classified as successful in the sense of being on time, on budget, and meeting user requirements. By 2006, the group reported that 35 per cent of projects could be so classified (Standish Group 2006), still leaving 65 per cent of IT projects classified as not wholly successful.

In addition to these IT project problems, there are also many examples of problems associated with the mishandling of data that have been accumulated on an organization's IT system, once operational (see website <http://www.privacyrights.org/ar/ChronDataBreaches.htm#CP> for a catalogue of data breaches). Some companies are careless in the extreme over the precautions they take in relation to personal data (Solove 2008), an issue of poor governance. As an example of a data breach, HM Revenues and Customs in the UK caused an unnecessary data interface when they sent, by courier, two CDs full of personal information (i.e. name, address, national insurance number, bank details) to the National Audit Office. Unfortunately, the CDs were intercepted, compromising the privacy and identity of 25 million Britons. As another example, TJX Companies, owner of retailer T.J. Maxx in the USA, maintained credit card information on unsecured wireless networks that were tapped into with the loss of a significant amount of customer data. These data breaches continue to happen despite the requirement of the US Sarbanes–Oxley Act of 2002 that companies put in place systems to protect data, through reducing the numbers of interfaces through which data must pass, thus reducing the opportunity for human error in the flow of data (Maurizio, Girolami, and Jones 2007). Under this law, public companies must also attest, annually, to the veracity of their internal controls over the privacy protections of this data and whether they have any material weaknesses in their systems frameworks (<http://www.sec.gov>). These examples of regular IT project and data-mishandling problems suggest that while IT may be generally important to most contemporary businesses, how it is exploited to support the business strategy (or not) will determine what value it has for an organization. In this sense, IT is very different to water or electricity—although current environmental concerns suggest that the use of water and electricity may itself become strategically important to environmental and social governance metrics.

Much research in IS has looked at what contributes to the poor performance of many IT projects and/or improper use of data produced by IT systems. This research has shown that organizational factors such as the available IT capabilities, support of top management, alignment between IT and business strategy, change management capabilities, and resources are crucial to ensuring healthy performance of IT (Holland and Light 1999; Holland, Light, and Gibson 1999; Markus, Tanis, and Fenema 2000; Markus et al. 2000; Parr and Shanks 2000; Sousa and Collado 2000; Sumner 2000; Nah, Lau, and Kuang 2001; Nah, Zuckweller, and Lau 2003; Bajwa, Garcia, and Mooney 2004). While research looking at the individual organizational factors that support IT implementation and use is important, we can also take a step back from this level of analysis and look at the ways decisions get made about IT in different organizations. Focusing on how decisions about IT—both current and future—are made, who makes these decisions and what rules and norms guide decisions is a fundamental first step as this will likely influence whether the necessary organizational structures are put in place to support the strategic adoption and use of IT. In looking at the allocation of IT 'decision rights' (how decisions are made and by whom), we are examining IT governance (Sambamurthy and Zmud 1999). In this chapter, we are also interested in broadening the notion of IT governance to look at the overall rights and responsibilities associated with the use, storage, retrieval, and collection of data.

In examining IT governance we draw upon the more general corporate governance literature as well as the specific IT governance literature. Corporate governance is concerned with ensuring that there is correspondence between the interests of managers, as decision makers, and the interests of shareholders, as owners (cf. Eisenhardt 1989). In other words, the focus is on how to ensure that managers make decisions that maximize the interests of shareholders, rather than merely their own self-interests. In this chapter, we combine aspects of the stakeholder and stockholder views of the firm, and consider governance to be about ensuring that IT decisions are made in the interests of the long-term sustainability of the organization. In this sense, governance relates to how to ensure ethical decision making and improved corporate social responsibility so that decisions are made which focus on the sustainability of a company. Sustainability is defined as meeting the needs of the present without compromising the ability of future generations to meet their own needs (Brundtland 1987). Sustainability, it is argued, is dependent on expanding the criteria used for measuring organizational success. A popular approach was articulated by John Elkington (1994) who coined the term 'triple-bottom line' to indicate that organizations should be measured according to three criteria—financial, social, and environmental performance (or profit, people, and planet)—rather than merely financial. In this chapter we discuss IT governance in relation to its ability to ensure such sustainability through balancing the need to make a profit with respect for the rights of people and the planet.[1] In other words, we focus on how the IT governance structures and processes ensure the interests of all stakeholders are taken into consideration with respect to the decisions that are made regarding IT and whether those decisions are in sync with the social, financial, and environment context within which the company does business.

EXAMINING TWO DIMENSIONS OF IT GOVERNANCE

Much has been written about IT governance and how it can influence the effective use of IT in an organization, supporting both the current and future strategy if done appropriately but creating major problems when IT governance is poor (Weill and Ross 2004). In exploring this issue of 'good' versus 'bad' IT governance the main focus has been on structural alignment. *Alignment* addresses the question of whether the IT governance structures, and the underlying rules and resources, adopted by an organization, match or align with the prevailing circumstances to ensure decisions are made that take into account interests of all the various stakeholders and so the overall sustainability of the business. (See also Chapter 22.) For example, here one could examine how far, if at all, the reward structures in place encourage CIOs to focus on making IT decisions that help organizations reduce their carbon footprint.

While structural alignment is an important issue, we argue in this chapter that there is a second dimension that needs to be considered, which we label *commitment*. Commitment refers to the manner in which those involved in IT governance follow the rules and use the resources that have been formalized in the governance structures. Thus, in some situations there may be low commitment so that compliance with the rules and use of resources (i.e. the governance structures) is superficial and dependent on sanctions, with what might be described as a check-box mentality. On the other hand, there may be other situations where those involved actively engage with the rules, because they are committed, believing in the underpinning values (i.e. following the spirit of the rules rather than merely the letter). Colyvas and Powell (2006), for example, distinguish between practices that simply conform to socio-political pressures, more of a check-box idea, versus practices that are driven by cultural-cognitive underpinnings, those that are laden with meaning and drive the sense-making process.

This second dimension of governance is becoming more influential. Enron, for example, was heralded as a bastion of good governance—it had all the appropriate structures in place to supposedly support ethical decision making. As we know, however, the way the structures were operationalized in practice meant that decisions were made which completely disregarded the spirit of the underlying rules (Kulik, O'Fallon, and Salimath 2008); and, indeed, included use of resources which was illegal. In Argyris' and Schon's (1974) terms there was a major disconnect between the espoused theories and the theories-in-use. In other words, commitment addresses whether those involved in IT governance comply with the governance structures for fear of sanction, without any ethical commitment to the implied rules, or fully support and believe in the underpinning ethical values. Its importance is demonstrated by prior research which has shown that top executives' values influence organizational outcomes because these executives possess the status necessary to influence vital organizational actions (Finklestein and Hambrick 1990). Managers who are committed to the values will invest in ethics programmes, policies, and structures in order to demonstrate their commitment to moral responsibility (Weaver, Trevino, and Cochran 1999).

In Figure 16.1 we outline these two dimensions of governance and their interaction. The alignment dimension contrasts organizations where the IT governance structures are in high alignment—with rules and resources provided that can, potentially, support decision making in the interests of sustainability—versus situations where IT governance structures are in low alignment—with rules and resources at odds with what is needed to support sustainability. The second dimension of commitment then relates to whether this potential is likely to be realized in practice based on actors' orientations to

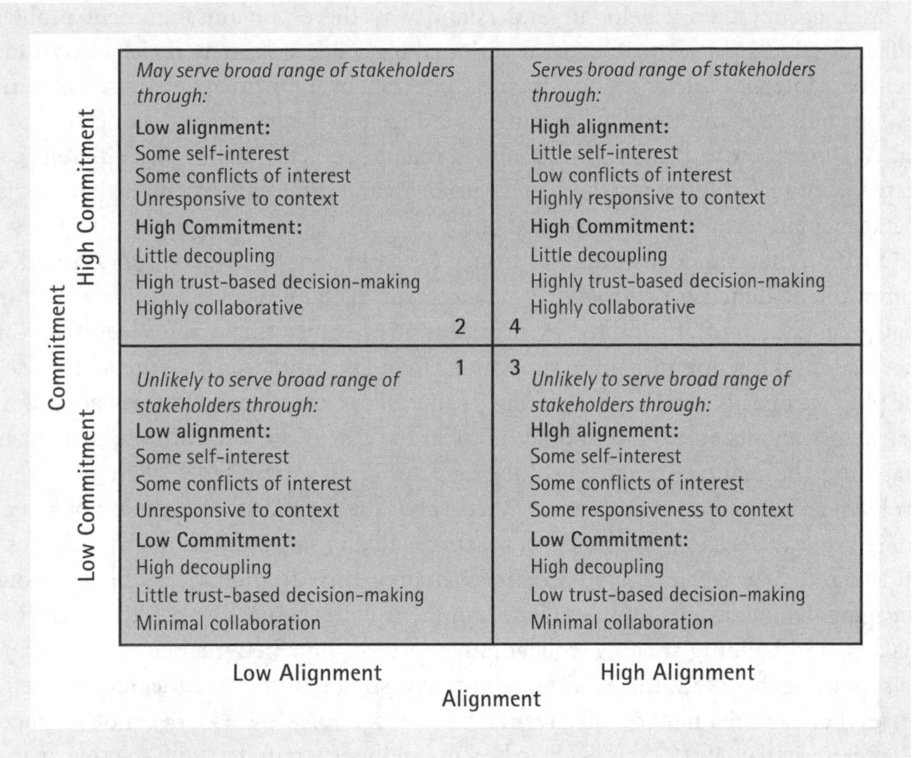

FIGURE 16.1 The alignment and commitment dimensions of (IT) governance

these rules and implied resource allocations. In this sense, we present the commitment dimension as a contrast between low commitment, which represents a compliance culture—where actors comply but only as long as they believe sanctions are in place that would be used if they got caught not complying—and high commitment, which represents a high level of top management engagement in the governance issues—where actors follow the spirit of the rule and use resources to benefit sustainability because it is what decision makers actually believe in. It should be noted that compliance can very easily become non-compliance where decision makers believe they can 'get away with it', as in Enron.

In understanding these two dimensions of IT governance, we will argue that it is necessary to take a multi-theoretic approach (Lynall, Golden, and Hillman 2003) since different theories throw light on different aspects of IT governance. In doing so, we take up the call by recent governance researchers suggesting that a single theory of governance is limiting (cf. Daily, Dalton, and Cannella 2003). A more holistic understanding of governance is derived from using different theoretical lenses to explore different aspects of governance. More specifically, we will use agency theory and contingency theory to explore the structural alignment dimension of governance, and institutional theory and stewardship theory to explore the commitment dimension of governance.

In brief, agency theory helps us understand why there is a misalignment problem, indicating that agents, those charged with making a decision, may make a decision in their best interests rather than in the best interests of the principals, those delegating responsibility for the decision making. Contingency theory, then, has been used to indicate how best to deal with this misalignment problem, identifying different contextual factors that influence this agency problem and different structures that alleviate the agency problem in different situations.

On the other hand, institutional theory (see Chapter 6) helps us understand the commitment dimension through the concept of decoupling. Decoupling recognizes that practices are often adopted by organizations because they confer legitimacy and that adoption is sometimes more important than appropriation (i.e. the actual use of the practice in daily work). This tendency can lead to a disconnect between adoption of a structure and its actual use in practice, as in the case of Enron, with the rhetoric not matching the reality. In this case, the structures may be aligned with the agency problem as suggested by contingency theory, but the formal structures do not actually guide the way decisions get made in practice. Finally, stewardship theory helps us to understand how we might be able to overcome this decoupling problem through engaging—rather than simply trying to control as with agency theory—the IT decision makers, and building trusting, collaborative relationships between agents and principals. In using these four theories we are not suggesting that they are the only theoretical lenses that can shed light on IT governance. For example, resource dependency theory (Pfeffer and Salancik 1978) is likely to be a useful theory to understand the role of an IT board governance structure, focusing not on the oversight and control role of a board but on the resources and advice that board members bring to the decision-making process (Daily, Dalton, and Cannella 2003). Rather, the objective of the paper is to demonstrate the importance of looking at the issue of IT governance from a multi-theoretic perspective if we are to understand what makes for effective IT governance in different organizational and institutional contexts. In developing this multi-theoretic approach we explore how to enable IS researchers to contribute to management and organizational literature on corporate governance rather than merely borrowing from it, thus addressing a concern that is repeatedly raised in the IS community (Baskerville and Myers 2002; Galliers 2003; Avison and Eliot 2006). Before we look at the different theories that can help us understand the two dimensions of IT governance explored here, however, we first need to define our terms.

Defining Governance and IT Governance

To think about governance one needs to analyse the purpose of an enterprise since one governs to fulfil a particular purpose, whether in a nation state or a business organization. In the literature there are opposing views about the purpose of a business enterprise. Sometimes this tension is simplified to a mere contrast between the stockholder and stakeholder views, which differ in terms of how they see corporate executives' obligations and responsibilities. The stockholder view maintains that the purpose of an enterprise is to provide the best returns for the owners of a firm, that is, the shareholders (at least of a publicly traded firm); other interests are subservient to this purpose as long as there is no rule breaking (Friedman 2004). On the other hand, the stakeholder view maintains that a firm should be managed to ensure that the best interests of all stakeholders are considered, with the shareholders given no particular priority in this process (Freeman and Reed 1983).

In reality, this contrast is over-pronounced because, as instrumental stakeholder theory argues, firms will be successful in conventional performance terms by addressing stakeholder interests (Donaldson and Preston 1995). This instrumental stakeholder view can be contrasted with the normative stakeholder view, which posits that there is an ethical obligation to respond to stakeholder claims regardless of whether doing so advances the interests of shareholders (Donaldson and Preston 1995). Thus, the instrumental view of stakeholder management emphasizes the fulfilment of traditional corporate objectives such as profitability and growth while the normative view stresses doing the right thing because the interests of stakeholders have intrinsic value. In this chapter we assume that it is important to take into account the interests of different stakeholders because this will ultimately be important for long-term sustainability; that is, we adopt an instrumental stakeholder perspective. Such a view is especially applicable to IT governance as it involves a set of processes and structures affecting all stakeholders unlike an equity investment made by shareholders alone. The instrumental stakeholder approach is generally associated with the expanded view of corporate responsibility discussed earlier, that is, the triple-bottom line, including social and environmental as well as financial responsibilities (O'Donovan and Gibson 2007).

Applied to IT governance, this debate reflects whether IT decisions should be made from a purely financial cost-benefit analysis or whether broader stakeholders' needs and interests should also be taken into consideration. For example, the IS literature emphasizes the importance of user participation to ensure that social as well as technical user needs are contemplated (Mumford 1983). From a normative stakeholder perspective user social needs are important in their own right—it is important to satisfy employees' social needs because this indicates a respect for human dignity. From an instrumental stakeholder perspective, participation would also be a concern if it was shown to increase the business value of IT. It could certainly be argued that taking into consideration the social context of IT—for example, constituents' privacy rights and concerns—would be important in relation to optimizing the exploitation of IT, which in turn would increase profits.

In reality, therefore, while there are opposing views of the purpose and responsibilities of a business enterprise, if one considers that the purpose of a firm is to sustain itself into the future then the interests of the shareholders can only be fully served if the interests of other stakeholders are taken into consideration (Watson 2006). Therefore, while a firm may increase short-term profits by adopting IT that alienates and deskills users or sells customer data without their knowledge and ignores their privacy rights in order to make money, its actions are not consistent with the stakeholder view of the firm, either normatively or instrumentally. In the long term such practices are likely to undermine the ability of an organization to maintain productive relationships with key constituents such as employees, green pressure groups, suppliers, customers, and regulators. Empirical evidence confirms this inference: Orlitzky, Schmidt, and Rynes (2003) conducted a meta-analysis which showed a significant positive effect of corporate social/environmental performance on corporate financial performance.

Given the above discussion, we can define corporate governance as being concerned with *the rights, responsibilities and balance of power among management and other parties who have a stake in the firm* so as to ensure that decisions are made about the use of resources that contribute to the *long-term financial, social and environmental sustainability* of an enterprise. This definition coincides with the definition provided by Daily and colleagues (2003: 371) in going beyond a narrow focus on executive self-interest and shareholder protection. Thus, our definition considers the rights and responsibilities of 'the myriad participants in an organization'.

Extending this to IT governance, we can define IT governance as being concerned with the rights and responsibilities and balance of power among management and other parties who have a stake in the IT processes and structures that are adopted and utilized within or across firms with the purpose of ensuring that IT is used to help promote the long-term financial, social, and environmental sustainability of a firm. This view is similar to the definition proposed by Weill and Ross (2004: 4): 'IT governance is the decision rights and accountability framework for encouraging desirable behaviours in the use of IT'. But it extends their definition in terms of what are 'desirable behaviours' in the light of our discussion of the purpose of business.

In relation to these rights and responsibilities, Weill and Ross (2004) identify five major IT governance decision areas: *IT principles* (the stated strategic role of IT in relation to business goals); *IT architecture* (the overall policies and procedures that define how IT will be used and new IT adopted to support the business); *IT infrastructure* (the overall framework of IT that reflects the strategy and the policies and procedures, including the network infrastructure that enables electronic communications within and across the enterprise, the hardware and software that supports transaction processing and analysis, the expertise available to support the adoption and management of IT, and the training infrastructure to support both IT professionals and IT users); *business application needs* (specific IT applications that will meet particular business needs); and *prioritization and investment* (decisions about what IT to invest in and the extent of investment). What is perhaps missing from this list is governance over data that are captured, stored, and shared through IT systems. That is, a company must determine the rights and responsibilities it has to consumers regarding the storage, use, retrieval, and mining of data beyond what the law requires. Given the concerns about privacy in general and the violations that are all too common in organizations of all types, as discussed above, this is arguably a distinct area that IT governance should cover, requiring leadership at the most senior levels.

This discussion emphasizes that IT governance is concerned with managing and controlling an organization's portfolio of IT systems, and the data that exist on these systems, to serve the business both currently and in the future (Brown 2006). There is, therefore, a direct link between IT and corporate governance—because both are geared to serving the business strategy of a firm (Van Grembergen 2002; Greenaway and Chan 2005) and are fundamentally about rights and responsibilities. Indeed, the goal of effective IT governance is that it creates the conditions that allow IT to be exploited to support the strategic value of IT investments while also considering the impact of technology on all the various stakeholders. We return to this important link between IT and corporate governance in the following sections because it suggests that the IT context offers a new understanding beyond what organization and management literature have contributed to date. Next, we turn to a review of the four selected theories to help us understand the source of the governance problems that we have defined—alignment and commitment—and the solutions to overcoming these problems.

AGENCY THEORY AND UNDERSTANDING THE ALIGNMENT PROBLEM

To recap, alignment refers to how far the IT governance framework is structured to ensure decisions are made that take into consideration the interests of all stakeholders—so decisions balance financial, social, and environmental risks. Alignment traditionally, in the corporate governance research literature, refers to the alignment between managers and shareholders (cf. Eisenhardt 1989). Here we are concerned with whether the IT governance structures and processes ensure the interests of the different stakeholders are taken into consideration in IT decisions so that decisions are made that are aligned with the social, financial, and environment context within which the company does business.

The first theoretical lens that we will explore is agency theory (Eisenhardt 1989) because agency theory helps us understand the basic decision-making dilemma in business organizations and reveals why there is the potential for discrepancy (i.e. misalignment) between IT decisions that get made and the interests of all stakeholders. IT governance, as we have discussed, relates to the rights and responsibilities of a firm's management to its owners and other constituents so as to ensure that decisions are made because they benefit the long-term sustainability agenda of the organization. That this does not always happen is due to the so-called agency problem—that is, that managers act opportunistically with self-interest and guile. It is this fundamental agency problem that governance is all about: how to ensure there are structures and processes in place to ensure that agents—those given responsibility for making decisions about something—act in the best interests of the principals, those who delegated responsibility, rather than in the best interests of the agents themselves.

In corporate governance terms, agents of a firm refer to those executives making decisions while principals refer to the owners/shareholders. More generally, agents are those responsible for making decisions and principals are those who have delegated the decision-making power. Applied to governance, from an agency theory perspective (Jensen and Meckling 1976) it is not that agents and principals do not both want high returns. Rather, the problem is that agents and principals may differ in how they want the returns allocated or in their time horizon. Often, too, the problem occurs due to conflicts of interest. When interests are virtually identical, the agency problem is small: executives do what is in principals' best interests. But, interests don't always overlap. As an example, when a company receives a purchase offer, shareholders (principals) might benefit because price assures a good return on their investment, while management (agents) may resist because they may lose their jobs. In agency theory terms there is incentive misalignment between agents and principals.

In many cases, these agency problems arise because of information asymmetry. The agent typically has access to information that the principal does not so that the principal is not able to evaluate the decisions that the agent is making on his/her behalf. The agent can, therefore, make decisions that prioritize his/her self-interests rather than the interests of the principal. Governance structures are put in place to try and reduce this agency problem with the goal of reducing the incentive misalignment, so creating a situation where the agent's best interests are served by fulfilling the interests of the principal.

As in the corporate governance literature the agency problem in IT is related to problems of incentive misalignment and information asymmetry (Gu, Xue, and Ray 2008). Incentive misalignment and information asymmetry can create a situation where business units make decisions about IT which are beneficial for them, but which are not the most sensible from the enterprise perspective or from the perspective of all stakeholders. For example, a decision may be made by the CIO to buy cheaper but more energy-intensive laptops because this decision will then allow her to achieve her goal of reducing the IT budget, for which she receives a bonus. As another example, selling client data may prove lucrative in the short term (and be reflected in executive bonuses) but may reduce client loyalty in the longer term, harming profits. These examples demonstrate how the alignment issue agency theory seeks to solve is very real in relation to IT governance.

This theoretical lens suggests that a useful research stream could focus on what kinds of incentive structures can encourage IT decision makers to focus on the broad social, environmental, and long-term financial implications of their decisions, rather than what might be most expedient for their own career success. It would also suggest that researchers might usefully examine whether organizations that do incentivize IT decision makers to adopt a broader perspective for evaluating their IT decisions, one that encourages them to balance the impacts on people and the planet as well as profits, are any better at exploiting the potential from their IT investments. In sum, agency theory emphasizes governance control—agents must be controlled to ensure that they make decisions in the interests of principals or more broadly in the interests of stakeholders. Contingency theory takes this notion a step further and helps us to understand what governance structures are needed in different circumstances, given that the agency problem will vary across contexts.

Contingency Theory and Understanding the Alignment Solution

Understanding the agency problem directs attention to finding ways to reduce or eliminate the problem. Governance structures are thus put in place that direct decision making so that it is in line with sustainability objectives, rather than allowing decisions to be made in an ad hoc way or, more specifically, in ways that are in line with decision makers' interests. In the agency theory literature, the key recommendations for addressing these concerns are to use incentives that help to align the interests of agents and principals and to embolden boards of directors to provide rigorous oversight of the decision-making process. Consistent with broader corporate governance research, the focus in IT governance is on ensuring that there are effective organizational structures in place in order to protect all those impacted by the IT (e.g. company users, customers, suppliers) from the self-interested actions of decision makers or from a focus on the short-term expedient rather than the long-term sustainable. In Table 16.1, we distinguish structures, processes, and mechanisms, as defined in the IT literature (e.g. Brown 2006). All, however, are part of the overall governance structure in the sense that they define the rules and resource allocation criteria that decision makers need to follow. IT needs to be governed in a transparent and effective way for all stakeholders with their diverse interests and needs in relation to information, recognizing that needs are

Table 16.1 Structures, processes, and mechanisms related to IT governance

Governance structures	Governance processes	Governance mechanisms
CIO on Board	Strategic information systems planning	Active participation of stakeholders
Executive management committee	Balanced scorecards	Partnership rewards and incentives
IT strategy committee	Service level agreements	Business/IT co-location
IT leadership committee	IT portfolio management	Cross-functional collaboration
IT steering committee	Demand management	IT training
IT coordinator	Security management	IT/business rotation

Source: Adapted from Peterson (2004).

context dependent. In other words, ensuring that rights and responsibilities are allocated to produce sustainability of a firm depends on having a set of structures, processes, and relational mechanisms that can facilitate it (Brown 2006) and the most appropriate structures and processes will depend on the circumstances. In Table 16.1, governance *structures* are the most visible consisting of committees and boards that are set up to deal with different types of IT decision making and oversight and roles that are assigned in relation to specified responsibilities. Important IT governance structures include:

1. IT strategy committee—comprises members of the corporate board who provide oversight and advice about the strategy and alignment of IT with the business (IT Governance Institute 2003). Having a board sub-committee dedicated to IT issues demonstrates commitment that IT is perceived as important to the success of the corporation; this committee can also be important in ensuring that necessary resources are available (Premkumar and King 1994).

2. IT steering committee— comprises senior management from across divisions and/or functions whose role is to support the planning and management of IT issues in the organization. The steering committee would, for example, be responsible for linking IT decisions with business strategy and helping to garner support for IT projects (IT Governance Institute 2003). The CIO would typically sit on the steering committee. The importance of an IT steering committee has been demonstrated by previous research (cf. Karimi et al. 2000; Vaswani 2003).

3. Head of IT role—organizations differ in terms of the seniority associated with the individual vested with overall responsibility for IT. This can range from having a CIO who reports directly to the CEO, thus having equal seniority alongside other functional heads like CFO and COO, to organizations where the head of IT is a departmental manager who reports to an executive member, often the CFO. Research has demonstrated that the closer the distance between CIO and the CEO the more successful the IT infrastructure tends to be (Law and Ngai 2007).

In Table 16.1, governance *processes* refer to management practices that relate to the actual development and use of IT, helping to ensure that IT is used in the ways that were intended by the structural entities. So, an enterprise-wide IT strategy committee might set a strategy that all business units adopt the same enterprise system, and management processes would then be in place to track and evaluate the impact of this decision. Important IT governance processes include:

1. Performance measure systems—such systems can provide information about how IT systems are performing relative to their stated objectives. An example of such a measurement system would be a balanced scorecard (Kaplan and Norton 1992).

2. Risk management systems—having appropriate processes in place to manage risk associated with IT is essential to ensure data security and privacy, as well, of course, as ensuring financial control of IT systems, both new and existing.

3. Planning systems—having methodologies that set out how to design a new IT system or how to maintain an existing one are an essential part of the IT governance process. Such systems set out the roles and responsibilities, the action steps, and the control processes for IT development and use.

Finally, governance *mechanisms* relate to how communication about IT policy, development, and use is effected in the organization so that there is stakeholder buy-in for IT decisions that are made. Mechanisms are thus relational; focused on ensuring stakeholders support and understand decisions related to IT (Weill and Ross 2004). Important IT governance mechanisms include:

1. Business/IT coordination—this is especially important in relation to IT governance, given what we know about the communication problems that exist between IT departments and the business functions. Mechanisms that establish good communication between business and IT will therefore be very important (De Haes and Grembergen 2005).
2. Participation—user participation is a long-established mechanism that influences user acceptance and use of IT (Mumford 1983; Wagner and Newell 2007).

Governance structures can be configured to be more or less centralizing. Weill and Ross (2004) suggest that centralized IT governance approaches are effective where the key organizational driver is low cost and efficiency since this enables the creation of standardized IT solutions that maximize economies of scale. Decentralized IT governance approaches are effective where the key organizational driver is innovation, flexibility, and local responsiveness. A centralized approach would vest significant power in the CIO and a central executive IT committee who would dictate a standard architecture and infrastructure to be used across the organization; governance processes would be standardized and mechanisms would focus on communication of the standards through for example centrally designed training programmes. A decentralized approach, on the other hand, might have multiple CIOs, one in each business unit, committees with considerable power at each business unit or function, and significant participation from local stakeholders in IT decisions.

While these central/dispersed structures do coincide with different business strategies supporting, respectively, efficiency/innovation, it is also clear today that many organizations need to be both efficient and innovative, and global and local; in short, they need to be ambidextrous (Adler, Goldoftas, and Levine 1999). In line with this strategic need to be ambidextrous, IS research has also identified hybrid forms of organizational governance that enable flexibility in IT decision-making authority depending on the type of decision being made and the strategic orientation that the particular IT supports. Thus, researchers have identified forms including matrixed IT governance (Weill and Ross 2005), hybrid IT governance (Brown 2006), and federal IT governance (Sambamurthy and Zmud 1999). In the federal form, for example, IT infrastructure decisions may be centralized to encourage efficiencies, while decisions about IT business applications may be decentralized to encourage flexible responsiveness to the local context.

This implies a contingency approach to IT governance and considerable research in the IS space has been done from this perspective (Sia, Soh, and Weill 2008). For example, Gu, Xue, and Ray (2008) developed a multiple contingency model that identified the appropriate IT governance structure given the particular circumstances of the firm (e.g. company size, degree of diversification, level of IT expertise available locally). The aim of the particular structures is to reduce information asymmetry and increase incentive alignment. They were able to contrast firms whose IT governance structure was either aligned or misaligned with this ideal. They found that firms that were misaligned obtained less value from their IT investment compared to firms that were aligned.

This work is clearly important and has practical value—aligning a company's IT governance framework with its particular organizational strategy is very important, as demonstrated by the study by Gu and colleagues (2008). More research can be done on identifying the key contingency variables and the appropriate governance design given the circumstances. Moreover, looking at these contingencies from a stakeholder perspective, the key issue is how IT governance structures can be selected to ensure that IT decisions and the follow-on behaviour meets the sustainability requirements of the particular organizational context. Doing so might suggest, for example, that IT principles reflecting sustainability concerns would need to be set by the board while decisions about particular business applications would be made locally, involving as many people as possible in order to generate innovative ideas about how to meet diverse needs of people and the environment. In other words, research is needed that identifies what configuration of IT governance structures supports sustainable IT decision making.

In undertaking such research it would be helpful for IS researchers to be more explicit about linking their contingency frameworks to the underlying agency problems in place in order to achieve high structural alignment. This would enable a clearer link with, and therefore contribution to, the management and organization literature on governance. Identifying what the particular agency problems are in relation to IT governance and how they can be overcome through contingency management can, then, contribute to the broader literature on governance. While some of the examples described above (e.g. Gu, Xue, and Ray 2008) do situate their contingency framework within the theoretical debate about agency, not all IS researchers do this, or indeed use any theoretical perspective. Yet there are ways that IT research can contribute to the broader governance discussions if the researchers involved engage with these broader debates and situate their studies using common language and common metrics such as incentive alignment and board composition. There may be differences between the contingency variables that influence IT governance as opposed to corporate governance and the agency problems may also be different. However, using common theoretical lenses will enable researchers to be explicit about these differences and thus, potentially, contribute to governance theory as well as IT governance practice.

INSTITUTIONAL THEORY AND UNDERSTANDING THE COMMITMENT PROBLEM

As already indicated, agency and contingency theory focus on the structural alignment problem of governance, helping us understand why misalignment is a common problem and what can be done to manage it. However, even where there is alignment—structures are in place that supposedly ensure that decisions are made that contribute to the long-term sustainability of the enterprise—it does not necessarily mean that the decisions actually will get made as the structures would suggest. Decisions continue to get made that are not aligned with the rules because organizations are composed of both formal and informal activity systems. As Suchman (1987) describes so neatly, plans—or formal procedures of work—do not equate to situated actions (i.e. how work actually gets done in practice). The formal structures describe how the system *should* work. It is individuals, however, who enact these structures (Weick 1980). In structuration theory terms (Giddens 1984)—see Chapter 5—structures constrain action but they also enable action, including generative action which breaks away from and changes the existing structures.

Formally, therefore, there may be a set of rules and resources embedded in the established governance structures—both externally imposed through legislation and internally imposed through corporate mandates. These may indicate how decisions should be made that are aligned to the business objectives. However, the enactment of these formal structures may create a set of norms and practices that influence decisions in ways that are very different to those indicated by the formal structures. Therefore, it is important to look at the second dimension of IT governance—the commitment dimension. In looking at commitment we are focusing on the interplay between the formal rules and resources embedded in the structures and the enactment of these in practice. Labelling this governance dimension commitment represents how actors' values and beliefs—their ethical compass—will influence this enactment process (see also Chapter 23).

When actors, especially upper echelon managers, are strongly committed to ethics they will create governance structures and other ethics programmes and policies in order to demonstrate their commitment (Weaver, Trevino, and Cochran 1999). When managers do not believe in the underpinning ethical values they are more likely to look for ways to avoid what they see as inappropriate constraints on their actions. When values and structures are in tune, there will be high engagement with the formal rules and routines. When they are opposed so that commitment is lacking, there may be a semblance of compliance, but actual decisions will get made in ways that are not in line with the spirit or intention of the formal rules (DeSanctis and Poole 1994). This suggests that we need to be aware of the policies that hold more weight in an organization—the way things are actually done—versus the stated procedures. In the case of Enron, there were many policies regarding governance that looked sound on paper, but the overriding policy that drove the company was the policy of eliminating poor performing employees, creating a culture of unethical behaviour in order to meet performance goals.

Commitment is thus an important issue, because even where there is alignment there may not be compliance. To understand this we can turn to institutional theory. Adopting formal governance reforms confers legitimacy on an organization because it indicates to the market that the agency problem is being addressed. For example, Greenaway and Chan (2005) showed that an organization's IT privacy behaviours can help a firm achieve legitimacy and can provide a strategic advantage to an organization. However, research indicates that this legitimacy can be earned even when the governance reforms are announced but not implemented (Westphal and Zajac 1998). This situation can be explained by institutional theory which suggests that 'the appearance rather than the fact of conformity is often presumed to be sufficient for the attainment of legitimacy' (Oliver 1991: 155). Such symbolic rather than substantive reform is explained in institutional theory terms by the concept of decoupling (Meyer and Rowan 1977)—formal structures are adopted in response to external pressures but actual practices are not reflected by these formal structures. Structures are adopted but do not constrain action in the ways intended, so that structure and practice are decoupled. Decoupling, it is argued, helps to buffer an organization from the uncertainties and rapid fluctuations of the external environment while still ensuring that organizations are conferred legitimacy by the external environment. For example, Westphal and Zajac (1998) found that companies that announced but did not implement long-term incentive plans for their CEO, nevertheless received a significant boost in firm market value. Moreover, this boost was enhanced where the announcement of the new plan was couched in agency terms, thus indicating that socially legitimating verbal explanations can be helpful even when it is mere rhetoric.

There is debate about whether it is possible to maintain such decoupling, especially in a competitive market context where institutional investors attempt to ensure that companies do behave in the long-term interests of their shareholders (Zuckerman 2004). This caveat is perhaps why in the original article by Meyer and Rowan (1977) they distinguish between public organizations and market-based organizations, suggesting that it is in the former that legitimacy through conformity to rules and regulations is more important since there are no external market mechanisms to control behaviour. In such organizations there are, therefore, stronger pressures towards institutional isomorphism (DiMaggio and Powell 1983). However, it is clear from research and from everyday experience that a significant number of companies do not 'practice what they preach' when it comes to governance structures.

Self-interested decision making does occur and includes decisions in relation to IT, as well as other types of corporate decisions. We can look, for example, at the literature on participation. User participation is advocated to help ensure that the needs of the users are taken into consideration in the design of a new IT system (Mumford 1983). User participation is prescribed as a fundamental part of the IT development methodology in many organizations (Howcroft and Wilson 2003). However, research has demonstrated that in some cases where user participation may be formally included, it is ultimately the IT professionals who actually make the final decisions. Avison and Fitzgerald (1995) refer to this as 'pseudo participation'. Wagner and Newell (2007) demonstrate that this pseudo participation can be both top-down and bottom-up. Bottom-up pseudo participation refers to the situation where users 'pretend' to be involved in the IT project in the pre-implementation phase but actually are not at all interested or engaged in the decisions that are being made. Users may be unengaged, for example, because of time constraints or simply a lack of salience as to the importance and relevance of the decisions being made, as noted in Chapter 15.

Because institutional theory is at its very fundamental level about control and coordination, it has been a natural setting for exploring corporate governance and the pressures that produce varying levels of conformity across cultures, political systems, and legal frameworks (Aguilera and Jackson 2003). Interestingly, a growing stream of recent research has pointed to the heterogeneity of actors and activities that underlie apparent conformity (Lounsbury 2007) and, specifically, the variation in governance practices as these practices are adapted to local country needs (Aguilera and Jackson 2003; Fiss and Zajac 2006; Lounsbury 2007). These variations tend to occur in the implementation stage following the diffusion of a unified set of institutional pressures (Fiss 2008) largely because implementation is a technical, cultural, and political process taking place within various country contexts. These studies drawing upon institutional theory and the concept of decoupling help to explain why the governance structures recommended by agency theory and contingency theory, such as having a majority of independent board members, separating the roles of CEO and Chairman or incentivizing executives with equity ownership, have not been found to be related to firm performance (Dalton et al. 1998; Dalton et al. 2003).

Institutional theory and ethical frameworks, however, have not been prevalent in the IS literature on governance, which may be why there is very little discussion about the issue of commitment (Greenaway and Chan 2005; Islamoglu and Liebenau 2007). It is true that there is discussion of the importance of governance mechanisms as part of the overall governance structure. These mechanisms are focused on ensuring that there is good communication about the governance framework being used and its underpinning rationale. Indeed, Weill and Ross (2004) found that a key factor influencing the effectiveness of IT in an organization was whether the top executives and managers understood and agreed upon the formal governance structure in the organization. Moreover, studies as described in the contingency theory section above seem to indicate that the presence of aligned structures, albeit contingent upon the specific context, does predict IT effectiveness in an organization. However, this does not mean that non-compliance due to low commitment is not an issue in the IT governance sphere (Carroll and Fitz-Gerald 2005). The very fact that there are so many failed IT projects and data breaches suggests that we should not be complacent about this issue. Moreover, the user participation example provided above suggests that commitment to the formal structures, as demonstrated by the gap between what should happen and what actually does happen, can be very tenuous.

However, while corporate governance scholars do use the institutional theory lens to demonstrate in broad theoretical terms that governance decoupling happens, there has been little qualitative research that has been able to study what happens in practice at corporate boards when decisions are taken that do not follow the formal rules. This is hardly surprising since board level discussions are generally proprietary so that allowing researchers to sit in and observe has not been possible. Such a situation is even more likely where decisions are sensitive, controversial, or rule bending in nature. However, qualitative research exploring IT governance may be much more possible and while we could find no such research which explicitly used an institutional theory lens, there are scholars who have been able to gain access to rich qualitative material about the IT governance process (e.g. Sia, Soh, and Weill 2008). This suggests that IT research may be able to actually contribute to the broader corporate governance literature by being able to conduct research that explores the interactions between formal governance structures and their enactment in practice. Undertaking research in organizations that have a clearly stated sustainability strategy and identifying when and why decisions get made that do not fit with this stated strategy would be particularly fruitful.

Studying the divide between the formal IT governance structure and where, how, and what decisions actually get made in practice is therefore an important area for future IS research. Such research needs to be in-depth, processual, and qualitative rather than quantitative research that simply relates the presence of governance structures to some dependent measure of IT effectiveness (Pettigrew 1992). Also, since governance is not static, but rather co-evolutionary (Lubatkin et al. 2007), with agents and principals responding recursively as they each engage in a sense-making process (Weick 1995) that is deeply embedded (Granovetter 1985) in the emergent institutional context, analysis of IT governance problems needs to be context specific. Moreover, given the diversity of stakeholders involved, we must examine how IT governance is embedded in a particular firm's social context (Aguilera and Jackson 2003). The importance of producing more of this type of research for studying governance decoupling is articulated in the corporate governance literature (Forbes and Milliken 1999; Daily, Dalton, and Cannella 2003).

Stewardship Theory and Understanding the Solution to Low Commitment

Agency theory often portrays agents (e.g. CEOs or CIOs) as villains mainly pursuing their own self-interest. However, this is not always the case. Thus, recent research has called for organizational theorists to investigate when shareholder returns, efficiency, stakeholder rights, and the amelioration of social issues all matter (Margolis and Walsh 2003) especially in the governance of a firm (Aoki 2001; Aguilera and Jackson 2003). In this section, we consider this state of affairs as we move to understand how to resolve the low commitment problem by looking at stewardship theory.

Stewardship theory is often contrasted with agency theory. Agency theory emphasizes governance control—agents (i.e. executives) must be controlled to ensure that they make decisions in the interests of principals (i.e. shareholders). On the other hand, we know that excessive control reduces trust and can lead to a self-reinforcing cycle that eventually reduces performance—the so-called paradox of control (Sundaramurthy and Lewis 2003). An alternative view of governance, therefore, emphasizes collaboration. Theoretically, this approach is based in stewardship theory (Davis, Schoorman, and Donaldson 1997) with sociological/psychological roots rather than the economic roots of agency theory. These opposing theories make different assumptions about human nature (Sundaramurthy and Lewis 2003): agency theory stressing individual opportunism, self-interest, and extrinsic motivation; stewardship theory stressing collectivist cooperation and intrinsic motivation. These different assumptions about human nature translate, then, into very different governance proposals. Agency theory stresses control and discipline mechanisms and stewardship theory stresses trust-developing and empowering collaborative mechanisms, such as building strong social ties between executives and IT board members. Such trust-based mechanisms would provide the context within which it would be less likely that lack of commitment undermined compliance with the formal rules, since the parties are collaborating rather than competing.

Sundaramurthy and Lewis (2003) point out the negative implications of both the control and collaboration perspectives on governance. Too much emphasis on control mechanisms leads to a self-reinforcing cycle that builds ever-greater distrust, as noted above in the paradox of control. On the other hand, too much emphasis on collaboration leads potentially to groupthink (Janis 1982). Thus, where the emphasis is on collaboration and trust, research has shown that in contexts of reducing performance, where there are strong groupthink pressures, rather than rethinking whether the decision was initially a good one, decisions are often made which exacerbate the failure (Kisvalfi 2000). As an example, Drummond (1998) illustrates how in the context of a large IT project in the Bank of England, which was not going well, executives infused greater resources into the failing project in order to 'save face' rather than admit that things were not going well.

To overcome the limitations of both approaches to governance, Sundaramurthy and Lewis (2003) advocate embracing the paradoxes between them and using both control and collaboration mechanisms simultaneously. This approach will benefit from the trust-enhancing effects of collaboration but at the same time ensure that some conflict is present in order to counter the possible negative effects of too much trust, that is groupthink. Finding ways to balance the trust-conflict paradox is, they argue, key to successful governance. In particular, they stress the importance of diversity to stimulate conflict. For example, in relation to the composition of the executive team and board, they argue, diversity must be coupled with approaches that can encourage shared understanding (Dougherty 1992) that can provide the context in which conflict can be used creatively rather than destructively (Leonard and Barton 1995). However, while

Sundaramurthy and Lewis (2003) suggest that they are advocating a system of governance that includes prescriptions from both agency and stewardship theory, it may be fairer to suggest that they are advocating a stewardship model, but with some mechanisms to prevent groupthink. Thus, in advocating a stewardship model, they recognize the potential problems of groupthink, including mechanisms that will help to ensure that the decision-making body does not get overly cohesive, and at the same time ensuring that varied stakeholders interests will be represented through diverse participation (Montgomery and Kaufman 2003). Stimulating productive conflict is not the same as imposing control mechanisms (as per agency theory), especially as they also point to the importance of creating a shared understanding. Indeed, their prescription for effective governance bears remarkable similarity to the long-established ideas about effective team working that very much comes from a paradigm of collaboration and trust building rather than externally imposed control (Hackman 1990).

Stewardship theory reminds us that effective IT governance depends ultimately on people and that without their willing cooperation (i.e. commitment) people are usually able to subvert rules and regulations, however complex these become and however many monitoring devices are used. If people believe in the rules and regulations they are much more likely to comply in substance rather than merely symbolically (Meyer and Rowan 1977). Rotvold (2008) endorses this view in her examination of IT security issues. As she indicates, security is achieved not simply by assigning roles and responsibilities associated with maintaining data security; it is also about creating a security culture through educating people about the importance of security and how, in their daily practice, they can ensure security (see also Chapter 17).

As another example, promoting IT to support environmental initiatives is unlikely to be effective unless there is real commitment to these issues (Jaffe and Stavins 1994). Gaining user commitment means that users might *want* to comply with new environmental rules (e.g. putting personal computers onto the energy-saving setting) because of personal beliefs in the importance of reducing climate change, rather than because of specific incentives they may (or may not) receive. Certainly, from a stewardship perspective, a key to green IT would be to work with the various stakeholders to develop a collective agreement about the importance of reducing energy use. Moreover, this collective intelligence is likely to be a significant source of ideas about reducing wasteful use of resources using IT (see also Chapter 22).

In the IS literature, although not always explicitly referring to stewardship theory per se, it is probably fair to say that this collaborative model of governance, as opposed to the agency control model, implicitly underpins much of the literature. In this sense, the IS literature may have something to offer the organization and management literatures on corporate governance—demonstrating how to achieve this more collaborative orientation to overcome different stakeholder interests and orientations. In particular, the long-standing research on how to bridge the divide between IT departments and other functional business departments can be important here (Jarvenpaa and Ives 1991). Indeed, the issue of IT-business cooperation is a key element identified in much of the IT governance literature, whether related to how to ensure senior corporate involvement in IT decisions about data security and privacy at the board level or how to ensure user requirements are captured accurately in the context of IT development. Using this past literature to inform the debate around governance stewardship more generally could prove a fruitful avenue for IS researchers. Thus, IS research has looked at how to move beyond a 'tick-box compliance' in the relationship between IT and business employees to a situation of real engagement between IT and Business where they work together as partners, enabling IT solutions that add real business value. This collaboration is an issue that IS research has been working on since the 1980s and it is highly relevant to the commitment governance problem.

ALIGNMENT AND COMMITMENT INTERACTIONS

Having explained the two dimensions of our IT governance model (see Figure 16.1), we look at their interactions in this final section of the chapter. Thus, Figure 16.1 depicts four unique quadrants, which depend on the joint operation of both alignment and commitment, each of which can be independently high versus low. Below we suggest some probable outcomes of this interaction while recognizing that a firm's position in each quadrant is not static as its commitment or alignment levels may change over time. Clearly research is needed to test these propositions.

Low Alignment and Low Commitment (Quadrant 1)

In this situation, it is least likely that IT decisions will be made that serve the interests of a broad range of stakeholders and most likely that decisions are made that serve the interests of only the decision makers. On the alignment dimension, interests are likely to be misaligned with conflicts of interest common. There is likely to be little effort to adapt to the contingencies through using appropriate structures, processes, and mechanisms that are presented in the particular firm context. On the commitment dimension, decoupling between rhetoric and practice is likely to be common with significant symbolic management action; trust between managers and IT professionals is likely to be low, and business managers are likely to show very little engagement in the IT function.

Low Alignment and High Commitment (Quadrant 2)

In this situation, decisions may be made that serve the interests of a broad range of stakeholders in spite of a lack of formal governance structures that are designed to facilitate it. Managers are likely to exhibit some evidence of conflicts of interest, some self-interested decision making, indicative of low alignment, but be highly committed to trust-based and collaborative IT procedures and mechanisms. Still, this situation presents the possibility of substantive change as committed executives have the power to make changes to the structural alignment issues in their particular context. Organizations in this quadrant are therefore likely to move to the high alignment/high commitment space over time.

High Alignment and Low Commitment (Quadrant 3)

In this situation, incentives and conflicts of interests may be under control and highly coordinated but the decision makers remain uncommitted to a trusting and value-driven set of processes and to the mechanisms and structures already in place—perhaps instituted by previous management. There is likely a high level of decoupling between these structures and the actual IT practices due to the low commitment. In this case, IT decisions may be made that serve the interests of a broad range of stakeholders only if there are monitoring mechanisms in place and sanctions that are seen as threatening if self-interested decisions are made. It may be possible to stay in this position for a considerable amount of time, since symbolic management can be a powerful illusion.

High Alignment and High Commitment (Quadrant 4)

In this situation, it is most likely that decisions are made that serve the interests of a broad range of stakeholders. There is high commitment by managers and board members for making IT decisions that are utilizing trust-based mechanisms and are collaborative in nature. On the alignment dimension, there are structures in place that ensure a high level of user coordination and control as well as a minimum of information asymmetry and conflicts of interest; these structures and the associated commitment also mean that there is likely to be collaboration between the IT suite and the broader corporate governance members.

The above provides an indication of what we would expect to find depending on the joint interactions between alignment and commitment. It is important to note, however, that an organization will not sit in a particular quadrant indefinitely. Taking the most extreme conditions, quadrants 2 and 3, we can demonstrate how movement between quadrants can occur. An example of quadrant 2 would be a board member who represents an IT organization putting pressure on decision makers to invest in IT from his/her own company even when the technology is not in the best interests of the stakeholders. This situation represents low alignment because it indicates a conflict of interest. Such low alignment may be a problem even when the company is committed to collaborative, trust-based decision making, indicative of high commitment. If the organization removes the board member or discloses the conflict of interest and makes it explicit that decisions will not be so prioritized, the alignment problem may be resolved. In this case, the organization would move to the high commitment/high alignment quadrant, *ceteris paribus*.

As an example of quadrant 3, an organization might have a diverse IT board, no conflicts of interest and principles that indicate IT decisions will be made in pursuit of sustainable business goals, indicative of high alignment. However, this organization might also have an informal compensation policy that steers people to prioritizing the short-term financial implications of decisions (e.g. linking annual bonuses to quarterly earnings). The subtext of this policy means that there is low commitment to the underlying governance values so that IT decisions only pay lip-service to the broad stakeholder concerns about the impact of IT decisions. In this situation, if the compensation policy is changed to encourage a longer-term perspective (e.g. removing bonus payments that are linked to short-term measures of financial success) then commitment to the IT principles might increase and the organization would move to the high alignment/high commitment quadrant.

CONCLUSION

We have argued that there are two important dimensions of IT governance—alignment and commitment—that are independent but that need to be considered holistically. It is also important to note that an organization's IT governance system is dynamic so that there will be movement in terms of strengths and weaknesses on both these dimensions depending on particular situations that are encountered and how these are responded to. Alignment is important because of the agency problem and suggests that decision-making structures need to be carefully aligned and contingent on the particular circumstances of the organization and the decision focus, to ensure the interests of all stakeholders are taken into consideration in IT decisions. Commitment is important because of the decoupling that we know exists between formal structures and the enactment of these in practice. Building trust-based, collaborative relationships can assist in overcoming this decoupling because it can help to ensure that decision makers believe in the underlying value systems implied by the structures.

In this chapter we have demonstrated the importance of looking at both dimensions and explored how different theoretical lenses are needed to understand both the causes and solutions to the alignment and commitment problems. A key point that we have tried to emphasize throughout the chapter is that IT governance research can make important theoretical contributions, as well as being highly relevant to practice.

We suggest that more explicitly engaging with the breadth of theoretical lenses that have been used in the broader governance literature will help IS researchers fulfil that potential and contribute to, rather than merely borrow from, the organization and management literatures. As a further example of this potential, Daily, Dalton, and

Cannella (2003) point to governance during organizational crises as an important area for future research and highly pertinent given the economic crises that companies of all sorts are facing across the globe in 2009. Given that so many IT projects are crisis ridden, there may be an excellent opportunity for IS researchers to contribute to the literature on governance. How establishing control (from an agency theory perspective) and/or effecting collaboration (from a stewardship perspective) can help to meet the challenges faced in a crisis is a question for future IS research. In turn, such research can inform broader corporate governance discussions related to the sustainability of the business itself.

Another area where IT governance research may be able to contribute to the broader governance literature is in the area of organizational collaborations. IT outsourcing (see Chapter 19) is now a well-known phenomenon and research has explored what factors influence how to govern such outsourcing arrangements (Islamoglu and Liebenau 2007). More generally, there is a trend towards networked organizational forms—organizations collaborating to achieve particular goals—whether this collaboration is designed to develop a new product or to service a particular type of customer. There has been little written about how to govern these networked organizational forms—i.e. how to align the rights, responsibilities, and power dynamics of the various parties involved in these collaborative relationships in order to ensure sustainability. Therefore, applying IT governance to networked organizations is potentially an area where IS researchers could comment on what types of governance arrangements might be most appropriate and theoretically why this is the case.

Note

1. This is not to say that all companies focus on sustainability; some companies may adopt a strategy of turning over a quick profit and then exiting. In this chapter, however, we consider governance as it relates to ensuring sustainability.

References

Adler, P., Goldoftas, B., and Levine, D. (1999). 'Flexibility versus Efficiency: A Case Study of Model Changeovers in the Toyota Production System', *Organization Science*, 10: 43–68.

Aguilera, R., and Jackson, G. (2003). 'The Cross-National Diversity of Corporate Governance: Dimensions and Determinants', *Academy of Management Review*, 28(3): 447–65.

Argyris, C., and Schön, D. (1974). *Theory in Practice*. San Francisco, CA: Jossey-Bass.

Aoki, M. (2001). *Towards a Comparative Analysis*. Cambridge, MA: MIT Press.

Avison, D., and Eliot, S. (2006). 'Scoping the IS Discipline', in J. King and K. Lyytinen (eds.), *Information Systems: The State of the Field*. Chichester: Wiley, 3–18.

——and Fitzgerald, G. (1995). *Information Systems Development: Methodologies, Techniques and Tools*, 2nd edn. London: McGraw-Hill.

Bajwa, D., Garcia, J., and Mooney, T. (2004). 'An Integrative Framework for the Assimilation of Enterprise Resource Planning Systems: Phases, Antecedents and Outcomes', *Journal of Computer Information Systems*, Spring: 81–90.

Baskerville, R., and Myers, M. (2002). 'Information Systems as a Reference Discipline', *MIS Quarterly*, 17(2): 209–26.

Brown, W. (2006). 'IT Governance, Architectural Competency and the Vasa', *Information Management and Computer Security*, 14(2): 140–54.

Brundtland, G. H. (1987). *Our Common Future: Report of the World Commission on Environment and Development*. Oxford: Oxford University Press.

Carroll, J., and Fitz-Gerald, L. (2005). 'Beyond an IT project: Governance in an ERP Driven Business Transformation', 16th Australasian Conference on Information Systems, Sydney.

Carr, N. (2003). 'IT Doesn't Matter', *Harvard Business Review*, May: 41–9.

Colyvas, J. A., and Powell, W. W. (2006). 'Roads to Institutionalisation: The Re-making of Boundaries between Public and Private Science', *Research in Organisational Behaviour*, 27: 305–53.

Computer Economics (2008/9). 'IT Spending, Staffing and Technology Trends'. Irvine, CA: Computer Economics.

Daily, C., Dalton, D., and Cannella, A. (2003). 'Corporate Governance: Decades of Dialogue and Data', *Academy of Management Review*, 28(3): 371–82.

Dalton, D. R., Daily, C. M., Ellstrand, A. E., and Johnson, J. L. (1998). 'Meta-analytic Reviews of Board Composition, Leadership Structure, and Financial Performance', *Strategic Management Journal*, 19: 269–2.

——— Certo, S. T., and Roengpitya, R. (2003). 'Meta-analyses of Financial Performance and Equity: Fusion or Confusion?', *Academy of Management Journal*, 46: 13–26.

Davis, J. H., Schoorman, F. D., and Donaldson, L. (1997). 'Toward a Stewardship Theory of Management', *Academy of Management Review*, 22: 20–47.

De Haes, S., and Grembergen, W. V. (2005). 'IT Governance Structures, Processes and Relational Mechanisms: Achieving IT/Business Alignment in a Major Belgian Financial Group', *Proceedings of the 38th Hawaii International Conference on System Sciences*.

DeSanctis, G. M., and Poole, M. S. (1994). 'Capturing the Complexity in Advanced Technology Use: Adaptive Structuration Theory', *Organization Science*, 5(2): 121–47.

Di Maggio, P., and Powell, W. (1983). 'The Iron Cage Revisited: Institutional Isomorphism and Collective Rationality in Organisational Fields', *American Sociological Review*, 48: 147–60.

Dougherty, D. (1992). 'Interpretive Barriers to Successful Product Innovation in Large Firms', *Organization Science*, 3: 179–202.

Donaldson, T., and Preston, L. E. (1995). 'The Stakeholder Theory of the Corporation: Concepts, Evidence, and Implications', *Academy of Management Review*, 20(1): 65–91.

Drummond, H. (1998). 'Is Escalation Always Irrational?', *Organization Studies*, 19: 911–29.

Eisenhardt, K. M. (1989). 'Agency Theory: An Assessment and Review', *Academy of Management Review*, 14: 57–74.

Elkington, J. (1994). 'Towards the Sustainable Corporation: Win-Win-Win Business Strategies for Sustainable Development', *California Management Review*, 36(2): 90–100.

Finkelstein, S., and Hambrick, D. C. (1990). 'Top-Management-Team Tenure and Organizational Outcomes: The Moderating Role of Managerial Discretion', *Administrative Science Quarterly*, 35(3): 484–503.

Fiss, P. C. (2008). 'Institutions and Corporate Governance', in R. Greenwood, C., Oliver, K. Sahlin, and R. Suddaby (eds.), *Handbook of Organizational Institutionalism*. Thousand Oaks, CA: Sage, 389–410.

——and Zajac, E. J. (2006). 'Symbolic Management of Strategic Change: Sensegiving via Framing and Decoupling', *Academy of Management Journal*, 49: 1173–93.

Forbes, D., and Milliken, F. (1999). 'Cognition and Corporate Governance: Understanding Boards of Directors as Strategic Decision-Making Groups', *Academy of Management Review*, 24: 489–505.

Freeman, R., and Reed, D. (1983). 'Stockholders and Stakeholders: A New Perspective on Corporate Governance', *California Management Review*, 25 (Spring).

Friedman, M. (2004). 'The Social Responsibility of Business is to Increase its Profits', reprinted in Tom L. Beauchamp and Norman E. Bowie (eds.), *Ethical Theory and Business*, 7th edn. Upper Saddle River, NJ: Pearson, 50–5.

Galliers, R. D. (2003). 'Change as Crisis or Growth? Toward a Trans-disciplinary View of Information Systems as a Field of Study: A Response to Benbasat and Zmud's Call for Returning to the IT Artifact', *Journal of the Association for Information Systems*, 4(6): 337–51.

Giddens, A. (1984). *The Constitution of Society*. Cambridge: Polity Press.

Granovetter, M. (1985). 'Economic Action and Social Structure: The Problem of Embeddedness', *American Journal of Sociology*, 91: 481–510.

Greenaway, K. E., and Chan, Y. E. (2005). 'Theoretical Explanations of Firms' Information Privacy Behaviors', *Journal of the Association for Information Systems*, 6(6): 171–98.

Gu, B., Xue, L., and Ray, R. (2008). 'IT Governance and IT Investment Performance: An Empirical Analysis', *ICIS Proceedings*.

Hackman, R. (1990). *Groups That Work (and Those That Don't): Conditions for Effective Teamwork*. San Francisco, CA: Jossey-Bass.

Holland, C., and Light, B. (1999). 'A Critical Success Factors Model for ERP Implementation', *IEEE Software* 16(3): 30–6.

————and Gibson, N. (1999). 'A Critical Success Factors Model For Enterprise Resource Planning Implementation', *Proceedings of the 7th European Conference on Information Systems*. Copenhagen, 273–87.

Howcroft, D., and Wilson, M. (2003). 'Participation: "Bounded Freedom" or Hidden Constraints on User Involvement', *New Technology, Work and Employment*, 18(1): 2–19.

Islamoglu, M., and Liebenau, J. (2007). 'Information Technology, Transaction Costs and Governance Structures', *Journal of Information Technology*, 22: 275–83.

IT Governance Institute (2005). 'The Governance Institute Home Page', available at: <http://www.governanceinstitute.com/>.

Jaffe, A., and Stavins, R. (1994). 'The Energy Paradox and the Diffusion of Conservation Technology', *Resource and Energy Economics*, 16(2): 91–123.

Janis, I. (1982). *Groupthink*. Boston, MA: Houghton Mifflin.

Jarvenpaa, S., and Ives, B. (1991). 'Executive Involvement and Participation in the Management of Information Technology', *MIS Quarterly*, 15(2): 204–27.

Jensen, M. C., and Meckling, W. F. (1976). 'Theory of the Firm: Managerial Behavior, Agency Costs, and Ownership Structure', *Journal of Financial Economics*, 3: 305–60.

Kaplan, R., and Norton, D. (1992). 'The Balanced Scorecard: Measures that Drive Performance', *Harvard Business Review*, January–February: 71–9.

Karimi, J., Bhattacherjee, A., Gupta, Y. P., and Somers, T. M. (2000). 'The Effect of MIS Steering Committees on Information Technology Management Sophistication', *Journal of Management Information Systems*, 17(2): 207–30.

Kisfalvi, V. (2000). 'The Threat of Failure, the Perils of Success and CEO Character: Sources of Strategic Persistence', *Organization Studies*, 21: 611–39.

Kulik, B., O'Fallon, M., and Salimath, M. (2008). 'Do Competitive Environments Lead to the Rise of Unethical Behaviour: Parallels from Enron', *Journal of Business Ethics*, 83: 703–23.

Law, C., and Ngai, E. (2007). 'IT Infrastructure Capabilities and Business Process Improvements: Association with IT Governance Characteristics', *Information Resources Management Journal*, 20(4): 25–47.

Leonard-Barton, D. (1995). *Well-springs of Knowledge: Building and Sustaining the Sources of Innovation*. Boston, MA: Harvard Business School Press.

Lounsbury, M. (2007). 'A Tale of Two Cities: Competing Logics and Practice Variation in the Professionalization of Mutual Funds', *Academy of Management Journal*, 50: 289–307.

Lubatkin, M., Lane, P., Collin, S., and Very, P. (2007). 'An Embeddedness Framing of Governance and Opportunism: Towards a Cross-nationally Accommodating Theory of Agency', *Journal of Organizational Behaviour*, 28: 43–58.

Lynall, M., Golden, B., and Hillman, A. (2003). 'Board Composition from Adolescence to Maturity', *Academy of Mangement Journal*, 28(3): 416–31.

Margolis, J. D., and Walsh, J. P. (2003). 'Misery loves Companies: Rethinking Social Initiatives by Business', *Administrative Science Quarterly*, 48: 268–305.

Markus, M. L., Tanis, C., and Fenema, P. C. (2000). 'Multisite ERP Implementations', *Communications of the ACM*, April, 43(4).

——Axline, S., Petrie, D., and Tanis, C. (2000). 'Learning from Adopters' Experiences with ERP: Problems Encountered and Success Achieved', *Journal of Information Technology*, 15: 245–65.

Maurizio, A., Girolami, L., and Jones, P. (2007). 'EAI and SOA: Factors and Methods Influencing the Integration of Multiple ERP Systems (in an SAP Environment) to Comply with the Sarbanes–Oxley Act', *Journal of Enterprise Information Management*, 20(1): 14–31.

Meyer, J., and Rowan, B. (1977). 'Institutional Organizations: Formal Structure as Myth and Ceremony', *American Journal of Sociology*, 83: 340–63.

Montgomery, C., and Kaufman, R. (2003). 'The Board's Missing Link', *Harvard Business Review*, 81(3): 86–93.

Mumford, E. (1983). 'Participative Systems Design: Practice and Theory', *Journal of Occupational Psychology*, 4(1): 47–57.

Nah, F. F., Lau, J. L., and Kuang, J. (2001). 'Critical Factors for Successful Implementation of Enterprise Systems', *Business Process Management*, 7(3): 285–96.

——Zuckweller, K., and Lau, J. (2003). 'ES Implementation: Chief Information Officers' Perceptions of Critical Success Factors', *International Journal of Human–Computer Interactions*, 16(1): 5–22.

O'Donovan, G., and Gibson, K. (2007). 'Corporate Governance and Environmental Reporting: An Australian Study', *Corporate Governance: An International Review*, 15: 944–56.

Oliver, C. (1991). 'Strategic Responses to Institutional Processes', *Academy of Management Journal*, 16: 145–79.

Orlitzky, M., Schmidt, F., and Rynes, S. (2003). 'Corporate Social and Financial Performance: A Meta-analysis', *Organization Studies*, 24(3): 403–41.

Parr, A., and Shanks, G. (2000). 'A Model of ES Project Implementation', *Journal of Information Technology*, 15: 289–303.

Peterson, R. (2004). 'Information Strategies and Tactics for Information Technology Governance', in *Strategies for Information Technology Governance*. Hershey, PA: Idea Group.

Pettigrew, A. (1992). 'On Studying Managerial Elites', *Strategic Management Journal* 13: 163–82.

Pfeffer, J., and Salancik, G. (1978). *The External Control of Organizations: A Resource Dependence Perspective*. New York: Harper and Row.

Premkumar, G., and King, W. R. (1994). 'The Evaluation of Strategic Information System Planning', *Information and Management*, 26: 327–40.

Rotvold, G. (2008). 'How to Create a Security Culture in your Organization', *Information Management Journal*, 42(6): 32–8.

Sambamurthy, V., and Zmud, R. W. (1999). 'Arrangements for Information Technology Governance: A Theory of Multiple Contingencies', *MIS Quarterly*, 23(2): 261–90.

Sia, S., Soh, C., and Weill, P. (2008). 'IT Governance in Global Enterprises: Managing in Asia', *ICIS Proceedings*, Paris, France.

Solove, D. J. (2008). 'The New Vulnerability: Data Security and Personal Information', in A. Chander, L. Gelman, and M. J. Radin (eds.), *Securing Privacy in the Internet Age*. Palo Alto, CA: Stanford University Press.

Sousa, J. E., and Collado, J. P. (2000). 'Towards the Unification of Critical Success Factors for ERP Implementations', in *10th Annual Business Information Technology (BIT) Conference*, Manchester.

Standish Group (2006). Chaos report. <http://www.standishgroup.com>.

Suchman, L. (1987). *Plans and Situated Actions: The Problem of Human/Machine Communication*. Cambridge: Cambridge University Press.

Sumner, M. (2000). 'Risk Factors in Enterprise-wide/ERP Projects', *Journal of Information Technology*, 15: 317–27.

Sundaramurthy, C., and Lewis, M. (2003). 'Control and Collaboration: Paradoxes of Governance', *Academy of Management Review*, 28(3): 397–415.

Van Grembergen, W. (2002). 'Introduction to the Minitrack, IT Governance and its Mechanisms', *Proceedings of the 35th Hawaii International Conference on System Sciences* (HICSS), IEEE.

Vaswani, R. (2003). 'Determinants of Effective Information Technology (IT) Governance', unpublished thesis, School of Business, University of Queensland, Australia.

Wagner, E., and Newell, S. (2007). 'Exploring the Importance of Participation in the Post-implementation Period of an Enterprise System Project: A Neglected Area', *Journal of the Association for Information Systems*, 8(10): article 32.

Watson, T. (2006). 'Organizing and Managing Work', *Financial Times Management*.

Weaver, G. R., Trevino, L. K., and Cochran, P. L. (1999). 'Corporate Ethics Programs as Control Systems: Influences of Executive Commitment and Environmental Factors', *Academy of Management Journal*, 42(1): 41–57.

Weick, K. E. (1995). *Sensemaking in Organizations*. Thousand Oaks, CA: Sage Publications.

Weill, P., and Ross, J. (2004), *IT Governance*. Boston, MA: Harvard Business School Press.

Westphal, J., and Zajac, E. (1998). 'The Symbolic Management of Stockholders: Corporate Governance Reforms and Shareholder Reactions', *Administrative Science Quarterly*, 43: 127–53.

Zuckerman, E. (2004). 'Towards the Social Reconstruction of an Interdisciplinary Turf War', *American Sociological Review*, 69(3): 458–71.

CHAPTER 17

RETHINKING
INFORMATION SYSTEMS
SECURITY

AMY W. RAY

INTRODUCTION

SURVEY reports on security practices indicate that spending on information security management is steadily increasing. However, a quick review of the chronology of security breaches updated and maintained by privacyrights.org reveals that security breaches are also increasing. If both security breaches and spending are increasing, it is time to rethink current approaches to information security management.

Typically, security management involves some combination of organizational security policies development and investment in security tools and technologies. These two approaches may be viewed as top-down and bottom-up, respectively, where top-down security policies and procedures are based on the expected, known use of organizational information systems by authorized users and the bottom-up technology management efforts involve identifying and securing the specific vulnerabilities associated with the technologies employed by the organization. Examples of commonly used top-down guidance include the Information Systems Audit and Control Organization's Control Objectives for Information and related Technology (COBIT) and the International Standards Organization's ISO17799. Examples of bottom-up guidance include procedures for securing a UNIX platform or an Oracle database, various encryption methods appropriate for different wireless standards, or appropriate password management techniques for a specific end-user application (Zviran and Haga 1999; Soderborg, Crawley, and Dori 2003; Hesseldahl 2004).

The combination of policy- and technology-based security management efforts has worked reasonably well in the past. However, information systems and their use have become considerably more complex in recent years as the volume and variety of both systems components and authorized users is continuously growing. Newer technologies, from large and powerful computers to inventory tags, are more feature rich and more intelligent and thus more inherently complex than ever. When all of the intelligent computing components are interconnected for use in an organization, the result is an information systems network that is quite complex in terms of features, capabilities, and access points. The advantage of these intelligent and feature-rich systems is that they enable new and creative uses of data that may improve organizational effectiveness or efficiency. However, the seemingly endless variety of possible uses also often leads to unexpected and sometimes unknown developments that can potentially result in unexpected and unknown risks. Keeping up with emergent security risks is a daunting task in this computing environment where both increased access and increased complexity prevail.

Current security management approaches are insufficient because they can overlook additional risks resulting from interactions among technologies as well as the growing variety of unexpected ways that users interact with the technologies. Practical research on how to address known vulnerabilities associated with specific technological components is very active in the professional communities as witnessed by the speed with which software companies such as Symantec or Microsoft respond when new hacker exploits are uncovered. Research related to theoretical development and improvement of strategic-level, top-down information security guidance is also growing (Nance and Straub 1988; Straub and Welke 1998; Alter and Sherer 2004; Deshmuhk 2004; Sherer and Alter 2004). However, research that looks into the processes and outcomes resulting from interactions among newer feature-rich systems and the growing diversity of authorized users is quite limited.

Another problem is that security policies and technology management practices tend to remain fairly static until there is a problem such as loss of data from new and insecure employee practices or identification of a new type of malware. This reactive approach to changes in security management has become problematic because the network of organizational information systems and devices is not only increasingly more complex but also highly dynamic, and changes in users and uses of those systems is more dynamic than ever as well. Accordingly, the volume and variety of risks and vulnerabilities is constantly growing, requiring a more proactive security management approach that goes beyond top-down policies and bottom-up plugging of individual technological vulnerabilities. We need to incorporate into our security management methods explicit consideration of the dynamic and complex interactions of more feature-rich technologies with each other and with their users. The first part of this chapter considers how the growing sophistication of newer technologies demands new security management thinking beyond addressing individual vulnerabilities. The next section describes some new complexities resulting from interactions among more feature-rich technologies and their use, along with consideration of related security risks. The following section presents some ideas for improving security management efforts and includes suggestions for more proactively identifying risks resulting from emergent use of these systems. Specifically, the potential role of logical models similar to those used for decades for information systems analysis and design is introduced as a method to more effectively identify and manage security risks and vulnerabilities that result from the interactions among more complex systems components as well as the risks from more diverse and complex systems use. In summary, this chapter presents an effort to bridge the gap between high-level policy-based security management and low-level technology-based security management to consider how more attention to technological and business processes may lead to improvements in information security management efforts.

CHANGING FEATURES AND CHARACTERISTICS OF TECHNOLOGY

Organizational boundaries are non-existent in business today as a result of electronic, interorganizational information-sharing systems for supply chain management or other business purposes. Systems components including computers, cellphones, and even inventory tags are now equipped with features that enhance their support of mobile and distributed organizational and interorganizational information systems. These features have enabled improvements in communications efficiencies but have also increased communications complexity and related security risks.

Six characteristics of technologies enhanced with features to improve mobility and distribution are explored in this section for their capacity to increase the vulnerability of systems to attack. The purpose of this exploration is to demonstrate the challenge of security management in these complex environments rather than to represent an all-inclusive list of characteristics and associated vulnerabilities. RFID (radio-frequency identification) examples are used for purposes of illustration because they epitomize the highly distributed, mobile technologies in use today. Also, investments in RFID are growing rapidly, and as a consequence, most readers will likely have some familiarity with the technology. However, the six characteristics presented apply generally to other distributed, mobile applications (see also Chapter 18).

Table 17.1 presents a summary of the six distributed, mobile systems characteristics and associated vulnerabilities discussed here.

More Access

Most mobile applications are extensions to existing applications rather than replacements for them. For example, one common use of RFID is tracking inventory items in warehouses. Electronic, wireless tag readers are either placed at fixed points in buildings, provided to authorized users as handheld devices, or both. Since data are collected electronically, most companies anticipate reductions in labour, and consequently,

Table 17.1 Mobile system characteristics and related security vulnerabilities

characteristics	Vulnerbilities
More Access	• More points to control • More authorized users • No clear interorganizational policy guidelines • Mobile systems for sharing critical/sensitive data hold great promise to organizations and great temptation to hackers
Standards-Based Communications	• Mobile devices designed to trust each other, including rogue devices • Knowledge of data format standards may be enough to delete or modify fields (data visibility not necessary)
Greater Data Storage Capacity	• More mobile data increases potential cost per incident • More mobile data increases rewards form theft • Programmable storage at greater risk
Remote Objects and Sensors	• Remote objects more vulnerable to attack • Recovery from attack on remote abjects may take longer • Less human monotoring • Risk to in-transit objects may be greater
New Data Types	• Increases security management complexity • New location data difficult to manage and secure
Use of Public Networks	• Attacks can come from anywhere • Data in transit may be more visible

reductions in human error as well as employee theft. However, replacing humans with electronic polling devices produces an *exchange* of risks rather than a reduction of risks, for several reasons. The polling devices are electronic access points that can support new methods of data theft or corruption, and because distributed, mobile systems are wireless, introducing rogue devices to create new, unauthorized access points is also possible. Examples of potential attacks enabled by the new access points include intercepting and modifying product price information on a tag using a rogue device, interrupting network communications by placing a barrier over either a reader or a tag, and collecting inventory status information sent over wireless communications between polling devices and corporate systems (see Figure 17.1). In the case of information interception, RFID systems may provide a false sense of security to management because tag readers will continue to automatically send reports that inventory items are safe and secure as long as tags remain readable, readers remain functional, and no material differences in reports are encountered during or after an unauthorized access occurrence. Similarly, intentional interference with signals may be interpreted by security personnel as an ordinary technical failure, especially if the interference is temporary. However, a hacker may only need to disrupt service temporarily to steal inventory or to otherwise prevent security managers from electronically viewing malicious activities.

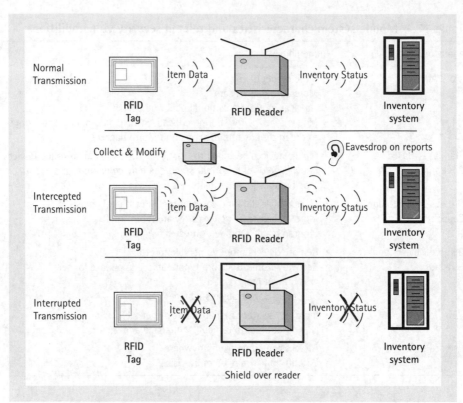

FIGURE 17.1 Access concerns

Since many RFID investments are in response to mandates for increased supply chain integration, there is increasing pressure to provide external access points to trading partners. Ensuring security of external connections from rogue access involves interorganizational agreement on security measures and trust that partners will comply. Coordinating interorganizational access controls is particularly important when the data exchanged across organizational boundaries are highly sensitive or valuable. In healthcare, for example, interorganizational use of RFID is growing in efforts to reduce administrative costs and medical errors through better and faster access to a variety of critical and sensitive data. Popular healthcare uses of RFID include using active tags to track patients in hospitals, using programmable tags to update patient care schedules, tagging medical equipment, devices, and pharmaceuticals to identify their location within facilities, and tagging and tracking hazardous waste. Clearly, giving authorized users distributed, mobile access to these types of data can improve healthcare management, but only if data thieves interested in anything from blackmail to asset theft to terrorism can be effectively deterred from using the same access points. Obtaining interorganizational consensus regarding who will be authorized users, how security policies and procedures will be developed and managed, and who is responsible for safeguarding infrastructure is challenging but essential where sensitive data are involved.

This is especially true in an environment like healthcare where the scope of authorized users can include personnel at hospitals, doctors' offices, laboratories, research facilities, pharmacies, and other locations.

Standards-Based Open Communications

The second characteristic of distributed mobile technologies affecting security risk is the growing dependence on standards. Data standards are applied to facilitate interpretation of information transmitted while transmission standards are applied to facilitate movement of data from one point to another. The ultimate goal is to apply data and transmission standards together for seamless, automatic information sharing across different systems without human intervention. For example, the Electronic Product Code (EPC) was developed at MIT as a data standard for assigning unique product identification codes to all items carrying an RFID tag. EPCglobal develops transmission standards to support the EPC data standard. Similarly, the Open Mobile Alliance has developed application-level protocols for retrieving the position of mobile devices independent of the underlying network technologies and the Open Geospatial Consortium (OGC) has worked with the OMA on frameworks for processing and transmitting location-based data. The Third Generation Partnership Project (3GPP), the Internet Engineering Task Force (IETF), the World Wide Web Consortium (W3C), and the Institute of Electrical and Electronics Engineers are also all working on various standards to facilitate sharing of mobile communications.

Standards-based applications are popular because they facilitate improved efficiency and effectiveness of mobile communications, but they can also facilitate the efforts of intruders. A standard, by definition, is well-documented and published, and is thus available to anyone interested in learning how to apply it. Communications and operations standards such as the OMA and OGC standards are designed to facilitate interoperability and compatibility of legitimate mobile systems but they also facilitate connection of rogue devices and applications to organizational systems. Where transmission standards are used to successfully obtain rogue systems connections, publicly available information on data standards such as the EPC may be used to understand how the data are structured on a tag, which can in turn be used to manipulate the data. At the 2004 Black Hat Conference, for example, a demonstration was given to show how a tool known as RFDump could display all metadata on programmable RFID tags and allow the user to modify the tag data using a simple text or hex editor (Hesseldahl 2004). Hackers may also use knowledge of mobile data standards to render objects unrecognizable to authorized readers, in turn making the object easier to steal or relocate. Security personnel must understand that weaknesses of each standard vary and recognize that hackers are studying standards to uncover associated vulnerabilities. In private sector applications, standards may be strategically manipulated to steal an inventory item or to change its value while more frightening scenarios may play out in public sector uses of these technologies, especially where tagged 'objects' include soldiers as well as weapons.

Greater Data Storage Capacity

The dynamic storage capacity of all sizes of mobile devices including notebooks, USB hard drives, mobile phones, PDAs, and RFID tags continues to grow, presenting its own set of security challenges. RFID tags typically have less storage capacity than other mobile objects, but some RFID tags are designed to store several thousand bits of information. As storage capacities continue to increase and prices continue to drop, the desire for greater efficiencies and profits will likely drive creative use of excess storage capacity on all mobile devices. For example, a business may start by using only EPC information in RFID tags but then subsequently elect to add static or even programmable information about items or transactions if it is considered profitable to do so. Item descriptions, source and destination information, useful life information, and other information that the tag encoder desires may be included on tags. While encryption may help secure data, it adds to tag costs while simultaneously reducing processing efficiencies, leading some companies to reject such security measures. Programmable (i.e. changeable) tags are at greater risk than read only tags because there is a risk that information about the object or the transaction may be changed by an unauthorized user to reflect a new state. The efficiency/security trade-offs associated with inclusion of rich information in tags must be carefully weighed in each situation. On one hand, adding more data to mobile devices can increase organizational efficiencies and effectiveness while on the other hand, successful hacks can result in greater cost per theft for organizations (e.g. more data stolen per theft). In addition, as the volume and richness of data carried on mobile devices grows, they will pose greater temptation to hackers since the potential rewards are greater.

Degree of Asset Remoteness

Risks to distributed assets may increase as the distribution and/or mobility of those assets increases. For example, handheld scanners carried on freight trucks may be more susceptible to theft or loss than handheld scanners used within a warehouse. Remotely located equipment such as RFID tag readers and other mobile sensors are vulnerable to physical attack and may be stolen, altered, or replaced with rogue equipment. Information transmitted to and from wireless, mobile devices is more vulnerable to interception than information transmitted over wired devices, so remotely located mobile devices present greater risks to organizations than remotely located wired equipment. Remotely located equipment is also vulnerable to intentionally distributed malicious code such as viruses, Trojan horses, and spyware as well as signal jamming through a variety of very low-tech means such as creating a temporary shield over remote equipment using a metal container. In addition, identifying the source of attacks on remotely located, highly distributed systems may take longer since they are typically not as well monitored as equipment more centrally located. Accordingly, greater damage to systems may be sustained and more data lost before attacks are discovered, consequently increasing the time required to recover from attacks.

In-transit mobile objects are at greater risk of being sensed by rogue equipment. Rogue readers can be placed anywhere along transportation routes and used to scan for interesting tagged objects en route. For example, a hacker could wander around trucks at a truck stop using a concealed handheld scanner to look for signals from trucks carrying tagged products. The goal may not be to read the tags but rather to simply pick up evidence that tagged objects are near, similar in concept to pinging a computer to identify its presence. The presence of a signal in conjunction with visual cues from the type of vehicle (e.g. armoured commercial truck, armoured military truck, delivery van, etc.) may provide enough intelligence to trigger a physical attack.

New Data Types

Many mobile technologies, including RFID and GPS (global positioning system), have location-sensing capabilities and thus introduce a new data type, location information, which must now be securely managed. Unlike other types of information that are simply read from a storage device, location information is derived either internally at the object level or externally at the reader level. It may be easier to control dissemination of location information that is internally generated as many such devices are programmed to remove location information from transmission, whereas externally derived location information cannot be controlled by the managing firm. Some devices, such as GPS-enabled cellphones, are locatable through internal as well as external means. For example, a GPS-enabled cellphone can be programmed to remove the GPS information from a transmission. However, the same cellphone can have its location externally derived using other positioning techniques simply because it is on a cellular network.

In addition to security efforts to control transmission of location information, companies need to consider the security implications of how location information is formatted and stored. For instance, the location of an object may be recorded as a physical location within a well-known spatial context such as the global coordinate system or, alternatively, as a symbolic location relative to some special context. For example, the location of a warehouse may be described by its longitude and latitude or by its proximity to a particular road or landmark. Physical location information is more vulnerable than symbolic location information when location data is transmitted over an insecure network. Once an information stream has been compromised, physical location information can be used to pinpoint the locations of objects with a degree of accuracy consistent with the location positioning technology. GPS-enabled tracking systems, for example, can report the locations of assets within a few metres in the global coordinate system. Once the physical location of an asset is captured, the information can be easily placed on a map. Further, as most tracking systems repeatedly report asset locations every few minutes or seconds, this information can be extrapolated to predict the future position of an asset.

The transmission of symbolic locations, on the other hand, is inherently more secure as the location information is coded within the context of the business application and can only be discovered by understanding the coding scheme. For example, an inventory item transmitted between a warehouse and a retail location might be encoded and have facility codes representing the symbolic location of assets. Only when the coding scheme is compromised can the symbolic locations be identified and interpreted.

Use of Ubiquitous, Public Networks

Perhaps the most readily apparent characteristic of mobile, distributed information technology that affects information security is that most distributed applications depend on the Internet for transferring information from one point to another. The Internet is designed to be open and available to every computer configuration, making it simultaneously ideal for information sharing and vulnerable to attack. Every computer connected to the Internet is theoretically connected to every other computer on the Internet. As a result, attacks on Internet-enabled applications can literally come from anywhere.

Prior to the Internet, organizations could avert most computer-related threats to information by implementing an effective enterprise risk management programme. However, as use of externally distributed systems grows, newer approaches are needed for identifying breaches, recognizing patterns of abuse from all internal and external authorized users, and for securing external connections to the extent possible. Accidental as well as intentional data entry errors can also have a greater negative impact over ubiquitous networks, since invalid data entered at one point may update multiple other data repositories.

In summary, evidence suggests that hackers are quickly learning how to exploit vulnerabilities associated with the mobile capabilities of computers and computing devices (Sullivan 2005). The distributed and mobile characteristics of systems today are attractive to hackers because of the increase in the inherent vulnerabilities of systems. Anticipated improvements in organizational efficiency and effectiveness have overshadowed concerns about the information security risks associated with these systems.

Given the growing volume and complexity of risks associated with employment of feature-rich technologies, a reactive approach to security management is increasingly problematic. First, patching systems in reaction to each new attack will be financially unsustainable with distributed, mobile systems because of the number and variety of possible attack strategies. Some evidence suggests that the bulk of corporate spending on information security is in reaction to external forces such as legislative mandates and threats from malware. Many companies react to legislative mandates by focusing on how they are going to provide evidence of compliance rather than focusing on the process of creating a more secure environment. To provide assurance of compliance with legislation, managers may create checklists of narrowly focused controls put into place to assure that each systems component is secure. For example, one checklist item might be that encryption is used for transmission of a particular type of sensitive data such as credit card information. While this approach to security management is clearly better than providing no security, it is ultimately suboptimal and can result in too much spending in one area while key vulnerabilities are missed in another area. Also, and as previously noted, changes in the way that technologies interact with each other has resulted in greater diversity of expected and unexpected uses of the systems, further exacerbating the challenges of security management. These additional concerns are discussed in the following section.

Systems Complexity and Use

Information security is dependent upon what we know about information systems and what we know about their use. While challenging, as discussed above, it is still easier to analyse systems components and their inherent weaknesses than it is to consider all the possible uses of interconnected information systems and associated devices and applications. This is an important consideration in light of the fact that most security breaches reveals are associated with unexpected and previously unknown uses of technology (privacyrights.org).

Findings from the IS literature (Truex, Baskerville, and Klein 1999) confirm that when complex systems are used by a diverse set of interorganizational users, opportunities for new, emergent uses of systems are created. For example, in healthcare, once a practice begins using an EHR system for patient visits, the care providers may decide to add new functionality (e.g. the ability to submit prescriptions electronically), new hardware (e.g. addition of handhelds for use in examination or hospital rooms), or simply change business practices (e.g. access records from a home computer as well as office computers). All of these are examples of emergent use of systems and data that can increase efficiency and effectiveness but may also have potential consequences for the security of the information that is accessed (Baskerville and Siponen 2002; Ray and Newell 2008). In particular, emergent use can increase the complexity of the system itself through the addition of features, functions, and component connections. As the volume and diversity of uses increases, the complexity of systems use will also increase. In turn, the complexity of systems and uses makes effective security management more challenging (Ray and Newell 2008). Approaches to the creation and maintenance of security policies that can keep up with contexts where there is a high level of system emergence are severely lacking, both in practice and in theory (Baskerville and Siponen 2002).

In situations where information systems are linked for interorganizational communications, an additional concern is that the needs of these different groups are likely to be contradictory so that competing needs must coexist rather than be resolved by tighter or more centralized control (Law 2000). As the diversity of users and uses increases, interorganizational system complexity increases. Interorganizational systems are made more complex due to their technologically sophisticated, organizationally and geographically dispersed nature. The complexity associated with interorganizational information systems stems from the interdependencies and interactions between the many different elements, managed by different organizations, with a large number of human actors attempting to accomplish diverse work processes in a variety of different organizational contexts. Such complex systems usually give rise to errors (social and technical), which can lead to failure (Perrow 1984), including a breach of security. Further, the complexity of large technical systems undermines the ability to plan and regulate them (LaPorte 1994) so that they constantly present threats of instability and security breaches, sometimes with dire consequences. Complexity typically involves an increase in the non-linearity of an environment, resulting in management complications where inputs lead to unexpected outputs (Daft and Lewin 1990). Non-linearity occurs when there is an interaction between two or more elements in a system that cannot be predicted at the time of design. Small changes in the behaviours of any one of the actors in the network can have multiple, small, secondary effects on the rest of the system that can ultimately lead to dramatic consequences. The result is that complex systems do not reach equilibrium states (Dooley and Van de Ven 1999) and can be upset by small unanticipated events (Arthur 1989). Complex systems, therefore, have emergent properties: 'They baffle us because we acted in terms of our own designs of a world that we expected to exist—but the world was different' (Perrow 1984: 75).

There are essentially two types of emergent use of an information system: intended and unintended. Intended emergent use is documented, planned use that results from efforts to exploit untapped potential in the data. One can see this emergent use in currently popular Enterprise Resource Planning (ERP) systems. (See also Chapter 15.) Initially ERP systems contained primarily financial and operational planning functions. Over time many new functions have been added, such as human resource and knowledge management functions that can exploit the integrated database that is the central characteristic of an ERP system (Newell, Huang, and Tansley 2004). In electronic health record (EHR) systems, emergent intended uses that have already arisen are e-prescribing and e-referral. Emergent intended use is, thus, planned based on the ideas of those involved in using, managing, or designing the system. Emergent intended use includes new functionality added to the system by software vendors, often based on feedback from users (Stefan and Von Hippel 2002).

On the other hand, unintended emergent use evolves organically as users appropriate a system and includes available functionality that is gradually adopted by a particular user or group of users. Cook and Brown (1999) refer to this as dynamic affordance. Dynamic affordance occurs through a process of situated learning as those using, managing, or designing an IT system learn about potential new opportunities to add to the functionality of the system to improve practice. This type of emergence is unplanned and often occurs without any knowledge of the system managers. Such unintended emergent use has been described as improvisation or tinkering, and research has shown that it is widespread as individuals learn to use new systems and identify ways to use a system that were not intended or anticipated by the system designers (Suchman 1987; Ciborra et al. 2000). Orlikowski (1996), for example, demonstrated how the customer support group in a software company appropriated the use of Lotus Notes technology. As she describes:

> In this organization, a series of subtle but nonetheless significant changes were enacted over time as organizational actors appropriated the new technology into their work practices, and then experimented with local innovations, responded to unanticipated breakdowns and contingencies, initiated opportunistic shifts in structure and coordination mechanisms, and improvised various procedural, cognitive, and normative variations to accommodate their evolving use of the technology. (p. 63)

Both intended and unintended emergent use is likely to pose increased security risks. Intended emergent use of highly distributed organizational or interorganizational information systems is likely to increase security risks because as functionality is added the number of users and organizations is increased, thus increasing the complexity of the system. Unintended emergent use is likely to further increase security risks because those involved may not be aware of the security implications of their improvisations; moreover, unintended emergence also increases complexity. Thus, there is a duality between emergence and complexity with emergence leading to complexity and complexity increasing the opportunities for emergence, while both complexity and emergent use have the potential to increase security risks.

As users work together and with technologies they establish 'normal' and 'unacceptable' behaviour (Gersick and Hackman 1990). These behaviours evolve into social structures encompassing the rules and norms that guide future behaviour (Giddens 1979). However, as the behaviours change so too do the structures. Thus, there is also a duality of interaction here as well, where action creates structures and structures constrain action (DeSanctis and Poole 1994). Action is 'conditioned by existing cultural structures and also creates and recreates those structures through the enactment process' (Walsham 1993: 34). This constant interplay of action and structure eventually settles into a somewhat stable state for most sets of users (DeSanctis and Poole 1994). However, as already noted, highly distributed organizational and interorganizational systems will involve multiple groups or communities of users across multiple settings, often with contradictory and conflicting needs and demands. So while a temporary equilibrium may be achieved within a set of users, the interdependencies between user groups means that any small alteration in use by one group can impact the structures governing the behaviour of other groups and can amplify across the whole system of use.

Email is an example of a technology that is currently used in a number of emergent ways, planned and unplanned. Email was an investment originally designed to simply facilitate rapid electronic communications. Organizations cost-justified investments in email systems through expectations that expenditures on traditional mail would fall, labour costs from routing external and internal mail would fall, and decision-making processes would be more efficient and effective than ever. Further, there was the expectation that use of email would be straightforward and the cost of the required software, server, and maintenance would be minimal. However, as a result of how quickly email was accepted by the business world, email vendors were soon offering enhanced applications with innovative capabilities such as support for attaching documents, and this led to a host of creative uses of email by users that were not originally anticipated when organizations initially invested in the software. For example, users began to use email as a backup for data storage, as a group decision support aid, as a document-sharing mechanism, as a method of advertising, as a method of collecting survey data, and as a source of non-business communications and entertainment. Email has become so embedded in our communications culture that new devices to support mobile access to email, for example Blackberries, emerged. While email has certainly fulfilled its promise as a rapid facilitator of communications, the inherent flexibility of email's structure led to the development of many other uses that were unforeseen at the time of the original investment. There have been a number of very positive outcomes from the alternative uses of email, but there have been numerous unforeseen costs. Immeasurable sums of time and money have been spent on efforts to control spam, malware, and non-work related use of email systems. Controlling access to only authorized users has become a daunting task as authorized users access sensitive business information through their email applications on various different computers and computing devices from virtually any location around the globe. Had there been a way to accurately forecast these additional costs and then include them in the decision model that included the time gained from efficiencies, would management have decided to invest in email? Another cost of email that was unforeseen in the early days is the cost of upgrading the networks to provide enough bandwidth for transmissions that continuously increase in volume and size. Foretelling the impact of email was impossible, but through examination of the evolution of feature-rich email applications that in turn led to a host of secondary positive and negative emergent uses, it becomes possible to consider some of the potential alternative uses of other feature-rich technologies.

For example, it is important to learn from our lessons with email that the same characteristics of systems that facilitate cost-effective improvements in business may also contribute to security management challenges. As with email, any highly distributed information technology that facilitates instantaneous sharing of information is harder to secure because perimeter controls are ineffective. Also, the wireless communications and mobile devices that we use in business today are inherently insecure and so increase the vulnerability of all systems connected via these networks and through these devices. A connection between any two computers can potentially put entire networks of computers at risk if, for example, unauthorized access into the system is obtained through just one improperly secured computer.

As systems and use evolve, it often becomes unclear who should own which part of the interorganizationally relevant data and thus who is responsible for securing the data. In healthcare, for example, different constituents (e.g. payers, physicians, laboratories, insurance agencies, and patients) require different levels of ownership and accessibility to health data. However, the heterogeneity and complexity of health data make it difficult to clearly define the ownership of data. Second, although healthcare systems are expected to enhance effectiveness and efficiency, the use of such systems also brings about legal risks. The sensitive and personal nature of the data associated with healthcare systems make these systems unique both in legal ramifications and their desirability for unwelcome guests to gain unauthorized access to them.

Additionally, because healthcare systems share information among multiple organizations, differences in organizational cultures and management processes further increase the security management challenges. Securing data that are used to support multiple types of processes and decisions makes identifying a complete set of potential security weaknesses across all processes challenging, especially given the fact that usage of the system and the data will change over time. Use of the system that was not anticipated at the time of system implementation and deployment may also lead to lawsuits in the future. Physicians and other health providers may hesitate to use the system due to the fear of lawsuits.

In summary, security against accidental and intentional destruction, and modification and misuse by the complete set of authorized and unauthorized users, is both critically important and managerially daunting. It will require an understanding of how the organizational and interorganizational processes interact with the supporting information technology infrastructure to appreciate the potential security risks to systems. How these factors collectively and individually influence security is not well understood and as a result, existing frameworks for security management, while helpful, are insufficient. Understanding how the interaction of the users, the organization, the work processes, and the technology will impact the system use will greatly enhance our ability to enhance effective security policies and practices. Research which explores the potential organizational and interorganizational uses of modern mobile and distributed systems will help us to understand how to leverage the systems' potential power without sacrificing security and privacy. In the following section, the potential uses of logical models, adapted from information systems analysis and design methods, are presented as an option for looking into the complex interactions among feature-rich technologies and users.

RETHINKING SECURE MANAGEMENT OF
COMPLEX SYSTEMS

Designing effective information system security requires an understanding of the range of relevant, possible attacks on any given system. The discussion thus far illustrates that in order to better understand information security vulnerabilities, it is imperative to understand the complex interactions among various technological elements of an information system, and thus understand the information structures and processes that are in place. The chapter began with a discussion on how most modern technologies today include mobile capabilities as well as many other features, rendering the technologies themselves inherently more complex than ever before. The following section addressed how interactions among these technologies and authorized users are creating new complexities in the organizational systems, and how these complexities are creating novel security challenges. As noted at the beginning of the chapter, these new security challenges are not fully addressed by the predominant approach to security management that employs a combination of top-down information security policy development and bottom-up 'plugging' of known technological vulnerabilities. The primary problem is that by simply considering known vulnerabilities of the technologies and expected use of the systems by the users, the risks that result from unexpected or unintended interactions are missed.

An additional issue that compounds these problems is that organizational information systems are heterogeneous, so learning about the unique complexities in one organizational information system typically will not be generalizable to other organizational systems. Further, research suggests that there is no 'best' IT architecture to use as a goal or a benchmark because IT architectures should be designed to support the uniquely complex decentralized organizational structures in place today (Agarwal and Sambamurthy 2002). As organizational structures increase in individuality as well as complexity, the information security challenges facing organizations become more voluminous as well as more complex. Accordingly, an important step in rethinking information security management is to develop systematic *processes* for identifying vulnerabilities and risks in our heterogeneous and highly complex organizational information systems. Providing processes for dealing with complexity will allow managers to address their unique security problems more effectively than creating evermore checklists and general policies.

Thus, it is proposed here that logical models, similar to the traditional, formal models used for decades in the analysis and design of complex information systems processes may be effectively adapted for analysis of security risks and vulnerabilities associated with the complex processes in modern organizational information systems and can lead to more effective design of security management strategies. Use of logical models to understand complex systems is not a new concept. However, in this age of packaged software and plug and play systems, decreasing attention has been paid to methods like logical modelling that are typically associated with custom development of programs and systems, although some research demonstrates that there may be a renewed interest in the possible use of logical and other models for understanding information technology activities in firms (Agarwal and Sambamurthy 2002). Additional research suggests that modelling techniques for complex systems should simply address the question of what are the primary functional capabilities of the systems and how can the information be used to better support organizational decision making. Using overly complicated diagramming techniques can confuse the readers of diagrams, thus defeating the purpose of creating the diagrams in the first place (Soderborg, Crawley, and Dori 2003). Accordingly, the diagramming technique used here for purposes of illustration is quite simple.

Returning to the concepts introduced in the section on the characteristics of modern technologies where RFID was used for illustration purposes, the examples used here will refer to location aware systems (LAS) technology generally, with some additional specific examples involving RFID, GPS, cellphones, or any other location aware technology. LAS technologies are used here for the same reasons that RFID was used earlier: they are growing in popularity and epitomize the organizational trend to invest in increasingly feature-rich and thus complex technology. LAS are also used because they are emerging as popular means for conducting a wide range of business transactions (Mitchell and Whitmore 2003). Location-based applications aim to determine with reasonable accuracy the relative position of one object, the object being located, to an object collecting the location information or external referencing scheme in order to provide value-added services at the point of the object being located. For example, cellphone applications to help locate the nearest gas and food, transportation management systems for optimizing routes and tracking assets, and inventory management of consumer goods as they move from manufacturing to warehousing to retail outlets are common uses of LAS in business. In addition, by using one type of technology to illustrate the use of logical modelling for security management, it is possible to provide more thorough examples of how alternative use result in different risks.

Two alternative ways that location aware systems are used in business are presented in this section. Mobile objects being located are referred to as *locatable objects*, and the objects performing location data collection as *location collection objects*. A locatable object is any object that can have its location derived using a *location collection process*. A location collection process is then an interaction between locatable objects and location collection objects and involves the transmission of *location data* from a locatable object to a location collection object (Figure 17.2).

The location data that are transmitted during a location process contain two fundamental properties: an *object reference* and a *location reference*. Additionally a *temporal reference* determining the time for which the location reference is valid can be sent in explicit or implicit form (Rodden et al. 2002). The object reference is used to denote uniqueness or class membership such as a product code, for the locatable object. In some cases, the object reference might be transmitted as actual data or conversely, implied within the properties of the signal itself (e.g. a specific radio signature). The

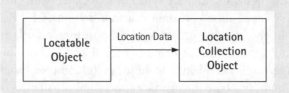

FIGURE 17.2 Logical model

location reference is defined within the spatial context of the location process and can consist of explicit, derivable, or implied location information. Explicit location references, such as a geographical coordinate, place the locatable object in an external spatial context such as the global coordinate system. A GPS-enabled transponder, for example, can transmit the actual geographic coordinate of the device. Derivable location references require the use of external positioning techniques to determine the location of the locatable object based on the physical properties of the transmission. A cellphone can be located with some degree of accuracy using triangulation methods, for example. Lastly, implied location references place the locatable object in the spatial context of a collection object based on a Boolean result of a collection process, i.e. the object is either there or it is not. The presence of an RFID tag, for example, can only be detected when it is within spatial proximity to a suitable reader.

A location collection process is initiated by a *location event*. A location event results in the transmission of location data and can originate from either locatable objects or location collection objects. When a locatable object initiates a location event, the collection process is a *push* system as location data are broadcast from the locatable object to any collection objects within range. When a location collection object initiates a location event, the collection process is a *pull* system and location data are shared through a specific request.

In push systems, locatable objects initiate location events. A locatable object transmits location data that can be received by location collection objects (Figure 17.3).

The transmission of location data in push systems requires the locatable object to carry an internally generated signal and have a power source. Data contained in the locatable object are generally broadcast based upon a particular event that is initiated by the locatable object. An example push event might be a periodic transmission from a mobile vehicle which is transmitted via a wireless system to a home base or an E-911 call from a cellular phone. While locatable objects in location-based system employing push models have the capability to initiate the dissemination of data, they have little or no control over the number and nature of collection objects that may receive the location data. Access controls on the collection infrastructure are then required to ensure security and integrity of any location data transmitted.

Technologies in this category include devices such as GPS-enabled transponders, cellphones that can be located via various triangulation methods and radio beacons such as those used to guide aircraft or locate aircraft black boxes. Active RFID tags also

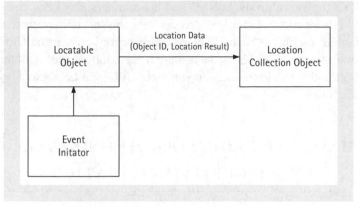

FIGURE 17.3 Push system

fall into this category as once activated, they can transmit location data without being in proximity to a reader until their power supply is exhausted.

In contrast to push systems, location event data in pull systems are transmitted in response to a query initiated by a location collection object. With pull systems, the location collection object queries locatable objects for location and other information contained within the object. During the location process, the location collection object broadcasts a query to which locatable objects within range respond with the requested data (Figure 17.4).

Data collection objects can only collect data from locatable objects that exist within the range of the collection objects capacity or range. An RFID scanner inventorying objects passing through a doorway, for example, will retrieve RFID identifiers and determine locations of objects relative to the scanner. The location context of the scanner is restricted to the scan tunnel and the concept of location in this example is a Boolean: the object is either present in the scanned space or it is not. Applying this

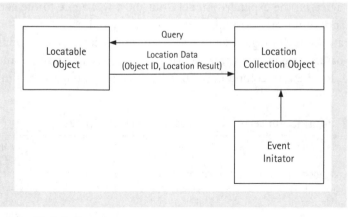

FIGURE 17.4 Pull system

concept, UPCs (universal product codes) and bar scanners may be placed in the same framework. The location of the UPC reader sets the location context of locatable objects (i.e. objects with bar codes). The only difference between the UPC and RFID technologies for purposes of this model is that UPCs require line of sight and therefore have a significantly restricted location context. UPC scanners can also inventory objects one at a time.

TECHNOLOGY PROCESSES, ALTERNATIVE USE, AND SECURITY IMPLICATIONS

Common to most strategic security frameworks is the balance of three security services: information integrity, confidentiality, and availability (Bishop 2003). Information integrity refers to the trustworthiness of data content and data sources, information confidentiality refers to protection of data from unauthorized users and uses, and information availability refers to assurance that data-sharing processes are protected from interruption. Table 17.2 provides examples of general information security threats in each of these three categories of security services. Note that some threats are against multiple security services. Consider further that each threat may be associated with multiple methods of attack. For example, categories of individuals who may attempt to intercept and collect (read) data include employees, former employees, random hackers, competitors, or terrorists. Similarly, methods employed for interception and collection of data may include stealing or hacking a password of a legitimate user, tapping into the communications medium, breaking into the database where desired information is stored, modifying an application program to change routing of information, or theft of a computer or device that will allow access to the desired information. While some efforts to expand categorization of security services beyond these three elements have been proposed, not all security professionals and researchers agree on the expanded models, but most will agree to the generalizability and importance of integrity, confidentiality, and availability.

To illustrate the use of logical models for analysing security vulnerabilities and risks in location-based systems, the three security services described above and the logical model of location aware computing defined earlier are applied to a simple example

Table 17.2 Information security services and security threats

Integrity	Confidentiality	Availability
Intercepting and modifying data	Intercepting and collecting data	Poaching network services
Poor data quality controls	Intercepting and modifying data	
Destruction of data	Malicious code	Denial of service
Malicious code		Malicious code

from electronic supply chain integration. The problem analysed requires providing visibility of pallets of goods as they move from manufacturer to warehouse. If the inventory management system employed active RFID on products and/or GPS on trucks in transit with the goods (i.e. using the push alternative for processing information), the basic process would involve periodic transmission of location information from the device, every fifteen minutes for example. These signals would pass the data onto an application in one or more organizations, which can use the data to update the location of the container.

Use of pull system processes for pallets might be implemented using passive RFID tags, where the tags are activated when in the presence of a suitable reader. The reader can record the time at which each tag was read and send the data to an application which can update the time at which the container was read by a specific reader. Readers are typically placed in a fixed location known a priori to the application: the exit gate of the manufacturer, an in-transit location, or the entrance to a storage facility, for example.

Results showing the different risks associated with alternative uses of LAS generally and RFID specifically are provided in Table 17.3. As the reader can see, the processes and use of technology significantly impact the risks associated with use of the technology, beyond the inherent characteristics of the technologies used.

Table 17.3 Application of push/pull model

	Push system	Pull system
Integrity issues	Loss or attenuation of signal due to 'blind spots', out-of-range, and system black-outs. Spurious location readings due to external effects on signal reception. Malicious use of technologies to confuse or jam signals (e.g. GPS jammers). Control of network to ensure data received and processed are not altered.	Recoding of RFID tags once they have been attached. Relocation of readers.
Confidentiality	Interception of signal by non-authorized systems. Ability to relate signal to physical object (i.e. the container). Ability to infer container content from signal. Ability to track container as it moves from source to destination and predict future location and time.	Controlled access to readers. Controlled access to proximity of container within 'scan range' of reader. Availability of technical specification of implementation e.g. RFID transmit frequencies, range, etc. Reconciliation of pallet contents to RFID tag.
Availability	Internal power source. Dependent on availability of network. Network traffic.	Access to readers. Power source for readers. Frequency interference.

The goal of this illustration is not to make technology recommendations or to determine the general benefit of one technology over the other. Rather, the intent is to illustrate how important considerations for ensuring information security are more readily apparent when using logical models to assess alternatives uses and processes.

CONCLUSIONS

To complement analysis of the inherent vulnerabilities in information systems components, consideration of electronic business processes and uses of information may reveal a broader and more complete set of vulnerabilities. By considering possible alternative unauthorized as well as authorized uses of information and systems, potential security risks and vulnerabilities may become clear that would not be visible otherwise.

Malicious attackers focus as much on how systems support electronic processes as they do on the inherent vulnerabilities of specific technologies used. If an attacker has access at any point in a system, she will consider how to use it to gain access elsewhere. Thus, a thorough analysis of all possible uses of a system prior to its implementation could help companies identify changes to systems architectures that will reduce security risks. This approach is proposed as particularly valuable where information architectures are complex and the number of possible electronic paths to data become too numerous to consider informally, as is the case with distributed, mobile systems.

Much research has focused on the efficiencies and effectiveness afforded companies through their investments in highly distributed, externally facing applications such as supply chain integration systems. The potential improvements in organizational efficiency and effectiveness are exciting to consider, but the information security risks associated with complex systems of feature-rich technologies must be addressed before systems can be fully trusted by their authorized users. This chapter presented reasons why we need to rethink information security management and demonstrated that the current guidelines for information security are increasingly insufficient for organizations with highly decentralized systems. More attention to how systems are employed is needed.

REFERENCES

Agarwal, R., and Sambamurthy, V. (2002). 'Principles and Models for Organizing the IT Function', *MIS Quarterly Executive*, 1(1).

Alter, S., and Sherer, S. (2004). 'A General But Readily Adaptable Model of Information Systems Risk', *Communications of the Association for Information Systems*, 14: 1–28.

Arthur, B. W. (1989). 'Positive Feedback in the Economy', *Scientific American*, 262(2).

Baskerville, R., and Siponen, M. (2002). 'An Information Security Meta-policy for Emergent Organizations', *Journal of Logistics Information Management*, 15(5/6): 337–46.

Bishop, M. (2003). *Computer Security: Art and Science*. Boston: Addison Wesley Publishing.

Ciborra, C., et al. (2000). *From Control to Drift: The Dynamics of Corporate Information Infrastructures*. Oxford: Oxford University Press.

Cook, S. D., and Brown, J. S. (1999). 'Bridging Epistemologies: The Generative Dance between Organizational Knowledge and Organizational Knowing', *Organization Science*, 10: 381–400.

Daft, R. L., and Lewin, A. R. (1990). 'Can Organization Studies Begin to Break out of the Normal Science Straight-jacket: An Editorial Essay', *Organization Science*, 1: 1–19.

DeSanctis, G., and Poole, M. S. (1994). 'Capturing the Complexity in Advanced Technology Use: Adaptive Structuration Theory', *Organization Science*, 5(2): 121–47.

Deshmukh, A. (2004). 'A Framework for Online Internal Controls', *Proceedings of the Americas Conference on Information Systems*, August: 4471–9.

Dooley, K., and Van de Ven, A. (1999). 'Explaining Complex Organizational Dynamics', *Organization Science*, 10(3): 358–72.

Gersick, C., and Hackman, J. R. (1990). 'Habitual Routines in Task-Performing Groups', *Organizational Behavior and Human Decision Processes*, 47(1): 65–97.

Giddens, A. (1979). *Central Problems in Social Theory: Action, Structure, and Contradiction in Social Analysis*. Berkeley and Los Angeles, CA: University of California Press.

Hesseldahl, A. (2004). 'A Hacker's Guide to RFID', Forbes, July. <http://www.rfdump.org/media/forbes.pdf>.

LaPorte, T. R. (1994). 'Large Technical Systems, Institutional Surprises and Challenges to Political Legitimacy', *Technology and Society*, 16(3): 269–88.

Law, J. (2000). *Ladbroke Grove, or How to Think about Failing Systems*. Centre for Science Studies, Lancaster University.

Mitchell, K., and Whitmore, M. (2003). 'Location Based Services: Locating the Money', in B. E. Mennecke and T. J. Strader (eds.), *Mobile Commerce: Technology Theory and Applications*. Hershey, PA: Idea Group Publishing.

Nance, W. D., and Straub, D. W. (1988). 'An Investigation into the Use and Usefulness of Security Software in Detecting Computer Abuse', *Proceedings of the Ninth International Conference on Information Systems*, 283–94.

Newell, S., Huang, J., and Tansley, C. (2004). 'Social Capital and Knowledge Integration in an ERP Project Team: The Importance of Bridging and Bonding', *British Journal of Management*, 15: 43–57.

Orlikowski, W. (1996). 'Improving Organizational Transformation over Time: A Situated Change Perspective', *Organization Science*, 7(1): 63–92.

Perrow, C. (1984). *Normal Accidents: Living with High Risk Technologies*. New York: Basic Books.

Ray, A., and Newell, S. (2008). 'Exploring Information Security Risks in Healthcare Systems', in *Encyclopedia of Healthcare Information Systems*. Hershey, Pa.: Idea Group Reference.

Rodden, T., Friday, A., Muller, H, and Dix, A. (2002). *A Lightweight Approach to Managing Privacy in Location-Based Services Technical Report Equator–02–058*. University of Nottingham, Lancaster University, and University of Bristol.

Sherer, S., and Alter, S. (2004). 'Information Systems Risks and Risk Factors: Are They Mostly about Information Systems?', *Communications of the Association for Information Systems*, 14: 29–64.

Soderborg, N. R., Crawley, E. F., and Dori, D. (2003). 'System Function and Architecture: OPM-Based Definitions and Operational Templates', *Communications of the ACM*, 46(10).

Stefan, T., and Von Hippel, E. (2002). 'Customers as Innovators: A New Way to Create Value', *Harvard Business Review*, 80: 74–81.

Straub, D. W. (1990). 'Effective IS Security: An Empirical Study', *Information Systems Research*, 1(3): 255–76.

——and Welke, R. J. (1998). 'Coping with Systems Risk: Security Planning Models for Management Decision-Making', *MIS Quarterly*, 441–69.

Suchman, L. (1987). *Plans and Situated Actions: The Problem of Human/Machine Communication*. Cambridge: Cambridge University Press.

Sullivan, B. (2005). 'Hacker Spies on T-Mobile Customers', MSNBC <http://msnbc.msn.com/id/6818785/>.

Truex, D., Baskerville, R., and Klein, H. (1999). 'Growing Systems in Emergent Organizations', *Communications of the ACM*, 42(8): 117–23.

Walsham, G. (1993). *Interpreting Information Systems in Organizations*. Chichester: Wiley.

Zviran, M., and Haga, W. J. (1999). 'Password Security: An Empirical Study', *Journal of Management Information Systems*, 15(4): 161–85.

CHAPTER 18

....

MOBILE IT

....

CARSTEN SØRENSEN

INTRODUCTION

....

THERE are in 2009 over 4.5 billion mobile phone connections globally and a growing number of other mobile information technologies permeate all aspects of life.[1] The around 1 billion mobile phones in developing countries is rapidly coming close to matching the global total of 1.5 billion Internet connections in 2008 (Kluth 2008). It is estimated that 6 billion mobile phone connections will be reached by 2013. The mobile phone offers a highly visible new information technology (IT) that has found its way into social and organizational life. A growing body of research studies this global socio-technical experiment of instant interactivity through the mobile phone. This significant strand of research uncovers a wealth of issues ranging from mobile phone usage across countries to the deeper cultural issues of instant touch between people. It generally provides a balanced discussion of how technological opportunities play out in social contexts. However, characteristic of most mobile IT research is its concern with one single technology in one particular sphere of life—the mobile phone in a general social context. Compared with this, little research has so far broadened the focus to include a range of mobile IT, mainly as such technological arrangements are not yet considered mainstream. It is, however, not uncommon to find people managing complex portfolios of mobile IT, for example, consisting of more than one mobile phone, a dedicated mobile email client, a notebook computer with wireless Internet access, and perhaps peripheral equipment interacting with the devices in Personal Area Networks (PANs) such as Bluetooth headsets, cameras, photo printers, and speakers. While the mobile phone offers a strikingly successful information technology, everyday life is for most people partially shaped by what Yoo (forthcoming) characterizes as 'experiential computing', i.e. activities involving everyday artefacts with embedded computing capabilities—mobile phones, iPods, cameras, GPS navigators, digital photo frames, toasters, ovens, etc.

There is, however, an even more striking lack of research into the organizational use of mobile IT, enterprise mobility. This issue is critical as both increased personalization and ubiquity of information technology at work raise important issues on the intersection between the individual experience at work, the coordination of work within teams, and the organizational concern for efficiency. The aim of this chapter is to outline the main issues of relevance for the understanding of mobile IT, such as the technological background, unpacking the issue of mobility, and contemporary research themes. The chapter also provides examples of discussions of enterprise mobility based on a series of case studies conducted 2001–7.

The following section characterizes mobile IT. The third section discusses mobility as a means of conceptualizing the use of mobile IT. The fourth section presents pertinent themes related to the study of mobile IT. The fifth section illustrates issues specific to the organizational use of mobile IT by way of results from a number of case studies. The sixth section concludes the chapter.

TECHNOLOGY

Mobile information technology relies critically on the combination of a number of technological developments discussed in this section. The miniaturization of computers has made them portable or embedded into the environment. Wireless connections to local or global information infrastructures have been established enabling widespread interconnectivity.

The Invention of Cellular Communication

When Lars Magnus Ericsson in 1910 built a telephone for his wife Hilda's car, this marked the beginning of a new era, even if its use required Hilda stopping the car and connecting the phone to telephone wires (Agar 2003: 8). However, it was two-way closed radio systems sharing frequencies that during the 1930s and 1940s became the first mobile IT of significant importance for the military and police forces. Two-way radio systems still play an important role in many contexts, such as in taxis and police vehicles. Harold S. Osborne forwarded in 1954 the prediction for a device similar to a mobile (or cell) phone with video connection and a phone number given to the owner at birth and which would follow him or her to their death (Ling 2004). However, the use of mobile communication systems beyond the police, military, and fire services was not possible until the 1970s invention of frequency reuse through a system of cells. During the 1980s first-generation (1G) mobile phone networks were established in cities around the world, gradually replaced in the 1990s with 2G GSM infrastructure and handsets. The first 3G network was established in Tokyo in 2001 and different 3G standards have since increasingly provided mobile phone users with fast data services. In 2003 the number of mobile phone subscriptions exceeded the number of fixed-line subscriptions (Castells et al. 2007).

Shrinking Computation to Portability

Intertwined with the global expansion of mobile telephony is the miniaturization and widespread diffusion of computational devices, of which the mobile phone of course is one. Making computers mobile and embedded has been a process of both significant technological achievements and of radical changes in the ways computation has been perceived. IBM's Chairman Thomas Watson in 1943 famously stated, 'I think there is a world market for maybe five computers.' Digital Equipment Corporation's co-founder Ken Olsen predicted in 1977, 'there is no reason for any individual to have a computer in his home.' Even Bill Gates's statement that 'Microsoft was founded with a vision of a computer on every desk, and in every home' no longer seems visionary. Already in the late 1960s and early 1970s, at the time of the large monolithic mainframes, Alan Kay and others from Xerox Parc formulated the conceptual design of the Dynabook, which in essence was a notebook or tablet computer. The Dynabook represented a conceptual leap in the understanding of how computers ought to support human activities. Another Xerox Parc researcher, Mark Weiser (1991), was later one of the first to properly formulate a vision of hundreds of computers becoming integrated into everyday life. Each such computer would be embedded in the environment or in portable objects providing a ubiquitous environment of everyday computational objects. The 1980s and 1990s produced a range of hand-held computers, Personal Digital Assistants (PDAs), supporting personal information management. These were subsequently equipped with wireless access capabilities accessing WiFi and GSM networks as well as Bluetooth technology for Personal Area Networks (PAN). The process of transforming PDAs into mobile phones is mirrored by the process of expanding the mobile phone with personal information management, document management, Internet access, etc. This began in the early 1990s and has resulted in the smart phone category converging the mobile phone and the PDA (Lind 2007).

Digital Convergence

The convergence between two distinct types of mobile technologies, the mobile phone and the PDA into the smart phone (Lind 2007), is a good example of the emerging convergence between the computing and the telecommunications industries where previous clear demarcations have become blurred. The duality of mobile IT in terms of complex infrastructures relying on global standards providing services through a variety of clients, handsets, and tags has shaped research in Mobile IT (Lyytinen and Yoo 2002b). The combined forces of mass-scale adoption of digitally converged mobile IT constitute emerging nomadic information environments that provide new challenges and opportunities for the development of infrastructures and services (Lyytinen and Yoo 2002b). Cultivating global mobile telecommunications infrastructures relies on a complex set of constantly evolving standards ensuring interoperability of services and handsets across countries. Research into processes of standardization of mobile tele-communications infrastructures seeks to understand how standards, policies, directives, and incentives relate to an innovation system, the marketplace, and regulatory regimes (Lyytinen and King 2002); for example, studies of international competition between standards (Funk 2002), understanding how innovation processes differ across countries (Yoo, Lyytinen, and Yang 2005; Tilson 2008), and interorganizational innovation based on standard infrastructures, such as mobile content services (Nielsen 2006).

The popularized technical understanding of digital convergence stipulates mergers of core functionalities from the computer (calculation), the telephone (point-to-point connection), and the television (broadcasting) (Yoffie 1997; Braa, Sørensen, and Dahlbom 2000). The concept of digital convergence has, however, been used as a broader conceptual clearing covering a range of possible interpretations, and through the lack of specific agreed meaning allow for an open-ended exploration with partici-pants who each may have varying and even conflicting understanding of its precise meaning. The most common interpretation of digital convergence is the digitization of previous analogue communications and data, thereby allowing processing of data across previously separated carriers through open standards (Lyytinen and Yoo 2002b). Convergence has also been used to describe convergence of the PDA and the mobile phone (Lind 2007); and the broader issue of converging the IT and telecom-munications industries (Kärrberg and Liebenau 2006). The concept has also been associated with much broader meaning beyond particular technical phenomena or specific industries, for example as the cornerstone in characterizing technological development (Schmidt 2008) or as a broad category of a number of phenomena, such as technical, economic, organic, global, and cultural convergence (Jenkins 2006). Studying the use of the concept of convergence within the Information Systems literature, Herzhoff (2009) finds that 317 articles in the top ten IS journals the past ten years have used the concept but also that only 48 of these (15 per cent) use the term in the context of technological change. The concept of digital convergence is essential for understanding phenomena related to mobile IT, but also as an emerging concept mirroring the dynamic reality of changing technologies, industries, and behaviour as digitization destabilizes established vertical industry arrangements (Tilson, Lyytinen, and Sørensen 2010).

Ubiquitous Computing

The term 'mobile' in mobile IT essentially refers to the client-part of the technology being portable and therefore implicitly supporting users who are geographically mo-bile. Although the client does not necessarily connect to a wireless infrastructure, this will often be the case. Characterizing wireless networking of portable information technology does, however, not fully cover the technologies considered here. Informa-tion technology can be characterized both in terms of the degree to which it is mobile and the extent to which it is pervasive, i.e. the technology has built-in capabilities of relating to its environment (Lyytinen and Yoo 2002a; Kourouthanassis and Giaglis 2008). The PDA and the notebook computer are both examples of information technologies that are mobile but not pervasive since they do not generally embed any understanding of the environment. A built-in sensor measuring the water level in a tank and sending a message to a server when the level is reduced below a certain point is an example of a stationary pervasive technology. Ubiquitous technologies display both characteristics of being mobile and pervasive (Lyytinen and Yoo 2002a). The mobile phone is a simple example of such a technology as it is only able to function due to a built-in ability to move across predefined cells. However, in terms of the user experience, the traditional mobile phone does not provide the user with ubiquitous services, for example, configuring services according to specific aspects of the environment. Contemporary location-based consumer services on GPS navigation devices or 3G mobile phones do, however, offer the user ubiquitous services. The Apple iPhone application Urbanspoon, for example, will suggest a restaurant near the user when the iPhone is shaken.[2]

Technology arrangements can also combine separate mobile and pervasive elements, where one part is embedded into the environment and the other is mobile. The best example of this is the large class of near field communication technologies used for contact-less cards and in RFID (radio-frequency identification) tags.[3] Tags and readers can both be mobile and stationary, for example, mobile pallets of goods with RFID tags passing by stationary readers (Arbin and Julander 2007), or RFID tags embedded in the environment patrolled by security guards carrying mobile phones with built-in readers (Kietzmann 2008). Expanding the perspective of mobile IT beyond handheld devices interacting with telecommunication networks offers a range of interesting opportunities for creating experiences by allowing the individual devices and the environment to interact (Mccullough 2004). This merger between the environment and client-devices has been characterized as augmented reality and originally emerged in the early 1980s when researchers experimented with wearable computing (Barfield and Caudell 2001).

Ubiquitous information technology raises serious issues of privacy as, for example, embedding tracking devices allow for subsequent inspections of human movement (Albrecht and McIntyre 2006). Registered contact less payment cards and mobile phones already constitutes opportunities for tracking either with proper legal authority or indeed without (Pamplin 2005). Steve Mann has since the late 1970s been experimenting with long-term use of wearable computing and advocates using such technology for counter-surveillance (Mann and Niedzviecki 2002). While the notion of the cyborg as a merger of the human body and wearable (Mann and Niedzviecki 2002) or bodily embedded technology (Warwick 2002) generates media interest and feeds into the collective imagination of strange futures, the mobile phone is through mass adoption and ubiquitous use in effect turning the global population into cyborgs. Augmented reality is no longer the dream of laboratory geeks, or reserved jetfighter pilots with head-up displays, but downloadable from the iPhone Store.[4]

MOBILITY

The primary aspect of mobile IT in use is obviously the ability to free the user from the constraints of engaging with technology in predetermined contexts, leading to the much-touted notion of anytime, anywhere interaction (Kleinrock 1996). The idea of simultaneously interacting with others or otherwise engaged in computing whilst mobile has inspired highly optimistic accounts of technological possibilities, such as Makimoto and Manners's (1997) early exposition of the 'digital nomad' who unhindered engages in fairly unproblematic global nomadic working. However, the issues are more complex than the initial technology-focused accounts of how the sheer technological opportunity in a linear manner alters behaviour, and these accounts tend to neglect the socially and organizationally situated nature of interaction (Wiberg and Ljungberg 2001; Pica and Kakihara 2003). This section discusses how the understanding of mobile IT can be situated in a context of social interaction and presents this in terms of: mobility as human movement; the mobilization of interaction; the paradoxes of technology in use: and the general notion of mobilities in society.

Human Movement

The term mobility is used to characterize a range of phenomena, such as: mobilization of armed forces, economic mobility, social mobility up and down the class system, and population mobility in terms of migration. Mobility as broadly related to the definition and use of physical space also relates to research within geography, architecture, sociology, organizational theory, and philosophy. Geographers have a long-standing interest in understanding everyday human movements (Hägerstrand 1975; Carlstein 1983), and in how social and economic development transform our understanding of space, for example, how social space is extended under globalization (Gregory and Urry 1985; Massey and Jess 1995). Nandhakumar (2002) applies time-geography techniques from the social geographers to understand locational and spatial aspects of software development work. Architects also seek to understand relationships between workplace design, social engagement, and working practices (Becker 2004). Within sociology, Goffman's (1959) detailed analyses of the use of space as means of reproduction of social routines and his spatial dramaturgical metaphor characterizing front- and backstage interaction has informed the study of mobile communications, for example, Ling's (2008) discussion of rituals. In organization studies, the issue of changing human geographical mobility and the role of space in organizational life in general, is largely under-researched (Felstead, Jewson, and Walters 2005). Dale and Burrell (2008) offer a critical analysis of the intertwined physical and symbolic role of space in organizations in terms of the shaping of identity and power. This work is partly based on Lefebvre's (1991) philosophical discussion of the meaning of space, in its broadest sense, as experienced in everyday life.

The understanding of how different mobile information technologies related to human physical movement can be characterized as the modalities of: (1) travelling and therefore being able to interact with a notebook computer; (2) visiting a place for a period of time and therefore having access to a desk, electricity, etc.; or (3) wandering within a local area, for example within a medical ward, or a manufacturing plant, thus rendering the use of any technology requiring two hands and a stable surface difficult or impossible (Kristoffersen and Ljungberg 2000). In addition to this simple classification of types of human movement and the subsequent evaluation of appropriate technological support, a more integrative approach can be illustrated by Luff and Heath's (1998) synthesis of three types of mobility in collaboration supported by technology. They distinguish between micro-, local, and remote mobility. Micro-mobility characterizes the way in which physical artefacts can be handled and managed at arms length between people. Local mobility signifies the ways in which people collaborate through moving around their place of work thereby using information and colleagues available to them where they are. Remote mobility implies the wider mobility of actors distributed across distance and moving between these. Here, the application of various artefacts and procedures will often support coordination of remote mobile activities. In terms of more comprehensive discussions of human movement and the use of a variety of ubiquitous information technologies, traditional categorizations of places are insufficient and further exploration of the tensions in the co-construction of everyday places and the ubiquitous technologies inhabiting these places (Bassoli 2010).

Mobilizing Interaction

Rather than merely categorizing and classifying modalities of human movement in time and space as the core aspect of mobility, further understanding can be gained by the more abstract notion of the mobilization of interaction through information technology in general and mobile information technology in particular (Kakihara 2003). This is similar to the concept of 'mobile communication' used by several researchers, such as Katz (2006) and Ling (2008) The essence of mobile IT is indeed a dramatic and interactive mobilization of interaction mediated by handsets, tags, readers, services, and associated infrastructures. The mobile phone enables personalized, situated, and thereby mobilized interaction between people and allows for new arrangements in the co-evolution of technological affordances and human practices, for example in terms of the temporal, spatial, and contextual aspects of interaction (Kakihara 2003). Mobilized interaction further challenges the notion of linear clock-time and supports social time with more flexible time disciplines (Lee and Liebenau 2002). Traditional spatial barriers for interaction are transcended allowing individual, social, or organizational concerns to influence the spatial aspects of interaction. Finally, mobile interaction alters the broader contextual aspects of interaction from being locally conditioned to flexible, coordinated by the participants in mobile interaction, for example in terms of who is engaged in the interaction, their moods, cultural context, and mutual recognition (Kakihara 2003).

John Urry suggests going even further than merely characterizing the mobilization of interaction and to include all mobilities in a mobile sociology (Urry 2000). This much broader sociological perspective is founded in the observation that global flows of people, objects, information, and images call for deeper inquiry than has been the case. Such a study involves understanding mobilities in terms of: corporeal travel of people; the physical movement of objects; the imaginative travel of images of places and people; virtual travel transcending geographical and social distance; and communicative travel through person-to-person messages (Urry 2007: 47).

Technology Paradoxes and Contrary Performances

The socio-technical relationship between the user and their mobile IT may be considered as a linear relationship of purposes being met by straightforward technological affordances, e.g. a person needs to obtain an address from a friend and therefore calls the person from their mobile phone. This, however, constitutes a techno-centric assumption of linear performances directly relating affordance to purpose without apparent contradictions and paradoxes (Mick and Fournier 1998; Arnold 2003). The use of technology can instead be conceptualized as a non-linear relationship between technical affordance and a diversity of contrary performances, partly where the user will engage coping mechanisms as a means of resolving the contradictions (Mick and Fournier 1998; Arnold 2003; Jarvenpaa and Lang 2005). Mobile IT will most often both follow the user and offer access to ubiquitous connections. The technology therefore follows the user in pockets and handbags while the user follows the technology by being disrupted when the phone rings. The mobile phone both facilitates the user's mobility and provides an uniquely fixed point of contact: 'We can move, but we are always there' (Arnold 2003: 243). It can render even the busiest person instantly available; yet provide an easy means for even the most available person to appear busy. The user is both liberated and leashed by the technology, which at the same time is deeply private and yet often making conversations into public events (Arnold 2003). Mobile IT offers an employee easy access to flexibly coordinate activities with a colleague on the fly but also his or her manager an instrument for instant control and micro-management. Technology performances emerge when technological affordance is socially situated thereby being thrown into a context of contradictions. Rudy Giuliani expressed this well when his wife had called him while he was addressing a large audience during the US presidential primaries: 'Well this is one of the great blessings of the modern age, being always available. Or maybe it isn't, I'm not sure' (Ling and Donner 2009: 108). Performances emerge from situated improvisation informed by individually cultivated coping strategies and can be stipulated by social and organizational practices (Schmidt 1999).

THEMES

This section outlines the main themes related to mobile IT and exemplifies these with contemporary research—primarily research monographs and edited books.[5] The research cited is concerned with socio-technical aspects of mobile IT and not primarily with purely technical aspects as this is an entirely separate technical field. Most of the work is not produced within Information Systems, although the use of mobile IT is a relevant area of concern for the Information Systems field. The study of mobile IT within Information Systems is an emerging field and there are relatively few articles published on this in the main Information Systems journals.[6]

The Social Aspects of Mobile Phone Use

Given the rapid diffusion of mobile phones across all regions of the world, and with the speed this particular technology has gained prominence in societies, it is natural that a large body of research engages in the social study of the mobile communication in everyday life. The relatively brief history and broad impact of the mobile phone in modern societies has been dealt with by a large number of books and edited collections, for example Brown, Green, and Harper (2001) and Agar (2003). As a truly global phenomenon, several efforts have documented the impact of the mobile phone across countries and regions, for example Katz and Aakhus (2002), Castells et al. (2007), Hjorth (2009), or specifically emphasizing the phenomenon in developing countries (Horst and Miller 2006; Donner 2008). The mobilization of interaction through technology raises a range of issues in everyday life, such as: the micro-coordination of social relationships, changing dynamics of family life, the reproduction of social rituals, the expression of identity, health, and safety, and disruptions (Ling 2004, 2008). Studies have explored: the relationship between the use of mobile phones and the development of language (Baron 2008); SMS practices (Harper, Palen, and Taylor 2005); the mobile phone as fashion and the relationship between the body and technology (Fortunati, Katz, and Riccini 2003); and the mobile phone and emotions (Vincent and Fortunati 2009).

It is also important to draw upon the lessons learnt from previous studies of fixed-line telephone use in order to compare and contrast findings (e.g. Pool 1997). Licoppe (2004) studies the use of fixed-line telephones, mobile phones, and SMS messages as means of managing social relations as a repertoire of connected relationships. The commercial aspects of mobile phone use have been the subject of substantial research, for example, mobile commerce in general (Urbaczewski, Valacich, and Jessup 2003), understanding the conditions for mobile data service usage (Blechar, Constantiou, and Damsgaard 2006), or the diffusion of wireless data services (Knutsen and Lyytinen 2007).

Mobile IT beyond the Mobile Phone

A smaller body of research outside the field of Human-Computer Interaction (HCI) and the technical fields has studied mobile and ubiquitous IT beyond the mobile phone, for example: a general theoretical understanding of embodied interaction using ubiquitous information technologies (Dourish 2001), the impact of RFID technology on consumer privacy (Albrecht and McIntyre 2006), or using mobile IT for learning (Kukulska-Hulme and Traxler 2005). The changing role of the city and the individual inhabiting this world of merging architectural and ubiquitous informational elements raises essential design issues (Mccullough 2004). The broader relationships between people, ubiquitous technologies, and the built environment are explored by emerging research conceptualized in terms of, for example, ambient information environments, or urban computing. Dourish and Bell (2007), for example, explore the everyday use of space as an infrastructure of experience.

Enterprise Mobility

Enterprise mobility, which is the use of mobile IT for the accomplishment, coordination, and management of organizational activities, is an emerging area of research and has received relatively little attention in research compared with the significant body of research on the impact of mobile communications on social life in general.[7] Technology-centric work on enterprise mobility emphasizes opportunities for changes to working practices through new technologies (Makimoto and Manners 1997; Lattanzi, Korhonen, and Gopalakrishnan 2006). Another strand of research emphasizes the work arrangements and changes in these, for example, characterized in terms of: homework; tele-work; remote work; mobile work; tele-commuting; Small Office Home Office; and virtual work (Daniels, Lamond, and Standen 2001). The fragmentation of workscapes into shared offices, home offices, and mobile working has implications for how work is managed and coordinated (Felstead, Jewson, and Walters 2005). A number of studies have explored mobile working, such as highly distributed photocopy repair engineers (Orr 1996), medical trial work and IT support (Ljungberg 1997), mobile journalists (Fagrell 2000), telephone engineers (Wiberg 2001), or equity investors (Mazmanian, Yates, and Orlikowski 2006); cab drivers (Skok and Kobayashi 2005), and policing (Manning 2008). These studies generally document changing working practices and the precarious balance between individuals and their supportive technologies. Generally, the issue of enterprise mobility still needs considerable research attention in order to shape a coherent research agenda emphasizing any unique aspects contributing to the general study of IT in organizational contexts.

Approaches for Studying Mobile IT

Any existing method discussion within Information Systems can be replayed and appropriated to the context of studying mobile IT, and current research of the social and organizational use of mobile IT also illustrates a diversity of approaches, for example: qualitative interviews (Kakihara 2003), remote recording of activities (Ela-luf-Calderwood, Kietzmann, and Saccol 2005) factor-based approaches for analysing survey data (Hong and Tam 2006), participant observation (Horst and Miller 2006), analysis of industry data (Castells et al. 2007), and action research (Kietzmann 2008). The specific characteristics of in-depth studies of enterprise mobility may call for approaches containing more than one data collection method, for example combining interviews and participant observation (Al-Taitoon 2005; Pica 2006) or remote record-ing of activities combined with interviews (Elaluf-Calderwood, Kietzmann, and Saccol 2005). Within human-computer interaction research it has been recognized that the unique characteristics of mobile IT requires new approaches to studying usability (Kjeldskov and Stage 2004). Similarly, it is important to invigorate a discussion within Information Systems of the relative strengths and weaknesses of the various elements in our methodological arsenal for the study of mobile IT.

Based on the experiences gathered during the past decade from studying enterprise mobility[8] it is clear that there are significant strengths associated with the interview-based approach for broadly understanding mobile activities and interviewee opinions about their socio-technical arrangements. It is, however, also evident that the often highly individually determined and emerging mobile activities make some form of observation an important source of primary data. The increased body closeness of most mobile IT potentially alters the perspective of the inquiry to encounter more for the individual that the traditional information systems approaches tend to do. In this sense, there is perhaps a need for a closer investigation of how to draw on lessons learnt within HCI research typically drawing upon theories from psychology. It can be argued that HCI research into usability must appreciate that the organizational usability is essential when the technology in question spans from the individual to service-layer and corporate and global infrastructures (Sørensen and Al-Taitoon 2008). Similarly, IS research must consider if the fact that our technological object of study is much more closely connected to individual discretionary actions also must lead to a re-appreciation of how best to study and analyse this phenomenon. This should also include discussions of the use of experimental approaches similar to much of HCI research; as well as the analysis of usage logs similar to Straub and Karahanna (1998) due to the difficulties in directly observing use. It is clear that it is a significant methodological challenge to comprehensively analyse the entire system spanning mobile or embedded technologies supporting mobile individual, distributed teams, the organization, concerns across organizations, and relying on organisational and global infrastructures. Table 18.1 illustrates the methodological diversity of a selection of the research efforts conducted at LSE in the period 2001–7.

Table 18.1 Selected examples of enterprise mobility studies 2001–7

#	Workers	Year	Location	Method	Extent	Topic	References
1	Professionals	2001–2	Japan	Interviews	63 interviews and in-situ observations	Mobilization of interaction for modern Tokyo professionals	(Kakihara 2003) (Kakihara and Sørensen 2004)
2	Off-premises foreign exchange traders	2003–4	Middle East	Interviews & observation	102 interviews plus observation of traders	Discretion and control in mobile working for off-premises foreign exchange traders	(Al-Taitoon 2005) (Sørensen and Al-Taitoon 2008)
3	London black cab drivers	2004–5	UK	Interviews & video observation	39 interviews and 14 hours of videotaped observations	The choice of location as core business strategy and the role of mobile technologies in pooling resources and informing individuals	(Elaluf-Calderwood 2008) (Elaluf-Calderwood and Sørensen 2008)
4	Police officers	2002–4	UK	Observation, interviews, & focus group	250+ hours' participant observation with 40+ officers and managers. 20+ interviews. 2 focus groups	The rhythms of interaction with mobile information technology by operational police officers	(Pica 2006) (Sørensen and Pica 2005)
5	Health professionals	2002–4	UK	Action research	Intensive collaboration with 16 students + others participating in project	Supporting situated and remote learning for medical professionals (Perioperative Specialist Practitioners) with mobile information technology	(Wiredu 2005) (Wiredu and Sørensen 2006) (Wiredu 2007)

6	Security guards	2004–5	UK	Action research	350 hours of meetings, interviews, & observation for Study 6 & 7	Real-life experimentation with RFID (radio-frequency ID) enabled mobile phone technology supporting new ways of working	(Kietzmann 2007) (Kietzmann 2008)
7	Industrial waste management workers	2004–5	UK	Action research	350 hours of meetings, interviews, & observation for Study 6 & 7	Real-life experimentation with RFID enabled mobile phone technology supporting new ways of working	(Kietzmann 2007) (Kietzmann 2008)
8	Delivery drivers	2006–7	UK	Observation & interviews	50+ people participating in interviews and participant observation	Establishing IT mediated control of work tasks with low degree of discretion through enterprise infrastructure and mobile information technology	(Boateng forthcoming)

WORK

This section provides illustrative examples of issues particularly relevant for the understanding of enterprise mobility. The section draws upon eight studies of enterprise mobility conducted 2001 to 2007 (Sørensen et al. 2008). Table 18.1 provides a brief overview of the eight cases, the empirical data collection approach applied, and references to key publications from each of the studies. The section emphasizes challenges, which although of possible general relevance for other socio-technical assemblages, gain particular importance when considering the organizational use of mobile IT. The following three aspects of mobile work are explored: Issues emerging for individual workers when supported by mobile IT; the challenges and opportunities for individuals engaged in the coordination of teamworking; and the interrelationships between individual mobile workers and broader organizational concerns for effectiveness.

Fluidity of Individual Mobile Performances

The introduction of mobile technology in the workplace signifies a closer and more intimate relationship between the individual worker and their everyday use of technology as a means of supporting decisions, managing information, and coordinating work with others. Contacting colleagues or accessing information may therefore be done immediately and be associated less with specific places. The straightforward discourse emphasizing technological opportunities rather than social and organizational realities, or indeed their interaction, leads to simplistic claims of mobile technology as a means of enabling work to be conducted anytime, anywhere, and with anyone (Kleinrock 1996; Makimoto and Manners 1997). Although mobile IT supports these opportunities, this does not imply that organizational realities and indeed the emerging operational demands are best satisfied through such fluidity as the requirements of work often will be organized under specific constraints (Wiberg and Ljungberg 2001; Cousins and Daniel Robey 2005). Characteristic for the studies listed in Table 18.1 was individuals facilitating fluid performances by carefully matching situational factors, individual preferences, and specific mobile IT affordances.

Hiro, the CEO of a small company developing various digital services for Internet-enabled mobile phones and television (Study 1), had extensive discretion regarding how he organized his day (Kakihara 2003). As a result he often engaged in one of his favourite pastimes: to find inspiration for new mobile services through immersing himself in Tokyo street life. He observed what people would do, what they would buy and wear. Being in the field of the Japanese consumer was a source of inspiration to Hiro, and he characterized this behaviour as 'being analogue' as opposed to surfing the Internet for inspiration. Wandering the streets of Tokyo was an important way for him to get new ideas for his company. Whilst traversing through Tokyo as a mobile age flaneûr (Kopomaa 2000) he is subjected to a large amount of requests for interaction through emails and calls to his mobile phone. His mobile phone was specially customized for him by one of his client companies—a mobile operator who also manufactures handsets. It represented significant symbolic value, as it was the only one of its kind. Hiro maintained a complex arrangement of alerts and ring-tones depending on who sought his attention. Hiro can be characterized as a digital nomad with extensive individual discretion, yet it is not the case that his working life is 'anytime, anywhere'. Hiro's extensive discretion to select and shape his workscapes (Felstead, Jewson, and Walters 2005) translated into specific choices for the purpose of getting inspiration. From a phenomenological point of view, situations always matter and the notion of anytime, anywhere can at most be translated into a discussion of the extent to which the constraints are imposed by the individual through exercising discretion, by necessities of work, or by organizational arrangements. Emphasizing the possibilities afforded by technological opportunities—interaction anytime, anywhere—favours the technological opportunities and not the emerging performances or indeed the human disposition (Pica and Kakihara 2003; Ciborra 2006). Hiro had very good reasons for going about his business as he did, and the mobile phone supported him in doing so. All the studies listed in Table 18.1 displayed complex interrelationships between the use of technology and the specifics of the situations users found themselves in.

Ray owned one of the 21,000 licensed London Black Cabs (Study 3). As an independent taxi driver, he also had extensive discretion regarding where and when he worked. Our interviews found that many cab drivers were motivated by a desire for flexible working arrangements in order to better balance work and family life (Elaluf-Calderwood 2008). However, choices regarding where and when to work were mostly informed by deep experiences in where to be located in order to make money as an independent business owner. The insights shaping Ray's choices were fashioned through extensive training and, as with Hiro, not merely a matter of choosing among seemingly open opportunities. Prior to becoming a licensed cab driver, Ray drove around the streets of London on a moped for several years in order to be able to pass a strict set of exams, 'The Knowledge', covering 25,000 streets in a six-mile radius from the centre of London. This exam has been largely unchanged since 1865. Having passed the exam and working as a black cab driver, Ray subsequently spent 5–6 years learning how to maximize his profit by choosing where and when to obtain cab fares. Gaining practical knowledge on how to use 'The Knowledge' allowed Ray to both be able to make immediate decisions based on his assessment of emerging situations as well as establishing a rhythm of working that both suited him and provided income. Explaining his work in terms of 'anytime, anywhere' would be misleading and simplify the underlying complexity.

Black cab drivers used mobile phones extensively as a means to get in touch with family and colleagues in order to socialize. Ongoing conversations with colleagues, furthermore, provide critical information about emerging events influencing the choice of location, such as particularly profitable work or essential traffic situations. In order to be able to meet steadily growing competition from minicabs where drivers are not required to pass 'The Knowledge' exam, London black cab drivers are turning to organizing themselves through joining computer-cab firms and accepting a certain quota of monthly jobs through an in-car terminal connected to a central dispatch office. This development is, in effect, almost the opposite of the traditional hierarchical organization seeking more flexible decision making through facilitating emerging mobile connections between its members.

The cases of Hiro and Ray both illustrate the paradox of mobile technology concurrently enabling flexibility and imposing constraints. Both were free to roam the streets of Tokyo and London respectively. However, they were also both constantly available through their mobile phones. Many of the cab drivers studied had more than one mobile phone in the cab. This naturally led to emerging contradictory performances as technological affordance of instant connectivity met the user's multiple contradictory dispositions. The intensification of the human-computer relationship by personalizing the technology and at the same time wirelessly connecting it to a variety of communication and information infrastructures also intensifies the technology paradoxes. Users engaged in coping strategies as a means of dealing with such paradoxes (Jarvenpaa and Lang 2005). Hiro dealt with the excessive demand on him wherever he was by customizing his mobile phone to filter incoming calls and emit a variety of subtle and less subtle sounds according to who was calling. This helped him make instant decisions of rejecting or accepting the call depending on the specific situation he found himself in. Ray would screen calls to his mobile phone and for example text a caller back with 'POB' explaining that he did not pick up the call as he had a 'passenger onboard'. However, both cab drivers and passengers equally used the mobile phone as means of absent presence when spending the cab ride on the mobile phone or doing email (Gergen 2002).

Characteristic for both examples above is that the performances, patterns of technology use, mainly emerge as complex individual responses to situations, personal preferences, and technological affordances. However, mobile work is of course not governed by such extensive individual discretion alone allowing for emerging performances to dominate. The role of mobile IT together with organizational procedures is also to stipulate specific sets of performances. For example, the requirements for cab drivers joining a computer cab organization to fulfil a specific quota of monthly fares through the computer system. The case of off-premises foreign exchange trading at a large Middle Eastern bank illustrates this (Study 2) (Al-Taitoon 2005). The traders spent their days trading on an ordinary trading floor. After normal hours a selective subset of traders continued trading using Reuters SmartWatches to follow the financial markets in London, New York, and Tokyo throughout the evenings and nights. They used their mobile phone for infrequent coordination of trading limits and to record trades on an answer machine inside the bank. Traders would largely engage in emerging performances and on their own decide how and when they engaged with the mobile technologies. This was essential as their working day implied extensive coordination of activities, something that was unrealistic to expect outside normal working hours. Indeed a previous configuration of off-premises trading based on trading stations set up in the traders' homes was not successful as it tied the traders to their homes (Sørensen and Al-Taitoon 2008). Off-premises trading stipulated, however, one specific mobile IT performance of documenting each trade separately by recording a message on a separate answer machine in the bank.

Late at night in an industrial estate in the outskirts of Manchester (Study 6), the security guard Simon was doing his nightly round at an electronics warehouse (Kietzmann 2007). At each checkpoint he waved his mobile phone, which had a built-in RFID (radio-frequency identification) reader, over a tag mounted on the wall and a message was automatically sent to a central server to update his whereabouts. The previous system was less interactive in reporting Simon's position immediately, but otherwise required him to touch tags on his rounds. The RFID reader mobile phone and associated back-end database further strengthens the remote control in a working arrangement where Simon engages in clearly stipulated performances with little room for emerging trade-offs.

Mobile IT can support the individual in managing information and in their interaction with others. An intimate relationship is fostered between the individual user and the mobile IT they engage with day in and day out. Combinations of emerging and stipulated technology performances express the mesh of situational characteristics, individual preferences, organizational arrangements, and technological affordances. The everyday cultivation of these performances through the years produce highly specialized skills dedicated to the socio-technical assemblage of mobile information and interaction management. In cases where individuals have extensive discretion and where they may be subjected to a range of conflicting demands, they will also cultivate individual coping mechanisms. Hiro stipulated relationships between expected disturbances and specific ring-tones in order to allow him to rapidly filter requests for his attention. Simon, on the other hand, was engaged in highly regulated work with the socio-technical assemblage of embedded tags, inspection routes, and recorded RFID tag-swipes establishing a regimented performance. Mobile IT will be experienced as providing either ubiquitous or opaque support for work depending on the extent to which the technology supports (Sørensen 2010): (1) a range of features enabling the user to establish priority of interaction if needed—Hiro's extensive email filters are an example of such prioritization, another example is the display of a mobile phone caller's identity; (2) and support for ongoing technology-mediated relationships as opposed to a series of individual encounters—for example the police radio supporting ongoing relationship between officers and the control room during incidents, as will be discussed in the following section. Mobile IT performances are, therefore, not only best described as an affordance subjected to contrary performances, but rather the process of cultivating the affordance to support appropriate counter-measures to complex demands is equally essential. Such interaction management mechanisms can, for example, support the negotiation of availability (Wiberg and Whittaker 2005), and hereby provide further individual experience of interaction ubiquity by embedding an individual coordination mechanism, without which the individual user would have had to carry the entire interactional burden on their own. This denotes an individualization of coordination mechanisms. The purpose is not exclusively the negotiation of mutual interdependencies but general interaction management in order to seek fluid interactivity.

Transparency in Team Collaboration

Carefully cultivated individual and organizational practices with mobile IT can serve a broad variety of purposes. One of the essential purposes is to support individuals participating in team collaboration. The coordination of work activities within teams implies managing their mutual interdependencies (Schmidt and Bannon 1992; Malone and Crowston 2001), which can be resolved through combinations of mutual adjustment, standardization, and direct supervision (Mintzberg 1983). Mobile IT can support both emerging and stipulated performances of mobile team members coordinating activities through: (1) lightweight support for mutual adjustments by affording direct access to synchronous and asynchronous connections; (2) the ability to push systems of standardization to the individual mobile worker allowing teams to operate based on shared understanding of these standards; and (3) offering extensive means for mediated supervision. Mobile IT offers through such support both the promise of increased transparency in distributed collaborative efforts as well as opportunities for rendering collaborative arrangements more opaque as both individuals and groups no longer may be able to gain an overview. From an analytical perspective, focusing on the coordination of mutual interdependencies emphasizes the cultivation of horizontal coordination of work amongst peers as opposed to the vertical aspects of managing work through command-and-control decision processes (Schmidt and Bannon 1992; Malone 2004). Such distinction is, however, analytical as the organization of individual teams can mix horizontal and vertical aspects depending on how dependent the team is on a project leader (Perlow, Hoffer Gittell, and Katz 2004).

In the south of England two operational police officers, John and Mary, drove at high speed towards a domestic disturbance incident (Study 4) (Pica 2006). Whilst driving to the incident they were in constant touch with the control room over the radio to report on their progress and to arrange for information about the incident and past incidents at the same address to be streamed from the control room to a small computer in the patrol vehicle—a Mobile Data Terminal. Mary read out the received information displayed on a detachable screen while at the same time supporting John in manoeuvring the car across intersections at high speed. As they arrived at the scene most mobile IT receded into the background. However, throughout the incident they kept in constant touch with the control room via their shoulder-mounted personal radios. Maintaining an overview of the collaborative arrangement was essential for both the highly distributed operational police officers and for control room staff and senior police officers. The two-way radio system was first used outside the military by the

Chicago Police Force in the 1930s Prohibition period of emerging organized crime (Agar 2003). Since then, police forces have embraced a diversity of mobile voice and data services as means of collecting intelligence, distributing information to officers in the field, and for coordination of efforts (Manning 2008).

The operational police officers studied had significant discretion when dealing with incidents and used a combination of emerging and stipulated performances with a portfolio of mobile IT. Using available information to translate a sense of uncertainty about the situations they were about to enter into a sense of calculated risks formed an essential part of their preparations for engaging. The Mobile Data Terminal installed in the vehicle offered several means for accessing both data and other officers to gain such understanding. The officers could search the national person and vehicle database, receive data from the control room, see the active queue of incidents, and send instant messages to other vehicles. In-car and personal two-way radios and mobile phones offered further means for direct point-to-point access to other police vehicles and to citizens. Officers were also held accountable for their actions and therefore subjected to a range of administrative measures ensuring this accountability in terms of following procedures, filling in forms and reporting progress. In the coordination of work, emerging performances continuously sought to balance the push of information to all officers with the dedicated pull of information from individual officers. The two-way radio system helped establish shared mutual aware-ness of the state of affairs but also offered a more limited resource for information. The Mobile Data Terminal offered a rich source of appropriated information pulled by individual officers before engaging with an incident, however, at the cost of providing other officers a chance to obtain awareness of the situation. This illustrates the constant balancing between rendering relevant aspects of the collaboration transparent and others opaque.

In the study of a team of truck drivers managing a flow of empty and full industrial waste containers between client organization sites and dumps (Study 7), the work had previously been conducted in a self-organized manner whereby several aspects of work were documented centrally (Kietzmann 2007). The team were, therefore, the only members of the organization with full insight into the exact whereabouts of containers as coping practices had emerged as a means of optimizing the overall performance of the team. These practices included temporarily storing empty contain-ers halfway between the customers to save on transport time, borrowing containers from or lending to colleagues from competing firms, or producing elaborate excuses to avoid being called to far-away emergencies. Extensive RFID tagging of containers was deployed and workers were equipped with RFID-reader enabled mobile phones auto-matically relaying information back to headquarters. This resulted in managers obtain-ing insight into the movement of containers through this direct link between the core elements in the common field of work (Schmidt and Simone 1996)—waste containers—and their symbolic representation in a central system. The movement of waste containers became visible beyond the team of truck drivers but the specific reasons for the workarounds did not. This was the cause of a conflict as local team discretion to organize work was challenged. The use of mobile IT can support transparency of activities beyond the immediate co-present group in similar ways as ordinary groupware technology, for example, the design team suddenly realizing that a remote group of top management are following their progress (Ciborra 1996). However, the central system directly modelling the interactive behaviour of the common field of work, containers, produced such transparency of teamworking allowing remote managers to not only question previously hidden mobile working practices, but also assume that all that was needed for effective teamworking was this transparency.

This section has mainly illustrated situations where a team is co-located, for example, two officers in one police vehicle or a team of waste disposal workers. In the cases of the Tokyo CEO (Study 1), off-premises traders (Study 2), and security guards (Study 6) mutual interdependencies were either resolved through mobile interaction or through predetermined stipulations of behaviour. The discussion of how coordination mechanisms can support not only distributed working needs to take into account the specific challenges of mobile working, for example, the opportunities and risks of rendering the actions, movements, and interactions of mobile workers visible for others to inspect. Increasing transparency of individual behaviour supports fluid negotiation of mutual interdependencies in collaboration as it allows remote inspection of the situation and thereby facilitates remote awareness of the state of affairs. For the police officers (Study 4), transparency was essential, as immediate assistance from colleagues required their awareness of what was going on. However, the design of collaborative working arrangements clearly needs to take into consideration the specific requirements for mutual awareness of mobile activities. This will relate directly to the extent of mobile worker discretion. Furthermore, as illustrated in the case of off-premises traders, it is not always optimal or indeed acceptable for mobile workers to be mutually interdependent and subjected to external inspection, for example when conducted outside normal working hours.

Efficiency in Managing Mobile Workers

This section is concerned with the management of mobile work emphasizing vertical processes of command-and-control rather than horizontal processes of coordination (Malone 2004). Managing mobile workers generally implies relying on technology mediation of direct supervision, mutual adjustments, and standardization. As argued by Yates (1989) in the case of early scientific management, control can be obtained through socio-technical systems collecting and aggregating operational data on organizational performance upstream and communicating decisions and values downstream. Information technology served as a means of satisfying increasing need for increased sophistication of control as industrial societies became more complex and faster (Beniger 1986). Similarly, enterprise mobility can be seen as a response to further fragmentation and intensification of information and interaction work.

At Foods International (Study 8) they provided food, drinks, and just about everything else needed to run small restaurants and fast-food outlets (Boateng, forthcoming). Jason worked as a delivery driver for the company and he had, like many of his
colleagues, only worked there for a relatively short period of time. However, the
systems he relied on in his daily work delivering goods to the customers were designed
to guide him through his working day. In the course of performing his duties, Jason
relied on the strength of technology-mediated interaction to update him on the
readiness of customers to collect their orders and any road diversions or blocks on
his routes. If he found a customer's shop closed at the time of delivery, Jason used the
company's mobile phone to find out from Customer Services the whereabouts of
the customer. The answer would determine if he would have to return at a later time
with the customer's purchased order. Jason's work was characterized by a low degree of
individual discretion and his activities were, similarly to the security guard in Study 6,
to a large extent stipulated and controlled by systems. Logistics technology carefully
orchestrated top down the flow of activities expected of Jason, but as GPS technology
was not yet implemented, the system critically relied on Jason to report his progress
and any emerging changes, for example, due to the unpredictable London traffic or
unavailable customers. The study demonstrated the use of mobile IT integrated with an
extensive organizational infrastructure allowing for replacement of emerging performances with stipulated ones. Mutual interdependencies between delivery drivers and
call-centre staff who took orders from customers, workers who picked items in the
warehouse, and those packing the lorry for delivery were largely mediated and stipulated by organizational systems. This illustrates the strength of an integrated station-
ary-mobile work support system for not only supporting highly distributed activities
but also as a viable tool to further limit individual discretion. However, the study also
revealed how improvised emerging technology performances could utilize the limitations of the control system to allow the mobile workers pockets of discretion to
organize their work.

The work-integrated training of sixteen National Health Service professionals
distributed across Great Britain (Study 5) sought to use mobile IT for the management
of the learning process (Wiredu 2005). This, however, resulted in significant conflict
and eventual abandonment of the technology for this purpose. The one-year process
involved the professionals engaging in on-the-job training at the hospital at which they
worked. An essential part of the theoretical learning and practical training was done at
one-week sessions every six weeks in London. Here, the main coordinator of the
programme was keen to follow and record the progress of each of the participants
when they were back at their respective hospitals. This was deemed essential both for
providing feedback on the learning and for documenting progress to ensure
subsequent certification. The students were therefore provided with a personal digital
assistant (PDA) with proprietary software to record conduct and outcomes of each
session back at their respective hospitals. The centrally stipulated technology performances of recording the learning process for the purpose of management, feedback,
and certification, ended up intrinsically being in the way of work being done both in

terms of the fluidity of individual activities and as a disruptive element in teamwork on the hospital wards. At the individual level, the participants, however, engaged in a rich set of emerging technology performances using the PDAs for personal information management, for reference using installed medical dictionaries, and for participants wirelessly exchanging documents when meeting up in London for sessions. The conflicts between the localized control of the participants at their hospitals and the desire for centralized influence and control through the technology from the central London-based learning-centre presented a significant barrier for using the mobile technology effectively. The aims for strong local control over activities locally clashed in territorial dispute with the attempts to exercise equally strong remote control from the central learning centre. As a result, the only useful aspect of the PDA was individual use.

A balanced approach to obtaining organizational control over mobile workers through stipulating technology performances was identified in the study of London black cab drivers (Study 3) who volunteered to join a computer-cab company in order to obtain more diverse access to fares. Each computer-cab company had its own rules for how many jobs were required of each driver, and for how jobs were allocated to drivers. Such stipulated technology performances through the allocation of jobs to mobile workers worked well from the perspective of the drivers as it was up to each of them where and when they decided to satisfy the quota. However, in terms of organizational efficiency of mobile working, the system could due to this discretion not guarantee the same performance as the minicab companies where drivers were much more centrally organized.

In terms of the management of mobile working, mobile IT can ensure that actors have sufficient information to engage localized discretion and thereby ensure emerging decision making suiting the specific situation. However, mobile IT performances also imply immediate access to exercise direct supervision. The degree to which the relationship between the assumed and real state of affairs is ambiguous, the individual mobile worker will be able to create spaces of freedom. However, with these increasingly easily being closed, the question is to what extent organizations will experience a further polarization into mobile work that is extensively based on individual discretion and work that is minutely observed and controlled. Several of the studies showed examples of mobile workers on purpose circumventing rules in order to gain small amounts of freedom. Study 2 also illustrated the limits to tightly coordinated work with traders being managed and engaging in tight coordination during the day and the subset of mobile traders being granted extensive discretion as a means of making off-premises out-of-hours trading possible at all.

For contemporary organizations enterprise mobility will raise a number of organizational issues regarding how to increase organizational effectiveness through enabling mobile working. In some cases this includes increasing the degree of centralized control and supervision, whilst other cases will demand increased cultivation of localized collaboration where mobile workers retain a high degree of individual discretion. Balancing the concern for direct supervision with the need for decentralized mutual adjustment will be an essential issue. The extreme examples of highly individualized executives, such as Hiro, or highly managed workers, such as Simon, only reveal the relatively simple part of the story as a large group between these two extremes still work from fixed locations, or engage in mobile working where organizations have yet to formulate how best to see mobilizing the workforce as a means of placing people where they matter and not only providing a perk to key members of the organization.

CONCLUSION

This chapter has explored the technical elements of mobile information technology and forwarded different interpretations of mobility as a way of conceptualizing the use of mobile IT. Subsequently, an overview of current research on mobile IT demonstrated that there is still a considerable gap between the possible research questions within MIS research of this significant technological phenomenon. Furthermore, it was argued that whilst the large majority of work has been concerned with the everyday use of mobile phones, there is much less research broadening the perspective to studying mobile and ubiquitous information technologies beyond the mobile phone. Even more significantly, it was argued that there is a dire need for comprehensive research on the use of mobile IT for enterprise mobility, despite a clearly formulated portfolio of research questions by Lyytinen and Yoo (2002b). To illustrate the emerging research in enterprise mobility, results from eight case studies were highlighted and discussed in terms of: the relationships of fluid interaction between user, task, situation, and technology; the challenges of managing mobile activities through increased discretion and by creating transparency of remote activities, and the effective organization of work through mobile IT.

A long list of issues could not be included, but mobile IT is still a phenomenon to be investigated, experimented with, and reflected upon. What is clear is that although most of the traditional classical concerns within information systems will be relevant to discuss in the context of this new technology, then it is also evident that the specific characteristics of the technology and of its individual, social, and organizational appropriation will give rise to uniquely new questions as well as nudging the classical ones in slightly different directions.

NOTES

1. Updated statistics from the GSM Association are available on <http://www.gsmamobileinfolink.com>.
2. See <http://www.urbanspoon.com/blog/27/Urbanspoon-on-the-iPhone.html>.
3. For more information on RFID, see <http://www.wikipedia.org/wiki/RFID>.

4. For example, Layar, <http://www.layar.com>.
5. There are just over sixty books on various aspects of mobile IT constituting a fairly exhaustive list of all the books written on mobile IT excluding the practitioner-oriented books on mobile commerce.
6. Searching all volumes of main IS journals for titles or abstracts containing either the term 'mobile' or 'cell' plus adding articles found manually, identified the following number of articles on mobile IT: MISQ 1, ISR 2, CAIS 1, JAIS 1, BIT 2, IT&P 2, JISM 2, SJIS 2, ISJ 3, JIT 5, JSIS 7, I&O 7, CSCW 8, ISM 10, and EJIS 11. The journals dedicated to mobile and ubiquitous computing, such as *IEEE Pervasive Computing, Personal and Ubiquitous Computing, Journal of Mobile Marketing*, as well as the HCI journals for obvious reasons have many more articles. However, the discourse in these journals will also often be remote from the core concerns within MIS, as for example illustrated by Sørensen and Al-Taitoon (2008) extending the usability concept to encompass organizational issues.
7. The total of 6 out of over 300 pages in Castells et al. (2007: 78–83) serves as a good illustration of this.
8. The research reported here has been conducted within the mobility@lse research unit established in 2001 at The London School of Economics and Political Science. For more information, see <mobility.lse.ac.uk>.

REFERENCES

Agar, J. (2003). *Constant Touch: A Global History of the Mobile Phone*. Cambridge: Icon Books.

Al-Taitoon, A. (2005). 'Making Sense of Mobile ICT-Enabled Trading in Fast Moving Financial Markets as Volatility-Control Ambivalence: Case Study on the Organisation of Off-Premises Foreign Exchange at a Middle-East Bank', Ph.D. dissertation, London School of Economics and Political Science.

Albrecht, K., and McIntyre, L. (2006). *Spychips: How Major Corporations and Government Plan to Track Your Every Move with RFID*. Nashville, TN: Nelson Current.

Arbin, K., and Julander, C.-R. (2007). 'Is RFID the Solution to Inventory Problems in the Retail Supply Chain?', in P. Andersson, U. Essler, and B. Thorngren (eds.), *Beyond Mobility*. Malmö: Studentlitteratur, 207–31.

Arnold, M. (2003). 'On the Phenomenology of Technology: The "Janus-Faces" of Mobile Phones', *Information and Organization*, 13: 231–56.

Barfield, W., and Caudell, T. (eds.) (2001). *Fundamentals of Wearable Computers and Augmented Reality*. Hillsdale, NJ: Lawrence Erlbaum Associates.

Baron, N. S. (2008). *Always On: Language in an Online and Mobile World*. Oxford: Oxford University Press.

Bassoli, A. (2010). 'Living the Urban Experience: Implications for the Design of Everyday Computational Technologies', Ph.D. thesis, London School of Economics and Political Science.

Becker, F. (2004). *Offices at Work: Uncommon Workspace Strategies That Add Value and Improve Performance*. San Francisco, CA: Jossey-Bass Business & Management.

Beniger, J. R. (1986). *The Control Revolution: Technological and Economic Origins of the Information Society.* Cambridge, MA: Harvard University Press.

Blechar, J., Constantiou, I. D., and Damsgaard, J. (2006). 'Exploring the Influence of Reference Situations and Reference Pricing on Mobile Service User Behaviour', *European Journal of Information Systems*, 15(3): 285–91.

Boateng, K. (forthcoming). 'ICT-Driven Interactions: On the Dynamics of Mediated Control', Ph.D. Dissertation, London School of Economics.

Braa, K., Sørensen, C., and Dahlbom, B. (eds.) (2000). *Planet Internet.* Lund: Studentlitteratur.

Brown, B., Green, N., and Harper, R. (eds.) (2001). *Wireless World.* Godalming: Springer-Verlag UK.

Carlstein, T. (1983). *Time Resources, Society and Ecology.* London: George Allen & Unwin.

Castells, M., Qiu, J. L., Fernandez-Ardevol, M., and Sey, A. (2007). *Mobile Communication and Society: A Global Perspective.* Cambridge, MA: MIT Press.

Ciborra, C. (ed.) (1996). *Groupware and Teamwork.* Chichester: John Wiley & Sons.

—— (2006). 'The Mind or the Heart? It Depends on the (Definition of) Situation', *Journal of Information Technology*, 21: 129–39.

Cousins, K. C., and Robey, D. (2005). 'Human Agency in a Wireless World: Patterns of Technology Use in Nomadic Computing Environments', *Information and Organization*, 15: 151–80.

Dale, K., and Burrell, G. (2008). *The Spaces of Organisation & the Organisation of Space: Power, Identity & Materiality at Work.* Basingstoke: Palgrave Macmillan.

Daniels, K., Lamond, D., and Standen, P. (2001). 'Teleworking: Frameworks for Organizational Research', *Journal of Management Studies*, 38(8): 1151–86.

Donner, J. (2008). 'Research Approaches to Mobile Use in the Developing World: A Review of the Literature', *The Information Society*, 24(3), June: 140–59.

Dourish, P. (2001). *Where the Action Is: The Foundations of Embodied Interaction.* Cambridge, MA: MIT Press.

—— and Bell, G. (2007). 'The Infrastructure of Experience and the Experience of Infrastructure: Meaning and Structure in Everyday Encounters with Space', *Environment and Planning B: Planning and Design*, 34(3): 414–30.

Elaluf-Calderwood, S. (2008). 'Organizing Self-Referential Taxi-Work with mICT: The Case of the London Black Cab Drivers', Ph.D. dissertation, London School of Economics and Political Science.

—— Kietzmann, J., and Saccol, A. Z. (2005). 'Methodological Approach for Mobile Studies: Empirical Research Considerations', in *4th European Conference on Research Methods in Business and Management*, Paris.

—— and Sørensen, C. (2008). '420 Years of Mobility: ICT Enabled Mobile Interdependencies in London Hackney Cab Work', in D. Hislop (ed.), *Mobility and Technology in the Workplace.* London: Routledge.

Fagrell, H. (2000). 'Mobile Knowledge. Gothenburg Studies in Informatics', Ph.D. dissertation, Department of Informatics, Gothenburg University, October.

Felstead, A., Jewson, N., and Walters, S. (2005). *Changing Places of Work.* London: Palgrave Macmillan.

Fortunati, L., Katz, J. E., and Riccini, R. (2003). *Mediating the Human Body: Technology, Communication, and Fashion.* Mahwah, NJ: L. Erlbaum.

Funk, J. L. (2002). *Global Competition between and within Standards: The Case of Mobile Phones.* Chippenham: Palgrave.

Gergen, K. J. (2002). 'The Challenge of Absent Presence', in J. E. Katz and M. Aakhus (eds.), *Perpetual Contact*. Cambridge: Cambridge University Press, 227–41.

Goffman, E. (1959). *The Presentation of Self in Everyday Life*. New York: Bantam.

Gregory, D., and Urry, J. (eds.) (1985). *Social Relations and Spatial Structures*. Basingstoke: Palgrave Macmillan.

Hägerstrand, T. (1975). 'Space, Time and Human Conditions', in A. Karlqvist, L. Lundqvist, and F. Snickars (eds.), *Dynamic Allocation of Urban Space*. Farnborough: House.

Harper, R., Palen, L., and Taylor, A. (eds.) (2005). *The Inside Text: Social, Cultural and Design Perspectives on SMS*. Dordrecht: Springer.

Herzhoff, J. (2009). 'The ICT Convergence Discourse in the Information Systems Literature: A Second-Order Observation', in *Proceedings of European Conference of Information Systems* (ECIS). Verona.

Hjorth, L. (2009). *Mobile Media in the Asia-Pacific*. Oxford: Routledge.

Hong, S.-J., and Tam, K. Y. (2006). 'Understanding the Adoption of Multipurpose Information Appliances: The Case of Mobile Data Services', *Information Systems Research*, 17(2): 162–79.

Horst, H., and Miller, D. (2006). *The Cell Phone: An Anthropology of Communication*. Oxford: Berg Publishers Ltd.

Jarvenpaa, S. L., and Lang, K. R. (2005). 'Managing the Paradoxes of Mobile Technology', *Information Systems Management*, 22(4): 7–23.

Jenkins, H. (2006). *Convergence Culture: Where Old and New Media Collide*. New York: New York University Press.

Kakihara, M. (2003). 'Emerging Work Practices of ICT-Enabled Mobile Professionals', Ph.D. thesis, London School of Economics and Political Science.

——and Sørensen, C. (2004). 'Practicing Mobile Professional Work: Tales of Locational, Operational, and Interactional Mobility', *INFO: The Journal of Policy, Regulation and Strategy for Telecommunication, Information and Media*, 6(3): 180–7.

Kärrberg, P., and Liebenau, J. (2006). 'IT and Telecoms Convergence: Mobile Service Delivery in the EU and Japan', in *Global Mobility Roundtable*. Helsinki.

Katz, J. E. (2006). *Magic in the Air: Mobile Communication and the Transformation of Social Life*. London: Transaction Publishers.

——and Aakhus, M. (eds.) (2002). *Perpetual Contact*. Cambridge: Cambridge University Press.

Kietzmann, J. (2007). 'In Touch out in the Field: Coalescence and Interactive Innovation of Technology for Mobile Work', Ph.D. dissertation, London School of Economics and Political Science and Political Science.

——(2008). 'Internative Innovation of Technology for Mobile Work', *European Journal of Information Systems*, 17(3): 305–20.

Kjeldskov, J., and Stage, J. (2004). 'New Techniques for Usability Evaluation of Mobile Systems', *International Journal of Human–Computer Studies*, 60: 599–620.

Kleinrock, L. (1996). 'Nomadicity: Anytime, Anywhere in a Disconnected World', *Mobile Networks and Applications*, 1: 351–7.

Kluth, A. (2008). 'Nomads at Last: A Special Report on Mobile Telecoms', *Economist*, 12 April, <http://www.economist.com/specialreports/displayStory.cfm?story_id=10950394>.

Knutsen, L. A., and Lyytinen, K. (2007). 'Messaging Specifications, Properties and Gratifications as Institutions: How Messaging Institutions Shaped Wireless Service Diffusion in Norway and Japan', *Information and Organization*, 17: 101–31.

Kopomaa, T. (2000). *The City in your Pocket: Birth of the Mobile Information Society*, trans. T. Snellman. Helsinki: Gaudeamus.

Kourouthanassis, P. E., and Giaglis, G. M. (eds.) (2008). *Pervasive Information Systems*. Armonk, NY: M. E. Sharpe.

Kristoffersen, S., and Ljungberg, F. (2000). 'Mobility: From Stationary to Mobile Work', in K. Braa, C. Sørensen, and B. Dahlbom (eds.), *Planet Internet*. Lund: Studentlitteratur, 41–64.

Kukulska-Hulme, A., and Traxler, J. (2005). *Mobile Learning: A Handbook for Educators and Trainers*. London: Routledge.

Lattanzi, M., Korhonen, A., and Gopalakrishnan, V. (2006). *Work Goes Mobile: Nokia's Lessons from the Leading Edge*. Chichester: John Wiley & Sons.

Lee, H., and Liebenau, J. (2002). 'A New Time Discipline: Managing Virtual Work Environments', in R. Whipp, B. Adam, and I. Sabelis (eds.), *Making Time: Time and Management in Modern Organizations*. Oxford: Oxford University Press, 115–25.

Lefebvre, H. (1991). *The Production of Space*. Oxford: Blackwell Publishing.

Licoppe, C. (2004). 'Connected Presence: The Emergence of a New Repertoire for Managing Social Relationships in a Changing Communication Technoscape', *Environment and Planning D: Society and Space*, 22: 135–56.

Lind, J. (2007). 'The Convergence Between the PDA and the Mobile Phone', in P. Andersson, U. Essler, and B. Thorngren (eds.), *Beyond Mobility*. Malmö: Studentlitteratur, 269–97.

Ling, R. (2004). *The Mobile Connection: The Cell Phone's Impact on Society*. Amsterdam: Morgan Kaufmann.

——(2008). *New Tech, New Ties: How Mobile Communication is Reshaping Social Cohesion*. Cambridge, MA: MIT Press.

——and Donner, J. (2009). *Mobile Communication*. Cambridge: Polity Press.

Ljungberg, F. (1997). 'Networking', Ph.D. thesis, Göteborg University, Gothenburg, Sweden.

Luff, P., and Heath, C. (1998). 'Mobility in Collaboration', in *Proceedings of ACM 1998 Conference on Computer Supported Cooperative Work*. New York: ACM Press.

Lyytinen, K., and King, J. L. (2002). 'Editorial: Around the Cradle of the Wireless Revolution. The Emergence and Evolution of Cellular Telephony', *Telecommunications Policy*, 26: 97–100.

——and Yoo, Y. (2002a). 'Issues and Challenges in Ubiquitous Computing', *Communications of the ACM*, 45(12): 62–5.

————(2002b). 'The Next Wave of Nomadic Computing: A Research Agenda for Information Systems Research', *Information Systems Research*, 13(4): 377–88.

Mccullough, M. (2004). *Digital Ground: Architecture, Pervasive Computing, and Environmental Knowing*. Cambridge, MA: MIT Press.

Makimoto, T., and Manners, D. (1997). *Digital Nomad*. Chichester: John Wiley & Sons.

Malone, T. W. (2004). *The Future of Work: How the New Order of Business Will Shape your Organization, your Management Style, and your Life*. Cambridge, MA: Harvard Business School Press.

——Crowston, K. (2001). 'The Interdisciplinary Study of Coordination', in G. M. Olson, T. W. Malone, and J. B. Smith (eds.), *Coordination Theory and Collaboration Technology*. Hillsdale, NJ: Lawrence Erlbaum Associates, Inc, 7–50.

Mann, S., and Niedzviecki, H. (2002). *Cyborg: Digital Destiny and Human Possibility in the Age of the Wearable Computer*. Toronto: Doubleday Canada.

Manning, P. K. (2008). *The Technology of Policing: Crime Mapping, Information Technology, and the Rationality of Crime Control.* New York: New York University Press.

Massey, D., and Jess, P. M. (eds.) (1995). *A Place in the World? Places, Cultures and Globalization.* Oxford: Oxford University Press.

Mazmanian, M., Yates, J., and Orlikowski, W. (2006). 'Ubiquitous Email: Individual Experiences and Organizational Consequences of Blackberry Use', in *Proceedings of the 65th Annual Meeting of the Academy of Management*, Atlanta, GA.

Mick, D. G., and Fournier, S. (1998). 'Paradoxes of Technology: Consumer Cognizance, Emotions, and Coping Strategies', *Journal of Consumer Research*, 25(September): 123–43.

Mintzberg, H. (1983). *Structure in Fives: Designing Effective Organizations.* Englewood Cliffs, NJ: Prentice-Hall.

Nandhakumar, J. (2002). 'Managing Time in a Software Factory: Temporal and Spatial Organization of IS Development Activities', *The Information Society*, 18(4): 251–62.

Nielsen, P. (2006). 'A Conceptual Framework of Information Infrastructure Building: A Case Study of the Development of a Content Service Platform for Mobile Phones in Norway', Ph.D. thesis, Oslo University, Oslo, Norway.

Orr, J. E. (1996). *Talking about Machines: An Ethnography of a Modern Job.* Ithaca, NY: Cornell University Press.

Pamplin, J. (2005). 'How to Track Any UK GSM Mobile Phone (Without the User's Consent)', *2600: The Hacker Quarterly*, 17.

Perlow, L. A., Hoffer Gittell, J., and Katz, N. (2004). 'Contextualizing Patterns of Work Group Interaction: Toward a Nested Theory of Structuration', *Organization Science*, 15(5): 520–36.

Pica, D. (2006). 'The Rhythms of Interaction with Mobile Technologies: Tales from the Police', Ph.D. thesis, London School of Economics and Political Science.

—— and Kakihara, M. (2003). 'The Duality of Mobility: Understanding Fluid Organizations and Stable Interaction', in *Proceedings of European Conference of Information Systems.* Naples.

Pool, I. D. S. (1997). *Social Impact of the Telephone.* Cambridge, MA: MIT Press.

Schmidt, K. (1999). 'Of Maps and Scripts: The Status of Formal Constructs in Cooperative Work', *Information and Software Technology*, 41(6): 319–29.

—— and Bannon, L. (1992). 'Taking CSCW Seriously: Supporting Articulation Work', *CSCW Journal*, 1(1 –2): 7–40.

—— and Simone, C. (1996). 'Coordination Mechanisms: Towards a Conceptual Foundation of CSCW Systems Design', *Computer Supported Cooperative Work: The Journal of Collaborative Computing*, 5(2–3): 155–200.

Schmidt, S. (2008). *The Coming Convergence: Surprising Ways Diverse Technologies Interact to Shape our World and Change the Future.* Amherst, NY: Prometheus Books.

Skok, W., and Kobayashi, S. (2005). 'An International Taxicab Evaluation: Comparing Tokyo with London, New York and Paris', *Knowledge and Process Management*, 14(2): 117–30.

Sørensen, C. (2010). 'Cultivating Interaction Ubiquity at Work', *The Information Society*, 26(4): 276–87.

—— and Al-Taitoon, A. (2008). 'Organisational Usability of Mobile Computing: Volatility and Control in Mobile Foreign Exchange Trading', *International Journal of Human–Computer Studies*, 66(12): 916–29.

—— and Pica, D. (2005). 'Tales from the Police: Mobile Technologies and Contexts of Work', *Information and Organization*, 15(3): 125–49.

——Al-Taitoon, A., Kietzmann, J., Pica, D., Wiredu, G., Elaluf-Calderwood, S., Boateng, K., Kakihara, M., and Gibson, D. (2008). 'Enterprise Mobility: Lessons from the Field', *Information Knowledge Systems Management Journal*, Special Issue on Enterprise Mobility, 7(1, 2): 243–71.

Straub, D., and Karahanna, E. (1998). 'Knowledge Worker Communications and Recipient Availability: Toward a Task Closure Explanation of Media Choice', *Organization Science*, 9(5): 160–75.

Tilson, D. (2008). 'The Interrelationships between Technical Standards and Industry Structures: Actor-Network Based Case Studies of the Mobile Wireless and Television Industries in the US and the UK', unpublished doctoral dissertation, Case Western Reserve University.

——Lyytinen, K., and Sørensen, C. (2010). 'Desperately Seeking the Infrastructure in IS Research: Conceptualization of "Digital Convergence" as the Co-evolution of Social and Technical Infrastructures', in *43rd Hawaii International Conference on System Science* (HICSS 43). Kauai, Hawaii.

Urbaczewski, A., Valacich, J. S., and Jessup, L. M. (2003). Special Issue: Mobile Commerce-Opportunities and Challenges, *Communications of the ACM*, 46(12): 31–2.

Urry, J. (2000). 'Mobile Sociology', *British Journal of Sociology*, 51(1): 185–203.

——(2007). *Mobilities*. Cambridge: Polity.

Vincent, J., and Fortunati, L. (eds.) (2009). *Electronic Emotion: The Mediation of Emotion Via Information and Communication Technologies*. Bern: Peter Lang Publishing.

Warwick, K. (2002). *I, Cyborg*. London: Century.

Weiser, M. (1991). 'The Computer for the Twenty-First Century', *Scientific American*, September: 94–110.

Wiberg, M. (2001). 'In between Mobile Meetings: Exploring Seamless Ongoing Interaction Support for Mobile CSCW', Ph.D. dissertation, Department for Informatics, Umeå University, Umeå, Sweden.

——and Ljungberg, F. (2001). 'Exploring the Vision of "Anytime, Anywhere" in the Context of Mobile Work', in Y. Malhotra (ed.), *Knowledge Management and Virtual Organizations*. Hershey, PA: Idea Group Publishing, 157–69.

——and Whittaker, S. (2005). 'Managing Availability: Supporting Lightweight Negotiations to Handle Interruptions', *ACM Transactions of Computer–Human Interaction*, 12(4): 1–32.

Wiredu, G. (2005). 'Mobile Computing in Work-Integrated Learning: Problems of Remotely Distributed Activities and Technology Use', Ph.D. dissertation, London School of Economics and Political Science.

——(2007). 'User Appropriation of Mobile Technologies: Motives, Conditions, and Design Properties', *Information and Organization*, 17: 110–29.

——and Sørensen, C. (2006). 'The Dynamics of Control and Use of Mobile Technology in Distributed Activities', *European Journal of Information Systems*, 15(3): 307–19.

Yates, J. (1989). *Control through Communication: The Rise of System in American Management*. Baltimore, MD: Johns Hopkins University Press.

Yoffie, D. B. (1997). *Competing in the Age of Digital Convergence*. Cambridge, MA: Harvard Business School Press.

Yoo, Y. (2010). 'Computing in Everyday Life: A Call for Research on Experiential Computing', *MIS Quarterly*, 34(2): 213–31.

——Lyytinen, K., and Yang, H. (2005). 'The Role of Standards in Innovation and Diffusion of Broadband Mobile Services: The Case of South Korea', *Journal of Strategic Information Systems*, 14: 323–53.

CHAPTER 19

A REVIEW OF THE IT OUTSOURCING LITERATURE: INSIGHTS FOR PRACTICE

MARY C. LACITY, SHAJI A. KHAN, AND
LESLIE P. WILLCOCKS

INTRODUCTION

THIS chapter provides substantial evidence that information technology outsourcing (ITO) research has meaningfully and significantly addressed the call by Lee (1999) and Westfall (1999) for academics to produce knowledge relevant to practitioners. The ITO academic literature that studies practice is widely cited and indicates that academics have clearly served to disseminate learning. In addition, thoughtful practitioners have published their IT outsourcing experiences in academic outlets (Huber 1993; Cross 1995), further fuelling the ability of academics to abstract lessons for practice. In several ways then, ITO research has been an exemplar of how information systems (IS) academics can study and inform practice.

ITO research aimed at studying and influencing practice has examined multiple aspects of the phenomena, from reasons why organizations outsource through to the long-term consequences of outsourcing from both client and supplier perspectives. The first published outputs from academic research appeared in 1991, which documented companies pursuing large-scale *domestic* IT outsourcing (Applegate and Montealegre 1991; Huber 1993). More quantitative research and multiple-case studies followed, focusing on why firms outsource (Loh and Venkatraman 1992a) and how firms benefit (or do not benefit) from IT outsourcing (Lacity and Hirschheim 1993; Willcocks and Fitzgerald 1993). Between 1994 and 2000, at least 79 other academic studies were published (Dibbern, Winkler, and Heinzl 2004), many geared towards practice. Since the beginning of 2009, we found 357 published papers on ITO.

The eighteen years of research on domestic IT outsourcing has generated a good understanding of the practice. Overall, we learned *why* firms outsource (mostly to reduce costs, access resources, and focus internal resources on more strategic work[1]), *what* firms outsource (mostly a portion of their overall IT portfolio), *how* firms outsource (mostly by formal processes), and IT outsourcing *outcomes* as measured by realization of expectations, satisfaction, and performance (Dibbern, Winkler, and Heinzl 2004). Overall, we know that client readiness, good strategy, good processes, sound contracts, and good relationship management are key success factors (Teng, Cheon, and Grover 1995; Feeny and Willcocks 1998; Cullen, Seddon, and Willcocks 2005a; Willcocks and Lacity 2006).

More recently, much of the academic research has focused on *offshore* outsourcing. Offshore outsourcing research addresses macroeconomic issues, supplier capabilities in developing countries, and specific client and supplier practices to ensure success. From the client perspective, researchers have found that offshore IT outsourcing poses additional challenges when compared to domestic IT outsourcing (Rottman and Lacity 2006). Some of these issues are so difficult to manage that, more recently, according to Carmel and Abbott (2007), practitioners are turning to nearshore alternatives.

There are many other emerging outsourcing trends that interest practitioners, including business process outsourcing (BPO), application service provision, freelance outsourcing, rural sourcing, certifications of outsourcing professionals, and global standards. Academics have already contributed to practice for the first two trends among this list. The remaining topics offer academics a chance for future research.

Our aim in this chapter is to extract the insights academics have identified for ITO practice. From an in-depth study of the literature, we classified 191 ITO research papers into six topics. Each topic is thoroughly reviewed in this paper (see Table 19.1). Each topic answers specific questions relevant to practice.

RESEARCH METHOD

Our study goal requires a complete review of past ITO research relevant to practice. To identify papers which adequately represent the topics above, we searched the full-text of articles within ABI/INFORM, EBSCOHost, and JSTOR databases with ITO-related keywords for articles published between 1990 and 2008. The preliminary search resulted in 765 papers. Perusal of abstracts resulted in the elimination of 408 articles which did not directly pertain to ITO. This resulted in a list of 357 papers related to ITO across 71 journals (see Appendix 19.1). Following this, we carefully examined each paper and categorized it into the six topics (see Table 19.1). Some papers cover more than one topic, thus the total number of papers considered for this review was 191. These papers are a rich mix of conceptual and empirical studies.

Table 19.1 ITO topics relevant to practice

Topic	Questions relevant to practice	Number of articles
1. Determinants of IT outsourcing	• Which types of firms are more likely to outsource IT?	73
2. IT outsourcing strategy	• What is the strategic intent behind IT outsourcing decisions? • What are the strategic effects of IT outsourcing decisions?	24
3. IT outsourcing risks	• What are the risks of IT outsourcing? • How are IT outsourcing risks mitigated?	34
4. Determinants of IT outsourcing success	• Which practices increase the likelihood that a client's outsourcing decision will be successful?	86
5. Client and supplier capabilities	• Which capabilities do client firms need to develop to successfully engage IT outsourcing suppliers? • Which capabilities do client firms seek in an IT outsourcing supplier?	64
6. Sourcing varietals	• How do practices differ when pursuing different types of outsourcing such as offshore outsourcing, application service provision, and business process outsourcing?	49
Total unique articles (topics overlap across articles)		191

As ITO researchers will well attest, there are few standard terms and definitions applied across ITO studies. For example, ITO outcomes have been measured as cost expectations realized (Lacity and Willcocks 1998), project duration, re-work, and quality (Gopal, Mukhopadhyay, and Krishnan 2002), perceptions of strategic, economic, and technical benefits (Grover, Cheon, and Teng 1996), and effects on stock price performance (Hall and Liedtka 2005). In order to compare findings across this vast body of literature, we coded the empirical findings[2] for both qualitative and quantitative articles using a unique grounded coding technique we developed and published in Jeyaraj, Rottman, and Lacity (2006).

The method works as follows. We first extracted the authors's terms and definitions for dependent and independent variables to begin building a master list. We then began to combine variables that had similar definitions, altering the master list with each pass through another article. For example, eighteen articles empirically examined the variable we call 'Access to Expertise/Skills'. The specific variable names in the articles were, for example, 'Technical expertise for new IT' (Kishore et al. 2003), 'Access to experts' (Al-Qirim 2003), and 'Access to a larger group of highly schooled professionals' (Sobol and Apte 1995). Each pass through a new article also triggered a reanalysis of the master list and a re-examination of previously coded articles, until all articles were coded against the master list of terms and definitions. In the end, we identified 174 variables of which 130 were independent variables, 17 were dependent variables, and 27 variables were used as both an independent and a dependent variable. We use these codes to report on the overall findings for practice for the six topic areas.

DETERMINANTS OF IT OUTSOURCING

As evidenced by Table 19.1, the category 'Determinants of IT Outsourcing' is one of the most researched areas in our database of ITO articles with 73 empirical articles. Researchers who study the determinants of IT outsourcing primarily ask:

- Which types of firms are more likely to outsource IT?

Researchers examine attributes of client organizations that engage in IT outsourcing. These client firm attributes include *financial attributes* (firm profitability, return on assets, earnings per share, operating expenses, and financial slack in the organization), *size attributes* (size of the client firm in terms of total revenues or number of employees or size of the IT department within the client firm), and *industry attributes*. Below we present the findings from the academic literature on the three types of determinants of ITO.

Financial Attributes

Concerning the client-firm's financial attributes, we coded fourteen relationships that examined financial attributes as determinants of IT outsourcing decisions. Five relationships were not significant. Among the nine significant relationships, eight found that poor financial performance was a determinant of IT outsourcing decisions. Thus, more than half the findings report that IT outsourcing is primarily done by firms with poor financial performance.

Practitioners became aware of this finding from Paul Strassmann's controversial 1995 article 'Outsourcing: A Game for Losers'. He looked at financial data and layoff data for thirteen companies with the largest IT outsourcing contracts. He concluded 'Strategy isn't driving outsourcing. Statistics show the real reason companies outsource is simple: They're in financial trouble.' In a 2004 publication, Strassmann conducted another statistical analysis on 324 companies and reached the same conclusion: 'My 1995 assertion that "outsourcing is a game for losers" still stood up in 2002.'

Academic research has generally found Stassmann's findings to be robust across time, from the most widely cited study by Loh and Venkatraman in 1992a to a more recent study by Mojsilovic et al. in 2007. This was particularly true for client-firms pursuing large-scale IT outsourcing because academic researchers primarily rely on outsourcing announcements in the trade press to identify a pool of outsourcing clients to study. (Small IT outsourcing contracts are unlikely to be announced in press releases.) For example, Loh and Venkatraman (1992a) is one of the first major articles on the determinants of IT outsourcing—it has been cited 341 times. Based on data from 55 large US firms, the authors found that high business cost structures, poor business performance in terms of reduced profits, high levels of debt, high annual IT costs, and poor IT performance determine large-scale outsourcing of IT in client firms. Thirteen years later, Hall and Liedtka (2005) found very similar findings. They examined the financial determinants of large-scale IT outsourcing decisions. They used secondary data to compare 51 firms doing large-scale outsourcing of IT with 1,261 control firms. The authors conclude that IT outsourcing is a practice of 'financial losers' in that the 51 firms had significantly lower profits, higher operating expenses, and less cash than control firms. Mojsilovic et al. (2007) studied 68 publicly traded firms and found that companies with lower profits and lower earnings per share were more likely to outsource IT.

Size Attributes

Concerning size of the client firm, the findings are mixed. Of the eleven relationships we found in the empirical ITO literature, six found that size of the client firm did not matter (e.g. Grover, Cheon, and Teng 1994), two found that larger client firms are more likely to outsource (e.g. Nam et al. 1996), and three found that smaller firms are more likely to outsource (e.g. Ang and Straub 1998). Studies of the size of the IT department also produced mixed results. Of the seven relationships we examined, three found that larger IT departments are more likely to outsource (e.g. Sobol and Apte 1995), two found that smaller IT departments were more likely to outsource (e.g. Barthélemy and Geyer 2004), and two found no relationship between size of IT department and IT outsourcing (e.g. Miranda and Kim 2006).

Industry Attributes

We coded fourteen relationships between client industry and IT outsourcing. Five relationships did not find that industry mattered (e.g. Barthélemy and Geyer 2005). Nine relationships found that industry mattered, but it is difficult to identify a clear pattern because of the variety of ways researchers operationalize 'industry'. Some researchers use Standard Industry Classification (SIC) codes (e.g. Oh, Gallivan, and Kim 2006). Some researchers use dichotomous classifications such as public versus private (e.g. Slaughter and Ang 1996) or service versus industrial (e.g. Loh and Venkatraman 1992a). Some researchers use categories of industries such as manufacturing, finance, and healthcare industries (e.g. Grover, Cheon, and Teng 1994).

Insights for Practice

For the practitioner, this body of research does not extract best practices, but instead provides a deeper understanding of the attributes of client firms that pursue IT outsourcing. Which types of firms are more likely to outsource IT? Overall, client firms that are more likely to pursue IT outsourcing—particularly large-scale IT outsourcing—are in poorer financial health compared to peer firms. Some industries are more likely to outsource than others, but because researchers have used so many different industry classifications, there is no clear list of particular industries to report. Size of the client firm and size of the client firm's IT function also have no clear pattern to report.

Academic research has also looked at the determinants of second generation outsourcing decisions (e.g. Lacity and Willcocks 2000; Cullen, Seddon, and Willcocks 2005b; Whitten and Leidner 2006). After a client firm outsourced IT, did the firm next decide to bring the IT function back in-house, renew the contract with the existing supplier, or continue outsourcing using a different supplier? For example, Whitten and Leidner (2006) found that both economic and relationship constructs are important determinants of second generation outsourcing decisions. Clients renewing contracts report high levels of product, service, and relationship quality, and higher switching costs. Clients that switched suppliers report high product and service quality but low relationship quality and switching costs. Clients that brought back IT in-house report low levels on all four variables.

IT OUTSOURCING STRATEGY

This topic examines ITO strategies and how IT outsourcing strategies either affect or are affected by firm strategies and firm performance. Researchers have addressed the questions:

- What is the strategic intent behind IT outsourcing decisions?
- What are the strategic effects of IT outsourcing decisions?

The Strategic Intent behind IT Outsourcing Decisions

As evident in the section on the determinants of IT outsourcing decisions, empirical results generally found that large-scale ITO decisions are driven by poor financial performance, suggesting that the 'strategic' intent of IT outsourcing is to reduce costs. To get a more thorough view on ITO strategy, we coded the motivations for IT outsourcing as assessed by client firm representatives. Research on what motivates client organizations to outsource ITO has uncovered a long list of motivations or expectations from outsourcing IT (see Table 19.2). By far, cost reduction was the most

Table 19.2 Motivations for IT outsourcing

Motivation for Outsourcing	Description	Number of Articles
Cost reduction	A client organization's need or desire to use outsourcing to reduce or control IS costs.	39
Focus on core capabilities	A client organization's desire or need to outsource in order to focus on its core capabilities.	24
Access to expertise/ skills	A client organization's desire or need to access supplier(s) skills / expertise.	18
Improve business/ process performance	A client organization's desire or need to engage a supplier to help improve a client's business, processes, or capabilities.	17
Technical reasons	A client organization's desire or need to gain access to leading-edge technology through outsourcing.	10
Flexibility	The ability to adapt to change.	7
Political reasons	A client stakeholder's desire or need to use an outsourcing decision to promote personal agendas such as eliminating a burdensome function, enhancing their career, or maximizing personal financial benefits.	5
Change catalyst	A client organization's desire or need to use outsourcing to bring about large-scale changes in the organization.	4
Commercial exploitation	A client organization's desire or need to partner with a supplier to commercially exploit existing client assets or form a new enterprise.	3
Scalability	A client organization's desire or need to outsource to be able to scale the volume of IS services based on demand.	3
Access to global markets	A client organization's desire or need to gain access to global markets by outsourcing to suppliers in those markets.	2
Alignment of IS and business strategy	The fit or congruence between a firm's business strategy (conceptualized as defenders, prospectors, analysers) and its outsourcing strategy (e.g. arm's length, independent, and embedded).	2
Cost predictability	A client organization's desire or need to use outsourcing to better predict IS costs.	2
Headcount reduction	A client organization's need or desire to use outsourcing to reduce the number of staff.	2
Need to generate cash	A client organization's desire or need to generate cash through the sale of IT assets to the supplier.	2
Rapid delivery	A client organization's desire or need to engage in outsourcing in order to speedup project delivery.	2
Innovation	A client organization's desire or need to use outsourcing as an engine for innovation.	1
Total articles		143

common motive identified by researchers. Despite all the rhetoric of using outsourcing strategically, cost reduction has remained an important driver for a majority of client firms, from the earliest studies (e.g. Lacity, Hirschheim, and Willcocks 1994) to more recent ones (e.g. Fisher, Hirschheim, and Jacobs 2008).

Some of the most interesting research, however, challenges practitioners to consider outsourcing for more strategic reasons other than just cost reduction. One of the most widely cited articles on this topic is by DiRomualdo and Gurbaxani (1998).[3] The authors addressed three strategic intents for IT outsourcing: IS improvement (including cost savings), business impact (such as improving business processes), and commercial exploitation. Their paper also suggested which types of contracts, incentives, measures, and pricing provisions should be used to match the strategic intent. The logic of their prescriptions is solid, but many of the examples cited in the article as exemplars of an IT strategy actually failed to deliver the expected benefits in the longer term, including Xerox, J. P. Morgan, Swiss Bank, and Delta Airlines. This suggests that realizing the strategic intent of IT outsourcing is exceedingly difficult and requires a high degree of managerial attention.

Other authors have also tried to challenge practitioners to use IT outsourcing more strategically. The main issue is that these papers rely on anecdotal evidence from a few exceptional firms. Most notable are three excellent papers by James Brian Quinn (Quinn and Hilmer 1994; Quinn 1999, 2000). His work, although based on anecdotal evidence and not focused on IT, celebrates the most innovative and strategic uses of outsourcing. Linder (2004), Ross and Beath (2006), and Lacity, Feeny, and Willcocks (2003, 2004) also wrote about a few companies using IT outsourcing to facilitate large-scale transformation. Some of their examples, however, pertain to BPO rather than IT outsourcing.

The Strategic Effects of IT Outsourcing Decisions

Researchers have also assessed the effects of IT outsourcing on firm-level performance using such metrics as stock price performance and financial performance. Concerning stock price, senior executives want to know how stockholders perceive their large-scale IT outsourcing decisions. Therefore, a number of academic event studies have examined how announcements of large-scale IT outsourcing decisions affect stock prices (Loh and Venkatraman 1992b; Smith, Mitra, and Narasimhan 1998; Hayes, Hunton, and Reck 2000; Farag and Krishnan 2003; Madison, San Miguel, and Padmanabhan 2006; Oh, Gallivan, and Kim 2006). In total, we coded thirteen effects of IT outsourcing on stock price performance. Six found significant positive effects on stock price (e.g. Agrawal, Kishore, and Rao 2006), four found no relationship (e.g. Florin, Bradford, and Pagach 2005), and three found a negative effect on stock price (e.g. Oh, Gallivan, and Kim 2006).

Oh, Gallivan, and Kim (2006) is the best paper to help understand these mixed results. These authors summarize all prior event studies and also present the results of their own event study. Their event study is unique because they did not just look at the overall change in stock market value, which tends to be very small. Instead, they looked at the differences between announcements that led to *above* Average Abnormal Returns (AAR) versus announcements that led to *below* AAR. The authors examined 192 IT outsourcing announcements during a nine-year period (1995 to 2003). On the day of an announcement, 97 announcements led to negative AAR and 95 announcements lead to positive AAR. The authors conclude that the content of ITO announcement matters. Investors reacted favourably to ITO announcements about smaller contracts, ITO contracts intending to reduce costs, transactions with low asset specificity (data centres and telecommunications), and contracts signed with larger supplier firms.

Concerning the effects of IT outsourcing on a client-firm's financial performance, we coded nine relationships. Again, the results were mixed. Four relationships found that the client's financial position improved (e.g. Mojsilovic et al. 2007), three relationships found that the financial performance worsened (e.g. Wang et al. 2008), and two found no effects on financial performance (e.g. Bhalla, Sodhi, and Son 2008).

Insights for Practitioners

For nearly twenty years of ITO research, client firms have primarily pursued outsourcing as a way to reduce ITO costs. Cost reduction drove domestic ITO decisions in the 1990s and continues to drive both domestic and offshore outsourcing in the 2000s. We are perplexed when practitioners argue with this seemingly ignominious finding. Indeed, some of the world's most respected thinkers—such as Oliver Williamson—argue that cost efficiency is the only long-term viable strategy a company should pursue:

> I furthermore aver that, as between economizing and strategizing, economizing is much the more fundamental . . . More importantly, I maintain that a strategizing effort will rarely prevail if a program is burdened by significant cost excesses in production, distribution, or organization. All the clever ploys and positioning, aye, all the king's horses and all the king's men, will rarely save a project that is seriously flawed in first-order economizing respects. (Williamson 1991: 75).

While both practitioners and academics are highly interested in more strategic uses of ITO (Galliers and Leidner 2009), the preponderance of evidence is based on single-case studies of exceptional firms. The strategic exploitation of IT outsourcing remains a minority pursuit. Furthermore, the effects of IT outsourcing on firm-level attributes are small, even when they are statistically significant. On average, most firms only spend 3 per cent of their annual revenues on IT; outsourcing even a large portion of IT may not be substantial enough to affect firm-level financial metrics such as profitability (Aubert et al. 2008). Another challenge is trying to isolate the true effects of IT outsourcing on firm-level performance.

IT OUTSOURCING RISKS

Another important topic for practitioners is managing IT outsourcing risks. Risks are generally defined as the probability that an action will adversely affect an organization. Risk management is a set of activities geared toward identifying, assessing, prioritizing, and addressing risks in order to minimize their probability or impact. ITO researchers address two questions relevant to practitioners:

- What are the risks of IT outsourcing?
- How are IT outsourcing risks mitigated?

In the ITO academic literature, we found 34 published papers on ITO risks and risk management, of which 18 were conceptual. Conceptual papers primarily identify lists of ITO risks (e.g. Jurison 1995; Earl 1996; Sakthivel 2007) or develop ITO risk models (e.g. Aron, Clemons, and Reddi 2005; Osei-Bryson and Ngwenyama 2006). The empirical papers primarily address specific risks and risk management strategies as they pertain to IT outsourcing in general (Currie and Willcocks 1998; Aubert et al. 1999; Willcocks and Lacity 1999; Willcocks, Lacity, and Kern 1999; Bahli and Rivard 2005), or as they pertain to specific types of outsourcing such as offshore outsourcing (Iacovou and Nakatsu 2008) or application service provision (Kern, Kreijger, and Willcocks 2002; Kern, Lacity and Willcocks 2002; Kern, Willcocks, and Lacity 2002). Measurement of risks has also been studied (e.g. Bahli and Rivard 2005; Whitten and Wakefield 2006).

The most cited paper on ITO risks is by Michael Earl (1996).[4] Earl discusses eleven risks of IT outsourcing: possibility of weak management, inexperienced staff, business uncertainty, outdated technology skills, endemic uncertainty, hidden costs, lack of organizational learning, loss of innovative capacity, dangers of an eternal triangle, technology indivisibility, and fuzzy focus. One of the reasons why this paper is so valuable is because it holds the client accountable for the success of outsourcing. Before IT outsourcing can work, 'a company must be capable of managing the IT services first' (p. 27).

In reviewing the body of literature, the number of identified ITO risks is quite intimidating. For example, we counted 43 unique ITO risks from just the first three sources we coded (Jurison 1995; Kern, Willcocks, and Lacity 2002; Lacity and Rottman 2008)! The most common risks are found in Table 19.3.

Concerning risk mitigation advice for practitioners, academic researchers have identified many specific practices designed to reduce risk and therefore increase the likelihood of ITO success. In general, we found as many risk mitigation practices as we found ITO risks. Advice, therefore, is tied to each specific ITO risk. For example, one ITO risk is 'supplier has too much power over the customer'. Many ITO practices mitigate this risk such as engaging multiple suppliers (Currie 1998), signing short-term contracts (Lacity and Willcocks 1998), outsourcing standard IT services for which there are many suppliers capable of delivering good services (Lacity and Hirschheim 1993; De Loof 1995; Apte et al. 1997), and insourcing highly specific assets (Watjatrakul 2005).

Table 19.3 Common ITO Risks

Backlash from internal IT staff	Loss of in-house capability
Biased portrayal by vendors	No overall cost savings
Breach of contract by the vendor	Perceived as unpatriotic (offshore)
Cultural differences between client and supplier	Poor supplier capability, service, financial stability, cultural fit
Difficulty in managing remote teams	Security/Privacy breech
Excessive transaction costs	Supplier employee turnover/burnout
Hidden costs	Supplier employees are inexperienced
Inability to manage supplier relationship	Supplier employees have poor communication skills
Inflexible contracts	Supplier goes out of business
Infringement of IP rights	Supplier has too much power over the customer
Lack of trust	Transition failure
Loss of autonomy and control over IT decisions	Treating IT as an undifferentiated commodity
Loss of control over data	Uncontrollable contract growth
Loss of control over vendor	Vendor lock-in (high switching costs)

Academics have also discussed risks specific to certain types of outsourcing, such as application service provision or offshore outsourcing (Kern, Lacity, and Willcocks 2002; Kern, Willcocks, and Lacity 2002; Sakthivel 2007). Kern, Willcocks, and Lacity (2002) examine specific risks and risk mitigation strategies for application service provision. Sakthivel (2007) identifies 18 risks and 18 risk control mechanisms specific to offshore systems development. As new IT sourcing models emerge, early adopters will always face more risks.

Insights for Practice

Facing so many risks may prompt clients to rephrase the IT sourcing question to 'Why should we not insource IT services?' (Earl 1996: 27). Although the number of ITO risks and risk mitigation practices are daunting, practitioners may find that the best way to mitigate risks is through experience. Clients cannot fully bypass the learning curve based on explicit risk mitigation practices identified from other organizations—there is no substitute for the tacit knowing that comes from actual experiences. Many researchers have found that learning curve effects and prior client experience are vital to ITO success (Lacity and Willcocks 1998; Barthélemy 2001; Carmel and Agarwal 2002; Kaiser and Hawk 2004; Rottman and Lacity 2006). Any organization that explores a new sourcing option in terms of new suppliers, new services, or new engagement models with existing suppliers must plan on false starts and many mistakes. Executives often manage learning by pilot testing new sourcing options. This is a risk-mitigating practice, but we also note that when pilot tests are too small, the learning is slow, supplier capabilities are not fully tested, and expected benefits are not often realized. Thus there is a trade-off between mitigating risks and achieving substantial benefits from outsourcing.

DETERMINANTS OF IT OUTSOURCING SUCCESS

We found 86 articles on the determinants of ITO success. Specifically, this body of research answers:

- Which practices increase the likelihood that a client's outsourcing decision will be successful?

Researchers have defined and measured ITO success using three units of analysis—the organization, the IT function, and the project. At an organizational level, we have already discussed the strategic impact of outsourcing decisions on firm-level performance using such metrics as stock price performance and financial performance (see above, section entitled 'Determinants of IT Outsourcing'). At the level of an IT function, researchers have examined the effects of ITO decisions on IS improvements such as reduced costs or increased service levels. At the level of a project, researchers have examined the effects of ITO decisions on cost, quality, and time to complete outsourced projects.

Concerning the determinants of ITO success, researchers have inspected three categories—the ITO Decision, Contractual Governance, and Relational Governance. These are very broad categories of determinants meant to capture the practices associated with ITO decisions, the practices associated with contracts, and the practices associated with managing supplier relationships.

The ITO Decision

Researchers have examined the relationships between the types of ITO decisions made and their subsequent outcomes. In particular, researchers have examined how the degree of outsourcing, top management commitment, and the evaluation process have affected ITO success.

The *degree of outsourcing* is the amount of outsourcing as indicated by percentage of IT budget outsourced and/or the type and number of IS functions outsourced. We coded nine relationships that looked at the effects of degree of outsourcing on ITO success. Seven relationships found that the degree of outsourcing mattered. In general, too much outsourcing was associated with lower levels of success (Currie 1998; Lacity and Willcocks 1998; Seddon 2001; Straub, Weill, and Schwaig 2008). As an example of 'too much', Lacity and Willcocks (1998) found that clients who outsourced more than 80 per cent of their IT budgets had success rates of only 29 per cent; clients who outsourced less than 80 per cent of their IT budgets had success rates of 85 per cent. Seddon (2001) provides another example of outsourcing 'too much'. He examined one of the most aggressive public sector ITO programmes in the world—the Australian federal government's Au$1.2 billion ITO programme. The Australian federal government experienced poor results, both financially and operationally. One reason for the disappointing financial results is that the Australian government clustered disparate IT functions in hopes of achieving cost savings through economies of scale. However, the increased coordination costs across disparate IT functions cancelled the intended effects of cost savings through economies of scale.

The types of IT functions outsourced also mattered. For example, Grover, Cheon, and Teng (1996) found clients had higher levels of satisfaction from outsourcing systems operations and telecommunications than they did from outsourcing applications development, end user support, and systems management.

Top management commitment/support in ITO initiatives is a critical factor for success. Ten out of the ten relationships we coded suggest top management's commitment and support are critical for client satisfaction (e.g. Lee and Kim 1999; Han, Lee, and Seo 2008), offshore project success (Iacovou and Nakatsu 2008), and overall outsourcing success (e.g. Quinn 1999; Seddon 2001; Koh, Ang, and Straub 2004). For example, Lacity and Willcocks (1998) report the positive effects of joint IT and non-IT senior management involvement in the ITO decision on cost savings realized. Smith and McKeen (2004) suggest top management's involvement in outsourcing decisions impact overall outsourcing success.

The client organization's *evaluation process* for selecting suppliers seems to be a rather consistent predictor of the contract price, the outsourcing decision, expected cost savings being realized, and the achievement of outsourcing success in general. Eight out of the nine relationships we coded for the evaluation process reported significant findings (e.g. Lacity and Willcocks 1998; Kern, Willcocks, and Lacity 2002; Cullen, Seddon, and Willcocks 2005a). For example, inviting internal and external bids has been identified as a proven practice (e.g. Lacity and Willcocks 1998; Smith and McKeen 2004).

Contractual Governance

In all, we coded 40 relationships between contractual governance and ITO success. Contractual governance was operationalized most frequently as contract detail (12 relationships), contract type (11 relationships), contract duration (6 relationships), and contract size (4 relationships).

Contract detail is the number or degree of detailed clauses in the outsourcing contract, such as clauses that specify prices, service levels, benchmarking, warranties, and penalties for non-performance. Overall, 10 of the 12 relationships found that higher levels of contractual detail led to higher levels of ITO success. For example, Poppo and Zenger (2002) found that contractual complexity (i.e. contract detail) was significantly related to ITO performance.

Contract type is a term denoting different forms of contracts used in outsourcing. Examples include customized, fixed, time and materials, fee for service, and partnership-based contracts. Out of 11 relationships, all 11 found that the type of contract affected the level of ITO success. For example, Gopal, Mukhopadhyay, and Krishnan (2002) found that fixed-fee contracts resulted in less rework than time and materials contracts.

Contract duration also produced consistent findings—all six studies that examined contract duration found that shorter-term contracts had higher frequencies of success than longer-term contracts. For example, Lacity and Willcocks (1998) found that contracts that were three years or less had a higher frequency of success than contracts greater than three years.

Somewhat counter to prior findings—all four relationships that studied the effects of *contract size* on ITO success found that the larger contracts had higher frequencies of success than smaller contracts. For example, Domberger, Fernandez, and Fiebig (2000) found that higher-valued contracts (price) were positively related to service quality. How can the contract duration and contract size findings be reconciled? Contract duration is measured in years and long-term relationships tend to lose their momentum and enthusiasm. Contract size is measured in dollars—larger-valued contracts lead to successful outcomes because suppliers are more motivated to allocate their best resources to clients with large contracts. Large contracts also spread the enormous transaction costs associated with outsourcing over more volume of work.

Relational Governance

Relational governance covers the softer issues of managing client-supplier relationships, including trust, norms, open communication, open sharing of information, mutual dependency, and cooperation. In total, we coded 44 relationships on relational governance. In ALL instances, the research shows that higher levels of all the relational governance attributes are associated with higher levels of ITO success. In some ways, the findings are obvious and trivial. Few people would argue that distrust, closed communication, or lack of cooperation would lead to better outsourcing relationships!

Some of the more interesting research in this area uses interviews and case studies rather than sample surveys (e.g. Kern and Willcocks 2002; Heiskanen, Newman, and Eklin 2008). These qualitative methods allow researchers to understand *why* factors are important or *how* relational governance develops over time. For example, Sabherwal (1999) studied eighteen outsourced IS development projects in seven client organizations to determine the role of trust in client-supplier relationships. The paper provides a good overview of the different types of trust, including (1) *calculus-based trust* that is rooted in rewards and punishments associated with a particular project,

(2) *knowledge-based trust* that depends on the two parties knowing each other well, (3) *identification-based trust* that follows from the two parties identifying with each other's goals, and (4) *performance-based trust* that depends on early project successes. The paper is one of the first to incorporate two important determinants of ITO success—trust (a form of relational governance) and structural control (a form of contractual governance). ITO success was measured by the quality and timeliness of project deliverables. The author found that relational governance and contractual governance must both be in place to ensure ITO success. More interesting, however, was the reciprocal relationships among trust, contractual governance, and ITO success. ITO success fuelled further trust among clients and suppliers. In contrast, projects that suffered from delays or poor performance led to decreased trust.

Since Sabherwal (1999), a number of researchers have begun to simultaneously study contractual and relational governance (Kern and Willcocks 2000; Poppo and Zenger 2002; Goo et al. 2009). Are they substitutes? Are they complements? Newer studies show them as complements. Kern and Willcocks (2000) used twelve case studies to argue the importance of both contractual and relational governance. Poppo and Zenger (2002) surveyed 151 US client firms and found that ITO success was greater when both contractual complexity and relational governance were greater. Goo et al. (2009) also found that formal contracts and relational governance function as complements, rather than as substitutes, in a sample of South Korean firms.

Researchers have also studied the interactions between ITO decision and contractual governance. Lee, Miranda, and Kim (2004) is a very interesting article that used the same dependent variable to measure ITO success as Grover, Cheon, and Teng (1996) and many of the same independent variables used in Lacity and Willcocks (1998) including ITO decision (degree of outsourcing) and contract governance (contract duration and contract type). The authors surveyed 311 South Korean firms. Instead of treating outsourcing decision scope, contract duration, and contract type as independent variables, they created three ideal profiles that integrate these constructs. For example, one ideal pattern is called 'arms-length' and has the ideal value of selective outsourcing for decision scope, detailed contract for contract type, and medium contract duration. The expected effect of 'arms-length' profile on ITO success is 'cost efficiency'. The other two patterns are 'independent' and 'embedded'. The authors found that two of the three profiles were significant—the arms-length and the embedded profiles. Overall, they show the importance of matching ITO decision and contractual governance to achieve higher levels of ITO success.

Insights for Practitioners

The three major categories of determinants of ITO Success are ITO decisions, contractual governance, and relational governance. These determinants are depicted as direct relationships to ITO success in Figure 19.1. Overall, we know ITO decisions that entailed

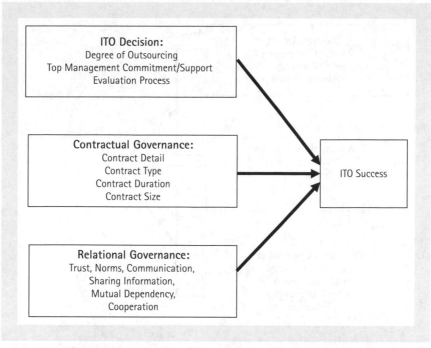

FIGURE **19.1** Three main categories of determinants of ITO success

selective use of outsourcing, the involvement of senior managers, and rigorous evaluation processes were associated with higher levels of ITO success. Contractual governance also positively affected ITO success. In general, more contract detail, shorter-term contracts, and higher-dollar valued contracts were positively related to ITO success. Such contracts maintain the balance of power between clients and suppliers, clearly define expectations, and motivate good supplier performance. Relational governance positively affected ITO outcomes. Trust, norms, open communication, open sharing of information, mutual dependency, and cooperation were always associated with higher levels of ITO success.

Recently, research has found that the interaction among these determinants is important. The *combination* of ITO decision and contractual governance are associated with higher levels of ITO success (Lee, Miranda, and Kim 2004) and the *combination* of contractual governance and relational governance are associated with higher levels of ITO success (Sabherwal 1999; Poppo and Zenger 2002; Goo et al. 2009).

Finally, what is also clear from the preponderance of evidence is that ITO success is not only caused by sound decisions and strong contractual and relational governance, but ITO success in turn caused better ITO decisions and stronger governance. Thus, the relationship between ITO success and its 'dependent variables' (sound decisions, contractual governance, and relational governance) is reciprocal. Specifically, ITO success fuelled higher levels of trust (relational governance), built stronger client and supplier capabilities, and determined the kinds of ITO decisions and ITO contracts clients made moving forward (Sabherwal 1999; Seddon 2001; Gopal et al. 2003; Levina

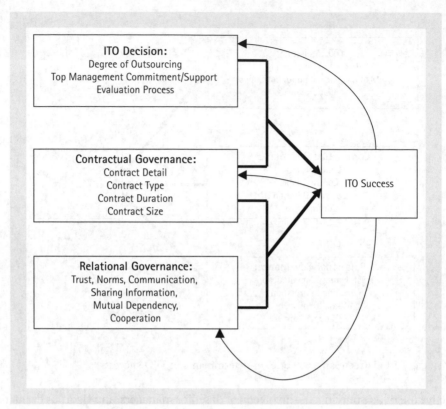

FIGURE **19.2** The complementary and reciprocal relationships of ITO success

and Ross 2003; Whitten and Leidner 2006). Conversely, ITO failure fuelled greater need for controls, monitoring mechanisms, tougher contracts, and determined the kinds of ITO decisions clients made moving forward (Lacity and Willcocks 1998; Sabherwal 1999; Choudhury and Sabherwal 2003). For practice, then, a more compli-cated but richer depiction of the relationships among ITO decision, contractual governance, relational governance, and ITO success is found in Figure 19.2.

CLIENT AND SUPPLIER CAPABILITIES

Organizational capability is defined as the previous experience, productive capacity, personnel, and other resources which indicate that the applying organization can carry out a proposal.[5] In general, this research topic asks:

- Which capabilities do client firms need to develop to successfully engage IT outsourcing suppliers?
- Which capabilities do client firms seek in an IT outsourcing supplier?

In Table 19.4, we list the overall capabilities found in the articles we reviewed sorted by frequency of occurrence. The most frequently mentioned capability was 'IS technical/ methodological capability' (e.g. Kishore et al. 2003; Levina and Ross 2003; Oza, Rainer, and Grey 2006; Ross and Beath 2006). This is an operational capability that is important to both client and supplier firms. For the outsourcing of new application development, research has found that it is important for clients and suppliers to have shared processes (Davenport 2005). For example, Rottman and Lacity (2006) interviewed 149 people from both client and supplier organizations. They found that ITO

Table 19.4 Client and supplier capabilities

Capability	Capability description	Number of Articles		
		For clients	For suppliers	Total
IS Technical/ Methodological Capability	An organization's level of maturity in terms of technical or process related standards including the Capability Maturity Model (CMM), Capability Maturity Model Integrated (CMMI), and the Information Technology Infrastructure Library (ITIL).	5	8	13
IS human Resource Management Capability	An organization's ability to identify, acquire, develop, and deploy human resources to achieve its organizational objectives.	1	9	10
Supplier Management Capability	The extent to which a client organization is able to effectively manage outsourcing suppliers.	10	0	10
Contract Negotiation Capability	The extent to which an organization is able to effectively bid, select, and negotiate effective contracts with suppliers.	7	0	7
Domain Capability	The extent to which a supplier has built a capability of the client organization's business and technical contexts, processes, practices, and requirements.	0	4	4
IS Change Management Capability	The extent to which an organization effectively manages change.	3	0	3
Transition Management Capability	The extent to which an organization effectively transitions services to outsourcing suppliers or integrates client services with supplier services.	2	0	2
Client Management Capability	The extent to which a supplier organization is able to effectively manage client relationships.	0	2	2
	Total	28	23	51

success was greater when both the client and supplier firms had at least CMMI[6] level 3 capabilities.

The most important capability for clients is the 'Supplier Management Capability'. This is defined as the extent to which a client organization is able to effectively manage outsourcing suppliers (e.g. Cross 1995; Michell and Fitzgerald 1997; Al-Qirim 2003; Ranganathan and Balaji 2007). For example, Michell and Fitzgerald (1997) found that among clients that disputed with vendors, nearly four-fifths said they would 'strengthen their ability to manage the vendor' (p. 232).

The most important capability for suppliers was the 'IS human resource management capability' (e.g. Gopal et al. 2003; Beulen and Ribbers 2003; Rao et al. 2006; Oshri, Kotlarsky, and Willcocks 2007a). This is an organization's ability to identify, acquire, develop, and deploy human resources to achieve its organizational objectives. Clients achieved higher levels of ITO success when supplier staff turnover was low and when the supplier assigned the most capable people to the client's account.

Insights for Practice

Our review treats these capabilities as independent, but the most widely cited and respected papers on this topic identify a *mix* of complementary capabilities that lead to ITO success (see Table 19.5). The first paper to meaningfully address this question is Feeny and Willcocks (1998).[7] The authors identified nine interrelated capabilities,

Table 19.5 The mix of complementary capabilities

Research study	Empirical base	Focus	Critical capabilities identified
Feeny and Willcocks (1998)	Analysis of over 100 sourcing decisions	Client	(1) IS leadership, (2) business systems thinking, (3) relationship building, (4) technical architecture, (5) making technology work, (6) informed buying, (7) contract facilitation, (8) contract monitoring, and (9) vendor development
Levina and Ross (2003)	Detailed case study of client/supplier relationship	Supplier	(1) IT personnel career development, (2) methodology development and dissemination, and (3) client relationship management
Feeny, Lacity, and Willcocks (2005)	Analysis of over 100 sourcing decisions	Supplier	(1) planning and contracting, (2) governance, (3) organizational design, (4) leadership, (5) business management, (6) customer development, (7) domain expertise, (8) behaviour management, (9) sourcing, (10) process re-engineering, (11) technology exploitation, and (12) programme management

depicted as three interlocking rings. Levina and Ross (2003) found that suppliers need three complementary capabilities: (1) IT personnel career development, (2) methodology development and dissemination, and (3) client relationship management. They showed how supplier capabilities were complementary in that engaging in one capability improved the other two capabilities. Feeny et al. (2005) developed a sister model to identify the twelve most important, interrelated capabilities clients seek in a supplier.

SOURCING VARIETALS: OFFSHORE, ASP, AND BPO

Thus far we have covered foundational issues associated with ITO practice, including strategy, risk management, best practices, and capabilities. The insights for practice have been primarily derived from the studies of domestic IT outsourcing. Recently, much of the academic research has focused on ITO using other sourcing models, including the offshore outsourcing of IT work, application service provision, and business process outsourcing. A common question for all these sourcing varietals is:

- How do practices differ when pursuing different types of outsourcing such as offshore outsourcing, application service provision, and business process outsourcing?

Offshore Outsourcing

Recently, academics have extracted important insights for practice about offshore outsourcing of IT work. We have coded 69 findings from 20 major papers in this area. Academics are beginning to have a good understanding of how offshore outsourcing differs from domestic outsourcing. So far, researchers have found that offshore outsourcing poses considerably more challenges than domestic outsourcing. Offshore outsourcing is more challenging because of time zone differences (Carmel 2006; Gokhale 2007), the need for more controls (Choudhury and Sabherwal 2003; Kotlarsky, van Fenema, and Willcocks 2008), problems transferring knowledge (Gupta et al. 2007; Oshri, Kotlarsky, and Willcocks 2007a), cultural differences (Smith and McKeen 2004; Carmel and Tjia 2005; Oza and Hall 2005; Rao et al. 2006; Iacovou and Nakatsu 2008), having to define requirements more rigorously (Gopal et al. 2003), and difficulties in managing dispersed teams (Zviran, Ahituv, and Armoni 2001; Oshri, Kotlarsky, and Willcocks 2007a, 2007b). The transaction costs of offshore outsourcing are considerably higher than domestic outsourcing (Dibbern, Winkler, and Heinzl 2008; Lacity and Rottman 2008).

Researchers are also identifying practices and capabilities that are specific to offshore outsourcing (Rottman and Lacity 2004; Ranganathan and Balaji 2007). Sample practices include the use of middlemen (Mahnke, Wareham, and Bjorn-Andersen 2008), the design of special interfaces between client and offshore supplier employees (Kaiser and Hawk 2004; Rottman and Lacity 2006; Oshri, Kotlarsky, and Willcocks 2007a; Leonardi and Bailey 2008), and the use of increased number of liaisons (Gopal et al. 2003; Lacity and Rottman 2008). Researchers have also studied up to ten capabilities required for offshore outsourcing (Ranganathan and Balaji 2007; Jarvenpaa and Mao 2008). Achieving total cost savings has been difficult in the context of offshore outsourcing because of all the additional challenges and practices needed to ensure success. Client organizations need to commit a high enough volume of work offshore to ensure total cost savings.

The recent economic downturn may predict a significant change in the way such offshore sourcing is organized and structured. Cash strapped organizations, both large and small, are selling off their captive centres to offshore suppliers which get lengthy offshore outsourcing contracts in return for purchasing an organization's captive centre assets. For example, Citigroup has reportedly sold its IT captive centre in India to Tata Consultancy Services (TCS) Ltd for (US) $505 million, and in turn got into an offshore outsourcing arrangement with TCS resulting in a (US) $2.5 billion, nine-year deal (*Wall Street Journal*, 8 June 2009).

Application Service Provision

Initially, application service provision (ASP) was a business model in which suppliers hosted and rented standard applications to clients over the Internet. ASP was one way small client firms could access expensive software—like enterprise resource planning software by SAP or Oracle—while avoiding high infrastructure costs, support costs, or hefty software licence fees. The ASP model flourished during the dot.com era, but although the value proposition to clients was solid, suppliers had difficulty generating revenues. Many ASP suppliers went bankrupt because the client contracts were too small, their duration too short, the marketing costs to educate clients about ASP too high, the margins from reselling propriety software too thin, and the transaction costs of serving so many needy clients too high (Kern, Kreijger, and Willcocks 2002; Kern, Lacity, and Willcocks 2002).

The ASP bubble burst by 2001, but has since been revived into what we call 'netsourcing'. Netsourcing uses the internet as the delivery mechanism, but the suppliers, clients, and services have changed. Netsourcing suppliers have new business models and are attracting larger-sized clients. Rather than reselling other vendors' software, the new netsourcing suppliers have developed net-native applications (proprietary applications designed and delivered specifically for Internet delivery) that are only available through ASP delivery (e.g. Salesforce.com). Traditional IT suppliers like

IBM and EDS (now part of HP) also incorporated netsourcing into their service options, offering a portfolio of application delivery options to their clients. Providers got the message: clients want customized services, even if the products are standardized. The need for customized services actually increases the service providers' viability because they can generate profits by charging for value-added services. Companies like Xchanging and Hewitt have highly customized service contracts but deliver many services in an ASP manner (Willcocks and Lacity 2006).

Kern, Willcocks, and Lacity (2002) provide a good overview of how ASP differs from traditional IT outsourcing. They conclude that the risks of ASP are similar to traditional IT outsourcing, but that the probabilities of occurrence for many risks are higher with ASP. In particular, the probabilities for risks increase with ASP because of immature suppliers, immature customers, and immature technologies.

Loebbecke and Huyskens (2006) examined the determinants of netsourcing decisions in 88 German companies. The authors found that the companies that netsource applications had significantly *lower* values for (1) competitive relevance of the software application, (2) strategic vulnerability of netsourcing, and (3) technical uncertainty. Thus, applications that were netsourced were perceived as non-strategic and technically certain and thus could be safely netsourced—very similar findings to traditional outsourcing. Susarla, Barua, and Whinston (2003) examine the determinants of ASP success as measured by ASP satisfaction and ASP supplier performance. Based on a sample of 256 client firms that netsource at least one software application, the authors found that the clients most satisfied with ASP (1) rated ASP supplier performance higher, (2) had more prior systems integration experience, (3) had higher a priori expectations about the ASP's functional capability, and (4) had lower gaps between a priori expectations and a posteriori perceptions of ASP performance. Like findings from research in traditional IT outsourcing, clients have more success with ASP when they have realistic expectations and have already conquered the learning curve through prior experience.

Business Process Outsourcing

Business process outsourcing (BPO) entails a supplier taking over the execution of a client's business processes within functions such as human resource management, finance, and accounting (Lacity, Feeny, and Willcocks 2003). BPO is a growing trend and, with increasing standardization of business processes, is expected to permeate the organizations of the future (Davenport 2005). Although research on BPO is still evolving, much in the way IT outsourcing research did, we do see some important patterns emerging.

As standards for processes become available, outsourced processes will become increasingly commoditized (Davenport 2005). This idea is supported by the current view that, in general, BPO is suitable for well-defined, self-contained, modular,

IT-enabled, and easily measurable processes (e.g. Borman 2006; Tanriverdi, Konana, and Ge 2007). Concerning IT enablement, IT may help reduce the transaction costs associated with BPO (Borman 2006). Based on data from 287 manufacturing plants, Bardhan, Whitaker, and Mithas (2006) report that plants with higher IT spending were more likely to engage in production process outsourcing. Also, when processes can be detached from the underlying IT infrastructure at a client organization they may be more suitable for offshoring. However, when processes are tightly coupled with IT, domestic sourcing or insourcing may be a better option (Tanriverdi, Konana, and Ge 2007).

As with IT outsourcing, cost savings, greater flexibility, and access to specialized process expertise remain key motivators of BPO (Lacity, Feeny, and Willcocks 2003; Davenport 2005). However, indicators of BPO success go beyond cost reduction and flexibility to include quality improvement, realized core competence focus, and realized strategic advantage (Wüllenweber et al. 2008). Wüllenweber et al. (2008) studied the impact of contractual and relational governance mechanisms on BPO success and report that process standardization, contract completeness, coordination, and consensus are directly associated with BPO success. Like Sabherwal (1999), Poppo and Zenger (2002), and Goo et al. (2009), Wüllenweber et al. (2008) also found that sound contracts (contract completeness) and relational governance (high values of coordination and consensus between client and supplier firms) are determinants of success.

We anticipate that future research will increasingly focus on the bundling of ITO and BPO because client firms are increasingly pursuing this practice. Thus, studies such as the one by Wüllenweber et al. (2008) maybe bellwethers for future research and practice.

Conclusion

In effect, research on practice has documented the 20-year rise to globalism of IT and business services outsourcing. The key quest for clients has been how to leverage the ever expanding services market for significant business advantage. The common denominator in the findings: researchers have uncovered no quick fix. Much depends on experiential learning and sheer hard work. Executives must conquer a significant learning curve and build key in-house capabilities in order to successfully exploit outsourcing opportunities. They need to accept that outsourcing is not about giving up management, but managing in a different way.

Suppliers have also faced learning curves in their attempts to differentiate their services, find new markets, and deal with new competition from potentially anywhere in the world. Maturing their ability to deliver fully on the promise of cost-effective service delivery, strong relationships and back-office transformation has been a constant challenge. As the 2007 economic downturn turned into 2008 recession, suppliers's abilities to develop and leverage requisite capabilities in ITO, BPO, and 'bestshoring' have become ever more critical.

The sheer dynamism of modern business and public sectors makes any lessons derived more important to learn and apply, and trends more important to watch and take suitable action on. Looking forward, McDonald (2007) suggests IT leaders need to develop an *enterprise capability*, comprising nine elements that are standardized, integrated, and operated together to achieve strategic goals. The nine elements address human capital, organization, processes, facilities and equipment technology, applications, information, rules and metrics, and specific tasks. Many of these elements will be sourced through a comprehensive portfolio of in-house workers, contract workers, and third party suppliers. Lacity, Willcocks, and Rottman (2008) predict thirteen trends about the size and growth of ITO and BPO markets, about suppliers located around the world, and about particular sourcing models including application service provision, insourcing, nearshoring, rural sourcing, knowledge process outsourcing, freelance outsourcing, and captive centres. They also identify five perennial, prickly, future challenges for practice pertaining to business back office alignment, client and supplier incentives, knowledge transfer, knowledge retention, and sustainability of outsourcing relationships.

As outsourcing spend increases, the alignment of business and sourcing strategy does indeed becomes a key issue, as does CEO and business executive involvement in outsourcing objectives, relationships, and implementation. This requires a further advance in client thinking and action. One way of looking historically at outsourcing practice research work is to say that it has documented how organizations have been learning, experientially and often painfully, how to *manage* back-office outsourcing. But the increased size, importance, complexity of the phenomena, and the risks they engender, suggest that in the next phase researchers will be examining how organizations seek to provide *leadership* in outsourcing. Leadership is about shaping the context and mobilizing resources to deal with the adaptive challenges organizations face. In glimpsing the future, it is pretty clear that changing business needs, the globalizing and technologizing of the supply of business services, and the much greater use of outsourcing, will provide challenges that will require this shift from management to leadership—if governance, control, flexibility, and superior business outcomes are to be the consequences of outsourcing practice.

Appendix 19.1 Distribution of ITO articles by journal

Journal Name	No. of Articles	Journal Name	No. of Articles
Academy of Management Journal	1	International Journal of Organizational Analysis	1
Academy of Management Review	3	Journal of Applied Business Research	1
ACM SIGMIS Database	1	Journal of Electronic Commerce in Organizations	3
BT Technology Journal	1	Journal of Global Information Management	4
California Management Review	2	Journal of Global Information Technology Management	5
Communications of the ACM	18	Journal of High Technology Management Research	1
Communications of the AIS	10	Journal of Information Systems	2
Computers & Operations Research	4	Journal of Information Systems Management	1
Database for Advances in Information Systems	2	Journal of Information Technology	22
Decision Sciences	3	Journal of Information Technology Case and Application Research	5
Decision Support Systems	1	Journal of Information Technology Cases and Applications	5
Engineering Management Journal	1	Journal of International Management Studies	1
European Journal of Information Systems	10	Journal of Management	1
European Journal of Operational Research	3	Journal of Management Information Systems	14
European Management Journal	2	Journal of Operations Management	2
Foreign Affairs	1	Journal of Purchasing & Supply Management	1
Harvard Business Review	8	Journal of Strategic Information Systems	10
IEEE Computer	1	Journal of Systems Management	5
IEEE Transactions on Engineering Management	2	Journal of the Association for Information Systems	3
Industrial Management & Data Systems	1	Management Science	8
Industrial Management + Data Systems	8	MIS Quarterly	18

Industry and Innovation	1	MIS Quarterly Executive	12
Information & Management	17	Omega	1
Information and Software Technology	1	Organization Science	1
Information Management & Computer Security	7	Public Personnel Management	1
Information Resources Management Journal	2	S.A.M. Advanced Management Journal	1
Information Systems Frontiers	12	Sloan Management Review	21
Information Systems Journal	2	Strategic Management Journal	3
Information Systems Management	35	Strategic Outsourcing: An International Journal	1
Information Systems Research	8	Technovation	1
Information Technology & People	1	The Academy of Management Executive	2
Information Technology and Management	2	The Academy of Management Review	1
International Journal of E-Business Research	1	The Journal of Applied Behavioral Science	1
International Journal of Information Management	11	The Journal of Computer Information Systems	12
International Journal of Logistics Management	1	The Journal of Management Development	1
International Journal of Management	1	TOTAL	357

Notes

1. Besides these rational reasons, some studies find personal agendas dominating large-scale outsourcing decisions (Lacity and Hirschheim 1993; Hall and Liedtka 2005).
2. The articles were coded by Mary C. Lacity, Shaji Khan, and Aihua Yan.
3. Cited 261 times by Summer 2009 according to Harzing' *Publish or Perish*.
4. Cited 399 times by Summer 2009 according to Harzing' *Publish or Perish*.
5. <http://www.broward.k12.fl.us/grants/old/html/resources/definitions.html>.
6. CMMI (Capability Maturity Model Integrated) defines five levels of software development maturity and specifies what processes must be in place to achieve those levels.

7. Their model has been adopted by many large organizations, including DuPont and Commonwealth Bank in Australia. As further evidence of this model' impact, the original paper has been cited 336 times as of 2009. The paper has been updated in Willcocks and Feeny 2006.

REFERENCES

Agrawal, M., Kishore, R., and Rao, H. R. (2006). 'Market Reactions to E-business Outsourcing Announcements: An Event Study', *Information & Management*, 43: 861–73.

Al-Qirim, N. A. (2003). 'The Strategic Outsourcing Decision of IT and eCommerce: The Case of Small Businesses in New Zealand', *Journal of Information Technology Cases and Applications*, 5(3): 32–56.

Ang, S., and Straub, D. (1998). 'Production and Transaction Economies and IS Outsourcing: A Study of the U.S. Banking Industry', *MIS Quarterly*, 22(4): 535–52.

Applegate, L. M., and Montealegre, R. (1991). 'Eastman Kodak Company: Managing Information Systems through Strategic Alliances', *Harvard Business School Case* 9-192-030.

Apte, U., Sobol, M., Hanaoka, S., Shimada, T., Saarinen, T., Salmela, T., and Vepsalainen, A. (1997). 'IS Outsourcing Practices in the USA, Japan, and Finland: A Comparative Study', *Journal of Information Technology*, 12: 289–304.

Aron, R., Clemons, E., and Reddi, S. (2005). 'Just Right Outsourcing: Understanding and Managing Risk', *Journal of Management Information Systems*, 22(2): 37–55.

Aubert, B. A., Dussault, S., Patry, M., and Rivard, S. (1999). 'Managing the Risk of IT Outsourcing', *Proceedings of the 32nd Annual Hawaii International Conference on System Sciences*.

——Beaurivage, G., Croteau, A. M., and Rivard, S. (2008). 'Firm Strategic Profile and IT Outsourcing', *Information Systems Frontiers*, 10(2): 129–43.

Bahli, B., and Rivard, S. (2005). 'Validating Measures of Information Technology Outsourcing Risk Factors', *Omega*, 33(2): 175–87.

Bardhan, I., Whitaker, J., and Mithas, S. (2006). 'Information Technology, Production Process Outsourcing, and Manufacturing Plant Performance', *Journal of Management Information Systems*, 23(2): 13–40.

Barthélemy, J. (2001). 'The Hidden Costs of IT Outsourcing', *Sloan Management Review*, 42 (3): 60–9.

——and Geyer, D. (2004). 'The Determinants of Total IT Outsourcing: An Empirical Investigation of French and German Firms', *Journal of Computer Information Systems*, 44(3): 91–8.

————(2005). 'An Empirical Investigation of IT Outsourcing versus Quasi-outsourcing in France and Germany', *Information & Management*, 42(4): 533–42.

Beulen, E., and Ribbers, P. (2003). 'International Examples of Large-Scale Systems—Theory and Practice II: A Case Study of Managing IT Outsourcing Partnerships in Asia', *Communications of the AIS*, 11: 357–76.

Bhalla, A., Sodhi, M. S., and Son, B.-G. (2008). 'Is More IT Offshoring Better? An Exploratory Study of Western Companies Offshoring to South East Asia', *Journal of Operations Management*, 26(2): 322–35.

Borman, M. (2006). 'Applying Multiple Perspectives to the BPO Decision: A Case Study of Call Centers in Australia', *Journal of Information Technology*, 21: 99–115.

Carmel, E. (2006). 'Building your Information Systems from the Other Side of the World: How Infosys Manages Time Zone Differences', *MIS Quarterly Executive*, 5(1): 43–53.

—— and Abbott, P. (2007). 'Why Nearshore Means That Distance Matters', *Communications of the ACM*, 50(10): 40–6.

—— and Agarwal, R. (2002). 'The Maturation of Offshore Sourcing of Information Technology Work', *MIS Quarterly Executive*, 1(2): 65–78.

—— and Tjia, P. (2005). *Offshoring Information Technology: Sourcing and Outsourcing to a Global Workforce*. Cambridge: Cambridge University Press.

Choudhury, V., and Sabherwal, R. (2003). 'Portfolios of Control in Outsourced Software Development Projects', *Information Systems Research*, 14(3): 291–314.

Cross, J. (1995). 'IT Outsourcing: British Petroleum's Competitive Approach', *Harvard Business Review*, 73(3): 94–103.

Cullen, S., Seddon, P., and Willcocks, L. (2005a). 'Managing Outsourcing: The Life Cycle Imperative', *MIS Quarterly Executive*, 4(1): 229–46.

—— —— —— (2005b). 'IT Outsourcing Configuration: Research into Defining and Designing Outsourcing Arrangements', *Journal of Strategic Information Systems*, 14(4): 357–87.

Currie, W. (1998). 'Using Multiple Suppliers to Mitigate the Risk of IT Outsourcing at ICI and Wessex Water', *Journal of Information Technology*, 13: 169–80.

—— and Willcocks, L. (1998). 'Analyzing Four Types of IT Sourcing Decisions in the Context of Scale, Client/Supplier Interdependency and Risk Mitigation', *Information Systems Journal*, 8(2): 119–43.

Davenport, T. (2005). 'The Coming Commoditization of Processes', *Harvard Business Review*, 83(6): 101–8.

De Loof, L. A. (1995). 'Information Systems Outsourcing Decision Making: A Framework, Organizational Theories and Case Studies', *Journal of Information Technology*, 10: 281–97.

Dibbern, J., Winkler, J., and Heinzl, A. (2008). 'Explaining Variations in Client Extra Costs between Software Projects Offshored to India', *MIS Quarterly*, 32(2): 333–66.

—— Goles, T., Hirschheim, R., and Bandula J. (2004). 'Information Systems Outsourcing: A Survey and Analysis of the Literature', *Database for Advances in Information Systems*, 34 (4): 6–102.

DiRomualdo, A., and Gurbaxani, V. (1998). 'Strategic Intent for IT Outsourcing', *Sloan Management Review*, 39(4): 67–80.

Domberger, S., Fernandez, P., and Fiebig, D. G. (2000). 'Modelling the Price, Performance and Contract Characteristics of IT Outsourcing', *Journal of Information Technology*, 15: 107–18.

Earl, M. (1996). 'The Risks of Outsourcing IT', *Sloan Management Review*, 37(3): 26–32.

Farag, N., and Krishnan, M. (2003). 'The Market Value of IT Outsourcing Investment Announcements: An Event-Study Analysis', *Proceedings of the 9th Americas Conference on Information Systems*, 1623–9.

Feeny, D., Lacity, M., and Willcocks, L. (2005). 'Taking the Measure of Outsourcing Providers', *Sloan Management Review*, 46(3): 41–8.

—— and Willcocks, L. (1998). 'Core IS Capabilities for Exploiting Information Technology', *Sloan Management Review*, 39(3): 9–21.

Fisher, J., Hirschheim, R., and Jacobs, R. (2008). 'Understanding the Outsourcing Learning Curve: A Longitudinal Analysis of a Large Australian Company', *Information Systems Frontiers*, 10: 165–78.

Florin, J., Bradford, M., and Pagach, D. (2005). 'Information Technology Outsourcing and Organizational Restructuring: An Explanation of their Effects on Firm Value', *Journal of High Technology Management Research*, 16(2): 241–53.

Galliers, R., and Leidner, D. (2009). *Strategic Information Management: Challenges and Strategies in Managing Information Systems*. 4th edn., London: Routledge.

Gokhale, A. A. (2007). 'Offshore Outsourcing: A Delphi Study', *Journal of Information Technology Case and Application Research*, 9(3): 6–18.

Goo, J., Kishore, R., Rao, H. R., and Nam, K. (2009). 'The Role of Service Level Agreements in Relational Management of Information Technology Outsourcing: An Empirical Study', *MIS Quarterly*, 33(1): 1–28.

Gopal, A., Mukhopadhyay, T., and Krishnan, M. (2002). 'The Role of Software Processes and Communication in Offshore Software Development', *Communications of the ACM*, 45(4): 193–200.

——Sivaramakrishnan, K., Krishnan, M., and Mukhopadhyay, T. (2003). 'Contracts in Offshore Software Development: An Empirical Analysis', *Management Science*, 49(12): 1671–83.

Grover, V., Cheon, M., and Teng, J. (1994). 'A Descriptive Study on the Outsourcing of Information Systems Functions', *Information & Management*, 27: 33–44.

————(1996). 'The Effect of Service Quality and Partnership on the Outsourcing of Information Systems Functions', *Journal of Management Information Systems*, 12(4): 89–116.

Gupta, A., Seshasai, S., Mukherji, S., and Ganguly, A. (2007). 'Offshoring: The Transition from Economic Drivers toward Strategic Global Partnership and 24-Hour Knowledge Factory', *Journal of Electronic Commerce in Organizations*, 5(2): 1–23.

Hall, J., and Liedtka, S. (2005). 'Financial Performance, CEO Compensation, and Large-Scale Information Technology Outsourcing Decisions', *Journal of Management Information Systems*, 22(1): 193–222.

Han, H., Lee, J., and Seo, Y. (2008). 'Analyzing the Impact of a Firm's Capability on Outsourcing Success: A Process Perspective', *Information & Management*, 45: 31–42.

Hayes, D., Hunton, J., and Reck, J. (2000). 'Information Systems Outsourcing Announcement: Investigating the Impact on the Market Value of Contract Granting and Receiving Firms', *Journal of Information Systems*, 14(2): 109–25.

Heiskanen, A., Newman, M., and Eklin, M. (2008). 'Control, Trust, Power, and the Dynamics of Information System Outsourcing Relationships: A Process Study of Contractual Software Development', *Journal of Strategic Information Systems*, 17(4): 268–86.

Huber, R. (1993). 'How Continental Bank Outsourced its "Crown Jewels"', *Harvard Business Review*, 71(1): 121–9.

Iacovou, C. L., and Nakatsu, R. (2008). 'A Risk Profile of Offshore-Outsourced Development Projects', *Communications of the ACM*, 51(6): 89–94.

Jarvenpaa, S., and Mao, J. (2008). 'Operational Capabilities Development in Mediated Offshore Software Service Models', *Journal of Information Technology*, 23(1): 3–17.

Jeyaraj, A., Rottman, J., and Lacity, M. (2006). 'A Review of the Predictors, Linkages, and Biases in IT Innovation Adoption Research', *Journal of Information Technology*, 21(1): 1–23.

Jurison, J. (1995). 'The Role of Risk and Return in Information Technology Outsourcing Decisions', *Journal of Information Technology*, 10: 239–47.

Kaiser, K., and Hawk, S. (2004). 'Evolution of Offshore Software Development: From Outsourcing to Co-Sourcing', *MIS Quarterly Executive*, 3(2): 69–81.

Kern, T., Kreijger, J., and Willcocks, L. (2002c). 'Exploring ASP as a Sourcing Strategy: Theoretical Perspectives, Propositions for Practice', *Journal of Strategic Information Systems*, 11(2): 153–77.

——Lacity, M., and Willcocks, L. (2002). *Netsourcing: Renting Business Applications and Services over a Network*. New York: Prentice Hall.

——and Willcocks, L. (2000). 'Exploring Information Technology Outsourcing Relationships: Theory and Practice', *Journal of Strategic Information Systems*, 9(4): 321–50.

————(2002). 'Exploring Relationships in Information Technology Outsourcing: The Interaction Approach', *European Journal of Information Systems*, 11: 3–19.

————and Lacity, M. (2002). 'Application Service Provision: Risk Assessment and Risk Mitigation', *MIS Quarterly Executive*, 1(2): 113–26.

Kishore, R., Rao, H., Nam, K., Rajagopalan, S., Chaudhury, A. (2003). 'A Relationship Perspective on IT Outsourcing', *Communications of the ACM*, 46(12): 86–92.

Koh, C., Ang, S., and Straub, D. (2004). 'IT Outsourcing Success: A Psychological Contract Perspective', *Information Systems Research*, 15(4): 356–73.

Kotlarsky, J., van Fenema, P., and Willcocks, L. (2008). 'Developing a Knowledge-Based Perspective on Coordination: The Case of Global Software Projects', *Information and Management*, 45(2): 96–108.

Lacity, M., Feeny, D., and Willcocks, L. (2003). 'Transforming a Back-Office Function: Lessons from BAE Systems' Experience with an Enterprise Partnership', *MIS Quarterly Executive*, 2(2): 86–103.

———— ——(2004). 'Commercializing the Back Office at Lloyds of London: Outsourcing and Strategic Partnerships Revisited', *European Management Journal*, 22(2): 127–40.

——and Hirschheim, R. (1993). 'The Information Systems Outsourcing Bandwagon', *Sloan Management Review*, 35(1): 73–86.

————and Willcocks, L. (1994). 'Realizing Outsourcing Expectations', *Information Systems Management*, 11(4): 7–18.

——and Rottman, J. (2008). *Offshore Outsourcing of IT Work*. Basingstoke: Palgrave.

——and Willcocks, L. (1998). 'An Empirical Investigation of Information Technology Sourcing Practices: Lessons from Experience', *MIS Quarterly*, 22(3): 363–408.

———— (2000). 'Survey of IT Outsourcing Experiences in US and UK Organizations', *Journal of Global Information Management*, 8(2): 5–23.

————and Rottman, J. (2008). 'Global Outsourcing of Back Office Services: Lessons, Trends and Enduring Challenges', *Strategic Outsourcing: An International Journal*, 1(1): 13–34.

Lee, A. (1999). 'Rigor and Relevance in Information Systems Research: Beyond the Approach of Positivism Alone', *MIS Quarterly*, 23(1): 29–34.

Lee, J., and Kim, Y. (1999). 'Effect of Partnership Quality on IS Outsourcing Success: Conceptual Framework and Empirical Validation', *Journal of Management Information Systems*, 15(4): 29–61.

——Miranda, S., and Kim, Y. (2004). 'IT Outsourcing Strategies: Universalistic, Contingency, and Configurational Explanations of Success', *Information Systems Research*, 15(2): 110–31.

Leonardi, P. M., and Bailey, D. E. (2008). 'Transformational Technologies and the Creation of New Work Practices: Making Implicit Knowledge Explicit in Task-Based Offshoring', *MIS Quarterly*, 32(2): 411–36.

Levina, N., and Ross, J. (2003). 'From the Vendor' Perspective: Exploring the Value Proposition in Information Technology Outsourcing', *MIS Quarterly*, 27(3): 331–64.

Linder, J. (2004). 'Transformational Outsourcing', *Sloan Management Review*, 45(2): 52–8.

Loebbecke, C., and Huyskens, C. (2006). 'What Drives Netsourcing Decisions? An Empirical Analysis', *European Journal of Information Systems*, 15(4): 415–23.

Loh, L., and Venkatraman, N. (1992a). 'Determinants of Information Technology Outsourcing: A Cross-Sectional Analysis', *Journal of Management Information Systems*, 9(1): 7–24.

——— (1992b). *Stock Market Reaction to IT Outsourcing: An Event Study*. Cambridge, MA: Sloan School of Management, MIT.

McDonald, M. (2007). 'The Enterprise Capability Organization: A Future for IT', *MIS Quarterly Executive*, 6(3): 179–92.

Madison, T., San Miguel, P., and Padmanabhan, P. (2006). 'Stock Market Reaction to Domestic Outsourcing Announcements by U.S. Based Client and Vendor Firms', *Journal of Information Technology Case and Application Research*, 8(4): 6–26.

Mahnke, V., Wareham, J., and Bjorn-Andersen, N. (2008). 'Offshore Middlemen: Transnational Intermediation in Technology Sourcing', *Journal of Information Technology*, 23(1): 18–30.

Michell, V., and Fitzgerald, G. (1997). 'The IT Outsourcing Market-Place: Vendors and their Selection', *Journal of Information Technology*, 12: 223–37.

Miranda, S., and Kim, Y. (2006). 'Professionalism versus Political Contexts: Institutional Mitigation and the Transaction Cost Heuristic in Information Systems Outsourcing', *MIS Quarterly*, 30(3): 725–53.

Mojsilovic, A., Ray, B., Lawrence, R., and Takriti, S. (2007). 'A Logistic Regression Framework for Information Technology Outsourcing Lifecycle Management', *Computers & Operations Research*, 34(12): 3609–27.

Nam, K., Rajagopalan, S., Rao, H. R., and Chaudhury, A. (1996). 'A Two-Level Investigation of Information Systems Outsourcing', *Communications of the ACM*, 39(7): 36–44.

Oh, W., Gallivan, M., and Kim, J. (2006). 'The Market's Perception of the Transactional Risks of Information Technology Outsourcing Announcements', *Journal of Management Information Systems*, 22(4): 271–303.

Osei-Bryson, K.-M., and Ngwenyama, O. K. (2006). 'Managing Risks in Information Systems Outsourcing: An Approach to Analyzing Outsourcing Risks and Structuring Incentive Contracts', *European Journal of Operational Research*, 174(1): 245–64.

Oshri, I., Kotlarsky, J., and Willcocks, L. (2007a). 'Managing Dispersed Expertise in IT Offshore Outsourcing: Lessons from Tata Consultancy Services', *MIS Quarterly Executive*, 6(2): 53–66.

——— (2007b). 'Global Software Development: Exploring Socialization and Face-to-Face Meetings in Distributed Strategic Projects', *Journal of Strategic Information Systems*, 16: 25–49.

Oza, N., and Hall, T. (2005). 'Difficulties in Managing Offshore Software Outsourcing Relationships: An Empirical Analysis of 19 High Maturity Indian Software Companies', *Journal of Information Technology Case and Application Research*, 7(3): 25–41.

————Rainer, A., and Grey, S. (2006). 'Trust in Software Outsourcing Relationships: An Empirical Investigation of Indian Software Companies', *Information and Software Technology*, 48: 345–54.

Poppo, L., and Zenger, T. (2002). 'Do Formal Contracts and Relational Governance Function as Substitutes or Complements?', *Strategic Management Journal*, 23: 707–25.

Quinn, J. B. (1999). 'Strategic Outsourcing: Leveraging Knowledge Capabilities', *Sloan Management Review*, 40(4): 9–21.

——(2000). 'Outsourcing Innovation: The New Engine of Growth', *Sloan Management Review*, 41(4): 13–28.

——and Hilmer, F. (1994). 'Strategic Outsourcing', *Sloan Management Review*, 35(4): 43–55.

Ranganathan, C., and Balaji, S. (2007). 'Critical Capabilities for Offshore Outsourcing of IS', *MIS Quarterly Executive*, 6(3): 147–64.

Rao, M. T., Poole, W., Raven, P. V., and Lockwood, D. L. (2006). 'Trends, Implications, and Responses to Global IT Sourcing: A Field Study', *Journal of Global Information Technology Management*, 9(3): 5–23.

Ross, J., and Beath, C. (2006). 'Sustainable IT Outsourcing: Let Enterprise Architecture be your Guide', *MIS Quarterly Executive*, 5(4): 181–92.

Rottman, J., and Lacity, M. (2004). 'Twenty Practices for Offshore Sourcing', *MIS Quarterly Executive*, 3(3): 117–30.

————(2006). 'Proven Practices for Effectively Offshoring IT Work', *Sloan Management Review*, 47(3): 56–63.

Sabherwal, R. (1999). 'The Role of Trust in Outsourced IS Development Projects', *Communications of the ACM*, 42(2): 80–6.

Sakthivel, S. (2007). 'Managing Risk in Offshore Systems Development', *Communications of the ACM*, 50(4): 69–75.

Seddon, P. B. (2001). 'The Australian Federal Government's Clustered-Agency IT Outsourcing Experiment', *Communications of the AIS*, 5: 1–33.

Slaughter, S. A., and Ang, S. (1996). 'Employment Outsourcing in Information Systems', *Communications of the ACM*, 39(7): 47–54.

Smith, H. A., and McKeen, J. D. (2004). 'Developments in Practice XIV: IT Outsourcing—How Far can you Go?' *Communications of the AIS*, 14: 508–20.

Smith, M., Mitra, S., and Narasimhan, S. (1998). 'Information Systems Outsourcing: A Study of Pre-Event Firm Characteristics', *Journal of Management Information Systems*, 15(2): 61–93.

Sobol, M., and Apte, U. (1995). 'Domestic and Global Outsourcing Practices of America's Most Effective IS Users', *Journal of Information Technology*, 10: 269–80.

Strassmann, P. (1995). 'Outsourcing: A Game for Losers', *Computerworld*, 21 August.

——(2004). 'Most Outsourcing is Still for Losers', *Computerworld*, 2 February.

Straub, D., Weill, P., and Schwaig, K. (2008). 'Strategic Dependence on the IT Resource and Outsourcing: A Test of the Strategic Control Model', *Information Systems Frontiers*, 10(2): 195–211.

Susarla, A., Barua, A., and Whinston, A. B. (2003). 'Understanding the Service Component of Application Service Provision: An Empirical Analysis of Satisfaction with ASP Services', *Management Information Systems Quarterly*, 27(1): 91–123.

Tanriverdi, H., Konana, P., and Ge, L. (2007). 'The Choice of Sourcing Mechanisms for Business Processes', *Information Systems Research*, 18(3): 280–302.

Teng, J., Cheon, M., and Grover, V. (1995). 'Decisions to Outsource Information Systems Functions: Testing a Strategy-Theoretic Discrepancy Model', *Decision Sciences*, 26(1): 75–103.

Wang, L., Gwebu, K. L., Wang, J., and Zhu, D. X. (2008). 'The Aftermath of Information Technology Outsourcing: An Empirical Study of Firm Performance Following Outsourcing Decisions', *Journal of Information Systems*, 22(1): 125–59.

Watjatrakul, B. (2005). 'Determinants of IS Sourcing Decisions: A Comparative Study of Transaction Cost Theory and the Resource-Based View', *Journal of Strategic Information Systems*, 14: 389–415.

Westfall, R. (1999). 'An IS Research Relevance Manifesto', *Communications of the AIS*, 2(14), <http://cais.asinet.org/articles/2-14/article.htm>.

Whitten, D., and Leidner, D. (2006). 'Bringing Back IT: An Analysis of the Decision to Backsource or Switch Vendors', *Decision Sciences*, 37(4): 605–21.

——and Wakefield, R. (2006). 'Measuring Switching Costs in IT Outsourcing Services', *Journal of Strategic Information Systems*, 15(3): 219–48.

Willcocks, L., and Feeny, D. (2006). 'IT Outsourcing and Core IS Capabilities: Challenges at Lessons at DuPont', *Information Systems Management*, 23(1): 49–56.

——and Fitzgerald, G. (1993). 'Market as Opportunity? Case Studies in Outsourcing Information Technology and Services', *Journal of Strategic Information Systems*, 2(3): 223–42.

——and Lacity, M. (1999). 'IT Outsourcing in Insurance Services: Risk, Creative Contracting, and Business Advantage', *Information Systems Journal*, 9(61): 1–18.

——— (2006). *Global Sourcing of Business and IT Services*. Basingstoke: Palgrave.

———and Kern, T. (1999). 'Risk Mitigation in IT Outsourcing Strategy Revisited: Longitudinal Research at LISA', *Journal of Strategic Information Systems*, 8(3): 285–314.

Williamson, O. (1991). 'Comparative Economic Organization: The Analysis of Discrete Structural Alternatives', *Administrative Science Quarterly*, 36(2): 269–96.

Wüllenweber, K., Beimborn, D., Weitzel, T., and Kőnig, W. (2008). 'The Impact of Process Standardization on Business Process Outsourcing Success', *Information Systems Frontiers*, 10(2): 211–24.

Zviran, M., Ahituv, N., and Armoni, A. (2001). 'Building Outsourcing Relationships across the Global Community: The UPS-Motorola Experience', *Journal of Strategic Information Systems*, 10(4): 313–33.

PART IV

··

RETHINKING MIS PRACTICE IN A BROADER CONTEXT

··

PART IV extends our coverage of Information Systems to consider a somewhat wider set of topics that are nonetheless central to our field of study in the twenty-first century. To recap, we introduced the book with a chapter from Lynne Markus that attempted to embrace the totality of the field of MIS, as we have construed it in this volume. We followed this with a historical account of how things have developed, through the eyes of Rudy Hirschheim and the late Heinz Klein. Building on these introductory contributions, Part II set the foundation for a consideration of MIS by providing a reprise of the various theoretical and methodological perspectives that exist to assist us in researching MIS phenomena—many of which are emerging as the technology, and our understanding of the subject matter, advances. Part III built on this foundation by considering key topics in the MIS domain. Some of these topics have been with us for some time, such as IS strategizing; business-IT alignment; IT for competitive advantage, and the like. Others have become more centre-stage in more recent years: enterprise systems; questions of IT governance; matters of security, and the emergence and impact of mobile IT, for example. Part IV expands the boundaries of MIS still further by considering such important topics as managing knowledge work; gender issues in IT; issues of sustainability and ethics; aspects of globalization, human development and the related topic of IT in developing countries, and—to bring things to a close—insights into questions of technological innovation and further emerging themes that are likely to attract our attention into the future.

We commence Part IV with Chapter 20, which focuses on the topic of managing knowledge work. Written by Jacky Swan, this chapter introduces the core concepts of knowledge, organizational knowledge, knowledge management, and—importantly—innovation. It draws from material that can be found in the second edition of *Managing Knowledge Work and Innovation* (Newell et al. 2009). Importantly, because this extends our understanding of why we wish to 'manage knowledge'; why it is that increasing attention is being paid to knowledge *creation* (e.g. von Krogh, Ichijo, and Nonaka 2000; Gourlay 2006) rather than the more static view that went with the earlier treatments of knowledge management that were more akin to the collection and reuse of existing 'knowledge', with terms like 'harvesting' and 'mining' being used liberally. The chapter draws on theory developed in the organizational behaviour and strategy literatures and shows how these concepts have been—and can be—applied to the world of Information Systems through knowledge management systems (e.g. Leidner 2000). While the philosophical debates about what exactly is knowledge (e.g. Tsoukas and Vladimirou 2001; Tsoukas 2003) and the implications for IS (e.g. Newell, Swan, and Scarbrough 2001; Galliers and Newell 2003) are left to others, the chapter, nonetheless, covers a great deal of territory. A working definition of knowledge is provided and aspects of knowledge sharing across organizational boundaries are also dealt with (Hansen 1999; Carlile 2004). The distinction between knowledge and knowing is also highlighted (Cook and Brown 1999), with organizational learning (e.g. Boisot 1995; Brown and Duguid 2001; Gheradi 2001) coming to the fore, and—with the impact of new technologies—networking concepts are introduced in addition (e.g. McAfee 2006).

We next turn our attention—in Chapter 21—to matters of gender in the field of MIS. Written by Eileen Trauth, this chapter begins by asking the question: 'Why should the MIS field be concerned about gender?' or rather, why should we be concerned with this question *now*? As she states, 'The rationale for the inclusion of gender among the "legitimate" topics of MIS attention is embedded within the larger rationale for the inclusion of the human resource dimension of the MIS field.' The chapter traces the evolution of research in the field of gender and information systems in the context of developments in and forces shaping the twenty-first century. Highlighting, for example, the impact of globalization in providing impetus for the IS academy to pay greater attention to human differences, she identifies increased opportunities for research in relation to gender and socio-cultural differences, building on the work of Lisa von Hellens and colleagues (e.g. von Hellens and Nielsen 2001; von Hellens, Nielsen, and Trauth 2001), for example, and on social inclusion (e.g. Huang et al. 2006). The chapter, therefore, provides some interesting links with subsequent chapters that deal with matters related to IT and globalization, and IT in developing countries.

The following chapter, by Pierre Berthon and colleagues, highlights some of the paradoxes associated with IT, noting that 'sometimes IT has done more to compound problems than create sustainable solutions'. Some of these paradoxes include the promise of efficiency gains, of cleanliness, of education, and of community, with each being questioned in turn (e.g. Sellen and Harper 2001; Grossman 2006; Sigman 2009). Unlike others before them, however, the authors of this chapter focus not on green information systems or green IT, but rather on the way in which we go about *thinking* about the topic. As a result, they identify three 'paradigms of sustainability' that lead to varying ways of using IT 'to achieve the goal of a viable planet', as opposed to the exploitative view of IT that has permeated much of the earlier treatment of the topic. Building their argument on the work of Heidegger (1977)—see also Chapters 9 and 10—they argue that (information) technology is 'a mode of revelation . . . a process of bringing forth . . . a way of seeing . . . '. Thus, rather than merely *exploiting* nature, they propose *viewing* IT in terms either of *preserving*, *returning to*, or *transforming* nature.

Already, then, we are considering ethical considerations when we talk of MIS, and this is the specific focus of Chapter 23. This chapter, written by Simon Rogerson, might usefully be read in combination also with Chapter 16, in which Sue Newell and Cynthia Williams consider questions of governance, sustainability, and the so-called 'triple-bottom line' (Elkington 1994): financial, social, and environmental performance. In this chapter, the author considers the many different definitions of what he terms 'computer and information ethics', with the aim of demonstrating the breadth and multi-disciplinarity of the field. Building on this introduction, the chapter then focuses on *application*: how to embed an ethical perspective into the way in which we develop information systems, and how to instil ethical professionalism into our practice. A series of challenges are identified, including privacy (see also questions of security covered by Amy Ray in Chapter 17), culture, and crime. This chapter leads nicely into the following chapter, by Geoff Walsham, as Rogerson concludes his chapter with a look into a future that involves a technology that 'continually increases choice in global interaction within a dispersed community and between different and geographically distant communities'.

Thus, in Chapter 24, Geoff Walsham reviews the literature on IT and globalization, and argues, in line with the likes of Grey and Willmott (2002), for 'critical research which addresses issues of IT and human development in our more globalized world'. This literature includes some of his own prior work (e.g. Walsham 2001, 2005), and the work of others including that of Manuel Castells (1996, 1997, 1998). First, though, he considers varying treatments of globalization itself, most notably, the work of Robertson (1992), and Beck (2000). This chapter, in turns, provides a useful segue into Chrisanthi Avgerou's treatment of information systems research in developing countries, in the chapter that follows. It does so by providing two examples of the critical research for which he argues: in relation specifically to health information systems (e.g. Braa and Hedberg 2002) and IT for the poor (cf. the so-called 'digital divide').

As indicated, Chapter 25 broadens our perspective to consider information systems in the context of developing countries. As Chrisanthi Avgerou points out, there is considerable literature on the topic, but this has more recently been extended to include 'the broader socio-economic context of the organizations hosting new technologies', rather than simply focusing on development and implementation issues per se. This is where her use of the term 'innovation' comes in: as she points out, 'even if the technologies implemented . . . are already common elsewhere . . . the local experience of technology implementation and socio-organizational change constitutes an innovation for the organization concerned and [possibly] . . . for its socio-economic context'. Her treatment of the innovation process focuses in the main on two perspectives: transfer and diffusion on the one hand, and socially embedded action on the other. In the former case, the local context means that one size does not fit all (cf. Bada 2002), and in the latter, incorporating such considerations as empowerment into the process (cf. Sahay and Walsham 2005). The chapter ends with a plea that echoes the arguments raised by Geoff Walsham in the preceding chapter: critical research that will have real impact in policy circles.

Our final chapter is by Rick Watson, Pierre Berthon, and Leyland Pitt. In it, the authors take an expansive view of the field of MIS and argue for a broadening of the field's traditional boundaries as we confront the issues of the twenty-first century. Traditional foci associated with information systems *within* organizations, or theories or approaches formed within the industrial as opposed to the information age constrain our research and are inappropriate as the field develops. Watson and colleagues argue that some of the recent debate as to what properly constitutes the field of Information Systems (cf. King and Lyytinen 2006) is potentially misplaced: research into instrumental design *and* research into emergent 'IS phenomena' is required, not one or the other.

We have covered a vast territory in this Handbook. We have done so, quite deliberately, with a view to demonstrating how the field of MIS has developed in recent years—and continues to do so. To echo the argument of the authors of Chapter 26: 'the instrumental and the emergent are inherent aspects of any technology—neither can be ignored for they feed each other . . . ' We have therefore attempted to cover some of the ground that has been the traditional haunt of MIS researchers in recent decades: the use and impact of IT in and between organizations. In addition, however, we have attempted to expand our focus to include managing knowledge, information systems and human development, and broader issues of ethics, sustainability, and globalization as they relate to IT. To do so, we need sound theoretical and methodological tools to guide our endeavours, and that is why we have provided what we hope to be a strong foundation for our treatment of this expanding universe in Part II. We conclude that issues or emergence and innovation are the very stuff of MIS as we attempt to address the many pressing issues of the twenty-first century—a century in which information and communication technologies will play an increasing, and as yet, only dimly perceived role.

References

Bada, A. O. (2002). 'Local Adaptations to Global Trends: A Study of an IT-Based Organizational Change Programme in a Nigerian Bank', *Information Society*, 18(2): 77–86.

Beck, U. (2000). *What is Globalization?* Cambridge: Polity Press.

Boisot, M. (1995). *Information Space: A Framework for Learning in Organizations, Institutions and Culture.* London: Blackwell.

Braa, J., and Hedberg, C. (2002). 'The Struggle for District-Based Health Information Systems in South Africa', *Information Society*, 18(2): 113–28.

Brown, J. S., and Duguid, P. (2001). 'Knowledge and Organization: A Social-Practice Perspective', *Organization Science*, 12(2): 198–213.

Carlile, P. (2004). 'Transferring, Translating and Transforming: An Integrative Framework from Managing Knowledge across Boundaries', *Organization Science*, 15(5): 555–68.

Castells, M. (1996). *The Rise of the Network Society.* Oxford: Blackwell.

——(1997). *The Power of Identity.* Oxford: Blackwell.

——(1998). *End of Millenium.* Oxford: Blackwell.

Cook, S., and Brown, J. (1999). 'Bridging Epistemologies: The Generative Dance between Organizational Knowledge and Organizational Knowing', *Organization Science*, 10(4): 381–400.

Elkington, J. (1994). 'Towards the Sustainable Corporation: Win-Win-Win Business Strategies for Sustainable Development', *California Management Review*, 36(2): 90–100.

Galliers, R. D., and Newell, S. (2003). 'Back to the Future: From Knowledge Management to the Management of Information and Data', *Information Systems and e-Business Management*, 1(1): 5–13.

Gherardi, S. (2001). 'From Organizational Learning to Practice-Based Knowing', *Human Relations*, 54(1): 131–9.

Gourlay, S. (2006). 'Conceptualizing Knowledge Creation: A Critique of Nonaka's Theory', *Journal of Management Studies*, 43(7): 1415–36.

Grey, C., and Willmott, H. (2002). 'Contexts of Critical Management Studies', *Organization*, 9(3): 411–18.

Grossman, E. (2006). *High Tech Trash: Digital Devices, Hidden Toxics, and Human Health.* Washington, DC: Shearwater.

Hansen, M. T. (1999). 'The Search Transfer Problem: The Role of Weak Ties in Sharing Knowledge across Organizational Sub-units', *Administrative Science Quarterly*, 44: 82–111.

Heidegger, M. (1977). *The Question Concerning Technology, and Other Essays.* New York: Harper & Row.

Huang, H., Quesenberry, J. L., Morgan, A. J., and Yeo, B. (2006). 'Where Have We Been and Where Are We Going? Social Inclusion in the Last Decade of IFIP WG 8.2 Research', poster presentation at IFIP 8.2 Conference (Limerick, June).

King, J. L., and Lyytinen, K. (2006). *Information Systems: The State of the Field.* Chichester: Wiley.

Leidner, D. E. (ed.) (2000). Special Issue: Knowledge Management and Knowledge Management Systems, *Journal of Strategic Information Systems*, 9(2–3): 101–261.

McAfee, A. (2006). 'Enterprise 2.0: The Dawn of Emergent Collaboration', *MIT Sloan Management Review*, 47(3): 21–8.

Newell, S., Swan, J., and Scarbrough, H. (2001). 'From Global Knowledge Management to Internal Electronic Fences: Contradictory Outcomes of Intranet Development', *British Journal of Management*, 12(2): 97–111.

Newell, S., Robertson, M., Scarbrough, H., and Swan, J. (2009). *Managing Knowledge Work and Innovation*, 2nd edn. Houndmills: Palgrave Macmillan.

Robertson, R. (1992). *Globalization: Social Theory and Global Culture*. London: Sage.

Sahay, S., and Walsham, G. (2005). 'Scaling of Health Information Systems in India: Challenges and Approaches', *Enhancing Human Resource Development through ICT*, IFIP WG9.4. Abuja-Nigeria.

Sellen, A., and Harper, R. (2001). *The Myth of the Paperless Office*. Boston, MA: The MIT Press.

Sigman, A. (2009). 'Technology and Community', *Biologist*, January.

Tsoukas, H. (2003). 'Do We Really Understand Tacit Knowledge?', in M. Easterby-Smith and M. A. Lyles (eds.), *The Blackwell Handbook of Organizational Learning and Knowledge Management*. Oxford: Blackwell, 410–27.

Tsoukas, H., and Vladimirou, E. (2001). 'What is Organizational Knowledge?', *Journal of Management Studies*, 38(7): 973–93.

von Hellens, L. A., and Nielsen, S. (2001). 'Australian Women in IT', *Communications of the ACM*, 44(7): 46–52.

——— and Trauth, E. M. (2001). 'Breaking and Entering the Male Domain: Women in the IT Industry', in M. Serva (ed.), *Proceedings of the 2001 ACM SIGMIS Conference on Computer Personal Research* (San Diego, April), 116–20.

von Krogh, G., Ichijo, K., and Nonaka, I. (2000). *Enabling Knowledge Creation: How to Unlock the Mystery of Tacit Knowledge and Release the Power of Innovation*. New York: Oxford University Press.

Walsham, G. (2001). *Making a World of Difference: IT in a Global Context*. Chichester: John Wiley.

——(2005). 'Development, Global Futures and IS Research: A Polemic', *Journal of Strategic Information Systems*, 14(1): 5–15.

CHAPTER 20

MANAGING KNOWLEDGE WORK

JACKY SWAN

INTRODUCTION

WITHOUT doubt amongst the most important applications of MIS to improving business performance in the last fifteen years has been via their central role in 'Knowledge Management' (KM). Even well before the term KM was used, the 'infor-mating' role of technologies for managers has been stressed over and above their ability to automate organizational processes (Zuboff 1988). However, the more recent surge of interest in KM has heightened the strategic importance afforded to MIS by business organizations, many of whom are now taking seriously the mantra that 'knowledge is our greatest asset' and making major investments in MIS as part and parcel of broader KM initiatives.

Attempts to manage organizational knowledge have also gone hand in hand with major advances in MIS design (social networking technologies, for example) and there are now a vast number of academic offerings on the subject of using MIS to improve knowledge sharing in organizations. Underpinning this interest in KM is the central notion that work tasks are relying more and more on knowledge and information. The management of knowledge work and knowledge workers, then, is seen as the single most important challenge being faced by all kinds of organizations and as essential to efforts to improve competitiveness and innovation through the deployment of MIS and other means.

Yet, we also know many attempts to manage knowledge and knowledge workers have failed, and continue to fail, to deliver promised improvements (Scarbrough and Swan 2001; Walsham 2002). More specifically, there have been numerous failures associated with attempts to mobilize knowledge flows using MIS. Hence the now well-versed critique of so-called 'first wave' approaches to KM, in the late 1990s, is that they failed because they were overly focused on generically applicable IT-based tools and methods to store and transfer 'knowledge' and information, and took little heed of the social, organizational, and cultural context needed to apply that knowledge and information and to support and enable knowledgeable work (McDermott 1999).

Whilst 'second wave' approaches—focused on generating the social and cultural conditions necessary for knowledge sharing—have been offered as an antidote to formerly overly deterministic technocratic approaches, these have been similarly criticized for leaving technologies 'black boxed' and for failing to acknowledge the subtleties of MIS design and their material effects on how work is actually done.

This see-sawing of attention to technical and social interests in KM—oddly reminiscent of earlier debates around determinism versus choice in socio-technical systems—is perhaps an inevitable consequence of the division of professional knowledge and interests (Scarbrough and Swan 2001). It has also been rather unhelpful as it has focused attention on how to increase knowledge stocks and flows (i.e. through technical or social means) and has diverted attention from what it is we are actually managing knowledge *for*. These criticisms aside, given the importance of the 'KM revolution' (or, at least evolution) as a backdrop to the enhanced strategic role of MIS, it is useful to take a broader look at the major approaches deployed in managing knowledge work, the challenges these entail, and the role of MIS in resolving (or perhaps creating) these challenges.

In this chapter, then, I first outline some reasons why, while the label may change, KM is rather unlikely to be another management fad that will quickly disappear. The chapter then provides a brief overview and critique of different approaches to managing knowledge work, and looks at how ideas in the 'field' have developed and the implications of these approaches for the development of MIS. The purpose is not to engage deeply in philosophical debates about the nature of knowledge—this has been done rather well elsewhere (Tsoukas and Vladimirou 2001; Tsoukas 2003). Rather, we outline and critique three broad approaches—termed here as structuralist, process, and practice—that have been developed in organizational theory and strategy and which help inform our understanding of what it is that firms are trying to do when they claim to be managing knowledge.

THE IMPORTANCE OF KNOWLEDGE WORK

Whilst it has been recognized for a very long time that applying knowledge to work tasks is crucial for economic performance, in recent decades a 'new' language has arisen around concerns that, in the 'knowledge society', it is knowledge, and not other resources, such as labour or capital, that is the main source of competitive advantage across sectors. This language is now deeply embedded in the rhetoric of politicians, management practitioners, and academic scholars, reflected in such terms as 'the learning organization', 'Knowledge Management', 'core competencies', 'dynamic capabilities', 'the knowledge-based view of the firm', 'knowledge-intensive firms', 'intellectual and social capital', talent management, and so forth.

Of course, popular fashions and associated rhetorics do come and go—for example, the corresponding chapter in the forerunner to this Handbook (Currie and Galliers 1999) used the term 'Knowledge Management', and this has largely lost ground as 'flavour of the month' (Scarbrough and Swan 2001). Yet, the rapid onset and demise of management fads is itself continued testimony to the phenomena which they address—that is, the importance of change and innovation for organizations facing increasingly turbulent environments, the impact of discourse on patterns and styles of management, and the seemingly endless importance of information systems (IS) on work and work relationships. These factors are not the product of fashion, then, but of history—a convergent set of forces which have unleashed fundamental patterns of change on advanced industrial economies. These forces have been the focus of ongoing concern across a number of different studies of industrial, occupational, and organizational change in recent decades (see e.g. Drucker 1969; Bell 1973; Drucker 1988; Gibbons et al. 1994; Castells 1996) and include:

- The importance of knowledge as a primary means of production, acting upon itself in 'an accelerating spiral of innovation and change'.
- The extent to which knowledge has been 'globalized', or freed up from material, physical, and geographic constraints.
- The convergence of computing power and communications technology, with a new generation of web-based technologies having major impacts on the structuring of work and occupations.
- An emphasis on normative, or cultural, rather than hierarchical forms of control so that knowledge workers effectively manage and discipline themselves (and each other).
- Fundamental changes in the ways knowledge itself is produced—no longer just in 'ivory tower' academic organizations or isolated R&D departments (i.e. 'Mode 1') but 'co-produced' by heterogeneous groups *as it is applied* to solving problems in new contexts ('Mode 2'—Gibbons et al. 1994; Nowotny, Scott, and Gibbons 2003).
- The rise of the 'service economy' and the economic value of intangibles, such as services, ideas, software, and network relationships.

It is also argued, moreover, that the challenges for managing knowledge work posed now are greater than ever. This is because the knowledge economy is also a service economy (Dankbarr 2003). Hence we have seen massive growth in the service sector and major changes in the ways knowledge and information are applied to new service delivery. The pressures to develop, not just new products and technologies, but also new ways of dealing with shifting user needs and demands, often on a global scale, are, it is argued, significantly greater now than in years past (Dankbarr 2003) and information systems have undoubtedly had an important role to play. In insurance and financial services, for example, forms of service delivery have changed drastically, with the worldwide web providing much greater information to consumers and on-line service providers such as Direct Line. This means more knowledgeable customers can 'shop around' much more easily. It is also the case that the boundaries traditionally seen between services and products are blurring. Indeed some scholars even argue that 'material products (e.g. computers, mp3 players, mobile phones) are themselves only material embodiments of the services they deliver' (Dankbarr 2003: 79). It can even be difficult to tell whether we are actually buying a service or a product—the iPhone is intrinsically linked to iTunes and 3 Mobile Media, for example.

The implications of the rise in information-intensive services for managing knowledge work are extensive. With services, relevant knowledge is nearly always distributed across a whole range of stakeholders including, on a much greater basis than before, the customer (Dodgson, Gann, and Salter 2005). Knowledge workers also need significant autonomy so that they can deal flexibly with more knowledgeable customers and actively match services to requirements. The deep frustration that many of us experience when we telephone service companies only to be met by inflexible, 'rote' responses is testament indeed to the need for worker autonomy. In short, in a service economy, managing knowledge is not a support function but, rather, is intrinsic to the work itself (Coombs 2003; Miles 2003).

Taking a more critical approach, it is of course important that we continue to ask questions about the extent to which the changes outlined above have been as widespread, or as inherently positive, as predicted by their proponents. There are still many types of works—call centres, for example—where hierarchy, strict top-down control, and standardization continue to be the norm. Web-based and increasingly mobile information technologies also create their own problems. On the one hand, they decentralize work and free people and activities from the constraints of physical location or even identity. At the same time, however, they may depersonalize the experience of work and generate social isolation, or intensify it by blurring the boundaries between home and work and shifting the home-work life balance toward the latter. Finally, they can increase opportunities for more subtle forms of the surveillance and control—normative pressures to respond more instantly to email, by way of example, than to hard copy forms of communication.

A final point of critique concerns the links between knowledge and innovation. These linkages—and the virtue of knowledge management for improving innovative capabilities—have been rarely questioned in the literature. For example, Nonaka's (1994) now widely cited work on 'the knowledge creating company' emphasized the need to accumulate knowledge to improve creativity and innovation. More recent literature on 'dynamic capabilities', similarly, highlights the importance of developing and managing knowledge processes—'experience accumulation', 'knowledge codification', and 'knowledge articulation'—in order to generate and modify operating routines in the pursuit of organizational innovation and improved competitiveness (Zollo and Winter 2002; Bjorkman, Barner-Rasmussen, and Li 2004). Similarly the 'Mode 1', 'Mode 2' thesis is underpinned by the quite normative proposition that accumulated knowledge, produced in more socially reflexive ways, will benefit society (Nowotny,

Scott, and Gibbons 2001). Indeed, increased knowledge has been roughly equated with more innovation. Yet, it is also important to retain a healthy scepticism about this rather straightforward, functionalist equation between (more) knowledge and (more) innovation (see debates in special issues of the *Journal of Management Studies* 2001; *Journal of Information Technology* 2001, for example). Arguably, innovation stems as much from breaks with knowledge (forgetting previous recipes, for example) as from its steady accumulation.

Positive or negative, the changes heralded by the 'Information Age' are, however, undoubtedly having a visible impact on organizational forms, with flatter, decentralized structures and more flexible, open-ended, fluid, and networked arrangements becoming the norm rather than the exception in many sectors. The rise of networked organizations (sometimes referred to as polycentric organizations), virtual modes of organizing, and more open-ended, collaborative forms of innovation and product development (Chesbrough 2004) illustrate the extent to which organization designs have evolved in pace with changes in information systems that break down traditional boundaries of time and space.

These changes in organizational design have brought with them new problems for managing knowledge. For example, outsourcing brings with it risks of knowledge 'loss' and more open, collaborative forms of innovation bring challenges around ownership and intellectual property (Chesbrough 2003). And, when organizations are stretched across time and space (global and networked organizations, for example), they inevitably lose opportunities for casual and easy sharing of knowledge and learning afforded by physical proximity and shared culture (Prusak 1997). Indeed, it has been suggested that one of the reasons that 'Knowledge Management' initiatives became so popular in the late 1990s was *because* of the profound problems posed by changes of organization in the 'information age' (Prusak 1997). Hence, even though the scope and positive impact of changes associated with the 'Knowledge Era' may indeed be over-claimed, fundamental changes in the way practices of work are actually carried out and in the primary means of production (and consumption) do suggest that the challenges on managing knowledge work are likely to persist for some considerable time.

What is Knowledge Work?

In outlining the challenges of managing knowledge work, it seems important to first define terms, especially because there is rather little agreement on what knowledge actually is. There is a whole branch of philosophy, 'epistemology'—from the Greek words 'episteme' (knowledge) and 'logos' (word/speech)—that deals with, and debates on, the nature, origin, and scope of knowledge. However, in studies of knowledge work in organizational settings two views stand out. These have been usefully summarized by Cook and Brown (1999) as the 'epistemology of possession' and the 'epistemology of practice'.

The epistemology of possession view treats knowledge as something people *have*—knowledge is seen as a possession of the human mind and treated as a mental (or cognitive) capacity, or resource, that can be developed, applied, and used to improve effectiveness in the workplace. Those adopting this view often describe knowledge along a kind of pyramid, or hierarchy, comprising data (the dots of ink on this page, for example), information (the words and sentences that are inscribed by data), and knowledge (and even wisdom) (Ackoff 1989). Whereas data and information are 'out there'—objective properties of the world, external to individuals, which can be searched, stored, sorted, transmitted, sent, and received—knowledge is a different kind of thing altogether. Knowledge, according to this view, is a personal property of the individual knower who confers meaning on data and information by drawing from his/her subjective experiences, perceptions, and previous understandings (or cognitive schema). This is the sense in which knowledge is 'possessed' by individuals. The sense you make of the words and sentences on this page is about knowledge. Moreover, because different people have different experiences and 'frames of reference', it is quite possible that they also infer different things from the same information.

The 'knowledge as possession' view is implicit in much of what is written about managing knowledge within contemporary organizations. For example, the oft-cited conversion of tacit knowledge into explicit knowledge, inspired by writers such as Nonaka (1994), is underpinned by a view of knowledge as something that needs to be grasped from the narrow confines of individual cognition, codified, and made more widely available. However, this view has also been heavily criticized by proponents of an 'epistemology of practice' who start from the rather different premiss that knowledge is something that people *do* (Lave and Wenger 1991; Lave et al. 1992; Brown and Duguid 2001; Gherardi 2001; Orlikowski 2002; Nicolini, Gherardi, and Yanow 2003). According to this view, knowledge is constructed and negotiated through social interaction. It is intrinsic to practices (including discursive practices) that people actually perform in specific local contexts and not something that can stand outside those practices.

Empirical studies from this viewpoint show how social groups as diverse as construction engineers, photocopier technicians, radiologists, ship builders, and alcoholics learn to do things, not by converting tacit knowledge into explicit knowledge, but, rather, by sharing and creating norms, stories, representations, tools, and symbols which enable the experience of individuals to be related to the knowledge of the wider community. Knowledge is, in effect, 'enacted' through the practices of social groups and inextricably bound up with the development of shared identities, beliefs, and systems of power. Some proponents of this 'knowledge as practice' view prefer to use the term 'knowing' rather than knowledge, precisely to underline this interweaving of what people know with what they do and who and where they are. The term 'knowing' (as a verb rather than a noun) draws our attention to the active, processual, social and negotiated nature of knowledge (or knowledge claims—Suchman 1987).

Yet others have attempted to reconcile these different epistemologies by arguing that it is possible to see processes of knowing and forms of knowledge as equally important and complementary. Thus, Cook and Brown (1999: 381) note: 'Organizations are better understood ... if knowledge and knowing are seen as mutually enabling (not competing). We hold that knowledge is a tool for knowing, that knowing is an aspect of our interaction with the social and physical world, and the interplay of knowledge and knowing can generate new knowledge and new ways of knowing'. Whilst, this 'happy marriage' of such different philosophical standpoints is somewhat controversial, the debate itself reminds us that we need to reflect on underlying assumptions about knowledge when we analyse and manage knowledge work because these do have a profound influence on the tactics, strategies, and analytical tools that we use. For example, a 'knowledge as possession' view will lead to efforts to manage knowledge by freeing tacit knowledge from the individual and making it explicit and more widely available as an organizational resource through the use of IT and other codified forms. A 'knowledge as practice' view, in contrast suggests that the challenge for KM is to provide an enabling context that allows people to do (and say) things differently and, hopefully, better.

Here, then, I refer to knowledge simply as 'the ability to discriminate within and across contexts' (Swan 2007). This working definition borrows from Tsoukas and Vladimirou (2001: 979) who theorize knowledge as 'the individual ability to draw distinctions within a collective domain of action, based on an appreciation of context or theory or both'. This approach is broad enough to encompass the individual cognitive aspects of knowledge as well as its social nature. It also suggests that it is important for to consider the roles of material artefacts in managing knowledge work—technologies, tools, computers, physical spaces, clocks, schedules, and the like—because the ability to discriminate is mediated by them (Barley 1986; Orlikowski and Yates 2002; Black, Carlile, and Repenning 2004; Schultze and Orlikowski 2004; Orlikowski 2007).

Following this line of reasoning, *knowledge work* refers to organizational activities and occupations that are characterized by an emphasis on using theoretical knowledge and analytical and social skills to discriminate across contexts and resolve problems. Finally, *organizational knowledge* can be understood as 'a learned set of norms, shared understandings and practices that integrates actors and artefacts to produce valued outcomes within a specific social and organizational context' (Scarbrough 2008). Organizational knowledge is thus reflected in what people say, the actions they take, and in the technologies, routines, and systems that they use.

Managing knowledge work, then, includes strategies, tools, and practices that enable actors in particular social and organizational contexts to understand and make sense of what it is that they, and others, are doing and to do things differently. Major theories and frameworks for managing knowledge work can be broadly grouped in three areas—structural perspectives, which essentially adopt a 'knowledge as possession' epistemology, and process and practice perspectives, which adopt a 'knowledge as practice' epistemology. These are reviewed and compared in brief next.

Structural Perspectives and Types of Knowledge

Structural perspectives on knowledge have drawn largely from the epistemology of possession, outlined above, and have focused on identifying different types, or forms, of knowledge that individuals and groups possess. Citing Polanyi's (1962) earlier work on 'personal knowledge', two forms or types of knowledge—tacit and explicit—are very often distinguished (e.g. Nonaka 1994). Tacit knowledge is associated with the personal skills or know-how that people develop through their own experience in specific contexts (e.g. *knowing how* to ride a bicycle) and, because of its personal nature, is hard to formalize or communicate. In contrast, explicit knowledge is that which has been 'spelled out' or codified, making it more communicable across contexts (e.g. *knowing what* components a bicycle needs to have to make it work and how they should be put together).

An important, but sometime neglected, aspect of tacit knowledge is that we know more than we can articulate or attend to at any point in time. Hence tacit knowledge is often referred to as 'know-how'—it resides in our heads *and* in practical skills and actions. An apprentice learning a new task, for example, does so through a combination of instruction and first-hand practical experience, including feedback from the practical action itself. However, if everything in organizations had to be learned from first-hand experience then learning in organizations—especially highly distributed organizations—would be greatly limited. Explicit knowledge, on the other hand, then, can be readily codified, articulated and communicated to others and is, therefore, seen by some as more useful for organizational learning (Teece, Pisano, and Shuen 1997; Zollo and Winter 2002). According to the structural perspectives, then, the way to create knowledge in organizations is to identify important tacit knowledge, find a way of making it explicit, and convert it back again into the tacit knowledge of others elsewhere in the organization so that it can be further applied (Nonaka 1994).

Structural perspectives have provided numerous frameworks that help us to understand what types of knowledge are involved in knowledge work and how knowledge can be expanded by converting one type to another. Nonaka's now well cited 'SECI' model, for example, sees knowledge creation as a spiralling process of interactions between tacit and explicit knowledge. He identified four distinct knowledge conversion processes: socialization (tacit/tacit); externalization (tacit/explicit); combination (explicit/explicit); and internalization (explicit/tacit). He suggested, further, that organizational knowledge creation stemmed from the individual. If we take socialization, for example, this rests on individuals interacting with others and reflecting on their own and others' experiences.

This is not to suggest, however, that managers of organizations do not have a role to play in knowledge creation. Nonaka also stressed that managers needs to design organizations in such a way as to provide the necessary enabling context for individuals to share and create knowledge. Thus in his more recent elaborations of the SECI model, Nonaka developed the notion of 'ba'—a concept originally developed by Japanese philosopher Kitaro Nishida, meaning 'a context which harbours meaning' (Nonaka and Konno 1998). According to Nonaka and Konno, 'ba' (roughly translated in English as 'place') is 'a shared space for emerging relationships. This space can be physical (e.g. office, dispersed business space), virtual (e.g. email, teleconference), mental (e.g. shared experience, ideas, ideals), or any combination of them' (p. 40). Relating back to the distinction between knowledge and information discussed earlier, knowledge is seen as embedded in 'ba' where it is acquired though individuals' experiences and reflections. Information, in contrast, is knowledge that is separated from ba and so able to be communicated independently—'Information resides in media and networks. It is tangible. In contrast knowledge resides in 'ba'. It is intangible' (ibid.).

The SECI model is not without critics. Not least, and despite the notion of 'ba', it presents an overly individualized view of knowledge and is a bit 'slippery' in how it treats knowledge. For example, on the one hand knowledge separated from 'ba' is not knowledge but information. At the same time, the model continues to classify knowledge as either tacit or explicit, leaving open the question of what explicit knowledge actually is. Others suggest that the whole idea of being able to convert essentially personal knowledge into explicit forms is a fundamental misreading of the original ideas of Polanyi, upon whom Nonaka draws (Gourlay 2006).The SECI model also significantly downplays the differences of interests, power, and political dynamics that knowledge creation processes in organizational contexts inevitably encounter. Instead the 'knowledge spiral'—the movement of knowledge from being the possession of an individual to becoming an organizational resource—is depicted as rather smooth, linear, uncontested, and unproblematic. These criticisms aside, the model has no doubt been very influential and has played an important part in channelling attention, not just to the cognitive, information processing aspects of knowledge creation in organizations, but also to the importance of values and the enabling context in which such values are shared, acquired, and played out.

Other structuralist perspectives share Nonaka's interest in tacit and explicit knowledge but argue that in order to understand where organizational knowledge comes from, we need to be concerned, not only with types of knowledge (i.e. epistemology), but also where it is rooted (i.e. ontology). For example, Spender (1998) incorporates tacit and explicit knowledge into his framework but also makes a distinction between individual and social (or collective) knowledge (see Figure 20.1). Combining concerns about what knowledge is (i.e. tacit or explicit) and where it resides (individual or social) means that the four, rather than two, types of knowledge are identified: (i) individual/explicit (conscious); (ii) individual/implicit (automatic); (iii) social/explicit (objectified); and (iv) social/implicit (collective).

Spender's framework makes an important additional point, then, which is that forms of knowledge exist beyond the individual. Hence it is possible to make a 'contrast between the explicit knowledge that individuals feel they possess and the collective knowledge on which this explicit knowledge actually stands, and the interaction of the two' (Spender 1998: 238). For example, the culture of an organization is a form of social knowledge that survives beyond the contribution of particular individuals.

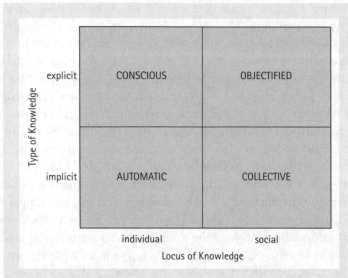

FIGURE 20.1 Forms of knowledge—Spender's framework

Critique of Structural Perspectives

Structuralist approaches assume, in the main, a 'knowledge as possession' view (Cook and Brown 1999) and because of this have been challenged for failing to take sufficient account of the more subjective, highly equivocal, and dynamic nature of knowledge (Bijker, Hughes, and Pinch 1987; Weick 1990). Other critics of structural approaches claim that the separation between tacit and explicit knowledge has been overstated and is not, in fact, a very accurate reflection of Polanyi's original idea (Gourlay 2006). Indeed Polanyi argued that all knowledge has an indispensable personal component but that, depending on the circumstances, we are only aware of certain aspects at particular points in time. Explicit knowledge, then, is merely that which we are aware of at any given moment, in much the same way as shining a spotlight highlights particular features of a landscape at that point in time. These explicit features are always connected, though, to the things that lie behind in the dark and that can come into view at any moment as the spotlight, and our focus, shifts. Taking this view we can see, in fact, that tacit and explicit knowledge are mutually 'constituted' (Boisot 1995; Tsoukas 1996; Gourlay 2006). In other words they define each other. By attending to something, and making it explicit, we automatically push other things into the background, or into tacitness, so to speak. Gourlay (2006) points out, then, that tacit knowledge may be better considered as a continuum where the degree of 'tacitness' and 'explicitness' is a function of the extent to which knowledge is communicated.

In the oft-used example of bicycle riding, it may be useful for the novice to be told to hold lightly onto the handle bars. This brings knowledge about how to hold the handle bars into focus, making it explicit. But, at the same time, it pushes other knowledge (e.g. on how to balance weight onto the pedals) further into the background. This is not a trivial point when it comes to managing knowledge and MIS design because it means that *any* explicit, codified knowledge will *always* be incomplete or partial. It is only by combining this explicit knowledge with tacit 'know-how' developed through experience (for example, about balance and hand-eye coordination) that tasks can be accomplished. This means that it is actually quite misleading to call an MIS a 'KM system', as only selected aspects of knowledge can ever be revealed.

By focusing on what knowledge is, structural approaches also tend to adopt what has been termed an 'entitative' view of knowledge (Hosking and Morley 1991). Hence knowledge is seen as 'thing-like'—an object or resource that can be moved around much like other resources such as money. Like other resources the aim is to accumulate it and move it around for the good of the organization. In short, more knowledge equals more profit. However, there is no particular reason, a priori, why benefit should automatically follow from having more and more knowledge. As seen with the widespread diffusion of email, it is quite conceivable that information overload might result and/or that existing, embedded knowledge might constrain attempts to do new things. Thus knowledge, unlike money, is not valuable in and of itself, but only where it is applied to specific tasks.

Another criticism of this approach lies in its largely functionalist view of organizations (Burrell and Morgan 1979). In other words organizations are depicted as a collection of interdependent parts (e.g. machines and people) that work in harmony toward a common, agreed-upon goal (e.g. organizational survival and profit). However, this assumes that common goals actually exist in organizations and, therefore, doesn't address important issues of power and conflict in organizations and in society at large (Foucault 1980). For example, encouraging individual employees to surrender their knowledge for the benefit of 'the organization' may actually benefit shareholders or senior managers but can, equally, be disempowering for the individuals themselves. This is one reason why individuals may choose to 'hoard' rather than share knowledge. Moreover, it is quite conceivable that those in power could use knowledge to further their own interests rather than the interests of the collective organization.

As well as theoretical objections, there are some very practical issues when it comes to using structural approaches to manage knowledge work. For one thing, understanding types of knowledge (e.g. tacit/explicit) and where it resides (e.g. individual/collective) doesn't actually tell us much about where it comes from or how to *use* it— knowing, in this sense of the word, does not equal doing (Pfeffer and Sutton 2000). Furthermore, there is now good evidence that Knowledge Management initiatives based solely on this kind of thinking often fail (Walsham 2002). For example, in an empirical study of an initiative to encourage knowledge transfer in a worldwide bank, Newell, Swan, and Scarbrough (2001) found that the introduction of a Knowledge Management system—a global intranet—designed to capture and share tacit knowledge across the organization had the opposite effect to that intended by senior management.

These points of critique have led people to develop more nuanced 'contingency' frameworks that show us how strategies for managing knowledge can be linked to specific aspects of the organizational tasks at hand. For example, Hansen (1999) studied innovation in a large electronics company and concluded that strong social relationships with a few people were beneficial for tasks that required the transfer of complex, highly tacit knowledge, whereas weak relationships with many people were more effective where the knowledge involved was less complex and more explicit. This approach is promising as it takes into account *purpose*—i.e. what knowledge is to be used for. However it still, fundamentally, sees knowledge as a thing or commodity that is valuable for its own sake and tells us relatively little about the processes involved in creating and using knowledge across contexts.

Process and Practice Perspectives: Knowledge and Knowing

The failure of many initiatives that have attempted to 'capture' and 'transfer' individuals' knowledge have helped fuel shifts towards accounts that take as their focus the development of *processes* and *enabling contexts* capable of supporting knowledge work. This shift can be seen in organization theories which focus on 'knowing' as a social and organizational activity, in contrast to 'knowledge', as a thing or object. Process, and more recently practice, perspectives draw, then, from an epistemology of practice (outlined above—Cook and Brown 1999).

Our working definition of knowledge—as the ability to discriminate within and across contexts—is based on this processual perspective in that it avoids notions of 'truth' and defines knowledge in dynamic terms as a practice of making distinctions (Tsoukas and Vladimirou 2001). Process approaches to managing knowledge work draw from theoretical traditions of 'social constructivism', seeing knowledge, or knowing, as a process of 'sensemaking', whereby actors interacting within particular social contexts come to negotiate understandings of the world (Berger and Luckman 1966; Weick 2001). Knowledge is, therefore:

- equivocal (subject to different meanings and interpretations);
- dynamic (accepted meanings can change as actors and contexts change); and
- context dependent (difficult, if not impossible, to separate from the context in which it is produced).

While structural approaches see a direct relationship between increased knowledge, knowledge transfer, and organizational performance, process approaches view this relationship as socially and politically mediated. Whether or not knowledge (or knowing) leads to improvement depends, then, on how tasks, actors, and contexts come together. For example, Clark (2003) describes how the US game of American Football originated from knowledge of the game of rugby in the UK. However, it was not simply a case of capturing knowledge about rugby and transferring this to the USA. His historical analysis showed how key stakeholders (including players, sports promoters, and the media) reinterpreted the British rules of the game and created 'pivotal modifications' that allowed it to be adapted to the particular context in the USA at the time. Hence, in order to generate advertising revenue through media breaks, they introduced shorter 'periods' (instead of halves) and 'time-outs'.

This example shows how the particular interests and interpretations of actors within and across different social and institutional contexts come to bear in reproducing and legitimating particular forms of knowledge and innovation. The process approach also highlights the central role of social networks in translating (not just transferring) knowledge across groups and contexts:

> knowing is not a static embedded capability or stable disposition of actors, but rather an ongoing social accomplishment, constituted and reconstituted as actors engage the world in practice. (Orlikowski 2002)

Managing knowledge work, then, is less about converting, capturing, and transferring different forms of knowledge and more about building an *enabling context* that connects different social groups and interests, identities, and perspectives to accomplish specific tasks or *purposes*. Management initiatives aimed at building so-called 'communities of practice' (Wenger and Snyder 2000; Thompson 2005) or social networks (Cross and Sproull 2004) reflect such a view.

PRACTICE PERSPECTIVES

In the last decade there has been a new surge of interest in 'practice perspectives' as a way of studying and analysing social and organizational life (Schatzki 2001). In terms of managing knowledge work, however, practice perspectives have had less attention. Even advocates of the so-called 'communities of practice' approach to managing knowledge within firms have emphasized the importance of communities and networks for improving knowledge flows but have left 'practice' relatively untouched (Bechky 2003).

Practice and process perspectives have more in common than not—both see knowing as a social activity and address process, context, and purpose, for example. However, practice perspectives emphasize in particular the links between knowledge and action, or practice. In short, knowledge is inextricably linked to practice—it flows where practice is shared (for example within specialist or functional groups) and sticks where practice is not shared (for example, across functional departments). It is useful to look at practice perspectives more closely because they help focus attention to aspects of managing knowledge work that have not been so commonly addressed to date.

Many different kinds of theorists have influenced practice perspectives, including social philosophers (e.g. Wittgenstein 1958; Dreyfuss 1991), and ethnomethodologists (e.g. Garfinkel 1967), cultural theorists (e.g. Lyotard 1988), and social theorists (e.g. Bourdieu 1990). It is impossible to do them justice here. Definitions of 'practice' include 'action informed by meaning drawn from a particular group context' (Cook and Brown 1999) and 'socially recognized forms of activity, done on the basis of what members learn from others, and capable of being done well or badly, correctly or incorrectly' (Barnes 2001: 19). However, it is perhaps useful to identify some general insights that practice perspectives offer over and above process perspectives to our understanding of knowledge work.

First, practice perspectives highlight that knowledge is 'sticky'—it sticks to practice and is therefore difficult to share where peoples' practices are not also shared. This helps to explain why sharing knowledge across specialist functions or disciplines within an organization, or from one organization to another, is so difficult—even where people appreciate others' ideas, they may not be able to apply them because it would be too difficult to change their current practices. This means that knowledge is not uniformly good but is actually quite paradoxical in relation to organizational performance. On the one hand, division of labour results in different groups performing different practices which means that valuable specialized knowledge can develop. On the other hand, the 'knowledge boundaries' created by specialization pose barriers to knowledge sharing across different groups of practitioners (Brown and Duguid 2001; Carlile 2004; Scarbrough et al 2004). As Carlile (2002: 442) puts it: 'the irony is that these knowledge boundaries are not only a critical challenge, but also a perceptual necessity because much of what organizations produce has a foundation in the specialization of different kinds of knowledge'.

Second, when we perform practice we use many kinds of material and physical objects, not just words and thoughts. Material objects are not just tools that people use to achieve ends, however, they also set limits around what practices are actually possible (Swan et al. 2007). For example, Orlikowski (2007) describes an on-line business meeting where laptop computers, internet connections, phone lines, cables, connectors, pens, mute buttons on telephones—in her terms, the 'stuff' of everyday life—serve to 'scaffold' the social activity of the people involved. She uses the metaphor of 'scaffolds' to highlight the ways in which temporary material arrangements help constitute particular kinds of social activity *in real time*. Practice perspectives on knowledge work draw attention, then, to the 'materiality' of social activity (Schatzki 2001; Orlikowski 2007). In other words they focus on the ways that all human activities, including knowledge work, are interwoven with non-human, material artefacts, objects, and physical arrangements. While there is considerable debate around exactly *how* this interweaving takes place (the importance of human versus non-human agency, being a particular bone of contention—Latour 1987), practice perspectives agree that the social world is: 'a field of embodied, materially interwoven practices centrally organized around shared practical understandings' (Schatzki 2001: 3).

This has important implications for managing knowledge work and MIS. On the one hand it means that the ability (or lack thereof) to transform knowledge and innovate depends, at least to some extent, on what Schatzki (2001: 3) describes as the 'solidifying inertia' of material layouts. Many computers rely fundamentally on the keyboard which is still laid out (in the Qwerty design) very much the same today as it was decades ago, for example. On the other hand, material objects (mobile technologies, drawings, prototypes, and so on) can also act as critical tools for Knowledge Management. An important point, however, is that this is not a one-way relationship—the design of material objects (e.g. the layout of the meeting room) influences human activity but also results from it.

Third, practice perspectives remind us that knowledge work actually takes place in a broader 'field of practices' (Schatzki 2001). For example, the practices of medical professionals are part of the broader field of scientific practice. This includes 'epistemic practices' (or 'knowledge cultures') that govern how knowledge is created and legitimated—in science via the rules of scientific method for example (Knorr-Cetina 1999). Therefore, to manage knowledge work, we also need to be sensitive to the broader institutional contexts and interconnected sets of practices in which that knowledge work is located. The notion of 'the field of interconnected practices' reminds us that change in one area of practice potentially disrupts a wide range of other practices. It is for this reason that creating and using knowledge in interdisciplinary settings can be so challenging since, 'unfortunately, interdisciplinary subjects have a way of escaping from any discipline whatever' (Drexler 1989).

Fourth, practice perspectives emphasize, not just the socially situated nature of knowledge, but also the *investment* of knowledge in peoples' practice (Carlile 2002). In other words, practices often take considerable time and effort to establish and, once established, can be reinforced by a whole range of other, interconnected practices. For this reason they are difficult to change, even where there is good evidence to do so and good intent. For example, new integrated IT systems are notoriously difficult to introduce into organizations because people find it very difficult to change from their current 'legacy' systems. Moreover, even if one group is willing to change, they may face challenges in introducing the system because other groups can't (or won't).

IMPLICATIONS FOR MIS

Table 20.1 provides a summary of the contrasts between structural, process, and practice perspectives on knowledge and managing knowledge work. This albeit brief review suggests that, if we want to design MIS that enable knowledge *work* (i.e. where people work with knowledge in order to accomplish tasks), rather than to manage knowledge for its own sake, then process and practice perspectives may be more a promising basis from which to start. This is because these: (a) take closer account of the core aspects of knowledge work—i.e. processes, purposes, and enabling contexts and; (b) balance attention to the social *and* the material/technological aspects of knowledge work. MIS may thus act, both as a technology that enables communication, and also as

Table 20.1 Perspectives on knowledge work compared

	Epistemology of possession	Epistemology of practice	
	Structural	Process	Practice
View of social life	Individuals navigate in an objective external world through cognitive processes	Individual and collective interpretations embedded in social interactions, roles, and structures	Materially interwoven (human and non-human) practices centrally organized around shared practical understandings
View of Knowledge	Knowledge as a cognitive entity—a resource to be accumulated, captured, transferred	Knowing as a social and organizational activity—socially constructed through interactions in particular contexts	Knowing as practice—constituted by and constituting fields of interconnected practices
Major locus of knowledge	Embedded and embodied in the skills and heads of individuals or organizations	Embedded and encultured in social context	Embedded, embodied and invested in practice
Link between knowledge and organizational performance	Knowledge directly related to, and functional (good) for performance	Relationship between knowledge and performance socially and politically mediated: reflecting interests of powerful groups	Relationship between knowledge and performance mediated through practice: Knowledge paradoxical for performance—sticks at practice boundaries
Major focus for managing knowledge work	Transfer/convert knowledge from one type (e.g. tacit to explicit) or location (individual, organizational) to another	Share, translate, and legitimate knowledge amongst interacting groups	Transform knowledge through overlapping practices
Major tasks of knowledge management	Capturing/transferring knowledge, e.g. using IT	Translating knowledge across social groups, e.g. by building social networks and trust	Transforming practice and transversing boundaries of practice e.g. using objects and creating communities of practice

a material fabric through which social practices and identities are woven, sustained, and dismantled (Orlikowski 2007).

Yet many MIS aimed at KM (KM systems) still assume a possession/structural view—valuable knowledge, located inside people's heads can be identified, captured, and processed via the use of ICT tools so that it can be applied in new contexts (Tseng 2007). Indeed, 'Knowledge Management' is frequently reduced to the implementation of ICTs for knowledge transfer (Jennex and Olfman 2003). Thus, surveys of firms introducing what they describe as 'Knowledge Management initiatives' show that these are dominated by ICT implementations. For example, a recent survey in Australia (Xu and Quaddus 2005) found that nearly 70 per cent of the 1,500 participants indicated that they had some type of IT-based KM system. Alavi and Tiwana (2003) categorized KM systems, further, in terms of the knowledge processes that they aim to enhance (knowledge creation, storage, transfer, and application), as depicted in Table 20.2. This is helpful in the sense that it recognizes that different types of IS will be more or less useful for different knowledge processes. At the same time, the Xu and Quaddus (2005) study demonstrates that, whilst the range of what is defined as a KM system has been expanded over time, it is the storage and transfer technologies which remain the most popular in terms of the types of KM systems actually used in practice.

In relation to the storage and transfer processes, we can contrast two different types of KMS: McAfee (2006) describes these as 'platform' and 'channel' technologies; while Alavi (2000) distinguishes between 'network' and 'repository' technologies. Channel or network technologies (e.g. email) can be used where it is clear that a particular individual or group needs specific information and knowledge from another individual—for example, a software project manager needing information from sales about the client requirements for a new system. Channel technologies are thus used to pass information and knowledge from a source to one or more recipients. In other cases, however, it is not known in advance who will need, or find useful, particular information and knowledge, either right now or in the future. In this situation some kind of platform or repository technology (e.g. an organizational intranet) is used so that people can store and search/retrieve information and knowledge as they need it. The fact that so many organizations have adopted these two types of KMS implies that decision makers believe that sophisticated ICT tools can help in the capture, storage, and transfer of knowledge.

Table 20.2 Knowledge processes featured in KM systems

Knowledge process	Knowledge creation	Knowledge storage	Knowledge transfer	Knowledge application
KMS	E-learning systems Collaboration support systems	Knowledge repositories (data warehousing and data mining)	Communication support systems (email) Enterprise information portals (intranets/ internets)	Expert systems Decision support systems

Source: After Alavi and Tiwana 2003.

Many commentators, however, are more sceptical about the utility of new ICTs for delivering organizational performance improvements (Blair 2002). Thus, many organizations have put a lot of effort into putting content on to their intranets—a type of platform technology (McAfee 2006) where documents can be stored and searched— but research has found that users do not always find these platform technologies useful. Davenport (2005) for example, found that only 44 per cent of survey respondents felt that it was easy to find information they needed by looking on the company intranet. The other very popular type of KMS involves channel technologies, such as email (McAfee 2006), which allow the sharing of documents between particular individuals, either one-to-one or one-to-many. This research finds that those involved in knowledge work rely more heavily on the channel (e.g. email) than the platform (e.g. intranets) technologies, reflecting the extent to which knowledge work is a social activity dependent on joint production of knowledge. However, even the channel tools have problems with regard to their ability to enhance knowledge processes. For example, Davenport (2005) found that 26 per cent of people in a survey felt that email was overused in their organization; 15 per cent felt that it reduced their productivity; and 21 per cent actually felt overwhelmed by the amount of email that they received.

One reason for the limitations of these KM systems is that they will not in themselves improve the capture, storage, and sharing of knowledge. As process/practice approaches tell us, it depends on how the KM system is perceived and materially enacted and used as part of people's everyday work practices. Thus practice/process views suggest that KM systems are limited by the very possession view of knowledge that they assume. In contrast, the knowledge-as-practice view highlights the importance of relationships and shared understandings and attitudes to knowledge formation and knowledge sharing (Kofman and Senge 1993). It is important to acknowledge these issues since they help to define the likely success or failure of attempts to implement KM systems. The knowledge-as-practice view suggests, moreover, that it is likely to be fairly easy to share knowledge between individuals who are relatively homogeneous in terms of their practice, because they are likely to share a common understanding, identity, and belief system. For example, globally distributed software engineers, with a similar training and education, may be able to work collaboratively without much difficulty and to share information via a KM system. However, it is extremely difficult for such globally distributed collaboration to occur where the individuals have heterogeneous beliefs and understandings. Yet, the sharing of knowledge across functional, organizational, and/or national boundaries is precisely the goal of most KM initiatives. Paradoxically, then, this means that attempts to manage knowledge work using KM systems may actually be most problematic in the very conditions where the need is greatest—i.e. where there are significant divisions of practice.

Developments in IS do, however, open up opportunities for managing knowledge work and knowledge workers from a practice perspective. In particular, new material properties of IS, in particular the development of so-called Web 2.0 and Enterprise 2.0, can facilitate the types of interaction that support knowing in practice. Web 2.0 software, then, can allow users themselves to create content and share directly with each other, whether through social networking sites like Facebook, MySpace, YouTube and LinkedIn, or through wikis and blogs. The internet has thus become a tool for collaboration through a shared social space and networking rather than a repository.

In the context of an organization, McAfee (2006) uses the term 'enterprise 2.0' to define these same kinds of technologies, but used within the firewall of an organization. The key characteristic of these 2.0 technologies, according to McAfee is that they not only allow the sharing of documents (i.e. outputs of knowledge work) but also make visible the *practices* of knowledge workers and interdependencies between practices (i.e. valuable process knowledge not just content or product knowledge). McAfee suggests that there are six key features of 2.0 technologies that differentiate them from traditional ICT:

- Search—new tools that make it possible to search for information rather than having to rely on navigation options.
- Links—dynamic links between content, reflecting how people have actually moved across pages and sites, make it possible to identify related content, thus facilitating users in finding useful content.
- Authoring—blogs (enabling individuals to author content that others can add to), wikkis (enabling groups to author content in an iterative fashion), and YouTube (enabling individuals or groups to produce multi-media content for others to view) provide everyone with the opportunity to author content that others can read or view—many people are now actively engaged in either producing or consuming this user-generated content.
- Tags—allow individuals to have control of categorizing the content of their digital material (e.g. del-icio.us allows users to tag websites with book marks). These user-generated categorization systems are called folksonomies—a folksonomy emerges over time depending on what users find useful to group together based on the information structures and relationships that are actually used in practice.
- Extensions—systems can also go beyond this tagging process to develop algorithms based on the pattern of use of different information which then allows for automatic referrals to individuals who have shown interest in a certain type of content. This is done by Amazon very effectively to make recommendations to their customers of other books they might enjoy reading, based on their pattern of consumption to date as compared to the millions of other customers.
- Signals—given the sheer amount of information that is digitally available, it can also be helpful to have certain information automatically pushed to users based on their interests. Signals are the means of doing this, alerting users to the fact that new information is available that they may be interested in. RSS (really simple syndication) is now a popular technology that provides this kind of signal.

McAfee (2006: 26), thus, argues, that

Enterprise 2.0 technologies have the potential to let an intranet become what the Internet already is—an online platform with a constantly changing structure built by distributed autonomous and largely self-interested peers. On this platform, authoring creates content; links and tags knit it together; and search, extensions, tags and signals make emergent structures and patterns in the content visible and help people stay on top of it all.

In reality, though, many organizations have yet to take advantage of 2.0 technologies. A major reason is that they can reduce managerial control and may be used by some to express negativity, which many senior managers want to avoid. For example, individuals can use blogs to broadcast weaknesses in a company's strategy or to deride organizational decision makers. Some may fear that chaos may rein if knowledge workers are allowed to add or change content on their departmental website without this being vetted by a central authority. Nevertheless, we can expect that KM systems will change over time in organizations as the potential of these new 2.0 technologies become more fully understood, especially in support of knowledge work, and more accepted in practice.

Conclusions

This albeit brief overview, and the points raised in this chapter, suggests that process/ practice approaches may be a more fruitful starting point from which to manage knowledge work and to design the systems used to support it. Process/practice approaches suggest that those attempting to manage knowledge, then, need be less concerned with capture and control of knowledge (i.e. from individuals into systems) and more concerned with providing an enabling context that supports employees in the processes and practices of applying knowledge for specific tasks and purposes. This is especially the case when talking about knowledge work because workers here demand significant autonomy. Returning to the definition of knowledge earlier, 'managing knowledge' from a process/practice perspective means, simply, enabling people to discriminate more readily within and across contexts and to engage in shared problem solving. In other words, managing means *coping* with the work at hand and not *controlling* the way that work is actually performed. Consequently, one can argue that a more promising avenue for MIS is not to capture and share 'knowledge' per se, but to allow people to cope with their work by being able to draw from a broader range of skills and resources and by providing opportunities for the sharing of practice and identity.

In terms of KM as a (changing) field of study, we have seen how 'first wave' approaches focused on codification of (tacit) knowledge, primarily through the development of IT systems, whereas 'second wave' approaches emphasized the development role of social relations, networks, and communities. Both approaches assume, however, that sharing knowledge is a good thing per se. If we really accept, however, that knowledge is only as useful as the ends to which it is applied, then simply increasing knowledge 'stocks' and 'flows' does not in itself add value and may, indeed, deflect attention from critical tasks.

More serious attention to practice suggests, in contrast, a 'third wave' of KM—one that focuses on purpose, not just process, and that takes account of the strategic intent of KM initiatives and the new capabilities that these afford in organizations (cf. Wenger 2009). As Wenger has noted recently, this 'third wave' might address such core issues as, how to identify business-critical knowledge domains, how to connect KM initiatives and organizational imperatives, how to make knowledge work a formal strategy, and how to assess the impact of KM on ground-level results. This means taking critical decisions with regard to the *purpose* of KM—is it to improve efficiency of current activities and/or to do things differently and innovate, for example? The role of MIS implied in this 'third wave' then, is neither to stock ever increasing quantities of knowledge in IT systems (the focus of the first wave), nor to use communication technologies to make knowledge flow between people (the focus of the second). Rather, it is to help knowledge workers cope with ever changing work demands by applying information (however sourced) to particular problems, and to inform decisions regarding core knowledge domains and future (not just past) capabilities and interests.

ACKNOWLEDGEMENT

Aspects of this chapter have been extracted and developed from: S. M. Newell, M. Robertson, H. Scarbrough, and J. Swan (2009). *Managing Knowledge Work and Innovation*, 2nd edn. Basingstoke: Palgrave Macmillan, with permission from the authors.

REFERENCES

Ackoff, R. L. (1989). 'From Data to Wisdom', *Journal of Applied Systems Analysis*, 16(1): 3–9.

Alavi, M. (2000). 'Managing Knowledge', in R. Zmud (ed.), *Framing the Domain of IT Management*. Cincinnati, OH: Pinnoflex Educational Resources Ltd., 15–28.

—— and Tiwana, A. (2003). 'Knowledge Management: The Information Technology Dimension', in M. Easterby-Smith and M. Lyles (eds.), *The Blackwell Handbook of Organizational Learning and Knowledge Management*. Oxford: Blackwell, 104–21.

Barley, S. R. (1986). 'Technology as an Occasion for Structuring: Evidence from Observation of CT Scanners and the Social Order of Radiology Departments', *Administrative Science Quarterly*, 31: 78–108.

Barnes, B. (2001). 'Practice as Collective Action', in T. Schatzki, K. Knorr-Cetina, and E. von Savigny (eds.), *The Practice Turn in Contemporary Theory*. London: Routledge, 17–28.

Bechky, B. A. (2003). 'Sharing Meaning across Occupational Communities: The Transformation of Understanding on a Production Floor', *Organization Science*, 14(3): 312–30.

Bell, D. (1973). *The Coming of Post-industrial Society*. New York: Basic Books.

Berger, P., and Luckmann, T. (1966). *The Social Construction of Reality: A Treatise in the Sociology of Knowledge*. New York: Doubleday Anchor Books.

Bijker, W. E., Hughes, T. P., and Pinch, T. J. (1987). *The Social Construction of Technological Systems*. Cambridge, MA: MIT Press.

Bjorkman, I., Barner-Rasmussen, W., and Li, L. (2004). 'Managing Knowledge Transfer in MNCs: The Impact of headquarters Control Mechanisms', *Journal of International Business Studies*, 35: 443–55.

Black, L. J., Carlile, P. R., and Repenning, N. P. (2004). 'A Dynamic Theory of Expertise and Occupational Boundaries in New Technology Implementation: Building on Barley's Study of CT Scanning', *Administrative Science Quarterly*, 49(4): 572–607.

Blair, D. (2002). 'Knowledge Management: Hype, Hope or Help', *Journal of the American Society for Information Science and Technology*, 53(12): 1019–28.

Boisot, M. (1995). *Information Space: A Framework for Learning in Organizations, Institutions and Culture*. London: Blackwell.

Bourdieu, P. (1990). *The Logic of Practice*. Cambridge: Polity.

Brown, J. S., and Duguid, P. (2001). 'Knowledge and Organization: A Social-Practice Perspective', *Organization Science*, 12(2): 198–213.

Burrell, G., and Morgan, G. (1979). *Sociological Paradigms and Organizational Analysis: Elements of a Sociology of Corporate Life*. London: Heinemann.

Carlile, P. (2002). 'A Pragmatic View of Knowledge and Boundaries: Boundary Objects in New Product Development', *Organization Science*, 13(4): 442–55.

——(2004). 'Transferring, Translating and Transforming: An Integrative Framework from Managing Knowledge across Boundaries', *Organization Science*, 15(5): 555–68.

Castells, M. (1996). *The Rise of Network Society*. Oxford: Blackwell.

Chesbrough, H. (2003). 'The Logic of Open Innovation: Managing Intellectual Property', *California Management Review*, 45(3): 33.

——(2004). 'Managing Open Innovation', *Research Technology Management*, 47(1): 23–6.

Clark, P. (2003). *Organizational Innovations*. London: Sage.

Cook, S., and Brown, J. (1999). 'Bridging Epistemologies: The Generative Dance between Organizational Knowledge and Organizational Knowing', *Organization Science*, 10(4): 381–400.

Coombs, R. (2003). 'The Changing Character of "Service Innovation" and the Emergence of "Knowledge Intensive Business Services" ', in B. Dankbarr (ed.), *Innovation Management in the Knowledge Economy*. London: Imperial College Press, 83–96.

Cross, R., and Sproull, L. (2004). 'More than an Answer: Information Relationships for Actionable Knowledge', *Organization Science*.

Currie, W. L. and Galliers, R. D. (eds.) (1999). *Rethinking Management Information Systems: An Interdisciplinary Perspective*. Oxford: Oxford University Press.

Dankbaar, B. (2003). *Innovation Management in the Knowledge Economy*. London: Imperial College Press.

Davenport, T. (2005). *Thinking for a Living*. Boston, MA: Harvard Business School Press.

Dodgson, M., Gann, D., and Salter, A. (2005). *Think, Play, Do: Technology, Innovation and Organization*. Oxford: Oxford University Press.

Drexler, K. E. (1989). *Engines of Creation*. New York: Doubleday.

Dreyfuss, H. (1991). *Being-in-the-World: A Commentary on Heidegger's Being and Time, Division One*. Cambridge, MA: MIT Press.

Drucker, P. (1969). *The Age of Discontinuity: Guidelines to our Changing Society*. London: Heinemann.

——(1988). 'The Coming of the New Organization', *Harvard Business Review*, Summer: 53–65.

Foucault, M. P. (1980). *Power/Knowledge: Selected Interviews and Other Writings 1972–1977*. Brighton: Harvester Press.

Garfinkel, H. (1967). *Studies in Ethnomethodology*. Englewood Cliffs, NJ: Prentice Hall.

Gherardi, S. (2001). 'From Organizational Learning to Practice-Based Knowing', *Human Relations*, 54(1): 131–9.

Gibbons, M., Limoges, C., Nowotny, H., Schwarzman, S., Scott, P., and Trow, M. (1994). *The New Production of Knowledge: The Dynamics of Science and Research in Contemporary Societies*. London: Sage.

Gourlay, S. (2006). 'Conceptualizing Knowledge Creation: A Critique of Nonaka's Theory', *Journal of Management Studies*, 43(7): 1415–36.

Hansen, M. T. (1999). 'The Search Transfer Problem: The Role of Weak Ties in Sharing Knowledge across Organizational Sub-units', *Administrative Science Quarterly*, 44: 82–111.

Hosking, D., and Morley, I. (1991). *A Social Psychology of Organizing*. London: Harvester Wheatsheaf.

Jennex, M., and Olfman, L. (2003). 'Organizational Memory', in C. Holsapple (ed.), *Handbook of Knowledge Management*, 2nd edn. New York: Springer, 207–34.

Knorr-Cetina, K. (1999). *Epistemic Cultures: How the Sciences Make Knowledge*. Cambridge, MA: Harvard University Press.

Kofman, F., and Senge, P. (1993). 'Communities of Commitment: The Heart of Learning Organizations', *Organizational Dynamics*, 22(2): 5–22.

Latour, B. (1987). *Science in Action*. Cambridge, MA: Harvard University Press.

Lave, J., and Wenger, E. (1991). *Situated Learning: Legitimate Peripheral Participation*. Cambridge: Cambridge University Press.

——Duguid, P., Fernandez, N., and Axel, E. (1992). 'Coming of Age in Birmingham: Cultural-Studies and Conceptions of Subjectivity', *Annual Review of Anthropology*, 21: 257–82.

Lyotard, J. F. (1988). *The Differend: Phrases in Dispute*, trans. G. van den Abbeele. Minneapolis, MN: University of Minnesota Press.

McAfee, A. (2006). 'Enterprise 2.0: The Dawn of Emergent Collaboration', *MIT Sloan Management Review*, 47(3): 21–8.

McDermott, R. (1999). 'Why Information Technology Inspired but Cannot Deliver Knowledge Management', *California Management Review*, 41: 103–17.

Miles, I. (2003). 'Services Innovation: Coming of Age in the Knowledge Based Economy', in B. Dankbarr (ed.), *Innovation Management in the Knowledge Economy*. London: Imperial College Press, 59–82.

Newell, S., Swan, J., and Scarbrough, H. (2001). 'From Global Knowledge Management to Internal Electronic Fences: Contradictory Outcomes of Intranet Development', *British Journal of Management*, 12(2): 97–111.

Nicolini, D., Gherardi, S., and Yanow, D. (eds.) (2003). *Knowing in Organizations: A Practice-Based Approach*. New York: M. E. Sharpe.

Nonaka, I. (1994). 'A Dynamic Theory of Organizational Knowledge Creation', *Organization Science*, 5(1): 14–37.

——and Konno, N. (1998). 'The Concept of "Ba": Building a Foundation for Knowledge Creation', *California Management Review*, 40(3): 40–54.

Nowotny, H., Scott, P., and Gibbons, M. (2001). *Rethinking Science: Knowledge and the Public in an Age of Uncertainty*. Cambridge: Polity Press.

——————(2003). '"Mode 2" Revisited: The New Production of Knowledge', *Minerva*, 41: 179–94.

Orlikowski, W. J. (2002). 'Knowing in Practice: Enacting a Collective Capability in Distributed Organizing', *Organization Science*, 13(3): 249–73.

——(2007). 'Sociomaterial Practices: Exploring Technology at Work', *Organization Studies*, 28(9): 1435.

——and Yates, J. A. (2002). 'It's about Time: Temporal Structuring in Organizations', *Organization Science*, 13(6): 684–700.

Pfeffer, J., and Sutton, R. I. (2000). *The Knowing–Doing Gap: How Smart Companies Turn Knowledge into Action*. Boston, MA: Harvard Business School Press.

Polanyi, M. (1962). *Personal Knowledge*. Chicago, IL: University of Chicago Press.

Prusak, L. (1997). *Knowledge in Organizations*. Oxford: Butterworth-Heinemann.

Scarbrough, H. (2008). 'Organizational Knowledge' entry in James R. Bailey and Stewart Clegg (eds.), *International Encyclopedia of Organization Studies*, vol. iii. London: Sage Publications.

——and Swan, J. (2001). 'Explaining the Diffusion of Knowledge Management: The Role of Fashion', *British Journal of Management*, 12(1): 3–12.

——————Laurent, S., Edelman, L., and Newell, S. (2004). 'Project-Based Learning: An Exploratory Study', *Management Learning*, 35(4): 491–506.

Schatzki, T. (2001). 'Practice Theory', in T. Schatzki, K. Knorr-Cetina, and E. von Savigny (eds.), *The Practice Turn in Contemporary Theory*. London: Routledge, 1–14.

Schultze, U., and Orlikowski, W. J. (2004). 'A Practice Perspective on Technology-Mediated Network Relations: The Use of Internet-Based Self-Serve Technologies', *Information Systems Research*, 15(1): 87–106.

Spender, J.-C. (1998). 'Pluralist Epistemology and the Knowledge-Based Theory of the Firm', *Organization*, 5(2): 233–56.

Suchman, L. (1987). *Plans and Situated Actions: The Problem of Human–Machine Communication*. New York: Cambridge University Press.

Swan, J. (2007). 'Knowledge', in James R. Bailey and Stewart Clegg (eds.), *International Encyclopedia of Organization Studies*. London: Sage Publications, vol. ii.

——Bresnen, M., Newell, S., and Robertson, M. (2007). 'The Object of Knowledge: The Role of Objects in Interactive Innovation', *Human Relations*, 60(12): 1809–37.

Teece, D. J., Pisano, G., and Shuen, A. (1997). 'Dynamic Capabilities and Strategic Management', *Strategic Management Journal*, 18(7): 509–33.

Thompson, M. (2005). 'Structural and Epistemic Parameters in Communities of Practice', *Organization Science*, 16(2): 151–64.

Tseng, S. (2007). 'The Effects of Information Technology on Knowledge Management Systems', *Expert Systems with Applications*, 35(1–2): 1–11.

Tsoukas, H. (1996). 'The Firm as a Distributed Knowledge System: A Social Constructionist Approach', *Strategic Management Journal*, 17(Winter Special Issue): 11–25.

——(2003). 'Do we Really Understand Tacit Knowledge', in M. Easterby-Smith and M. A. Lyles (eds.), *The Blackwell Handbook of Organizational Learning and Knowledge Management*. Oxford: Blackwell, 410–27.

——and Vladimirou, E. (2001). 'What is Organizational Knowledge?', *Journal of Management Studies*, 38(7): 973–93.

Walsham, G. (2002). 'What can Knowledge Management Systems Deliver?', *Management Communication Quarterly*, 16(2): 267–73.

Weick, K. E. (1990). 'Technology as Equivoque: Sensemaking in New Technologies', in P. S. Goodman, L. S. Sproull et al. (eds.), *Technology and Organizations*. Oxford: Jossey-Bass.

——(2001). *Making Sense of the Organization*. Oxford: Blackwell Business.

Wenger, E. (2009). 'Communities of Practice', presentation at the 'Knowledge and Innovation Quarterly' Workshop, University of Warwick, September.

——and Snyder, W. M. (2000). 'Communities of Practice: The Organizational Frontier', *Harvard Business Review*, January–February: 139–45.

Wittgenstein, L. (1958). *Philosophical Investigations*, trans. G. E. M. Anscombe, 3rd edn. Oxford: Blackwell.

Xu, J., and Quaddus, M. (2005). 'Adoption and Diffusion of Knowledge Management Systems: An Australian Survey', *Journal of Management Development*, 24(4): 335–61.

Zollo, M., and Winter, S. G. (2002). 'Deliberate Learning and the Evolution of Dynamic Capabilities', *Organization Science*, 13(3): 339.

Zuboff, S. (1988). *In the Age of the Smart Machine: The Future of Work and Power*. Oxford: Heinemann.

CHAPTER 21

RETHINKING GENDER AND MIS FOR THE TWENTY-FIRST CENTURY

EILEEN M. TRAUTH

INTRODUCTION

A reasonable starting point for this chapter might be to ask the question: why should the MIS field be concerned about gender? Indeed, as various reviews of the MIS literature reveal, it does not appear to have been all that concerned about gender until quite recently. Hence, an additional question might be: why should the MIS field be concerned about gender *now*? This chapter considers these questions by tracing the evolution of research and thinking about gender and MIS against the background of forces that are shaping the twenty-first century. It begins by addressing the question of why gender should be part of our thinking about MIS. It then moves on to consider the evolution of research on gender and MIS. It ends with some thoughts about the topic of gender and MIS in the future. It is important to note that this is by no means a review of the entire body of gender and MIS literature, but merely signposts along the way.

THE ARGUMENT FOR RESEARCH ON GENDER AND MIS

The rationale for the inclusion of gender among the 'legitimate' topics of MIS attention is embedded within the larger rationale for the inclusion of the human capital dimension in the MIS field. Counter to the stereotype of the computing field as not being concerned about humans, 'computer personnel' has been recognized as a component of the computing field almost since its inception. For example, the Association for Computing Machinery (ACM) has held conferences that focus on computer personnel research since the early 1960s.[1] In addition to this dedicated conference, 'air time' is also given to this topic in generic information systems research conferences such as the International Conference on Information Systems, the European Conference on Information Systems, the Americas Conference on Information Systems, and the Pacific Asia Conference on Information Systems, all of which regularly have papers and tracks devoted to human resource aspects of the MIS field.[2]

In addition to conference venues, an increased interest over the past decade in human capital in MIS has spawned special issues of journals such as *Communications of the ACM*,[3] *Human Resources Management Journal*,[4] *European Journal of Information Systems*,[5] and *The Database for Advances in Information Systems*.[6] Further, in research books, the topic of human resources, human capital, or IT workforce has been the focus of attention.[7] It has also been included as a topic in overview books. For example, the final chapter of *Rethinking Management Information Systems*, the forerunner of this Handbook, is a discussion of the management of knowledge workers (Scarbrough 1999). Likewise, the *Oxford Handbook of Information and Communications Technologies* (Mansell et al. 2007) contains two chapters that are directly focused on personnel topics (the global labour force, and inequality), and several more that indirectly focus on personnel (e.g. productivity, digital divide, sourcing, and ICT literacy).

From this quick tour of human capital in MIS literature we can see that a trend toward investigation of these aspects of MIS is clearly present. So we can now rephrase the question that introduced this chapter: given the interest in human capital within the MIS field, why should there be (or why is there) a particular focus on gender? The rationale for including gender among the human capital topics of MIS attention can be viewed as part of the overall argument for the inclusion of diversity as a topic in the MIS field. So, in addressing the topic of 'why study gender', we can approach it as an aspect of the broader question of 'why study diversity'.

Overall, one can observe that as IT has spread throughout all aspects of personal and work life, so too has grown an interest in understanding more about the people who use and develop IT, as well as those who are affected by it at both the organizational and the societal levels. Thus, in the twenty-first century, the task of ensuring a supply of qualified IT personnel is increasingly bound up with issues of diversity. This has led to increasing interest in the demographic characteristics of those who are the consumers and developers of IT products. As the appetite for IT continues to grow, the IT profession is challenged with meeting the demand to enlarge the IT workforce by recruiting and retaining personnel from historically under-represented groups. Gender is one such type of demographic diversity of interest.[8] Hence, we can reframe the generic diversity argument (Trauth et al. 2006) and focus it on the topic of gender diversity.

The first argument for including gender diversity in studies of the MIS field can be called the *consumer argument*. In an information society, in which all citizens are engaged in the consumption of information products, it is crucial that the varying needs of the entire consumer base be represented. The airbag story is now given as a classic example of the failure to include diverse perspectives in design considerations. The problem with the airbag is that it was designed with a typical Euro-American man's physique in mind as the generic 'person', without sufficient consideration being given to the effect of the deployed airbag on someone of a lighter and slighter build, with the tragic consequences that have resulted. Other examples include the artificial knee that was designed by men for a man as the generic 'person' with similarly negative consequences (Smith 2009).

The second argument for considering gender diversity is the *demographic argument*. In much of the Western world, demographic changes add urgency to the desire to create a more diverse MIS labour force. The impending retirement of baby boomers is being compounded by the shift in countries such as the United States from a white majority (Frey 2008). These two trends coupled with projected growth in the IT sector over the next ten years will produce an MIS labour force demand that cannot be satisfied by white men alone. Yet, women typically make up less than 25 per cent of the IT labour force of many countries (Panko 2008).

The third argument for gender diversity can be termed the *innovation economy argument*. The post-industrial or information society is also described as a service economy. In this economy there is greater emphasis on innovation. This is because in the knowledge economy information *services* become emphasized over information *technology*. As technology becomes a commodity it is likely to move offshore to lower wage economies. Therefore, advanced economies such as the USA need to focus on what cannot be easily offshored: continuous innovation. In such an economy 'talent' or human capital development is prized. Florida (2002) argues that the recruitment and retention of technology talent to a particular region is intimately bound up with tolerance of diversity. This is because it is brainpower and creativity that fuels innovation. And the 'best brains' can come in a variety of bodies: female, male, Black, White, gay, straight, etc.

The final argument for gender diversity in the IT field is the *equity argument*. Simply put, women should have the same opportunity to pursue a career as men. However, the data show that that is not the case in the information technology field. A new study in the USA, *The Athena Factor: Reversing the Brain Drain in Science, Engineering and Technology* (Hewlett et al. 2008), examined factors influencing the career trajectories of women in the science, engineering, and technology fields (which would include IT jobs) in private sector companies. The findings point to a troubling rate of attrition among women as many of them reach a 'breaking point' in their careers. The report's authors characterize their findings about the sources of this retention crisis as 'antigens' in the culture of these technical organizations that include: a hostile macho culture, isolation in the workplace, mysterious career paths, systems of risk and reward, and extreme work pressures (pp. i–ii). These findings about gender equity issues in industry are consistent with the situation in the academy. Similar findings about gender equity issues in higher education were published in the report from The National Academy of Sciences (2006) study: *Beyond Bias and Barriers: Fulfilling the Potential of Women in*

Academic Science and Engineering. In the UK an investigation by Tattersall et al. (2006) of the working conditions and the cultural barriers of women in the information technology industry in North West England produced similar findings about causes of female attrition from the field.

These findings about female attrition in the information technology field can be viewed as a part of a larger mosaic of challenges being posed to the IT field. Female attrition, combined with the labour force projections and the other arguments for gender diversity, have presented a compelling argument for considering gender as an important topic to be examined in MIS research. Indeed, one could argue that in response to this situation scholars in the MIS field are being *compelled* to consider gender and IT insofar as their societies are requiring it. In some places, gender and IT research has been motivated by government demands for more equal representation of women in the information society. For example the European Union's Commission on Women's Rights and Equal Opportunities (2003) report recognizes the unequal and gendered path into the information society, and the under-representations of women in the European ICT sector. For this reason it recommends the continuation of gender mainstreaming policies and the undertaking of new initiatives to increase the representation of women. In other countries, funding agencies are motivating research into the gender imbalance in the IT field. For example, the United States' National Science Foundation funds a variety of research programmes aimed at increasing the participation of women in science, technology, engineering, and mathematics (STEM) fields, which include IT. It also funds action-oriented research directed at facilitating broader participation in computing fields. These examples give evidence that the topic of gender and IT will increasingly shift from the periphery of the field to its core. The argument developed in this section concludes that for these reasons, managerial perspectives on the use and management of information systems and technology in the twenty-first century need to take gender into account.

THE STATUS OF GENDER RESEARCH IN MIS

Despite the case that can be made for the importance of gender research in the MIS field, the reality is that there hasn't been that much published. Thus, not only is there a gender imbalance in the MIS labour force, but there is also an imbalance in terms of what research is being conducted. This conclusion has been supported by several meta studies of gender and MIS research. Trauth, Quesenberry, and Huang (2006) conducted an investigation of papers presented at the ACM SIGMIS computer personnel research conference between 1961 and 2005. A search of 862 papers yielded 29 that were about gender and the IT workforce or gender and preparation for the IT workforce. The first paper was presented in 1988. The majority of the papers (10) were published in 2003 when the conference theme was 'difference and diversity'.[9] These findings also indicate that this body of research is of fairly recent vintage: only 6 out of 29 articles on gender issues in the IT workforce and education were presented before 2000. Adam, Howcroft, and Richardson (2004) also conducted an investigation of gender and MIS research. But whereas Trauth et al. looked at the gender research in a single conference, Adam et al. examined top MIS journals over a ten-year period from 1993 to 2002. Their results shown in Table 21.1 indicate that only nineteen papers on gender were published in this time period.

Kvasny, Greenhill, and Trauth (2005) conducted a similar examination of gender and IS research using publications in top MIS journals stretching back to the 1970s. Their search of abstracts for papers that use gender as a central construct in the analysis yielded the results shown in Table 21.2. The difference in journals selected in these two studies reflects their regional origins: Adam, Howcroft, and Richardson (2004) reflects more of the European ranking of top journals whereas Kvasny, Greenhill, and Trauth (2005) reflects more of the American ranking. Finally, a review of gender articles published recently in top MIS journals was done for this chapter. As Table 21.3 shows, the publication trend between 2003 and 2009 is consistent with earlier conclusions that there is a dearth of gender papers in influential MIS journals.

Table 21.1 Gender papers published in IS journals 1993–2002

Journal	Number of papers	Methodology
MIS Quarterly	4	Quantitative
Information Systems Research	1	Quantitative
Communications of the ACM	3	Quantitative
Information Technology & People	1	Quantitative
	4	Qualitative
Information Systems Journal	2	Qualitative
European Journal of Information Systems	1	Mixed methods
	1	Theoretical
Journal of Information Technology	1	Theoretical
Information and Organization	1	Theoretical

Source: Adam, Howcroft, and Richardson 2004: 226.

Table 21.2 Gender papers published in IS journals 1976–2004

Journal	Number of papers
MIS Quarterly	5
Communications of the ACM	33
Information Systems Research	0
Journal of Management Information Systems	3
Management Science	1

Source: Kvasny, Greenhill, and Trauth 2005: 10.

Table 21.3 Gender papers published in IS journals 2003–9

Journal	The number of the papers by year							
	2003	2004	2005	2006	2007	2008	2009	Total
MIS Quarterly(MISQ)	0	0	1	0	1	0	0	2
Information Systems Research (ISR)	0	0	0	0	0	0	0	0
Communication of the ACM (ACM)	1	0	0	1	0	1	1	4
Information Technology & People (ITP)	0	2	1	1	2	0	0	5
Information System Journal (ISJ)[a]	0	0	0	0	0	1	0	1
European Journal of Information Systems (EJIS)	0	0	0	1	1	0	1	3
Journal of Information Technology (JIT)	0	1	0	0	0	0	0	1
The DATA BASE for Advances in Information Systems (DB)	0	1	1	5[b]	1	1	1	10
Information and Organization (IO)	0	0	0	0	0	0	0	0
Journal of Management Information Systems (JMIS)	0	0	0	0	0	1	0	1
Management Science (MS)	0	0	0	0	0	0	0	0

[a] It should be noted that as this chapter is being written the development of a special issue of *Information Systems Journal* on *Women and IT* is underway (see von Hellens, Fisher, and Trauth, forthcoming).
[b] One issue this year was devoted to articles on diversity in the IT workforce, all of which were about gender (see Trauth and Niederman 2006).

THE EVOLUTION OF THINKING
ABOUT GENDER AND MIS

The evolution of research on gender and MIS can be represented as occurring through several phases. The criteria used for aligning research with these different phases include: methodology, epistemology, and gender theory. As this analysis will demonstrate, it has not been a linear evolution; phases of research overlap and influence each other.

Positivist Thinking: Observing Gender and MIS

The first phase of research on the topic of gender and MIS began in the 1970s and continues today. It can be characterized as positivist and quantitative. The goal of this phase of gender and MIS research is to document gender as a phenomenon of interest in investigations of the design, use, and effect of information technology and systems. Adam, Howcroft, and Richardson (2004) note that the bulk (47 per cent) of the gender papers published in the journals they reviewed employed positivist and quantitative methodology. Kvasny, Greenhill, and Trauth (2005) found that every paper in their study that was published in *Management Science*, *MIS Quarterly*, and *Journal of MIS* was positivist in its epistemological orientation and utilized quantitative methods to test hypotheses. Ahuja's (2002) review of the gender and MIS literature agreed that, at the time of her research, it was dominated by quantitative/positivist studies.

The approach taken in these papers is typically to measure gender differences along a variety of factors related to information technology use and participation in the IT profession. One category of papers looks at gender as a variable in studies of technology adoption and use. For example, Venkatesh and Morris (2000) and Venkatesh, Morris, and Ackerman (2000) employed the technology acceptance model (TAM) for theoretical insights as they measured gender differences in computer usage in a workplace setting. Gefen and Straub (1997) used TAM to study gender differences in perceptions about email usage. Gender differences in measures of computer playfulness were taken by Webster and Martocchio (1992). Ahuja and Thatcher (2005) employed the theory of reasoned action to examine the influence of work environment and gender on trying to innovate with information technology. The findings show that work overload interacts with autonomy to affect trying to innovate with IT and that these relationships vary by gender.

The other category contains research that examines gender differences in membership in the IS profession. With respect to gender differences in the workplace Frenkel (1990) and Igbaria and Baroudi (1995) examined job performance and career advancements. Pay disparity was examined by Truman and Baroudi (1994) and participation rate was measured by Carayon et al. (2003). Quite recently, McKinney et al. (2008) reported on a quantitative study that collected data about gender differences with respect to the IT profession, including: motivations for entering the field, professional socialization, work experiences, and attitudes about the profession. Wardell et al. (2006) followed the career trajectory of 2,823 male and female IT professionals and found that women are nearly two and a half times more likely than men to leave the IT labour force. Ahuja's (2002) overview of the gender and MIS literature hypothesized that IT career choice, persistence, and advancement are determined by a set of social factors (such as social expectations, work family conflict, informal networks) and structural factors (such as lack of role models and mentors, the culture of IT education and industry).

A related stream of research focuses on recruitment and retention in the computer fields. For example, Katz et al. (2006) investigated factors related to persistence in an undergraduate computer science programme in the USA. They found that female students who received a grade lower than a B in the introductory computing course were much less likely than male students to take the next course in the curriculum. They speculate that the female students interpreted an average or below average grade as validating the societal stereotype that women do not belong in the IT field. Joshi and Schmidt (2006) found that gender stereotypes that have plagued computer science have pervaded information systems education as well. They surveyed students' perceptions of the gendered nature of tasks associated with the information systems profession. These findings are consistent with the prevailing gender stereotype that most of the traits and abilities associated with IS careers were perceived as masculine rather than feminine or gender neutral. Gallivan (2004) examined the challenge of adapting to technological changes in IS departments using hypotheses about the linkage between personal attributes (tolerance of ambiguity and openness to experience) and IT professionals' ability to adapt to a technological innovation. The findings revealed that the women in the study had lower job satisfaction on a dimension that captured job stress, and this effect was exacerbated for the women working at the firm that expected its IT employees to develop mastery of the innovation on their own time (i.e. outside the normal work day). In many of these quantitative gender and MIS papers—particularly the early ones—gender theory is not explicitly used to guide the research. Rather, the papers published in top MIS journals—the journals that typically require theoretically informed research—tend to employ 'implied' gender essentialism in conjunction with a theory about technology adoption and/or organizational change. That is, they assume the categorization of individuals into two clearly delineated gender categories, masculine and feminine, and that homogeneity exists within them. This theoretical lens is then used to interpret observed quantitative gender differences. The reader is left to infer from this gender essentialism that men and women are fundamentally different in ways that matter with respect to interaction with information systems. The source of this gender essentialism is sometimes revealed as resulting from social construction of gender and IT; other times it is left to the reader to decide whether statistically documented gender differences are biological or sociological in origin.

The review of papers from the ACM SIGMIS computer personnel research conference (Trauth, Quesenberry, and Huang 2006) revealed a similar pattern of 'implied' gender theory, though it falls heavily in the social construction rather than the biological essentialism camp. Articles were coded into four categories: gender essentialist theory, gender social construction theory, individual differences theory of gender, and non-gender theories. This categorization reflects the common theoretical anchor points on the landscape of gender and IT research. The *essentialist theory* invokes biological differences between men and women to explain differences in their relationship to technology. This theoretical position is based on the assertion that such differences are fixed and unified (see critiques by De Cecco and Elia 1993; and Adam, Howcroft, Richardson 2001). The *social construction theory* argues that various socio-cultural factors are the primary constructs that shape individuals and their relationship to IT (see Berger and Luckmann 1966; Marini 1990). Hence, since IT has been socially shaped as 'men's work', IT careers are placed outside the female domain (Wajcman 1991; Webster 1996; von Hellens et al. 2000; von Hellens, Nielsen, and Trauth 2001). The *individual difference theory of gender and IT* is situated between the essentialist theory and social construction theory and is based upon the premiss that gender groups are neither dichotomous nor homogeneous. It argues that there are a variety of expressions of gender identity and, hence, relationships between gender and IT.

Analysis of the twenty-nine papers presented at the ACM SIGMIS CPR conference shows that the dominant theoretical perspective is social construction theory: 21 of the papers (75.9 per cent) use the lens that information technology is socially constructed as a male domain. However, this theoretical alignment did not come from the authors themselves. In 11 of the papers (52 per cent) there was no explicit mention of gender theory. Ten of the papers were subsequently classified by Trauth, Quesenberry, and Huang (2006) as 'social construction' and one was classified as 'no explicit theory'. Hence, in half of the papers the authors did not explicitly identify any gender theory. Also, consistent with the examinations of gender and IT research published in the MIS journals that were discussed above, three of the papers employed non-gender related theories. These results are shown in Table 21.4.

The conclusion from this review of the first phase of research on gender and MIS is that these studies are primarily concerned with tracking the gender variable in quantitative measurement of business information systems. In general, this research is about *observing* gender differences in IT but not *understanding* them. A further and more political interpretation of this phase of gender research is offered by Adam, Howcroft, and Richardson (2004: 223). They posit that in the effort to obtain legitimacy as a

Table 21.4 Treatment of theory in gender papers published in ACM SIGMIS Conference 1988–2005

Number	Theoretical perspective	Theoretical analysis
2	Individual Difference Theory	Explicit
1	Individual Difference Theory / Social Construction Theory	Explicit
9	Social Construction Theory	Explicit
10	Social Construction Theory	Implied
1	Social Construction Theory / Essentialism	Explicit
1	Essentialism	Explicit
1	Social Construction Theory / Organizational Culture Theory	Implied
1	Institutional Discourse Theory	Explicit
1	Structuration Theory	Explicit
1	Theory of Reasoned Action	Implied
1	No Theory	

Source: Trauth, Quesenberry, and Huang 2006: 19.

discipline, information systems has been conservative and narrow in its definition of 'proper' research topics, an approach that has generally excluded gender. They observe that from the limited gender research that has been conducted it can be concluded that 'the concept of gender in IS research largely lacks theorization' (p. 222). They conclude that if we are to adequately understand information technologies we must also understand gender.

Interpretive Thinking: Understanding Gender and MIS

When a positivist approach has been applied to studying gender and MIS, the objective has typically been to discover *whether* and *where* there are gender differences. The purpose of increasing gender diversity would be to further managerial objectives such as increased effectiveness and productivity. The criticism of this research is that such studies remain on the surface of observable and documentable differences and run the risk of engaging in a superficial and unproblematic treatment of gender. In reaction to a view of gender as a variable to be counted and contrasted in studies of technology adoption or the IT workforce, an alternative approach to gender research began to emerge in the final years of the twentieth century. This second phase of gender and MIS research—one that employs qualitative methods and interpretive epistemology—is gaining momentum in the gender and MIS research community. However, this approach remains more dominant outside the United States; in the USA quantitative/positivist studies still dominate.

The limitations of quantitative/positivist studies are addressed in qualitative/interpretivist gender and MIS research. This latter type of research focuses on developing a better understanding of the forces at work that bring about the observed gender differences. The goal is to develop a better understanding of *how* these gender differences in IT use and careers have come about. It does this through the inclusion of context into the scope of study. In this view, gender is among the important social factors shaping both personal and professional spheres. That is, the tension between dichotomizing people into feminine and masculine, on the one hand, and the recognition of variation among and within gender categories, on the other, reveals much about social organization, hierarchies, power, etc. Hence, it is an important factor to be taken into account whether one is studying the producers or consumers of IT.

Consistent with this research movement that goes beyond measuring gender differences in IT use or occupations towards understanding the mutual shaping of technology and gender has been a methodological shift. Because this phase of research seeks not so much to *measure* as to *understand* the gender factor in IT adoption, use, and careers, it has gravitated towards an interpretive epistemology and qualitative methods. The effect of epistemology on the study of a phenomenon was demonstrated in Trauth and Jessup's study of group support systems (2000). They showed how the shift from a positivist to an interpretive analysis of a group support system revealed a considerably different and much more nuanced understanding of the same data. Likewise, qualitative methods, which provide the opportunity to introduce nuance and unanticipated themes, have dominated. Much of the data in this research comes directly from women themselves, through such methods as: open-ended interviews, case studies, focus groups, or ethnographic research. In this way, the subjective reality being experienced by the women who are the object of the statistical studies is being revealed. Statistics tell one story. This type of research is able to tell the story behind the statistics by exploring, in depth, the voices of those women.

This body of gender and MIS research takes as a given that there is a gender imbalance with respect to IT design, use, and professional involvement. In this sense, it is building upon the research findings from the first phase of gender and MIS research. It signifies a desire to go beyond statistical documentation of gender differences towards a deeper understanding of those statistics. In doing so, there is also recognition of the need for relevant theory to guide the interpretations. Thus, whereas some quantitative/positivist gender and MIS research uses no theory, or at least no gender theory to guide the collection and analysis of data, the role of theory in qualitative/interpretive gender and MIS research is heightened. Much of this research employs social construction theory to interpret the subtleties of women's interaction with IT and the IT profession.

The publication of the special issue of *Information Technology & People* on gender and information systems (Adam, Howcroft, and Richardson 2002) signalled a definite movement into this next phase of gender and MIS research. In introducing this special issue, the editors articulated their agenda: to move gender and IS research forward both theoretically and methodologically. In doing so, they also summarized the research gaps present in the first phase of gender and MIS research. They note that as the field of IS has attached increasing importance to the social context and content of systems that are developed, gender has remained largely neglected. In this regard, they suggest, the IS discipline is behind other disciplines, where gender is present and gender analysis is an influencing factor. Further, they note that the little bit of gender research in IS that has been published is under-theorized and, consequently, tends to base analyses on gender stereotyping rather than on gender theorizing.

By way of explaining the papers that were chosen for publication in this issue, the editors explained that the direction of their gaze was shifting away from papers that focused primarily on documenting the low participation of women in the IS profession. In doing so, they signalled the need for gender and MIS research to move beyond a simplistic view of the gender imbalance as simply 'add more women' without probing deeper into why so few women want to enter the IS arena to begin with. Thus, the papers that were featured in this issue did more than meet the standard of high-quality gender and IS research. They also revealed a new *type* of gender and IS research. These papers all see gender as a social rather than as a biological construction and they moved beyond dualist thinking that dichotomized men and women based on gender stereotypical characteristics and behaviours. According to the editors, these papers combine empirical study with gender theorizing so as to advance a deeper understanding of the gender imbalance in MIS.

Habib and Cornford (2002) investigated the themes of domestication, gender, and technology through an ethnographic study of computers in the home. They found that IT is situated within a web of values, relationships, symbols, and routines. Woodfield (2002) begins with the premiss that women bring a different approach to IS work. She then wonders whether a quantitative increase in the number of women in the MIS workforce would result in an accompanying change in the nature of systems development work. Her analysis of interviews conducted with developers revealed that processes by which skills are recognized tend to privilege the 'masculine work' and competencies of male workers. Hence, she remains sceptical about a quantitative change in the gender imbalance resulting in a qualitative change in the way IS work is accomplished. Wilson (2002) employed an empirical study of an automated care planning system that was resisted by nurses as a setting for her theoretical work that combines feminist theory with social shaping of technology theory. Trauth's paper (2002) contributes to the movement toward greater theorizing about gender and IT in that it initiated a programme of interpretive research directed at developing new theory about within-gender variation to guide research about gender in MIS.

The contribution of qualitative/interpretive research is that it has taken a significant step forward in helping to explain the gender factor in MIS adoption, use, and professional affiliation, etc. However, while this phase of gender and MIS research has contributed a better understanding of the phenomena, qualitative/interpretive studies of gender and MIS have also been taken to task on the basis of epistemology and gender theory. Hence, Kvasny, Greenhill, and Trauth (2005: 10) observe that it suffers from some of the same drawbacks as quantitative/positivist research:

> What is lost is inclusion of the critical, radical, and problem-posing nature of feminist theory and practice as an anti-paternalistic discourse. Gender as operationalized in 'mainstream' MIS escapes intensive probing and questioning; it is simply taken as a given dimension for determining differences between men and women. It remains a challenge to get those who conduct gender research to move from the center, the place of safety which excludes the lives, identities and experience of the 'other.' Consequently, the most privileged discourse community, the premiere academic journals, has not, to date, contended with feminist projects in MIS.

TWENTY-FIRST CENTURY RETHINKING OF GENDER AND MIS

In the twenty-first century gender and MIS research is continuing to evolve even as the MIS field, itself, is evolving. Hence, we now have evidence of the emergence of the third phase of gender and MIS research. This new phase is marked by the introduction of critical epistemology, the new ways in which positivist and quantitative tools are being used, and the treatment of theory in this research.

Rethinking Epistemology

The past decade has witnessed epistemological evolution via the emergence of critical theory in MIS research. Though not nearly as 'mainstream' as positivist and interpretive research, there are clear signs that critical IS research (and critical gender and IS research as well) is moving in that direction. One indication is the attention given to critical research in MIS research books, dedicated conferences, and special issues of journals.[10] Whereas the contribution of interpretive gender and IS research has been to enable more nuanced understanding of gender relations in the IS field, in the new century momentum is gathering around critical gender and IS research. The research objective is to challenge existing assumptions about gender relations in order to address the question of *why* gender relations exist as they do. The ultimate objective is to change gender relations in society so as to achieve greater gender equality. Thus, this goal is pursued by reaching beyond an understanding of *how* gender relations emerge, to look at *why* they exist. In doing so, this gender research enters the unstable territory of power, control, resistance, and inequality.

But what, exactly, does critical gender and IS research look like? For illustrative purposes, consider the series of papers[11] by Trauth and Howcroft. They began by framing gender and IS research as a continuum according to epistemological orientation: from 'that there is a gender difference' (positivist) to 'how the current status of gender relations has come to occur' (interpretive) to 'why is gender constructed as it is and whose interests are being privileged' (critical). They begin by considering how the understanding of the gender and IS research topic changes when the epistemology shifts from interpretive to critical. The example is Trauth's research programme to investigate the individual and environmental factors that explain the way American women are influenced by and react to the social shaping of both gender identity and IT. The goal of this research is to develop a better understanding of factors that are enhancing or inhibiting women's participation in the IS profession. This overall goal has embedded within it two specific objectives. One is to gain a better understanding of the particular individual and environmental factors at play. The other is to develop interventions to be implemented by public policy makers, parents, educators, and employers. At the outset, the research methods consisted of interpretive field interviews with women IT professionals. The *individual differences theory of gender and IT* is used as a sensitizing device to guide both data collection and analysis.

Howcroft and Trauth then show how this research would be enacted differently when the epistemological lens shifts from interpretive to critical. First, the goal would change from investigating the reasons for the under-representation by exploring the ways in which women are influenced by and react to the social shaping of both gender identity and IT. It would change to an investigation of the wider systems of repression at work and an exploration of how the social construction of gender identity is seen as being incompatible with IT. And the research, itself, would also change to enable exploration of the interests being served by creating and maintaining the existing power structure. It would shift away from detailed and comprehensive interpretations of interview transcripts which illustrate individual women's responses to the environmental influences they experience. Instead, it would move towards an attempt to better understand the wider economic, social, and political forces that shape this particular construction of differential power.

For example, in the interpretive study the focus is on the story of women who 'overcame the odds' and how they did so; in the critical study the focus would be on why the odds are stacked against women to begin with. Whereas with the interpretive study the results are intended for use in supporting and evaluating interventions directed at women and their societal context, a critical study shifts the focus from how an individual woman copes to uncovering the systems of gender relations at work that create the *need* for women to cope. Hence the critical understanding of the research topic would move beyond articulating key influencing factors affecting women and the within-gender variation in how they overcome them. It would change to showing issues of a structural and ideological nature that may frame the experiences that hold women back and serve to reproduce inequality.

Rethinking Methodology

Trauth and Howcroft, then, consider the ways in which the data collection and analysis methods are altered by this change in epistemological orientation. In a critical field study the focus shifts from emphasis on eliciting the participant's subjective representation of her career history to encouraging critical reflection upon her experiences as she recounts them. Sometimes this is achieved by encouraging development of awareness of the contradictions between her accounts of her behaviour, on the one hand, and her self-characterizations on the other. Like an interpretive interview, the focus of a critical interview remains the subjective representation of the participant's experience. But what is added is the subjective representation of the participant's own *critical thinking* about her experience. In the data analysis phase of the research, a critical reading of the interview transcript will yield insights not only by what is said, but also by what is *not said*. Other insights are garnered from non-verbal communication and contradictions that are observed during the interview. The researcher is also on the alert for instances of the exercise of power experienced by the women and their responses to this as manifested in their narratives. Finally, the researcher engages in reflexive analysis by consciously incorporating her or his own subjective experiences into the process. Thus, critical gender and IS research seeks to do more than merely observe and explain; it also seeks to challenge and change the status quo of gender relations. Hence, there is a close linkage between a critical epistemology and an action research methodology in that the researcher does not remain aloof from the phenomenon and is invested in bringing about change.

In addition to the influence of critical epistemology on research methods, what is also evident in this third phase of gender and MIS research is a new sophistication that is being brought to positivist and quantitative studies. While there continues to be positivist/quantitative research being published that limits itself to documenting gender differences, increasing numbers of gender researchers are using these research tools—sometimes in combination with qualitative methods—to develop a deeper and more nuanced understanding of gender issues in the MIS field. Armstrong et al. (2007) employed revealed causal mapping, a highly detailed qualitative method, to conduct positivist examinations of cognitive linkages that female MIS professionals make among workplace issues that influence voluntary turnover and perceived promotion opportunities. Riemenschneider, Moore, and Armstrong (2006) studied barriers facing women in the IT workforce of a Fortune 500 firm using revealed causal mapping. They found that two of the four workplace barriers women had faced that had influenced voluntary turnover decisions or those of their female co-workers were linked to perceptions about family responsibilities and flexibility to determine work schedule. Kuhn and Joshi (2009) argued that in the absence of research demonstrating gender group-level differences in what employees want from their work, any attempt at targeted recruitment strategies is at best based on anecdotal evidence and at worst on mistaken premises and potentially invalid gender stereotypes. They supported their argument through a quantitative examination of gender similarities and differences in job attribute preferences among prospective IT professionals. In some cases, observed results were contrary to gender differences reported in prior research, suggesting that commonly accepted stereotypes do not necessarily apply. For instance, the men in this study were actually somewhat more averse to lengthy work weeks than the women, and the women did not place any less weight on income than did the men.

Adya and Kaiser (2005) make a contribution to bridging the positivist-interpretive gap by employing qualitative methods to develop a model of females' career choices in technology fields that resulted in a set of hypotheses that can be employed in subsequent positivist studies. Similarly, Trauth et al. (2007) are building upon the results of their prior qualitative/interpretive research on gender, race, and ethnicity to develop and test hypotheses about the intersectionality of these identity characteristics and their influence on IT career choice.

Rethinking Theory

Accompanying the need for new methods to support a deeper and more critical examination of gender relations in MIS is the need to peer inside the 'black box' of gender. Therefore, developing a better understanding of existing gender relations also requires the use of appropriate gender theories. As noted earlier, much of the published work on gender and MIS does not employ gender theory to inform the design of the research, to interpret the findings, or to develop implications emanating from them. Consequently, it has been characterized by Adam, Howcroft, and Richardson (2004) as under-theorized.

Trauth (2006b) has identified three different forms of under-theorization. One occurs when no gender theory is used in the research. Hence, while some other theory (such as about technology or organizational behaviour) might be employed, there is no gender lens to guide the conceptualization of the gender dimension of the research, or to inform the data collection and analysis. The focus is limited to compiling and representing statistical data regarding the differences between men and women with respect to technology adoption, use, or organizational impact. This form of under-theorization is labelled *pre-theoretical research* insofar as it provides limited opportunity for future work that could test, refute, or extend it. The second category of gender and MIS research also employs theories about technology and organizations. And while it does not explicitly articulate a particular gender theory it, nevertheless, is guided by a gender theory-in-use. This has been most prevalent in the positivist, quantitative studies that dominated the early gender and MIS literature. The theory-in-use most often employed is gender essentialism that espouses fundamental, inherent differences between men and women that are applicable to the context of IT. While not explicitly declared as such, this theory-in-use has been used to guide the interpretation of findings in a gender essentialist direction. This form of under-theorization is labelled *implicit-theoretical research*. It is a type of under-theorization because the failure to explicitly articulate the gender lens being used to interpret the data makes it difficult for others to discuss, challenge, or extend the research. Finally, even the corpus of gender and MIS research that explicitly employs gender theory reveals gaps in the theoretical landscape. It has been argued that current theories about gender and IS do not fully account for the observed differences in men's and women's relationships to information technology and the IT field. This form of under-theorization is labelled *insufficient-theoretical research*. It is this third condition that signals the need for new theoretical insights to guide our effort to understand the gender imbalance in the MIS discipline.

A promising area of new gender theorizing is about within-gender variation as it relates to women and men in the IT profession. For example Allen et al. (2006) employed standpoint theory and causal mapping in their examination of mentoring. They showed that mentoring can serve as an important intervention to enhance the retention of women in the IT workforce because of its correlation with professional advancement. And several studies (Nielsen et al. 1997; Adya and Kaiser 2005; Adya 2008; Soe and Yakura 2008) have addressed the topic of varied cultural influences in analyses of gender and IT.

The *individual differences theory of gender and IT* has been developed to provide a theoretical lens that focuses explicit attention on with-gender rather than between-gender variation in the ways that individuals are exposed to, experience and respond to gender relations in the IT profession (Trauth and Quesenberry 2006, 2007). This theory conceptualizes gender relations in the IT field at two different levels of analysis. One level—the societal level—is concerned with gender group biases that women encounter. The other level of analysis—the individual level—deals with the variation among women with respect to how they respond to gender group biases. This variation is posited as resulting from differences in demographic traits, personalities, and individual and socio-cultural influences.

This theory comprises three constructs. The *individual identity* construct includes both personal demographics (e.g. age, race, nationality, socio-economic class, and parenthood), and career items (e.g. industry in which one works). The *individual influence* construct includes personal characteristics (e.g. educational background, personality traits, and abilities) and personal influences (e.g. mentors, role models, and significant life experiences). Finally, the *environmental influence* construct which relates to the geographic region in which an individual lives and works, includes four items. These are: cultural influences (e.g. national, regional, or organizational attitudes about women or about women and IT); economic influences (e.g. cost of living); policy influences (e.g. laws about gender discrimination, and policies about maternity leave); and infrastructure influences (e.g. the existence of childcare facilities). The *individual differences theory of gender and IT* argues that, collectively, these constructs account for the differences among women in the ways they relate to the IT field, and respond to gendered discourses about IT.

Theorizing in this way is intended to help the effort to identify those individual and societal factors that serve to both enhance and inhibit women's participation in the IT field. Research to date has investigated: the intersectionality of gender, race, ethnicity, and class in the choice of an IT career (Kvasny, Trauth, and Morgan 2009); varied responses to exclusion from social networks in the workplace (Morgan, Quesenberry, and Trauth 2004); regional economic and cultural factors that help to explain variation in women's participation in the IT sector (Trauth, Quesenberry, and Yeo 2008); the influence of motherhood on IT careers (Quesenberry, Trauth, and Morgan 2006); the effects of ubiquitous IT on work life balance (Quesenberry and Trauth 2005); variation in career motivations among women in the IT profession (Quesenberry and Trauth 2007, 2008); national cultural influences on women in the IT field (Trauth, Quesenberry, and Huang 2008); and the influence of organizational factors on the retention of women in the IT workforce (Trauth, Quesenberry, and Huang 2009). This theory provides a robust way in which to focus on the differences *within* rather than *between* the sexes, thereby adding to the 'toolbox' of theoretical perspectives to guide investigations of gender and MIS.

In order to serve as a bridge to feminist, gender, and women's studies literature, gender and MIS theories need to provide links to feminist theory. For example, employing Rosser's (2006) classification of feminist theories related to gender and technology, the *individual differences theory of gender and IT* has theoretical linkages to: liberal feminism, socialist feminism, feminist standpoint theory, postmodern feminism, and post-structuralist feminism. Consistent with liberal feminism, it is concerned with removing gender barriers to equal access. But it relates to socialist feminism's recognition of gender along with class as societal factors that explain the social shaping of technology and technology professions. The recognition in the *individual difference theory of gender and IT* on individual characteristics and experiences aligns it with feminist standpoint theory (FST) which emphasizes the situated knowledge of marginalized individuals (Harding 2004). The influence of postmodern and post-structuralist feminism are evidenced in the recognition that women do not all speak with a unified voice. Postmodern feminism believes that the variation in women's national, class, and cultural identities means that the category of 'woman' can no longer be regarded as smooth, uniform, and homogeneous (Brooks 1997).

As more of the feminist theories currently present in the broader gender and technology literature migrate into MIS research, gender and MIS theorizing in the twenty-first century will take on a decidedly critical tone. A return to essentialism accompanies ecofeminism, which bases its arguments on the belief that all women work and learn differently from men (Cockburn 1985; Faulkner and Arnold 1985; Hacker 1990), have a different voice (Gilligan 1982) and, therefore, design and use technology differently from men. But in contrast with more traditional versions of essentialism which would conclude with women's inferiority, ecofeminism argues for women's superiority. Women would design technology differently, and presumably better than men.

Whereas cyberfeminism focuses on the ways in which the Internet can be used to both liberate and oppress women, it is utopian in its vision of a new, electronic world in which disembodied individuals can gain greater equality. In this way, cyberspace is seen as a realm in which the playing field is levelled (Plant 1996). However, its critics argue that cyberfeminism is a bit naive in the belief that the structures of patriarchy and oppression that inhabit the real world do not inhabit the virtual world as well. Wajcman's (2007) response is technofeminism, a theoretical stance that rejects the inherent essentialism of ecofeminism and cyberfeminism. Instead, it draws upon science and technology studies (STS) to reassert the social construction argument: the relationship between gender and technology is one of mutual shaping.

As these feminist debates show, a theoretical tension along the essentialist–constructivist continuum will continue in the twenty-first century. But in addition to debates about ways of theorizing gender and MIS, are coming new discussions that challenge our basic assumptions about how gender is conceptualized in MIS research. Whereas 'gender' in MIS research, to date, has been understood to mean 'woman', the field is beginning to see research on men and masculinity (e.g. Light 2007). The questioning of heteronormativity and the automatic binding of gender to biological sex in gender and MIS research can also be expected to appear. These challenges will take on new forms as the research domain increasingly includes the virtual world.[12]

CONCLUSION

The evolution in gender research during this century will occur against a backdrop of important trends and will be accompanied by challenges within the MIS field itself. The very confusion over the labels used—MIS, IS, IT, ICT—is but one indication of this tension. Some of these trends will have a direct effect on the conduct and prominence of gender and MIS research in this century. One such trend that will intensify is the globalization of MIS (see also Chapter 24 in this volume). As the professional and academic communities in the information professions globalize they will bring with them the research and practice challenges associated with socio-cultural differences. Accompanying the general set of issues related to a global IT workforce and consumer base will be the particular challenges associated with gender differences in the IT workforce and consumer base. Globalization will provide significant impetus for paying greater attention to human differences. Further, it will challenge the hegemony of the Western white man as the prototypical 'IT worker' or 'IT consumer'. Hence, we can expect to see increased interest in the topic of gender and socio-cultural differences and a need for more research on the influences of cultural context on gender and MIS.

A second trend influencing MIS that will have an impact on gender research is the movement toward social inclusion in the MIS field. This term refers to the consideration of the 'haves' and the 'have nots' in the information age: who is invited to participate in the digital revolution; who cannot afford to do so; who is deliberately kept away; who has never heard of the information age. Perhaps because of MIS's origins in business, this is a topic that until quite recently has not been considered a relevant topic within MIS. For example, Huang et al.'s (2006) meta-analysis of the treatment of this theme at the IFIP 8.2 conferences since 1997 revealed that 16 per cent of the 286 papers presented during this time period dealt with this topic. But in sharp contrast, the past few years have seen an explosion of venues for the presentation of this research. Huang's paper was presented the year that the IFIP 8.2 conference theme was social inclusion. This was followed in 2007 by the ICIS conference theme of 'underserved groups'. In 2008 a special issue of *Information Technology & People* (Cushman and McLean 2008) was published. In 2009 a special issue of *Journal of Information, Communication & Ethics in Society* (Urquhart and Underhill-Sem 2009) was published, and a new special interest group within the Association for Information Systems—SIG Social Inclusion—was established. The theme of the 2010 ECIS conference, held in South Africa for the first time, was 'IT to Empower'. As the concept of social inclusion becomes embedded within the MIS consciousness, the subtheme of 'gendered social inclusion' can be expected to become more prominent and commonplace as well.

As the global economy expands in the twenty-first century, and CIOs are faced with managing an increasingly geographically dispersed and culturally disparate IT labour force, new questions arise about the professional development of the IT workforce. Among them are questions about gender in the IT labour force. Should there be special recruitment and retention strategies for women in the MIS profession? What can be done to recruit and retain more women in the IT field? What are the management challenges associated with a more gender-balanced MIS workforce? Should gender balance only be seen as a social goal or can it also be seen as a resource to be leveraged for competitive advantage? These and other questions about possible interventions (Klawe, Whitney, and Simard 2009) require that gender and MIS research remain an important component of the MIS field. All three different approaches to gaining more knowledge about gender and MIS—positivist, interpretive, critical—and their associated methods, will no doubt continue to appear in the gender and MIS literature. This can result in a productive tension regarding the types of knowledge produced by each different approach and whether/how they further the goal of a gender balance in the MIS field.

Notes

1. That conference is now called the ACM SIGMIS Computer Personnel Research Conference.
2. For example, the 2010 ICIS conference has a dedicated track on human capital and IS.
3. See Arnold and Niederman (2001).
4. See Niederman et al. (2007).
5. See Riemenschneider, Moore, and Armstrong (2009).
6. See Mandviwalla and Niederman (2004).
7. See e.g. Niederman and Ferratt (2006); Lowry and Turner (2007); Yoong and Huff (2007).
8. Evidence of this is the publication of the two-volume *Encyclopedia of Gender and IT* in 2006. (See Trauth 2006a.)
9. See Trauth (2003).
10. See e.g. Adam et al. (2001); Howcroft and Trauth (2005); Richardson and Kvasny (2006); Cecez-Kecmanovic, Klein, and Brooke (2008).
11. See Howcroft and Trauth (2004); Trauth and Howcroft (2006); Howcroft and Trauth (2008).
12. See e.g. Blodgett, Xu, and Trauth (2007).

References

Adam, A., Howcroft, D., and Richardson, H. (2001). 'Absent Friends? The Gender Dimension in Information Systems Research', in N. L. Russo, B. Fitzgerald, and J. DeGross (eds.), *Realigning Research and Practice in Information Systems Development: The Social and Organizational Perspective*. Boston, MA: Kluwer, 333–52.

—— —— ——(2002). 'Guest Editorial', *Information Technology & People*, Special Issue on Gender and Information Systems, 15(2): 94–118.

Adam, A., Howcroft, D., and Richardson, H. (2004). 'A Decade of Neglect: Reflections on Gender and IS', *New Technology, Work and Employment*, 19(3): 222–40.

—— —— —— and Robinson, B. (eds.) (2001). *Proceedings of the Critical Research in Information Systems (CRIS) Workshop* (Salford, July).

Adya, M. P. (2008). 'Women at Work: Differences in IT Career Experiences and Perceptions between South Asian and American Women', *Human Resources Management*, 47(3): 601–35.

—— and Kaiser, K. M. (2005). 'Early Determinants of Women in the IT Workforce: A Model of Girls' Career Choices', *Information Technology & People*, 18(3): 230–59.

Ahuja, M. (2002). 'Women in the Information Technology Profession: A Literature Review, Synthesis and Research Agenda', *European Journal of Information Systems*, 11: 20–34.

—— and Thatcher, J. B. (2005). 'Moving Beyond Intentions and Toward the Theory of Trying: Effects of Work Environment and Gender on Post-adoption Information Technology Use', *MIS Quarterly*, 29(3): 427–59.

Allen, M. W., Armstrong, D. J., Riemenschneider, C. K., and Reid, M. F. (2006). 'Making Sense of the Barriers Women Face in the Information Technology Workforce: Standpoint Theory, Self-Disclosure, and Causal Maps', *Sex Roles*, 54: 831–44.

Armstrong, D. J., Riemenschneider, C. K., Reid, M., and Allen, M. (2007). 'Advancement, Voluntary Turnover and Women in IT: A Cognitive Study of Work–Family Conflict', *Information and Management*, 44(2): 142–53.

Arnold, D., and Niederman, F. (eds.) (2001). *Communications of the ACM*, Special Issue on the Global IT Workforce, 44(7).

Berger, P. L., and Luckmann, T. (1966). *The Social Construction of Reality: A Treatise in the Sociology of Knowledge*. New York: Doubleday.

Blodgett, B. M., Xu, H., and Trauth, E. M. (2007). 'Lesbian, Gay, Bisexual and Transgender (LGBT) Issues in Virtual Worlds', *The Data Base for Advances in Information Systems*, 38(4): 97–9.

Brooks, A. (1997). *Postfeminisms: Feminism, Cultural Theory and Cultural Forms*. New York: Routledge.

Carayon, P., Hoonakker, P., Marchand, S., and Schwarz, J. (2003). 'Job Characteristics and Quality of Working Life in the IT Workforce: The Role of Gender', *Proceedings of the ACM SIGMIS Computer Personnel Research Conference* (Philadelphia, April), 58–63.

Cecez-Kecmanovic, D., Klein, H. K., and Brooke, C. (eds.) (2008). *Information Systems Journal*, Special Issue on Exploring the Critical Agenda in Information Systems Research 18(2).

Cockburn, C. (1985). *Machinery of Dominance: Men, Women and Technical Know-How*. London: Pluto Press.

Commission on Women's Rights and Equal Opportunities (2003). *Report on Women in the New Information Society*, <http://www.europarl.europa.eu/sides/getDoc.do?pubRef=-//EP//NONSGML+REPORT+A5-2003-0279+0+DOC+PDF+V0//EN>, accessed 10 April 2009.

Cushman, M., and McLean, R. (eds.) (2008). *Information Technology & People*, Special Issue on Living and Functioning in the E-society: Issues of Inclusion and Exclusion, 21(3).

DeCecco, J. P., and Elia, J. P. (1993). 'A Critique and Synthesis of Biological Essentialism and Social Constructionist Views of Sexuality and Gender', *Journal of Homosexuality*, 24(3–4): 1–26.

Faulkner, W., and Arnold, E. (eds.) (1985). *Smothered by Invention*. London: Pluto Press.

Florida, R. (2002). *The Rise of the Creative Class*. New York: Basic Books.

Frenkel, K. A. (1990). 'Women and Computing', *Communications of the ACM*, 33(11): 34–46.

Frey, H. W. (2008). 'The Census Projects Minority Surge'. *The Brookings Institution, Metropolitan Policy Program*, <http://www.brookings.edu/opinions/2008/0818_census_frey.aspx>, accessed 20 March 2009.

Gallivan, M. (2004). 'Examining IT Professionals' Adaptation to Technological Change: The Influence of Gender and Personal Attributes', *The Data Base for Advances in Information Systems*, 35(3): 28–49.

Gefen, D., and Straub, D. (1997). 'Gender Differences in the Perception and Use of E-mail: An Extension to the Technology Acceptance Model', *MIS Quarterly*, 21(4): 389–400.

Gilligan, C. (1982). *In a Different Voice*. Cambridge, MA: Harvard University Press.

Habib, L., and Cornford, T. (2002). 'Computers in the Home: Domestication and Gender', *Information Technology & People*, Special Issue on Gender and Information Systems, 15(2): 159–74.

Hacker, S. (1990). *Doing it the Hard Way: Investigations of Gender and Technology*. Winchester, MA: Unwin Hyman.

Harding, S. (ed.) (2004). *The Feminist Standpoint Theory Reader*. New York: Routledge.

Hewlett, S. A., Luce, C. B., Servon, L. J., Sherbin, L., Shiller, P., Sosnovich, E., and Sumberg, K. (2008). *The Athena Factor: Reversing the Brain Drain in Science, Engineering, and Technology*. Boston, MA: Harvard Business Review Research Report.

Howcroft, D., and Trauth, E. M. (2004). 'The Choice of Critical IS Research', in B. Kaplan, D. P. Truex, D. Wastell, A. T. Wood-Harper, and J. I. DeGross (eds.), *Relevant Theory and Informed Practice: Looking Forward from a 20 Year Perspective on IS Research*. Boston, MA: Kluwer Academic Publishers, 195–211.

————(eds.) (2005). *Handbook of Critical Information Systems Research: Theory and Application*. Cheltenham: Edward Elgar Publishing.

————(2008). 'The Implications of a Critical Agenda in Gender and IS Research', *Information Systems Journal*, Special Issue: Exploring the Critical Agenda in IS research 18(2): 185–202.

Huang, H., Quesenberry, J. L., Morgan, A. J., and Yeo, B. (2006). 'Where Have We Been and Where Are We Going? Social Inclusion in the Last Decade of IFIP WG 8.2 Research', *Poster Presentation at IFIP 8.2 Conference* (Limerick, June).

Igbaria, M., and Baroudi, J. (1995). 'The Impact of Job Performance Evaluations on Career Development Prospects: An Examination of Gender Differences in the IS Workplace', *MIS Quarterly*, 19(1): 107–23.

Joshi, K. D., and Schmidt, N. L. (2006). 'Is the Information Systems Profession Gendered? Characterization of IS Professionals and IS Careers', *The Data Base for Advances in Information Systems*, 37(4): 26–41.

Katz, S., Allbritton, D., Aronis, J., Wilson, C., and Soffa, M. L. (2006). 'Gender, Achievement and Persistence in an Undergraduate Computer Science Program', *The Data Base for Advances in Information Systems*, 37(4): 42–57.

Klawe, M., Whitney, T., and Simard, C. (2009). 'Women in Computing—Take 2', *Communications of the ACM*, 52(2): 68–76.

Kuhn, K., and Joshi, K. D. (2009). 'The Reported and Revealed Importance of Job Attributes to Aspiring Information Technology: A Policy-Capturing Study of Gender Differences', *The Data Base for Advances in Information Systems*, 40(3): 40–60.

Kvasny, L., Greenhill, A., and Trauth, E. M. (2005). 'Giving Voice to Feminist Projects in Management Information Systems Research', *International Journal of Technology and Human Interaction*, 1(1): 1–18.

——Trauth, E. M., and Morgan, A. (2009). 'Power Relations in IT Education and Work: The Intersectionality of Gender, Race and Class', *Journal of Information, Communication and Ethics in Society*, Special Issue on ICTs and Social Inclusion, 7(2/3): 96–118.

Light, B. (2007). 'Introducing Masculinity Studies to Information Systems Research: The Case of Gaydar', *European Journal of Information Systems*, 16(5) 658–65.

Lowry, G., and Turner, R. (eds.) (2007). *Information Systems and Technology Education: From the University to the Workplace*. Hershey, PA: Idea Group, Inc.

McKinney, V. R., Wilson, D. D., Brooks, N., O'Leary-Kelly, A., and Hardgrave, B. (2008). 'Women and Men in the IT Profession', *Communications of the ACM*, 51(2): 81–4.

Mandviwalla, M., and Niederman, F. (2004). *The Data Base for Advances in Information Systems*, Special Issue on Computer Personnel Research, 35(3).

Mansell, R., Avgerou, C., Quah, D., and Silverstone, R. (eds.) (2007). *The Oxford Handbook of Information and Communications Technologies*. Oxford: Oxford University Press.

Marini, M. M. (1990). 'Sex and Gender: What Do We Know?', *Sociological Forum*, 5(1): 95–120.

Morgan, A. J., Quesenberry, J. L., and Trauth, E. M. (2004). 'Exploring the Importance of Social Networks in the IT Workforce: Experiences with the "Boy's Club"', *Proceedings of the Americas Conference on Information Systems* (New York, August).

Naivinit, S. (2009). 'Gender, Access to Community Telecenter and Livelihood Asset Changes', *Journal of Information, Communication & Ethics in Society*, Special Issue on ICTs and Social Inclusion, 7(2/3): 128–35.

National Academy of Sciences (2006). *Beyond Bias and Barriers: Fulfilling the Potential of Women in Academic Science and Engineering*. Committee on Maximizing the Potential of Women in Academic Science and Engineering, National Academy of Sciences, National Academy of Engineering, Institute of Medicine. Washington, DC: National Academy of Sciences.

Niederman, F., and Ferratt, T. (eds.) (2006). *IT Workers: Human Capital Issues in a Knowledge-Based Environment*. Hershey, PA: Information Age Publishing.

——Maertz, C. P., Kaplan, D. M., and LeRouge, C. (2007). *Human Resource Management Journal*, Special Issue on Human Resource Management of Information Technology Employees, 46(3).

Nielsen, S. H., von Hellens, L. A., Greenhill, A., and Pringle, R. (1997). 'Collectivism and Connectivity: Culture and Gender in Information Technology Education', *Proceedings of the ACM Computer Personnel Research Conference* (San Francisco), 9–13.

Panko, R. R. (2008). 'IT Employment Prospects: Beyond the Dotcom Bubble', *European Journal of Information Systems*, 17: 182–97.

Plant, S. (1996). 'On the Matrix: Cyberfeminist Simulations', in R. Shields (ed.), *Cultures of the Internet: Virtual Spaces, Real Histories, Living Bodies*. London: Sage.

Quesenberry, J. L., and Trauth, E. M. (2005). 'The Role of Ubiquitous Computing in Maintaining Work–Life Balance: Perspectives from Women in the IT Workforce', in C. Sorensen, Y. Youngjin, K. Lyytinen, and J. I. DeGross (eds.), *Designing Ubiquitous Information Environments: Socio-Technical Issues and Challenges*. New York: Springer, 43–55.

——— (2007). 'What Do Women Want? An Investigation of Career Anchors among Women in the IT Workforce', *Proceedings of the ACM SIGMIS Computer Personnel Research Conference* (St Louis, April): 122–7.

——— (2008). 'Revisiting Career Path Assumptions: The Case of Women in the IT Workforce', *Proceedings of the International Conference on Information Systems* (Paris, December).

——— and Morgan, A. (2006). 'Understanding the "Mommy Tracks": A Framework for Analyzing Work–Family Issues in the IT Workforce', *Information Resources Management Journal*, 19(2): 37–53.

Richardson, H., and Kvasny, L. (eds.) (2006). *Information Technology & People*, Special Issue on Critical Research in Information Systems, 19(3).

Riemenschneider, C., Moore, J. E., and Armstrong, D. (2009). *European Journal of Information Systems*, Special Section on Meeting the Renewed Demand for IT Workers, 18(5): 458–61.

——— Armstrong, D., Allen, M., and Reid, M. (2006). 'Barriers Facing Women in the IT Workforce', *The Database for Advances in Information Systems*, 37(4): 58–78.

Rosser, S. V. (2006). 'Using the Lenses of Feminist Theories to Focus on Women and Technology', in M. F. Fox, D. G. Johnson, and S. V. Rosser (eds.), *Women, Gender and Technology*. Chicago, IL: University of Illinois Press, 13–46.

Scarbrough, H. (1999). 'The Management of Knowledge Workers', in W. Currie and R. Galliers (eds.), *Rethinking Management Information Systems*. Oxford: Oxford University Press, 474–96.

Soe, L., and Yakura, E. K. (2008). 'What's Wrong with the Pipeline? Assumptions about Gender and Culture in IT Work', *Women's Studies*, 37(3): 176–201.

Smith, D. (2009). 'The Imperative of Diversity for Institutional Viability: Building Capacity for a Pluralistic Society', presentation at The Pennsylvania State University (University Park, PA, 27 March).

Tattersall, A., Keogh, C., Richardson, H. J., and Adam, A. (2006). 'Women and the IT Workplace: Issues from North West England', in E. M. Trauth (ed.), *Encyclopedia of Gender and Information Technology*. Hershey, PA: Idea Group Publishing, 1252–7.

Trauth, E. M. (2002). 'Odd Girl Out: An Individual Differences Perspective on Women in the IT Profession', *Information Technology and People*, Special Issue on Gender and Information Systems, 15(2): 98–118.

——— (ed.) (2003). *Freedom in Philadelphia: Leveraging Differences and Diversity in the IT Workforce. Proceedings of the ACM SIGMIS Computer Personnel Research Conference*. New York: ACM Press.

——— (ed.) (2006a). *Encyclopedia of Gender and IT*. Hershey, PA: Idea Group Publishing.

——— (2006b). 'Theorizing Gender and Information Technology Research', in E. M. Trauth (ed.), *Encyclopedia of Gender and Information Technology*. Hershey, PA: Idea Group Publishing, 1154–9.

——— and Howcroft, D. (2006). 'Critical Empirical Research in IS: An Example of Gender and IT', *Information Technology and People*, Special Issue on Critical Research in Information Systems, 19(3): 272–92.

——— and Jessup, L. (2000). 'Understanding Computer-Mediated Discussions: Positivist and Interpretive Analyses of Group Support System Use', *MIS Quarterly*, Special Issue on Intensive Research, 24(1): 43–79.

——— and Niederman, F. (2006). *The Data Base for Advances in Information Systems*, Special Issue on Achieving Diversity in the IT Workforce, 37(4).

Trauth, E. M., and Quesenberry, J. (2006). 'Are Women an Underserved Community in the Information Technology Profession?', *Proceedings of the International Conference on Information Systems* (Milwaukee, December).

——— (2007). 'Gender and the Information Technology Workforce: Issues of Theory and Practice', in P. Yoong and S. Huff (eds.), *Managing IT Professionals in the Internet Age*. Hershey, PA: Idea Group Publishing, 18–36.

——— and Huang, H. (2006). 'Cross-Cultural Influences on Women in the IT Workforce', *Proceedings of the ACM SIGMIS Computer Personnel Research Conference* (Claremont, Calif., April), 12–19.

——— ——— (2008). 'A Multicultural Analysis of Factors Influencing Career Choice for Women in the Information Technology Workforce', *Journal of Global Information Management*, 16(4): 1–23.

——— ——— (2009). 'Retaining Women in the U.S. IT Workforce: Theorizing the Influence of Organizational Factors', *European Journal of Information Systems*, Special Issue on Meeting the Renewed Demand for IT Workers, 18: 476–97.

——— and Morgan, A. J. (2004). 'Understanding the Under Representation of Women in IT: Toward a Theory of Individual Differences', in *Proceedings of the ACM SIGMIS Computer Personnel Research Conference* (Tucson, AZ, April), 114–19.

——— and Yeo, B. (2008). 'Environmental Influences on Gender in the IT Workforce', *The Data Base for Advances in Information Systems*, 39(1): 8–32.

——— Huang, H., Morgan, A., Quesenberry, J., and Yeo, B. J. K. (2006). 'Investigating the Existence and Value of Diversity in the Global IT Workforce: An Analytical Framework', in F. Niederman and T. Ferratt (eds.), *IT Workers: Human Capital Issues in a Knowledge-Based Environment*. Hershey, PA: Information Age Publishing, 331–60.

——— Kvasny, L., Joshi, K. D., Mahar, J., and Kuturel, S. (2007). *Exploration of the Effects of Race, Ethnicity and Socio-economic Class on Gender Stereotyping of STEM Disciplines*. National Science Foundation #0733747.

Truman, G. E., and Baroudi, J. J. (1994). 'Gender Differences in the Information Systems Managerial Ranks: An Assessment of Potential Discriminatory Practices', *MIS Quarterly*, 18(2): 129–41.

Urquhart, C., and Underhill-Sem, Y. (2009). *Journal of Information, Communication & Ethics in Society*, Special Issue on ICTs and Social Inclusion, 7(2/3).

Venkatesh, V., and Morris, M. (2000). 'Why Don't Men Ever Stop to Ask for Directions? Gender, Social Influence, and their Role in Technology Acceptance and Usage Behavior', *MIS Quarterly*, 24(1): 115–39.

——— and Ackerman, P. L. (2000). 'A Longitudinal Field Investigation of Gender Differences in Individual Technology Adoption Decision Making Processes', *Organizational Behavior and Human Decision Processes*, 83(1): 33–60.

von Hellens, L. A., Fisher, J., and Trauth, E. M. (forthcoming). *Information Systems Journal*, Special Issue on Women and IT: Increasing the Representation of Women in Information and Communications Technology—Research on Interventions.

——— and Nielsen, S. (2001). 'Australian Women in IT', *Communications of the ACM*, 44(7): 46–52.

——— and Trauth, E. M. (2001). 'Breaking and Entering the Male Domain: Women in the IT Industry', in M. Serva (ed.), *Proceedings of the 2001 ACM SIGMIS Conference on Computer Personal Research* (San Diego, April), 116–20.

——Pringle, R., Nielsen, S., and Greenhill, A. (2000). 'People, Business and IT Skills: The Perspective of Women in the IT Industry', in W. Nance (ed.), *Proceedings of the 2000 ACM SIGCPR Computer Personnel Research Conference: Electronic Commerce and Internet Business. Roles, Relationships, Skills and Strategies for the New Millennium*, Chicago, 6–8 April, 152–7.

Wajcman, J. (1991). *Feminism Confronts Technology*. University Park, PA: Pennsylvania State University Press.

——(2007). 'ICTs and Inequality: Net Gains for Women?', in R. Mansell, C. Avgerou, D. Quah, and R. Silverstone (eds.), *The Oxford Handbook of Information and Communications Technologies*. Oxford: Oxford University Press, 581–99.

Wardell, M., Sawyer, S., Reagor, S., and Mitory, J. (2006). 'Women in the United States' IT Workforce: Current Status and Issues', *Labor & Industry*, 16(3): 39–58.

Webster, J. (1996). *Shaping Women's Work: Gender, Employment and Information Technology*. London: Longman.

——and Martocchio, J. (1992). 'Microcomputer Playfulness: Development of a Measure with Workplace Implications', *MIS Quarterly*, 16(2): 201–26.

Wilson, M. (2002). 'Making Nursing Visible? Gender, Technology and the Care Plan as Script', *Information Technology & People*, Special Issue on Gender and Information Systems, 15(2): 139–58.

Woodfield, R. (2002). 'Woman and Information Systems Development: Not Just a Pretty (Inter) Face?', *Information Technology & People*, Special Issue on Gender and Information Systems, 15(2): 119–38.

Yoong, P., and Huff, S. (eds.) 2007. *Managing IT Professionals in the Internet Age*. Hershey, PA: Idea Group Publishing.

CHAPTER 22

GREEN DIGITS: TOWARDS AN ECOLOGY OF IT THINKING

PIERRE BERTHON,* PHILIP DESAUTELS,
BRIAN DONNELLAN, AND
CYNTHIA CLARK WILLIAMS

'The most thought-provoking thing in our thought-provoking time is that we are still not thinking'

(Heidegger)

INTRODUCTION

THE world faces an ecological crisis: population, pollution, and planetary perturbation. Despite years of industry-funded propaganda, the scientific evidence for the unsustainable nature of modern living has become overwhelming. As humans, we are faced with a stark choice: change or face the possibility of extinction. There are differing opinions as to the causes of our ecological crisis, but there are many symptoms: on the abiotic front we are faced with rising temperatures, decreased rainfall, desertification, rising sea levels, vast toxic wastelands, and acidification of the oceans. On the biotic front we are faced with overpopulation, de-speciation, extinctions, and decreasing biodiversity in terms of both species and ecosystems. Hart (1997) argues that humans have contributed to the ecological crisis in three ways: population, lifestyle, and technology. Increased human population, living an unsustainable, environmentally destructive lifestyle has drained the earth of resources and flooded it with pollutants. The enabling mechanism for both the increase in population and the increase in affluence has been technology. Technology is the multiplier effect for every human action: and to date our technology has been focused on human needs without thought for the environment. The ecological crisis is forcing us to change our myopic views of both the environment and technology. Indeed the irony is that technology may well be the mechanism for our saviour as it has been the instrument of our plight.

To say we are still learning about our relationship with nature is palpable, however what is less obvious is that we are still learning about our relationship with technology. Indeed we have been as unconscious in our relationship with technology as we have been in our relationship with nature. We tend to think of both nature and technology as 'other': something out there; something separate from us. The difference being that we *find* the former and *create* that latter—but we treat them both the same: *instrumentally*. That is we *use* both technology and nature for our own ends. The ecological crisis has alerted us to the fact that our use of technology is causing us to consume and alter nature in unsustainable ways. While our ecological awareness has increased, our relationship with technology is more ambivalent. Indeed our use of technology for instrumental purposes has been plagued by paradoxes of intent and result.

IT Paradoxes

Much has been written about the information technology paradox (cf. Thatcher and Pingry 2007)—IT was meant to be the solution to inefficiency, yet in many ways, IT has failed to deliver the productivity gains promised. IT has done more to shift business practices than make industry more efficient. Further, IT has not delivered on its promise of increased leisure and freedom, but has rather blurred the boundaries of personal and work time, to the extent that many are always working. More recently, with the emerging climate and energy crises, IT is once again being touted as a solution: can it deliver this time? We argue that it can, but will require (1) a deeper understanding of our relationship with technology; and (2) a more thoughtful reflection on what it means to be green: there are many shades of green.

Information systems, that is, the design and implementation of entire systems of storage and retrieval, have promised the world—but more soberly have done more to change it than deliver it. IT, or the software and hardware that enables us to do more, faster; but to what end? Indeed the history of information technology has been beset by paradoxes. A few are summarized below, under the headings of: the promise of efficiency, the promise of cleanliness, the promise of education, the promise of satisfaction, and the promise of community.

Like some great thaumaturge IT's primary promise was that of making the world a better and less onerous place in which humans could live. At the core of this claim is the promise of efficiency—more for less. However, from the simple promise of the paperless office, where advances in IT have contributed to a massive explosion in the use of paper and concomitant deforestation (Sellen and Harper 2001), through the utopia of reduced energy consumption, where although IT has increased local energy efficiency, overall energy consumption has skyrocketed, with IT installations being one of the highest consumers of energy per unit of space occupied (Thatcher and Pingry 2007), IS has been conspicuous in its failure to manifest large-scale, systemic efficiencies.

In terms of making the world a less onerous place to live, IT contributions are once again paradoxical. For example, computers and robots were originally envisaged to reduce work—they were labour-saving devices; however, research suggests that this has not been the case. Indeed in many countries automation, although changing the types of jobs people do, has been accompanied by an increase in the number of hours humans work each week (Jackson 2008); machines that work tirelessly around the clock, around the world, and around the year need humans to do the same. The same goes for leisure: rather than increase leisure time, IT has blurred the distinction between work and the personal, such that the latter is increasingly eroded (Rubery et al. 2005). The irony here is that the very machines that we created are recreating us in their own image.

The next promise is that of cleanliness: IS has promised a cleaner, less wasteful world; the felicity of such claims is once again equivocal. For example, server farms appear the epitome of high-tech cleanliness (especially when compared to heavy industry such as steel); however, the disposal of IT equipment has become a major environmental problem: toxic materials in components have been found to be detrimental to many forms of life—including humans (Grossman 2006). Indeed, approximately 93 per cent of the materials used in the production of computers and electronics never end up in salable products and an estimated 99 per cent of the materials in products used in their manufacture end up as waste within six weeks of their sales (Weizsacker, Lovins, and Lovins 1997). Likewise, most products have been deliberately designed for obsolescence (Slade 2006), a condition that has existed for decades (Packard 1960).

Perhaps the most insidiously redolent of promises has been that of IT's potential to enhance and even transform education. It's insidious because it's so intuitively appealing. Education is all about information and thus information systems must by definition enhance the endeavour. Yet research suggests the very opposite: information systems can be inimical to education.

Consider the recent poster-child of IS enabled education: the one laptop per child initiative. Laudable in its ideals (to bring IS to the poor), longitudinal research suggests that such initiatives are detrimental to student learning (Cuban 2001; Malamud and Pop-Eleches forthcoming), matched groups of students with and without laptops clearly showing that those without laptops outperform (across subjects) those with laptops. Indeed, not only is IS intensive education less effective than traditional, but it also has a wider environmental footprint (Smith 2004); for example the environmental cost of manufacturing, running, and disposing of laptops is greater than traditional paper textbooks.

Moreover the more general relationship between ubiquitous information systems and a more informed and better educated populace is being questioned. There is growing concern that more information can result in less knowledge, or more facts can result in confusion rather than clarity (Manjoo 2008). Consider the debate over global warming; despite growing evidence and widespread promotion of the facts, the number of Americans believing in climate change is decreasing (Eilperin 2009)! How might this be? Procter (1991, 2001) argues that information ubiquity can be accompanied by a corresponding decrease in knowledge, or *agnosis* (from the Greek 'without knowledge') amongst the general population; *agnosis* is a social process whereby alternative narratives are constructed, typically by ideologically or financially driven groups, around a small subset of the available facts. Ideas (ideology) or money drives the collection and interpretation of facts, rather than facts driving ideas. This inversion of facts and knowledge is further compounded by the ease of selective search in advanced information systems: ideology replaces knowledge both as the container and driver of facts.

Indeed the wider iatrogenic effects of IS on human cognition are becoming apparent. There is increasing concern that ubiquitous information systems are rewiring the human brain with unforeseen consequences (see Rosen 2008). Research suggests that information overload is destroying our ability to focus attention; nuanced reasoning is replaced by simplistic black and white thinking; and reflection and creative thinking is replaced by distraction and bounded and shallow cognition (Keim 2009). Obviously more research is needed, but there is little doubt that IS tools are changing their makers in unforeseen ways.

Allied with the promise of increased efficiencies has been the promise that IS will deliver enhanced consumer satisfaction (cf. Day 1991). Yet the irony is that in recent years, despite accelerated investment in service industries such as banking, both productivity and customer satisfaction have deteriorated (Olazabal 2002). More broadly technology, and IS specifically, offers the promise of a better and easier life, yet paradoxically, as the rate of technological change in modern life has increased, happiness and societal health have decreased. Rather than yielding their promise of happiness, the technology has delivered a negative result (Toffler 1970; Miringoff, Miringoff, and Opdycke 1999).

Finally, there is little doubt that the apophthegm 'global village' is the corollary of the connectivity. However, this connectivity is once again replete with contradictions. IS has delivered the dream of instant communication between people and groups almost anywhere on the planet: we live in a hyperconnected, socially networked world—contact is only a click, swipe, or call away. Yet despite this, study after study has demonstrated that it is precisely this technology of connection that is resulting in increased isolation. As people spend more and more time in mediated interaction, unmediated interaction is declining, resulting in a potential epidemic of loneliness, depression, and concomitant diseases (Sigman 2009).

The point here is not to present some dystopian, Malthusian picture of technology, but highlight the fact that intention and manifestation are typically at odds; and it is the acknowledgement of this that may be critical if we are to use information systems to help us out of the ecological predicament in which we find ourselves.

In this chapter we explore the paradox of IT and IS and the promise of these as one of the solutions to our ecological predicament. We explore Green IT by focusing on a third, neglected level of information systems analysis: Information Views, or 'ways of *thinking*' about information technology and systems. We suggest that it is this ignored conceptual level that has in part contributed to the IT paradoxes. Specifically we differentiate instrumental versus emergent thinking about technology, and identify three paradigms that suggest very different uses of information technology to achieve the goal of Green IT in the service of sustainability.

GREEN IT

Terms such as green computing, Green IT, and Green IS have been used loosely and interchangeably in government and industry for some years; all are closely linked to the concept of sustainability. This latter term is generally considered to mean a strategy of meeting the needs of the present without compromising the ability of future generations to meet their own needs (Brundtland 1987: 8). This somewhat ambiguous definition, privileges society over the environment, conflates fact, intent, and value, and leaves a high degree of latitude for interpretation. Others have tried to operationalize the definition for practical implementation. Marshall and Toffel (2005) identify four such frameworks of sustainability: the ecological footprint (Wackernagel and Rees 1996), the triple bottom line (Elkington 1998), the natural step (Nattrass and Altomare 1999), and the sustainable emissions and resource usage (Graedel and Klee 2002). These are summarized in Table 22.1.

FROM INFORMATION TECHNOLOGY
TO INFORMATION VIEWS

Watson et al. (2008) differentiate Green information technology from Green information systems. The former focuses primarily on the matter and energy embodiment of information technology. It is concerned with issues such as efficiency, recycling of materials, reduction or elimination of toxic compounds in manufacturing, renewable energy, etc. In contrast Green IS focuses on the design and implementation of information systems—the linking together of components into purposeful organizations. Here the focus is on systemic initiatives to manage the transport of matter, energy, and information for optimum efficiency and effectiveness. Examples include systems to manage the energy consumption of an airline fleet, systems to manage traffic flow, systems to optimize information streams over the internet, etc. However the

Table 22.1 Sustainability frameworks

The triple bottom line	The natural step	The ecological footprint	Sustainable emissions and resource usage
Organizations pursuing sustainability make decisions based on three criteria: economic returns, environmental protection, and social equity. These three elements can be combined: eco-efficiency balances economic and environmental goals; fair trade balances economic activities with social justice; and environmental justice balances social equity with environmental protection.	A sustainable society is one in which human needs worldwide are met, but nature is not subject to systematically increasing concentrations of substances extracted from the earth's crust, concentrations of substances produced by society, and degradation by physical means.	Sustainability is calculated by comparing the environmental impact of specific actions to the limitations of the earth's natural resources and ecosystem functionality: the ratio of 'how many earths' would be required to provide enough biologically productive land area to maintain the flows of resources and wastes, if everyone lived like a specific person or group of people.	A sustainable rate of resource use can be determined by: (i) calculating the available supply of virgin materials (mass); (ii) allocating consumption of this supply over a specific time scale and among the global population (mass per person per year); (iii) accounting for recycling and for existing stockpiles and then updating the allocated consumption rate; and (iv) considering this rate to be the maximum sustainable consumption rate and comparing it to the current usage rate.

question must be asked: how do we decide the purpose of an information system? What does it mean to produce an efficient and effective technology or system? We propose that what has been lacking in the debate around Green IT is not the technology or the systems, but the ways of *thinking* that underpin each. The paradoxes outlined above all too clearly show that despite the best intentions of designers and managers, information technology has had a poor ecological track record. Why? Perhaps because of our naive relationship to technology and our simplistic understanding of what it means to be sustainable.

Green information views (Green IV) has two important elements—how we think about technology and how we think about the environment. We discuss each in turn.

RE-VIEWING TECHNOLOGY

Heidegger (1977) notes that the common view of technology is twofold: first technology is instrumental—i.e. it is a means to an end; a means of getting something done. Second, it is anthropological—i.e. the product of human activity; simply, humans create technology. Whilst this view is undoubtedly correct, it is also partial and misleading. Technology, Heidegger (1977) points out, stems from the Greek τέχνη, *techne*. There are two aspects to this term. First, *techne* is more than the Greek for the activities and skills of the craftsperson, it also means the art of the mind; techne is a 'bringing forth', a 'revealing'; it is a form of poiesis, a poetic creation. Second, from early Greek times, the word *techne* is linked with episteme. Both words are essential parts of knowing. Aristotle unites and differentiates thus: episteme and *techne*—the 'what' and 'how' of revelation. Heidegger's etymological review of the word technology suggests a very different meaning from the popular, instrumental view of technology as a means to an end: technology is also a mode of revelation. Here Heidegger employs the Greek word ἀλήθεια, *aletheia* which literally means 'unveiling' or 'revealing' and is also the Greek word for 'truth.' Thus technology is a mode of *aletheia*, an act of revelation, a process of bringing forth. The compass brings forth a world of magnetic fields; just as the chronograph reveals a world of abstract time.

Once brought forth Heidegger argues that technology becomes a way of seeing: in this context he uses the word *gestell*, best translated as enframing. Technology becomes a frame of mind, a way of viewing the world: technology becomes a way of seeing. Thus to the stem cell researcher, embryos become a resource for harvest, to the recycler, trash becomes gold. Technology has both a physical and a conceptual dimension—and it the conceptual dimension of enframing which Heidegger sees as the essence of technology.

To the dominant views of technology as instrumental and anthropologic, we might add the views of technology as *aletheia* and *gestell*—technology as revelation and enframing (cf. Berthon, Hulbert, and Pitt 2005). Technology can, therefore, be seen as both emergent and anthropoetic—it creates new ends and shapes the humans that created it— for the essence of technology is not the physical, it is the conceptual. Technology is a frame of mind that shapes both the viewer and the viewed, the actor and the acted. Our technology empowers and possesses us.

Conventionally, technology is seen as a neutral object, the product of people and a tool to enable them to achieve specified ends. To this we can now add technology as an active subject, a shaper of people and a revealer of new worlds. These four modes of technology can be mapped by two axes. Technology can either be seen as a passive or neutral object or an active subject or force; and technology is always viewed in relation to the people who created it and to the wider environment or world. This is summarized in Figure 22.1.

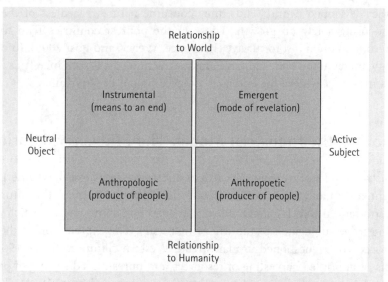

Relationship
to World

Instrumental (means to an end)	Emergent (mode of revelation)
Anthropologic (product of people)	Anthropoetic (producer of people)

Neutral
Object

Active
Subject

Relationship
to Humanity

FIGURE 22.1 Four views of technology

RE-VIEWING THE ENVIRONMENT

The relationship between the environment and technology is confounded. In the traditional view, technology is a neutral object produced by people as a means to an end, nature a resource to be exploited. From this perspective, nature is subjugated as a resource which technology can unlock, transform, and store for future use as needed (Heidegger 1977). Technology applied in this way to transform and leverage nature to our own ends does not remain merely a neutral object, but rather becomes an active subject in shaping our view of nature and of technology itself. Through this shifting of views, technology has become more than a tool to transform; it has become a means to reveal our impact on the environment and it has become a producer of successive generations of people who are more attuned to the environment and our technological impact on it. As technology has moved from a neutral, passive state to an active participatory state, our paradigm of interaction with nature has also shifted drastically.

The world's market economy encompasses approximately half of the world population, with one billion people in developed nations and two billion in emerging ones (Hart 1997). In emerging nations, technology is used naively as the engine of growth to enable rapid industrialization (and its associated urbanization) and through this industrialization there is movement towards a more developed state. In much the same way as their developmental predecessors, industrial cultures see nature as an inexhaustible resource to be exploited at all costs to increase the standard of living to that of the 'developed' world. Thus, they consume nature regardless of the cost or impact, focusing solely on growth. Those in the poorest countries tend to misuse natural resources often just to survive (Lawrence, Weber, and Post 2005). Information technology, much in the same light as industrial technology, is seen merely as a tool for growth, a means to achieve the end goal of development or survival.

Questioning the Industrial Model: The Efficiency Solution

The industrial model of treating the earth as a resource to be exploited emerged from the Enlightenment and the rise of modern science; these 'objectified' the natural world in a hitherto radical way. Human kind was set apart and above nature, which was seen as needing to be subjugated to the will of man (*sic*). The exploitation of the natural world proceeded unquestioned in mainstream Western culture until the 1960s when the effects of unbridled harvesting of resources and unrestrained sowing of pollutants became manifest to all but the most myopic denizens (Carson 1964). Thus, the industrial model gave way to the post-industrial model.

While the ecological impact of the world's emerging economies is evident (deforestation, desertification, mass urbanization), it is the ecological footprint of the developed world's post-industrial consumer cultures which imparts the predominant planetary impact. In these cultures, while the importance of nature is evident, society and nature are separate. It is the responsibility of society to manage and exploit nature, but to do so responsibly. The realization of the finality of nature has shifted the human–nature relationship to one of stewardship in order to maintain the status quo of life and the environment. Technology holds no more than a neutral role in achieving this goal. The predominant mechanism employed is relentless technocratic efficiency—doing more with less, reducing and reusing waste, and minimizing the impact that technology has on nature. Information technology is viewed as an end unto itself and faces the same demands for efficiency that all other technology faces.

Questioning the Efficiency Solution: The Simplify Model

Despite the fact that the efficiency model dominates much of current thinking (see Forester Report 2009 for IT and Hawken, Lovins, and Lovins 1999 for industry), its efficacy is coming under increasing scrutiny. For example Price (2008) starts with an interesting question: is modern efficiency inefficient—does its constant quest to pare down 'extraneous' elements in fact make life unsustainable—literally compromising the ability of future generations to meet their own needs? The issue is that efficiency is typically anthropocentrically defined and over too short a time period. Efficiency for whom and over what time period is seldom asked on the planetary level. The questioning of the efficiency or management paradigm and the concomitant questioning of the Enlightenment legacy of viewing humans separate and above their environment has led to radical rethinking.

Out of this arose the deep ecology movement which sees humans as fundamentally and indeed spiritually a product of the earth. Its proponents champion a return to more natural ways of living, reducing our dependence on high-tech solutions in favour of simple, appropriate technology and a more harmonious and spiritual way of life. The Amish might be illustrative of this model. This counterculture has developed across both emerging and developed economies. This romantic desire to return to nature produces a paradoxical relationship with technology. Technology is treated with distrust and it is seen as the primary cause of society's ecological and social problems (pollution, globalization, conflict, poverty) but it also serves as an enabling tool of the movement. Information technology is applied to higher purposes to enable the goals of the movement.

Questioning the Simplification Solution: The Transformation Model

Despite the neutral (or ambivalent) role that technology has taken in the paradigms described thus far, the anthropoetic impact of technology on society has resulted in the emergence of a fourth wave or way of green that is itself a product of technology. It rejects both the efficiency model as misguided and 'back to nature' as simply untenable. It is epitomized in movements such as Viridian Design (cf. Steffen 2006). The perspective here is that what we think of as the 'natural' world is a myth; for there is not a drop of water, a grain of soil, or a molecule of air that is unaltered by humanity. As Sterling of Viridian Design argues:

> 'Nature' is over. The twentieth century did it in. There's not a liter of seawater anywhere without its share of PCB and DDT. An altered climate will reshuffle the ecological deck for every creature that breathes. You can't escape industrialism and hide from the sky. It's over. (Quoted in Roberston 2008)

This movement embraces the fact that humans are an intrinsic part of nature, but inverts the relationship arguing that nature is now fundamentally 'human'. Nature thus transformed itself into a product of humanity rather than an entity unto itself. To them, technology is no longer a tool to be leveraged, but rather a means to achieving a post-human cybernetic existence. Information technology is fundamental to this culture and serves a higher purpose, enabling the transformation of both society and the planet.

Each of the four paradigms of the human–nature interaction presented here—Exploitative, Technocratic, Romantic and Transformative, is summarized in Table 22.2. The first two of these present a view of technology as neutral object while in the latter two, technology is an active subject. In the last of these paradigms, Transformative, the impact

Table 22.2 Paradigms of human–nature interaction

	Naive Exploitative	Efficiency Technocratic	Simplify Romantic	Evolve Transformative
Strategy	EXPLOIT Exploit nature	MANAGE Preserve nature	RETURN Return to nature	TRANSFORM Transform nature
Culture Primary goal	Industrial culture. Growth—at all costs Increase standard of living— regardless of costs	Consumer culture. Maintain the status quo: standard of living whilst minimizing impact	Counter-culture. Devolve Return to a simpler way of living	Cyber-culture. Evolve; create new world
Examples	Industrial: Industrial countries such as China, India, etc.	Post-industrial Europe; emerging paradigm in Western business today	Deep Ecology: Arne Naess, Gandhi, E. F. Schumacher's *Small is Beautiful* and Meadows's *Limits to Growth*; Honore's *In Praise of Slow*	Bright Green, Bruce Stirling, Viridian Green, etc.
Relationship with nature	Separate: Nature is seen as an inexhaustible resource to exploit	Separate: Nature is a finite resource to manage; humans as stewards of the natural world	Part: We are a product of nature, but have lost touch with it— we need to return. Stresses our deep spiritual relationship with nature. Return to Eden	Part: 'Nature is over'—nature is a *product* of humanity; Idealistic, Creative, Entrepreneurial
Relationship with technology	Naive: Technology seen as the unproblematic engine of growth	Neutral: Technology seen as neutral. Focus on efficiency— minimizing the impact of technology	Ambivalent: Ambivalence, even mistrust of technology. Technology is seen as a primary cause of the problem	Utopian: Belief in the power of technology to transform, post-human
View of IT	Internalist: Bigger, more powerful; IT an end in itself	Internalist: More efficient; do more with less; IT an end in itself	Telos: Do less with less— de-complexify; IT used for a higher purpose	Telos: Use IT to transform ourselves and the planet; IT used for a higher purpose

of technology on the culture is so profound that the very frame of reference for the culture has been shifted.

CONCLUSION

At the start of this chapter we argued for a third level of IT: to information *technology* and information *systems* we need to add an integrating framework of information *views*—or ways of thinking about technology and systems. We suggest that this new level is particularly important as we contemplate technological solutions to the problem of global warming and planetary change, as IT solutions have in the past been characterized by an etiology of opposite effects. For local problems this may have been overlooked, but in an increasingly strongly interlinked and critically interdependent world *there are no local problems*.

Drawing on the work of Heidegger we uncover two underappreciated aspects of technology. To the mainstream views of technology as a product of people, created and employed for instrumental ends, we must add a complementary view: technology as the producer of people and as an emergent, evolving entity in and of itself. For this view we realize that technology cannot be confined to the instrumental—it will always escape our control and change us and how we think of ourselves and our environment in the process.

Turning to the environment, we see that our position towards nature has remarkable parallels with our stance towards technology. Nature has been used instrumentally—as a resource to be exploited. Even humanity's genesis has until recently been thought of as somehow apart from nature (e.g. Rosenstand 1994). Ironically, it has been technology that has changed our relationship with nature: technology has revealed our dependence upon our environment through our instrumental use of the environment. This re-framing of our view of nature has produced a variety of different perspectives on sustainability. Each offers us a very different vision of sustainability and the role of Green IT.

The Technocratic solution presents a paradigm of thought focused on efficiency: doing more with less. This level, we argue, is where the bulk of Green IT thinking is at present, and will be a critical element to any ongoing strategy. It recognizes the finite nature of resources and the importance of getting the maximum out of a given resource; however, in and of itself the Technocratic perspective is incomplete. The Romantic solution recasts the question of our relationship with the environment as a 'losing touch' with our natural being. This 'fall' is no *felix culpa* but rather a tragedy of a spiritual dimension. Indeed it is this insight that can help inform Green IT: technology and nature are more than value imbued—they are fundamental aspects of ourselves. Nature and technology are the mirrors in which we discover ourselves; at the moment what we see is not pretty. Finally, the Transformative solution offers us the compelling vision of a mutual evolution. It flips the Romantic perspective of 'we are children of nature' to 'nature is now our product'. It stresses radical innovation and entrepreneurial solutions—rather than step back and let nature 'heal' itself, it argues for new forms of nature and humanity.

We argue that Green IV needs to integrate insights from each of these paradigms. From the naive industrial perspective we take the pragmatic instrumental perspective that humanity will always 'use' nature to some extent, and, to some degree, all societies must. Moreover, we need the Romantic to balance the Transformative, lest hubris become our nemesis. Indeed the emergent aspect of technology should lead us to value what the ancient Greeks termed *sophrosyne*, self-restraint, through a reflexive awareness of self-limitations; clearly our ability to predict the future is severely compromised.

So in conclusion, what can we learn from Green IV? First, we cannot treat technology in the way we have nature—instrumentally. Technology manifestly has emergent properties in exactly the same way nature has. Second, any technological solution to manage nature will escape our intentions. Third, every technological solution to manage nature will transform us—radically. Fourth, rather than try to control nature *and* technology we must build flexibility into our responses to its emergence—and ours. Fifth, rather than try to limit technological repercussions we need to instil *values* into it, just as nature is now instilling values into us—this is particularly pressing as machines reach and exceed humans. Finally, our future may be more determined by our ecological mindsets than our ecological footprints.

NOTE

* Corresponding author; co-editor of 'The Greening of IT', Special Issue of the *Journal of Strategic Information Systems*, 20(1), March 2011: 3–79.

REFERENCES

Berthon, P., Hulbert, J., and Pitt, L. (2005). 'Consuming Technology: Why Marketers Get It Wrong', *California Management Review*, 48(1): 110–28.

Braungart, M., and McDonough, W. (2008). *Cradle to Cradle: Remaking the Way we Make Things*. London: Jonathan Cape.

Brundtland, G. H. (1987). *Our Common Future: Report of the World Commission on Environment and Development*. Oxford: Oxford University Press.

Carson, R. (1964). *Silent Spring*. New York: Houghton Mifflin.

Cuban, L. (2001). *Oversold and Underused: Computers in the Classroom*. Cambridge, MA: Harvard University Press.

Day, G. S. (1991). 'Learning about Markets. Report No. 91-117', Marketing Science Institute, Cambridge, MA.

Eilperin, J. (2009). 'Fewer Americans Believe in Global Warming, Poll Shows', *Washington Post*, 25 November: 1.

Elkington, J. (1998). *Cannibals with Forks: The Triple Bottom Line of 21st Century Business*. Gabriola Island, BC: New Society Publishers.

Forester Report (2009). *Global IT Market Outlook*. Forrester Research <http://www.forrester. com/rb/Research/global_it_market_outlook_2009/q/id/46676/t/2>.

Graedel, T. E., and Klee, R. J. (2002). 'Getting Serious about Sustainability', *Environmental Science and Technology*, 36: 523–9.

Grossman, E. (2006). *High Tech Trash: Digital Devices, Hidden Toxics, and Human Health*. Washington, DC: Shearwater.

Hart, S. L. (1997). 'Beyond Greening: Strategies for a Sustainable World', *Harvard Business Review*, 75(1): 66–76.

Hawken, P., Lovins, A. B., and Lovins, L. H. (1999). *Natural Capitalism: Creating the Next Industrial Revolution*. Boston, MA: Little, Brown & Co.

Hayes, B. (2009). 'Automation on the Job', *American Scientist*, 97(1): 34–40.

Heidegger, M. (1977). *The Question Concerning Technology, and Other Essays*. New York: Harper & Row.

Jackson, M. (2008). *Distracted: The Erosion of Attention and the Coming Dark Age*. New York: Prometheus Books.

Keim, B. (2009). 'Digital Overload Is Frying Our Brains', *Wired*, February 06: 43–7.

Laitner, J., and Ehrhardt-Martinez, K. (2008). 'Information and Communication Technologies: The Power of Productivity—How ICT Sectors are Driving Gains in Energy Productivity'. Report No. E081, American Council for an Energy Efficient Economy, February.

Lawrence, A. T., Weber, J. E., and Post, J. (2005). *Business & Society: Stakeholders, Ethics and Public Policy*. New York: McGraw Hill.

Malamud, O., and Pop-Eleches, C. (2008). 'The Effect of Computer Use on Child Outcomes', University of Chicago, Working Paper No. wp.08.12.

—— —— (forthcoming). 'Home Computer Use and the Development of Human Capital', *Quarterly Journal of Economics*.

Manjoo, F. (2008). *True Enough: Learning to Live in a Post-Fact Society*. New York: Wiley.

Marshall, J. D., and Toffel, M. W. (2005). 'Framing the Elusive Concept of Sustainability: A Sustainability Hierarchy', *Environmental & Scientific Technology*, 39(3): 673–82.

Miringoff, M. L., Miringoff, M.-L., and Opdycke, S. (1999). *The Social Health of the Nation: How America is Really Doing*. New York: Oxford University Press.

Nattrass, B., and Altomare, M. (1999). *The Natural Step for Business: Wealth, Ecology and the Evolutionary Corporation*. Gabriola Island, BC: New Society Publishers.

Olazabal, N. G. (2002). 'Banking the IT Paradox', *McKinsey Quarterly*, 1: 47–51.

Packard, V. (1960). 'Progress through Planned Obsolescence', in V. Packard, *The Waste Makers*. New York: Pocket, 45–57.

Price, A. (2008). *Slow-Tech: Manifesto for an Over-wound World*. New York: Atlantic.

Proctor, R. (1991). *Value-Free Science? Purity and Power in Modern Knowledge*. Cambridge, MA: Harvard University Press.

——(2001). 'Anti-Agate: The Great Diamond Hoax and the Semiprecious Stone Scam', *Configurations*, 9: 381–412.

Robertson, R. (2008). 'A Brighter Shade of Green: Rebooting Environmentalism for the 21st Century', *Wired*, June: 158–65.

Rosen, C. (2008). 'People of the Screen', *New Atlantis: Journal of Technology and Society*, Fall: 20–32.

Rosenstand, N. (1994). *The Moral of the Story: An Introduction to Questions of Ethics and Human Nature*. Mountain View, CA: Mayfield.

Rubery, J., Ward, K., Grimshaw, D., and Beynon, H. (2005). 'Working Time, Industrial Relations and the Employment Relationship', *Time & Society*, 14: 89–111.

Sellen, A., and Harper, R. (2001). *The Myth of the Paperless Office*. Boston, MA: MIT Press.

Sigman, A. (2009). 'Technology and Community', *Biologist*, January.

Slade, G. (2006). *Made to Break: Technology and Obsolescence in America*. Cambridge, MA: Harvard University Press.

Smith, G. R. (2004). 'How Green is Technology? The Paradox of Online Sustainable Education', *International Journal of Sustainable Development & World Ecology*, 11(3): 262–70.

Steffen, A. (2006). *Worldchanging: A User's Guide for the 21st Century*. New York: Abrams, Inc.

Thatcher, M., and Pingry, D. (2007). 'Modeling the IT Value Paradox', *Communications of the ACM*, 50(8): 41–52.

Toffler, A. (1970). *Future Shock*. New York: Random House.

Wackernagel, M., and Rees, W. (1996). *Ecological Footprint: Reducing Human Impact on the Earth*. Gabriola Island, BC: New Society Publishers.

Watson, R., Boudreau, M.-C., Chen, A., and Huber, M. (2008). 'Green IS: Building Sustainable Business Practices', The Global Text Project, <http://docs.globaltext.terry.uga.edu:8095/anonymous/webdav/Information%20Systems/Green%20IS.pdf>.

Weizsäcker, E. U. V., Lovins, A. B., and Lovins, L. H. (1997). *Factor Four: Doubling Wealth, Halving Resource Use: The New Report to the Club of Rome*. London: Earthscan.

CHAPTER 23

ETHICS AND ICT

SIMON ROGERSON

INTRODUCTION

INFORMATION has increasingly become the new lifeblood of society, its organizations and its peoples. The dawn of the Information Society offers huge potential benefits for us all. Our dependence on information grows daily with the advance of information and communication technologies (ICT) and its global application. ICT now influences the way we live, work, socialize, learn, interact, and relax. We expect the information on which we rely to be correct. The integrity of such information relies upon the development and operation of computer-based information systems. Those who undertake the planning, development, and operation of these information systems have obligations to assure information integrity and overall contribute to the public good (Rogerson 2001).

The Information Society can be a dangerous world. Indeed Johnson (1997) explains that the potential benefit of the Information Society is being devalued by antisocial behaviour such as unauthorized access, theft of electronic property, launching of viruses, racism, and harassment. Add to that list identity theft, spam, electronic snooping, and aggressive electronic marketing, and it is clear that this new society is not problem free (see also Chapter 17). Such issues raise new ethical, cultural, economic, and legal questions. It is questionable whether legal or technological counter-measures are and ever will be very effective in combating the ever changing antisocial behaviour in the Information Society. The absence of effective formal legal or technological controls presents grave dangers for us all (Rogerson 2004a). Even when controls are implemented the ICT has moved on and facilitated new ethical issues. In the absence of effective controls we must rely upon ethics coupled with education and awareness. The added advantage of this approach is that it not only addresses problematic issues within the Information Society but also promotes its positive attributes.

This chapter focuses on the ethical perspective of ICT, which will be termed *computer and information ethics* from now on in this chapter. The discussion starts with a brief look at the roots of computer and information ethics focusing on the work of Norbert Wiener. There then follows an overview of the many definitions of computer and information ethics where the aim is to illustrate the breadth of this multidisciplinary field. Having laid some foundations, the chapter turns to application. The section on practice considers two distinct issues. The first is how to embed an ethical perspective into information systems development and the second is to consider the nature of ICT professionalism within the Information Society. A series of Information Society challenges are then considered in turn. These include privacy, property, culture, and crime. The final substantive section looks at the future, paying particular attention to how ICT continually increases choice in global interaction within a dispersed community and between different and geographically distant communities (see also Chapter 24).

ROOTS

It may seem surprising but the roots of computer and information ethics are to be found in the mid-1940s. This foundation lay unappreciated for many decades and has only recently become widely accepted primarily through the scholarship of Terrell Ward Bynum (see e.g. Bynum 2004, 2008) who has undertaken a detailed analysis of the writings of Norbert Wiener. This section relies heavily upon Bynum's work as it is considered an appropriate interpretation of Wiener for today's Information Society.

Wiener was a professor of mathematics and engineering at MIT in the USA. He worked on electronic computer advances during the Second World War and with colleagues created a new branch of applied science called cybernetics. Through his work Wiener became aware of the huge social and ethical impacts this fledgling ICT would have. Bynum (2008) explains that Wiener 'predicted that after the War, the world would undergo a second industrial revolution—an *automatic age* with enormous potential for good and for evil that would generate a staggering number of new ethical challenges and opportunities'. Bynum's analysis shows that Wiener discussed a range of computer and information ethics related topics which are still very relevant today. These include computers and security, computers and unemployment, responsibilities of computer professionals, computers for persons with disabilities, computers and religion, information networks and globalization, virtual communities, teleworking, merging of human bodies with machines, robot ethics, and artificial intelligence. Wiener (1950) had the insight to see ICT in the context of fundamental human values such as access, freedom, happiness, health, knowledge, life, and opportunity. This concept of core human values has been developed further by Moor (1998) where he suggests this is the essential grounding for ethical judgement related to ICT. Bynum (2008) suggests that the metaphysical ideas and analytical methods that Wiener employed are so powerful and wide-ranging that they could help in identifying, analysing, and resolving social and ethical problems associated with all kinds of ICT.

These quotations from *The Human Use of Human Beings* (1950, 1954) illustrate the significance of Wiener's work to computer and information ethics. Wiener wrote, 'It is the thesis of this book that society can only be understood through a study of the messages and the communication facilities which belong to it; and that in the future . . . messages between man and machines, between machines and man, and between machine and machine, are destined to play an ever-increasing part' (1954: 16). 'To live effectively is to live with adequate information. Thus communication and control belong to the essence of man's inner life, even as they belong to his life in society' (1954: 18); ' . . . communications in society . . . are the cement which binds its fabric together' (1954: 27). Wiener warned, 'The choice of good and evil knocks at our door' (1954: 186).

The field of computer and information ethics is relatively new. 'It has existed only since the late 1940s when Norbert Wiener created it. During the first three decades, it grew very little because Wiener's insights were far ahead of everyone else's' (Bynum 2008). The start of a growing consciousness is illustrated by two important events. In 1976, Joseph Weizenbaum, the eminent MIT computer scientist, published his influential book *Computer Power and Human Reason* in which he examined the dangers of ICT and suggested that computers should never be allowed to make important decisions because computers will always lack human qualities such as wisdom and compassion. In October 1981 a group of concerned computer professionals from Xerox/PARC and Stanford University started to have meetings articulating concerns over the increasing role of computers in nuclear war and how the misuse of computers would increase the risk of nuclear war. They adopted the name 'Computer Professionals for Social Responsibility' (CPSR). During the next year other CPSR groups formed in other cities around the USA. Early in 1983 President Reagan announced plans for the Strategic Defence Initiative (SDI). CPSR's policy advice against SDI swelled its membership ranks. CPSR quickly addressed other issues of professional responsibility such as privacy and voting. CPSR is now an international organization with chapters in over thirty countries. 'In the past 25 years, information and computer ethics has grown exponentially in the industrialised world, and the rest of the world has begun to take notice' (Bynum 2008). In the next section definitions from some of the key players are considered.

DEFINITIONS

According to van Luijk (1994) ethics comprises both practice and reflection. Ethical practice is the conscious appeal to norms and values to which individuals are obliged to conform, whilst reflection on practice is the elaboration of norms and values that colour daily activity. Norms are collective expectations regarding a certain type of behaviour whilst values are collective representations of what constitutes a good society. The computer and information ethics field considers both practice and reflection related to the development and application of ICT within society. It is a field of contrasting views which reflect differences in both discipline and experience of those working in the field. Bynum and Rogerson (2004: 17–20) discuss five different definitions which have credibility and together have helped shape the field.

Maner's Definition

The name 'computer ethics' was not commonly used until the mid-1970s when Walter Maner (1980) began to use it. He defined this field of study as one that examines 'ethical problems aggravated, transformed or created by computer technology'. Some old ethical problems, he said, were made worse by computers, while others came into existence because of computer technology. Maner (1996) showed how the key characteristics of computers have led to a series of significant ethical challenges. He suggested that we should use traditional ethical theories of philosophers, such as the *utilitarian* ethics of the English philosophers Jeremy Bentham and John Stuart Mill, or the *rationalist* ethics of the German philosopher Immanuel Kant.

Johnson's Definition

In her book, *Computer Ethics* Deborah Johnson (1985) claims that computer ethics studies the way in which computers 'pose new versions of standard moral problems and moral dilemmas, exacerbating the old problems, and forcing us to apply ordinary moral norms in uncharted realms'. Like Maner before her, Johnson adopted the 'applied philosophy' approach of using procedures and concepts from utilitarianism and Kantianism. But, unlike Maner, she did not believe that computers create wholly new moral problems. Rather, she thought that computers gave a 'new twist' to ethical questions that were already well known. Johnson (2004) later argues that as ICT evolves it will become increasingly integrated into the human and natural world, and consequently new profound ethical issues will arise. Johnson (2004: 74) claims that, 'as we become more and more accustomed to acting with and through [ICT], the difference between ethics and computer [and information] ethics may well disappear'.

Moor's Definition

In his seminal paper 'What Is Computer Ethics?', James Moor (1985) provided a definition of computer ethics that is much broader and more wide-ranging than that of Maner or Johnson. It is independent of any specific philosopher's theory; and it is compatible with a wide variety of approaches to ethical problem solving. Since 1985,

Moor's definition has been the most influential one. He defined computer ethics as a field concerned with 'policy vacuums' and 'conceptual muddles' regarding the social and ethical use of information technology. Moor (1985: 266) wrote,

> A typical problem in Computer Ethics arises because there is a policy vacuum about how computer technology should be used. Computers provide us with new capabilities and these in turn give us new choices for action. Often, either no policies for conduct in these situations exist or existing policies seem inadequate. A central task of Computer Ethics is to determine what we should do in such cases, that is, formulate policies to guide our actions. . . . A difficulty is that along with a policy vacuum there is often a conceptual vacuum. Although a problem in Computer Ethics may seem clear initially, a little reflection reveals a conceptual muddle. What is needed in such cases is an analysis that provides a coherent conceptual framework within which to formulate a policy for action.

Moor (1985: 269) explained that computer technology is genuinely revolutionary because it is 'logically malleable':

> Computers are logically malleable in that they can be shaped and moulded to do any activity that can be characterised in terms of inputs, outputs and connecting logical operations. . . . Because logic applies everywhere, the potential applications of computer technology appear limitless. The computer is the nearest thing we have to a universal tool. Indeed, the limits of computers are largely the limits of our own creativity.

Bynum's Definition

In 1989 Terrell Ward Bynum developed another broad definition of computer ethics following a suggestion in Moor's 1985 paper. According to this view, computer ethics identifies and analyses the impacts of information technology on social and human values like health, wealth, work, opportunity, freedom, democracy, knowledge, privacy, security, and self-fulfilment. Solution generation is not covered by this definition. This very broad view of computer ethics employs applied ethics, sociology of computing, technology assessment, computer law, and related fields. It employs concepts, theories, and methodologies from these and other relevant disciplines. This conception of computer ethics is motivated by the belief that, eventually, information technology will profoundly affect everything that human beings hold dear.

Gotterbarn's Definition

In the 1990s, Donald Gotterbarn became a strong advocate for a different approach to computer ethics. From his perspective, computer ethics should be viewed as a branch of *professional ethics*, concerned primarily with standards of good practice and codes of conduct for computing professionals. Gotterbarn (1991) wrote:

'There is little attention paid to the domain of professional ethics—the values that guide the day-to-day activities of computing professionals in their role as professionals. By computing professional I mean anyone involved in the design and development of computer artefacts . . . The ethical decisions made during the development of these artefacts have a direct relationship to many of the issues discussed under the broader concept of computer ethics.

With this 'professional ethics' approach to computer ethics, Gotterbarn co-authored the 1992 version of the ACM Code of Ethics and Professional Conduct and led a team of scholars in the development of the 1999 ACM/IEEE Software Engineering Code of Ethics and Professional Practice.

A definition for ICT

Given these differing definitions it would be useful to derive a common definition which is applicable to the discussions in this chapter. Therefore computer and information ethics is defined as integrating ICT and human values in such a way that ICT advances and protects human values, rather than doing damage to them which therefore must include the formulation and justification of policies for the ethical use of ICT and carefully considered, transparent, and justified actions leading to ICT products and services.

This definition provides a foundation on which to build some clear guidance. ICT is a practical pursuit whose participants are significantly affected by ethically volatile situations (Rogerson, Weckert, and Simpson 2000). The practice element of ethics mentioned earlier manifests itself in methods and procedures adopted in the development of, for example, information systems, whereas the reflection element of ethics manifests itself in, for example, professional codes of conduct which are concerned with establishing what are the generalized ways of working that are acceptable to a wider community. These two elements are now considered in more detail.

PRACTICE

The ethical dimension of the ICT practice has two distinct elements: process and product. Process concerns the activities of ICT professionals when undertaking research, development, and service/product delivery. The ethical focus is professional conduct. It is this focus which is typically addressed by professional bodies in their codes of conduct. The aim is for professionals to be virtuous in Aristotelian terms. In other words a professional knows that an action is the right thing to do in the circumstances and does it for the right motive. For example, cutting profit so that more development time can be spent on making systems more accessible to those with limited ability, such as dexterity, is a virtuous action if it helps to overcome social exclusion. Process is considered in the professionalism section below.

Product concerns the outcome of professional ICT endeavour. One of the issues of ICT is to avoid systems being used for inappropriate secondary reasons, for example, a security system which has been implemented to reduce the risk of property theft being used additionally to monitor employee movement. Another issue is the thirst of the ICT industry to add more and more facilities in future system releases. Both issues are illustrations of unwarranted function creep. The emphasis should be on accessibility and transparency of information systems so people can use them more easily and can understand, where necessary, how such systems work internally. One final issue regarding product is to do with the increasing use of non-human agents based on complex systems. Such agents might interact with humans, for example, those used on the Internet to enable e-trading, or they might interact with each other, for example agents which monitor the environment and *order* other agents to take remedial action if necessary.

The ethics focus of the product element is technological integrity from, for example, a Kantian or utilitarian perspective. This can be addressed by embedding ethics within ICT products themselves. This might be as simple as building in 'opt-in' facilities in service provision via the Internet whereby a person must ask to be informed of future service offerings rather than having to request explicitly not to receive such informa-tion by default. They might be more complex, for example, whereby a non-human agent in telecare is programmed with defined ethical principles so that it will only instigate actions which are deemed to be societally acceptable. Product is considered in the development section below.

Development

ICT applications are about satisfying a particular requirement or need so that people can realize for example some economic and/or social and/or leisure objective. Consid-eration of stakeholders should not be limited to those who are financing the develop-ment project or politically influential or using the developed information system but broadened to be consistent with models of ethical analysis. Stakeholder must include individuals or groups who may be directly or indirectly affected by the information system and thus have a stake in the development activities. For example, the unelected political candidate due to a poor voting machine interface is a stakeholder in the development of an electronic voting system. Similarly, anyone who suffers identity theft through a security flaw in an information system is a stakeholder, albeit indirect, of that system (Gotterbarn, Clear, and Kwan 2008: 435). Those stakeholders who are negatively affected are particularly important regarding ethical sensitivity because they are often the ones overlooked.

Information systems developers must guard against the design principles where users must adapt to ICT rather than ICT being moulded to users. The Design for All (DfA) approach is a way forward. This is because DfA's perspective is one of individualism and acceptability (Stary 2001). Roe (2007: 1) explains that DfA is not a one-off effort but an ongoing and permanent commitment over the longer term so that throughout the design cycle of products and services the focus is always on ensuring use by the broadest possible section of the population. DfA principles must focus on understanding the potential impact on people. These people include those whose behaviour/work process will be affected by the development or delivery of ICT systems or whose circumstance/job will be affected by the development or delivery of ICT systems or whose experiences will be affected by the development or delivery of ICT systems (Gotterbarn and Rogerson 2005: 741). Such principles are found, for example, in advice for designing for the elderly which includes: putting users centre stage, respecting individuals' wishes, realizing needs change, integrating social care and healthcare (European Commission—Information Society and Media 2006: 6–7). However, it is important to recognize that identified needs are often difficult to turn into feasible and realistic design requirements and subsequent specifications (Roe 2007: 3). Roe (2007: 133) cites the example of smart homes which include devices and services that may have an impact on the privacy and the autonomy of users. Often these effects are deeply embedded in the technology used to develop them and cannot be removed when the system is finished. However, designers are predisposed to ignore these issues, due frequently to the lack of knowledge and supporting methodologies, guidelines, and tools. Therefore, Roe (2007: 200) argues that in order to prevent undesired ethical impacts, it is necessary to provide designers with ethical or moral guidelines. This is not a new call. For example, Gotterbarn (1992) suggests that professionals must be aware of their professional responsibilities, have available methods for resolving non-technical ethics questions, and develop proactive skills to reduce the likelihood of ethical problems occurring.

One such approach is the Software Development Impact Statement (SoDIS) process which belongs to the family of issues-oriented approaches (see e.g. Hirscheim and Klein 1989) used in information systems development. SoDIS takes a comprehensive stakeholder perspective of the whole development cycle through considering each development task within the structured/defined plan of the information system project (Gotterbarn and Rogerson 2005: 738) It expands existing information systems development quantitative risk analysis methods by explicitly addressing a range of qualitative and ethically grounded questions about the impacts of the information system from a stakeholder perspective. 'The use of qualitative best practice questions associates a full range of stakeholders with the [information system] project tasks providing a comprehensive risk analysis which helps identify social, professional and ethical risks for a project. SoDIS is the first fully-developed approach of this kind. It points the way to achieving successful [information system] development . . .' (Gotterbarn and Rogerson 2005: 746). As Gotterbarn, Clear, and Kwan (2008: 442) explain, 'The process of developing a SoDIS requires the consideration of ethical development and the ethical impacts of [an information system] product. The SoDIS analysis process also facilitates the identification of new requirements or tasks that can be used as a means to address the ethical issues.' It is this type of explicit ethical consideration from a stakeholder perspective which will reduce the risk of information system failure during implementation and/or operation. It will increase the chance of fit for purpose systems which are acceptable and adopted.

Professionalism

ICT professionals have specialized knowledge and often have positions with authority and respect in the community. Their professional activity spans the management, development, and operation of all kinds of applications. For this reason, they are able to have a significant impact upon the world, including many of the things that people value. Along with such power to change the world comes the duty to exercise that power in a socially responsible manner. Six social responsibility principles (Rogerson 2004b) establish an ethos of professionalism within ICT. These principles are as follows:

- Develop a socially responsible culture within work which nurtures moral individual action
- Consider and support the well-being of all stakeholders
- Account for global common values and local cultural differences
- Recognize social responsibility is beyond legal compliance and effective fiscal management
- Ensure all business processes are considered from a social responsibility perspective
- Be proactive rather than reactive.

Adherence to such principles can be problematic because of ICT professional relationships. ICT professionals find themselves in a variety of professional relationships with other people (Johnson 1994), including: employer-to-employee; client-to-professional; professional-to-professional; and society-to-professional. These relationships involve a diversity of interests, and sometimes these interests can come into conflict with each other. Socially responsible ICT professionals, therefore, have to be aware of possible conflicts of interest and try to avoid them thereby adhering to the six principles. In line with the six social responsibility general principles, specific guidance has been provided in the codes of conduct of professional bodies such as the British Computer Society (BCS), the Institute for the Management of Information Systems (IMIS), the Australian Computer Society (ACS), the Association of Computing Machinery (ACM), and the influential Software Engineering Code of Ethics and Professional Practice (Gotterbarn, Miller and Rogerson 1999). In addition to such codes, professional bodies have established curriculum guidelines and accreditation requirements to help ICT professionals understand and manage ethical responsibilities.

This is because there are many ethical issues surrounding the decisions and actions within the information systems field and there are limitations on professional time to respond to such issues. An ICT professional educated in ethical responsibilities will be better placed to respond in a socially responsible manner. It is important to prioritize these issues on the basis of impact on the public good and so focus effort on the ethical hotspots (Rogerson 1997). It is some of these issues which are now considered in the remaining sections of this chapter.

SOME CHALLENGES

Privacy

Privacy is one of the earliest computer and information ethics issues to capture public interest both across Europe and in the USA from the mid-1960s onwards. It continues to be a hot topic because privacy is a fundamental right of individuals and is an essential condition for the exercise in self-determination and the advances in technology have facilitated more incursions into privacy. Much has been written about privacy as it relates to ICT. Before ICT, privacy primarily referred to non-intrusion and non-interference but that has now changed. There are those who propose that privacy is about control over personal information (see e.g. Westin 1967; Miller 1971; Fried 1984; Elgesem 1996). This is countered by an argument that control of personal information is insufficient to establish or protect privacy and that privacy is best defined in terms of restricted access rather than control (Tavani and Moor 2001). Privacy even extends to our presence in public spaces or circumstances (Nissenbaum 1998) with the advent of, for example, CCTV, electronic voting, and government-operated data matching. The ability to restrict access to or control personal information is certainly an important factor in sustaining privacy. Collste (2008) argues that the right to privacy exists, albeit in varying degrees, across cultures as it is seen as an instrument for sustaining autonomy, freedom, and personal relationships.

Organizations are increasingly computerizing the processing of personal information. This may be without the consent or knowledge of the individuals concerned. There has been a growth in databases holding personal and other sensitive information in multiple formats of text, pictures, and sound. The scale and type of data collected and the scale and speed of data exchange have changed with the advent of computers. The potential to breach people's privacy at less cost and to greater advantage continues to increase. It is situations like this that have led to a growing unwillingness to submit personal data to information systems. Furthermore, there is growing public discernment and demand for evaluation of ICT trustworthiness (Camp, McGrath, and Nissenbaum 2001).

ICT privacy is a new twist on an old ethical problem, as Johnson (1985) would put it, and involves issues not previously raised or that cannot be predicted. For example, advances in genetic data have led to some interesting ethical questions as it can accurately define genetic relatives and thus establish hereditary traits and diseases. Individuals have certain rights to how and where that information is distributed but in order to exercise those rights they will undoubtedly learn of their genetic profiles and that is the new twist. Knowledge of one's genetic profile will undoubtedly affect the individual's self-perception, self-esteem, and lifestyle. Thus privacy in this situation must also include an individual's right not to know.

Balancing the rights and interests of different parties in a free society is difficult. The acceptable balance will be specific to the context of a particular relationship and will be dependent upon trust between concerned parties and subscription to the principle of informed consent. This balance might incur the problem of protecting individual privacy while satisfying government and business needs. For example, a social services department might hold sensitive information about individuals that provides an accurate profile of individual tendencies, convictions, and so on. The sharing of these data with, for example, the local education authority in cases of child sex offenders living in the area might be considered morally justified even though it might breach individual privacy. Furthermore, once personal information is digitized and entered into a computer on a network the information becomes *greased data* that can easily slip across networks and into many different computers (Moor 1997). It leaves data shadows across the whole network. As a result, personal information may no longer be controlled and people may have unauthorized access to it. Unlike ordinary shadows, our data shadows remain long after (and often permanently after) we have passed through the network of conduits in the Information Society. Such problems are indicative of the Information Society, where it is the norm to hold electronic personal information about health, lifestyle, finance, buying habits, relationships, ethnicity, gender, religion, genetic make-up, and much more.

Property

Ownership is having control of one's property with the right to use it and the right to decide whether and how others can use it. Ownership extends to intellectual property which includes, for example, stories, poems, drawings, watercolour paintings, musical recordings, paintings, photographs, computer programs, films, and television programmes. Most forms of intellectual property can now have digital forms. Thus intellectual property ownership is an important computer and information ethics topic. At least four theories can be used when considering intellectual property rights. Locke's theory of labour argues that a person who mixes his/her labour with resources that are not owned by others, and thereby creates a product, has gained the right to own and control the resulting product. Hegel's theory of personality argues that intellectual property is an expression or extension of the creator's personality and therefore the creator has the right to control it. Utilitarian theory of ownership argues that property rights should be recognized, promoted, and protected as they provide incentives for creative people to generate a continuous flow of new creations, which in turn will contribute to the greatest happiness for the greatest number of people. Finally, social contract theory views ownership as a social agreement whereby the community agrees to pass laws and create conditions that are conducive to property ownership and in return owners agree to use their property in ways that society consider appropriate.

Software ownership continues to be controversial. Johnson (1994) argues that a utilitarian framework is best for analysing software intellectual property rights because it puts the focus on deciding ownership in terms of affecting continued creativity and development of software. She argues that software developers would not invest the necessary time and significant funds if they could not get the investment back in the form of licence fees or sales of software. In contrast, Stallman (1992) claims that current forms of software ownership are unjust and immoral, inflict many kinds of harm on society, and should be eliminated. Using utilitarian theory of ownership he concludes that current laws restrict and discourage creativity and invention and therefore should be abandoned in favour of free software. Stallman's position led to the open source movement. These two opposing positions are described by de Laat (2005) as the private regime and public regime. The private regime is based on exclusion of outsiders. Organizations use secrecy, copyright, and patents to protect their intellectual properties from imitation and theft by others. The public regime is based upon property rights being used to include others through open source licences and regulated commons where intellectual property is freely exchanged and discussed.

Copies of digital intellectual property are identical to the originals. Owners of intellectual property can easily find they are unable to sell, lease, or rent their property, thereby making a profit, because of the ease and trivial cost of creating digital copies which can then be easily distributed and sold cheaply or even disseminated for free as was the case with Napster music file swapping and Morpheus movie swapping. This latter case of peer-to-peer software has been ethically scrutinized by Spinello (2005). He argues that those who provide peer-to-peer software are accomplices in wrongdoing if they deliberately design their software to enable illicit copying of copyrighted music and movie files.

Overall, where software contains ideas and knowledge that can benefit society as a whole, clashes can occur between the owner, who has the right to exploit the product commercially, and society which has a general right to access and benefit from it. An equitable balance must be found that takes into account these competing rights. From an ethical perspective there are two fundamental questions that summarize this debate and that need to be answered regarding software. Who owns the software? Who has the right to modify, distribute, or use it?

Culture

Culture can be defined as the totality of shared meanings and interpretations of a given group or community. Groups or communities can align with, for example, countries or geographical regions, faiths, political ideologies, organizations, or social interests. They can be physically or virtually constructed. Cultures possess a normative element which lays out how things ought to be and how community members are expected to behave. These norms are the culture's ethics from which implicit cultural values can be derived (Stahl, Rogerson, and Kashmeery 2007). Common core values do exist that we all share such as life, happiness, ability, freedom, knowledge, resources, and protection (Moor 1998). It is this which enables alignments among differing cultural traditions to prevail which Hongladarom and Ess (2007) term harmonies. For instance, it is an ethical harmony that Collste (2008) is drawing upon when he suggests that privacy exists in all cultures but that they might differ when it comes to the question of how to balance a right to privacy against other social goods. In some cultures privacy is given more weight, in others less.

Everyone belongs to one or more cultural communities and so, as Hongladarom and Ess (2007) point out, it is impossible to consider ICT from a culturally neutral perspective. For example, Brey (2006) describes a positive view of the Internet from a libertarian ideology which is in marked contrast with the negative view he describes from the perspective of Orthodox Judaism. This cultural variability has been explored by Nance and Strohmaier (1994). They suggest there are two important dimensions to consider regarding cultural variability. The first dimension is the continuum from individualism to collectivism. Individualism emphasizes self-interest and promotes the self-realization of talent and potential. Its demands are universal. Collectivism emphasizes pursuit of common interests and belonging to a set of hierarchical groups where, for example, the family group might be placed above the job group. The demands on group members are different to those on non-group members. The second dimension concerns cultural differences in communication referred to as low context communication and high context communication. In the former the majority of the information resides in the message itself whilst in the latter the communication is implicit. Nance and Strohmaier (1994) suggest that the USA utilizes low-context communication whilst Japan uses high context. So even with a shift towards cultural homogenization through ICT usage, the variability that remains makes it very challenging to provide information or conduct a debate in a way that is acceptable to all (Fairweather and Rogerson 2003). It involves establishing a set of common behavioural standards whilst ensuring that there is no dominant participant. The current Internet seems a long distance from this position.

It is clear from this discussion that computer and information ethics must embrace a cultural perspective. The cultural groups and communities we live in are characterized by their relationship to ICT. Terms such as Information Society and Global Village are indicative of our awareness of the importance of ICT on our cultures (Stahl, Rogerson, and Kashmeery 2007). For example, on the one hand ICT enables social institutions to function whilst on the other hand social institutions accepts the use and development of ICT in their midst. There is a two-way relationship between ICT and culture in which ICT must be adaptable to culture and culture must be tolerant of ICT. The social and cultural consequences of ICT must be considered within this relationship. Brey (2006) suggests that there are three ways to change the social and cultural consequences of ICT: technological delegation which involves ICT redesign to realize a different outcome, structuration which changes the social context in which ICT is used, and signification which changes the way ICT is described, presented, and understood. An ICT professional primarily impacts the first, might impact the third, but has little influence on the second.

Those working in ICT must be culturally and ethically sensitive as well as having the moral desire to deliver ICT products and services are culturally acceptable either through the ethical harmonies of Hongladarom and Ess (2007) or Brey's cultural adaptability (Brey 2006). Whichever way it is achieved it is clear that an ICT-dependent Information Society must be tolerant of the global moral pluralism (Vedder 2001). This has yet to be covered explicitly in professional practice guidelines.

Crime

As ICT becomes more widely used and is used in more domains, the risk of misuse increases and the detrimental impacts of such acts are likely to be greater for society, organizations, and individuals. The laws around the world have struggled to address these new forms of criminal activity. It is a classic Moorian policy vacuum which is slowly being addressed. The Convention on Cybercrime is the first international treaty seeking to address ICT-related crime. It was drawn up by the Council of Europe (2001) in cooperation with Canada, Japan, and the USA, and adopted on 8 November 2001. The Convention lays out a framework within which ICT-related crime can be addressed. This framework is summarized as:

> Offences against the confidentiality, integrity and availability of computer data and information systems

Illegal access
Illegal interception
Data interference
System interference
Misuse of devices
Computer-related offences
Computer-related forgery
Computer-related fraud
Content-related offences

Offences related to child pornography
Offences related to infringements of property ownership
Offences related to infringements of copyright and related rights.

The framework provides good coverage but there are some omissions. For example, under content-related offences, it is unclear why all pornography or content which incites hatred are not included. Nevertheless, it is possible to categorize most of incidents of ICT misuse. The Parliamentary Office of Science and Technology (2006) suggests there are two types of incidents: old crimes conducted using computers as a tool and new types of crime made possible by specific types of ICT. Examples of old crimes are storage of illegal images on a hard disk instead of in print, harassment using mobile telephones, illegal downloads of music, and confidence tricks involving spoof emails and fraudulent websites to acquire sensitive information known as phishing. Examples of new crimes are denial of service attacks which prevent ICT resources being available to intended users, gaining unauthorized access to an ICT system through hacking, and releasing a virus to delete stored data.

Whilst ICT-related crime is a legal consideration it is also an ethical consideration. In creating laws account must be taken of civil liberties. This is particularly important within the Information Society. There are civil liberties concerns about the Convention on Cybercrime. For example, the treaty allows information to be exchanged between all the national governments signing up to the treaty thus creating seamless monitoring of activities using electronic networks across Europe. The treaty's common approach fails to take into account cultural differences. An act deemed criminal in the country of the target of the crime may not be considered so in the country from which the offending act was launched. For example, the attitude towards nudity is different across cultures and this has led to different legal positions on the availability of images of nudes over the Internet.

Spinello (1995) argues that organizations and individuals are ethically obliged to protect the systems and information entrusted to their care and must strive to prevent or minimize the impact of computer misuse incidents. He suggests that those stakeholders at greatest risk from a computer misuse incident might be party to decisions made concerning security arrangements. He argues that computer misuse offences should not be treated lightly, even if the detrimental outcome is negligible, because, at the very least, valuable resources will have been squandered and property rights violated. Spinello also points out that a balance has to be struck regarding stringent security measures and respect for civil liberties. Threats to business and personal computers and information assets are an everyday menace. It is essential that organizations and individual users identify the vulnerabilities and plan for corrective action to thwart these threats. Indeed, there is a dual responsibility regarding computer misuse. Organizations have a duty to minimize the temptation of perpetrating computer misuse whilst individuals have a responsibility to resist such temptations. ICT professionals have a responsibility not to facilitate computer crime. For example, it is unacceptable to use programming languages which easily allow buffer overloading because this is the most common way to break into computer systems and commit offences against confidentiality and integrity.

THE FUTURE

Those who have tried to forecast the next technological advances are usually incorrect. ICT has a track record of unpredictability in the specific nature and consequent impact of these future advances. The only certain thing is that there will always be significant advances and these will always impact upon society and its people. For this reason the ethical input from the onset of ICT development is essential. Consider just three views of the future.

Vaughn (2006: 8–14) suggests that there are four key ICT trends; ever-increasing computational power plus decreasing size and cost; technology advances enabling new types of interfaces; ability to be connected anywhere, anytime with services on demand; and creation of virtual places, service providers, and products. These general trends can be seen in the topics of new developments and dramatic inputs discussed by Baase (2009: 20–37) which include amateur creative works using blogs and video sharing; human connections through email, cell phones, and social networking; collaborative efforts among strangers using wikis; artificial intelligence, robotics, and motion sensing; tools for people with disability; and finally wearable and invasive ICT. The FP7 European funded project, ETICA looks at ICT in ten to fifteen years's time in an attempt to identify the ethical issues in advance. The landscape of ICT looks very different with the following advances suggested: concurrent terra-device computing; quantum information foundations and technologies; bio-chemistry-based ICT; human-computer confluence; self-awareness in autonomous systems; molecular-scale devices and systems; and, finally, brain-inspired ICT which focuses on how the brain processes information and/or how it communicates with the peripheral nervous system, and to explore potential ICT applications of this (Stahl and Rogerson 2009).

Two broad issues which are likely to continue to impact on the peoples of the world are ICT in the context of globalization and ICT in the context of inclusion.

Global

One of the biggest changes to occur with the advent of ubiquitous ICT is the arrival of what is often called the global village. Indeed Moor (1998) explains that 'The prospects of a global village in which everyone on the planet is connected to everyone else with regard to computing power and communication is breathtaking. What is difficult to comprehend is what impact this will have on human life. Surely some of the effects will be quite positive and others quite negative.' Once people had to go to a particular place in order to communicate but now communication comes to people. Through such communication the global village has a global reach but yet must still be locally sensitive if it is to be an acceptable space, albeit virtual space, in which to exist.

Traditional borders and barriers between countries have now become less meaningful because people and organizations in most countries are interconnected by the Internet. Different kinds of social processes occur which are neither locally limited nor territorially limited (Collste 2008). For this reason, individuals, companies, and organizations in every culture can engage in global business transactions, distance education, remote employment, on-line discussions of social and political issues, sharing and debating of values and perspectives. The question is whether this global dialogue brings about better understanding between peoples and cultures resulting in new shared values and goals or new national and international laws and policies. Some argue that the individual cultures will become diluted, leaving a global homogenized society. Others argue that the global heterogeneous demography will remain. If so it is likely that the remaining cultural diversity will result in great national differences which in turn lead to variability in ICT acceptance (Roe 2007). This is problematic for on-line infrastructures such as the Internet as there is a tendency towards a one-service provision which is culturally neutral. Consider these three examples related to publication, commerce, and medicine.

Publication. If sexually explicit materials are provided on a website in a culture in which they are permitted, and then they are accessed by someone in a different culture where such materials are outlawed as obscene, whose laws and values should apply? Should the offending person in the first culture be extradited to the second culture and prosecuted there as a purveyor of pornography? Should the values of the first culture be permitted to undermine those of the second culture via the Internet? How can such cultural clashes be reasonably resolved? One suggestion that is sometimes offered to help avoid or resolve cultural clashes on the Internet is to avoid doing anything that might offend someone—to be sensitive to the values and beliefs of cultures other than one's own. But how does one know what could be offensive to others? Almost anything could offend somebody somewhere; so does this mean that we should simply stop using the Internet?

Commerce. When people in one country purchase goods and services from vendors in another country, who should regulate or tax the transactions? Will electronic commerce in a global market detrimentally affect local business or local tax collections? What new laws, regulations, rules, practices should be adopted, and who should create or enforce them? How will global electronic commerce affect the gap between rich nations and poor nations? Will that gap get even wider? Will the Internet lead to a new form of colonialism in which the information rich hold power over the information poor? (See also Chapter 24.)

Medicine. Medical advice and psychological counselling on the Internet, keyhole surgery conducted at a distance, medical tests and examinations over the net, on-line prescriptions for medicine written by doctors in one part of the world for patients in other parts of the world are just a few of the medical services and activities that already exist via the Internet. How safe is on-line medicine? Who will have access to sensitive information held in electronic patient records? Who should regulate, license, and control cyber medicine?

These global issues demand global ethical consideration. For the first time in history, efforts to develop mutually agreed standards of conduct, and efforts to advance and defend human values, are being made in a truly global context (Gorniak-Kocikowska 1996). Ethics and values will be debated and transformed in a context that is not limited to a particular geographic region, or constrained by a specific religion or culture. This may very well be one of the most important social developments in history. Indeed Collste (2008: 76) argues,

> When societies exist isolated from each other, they will develop different moral standards. However, when there is interaction between individuals belonging to different societies one can . . . expect an interchange of moral norms and values . . . With increasing interactions of individuals belonging to different societies one can expect a convergence of moral standards in the direction towards universal values.

Inclusion

Specific attention needs to be given to those groups in society that are at high risk of being excluded, due to a wide variety of reasons such as location, age, gender, disability, literacy, and culture (European Commission—Information Society and Media 2006). Despite the many new opportunities for improvement in the daily lives of individuals with disabilities, including work, education, travel, entertainment, healthcare, and independent living, there is a risk that ICT could set people apart, create new barriers, and increase social exclusion. Indeed, ICT advances can pose new barriers to people with disabilities, including loss of access to products they had access to before the advances in technology (Vaughn 2006: 21–36). For example, the advent of electronic hand-held readers for books is changing the process of publication and could result in inaccessibility of books and other printed material by those people without a suitable reader. Whilst ICT means for many of us increased comfort and improved functioning, the same issues can mean for disadvantaged people the difference between dependency and autonomous living (Roe 2007: 188). For example, the advances in Internet shopping with facilities to buy and arrange delivery of groceries might lead to both fewer supermarkets and increased prices in shops, both of which have a greater impact on poorer members of society than on richer ones.

Computer and information ethics demands we look beyond legal compliance to moral requirements when planning, developing, and implementing ICT systems. This is particularly so regarding e-inclusion. Törenli (2006: 435) argues that if the utilization of ICT opportunities in disadvantaged groups is left purely to time or market forces, e-exclusion will continue to increase rapidly. Indeed he points out that market-led ICT strategies take too little account of the plight of the disadvantaged groups (Törenli

2006: 452). He suggests that under these conditions the problems caused by the present inequalities in society would reach new proportions. Warren (2007) discusses this in relation to those living in rural areas and their access to the Internet. He argues that 'The Internet is becoming embedded in society so rapidly that it is becoming a default medium for anyone wishing to provide information, to perform transactions, to create civic engagement' (2007: 385). There is an increasing cost-effectiveness of producing information only in electronic form. Those without access to the Internet, or intermittent access while travelling, will be penalized and indeed excluded as more and more information, which is essential to our lives, is available only via the Internet. Warren (2007) explains that the Internet offers significant benefits for rural dwellers in that it helps to overcome the barriers of distance and social dispersion. Therefore, he argues that the loss for those without Internet access in rural areas is greater than for those in urban areas.

And Finally . . .

In the Information Society individuals are subjected to e-junkmail, e-money, e-commerce, e-library, e-identity, e-education to mention but a few. Whether these are beneficial depends on a number of factors, some of which have been discussed here. An Information Society that empowers everyone including those with disabilities and less fortunate members of society, and sustains equality of opportunity regardless of race, colour, or creed is achievable. Governments, policy makers, developers, and service providers of the Information Society, have the wherewithal to balance global common values and local cultural differences. They must have the commitment as well, else apocalypse beckons.

REFERENCES

Baase, S. (2009). *A Gift of Fire: Social, Legal and Ethical Issues for Computing and the Internet*, 3rd edn. New York: Pearson Education.

Brey, P. (2006). 'Evaluating the Social and Cultural Implications of the Internet', *Computers and Society*, 36(3): 41–8.

Bynum, T. W. (2004). 'Ethical Challenges to Citizens of "The Automatic Age": Norbert Wiener on the Information Society', *Journal of Information, Communication and Ethics in Society*, 2(2): 65–74.

——(2008). 'Computer and Information Ethics', in Edward N. Zalta (ed.), *The Stanford Encyclopedia of Philosophy* (Winter edn.), accessed at <http://plato.stanford.edu/archives/win2008/entries/ethics-computer/> on 5 April 2009.

——and Rogerson, S. (eds.) (2004). *Computer Ethics and Professional Responsibility*. Oxford: Blackwell Publishing.

Camp, J., McGrath, C., and Nissenbaum, H. (2001). 'Trust: A Collision of Paradigms', Faculty Research Working Papers Series, John F. Kennedy School of Government, Harvard University, Cambridge, MA.

Collste, G. (2008). 'Global ICT-ethics: The Case of Privacy', *Journal of Information, Communication and Ethics in Society*, 6(1): 76–87.

Council of Europe (2001) ETS No. 185—Convention on Cybercrime, <http://conventions.coe.int/Treaty/EN/Treaties/Html/185.htm>, accessed 26 April 2009.

de Laat, P. B. (2005). 'Copyright or Copyleft? An Analysis of Property Regimes for Software Development', *Research Policy*, 34(10): 1511–32.

Elgesem, D. (1996), 'Privacy, Respect for Persons, and Risk', in C. Ess (ed.), *Philosophical Perspectives on Computer-Mediated Communication*. Albany, NY: SUNY Press, 45–66.

European Commission—Information Society and Media (2006). *Information Society and Inclusion: Linking European Policies*. Brussels: European Communities.

Fairweather, N. B., and Rogerson, S. (2003). 'The Problems of Global Cultural Homogenisation in a Technologically Dependent World', *Information, Communication & Ethics in Society*, 1(1): 7–12.

Fried, C. (1984). 'Privacy', in F. D. Schoeman (ed.), *Philosophical Dimensions of Privacy*. Cambridge: Cambridge University Press, 203–22.

Gorniak-Kocikowska, K. (1996). 'The Computer Revolution and the Problem of Global Ethics', *Science and Engineering Ethics*, 2(2): 177–90.

Gotterbarn, D. (1991). 'Computer Ethics: Responsibility Regained', *National Forum: The Phi Beta Kappa Journal*, 71: 26–31.

——(1992). 'The Use and Abuse of Computer Ethics', *Journal of Systems and Software*, 17: 75–80; reprinted in J. Weckert (2007) *Computer Ethics*. Aldershot: Ashgate, 57–62.

——Clear, T., and Kwan, C. (2008). 'A Practical Mechanism for Ethical Risk Assessment: A SoDIS Inspection', in K. E. Himma and H. T. Tavani (eds.), *The Handbook of Information and Computer Ethics*. New York: John Wiley & Son.

——Miller, K., and Rogerson, S. (1999). 'Software Engineering Code of Ethics is Approved', *Communications of the ACM*, 42(10): 102–7.

——and Rogerson, S. (2005). 'Next Generation Software Development: Responsible Risk Analysis Using SoDIS', *Communications of the Association for Information Systems*, 15 (May): 730–50, <http://aisel.aisnet.org/cgi/viewcontent.cgi?article=3162&context=cais>.

Hirschheim, R., and Klein, H. (1989). 'Four Paradigms of Information Systems Development', *Communications of the ACM*, 33(10): 1199–216.

Hongladarom, S., and Ess, C. (eds.) (2007). *Information Technology Ethics: Cultural Perspectives*. Hershey, PA: Idea Group Inc.

Johnson, D. G. (1985). *Computer Ethics*. Englewood Cliffs, NJ: Prentice-Hall (2nd edn. 1994, 3rd edn. 2000, 4th edn. 2009).

——(1994). *Computer Ethics*, 2nd edn. Englewood Cliffs, NJ: Prentice-Hall.

——(1997). 'Ethics Online', *Communications of the ACM*, 40(1): 60–5.

——(2004). 'Computer Ethics', in L. Floridi (ed.), *Philosophy of Computing and Information*. Oxford: Blackwell Publishing, 65–75.

Maner, W. (1980). *Starter Kit in Computer Ethics*. Zurich: Helvetia Press (published in cooperation with the National Information and Resource Center for Teaching Philosophy) (originally self-published by Maner in 1978).

——(1996). 'Unique Ethical Problems in Information Technology', *Science and Engineering Ethics*, 2(2): 137–54.

Miller, A. (1971). *The Assault on Privacy: Computers, Data Banks, and Dossiers.* Ann Arbor, MI: University of Michigan Press.

Moor, J. H. (1985). 'What Is Computer Ethics?', *Metaphilosophy*, 16(4): 266–75.

—— (1997), 'Towards a Theory of Privacy in the Information Age', *Computers and Society*, 27 (3): 27–32.

—— (1998). 'Reason, Relativity, and Responsibility in Computer Ethics', *Computers and Society*, 28(1): 14–21.

Nance, K. L., and Strohmaier, M. (1994). 'Ethical Accountability in the Cyberspace', *Ethics in the Computer Age.* Gatlinburg, TN: ACM, 115–18.

Nissenbaum, H. (1998). 'Protecting Privacy in an Information Age: The Problem of Privacy in Public', *Law and Philosophy*, 17: 559–96.

Parliamentary Office of Science and Technology (2006). 'Computer Crime', *Postnote*, October (271).

Roe, P. R. (ed.) (2007). *Towards an Inclusive Future: Impact and Wider Potential of Information and Communication Technologies*, a COST 219ter Report. Brussels: COST.

Rogerson, S. (1997). 'Software Project Management Ethics', in C. Myers, T. Hall, and D. Pitt (eds.), *The Responsible Software Engineer.* Berlin: Springer-Verlag, 100–6.

—— (2001). 'A Practical Perspective of Information Ethics', in P. Goujon and B. H. Dubreuil (eds.), *Technology and Ethics: A European Quest for Responsible Engineering.* Leuven: Peeters, 305–25.

—— (2004a). 'The Virtual World: A Tension between Global Reach and Local Sensitivity', *International Journal of Information Ethics*, November, 2(002-01), <http://www.i-r-i-e.net/inhalt/002/ijie_002_22_rogerson.pdf>, accessed 5 April 2009.

—— (2004b). 'Aspects of Social Responsibility in the Information Society', in G. I. Doukidis, N. A. Mylonopoulos, and A. Pouloudi (eds.), *Social and Economic Transformation in the Digital Era.* Hershey, PA: IDEA Group Publishing, 31–46.

—— Weckert, J., and Simpson, C. (2000). 'An Ethical Review of Information Systems Development: The Australian Computer Society's Code of Ethics and SSADM', *Information Technology and People*, 13(2): 121–36.

Spinello, R. A. (1995). *Ethical Aspects of Information Technology.* Englewood Cliffs, NJ: Prentice-Hall.

—— (2005). 'Secondary Liability in the Post Napster Era: Ethical Observations on MGM v. Grokster', *Journal of Information, Communication and Ethics in Society*, 3(3): 121–30.

Stahl, B. C., and Rogerson, S. (2009). 'Landscapes of Ethical Issues of Emerging ICT Applications in Europe', *CEPE (Computer Ethics Philosophical Enquiry) 2009.* Corfu: Ionian University, 26–8 June.

—— —— and Kashmeery, A. (2007). 'Current and Future State of ICT Deployment and Utilisation in Healthcare: An Analysis of Cross-cultural Ethical Issues', in S. Hongladarom and C. Ess (eds.), *Information Technology Ethics: Cultural Perspectives.* Hershey, PA: Idea Group Inc., 169–83.

Stallman, R. (1992). 'Why Software should be Free', in T. W. Bynum, W. Maner, and J. L. Fodor (eds.), *Software Ownership and Intellectual Property Rights.* New Haven, CT: Research Center on Computing and Society, Southern Connecticut State University, 35–52.

Stary, C. (2001). 'User Diversity and Design Representation: Towards Increased Effectiveness in Design for All', *Universal Access in the Information Society*, 1(1): 16–30.

Tavani, H. T., and Moor, J. H. (2001). 'Privacy Protection, Control of Information, and Privacy-Enhancing Technologies', in R. A. Spinello and H. T. Tavani (eds.), *Readings in CyberEthics*. Sudbury, MA: Jones & Bartlett, 378–91.

Törenli, N. (2006). 'The "Other" Faces of Digital Exclusion: ICT Gender Divides in the Broader Community', *European Journal of Communication*, 21: 435–55.

van Luijk, H. (1994). 'Business Ethics: The Field and its Importance', in B. Harvey (ed.), *Business Ethics: A European Approach*. Englewood Cliffs, NJ: Prentice Hall.

Vaughn, J. R. (2006). *Over the Horizon: Potential Impact of Emerging Trends in Information and Communication Technology on Disability Policy and Practice*. Washington, DC: National Council on Disability.

Vedder, A. (2001). 'Misinformation through the Internet', *ETHICOMP 2001 Conference Proceedings*, 2: 35–41.

Warren, M. F. (2007). 'The Digital Vicious Cycle: Links between Social Disadvantage and Digital Exclusion in Rural Areas', *Telecommunications Policy*, 31(6–7): 374–88.

Westin, A. (1967). *Privacy and Freedom*. New York: Atheneum.

Wiener, N. (1950, 1954). *The Human Use of Human Beings: Cybernetics and Society*. Boston, MA: Houghton Mifflin, (2nd edn. rev. 1954).

CHAPTER 24

IT, GLOBALIZATION, AND HUMAN DEVELOPMENT: A PERSONAL VIEW

GEOFF WALSHAM

INTRODUCTION

THIS chapter addresses the relationship between IT, globalization, and human development, and discusses how IS research can inform our understanding of this relationship. The topic area is of such wide scope that it could be considered impossible to say anything meaningful in the limited space of a book chapter. However, I have included the phrase 'a personal view' in the chapter title to emphasize that no attempt will be made here to survey in any depth the massive literature on concepts such as globalization and development. The chapter will try, instead, to condense some of my own thoughts on the broad topic area, using a relatively limited set of literature to support my arguments, and drawing on some of my earlier publications (Walsham 2001, 2005a, 2005b).

The term globalization has achieved the unusual status, in a relatively short time, of becoming fashionable in academic debates in the social sciences, in the business world, and to some extent in the popular media. However, even a cursory examination of these sources would demonstrate that the term is highly ambiguous, and that it masks a wide variety of opinions on what is happening in the world. Most writers on the subject would agree that information and communication technologies are of crucial importance to globalization processes, but again there is no clear consensus on the precise nature of this connection.

The next section of the chapter will summarize some key literature on globalization through the eyes of various well-known scholars of the contemporary world. Whilst their analyses are not the same, all of them argue the need for increasing reflection and changed action in order to make a better world or, to put it another way, to support human development in its broadest sense. I will follow the material on globalization with a brief discussion of 'human development' arguing that this is needed by all people and countries, not just by the developing countries. But what can IS researchers offer to this broad agenda? The argument will be made that IS researchers can contribute by addressing their research explicitly to issues of human development through a critical approach, and the rest of the chapter will be devoted to the question of how to go about doing this. Two illustrations will be given of critical research on IT in a globalized world, namely health information systems and IT for the poor. Finally, some conclusions will be drawn.

WHAT IS GLOBALIZATION?

Robertson (1992) wrote an early influential book on globalization in which he said that: 'Globalization as a concept refers both to the compression of the world and the intensification of consciousness of the world as a whole' (p. 8). The first of these two points relates directly to time-space compression, largely mediated through information and communication technologies. The second point refers to people's awareness of the world and applies quite generally, not only to the well educated. The widespread accessibility of communications media such as television, even in remote rural villages in the Third World or underprivileged urban communities anywhere, means that news of happenings in the world as a whole are available to the great majority of the world's population. This does not necessarily imply a well-informed world, since the 'news' is chosen, condensed, filtered, and manipulated by a host of complex mechanisms. However, it does mean that remoteness and isolation are not the same in the contemporary age, and that most people are more aware than they were of a wider global arena within which their own community forms only a small part.

Beck (2000: 10) referred to this change in global consciousness using the term 'globality', defined as follows: 'Globality means that we have been living for a long time in a world society, in the sense that the notion of closed spaces has become illusory. No country or group can shut itself off from others.' Beck reserved the term globalization for processes of interconnection and influence between national states and international actors such as the transnational corporations (TNCs). Beck argued that the TNCs are 'bidding farewell to the framework of the national state and refusing loyalty to its actors', through such devices as minimizing their taxes, but externalizing the costs of unemployment to the nation states.

Giddens (1999) argued that global financial flows are a key element of these globalization processes:

> Geared as it is to electronic money—money that exists only as digits in computers—the current world economy has no parallels in earlier times. In the new global electronic economy, fund managers, banks, corporations, as well as millions of individual investors, can transfer vast amounts of capital from one side of the world

to another at the click of a mouse. As they do so, they can destabilise what might have seemed rock-solid economies—as happened in East Asia.

This chapter is being written at the time of the global financial crisis in 2009 and Giddens' words of a decade earlier seem quite prophetic.

Global financial flows are one element in trends towards more global business as a whole, although we need to be wary of simplistic generalizations here. Although there is much talk in the business world, and the management schools, of global businesses, global markets, and global supply chains, the degree to which this has occurred to date, and the degree to which it might occur in the future, remain in dispute. For example, Doremus et al. (1998) investigated a range of multinational corporations, mainly in Germany, Japan, and the USA, and argued that such companies, who after all should surely be at the forefront of the move towards globally minded enterprises, remained tied to approaches derived from their unique national identities: 'However lustily they sing from the same hymn book when they gather together in Davos or Aspen, the leaders of the world's great business enterprises continue to differ in their most fundamental strategic behaviour and objectives' (quoted in Kogut 1999).

Cultural Diversity

This leads on to one of the most controversial issues in the globalization debate, namely the issue of homogenization and diversity. The broad question is whether the globalization phenomena that we have outlined above, such as time-space compression, an increased awareness of the world as a whole, and movements toward global business, will inevitably lead to a decrease in cultural difference among nations, companies, and/ or individuals. There is a school of thought, prevalent amongst the Western business community for example, which takes this for granted. The argument runs that there is only one economic system now, capitalism, and that enterprises need to compete globally under this one set of rules. Therefore, all companies that wish to survive will need to adopt the practices of the winners, leading towards more homogeneous ways of doing things and, by extension to the wider society, to a less diverse cultural world.

A range of writers have taken exception to this conclusion of the inevitability of homogenization. For example, Robertson (1992) discussed the way in which imported themes are 'indigenized' in particular societies, with local culture constraining the receptivity to some ideas rather than others, and adapting them all in specific ways. He cited Japan as a good example of this blending of the 'native' and the 'foreign' as an ongoing process. Whilst accepting the idea of time-space compression facilitated by information technology, Robertson argued that one of its main consequences is an exacerbation of collisions between global, societal, and communal attitudes.

Beck (2000: 9) defined the ideology of global homogenization as 'globalism': 'By globalism, I mean the view that the world market eliminates or supplants political action—that is, the ideology of the rule by the world market, the ideology of neoliberalism'. Beck argued strongly against this ideology, citing many different reasons. For example, he argued that globalism reduces the complexity of globality and globalization to a single economic dimension, showing no understanding of the importance of specific political and cultural meanings in particular contexts. Globalism also 'sings the praises' of worldwide 'free trade', but Beck argued that we live in a world far removed from any fair model of free trade due to enormously skewed initial conditions.

Appadurai (1996), coming from a non-Western background, argued against the global homogenization thesis on the basis of cultural considerations. Societies have different cultural histories and will appropriate global trends in a local way:

> ... globalization is itself a deeply historical, uneven and even *localizing* process. Globalization does not necessarily or even frequently imply homogenization or Americanization, and to the extent that different societies appropriate the materials of modernity differently, there is still ample room for the deep study of specific geographies, histories, and languages. (p. 17)

The term 'glocalization' reflects the ways in which the global, macroscopic aspects of contemporary life are appropriated locally. According to Robertson (1992), the term originated in Japan as a translation of the Japanese word *dochakuka*, roughly meaning global localization.

Globalization and the Self

The debate about the extent to which various processes linked to globalization may lead to homogenization in terms of business processes or national cultures rests to a significant extent on the effect of the processes on the individual member of society, whether in the Western or developing world. The argument will be made here that there is no strong evidence of any simple standardization of humanity, and indeed that global forces may, somewhat paradoxically perhaps, have some effects which tend towards the exact opposite.

Going back to the work of Giddens and Beck, both these writers about contemporary Western society talk about the need for individual life projects, specific to a person's own past history and context, and to his or her future trajectory and aspirations. The world of relatively set rules, traditions, social classes, and job roles has been undermined. The new uncertain world requires active navigation. Authors such as these have sometimes been criticised as emphasizing individual freedom of action, in societies where the underprivileged can be thought to have little choice. It is certainly true that some people's choices are more constrained than others, and that life chances are very different at birth dependent on one' parentage and background. Nevertheless, any individual growing up and working in the twenty-first century will need to chart their own course with some vigour, within the range of possibilities available to them, or risk being carried away by the waves of change which will undoubtedly continue to roll.

Robertson (1992) talked about this issue related specifically to globalization, and he added a subtle distinction regarding concepts such as life projects themselves, which can be seen to be Western individualistic constructs. More group-oriented societies such as many of those in Asia, and religions such as Islam which place great emphasis on community, would tend not to see the world as composed of distinct individuals with discrete life goals, opportunities, and problems.

Appadurai (1996) took these arguments on cultural difference further, with specific reference to self-identity, and in particular using the concept of imagination. He argued that people draw on contemporary sources, such as the media, and their own cultural histories, to 'annex the global' into their own 'practices of the modern' through their imagination. Thus, even conventional objects such as T-shirts and music become transformed differently in different contexts: 'T-shirts, billboards, and graffiti as well as rap music, street dancing, and slum housing all show that the images of the media are quickly moved into local repertoires of irony, anger, humor and resistance' (p. 7).

Gopal (1997) quoted Appadurai's arguments against global homogenization, and the role of imagination, with a specific focus on IT. He argued that the vision of an IT-driven world of progress, efficiency, unlimited markets, individualism, and the superiority of the Western developmental trajectory needs to be challenged, not least because the effects of the use of IT in the West itself have not always been benign. He argued that each developing country must forge its own path in the future, and not try to imitate inappropriate western models:

> They (developing countries) have different pasts; their historical trajectories have led to different configurations of valences, patterns of trust, responsibilities, and allegiances. They have, as a result, different presents: priorities, voices, capabilities, and capacities are arranged in patterns quite unlike those of the societies from which the technologies originate. And, in spite of the attempts of a few to sediment in the popular imagination a singular vision of prosperous IT-driven existence, they have different imagined futures (Appadurai, 1996); their varieties of aspirations and expectations bear little resemblance to the visions embedded in the technology. (p. 140)

The Role of the Nation State

A key topic identified by many writers about globalization concerns the changing role of the nation state in an increasingly globalized world. Is the nation state a redundant entity, at the mercy of international forces that it cannot control, to be replaced by large federal groupings or even world government? What policy measures and other action remain within the control of the individual nation state, and can these be effective in improving the lives of the citizens of that country, and protecting them from the worst effects of the cold winds of global competition and the actions of the transnational corporations?

The answer to the first of these questions is a qualified no, in my view, leading us to the details and complexities of the second question, which will be country and context specific. The nation state is not redundant, although its influence is more conditional than in some previous eras. Hirst and Thompson (1996) adopted the stronger view that the rhetoric of globalization is often used to attack the concept of the nation state as a strategy from the right of the political spectrum to undermine the welfare gains that have been achieved in most Western economies. They argued that this rhetoric should be opposed, and that the state should continue to pursue approaches to counter asymmetries of privilege within its borders.

Clark (1997) also supported the importance of the nation state, and argued that globalization tendencies should be analysed in conjunction with tendencies towards fragmentation, the latter referring to the multiplicity of diverse interests within the state which need to be accommodated. In addition to challenges to the welfare state, globalization brings with it political costs such as high levels of unemployment in a country as a whole, or in particular regions. The state is required to mediate between increasingly potent international pressures and heightened levels of domestic discontent from those affected negatively as a result of such pressures. Clark argued:

> In the circumstances, it is to be expected that fragmentationist policies will have renewed appeal amongst the motley groups and peoples who have most to lose by continuing globalization: employment sectors in the First World felt to be threatened by the 'export' of jobs to low-wage areas of globalized production; embattled politicians who see globalization eroding their own sources of power and control; traditionalist societies within the Third World disenchanted by the empty promises of development but subject none the less to its seemingly pervasive effects; ethnic identities which may seem to be the only stable anchors in the fast-moving tides of cultural change.' (p. 202)

Beck (2000) was deeply concerned with the type of issues raised in the above quotation, and he placed great emphasis on the need for new forms of political action that cross national borders as a means of moulding 'responsible globalization'. He argued the need for collaboration among nation states, for example to limit or obstruct the 'horse trading' whereby global firms minimize their tax obligations and maximize state subsidies. Using Europe as an example, he argued that a new transnational federalism would enable states to have a new life as 'individual glocal states', limiting the power of transnational centres. Turning to the wider world, Beck pointed to the need for political action in the form of a social contract against exclusion, and a sense of global responsibility in the face of enormous inequity:

> The share of the poorest fifth of humanity in world income fell from 4 to 1 per cent between 1960 and 1990. By contrast, 358 dollar billionaires possess more than what a half of humanity put together currently earns. (p. 153)

Beck's overall argument, therefore, was the need to oppose the hegemony of 'globalism', and to develop a new transnational politics that engages with the issues of globalization, particularly those concerned with social consequences.

The Information Age

A major analysis of contemporary society is contained in the three-volume magnum opus of Manuel Castells (1996, 1997, 1998). It draws on a wide range of empirical data, much of it collected by the author and his research collaborators over a period of more than a decade. The geographical coverage of the work is impressive, with major material on Latin America and Asia, for example, in addition to Europe and the USA.

Castells assigned a central role to information and communications technologies in the societal transformations that have taken place in the modern world. The basic thesis of Volume I, Castells (1996), is that a new 'network society' is emerging from current processes of change that is both capitalist and informational. The latter is defined as follows:

> ... the term informational indicates the attribute of a specific form of social organization in which information generation, processing and transmission become the fundamental sources of productivity and power, because of new technological conditions emerging in this historical period. (p. 21)

Castells believed that globalization is real, in the sense that the markets for goods and services are becoming increasingly globalized. This does not mean that all firms sell worldwide, but that the strategic aims of all firms, large and small, is to sell wherever they can throughout the world, either directly or via their linkage with networks that operate in the world market.

However, in the informational economy, there is complex interaction between historically rooted political and social institutions, and increasingly globalized economic agents. There is, thus, wide variety in the way in which individual countries and regions act as part of the globalized world. Castells argued that the global economy is characterized by its interdependence, but also by its asymmetry, and the increasing diversification within each region. In this sense, Castells supported the theory of glocalization, discussed earlier.

Castells placed great emphasis on networking, and indeed argued that firms have become network enterprises, and that we are in the era which forms the title of Volume I, namely the network society. Information technology is assigned a key role: 'While the networking form of social organization has existed in other times and spaces, the new information technology paradigm provides the material basis for its pervasive expansion throughout the entire social structure' (p. 469). It is interesting to note that this first volume was published in 1996, and that no doubt the material was developed rather earlier. Although the Internet has existed for a relatively long time, it is only in the last decade or so that its enormous potential impact has started to be exploited. Castells anticipated the network society before these developments, and the growth of the internet lends further support to his thesis here.

The processes of change to a network society have been accompanied by a transformation of work and employment but not to a unified global labour market. However, according to Castells, there is increasing interdependence of the labour force on a global scale, through three mechanisms. These are global employment in the multinational corporations and their associated cross-border networks; the impact of international trade on employment conditions, both in the North and in the South; and the effects of global competition and of the new mode of flexible production on each country's labour force. Castells argued that information technology is deeply implicated in these change processes, but that there is no simple structural relationship between the diffusion of IT and the evolution of employment levels in a particular economy taken as a whole.

Finally, in keeping with his roots in urban geography, Castells argued that the 'global city' plays a key role in the network society. However, he defines the global city not as a place, but as a process. This process connects centres of production and consumption of advanced services, and their ancillary local societies, in a global network, whilst simultaneously downplaying the linkages with their hinterlands. The megacities, in particular, provide a linkage for informational networks and concentrate the world's power. However, they also provide a depository of all those segments of the population who fight to survive, as well as those groups who want to make visible their dereliction.

Castells (1997) started Volume II with an impassioned plea for a multicultural world view of globalization:

> There is in this book a deliberate obsession with multiculturalism . . . This approach stems from my view that the process of techno-economic globalization shaping our world is being challenged, and will eventually be transformed, from a multiplicity of sources, according to different cultures, histories and geographies . . . I would like also . . . to break the ethnocentric approach still dominating much social science at the very moment when our societies have become globally interconnected and culturally intertwined. (p. 3)

The challenges to techno-economic globalization come from people's search for communal or collective identity, according to Castells. Reflexive life planning, of the type discussed earlier in the work of Giddens, is only possible for the elite, or the 'globapolitans'. For those people excluded from the global networks of power and wealth, cultural communes of religious, national or territorial foundation provide the main alternative for the construction of meaning in society.

There are clear links here with Appadurai's arguments on the diversity of imagination, and Castells (1997) provided detailed material on 'resistance movements' to the global order, both within particular national contexts, and in wider arenas. With respect to the former, three examples are given. First, the role of the Zapatistas in Mexico in fighting what they defined as a conjunction of American imperialism and corrupt, illegitimate national government. It is interesting to note their use of the media and Internet-based alliances to publicize and support their resistance. The second example is of the American militia of the far right opposing what they see as the excessive power of the US federal government, with the Oklahoma bombing as a stark example of their resistance. Finally, the Japanese movement Aum Shinrikyo, responsible for the Tokyo subway nerve gas attack, defined the global opposition as unified world government representing the interests of the multinational corporations, and enforced by the Japanese police.

In addition to these dramatic and violent examples of social resistance to the perceived global order in particular national contexts, Castells also analysed more cross-cultural resistance movements, who use largely peaceful means to pursue their opposition. The first of these is the environmental movement, representing the widespread fear of the people concerning the uncontrolled pursuit of science and technology without an adequate consideration of long-term consequences:

> The ecological approach to life, to the economy, and to the institutions of society emphasises the holistic character of all forms of matter, and of all information processing. Thus, the more we know, the more we sense the possibilities of our technology, and the more we realise the gigantic, dangerous gap between our enhanced productive capacities, and our primitive, unconscious and ultimately destructive social organization. (p. 133)

The second widespread opposition to the established order, cited by Castells, is feminism or, more generally, the transformation of women's work and women's consciousness (see also Chapter 21). Castells argued that the decline of patriarchalism, coupled with the change in women's roles and attitudes, requires a reconstruction of the family under more egalitarian relations. However, organizations and institutions have not in general adapted to this new world.

This leads on to Castells' analysis of the role of the state. He argued that the state is losing its power, in comparison to earlier eras, but not its influence. Nation states have been transformed from sovereign subjects into strategic actors. There is a paradox in their role, in that the more they emphasize communal identity, the less effective they become as co-agents of a global system of shared power. However, the more they triumph in the planetary sphere, in close partnership with the agents of globalization, or what Beck would call globalism, the less they represent their national constituencies. In particular, they must cope with the those groups who are largely excluded from the power and resources of the globalized production networks, whether as producers or as consumers. There are strong echoes here with the arguments of Beck on the role of the nation state, although Beck is perhaps more positive about what could be done to counteract the power of globalism and its agents.

Castells does, however, end Volume II on a relatively optimistic note concerning the possibilities for 'informational politics' in the information age. He argued for the recreation of the local state, using the opportunity offered by electronic communication to enhance political participation and horizontal communication among citizens. He believed that we have entered the era of 'symbolic politics' in which 'The new power lies in the codes of information and in the images of representation around which societies organise their institutions, and people build their lives, and decide their behaviour. The sites of this power are people's minds' (p. 359). Castells' analysis of the excluded 'Fourth World' is an important feature of Volume III. He argued that the development of the complex set of linkages of informational capitalism has been accompanied by the rise of inequality, social polarization, poverty, and misery in much of the world. Globalization proceeds selectively, including and excluding segments of economies and societies in and out of the networks of information, wealth, and power that characterize the new dominant system:

> ...a new world, the Fourth World, has emerged, made up of multiple black holes of social exclusion throughout the planet. The Fourth World comprises large areas of the globe, such as much of sub-Saharan Africa, and impoverished rural areas of Latin America and Asia. But it is also present in literally every country, and in every city, in this new geography of social exclusion. It is formed of American inner-city ghettos, Spanish enclaves of mass youth unemployment, French banlieues ware-housing North Africans, Japanese Yoseba quarters, and Asian megacities' shanty towns. (pp. 164–5)

Castells ended Volume III, and the work as a whole, with an appeal for conscious, purposive social action, supported by information, in order to address the many problems and challenges identified in the books.

> ...if people are informed, active and communicate throughout the world; if business assumes its social responsibility; ...if political actors react against cynicism, and restore faith in democracy; ...if humankind feels the solidarity of the species across the globe; if we assert intergenerational solidarity by living in harmony with nature ... then, we may, at last, be able to live and let live, love and be loved. (p. 360)

HUMAN DEVELOPMENT

The material in the previous section reflects the complexity of the globalization phenomenon itself and is not easily summarized. However, some key themes can be discerned from the work of these various scholars. Firstly, *the contemporary world is undergoing major processes of change.* In addition to the evident increase in interconnection between societies, there is an increased consciousness of the world as a whole, which Beck called globality. This consciousness includes an awareness of the production of global risks that transcend national boundaries, of which global warming and the current global financial crisis provide graphic examples. The transnational corporations have increased their power in this new globalized world, a cause of major concern to writers such as Giddens and Beck.

A second key argument is that *information and communication technologies are deeply implicated in the global changes that are taking place*, through their ability to enable new modes of work, communication, and organization across time and space. For example, Castells argued that we are in the 'information age' where information generation, processing, and transmission are fundamental to organizational and societal change. IT enables pervasive expansion of networking throughout the social structure, and is intimately involved in changes in economic and social activity. These change processes can have profound effects on self-identity, the nature of work and employment, organizational structure, and the nature and governance of the nation state.

However, thirdly, *the change processes are not uniform in their effects*, and organizations and societies will remain distinct and differentiated, although increasingly interconnected, though a process which has been labelled as glocalization. This arises through the selective appropriation and variable use of new ideas by different individuals, organizations, and societies. We are entering an age of globalization and interconnection, but also one of multiculturalism, in the sense that many cultures with specific geographies, histories and languages will be involved, and will affect the nature of the future world. Unfortunately, there are many excluded segments of all societies, referred to as the 'Fourth World' by Castells, who do not have adequate access to the networks of information, wealth, and power that characterize the new world order.

All the writers cited above were united that these changed conditions and uneven effects, brought about in part through the use of IT, imply an increased need for reflection and action. For example, Beck argued the need to oppose the ideology of rule by world markets, which he calls globalism. Castells talked about the power of 'resistance movements' such as environmentalism, feminism, and various religious movements. The goal of reflection and action is to make a better world or, to put it another way, to support human development in its broadest sense. But what can IS researchers contribute to this broad agenda? I would argue that *IS researchers can contribute by addressing their research explicitly to issues of human development*. The remainder of the chapter will be devoted to the question of how to go about doing this. The rest of this section will expand a little on the meaning of human development in this context.

The term 'development' is often associated only with the so-called developing countries. This contrasts with the term 'developed countries' which is the label often used to describe the rich countries of the world in terms of GDP per capita. This latter term is most unfortunate since it carries two implications, both of which I wish to argue against. First, that our sole measure of 'development' should be economic, calculated in terms of average income. However, there are many other non-material aspects of human development which we all recognize in other people, such as selflessness, courage, and kindness. Many people, for example, would accept that Mahatma Gandhi (1949) and Nelson Mandela (1994) travelled further on the path of individual development than most of the rest of us, even though they came from 'developing countries'.

The second reason why I do not like the term 'developed countries' is that it appears to ignore the myriad of individual, social, and political problems which beset the rich countries of the world. Examples include drug abuse, discrimination against women and ethnic communities, crime of all types, child pornography, and neglect of the elderly. Less dramatically, but equally important, problems at the workplace include feelings of dissatisfaction and alienation, concerns about inappropriate surveillance and monitoring methods, excessive working hours, and fears of job loss. All of these problems call for approaches that respect the need for human development in its broadest sense.

My argument that the rich countries also need to work at human development issues is not an argument that we should ignore the very different economic living standards in different countries, or the different standards within a given country. It is a global scandal, of which we should all be ashamed, that the world is so dramatically uneven and unfair. The Millennium Development goals (United Nations 2009) are laudable in themselves but it is appalling that these basic levels of provision in areas such as health services, education, and clean water are currently not achieved in large parts of the world and progress in this direction is so desperately slow. In terms of disparity within countries, a good example is India, where the high economic growth rates for the last fifteen years or so have not 'trickled down' to the poor in any major way, as evidenced by the statistics that roughly one in two children in India under the age of 5 is malnourished and one in two Indian women is illiterate (UNICEF 2004; World Bank 2007). The development economist Sen (1999) points out that poverty of such people is not simply material, but also relates to the capabilities that people have to make choices and take action in their lives.

So, in summary, human development is a complex multi-level ongoing process for all individuals, groups, organizations, societies, and the world as a whole. This applies to the rich as well as the poor countries, although the importance of particular problems will vary across different contexts. It is right that global attention should be directed towards the economically poor, but not to the exclusion of other issues of human development throughout our more globalized world. A further human development goal for all of us concerns the reduction of conflict within and between different societies and ethnic groupings, something which touches us all in our global interconnectedness: wars in Iraq and Afghanistan, the continuing Israeli-Arab conflict, global terrorism, and intra-society conflict such as in Darfur.

What about the role of IT in human development? It was argued earlier that information and communication technologies are deeply implicated in global changes that are taking place. However, they are not a silver bullet to solve human development problems whether these are wars or global poverty or, at a less dramatic level, concerns about surveillance or work-life balance. Nevertheless, in all these situations, IT is invariably present, whether to target bombs in war zones, to try to bridge the 'digital divide' for the poor, or to enable workplace monitoring. The role of IS researchers interested in issues of human development is, therefore, to catalogue and analyse particular situations in order to provide insight into whether IT is contributing, in this context, to making a better world. I turn now to how IS researchers can try to do this.

RESEARCH WITH A CRITICAL EDGE

I wish to argue that IS research that focuses on exploring the role of IT in making a better world needs to have a critical edge to it. To simplify somewhat, a critical stance is concerned with what is wrong with the world rather than what is right. It tends to focus on issues such as asymmetries of power, alienation, disadvantaged groups, or structural inequity. This fits well with an agenda focused on human development. A more precise definition of critical research in the IS field was given in the early seminal article by Orlikowski and Baroudi (1991) on different research traditions. They describe the critical researcher' beliefs about reality, knowledge, and the role of research as follows:

> ... social reality is historically constituted ... everything possesses an unfulfilled potentiality, and people, by recognizing these possibilities, can act to change their material and social circumstances ... knowledge is grounded in social and historical practices ... the role of the researcher is to bring to consciousness the restrictive conditions of the status quo, thereby initiating change in the social relations and practices, and helping to eliminate the bases of alienation and domination. (pp. 19–21)

This is a clear anti-establishment agenda and therefore it is not surprising that Orlikowski and Baroudi recorded that critical studies in four 'major information systems outlets' were non-existent. Nearly two decades later, the position would not be dissimilar in the more conservative journals, but overall the position has changed somewhat. There is an increasing interest in critical studies in IS research, as evidenced by focused conferences (e.g. Adam et al. 2004), books (e.g. Howcroft and Trauth 2005), special issues of journals (e.g. *Information Systems Journal*, 19(2), 2009), and a whole range of individual contributions. In the latter category, a wide range of topics have been addressed from a critical stance including the life of call centre workers (Richardson 2003), gender discrimination in the IS field (Woodfield 2002), the ethics of the UK government' identity card scheme (Whitley 2009), and a range of issues concerned with information systems in developing countries (Walsham, Robey, and Sahay 2007). It is also noticeable that the editors of this handbook have chosen to include several chapters with an explicit critical focus, such as that on critical social theory and the later contributions on IT and gender, green issues, ethics and IT, and the digital divide.

Why has critical IS research increased in scope and range over the last decade or so? A full discussion of this is beyond the remit of the present chapter but I would like to argue, to support the theme of this chapter, that our more globalized world has thrown up many issues that cry out for a critical approach which is focused on human development in the broadest sense. Our increased consciousness of the world as a whole, which Beck called globality, leads us to increased awareness of the enormous asymmetries of wealth and power in the world. The 'restrictive conditions of the status quo' and 'bases of alienation and domination' noted in Orlikowski and Baroudi's definition of critical research are highly relevant to the contemporary world. The next two sections will aim to support this assertion, and more generally to illustrate critical IS research in action in the world, aimed at human development goals.

HEALTH INFORMATION SYSTEMS

This section describes work which has been carried out over the last fifteen years under the label of HISP (Health Information Systems Programme). A summary and analysis of the work from 1994 to 2001 is given in Braa and Hedberg (2002) and later work is described in Braa, Monteiro, and Sahay (2004) and Braa et al. (2007). The basic objective of the work has been to develop locally relevant health information systems for public health administrations in developing countries, together with associated data collection procedures, linked to a national strategic approach to improving health standards across the country as a whole. The HISP approach was pioneered in South Africa but has been extended to a range of other African countries such as Mozambique and developing countries in other regions such as India. The main focus here will be on the work in South Africa, but the programme as a whole has a much wider global focus.

The initiation of the work needs to be viewed within the political context of post-apartheid South Africa. Following an armed struggle and international pressure, the notorious apartheid system was ended in South Africa in the early 1990s. A democratically elected government of national unity was formed in 1994 under the leadership of Nelson Mandela. The government brought with it a new policy agenda, and health was regarded as a key area. Government health policy stated that the health system would be decentralized to focus on districts, subdivisions of the country containing between 50,000 and 500,000 people. Part of the plan was the development of a new national health information system to support the changed focus, and work on HISP formed part of this.

The HISP Approach and Achievements

In its first phase up to 1998, HISP aimed at supporting the emerging decentralized structures in three pilot districts in Cape Town, the main town in the province of the Western Cape. A key goal of the approach was the empowerment of local health workers. In terms of data collection and related computer-based IS, this translates into the need to create, analyse, and use data at the same level at which it is collected.

This contrasts with the 'typical' approach in many developing countries, and certainly in apartheid South Africa, where the health data collected by local level workers are passed up the hierarchy, and data collection is perceived as a burden by local workers, irrelevant to their work with sick people. As an illustration of work under HISP to address such issues, Thompson (2002) described changed data collection approaches in some large Cape Town clinics in the poorest areas of the city. These were based on the use of simple tools such as hand-held counters (e.g. for patients arriving at the clinic) and simplified and more transparent procedures and forms for data collection.

One metaphor used by the researchers to describe their approach to the development of locally relevant information systems is that of 'cultivation'. The argument is that particular information systems (hardware/software/standards) may be planted in specific locations, so that the seeds are similar, but local growing conditions are infinitely variable. Thus the developing plant needs to be tended and nurtured through people at the lower level who have ownership and commitment towards it. Braa (1997) argued that a participatory design process is crucial in helping to create such ownership, and thus a bottom-up approach to IS development is essential.

However, although local empowerment and commitment is crucial, there is a need at the higher policy levels, both in districts and nationally, to create standardized data. A key rationale for this is to identify and target areas of need as described by Braa and Hedberg (2002: 114): 'striving for equity between geographical areas and racial groups will require a system of national standards to measure and monitor the extent to which this policy is being achieved and to pinpoint areas where more resources and efforts are needed'. Braa and Hedberg discuss a tension between this need for standardization and the flexibility needed for effective localization. They describe their approach to resolving this tension through a hierarchy of standards, where each level in the health system has freedom to define its own standards as long as they align with the standards of the level above.

With respect to the progress of HISP following the Cape Town pilot projects, the South African Department of Health adopted the strategies, processes, and software developed in the pilot districts as a national standard. Braa, Monteiro, and Sahay (2004) reported that these were rolled out to all districts in South Africa in 2003. Other countries are experimenting with the HISP approach (Braa, Monteiro, and Sahay 2004; Braa et al. 2007), and it is worth noting that the HISP software has been deliberately designed as open source, based on the political view that such systems should be freely available to other developing countries.

Critical Engagement of the Researchers

The action research on HISP has been a collaborative endeavour, initially involving the University of Oslo in Norway, the University of the Western Cape in South Africa, and the Department of Health in South Africa. More recently, a wide range of other individuals and institutions have been included. However, a core team has worked on the project since its inception. This core team offers a classic example of critical IS research and what I have called critical engagement (Walsham 2005c), as discussed below.

Orlikowski and Baroudi's definition of critical research emphasized the importance of recognizing *unfulfilled potential* and therefore the possibility of people acting *to change their material and social circumstances*. The unfulfilled potential in South Africa can be related directly to the oppression of non-white people during the apartheid years and, in the specific context of the health system, change includes the need to provide improved health services through decentralization and locally relevant information systems. This was a key motivation for the core team, as described by Braa and Hedberg (2002: 113):

> As a legacy of apartheid, the new South Africa (post-1994) inherited one of the least equitable health care systems in the world ... the new government launched the Reconstruction and Development Program ... with a title that clearly expressed its intent: the reconstitution and development of communities that suffered under apartheid. The restructuring of the health sector ... is based on a decentralized system of health districts. Development of new national health information systems to support the restructuring of the health sector is part of this plan.

A second feature of Orlikowski and Baroudi's definition of critical research is the recognition that *knowledge is grounded in social and historical practices*. The South African health system provides an excellent example of this, where the data collected during the apartheid years, and thus the 'knowledge' concerning the health of the overall population, were subordinated to the need to discriminate between the various races. Again, this is well recognized and articulated by Braa and Hedberg (2002: 113):

> The politics of apartheid—segmentation, centralism and exclusion of 'black' South Africans—have all been deeply inscribed into all the bits and pieces of the information systems in which standards for data collection are basic elements.

Finally, Orlikowski and Baroudi's definition suggests the role of the critical researcher as bringing to consciousness the restrictive conditions of the status quo, initiating changes in social relations and practices and thus *helping to eliminate the bases of alienation and domination*. The whole HISP activity has been geared to achieving such ends by the development of decentralized systems through local prototyping, the empowerment of local level health workers, and the improved ability to target poor areas and disadvantaged parts of the population by comparing standards across districts and the country as a whole.

I argued in an earlier publication (Walsham 2005c) for the use of the term 'engagement' as a valuable characteristic of critical IS researchers, and its meanings as an *undertaking*, a *battle*, and a *duty or commitment*. With respect to the first of these meanings, an undertaking implies a long-term approach in order to address complex and deep-seated problems and inequities. HISP has been operating for fifteen years already and its scope has widened rather than narrowed. The researchers have engaged with the complexity of the area across a wide range of activities as noted by Braa and Hedberg (2002: 116): 'The authors have been deeply and directly involved in strategic planning, daily implementation, political brokering, software prototyping, institutional development, and training at all levels'.

Turning to the metaphor of engagement as a battle, it is notable that Braa and Hedberg entitle their 2002 paper 'The Struggle for District-Based Health Information Systems in South Africa'. They articulate their political motives for engaging in this struggle as follows:

> It is important to note that the original key members of the HISP team have background as social/political activists in the antiapartheid struggle and other social movements, and that we have always explicitly and implicitly seen ourselves as political actors in a larger development process. (p. 114)

Engagement as a 'duty or commitment' is also captured in the above quote from the long-term members of the core HISP team.

IT FOR THE POOR

This section describes IS research carried out to investigate whether and how IT can be used to support better lives for people who are poor in economic terms. Unlike the previous section, this is not a unified body of work carried out by a particular team of researchers, but rather reflects the work of a variety of people. The uniting feature is their adoption of a broadly critical approach. In order to restrict the scope of this section, the work which is described here is focused on India. The section discusses research on three areas of IT application in India, namely telecentres, mobile phones, and e-government services to see to what extent the development objective of being pro-poor was achieved in particular projects.

Telecentres

A direct approach to the use of IT aimed at bettering the lives of the poor is through the setting up of telecentres. Many telecentre projects were started in India over last decade or so and there is a sizeable research literature on the topic. For example, Kumar and Best (2006) described the SARI (Sustainable Access in Rural India) project in the state of Tamil Nadu. Some 80 telecentre kiosks were set up offering a range of services including basic computer education, e-mail, web browsing, and various e-government services including the provision of certificates. Although the kiosks succeeded initially in delivering the e-government services, many failed subsequently. Kumar and Best identify a range of reasons for the failure including lack of trained staff, movement of key officials, and, at a deeper level, opposition from government officials at the local level who perceived a threat from the kiosks to their role, authority, and influence in the community and, more darkly, to their opportunities for corruption.

Gollakota (2008) analysed a telecentre kiosk initiative, also in Tamil Nadu, by the sugar manufacturer EID Parry aimed at providing information to farmers, with some of the kiosks being company owned but some operating through kiosk franchisees who were also able to offer more general computer-based services such as Internet browsing, communication services, and desk top publishing. Gollakota concluded that better relationships between local farmers and the company were achieved through the project, which had 36 kiosks by 2006, but there were also problems. There were concerns that caste, community, and gender influenced access to the kiosks and therefore that the poor and disadvantaged were often not reached by the initiative. In addition, there were serious problems of financial viability for the franchisees since, in poor rural areas, it is difficult to generate adequate revenue to make such a business viable. Rao (2008) examined a wide range of telecentre projects throughout India and echoed this concern about financial viability in addition to issues such as staff capability, community acceptance, and adequate service delivery. Kuriyan, Ray, and Toyama (2008) examined the extensive Akshaya telecentre project in the state of Kerala, and argued that it is problematic to achieve the twin goals of commercial profitability of telecentres with social development for those at the bottom of the pyramid.

It is clear that telecentre projects are not a simple way to bridge the so-called digital divide for poor people, but nevertheless many authors writing on the topic do not wish to see their abandonment but look for a more sophisticated way of thinking about and addressing the problems of telecentres. Kanungo (2004) drew on empirical data from a telecentre project in the union territory of Pondicherry to argue the need for social processes that bring together an alliance of funding agencies, government organizations, non-governmental organizations, villagers, scientists, etc. This focus on actors and governance processes of telecentre projects was also addressed by Madon (2005), drawing on her own field research on the Akshaya project mentioned above. Madon suggested a 'sociology of governance' approach to analysing telecentre projects and processes, focusing on how interactions are managed between a host of players including the government, private entrepreneurs, international donors, telecommunications suppliers, local companies, civil society organizations, and individual community members.

Mobile Phones

There are currently over three billion mobile phones in the world and there are more than twice as many in the poorer compared to the richer countries (Heeks and Jagun

2007). Of course, mobile phone ownership is skewed towards the wealthier groups in poorer societies but nevertheless mobile phone usage amongst the poor is not negligible, in India or elsewhere. Mobile phone ownership in India was estimated to be around 340 million at the end of 2008 with mobile operators currently targeting smaller villages and towns to attract new users. It is also a remarkable bottom-up phenomenon, in that mobile phone ownership and usage results primarily from the aggregate of individual purchasing and use decisions (see also Chapter 18).

The rapid spread of this new technology across the planet has, in large measure, outstripped research on the topic. Nevertheless, Donner (2008) was able to review around 200 studies of mobile phone use in the developing countries. He noted that there were still relatively few detailed studies of rural users and he called for further research which provided a better understanding of linkages between richer and poorer communities, and between rural and urban users. The same author (Donner 2007) provided an example of such work in an Indian context through a study of small businesses in the town of Hyderabad, and the role played by the mobile phone in customer acquisition and retention. He concluded that mobile phones were still not crucial to these small businesses in customer acquisition and retention, and that we should be careful to ascribe major transformative benefits to the mobile phone without hard evidence of how this is achieved.

It is clear that we are at a very early stage in our understanding of the impact of the mobile phone on the lives of the poor, in India and elsewhere in the developing world. An example of work that increases such understanding was provided by Abraham (2007) in his detailed case study of the extensive use of mobile phones in the fishing industry in Kerala. He concluded that there were clear benefits to the fishermen in areas such as responding to market demand, wasting less time and resources, and being less isolated and at risk in emergencies. Abraham argued more generally that demand-driven bottom-up interventions are more likely to succeed in developing countries than are top-down ones, and that technologies such as the mobile phone which reduce transaction costs are likely to be better investments than amorphous, ill-defined attempts to bridge the 'digital divide'. Jensen (2007) studied the same fisheries case using different field data and an economics lens, and he also concluded that there were measurable benefits from the mobile phone technology including the complete elimination of waste, a dramatic reduction in price dispersion, and an increase in both consumer and producer welfare.

e-Government Services

Many of the states in India have embarked on e-government programmes and initiatives. For example, Krishna and Walsham (2005) described two systems in the state of Andhra Pradesh. The first of these was the Computer-Aided Administration of Registration Department (CARD) system which computerized the registration of property transfers, resulting in significant reductions in processing time. The second was the e-Seva project which set up computerized centres where citizens can pay bills to multiple agencies, register births and deaths, get a passport, and so on. The previous manual processes had to be done in different places, involved large amounts of citizen time and often bribery to the desk officials to speed things up.

Krishna and Walsham described these as 'success stories' for e-government and attributed the success to a variety of factors including the hands-on leadership provided by the Chief Minister of Andhra Pradesh, Chandrababu Naidu, the involvement of multiple stakeholder groups such as consultants, government staff, and private firms, and the willingness to persist and learn over time. Whilst undoubtedly beneficial to some Indian citizens, the term 'success' is problematic. Dabla (2004) carried out extensive empirical work in Andhra Pradesh and concluded that projects such as CARD and e-Seva were mainly of benefit to urban dwellers and the relatively well off with few benefits to poor and rural social groups. One of the objectives of the e-government projects was to reduce corruption, namely the payment of bribes to government officials for preferential treatment. However, Caseley (2004) argued that, ironically, CARD reforms had made corruption easier since staff no longer had to find and copy documents by hand, freeing them up to concentrate on extracting additional money from citizens.

Other states in India have substantial e-government initiatives and Vasudevan (2007) described the STAR project in the state of Tamil Nadu, whose objectives and core technologies were similar to those of the CARD project in Andhra Pradesh. A complementary initiative in Tamil Nadu was REGiNET, a citizen accessible website to find the guideline value of any property in the State. Officials of the Tamil Nadu government claimed that STAR and REGiNET were superior to CARD since they enabled data entry and retrieval in both Tamil, the local language in the state, and English, whereas CARD used only English. In addition, CARD did not provide the on-line services enabled by REGiNET. However, Vasudevan (2007) qualified this claimed success in Tamil Nadu with the observation that the core processes of document registration were unreformed and that government officials persisted with citizen-unfriendly practices such as not allowing people to sit in government offices, not making prior appointments resulting in long queues, and continuing to solicit bribes.

A further case study of e-government, aimed specifically at poor communities, was provided by the Gyandoot project in the drought-prone rural Dhar district of the state of Madhya Pradesh. Sreekumar (2007) described how this started in 2000 with the objective of enhancing participation by citizens and government together in community affairs through creative uses of IT, and of ensuring equal access to emerging technologies for the oppressed and exploited segments of society. Forty kiosks were set up in different parts of the Dhar district and they offered a wide set of services such as agricultural prices, on-line registration of applications, rural email, information regarding government programmes, etc. However, Sreekumar observed that the kiosks were mainly used by the literate and middle-income groups and he described three particular case studies on how the complex layers of social power that characterize

Indian village society severely limit the potential of an initiative like Gyandoot to provide empowerment for the poor and disadvantaged. An earlier paper by Cecchini and Raina (2004) also concluded that the poor were not participating in the project, and that usage was low. They argued the need for pro-poor services rather than financial viability as a criterion for success, the important role for intermediaries to enable poor people to access e-government applications, and campaigns to raise awareness.

The Critical Agenda of the Researchers

It is clear that all of the researchers described above felt a *commitment* to investigate the *unfulfilled potential* of the poor and how IT could support their actions to *change their material and social circumstances*. With respect to the objective of *helping to eliminate the bases of alienation and domination*, the emphasis of some of the work on the embedded problems of caste or gender is a first step towards trying to address such problems in future initiatives. Corruption was also explicitly addressed in a number of the research studies. The mobile phone research contains some optimistic notes of IT providing valuable support in improving the livelihoods of relatively poor fishermen and their families. On the other hand, research is at a very early stage on the remarkable growth, even in poor communities, of mobile technology, and more research with a critical edge is needed to investigate whether and to what extent the mobile phone is effective in helping the poor to better their lives.

CONCLUSIONS

The examples of critical IS research given above are interesting illustrations of globalization processes in themselves. Both HISP in South Africa and IT for the poor in India reflect a complex network of actors and alliances which reach across the world. Local actions in a health district in a poor part of South Africa, or in a telecentre project in an Indian village, are influenced by many forces outside the individual location and they, in turn, affect our global view. The fact that I am writing about them in this chapter is an illustration of the latter point. Globalization is not a one-way top-down process but a complex, multi-level, multifaceted, and changing phenomenon.

The two examples I have given were both from the context of so-called developing countries (see also Chapter 25). This reflects my personal research interests to some extent. However, I wish to emphasize that IS research with a critical edge, focused on human development, is important in all countries and contexts. I briefly mentioned examples such as the life of call centre workers, gender discrimination in the IS field, and the ethics of identity card schemes, but these are only the tip of the iceberg, since IT is deeply implicated in a very wide range of human contexts and issues in the contemporary world.

Am I arguing that all IS researchers should pursue critical IS research aimed explicitly at human development issues? I would not go this far. Indeed I would support the assertions of Grey and Willmott (2002), both well-known critical researchers in the field of management studies, who argue that critical management studies is concerned with knowledge *of* management whereas a primary function of a business school is also to provide relatively non-critical knowledge *for* management. Nevertheless, I would like to end this chapter with my personal view that the balance in IS research is still weighted too heavily towards non-critical work, and that we need more critical IS research in the future that investigates IT for human development in the context of our more globalized world.

References

Abraham, R. (2007). 'Mobile Phones and Economic Development: Evidence from the Fishing Industry in India', *Information Technologies and International Development*, 4(1): 5–17.

Adam, A., Basden, A., Richardson, H., and Robinson, B. (eds.) (2004). *Critical Reflections on Critical Research in Information Systems*. Salford: University of Salford.

Appadurai, A. (1996). *Modernity at Large: Cultural Dimensions of Globalization*. New Delhi: Oxford University Press.

Beck, U. (2000). *What is Globalization?* Cambridge: Polity Press.

Braa, J. (1997). 'Use and Design of Information Technology in Third World Contexts with a Focus on the Health Sector: Case Studies from Mongolia and South Africa', Ph.D. thesis, Department of Informatics, University of Oslo, Norway.

—— and Hedberg, C. (2002). 'The Struggle for District-Based Health Information Systems in South Africa', *Information Society*, 18(2): 113–28.

—— Monteiro, E., and Sahay, S. (2004). 'Networks of Action: Sustainable Health Information Systems across Developing Countries', *MIS Quarterly*, 28(3): 337–62.

—— Hanseth, O., Heywood, A., Mohammed, W., and Shaw, V. (2007). 'Developing Health Information Systems in Developing Countries: The Flexible Standards Strategy', *MIS Quarterly*, 31(2): 381–402.

Caseley, J. (2004). 'Public Sector Reform and Corruption: CARD Façade in Andhra Pradesh', *Economic and Political Weekly*, 39(11): 1151–6.

Castells, M. (1996). *The Rise of the Network Society*. Oxford: Blackwell.

—— (1997). *The Power of Identity*. Oxford: Blackwell.

—— (1998). *End of Millenium*. Oxford: Blackwell.

Cecchini, S., and Raina, M. (2004). 'Electronic Government and the Rural Poor: The Case of Gyandoot', *Information Technologies and International Development*, 2(2): 65–75.

Clark, I. (1997). *Globalization and Fragmentation: International Relations in the Twentieth Century*. Oxford: Oxford University Press.

Dabla, A. (2004). 'The Role of Information Technology Policies in Promoting Social and Economic Development: The Case of the State of Andhra Pradesh, India', *Electronic Journal of Information Systems in Developing Countries*, 19(5): 1–21.

Donner, J. (2007). 'Customer Acquisition among Small and Informal Businesses in Urban India: Comparing Face-to-Face and Mediated Channels', *Electronic Journal of Information Systems in Developing Countries*, 32(3): 1–16.

——(2008). 'Research Approaches to Mobile Use in the Developing World: A Review of the Literature', *Information Society*, 24(3): 140–59.

Doremus, P. N., Keller, W. W., Pauly, L. W., and Reich, S. (1998). *The Myth of the Global Corporation*. Princeton, NJ: Princeton University Press.

Gandhi, M. (1949). *An Autobiography: The Story of my Experiments with Truth*. London: Phoenix Press.

Giddens, A. (1999). *Reith Lectures 1999*, <http://news.bbc.co.uk/hi/english/static/events/reith_99>.

Gollakota, K. (2008). 'ICT Use by Businesses in Rural India: The Case of EID Parry' Indiagriline', *International Journal of Information Management*, 28(4): 336–41.

Gopal, A. (1997). 'Information Technology and Globalization: Exploring the Underbelly', in M. Barrett, D. Cooper, C. R. Hinings, G. Lowe, H. Krahn, and K. Hughes (eds.), *Proceedings of Workshop on Understanding Information Technology, Globalization, and Changes in the Nature of Work*. Edmonton: University of Alberta.

Grey, C., and Willmott, H. (2002). 'Contexts of Critical Management Studies', *Organization*, 9(3): 411–18.

Heeks, R., and Jagun, A. (2007). 'Mobile Phones and Development,' <http://www.id21.org/insights/insights69/insights69.pdf>.

Hirst, P., and Thompson, G. (1996). *Globalization in Question: The International Economy and the Possibilities of Governance*. Cambridge: Polity Press.

Howcroft, D., and Trauth, E. A. (eds.) (2005). *Handbook of Critical Information Systems Research*. Cheltenham: Edward Elgar.

Jensen, R. (2007). 'The Digital Provide: Information (Technology), Market Performance, and Welfare in the South Indian Fisheries Sector', *Quarterly Journal of Economics*, 122(3): 879–924.

Kanungo, S. (2004). 'On the Emancipatory Role of Rural Information Systems', *Information Technology & People*, 7(4): 407–22.

Kogut, B. (1999). 'What Makes a Company Global', *Harvard Business Review*, January–February: 165–70.

Krishna, S., and Walsham, G. (2005). 'Implementing Public Information Systems in Developing Countries: Learning from a Success Story', *Information Technology for Development*, 11(2): 123–40.

Kumar, R., and Best, M. L. (2006). 'Impact and Sustainability of e-Government Services in Developing Countries: Lessons Learned from Tamil Nadu, India', *Information Society*, 22(1): 1–12.

Kuriyan, R., Ray, I., and Toyama, K. (2008). 'Information and Communication Technologies for Development: The Bottom of the Pyramid Model in Practice', *Information Society*, 24(2): 93–104.

Madon, S. (2005). 'Governance Lessons from the Experience of Telecentres in Kerala', *European Journal of Information Systems*, 14(4): 401–16.

Mandela, N. (1994). *Long Walk to Freedom: The Autobiography of Nelson Mandela*. London: Little, Brown.

Orlikowski, W. J., and Baroudi, J. J. (1991). 'Studying Information Technology in Organizations: Research Approaches and Assumptions', *Information Systems Research*, 2(1): 1–28.

Rao, S. S. (2008). 'Social Development in Indian Rural Communities: Adoption of Telecentres', *International Journal of Information Management*, 28(6): 474–82.

Richardson, H. (2003). 'CRM in Call Centres: The Logic of Practice', in M. Korpela, R. Montealegre, and A. Poulymenakou (eds.), *Organizational Information Systems in the Context of Globalization*. Boston, MA: Kluwer Academic Publishers.

Robertson, R. (1992). *Globalization: Social Theory and Global Culture*. London: Sage.

Sen, A. (1999). *Development as Freedom*. Oxford: Oxford University Press.

Sreekumar, T. T. (2007). 'Decrypting e-Governance: Narratives, Power Play and Participation in the Gyandoot Intranet', *Electronic Journal of Information Systems in Developing Countries*, 32(4): 1–24.

Thompson, M. P. A. (2002). 'Cultivating Meaning: Interpretive Fine-Tuning of a South African Health Information System', *Information and Organization*, 12(3): 183–211.

UNICEF (2004). <http://www.unicef.org>.

United Nations (2009). <http://www.un.org/millenniumgoals/poverty.shtml>.

Vasudevan, R. (2007). 'Changed Governance or Computerized Governance? Computerized Property Transfer Processes in Tamil Nadu, India', *Information Technologies and International Development*, 4(1): 101–12.

Walsham, G. (2001). *Making a World of Difference: IT in a Global Context*. Chichester: Wiley.

—— (2005a). 'Learning about Being Critical', *Information Systems Journal*, 15(2): 111–17.

—— (2005b). 'Development, Global Futures and IS Research: A Polemic', *Journal of Strategic Information Systems*, 14(1): 5–15.

—— (2005c). 'Critical Engagement: Why, What and How?, in D. Howcroft and E. M. Trauth (eds.), *Handbook of Critical Information Systems Research: Theory and Application*. Cheltenham: Edward Elgar.

—— Robey, D., and Sahay, S. (2007). 'Foreword: Special Issue on Information Systems in Developing Countries', *MIS Quarterly*, 31(2): 317–26.

Whitley, E. (2009). 'Perceptions of Government Technology, Surveillance and Privacy: The UK Identity Cards Scheme', in D. Neyland and B. Goold (eds.), *New Directions in Privacy and Surveillance*. Cullompton: Willan Publishers.

Woodfield, R. (2002). 'Women and Information Systems Development: Not Just a Pretty (Inter)face?', *Information Technology and People*, 15(2): 119–38.

World Bank (2007). 'India Country Overview', <http://www.worldbank.org.in>.

CHAPTER 25

DISCOURSES ON INNOVATION AND DEVELOPMENT IN INFORMATION SYSTEMS IN DEVELOPING COUNTRIES RESEARCH

CHRISANTHI AVGEROU

INTRODUCTION

THERE is a fairly large literature on Information Systems in Developing Countries (ISDC) research.[1] Being nurtured within the field of Information Systems, ISDC research tends to focus on the development and implementation of information technology applications and the organizational changes associated with them. Nevertheless ISDC research has extended the IS research domain to consider the broader socio-economic context of the organizations hosting new technologies. I will refer to this object of study of ISDC research as 'IS innovation' to convey the notion of novelty of experiences of IS implementation and the associated changes within the hosting organization and beyond it. The rationale for using the term innovation is that, even if the technologies implemented in an IS project are already common elsewhere and widespread, the local experience of technology implementation and socio-organizational change constitutes an innovation for the organization concerned and may well constitute innovation for its socio-economic context. Seeing IS implementation as innovation sensitizes the researcher to consider the effort of technology and organizational change and the value of such change in relation to an organization's context. As I argue in this chapter, this is particularly important in ISDC research.

ISDC research is premissed on the potential of ICT to contribute to the improvement of socio-economic conditions in developing countries (Sahay 2001; Walsham, Robey, and Sahay 2007). It aspires to the realization of perceptions of desirable world orders, such as Sen's theory of capabilities (Madon 2004) or the United Nations' Millennium Goal (Gilhooly 2005) vision of eradicating poverty. It is also guided by conceptual models of transformations happening in the contemporary world that necessitate ICT infrastructures, such as Castells' ideas of society and economy as networks (Braa, Monteiro, and Sahay 2004). But beyond these very general premises and aspirations, every ISDC study also makes assumptions about the way IS innovation happens in the context of developing countries and about the notion and process of 'development' towards which IS innovation is intended to contribute.

The existence of alternative assumptions and theoretical perspectives regarding IS innovation are a feature of the epistemological state of IS research in general, and has been extensively discussed in the IS literature (Hirschheim and Klein 1989; Orlikowski and Baroudi 1991; Robey and Boudreau 1999). To some, this state of diversity of research questions, theoretical foundations, and research method is a weakness that needs to be corrected with stricter 'disciplinary' mechanisms (Banville and Landry 1992; Benbasat and Weber 1996; Benbasat and Zmud 2003). But others have argued that that plurality in IS research stems from the nature of IS innovation as a social endeavour, and reflects deeper epistemological perspectives within the social sciences. Rather than seeking to eliminate alternative perspectives, IS research can strengthen its contributions by making explicit their underlying conceptual and theoretical differences (Hirschheim and Klein 1989; Robey 1996). I take this latter view and in this chapter I seek to explore the different underlying perspectives regarding IS innovation within the broader socio-economic context of developing countries.

Development is a contested notion too, and it has been subject to a long theoretical debate. Moreover, development policy and action are entangled with the conflicting interests and power relations in the contemporary global and national politics. The international agencies' policies for economic growth and institutional reform are widely contested in developing countries. Most ISDC studies avoid engaging with controversies on 'development' and tend not to discuss what constitutes development. However, some ISDC authors addressed the question of development more explicitly. For example, Thompson (2004) drew from Escobar's Foucauldian critiques of the discourse on development and voiced suspicion about the development policies IS innovation interventions are intended to support (Thompson 2004). Some authors have taken a critical stance to the currently prevailing development ideas that drive the discourse on digital divide and justifies IS innovation in terms of creating a country's competitiveness capabilities in a global free market (Warschauer 2003; Wade 2004a). Others pointed out the ongoing controversies about the validity of this theoretical position and suspicions on the motives of the agencies that promote them (Heeks and Kenny 2002; Avgerou 2003b; Ciborra 2005; Westrup and Al-Jaghoub forthcoming).

The combination of assumptions regarding the nature of IS innovation effort and development as the aim for IS innovation gives rise to different discourses in ISDC research. I use the term 'discourses' to refer to research approaches stemming from these assumptions on the fundamental nature and consequences of IS innovation. Approach is too vague a term, while 'discourse' indicates more specifically the research language of concepts, theories, and methods, through which researchers form the object of a research study and construct arguments about it.

My main literature sources for this chapter are the specialist journals on ISDC, namely *Information Technology for Development, Information Technologies and International Development,* and the *Electronic Journal of Information Systems in Developing Countries*; and the proceedings of the series of conferences on ICT in developing countries organized by the IFIP WG9.4, published in books and journal special issues (Bhatnagar and Bjørn-Andersen 1990; Bhatnagar and Odedra 1992; Odedra-Straub 1996; Roche and Blaine 1996; Avgerou and Walsham 2000; Krishna and Madon 2002; Sahay and Avgerou 2002; Krishna and Madon 2003). In addition, I reviewed articles on developing countries published in the general IS journals, some of them in special issues on ISDC research.[2]

In the next section I present two perspectives regarding the nature of the IS innovation process: as transfer and diffusion and as socially embedded action; I draw relevant examples from the literature on IS implementation and IS and culture to demonstrate them. In the following section I distinguish between two perspectives on the nature of development transformation towards which ICT is understood to contribute: progressive transformation and disruptive transformation. I draw examples from various research themes and, more specifically, from the literature on telecentres. I then discuss the four discourses formed by combining the perspectives on the nature of IS innovation process and on the nature of development transformation process, and demonstrate them with examples from the literature on software industries in developing countries. Finally, in the conclusions, I argue for the need to develop theoretical capabilities for studying IS innovation in relation to socio-economic contexts and to increase awareness and use of socio-economic development theory.

IS INNOVATION IN DEVELOPING COUNTRIES

ISDC research has been shaped with acute awareness of the relentless ICT and organizational innovation taking place in advanced economies of the world—primarily North America and Europe—and of the increasing socio-economic interconnectedness of all countries and regions in the condition named globalization. With such awareness, an assumption permeating most ISDC research is that developing countries are at a disadvantage in relation to the IS innovation experiences in the context of the origin of new technologies and related new organizational models. This sense of disadvantage is manifested in various ways. To begin with, emphasis has been given to the limited technology and skills available in developing countries or regions. This culminated in the notion of 'digital divide' signifying a new form of inequality and source of socio-economic disadvantage. Some research focused on the significance of this problem and sought to monitor progress in reducing it (Wresch 1998; Kenny 2000; Mbarika et al. 2003). Most ISDC research, though, tends to focus on the experiences and conse-quences of IS innovation, rather than the limitations of technical resources that inhibit it. Such research too tends to be grounded on the assumption that technological and institutional trends are set elsewhere and conveys a sense of urgency to engage with these trends. Difficulties met in following trends and standards of ICT-enabled global-ization and in practising IS innovation effectively feature frequently in research ques-tions and findings of ISDC research (see e.g. Heeks 2002).

Thus, invariably, research on how IS innovation happens in developing countries and with what consequences acknowledges and addresses distinctions of context. The context where a new technology artefact and business model first took shape (usually in an advanced economy) may be different from the context where this combined artefact and model are implemented as part of IS innovation practice in a developing country. Moreover, the socio-organizational settings of IS innovation within sectors, countries, or regions may differ substantially from each other—for example e-government is practised differently and with different results in countries with different public administration sectors.

General IS research has rarely addressed explicitly questions of the socio-economic context in IS innovation and is weak in relevant theoretical guidance. Nevertheless two different orientations towards addressing issues of context are implied in the *universalistic* and *situated* research traditions of general IS research and influenced ISDC research (Avgerou 2002; Avgerou and Madon 2004). Universalistic perspectives elaborate on the value of ICT and information and on the processes of IS innovation through which such value can be realized in terms of general techno-economic reasoning, independently from the particular circumstances of the social actors involved. For example they look for 'best practice', or for the most suitable new organizational form for the information age (Scott Morton 1991; Fulk and DeSanctis 1999). They often acknowledge contextual contingencies, but assume an overriding rationality that determines universal goals of IS innovation and the logic of action towards their satisfaction (Porter and Millar 1984). In contrast, situated perspectives consider IS innovation as enacted by social actors and tend to place emphasis on meaning making and practice within the power dynamics of the *immediate setting* of the innovating organization (Suchman 1994; Orlikowski et al. 1996). These perspec-tives are discernible in two different ways of addressing issues of context in ISDC research, either in terms of *transfer and diffusion* processes or in terms of *socially embedded* processes.

Transfer and Diffusion

The transfer and diffusion perspective examines IS innovation as the diffusion of IS knowledge transferred from advanced economies and adapted to the conditions of developing countries. This perspective assumes that the material/cognitive entities that comprise IS technologies and associated practices of organizing are adequately independent from the social circumstances that give rise to their being transferable, more or less intact, into any other society. Consequently, subject to suitable adaptation, these entities can make a desirable impact. Such research, therefore, traces the particular factors that capture the differences of the recipient country and organization that are likely to affect the innovation process—such as economic conditions, technology competences, people's attitudes to IT, institutionalized work place habits. Consequently it designs modifications of the technologies and interventions in the recipient institutions to make them hospitable to the intended innovation.

In studies of IS development and implementation, authors following the transfer and diffusion approach assume and endeavour to show the relevance of general IS research knowledge and good practice models (methods, analytical approaches, or theories) in particular developing countries or regions and to work out adaptations appropriate for them. They often shape their research in the conceptual terms of the theories of technology diffusion and technology acceptance (Davis 1989; Rogers 1995). For example Rose and Straub (1998) and Al-Gahtani (2003) use Davis's technology acceptance model to study IT use in the Arab world, and identify empirically the particular factors of the social and organizational context of the Arab countries that affect their take-up of ICT (Rose and Straub 1998; Al-Gahtani 2003).

Many studies have sought to transfer and adapt systems development methodologies to accommodate analyses of the socio-organizational conditions of developing countries (Bell and Wood-Harper 1990; Korpela 1996; Korpela et al. 2000; Mursu, Soriyan, and Korpela 2003). Similar method adaptation efforts have addressed the implementation of ERP technologies and IS-driven organizational change (Jarvenpaa and Leidner 1998; He 2004). Such studies enrich IS implementation knowledge and professional practice by working out modifications appropriate to accommodate various local circumstances. They avoid an a-contextual 'best practice' view and adopt a notion of 'appropriate', context-specific practice (Avgerou and Land 1992; Bada 2002). They challenge the feasibility of 'transferring' generic technical know-how into developing countries organizations with the expectation of the same organizational practices and outcomes as in their context of origin (Avgerou 1996). Yet, they retain the general assumptions on the validity of purpose of the attempted innovation as well as the validity of the underlying objectives and rationality of the transferred methods in their new context of practice.

Social Embeddedness

The *social embeddedness* perspective takes the view that IS innovation in developing countries is about constructing new techno-organizational structures within a given local social context. It focuses attention on the embeddedness of IS innovation in the social context of various organizational settings of developing countries. The socially embedded innovation research approach finds the assumption of the transfer and diffusion perspective about the nature of information systems oversimplifying and misleading. It has developed more elaborate ontologies of IS innovation as socially constructed entities, and therefore contingent in their perceived significance and their interplay with human actors and their social institutions. The focal point of the research is the process of innovation *in situ*, thus tracing the cognitive, emotional, and political capacities that individuals nurtured in their local social institutions bring to bear on unfolding innovation attempts. Through this approach the socially embedded innovation discourse sheds light on what, regarding an attempted innovation, is locally meaningful, desirable, or controversial, and therefore how innovation emerges (or is retarded) from the local social dynamics. With attention to local concerns, situated meanings of ICT, and courses of reasonable action that often differ from the taken-for-granted rationality of IS innovation, ISDC studies reveal a much more complex picture of the IS innovation effort than the general IS field has constructed (see e.g. Miscione 2007).

Studies of IS implementation that follow the social embeddedness approach see the purpose of innovation as arising from local problematizations and its course as being determined by the way local actors make sense of it and accommodate it in their lives (Avgerou 2002). To that end, this perspective found theoretical grounding in contemporary social theory, such as Actor Network Theory, structuration theory, organizational institutionalism. (See Part II for a discussion of such theories as these, as applied to the field of IS.) These provided insights and vocabularies to address conceptual relationships such as technology/society, agency/structure, technical reasoning/institutional dynamics. The main objective of contextualist ISDC studies has been the development of theoretical capacity for addressing questions concerning the way specific categories of technologies and social actors clusters are formed, shape each other, and construct particular socio-economic effects.

In comparison to situated studies in the general IS field, ISDC studies following the social embeddedness approach broadens research perspective beyond the particular circumstances of work within an organization—see for example (Orlikowski 1996; Ciborra and Associates 2000; Orlikowski 2000). Early efforts to account for IS innovation in relation to its context built on Pettigrew's contextualist theory, which views particular instances of organizational interventions as processes unfolding through time in relation to layers of context: typically, the organizational setting and its national environment (Pettigrew 1985; Walsham 1993). Madon, for example, followed Pettigrew's contextualist analysis to study the introduction of computers for the management of a rural development programme in India's local administration districts. Her analysis encompassed work norms within the district bureaucracies as well as cultural aspects of the Indian rural setting within which the rural development initiative and its administration was embedded (Madon 1993). While Pettigrew's contextualist approach continues to be followed in ISDC studies (Braa et al. 2007a), several other theoretical approaches have been introduced to explore IS innovation in the developing countries' context, including neo-institutionalist and social constructionist analyses (Avgerou 2001; Avgerou 2003a; Miscione 2007; Silva 2007).

An example of research that takes such a socially embedded view of IS innovation is the series of publications on an extensive action research programme aiming to contribute to the development and implementation of healthcare information systems (HISP) in African, Asian, and Latin American countries (Braa et al. 2007a; Braa, Monteiro, and Sahay 2004). (See also Chapter 24.) Authors analysing the HISP efforts have used a variety of complementary socio-theoretical approaches—structuration, ANT, Castells' networks of action model, complexity theory. They have not attempted to capture the healthcare context of developing countries in a 'best practice' general model. Instead, they have aimed to develop a conceptual analytical capacity to guide context-specific sense making and practice in countries with different healthcare systems and practices. This has led them to consider a range of issues, including standards that are sensitive to the local context (Braa et al. 2007a), and multiple country collaboration across north (technologically and economically advanced) and south (developing) regions (Braa et al. 2007b).

Another example of the social embeddedness perspective is a study of a ten-year effort to implement a data infrastructure for land administration in Guatemala by Silva (2007). His study traces the unfolding of power dynamics within the institutional context of the country and focuses on the historically formed lack of inter-institutional cooperation in the country that created conditions unfavourable to sharing data.

Transfer and Diffusion and Social Embeddedness Perspectives in Research on IS and Culture

In ISDC studies of culture the transfer and diffusion approach frames the relationship of IS and culture in terms of transferring ICT applications into a non-Western national culture, which is usually seen as posing obstacles to innovation and as being a source of resistance (Straub, Loch, and Hill 2001). Hofstede's model of national culture variables and cultural difference (Hofstede 1984) is often used to analyse conflicts between values embedded into and behaviours required by ICT and the national culture of developing countries (Leidner and Kayworth 2006).

Such studies have been criticized as oversimplifying cultural difference (see e.g. Myers and Tan 2002); they 'sweep the subtleties of cultural difference under the universal carpet' as Walsham put it in his extensive discussion of examples of ISDC studies of IS innovation and culture (Walsham 2001). In contrast, research taking the socially embedded and transformative perspective has led many authors to highlight distinct features of historically formed collective behaviour that require attention when designing appropriate ICT systems, or when organizing the innovation process, such as attitude to hierarchy, arranging action in time, sense of space and geography (Sahay 1998; Rohitratana 2000; Zakaria, Stanton, and Sarker-Barney 2003). It has also drawn attention to cross-cultural interactions. In effect, such studies avoid the juxtaposition of IS innovation—assumed to be inscribed with Western culture—with DC culture—assumed to be bent to accommodate it (Walsham 2002).

Particularly promising is the research that suggests a concept of culture which is dynamic and emergent, 'constantly being maintained and changing', an ongoing accomplishment (Westrup et al. 2003). Such research transcends the ICT/culture fit or conflict. Neither ICT nor culture are taken to be uni-dimensional determinants of values and behaviours. ICT, seen as a hybrid network of artefacts, people, and institutions, is subject to negotiation and local IS innovation shaping. Cultural influence on IS innovation, seen as a historically formed disposition for a particular behaviour, may stem from the innovating organization, its national or regional environment, or the social class of individual actors. And rather than IS innovation fitting in or conflicting with the culture of its social context, of particular interest is the mutual reconstitution of IS innovation and the cultures that influence it.

THE QUESTION OF DEVELOPMENT IN ISDC RESEARCH

The main motivation for ISDC research is the belief that ICT has, potentially, the capacity to contribute towards the improvement of many different aspects of life, from alleviating poverty to strengthening the democratic polity. But not all IS research in developing countries engages explicitly with questions of 'development' as action to transform the socio-economic conditions that have been historically formed in the so-called 'developing countries'. In this chapter I am interested in the research that concerns developing countries and is conscious of development as a purposeful and contested endeavour. Therefore, I examine that part of the literature that goes beyond a declaration of an assumption that ICT may serve good causes—e.g. the elimination of poverty—and at least implicitly takes a position regarding the socio-economic transformation process through which ICT will deliver its potential benefit.

Such transformative ISDC research often focuses on specific developmental aims, such as enhancement of livelihoods in rural areas (Duncombe and Heeks 2002), or improved government services (Krishna and Walsham 2005), and seeks to understand the effort it takes for IS innovation to take place successfully and deliver expected benefits. More often than not, though, ISDC research, confronted with the complex and highly political challenges of development endeavours, takes a critical stance to the role of ICT and development. I distinguish two perspectives of ICT-enabled development. The *progressive* perspective considers ICT as enabling transformations in multiple domains of human activities, but they can be accommodated within the existing international and local social order. The *disruptive* perspective is premised on the highly political and controversial nature of development, both as a concept and as an area of policy for international and local action, and reveal conflicts of interest and struggles of power as a necessary part of IS innovation in developing countries.

Progressive Transformation

The progressive transformation perspective in ISDC research reflects a much more widespread understanding of ICT as an instrument for economic and social gains that has been promoted since the mid-1990s by major international development agencies, including the World Bank (World Bank 1999), the United Nations Development Programme (United Nations Development Programme 2001), the World Economic Forum (Dutta and Mia 2009). UNDP's 2001 Human Development Report (United Nations Development Programme 2001: 29) is a good example of the association international organizations make between ICT and development, not least because this series of UNDP reports takes a broad view of development as a socio-economic condition that goes beyond a narrow consideration of economic growth. The 2001 UNDP report seeks to present a clear association between technology and desirable development effects, giving special attention to ICT—particularly the Internet. Indicatively, it quotes a World Bank study (Wang et al. 1999) that showed 'technical progress accounted for 40–50% of mortality reductions between 1960 and 1990—making technology a more important source of gains than higher incomes or higher education levels among women' (United Nations Development Programme 2001: 29). It asserts that '[c]ross-country studies suggest that technological change accounts for a large portion of differences in growth rates' (ibid.).

Central in this perspective is the view that 'investment in ICT and effective use do matter for the economic development of a country' (Mann 2004: 67). It is acknowledged that other changes matter too, particularly because ICT needs to be accompanied by organizational restructuring to deliver productivity gains (Dedrick, Gurbaxani, and Kraemer 2003; Draca, Sadun, and Van Reenen 2007). Moreover, development requires effective government, and e-government is considered to be an important tool for achieving efficiency, transparency, and responsiveness. International development agencies have emphasized also the potential of ICT to improve the performance of state institutions, the delivery of health and education services, as well as democratic participation (United Nations Development Programme 2001).

Some ISDC research has sought to corroborate this thesis on the economic significance of ICT for development (Ngwenyama et al. 2006; Mbarika et al. 2007), addressing concerns of sceptics who doubt the appropriateness of ICT for poor countries and point out their pressing necessity to provide for the basic life needs of a large part of their population, alleviate extreme poverty, and fight endemic diseases and illiteracy. But on the whole ISDC research in the progressive transformation perspective tends to accept without testing the assumption that ICT potentially contributes to economic growth and to investigate the features of the ICT-based economy in particular countries or regions (Molla 2000) or the way ICT contributes to the competitiveness of organizations or regions (La Rovere 1996; Jarvenpaa and Leidner 1998; Goonatilake, Maizza-Neto, and Jayawardene 2000; La Rovere and Pereira 2000; Munkvold and Tundui 2005). Some research from the progressive transformation perspective elaborated on the conditions under which ICT-mediated business models and practices, which are considered necessary for participating in the global economy, are diffused or the conditions under which IT-enabled niche industries are fostered (Davis, McMaster, and Nowak 2002).

The progressive transformation perspective is discernible also in research studying IS innovation in non-commercial organizations, such as in the development of national health data infrastructures (Braa et al. 2007a). The fundamental assumption is that IS innovation in the institutions responsible for the provision of social services can empower them to improve their services and work conditions (Puri 2007).

Disruptive Transformation

The disruptive transformation perspective considers development, including ICT-enabled development, as a contested endeavour or as involving action that affects differently different populations, and thus laden with conflict. Research taking this perspective often expresses doubts about the effectiveness and even the intentions of international or national policies regarding ICT and development. At the international level, analysis manifests suspicion of the developmental intentions of the so-called Washington Consensus as well as the effectiveness of the policies for development that comply with the institutions that comprise it—World Bank, IMF, WTO. At the local level they see the established social order as harbouring inequalities of wealth and power—for example in relation to castes, gender, or ethnic origin—and the ICT-enabled interventions as affecting differently categories of citizens. This approach tends to draw from heterodox economic ideas and critics of globalization (Wade 2004b) and often applies critical theoretical analyses (Kanungo 2003). The researcher is not a neutral observer of the way IS innovation contributes to socio-economic transformations; he or she takes the side of a particular category of people (e.g. the poor, women, children of the world or of a particular developing region) who are weak and vulnerable in the socio-economic regimes of their milieu, and who are at risk to lose out (or at least not benefit) from IS innovation initiatives. Research from the disruptive transformation perspective reveals hidden intentions and power dynamics which maintain or worsens current unevenness of wealth and opportunities for fulfilled lives among countries and categories of people.

A good example of the disruptive transformation perspective is Ciborra's study of the computerization of driving licences in Jordan (2005). In his analysis, Ciborra identifies an international socio-political significance of e-government interventions. Although the declared objectives of e-government projects, such as the computerization of the issuing of driving licences, are improvements of efficiency of citizen services, Ciborra's study shows that such an innovation stumbles upon the complex network of state government controlling mechanisms. Indeed Ciborra, drawing from Heidegger's treatise on technology, points out the ordering character of information technology. The order sought in this case study, he argues, does not concern only the Jordanian government, but the world order at large. He traces the origin of the rationale of e-government in developing countries in the Washington Consensus and the security interests of the US government (Ciborra 2005), thus critically revealing a disruptive logic of IS innovation.

Progressive vs Disruptive Transformation Perspectives in Research on Telecentres

The difference between these two perspectives is manifested in the research on telecentres, most of which acknowledges and discusses developmental aims. The rationale for the creation of telecentres is that countries or regions which do not have access to internet-based services are 'excluded' not only from global economic opportunities but also from modern society's information channels for education, health, and democratic participation. Poverty in many developing country areas, particularly the rural regions, prohibits the diffusion of ICT and telecommunication connectivity to any extent comparable to that of advanced economies. A solution appeared to be the development of community information services, often called telecentres, equipped with computers, Internet connection, as well as fax machines. Many initiatives to introduce telecentres in poor rural communities in developing countries have been taken by international NGOs, such as the Canadian IDRC's Acacia[3] programme in Africa, or by country governments. Although their services vary, most of them run software applications of local interest, such as providing information on health, agricultural product prices, educational material, or the issuing of government certificates.

Early research in the 1990s presented promising initiatives, highlighting the perceived potential of local empowerment through information and communication. Authors that heralded the developmental opportunities of telecentres gave examples of possibilities of overcoming extreme poverty or bureaucratic obstacles, of participating in public sector decisions and actions, and of overcoming corruption (Beilur 2007). Later, research indicated a more nuanced picture of some impressive cases of economic gain and social empowerment, widespread failure and closure, and increasing frustration among key actors such as the entrepreneurs who owned the telecentres, users/customers, and donors (Beilur 2007; Madon et al. 2007). Of interest to the discussion in this chapter is the researchers' assumptions about the way telecentres are expected to contribute their developmental promise.

Much of the research on telecentres assumes that they are introduced in the existing socio-economic structures and practices of disadvantaged communities and can have a positive impact on lessening the gap between them and the advanced industrialized societies. A common expectation in the telecentres initiatives by many NGOs and governments, even in very poor communities, has been that, after investing some seed money, telecentres would form viable enterprises, able to cover the costs of their operations and to sustain a profitable business for local entrepreneurs (Harris, Kumar, and Balaji 2003). Consequently, research on telecentres attempts to fit and adapt the economic rationality of profitable business, even though, as research shows, there is not much potential for profit making from telecentre 'customers' who live in extreme poverty and most of whom have little appreciation of the benefits they may gain from using ICT services (Madon et al. 2007).

Some research that attempted to explain why so often telecentres prove unsustainable raised fundamental questions of effective mechanisms for development, such as public/private partnership mechanism of governance for development (Madon 2005). Kanungo's (2003) analysis of the sustainability of an initiative that uses IT to create 'knowledge centers' in Indian villages places emphasis on the value of these centres 'in terms of a better informed and liberated society'. His Habermasian approach focuses on the disruptive mechanisms enabled by IT that may form a basis for empowerment for the rural poor.

FOUR DISCOURSES ON IS INNOVATION AND DEVELOPMENT

The combination of the two perspectives regarding the nature of the IS innovation process and the nature of the development transformation process give rise to distinctive discourses about ICT and development, see Figure 25.1. I don't mean that ISDC publications can be classified unambiguously on the four squares of a matrix. Indeed, some of the examples I draw from the ISDC literature could be positioned elsewhere on the plane of the matrix if a discussant chose to focus on some line of argument of a research article other than the one I chose to bring to the readers' attention. But my aim is not to classify existing research in rigid categories. It is to show the streams of argumentation about ICT and development that result from taking—most often in an unacknowledged way—these particular views about IS innovation and about development.

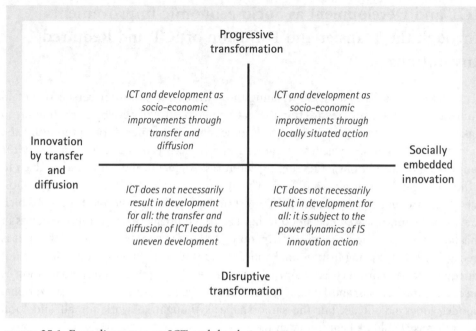

FIGURE 25.1 Four discourses on ICT and development

I find it easier to distinguish between the transfer and diffusion from the social embeddedness perspective of IS innovation and more difficult to do so for authors' perspectives regarding development. This is because ISDC research rarely adequately defines and discusses development perspectives and rarely draws from socio-economic development theory in its analysis. Moreover, quite frequently authors mix progressive transformation and disruptive transformation perspectives. For example, they may adopt the progressive transformation view of ICT and development at the global context by grounding their analysis on publications of indicator tables and policies of international agencies that follow neoclassical economic reasoning, and they may include a disruptive transformation view in their arguments that challenge existing power orders in domestic efforts of harnessing ICT (Brown and Brown 2009). Differences of perspective on the development process at different levels of context may indicate either complementarities or inconsistencies in the argumentation of an author. A point I wish to make in this chapter is that ISDC research can improve its contributions if authors extend the theoretical grounding of their research to draw from debates on development theory and policy.

ICT and Development as Socio-economic Improvements through the Transfer and Diffusion of ICT and Required Institutions

This discourse is formed by intertwining the transfer and diffusion perspective of IS innovation with the progressive transformation perspective of development. It tends to take the form of technical rational techno-economic argumentation, presenting the adoption of ICT-based practices pioneered in advanced economies as a necessity for improving life conditions in developing countries. A great deal of emphasis is given to efficiency gains resulting from ICT. The discourse uses the 'catch up' metaphor: developing countries should adopt the technologies and institutions through which developed countries are understood to have achieved prosperity and improvements in health, education, and political participation to close the gap that separates them. It is recognized that existing institutional conditions in most developing countries are not adequate to support such a vision, and therefore, the argument goes, adaptation is needed (Straub, Loch, and Hill 2001; Bada 2002). One size of ICT and organizational models does not fit all, but the same shape is thought to work for all and local institutions should be bent to match it.

ICT and Development as Socio-economic Improvements through Locally Situated Action

This discourse is formed by the social embeddedness perspective of IS innovation with the progressive transformation perspective of development. It assumes the capacity of ICT to contribute towards improving life conditions, but sees the form and processes of improvements as primarily locally decided in accordance with historically shaped meanings and power relations. Its core argument is that socio-economic change should make sense to the local people, who should be comfortable with the processes of change. There may be obstacles in the harnessing of the developmental potential, stemming from historically developed social orders, such as overcentralized public administration and authoritarian hierarchies, but the belief expressed in this discourse is that these can be addressed with empowering democratic ICT policies and appropriate professional practices, such as allowing for user participation (Braa, Monteiro, and Sahay 2004; Sahay and Walsham 2005; Puri 2007). This discourse acknowledges influences from global actors. It is cautious, but not confrontational about prevailing development ideologies and policies of international organizations. It often has a pragmatic character: technologies and methods transferred from technologically advanced societies do not work. Local improvisations are necessary to close the gap between theory and actual developing countries conditions. An example is Heeks's paper which suggests improvisations in systems development to avoid failure seen as caused by the inappropriateness of general IS design methods (Heeks 2002).

ICT does not Necessarily Result in Development for All: The Transfer and Diffusion of ICT Leads to Uneven Development

This discourse combines the transfer and diffusion perspective of IS innovation with the disruptive transformation perspective of development. Its argumentation accepts the logic of ICT as a force for socio-economic change, but finds that it entails risks of reinforcing domination and inequality. Thus, it uncovers distorting effects of ICT and institutional transfer and diffusion, and interests in preserving historically formed privileges (Wade 2004a; Ciborra 2005). It tends to be confrontational, challenging the evidence on the generally seen as beneficial effects of development policies such as globalization, liberalization, ICT, and productivity gains (Wade 2004b), and doubting the motives of powerful actors, such as the international development agencies, national policy makers, and corporate managers.

ICT does not Necessarily Result in Development for All: It is Subject to the Power Dynamics of IS Innovation Action

This discourse intertwines the social embeddedness perspective of IS innovation with the progressive transformation perspective of development. It is a critical discourse in the sociological sense of critical theory, and is concerned with particular biases of power and inequalities in specific socio-economic conditions of a country or a community. The starting position is the local context, with its historically formed patterns of privileges, and may extend its analysis to the biased influences exerted from the power-laden inscriptions carried by particular technologies or institutional reform models and policies. In a study of the potential use of ICT by Egyptian craftswomen, Hassanin points out various structural challenges that inhibit their capacity to trade in global markets (Hassanin 2008). In effect, the socially embedded and disruptive discourse deconstructs the dominant view about ICT and development, juxtaposing it to the local interests and imaginaries of a better life. Its critiques question not only the effectiveness of ICT and development to lead to life improvements, but also the desirability of their projected visions (Thompson 2004; Stahl 2008).

The Four Discourses in ISDC Research on the Software Industry

Prominent amidst the ISDC literature is a stream of studies focusing on the software industries that emerged in a number of developing countries and compete at the global market, thus forming a substantial part of the 'global outsourcing' or 'offshore outsourcing' phenomenon (Carmel and Agarwal 2002). India is the most successful country in this business, and the efforts of its software firms have been studied within the ISDC subfield since its early days nearly twenty years ago (Heeks 1990; Sahay, Nicholson, and Krishna 2003; Nicholson and Sahay 2004).

Most research on developing countries' software industries argue about ICT and development as socio-economic improvements through the transfer and diffusion of ICT capabilities and required institutions. They see the developmental potential of these industries in their capability to compete in global markets. Their achievement lies in being able to master software production techniques and business models that allow them to compete. Thus, many such studies examined the factors that account for software industry success within the global market of services and products of IS innovation (Carmel 2003a; Adelakum 2005). Success factors include technology and project management skills, labour costs, telecommunications infrastructures, English language skills, copyright legislation, and government industrial policy. There are also ongoing studies that assess and compare the relative advantages among developing countries competing for the lucrative markets of industrialized countries (Carmel 2003c). For example, while India is so far considered the most successful DC software exporter, competition from China on the basis of lower salaries may erode its advantage in some important markets, such as Japan.

Some research has focused on the micro-societal processes that constitute the practices of global outsourcing services, highlighted the difficulties of cross-cultural collaboration and the surfacing of multiple political conflicts (Barrett and Walsham 1995; Nicholson and Sahay 2001), and emphasized the significance of organizational identity and the intrinsically tacit nature of the knowledge of software developers (Sahay, Nicholson, and Krishna 2003; Nicholson and Sahay 2004). For example, Nicholson and Sahay's study of the policy efforts of the Costa Rican government to promote an export-oriented industry highlighted the implications of historically formed vested interests in the country, power structures, and attitudes towards development (Nicholson and Sahay 2007). Nevertheless the discourse of such research does not challenge an implicit progressive transformation view of ICT as an enabler of economic development by participating competitively in the global free market.

Both these discourses—stemming from the transfer of skills and socially embedded practice perspectives—on the software industry in developing countries tend to focus on their capacity for export of software products and services, taking such exports to be an important source of income and of national prestige. Some comparative analyses of the software industries of major developing countries suggest that there may be trade-offs between efforts to foster an export-oriented software industry and IS innovation in domestic organizations (Carmel 2003b; Commander 2005). For example, although successful in exporting software products and services, India's software industry is much less successful in contributing to domestic organizations' IS innovation. The 'trickle down' effect is too slow to make a difference for the rest of the economy so far.

Indeed there is research from the transfer and diffusion and disruptive transformation perspectives that engages in a critical discourse about the developmental role of the developing countries' software industry. D'Costa discusses the Indian software sector as a case of 'uneven and combined development', that is, as coexisting with stagnating sectors such as heavy industry and giving rise to tensions that stem from competing modes of production, inequality, and differential growth rates among different regions (D'Costa 2002). D'Costa's argumentation leads to the suggestion of state action for a balanced development of the economy, by assisting the development of other sectors and thus minimizing the social problems of uneven development.

Madon and Sahay focused on changes in the social fabric of the city of Bangalore caused by its booming software industry, and formed arguments from the social embeddedness and disruptive transformation perspectives (Madon and Sahay 2000). They point out that the city has not attracted only affluent professionals but also the very poor, seeking works at the margins of the official economy and living in slums at the borders of the city, and their research concern is how the lives of this section of the population can be improved.

CONCLUSIONS

ISDC has a lot to contribute by engaging with the ongoing research and debate regarding development that produce theoretical views about the role of ICT and underpin policy action, such as international political economy and institutional economics. To that end, empirical ISDC research needs to develop epistemological capacity to associate the study of IS innovation with the particular socio-economic rationale and policies of development that provide its underlying justification and targets. If it does so, ISDC research faces two major challenges as a subfield of information systems. The first is methodological/theoretical and is related with its recognition of the significance of contextual contingency, that both the diffusion and the social embeddedness discourses share. ISDC studies need to identify the context that matters and develop theory capable of addressing the interrelationship of context with IS innovation. To my judgement the social embeddedness discourse is in a better position to do so. As it has been developed in close association with contemporary social theory, its elaborate socio-technical concepts address more effectively the dynamic interplay between the artefacts/cognitive constructs of IS innovation and the multiple and changing social dimensions in developing countries.

The second challenge is related with the legitimacy of discourses that openly address contemporary political issues. In particular, the disruptive transformation discourses of ISDC research have a kind of criticality that is unprecedented in the IS field. The literature that discusses the developmental potential of ICT and associates IS innovation initiatives with social, political, and economic change articulates critical views about the power relations within specific developing countries and the world at large. The IS field, though familiar with critical discourses, mainly regarding the organizational level politics of the work place (Howcroft and Trauth 2005), has rarely engaged with macro-political analyses regarding ICT and institutional change. ISDC studies that concern the role of ICT in the struggle for the transformation of the life conditions of the billions of poor—with implications for the lives of the affluent—inevitably come to refer to political ideologies of development (such as the 'Washington consensus' or 'basic needs' views), and to policies and actions of development institutions (such as the World Bank, the aid agencies of 'Western' countries, international NGOs). Analyses of the IS innovation context include controversial government policies, such as liberalization of telecommunications for extending connectivity, or the filtering of Internet information by national governments.

This is where, I believe, theoretical strengthening is mostly needed. Without diligent theoretical grounding critical discourses on ICT and development run the risk of having a polemic character, unworthy of scholarly attention and unconvincing in policy circles. ISDC research has a great deal to gain from studying theories pertaining to argumentation of development in economics and political sciences, in a similar way that IS research gained strength in its argumentation about the nature of IS innovation from studying theories of technology in sociology.

NOTES

1. For a review, see Avgerou (2008).
2. See *The Information Society*, 19(1), 2003; *Information Technology and People*, 16(1), 2003; *MISQ*, 31(2), 2006.
3. For information about IDRC's telecentre initiative, see <http:www.idrc.ca/acacia/index.html>. Other initiatives for the creation of community telecentres by international development organizations include ITU's <http:www.itu.int/ITU-D/index.html>; UNESCO's <http:www.unesco.org/websowlr/iip/#funding>, and the World Bank's <http:worldbank.org/html/fpd/telecoms/subtelecom/selected_projects.htm>.

REFERENCES

Adelakum, O. (2005). 'Offshore IT Outsourcing to Emerging Economies: Analysis of Readiness vs Attractiveness', in A. O. Bada and A. Okunoye (eds.), *Proceedings of the 8th International Working Conference of IFIP WG9.4: Enhancing Human Resource Development through IC.* Abuja.

Al-Gahtani, S. S. (2003). 'Computer Technology Adoption in Saudi Arabia: Correlates of Perceived Innovation Attributes', *Information Technology for Development*, 10(1): 57–69.

Avgerou, C. (1996). 'Transferability of Information Technology and Organisational Practices', in M. Odedra-Straub (ed.), *Global Information Technology and Socio-Economic Development.* Nashua, NH: Ivy League, 106–15.

——(2001). 'The Significance of Context in Information Systems and Organisational Change', *Information Systems Journal*, 11: 43–63.

——(2002). *Information Systems and Global Diversity.* Oxford: Oxford University Press.

——(2003a). 'IT as an Institutional Actor in Developing Countries', in S. Krishna and S. Madon (eds.), *The Digital Challenge: Information Technology in the Development Context.* Aldershot: Ashgate, 46–62.

——(2003b). 'The Link between ICT and Economic Growth in the Discourse of Development', in M. Korpela, R. Montealegro, and A. Poulymenakou (eds.), *Organizational Information Systems in the Context of Globalization.* Dordrecht: Kluwer, 373–86.

——(2008). 'Information Systems in Developing Countries: A Critical Research Review', *Journal of Information Technology*, 23(3): 133–46.

——and Land, F. (1992). 'Examining the Appropriateness of Information Technology', in S. Bhatnagar and M. Odedra (eds.), *Social Implications of Computers in Developing Countries.* New Delhi: Tata McGraw-Hill, 26–42.

——and Madon, S. (2004). 'Framing IS Studies: Understanding the Social Context of IS Innovation', in C. Avgerou, C. Ciborra, and F. Land (eds.), *The Social Study of Information and Communication Technology: Innovation, Actors, and Contexts.* Oxford: Oxford University Press, 162–82.

——and Walsham, G. (eds.) (2000). *Information Technology in Context: Studies from the Perspective of Developing Countries.* London: Ashgate.

Bada, A. O. (2002). 'Local Adaptations to Global Trends: A Study of an IT-Based Organizational Change Programme in a Nigerian Bank', *Information Society*, 18(2): 77–86.

Banville, C., and Landry, M. (1992). 'Can the Field of MIS be Disciplined?', in R. Galliers (ed.), *Information Systems Research.* Oxford: Blackwell, 61–88.

Barrett, M., and Walsham, G. (1995). 'Managing IT for Business Innovation: Issues of Culture, Learning, and Leadership in a Jamaican Insurance Company', *Journal of Global Information Management*, 3(3): 25–33.

Beilur, S. (2007). 'Using Stakeholder Theory to Analyze Telecenter Projects', *Information Technologies and International Development*, 3(3): 61–80.

Bell, S., and Wood-Harper, A. T. (1990). 'Information Systems Development for Developing Countries', in S. C. Bhatnagar and N. Bjørn-Andersen (eds.), *Information Technology in Developing Countries.* Amsterdam: North-Holland, 23–40.

Benbasat, I., and Weber, R. (1996). 'Rethinking "Diversity" in Information Systems Research', *Information Systems Research*, 7(4): 369–99.

——and Zmud, R. W. (2003). 'The Identity Crisis within the IS Discipline: Defining and Communicating the Discipline's Core Properties', *MIS Quarterly*, 27(2): 183–94.

Bhatnagar, S. C., and Bjørn-Andersen, N. (eds.) (1990). *Information Technology in Developing Countries*. Amsterdam: North-Holland.

——and Odedra, M. (eds.) (1992). *Social Implications of Computers in Developing Countries*. New Delhi: Tata McGraw-Hill.

Braa, J., Monteiro, E., and Sahay, S. (2004). 'Networks of Action: Sustainable Health Information Systems across Developing Countries', *MIS Quarterly*, 28(3): 337–62.

——Hanseth, O., Heywood, A., Mohammed, W., and Shaw, V. (2007a). 'Developing Health Information Systems in Developing Countries: The Flexible Standards Strategy', *MIS Quarterly*, 31(2): 381–402.

——Monteiro, E., Sahay, S., Staring, K., and Titlestad, O. (2007b). 'Scaling up Local Learning: Experiences from South–North Networks of Shared Software Development', IFIP WG9.4 9th international conference 'Taking Stock of E-Development', São Paulo.

Brown, W., and Brown, I. (2009). *Towards a Research Framework for a Human Development-Based 'Bottom of the Pyramid' ICT Development Strategy in South Africa*. Verona, Italy: ECIS Proceedings.

Carmel, E. (2003a). 'The Globalization of Software Outsourcing to Dozens of Nations: A Preliminary Analysis of the Emergence of 3rd and 4th Tier Software Exporting Nations', in S. Krishna and S. Madon (eds.), *The Digital Challenge: Information Technology in the Development Context*. Aldershot: Ashgate, 359–67.

——(2003b). 'The New Software Exporting Nations: Impacts on National Well Being Resulting from their Software Exporting Industries', *Electronic Journal on Information Systems in Developing Countries*, 13(3).

——(2003c). 'Taxonomy of New Software Exporting Nations', *Electronic Journal on Information Systems in Developing Countries*, 13(2).

—— and Agarwal, R. (2002). 'The Maturation of Offshore Sourcing of Information Technology Work', *MIS Quarterly Executive*, 1(2).

Ciborra, C. (2005). 'Interpreting e-Government and Development: Efficiency, Transparency or Governance at a Distance?', *Information Technology & People*, 18(3): 260–79.

——et al. (eds.) (2000). *From Control to Drift*. Oxford: Oxford University Press.

Commander, S. (2005). *The Software Industry in Emerging Markets*. Cheltenham: Edward Elgar.

Davis, C., McMaster, J., and Nowak, J. (2002). 'IT-Enabled Services as Development Drivers in Low-Income Countries: The Case of Fiji', *Electronic Journal on Information Systems in Developing Countries*, 9.

Davis, F. D. (1989). 'Perceived Usefulness, Perceived Ease of Use, and User Acceptance of Information Technology', *MIS Quarterly*, 13(3): 319–40.

D'Costa, A. P. (2002). 'Uneven and Combined Development: Understanding India's Software Exports', *World Development*, 31(1): 211–26.

Dedrick, J., Gurbaxani, V., and Kraemer, K. L. (2003). 'Information Technology and Economic Performance: A Critical Review of the Empirical Evidence', *ACM Computing Surveys*, 35(1): 1–28.

Draca, M., Sadun, R., and Van Reenen, J. (2007). 'Productivity and ICTs: A Review of the Evidence', in R. Mansell, C. Avgerou, D. Quah, and R. Silverstone (eds.), *The Oxford Handbook of Information and Communication Technologies*. Oxford: Oxford University Press, 100–47.

Duncombe, R. A., and Heeks, R. B. (2002). 'Entreprise across the Digital Divide: Information Systems and Rural Micro-enterprise in Botswana', *Journal of International Development*, 14 (1): 61–74.

Dutta, S., and Mia, I. (2009).'The Global Information Technology Report 2008–2009: Mobility in a Networked World'. World Economic Forum, Geneva, Switzerland.

Fulk, J., and DeSanctis, G. (1999). 'Articulation of Communication Technology and Organizational Form', in G. DeSanctis and J. Fulk (eds.), *Shaping Organization Form: Communication, Connection, and Community*. Thousand Oaks, CA: Sage, 5–32.

Gilhooly, D. (2005). 'Innovation and Investment: Information and Communication Technologies and the Millennium Development Goals'. Report prepared for the United Nations ICT Task Force in Support of the Science, Technology & Innovation Task Force of the United Nations Millennnium Project.

Goonatilake, L., Maizza-Neto, O., and Jayawardene, P. (2000). 'Enhancing Enterprise Competitiveness in Developing Countries through the Promotion of Management Information and Benchmarking Tools', in S. Sahay, J. Miller, and D. Roode (eds.), *Proceedings of the 6th International Working Conference of IFIP WG 9.4: Information Flows, Local Improvisations and Work Practices*. Cape Town: STS Conferences.

Harris, R. W., Kumar, A., and Balaji, V. (2003). 'Sustainable Telecentres? Two Cases from India', in S. Krishna and S. Madon (eds.), *The Digital Challenge: Information Technology in the Development Context*. Aldershot: Ashgate, 124–35.

Hassanin, L. (2008). 'Egyptian Women Artisans: ICTs are Not the Entry to Modern Markets', in C. Avgerou, M. L. Smith, and P. Van den Besselaar (eds.), *Social Dimensions of Information and Communication Technology Policy*. New York: Springer.

He, X. (2004). 'The ERP Challenge in China: A Resource-Based Perspective', *Information Systems Journal*, 14: 153–67.

Heeks, R. (1990). 'Fourth Generation Languages (4GLs) and the Indian Software Industry', in S. C. Bhatnagar and N. Bjørn-Andersen (eds.), *Information Technology in Developing Countries*. Amsterdam: North-Holland, 251–64.

——(2002). 'Information Systems and Developing Countries: Failure, Success and Local Improvisations', *Information Society*, 18(2): 101–12.

——and Kenny, C. (2002). 'ICTs and Development: Convergence or Divergence for Developing Countries?' *Bangalore: Information and Communication Technologies and Development: New Opportunities, Perspectives and Challenges*, 29–44.

Hirschheim, R., and Klein, H. K. (1989). 'Four Paradigms of Information Systems Development', *Communications of the ACM*, 32(10): 1199–216.

Hofstede, G. (1984). *Culture's Consequences: International Differences in Work Related Values*. London: Sage.

Howcroft, D., and Trauth, E. M. (eds.) (2005). *Handbook of Critical Information Systems Research*. Cheltenham: Edward Elgar.

Jarvenpaa, S. L., and Leidner, D. E. (1998). 'An Information Company in Mexico: Extending the Resource-Based View of the Firm to a Developing Country Context', *Information Systems Research*, 9(4): 342–61.

Kanungo, S. (2003). 'Information Village: Bridging the Digital Divide in Rural India', in S. Krishna and S. Madon (eds.), *The Digital Challenge: Information Technology in the Development Context*. Aldershot: Ashgate, 104–23.

Kenny, C. J. (2000). 'Expanding Internet Access to the Rural Poor in Africa', *Information Technology for Development*, 9(1): 25–32.

Korpela, M. (1996). 'Computer Systems Development for "Delinking" in Nigeria', in M. Odedra-Straub (ed.), *Global Information Technology and Socio-Economic Development*. Nashua, NH: Ivy League, 116–29.

Korpela, M., Soriyan, H. A., Olufokunbi, K. C., and Mursu, A. (2000). 'Made-in-Nigeria Systems Development Methodologies: An Action Research Project in the Health Sector', in C. Avgerou and G. Walsham (eds.), *Information Technology in Context: Studies from the Perspective of Developing Countries*. Aldershot: Ashgate, 113–33.

Krishna, S., and Madon, S. (2002). 'Information & Communication Technologies and Development: New Opportunities, Perspectives & Challenges', Seventh International Working Conference of IFIP WG 9.4, Bangalore: Indian Institute of Management Bangalore.

——(eds.) (2003). *The Digital Challenge: Information Technology in the Development Context*. Aldershot: Ashgate.

——and Walsham, G. (2005). 'Implementing Public Information Systems in Developing Countries: Learning from a Success Story', *Information Technology for Development*, 11 (2): 1–18.

La Rovere, R. (1996). 'Diffusion of IT and the Competitiveness of Brazilian Banking', in E. M. Roche and M. J. Blaine (eds.), *Information Technology, Development and Policy*. Aldershot: Avebury, 95–112.

——and Pereira, M. V. R. (2000). 'Adoption of ICT and Competitiveness in the Tourism Sector: The Case of Brazilian Travel Agencies', in S. Sahay, J. Miller, and D. Roode (eds.), *Proceedings of the 6th International Working Conference of IFIP WG 9.4: Information Flows, Local Improvisations and Work Practices*. Cape Town: SBS Conferences.

Leidner, D. E., and Kayworth, T. (2006). 'A Review of Culture in Information Systems Research: Toward a Theory of Information Technology Culture', *MIS Quarterly*, 30(2): 357–99.

Madon, S. (1993). 'Introducing Administrative Reform through the Application of Computer-Based Information Systems: A Case Study in India', *Public Administration and Development*, 13: 37–48.

——(2004). 'Evaluating the Developmental Impact of e-Governance Initiatives: An Exploratory Framework' *Electronic Journal on Information Systems in Developing Countries*, 20 (5): 1–13.

——(2005). 'Governance Lessons from the Experience of Telecentres in Kerala', *European Journal of Information Systems*, 14(4): 401–16.

——and Sahay, S. (2000). 'Democratic Governance and Information Flows: A Case Study in Bangalore', *Information Communication and Society*, 3(2).

——Reinhard, N., Roode, D., and Walsham, G. (2007). 'Digital Inclusion Projects in Developing Countries: Processes of Institutionalisation', IFIP WG9.4 9th international conference 'Taking Stock of E-Development', São Paulo, Brazil.

Mann, C. L. (2004). 'Information Technologies and International Development: Conceptual Clarity in the Search for Commonality and Diversity', *Information Technologies and International Development*, 1(2): 67–79.

Mbarika, V. W., Kah, M. M. O., Musa, P. H., Meso, P., and Warren, J. (2003). 'Predictors of Growth of Teledensity in Developing Countries: A Focus on Middle and Low-Income Countries', *Electronic Journal on Information Systems in Developing Countries*, 12(1): 1–16.

——Payton, F. C., Kvasny, L., and Amadi, A. (2007). 'IT Education and Workforce Participation: A New Era for Women in Kenya?', *Information Society*, 23(1): 1–18.

Miscione, G. (2007). 'Telemedicine in the Upper Amazon: Interplay with Local Health Care Practices', *MIS Quarterly*, 31(2): 403–25.

Molla, A. (2000). 'Downloading or Uploading? The Information Economy and Africa's Current Status', *Information Technology for Development*, 9: 205–21.

Munkvold, B. E., and Tundui, H. P. (2005). 'The Role of IT in Supporting Women Entrepreneurs in Urban Tanzania', in A. O. Bada and A. Okunoye (eds.), *Proceedings of the 8th International Working Conference of IFIP WG9.4: Enhancing Human Resource Development through ICT.* Abuja, Nigeria.

Mursu, A., Soriyan, H. A., and Korpela, M. (2003). 'Risky Business: A Case Study on Information Systems Development in Nigeria', in S. Krishna and S. Madon (eds.), *The Digital Challenge: Information Technology in the Development Context.* Aldershot: Ashgate, 318–39.

Myers, M. D., and Tan, F. B. (2002). 'Beyond Models of National Culture in Information Systems Research', *Journal of Global Information Management,* 10(1): 24–32.

Ngwenyama, O., Andoh-Baidoo, F. K., Bollou, F., and Morawczynski, O. (2006). 'Is there a Relationship between ICT, Health, Education and Development? An Empirical Analysis of Five West African Countries from 1997–2003', *Electronic Journal on Information Systems in Developing Countries,* 23(5).

Nicholson, B., and Sahay, S. (2001). 'Some Political and Cultural Issues in the Globalisation of Software Development: Case Experience from Britain and India', *Information and Organization,* 11: 25–43.

————(2004). 'Embedded Knowledge and Offshore Software Development', *Information and Organization,* 14: 329–65.

————(2007). 'Software Exports Development in Costa Rica: Contradictions and the Potential for Change', IFIP WG9.4 9th international conference 'Taking Stock of E-Development', São Paulo, Brazil.

Odedra-Straub, M. (ed.) (1996). *Global Information Technology and Socio-economic Development.* Nashua, NH: Ivy League,.

Orlikowski, W. J. (1996). 'Improvising Organizational Transformation over Time: A Situated Change Perspective', *Information Systems Research,* 7(1): 63–92.

——(2000). 'Using Technology and Constituting Structures: A Practice Lens for Studying Technology in Organizations', *Organization Science,* 11(4): 404–28.

——and Baroudi, J. J. (1991). 'Studying Information Technology in Organizations: Research Approaches and Assumptions', *Information Systems Research,* 2(1): 1–28.

——Walsham, G., Jones, M. R., and DeGross, J. I. (eds.) (1996). *Information Technology and Changes in Organizational Work.* London: Chapman & Hall.

Pettigrew, A. M. (1985). 'Contextualist Research and the Study of Organisational Change Processes', in E. Mumford, R. Hirschheim, G. Fitzgerald, and A. T. Wood-Harper (eds.), *Research Methods in Information Systems.* Amsterdam: North-Holland, 53–78.

Porter, M., and Millar, V. (1984). 'How Information Gives you Competitive Advantage', *Harvard Business Review,* 63(4): 149–60.

Puri, S. K. (2007). 'Integrating Scientific with Indigenous Knowledge: Constructing Knowledge Alliances for Land Management in India', *MIS Quarterly,* 31(2): 355–79.

Robey, D. (1996). 'Diversity in Information Systems Research: Threat, Promise and Responsibility', *Information Systems Research,* 7(4): 400–8.

——and Boudreau, M. C. (1999). 'Accounting for the Contradictory Organizational Consequences of Information Technology: Theoretical Directions and Methodological Implications', *Information Systems Research,* 10(2): 167–85.

Roche, E. M., and Blaine, M. J. (eds.) (1996). *Information Technology, Development and Policy.* Aldershot: Avebury.

Rogers, E. M. (1995). *Diffusion of Innovations,* 4th edn. New York: The Free Press.

Rohitratana, K. (2000). 'The Role of Thai Values in Managing Information Systems: A Case Study of Implementing an MRP System', in C. Avgerou and G. Walsham (eds.), *Information Technology in Context: Implementing Systems in the Developing World*. Aldershot: Ashgate, 23–39.

Rose, G., and Straub, D. (1998). 'Predicting General IT Use: Applying TAM to the Arabic World', *Journal of Global Information Management*, 6: 39–46.

Sahay, S. (1998). 'Implementing GIS Technology in India: Some Issues of Time and Space', *Accounting, Management and Information Technologies*, 8: 147–88.

——(2001). 'Introduction to the Special Issue on "IT and Health Care in Developing Countries"', *Electronic Journal on Information Systems in Developing Countries*, 5: 1–6.

——and Avgerou, C. (2002). 'Special Issue on IS in Developing Countries', *Information Society*.

——Nicholson, B., and Krishna, S. (2003). *Global IT Outsourcing: Software Development across Borders* Cambridge: Cambridge University Press.

——and Walsham, G. (2005). 'Scaling of Health Information Systems in India: Challenges and Approaches', *Enhancing Human Resource Development through ICT*, IFIP WG9.4. Abuja, Nigeria.

Scott Morton, M. S. (1991). *The Corporation of the 1990s: Information Technology and Organizational Transformation*. New York: Oxford University Press.

Silva, L. (2007). 'Institutionalization does not Occur by Decree: Institutional Obstacles in Implementing a Land Administration System in a Developing Country', *Information Technology for Development*.

Stahl, B. C. (2008). 'Empowerment through ICT: A Critical Discourse Analysis of the Egyptian ICT Policy', in C. Avgerou, M. L. Smith, and P. Van den Besselaar (eds.), *Social Dimensions of Information and Communication Technology Policy*. New York: Springer.

Straub, D., Loch, K. D., and Hill, C. E. (2001). 'Transfer of Information Technology to the Arab World: A Test of Cultural Influence Modeling', *Journal of Global Information Management*, 9(4): 6–48.

Suchman, L. (1994). 'Working Relations of Technology Production and Use', *Computer Supported Cooperative Work*, 2: 21–39.

Thompson, M. P. A. (2004). 'ICT, Power, and Developmental Discourse: A Critical Analysis', *Electronic Journal on Information Systems in Developing Countries*, 20(4): 1–26.

United Nations Development Programme (2001). 'Making New Technologies Work for Human Development'. New York: UNDP.

Wade, R. (2004a). 'Bridging the Digital Divide: New Route to Development or New Form of Dependency?', in C. Avgerou, C. Ciborra, and F. Land (eds.), *The Social Study of Information and Communication Technology: Innovation, Actions, and Contexts*. Oxford: Oxford University Press, 185–206.

——(2004b). 'Is Globalization Reducing Poverty and Inequality?', *World Development*, 32(4): 567–89.

Walsham, G. (1993). *Interpreting Information Systems in Organizations*. Chichester: John Wiley.

——(2001). *Making a World of Difference: IT in a Global Context*. Chichester: John Wiley.

——(2002). 'Cross-cultural Software Production and Use: A Structurational Analysis', *MIS Quarterly*, 26(4): 359–80.

——Robey, D., and Sahay, S. (2007). 'Foreword: Special Issue on Information Systems in Developing Countries', *MIS Quarterly*, 31(2): 317–26.

Wang, J., Jamison, D. T., Bos, E., Preker, A., and Peabody, J. (1999). 'Measuring Country Performance on Health: Selected Indicators for 115 Countries'. Washington, DC: World Bank.

Warschauer, M. (2003). 'Dissecting the "Digital Divide": A Case Study in Egypt', *Information Society*, 19(4): 297–304.

Westrup, C., and Al-Jaghoub, S. (forthcoming). 'Nation States and Networks of Flows: The Role of the State in Jordan's ICT Enabled Development'.

——Liu, W., El Sayed, H., and Al Jaghoub, S. (2003). 'Taking Culture Seriously: ICTs, Cultures and Development', in S. Madon and S. Krishna (eds.), *The Digital Challenge: Information Technology in the Development Context*. Aldershot: Ashgate.

World Bank (1999). *World Bank Development Report: Knowledge for Development*. New York: Oxford University Press.

Wresch, W. (1998). 'Information Access in Africa: Problems with Every Channel', *Information Society*, 14(4): 295–300.

Zakaria, N., Stanton, J. M., and Sarker-Barney, S. T. M. (2003). 'Designing and Implementing Culturally-Sensitive IT Applications: The Interaction of Culture Values and Privacy Issues in the Middle East', *Information Technology & People*, 16(1): 49–75.

CHAPTER 26

....

FROM INSTRUMENTALITY TO EMERGENCE IN INFORMATION SYSTEMS

....

RICHARD T. WATSON,[*] PIERRE BERTHON,
AND LEYLAND F. PITT

THE NATURE OF INNOVATION

....

FRAMEWORKS that explain the dispersion of technological innovations are useful navigational aids for mapping future directions and understanding roadblocks and diversions. There are two aspects to *techne*, the term from which the word technology stems. First, *techne* is the Greek word for the activities and skills of the craftsperson, and also describes the art of the mind; *techne* is a 'bringing forth', a 'revealing'. Second, from early Greek times, the word *techne* is linked with *episteme*. Both words are essential parts of knowing. Aristotle unites and differentiates thus: *episteme* (the what) and *techne* (the how) of the emergence of new thoughts, or the revelation of fresh insights. This review of the origin of the term technology proposes an alternative to the *instrumental* view of technology as a means to an end: technology is also a mode of *emergence* (Berthon, Pitt, and Watson 2008). Organizations frequently think of technology as a means to achieving corporate strategies, and the IS field has concerned itself with aligning corporate and IS strategy. In many instances, however, information systems result in emergent organizational strategies. (See also Chapter 12.) The classic case of American Hospital Supplies (Vitale 1988) exemplifies this phenomenon. AHS set out to solve a data entry problem by placing terminals in hospitals for on-line order entry. It emerged that its easy to use system generated additional sales without an increase in the sales force. As a result, Information Systems were rebadged as competitive weapons (Ives and Learmonth 1984). (See also Chapter 14.) This creative, emergent nature of IS is not limited to the organizational arena, but can occur with any IS product, such as an iPod.

Organizations don't only use information systems to *implement* strategies, in many instances information systems *create* new emergent strategies for firms. Similarly, while information systems may be used to *satisfy* the needs and wants of organizational customers, just as frequently they *create* new needs and wants, maybe even more.

IS research on emergent phenomena has been almost exclusively confined to the hierarchical environment of the organization. Yet the hierarchy is only one of four domains of economic activity. Transaction cost economics's original identification of firms and markets as two approaches to organizing economic activity (Arrow 1974) was extended to embrace networks (Uzzi 1996). More recently, as a result of the emergence of open source, a fourth sector has been identified, which is variously labelled bazaar, peer production, or community (Watson et al. 2005). The three other domains (i.e. markets, networks, and communities) are not subject to the same intensity of control that exists within the bureaucratic confines of a hierarchy. The greater freedom means that they are potentially much richer environs for reinvention and studying the technology diaspora from genesis to revelations (Berthon, Pitt, and Watson 2008).

THE EVOLUTION

In order to better understand the trajectories that an IS might assume in and beyond the confines of the organization, we propose the model shown in Figure 26.1. The possible categories of how technology relates to the developer's original intentions are: extension, conversion, subversion, diversion, emersion, and aspersion (Berthon, Hulbert, and Pitt 2005). Our choice is to focus on intentions, because actions in a social setting are guided by an individual's goals. Inventors have a purpose and those who repurpose a technology also have intentions, even if they are at variance with those of the original designer.

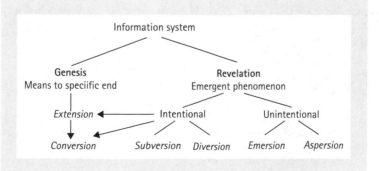

FIGURE **26.1** Information system evolution (adapted from Berthon, Hulbert, and Pitt 2005)

Genesis

From an instrumentality perspective, innovation is inspired by a perceived need. The invention is designed to solve a specific need, and the innovators typically have a particular goal in mind. Generally, the goal is highly specific and the potential consequences thus myopically constrained. In contrast is the contextual design approach epitomized by the Finnish architect, Eliel Saarinen, who averred,[1]

> Always design a thing by considering it in its next larger context—a chair in a room,
> a room in a house, a house in an environment, an environment in a city plan.

However, the shift from design for a specific task to contextual design is, we argue, only partially illuminating. We suggest that there are three dimensions to Information Systems design. Design for goal, design for context, and design for emergence (see Figure 26.1). Design for goal is the classic design paradigm: an information system is design to accomplish a specific task, meet a specific need, or reach a specific goal—the design criterion 'efficiency'. Design for context is thinking about the system in its operational context; this goes beyond the specific design goal, to consider the context or contexts of use; this includes such factors as ergonomics, experiential frame, social milieu, and so forth. The design criterion is 'fit'. Design for emergence is the realization that no *a priori* technology can be entirely pre-specified in its task or context. It is design by being cognizant of the emergent trajectories that a technology can and will take once it is released into a larger social, economic, and environmental system with which it interacts—changing and being changed in unpredictable ways. Here the design criterion is: to what extent should *emergent flexibility* be designed into the system? The characteristics of emergent flexibility are discussed later.

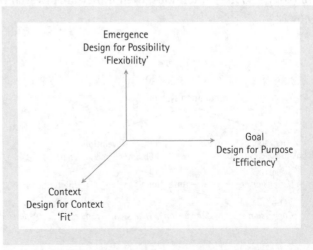

FIGURE **26.2** The three dimensions of Information Systems design

Whilst most information systems are designed with a specific goal in mind, relatively few take into account the context. The One Laptop Per Child (OLPC) project is an exception. It was designed with a specific goal in mind (to provide a laptop to children in developing countries), and designed with its wider operational context in mind. Where it failed was in the design for emergence. Its mission: 'To create educational opportunities for the world's poorest children by providing each child with a rugged, low-cost, low-power, connected laptop with content and software designed for collaborative, joyful, self-empowered learning. When children have access to this type of tool they get engaged in their own education. They learn, share, create, and collaborate. They become connected to each other, to the world and to a brighter future.'[2] This noble project identifies education as the major problem of children in the developing economies. The proposed solution is to provide each child with a laptop computer. The problem with laptop computers is that they are costly—expensive components and expensive operating systems. So the innovator's goal is to design and manufacture an inexpensive laptop, with a free, open source operating system. Initially the aim was to be able to sell the product at a price of US$100. The OLPC designers were conceptually expansive, and saw their product as fitting in a classroom, within a school, and as part of a national education system (Markoff 2005). As we will see, while the vision had distance, it did not embrace all the potential outcomes, which is not surprising. What is surprising is that the initial vision was so expansive, and our observations suggest that most innovators do not see the larger space they potentially influence. The root cause of this myopia is that information technologies are typically flexible and can usually be hacked to create further opportunities for retargeting. The more a system can be reprogrammed, the more it can be reinvented and drift from serving its original purpose. In Figure 26.1, we specify a conceptual framework for thinking about what happens to technology beyond its genesis. Thus, to paraphrase Saarinen, we would proclaim: always design an information technology by considering how it might change its larger context—reflect on the possibilities for conversion, subversion, diversion, emersion, and aspersion.

We now discuss each of these possibilities and explain the ideas illustrated by Figure 26.1 by drawing upon the One Laptop Per Child (OLPC) project to illustrate the conceptual foundations of our thinking.

Extension

In May 2008, OLPC announced plans for a second-generation device, which is an extension of the original design. The XO-2[3] is now presented foremost as a device following the format of a book. It is described as a notebook or a book reader. In addition, while still described as a laptop, it is also put forward as a tablet. In essence, XO-2 has been extended from a laptop to a multifunctional information appliance. In line with this rethinking, one alternative discussed is the provision of a piano keyboard, so that XO-2 can also be a musical instrument.

Conversion

Conversion describes the process by which an information technology is reconceived to meet different goals. The OLPC was originally conceived as a platform for freely available open source software with Sugar, the operating system, based on Linux.

Microsoft opposed the concept of the OLPC and open source software for some years, but by mid-2008 Microsoft had modified Windows XP to run on the OLPC and support its ebook reader, writing pad, and camera (Lohr 2008). The Ministries of Education who purchased the laptops believe that Windows-based skills would improve job prospects, an outlook that Microsoft undoubtedly encouraged. Thus, the original notion of a machine for learning had been converted to a tool for training in Microsoft software.

Revelation—Intentional

Consumers and other social actors through their interaction with new technologies envisage new opportunities. New applications emerge because of the deliberate acts of firms, competitors, and consumers. A technology can be complemented, imitated, and reinvented. In our terms, consumers *subvert* and third parties *divert* the innovator's plans for the use of the technology. Intentional revelations result from people changing the technology.

Subversion

San Francisco's Good Hotel is slated as a hotel with a conscience. Its philanthropic and positive outlook is meant to surface the 'good in all of us'.[4] Not surprisingly, it has a green OLPC computer in its business centre because of the 'goodness' aura of the OLPC project. Through the 'Give One, Get One' programme,[5] citizens in advanced economies who purchase one laptop also pay for another for a child in a developing economy. Thus, owning an OLPC laptop is a symbol of one's principles and can evoke the similar good feelings to driving a Prius. It has been diverted to become a conspicuous sign that one cares about the education of the less privileged.

Diversion

Information technologies because of their designed flexibility can be consciously diverted to meet other goals. Third parties can repurpose the use of a technology through political, social, technological, or legal interventions. The openness of the OLPC makes it a hacker's dream (Fogie 2008a, 2008b). The instructions are readily available (Fogie 2008b) to install a range of tools that most hackers find necessary, such as network mapping and application vulnerability scanning. These tools can be used by security experts for checking the shortcomings of corporate systems, as well as by those with sinister goals, who can use it to crack a corporation's electronic security. The size and friendly green of the OLPC gives it an appearance of innocence, but it can be easily diverted into a powerful tool for intrusion, for both good and bad. (See also Chapter 17.)

Revelation—Unintentional

The designer of any technology cannot foresee all the potential outcomes of a new product, and some of these outcomes can have a significant impact on society and human behaviour. Unintentional revelation changes roles and structures in a way the original inventor had not conceived. *Emersion* occurs when a technology is widely adopted and produces primary positive changes for consumers and society.

On the other hand, some emergent reinventions create negative societal effects. *Aspersion*,[6] our term for these outcomes, results in undesirable consequences and even in some cases the opposite of the designer's larger purpose. For example, we will shortly report evidence that laptops for students result in lower grades.

Emersion

Emersion describes the degree to which a technology morphs into a different form that influences economic and social life. The OLPC concept of a small and highly portable computer of limited processing power but with connectivity has spawned the netbook computer (Thompson 2009). The design specifications presented to Mary Lou Jepsen by OLPC forced an innovative approach. The result was a computer with flash memory, an open source operating system, a low-power low-speed processor, and an energy-efficient LCD panel—all for less than US$200.

The design of the OLPC inspired traditional laptop makers because these low-cost, low-performance computers were a potential threat to their laptop market. The manufacturers soon discovered there was a market for such a product among the middle class in Western Europe and the USA. Over 10 million netbooks have been sold and it is estimated that in 2010, netbooks will be 12 per cent of the laptop market (Thompson 2009). Netbooks align with the move to cloud computing in which all data and applications are stored on servers and accessed via networks (e.g. WiFi, WiMax, G4). There is no need for a powerful computer when it need only run a browser to give a high level of functionality. The OLPC has given rise through the process of emersion to a highly portable, low-cost, simple machine that serves the middle class in the developed economies, who are a far cry from the classroom in a poor country.

Aspersion

Aspersion occurs when a technology produces undesirable social outcomes. The central belief of the founders and funders of the OLPC is that laptops improve education. However, there is considerable evidence, which was available at the time the project commenced, that computers in the classroom have not transformed education (Cuban 2001). Recent research shows no evidence that computers in the home lead to better educational outcomes. Indeed, it appears that computers result in students doing less homework, with a consequent impact on learning (Malamud and Pop-Eleches 2008). Computers are a distraction for many children because they provide access to much more than educational material, in particular games (Fisman 2008). Thus, when developing economies divert very scarce resources into laptop programmes there is a strong likelihood that they get no educational gains. Furthermore, funding for other educational needs (e.g. textbooks) or infrastructure projects (e.g. sewage and electrification) is likely to be reduced so that beneficial gains from proven investments are lost. For example, the World Bank reports that the return on basic educational materials, such as textbooks, is very high (Filmer and Pritchett 1997). The net effect is that a country loses rather than gains from a large-scale investment in laptops. As one critic noted: 'I've thought for a while that sending laptops to developing countries is simply the 21st century equivalent of sending bibles to the colonies.'[7]

Factors Affecting the Emergent Flexibility

Technologies vary in their degree of emergent flexibility. Some technologies stray little from their intended goal (e.g. the disk drive). Others drift slowly from the inventor's original purpose (e.g. the cellphone). Finally, some technologies morph in ways that their designers never imagined (e.g. the Internet). Three factors—openness, programmability, and self-organization—can help us understand emergent flexibility (Berthon, Pitt, and Watson 2008).

Openness

Technologies are frequently the playthings of technologists, nerds, and hackers. The more they can learn about the technology, the more likely that we will reinvent. The open source software movement typifies the power of openness. Releasing a program's code is one of the highest levels of openness. The success of Linux, augmented by many programmers, is one of the most powerful demonstrations of openness on emergent flexibility.

> Proposition 1: The more open a technology the faster and more expansive will be the level of emergent flexibility.

Programmability

Customization and reinvention are facilitated by programmability. Computers are in many ways the ultimate demonstration of the power of emergent flexibility because the notion of what you can do with a computer has been reinvented over and over again—from the computer as a calculator to the computer as a social networking tool.

> Proposition 2: The ease of programming a technology determines its emergent flexibility.

Self-organizing Mechanisms

Emergence flexibility requires mechanisms that support self-organizing. The spread of reinvention of a new technology depends on an infrastructure that allows talented consumers, who might be globally distributed, to collaborate collectively. The Internet and associated cooperative technologies (e.g. cloud computing, websites, Skype) enable those with a common interest to participate in the reinvention of a technology and the dispersion of innovative applications. Global communication networks facilitate self-organizing groups to emerge among a technology's aficionados no matter where individual participants might live provided they have an Internet connection with sufficient bandwidth. Self-organization is one of the emergent outcomes of the Internet and cellphones. We can organize in ways that were inconceivable a few decades ago.

> Proposition 3: Technologies that support self-organizing mechanisms will support emergent flexibility.

> Proposition 4: Technologies that support self-organizing mechanisms will support emergent technologies for increased self-organization.

CONCLUSION

Information systems have existed since the emergence of modern humans. As our distant ancestors learned how to use simple technologies (e.g. hammerstones), they also developed techniques to transmit their skills and knowledge within and across generations. Humans have a long history of building highly flexible information technologies to support their need to share information. Speech, writing, printing, and algebraic symbols are all examples of technologies that have high emergent flexibility because of their openness, programmability (in the sense of supporting infinite combinations), and an ability to enable self-organizing mechanisms.

If one reflects on the historical development of information technology, and the information systems they enable, the predominant pattern is emergence. Our forebears did not plan speech, grammar, writing, alphabets, and ideograms. These fundamental elements of information technology emerged and generated a myriad of emergent information systems. The idiosyncrasies of many of our fundamental technologies, grammar for example, are abundant evidence of the lack of planning or control driving these technologies.

For a short period, when information systems were primarily the product of mainframe computers and corporate bureaucracies, the great majority of computer-based information systems were planned and controlled. They were developed in a systematic manner following the principles of systems analysis and design and project management. This is no longer the case. Personal computers, browsers, and smart cellphones have broken the dyke of corporate control. Personal computers breached the wall, web browsers overwhelmed it, and who knows at this point what smart cellphones will do. What we do know is that the level of innovation and creativity has exploded recently with Apple's release of a software development kit for the cellphone. In a little over six months, 30,000 apps have been released.[8] Who would have expected that the iPhone could be a level or panoramic camera, let alone a seismometer?[9] (See also Chapter 18.)

The dominance of emergence in the landscape means that IS researchers will need to widen their approaches to studying IS phenomena. First, the traditional focus has been on corporate domains but now so much more happens in personal spaces and information systems are the fabric of everyday life. In many ways, we are returning to the status quo as information systems have always been integrated into the texture of civilization (e.g. books, newspapers, and television), and now it is Facebook, iPods, smart phones, and the web as advances in information technologies have enabled computers to be embedded in consumer appliances.

Second, technological change has made so many new sources of data available to study. When the vast majority of data are borne digital, huge repositories of data are created. So the trusted and traditional approaches, like surveys, experiments, and qualitative approaches will now need to be expanded to things like text analysis, social network analysis, ethnography in virtual environments, and data mining. The logged interactions of the open source community alone, in their never-ending search for perfection through continuous modification, could provide sufficient data for a team of researchers over entire careers (cf. Pitt et al. 2006). In the old world of research, small n and unrepresentative samples are often a problem. In the new world, these problems can disappear. Imagine when you have all the data for transactions with a hotel website for a year, then large n becomes the problem because you might lack the computing power to process these data.

Third, much of our theory base was built in the industrial era (e.g. Porter's five forces model) of planning and control. We might need to build new theory for the information age of emergence. Is the e-consumer the same as the traditional consumer? Are e-relationships the same? Should we build theory in the same way when we no longer have a paucity of data? Should we be so focused on theory when we have vast amounts of data to explore? Maybe this is a time to put theory development aside for a while, and just focus on reporting findings revealed from innovative exploration of massive data sets. The straitjacket of applying old theories to a new environment might be limiting creative thinking. Force fitting the old to explain the new constrains new thinking. Of course, our traditional publication outlets will have to forsake some of their prior era practices to nurture the new, though it is more likely we will need an entirely new knowledge management system to emerge (e.g. Social Science Research Network) to really break away from our slavish attachment to a system that can't shake its paper and postal system inheritance.

One can argue that global warming is the most important emergence-related research issue. A phenomenon that threatens the survival of our species and many others should dominate the research agenda of many scholars, including those in information systems. Critically, we need to address the issue of how do we harness our understanding of emergence to change human behaviour in an ecologically and sustainable direction. Emergence is a different diffusion mechanism in its speed and effect than traditional plan and control. When you don't have a lot of time, and we might be too late already, then you need to find the fastest methods of change. Is it ethical for the majority of IS researchers to ignore global warming as an IS research issue? We don't believe it is, but if action is a sign of agreement, then few are in accordance with us. (But see also Chapter 22.) Waves of generations of innovators have given successive generations a legacy of technologies. An expansive understanding of these technologies, one that spans eons, sees the development of technology as a vast diverging tree of instrumentality and emergence that in many ways mirrors the tree of species's emergence. If we want this tree to continue to branch, rather than wither, then we need to understand how emergence can help us solve civilization's most pressing problem of today.

Notes

* Corresponding author, <rwatson@terry.uga.edu>.
1. *Time*, 2 July 1956.
2. <http://laptop.org/en/vision/index.shtml>.
3. <http://wiki.laptop.org/go/XO-2>.
4. <http://www.jdvhotels.com/hotels/sanfrancisco/good>.
5. <http://laptop.org/en/participate/give-one-get-one.shtml>.
6. Aspersion stems from the Latin 'aspergere', meaning to spread or scatter, typically in a negative sense.
7. <http://www.humanitarian.info/2008/05/19/olpc-a-different-type-of-disaster/>.
8. <http://148apps.com/10000/>.
9. <mac.blogdig.net/archives/articles/September2008/01/Seismometer_iPhone_app.html>.

REFERENCES

Arrow, K. J. (1974). *The Limits of Organization*. 1st edn., New York: Norton.

Berthon, P., Hulbert, J., and Pitt, L. F. (2005). 'Consumers and Technology: Why Marketers Sometimes Get it Wrong', *California Management Review*, 48(1): 1–19.

——Pitt, L. F., and Watson, R. T. (2008). 'From Genesis to Revelations: The Technology Diaspora', *Communications of the ACM*, 51(12): 151–4.

Chandler, A. D. J. (1962). *Strategy and Structure: Chapters in the History of the American Industrial Enterprise*. Cambridge, MA: MIT Press.

Cuban, L. (2001). *Oversold and Underused: Computers in the Classroom*. Cambridge, MA: Harvard University Press.

Filmer, D., and Pritchett, L. (1997). 'What Educational Production Functions Really Show: A Positive Theory of Education Funding', World Bank Policy Research Paper 1795.

Fisman, R. (2008). 'The $100 Distraction Device: Why Giving Poor Kids Laptops Doesn't Improve their Scholastic Performance', *Slate*, 5 June.

Fogie, S. (2008a). 'Turning the OLPC into a Hacker's Toolkit: Give One, Get Owned, Part 1', *InformIT*, 19 May.

——(2008b). 'Turning the OLPC into a Hacker's Toolkit: Give One, Get Owned, Part 2', *InformIT*, 26 May.

Ives, B., and Learmonth, G. P. (1984). 'The Information Systems as a Competitive Weapon', *Communications of the ACM*, 27(12): 1193–201.

Keoner, B. I. (2006). 'Geeks in Toyland', *Wired*, 14(2).

Lohr, S. (2008). 'Microsoft Joins Effort for Laptops for Children', *New York Times*, 16 May, from <http://www.nytimes.com/2008/05/16/technology/16laptop.html?_r=2&ref=technology&oref=slogin&oref=slogin>.

Malamud, O., and Pop-Eleches, C. (2008). *The Effect of Computer Use on Child Outcomes*. Chicago, IL: Harris School of Public Policy Studies, University of Chicago.

Markoff, J. (2005). 'Taking the Pulse of Technology at Davos', *New York Times*, 31 January, from <http://www.nytimes.com/2005/01/31/technology/31newcon.html?_r=1&scp=1&sq=%24100+laptop+negroponte&st=nyt>.

Pitt, L. F., Watson, R. T., Berthon, P. R., Wynne, D., and Zinkhan, G. (2006). 'The Penguin's Window: Corporate Brands from an OS Perspective', *Journal of the Academy of Marketing Science*, 34: 115–27.

Thompson, C. (2009). 'The Netbook Effect', *Wired*, 60–70.

Uzzi, B. (1996). 'The Sources and Consequences of Embeddedness for the Economic Performance of Organizations: The Network Effect', *American Sociological Review*, 61: 674–98.

Vitale, M. R. (1988). *American Hospital Supply Corp.: ASAP System (A)* (No. 9-186-005). Boston, MA: Harvard Business School.

Watson, R. T., Boudreau, M.-C., Greiner, M., Wynn, D., York, P., and Gul, R. (2005). 'Governance and Global Communities', *Journal of International Management*, 11(2): 125–42.

INDEX

RFDump tool 449
RFID (radio-frequency identification)
    446–51, 459–63, 471, 483, 485
  impact on consumer privacy 476
Ribbers, P. 514
Riccini, R. 475
Richardson, H. 204, 210, 218, 292, 564,
    566–70, 575, 635
Rickards, T. 120
Ricoeur, P. 231, 235, 239, 247–8, 251, 280
Riemenschneider, C. 574
Riley, M. J. 26
Riley, P. 123
risk analysis 608
risk management 452
risk mitigation 505–7
rituals 472, 475
Rivard, S. 337, 349–50, 505
Rivett, P. 106
Roach, S. S. 32
Roberts, J. 123
Robertson, R. 595, 625–7
Robey, D. 18–19, 27, 32, 37, 45, 126, 153, 155,
    212, 295, 336–7, 353, 394–5, 402–3, 410,
    480, 635, 648
Robins, K. 186–7, 192
Robinson, B. 204, 209–10, 218
robots 588
Robson, W. 182
Rockart, Jack 38
Roe, P. R. 608, 617–18
Rogers, E. 33
Rogers, E. M. 651
Rogers, M. F. 279
Rogerson, S. 601, 604, 606, 608–10, 613–14,
    616
rogue devices 447
ROI (return on investment) 32
Romantic paradigm 595, 597–8
Rondinelli, D. 358–9
Root Definitions 100–3
Rose, G. 651
Rose, N. 175, 185
Rosemann, M. 44–6
Rosen, B. 358–9
Rosen, C. 589

Rosenberg, D. 17
Rosenblueth, A. 90
Rosenstand, N. 597
Ross, A. 154
Ross, J. 334, 417, 422, 427, 431, 503, 511,
    513–15
Ross, J. W. 380, 394, 410
Rosser, S. V. 576
rote learning 410
Rottman, J. 380, 497–8, 505–6, 513–16,
    519
Rotvold, G. 434
Rouse, Robert 41
routinization 119, 132
Rowan, B. 139, 144–5, 400, 430, 434
Rowe, F. 218
Rowlinson, M. 186
Royal Institute of Technology (Sweden) 21
Royal Military College of Science,
    Shrivenham 29
RSS (really simple syndication) 553
rugby 546–7
Ruhleder, K. 330, 334, 336
rules 147, 181, 219, 232, 419
  alternatives to 180
  breaking 421
  codified interpretations of 116
  compliance undermined 433
  conformity to 430
  decisions which completely disregarded the
    spirit of 418
  formal and informal 143
  formulated 116
  high engagement with 429
  institutional(ized) 139, 142, 144–5, 150
  intersubjective 312
  legitimated 137, 430
  moral 216
  particular meaning of 116
  people usually able to subvert 434
  rationalized 139, 144
  resources and 117, 127
  social 118
rural sourcing 497, 519
Russia 44
Rynes, S. 422

Watson, M. 185
Watson, R. 39, 379, 388
Watson, R. T. 672–3, 678
Watson, Thomas 469
wearable computing 471
Weaver, G. R. 120, 418, 429
Weaver, Warren 108
Web 2.0 technologies 552–3
Weber, Max 24, 114, 146, 176, 189–90
Weber, R. 17–19, 34, 39, 47 n. 218, 648
Webster, F. 186–8, 192
Webster, J. 333, 566, 568
Weckert, J. 606
Wei, K. K. 39, 155
Weick, K. E. 330, 338, 429, 432, 544, 546
Weill, P. 334, 417, 422, 427–8, 431–2, 507
Weir, D. 404
Weiser, Mark 469
Weizenbaum, Joseph 603
Wenger, E. 331, 335–6, 408, 540, 547
Wennberg, L. 72
Western Cape 636
Westfall, R. 496
Westin, A. 610
Westphal, J. 430
Wetherbe, J. C. 18, 31
Whinston, A. B. 517
Whitaker, J. 518
Whitley, E. 21, 40, 46, 281, 285 n., 635
Whittaker, L. 210, 285 n.
Whitten, D. 501, 505, 512
Whittington, R. 123–4, 130, 132, 358
Wieder, B. 337
Wiener, Norbert 90–1, 602–3
WiFi 469, 677
Wijnhoven, T. 333
Wilensky, H. 17
Wilkie, F. 73
Wilkinson, B. 186
Willcocks, L. P. 5, 37–8, 48 n., 74, 175–6, 180, 185, 195 n., 214, 292, 300, 331, 335, 337, 380, 496–8, 501, 503, 505–10, 512, 514–19
Williams, Cynthia Clark 10
Williamson, O. E. 17, 146, 504

Willmott, H. 122–3, 175, 186–7, 202, 310–11, 334, 644
Wilson, D. 185
Wilson, F. 337
Wilson, M. 74, 203, 210, 292, 313, 404, 406, 430, 571
Winkler, J. 515
Winograd, T. 230–1, 281–2, 285 n.
Winokur, M. 193
Winter, S. 334
Winter, S. G. 538, 542
wireless communications 447, 457, 468–70, 475, 482, 488
Wittgenstein, L. 236–9, 246–7, 273, 287, 547
women 562–3, 567
  illiterate 634
  low participation in IS 570
  recruitment/retention in IT
    workforce 575–6, 579
  variation in career motivations 576
  see also feminism; gender
Wong, P.-K. 336
Wood, B. 201
Wood-Harper, A. T. 25, 73, 201, 213, 407
Woodfield, R. 571, 635
Woodger, J. H. 90
Woodhouse, E. 310
Wood-Harper, A. T. 651
Woolgar, S. 295, 298, 300
Woolridge, B. 351, 355
work 480–9, 535–59
working conditions 563
World Bank 634, 655–6, 664, 678
World Economic Forum 655
world income 628
World Wide Web 282, 380, 538
World Wide Web Consortium (W3C) 449
WorldCom 7
Wüllenweber, K. 518

Xchanging 517
Xerox 503